Treat this book with care and respect.

*It should become part of your personal
and professional library. It will
serve you well at any number
of points during your
professional career.*

COST
ACCOUNTING
planning and control

Sixth Edition

ADOLPH MATZ, PhD

Professor Emeritus of Accounting
The Wharton School
University of Pennsylvania

MILTON F. USRY, PhD, CPA

Regents Professor of Accounting
College of Business Administration
Oklahoma State University

Published by

A85 **SOUTH-WESTERN PUBLISHING CO.**

CINCINNATI   WEST CHICAGO, ILL.   DALLAS   PELHAM MANOR, N.Y.
PALO ALTO. CALIF.   BRIGHTON, ENGLAND

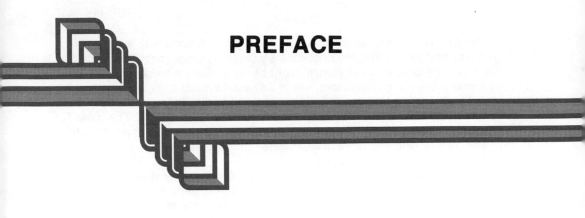

PREFACE

Management's efforts to achieve company objectives rest upon the twin functions of planning and control. The *planning function* is essentially a decision-making process dealing with the establishment of a desired profit; the preparation and availability of materials, labor force, and plant and equipment for the anticipated volume; and the creation of a communication system that permits reporting and controlling actual results against predetermined plans. The *control function* deals with management's task of organizing and marshaling natural forces, human behavior, and material objects into a coordinated unit in order to attain the desired results. The connecting link between the originating planning function and the terminating control function is the cost accounting information system that permits effective communication, continuous feedback, responsibility accounting, and managerial flexibility. Modern cost accounting is rightly termed a tool of management, with emphasis on management. The processing and reporting of a firm's historical and projected microeconomic data assist management in developing new potentials, improving present opportunities, establishing more aggressive yet flexible control of operations, and enhancing the management process through objective evaluation of the feedback data.

The importance of cost accounting to the performance and success of any level of management in both problem identification and problem solving is emphasized throughout the Sixth Edition. While planning is essentially a decision-making activity, control intends to ensure realization of the planner's goals. Although the information and underlying data required for these two functions are often quite different, one expects the cost accounting system to provide the answers and respond to the needs of both functions. This dual responsibility of the cost accounting information system to both functions strongly influenced the authors in structuring the presentation followed in this textbook.

Parts I and II of the textbook fuse planning and control into a harmonious whole by first presenting the cost data accumulation methods. The study of a job order or a process cost system might be considered a mechanical exercise by some accounting instructors; yet in any cost system they deserve primary attention if routine employee performance and computerized accounting are to furnish reliable data for management's tasks and decisions. The need for improving cost accounting instruction is recognized; but an orderly growth is still necessary, and the value of established practices as well as the lessons of the past should not be discarded.

Part III deals essentially with responsibility accounting and reporting of factory overhead. The text discussion shows that these steps outlined for a manufacturing concern are equally important and adaptable to nonmanufacturing businesses and nonprofit organizations. Part IV considers the other two cost elements, materials and labor, each from both the planning and cost control phases. Part V is the heart of the planning function — budgeting. Long- and short-range budgets as well as the flexible budget are discussed. Part VI treats not only standard costs basic to the control of costs and profits but also gross profit analysis and direct costing with its contribution margin. The final section, Part VII, covers the entire spectrum of cost and profit analysis, culminating in a chapter on linear programming for planning and decision making.

The concepts and techniques presented in this textbook are mainly in the context of manufacturing business organizations. However, it is important to note their wide, virtually universal applicability to many dimensions of organizations including: (1) small business organizations of all types; (2) nonmanufacturing businesses such as wholesale and retail stores and such service organizations as banks, insurance companies, hotels, and motels; and (3) nonprofit institutions such as churches, fraternal and charitable organizations, hospitals, libraries, public school systems, colleges and universities, and last, but not least, local, county, state, and federal governmental units and agencies. Indeed, any organization charged with the responsibility of efficient use of resources could and should utilize cost accounting concepts and techniques.

Like many other disciplines, cost accounting has in recent years been influenced by significant advances made in the development of quantitative management techniques and decision models. Topics retained — modernized where appropriate — from earlier editions include such mature techniques as economic buying quantity, the method of least squares for regression analysis, differential cost analysis, the discounted cash flow method, as well as the application of the modern techniques of PERT/Cost, probability analysis, risk and sensitivity analysis, statistical correlation analysis, and the simplex method for profit maximization and cost minimization.

This Sixth Edition has expanded and modernized nearly every chapter with its presentation and discussion of such new methods and techniques as the journal voucher control system for electronic data processing, computerized materials and payroll procedures, human resource accounting, learning curve theory, the Pension Reform Act of 1974, productivity and performance standards, zero-base budgeting, probabilistic budgets, modern marketing concepts and terminology, new transfer pricing theory, and shadow prices.

These mathematical and decision-making models together with a computerized information system combined with fundamental theoretical and practical aspects of cost accounting and relevant behavioral science concepts provide wide flexibility for classroom usage. In addition to its applicability to the traditional two-semester or three-quarter course, the textbook may be used in a one-semester cost or managerial accounting course or in a cost course with emphasis on profit planning and cost analysis. A suggested course outline, by chapter numbers, for each of these one-semester courses follows:

Cost or Managerial Accounting	Profit Planning and Cost Analysis
Chapters 1–15	Chapters 1–4
Chapters 18–20	Chapter 13
Chapter 27	Chapters 16–28

Many other chapter mixes can be used effectively, depending on students' needs; for example, the instructor may cover Chapter 28 immediately following Chapter 25.

End-of-chapter materials total 390 discussion questions, 270 exercises, 225 problems, and 42 cases. These materials include 50 questions and over 100 exercises, problems, and cases from the Uniform CPA Examinations of the American Institute of Certified Public Accountants (designated AICPA adapted), from the examinations for the Certificate in Management Accounting given by the Institute of Management Accounting of the National Association of Accountants (designated NAA adapted), and from the Uniform Final Examinations of the Canadian Institute of Chartered Accountants (designated CICA adapted). In addition to a significant number of new end-of-chapter materials, other situations have been updated to reflect increasing materials and labor costs and to incorporate metric measurements. Exercises and problems included for each topic afford coverage of relevant concepts and techniques at progressive levels in the learning hierarchy, thereby providing a significant student-learning benefit.

Three separately printed practice cases are available: a job order cost case, a process cost case, and a standard cost analysis case. Each case acquaints students with basic procedural characteristics without involving them in time-consuming details.

Instructors adopting the Sixth Edition are supplied with a solution manual that has been carefully prepared to improve the effective use of the textbook, to reduce the time the instructor must spend in checking problems, and to help the instructor plan his class periods more efficiently. The major portion of this manual is devoted to detailed solutions of the end-of-chapter materials. Wherever computations, supporting entries, schedules, or analyses are of a detailed or involved nature, the computations are given in full. Instructors are also entitled to practice case solutions, an Examinations Booklet (including both multiple-choice questions and problems), and multiple copies of Student Check Sheets for the problems.

The authors are indebted for the use of materials included in the publications of the National Association of Accountants (NAA), the American Institute of Certified Public Accountants (AICPA), the American Accounting Association (AAA), the Financial Executive Institute (FEI), the Canadian Institute of Chartered Accountants (CICA), and numerous other publication sources. Materials from these various sources are acknowledged by footnotes.

The authors wish to express appreciation to the many users of the previous editions who offered helpful suggestions. Special thanks are given the students of the Wharton School of the University of Pennsylvania and of Oklahoma State University who class-tested the new exercises, problems, and cases and made suggestions for improvements. The cooperation and valuable assistance of Professors John H. McMichael of the University of Pennsylvania, G. M. F. di Roccaferrera of Syracuse University, and Edward B. Deakin of The University of Texas at Austin are greatly appreciated.

Finally, we wish to express our heartfelt appreciation to our wives Trean Benfer Matz and Dona White Usry for their patience, understanding, and assistance in typing, editing, and proofreading the many pages for this Edition.

ADOLPH MATZ

MILTON F. USRY

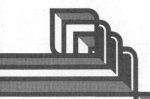

CONTENTS

Chapter 24   Break-Even and Cost-Volume-Profit Analysis

Chapter 25   Differential Cost Analysis

Chapter 26   Capital Expenditure Planning, Evaluating, and Control

Chapter 27   Profit Performance Measurements, Intracompany Transfer Pricing, Product Pricing Methods

Chapter 28   Linear Programming for Planning and Decision Making

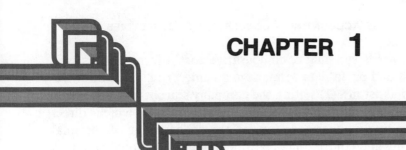

CHAPTER 1

CONCEPT OF MANAGEMENT
AND FUNCTION OF
THE CONTROLLER

The management of a business enterprise is based upon a structure of individuals that belong to one of three groups: (1) the operating management group, consisting of foremen and supervisors; (2) the middle management group, represented by department heads, division managers, and branch managers; and (3) the executive management, consisting of the president, the executive vice-presidents, and the executives in charge of the various functions of marketing, purchasing, engineering, manufacturing, finance, and accounting. The existence of these three levels suggests that management consists basically of people whose activities must be planned and controlled through top-level directives, decisions, and instructions. Plans and directives should be considered under the all-inclusive term "planning," and the continuous observation of the plans under the term "control." *Planning* refers to the construction of an operating program, comprehensive enough to cover all phases of operations and detailed enough so that specific attention may be given to the program's fulfillment in controllable segments. *Control* is that force which guides the business to the predetermined objective(s) by means of comparison of performance with predetermined policies and decisions. Planning is and remains basically an executive management attribute even though participation at all management levels is needed. The control phase reaches through all the levels of the management team.

Management needs systematic, comparative cost information as well as analytical cost and profit data to manage an enterprise. This information is needed to assist in: (1) setting the company's profit goal by executive management, (2) establishing departmental targets which direct middle and operating management toward the achievement of the final goal, (3) measuring and controlling departmental and functional activities with the aid of budgets and standards, and (4) analyzing and deciding on adjustments and improvements to keep the entire organization moving forward in balance toward established profit and other company objectives.

THE CONCEPT "MANAGEMENT"

A comprehensive explanation of the concept "management" poses innumerable difficulties. Invariably it leads to descriptive phrases such as "making decisions, giving orders, establishing policies, providing work and rewards, and hiring people to carry out policies." Management sets certain objectives which it tries to accomplish through the efforts of the people it directs. In this sense, it looks toward a final goal through a series of steps and processes. To be successful, management requires the integration of its own knowledge, skills, and practices with the know-how and experience of those who are entrusted with the task of carrying out the objectives. These objectives can be achieved by management, together with the efforts of all employees and workers, through performance of the two basic management functions: (1) planning and (2) controlling, both of which are basic to this textbook.

Planning. Planning is basic to the management process, a process of sensitizing an organization to external opportunities and threats, of determining desirable and possible objectives, and of deploying resources to match the objectives. Without planning there is no basis for controlling, for planning provides the foundation upon which the control function operates. Effective corporate planning is based on facts collected and analyzed. Reflective thinking, imagination, and foresight are of invaluable help. The planner should be able to visualize the proposed pattern of activities individually and collectively, internally and externally. Planning is looking ahead — preparing for the future. It involves a choice of several possible alternatives, a matter of making a decision. Planning must precede the doing.

One kind of plan, among several, is the budget. The budget is not only the most important plan of an enterprise, but also the basic link of cost accounting with management. The use of budgets, particularly in connection with the control phase of management, has been termed "budgetary control." In a budget, anticipated results, as envisioned by the planners, are expressed in quantitative data such as dollars, man-hours, number of employees, units of input and output, and products made and sold.

For the budget or any other kind of plan to operate effectively, an integrated balance must be maintained among the various plans and programs. Engineering, manufacturing, marketing, research, finance, and accounting participate in the establishment of the corporate plan. No single function should plan and act individually or independently from other functions, for all are interdependent. Failure to recognize this fundamental truth can cause unnecessary complexity and difficulty in planning and can result in disaster for the organization.

Closely allied with proper planning are the determination and establishment of company objectives. An objective is a target, an end result. Corporate planning includes such areas of investigation as the nature of the company's business, its objectives and major policies, the timing of major steps in the plan, and other factors related to long-range plans.

When asked to state the objectives of a business enterprise, many businessmen reply, "To realize a profit." However, in the last few years, some businessmen have tended more frequently to soft-pedal profit maximization and to emphasize the modern corporation's growing list of social obligations. Yet, the phrase "social responsibilities," rarely defined, remains a hazy concept. Profits are the indispensable element in a successful business enterprise. A firm making inadequate profits will not only not survive but will perhaps become a social or economic disaster to the very society it is expected to support. Social responsibility is a fair-weather concept; management cannot begin to think in terms of philanthropy unless profits are adequate. However, profit cannot remain the sole objective of the company and its management. It is a limited concept in today's economic society and does not give the whole answer. Management must execute a series of thinking processes and actions which will guide it to produce specific products or render service in a definite manner or method, in a volume, at a time, at a cost, and at a price that will, in the long run, assure a profit and also win the cooperation of employees, gain the goodwill of customers, and meet social responsibilities.[1] Such a company will be able to make the strongest case for profit maximization. Business logic and changing public expectations suggest that plans should be formulated within a framework of four major parameters — economic, technological, social, and political. Organizational objectives and performance criteria must be broader and more sophisticated.

---

[1]See "The Executive As Social Activist," *Time*, Vol. 96, No. 3, pp. 62–68.

Controlling. Management control is the systematic effort by business management to compare performance to plans. The control function is of prime importance in the accomplishment of objectives. The need for control increases with the size and complexity of the organization. Continuous supervision of an activity, task, or job is required to keep it within previously defined boundaries. These boundaries, termed "budgets and/or standards," are set up for manufacturing, marketing, finance, and all other activities. The actual results are measured against plans; and if significant differences are noted, remedial actions are taken. Diagrammatically, the control practice can be pictured in the manner illustrated by the chart below.

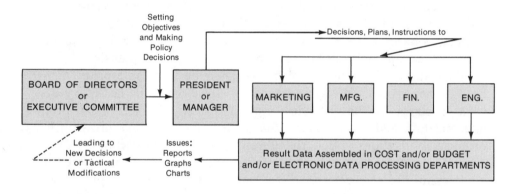

Control Circuit

Planning and Control Responsibilities of the Middle and Operating Management Levels. In a small company, planning and control activities often tend to be performed by a single person. The owner or the general manager of a small company can often perform these tasks without elaborate fact-finding and analysis due to his intimate knowledge of men, materials, money, and customers. In a large concern with numerous divisions and a variety of products or services, planning and control responsibilities are not combined in the same person or group of persons. In fact, the larger the business organization the greater the problem of planning, and the more involved the process of controlling the activities of individual units scattered throughout the United States and foreign countries. For this reason many firms have initiated the decentralization of certain planning and control functions in order to place the reports and necessary corrective actions closer to the scene of activity.

Overall responsibility for control rests with executive management or, in the final analysis, with the president of the company. Because the president cannot attend to every aspect of the control program, he must delegate authority and assign responsibilities to the middle and operating echelons of management. The delegation of authority and the assignment of responsibility are fundamental requirements if management's plans are to succeed and control is to be exercised.

Authority is the key to the managerial job and the basis for responsibility. It is not only the force that binds the organization together, but also the power to command others to perform or not perform certain activities. Managers work through people. Authority vested in a division manager, a department head, a supervisor, or a foreman enhances compliance with the plans and objectives of the organization. Authority originates with executive management which delegates it to the various managerial levels. Delegation of authority is essential to the existence of an organizational structure. By means of delegation, the chief executive extends his area of operations. However, he will always retain the overall authority for the assigned functions since delegation does not mean a permanent release from obligations.

Closely related to authority is *responsibility*. The essence of responsibility is obligation. It arises particularly in the superior-subordinate relationship due to the fact that the superior has the authority to require specified work or services from another person. As this other person accepts the obligation to perform the work, he creates his own responsibility. However, since responsibility cannot be delegated, the superior is, in the last analysis, responsible for performance or nonperformance by the individual.

Responsibility is often considered to have two facets. In addition to securing results, another aspect of responsibility is accountability — reporting back to higher authority of results achieved. The reporting phase is an important function of budgetary control and standard cost accounting. It makes possible the comparison of actual performance with predetermined plans and the measurement — in terms of quantity, quality, time, or cost — of the extent to which objectives were reached.

Accountability is basically an individual rather than a group problem, and the principle of single accountability has become well established in business organizations. Divided authority and responsibility result in divided accountability. The organizational structure must avoid duality or pooling of judgment, for this diffuses responsibility and nullifies accountability. Without single accountability, control reports would not only be meaningless, but corrective actions would be delayed or not forthcoming at all.

ORGANIZING

Organizing is essentially the establishment of the framework within which required activities are to be performed and a designation of who should do them. Without proper organization a person cannot function as a manager.

The terms "organize" or "organization" refer to the systematization of various interdependent parts and units into one whole. Considered in this sense, organizing requires: (1) bringing the many functional units of an enterprise into a well-conceived structure and (2) assigning authority and responsibility to certain individuals. These organizational efforts include the task of getting people to work together for the good of the company. Because of the attitudes, ambitions, and ideas of the many persons involved, indoctrination, instruction, and patience are needed to arrive at the desired organizational structure.

Creation of an organization involves the establishment of organizational or functional units generally known as divisions, departments, sections, branches, etc. These units are created for the purpose of breaking the tasks into workable parts leading to division and to specialization of labor. A manufacturing enterprise usually consists of at least three large, fundamental activities: manufacturing, marketing, and administration. Within these three basic organizational units, numerous departments or sections are formed according to the nature and the amount of work, the degree of specialization, the number of employees, and the location of the work.

After organizational units have been created, management must assign the work to be done within each unit. Appropriate division and distribution of work among the employees combined in organizational units are vital to the attainment of company objectives. Of still greater importance are the relationships between superior and subordinate on the one hand and among managers within the management team on the other. For ultimate success, the authority relationship binds the units into one whole.

THE ORGANIZATION CHART

The *organization chart* sets forth each principal management position and helps to define authority, responsibility, and accountability. The accountant's reports must help management evaluate the effectiveness of its plans, must pinpoint successes or failures in terms of specific responsibilities, and must establish the conditions that will lead to corrective action.

An organization chart is essential to the development of a cost system and cost reports which parallel the responsibilities of individuals for

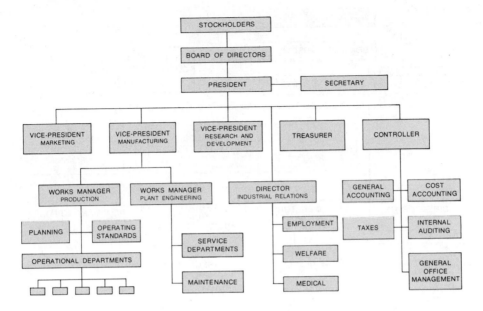

Organization Chart
Based on Line-Staff Concept

implementing management plans.   The coordinated development of a company's organization with the cost and budgetary system will lead to an approach to accounting and reporting called "responsibility accounting." (See Chapter 11.)

Generally, an organization chart is shown in the form illustrated at the top of this page.   This type of organization chart is based on the line-staff concept, a concept that is particularly useful when a company's product lines are simple and not subject to frequent changes over the years. The fundamental assumption is that all positions or functional divisions can be simply categorized into two groups: one group — the line — makes decisions and performs the true management functions; the other group — the staff — gives advice or performs any technical functions.

Another type of organization chart, based on the functional-teamwork concept of management, appears on page 8.   The functional-teamwork concept[2] is structured to place proper emphasis and balance on the truly important functions of any enterprise.   These business functions can be grouped around *resources, processes,* and *human interrelations.*   The resources function involves the acquisition, disposal, and husbanding of a wide variety of resources — tangible and intangible, human and physical.   The processes function deals with activities such as product design,

---

[2]Gerald G. Fisch, "Line-Staff is Obsolete," *Harvard Business Review*, Vol. 39, No. 5, pp. 67–79.

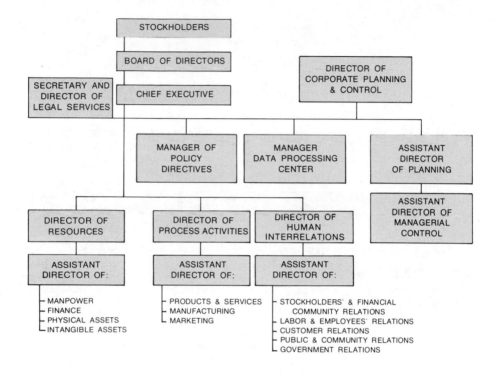

Organization Chart
Based on Functional-Teamwork Concept

research and development, purchasing, manufacturing, advertising, marketing, and billing. The human interrelations function directs the company's effort toward the behavior of people inside and outside the company.

ACCOUNTING — THE FRAMEWORK FOR PLANNING AND CONTROLLING MANAGEMENT ACTIVITIES

The effective use of company capital is one of management's chief concerns. This capital is invested in the form of productive facilities such as factory buildings, factory machinery, tools, and equipment (called property, plant, and equipment in accounting terminology) as well as in the form of circulating capital called current assets. The use of this capital is determined by management's plans for the immediate future and by plans for two to five years ahead. The budget emerges as the result of management's planning and plays an important role in controlling operations. Constant comparison of the budget plan with actual results not only provides a measure of the amount of deviation but also reflects the reasons for variances or differences.

The effectiveness of the control of costs depends upon proper communication through control and action reports from the accounting function to the various levels of management. Accounting and cost control reports are directed to three levels of management: executive, middle, and operating. Each managerial level requires data for deciding and solving varied and difficult problems, and data assembled for one purpose may not be usable for another purpose. For example, figures collected and assembled for measuring and reporting to operating management the past use of materials, labor, machines, and money are often irrelevant for future price and output decisions made by executive management.

Inasmuch as classifying and reporting data are essential to the proper discharge of the accounting function, the controller must devise an information system into which past, present, and future data are marshalled to fit the multitude of problems confronting company management. The accountant's means of classifying costs and expenses, called the chart of accounts (Chapter 4), must be closely associated with management's own fundamental classification, the organization chart.

THE CONTROLLER'S PARTICIPATION IN PLANNING AND CONTROL

The controller, a member of the management team, assists management in both planning and control. In planning he assembles, classifies, and presents the economic and financial data concerning men, money, materials, machines, and methods into a coordinated plan or plans for management's considerations and decisions. The data are based on (1) the company's own historical, experienced, or past costs and revenues modified by management's own evaluation of the future and (2) other economic forecast information originating outside the company. To coordinate the internal and external information and to chart for management a course of expected trend levels constitutes the controller's most formidable contribution to planning.

In recent years the controller and his staff have become the nerve centers of many large corporations. Their knowledge and control of the basic communication network — the electronic data processing system — permit them to extract diverse data from computer storage and to suggest to executive management alternative plans and sound decisions in certain crucial areas of operations.

In the control phase, the controller's function is the result of a need for checks and balances within the business. Actually, the controller does not control but, through the issuance of performance reports, advises all levels of management where and what jobs or tasks require corrective action.

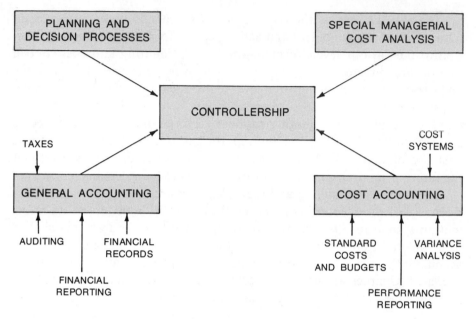

The Controllership Cluster[3]

These reports should make possible *management by exception*. Emphasizing the exceptions to or deviations from a predetermined plan expedites managerial control.

The functions of the controllership sector of a business are depicted in the diagram illustrated above.

THE NATURE OF COST ACCOUNTING

Cost accounting, sometimes called management or managerial accounting, should be considered the key managerial partner in the planning and control activities, furnishing management with the necessary accounting tools to plan, control, and evaluate operations.

In the *planning* phase, cost accounting deals with the future. It helps management to budget the future or predetermined materials costs, wages and salaries, and other costs of manufacturing and marketing products. These costs might be used to set prices or to assist in disclosing the profit that will result with the existence of these costs and expenses, considering competition and other economic conditions. Cost information is also provided to assist management with problems such as product pricing, capital expenditures decisions, expansion of facilities for increased sales or production, make-or-buy decisions, or purchase-or-lease decisions.

[3]Adapted from John P. Fertakis, "Toward a Systems-Oriented Concept of Controllership," *Management Accounting*, Vol. L, No. 6, p. 8.

In the *control* phase, cost accounting deals with the present, comparing current results with predetermined standards and budgets. Cost control, to be effective, depends upon proper cost planning for each activity, function, and condition. Via the cost accounting media, management is informed frequently of those operating functions that fail to contribute their share to the total profit or that perform inefficiently, thereby leading to profit erosion. Periodically, generally at the end of the fiscal period, cost accounting deals with past costs for the purpose of profit determination and thereby with the allocation of historical costs to periods of time. At this point cost accounting procedure is particularly concerned with the application of manufacturing cost to units of products to be capitalized in the ending inventory and transferred to cost of goods sold as shipments are made.

More specifically, cost accounting is charged with the tasks of:

1. Aiding and participating in the creation and execution of plans and budgets.
2. Providing management with information in connection with problems that involve choice from among two or more alternative courses (decision making).
3. Establishing methods and procedures that permit control and, if possible, reduction or improvement of costs.
4. Creating inventory values for costing and pricing purposes and, at times, controlling physical quantities.
5. Determining costs and profit for an accounting period.

SCOPE OF COST ACCOUNTING

Cost accounting is generally considered and discussed as being applicable only to manufacturing operations. This is not the case; every type and kind of activity, regardless of size, in which monetary value is involved should consider the use of cost accounting concepts and techniques. Nonmanufacturing activities of manufacturing firms, wholesale and retail businesses, banks and other financial enterprises, insurance companies, transportation companies, railroads, airlines, shipping companies, bus companies, schools, colleges and universities, hospitals, governmental units on local, state, or federal levels, churches, and welfare organizations — all should employ cost accounting in order to operate efficiently. These many types are not considered individually in this text; however, at appropriate places mention will be made regarding the use of specific costing concepts and techniques in certain of these activities. In other cases it is a matter of recognition by the management and its accounting staff of the applicability of these concepts and techniques to their own special nonmanufacturing and nonprofit fields of endeavor.

GOVERNMENTAL AND PRIVATE ORGANIZATIONS INFLUENCING COST ACCOUNTING PRINCIPLES AND PRACTICE

Cost Accounting Standards Board. Created as an agent of Congress in August 1970 by an amendment to the Defense Production Act of 1950, the Cost Accounting Standards Board (CASB) was formally organized in January 1971. The Controller General of the United States serves as chairman of the five-member board.

The Board's purpose is to promulgate standards, rules, and regulations to achieve uniformity and consistency in the cost accounting practices followed by contractors in the pricing, administration, and settlement of covered negotiated federal government contracts in excess of $100,000 after the contractor has first received a covered contract in excess of $500,000. Originally, these pronouncements were to be applied to negotiated national defense procurement contracts. By virtue of an amendment to the Federal Procurement Regulation, they also apply to nondefense federal government contracts.

The CASB defines a *cost accounting standard* as a formal statement that (1) enunciates a principle or principles to be followed, (2) establishes practices to be applied, or (3) specifies criteria to be employed in selecting from alternative principles and practices in estimating, accumulating, and reporting costs of contracts subject to the rules of the Board.

Because so many companies engage in federal government contract work, the CASB's pronouncements are significant in terms of their impact on cost accounting. These pronouncements thus far have been in general harmony with sound cost accounting concepts and techniques.

Financial Accounting Standards Board (FASB), Securities and Exchange Commission (SEC), and Others. These first two groups, the former in the private and the latter in the public sector, focus on the promulgation of standards and regulations dealing with financial reporting by companies. Although their concern is primarily with published financial statements, their pronouncements influence the concepts and techniques used in the cost accounting domain.

In the private sector, research and pronouncements by professional organizations including the American Institute of Certified Public Accountants, the National Association of Accountants, the American Accounting Association, and the Financial Executives Institute contribute to the development of both financial and cost accounting theory and practice. Contributions are also made by companies, nonprofit organizations, public accounting firms, and individuals.

Internal Revenue Service (IRS). IRS regulations are designed primarily to determine federal income tax liability. Their influence on financial statements and on cost accounting cannot be ignored.   Likewise, any meaningful analysis for planning and decision making must carefully consider federal as well as applicable state and local income tax conse- quences, for this is the very essence of intelligent tax and profit planning.

DISCUSSION QUESTIONS

1. Webster includes in the definition of management "judicious use of means to accomplish an end"; planning is described as "the establishment of goals, policies, and procedures for a social or economic unit"; and control is defined as "the exercise of restraining or directing influence through checks and tests and verification by counter or parallel evidence." In our modern economy these definitions might be paraphrased to describe management planning and control as a concept of doing business.
   (a) State the premises on which these management functions might be based.
   (b) The concept of management planning and control varies among com- panies. Why?

2. (a) What should be considered the fundamental task in planning and con- trolling the activities of a company?
   (b) A sound organization is often the product of a positive and dynamic program of planning and control. Name some fundamental steps needed to achieve a sound organization.

3. (a) What is meant by "responsibility accounting"?
   (b) Is "responsibility accounting" identical with the concept of "account- ability"?

4. Explain the relationship between assignment of responsibility and control.

5. What does reassignment of responsibility mean?

6. In what manner does the controller exercise control over the activities of other members of management?

7. Why must the controller be aware of the latest developments in the field of communications?

8. Enumerate some social responsibilities of which management should be aware.

9. A company should create a good relationship with its personnel. State some possible ways of achieving this goal.

10. The budget has been cited as the most essential tool in cost planning. Why?

11. When an organization or business outgrows direct supervision and man- agement by its owner, authority must be delegated to subordinate managers, and some form of accountability on their part must be provided. Discuss.

12. The principle of management by exception is followed by a company in which a major item showed the following percentage relationship to the budgeted figures for six consecutive months: 92%, 95%, 96%, 99%, 103%, 108%. Does the item need attention?

13. As a member of the management advisory service division of a certified public accounting firm, you visit a client's office and find the following situation:

   Mr. Gonzalez is President and also Sales Manager of the company. Mr. Kern is Vice-President in Charge of Purchasing — he also prepares weekly production schedules and maintains inventories of materials and work in process. Mr. Troop is the Assistant Purchasing Agent; Miss Clark is Vice-President in Charge of Sales; and Mr. Graham, the Product Engineer, is responsible for design and engineering development. The accounting department and general office are under the supervision of Mr. Hanna who reports directly to the President. Office help consists of two full-time and one part-time bookkeeper, one typist, and one clerk. The company's factory is divided into four producing departments employing about 175 workers. The president requests:

   (a) An organization chart.

   (b) An opinion regarding certain duties that apparently have not been sufficiently delegated.

   (c) A report as to additional information needed to prepare a more satisfactory organization chart.

14. The number of factory workers mentioned in discussion question 13 indicates that this company falls into the category of "small business."

   (a) Would the consultant's answer be different if he were told that the company employs 2,000 factory workers?

   (b) What additional managerial positions might have to be set up?

   (c) In what manner would the accounting department and general office have to be reorganized?

15. The management of the Kringle Company, interested in an improved organization, created a Control Division with a controller as its chief executive. As one of his first steps the controller prepared the organization chart shown below and invited staff members to comment on the chart with respect to:

   (a) organization; (b) possible improvements; (c) a new chart.

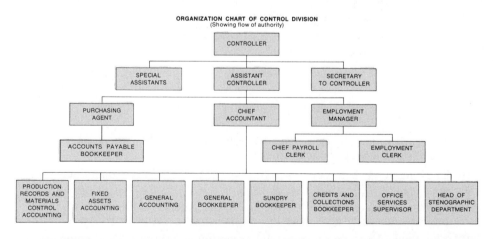

ORGANIZATION CHART OF CONTROL DIVISION
(Showing flow of authority)

16. Name governmental and private groups whose pronouncements influence cost accounting methods and procedures.

17. Explain the activities of the Cost Accounting Standards Board (CASB).

CHAPTER 2

FUNDAMENTAL COST REPORTS
AND ANALYSIS FOR
PLANNING AND CONTROL

The previous chapter has presented the duties and responsibilities of the controller in connection with management's request and need for cost and economic data to plan the future and to control day-by-day activities. The subject matter is continued in this chapter by presenting first the organizational unit: the cost department itself and its relation to other departments and functions in order to fulfill its obligations to all parties concerned. Second, the cost department is pictured as a part of the information system, a large data and record-keeping unit, which in turn provides past, present, and future data. Third, the discussion leads to accounting's basic information models, the balance sheet and the income statement. Any company, with or without a cost system or cost department, will and must prepare these two financial statements at the end of the fiscal year. The system should, however, make possible the production of monthly income statements which are of utmost importance to top executives and middle management for control purposes. Such statements need comparative cost figures — planned vs. actual — to be of value. Finally, this chapter deals briefly with some planning and control devices particularly applicable for management's overall review of the company's profit goal.

THE COST DEPARTMENT

The cost department is responsible for keeping records associated with the accounting for manufacturing and nonmanufacturing activities. To attain the greatest usefulness, the cost department must not only record but also analyze all costs of manufacturing, marketing, and administration for use by management in planning and control. It must, in addition, issue significant control reports and other decision-making data to executives, superintendents, department heads, and foremen which assist in controlling and in improving costs and operations. The need for the prompt issuance of reports and statements must alert the accountant to modern developments and techniques in the field of communications. Information transmittal problems have too often been overlooked or neglected. Cost control needs or profit opportunities have been delayed or missed because of poor communications. The analysis of costs and the preparation of reports are greatly facilitated through proper sectioning of functions generally listed under the cost department. Proper coordination is also needed with other functions closely allied with cost accounting for which separate departments or sections are often set up; namely, planning and cost analysis and general accounting activities. These functional units should come under the supervision of the controller.

The performance of the functions of the cost department involves the past, present, and future. In profit measurement, as evidenced in the income statement, the accountant is primarily concerned with the proper recording and presentation of costs and revenues for operations and transactions already experienced. When issuing cost control reports, he is working in the present rather than in the past. In developing costs for planning and decision-making purposes, the accountant is concerned with the future.

RELATIONSHIP OF COST DEPARTMENT TO OTHER DEPARTMENTS

The *manufacturing departments,* under the direction of factory superintendents and engineers, design, plan, and control products to their finished stage. In research and design, cost estimates are needed for each type of material, each item of labor, and each machine process before an intelligent decision can be reached in accepting or rejecting a design. Likewise, the scheduling, producing, and inspecting of jobs and products by the manufacturing departments are measured for efficiency in terms of the costs incurred.

The *personnel department* interviews, screens, and selects employees for various job classifications. It keeps workers' personnel records and is interested in keeping efficient and satisfied employees. The wage rates and the methods of remuneration agreed upon with the employee form the basis for the computation of the payroll.

The *treasury department*, responsible for the financial administration, relies upon accounting, budgeting, and related reports in scheduling cash requirements and expectations.

The *marketing department* needs a good product at a competitive price in its dealings with customers. While prices should not be set merely by adding a predetermined percentage to cost, cost cannot be ignored. Pertinent cost data give marketing managers information as to which products are most profitable and assist them greatly in determining sales policies.

The *public relations department* has the primary function of maintaining good relations between the company and the public in general, especially customers, stockholders, and employees. Points of friction are most likely to be prices, wages, profits, and dividends. The cost department is often called on to provide basic information for public releases concerning these policies and practices.

The *legal department* finds cost accounting helpful in keeping many affairs of the company in conformity with the law. The Wages and Hours Law, terms of industry-wide union contracts, the Robinson-Patman Act, social security taxes, unemployment compensation taxes, as well as income taxes, are some of the areas where the legal and cost departments need to cooperate.

SOURCES OF COST ACCOUNTING DATA

Much of the source data for cost accounting originates outside the accounting function. In addition to invoices and documents supporting transactions of materials purchased, consumed, or transferred between departments, the accountant requires reports of time studies, records of workers' actual time, bills of material, and lists of operating and planning schedules. Capacity studies, machine-tool requirements, and statistics regarding floor space, machine capacities, and power ratings or power consumption constitute additional source data required. The accountant's dependence upon information furnished by *outsiders* necessitates source data that are accurate, reliable, and available at the proper time.

The accountant evaluates and uses such data in a manner that will channel out essential facts for management. Since these cost data depend upon proper, correct, and timely information from all levels of the organization, cost accounting becomes a cooperative venture involving all departments of the company. It is an educational problem of executive management, the controller, and the controller's staff to make all employees cost conscious. Employees must be taught to observe and execute cost procedures to promote cost control.

INFORMATION SYSTEM

With the aid of the supervisors in charge of the functions shown on page 10 of the first chapter, the controller coordinates participation in planning and control by consulting with various segments of management concerning any phase of the operation of the business as it relates to the attainment of objectives, the effectiveness of policies, and the creation of organizational structures and procedures. It is also his responsibility to observe the method of planning and control throughout the enterprise in order that he may propose improvements in the planning and control system. To discharge these duties, the controller's function is immeasurably assisted by an electronic data processing system. Depending on the progress made in the use of computers, the assistance offered will generate the effective development of a new information technology which requires the use of these modern computer-communication facilities.

An integrated and coordinated information system should provide exactly the data and other information needed, and no more, to each responsibility head in accordance with his needs. A good information system requires the establishment of: (1) long-range objectives, (2) an organization plan showing delegated responsibilities in detail, (3) detailed plans for future operations, both long- and short-term, and (4) procedures for implementing and controlling achievement of these plans.

A comparison of the characteristics of the three management levels highlights the similarities, differences, and interrelationships among these groups. Executive management is principally concerned with long-range decisions, middle management with decisions of medium-range impact, and operating managers with short-range decisions. The information requirements for each level of planning and control vary significantly. Executive management, engaged in strategic planning, sets objectives and determines the resources to be applied in meeting these objectives. For these tasks essential information ingredients should consist of long-term trends, extensive staff studies, external situation information, and reports of achievements. The middle management, engaged in tactical planning and control decision making, relies upon summaries, exceptions, operating results, and estimates relating to internal information of the enterprise. The operating management requires data on internal events relating to daily, weekly, or monthly transactions to fulfill its operational duties and responsibilities.

THE REPORTING FUNCTION

Accounting information is the chief means of communicating the results of management's stewardship to external and internal users. The external users receive their information in the annual report, which includes the balance sheet, the income statement, and the statement of changes in financial position. Additionally, effects of price-level changes and/or current values may be presented as supplemental information to these historical-dollar financial statements. These reports lack a considerable amount of detail, for it is impossible to include all the data relevant to the external users' many needs. The internal users, executive management and all other levels of management, have access to many sources of information required for the execution of the planning and control tasks. Management's needs are answered by information provided by the conventional accounting system models — balance sheet, income statement, statement of changes in financial position — and by information outside these models but most likely also obtained from the total computerized information system.

FINANCIAL STATEMENTS IN ANNUAL REPORTS

The reporting function is initially illustrated here with two historical-dollar financial statements, the balance sheet and the income statement based on the annual report of a manufacturing concern. These statements and their individual items are analyzed to indicate their fundamental value for planning and control. Not illustrated here is the statement of changes in financial position which is also found in published annual financial reports to stockholders. Such a statement is designed to "(1) summarize the financing and investing activities of the entity, including the extent to which the enterprise has generated funds from operations during the period, and (2) complete the disclosure of changes in financial position during the period."[1]

Although the balance sheet of The Seabright Manufacturing Company is utilized in the discussion of financial ratios beginning on page 23, it is not discussed in as much depth as the income statement because, as is the case with the statement of changes in financial position, its discussion is better left to financial accounting textbooks.

The income statement, however, is supported with schedules of cost of goods sold, marketing (sometimes called selling or distribution) expenses, and administrative expenses. These supporting statements are generally made available to executive management, not to external users. They are included here to (1) indicate the difference existing in the information provided and (2) permit the subsequent discussion of additional cost accounting theory, procedures, analytical steps, and methods necessary to succeed in the planning and control task.

[1]AICPA Accounting Principles Board, *APB Opinion No. 19, Reporting Changes in Financial Position*, March 1971, p. 372.

THE SEABRIGHT MANUFACTURING COMPANY, INC.
INCOME STATEMENT
FOR YEAR ENDED DECEMBER 31, 19—

			%
Sales (4,500,000 units @ $5.50 per unit).....................		$24,750,000	100.0
Less cost of goods sold (see Schedule 1).................		21,285,000	86.0
Gross profit on sales......................................		$ 3,465,000	14.0
Less commercial expenses:			
Marketing expenses (see Schedule 2).........	$580,000		
Administrative expenses (see Schedule 3)......	533,750	1,113,750	4.5
Net income from operations.............................		$ 2,351,250	9.5
Other income and expense items:			
Royalties and dividends......................	$167,000		
Gain from sales of fixed assets................	12,000		
	$179,000		
Interest and debt expenses...................	129,500		
Net addition.......................................		49,500	0.2
Net income before estimated income tax...................		$ 2,400,750	9.7
Less estimated income tax.............................		1,064,250	4.3
Net income after estimated income tax....................		$ 1,336,500	5.4

The cost of goods sold section of the income statement of The Seabright Manufacturing Company or of any other manufacturing business can be divided into five distinct parts:

1 Direct materials section, comprised of opening inventory, purchases, any purchases returns or allowances, and the final inventory.

2 Direct labor section, indicating the cost of those employees whose work can be identified directly with the product manufactured.

3 Factory overhead, comprised of all those costs that assist in an indirect manner in the manufacturing of the product; e.g., factory supplies and depreciation of machinery. The factory overhead section does not indicate the amount of fixed and variable factory overhead, an extremely important requisite in the analytical uses of cost data. Furthermore, it must be assumed that the items are stated at actually experienced costs. Generally, as introduced in Chapter 4 and discussed in great detail in the factory overhead Chapters 9, 10, and 11, a predetermined factory overhead rate is used to charge overhead to work in process. The Seabright Manufacturing Company applies factory overhead on a unit of production basis ($.90 per unit). Factory overhead could also be applied as a rate based on percentage of direct labor cost, or on direct labor hours or some other representative method. (See Chapter 9 for details.) With 4,430,000 units being manufactured and assuming a factory over-

head rate of $.90 per unit $\left(= \dfrac{\$3,960,000 \text{ predetermined factory overhead}}{4,400,000 \text{ planned units}} \right)$, total

THE SEABRIGHT MANUFACTURING COMPANY, INC.
SCHEDULE 1

STATEMENT OF COST OF GOODS SOLD
FOR YEAR ENDED DECEMBER 31, 19—

1 Direct materials:

Materials inventory, January 1, 19—...............		$1,572,400	
Purchases.........................	$8,420,000		
Less purchases returns and allowances.	42,000	8,378,000	
Materials available for use.......................		$9,950,400	
Less materials inventory, December 31, 19—......		1,270,600	
Direct materials consumed...............................			$ 8,679,800

2 Direct labor... | | | 7,346,400 |

3 Factory overhead:

Indirect labor....................................	$1,329,300
Salaries..	972,000
Payroll taxes....................................	489,000
Power...	112,000
Heat..	69,200
Light...	44,300
Factory supplies.................................	50,000
Depreciation — factory building..................	68,300
Depreciation — machinery......................	403,000
Repairs and maintenance.........................	145,800
Patent amortization.............................	33,200
Tools and dies used.............................	178,600
Insurance on building and machinery..............	21,200

Total factory overhead.....................................	3,915,900
Total manufacturing costs.....................................	$19,942,100
4 Add work in process inventory, January 1, 19—...............	2,338,000
	$22,280,100
Less work in process inventory, December 31, 19—.............	1,303,200
Cost of goods manufactured................... (4,430,000 units)	$20,976,900
5 Add finished goods inventory, January 1, 19—. (210,000 units)	966,100
	$21,943,000
Less finished goods inventory, December 31, 19— (140,000 units)	658,000
Cost of goods sold......................... (4,500,000 units)	$21,285,000

applied factory overhead would amount to $3,987,000. Deducting the actual overhead of $3,915,900 shows that $71,100 was overapplied; i.e., actual factory overhead was less than the overhead charged to production. In The Seabright Manufacturing Company's statement of cost of goods sold the accountant might have shown the difference in this manner:

Applied factory overhead......................	$3,987,000	
Less overapplied factory overhead.............	71,100	
Actual factory overhead, as per schedule......		$3,915,900

4 Work in process inventories, representing costs in process at the beginning and costs still in process at the end of the fiscal period.

5 Finished goods inventories, beginning and ending.

THE SEABRIGHT MANUFACTURING COMPANY, INC.

SCHEDULE 2

MARKETING EXPENSES
FOR YEAR ENDED DECEMBER 31, 19—

Sales salaries and commissions	$330,500
Travel expenses	43,000
Payroll taxes	16,850
Advertising	125,000
Telephone and telegraph	11,800
Entertainment	21,000
Donations and dues	4,000
Depreciation — furniture and fixtures	7,500
Stationery and office supplies	13,500
Postage	6,850
Total	$580,000

THE SEABRIGHT MANUFACTURING COMPANY, INC.

SCHEDULE 3

ADMINISTRATIVE EXPENSES
FOR YEAR ENDED DECEMBER 31, 19—

Salaries — officers and executives	$290,200
Salaries — general office employees	77,250
Travel expenses	22,450
Payroll taxes	17,500
Depreciation — furniture and fixtures	6,200
Stationery and office supplies	5,450
Telephone and telegraph	7,800
Postage	3,650
Subscriptions, dues, and association activities	4,750
Legal and accounting fees	46,000
Donations	52,500
Total	$533,750

EVALUATING ANNUAL RESULTS TO ORIENT THE OUTSIDER

The income statement (page 20) follows a functional classification. The various costs incurred are grouped according to the function served by their incurrence: manufacturing, marketing, administrative, and non-operating. The relationship between the various items in the income statement is a criterion for judging the efficiency with which the profit-earning process is conducted. Using the sales figure as a base, or 100 percent, absolute differences become more meaningful when they are reduced to percentage relationships, as indicated in the final column of the preceding income statement. Today's annual reports are made still more useful by adding financial ratios. The more prevalent ratios are:

THE SEABRIGHT MANUFACTURING COMPANY, INC.
BALANCE SHEET
DECEMBER 31, 19—

ASSETS

Current assets:

Cash..	$ 2,320,000
Marketable securities......................................	820,000
Accounts receivable (net).................................	2,661,000
Inventories (materials, work in process, finished goods)............	3,231,800
Prepaid insurance, taxes, and miscellaneous expenses..............	220,000
Total current assets..	$ 9,252,800

Property, plant, and equipment:

Land.......................................		$ 289,000	
Buildings.............................	$ 3,406,100		
Machinery and equipment.............	12,529,000		
	$15,935,100		
Less accumulated depreciation.......	8,118,000	7,817,100	
Total property, plant, and equipment.......................			8,106,100
Total assets..			$17,358,900

LIABILITIES

Current liabilities:

Accounts payable...		$ 990,800
Accrued payroll, taxes, interest, etc..........................		1,045,000
Estimated income taxes....................................		190,700
Due on long-term debt.....................................		200,000
Total current liabilities.....................................		$ 2,426,500
Long-term debt...		2,677,500
Total liabilities..		$ 5,104,000

STOCKHOLDERS' EQUITY

Common stock..	$ 4,258,000	
Retained earnings...................................	7,996,900	
Total stockholders' equity.......................................		12,254,900
Total liabilities and stockholders' equity...........................		$17,358,900

1. Current Ratio
2. Acid-Test Ratio
3. Net Income as a Percentage of Sales
4. Ratio of Gross Profit to Sales
5. Rate of Return on Capital Employed

On the basis of the data available in the preceding financial statements, these ratios would be computed as shown on page 24.

1. Current Ratio $= \dfrac{\text{Current Assets}}{\text{Current Liabilities}} = \dfrac{\$9,252,800}{\$2,426,500} = \underline{\underline{3.81}}$,

   indicating that $3.81 is available in current assets for every $1 of current liabilities.

2. Acid-Test Ratio $= \dfrac{\$5,801,000}{\$2,426,500} = \underline{\underline{2.39}}$,

   indicating that without inventories and prepaid items, $2.39 in current assets is available for every $1 of current liabilities.

3. (a) Net Income (before estimated income tax) $= \underline{\underline{9.7\%}}$,

   calculated as a percentage of sales $\left(\dfrac{\$\,2,400,750}{\$24,750,000} \right)$.

   (b) Net Income (after estimated income tax) $= \underline{\underline{5.4\%}}$,

   calculated as a percentage of sales $\left(\dfrac{\$1,336,500}{\$24,750,000} \right)$.

   The difference of 4.3% between the two percentages indicates the portion of net income claimed by the government and unavailable to the stockholder.

4. Ratio of Gross Profit to Sales $= \underline{\underline{14\%}}$

   This ratio indicates the percentage available for operating expenses (marketing and administrative), other income and expense items, income taxes, and net income. The gross profit and its percentage are significant to management's planning and are discussed in depth in Chapter 21.

5. Rate of Return on Capital Employed $=$

$$\dfrac{\text{Net Income (after estimated income tax)}}{\text{Capital Employed (total assets)}} = \dfrac{\$1,336,500}{\$17,358,900} = \underline{\underline{7.7\%}}$$

   This ratio reveals the percentage earned on the assets employed in the business. It should not be confused with the net income to sales ratio of No. 3 above. The numerator may be more generally described as "profit." The rate of return on capital employed is presented in detail in Chapter 27.

EVALUATING RESULTS TO ORIENT THE INSIDER

Cost accounting adds no additional steps to the familiar accounting cycle, which is illustrated on page 25.

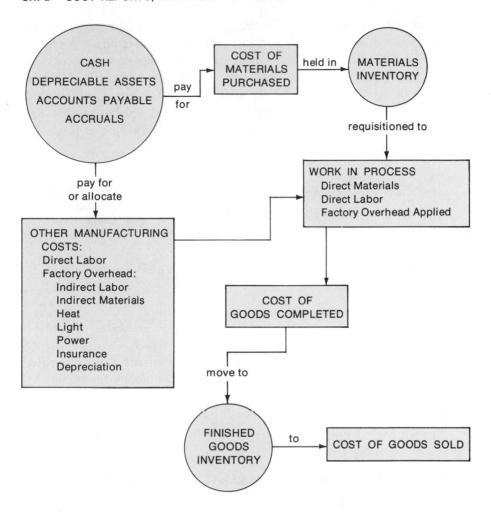

Flow of Manufacturing Costs

As materials are purchased, they are first held in the inventory account, an asset, from which they move to the work in process account, an asset, as needed. There labor and factory overhead are added. When completed, these costs move into the finished goods inventory account, an asset. When sold, the asset, finished goods, moves to the income statement as costs of goods sold. What is an asset one moment becomes an expense the next.

Cost accounting does not discard the principles and procedures studied in financial accounting. Cost accounting consists of a system which is concerned with a more adequate, detailed, and precise recording and measurement of cost elements as they originate and flow through the productive processes. Cost accounting has as one of its purposes the determination of a unit cost figure to be utilized in assigning costs to inventories included in the balance sheet and in the income statement.

For example, using the illustrative statements and assuming that 4,500,000 units were sold and that 4,430,000 units were manufactured, with 210,000 units in the beginning inventory of finished goods and 140,000 units in the ending inventory of finished goods, the following unit costs can be calculated:

$$\frac{\text{Cost of Goods Manufactured}}{\text{Units Manufactured}} = \frac{\$20,976,900}{4,430,000} = \begin{array}{l}\$4.735 \text{ Average Cost} \\ \text{per Unit Manufactured}\end{array}$$

$$\frac{\text{Cost of Beginning Finished Goods Inventory}}{\text{Units in Beginning Finished Goods Inventory}} = \frac{\$966,100}{210,000} = \begin{array}{l}\$4.60 \text{ Average Cost} \\ \text{per Unit in Beginning} \\ \text{Finished Goods Inventory}\end{array}$$

$$\frac{\text{Cost of Ending Finished Goods Inventory}}{\text{Units in Ending Finished Goods Inventory}} = \frac{\$658,000}{140,000} = \begin{array}{l}\$4.70 \text{ Average Cost} \\ \text{per Unit in Ending} \\ \text{Finished Goods Inventory}\end{array}$$

$$\frac{\text{Cost of Goods Sold}}{\text{Units Sold}} = \frac{\$21,285,000}{4,500,000} = \begin{array}{l}\$4.73 \text{ Average Cost} \\ \text{per Unit Sold}\end{array}$$

Such calculations merely fill the gaps in financial accounting created by the fact that an enterprise seldom sells all the goods manufactured during the year. Financial statements are basically of a long-run nature based on historical or past costs. The insiders (i.e., the various levels of management) also need present and future costs for planning and control.

COST ACCOUNTING FULFILLING MANAGEMENT'S NEEDS FOR PLANNING AND CONTROL INFORMATION

While financial accounting with its annual reports relates to the overall progress of the enterprise, cost accounting must concern itself with the details of the progress and the contributive efforts and effect of the enterprise's divisions, subdivisions, departments, and manufacturing/marketing units and centers. The details are generally attuned to a short-run point of view with its related categories and classifications of costs described in the next chapter.

PLANNING AND CONTROL MODELS

The Budget—A Planning and Control Model. Conventional accounting models — namely, the balance sheet and the income statement — used to evaluate the past, are also useful in planning the future of the enterprise.

As explained in the budget chapters, the planning process is best started by an examination of the past, particularly with regard to trends and directions, and then forecasting the future course by projecting and pre-determining costs and revenues, profits and rates of return based on numerous alternatives. The projected data as well as the process of setting long- and short-term goals for the subdivisions of the enterprise allow management to test the feasibility and degree of possible success of the forecast outcome of the operations. The budget is not only the widely used instrument for management planning but is also the fundamental accounting model for management control. The development of the budget requires the participation of many individuals within a company who are made responsible for the control of their planned costs. This phase of cost planning is expressed as "responsibility accounting," details of which are reserved for Chapter 11. Since plans are based primarily on forecasts of future conditions, it is necessary to consider costs as they most likely will be at such future times. For planning purposes, costs must be considered in terms of their relationship to volume as well as in terms of future prices, plant capacities, and labor efficiencies.

Standard Costs for Planning and Control. The ever-increasing use of standard costs provides a necessary measure of what costs should be. These standard costs permit an early preparation and presentation of financial statements to executive management, highlighting deviations from the planned goals. Financial statements in which actual year-end results are compared with the planned or budgeted figures based on standard costs bring to management not only the information regarding the profits already made, but also information as to what happened to the profits that should have been made. Standard costs should ideally be made an integral part of the budget, not only in its preparation but also in its use as a control device.

Break-Even Analysis — A Check on Planning. Cost accounting can assist management levels in planning and control duties by providing information via analytical tools that express more vividly and forcefully the multidimensional aspects of managerial problems. The return-on-capital-employed ratio has been illustrated in connection with the analysis of the financial statements. Break-even analysis offers another method that permits management to judge the overall plan on a very pragmatic and convenient basis. To calculate the break-even point, it is first necessary to observe the behavior of costs as to their fixed or variable nature. For the present it suffices to say that direct materials and direct labor are fundamentally considered variable costs. Factory overhead as well as marketing and administrative expenses contain elements of fixed and variable costs. These costs must be analyzed to establish a clear-cut division between fixed and variable segments. Detailed procedures and mathematical and statistical methods to establish this cost variability are described in Chapter 18.

The break-even point can be computed by the following formula:

$$\text{Break-Even Sales Volume in Dollars} = \frac{\text{Fixed Costs}}{1 - \dfrac{\text{Variable Costs}}{\text{Sales}}}$$

Other variations used to compute the break-even point are discussed in Chapter 24. Assume, for the sake of illustration, that the fixed and variable operating costs of The Seabright Manufacturing Company were established by statistical methods as follows:

Variable costs...	$19,898,750
Fixed costs...	2,500,000
Sales dollar volume....................................	24,750,000

The break-even sales dollar volume would then be $12,755,102, determined by this method:

$$\frac{\$2,500,000 \text{ Fixed Costs}}{1 - \dfrac{\$19,898,750 \text{ Variable Costs}}{\$24,750,000 \text{ Sales Volume}}} = \frac{\$2,500,000}{1 - .804} = \frac{\$2,500,000}{.196} = \underline{\$12,755,102}$$

The break-even sales dollar volume indicates the amount of sales needed to break even; i.e., to make neither a profit nor a loss. The result can be checked by making this statement:

Break-even sales volume.................................	$12,755,102
Variable costs (80.4% of break-even sales volume)...........	10,255,102
Contribution margin to cover fixed costs and profit..........	$ 2,500,000
Fixed costs...	2,500,000
Profit or (loss).......................................	$ 0

The answers to break-even calculations suggest to management the level of operations at which it is profitable to operate. The above illustration indicates that a level above $12,755,102 sales is needed if the company is to make a profit. Expressed in terms of units, the break-even point would be approximately 2,319,109 units ($12,755,102 ÷ $5.50, the unit sales price according to the income statement).

COST-AND-PROFIT ANALYSIS

Break-even techniques provide but one example of the ever-widening application of cost-and-profit analysis and an understanding of the behavior of costs in the use of making rational decisions. Decisions involving cost-profit-price-volume levels offer still another example of meaningful analysis. The multiplicity of causes and effects of these four factors is dramatically emphasized with the aid evolving from electronic computers that quickly and economically collect and process data from a variety of sources for a variety of end-products. These mechanical influences together with inventory models to project future materials requirements based on orderly planning and control procedures, the use of time-adjusted cash flow projections for capital expenditures, and the technique of linear programming for profit maximization or cost minimization are examples of an ever-growing number of decision-aiding models that have become part and parcel of the information system available to management for the execution of its planning and control responsibilities.

DISCUSSION QUESTIONS

1. Discuss the functions of the cost department.
2. Numerous nonaccounting departments require cost data and must also feed basic data to the cost department. Discuss.
3. What are the requirements of a good information system?
4. The cost of goods sold section of the income statement is divided into five distinct parts. Enumerate.
5. Distinguish between actual and applied factory overhead.
6. State some ratios that assist outsiders with the evaluation of the company's annual results.
7. Give the formula to calculate the break-even point in dollars.
8. An understatement of work in process inventory at the end of a period will (a) understate cost of goods manufactured in that period; (b) overstate current assets; (c) overstate gross profit from sales in that period; (d) understate net income for that period. Which of the above is correct?

    (AICPA adapted)

9. If the work in process inventory has increased during the period, (a) cost of goods sold will be greater than cost of goods manufactured; (b) cost of goods manufactured will be greater than cost of goods sold; (c) manufacturing costs for the period will be greater than cost of goods manufactured; or (d) manufacturing costs for the period will be less than cost of goods manufactured. Which of the above is correct?

    (AICPA adapted)

10. The gross profit of the Garrard Company for 19— is $56,000; the cost of goods manufactured is $300,000; the beginning inventories of work in process and finished goods are $18,000 and $25,000, respectively; and the ending inventories of work in process and finished goods are $28,000 and $30,000, respectively. Determine the company's sales for 19—.

    (AICPA adapted)

11. A corporation's annual financial statements and reports were criticized because it was claimed that the income statement does not by any means give a clear picture of annual earning power, and the balance sheet does not disclose the true value of the fixed assets. Considering the criticism made, offer an explanation of the nature and purpose of the income statement and of the balance sheet, together with comments on their limitations.

(AICPA adapted)

12. The president of the New Haven Products Co., Inc. requests your advice with respect to the following situation:

The company's chief accountant has been telling the president each year that "the business has just about been breaking even." This statement has been puzzling to the president because inventories, receivables, and payables have not varied much since the company was organized over ten years ago. In fact, cash has been increasing constantly. The president thinks that the business has been making money and that the chief accountant is wrong. Furthermore, no sale of assets, no refinancing of indebtedness, nor any change in the corporate structure, such as a sale of stock, has taken place in these years.

Required: (1) An explanation to the president for the continued increase in cash.

(2) Examples of transactions that illustrate the explanation given in (1).

(3) A recommendation for any additional financial statements for the use of the president.

(AICPA adapted)

EXERCISES

1. **Income Statement.** Kingsley Inc. submits the following data for September:

Direct labor cost, $30,000.
Cost of goods sold, $111,000.
Factory overhead is applied at the rate of 150% of direct labor cost.

Inventory accounts showed these opening and closing balances:

	Sept. 1	Sept. 30
Raw materials	$ 7,000	$ 7,400
Work in process	9,600	13,000
Finished goods	15,000	17,500

Other data:

Marketing expenses	$ 14,100
General and administrative expenses	22,900
Sales for the month	182,000

Required: An income statement with schedule showing cost of goods manufactured and sold.

2. **Income Statement; Profit Percentage.** The Cherokee Manufacturing Company submits the following information on December 31, 19—:

Sales for the year: $314,000

Inventories at the beginning of the year:
    Work in process: $4,600
    Finished goods: $5,900

Purchases of materials for the year: $140,000

Materials inventory:
    Beginning of the year: $3,800
    End of the year: $4,300

Direct labor: $67,350

Factory overhead: one half of the labor cost

Inventories at the end of the year:
    Work in process: $6,200
    Finished goods: $9,270

Other expenses for the year:
    Marketing expenses: $23,115
    Administrative expenses: $17,650

Required: (1) An income statement for the year ended December 31, 19—.
(2) The percentage of net income to sales, before income taxes.

3. Statement of Cost of Goods Sold. The accountant of the Sonnenberg Corporation has submitted the following summary to the executive management:

Inventories at September 1,19—:

Raw materials	$36,000	
Work in process	15,000	
Fuel	3,400	
Factory repair parts	2,600	
Finished goods	12,000	$ 69,000

Raw materials purchases	$58,000	
Fuel purchases	5,200	
Direct labor	83,100	
Miscellaneous factory overhead	2,300	
Repairs to factory (including purchase of parts)	4,200	
Depreciation of plant	2,700	
Superintendence	2,200	
Transportation out	1,100	
Purchases discounts lost	800	
Indirect factory labor	2,000	161,600

Total costs		$230,600

Inventories at September 30, 19—:

Raw materials	$40,000	
Work in process	12,000	
Fuel	2,000	
Factory repair parts	2,800	
Finished goods	14,000	70,800

Total		$159,800

Required: The management returns the summary with the request for a statement showing cost of goods sold in proper form.

4. Statement of Cost of Goods Sold. The following data relate to the Shirley Company:

	Inventories	
	Ending	*Beginning*
Finished goods.....................................	$95,000	$110,000
Work in process....................................	80,000	70,000
Direct materials....................................	95,000	90,000

Costs incurred during the period:

Costs of goods available for sale............................	$684,000
Total manufacturing costs...................................	584,000
Factory overhead...	167,000
Direct materials used.......................................	193,000

Required: Statement of cost of goods sold, including all beginning and ending inventories.

(AICPA adapted)

5. Cost of Goods Sold Statement; Unit Cost. The records of the Rein Corporation show the following information as of March 31, 19B:

Raw materials used...	$440,000
Direct factory labor..	290,000
Indirect factory labor.......................................	46,000
Light and power..	4,260
Depreciation..	4,700
Repairs to machinery.......................................	5,800
Miscellaneous factory overhead..............................	29,000
Work in process inventory, April 1, 19A......................	41,200
Finished goods inventory, April 1, 19A.......................	34,300
Work in process inventory, March 31, 19B.....................	42,500
Finished goods inventory, March 31, 19B.....................	31,500

During the year 18,000 units were completed.

Required: (1) A cost of goods sold statement for the year ended March 31, 19B.

(2) The unit cost of goods manufactured.

(3) The company applies factory overhead on the basis of 30% of direct factory labor cost. Determine the amount of over- or underapplied factory overhead.

6. Income Statement; Cost and Profit Ratios. The records of the Algarve Refrigerator Company show the following information for the three months ended March 31, 19—:

Materials purchased.......................................	$1,946,700

Inventories, January 1, 19—:

Materials...	268,000
Finished goods (100 refrigerators).........................	43,000
Direct labor...	2,125,800
Factory overhead (40% variable).............................	764,000
Marketing expenses (all fixed)................................	516,000
General and administrative expenses (all fixed).................	461,000
Sales (12,400 refrigerators).....................................	6,634,000

Inventories, March 31, 19—:

Materials.......................................   167,000
Finished goods (200 refrigerators), costed at $395 each.
No unfinished work on hand.

Required: (1) An income statement for the period.
(2) The number of units manufactured.
(3) The unit cost of refrigerators manufactured.
(4) The gross profit per unit sold.
(5) The net income per unit sold.
(6) The ratio of gross profit to sales.
(7) The net income to sales percentage.
(8) The break-even point in sales dollars.

7. Unit Cost; Inventory Valuation; Cost of Goods Sold. The cost department of the Swartz Corporation made the following data and costs available for the year 19—:

Inventories:	*Jan. 1*	*Dec. 31*		*Dec. 31*
Raw materials.....	$34,200	$49,300	Raw materials purchased........	$364,000
Work in process....	81,500	42,350	Direct labor...................	162,500
Finished goods.....	48,600	?	Indirect labor.................	83,400
Depreciation —			Freight-in.....................	8,600
factory equipment....		21,350	Miscellaneous factory overhead..	47,900
Interest earned........		6,300	Purchases discounts	5,200

Finished goods inventory: January 1: 300 units; December 31: 420 units, all from current year's production.

Sold during 19—: 3,880 units at $220 per unit.

Required: (1) The unit cost of the finished goods inventory, December 31.
(2) The total value of the finished goods inventory, December 31.
(3) The cost of goods sold.
(4) The gross profit total and the gross profit per unit.

8. Income Statement. In an accounting conference, discussion turned to the possibility of preparing financial statements from a few key accounts together with financial or cost ratios.

The assistant controller of a participating firm provided the following data: before-tax income for the year, $1,200,000; before-tax income rate on sales, 10%; gross profit rate on sales, 40%; rate of marketing expenses to sales, 15%; 5% bonds payable represent 37.5% of the total liabilities of $2,000,000.

Required: An income statement for the year based on the above information.

9. Rate of Return on Capital Employed. During the past year a company had a net income after taxes of $40,000. Sales were $200,000, and total capital employed was $400,000.

Required: Rate of return on capital employed.

10. Operating Data Analysis. The 19B annual report of the Columbia Gas Company contains the following statistics regarding operating revenues:

	19A	19B	Increase (Decrease)
Average number of customers.........	27,000	26,000	(1,000)
Sales in 1,000 cubic feet (MCF).......	486,000	520,000	34,000
Revenue...........................	$1,215,000	$1,274,000	$59,000

Required: An analysis accounting for the effect of changes in (a) average number of customers, (b) average gas consumption per customer, and (c) average rate per thousand cubic feet (MCF) sold.

(AICPA adapted)

PROBLEMS

2-1. Statement of Cost of Goods Sold. The records of the Levitz Manufacturing Company for the six months ended June 30, 19B provided the following data:

Inventories	Dec. 31, 19A	June 30, 19B
Raw materials..........	$117,000	$ 41,600
Factory supplies........	320	560
Work in process........	30,400	51,380
Finished goods.........	113,500	121,300

Other Data:

Direct labor....................	$101,000	Depreciation — machinery........	$ 3,800
Indirect labor.................	6,900	Depreciation — factory building...	1,100
Power and light...............	3,200	Tool expenses...................	1,645
Heat.........................	1,750	Factory supplies purchased........	3,100
Fire insurance.................	600	Raw materials purchased.........	314,000
Superintendence...............	11,200	Compensation insurance.........	1,900

Required: A statement of cost of goods manufactured and sold for the six months with a separate schedule for factory overhead and a calculation of the over- or underapplied factory overhead. The company applies factory overhead based on 35% of direct labor cost.

2-2. Income Statement. The Della Valla Company began business on April 1 and produced by the end of the month of June 40,000 units of its single product, called Ken-Del. The product requires three basic raw materials, A, B, and C, which were purchased during the first three months at the following prices and quantities:

	Purchase Price	Quantities Purchased	Quantities on Hand, June 30
Material A	$.35	35,000	4,000
Material B	.30	10,000	6,000
Material C	.60	8,000	5,000

Factory wages and other salaries paid and accrued were:

	Paid	Accrued
Direct labor...	$18,000	$750
Indirect labor...	2,625	175
Supervision...	3,000	–0–
Marketing and administrative salaries	18,200	1,800

Overhead consisted of:

	Factory Overhead	Marketing and Adm. Expenses
Supplies......................................	$1,400	$ 800
Repairs and maintenance.......................	900	400
Depreciation.................................	1,000	350
Utilities.....................................	1,740	310
Insurance....................................	560	280
Delivery expenses.............................	–0–	2,460

At the end of the three months, finished goods inventories contained 1,500 units. 38,500 units were sold at an average sales price of $2.25 per unit.

Required: (1) An income statement.
(2) Ratio of gross profit to sales.
(3) Net income as a percentage of sales.

2-3. Income Statement. McCafferty Products, Inc. produces a household appliance that sells for $90. The basic patent is held by the inventor who is paid a royalty of $5 on each unit sold. The royalty is considered a marketing expense.

The data taken from the books and other records of the company on December 31, 19— are shown below:

	Jan. 1	Dec. 31		Dec. 31
Inventories:				
Raw materials.........	$3,420	$ 7,130	Rent	$ 5,000
Work in process........	8,159	4,002	Sales salaries...................	28,000
Finished goods.........	4,584	7,518	Royalties paid..................	21,500
Sales........................		387,000	Freight-out.....................	1,860
Raw materials purchased........		90,563	Miscellaneous marketing expenses.	11,380
Freight-in......................		477	Office salaries..................	24,790
Direct labor....................		62,522	Bad debts expense...............	280
Indirect labor..................		5,026	Miscell. administrative expenses..	8,700
Depreciation — factory equipment.		2,135	Interest earned	130
Miscellaneous factory overhead...		17,908	Purchases discounts.............	840

There were 120 finished units in the inventory of finished goods on January 1 and 179 in the inventory on December 31. All units held on January 1 were sold during the year. Rent is to be apportioned 80% to manufacturing, 10% to marketing, and 10% to administration.

Required: (1) An income statement for the year ended December 31, 19—, supported by a schedule of cost of goods sold.
(2) Figures to prove the cost of the inventory of finished goods on December 31, 19—.

2-4. Income Statement; Cost of Goods Sold Statement; Factory Overhead Analysis On October 1, 19—, the accountant of the Adelaide Manufacturing

Company, Inc. had prepared a trial balance from which these accounts were extracted:

	Debits	Credits
Materials and Supplies Inventory......................	$40,700	
Work in Process Inventory (1,200 units)................	4,070	
Finished Goods Inventory (2,800 units).................	9,800	
Buildings..	48,000	
Accumulated Depreciation — Buildings..................		$ 6,000
Machinery and Equipment............................	96,000	
Accumulated Depreciation — Machinery and Equipment..		37,500
Office Equipment....................................	3,200	
Accumulated Depreciation—Office Equipment		1,000
Accrued Payroll.....................................		650

For the month of October, the following transactions and other data have been made available:

Purchased materials and supplies................................	$ 24,800
Paid factory overhead...	20,100
Paid marketing expenses.......................................	25,050
Paid administrative expenses...................................	19,700

Requisitions for:
Direct materials...	29,800
Indirect materials..	3,950

Depreciation:
Building, 5% (75% to manufacturing, 15% to
               marketing, and 10% to admin-
               istrative expenses)
Machinery and equipment, 10%
Office equipment, 15% (40% to marketing and
               60% to administrative expenses)

Sales on account (20,700 units).................................	144,900
Sales returns and allowances...................................	1,300

Cash payments for:
Accounts payable..	75,000
Payroll...	21,800

Distribution of payroll earned:
Direct labor..	18,600
Indirect labor...	4,400

Cash collected from customers..................................	116,900
Factory overhead applied......................................	27,450

20,400 units are transferred to finished goods.
Cost of goods sold figure is calculated on the fifo basis.
1,200 units are in work in process inventory on October 31, 19—.

Required: (1) The cost of goods sold section of the income statement in detail. Any over- or underabsorbed factory overhead is deferred until the end of the fiscal period.

(2) The income statement for the month of October.

(3) The amount of over- or underapplied factory overhead.

2-5. Profit Planning via Income Statement. The controller of the Wellington Corporation presented the following income statement for the year ending June 30, 19A to the board of directors:

Sales..		$12,000,000
Cost of goods sold:		
Direct materials........................	$3,800,000	
Direct labor.............................	2,900,000	
Factory overhead........................	2,450,000	9,150,000
Gross profit....................................		$ 2,850,000
Commercial expenses:		
Marketing expenses......................	$1,350,000	
Administrative expenses..................	1,000,000	2,350,000
Net income.....................................		$ 500,000

The board discussed the ratio of net income to sales and decided that for the year 19B an increase of at least 25% of the present profit was desirable. While the sales volume is expected to increase about 20%, all costs and expenses point to considerable advances in costs; e.g., direct materials up 8%; direct labor up 10%; factory overhead up 3%; marketing expenses up 4%; and administrative expenses up 2%. The 3% increase of factory overhead applies to the variable overhead only. Fixed factory overhead is considered to remain at the present level of $1,250,000. Volume will not cause an increase in marketing and administrative expenses. Ignore income tax.

Required: (1) A forecast income statement for the year 19B incorporating all cost increases as well as management's goal for a higher net income.

(2) How much will the percentage of net income to sales change from the previous year?

2-6. Price Determination. The Fortunato Manufacturing Company produces a single product which is sold to fabricators of electronic equipment. Since the company is relatively small, it does not utilize involved cost accounting techniques in determining inventory values. A simplified job order system is used with direct materials and direct labor being identified with specific lots of product. Factory overhead rates are not used; the company waits until the end of the accounting period for which statements are required and then assigns overhead to inventory and to cost of goods sold on a unit of production basis.

During 19— the company produced its regular year's output by December 15 at which time it planned to shut down for the last two weeks of the year, re-opening after the new year. As of December 15, the following income statement which included all 19— costs was prepared:

FORTUNATO MANUFACTURING COMPANY

INCOME STATEMENT
DECEMBER 31, 19—

Sales (20,000 units)...........................		$100,000
Cost of goods sold:		
Inventory, January 1, 19—..............	—0—	
Production costs for an output of 22,000 units:		
Direct materials.......................	$13,500	
Direct labor..........................	30,500	
Factory overhead......................	35,200	
Total.................................	$79,200	
Inventory, December 31, 19— (2,000 units).........	8,220	70,980
Gross profit on sales...........................		$ 29,020
Marketing and administrative expenses (all fixed)...............		10,000
Net income for the period (before income taxes)................		$ 19,020

On December 18, 19—, a department of the United States government placed an order with the company for 4,000 units of product. The company accepted the order which stipulated that delivery was to be made by December 31, 19—, and that the company should be permitted to earn a gross profit on the order calculated as 20% of selling price. The company called back its production personnel and completed 2,000 units by the end of the year which, with its inventory, made up the total of the government's order. During this period it expended additional costs as follows: direct materials, $1,300; direct labor, $2,800; and factory overhead, $800.

In accordance with the terms of the order, the government was billed at a price of $4.85 per unit. The government auditor who reviewed the company's invoice complained that at this price the company would earn a profit calculated on sales of 32.4% and that the unit sales price should have been $4.10 in order to comply with the terms of the order.

Required: (1) Calculations to show (a) how the company arrived at its price of $4.85 and (b) how the government reached a price of $4.10.

(2) A critical evaluation of the two pricing methods. Could acceptable accounting procedures be utilized to arrive at a third price for the order? Explain this third method and indicate which of the three methods is preferable in this instance.

2-7. Ratio and Break-Even Analyses. The condensed financial statements of the Tournado Watch Company for the year ended December 31, 19—, appeared as:

TOURNADO WATCH COMPANY

CONDENSED BALANCE SHEET AS OF DECEMBER 31, 19—

Assets		*Liabilities and Capital*	
Cash......................	$ 750,000	Accounts and notes payable.	$1,494,000
Receivables...............	3,508,000	Accruals payable..........	368,000
Inventories...............	2,217,000	Capital stock.............	4,387,000
Plant and equipment.......	1,353,000	Retained earnings.........	1,579,000
	$7,828,000		$7,828,000

CONDENSED INCOME STATEMENT FOR THE YEAR 19—

Sales....................................	$6,491,000
Cost of goods sold......................	4,676,000
Gross profit............................	$1,815,000
Marketing and administrative expenses......	804,000
Net operating income before income taxes...	$1,011,000

Required: (1) The current ratio.
(2) The acid-test ratio.
(3) The net operating income as a percentage of sales.
(4) The rate of return on capital employed.

(5) The break-even point in dollars if 75% of the cost of goods sold figure consists of variable costs, and 80% of the marketing and administrative expenses consists of fixed costs.

2-8. Statement of Cost of Goods Sold; Income Statement; Balance Sheet; Ratio Analysis. On September 30, 19B the trial balance of The Kissling Company appeared as follows:

THE KISSLING COMPANY

TRIAL BALANCE
SEPTEMBER 30, 19B

Cash in Banks and on Hand	$ 23,400	
Notes Receivable	2,180	
Accounts Receivable	44,400	
Raw Materials Inventory, October 1, 19A	38,200	
Work in Process Inventory, October 1, 19A	44,500	
Finished Goods Inventory, October 1, 19A	60,000	
Prepaid Expenses	3,550	
Land	15,000	
Buildings	125,000	
Accumulated Depreciation — Buildings		$ 15,000
Machinery	165,000	
Accumulated Depreciation — Machinery		66,000
Office Furniture and Fixtures	2,600	
Accumulated Depreciation — Office Furniture and Fixtures		500
Notes Payable		50,000
Accounts Payable		40,000
Accrued Wages Payable		5,000
Accrued Interest on Mortgage		500
Mortgage on Plant		75,000
Capital Stock		100,000
Earnings Retained in Business		130,830
Sales		360,000
Sales Allowances	6,000	
Raw Materials Purchased	50,000	
Direct Labor	100,000	
Patterns and Drawings Expenses	3,500	
Miscellaneous Factory Overhead	90,000	
Freight and Postage on Sales	1,000	
Miscellaneous Marketing Expenses	35,000	
Miscellaneous Administrative Expenses	25,000	
Interest Earned		2,500
Interest Paid	6,000	
Discounts on Sales	5,000	
Total	$845,330	$845,330

The following information is also available:

Inventories on September 30, 19B:
  Raw materials, $38,000
  Work in process, $48,000
  Finished goods, $82,000

Allowances for depreciation:
  3% on buildings (80% to factory, 20% to administration)
  10% on machinery (100% to factory)
  5% on office furniture and fixtures (100% to administration)

Ignore income tax.

Required: (1) A cost of goods sold statement for the year ended September 30, 19B:

(2) An income statement for the year ended September 30, 19B.

(3) A balance sheet as of September 30, 19B.

(4) The following ratios and percentages:

    (a) Current ratio.

    (b) Acid-test ratio.

    (c) Net income to net sales percentage.

    (d) Ratio of gross profit to net sales.

    (e) Rate of return on capital employed.

2-9. Balance Sheet; Income Statement. On December 31, 19A the Atlantic Seaboard Company with outstanding capital stock of $30,000 had the following assets and liabilities:

Cash..	$ 5,000
Accounts Receivable...	10,000
Materials..	4,000
Work in Process...	2,000
Finished Goods..	6,000
Prepaid Expenses..	500
Fixed Assets (net)..	30,000
Current Liabilities..	17,500

During the year 19B the retained earnings account increased 50% as a result of the year's business. No dividends were paid during the year. Balances of accounts receivable, prepaid expenses, current liabilities, and capital stock were the same on December 31, 19B as they had been on December 31, 19A. Inventories were reduced by exactly 50%, except for the finished goods inventory which was reduced by $33\frac{1}{3}\%$. Fixed assets (net) were reduced by depreciation of $4,000, charged $\frac{3}{4}$ to factory overhead and $\frac{1}{4}$ to administrative expenses. Sales of $60,000 were made on account of finished goods costing $38,000. Direct labor cost was $9,000. Factory overhead was applied at a rate of 100% of direct labor cost, leaving $2,000 unapplied that was closed into the cost of goods sold account. Total marketing and administrative expenses amounted to 10% and 15%, respectively, of the gross sales.

Required: (1) A balance sheet as of December 31, 19B.

(2) An income statement for the year 19B with details of the cost of goods manufactured and sold.

(AICPA adapted)

CHAPTER 3

CONCEPTS, USES, AND CLASSIFICATIONS OF COSTS

Cost accounting measures cost in accordance with the plans and needs of management. Costs must be based on relevant facts, competently observed and significantly measured to enable management to make valid decisions. A diagnosis of this requirement reveals that there is a wide diversity in the use of terms and concepts employed in cost computations and that this diversity is the result of a variety of causes. Costs may have to be computed under different conditions, for different purposes, by different people. Cost accounting is a means to an end, not an end in itself.

THE CONCEPT "COST"

Accountants, economists, engineers, and others facing cost problems have developed cost concepts and cost terminology according to their needs. Basically, a concept should be stated in the terms in which it has become generally familiar. It is not easy to define or explain the term "cost," leaving no doubt concerning its meaning. The Committee on Cost Concepts and Standards of the American Accounting Association wrote: "Cost is a foregoing, measured in monetary terms, incurred or potentially to be incurred to achieve a specific objective."[1] In "A Tentative

[1]Report of the Committee on Cost Concepts and Standards, *The Accounting Review*, Vol. XXVII, No. 2, p. 176.

Set of Broad Accounting Principles for Business Enterprises," cost is defined as "an exchange price, a foregoing, a sacrifice made to secure benefit. In financial accounting, the foregoing or sacrifice at date of acquisition is represented by a current or future diminution in cash or other assets."[2]

AICPA Accounting Research Study No. 3 considers expense to be:

> ... the decrease in net assets as a result of the use of economic services in the creation of revenues or of the imposition of taxes by governmental units. Expense is measured by the amount of the decrease in assets or the increase in liabilities related to the production and delivery of goods and the rendering of services. ... In its broadest sense *expense* includes all expired costs which are deductible from revenues. In income statements, distinctions are often made between various types of expired costs by captions or titles including such terms as cost, expense, or loss; e.g., cost of goods or services sold, operating expenses, marketing and administrative expenses, and loss on sale of property.[3]

Frequently the term "cost" is used synonymously with the term "expense." Yet the term "cost" is used for both assets and expenses. Cost means, at one time, the amount paid for something; at another time, the fair market value of the item given in exchange for the item received. The term "expense" refers to the sacrifice, the renouncing aspect of the revenue transaction. Expenses are the measured outflow of goods and services that are matched with revenue to determine income.

When the term "cost" is used specifically, it should be modified with reference to the object costed by such descriptions as direct, prime, conversion, indirect, fixed, variable, controllable, product, period, joint, estimated, standard, future, replacement, opportunity, imputed, sunk, differential, and out-of-pocket. Each modification implies a certain attribute which is important in computing and measuring the cost which is to serve the management levels in achieving the basic objectives of planning and control.

These modifications or cost attributes are, as the text will show, applicable to many objectives. A definition of each will not be offered at this point but will be found at the appropriate place within the textbook. Many of them are used in connection with the accumulation of cost data necessary for the assignment of costs to inventories and the preparation of general financial statements and the planning and control of costs by the various levels of management. In most cases they find their way into the books and records and as such constitute typical cost attributes. However, for planning, analytical, and decision-making purposes, the accountant often must abandon his "book" costs and deal with future, imputed, differential, or opportunity costs which must be based on other

---

[2]Robert T. Sprouse and Maurice Moonitz, *A Tentative Set of Broad Accounting Principles for Business Enterprises, AICPA Accounting Research Study No. 3* (New York: American Institute of Certified Public Accountants, 1962), p. 25.
[3]*Ibid.*, p. 49.

than the recorded past costs. It is a fundamental axiom that a cost must be understood in its relationship to the aims or purposes which it is to serve. A request for cost data must be accompanied by a description of the situation in which the data are to be used, for the same cost data cannot serve all purposes equally well.

USES OF COST DATA

The collection, presentation, and analysis of cost data should serve the following essential uses or aims:

1. Planning profit by means of budgets
2. Controlling costs via responsibility accounting
3. Measuring annual or periodic profit, including inventory costing
4. Assisting in establishing selling prices and a pricing policy
5. Furnishing relevant cost data for analytical processes for decision making

Planning Profit by Means of Budgets. The planning phase deals with the future — the next year or years — of the company. Cost accounting provides or budgets the contemplated materials costs, wages and salaries, and other costs of producing and marketing the products. Management is concerned with the ultimate profit arising from these costs and planned revenues or sales. Budgeting is the forecast of the effects on profits of varying volumes of activity. Budgeted materials costs and quantities and labor costs and predetermined quantities of time required to manufacture each product are basic for these cost elements. These costs plus all factory overhead and nonmanufacturing costs that fluctuate with activity must be determined first in order to establish the profit base for budgeted sales. Some operating costs vary directly in relationship to volume; other costs and expense items are either wholly or partially fixed in character. The final budget should represent a conservative operating forecast. If the contemplated volume seems attainable and management decides to operate on such a cost-volume-profit relationship, it becomes imperative for all levels of management to strive to control their costs accordingly.

Controlling Costs via Responsibility Accounting. To control costs, these fundamentals should be observed: (a) fixing responsibility for control, (b) limiting the individual's control effort to his controllable costs, and (c) reporting the performance of the individual.

Fixing responsibility for the control of costs requires the establishment of definite lines of authority. The organization chart presents the organizational structure and, following these lines of authority, allows the assignment of cost control responsibility to specific individuals. These individuals should also have had a hand in determining the planned or budgeted costs under their control. Not only costs but also sales revenue and profits are made the responsibility of certain executives. Cost and revenue responsibility becomes profit responsibility.

Limiting the individual's control effort to his controllable costs is a necessary aspect of responsibility accounting. Any report should specifically identify the manager's controllable costs. Of course, each cost should be someone's responsibility. This responsibility phase often becomes lost in a maze of cost classifications as shown later in the chapter.

The reporting and measuring phase has already been touched upon. It is important that each individual's budget be considered as an integral part of the overall company budget. The greater each supervisor's effort and succcess in controlling the costs for which he is responsible, the greater the chance for the entire company to reach the planned profit goal.

The control of costs requires a basis for comparison. Budgeted costs constitute one basic foundation for comparison; standards or predetermined costs and expenses provide the cornerstone for cost control procedures. A comparison of actual or experienced costs and expenses with these standards reveals an out-of-line performance. These exceptions form the basis for an investigation into the reasons, resulting hopefully in remedy and correction.

Measuring Annual or Periodic Profit, Including Inventory Costing.   The measuring of an annual or periodic profit for the entire enterprise involves the matching of expired costs with revenues on some consistent basis. This matching process requires distinguishing between short-run and long-run costs. The longer the period, the greater the accuracy of the matching process. A company's annual reports reflect the results of separating the costs applicable to the units sold from the costs applicable to the units remaining in inventories. This separation procedure has always been a distinctive feature of cost accounting. The costs reported thereby are historical or past costs.

Short-run, interim, or periodic reports are useful for purposes of internal control and for the solution of particular managerial problems. In such cases a product's variable costs are assigned first to the units manufactured and are then matched with the units sold. The fixed costs, however, require an arbitrary allocation to the units and consequently lead to the possibility of three alternative matching processes:[4]

> (a) To match fixed (capacity) costs assigned to each period in total with revenues of that period (direct costing).

---

[4]Walter B. McFarland, *Concepts for Management Accounting* (New York: National Association of Accountants, 1966), p. 134.

(b) To match manufacturing fixed (capacity) costs on a product unit basis and to match all other fixed costs in total each period (absorption costing).

(c) To match *all* fixed costs, manufacturing as well as nonmanufacturing, on a long-run sales unit basis.

Over a long enough period these methods give the same result but yield a different profit for individual short periods, when cost incurring activities are out of phase with revenues. Because all methods are arbitrary to some extent, no one method gives consistently useful results under all conditions. Different circumstances may call for different methods.[5]

Assisting in Establishing Selling Prices and a Pricing Policy. The establishment of a profitable sales price workable over a period of time requires the combined knowledge of costs and their volume. In the planning phase, a knowledge of future costs and allowances for fluctuating production and sales might permit management to agree on a pricing policy that assures not only the recovery of all costs but also the securing of a profit even under adverse conditions. Supply and demand are still considered the cornerstones for pricing. However, costs and their proper application to the company's pricing efforts must never be forgotten.

Furnishing Relevant Cost Data for Analytical Processes for Decision Making. Managerial planning as evidenced by long-range budgeting involves business strategies covering one or more years. To implement long-range strategy, management must make tactical changes and decisions involving a choice of alternative courses of action. Different costs and different revenues may have to be determined and presented by the accountant. Changes in production methods, making or buying a component part, replacing equipment, substituting materials, accepting or rejecting a price or an order — each situation calls for new expected actual costs and a new set of revenues related to these specific situations.

COST DATA: IMPORTANCE OF PAST, PRESENT, FUTURE

Measuring annual or periodic profit, including inventory costing, pertains mainly to events of the *past*. Cost control relates to the *present*. Planning, pricing, and analyzing data for decision making are *future*-oriented. These time-frame-oriented views of cost data intertwine; e.g., (1) inferences may be drawn from the past as plans and decisions are made

---

[5] *Ibid.*, pp. 134–135.

about the future and (2) cost control should be designed to monitor the accomplishments of plans.

Ranking these time-frame categories as to their relative importance would certainly place the organization's future as most important, followed by what is presently occurring and, lastly, by what has happened in the past. This ranking does not mean that data about the past are unimportant nor that they should be neglected, because past data may aid in future decision making. Past performance must be reported to internal management as well as to external groups such as stockholders, creditors, the Internal Revenue Service, and the general public. The point is not that past performance is unimportant but rather that the cost accounting information system often does little more than account for the past without being adequately designed and utilized to focus on the present and future time-frames.

Optimum attention to the past, present, and future, at a reasonable cost, should be the primary objective of the cost data provided by the information system.

CLASSIFICATIONS OF COSTS

Cost classifications are needed for the development of cost data that are useful to management with regard to the five purposes or aims described on pages 43–45. Therefore, costs are classified:

1. By the nature of the item (a natural classification).
2. With respect to the accounting period to which they apply.
3. By their tendency to vary with volume or activity.
4. By their relation to the product.
5. By their relation to manufacturing departments.
6. For planning and control.
7. For analytical processes.

Natural Classification of Costs. The process of classifying costs and expenses can begin with a simple grouping of all manufacturing costs according to the three main elements of cost: materials, labor, and factory overhead. *Total cost* may be considered as all costs or deductions from sales revenue before federal income tax. In a manufacturing concern, total *operating* cost is divided into two groups: (1) manufacturing cost and (2) commercial expenses.

Manufacturing cost, often named "production cost" or "factory cost," is the sum of the cost of direct materials, direct labor, and factory overhead. During the accounting period, that part of manufacturing cost which represents work completed is transferred to Finished Goods Inventory, while incomplete work remains in Work in Process.

Commercial expenses also fall into two large classifications: (1) marketing (or distribution or selling) expenses and (2) administrative (general and administrative) expenses. *Marketing expenses* begin at the point where the factory costs end; that is, when manufacturing has been completed and the product is in salable condition. Marketing expenses cover the expenses of making sales and delivering products. *Administrative expenses* include expenses incurred in the direction, control, and administration of the organization. Some of these items, such as executive salaries, are often allocated to manufacturing and marketing and included in factory and marketing cost. The sum of the expired factory cost and commercial expenses is the "cost to make and sell."

This basic classification of costs must be expanded into numerous subclasses, groups, or divisions. The chart below illustrates the results of dividing further the total operating cost and individual cost elements.

ANALYSIS OF TOTAL OPERATING COST

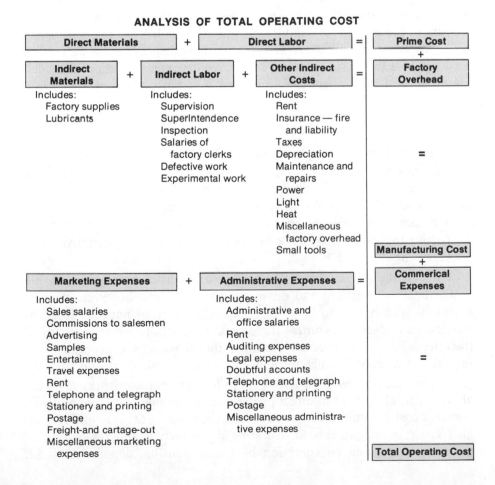

Costs with Respect to the Accounting Period to Which They Apply.
Expenditures can be divided into two broad classes: (1) capital expenditures and (2) revenue expenditures. A *capital expenditure* is intended to benefit future periods and is classified as an asset; a *revenue expenditure* benefits the current period and is termed an expense. An expenditure classified originally as an asset will flow into the expense stream when the asset is either consumed or charged off.

The distinction between capital and revenue expenditures is essential to the proper matching of costs and revenue and to the accurate measurement of periodic income. While the distinction between a capital or revenue expenditure is generally observed, a precise interpretation and application is not always feasible or practical. The initial classification depends in many cases upon: (1) the attitude and action taken by the management toward these expenditures and (2) the character of the company's operations. Management's decision on classification is often influenced by the ease and accuracy with which costs may be allocated among products, departments, territories, or any other desirable division. The amount of the expenditure and the number of detailed records and underlying documents required are also factors that determine the distinction between these two basic classes of costs. Whatever classification is decided upon can and does affect the computed unit costs and reported profit figures of a fiscal period.

Costs in Their Tendency to Vary with Volume or Activity. Some costs vary directly in relation to changes in the volume of output (production), while others, as they are incurred in relation to time, remain more or less fixed in amount. Unless a cost system pays due regard to this distinction, costs accumulated and reported for planning the company's strategy or for costing individual products or services will not be of material value to management.

Direct materials and direct labor are generally listed among the variable costs. Factory overhead and nonmanufacturing costs, however, must be examined with regard to items of a variable *and* fixed nature. It is impossible to budget and control these costs successfully without regard to their tendency to be fixed or variable; the division is a necessary prerequisite to successful budgeting and intelligent cost planning and analysis.

In general, *variable costs* show the following characteristics: (1) variability of total amount in direct proportion to volume; (2) comparatively constant cost per unit in the face of changing volume; (3) easy and reasonably accurate assignments to operating departments; and (4) control of their incurrence and consumption by the responsible department head.

The following costs fall into this category:

VARIABLE FACTORY OVERHEAD

Supplies	Receiving costs
Fuel	Hauling within plant
Power	Royalties
Small tools	Factory traveling costs
Spoilage, salvage, and reclamation	Communication costs
expenses	Overtime premium

The characteristics of *fixed costs* are: (1) fixed amount within a relevant output range; (2) decrease of fixed cost per unit with increased output; (3) assignment to departments often made by arbitrary managerial decisions or cost allocation methods; and (4) control for incurrence in most cases rests with executive management rather than operating supervisors.

The following are examples of fixed costs:

FIXED FACTORY OVERHEAD

Salaries of production executives	Wages of watchmen, janitors, and
Depreciation	firemen
Taxes on real estate	Maintenance and repairs of buildings
Taxes on plant equipment	and grounds
Patent amortization	Insurance — property and liability
	Rent

Whether or not a cost is classified as fixed or variable may well be the result of management decision. For example, management may decide to (1) rent a truck at a rate per mile driven (a variable cost) or (2) buy a truck and depreciate it by the straight-line method of depreciation (a fixed cost).

Some factory overhead items are *semivariable* in nature, containing both fixed and variable elements. A semivariable expense is often characterized by a fixed dollar element below which it will not fall, at all relevant levels of output. The variable element, as defined above, changes at a constant amount per unit of output. Electricity cost, for example, may be used to furnish both lighting for the plant as well as power to operate the equipment. The electricity used for lighting tends to be a *fixed* cost because if the plant is in use, the building will be lighted regardless of the level of output. Conversely, electricity used to operate the equipment will *vary* depending on how much use is made of the equipment.

The following items generally contain both fixed and variable elements:

SEMIVARIABLE FACTORY OVERHEAD

Supervision	Maintenance and repairs of machinery
Inspection	and plant equipment
Payroll department services	Compensation insurance
Personnel department services	Health and accident insurance
Factory office services	Social security taxes
Materials and inventory services	Industrial relations and welfare expenses
Cost department services	Heat, light, and power

For practical purposes it is desirable to classify all manufacturing and nonmanufacturing costs as fixed and variable costs. Semivariable expenses must therefore be divided into their fixed and variable elements. Methods to accomplish this are discussed in Chapter 18.

Costs in Their Relation to the Product. The elements of manufacturing costs are direct materials, direct labor, and factory overhead. Direct materials and direct labor are combined into another classification called *prime cost*. Direct labor and factory overhead can be combined into a classification called *conversion cost*, representing the costs of converting direct materials into finished products.

Direct materials refers to all materials that form an integral part of the finished product and that can be included directly in calculating the cost of the product, such as the lumber to make furniture, the steel to make automobile bodies, and the crude oil to make gasoline. The ease and feasibility with which the materials items can be traced to the final product are major considerations in their designation as direct materials. Glue and tacks to build furniture undoubtedly form part of the finished product, but for costing purposes such items may be classified as indirect materials for expediency.

Direct labor is labor expended directly upon the materials comprising the finished product. The cost of wages paid to skilled or unskilled workers alike that can be assigned to the particular unit produced is termed "direct labor."

Factory overhead — also called manufacturing overhead, manufacturing expenses, or factory burden — may be defined as the cost of indirect materials, indirect labor, and all other manufacturing costs that cannot conveniently be charged directly to specific units, jobs, or products. Simply stated, factory overhead includes all manufacturing costs except direct materials and direct labor.

Indirect materials refers to materials needed for the completion of the product but whose consumption with regard to the product is either so small or so complex that it would be futile to treat it as a direct materials item. Glue, thread, nails, tacks, rivets, and other such items usually belong in this category. *Factory supplies*, a form of indirect materials, consist of items such as lubricating oils, grease, cleaning rags, and brushes needed to maintain the working area and machinery in workable and safe condition.

Indirect labor may be defined, in contrast to direct labor, as that labor expended which does not affect the construction or the composition of the finished product. The term includes the labor cost of foremen, shop clerks, general helpers, cleaners, and those employees engaged in maintenance work or other service work not directly related to physical production.

Costs in Their Relation to Manufacturing Departments. A factory is generally organized along departmental lines for production purposes. This factory departmentalization is the basis for the important classification and subsequent accumulation of costs by departments to achieve (1) cost budgeting with responsibility accounting and control and (2) a greater degree of reliable costing.

Producing and Service Departments. The departments of a factory generally fall into two categories: (1) producing departments and (2) service departments.

A *producing department* is one in which manual and machine operations are performed directly upon any part of the product manufactured. More specifically, producing departments are those whose costs may be charged to the product because they have contributed directly to its production, such as the machining, forming, upholstering, or assembling departments.

In many cases producing departments are further subdivided into cost centers. Where two or more different types of machines perform operations on a product within the same department, a breakdown into cost centers increases the accuracy of product costs. For example, in the manufacture of cotton yarn and cloth, the producing department "Carding" can be broken up into the cost centers: opening cotton bales, picking, carding, drawing, and slubbing.

A *service department* is one that is not directly engaged in production but renders a particular type of service for the benefit of other departments. In some instances the services furnished benefit other service departments as well as the producing departments. The cost incurred in the operation of service departments represents a part of the total factory overhead and must be absorbed in the cost of the product by means of the factory overhead rate. Some service departments common to many industrial concerns are receiving, inspection, storerooms, maintenance, timekeeping, payroll, cost accounting, budgeting, data processing, general office, cafeteria, and plant protection.

Departmentalization for Product Costing and Responsibility Accounting. The organization chart divides a business into departments, segments, or functions. Although the division is often made primarily for administrative purposes, departmentalization or segmentation is significant and important for (1) the costing of a product and (2) the control of costs by means of departmental budgets.

For product costing, the factory may be divided into departments; and departments may be further subdivided into cost centers. As a product passes through a department or cost center, it is charged with (1) direct materials, (2) direct labor, and (3) a share of factory overhead on the basis of a departmental factory overhead rate.

For cost control, budgets are established for departments and cost centers with the active participation of operating management in order to achieve a sense of commitment on the manager's part. Each manager should be made to feel that he is responsible for the control of those costs he helped to develop. The crux of the matter rests in the controllability. A departmental budget should clearly identify those costs about which the manager can make decisions. This identification of costs by areas of responsibility and therewith of their controllability depends on the time frame and the level in the organization; i.e., the degree of segmentation reported upon. All costs should be controllable at some level of management over some time frame; no cost can remain in a noncontrollable category. The comparison of actual costs with budget allowances at the end of a weekly, monthly, or annual reporting period permits evaluation and judgment regarding the efficiency of a department or cost center and measures the manager's success in controlling the expenses for which he accepted responsibility.

Direct and Indirect Departmental Charges. In connection with the charging of expenses to departments, it is important that the term "direct" as applied to factory overhead be clearly understood. In the preceding discussion of production costs, the terms "direct materials" and "direct labor" were introduced. The word "direct," in that discussion, referred to costs which were chargeable directly to the product produced and which, therefore, needed no further allocation.

Factory overhead, however, is considered indirect with regard to a product or job. As actual factory overhead expenses are incurred and charged to either a producing or a service department, the expense is referred to as a *direct* departmental charge if it is readily identifiable with the originating department. Expenses such as rent and depreciation of a building may be shared by several departments; they are described as *indirect* because they must be prorated to benefiting departments. The same notion of direct and indirect charges is equally applicable to nonmanufacturing activities and organizations.

Service department expenses are prorated to producing departments and/or service departments. These prorated costs are also termed "indirect departmental charges." When all service department expenses have been prorated to the producing departments, each producing department's overhead will consist of its own direct and indirect departmental expense and the prorated or apportioned charges from service departments to form the toal factory overhead for the department. This total actual cost is then compared with the amount charged to production on the basis of each producing department's predetermined factory overhead rate (see Chapter 10).

Departmentalization of a factory is of even greater importance in connection with budgeting and control of costs. Factory overhead is charged to the product on the basis of a predetermined departmental overhead rate based on budgeted or estimated costs and planned production. During the year it becomes quite necessary for all individuals to make every effort to keep costs at the predetermined budget level. Department heads are made responsible and accountable for the actual controllable costs incurred in their departments. Cost responsibility is assigned to operating management in accordance with the authority delegated to them. Keeping actual costs in line with budgeted cost aids in attaining the organization's profit objective.

Costs for Planning and Control. A company's cost information system provides the data required for the preparation and operation of a budget and for establishing standard costs.

Budgets. In many companies the predetermination or estimating of factory overhead constitutes the initial step toward a budget program. When all phases of a business — sales, engineering, manufacturing, marketing, and administration — have been coordinated into a well-thought-out budget program, the budget becomes the written expression of management's plan for the future. The budget program enlists all members of management in the task of creating a workable and acceptable plan of action, welds the plan into a homogeneous unit, communicates to all managerial levels differences between planned activity and actual performance, and points out unfavorable conditions which need corrective actions. No person intimately connected with the affairs of a company in which budgeting is used can be unaffected or disinterested. The budget will not only help promote coordination of people, clarification of policy, and crystallization of plans, but with successful use will create greater internal harmony and unanimity of purpose among managers and workers.

Standard Costs. Closely allied with the budget are standard costs. *Standard costs* are predetermined costs for direct materials, direct labor, and factory overhead. They are established by using information accumulated from past experience and data secured from research studies. The established standard costs for materials, labor, and factory overhead form the foundation for the budget. Since standard costs are an invaluable aid in the process of setting prices, it is essential to set these standard costs at realistic levels.

A standard states the cost under given conditions which are held constant in order to observe and measure fluctuations. The measurement of deviations from established standards or norms is accomplished with the aid of variance accounts. These deviation measurements arc similar to budget comparisons in that they compare actual with predetermined data. The deviation measurements and budget comparisons are also alike in that both relate to the idea of responsibility accounting. It should be noted, however, that standards with their variance analyses go beyond the mere comparative level.

Standard costs constitute a basic accounting tool which aids in the solution of managerial problems. The accounting measurement of variances provides management with necessary information; and to be complete, standard costs' service to management should include systematic, day-by-day reports relaying deviation information which requires the attention of management.

Costs for Analytical Processes. Costs as a basis for analysis are estimated costs which may be incurred if any one of several alternative courses of action is adopted. Different types of costs involve varying kinds of considerations in managerial analysis for decision making. For example, differential and out-of-pocket costs are types of costs which attempt to envision and evaluate future conditions in the light of the current situation. When management is faced with the problem of abandoning one product and substituting another, the decision will demand the consideration of opportunity costs. If expansion of operating facilities is contemplated, the relevant costs are future costs to be incurred. Should a project be abandoned or capital costs never fully recovered through revenues, the company's management will face a cost situation that is termed a sunk cost. The measure of a sunk cost is the difference between book value at any time and the disposal value of the facilities.

While these isolated illustrations stress the managerial aspect of accounting, it must be realized that, in the final analysis, all accounting is management accounting. For a long time the major reporting emphasis was on the balance sheet, but more and more importance has been placed on the income statement. The rapid rise and growth of business units into large-scale enterprises caused cost accounting to develop as a separate division of the accounting function. Cost accounting should be regarded as the first step in distinguishing a major part of accounting as managerial accounting. It instituted the concepts of cost planning and cost control, both of which are essential to managing successfully the multiple divisions and interests of a modern organization. Cost accounting's importance necessitates the establishment of that type of cost system which best fulfills the needs of management.

DISCUSSION QUESTIONS

1. Enumerate the various classifications of costs.

2. Conversion cost is equal to the total of (a) direct labor and raw materials; (b) direct labor and factory overhead; (c) indirect labor and factory overhead; or (d) factory overhead and raw materials. Select the answer which correctly completes the statement.

   (AICPA adapted)

3. Which of the following is the best example of a variable cost? (a) property taxes; (b) the corporate president's salary; (c) the controller's salary; (d) interest charges; or (e) material in a unit of product?

   (NAA adapted)

4. The statement has often been made that an *actual* product cost in the sense of absolute authenticity and verifiability does not exist. Why?

5. The division of costs between inventory charges and profit and loss charges is not uniform throughout industries.
   (a) Name two broad classifications of costs that find different treatments.
   (b) Give reasons for the existence of these differences.

6. Expenditures may be divided into two general categories — (1) capital expenditures and (2) revenue expenditures.
   (a) Distinguish between these two categories of expenditures and between their treatments in the accounts.
   (b) Discuss the impact on both present and future balance sheets and income statements of improperly distinguishing between capital and revenue expenditures.
   (c) What criteria do firms generally use in establishing a policy for classifying expenditures under these two general categories? Discuss.

   (AICPA adapted)

7. (a) What is a service department? Name a few.
   (b) What are some characteristics of a service department in connection with the establishment of a product cost?

8. The board of directors of the Sebal Manufacturing Company had just received the company's financial statements. While reading them, one director asked, "What are the precise meanings of the terms 'cost,' 'expense,' and 'loss'? These terms sometimes seem to identify similar items and other times dissimilar items."

Required: (1) An explanation of the meanings of the terms (a) "cost," (b) "expense," and (c) "loss" as used for financial reporting in conformity with generally accepted accounting principles. The explanation should indicate distinguishing characteristics of the terms, their similarities and interrelationships.

(2) A classification of each of the following items as a cost, expense, loss, or other category with an explanation of how the classification of each item may change: (a) cost of goods sold; (b) bad debts expense; (c) depreciation expense for plant machinery; (d) organization costs; (e) spoiled goods.

(3) The terms "period cost" and "product cost" are sometimes used to describe certain items in financial statements. Define these terms and distinguish between them. To what types of items does each apply?

(AICPA adapted)

EXERCISES

Exercises 1 through 4 inclusive deal with definitions and cost classifications.

1. (1) What is meant by fixed overhead costs?

(2) What is meant by variable overhead costs?

(3) How will increases in production affect the variable and the fixed overhead in the cost per unit?

(4) Why should any distinction be recognized between fixed and variable costs?

2. Classify the following costs as fixed, variable, or semivariable. Explain the reasons for your classification of the semivariable costs.

(a) Depreciation — straight-line method	(f) Rent
(b) Direct materials	(g) Repairs to machinery
(c) Factory insurance	(h) Social security taxes
(d) Heat, light, and power	(i) Superintendence
(e) Indirect labor	(j) Washroom supplies

3. Under which subheadings of the elements of cost should the following costs be classified?

(a) Cutting tools	(f) Inspector's salary
(b) Depreciation of factory	(g) Legal expenses
(c) Earnings of machinist	(h) Lubricating oil
(d) Foreman's wages	(i) Salary of factory stores clerk
(e) Maintenance parts for factory equipment	(j) Wages of factory crane operator

4. Classify the following items as direct or indirect materials:

(a) Quench oil in heat treating.
(b) Copper band on an 8-inch artillery shell.
(c) Ailerons on an airplane.
(d) 1-oz. perfume bottle.
(e) Sanding material in furniture making.
(f) Bags in flour mills.
(g) Ingots used by a foundry for making castings.

(h) Seats to be installed in a railway car.
(i) Stainless steel cone that holds the mirror in a color television set.
(j) Milk to make ice cream.

5. Cost Computations.   The Kleinschmidt Company submits the following data on October 31, 19—: raw materials put into process, $42,300; direct labor is paid at the rate of $3.90 and $4.20 per hour in Departments A and B respectively; Department A worked 12,250 hours and Department B reported 19,750 hours. Factory overhead is applied on the basis of direct labor hours at the rate of $2.50 per hour in Department A and $2.10 per hour in Department B.

	Inventories	
	Oct. 1	*Oct. 31*
Raw materials	$15,000	$19,200
Work in process	17,300	19,425
Finished goods	11,300	9,400

Required: Without preparing a formal income statement:

(a) Total costs put into process.
(b) Cost of goods manufactured.
(c) Cost of goods sold.

6. Gross Profit Determination.   The Gary-Elliott Corporation manufactures a kitchen appliance to sell for $280. Last year the company sold 2,000 of these appliances, realizing a gross profit that amounted to 25% of the cost of goods sold. Of this total cost of goods sold, materials accounted for 40% of the total and factory overhead for 15%.

During the coming year it is expected that materials and labor costs will each increase 25% per unit and that factory overhead will increase 12½% per unit. To meet these rising costs, a new selling price has to be set.

Required: The number of units that must be sold to realize the same total gross profit in the coming year as realized last year if the new selling price is set at (1) $300; (2) $325; (3) $350.

7. Cost of Goods Manufactured and Sold.   Guy M. Cooper, Inc. incurred direct labor costs of $205,000 and factory overhead costs of $173,000 during 19B. During the year direct materials purchased totaled $198,000. Inventories were counted and costed as follows:

	Dec. 31, 19B	*Dec. 31, 19A*
Inventory of direct materials.........................	$39,700	$32,850
Inventory of work in process.........................	74,350	72,180
Inventory of finished work...........................	22,400	24,320

Required: (1) The cost of goods manufactured for 19B.
(2) The cost of goods sold for 19B.

8 New Sales Price   In June, 19—, the Rolon Corporation sold 50 air conditioners for $200 each. Costs included: materials costs of $50 per unit, direct labor costs of $30 per unit, and factory overhead at 100% of direct labor cost. Interest expense on an 8% bank loan was equivalent to $2 per unit. Federal income tax at a 30% rate was equivalent to $15 per unit.

Effective July 1, 19—, materials costs decreased 5% per unit and direct labor costs increased 20% per unit. Also effective July 1, 19—, the interest rate on the bank loan increased from 8% per annum to 9% per annum.

Assume in requirements (1) and (2) that the expected July sales volume is 50 units, the same as for June.

Required: (1) The sales price per unit that will produce the same ratio of gross profit, assuming no change in the rate of factory overhead in relation to direct labor costs.

(2) The sales price per unit that will produce the same ratio of gross profit, assuming that $10 of the June, 19—, factory overhead consists of fixed costs and that the variable factory overhead ratio to direct labor costs is unchanged from June, 19—.

(AICPA adapted)

9. Fire Loss Calculation. The Walker Products Company, Inc., a small manufacturing company, produces a highly flammable cleaning fluid. On May 31, 19F the company had a fire which completely destroyed the processing building and the work in process inventory; some of the equipment was saved.

After the fire a physical inventory was taken. The raw materials were valued at $30,000, the finished goods at $60,000, and supplies at $5,000.

The inventories on January 1, 19F consisted of:

Raw materials	$ 15,000
Work in process	50,000
Finished goods	70,000
Supplies	2,000
Total	$137,000

A review of the accounts showed that the sales and gross profit for the last five years were:

	Sales	Gross Profit
19A	$300,000	$ 86,200
19B	320,000	102,400
19C	330,000	108,900
19D	250,000	62,500
19E	280,000	84,000

The sales for the first five months of 19F were $150,000; raw materials purchases were $50,000; freight on purchases was $5,000; direct labor for the five months was $40,000. For the past five years, factory overhead was 50% of direct labor cost.

Required: The value of the work in process inventory lost by fire.

(AICPA adapted)

PROBLEMS

3-1. Bid Calculations. The Meredith Equipment Company manufactures machines to customers' specifications. Two requests for bids have been received, each calling for the delivery of one machine with the following shop and cost specifications:

	Bid No. 1	Bid No. 2
Parts to be purchased	$275	$450
Materials: bar, strip, and sheet metal	65	95
Pig metal for castings	28	40

	Bid No. 1	Bid No. 2
Direct labor hours, foundry	6 hrs.	8 hrs.
Direct labor hours, machining....................	8	20
Direct labor hours, electroplating and painting.......	6	12
Direct labor hours, assembly.....................	40	70
Direct labor hours, installing....................	0	16

Labor and overhead hourly rates:

	Foundry	*Machining*	*E & P*	*Assembly*	*Installing*
Direct labor rate per hour...........	$7.25	$5.50	$4.40	**$6.00**	$4.00
Factory overhead rate per direct labor hour..	3.25	3.00	2.50	2.60	1.80

Allowance for spoilage and estimating error, 5% of direct labor and materials cost (including parts purchased).

Allowance for marketing and administrative expenses and profit, 35% of sales.

Required: The bids for the two possible orders, calculated to the nearest $1.

3-2. Influence of Fixed and Variable Costs on Price and Profit. In 19A, The Keswick Products Company produced a machine that sold for $600, of which amount $450 represented cost of goods sold and $50 represented marketing and administrative expenses. The cost of goods sold was comprised of 40% materials cost, 40% labor cost, and 20% factory overhead. During 19A, 2,000 machines were sold. During 19B, an increase of 20% in the cost of materials and an increase of 25% in the cost of labor are anticipated. The company plans to raise the selling price to $675 per unit with a resulting decrease of 40% in the number of units to be sold.

Required: (1) An income statement for the year 19B indicating the new costs per unit. Assume that materials and labor costs will still equal 80% of the cost of goods sold for 19B and marketing and administrative expenses are still $50 per unit.

(2) After the statement required in (1) was prepared, it was ascertained that the 20% factory overhead in 19A consisted of $100,000 fixed expenses and $80,000 variable expenses. The decrease in the number of units to be sold in 19B does not influence the fixed costs. Prepare a revised income statement for 19B disregarding the 80% relationship of materials and labor costs to cost of goods sold.

CASE

Accounting Conventions. The general manager of the Pocono Mountain Manufacturing Company examined and discussed the company's annual income statement with the controller. She remarked that while the company earned two million dollars last year, its value is not much more than it was a year ago. The controller replied that this observation is quite correct. However, certain factors in accounting prevent reported operating results from reflecting the change in the value of the company.

Required: A detailed explanation of the accounting conventions to which the controller referred. Include justification, to the extent possible, for the generally used accounting methods.

CHAPTER 4

THE COST ACCOUNTING INFORMATION SYSTEM: DESIGN AND OPERATION

Timely and meaningful information on revenues, costs, and profits is vital for management's effective and competent planning and control. The cost accounting information system — a part of the total integrated, computerized type of information developed by accounting techniques — should bring executive management significant planning data to aid in understanding the specific problems facing the company, indicating alternative ways and methods for the best possible solutions. Periodically, information must be communicated to middle and operating management in the form of control reports to show the individual manager, department head, supervisor, or foreman the success or failure of the objective and the cost of his accomplishment. These cost reports should motivate responsible people to corrective action and new decisions. The accumulation of accounting data requires many forms, methods, and systems due to the varying types and sizes of businesses. A successful system is tailored to give the blend of sophistication and simplicity that is most efficient and economical for a specific organization. In recognition of these facts, the chapter is divided into five parts:

1. Fundamentals of a cost accounting information system
2. Data processing by means of the journal voucher control system
3. The manufacturing cost accounting cycle
4. The factory ledger
5. Integrated electronic data processing system

FUNDAMENTALS OF A COST ACCOUNTING INFORMATION SYSTEM

The construction of a cost accounting information system requires a thorough understanding of: (1) the organizational structure of the company, (2) the manufacturing procedure or processes, and (3) the type of cost information desired and required by all levels of management.

The cost accounting information system with its operating accounts must correspond to the organizational division of authority so that the individual foreman, supervisor, department head, or manager can be held accountable for the costs incurred in his department. The concept of authority and responsibility is closely allied with accountability which recognizes the need for measuring a manager's discharge of his responsibilities. The organization charts on pages 7 and 8 depict the authority and responsibility relationships among managers, superintendents, department heads, and foremen who are responsible for:

1. Providing detailed information needed by the accounting department in order to install a successful system.

2. Incurring expenditures for materials, labor, and other costs which the accountant must segregate and report to those in charge.

The system must reflect the manufacturing procedure, processes, shop methods, and the marketing and administrative organization and processes of the particular company for which it is designed. The accountant designing the system must know the type of pay (piece-rate, incentive, day-rate, etc.); the method of collecting hours worked; the control of inventories; the costing of tools, dies, jigs, and machinery; and other information related to operations.

A satisfactory system results from a meeting of minds between the accountant and management. The service rendered by the accountant is by prompt presentation of meaningful cost reports and statements to management. The reports indicate the success or failure of a preestablished course of action. Deviations from the course, if significant, are of interest to management. The cost control presentation should be made so that management by exception is possible; that is, it should enable management to take prompt remedial action based on compact information regarding the activities of the various divisions and departments of the company.

While details for analyzing and reporting may be different for different businesses, each system should be perfected in a manner that will:

1. Aid in planning the future and controlling the present.
2. Provide a means of costing inventories.
3. Compute the cost of sales.
4. Measure the efficiency of men, materials, and machines.

5. Aid in establishing selling prices.

6. Furnish data for various other analytical processes.

It is important to recognize that the accounting records do not provide all the information necessary for effective management. Other quantifiable as well as nonquantifiable information, much of which may involve estimates as to the future, may provide vital information especially with respect to the decision-making process. With the advent of electronic computers and their large memory storage, it has become popular to speak of a total information system in which all data — past, present, and future, accounting and nonaccounting — will be stored for quick retrieval.

It is equally important to weigh the cost of the system against its value. There are certain external requirements imposed on an organization that necessitate the establishment of minimum systems requirements. For example, the Internal Revenue Code prescribes certain record-keeping and reporting requirements, as does the Federal Insurance Contributions Act, the 1974 Pension Reform Act, the Securities and Exchange Commission, the Federal Power Commission for public utilities, and various other governmental regulatory agencies and taxing authorities at local, state, and federal levels. Also, stockholders, creditors, labor unions, and others may impose requirements on the information system. These many legal or contractual requirements must be met, but in meeting them the system should be designed in a cost-conscious manner. Beyond these external requirements, any additional sophistication in the system should be justified *solely* on the basis of its value to management.

The Chart of Accounts. Every organization, irrespective of its size and complexity, whether organized for profit or nonprofit, must maintain some type of general ledger accounting system. Data must be collected, identified, and coded for recording in journals and posting to ledger accounts for subsequent reporting. The prerequisite for accomplishing these tasks is a properly established account structure. A company's chart of accounts constitutes the fundamental means for budgetary and control accounting. It provides control accounts for the recognized elements of cost, and it segregates and details all expenses not included in prime cost. The coding system should permit the flow and charge of costs and expenses directly to the individual responsible and accountable for their incurrence.

In constructing a chart of accounts, the following basic considerations should be observed:

1. Accounts should be arranged and designated to give maximum information with the least need for supplementary analysis consistent with a reasonable degree of economy in performing the accounting function.

2. Account titles should reflect as far as possible the purpose rather than the nature of the expenditure.

3. Manufacturing, marketing, and administrative cost accounts should receive particular attention as these accounts are used to bring efficiency variations to management's attention. These costs should be classified further so as to identify them with the responsible department managers. Discussion of this added dimension of cost accumulation is illustrated in subsequent chapters.

A chart of accounts is divided into: (1) balance sheet accounts for assets, liabilities, and capital, and (2) income statement accounts for sales, cost of goods sold, commercial, and other expenses and income.

Assignment of codes in the form of numbers, letters, or other symbols is essential to facilitate the processing of the information. Today's modern data processing equipment makes coding an essential technique. The rapid handling of data by accounting machines, tabulating equipment, and electronic computers necessitates a high degree of planning, organization, and integration of the classification and coding of business data. A typical chart of accounts for a manufacturing concern follows:

CHART OF ACCOUNTS FOR A MANUFACTURING BUSINESS
BALANCE SHEET ACCOUNTS (100–299)
Assets (100–199)

Current Assets (100–129)
101   Cash in Bank
102   Cash on Hand
103   Petty Cash
104   Marketable Securities
106   Customers' Notes Receivable
106.1 Notes Receivable Discounted
109   Customers' Accounts Receivable
109.1 Allowance for Doubtful Accounts
115   Materials
115.1 Inventory Adjustments
116   Work in Process
117   Finished Goods
120   Prepaid Taxes
121   Prepaid Insurance
122   Other Prepaid Items

Land, Plant, and Equipment (130–159)
130   Land
132   Buildings
133   Structures

133.1 Accumulated Depreciation — Buildings
    and Structures
135   Machinery and Equipment — Factory
135.1 Accumulated Depreciation — Machinery
    and Equipment — Factory
143   Automobiles
143.1 Accumulated Depreciation —
    Automobiles
146   Office Furniture and Fixtures
146.1 Accumulated Depreciation — Furniture
    and Fixtures — Office

Intangible Assets (170–179)
170   Goodwill
171   Patents
172   Franchises, Licenses, and Other
    Privileges

Other Assets (180–189)

Sinking Funds (190–199)

Liabilities and Capital (200–229)

Current Liabilities (200–219)
201   Notes Payable
203   Accounts Payable
206   Accrued Payroll
207   Accrued Interest Payable
208   Accrued Payroll Taxes
209   Other Accrued Liabilities
211   Estimated Federal Income Tax Payable
216   Long-Term Debt (due within one year)
218   Dividends Payable
219   Other Current Liabilities

Long-Term Liabilities (220–229)
220   Bonds Payable
222   Mortgage Payable
224   Other Long-Term Debt

Capital (250–279)
250   Capital Stock
250.1 Treasury Stock
255   Paid-In Capital in Excess of Par Value
260   Earnings Retained in Business

(Continued)

CHART OF ACCOUNTS FOR A MANUFACTURING BUSINESS
(Concluded)
INCOME STATEMENT ACCOUNTS (300–899)

Sales (300–349)
301   Sales
301.1 Sales Returns
301.2 Sales Allowances

Cost of Goods Sold (350–399)
351   Cost of Goods Sold
356   Materials — Price Variance
357   Materials — Quantity Variance
366   Labor — Rate Variance
367   Labor — Efficiency Variance
372   Applied Factory Overhead
376   Factory Overhead — Spending Variance
377   Factory Overhead — Idle Capacity
        Variance
378   Factory Overhead — Efficiency
        Variance
379   Factory Overhead — Overapplied or
        Underapplied
390   Development Expenses

Factory Overhead (400–499)
400   Factory Overhead Control
401   Salaries
411   Indirect Materials
412   Indirect Labor
414   Freight and Cartage In
417   Training
420   Overtime Premium
422   Payroll Taxes
425   Vacation Pay
427   Compensation Insurance
434   Fuel — Factory
436   Light and Power
438   Telephone and Telegraph
440   Tools
442   Defective Work
460   Depreciation — Machinery and
        Equipment
461   Depreciation — Buildings and
        Structures
462   Rent of Equipment
463   Repairs and Maintenance of Machinery
        and Equipment
480   Repairs and Maintenance of Buildings
481   Repairs and Maintenance of Roads
482   Repairs and Maintenance of
        Transportation Facilities
486   Amortization of Patents

Marketing Expenses (500–599)
500   Marketing Expenses Control
501   Salaries — Sales Supervision
503   Salaries — Salesmen
504   Salaries — Clerical Help
507   Salesmen's Commissions
515   Freight Out

522   Payroll Taxes
530   Supplies
534   Fuel
536   Light and Power
538   Telephone and Telegraph
546   Postage
548   Travel Expenses
560   Depreciation — Automobiles
562   Rent of Equipment
565   Advertising
567   Display Materials
568   Conventions and Exhibits
580   Repairs and Maintenance of Buildings

Administrative Expenses (600–699)
600   Administrative Expenses Control
601   Salaries — Administrative
604   Salaries — Administrative Clerical
        Help
620   Overtime Premium
622   Payroll Taxes
630   Supplies
634   Fuel
636   Light and Power
638   Telephone and Telegraph
646   Postage
648   Travel Expenses
660   Depreciation — Furniture and
        Fixtures
661   Depreciation — Buildings and
        Structures
662   Rent of Equipment
670   Legal and Accounting Fees
680   Repairs and Maintenance of Buildings
691   Donations
693   Bad Debts Expense

Other Expenses (700–749)
701   Interest Paid on Notes Payable
703   Interest Paid on Mortgage
707   Interest Paid on Bonds
708   Discount on Sales
731   Operating Expenses on Excess
        Facilities

Other Income (800–849)
801   Income from Investments
808   Discount on Purchases
816   Interest Earned on Notes and
        Accounts Receivable
817   Rental Income
818   Miscellaneous Income

Income Deductions (890–899)
890   Federal Income Tax
891   State Income Tax

DATA PROCESSING BY MEANS OF THE JOURNAL VOUCHER CONTROL SYSTEM

Every company designs an accounting system that will meet its own particular needs. Since a knowledge of costs is of key importance to management, the system should make pertinent cost information available to the right person at the right time. To assure the flow of needed cost information into control accounts and subsidiary records, the original transaction must first be account-classified and coded.

DATE		JOURNAL VOUCHER	NO.
MONTH	DAY		**123**
MAR.	31		APPROVED
			EJY

ACCOUNT	ACCT. NO OR CODE	AMOUNT	
		DEBIT	CREDIT
Materials	115	25,000	
Accounts Payable	203		25,000

Journal Voucher Evidencing Purchase of Materials on Account

Throughout the fiscal year the accounting staff assembles and analyzes source documents related to numerous financial transactions. Source documents, often referred to as transaction documents, constitute the fundamental evidence for an accounting event. Source documents — such as sales slips, checks received, checks mailed out, purchase invoices, payroll clock or time cards, materials requisitions, production reports, and shipping records — indicate the occurrence of a transaction. Properly approved transaction documents generate the flow of accounting events into the accounting system. The system itself then depends upon the type and size of a business and the part accounting plays in its management.

Accounting systems often facilitate the flow of accounting by the use of the *journal voucher control system*, consisting of journal vouchers, supported by the original transaction documents. In such systems, journal entries are made via the journal voucher which represents the transactions that have occurred during a given period and that have been identified with the chart of accounts. Essential to a journal voucher control system[1] is the voucher itself. Whether a manual, mechanized, or computerized accounting information system is utilized, the journal voucher is prepared for the purpose of summarizing the transactions in journals and posting them to the accounts.

The journal voucher format used is generally quite similar among organizations. Basically, it should indicate the voucher number, the date, the accounts with their account numbers or codes, the amounts to be debited and credited, and approval (as illustrated above). When subsidiary ledgers or cost ledgers are involved, columns are added to meet the needs of the detailed expense and cost subsidiary ledger requirements at the same time; subsidiary details may also be posted directly from the transaction documents.

---

[1]The journal voucher control system should not be confused with the voucher register, a basic journal for classifying and summarizing expenditures. The voucher register, also called an "accounts payable register," could be a part of the system, particularly under a manual system. Mechanization and computerization have eliminated the need for the voucher register; therefore it is not presented in this textbook.

THE MANUFACTURING COST ACCOUNTING CYCLE

The manufacturing process and the physical arrangement of a factory constitute the skeleton upon which the cost system and cost accumulation procedures for the manufacturing function are built. A knowledge of the flow of products through their various productive steps determines the nature of the costing techniques. Since cost accounts are an expansion of general accounts, they should, as a basic accounting procedure, be related to them. This relationship leads to the concept of the *tie-in* of cost accounts with general accounts as illustrated below:

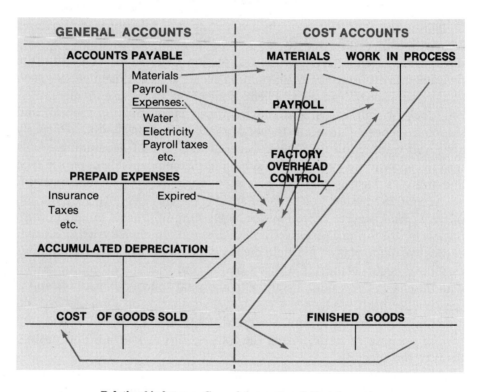

Relationship between General Accounts and Cost Accounts

Accounts describing manufacturing operations are: Materials, Payroll, Factory, Overhead Control, Work in Process, Finished Goods, and Cost of Goods Sold. Each fiscal period these accounts recognize and measure the flow of costs — from the acquisition of materials, through factory operations, to the cost of products sold.

Cost accounting makes extensive use of control accounts. To illustrate, the materials account controls hundreds of different materials items; and the factory overhead account controls indirect labor, supplies, rent, insurance, taxes, repairs, and other factory expenses. The following schedule lists the generally used control accounts with their subsidiary ledgers or records:

COST CONTROL ACCOUNTS AND THEIR SUBSIDIARY LEDGERS OR RECORDS	
Materials	Materials cards — perpetual inventory
Factory Overhead	Expense ledger or departmental expense analysis sheets
Work in Process	{ Cost sheets — job order costing { Production reports — process costing
Finished Goods	Finished Goods ledger cards
Machinery and Equipment	Plant ledger

The control account-subsidiary record format is used when it is desirable to maintain detailed information about general ledger accounts.

Use of control accounts in cost accounting is based on the same principles as those used in financial accounting. For instance, an entry is made in the purchases journal for materials purchased — debiting Materials and crediting Accounts Payable. The total of the Materials column is posted at the end of the period. The individual items purchased are also entered on materials ledger cards. The total of the individual balances on the materials ledger cards must agree with the balance in the materials account in the general ledger.

A company's cost procedure determines the type of subsidiary record which supports the work in process control account. With job order costing, job order cost sheets prepared for each job (or work order) receive the details that are posted in totals to the work in process account at the end of the month. With process costing, cost of production reports indicate the daily or weekly figures that appear in Work in Process.

Illustrative Cycle Problem. The flow of costs through factory operations of the Shamrock Manufacturing Company is shown on page 68. Debit items in the materials, payroll, and factory overhead control accounts represent purchases and other charges during the month. Balances remaining in Materials, Work in Process, and Finished Goods are ending inventories. Credits to Materials and to Payroll represent amounts used in production during the period. In the factory overhead control account, actual expenses incurred — including indirect materials, indirect labor, payroll taxes,[2] depreciation, and other prepaid items and accruals (Expired Insurance in this illustration) — comprise the total debit of $14,050.

---

[2]The amount of $2,852 for payroll taxes consists of:

$1,860 — 6% FICA Tax on $31,000 ($27,000 direct labor plus $4,000 indirect labor)
   155 — .5% Federal Unemployment Tax on $31,000
   837 — 2.7% State Unemployment Tax on $31,000
$2,852 — total payroll taxes

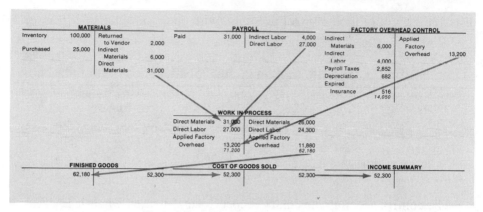

MATERIALS			
Inventory	100,000	Returned	
		to Vendor	2,000
Purchased	25,000	Indirect	
		Materials	6,000
		Direct	
		Materials	31,000

PAYROLL			
Paid	31,000	Indirect Labor	4,000
		Direct Labor	27,000

FACTORY OVERHEAD CONTROL			
Indirect		Applied	
Materials	6,000	Factory	
Indirect		Overhead	13,200
Labor	4,000		
Payroll Taxes	2,852		
Depreciation	682		
Expired			
Insurance	516		
	14,050		

WORK IN PROCESS			
Direct Materials	31,000	Direct Materials	26,000
Direct Labor	27,000	Direct Labor	24,300
Applied Factory		Applied Factory	
Overhead	13,200	Overhead	11,880
	71,200		62,180

FINISHED GOODS		COST OF GOODS SOLD		INCOME SUMMARY	
62,180	52,300	52,300	52,300	52,300	52,300

Flow of Costs Through Factory Operations

By means of a predetermined factory overhead rate, it is estimated that for each direct labor hour used in production, $2.20 of factory overhead should be charged to production. The credit of $13,200, based on 6,000 direct labor hours, is the applied factory overhead charged to production during the month. The debit balance of $850 remaining in Factory Overhead Control represents the amount of underapplied factory overhead. The disposition of such a balance, be it either over- or underapplied, is discussed in Chapter 9.

Cost of all production during the month consists of direct materials, $31,000; direct labor, $27,000; and applied factory overhead, $13,200 — a total production cost of $71,200. Units completed during the period cost $62,180 (direct materials, $26,000; direct labor, $24,300; and applied factory overhead, $11,880). The total cost of goods completed, $62,180, is transferred from the work in process account to the finished goods account. Finally, cost of goods sold of $52,300 is transferred from Finished Goods to Cost of Goods Sold. Cost of Goods Sold is closed to Income Summary at the end of each accounting period.

Underlying Documents. The ledger accounts with the transactions posted therein should be looked upon as the *storage* space or data-bank mentioned in computerized accounting systems. The flow of costs to these *memories* is based on originating documents that must be checked, verified, vouchered, journalized, and posted. Documents may be for:

Materials: purchase invoice, materials requisitions, materials returned slips, etc.

Labor: time tickets or time sheets, clock cards, job tickets, etc.

Factory Overhead: vouchers prepared to set up depreciation or prepaid expenses; vendors' invoices, utility bills, etc.

THE FACTORY LEDGER

The accounting system, and especially the cost accounting cycle problem based on the factory operations of the Shamrock Manufacturing Company, assumes that the entire business is under one roof or that little distance separates the factory and the general offices. It is not uncommon for administrative, marketing, and accounting offices to be far removed from factory sites; and, of course, the same company may operate several factories or marketing offices in different parts of the country. If the factory is some distance from the offices or if the manufacturing requires many accounts, it is practical to do some accounting at the factory.

Transactions recorded at the factory should be posted to a factory ledger. The factory ledger includes a control account entitled General Ledger that shows the equity of the general office in the factory. A reciprocal control account entitled Factory Ledger is maintained in the accounting records kept at the general office. When General Ledger is debited in the factory books, Factory Ledger is credited in the general office books; when General Ledger is credited, Factory Ledger is debited.

Just how much of the accounting may be done at the factory depends upon the organization and operation of a business. If sales are made, invoices prepared, and statements rendered from the factory, Cash, Accounts Receivable, Sales, and related accounts will appear in the factory ledger. If sales invoices, billings, and collections are made at the general office, only a petty cash account along with the various manufacturing accounts would be needed on the factory books.

At one factory it may be advantageous to meet payrolls locally, thereby requiring a bank account and payroll accounts. In another factory, the payroll summary might be sent to the general office which would prepare the payroll checks or envelopes and mail or deliver them to the factory. The liability for payroll taxes and income taxes withheld from employees is either kept in the general ledger or transferred from the factory ledger to the general ledger. For efficient management and control, one firm may keep detailed equipment accounts in the factory books, while another may keep them with accumulated depreciation accounts in the general office books.

Illustrative Problem. With the data of the Shamrock Manufacturing Company as the basis for the illustration (page 68), the following entries would be recorded assuming that (1) the materials account is kept at the factory while all invoices are vouchered and paid from the general office, (2) the payroll with its deductions is prepared at the factory while pay checks and tax liabilities are the treasurer's responsibility at the main office, and (3) the finished goods account is kept at the factory and the cost of goods sold account at the general office.

GENERAL OFFICE		FACTORY OFFICE			

Entries for the purchase of the materials:

	Dr.	Cr.		Subsidiary Record	Dr.	Cr.
Factory Ledger...........	25,000		Materials..........		25,000	
Accounts Payable........		25,000	General Ledger....			25,000

Entries for the requisitioning of direct and indirect materials:

NO ENTRY			Work in Process....		31,000	
			Materials.........			31,000
NO ENTRY			Factory Overhead Control..........		6,000	
			Indirect Materials.	6,000		
			Materials.........			6,000

Entries for the return of materials to the vendor:

Accounts Payable..........	2,000		General Ledger.....		2,000	
Factory Ledger...........		2,000	Materials.........			2,000

Entries to prepare the payroll at the factory and to set up payroll liability and pay employees at the main office: (Employees' payroll deductions consist of 15% for federal income taxes and 6% for FICA taxes. The tax liabilities are transferred to the general office.)

Factory Ledger...........	24,490		Payroll............		31,000	
Accrued Payroll..........		24,490	General Ledger....			24,490
			Federal Income Tax Payable.........			4,650
Accrued Payroll...........	24,490		FICA Tax Payable.			1,860
Cash...................		24,490				
Factory Ledger...........	6,510		Federal Income Tax Payable.........		4,650	
Federal Income Tax Payable............		4,650	FICA Tax Payable..		1,860	
FICA Tax Payable........		1,860	General Ledger....			6,510

Entries for the company's payroll tax liability:

Factory Ledger...........	2,852		Factory Overhead Control..........		2,852	
FICA Tax Payable........		1,860	FICA Tax.......		1,860	
Federal Unemploy. Tax Payable................		155	Federal Unempl. Tax............		155	
State Unemploy. Tax Payable...................		837	State Unempl. Tax............		837	
			General Ledger....			2,852

Entries to distribute payroll to work in process for direct labor costs and to factory overhead control for indirect labor:

NO ENTRY			Work in Process....		27,000	
			Factory Overhead Control..........		4,000	
			Indirect Labor....	4,000		
			Payroll..........			31,000

GENERAL OFFICE				*FACTORY OFFICE*		

Entries to charge factory overhead to work in process based on 6,000 direct labor hours worked at a factory overhead rate of $2.20 per hour:

	Dr.	Cr.		Subsidiary Record	Dr.	Cr.
NO ENTRY			Work in Process....		13,200	
			Factory Overhead			
			Control.........			13,200

Entries to charge expense accounts in the factory office with credits in the general office books for writing off prepaid insurance and accruing depreciation: (Prepaid expenses and accumulated depreciation accounts are kept in the general office ledgers.)

Factory Ledger	1,198		Factory Overhead			
Prepaid Insurance.........		516	Control.........		1,198	
Accumulated Depreciation.		682	Expired Insurance.	516		
			Depreciation.....	682		
			General Ledger....			1,198

Entry to transfer work in process to finished goods:

NO ENTRY			Finished Goods....		62,180	
			Work in Process...			62,180

Entries to transfer the cost of the goods sold to the general office books when notice is received that shipments were made to customers:

Cost of Goods Sold	52,300		General Ledger.....		52,300	
Factory Ledger		52,300	Finished Goods...			52,300

In the general office a second entry is necessary for the sales transaction. Entry assuming the above shipment was sold for $88,000:

Accounts Receivable........	88,000		NO ENTRY	
Sales....................		88,000		

In this illustrative problem subsidiary record detail is shown for factory overhead only. Similar detail, often posted to subsidiary records directly from transaction documents, must be available for all ledger accounts for which subsidiary records are maintained; e.g., materials and finished goods.

INTEGRATED ELECTRONIC DATA PROCESSING SYSTEM

The term "data processing" applies to the accumulation, classification, analysis, and summary reporting of large quantities of information. The procedures, forms, and equipment used to process and communicate data are called a *data processing unit*. Any accounting system, even a cash register in a supermarket, is basically a data processing system designed to make pertinent and timely information available to personnel responsible for various functions. Every purchase transaction requires a purchase requisition, a purchase order, verification of receipt of the order, voucher preparation, journalizing, posting, and a check to make payment. Multiple copies of the forms are prepared for the departments concerned, and it is necessary to rewrite the data perhaps several times — a time-consuming procedure almost certain to generate errors.

Integrated data processing is a system for recording and processing information without rerecording of repetitive data. For instance, payables data of all kinds — from purchase orders, receiving reports, credits and allowances, cash discounts, to invoices and payrolls — can be processed through the accounting procedures with summary reports monthly, weekly, and daily where needed. The results of computer processing are verification of accuracy, automatically written checks and remittance statements, classified and stored data files, preparation and posting to general and subsidiary records, and analytical reports.

In the course of recording and evaluating information, the computer will recognize and report any circumstances deviating from the routine or standard. This makes possible more efficient use of the concept of management by exception. Executives can examine and act upon only those situations requiring attention, allowing all normal operations to flow unimpeded.

The punched card is still one of the fastest and most efficient methods yet devised for posting source information. Depending upon the procedures, the original punched cards are prepared from either transaction documents or from journal vouchers showing the details provided by the source documents. After verification for accuracy, the punched cards are entrusted to extremely fast, accurate, and self-verifying machines for further processing. For business uses, the processing is usually done by a digital computer which basically is a calculating machine with extraordinary capabilities. At very high speeds it can perform basic arithmetic functions, compare numbers as to size, and make many *yes* or *no* decisions as called for in solving problems or processing an established routine. In addition, the computer can communicate with other machines in a system such as a magnetic ink reader, or another computer, which could be located in another city.

Major Computer Activities. All digital computers provide for four major activities: (1) *input-output* for transferring information into and out of the computer, (2) *storage* or *memory* where figures and facts are accessible, (3) *processing* or *calculating*, the *arithmetic and logic unit*, where operations are performed on the stored data, and (4) *control* for coordinating other units in the system to perform the instructions and desired sequence of operations.

The diagrams shown on pages 73 and 74 illustrate basic information flow through a typical computer accounting system and the functional parts of a computer.

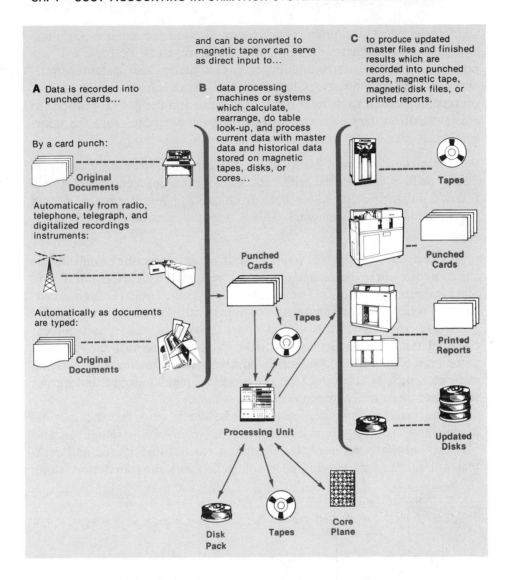

A Data is recorded into punched cards...

and can be converted to magnetic tape or can serve as direct input to...

C to produce updated master files and finished results which are recorded into punched cards, magnetic tape, magnetic disk files, or printed reports.

B data processing machines or systems which calculate, rearrange, do table look-up, and process current data with master data and historical data stored on magnetic tapes, disks, or cores...

By a card punch:

Original Documents

Automatically from radio, telephone, telegraph, and digitalized recordings instruments:

Automatically as documents are typed:

Original Documents

Punched Cards

Tapes

Processing Unit

Disk Pack

Tapes

Core Plane

Tapes

Punched Cards

Printed Reports

Updated Disks

Basic Information Flow Through a Typical Computer Accounting System

Input-Output. An input unit working from punched cards, punched paper tape, magnetic tape, magnetic ink, or other media feeds the data and processing instructions into the storage unit. The original data may come from purchase requisitions, invoices, time tickets, sales tickets, as well as from journal vouchers. The output system, a printer, prints out results at the conclusion of processing as instructed in the program, thereby providing rapid feedback to managerial personnel.

Storage. The computer stores information on magnetic tapes, magnetic cores, or magnetic disks. Computer storage can be regarded as a completely indexed electronic filing cabinet in many cases instantaneously accessible to the computer. Characters or digits of information are stored on tiny magnetized spots or cores in code form, and the data are processed electronically at very high speed to provide the computer with the information it seeks.

Arithmetic and Logic Unit. From its almost unbelievably complete electronic filing cabinet, the arithmetic and logic unit of a computer system follows instructions to select data from storage and to make desired computations or arrangements. This is done by electronic circuits at the speed of light.

Control Unit. A control panel or unit *reads* instructions and informs the computer where the desired data are stored, what data are required, and what sequence to follow. The computer can guide itself through a continuous series of instructions or programs, call data from storage and process it, return it to storage, and direct the output printer to print out the final results or report as directed. A console permits the operator to communicate with and manually control certain functions of a digital computer, such as start and stop the machine, regulate input and output units, and direct other operations of the system.

In essence, a computer system immediately converts the original document from every business transaction to computer language and files it. Then, as instructed, the computer reaches into its file and completes all further actions required in connection with the transaction, along

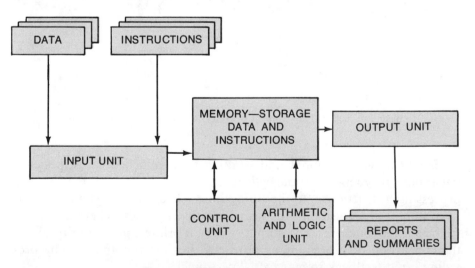

Functional Parts of a Computer System

with summary reports of all transactions classified in any way most useful to management.

Large businesses have converted their basic data accumulation procedures to an electronic system of some sort. Ledgers are now replaced by cards, reels of magnetic tape, or disks as media for recording and storing account data. Ledgers in the form of punched cards, for example, offer a high degree of economy and flexibility; i.e., posting can be accomplished simply by merging accounts payable cards into a master file (arranged in sequence by account number) at machine speeds. The same cards can be converted into the accounts payable ledger file by the computer. Any card that goes into the file is prepared and verified from the source document. The card is immediately available for use in any phase of the accounting procedures. None of the accounts or documents has to be handled individually (except source documents); and each item of data can be used as a unit, rather than as a fixed part of a rigid record.

As an example, at the end of each week or month, the accounts payable cards accumulated from daily processing of invoices or other source documents are withdrawn from the file, machine sorted into account number sequence, and then listed by a printer to produce the accounts payable distribution summary. Furthermore, these same cards can be machine sorted into categories of purchases and expenses. Summaries can be prepared for each class of expenditure or for each department manager responsible for cost control.

Electronic Data Processing and the Information System. Successful management of a business is essentially a continuous process of decision making. The decision making becomes even more complex with multiple plants located throughout the nation and in foreign countries; multiple product lines with an array of sizes, colors, and options; reports necessary for taxes, regulatory agencies, employees, and stockholders; and the necessity to communicate policies and objectives from executive management to all operating levels. With the speed and flexibility of computers, an information system may collect and analyze business data into categories for different levels of management, such as: (1) data from routine business transactions, (2) control totals, (3) control ratios, and (4) statistically tested mathematical models or simulation.

Data from Repetitive Transactions. These data originate with source documents necessary to verify the transaction in accordance with good business practice or to comply with legal requirements. Clock cards or time tickets, purchase orders and invoices, sales invoices, and derived documents (such as journal vouchers, materials cards, social security records, employee earnings records, payrolls, checks, production reports, inventory records, and other prepared documents and reports) constitute routine business data. Each document serves a simple and specific purpose without which a business cannot operate. Approximately 75 percent of all digital computers are being utilized for handling routine business data.

Control Totals.   Control totals arise because a business functions through departments, branches, and operating divisions; and data generated in one phase of operations flows into another phase. Or for internal control it may be necessary for different individuals or departments to report on the same transactions. Checks written in payment to creditors must show a total that agrees with amounts recorded in the cash payments journal; the total of materials purchased must agree with combined entries on materials cards; daily receipts from credit customers must show a total in agreement with amounts deposited and credited to customer accounts; materials issued totals need to agree with amounts entered on job or production cost sheets; and so on. In each case there is an accounting control total, and the separately derived totals must be identical. One with even a slight familiarity with business knows of the time and effort often required to locate errors in order to bring control totals into agreement. The electronic computer readily provides control totals and its use often releases supervisory personnel for more creative effort.

Control Ratios.   Control ratios provide management with information necessary for decisions and action. Cost control is basically a process of watching figures and taking action that will increase or decrease the figures if they become too small or too large. These figures may be totals — total sales, total materials cost, total labor hours, total labor cost, total overhead, total variable cost, total spoilage cost, etc. For management purposes, as control totals are obtained each day, week, month, and quarter, these totals are compared with previous time periods, with budgets, and with standards. From control totals other ratios meaningful to management are possible, such as inventory turnover, sales per dollar of variable cost, sales per dollar of assets, earnings per dollar of sales, and each cost element as a ratio to sales or to total costs.

Mathematical Models.   Mathematical models are now used by management as a tool to describe and help control operations. For example, models or simulations make it possible to test out various inventory control policies and forecasting techniques based on past experience and to select the method that best meets management objectives. By using the computer, it is possible to simulate a complete operating budget and manipulate product mix, price, cost factors, and the marketing program. By studying alternative combinations of the variables, it is possible to reduce the area of uncertainty in making decisions.

The linear programming chapter (Chapter 28) presents problems that can be attacked effectively by computer programming. These illustrations are realistic to the extent that management does face such problems, but often with more complexities and variables. Imagine an oil refinery that blends some combination of materials to produce a considerable array of products. If the goal is maximum earnings per barrel of crude refined and there are dozens of products and product variations with possibly 50 constraints, a computer solution is the only accurate and feasible way. Naturally, oil refineries were in operation before computers came into being; and refinery managers have been making decisions on these matters for years. The value of computer solutions in such work lies in the substantial financial effect of small improvements. The managers' decisions reached by previous methods may have been close to the optimum, but a few cents a barrel is a great deal of money when multiplied by production runs in the tens of thousands of barrels per day.

The amazing speed of the computer as a data processing device and its value in an updating or posting application (payrolls, accounts receivable, inventories, etc.) can readily be seen. The opportunities and applications in preparation and analysis of operating and financial information are not so obvious. There exist *program libraries* in machine readable form for various related companies where the data for each company, plant, or operating division appear in *standardized format*. It is feasible to have computer programs which will analyze data for all or any part of the related companies for any number of accounting periods.

DISCUSSION QUESTIONS

1. How may a cost system be defined?

2. A principal point in connection with the creation of a cost system is a knowledge of the company's plant, machinery, methods, layout, and flow of work. With this knowledge the accountant possesses the essential background information to develop the necessary cost procedures. Explain how the accountant would use this information.

3. A chart of accounts, accompanied by adequate instructions, is a great aid to better accounting, costing, and controlling. Explain.

4. The journal voucher control system is said to be one of the most effective means of internal control when designed to fit a specific enterprise and properly administered.
   (a) Explain how the voucher can be a means of internal control.
   (b) How does a voucher serve as a connecting link between general accounting and cost accounting?

5. If a factory is located in one city or state and the general office in another, it is desirable to separate a portion of the records.

(a) Name four control accounts and the subsidiary ledgers that would likely be kept at the factory.

(b) How are ledgers kept in balance between the factory and the general office?

(c) What entry would be made on the factory books when goods are shipped directly to a customer? Assume inventory records are maintained at the factory.

(d) What entry would be made on the home office books for transaction (c)?

(e) A factory sends goods it has produced to another branch factory. What entry would be made on the producing factory's books?

6. (a) Where a portion of the accounting is done at the factory and a factory ledger is maintained, what accounts are most likely to be in the factory ledger?

(b) What is the principal reason for maintaining accounts at the factory?

7. (a) What are the four major activities provided by a digital computer?

(b) A computer system may collect and analyze business data in different ways for different levels of management. Discuss.

8. What advantages does the electronic data processing system offer for cost accounting record keeping?

EXERCISES

1. T Accounts Showing Flow of Cost. The Baton Rouge Chemical Company had the following inventories on September 1:

Raw materials	$40,000	Work in process — materials.......	$15,000
Finished goods....	25,000	Work in process — labor	18,000
		Work in process — factory overhead.	13,500

During the month of September the cost of materials purchased was $100,000, direct labor cost incurred was $90,000, and factory overhead applicable to production was 75% of the direct labor cost. The September 30 inventories were:

Raw materials	$30,000	Work in process — materials.......	$12,000
Finished goods....	47,000	Work in process — labor	20,000
		Work in process — factory overhead.	15,000

Required: Using three accounts for work in process, prepare T accounts showing the flow of the cost of goods manufactured and sold.

2. Factory Overhead Rate and Relationship of Cost Elements. A schedule of cost of goods manufactured shows:

Materials used...	$150,000
Direct labor..	400,000
Overhead costs...	300,000
Work in process, ending inventory........................	120,000

Required: (1) The rate of factory overhead to direct labor cost.

(2) The cost of direct materials included in the work in process ending inventory, assuming that the direct labor cost included in the inventory of work in process is $40,000.

3. Journal Entries for the Cost Accounting Cycle. On October 1, the trial balance of the Durable Company showed:

Accounts	Dr.	Cr.
Cash on Hand and in Bank.........................	$ 25,800	
Accounts Receivable.............................	47,740	
Materials..	44,880	
Work in Process..................................	85,400	
Finished Goods...................................	78,700	
Plant and Machinery..............................	237,240	
Accounts Payable.................................		$ 54,270
Accrued Payroll..................................		6,600
Accumulated Depreciation — Plant & Machinery......		115,210
Allowance for Doubtful Accounts..................		2,825
Capital Stock....................................		80,000
Retained Earnings................................		260,855
	$519,760	$519,760

During October these transactions took place:

(a) Materials purchased (on account)......................... $ 40,000
(b) Materials issued (direct)............................... 65,000
      "   " (indirect)............................... 3,500
(c) Materials returned to supplier............................ 900
(d) Total payroll for month (direct).......................... 80,000
      "   "   "   " (indirect)......................... 9,500
    (*Assume there are no payroll deductions.*)
(e) Wages paid during October............................... 75,000
(f) Sundry manufacturing expenses incurred during October...... 12,000
(g) Marketing and administrative expenses incurred during October.. 8,500
(h) Accounts receivable collected............................ 300,000
(i) Accounts payable paid.................................... 135,000
(j) Depreciation to be provided for October on plant and machinery at the rate of 10% per annum.................... ?
(k) Factory overhead applied to production.................... 14,200
(l) Work in process, October 31............................. 75,000
(m) Cost of finished goods sold during October................. 205,000
(n) Sales made on account................................... 285,000

Required: Journal entries for the above transactions.

4. Cost Accounting Cycle Entries in T Accounts. At the beginning of October, the ledger of the Highlander Company contained (among other accounts) the following: Materials, $35,000; Work in Process, $40,000; Finished Goods, $25,000. During October the following transactions were completed:

(a) Materials were purchased on account at a cost of $18,500.
(b) Materials in the amount of $22,000 were issued from the storeroom for use in production.
(c) Requisitions for indirect factory materials and supplies amounted to $2,000.
(d) The total payroll for the month was $35,000 including salesmen's salaries of $5,000 and office salaries of $5,000. Labor time tickets show that $20,000 of the payroll was direct labor. Income taxes were withheld at the rate of 10% of wages earned, and employees' FICA taxes of $1,440 were deducted. The payroll due the employees was paid during the month.
(e) The employer's payroll taxes consist of $1,440 FICA, 1.4% state unemployment insurance, and .5% federal unemployment insurance tax. Two hundred

and seventy dollars of the taxes apply to salesmen's salaries and $180 to office salaries.

(f) Sundry manufacturing expenses requiring an outlay of $10,000 were paid.

(g) Factory overhead of 90% of the direct labor cost is charged to production.

(h) Cost of production completed for the month totaled $75,000, and finished goods in the shipping room at the end of October totaled $10,000.

(i) Customers were billed for $122,000 for shipments made during October.

(j) Customers paid $68,000 on account.

Required: (1) Record in T accounts the transactions for October using one work in process account.

(2) Close the income statement accounts to Income Summary. Close under-applied factory overhead to Cost of Goods Sold.

5. Cost Accounting Cycle Entries. Bayside Company completed transactions during the first half of September:

Sept. 1. Purchased grease, oil, and cleaning compound for factory use from Deaton Supply Company, $400. Terms 1/10, n/30.

       3. Purchased an electric motor from Lee Electrical Manufacturing Company listed at $3,400. Freight charges amounted to $225 and testing and installation charges were $175. Terms of sale were: one half down plus freight and installation charges with a cash discount of 2% on the list price; balance due in two equal monthly installments with a 2% discount on the first installment if paid by October 1.

       5. Paid Terrell Service Company for repairs to factory machinery, $125.

       6. Purchased raw materials from Ramel & Ruble Assembling Company, $5,000. Terms: 2/10, n/30.

       8. Recorded payroll for the week, $1,900. Payroll was distributed as follows:

	Federal Income Tax Withheld	FICA Tax
Factory (indirect labor) $1,200	$180	$72
Marketing......... 400	60	24
Administrative...... 300	45	18

      11. Returned $180 of water damaged cleaning compound for credit — purchased on September 1 from Deaton Supply Company.

      13. Paid account of Ramel & Ruble Assembling Company.

      15. Paid rent bill from Highside Realtors, $300. Of this amount, 10% is for administrative office and 30% for sales office.

Required: Record the above transactions by means of journal entries.

6. Factory Ledger Entries. The Henderson Company uses a general ledger and a factory ledger. The following transactions took place:

Nov. 2. Purchased raw materials for the factory, $20,000. Terms 1/10, n/60.

       4. Requisitions of $4,000 of direct materials and $2,000 of indirect materials were filled from the stockroom.

       8. Factory payroll of $2,000 for the week was made up at the home office; $1,730 in cash was sent to the factory. FICA tax was $90, and income tax was $180 ($1,880 direct labor; $120 factory repair).

      14. Depreciation of $200 for factory equipment was recorded. (Assets and accumulated depreciation accounts are kept on the general office books.)

      14. A job was completed in the factory with $960 direct labor and $450 of materials being previously charged to the job. Factory overhead is to be applied at an overhead rate of 66⅔% of direct labor.

Nov. 15. Miscellaneous factory overhead amounting to $800 was paid by the home office and transferred to the factory.

16. The job completed on the 14th was shipped to Sully Marx on instructions from the home office. Customer was billed for $2,300.

Required: Journal entries on the factory books and the general office books.

7. Factory Ledger Entries. The Emco Plastic Company has its general office in Louisville, but has a major plant in Evansville. A separate set of records is kept at the home office and at the factory. On November 1 the factory trial balance showed the following:

Accounts	Dr.	Cr.
Materials......................................	$ 3,500	
Work in Process..............................	7,800	
Finished Goods...............................	6,400	
General Ledger...............................		$17,700
Total......................................	$17,700	$17,700

For the month of November the following transactions occurred:

(a) Materials purchased on account, $23,000.

(b) Direct materials of $12,000 were requisitioned, along with indirect materials of $6,500 and $2,500 of supplies.

(c) Total payroll for November was $30,000. The home office prepared the payroll and the checks and also deducted 6% for FICA tax and 10% for federal income tax. The liability for employer payroll taxes is kept on the home office books. The state unemployment insurance tax rate is 2.1%; the federal unemployment insurance tax rate is .5%. The Evansville payroll consisted of: $3,000, office salaries; $8,000, sales salaries; $6,000, indirect labor; and $13,000, direct labor.

(d) Factory overhead is applied at a rate of 210% of direct labor cost.

(e) Materials costing $275 were defective and were returned to the supplier.

(f) Payments made to vendors on account, $21,500.

(g) $12,000 of various factory overhead expenses is recorded, including $2,000 depreciation on factory machinery.

(h) Goods completed totaled $48,300.

(i) Goods costing $45,000 were sold for $60,000.

Required: Journal entries on the books of the general office and the factory to record the above transactions.

8. Factory Ledger Entries. Electronics Incorporated maintains its factory in Stillwater, Oklahoma, but has its main office in Tulsa. On September 1, the factory trial balance appeared as follows:

Accounts	Dr.	Cr.
Materials..	$ 19,500	
Work in Process.................................	68,250	
Finished Goods..................................	23,000	
Factory Overhead Control........................	540,000	
Factory Machinery...............................	120,000	
Applied Factory Overhead........................		$536,400
Accumulated Depreciation — Factory Machinery......		36,000
General Ledger..................................		198,350
Total.......................................	$770,750	$770,750

The following transactions were completed during September:

(a) Direct materials purchased on terms of 2/10, n/30, $120,000.

(b) The factory payroll for $45,000 direct labor and $9,000 indirect labor was mailed to the home office. The home office payroll was $15,000 for sales salaries and $21,000 for office salaries. Employee payroll deductions were recorded at the home office at these rates: 6% of gross earnings for FICA tax; 18% of gross earnings for federal income tax.

(c) Indirect materials and supplies amounting to $26,250 were purchased; terms 2/10, n/30.

(d) Employer payroll tax expense is recorded on the home office books. State unemployment rate, 1.8%; federal unemployment, .5%; FICA tax, 6%.

(e) Analysis of the materials requisitions (all supplies are kept at the factory):

Production orders..................	$60,000
Maintenance and repairs............	15,000
Shipping supplies..................	4,500

(f) Defective shipping supplies returned to the vendor, $900.

(g) Accounts payable totaling $142,500, including the accrued payroll, were paid.

(h) Depreciation at an annual rate of 10% of the original cost was recorded on the factory machinery.

(i) Sundry factory expenses of $6,900 were recorded as liabilities.

(j) Factory overhead was applied to production at the rate of $3 per direct labor hour; the factory worked 12,000 hours in September.

(k) Goods completed with a total cost of $126,000 were transferred to finished goods.

(l) Sales for September were $150,000 which cost $96,000 to produce.

(m) At the end of September the factory overhead accounts are closed, and any over- or underapplied balance is closed to the cost of goods sold account. Draw up the two factory overhead accounts; post applicable transactions therein and determine the over- or underapplied amount.

Required: Journal entries to record the above transactions on the general office books and on the factory books.

PROBLEMS

4-1. Cost Accounting Cycle; Cost of Goods Sold and Income Statements. Baker Co., a manufacturer, had these beginning and ending inventories at the end of its current year:

	Beginning	Ending
Raw materials.....................................	$22,000	$30,000
Work in process..................................	40,000	48,000
Finished goods...................................	25,000	18,000

During the year the following transactions occurred:

Raw materials purchased.....................................	$300,000
Indirect materials and supplies purchased......................	50,000
Direct labor cost...	120,000*
Indirect factory labor.......................................	60,000*
Property taxes and depreciation on factory building............	20,000
Property taxes and depreciation on salesroom and office (shared on a 50%–50% basis).......................................	15,000

*Assume no payroll deductions are made.

Utilities (60% to factory, 20% to salesroom, and 20% to office)...	$ 50,000
Indirect materials issued to factory...........................	40,000
Factory overhead applied on the basis of 120% of direct labor cost..	?
Salesmen's salaries...	40,000*
Office salaries...	24,000*
Sales on account..	730,000

Over- or underapplied factory overhead is deducted from or added to cost of goods sold.

---

*Assume no payroll deductions are made.

Required: (1) Draw up T accounts, and post the data therein.   (Credit purchases and payroll to Accounts Payable.)

(2) A cost of goods sold statement.

(3) An income statement.   (AICPA adapted)

4-2. Cost Accounting Cycle Entries.   During September these transactions took place at the Grand Rapids Manufacturing Company:

Sept.   1. Purchased raw materials from Harvey Manufacturing Company, $5,500. Terms: 2/10, n/60. Purchases are recorded at the gross amount.

   1. Received a $2,500 invoice for factory equipment from Becker & Company. Terms: net 90 days.

   3. Sent C. E. Olsen, a company salesman, a $205 check for traveling expenses.

   5. Paid and distributed weekly payroll:

	Gross Earnings	Federal Income Tax Withheld	FICA Tax
Factory (20% of the factory payroll is indirect labor)........................	$3,200	$320	$192
Marketing............................	1,400	140	84
Office...............................	1,200	120	72

   5. Employer's payroll taxes on weekly payroll: FICA tax, 6%; state unemployment tax, 2.7%; federal unemployment, .5%. Charge factory payroll taxes to factory overhead.

   8. Paid Lackawanna Railroad Company $105 for freight on a machine bought on September 1.

   9. Paid Becker & Company $340 for installing machinery bought on September 1.

   10. Paid Harvey Manufacturing Company for September 1 invoice.

   11. Received advertising bill from the Ayres Advertising Agency, $300. Terms: net 30 days.

   12. Paid and distributed weekly payroll:

	Gross Earnings	Federal Income Tax Withheld	FICA Tax
Factory (25% of the factory payroll is indirect labor)....................	$3,280	$328	$196.80
Marketing..........................	1,350	135	81.00
Office.............................	1,200	120	72.00

   12. Employer's payroll taxes on weekly payroll (see Sept. 5 transaction for instructions).

   14. Purchased factory supplies from Haines & Company, $1,560. Terms: 2/10, n/30. Charge factory overhead.

Sept. 16. Bought tools for factory use from Tower Machinery Company for cash, $60. Charge factory overhead.

17. Paid Brown Garage Company for service and repair of trucks, $800. Of this amount, charge 60% to the factory and the balance to marketing.

18. Paid the bill of the Ayres Advertising Agency.

18. Bought raw materials from Clark Manufacturing Company, $7,500. Terms: net 30 days.

19. Paid and distributed weekly payroll:

	Gross Earnings	Federal Income Tax Withheld	FICA Tax
Factory (20% of the factory payroll is indirect labor).....................	$3,250	$325	$195.00
Marketing.........................	1,320	132	79.20
Office.............................	1,190	119	71.40

19. Employer's payroll taxes on weekly payroll.

21. Returned to Clark Manufacturing Company the raw materials received in damaged condition on the 18th; billed price, $600.

22. Purchased raw materials from Boyer Manufacturing Company for cash, $3,000.

23. Paid Haines & Company for September 14 invoice.

24. Paid Apex Service Company for repairs to factory building, $575. Charge factory overhead.

25. Paid Reading Railroad Company for freight as follows: freight-in, $145; freight-out, $120.

25. Paid Franklin Insurance Agency $960 for a 3-year fire insurance premium.

26. Paid and distributed weekly payroll:

	Gross Earnings	Federal Income Tax Withheld	FICA Tax
Factory (20% of the factory payroll is indirect labor).....................	$3,300	$330	$198.00
Marketing.........................	1,330	133	79.80
Office.............................	1,200	120	72.00

26. Employer's payroll taxes on weekly payroll.

26. Paid Clark Manufacturing Company for Sept. 18 invoice less damaged materials returned.

30. Paid Central Telephone Company bill, $210 (charge 10% to factory, 60% to marketing, and 30% to office).

30. The beginning raw materials inventory was $2,000; the ending inventory is $2,200. Transfer the difference to Work in Process after posting the purchase transactions.

30. Factory overhead for September to be applied based on a rate of 70% of direct labor cost.

30. The following information relates to expiration of insurance and accrual of depreciation for September:

Depreciation on factory equipment..........	$420
Depreciation on delivery equipment.........	330
Depreciation on office equipment............	210
Insurance expired on factory...............	350
Insurance expired on delivery equipment.....	430
Insurance expired on office equipment.......	180

Sept. 30. Other necessary end-of-month information is as follows:

Costs transferred from Work in Process to Finished Goods...	$31,927
Opening inventory, Work in Process......................	3,500
Cost of goods sold......................................	32,085
Opening inventory, Finished Goods......................	3,875
Sales on account.......................................	61,320

  30. Determine the amount of over- or underapplied factory overhead, and transfer the balance to Cost of Goods Sold.

Required: Record the preceding transactions in general journal entry form.

4-3. Factory Ledger Entries.   The following transactions were completed by The Sullivan Corporation, which maintains both a factory ledger and a general ledger:

  (a) Materials purchased and received at the factory: $13,500
  (b) Requisitions received and filled in the storeroom:

For direct materials.................	$12,300	
For manufacturing supplies...........	4,000	$16,300

  (c) Paid the factory payroll for the week, as follows:

Direct labor.........................	$10,000	
Indirect labor.......................	3,200	
Superintendence.....................	1,000	$14,200

  (A factory payroll book is maintained at the factory. At the end of each week the factory payroll is reported to and paid by the general office. Provision for employees' FICA tax in the amount of $639 and 10% income tax is made on the general office books. The only payroll entry on the factory books is one distributing the payroll to the appropriate accounts and crediting General Ledger. The employer's factory payroll taxes are treated as factory overhead. The state unemployment insurance rate is 1.8%, the federal unemployment insurance rate is .5% and the employer's FICA tax is $639.)

  (d) Direct materials returned to the storeroom, $800.

  (e) A transfer voucher from the general office showed the following expenses to be recorded:

Insurance on factory building and equipment (prepaid account on general books)........	$250	
Heat, light, and power.....................	325	
Taxes on factory building.................	75	
Depreciation of machinery.................	240	
Depreciation of factory building...........	100	$990

  (f) Factory overhead is applied to production at the rate of 125% of direct labor cost.

  (g) Work completed during the week, $28,000.

  (h) Goods costing $32,500 to produce were sold for $42,000.

Required: Journal entries to record the above transactions on the general office books and on the factory books. Use only one work in process account. All inventory accounts and Factory Overhead are a part of the factory ledger; liability accounts, Sales, and Cost of Goods Sold are a part of the general ledger.

4-4. Factory Ledger Entries.   Spacecraft Corporation has its general office in Philadelphia, Pennsylvania, and its factories in nearby Trenton, New Jersey, and Pottstown, Pennsylvania.   A separate set of records is kept at the general office and at the factories.

On January 1 the factory books showed the following:

	Trenton		Pottstown	
Materials.....................	$25,000		$24,000	
Work in Process...............	13,500		15,000	
Finished Goods................	9,000		10,000	
General Ledger................		$47,500		$49,000
Total........................	$47,500	$47,500	$49,000	$49,000

The following transactions were completed during the month:

	Trenton	Pottstown
(a) Materials purchases...........................	$29,000	$26,000
(b) Materials requisitions:		
Direct......................................	35,000	32,000
Indirect....................................	6,000	4,000
(c) Return of materials to suppliers.................	400	550
(d) Payments to vendors (less 2% discount)..........	30,000	25,000

(e) Payrolls for the month:

		Trenton	Pottstown
Direct labor ($3 per hour)...................		15,000	11,400
Indirect labor.............................		3,500	2,900
Sales salaries.....................	$2,800		
Office salaries.....................	2,300		

(Deduct 6% for FICA tax and 10% for federal income tax.)
(Liability for the payrolls and payroll taxes is kept on the home office books.)

(f) Workers are paid, and employer's payroll taxes are recorded. The state unemployment insurance rate is 2%, the federal unemployment insurance rate is .5%, and employer FICA tax is 6%.

	Trenton	Pottstown
(g) Sundry factory overhead expenses.............	$17,000	$15,000

(h) Factory overhead applied to production at $5 per direct labor hour.

(i) Goods completed amounted to 80% of the total cost in the work in process accounts.

(j) Finished goods amounting to $114,000 were shipped to customers — $65,000 from the Trenton plant and $49,000 from the Pottstown plant. (A gross profit of 25% of the sales price is made on these shipments.)

Required: Using three parallel vertical columns headed General Office, Trenton Plant, and Pottstown Plant, prepare entries in journal form to record the January transactions. Use one work in process account for each plant.

4-5. Factory Ledger Accounts, Journal Entries, and Trial Balances. The Colorado Manufacturing Company has a cost accounting system using both general and factory ledgers. On December 31, 19A, after closing, the ledgers contained the following account balances:

Cash.....................	$20,000	Accounts Payable........	$15,500
Accounts Receivable......	25,000	Accrued Payroll..........	2,250
Materials................	10,000	Capital Stock............	60,000
Work in Process..........	4,500	Retained Earnings........	21,250
Finished Goods..........	9,500	Factory Ledger..........	24,000
Machinery...............	30,000	General Ledger..........	24,000

Inventory accounts are kept in the factory ledger.

During the month of January, 19B, the following transactions were completed:

(a) Materials purchased, $92,000.

(b) Sundry factory overhead incurred, $18,500.

(c) Labor was consumed as follows: for direct production, $60,500; indirect labor, $12,500; sales salaries, $8,000; administrative salaries, $5,000. Credit Accrued Payroll for total gross wages. The employer's payroll tax cost is based on labor purchased. The state and federal unemployment insurance tax rates are 1.6% and .5%, respectively; and the employer's FICA tax is $5,160. Of the FICA tax, $480 pertained to sales and $300 to administrative salaries.

(d) Gross payrolls totaling $75,750 were paid (10% of wages paid was withheld for income taxes, and $4,545 for FICA taxes). Debit Accrued Payroll for total gross wages of $75,750. Credit Accounts Payable for employee earnings after deductions; then record the cash payment to employees.

(e) Materials were consumed as follows: direct materials, $82,500; indirect materials, $8,300.

(f) Factory overhead applied to production was 76% of the direct labor cost.

(g) Work finished and placed in stock cost $188,000.

(h) All but $12,000 of the finished goods were sold, terms 2/10, n/60. The markup was 30% above production cost.

(i) 80% of the accounts receivable was collected, less 2% discount.

(j) Various marketing and administrative expenses, 60% marketing, 40% administrative, incurred during the month amounted to $30,000, the credit being to Accounts Payable.

(k) The check register showed payments of accounts other than for payrolls in the amount of $104,000.

Required: (1) Set up trial balances of the general ledger and of the factory ledger as of January 1, 19B.

(2) Open general ledger and factory ledger accounts from the January 1 trial balances and record the balances.

(3) Post the January transactions directly into the ledger accounts without journal entries. Open new accounts whenever necessary.

(4) Prepare trial balances of the general ledger and the factory ledger as of January 31, 19B.

CASE

Chart of Accounts — Coding System.   Ollie Mace has recently been appointed controller of a family-owned manufacturing enterprise. The firm, S. Dilley & Co., was founded by Mr. Dilley about 20 years ago, is 78% owned by Mr. Dilley, and has served the major automotive companies as a parts supplier. The firm's major operating divisions are Heat Treating, Extruding, Small Parts Stamping, and Specialized Machining. Sales last year from the several divisions ranged from $150,000 to over $3,000,000. The divisions are physically and managerially independent except for Mr. Dilley's constant surveillance. The accounting system for each division has evolved according to the division's own needs and to the abilities of its accountants. Mr. Mace is the first controller in the firm's history to have responsibility for overall financial management. Mr. Dilley expects to retire within six years and has hired Mr. Mace to improve the firm's financial system.

Mr. Mace decides that he must design a financial reporting system that will:

1. Give managers uniform, timely, and accurate reports on business activity. Monthly divisional reports should be uniform and available by

the 10th of the following month. Company-wide financial reports also should be prepared by the 10th.

2. Provide a basis for measuring return on investment by division. Divisional reports should show assets assigned each division and revenue and expense measurement in each division.

3. Generate meaningful budget data for planning and decision-making purposes. The accounting system should provide for the preparation of budgets which recognize managerial responsibility, controllability of costs, and major product groups.

4. Allow for a uniform basis of evaluating performance and quick access to underlying data. Cost center variances should be measured and reported for operating and nonoperating units including headquarters. Also questions about levels of specific cost factors or product costs should be answerable quickly.

It appears to Mr. Mace that a new chart of accounts is essential to attacking other critical financial problems. The present account codes used by divisions are not standard.

Mr. Mace sees a need to divide asset accounts into six major categories; i.e., current assets, plant and equipment, etc. Within each of these categories, he sees a need for no more than 10 control accounts. Based on his observations to date, 100 subsidiary accounts are more than adequate for each control account.

No division now has more than five major product groups. The maximum number of cost centers Mr. Mace foresees within any product group is six, including operating and nonoperating groups. He views general divisional costs as a nonrevenue producing product group. Altogether, Mr. Mace estimates that about 44 natural expense accounts plus about 12 specific variance accounts would be adequate.

Mr. Mace is planning to implement the new chart of accounts in an environment that at present includes manual records systems and one division which is using an EDP system. Mr. Mace expects that in the near future most accounting and reporting for all units will be automated. Therefore, the chart of accounts should facilitate the processing of transactions manually or by machine. Efforts should be made, he believes, to restrict the length of the code for economy in processing and convenience in use.

Required: (1) Design a chart of accounts coding system that will meet Mr. Mace's requirements. Your answer should begin with a digital layout of the coding system. You should explain the coding method you have chosen and the reason for the size of your code elements. Explain your code as it would apply to asset and expense accounts.

(2) Use your chart of accounts coding system to illustrate the code needed for the following data:

    (a) In the Small Parts Stamping Division, $100 was spent on cleaning supplies by Foreman Bill Shaw in the Polishing Department of the Door Lever Group. Code the expense item using the code you developed above.

    (b) A new motorized sweeper has been purchased for the Maintenance Department of the Extruding Division for $3,450. Code this asset item using the code you developed above.

(NAA adapted)

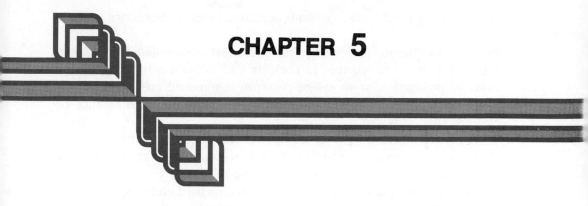

CHAPTER 5

JOB ORDER
COSTING

An enterprise seeks to profit by providing customers with goods and services. To realize this profit, it is continuously necessary to make decisions based upon appropriate and timely information provided by accounting procedures and reports. In fulfilling the needs of management, cost accounting consists of three basic phases: (1) cost accounting in the sense of cost determination and measurement, (2) cost planning and control through budgets and standards, and (3) cost analysis for decision-making purposes.

The cost finding or cost determination phase for the manufacturing function is discussed in this and subsequent chapters. Costing involves systems and procedures which lead to accounting entries and summary reports designed to enable management to control the cost of materials, labor, and factory overhead. The previous chapter presented an overall view of the flow of costs and expenses, generally known as the manufacturing cost accounting cycle. The greater part of this chapter is devoted to the cost accumulation procedures utilized in job order costing. Before entering into this discussion, it seems advisable to differentiate briefly between cost systems and cost accumulation procedures.

COST SYSTEMS: HISTORICAL OR STANDARD

Determination of a product's cost is a basic objective of cost accounting. After the cost unit has been selected (see discussion on page 91), the obvious question arises: How are these costs accumulated? A decision must be made as to whether to compile and allocate actual costs to the units of production or to assign costs on a standard cost basis. If the latter method is chosen, variance accounts will set off the difference between actual costs and standard costs.

An *actual* or *historical* cost system collects the costs as they occur but delays the presentation of results until manufacturing operations have been performed or services rendered. While the job or the process is charged with the actual quantities and costs of materials used and labor expended, the factory overhead in most cases is allocated on the basis of a predetermined overhead rate. Thus, even so-called "actual" cost systems are not predicated entirely on actual costs.

In a *standard* cost system all costs are predetermined in advance of production. Products, operations, and processes are costed using standards for both quantities and dollar amounts. Accounts are designed to collect actual costs. Differences between actual costs and standard costs, called variances, are collected in separate accounts. These variances are analyzed, and management is expected to move quickly to check unfavorable trends and departures from predetermined standards as well as from the desired overall profit goal.

COST ACCUMULATION PROCEDURES: JOB ORDER OR PROCESS

Both the actual (historical) cost system and the standard cost system may be used in connection with either job order or process costing.

The Job Order Cost Procedure. The job order cost procedure, discussed in detail in this chapter, keeps the costs of various jobs or contracts separate during their manufacture or construction. The method is applicable to job order work in factories, workshops, and repair shops as well as to work by builders, construction engineers, shipbuilders, and printers. The cost unit is the job, the work order, or the contract; and the records will show the cost of each. The method presupposes the possibility of physically identifying the jobs produced and of charging each with its own cost.

A variation of the job order cost method is that of costing orders by lots. A lot constitutes the quantity of product which can be conveniently and economically produced and costed. For example, in the shoe manufacturing industry a contract is divided into lots, each lot being from 100 to 250 pairs of one size and style shoe. The costs are then accumulated for each lot.

The Process Cost Procedure. The process cost procedure discussed in Chapters 6, 7, and 8 consists of computing an average unit cost for production by dividing the total manufacturing cost by the total number of units produced in the factory over a specific period of time. This method is used when units are not separately distinguishable from one another during one or more manufacturing processes.

The following conditions may also exist:

1. The product of one process becomes the material of the next process.

2. Different products, or even by-products, are produced by the same process.

A process cost method is applicable to industries such as flour mills, breweries, chemical industries, textile factories, and many others. Because of the nature of the output, it is necessary to compute a unit cost for each process. A process is often identifiable with a department. Such a computation is prepared on a process cost sheet or a cost of production report.

Many companies use both the job order and the process cost method in their product costing. For example, a company manufacturing a railway car built according to the customer's specifications uses job order costing to collect the cost per railway car. However, the multiple small metal stampings required are manufactured in a department which uses fast and repetitive stamping machines. The cost of these stampings is accumulated by the process cost method.

Both the job order and process costing procedures can also be used for service organizations. For example, an automobile repair shop uses order costing to accumulate the costs associated with work performed on each automobile. An airline or a hospital can utilize the notion of process costing to accumulate costs per passenger mile or per patient day, respectively. The textbook discussion of job order and process costing emphasizes manufacturing activity; however, the broad applicability of cost accumulation methods, including both actual and standard costs, should be realized.

Cost Units. Determination of unit costs and assignment of inventory costs for the purpose of profit determination is fundamental to cost accounting. The accumulation of costs poses a problem regarding the unit in which the product cost is to be stated. Because the total cost figure is considered unsatisfactory from a control point of view, a cost unit must be found that most adequately conforms both to the type of product and the manufacturing processes. The cost unit used is by no means uniform. While coal is measured by the ton, oil by the barrel, and lumber by board feet, products such as machines, airplanes, automobiles, shoes, shirts, or stockings are measured either by the individual unit or by multiples thereof, such as a dozen or a gross.

In selecting the cost unit, care must be taken that it is neither too large nor too small. If the unit is too large, significant cost trends may pass unnoticed due to averaging of costs. If the unit is too small, it may necessitate detailed and expensive clerical work. After the cost unit has been established, data can be marshaled to determine unit costs and to assign inventory costs.

JOB ORDER COST ACCUMULATION PROCEDURES

Job order and process costing procedures are employed by many types of manufacturing and service businesses. It should be remembered that job order and process costing represent two methods of cost accumulation, both of which follow the basic manufacturing cost cycle. In job order costing, each job is an accounting unit to which materials, labor, and factory overhead costs are assigned by means of job order numbers. The cost of each order produced for a given customer or the cost of each lot to be placed in stock is recorded on a summary sheet called a *job order cost sheet*, or merely a *cost sheet*. This master sheet is designed to collect the cost of materials, labor, and factory overhead applicable to a specific job.

Several jobs or orders may be going through a factory at the same time. Each cost sheet is given a job number which is placed on each materials requisition and labor time ticket used in connection with the job. These forms used for materials and labor, numbered for the job to which they apply, are totaled daily or weekly and entered on the cost sheets. The cost sheet eventually becomes a summary of all the costs, including factory overhead, involved in completing a job. The cost sheets are subsidiary records and are controlled by the work in process account.

Jobs performed on the basis of customer specifications allow the computation of a profit or loss on each order. If jobs constitute production of a specific quantity for inventory, job order costing permits computation of a unit cost for inventory costing purposes.

The discussion that follows deals with job order cost accumulation procedures using the data for Shamrock Manufacturing Company presented on pages 67 and 68 (Ch. 4). The data are expanded in this chapter for purposes of introducing the many detailed procedures that are so essential to adequate accounting for costs.

Cost Accounting Procedures for Materials. Merchandise Inventory and Purchases are familiar accounts in trading concerns. In manufacturing enterprises, it is common practice to record all materials and supplies in one control account titled Materials. Procedures that affect the materials account involve the:

1. Purchase of materials
2. Issuance of materials for factory use

These procedures are discussed in greater detail in Chapters 12 and 13.

Recording the Purchase of Materials. Accounting techniques used for the purchase of materials vary little from those studied in general accounting. The account debited is Materials or Materials Inventory (now used in place of the account Purchases), and the credit is made to Accounts Payable as materials are received. However, a posting to the materials account is not sufficient. Each purchase is also entered on an individual materials ledger card (a separate card being used for each materials item) showing quantity received, unit price, and amount. The amount posted to each materials ledger card is added to the previous balance which provides a perpetual inventory.

When materials are purchased, the approved invoice is recorded as:

Materials... 25,000
    Accounts Payable.....................................   25,000

Materials returned to the vendor are recorded as follows:

Accounts Payable..................................... 2,000
    Materials...   2,000

An entry for the returned materials is also made on the appropriate materials ledger cards.

Recording the Issuance of Materials. When a job is started, the materials necessary for the work are issued to the factory on the basis of materials requisitions prepared by production scheduling clerks or other employees. A copy of the requisition goes to the storekeeper who assembles the materials called for on the requisition. The materials requisition bears the job order number and specifies the type and quantity of materials required. The unit costs and the total costs of the materials are entered later on the requisition and posted to the materials ledger card.

The flow of materials from storerooms to factory results in a transfer of raw materials from the materials account to the work in process account. Essentially, each requisition results in a debit to Work in Process and a credit to Materials. Materials requisitions are summarized and recorded as follows:

Work in Process..................................... 31,000
    Materials...   31,000

A copy of each requisition goes to the cost department. These requisitions are sorted by job numbers, totaled, and entered in the materials section of the cost sheet bearing the same number. This basic costing technique accumulates the quantity and cost of materials used in each job.

When materials originally requisitioned for a job are not used and are returned to the storeroom accompanied by a returned materials report, Materials is debited and Work in Process is credited. The return to Materials requires entries on the materials ledger card as well as on the job order cost sheet.

Materials requisitions are also used to secure indirect materials or supplies from the storerooms. These requisitions are charged to the factory overhead control account and to departmental expense analysis sheets which constitute a subsidiary ledger for the departments using the supplies. Supplies issued might also be charged to marketing or administrative expense accounts.

Requisitions for indirect materials result in the entry:

	Subsidiary Record	Debit	Credit
Factory Overhead Control....................		6,000	
Indirect Materials.....................	6,000		
Materials................................			6,000

It is important to note that the above entry is made when indirect materials are issued and not when purchased. At the time of purchase, indirect materials are charged to Materials or to separate accounts such as Indirect Materials or Supplies.

The effect of all the preceding transactions on the materials account is shown below.

MATERIALS							
Mar.	1	Inventory	100,000	Mar.	31	Return	2,000
	31	Purchase	25,000		31	Direct Materials Requisitions	31,000
		86,000	125,000		31	Indirect Materials Requisitions	6,000
							39,000

The accounting entries required when materials are purchased and used are illustrated at the top of the next page. Stage 1 assumes that an invoice for materials purchased in the amount of $500 is recorded. A materials ledger card is required for each kind of material. In Stage 2 a materials requisition calls for $400 of materials for use on one order.

Cost Accounting Procedures for Labor. The entire payroll procedure may be divided into two distinct phases:

1. Collection of payroll data, computation of earnings, calculation of payroll taxes, and payment of the wages.
2. Distribution and allocation of labor costs to jobs, departments, and other cost classifications.

STAGE 1: MATERIALS PURCHASED	STAGE 2: MATERIALS USED	

Journal Entry:
Materials 500
   Accounts Payable...............500
	Journal Entry:
	Work in Process 400
	   Materials 400	

General Ledger:	**General Ledger:**	
MATERIALS	MATERIALS	WORK IN PROCESS
500	500 | 400	400 |

Subsidiary Record:
MATERIALS LEDGER CARD

Received	Issued	Balance
500		500

Subsidiary Records:
MATERIALS LEDGER CARD

Received	Issued	Balance
500		500
	400	100

JOB ORDER COST SHEET
Direct Materials Section

Date	Dept.	Req. No.	Cost
3/24	2	495	400

Entries Required for Materials Purchased and Used

To compute the labor cost of a given order, each worker must record on a labor time ticket the time spent on each job during a day. These time or job tickets collect the amount of labor used on each job. The time tickets, in turn, are priced in the payroll department to permit computation of employees' gross and net earnings.

In most factories the worker punches a time clock when entering and leaving the plant. The timekeeper makes periodic checks and records the days or hours worked by each employee. The clock card registers time "In" and "Out." Clock card hours should be reconciled with time ticket hours. When wages are paid on an hourly basis, the employee's clock card is often used by payroll clerks to compute gross wages, deductions, and net pay.

Time tickets for the various jobs worked on each day are sorted, priced, and summarized; at regular intervals, usually at the end of the payroll period, the labor time and labor cost for each job are entered in the space provided on the job order cost sheets. Posting to the cost sheets constitutes the distribution of the direct labor payroll. A summary of time ticket data facilitates journalzing, general ledger posting, and preparation of reports. For each payroll period — weekly, every two weeks, or monthly — a record of the labor cost and the liability for payment is summarized by journalizing and posting to the general ledger accounts. A full explanation of labor costing and payroll accounting is deferred to Chapters 14 and 15.

To simplify this discussion, reference will be made only to deductions from the gross earnings of employees for federal income taxes and for

Federal Insurance Contributions Act taxes of 6 percent[1] (the employees' share of the premium for Old Age and Survivors' Insurance and for Medicare). However, it should be realized that an employee's gross earnings are subject to other deductions such as state income taxes, city earnings taxes, pension payments, personal insurance policies, savings bonds, union dues, and United Fund contributions.

To illustrate the recording of labor cost, assume that the Shamrock Manufacturing Company met two payrolls during the month: $12,000 of direct labor and $1,800 of indirect labor on the 15th; and $15,000 of direct labor and $2,200 of indirect labor on the 31st. Assuming an average of 10 percent for income taxes withheld, the journal entry would show:

15th			*31st*		
Payroll[2]............	13,800		Payroll..............	17,200	
Federal Income Tax			Federal Income Tax		
Payable........		1,380	Payable........		1,720
FICA Tax Payable[3].		828	FICA Tax Payable..		1,032
Accrued Payroll....		11,592	Accrued Payroll....		14,448

At each payroll date the entry to record the payment to the workers would be:

Accrued Payroll......	11,592		Accrued Payroll......	14,448	
Cash.............		11,592	Cash.............		14,448

To distribute the total cost incurred, the following month-end summary entry would be in order:

	Subsidiary Record	Debit	Credit
Work in Process...........................		27,000	
Factory Overhead Control..................		4,000	
Indirect Labor......................	4,000		
Payroll................................			31,000

The above example was simplified for illustrative purposes. The entries are usually recorded on a weekly basis, so that labor cost remains current on the job order cost sheets made available to operating management. The details supporting the $27,000 Work in Process debit should be found in the labor cost section of the job order cost sheets.

---

[1]For convenience in computations, a rate of 6 percent for FICA (OASI and Medicare) on annual wages up to $15,000 paid each employee is used in the illustrations and problems of this textbook. Similarly, a maximum state unemployment tax of 2.7 percent and a federal unemployment tax of .5 percent on annual wages up to $4,200 are used.

[2]Payroll is the labor cost clearing account kept in the records as a convenience pending analysis of the labor time tickets and distribution of the labor cost to the proper accounts.

[3]The employees' share of the FICA tax is withheld at the time the employees are paid. At the same time or a later time the employer's share is recorded. For convenience, the FICA tax liability of both the employer and the employees is commonly recorded in one account, FICA Tax Payable.

The employer's payroll taxes are commonly recorded at the end of each month or sooner if necessary. Assuming the FICA tax to be 6 percent, the state unemployment tax to be 2.7 percent, the federal unemployment tax to be .5 percent, and that payroll taxes for direct and indirect factory labor are treated as factory overhead, the entry would be:

	Subsidiary Record	Debit	Credit
Factory Overhead Control...................		2,852	
Payroll Taxes........................	2,852		
FICA Tax Payable......................			1,860
State Unemployment Tax Payable.........			837
Federal Unemployment Tax Payable.......			155

Indirect labor is also accounted for through the use of clock cards and entered in the factory overhead control account and on the departmental expense analysis sheets in the same manner as indirect materials. The payroll account and employer payroll taxes accounts may also include amounts applicable to marketing and administrative personnel. Such costs would be charged to marketing and administrative expense accounts.

On page 98 is a summary of the entries required in recording labor cost. Stage 1 represents the record for each payroll period. Stage 2 shows the financial accounting phase for payments to the workers each payroll period. Stage 3 shows the cost accounting phase resulting from the labor used.

Cost Accounting Procedures for Factory Overhead. The quantity and the cost of materials and labor used on a given order can generally be measured in a straightforward and reasonably exact manner. The remaining cost element, factory overhead, presents a more involved problem.

If a planing mill contracts to make fifty cabinet assemblies for an apartment complex, the materials used and the labor expended can be entered on the requisitions and time tickets. But how much depreciation of the factory should be charged to the fifty cabinet assemblies; how much depreciation of saws, planers, and sanders; how much lubricating oil for the machines; how much power, light, heat, insurance, taxes, machine repairs, cutting tools, idle time, night watchman's salary, janitor's wages, plant foreman's salary, payroll taxes, and cost accountant's salary; and how much for other costs necessary to productive operations? A contributing difficulty is the fact that some of the expenses — such as rent, insurance, taxes, and night watchman's salary — are fixed regardless of the amount of production, while other expenses — such as lubricating oil, power, and cutting tools — vary with the quantity of goods manufactured. How, then, is it possible to charge a finished job at the time it is completed with a reasonable share of factory overhead when the actual amount of these expenses is often not known until the end of the fiscal period?

STAGE 1: PAYROLL COMPUTED WITH DEDUCTIONS	STAGE 2: PAYROLL PAID	STAGE 3: PAYROLL COSTS DISTRIBUTED
Journal Entries *15th*	*Journal Entries* *15th*	*Journal Entries* *31st*

Payroll 13,800
   Federal Income
     Tax Payable.....   1,380
   FICA Tax
     Payable   828
   Accrued Payroll ... 11,592
	Accrued
	   Payroll 11,592
	     Cash.......... 11,592
		Work in Process
		   27,000
		 Factory Overhead
		   Control....... 4,000
		   (Ind. Labor
		   4,000)
		     Payroll 31,000

31st	*31st*	Factory Overhead
		   Control....... 2,852
		   (Payroll Taxes,
		   2,852)
		   FICA Tax
		     Payable 1,860
		   State Un. Tax
		     Pay.......... 837
		   Federal Un. Tax
		     Pay.......... 155

Payroll 17,200
   Federal Income
     Tax Payable.... 1,720
   FICA Tax
     Payable 1,032
   Accrued Payroll .. 14,448
	Accrued
	   Payroll 14,448
	     Cash.......... 14,448	

Subsidiary Records		*General Ledger*
Employees' earnings records, tax, and other deduction records.		**WORK IN PROCESS** 27,000 |
		FACTORY OVERHEAD CONTROL 4,000 | 2,852 |
		Subsidiary Records:
		JOB ORDER COST SHEETS[1]
		DIRECT LABOR SECTION
		<table><tr><td>Date</td><td>Hours</td><td>Amount</td></tr><tr><td>31st</td><td>xx</td><td>27,000</td></tr></table>
		DEPARTMENTAL EXPENSE ANALYSIS SHEETS[2]
		<table><tr><td>Classification</td><td>Amount</td></tr><tr><td>Indirect Labor ......</td><td>4,000</td></tr><tr><td>FICA Tax ....</td><td>1,860</td></tr><tr><td>State Unemp. Tax.............</td><td>837</td></tr><tr><td>Federal Unemp. Tax.............</td><td>155</td></tr></table>

[1] There is a separate cost sheet for every job. Entries in the direct labor section of all jobs worked on during the period total $27,000 as shown by the work in process account.
[2] There is an analysis sheet for each department or cost center.

Entries Required in Recording Labor Cost

Estimated Factory Overhead. Factory overhead is entered on the job order cost sheets on the basis of a predetermined factory overhead rate based on direct labor hours, direct labor cost, machine hours, or other appropriate bases. Although a comprehensive study of estimating factory overhead is presented in Chapters 9, 10, and 18, a brief explanation of the procedure is advisable here to complete the picture of the cost cycle. In principle, the accountant determines a causal relationship between two factors, such as the direct labor hours and factory overhead, and uses this relationship as the means of charging factory overhead to jobs. For example, suppose direct labor hours for the Shamrock Manufacturing Company were *estimated* to be 12,000 hours and factory overhead to be $26,400. These estimates lead to the assumption that for each hour of direct labor there is $2.20 of factory overhead ($\frac{\$26,400}{12,000 \text{ hours}} = \$2.20$). The job order cost sheet for any job done during the period would disclose the factory overhead applicable to the job (direct labor hours worked on the job times the factory overhead rate).

Factory Overhead Applied Account. The applied factory overhead entered on the job order cost sheet for each job is the basis for this entry: (Again, figures used are from the illustration on page 68.)

Work in Process......................................	13,200	
Factory Overhead Applied (6,000 direct labor hours × $2.20)..		13,200

The factory overhead applied account is closed to the actual factory overhead control account at the end of the accounting period:

Factory Overhead Applied............................	13,200	
Factory Overhead Control..........................		13,200

It is common practice, as in the Shamrock Manufacturing Company, to use a factory overhead applied account because it keeps applied costs and actual costs in separate accounts. Some companies do not use the factory overhead applied account and post the credit directly to Factory Overhead Control:

Work in Process......................................	13,200	
Factory Overhead Control..........................		13,200

This entry eliminates the transfer of applied expenses to actual expenses.

Actual Factory Overhead. While job order cost sheets receive factory overhead on the basis of a predetermined factory overhead rate, actual factory overhead (consisting of indirect materials, indirect labor, payroll taxes, invoices received for overhead items, and the monthly adjusting entries such as depreciation and expired insurance) is charged to Factory Overhead Control and to departmental expense analysis sheets. These procedures are discussed in greater detail in the factory overhead chapters.

Representative examples of factory overhead costs involving adjusting entries are given on the next page.

	Subsidiary Record	*Debit*	*Credit*
Factory Overhead Control...................		682	
Depreciation........................	682		
Accumulated Depreciation — Machinery....			682
Factory Overhead Control...................		516	
Expired Insurance....................	516		
Prepaid Insurance......................			516

For the Shamrock Manufacturing Company, $6,000 of indirect materials were requisitioned from storerooms, $4,000 of indirect labor was used, and payroll taxes on factory labor totaled $2,852. Other factory expenses comprised of depreciation ($682) and insurance ($516) were prorated through month-end adjusting entries totaling $1,198. The factory overhead control account would reflect these facts as shown below.

FACTORY OVERHEAD CONTROL

Mar.	31	Indirect Materials	6,000	Mar.	31	Overhead Applied	13,200
	31	Indirect Labor	4,000			to Work in	
	31	Payroll Taxes	2,852			Process	
	31	Depreciation	682				
	31	Expired Insurance	516				
			14,050				

The balance of $850 remaining in the factory overhead control account indicates that actual expenses exceeded the overhead applied to the job orders; stated differently, overhead was underapplied. Further explanations and analyses of this balance are made in Chapters 9 through 11. The above control account was debited with all actual factory overhead items and credited with the factory overhead applied amount. In practice, the details of the actual factory overhead items are recorded in a subsidiary ledger called *departmental expense analysis sheets* or *factory overhead analysis sheets*.

The flow of factory overhead through accounting records is illustrated on the next page.

Accounting Procedures for Jobs Completed and Products Sold. During a month's operations, the materials placed in process are accounted for through materials requisitions for the jobs, the labor in process is evidenced by time tickets, and the factory overhead is applied. The figures charged to the work in process account represent the total factory cost for a month's operations.

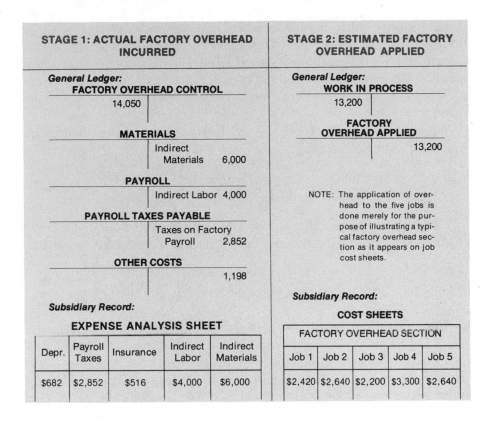

Flow of Factory Overhead Through Accounting Records

As jobs are completed, cost sheets are moved from the in process category to a finished work file. Completion of a job results in a debit to Finished Goods and a credit to Work in Process. If the completed job is undertaken for the purpose of replenishing stock, quantity and cost are recorded on finished goods ledger cards, which are the subsidiary record of the finished goods account. The journal entry to record all the work completed during the month for the Shamrock Manufacturing Company is:

Finished Goods.....................................	62,180	
Work in Process...................................		62,180

Or, if a separate work in process account is used to accumulate each cost element, the entry is:

Finished Goods.....................................	62,180	
Work in Process — Materials......................		26,000
Work in Process — Labor.........................		24,300
Work in Process — Factory Overhead..............		11,880

In factories with departmentalized operations, separate work in process accounts may be maintained for each producing department, and accumulated costs may be transferred from one department to the next based on the sequential work flow; or costs may be accumulated yet not transferred to subsequent departments until the job or the work is completed.

When finished products are delivered to customers, sales invoices are prepared, leading to an entry:

Accounts Receivable...............................	88,000	
Sales..		88,000

Each delivery necessitates a debit to Cost of Goods Sold and a credit to Finished Goods, using the cost figures recorded on the ledger cards:

Cost of Goods Sold.................................	52,300	
Finished Goods...................................		52,300

Job Order Cost Sheets.   A cost sheet is designed to summarize the amount of materials, labor, and factory overhead charged to a specific job. Cost sheets differ in form, content, and arrangement in each business. The illustrations on pages 103 and 104 show simple forms. In each form the upper section provides space for the job number, the name of the customer, a description of the items to be produced, the quantity, the date started, and the date completed. In factories with departmentalized operations, the cost sheet will show the materials, labor, and factory overhead applied in each department or cost center as is illustrated on page 104.

DISCUSSION QUESTIONS

1. Cost accounting is said to consist of three different phases. Name them.

2. Name five control accounts concerned primarily with cost finding.

3. What subsidiary record or ledger supports each of the control accounts mentioned in answering Question 2?

4. What is the primary objective in job order costing?

5. What is meant by a cost sheet?

6. What is the meaning of factory overhead?

Doran manufacturing co.   JOB ORDER NO. 978

FOR: Evans Construction Company   DATE ORDERED: 3/10/--

PRODUCT: #14 Maple drain boards   DATE STARTED: 3/14/--

SPECIFICATION: 12' x 20" x 1" clear finished   DATE WANTED: 3/22/--

QUANTITY: 2   DATE COMPLETED: 3/20/--

MATERIALS COSTS		DIRECT LABOR COSTS		FACTORY OVERHEAD APPLIED RATE: 125% of direct labor costs	
DATE	AMOUNT	DATE	AMOUNT	DATE	AMOUNT
3/14	$85.00	3/14	$45.00	3/20	$125.00
3/19	8.00	3/17	22.00		
3/20	3.00	3/18	12.00		
		3/19	15.00		
		3/20	6.00		
TOTAL →	$96.00	TOTAL →	$100.00	TOTAL →	$125.00

MATERIALS COSTS .... $ 96.00   SELLING PRICE $400.00
DIRECT LABOR COSTS 100.00
FACTORY OVERHEAD APPLIED .... 125.00   FACTORY COST $321.00
                                                          MARKETING EXPENSES .. 24.00
TOTAL FACTORY COST .... $321.00   ADMIN. EXPENSES 15.00

                                                          COST TO MAKE AND SELL 360.00

                                                          PROFIT .... $ 40.00

Cost Sheet for a Nondepartmentalized Plant

7. Explain briefly: (a) incurred factory overhead; (b) applied factory overhead.

8. When a sale is made, an asset is debited and Sales is credited. If a cost system, including perpetual inventory accounts, is used, what additional entry is required for this transaction?

9. Select the answer which best completes the following statement. Under job order cost accumulation, the dollar amount of the entry involved in the transfer of inventory from Work in Process to Finished Goods is the sum of the costs charged to all jobs (1) started in process during the period; (2) in process during the period; (3) completed and sold during the period; (4) completed during the period.

(AICPA adapted)

swenson furniture mfg. co.

JOB ORDER NO. 2706

FOR: Ellison Department Stores

PRODUCT: #120--recliners

SPECIFICATIONS: Attached drawings & blueprints

QUANTITY: 500

DATE ORDERED: 9/22/--

DATE STARTED: 11/21/--

DATE WANTED: 12/10/--

DATE COMPLETED: 12/5/--

DIRECT MATERIALS

DATE	DEPARTMENT	REQ. NO.	DESCRIPTION OR STORES NO.	QUANTITY	COST PER UNIT	TOTAL
11/12	Cutting	2947	Support lumber oak, 10 feet	500 pieces	$5.80	$2,900.00
		2948	Support lumber pine, 8 feet	250 pieces	3.50	875.00
11/15	Assembly	3080	Glue, pegs, and screws (standard)	500	2.20	1,100.00
11/27	Upholstery	3407	Upholstery cloth	3,000 yds.	4.00	12,000.00
			Total Materials Cost			$16,875.00

DIRECT LABOR

DATE	DEPARTMENT	TIME REPORT NO.	DESCRIPTION OF LABOR OR PROCESS	HOURS	RATE	COST
11/12-14	Cutting	867-901	Power saw cutting	120	$4.75	$ 570.00
11/14	Planing	1125-1130	Planing	50	5.50	275.00
11/15-21	Assembly	1360-1397	Assembling frames	200	5.25	1,050.00
11/25-27	Upholstery	1480-1505	Padding and upholstery	250	6.00	1,500.00
			Total Labor Cost			$ 3,395.00

APPLIED FACTORY OVERHEAD

DATE	DEPARTMENT	BASIS OF APPLICATION	HOURS	RATE	COST
11/15	Cutting	$3 per direct labor hour	120	$3.00	$ 360.00
11/15	Planing	$4 per direct labor hour	50	4.00	200.00
11/22	Assembly	$2 per direct labor hour	200	2.00	400.00
11/29	Upholstery	100% of direct labor cost	--	--	1,500.00
		Total Factory Overhead Applied			$ 2,460.00

DIRECT MATERIALS $16,875.00
DIRECT LABOR................................ 3,395.00
APPLIED FACTORY OVERHEAD 2,460.00

TOTAL FACTORY COST $22,730.00

SELLING PRICE.. $35,000.00

FACTORY COST $22,730.00
MARKETING EXPENSES 4,206.00
ADMIN. EXPENSES 2,905.00

COST TO MAKE AND SELL 29,841.00

PROFIT .... $ 5,159.00

Departmentalized Cost Sheet

Unless otherwise directed, use these rates in the exercises, problems, and cases that follow: FICA tax, 6%; federal unemployment insurance tax, .5%; state unemployment insurance tax, 2.7%.

EXERCISES

1. Cost Accumulation Procedure Determination. Classify these industries with respect to the type of cost accumulation procedure generally used — job order costing or process costing.

(a) Meat
(b) Sugar
(c) Steel
(d) Breakfast cereals
(e) Paper boxes
(f) Wood furniture
(g) Toys and novelties
(h) Coke
(i) Cooking utensils
(j) Caskets

(k) Pianos
(l) Linoleum
(m) Leather
(n) Nylon
(o) Baby foods
(p) Locomotives
(q) Office machines and equipment
(r) Luggage
(s) Paint
(t) Tires and tubes

2. Job Order Cost Sheet. Eddystone Machine Works, Inc. collected its cost data by the job order cost accumulation procedure. For Job No. 642, the following data are available:

Direct Materials	*Direct Labor*
9/14 Issued......$1,200	Week of Sept. 20 — 180 hrs @ $4.80/hr
9/20 Issued...... 620	Week of Sept. 26 — 140 hrs @ 5.25/hr
9/22 Issued...... 480	

Factory overhead is applied at the rate of $3.50 per direct labor hour.

Required: (1) The appropriate information entered on a job order cost sheet.

(2) The selling price of the job, assuming that it was contracted with a markup of 40% of cost.

3. Job Order Cycle Entries. Cleaver Manufacturing Company provided the following data for the month of January, 19B:

Raw Materials and Supplies:

Inventory, January 1, 19B....................................	$10,000
Purchases (all on credit) during January, 19B....................	30,000

Labor:

Accrued, January 1, 19B.......................................	$ 3,000
Paid during January, 19B (ignore payroll taxes)................	25,000

Factory Overhead Costs:

Supplies (issued from materials).............................	$ 1,500
Indirect labor...	3,500
Depreciation...	1,000
Other factory overhead costs (all from outside suppliers on credit)..	14,500

Work in Process:	Job #1	Job #2	Job #3	Total
Work in process January 1, 19B..	$1,000			$ 1,000
Job costs during January, 19B:				
Direct materials.............	4,000	$6,000	$5,000	15,000
Direct labor................	5,000	8,000	7,000	20,000
Factory overhead applied.....	5,000	8,000	7,000	20,000

Job #1 (started in December, 19A) was finished during January, 19B, and has been
   sold to a customer for $21,000 cash.

Job #2 (started in January, 19B) has not yet been finished.

Job #3 (started in January, 19B) was finished during January, 19B, and is in the
   finished goods warehouse awaiting customer's disposition.

Finished Goods:

Inventory, January 1, 19B................................. $ –0–

Required: Journal entries, with detail for the respective job orders and
factory overhead subsidiary records, to record these transactions:

(a) Purchases of materials during January on credit.
(b) Labor paid during January.
(c) Labor cost distribution for January.
(d) Materials issued during January.
(e) Depreciation for January.
(f) Acquisition of other overhead costs on credit during January.
(g) Overhead applied to production during January.
(h) Jobs completed and transferred to finished goods during January.
(i) Sales revenue for January.
(j) Cost of goods sold for January.

4. Job Order Costing. Williamstown Manufacturing Company had the following inventories on March 1:

Materials	$14,000
Work in process — materials	8,000
Work in process — labor	4,000
Work in process — factory overhead........................	3,200
Finished goods	15,000

The three work in process accounts control three jobs with this information:

	Job No. 621	Job No. 622	Job No. 623
Materials.........	$2,800	$3,400	$1,800
Labor............	1,600	1,500	900
Factory overhead...	1,280	1,200	720
Total.......	$5,680	$6,100	$3,420

The following information pertains to March operations:

(a) Materials purchased and received, $22,000; terms, n/30.

(b) Materials requisitioned for production, $21,000. Of this amount, $2,400 were
   for indirect materials; the difference was distributed: $5,300 to Job No. 621,
   $7,400 to Job No. 622, and $5,900 to Job No. 623.

(c) Materials returned to the storeroom from the factory, $600, of which $200
   were for indirect materials, the balance from Job No. 622.

(d) Materials returned to vendors, $800.

(e) Payroll, after deducting 6% for FICA tax and 12% for federal income tax,
   was $31,160. The payroll amount due the employees was paid during March.

(f) Of the payroll, direct labor represented 55%; indirect labor, 20%; sales salaries, 15%; and administrative salaries, 10%. The direct labor cost was distributed: $6,420 to Job No. 621; $8,160 to Job No. 622, and $6,320 to Job No. 623.

(g) An additional 9.2% is entered for employer's payroll taxes, representing the employer's 6% FICA tax, 2.7% state unemployment insurance contribution, and .5% federal unemployment insurance tax. Employer's payroll taxes related to direct labor are charged to the factory overhead control account.

(h) Factory overhead, other than any previously mentioned, amounted to $5,500. Included in this figure were $2,000 for depreciation of factory building and equipment and $250 for expired insurance on the factory. The remaining overhead, $3,250, was unpaid at the end of March.

(i) Factory overhead applied to production; 80% of the direct labor cost to be charged to the three jobs based on the labor cost for March.

(j) Jobs No. 621 and No. 622 were completed and transferred to the finished goods warehouse.

(k) Both Jobs No. 621 and No. 622 were shipped and billed at a gross profit of 40% of the cost of goods sold.

(l) Cash collections from accounts receivable during March were $65,450.

Required: (1) Job order cost sheets to post beginning inventory data.

(2) Journal entries to record the March transactions with current postings to job order cost sheets.

(3) A schedule of inventories on March 31.

5. Job Costing and Journal Entries for the Cost Accounting Cycle of a Municipality. The Intragovernmental Service Fund of Reading Township manufactures: (1) street and traffic signs for the Sanitation and Street Funds and (2) historical markers, information signs, and danger signs for the General Fund and Utility Fund. Each job is charged to these funds at prime costs (materials and labor) plus applied job overhead of 10% of prime costs. On November 1 there were no jobs-in-process inventories. During November these transactions occurred:

(a) Materials purchased on account from nongovernmental agencies, $8,000; materials transferred in from the Special Revenue Fund, $2,000 (credit Due to Special Revenue Fund).

(b) Actual job overhead, vouchered, $1,500. (The account is called Job Overhead Control instead of Factory Overhead.)

(c) Total production costs incurred on jobs during November:

Jobs for	Materials	Labor
Sanitation and Street Fund....	$5,000	$7,500
General Fund...............	3,000	4,500
Utility Fund...............	1,000	2,000

(d) From the payroll in (c), these deductions were made: FICA tax, $700; employee's federal income tax withheld, $1,600; union dues, $100; and employees' group insurance, $100.

(e) Recorded the employer's payroll taxes for November. The city has achieved a merit rating that enables it to pay only 1.5% for state unemployment tax.

(f) All jobs were completed and billed to the proper funds (for receivables, debit Due from _____ Fund).

(g) Close over- or underapplied job overhead to Cost of Jobs Billed.

(h) Paid amount owed to the Special Revenue Fund.

(i) Collected $10,000 from the Sanitation and Street Fund; $5,000 from the General Fund; and $3,000 from the Utility Fund.

Required: General journal entries for the preceding transactions, using separate "jobs in process" accounts for each fund.

PROBLEMS

5-1. Job Order Cost Sheet. Tedyuscung Manufacturing Company produces special machines made to customer specifications. The following data pertain to Job Order No. 1106:

Customer: Markem Machine Shop	Date started: 11 / 4 /19--
Customer's Order No.: C696	Date finished: 11 /18 /19--
Dated: October 27	Total cost to manufacture: ?
Description: 18 drilling units	Sales price: $20,425

	Week Ending 11/11	Week Ending 11/18
Materials used, Dept. 1...........	$2,400	$1,300
Direct labor rate, Dept. 1.........	$4.10 per hour	$4.10 per hour
Labor hours used, Dept. 1.........	600	400
Direct labor rate, Dept. 2.........	$4.00 per hour	$4.00 per hour
Labor hours used, Dept. 2.........	300	140
Machine hours, Dept. 2...........	200	120
Applied factory overhead, Dept. 1..	$2.00 per labor hour	$2.00 per labor hour
Applied factory overhead, Dept. 2..	$1.80 per machine hour	$1.80 per machine hour

Marketing and administrative costs are charged to each order at a rate of 25% of the cost to manufacture.

Required: A suitable cost sheet showing the above data. Did the company make an adequate profit margin on this order?

5-2. Job Orders; Factory Overhead Subsidiary Ledger; Cost of Goods Manufactured Statement. At the beginning of September certain ledger accounts in the books and records of the Mayfair Products Company, Inc. had these balances:

	Debit	Credit
Work in Process.....................................	$ 1,010	
Materials...	3,690	
Accrued Payroll.....................................		$ 436

The balance in the work in process account is supported by these details appearing in the job order cost sheets:

Direct materials.....................................	$ 320	
Direct labor (150 hours).............................	450	
Factory overhead applied............................	240	
Total...	$ 1,010	

Certain columnar totals in the accounts payable register at the end of September show:

Accounts payable..................................	$13,820 (credit)
Purchase discounts lost............................	108 (debit)
Materials...	5,300 (debit)
Accrued payroll...................................	4,352 (debit)
Income taxes withheld.............................	478 (credit)

Materials requisitions indicate:

For production....................................	$ 4,270
For repairs and maintenance.......................	250
For factory supplies..............................	600

The labor distribution sheet shows:

Direct labor (for job orders), 2,000 hours..............		$ 6,000
Factory overhead:		
Foreman's salary.................................	$ 800	
Repairs and maintenance..........................	180	
Indirect labor...................................	600	1,580
Total...		$ 7,580

The finished orders for the month consist of:

Direct materials..................................	$ 4,030
Direct labor (1,910 hours)........................	5,730
Factory overhead applied..........................	3,056
Total...	$12,816

The following subsidiary accounts and their balances controlled by the factory overhead control account appear in the ledger as of September 30:

Foreman's Salary............	$ 800	Factory Insurance............	$ 150
Repairs and Maintenance.....	430	Light and Power.............	160
Indirect Labor..............	600	Water and Heat.............	150
Factory Supplies............	600	Payroll Taxes	1,137
Depreciation — Factory		Rent — Factory.............	200
Equipment...............	120		

At the end of the month the three incomplete production (job) orders can be summarized as follows:

Materials..	$ 560
Direct labor (240 hours)..........................	720
Factory overhead applied..........................	384
Total...	$1,664

Required: (1) A statement of the cost of goods manufactured for the month of September.

(2) A calculation of the over- or underapplied factory overhead for the month of September.

5-3. Job Order Cost Accumulation and Accounting for Factory Overhead. The Clementon Manufacturing Company builds construction machinery to customer specifications. On December 31, the following inventories appeared on the company's balance sheet:

Materials and factory supplies................................	$32,300
Work in process..	55,115
Finished goods...	14,800

The work in process consisted of two partly completed construction jobs: Jobs No. LP4422 and OK5000 on which these costs had been incurred in previous months:

Job No.	Materials	Labor	Factory Overhead	Total
LP4422	$14,800	$12,300	$10,455	$37,555
OK5000	7,200	5,600	4,760	17,560
	$22,000	$17,900	$15,215	$55,115

The finished goods inventory consisted of one job: Job No. DU3750. The company has always applied factory overhead on a rate based on direct labor cost. Fluctuating labor costs and an attempt to attain greater control over indirect costs have led management to set up an overhead rate based on direct labor hours. The cost department estimates the total factory overhead for next year at $135,000 for 75,000 direct labor hours.

In January two new orders were started: No. MA4440 and No. HA5001. For these two orders and the other work in process, the following costs were incurred during January:

Job No.	Materials Cost	Labor Hours	and Cost
LP 4422	$ 2,300	825	$1,980
OK 5000	5,300	2,000	4,500
MA 4440	11,200	2,600	5,980
HA 5001	9,280	2,400	5,400

During January $16,400 of materials and factory supplies were purchased. The January 31 inventory of materials and supplies was $17,040. The factory payroll for the month totaled $20,834. Other factory overhead costs for the month were:

Power...........	$ 400		Repairs............	$3,200
Depreciation.....	1,600		Taxes.............	350
Insurance........	900			

Jobs LP4422 and OK5000 were completed and billed at $75,000 and $52,000. Jobs MA4440 and HA5001 were still in process on January 31.

Required: (1) The overhead rate used for the application of overhead to the jobs in process on December 31.

(2) The new overhead rate based on estimated direct labor hours.

(3) The journal entry to apply factory overhead to all jobs worked on during January (in total, not individual jobs).

(4) The amount of over- or underapplied factory overhead for January.

(5) The total cost and the gross profit on Jobs LP4422 and OK5000.

(6) The amount of the work in process inventory on January 31.

5-4. Journal Entries and Ledger Accounts Covering Cost Accounting Cycle.
During November, these transactions took place in the Sanger Manufacturing
Company:

(a) Materials purchased on account, $35,600.
(b) Materials issued during the month as follows: to fill requisitions on job orders,
$25,250; supplies issued to the factory, $1,300.
(c) Materials issued to complete defective units, $200.
(d) Freight paid for materials received, $850. (Freight is not added to unit costs on
materials inventory cards.)
(e) Materials returned to the vendor during the month, $225.
(f) Scrap materials received in the storeroom were set up at a value of $175, and
credit was given to Factory Overhead Control for that amount. A separate
general ledger account, Scrap Materials, is used.)
(g) Materials returned to the storeroom during the month as follows: from job
orders, $1,090; from supplies issued to the factory, $175.
(h) Total payroll for the month was as follows:
Recorded and then paid liability for net pay to workers, $41,503.
Withheld for federal income tax, $7,780.
Withheld for hospitalization plan, $950.
Withheld for FICA tax, $2,367.
(i) Taxes were recorded for the employer's FICA tax. State unemployment insurance for the Sanger Manufacturing Company is 1.5% of total payroll, and the
federal unemployment insurance rate is .5%. These taxes were charged to
Factory Overhead Control.
(j) The payroll was distributed as follows: direct labor, $40,200; indirect labor,
balance of payroll.
(k) Depreciation for the month: buildings, $3,000; machinery, $4,800.
(l) Property taxes accrued during the month, $750; insurance expired with a credit
to the prepaid account, $850.
(m) Factory overhead is charged to production at a rate of $1.40 per direct labor
hour. Records show 19,200 direct labor hours used during the month.
(n) Close out the over- or underapplied factory overhead to Cost of Goods Sold.
(o) Cost of goods completed during the month, $81,750.
(p) Goods costing $75,500 were sold on account during the month at a sales price
of $90,000.

Required: (1) Journal entries to record these transactions. Indicate the
subsidiary records to which the entries would also be posted.

(2) Ledger accounts for Work in Process, Factory Overhead Control, Materials, and Finished Goods. The November 1 balances were: Work in Process,
$9,750; Materials, $6,180; Finished Goods, $5,660.

(3) What is the effect of closing over- or underapplied overhead to Cost of
Goods Sold?

**5-5. Ledger Accounts Covering Cost Accounting Cycle and Job Cost Accumula-
tion.** The following is information regarding the operations for March of the
Goodfield Products Company:

The books show these account balances as of March 1:

Raw Materials.......	$ 65,000	Over- or Underapplied	
Work in Process.....	292,621	Factory Overhead.....	$12,300 (cr.)
Finished Goods......	78,830		

The work in process account is supported by these job order cost sheets:

Job No.	Item	Direct Materials	Direct Labor	Factory Overhead	Total
204	80,000 Balloons	$ 15,230	$ 21,430	$ 13,800	$ 50,460
205	5,000 Life Rafts	40,450	55,240	22,370	118,060
206	10,000 Life Belts	60,875	43,860	19,366	124,101
		$116,555	$120,530	$ 55,536	$292,621

During March these transactions occurred:

(a) Purchase of raw materials, $42,300.

(b) Purchase of special materials for new Job No. 207, $5,800.

(c) Job No. 207 calls for 4,000 life jackets.

(d) Payroll data for March:

Job No.	Amount	Hours
204	$13,422	6,711
205	14,630	6,500
206	14,075	7,230
207	12,948	5,820

Indirect labor cost, $9,480; factory superintendence, $1,500.
Payroll deductions: FICA tax, 6%; federal income tax, 12%.

(e) Employer's payroll taxes: FICA, 6%; state unemployment insurance, 1.6%; federal unemployment insurance, .5%. These taxes were charged to Factory Overhead Control.

(f) Raw materials issued:

Job No. 204..... $ 9,480
Job No. 205..... 11,320
Job No. 206..... 10,490
Job No. 207..... 16,640 (excluding special purchases of $5,800 which are also issued at this time)

(g) Other factory overhead incurred or accrued:

Insurance on factory........	$ 830	Coal expense..............	$1,810
Taxes on real estate.........	2,345	Power.....................	3,390
Depreciation — machinery...	4,780	Repairs and maintenance....	2,240
Depr. — factory building....	2,840	Indirect supplies...........	1,910
Light....................	1,260		

(h) Factory overhead is applied at the rate of $1.15 per direct labor hour.

(i) Shipped and billed Job No. 204 at a contract price of $97,500.

Required: (1) Ledger accounts, inserting beginning balances and entering transactions for March. (Factory overhead is to be posted to the control account only with a credit to Various Credits.)

(2) In itemized form, the total cost of each job at the end of March.

(3) The amount remaining in the over- or underapplied factory overhead account.

5-6. General and Subsidiary Ledger Accounts Covering Cost Cycle Using Job Order Cost Accumulation. The Leyden Company makes two types of storage batteries: Dependable Senior and Dependable Junior. General and subsidiary ledger balances as of May 1 were:

	Debit	*Credit*
Cash......................................	$ 35,000	
Accounts Receivable.......................	25,000	
Raw Materials.............................	35,000	
Work in Process...........................	15,000	
Finished Goods............................	25,000	
Factory Equipment.........................	20,000	
Accumulated Depreciation — Factory Equipment......		4,000
Accounts Payable..........................		46,000
Capital Stock.............................		80,000
Retained Earnings.........................		25,000
Total.................................	$155,000	$155,000

Raw materials:		Finished goods inventory:	
Cases.........	$17,500	Dependable Senior....	$15,000
Zinc..........	12,000	Dependable Junior....	10,000
Fluid.........	5,500	Total...............	$25,000
Total.........	$35,000		

	Dependable Senior *Job Order #84* *for Stock*	*Dependable Junior* *Job Order #85* *for Stock*
Work in process inventory:		
Materials.......................	$5,000	$4,000
Labor...........................	2,500	1,500
Factory overhead.................	1,250	750
Total...........................	$8,750	$6,250

The figures in the subsidiary ledgers are expressed in dollars only. The company buys cases, zinc, and fluid but assembles the batteries.

(a) Summary of accounts payable register:

Raw materials purchases:		
Cases.....................................	$10,000	
Zinc......................................	5,000	
Fluid.....................................	5,000	$20,000
Payroll....................................		18,000
Factory overhead............................		3,000
Marketing expenses..........................		20,000
Administrative expenses.....................		10,000
Financial expenses..........................		4,000
		$75,000

(b) Summary of materials requisitions:

	Total	*Job Order #84*	*Job Order #85*
Cases...................	$21,000	$11,000	$10,000
Zinc....................	16,000	8,000	8,000
Fluid...................	8,000	5,000	3,000
	$45,000	$24,000	$21,000

(c) Payroll analysis:

Direct labor:		
Job Order #84..........	$7,000	
Job Order #85..........	7,500	$14,500
Indirect labor...........		3,500
		$18,000

(d) The overhead rate is 50% of direct labor cost. Charge the two orders.

(e) Job #84 is finished.

(f) Summary of sales on account:

	Sales Price	Cost Price
Dependable Senior........................	$ 80,000	$ 45,000
Dependable Junior.......................	22,000	8,000
Total..................................	$102,000	$ 53,000

(g) Summary of cash transactions:

Received on account...................................	$118,000
Paid creditors and other liabilities.......................	105,000

(h) Depreciation on factory equipment is $1,250.

Required: (1) The posting of all transactions to ledger accounts to record the above data.

(2) The amount of over- or underapplied factory overhead — transferring the balances to the cost of goods sold account.

(3) The checking of the control account balances with the balances of the related subsidiary ledger balances.

(4) A trial balance.

CASES

A. Job Order Costing; General and Factory Ledger. On December 31, 19A, after closing, the ledgers of the Palmer-Travis Company contained these accounts and balances:

Cash.................	$47,000	Accounts Payable..........	$ 59,375
Accounts Receivable...	50,000	Capital Stock..............	100,000
Materials*..........	22,000	Retained Earnings..........	34,925
Work in Process*.....	7,500	Factory Ledger............	62,000
Finished Goods*......	32,500	General Ledger*...........	62,000
Machinery..........	35,300		

*Maintained in the factory ledger.

Details of the three inventories are:

Materials inventory:

Material A — 2,000 units @ $5.00........	$10,000
Material B — 4,000 units @ 3.00........	12,000
Total....................	$22,000

Finished goods inventory:

Item X — 1,000 units @ $12.50........	$12,500
Item Y — 2,000 units @ 10.00........	20,000
Total....................	$32,500

Work in process inventory:

	Job No. 101	Job No. 102
Direct materials:		
500 units of A @ $5.00.............	$2,500	
200 units of B @ 3.00.............		$ 600
Direct labor:		
500 hours @ $4.00.................	2,000	
200 hours @ 5.00.................		1,000
Factory overhead applied at the rate of		
$2.00/hour.....................	1,000	400
Total........................	$5,500	$2,000

During January, 19B, these transactions were completed:

(a) Purchases on account: Material A, 10,000 units @ $5.20; Material B, 12,000 units @ $3.75; indirect materials amounting to $17,520.

(b) Payroll totaling $110,000 was paid. $20,000 of the total payroll was for marketing and administrative salaries. Payroll deductions consisted of $15,500 for federal income tax withheld and 6% for FICA tax.

(c) Payroll to be distributed as follows: Job No. 101, 5,000 direct labor hours @ $4.00; Job No. 102, 8,000 direct labor hours @ $5,00; Job No. 103, 6,000 direct labor hours @ $3.00; indirect labor, $12,000; marketing and administrative salaries, $20,000. Employer's payroll taxes are: FICA tax, 6%; state unemployment insurance tax, 2.7%; federal unemployment insurance tax, .5%.

(d) Materials were issued on a fifo basis as follows: Material A, 10,000 units (charged to Job No. 101); Material B, 12,000 units (charged to Job No. 102); Material A, 1,000 units, and Material B, 2,500 units (charged to Job No. 103). (*Note:* Transactions to be taken in consecutive order.) Indirect materials amounting to $7,520 were issued.

(e) Factory overhead was applied to Jobs No. 101, 102, and 103 based on a rate of $2 per direct labor hour.

(f) Jobs No. 101 and 102 were completed and sold on account for $120,000 and $135,000, respectively.

(g) After allowing a 5% cash discount, a net amount of $247,000 was collected on accounts receivable.

(h) Marketing and administrative expenses paid during the month amounted to $15,000. Miscellaneous factory overhead amounting to $10,800 was paid and transferred to the factory. Depreciation on machinery was $2,000.

(i) Payments on account, other than payrolls paid, amounted to $85,000.

(j) Over- or underapplied factory overhead is to be closed to the cost of goods sold account.

Required: (1) Trial balances of the general ledger and of the factory ledger as of January 1, 19B.

(2) Open general ledger and factory ledger accounts from the January 1 trial balances and record the balances.

(3) Journalize the January transactions.

(4) Post the January transactions to the general ledger, factory ledger, and subsidiary ledgers for materials, work in process, finished goods, and factory overhead incurred.

(5) Trial balances of the general ledger and the factory ledger as of January 31, 19B, reconciling control accounts with subsidiary ledgers.

(6) A statement of cost of goods sold for January, 19B.

B. Job Lot Costing; Factory Ledger; Income Statement. The manufacturing process of the Pepper Products Company consists of assembling its product from parts supplied by four prime contractors. These parts are accepted by the Pepper Products Company only when they prove acceptable for use in the finished product.

The company pays its direct labor on a piecework basis, paying only for completed units which prove to be acceptable upon inspection. Although the company does not employ a cost accounting system, it normally schedules production in lots of 100 units each. Thus, at the end of a month some lots may still be in process. These lots may have all the necessary materials already issued, or only a portion of the materials may have been issued. Any direct labor costs incurred for these lots will be restricted to the labor for units already completed and accepted by inspection but not transferred to finished goods.

On September 30, 19—, the trial balance appeared as follows:

Assets (including a petty cash fund of $400 maintained at the plant)......................................	$133,700	
Liabilities...		$ 20,000
Capital Stock.......................................		100,000
Retained Earnings..................................		40,000
Materials...	53,200	
Direct Labor..	18,900	
Factory Overhead...................................	12,400	
Marketing Expenses.................................	8,000	
Administrative Expenses.............................	4,000	
Sales...		70,200
Total.......................................	$230,200	$230,200

Of the completed lots for September, one lot of 100 units is in the storeroom; and the remaining lots were sold to the National Mail Order Company under a contract which called for the purchaser to pay a price equal to cost (including a reasonable allowance for normal overhead) plus a markup equal to 30% of cost. This contract accounted for all of the company's sales in September. Since the Pepper Products Company has no cost accounting system, the National Mail Order Company cost accountant made an analysis of the Pepper Products Company's records and developed these figures pertinent to the contract:

	Unit Cost	*Basis of Calculation*
Direct materials cost........	$60	Cost to company of all components
Direct labor cost..........	30	Total piece rate per completed unit
Factory overhead.........	18	Percentage of prime cost

The Pepper Products Company now seeks to establish a cost accounting system for its plant. Since the home office and the plant are separated by a distance of 100 miles, the company also desires to maintain the cost accounts at the plant and the financial accounts on the books of the home office.

An inventory of materials on September 30 totals $12,100.

Required: Assuming the calculations of the cost accountant of the National Mail Order Company to be correct, prepare:

(a) Entries both on the books of the home office and on the books of the plant to change the company's accounts to reflect the use of a job-lot accounting system as desired by the management. (Assume that no inventories were on hand on September 1, 19—, and that the company closes its books on August 31, the end of its fiscal year.)

(b) An income statement for September. (Applied factory overhead is closed to the actual overhead account at the end of the fiscal year.)

C. Determination of Cost. The president of the Nola Cola Bottling Company has heard rumblings of dissatisfaction among the board of directors about the relatively low net earnings of the company. Several directors are not satisfied with the accounting reports being issued.

They believe, it appears, that the shipping and delivery expenses are reasonable, that advertising is in line, and that administrative expenses, although possibly somewhat above normal, are not out of control. Their primary criticism seems leveled at manufacturing costs.

Consequently, a meeting of the board of directors has been called in order to examine critically the accounting system in use for determining manufacturing costs; that is, in essence, the cost of a Nola Cola bottle ready for delivery as it comes from the last operation of the bottling process.

Sensing some of the problems involved, the president has adopted a recognized technique of executive strategy; before having the controller explain the accounting system in use, the president has decided to ask for an opinion as to what items should be included in the proper determination of the cost of a bottle of Nola Cola. For example, the president believes there is mutual agreement that such items as syrup, water, carbonation, and bottle caps are properly part of manufacturing costs.

Required: A list of other items that should be included, and to what extent.

D. Improving a Cost Information and Accumulation System. An examination of costing methods and procedures in the Zodiac Printing Company reveals the following:

(a) Costing formulas and ratios prepared a long time ago are still being used by estimators even though prices for materials have increased, overhead is higher, and new machinery has been installed.

(b) An estimator in the production department and a cost clerk in the cost department prepare estimates independently from one another, resulting in widely divergent cost figures.

(c) A profit per individual job or order can never be determined.

(d) Each job or order is sold with a definite markup. Yet instead of a profit of $100,000 as the president hoped for, the chief accountant prepared an income statement showing only a $48,000 profit.

(e) Determining departmental efficiency and control over expenses is not possible.

Required: A statement outlining: (a) possible causes of the existing conditions and (b) possible steps to remedy the situation.

E. Revising a Cost Information and Accumulation System. The Ackerman Thread Company produces a standardized, high-quality cotton thread. Recently the firm accepted the offer of a large distributor to produce small lots of high-quality thread with special characteristics at a relatively high margin of profit. Heretofore, controls on costs were maintained by processes because of the standardized nature of the product. It is now believed that the old system is no longer satisfactory because a knowledge of the profitability of each job lot is needed.

In order to produce these small lots, skilled workers in several of the departments have been assigned to work on the special orders; in some instances, even special locations for this type of work have been established. However, in some phases of the production processes the special threads are processed in the same way and by the same workers and facilities as the present, regular line.

Required: (1) Adjustments that are advisable in the present system and the reasons for them.

(2) Problems which the company may face because of these adjustments.

F. Installing a Cost Information and Accumulation System. A textile manufacturer asks your advice concerning the advisability of installing a cost system.

He explains briefly that he manufactures many different cloths, starting with scoured wool that passes through the following processes before becoming finished cloth: picking and blending, carding, spinning, weaving, finishing, and dyeing. The company's salesmen take orders considerably in advance of the actual production of the cloth, using samples produced during a special period set aside each season for the manufacture of samples. Competition is keen and the profit margin is low. Financing is received through bank loans.

Required: (1) The principal advantages of installing a cost system.

(2) The principal additions or alterations necessary to operate a cost system. (The present accounting system is designed for the purpose of preparing annual financial statements.)

(3) An explanation of how matters can be arranged in order to find the cost of the principal stages of manufacture, such as carding, spinning, weaving, etc. (The carding machines operate three shifts per day; the spinning machines, two shifts; and the weaving machines, one shift.)

G. Designing Cost Accumulation Procedures. You are asked by a client to advise him as to a satisfactory system of factory costs. You find that his factory is divided into two main divisions:

    (a) *Machine Shop.* This division makes steel molds used in the manufacture of plastic articles. These molds require careful precision work; and frequently, one man is employed at machining one mold for several weeks. The finished molds are used by the Plastics Division of the company. In addition, some other machine work is done for customers although this forms the smaller portion of the shop's output.

    (b) *Plastics Division.* This division manufactures plastic articles including ash trays, buttons, knobs, etc. The process of manufacture consists of placing chemical powders in a mold, which is then placed under a steam press where pressure is applied for a few minutes. The chemical powders are the only raw materials used and are not processed before being placed in the mold. After being pressed, a certain amount of finishing and inspection labor is necessary to complete the articles.

You also ascertain that:

    (a) The company has had no previous cost records.

    (b) Production in both divisions is controlled by job order tickets.

    (c) Raw materials are kept in one place, but no record has been kept of withdrawals.

    (d) Labor is paid at hourly rates, and a time clock at the factory entrance is used for determining the hours worked in any day.

    (e) Employees have been preparing satisfactory time tickets showing the hours worked on each job and, in the case of the Plastics Division, the number of units produced; but this record has never been balanced against the wages paid nor the record of production.

    (f) Spoilage is a substantial factor in both divisions.

    (g) The Machine Shop and the Plastics Division are in separate parts of the one building.

    (h) The company has a satisfactory system of general ledger accounting.

Required: A method or methods for obtaining factory costs, explaining why you consider them the most satisfactory under the circumstances.

(CICA adapted)

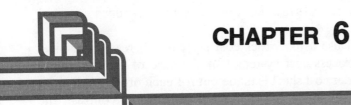

CHAPTER 6

PROCESS COSTING

Cost accumulation procedures used by manufacturing concerns are classified as either (1) job order costing or (2) process costing. The preceding chapter discussed procedures applicable to job order costing. It is important to understand that, except for some modifications, the accumulation of materials costs, labor costs, and factory overhead also applies to process costing.

Process costing methods are used for industries producing chemicals, petroleum, textiles, steel, rubber, cement, flour, pharmaceuticals, shoes, plastics, sugar, or coal. This type of costing is also used by firms manufacturing items such as rivets, screws, bolts, and small electrical parts. A third type of industry using process costing methods is the assembly-type industry which manufactures such things as typewriters, automobiles, airplanes, and household electric appliances (washing machines, refrigerators, toasters, electric irons, radios, television sets, etc.). Finally, certain service industries such as gas, water, and heat cost their products by using process costing methods. Thus, a process costing system is used when products are manufactured under conditions of continuous processing or under mass production methods; in fact, process costing procedures are often termed "continuous or mass production" cost accounting procedures.

The type of manufacturing operations performed determines the type of cost system that must be used. For example, a company manufacturing custom machinery will use a job order cost system, whereas a chemical company will use a process cost system. In the case of the machinery manufacturer, a job order cost sheet is made out for each order to accumulate the cost of materials, labor, and factory overhead. In contrast, the chemical company cannot identify materials, labor, and factory overhead with each order, for each order is part of a batch or of a continuous process. The individual order identity is lost, and the cost of a completed unit must be computed by dividing total cost incurred during a period by total units completed. The summarization of the costs takes place via the cost of production report which is an extremely efficient, economical, and timesaving device for the collection of large amounts of data.

The entire process-costing discussion is presented in this and the following two chapters. This chapter considers (1) the cost of production reports of departments originating products, (2) calculation of departmental unit costs, (3) costing of work in process, (4) computation of costs transferred to other departments, and (5) effect of lost units on unit costs. The cost reports of departments other than the originating department are also reviewed with emphasis on the costing of closing work in process inventories and the recalculation of preceding department unit costs due to lost units.

Chapter 7 deals with (1) special problems involved in adding materials in departments other than the first, (2) problems connected with opening work in process, and (3) the possibility of using costing methods other than those previously discussed.

Chapter 8 discusses the costing of by-products and joint products inasmuch as many industrial concerns using process cost systems are confronted with the difficult and often rather complicated task of assigning costs to their by-products and/or joint products.

CHARACTERISTICS AND PROCEDURES OF PROCESS COSTING

The characteristics of process costing are:

1. A cost of production report is used to collect, summarize, and compute total and unit costs.
2. Costs are charged to departmental work in process accounts.
3. Production is accumulated and reported by departments.
4. Production in process at the end of a period is restated in terms of completed units.
5. Total cost charged to a department is divided by total computed production of the department to determine an average cost for a specific period.
6. A cost for lost or spoiled units is computed and added to the cost of satisfactory units completed.

7. Costs of completed units of a department are transferred to the next processing department in order to arrive eventually at the total costs of the finished products during a period.

The procedures of process costing are designed to:

1. Accumulate materials, labor, and factory overhead costs by departments.
2. Determine a unit cost for each department.
3. Transfer costs from one department to the next and to finished goods.
4. Assign costs to the inventory of work still in process.

If accurate unit and inventory costs are to be established by process costing procedures, costs of a period must be identified with units produced in the same period.

COSTING BY DEPARTMENTS

The nature of manufacturing operations in firms using process or job order cost systems is usually such that work on a product takes place in several departments. In either system departmentalization of materials, labor, and factory overhead costs facilitates application of responsibility accounting. Each department performs a specific operation or process towards the completion of the product. For example, after the Mixing Department has completed the starting phase of work on the product, units are transferred to the Refining Department, after which they may go to the Finishing Department for completion and transfer to the finished goods storeroom.

Both units and costs are transferred from one manufacturing department to another. Separate departmental work in process accounts are used to charge each department for the materials, labor, and factory overhead used to complete its share of a manufacturing process.

Process costing involves averaging costs for a particular period in order to obtain departmental and cumulative unit costs. The cost of a completed unit is determined by dividing the total cost of a period by the total units produced during the period. However, determining departmental production for a period also involves evaluating units still in process which, in turn, requires the accumulation of total and unit costs by departments. The breakdown of costs for the computation of total unit costs and for costing departmental work in process inventories is also desirable for cost control purposes.

Departmental total and unit costs are determined by the use of the cost of production report which is described and illustrated in detail in later sections of this chapter. Most of the activity in a process cost system involves the accumulation of data needed for the preparation of these cost reports.

PRODUCT FLOW

A product can flow through a factory in numerous fashions. Three product flow formats associated with process costing — sequential, parallel, and selective — are illustrated here to indicate that basically the same costing procedures can be applied to all types of product flow situations.

Sequential Product Flow. In a sequential product flow, each item manufactured goes through the same set of operations. Graphically, this might be shown as:

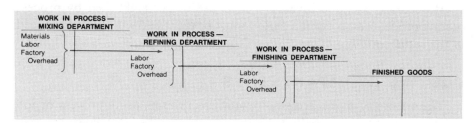

Materials are started in the Mixing Department. Labor and factory overhead are added; when the work is finished in the Mixing Department, it moves to the Refining Department. This second process, and any succeeding processes, may add more materials or simply work on the partially completed input from the preceding process, adding only labor and factory overhead, as in this example. After the product has been processed by the Finishing Department, it is a completed product and becomes a part of Finished Goods.

Parallel Product Flow. In a parallel product flow, certain portions of the work are done simultaneously and then brought together in a final process or processes for completion and transfer to Finished Goods. Graphically, this might be shown as:

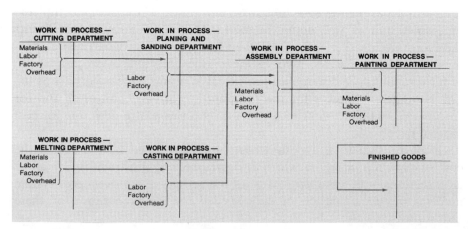

As in the previous illustration, materials may be added in processes subsequent to the first ones.

Selective Product Flow. In a selective product flow the product moves to different departments within the plant, depending upon the desired final product. For example, in meat processing, after the initial butchering process, some of the product goes directly to the Packaging Department and then to Finished Goods; some goes to the Smoking Department and then to the Packaging Department and finally to Finished Goods; some to the Grinding Department, then to the Packaging Department, and lastly to Finished Goods.

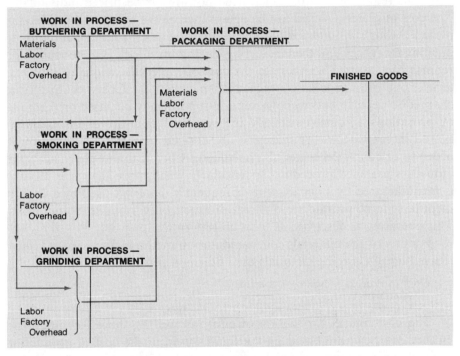

Transfer of costs from the Butchering Department involves consideration of joint cost allocation and is discussed and illustrated in Chapter 8.

PROCEDURES FOR MATERIALS, LABOR, AND FACTORY OVERHEAD COSTS

In a process cost system, materials, labor, and factory overhead costs are accumulated in the usual accounts using normal cost accounting procedures. Costs are then analyzed by departments or processes and charged to departments by appropriate journal entries. The details involved in a process cost system are usually fewer than those of a job order system where accumulation of costs for many orders can become unwieldy.

Materials Costs. In a job order cost system, materials requisitions are used to charge jobs for materials used. If requisitions are used in a process cost system, the details are considerably reduced because materials are charged to departments rather than to jobs, and the number of departments using materials is usually less than the number of jobs a firm might handle at a given time. Frequently materials are issued only to the process-originating department; subsequent departments add labor and factory overhead. If materials are needed in a department other than the first, they are charged to that department performing the specific operation.

For materials control purposes, it may still be desirable to require materials requisition cards which need not always be priced individually. The cost of materials used can be determined at the end of the production period through *inventory difference* procedures; i.e., adding purchases to opening inventory and then deducting closing inventory. Or, consumption reports can be used which state the cost of materials or quantity of materials put into process by various departments. Costs or quantities charged to departments by consumption reports may be based on formulas or prorations. Formulas specify the type and quantity of materials required in the various products and are applied to finished production in order to calculate the materials consumed. Chemical and pharmaceutical industries use such procedures, particularly when more than one product is manufactured by a department. Frequently materials used by a department have to be prorated to different products on various estimated bases. This proration is described as joint costing in Chapter 8.

For any of the materials cost computation methods discussed, a typical journal entry charging materials used during a period is:

```
Work in Process — Mixing Department.................  24,500
    Materials ..........................................        24,500
```

The cost figures for the above entry as well as those for labor and factory overhead are based on the figures used in the cost of production reports, the discussion of which begins on page 126.

Labor Costs. Labor costs are identified by and charged to departments in a process cost system, thus eliminating the detailed clerical work of accumulating labor costs by jobs. Daily time tickets or weekly time clock cards are used instead of job time tickets. Summary labor charges are made to departments through an entry which distributes the payroll:

```
Work in Process — Mixing Department.................  29,140
Work in Process — Refining Department...............  37,310
Work in Process — Finishing Department..............  32,400
Marketing Expenses Control..........................  16,600
Administrative Expenses Control.....................   4,550
    Payroll.............................................       120,000
```

Factory Overhead Costs. Factory overhead incurred in a process cost system, as well as in a job order cost system, is preferably accumulated in the factory overhead subsidiary ledger for producing and service departments — a procedure that is consistent with requirements for responsibility accounting and responsibility reporting.

The factory overhead chapters emphasize and recommend the use of predetermined overhead rates for charging overhead to jobs and products. However, in various process and job order cost systems, actual overhead rather than applied overhead is sometimes used for product costing. This practice is feasible when production remains comparatively stable from period to period, for factory overhead will then remain about the same from one month to the next. The use of actual overhead can also be justified when the influence of factory overhead is not an important part of total cost. However, departmental predetermined overhead rates should be used if:

1. Production is not stable.
2. Factory overhead, especially fixed overhead, is a significant cost.

Fluctuations in production can lead to the unequal incurrence of actual factory overhead from month to month. In such cases, factory overhead should be applied to production using predetermined rates so that units produced receive proper charges for factory overhead. Similarly, if factory overhead — especially fixed factory overhead — is significant, it is desirable to allocate factory overhead on the basis of normal or uniform production, using a predetermined rate. Indeed, the use of a predetermined rate is highly recommended for improving cost control and facilitating cost analysis.

Prior to charging factory overhead to departments via their respective work in process accounts, expenses must be accumulated in a factory overhead control account. As expenses are incurred, the entry is:

```
Factory Overhead Control.............................  xxxxx
    Accounts Payable......................................         xxxxx
    Accumulated Depreciation — Machinery.................         xxxxx
    Prepaid Items.........................................         xxxxx
```

The use of a factory overhead control account requires a subsidiary ledger for factory overhead with departmental expense analysis sheets to which all expenses are posted (see Chapter 10). Service department expenses are kept in like manner and distributed later on to producing departments. At the end of each period, departmental expense analysis sheets are totaled. These totals, which also include distributed service department costs, represent factory overhead for each department. The entry charging these expenses to Work in Process, either by debiting the actual cost incurred or by using the predetermined rates multiplied by the respective actual activity base for each producing department (e.g., direct labor hours), is:

```
Work in Process — Mixing Department.................. 28,200
Work in Process — Refining Department................ 32,800
Work in Process — Finishing Department............... 19,800
    Factory Overhead Control..........................         80,800
```

THE COST OF PRODUCTION REPORT

A departmental cost of production report receives all costs chargeable to a department. The cost of production report is not only the source for summary journal entries at the end of the month but also a most convenient vehicle for presenting and disposing of costs accumulated during the month.

A cost of production report shows (1) any cost, total and unit, transferred to it from a preceding department; (2) materials, labor, and factory overhead added by the department; (3) unit costs added by the department; (4) cumulative costs, total and unit, to the end of operations in the department; (5) the cost of opening and closing work in process inventories; and (6) cost transferred to a succeeding department or to a finished goods storeroom.

It is customary to divide the cost section of the report into two parts: one showing costs for which the department is accountable including departmental and cumulative total and unit costs, the other showing the disposition of these costs.

A quantity schedule showing the total number of units for which a department is held accountable and the disposition made of these units is also part of each department's cost of production report. Information in this schedule is used to determine the unit costs added by a department, the costing of closing work in process inventory, and the cost to be transferred out of the department.

A cost of production report determines periodic total and unit costs. However, a report that would merely summarize the total costs of materials, labor, and factory overhead and show only the unit cost for the period would not be satisfactory for controlling the costs. Total figures mean very little; cost control requires detailed data. Therefore, in most instances, total costs are broken down by cost elements for each department head held responsible for the costs incurred. Furthermore, detailed departmental figures are needed because of the various completion stages of the work in process inventories.

Either in the cost of production report itself or in the supporting schedules, each item of material used by a department is listed; every labor operation is shown separately; factory overhead components are noted individually; and a unit cost is derived for each item. To condense any of the illustrated cost of production reports, only total materials, labor, and factory overhead charged to departments are considered; and unit costs are computed only for each cost element rather than for each item.

The reports of The Carson Chemical Company, which manufactures one product in three producing departments (Mixing, Refining, and Finishing), are used to illustrate the details involved in the preparation of cost of production reports.

Mixing Department.   The cost of production report of the Mixing Department, the originating department of The Carson Chemical Company, is shown on page 128.   It illustrates the detailed computations needed to complete a cost of production report.

The quantity schedule of the cost report shows that the Mixing Department put 50,000 units in process, with units reported in terms of finished product.   Finished units can be pounds, feet, gallons, barrels, etc. If raw materials issued to a department are stated in pounds and the finished product is reported in gallons, units in the quantity schedule will be in terms of the finished product, gallons.   A product conversion table would be used to determine the number of units for which the department is accountable.   The quantity schedule of the Mixing Department's report shows that of the 50,000 units for which the department was responsible, 45,000 units were transferred to the next department (Refining), 4,000 units are still in process, and 1,000 units were lost in processing.

Equivalent Production.   Costs charged to a department come from an analysis of materials used, payroll distribution sheets, and departmental expense analysis sheets.   The Mixing Department's unit cost amounts to $1.72 — $.50 for materials, $.62 for labor, and $.60 for factory overhead.

Computation of individual unit costs requires an analysis of closing work in process to determine its stage of completion.   This analysis is usually made by a foreman or is the result of using predetermined formulas. Materials, labor, and factory overhead have been used on the 4,000 units in process but not in an amount sufficient to complete them.   To assign costs equitably to in-process inventory and transferred units, units still in process must be restated in terms of completed units, which is 4,000 units for materials costs but less than 4,000 for labor and overhead costs. The figure for partially completed units in process is added to units actually completed to arrive at the equivalent production figure for the period. This equivalent production figure represents the number of units for which sufficient materials, labor, and overhead were issued or used during a period.   Materials, labor, and overhead are divided by the appropriate equivalent production figure to compute unit costs by elements.   Should a

THE CARSON CHEMICAL COMPANY

MIXING DEPARTMENT

COST OF PRODUCTION REPORT

FOR THE MONTH OF JANUARY, 19—

QUANTITY SCHEDULE:

Units started in process.....................................		50,000
Units transferred to next department..........................	45,000	
Units still in process (all materials — ½ labor and factory overhead)	4,000	
Units lost in process......................................	1,000	50,000

COST CHARGED TO THE DEPARTMENT:

Cost added by department:

	Total Cost	Unit Cost
Materials..	$24,500	$ .50
Labor.......	29,140	.62
Factory overhead...	28,200	.60
Total cost to be accounted for...........................	$81,840	$1.72

COST ACCOUNTED FOR AS FOLLOWS:

Transferred to next department (45,000 × $1.72)...............		$77,400
Work in process — closing inventory:		
Materials.... (4,000 × $.50).............................	$ 2,000	
Labor....... (4,000 × ½ × $.62).........................	1,240	
Fac. overhead (4,000 × ½ × $.60).........................	1,200	4,440
Total cost accounted for...............................		$81,840

ADDITIONAL COMPUTATIONS:

Equivalent production — Materials $= 45,000 + 4,000 = 49,000$ units

$$\text{Labor and Factory Overhead} = 45,000 + \frac{4,000}{2} = 47,000 \text{ units}$$

Unit costs — Materials $= \dfrac{\$24,500}{49,000} = \$.50$

Labor $= \dfrac{\$29,140}{47,000} = \$.62$

Factory overhead $= \dfrac{\$28,200}{47,000} = \$.60$

cost element be at a different stage of completion with respect to units in process, then a separate equivalent production figure must be computed.

In many manufacturing processes all materials are issued at the start of production. Unless stated otherwise, the illustrations in this discussion assume such a procedure. Therefore, the 4,000 units still in process have all the materials needed for their completion. This is not true for labor and factory overhead, for only one half, or 50 percent, of the labor and factory overhead needed to complete the units has been used. In terms of equivalent production, labor and factory overhead in process are sufficient to complete 2,000 units.

Unit Costs. Departmental cost of production reports indicate the cost of units as they leave each department. These individual departmental unit costs are accumulated into a completed unit cost for the period. The report for the Mixing Department shows a materials cost of $24,500, labor cost of $29,140, and factory overhead of $28,200. The materials cost of $24,500 is sufficient to complete 49,000 units (the 45,000 units transferred out of the department as well as the work in process for which enough materials are in process to complete 4,000 units). The unit materials cost is, therefore, $.50 ($\frac{\$24,500}{49,000}$). A similar computation is made to determine the number of units actually and potentially completed with the labor cost of $29,140 and the factory overhead of $28,200. The 2,000 equivalent units in process are added to the 45,000 units completed and transferred to secure a total equivalent production figure of 47,000 units for both labor and factory overhead. When the equivalent production figure of 47,000 units is divided into the labor cost for the month of $29,140, a unit cost for labor of $.62 ($\frac{\$29,140}{47,000}$) is computed. The unit cost for factory overhead is $.60 ($\frac{\$28,200}{47,000}$). The departmental unit cost is $1.72, computed by adding materials, labor, and overhead unit costs — $.50, $.62, and $.60. This is the unit cost added by the department. This departmental unit cost figure cannot be determined by dividing total departmental costs of $81,840 by a single equivalent production figure, because no such figure exists; units in process are at different stages of completion as to materials, labor, and factory overhead.

Disposition of Departmental Costs. In the departmental cost report, the section titled "Cost Charged to the Department" shows a total departmental cost of $81,840. The lower part of the report shows the disposition of this cost. The 45,000 units transferred to the next department have a cost of $77,400 (45,000 units multiplied by the completed departmental unit cost of $1.72). The balance of the cost to be accounted for, $4,440 ($81,840 − $77,400), is the cost of work in process.

The inventory figure must be broken down into its component parts: materials, labor, and factory overhead. These individual costs are easily determined. The cost of materials in process is obtained by multiplying total units in process, 4,000, by the materials unit cost of $.50 (4,000 × $.50 = $2,000). The costs of labor and factory overhead in process are similarly calculated. The amount of labor and overhead in process is sufficient to complete only 50 percent, or 2,000, of the units in process. Therefore, the cost of labor in process is $1,240 (2,000 × $.62) and that of factory overhead in process is $1,200 (2,000 × $.60).

Lost Units. Continuous operating and processing leads to the possibility of waste, seepage, shrinkage, and other factors which cause loss or spoilage of production units. Management is interested not only in the quantities reported as completed production, units in process, and lost units but also in a comparison of planned and actual results. In verifying reported figures, the accountant will reconcile quantities put into process with quantities reported as completed and lost. One method of making such reconciliations is to establish process yields; i.e., the finished production that should result from processing various raw materials. These yields are computed as follows:

$$\text{Percent Yield} = \frac{\text{Weight of Finished Product}}{\text{Weight of Raw Materials Charged In}} \times 100$$

The yield figure is a useful managerial control of materials consumption. Various yields are established as normal. Yields below normal are measures of inefficiencies and are sometimes used to compute lost units.

The correct measurement of completed production and accurate determination of lost units ties in closely with a firm's quality control procedures. Frequently quality control data are used to compute production costs since the use of incorrect quantities would result in incorrect unit costs.

Units Lost in the First Department. Lost units reduce the number of units over which total cost can be spread, causing an increase in unit costs. The one thousand units lost in the Mixing Department increase the unit cost of materials, labor, and factory overhead. Had these units not been lost, the equivalent production figure would be 50,000 units for materials and 48,000 for labor and factory overhead. The unit cost for materials would be $.49 instead of $.50, labor $.607 instead of $.62, and factory overhead $.588 instead of $.60. In a first department, the only effect of losing units is an increase in the unit cost of the remaining good units.

Refining Department. The Mixing Department transferred 45,000 units to the Refining Department for further processing. Labor and factory overhead were added in the Refining Department before the units were transferred to the Finishing Department. Costs incurred by the Refining Department resulted in additional departmental as well as cumulative unit costs.

The cost of production report of the Refining Department, shown on page 131, differs from that of the Mixing Department in several respects. Several additional calculations are made for which space has been provided on the report. The additional information deals with (1) costs received from the preceding department, (2) adjustment of preceding department's unit cost because of lost units, and (3) costs received from the preceding department to be included in the cost of closing work in process inventory.

The quantity schedule for the Refining Department shows that 45,000 units were received from the Mixing Department. These units were accounted for as follows: 40,000 units sent to the Finishing Department, 3,000 units still in process, and 2,000 units lost. An analysis of the work in process indicates that units in process are but one third complete as to labor and factory overhead. Unit costs, $.91 for labor and $.80 for factory overhead,

THE CARSON CHEMICAL COMPANY

REFINING DEPARTMENT

COST OF PRODUCTION REPORT

FOR THE MONTH OF JANUARY, 19—

QUANTITY SCHEDULE:

Units received from preceding department......................		45,000
Units transferred to next department............................	40,000	
Units still in process ($\frac{1}{3}$ labor and factory overhead).............	3,000	
Units lost in process...	2,000	45,000

COST CHARGED TO THE DEPARTMENT:	Total Cost	Unit Cost
Cost from preceding department:		
Transferred in during the month (45,000)......................	$ 77,400	$1.72
Cost added by department:		
Labor..	$ 37,310	$ .91
Factory overhead...	32,800	.80
Total cost added...	$ 70,110	$1.71
Adjustment for lost units..................................		.08
Total cost to be accounted for	$147,510	$3.51

COST ACCOUNTED FOR AS FOLLOWS:		
Transferred to next department (40,000 × $3.51)................		$140,400
Work in process — closing inventory:		
Adjusted cost from preceding department [3,000 ×($1.72 + $.08)]	$5,400	
Labor....... (3,000 × $\frac{1}{3}$ × $.91).........................	910	
Fac. overhead (3,000 × $\frac{1}{3}$ × $.80).........................	800	7,110
Total cost accounted for.................................		$147,510

ADDITIONAL COMPUTATIONS:

Equivalent production — Labor and Factory Overhead $= 40,000 + \dfrac{3,000}{3} = 41,000$ units

Unit costs:

$$\text{Labor} = \frac{\$37,310}{41,000} = \$.91 \qquad\qquad \text{Factory overhead} = \frac{\$32,800}{41,000} = \$.80$$

Adjustment for lost units:

Method No. 1 — $\dfrac{\$77,400}{43,000} = \$1.80$.................$1.80 — $1.72 = $.08 per unit

Method No. 2 — 2,000 units × $1.72 = $3,440............. $\dfrac{\$3,440}{43,000} = \$.08$ per unit

were calculated as follows: the $37,310 labor cost completed 40,000 units transferred and is sufficient to complete 1,000 of the 3,000 units still in process. Therefore, equivalent production of the Refining Department is 41,000 units (40,000 + 1,000), the labor unit cost is $.91 ($\frac{\$37,310}{41,000}$), and the factory overhead unit cost $.80 ($\frac{\$32,800}{41,000}$). There is no materials unit cost as no materials were added by the department. The departmental unit cost is $1.71, the sum of the labor unit cost of $.91 and the factory overhead unit cost of $.80.

The Refining Department is responsible for labor and factory overhead used as well as for the cost of units received from the Mixing Department. This latter cost is inserted as a cost charged to the department under the title "Cost from preceding department," which is immediately above the section of the report dealing with costs added by the department. The cost transferred in was $77,400, previously shown in the cost report of the Mixing Department as cost transferred out of that department by this entry:

<pre>
Work in Process — Refining Department................. 77,400
     Work in Process — Mixing Department..............   77,400
</pre>

The work in process account of the Refining Department is charged with costs received from the preceding department and with $70,110 of departmental labor and factory overhead, a total cost of $147,510 to be accounted for by the department.

Units Lost in Departments Subsequent to the First. The Mixing Department's unit cost was $1.72 when 45,000 units were transferred to the Refining Department. However, because 2,000 of these 45,000 units were lost during processing in the Refining Department, the $1.72 unit cost figure has to be adjusted as it no longer applies. The total cost of the units transferred remains at $77,400, but 43,000 units must now absorb this total cost, causing an increase of $.08 in the cost per unit due to the loss of 2,000 units in the Refining Department.

The lost unit cost can be computed by either of two methods: Method No. 1 determines a new unit cost for work done in the preceding department and subtracts the preceding department's old unit cost figure from the adjusted unit cost figure. The difference between the two figures is the additional cost due to lost units. The new adjusted unit cost for work done in the preceding department is obtained by dividing the remaining good units, 43,000 (45,000 − 2,000), into the cost transferred in, $77,400. The old unit cost figure of $1.72 is subtracted from the revised unit cost of $1.80 ($\frac{\$77,400}{43,000}$) to arrive at the adjustment of $.08.

Method No. 2 determines the lost units' share of total cost and allocates this cost to the remaining good units. Total cost previously absorbed by the units lost is $3,440, which is the result of multiplying the 2,000 lost units by their unit cost of $1.72. The $3,440 cost must now be absorbed by the remaining good units. The additional cost to be picked up by each remaining good unit is $.08, computed by dividing the cost to be absorbed, $3,440, by the 43,000 remaining good units.

The lost unit cost adjustment must be entered in the cost of production report. The $.08 is entered on the "Adjustment for lost units" line. The departmental unit cost of $1.71 does not have to be adjusted for units lost. In the Refining Department the cost of any work done by the department on lost units has automatically been absorbed in the departmental unit costs with the equivalent production figure of 41,000 instead of 43,000 units. The unadjusted unit cost for work done in the preceding department, the departmental unit cost, and the adjustment for lost units are totaled to obtain the cumulative unit cost for work done up to the end of operations in the Refining Department. The unit cost figures are $1.72, $1.71, and $.08 for a total unit cost of $3.51.

Units are lost through evaporation, shrinkage, poor yields, or spoiled work. In many instances the nature of operations is such that certain losses cannot be avoided or are within normal tolerance limits for human and machine error. Therefore, a common method of accounting for lost units does not show the cost of lost units as a separate item of cost but spreads it over the remaining good units. This method does not require a separate journal entry to charge a *spoilage* or *units lost* or some other current period expense account with the cost of units lost, as should be done for any avoidable (abnormal) loss that is beyond normal tolerance limits.

Lost units may occur at the beginning, during, or at the end of a process. Ordinarily, for purposes of practicability and simplicity, it is assumed that units lost at the beginning or during a process were never put in process. This assumption has been made in the preceding discussion, and the cost of units lost is spread over the equivalent production of units produced; that is, units completed and units still in process.

When lost units occur at the end of a process and a firm's process cost system is designed to account for this possibility, the cost of lost units is charged to completed units only. No part of the loss is charged to units still in process. If the 2,000 units lost by the Refining Department were the result of a spoilage found at final inspection by the Quality Control Department, the cost of these lost units would be charged only to the 40,000 finished units; and the cost of production report for The Carson Chemical Company's Refining Department would appear as illustrated on page 134.

A comparison of the differences between the two cost of production reports for the Refining Department of The Carson Chemical Company as to amounts for costs of units transferred and work in process inventory appear as shown below. (Note the offsetting increases and decreases.)

Cost of units transferred:	Work in process inventory:
On page 131.... $140,400	On page 131.... $7,110
On page 134.... 140,720	On page 134.... 6,790
Increase.....+$ 320	Decrease....−$ 320

If lost unit costs are to be charged off as a current period expense, as in the case of avoidable, abnormal loss (see first paragraph on this page), the

THE CARSON CHEMICAL COMPANY
REFINING DEPARTMENT
COST OF PRODUCTION REPORT
FOR THE MONTH OF JANUARY, 19—

QUANTITY SCHEDULE:

Units received from preceding department...................... | | 45,000

Units transferred to next department........................... | 40,000 |
Units still in process (⅓ labor and factory overhead)............. | 3,000 |
Units lost in process (at end of process)........................ | 2,000 | 45,000

COST CHARGED TO THE DEPARTMENT:		Total	Unit
Cost from preceding department:		Cost	Cost
Transferred in during the month (45,000).....................		$ 77,400	$1.72
Cost added by department:			
Labor..		$ 37,310	$ .87
Factory overhead...		32,800	.76
Total cost added...		$ 70,110	$1.63
Total cost to be accounted for.............................		$147,510	$3.35

COST ACCOUNTED FOR AS FOLLOWS:

Transferred to next department [40,000 units × ($3.35 + $.1675)]*		$140,720
Work in process — closing inventory:		
From preceding department (3,000 × $1.72)....................	$ 5,160	
Labor (3,000 × ⅓ × $.87)...................................	870	
Factory overhead (3,000 × ⅓ × $.76)........................	760	6,790
Total cost accounted for...................................		$147,510

ADDITIONAL COMPUTATIONS:

$$\text{Equivalent production} - \text{Labor and Factory Overhead} = 40,000 + \frac{3,000}{3} + 2,000 \text{ lost units}$$

$$= 43,000 \text{ units}$$

Unit costs:

$$\text{Labor} = \frac{\$37,310}{43,000} = \$.87; \text{ Factory overhead} = \frac{\$32,800}{43,000} = \$.76$$

Lost unit cost = $3.35 × 2,000 units = $6,700 ÷ 40,000 units = $.1675 per unit to be added to $3.35 to make the transfer cost $3.5175.

---

*40,000 units × $3.5175 = $140,700. To avoid a decimal discrepancy, the cost transferred is computed: $147,510 − $6,790 = $140,720.

same pattern of computations could be used regardless of when the loss occurs, except that costs would be distinguished as follows:

Transferred to next department (40,000 units × $3.35).................. | $134,020*
Transferred to a lost units expense account (40,000 units × $.1675)...... | 6,700

Total............. | $140,720

---

*40,000 units × $3.35 = $134,000. To avoid decimal discrepancy, the cost transferred is computed: $147,510 − [$6,790 (closing inventory) + $6,700] = $134,020.

Furthermore, if one part of this loss is normally unavoidable and another part is avoidable (abnormal), the former loss is treated as discussed previously with consideration of the time when the loss was incurred; i.e., beginning, during, or end of process. The avoidable loss part is charged to an expense account, Lost Units.

Disposition of Refining Department Costs.   The cost of production report on page 131 shows total cost to be accounted for by the Refining Department to be $147,510. The department completed and transferred 40,000 units to the Finishing Department at a cost of $140,400 (40,000 × $3.51). The remaining cost is assigned to the work in process inventory. This balance is broken down by the various costs in process. When computing the cost of closing work in process inventory of any department subsequent to the first, costs received from preceding departments must be included.

The 3,000 units still in process completed entirely by the Mixing Department at a unit cost of $1.72 were later adjusted by $.08 (to $1.80) because of the loss of some of the units transferred. Therefore, Mixing Department cost of the 3,000 units still in process is $5,400, the result of multiplying the 3,000 units by the $1.80 adjusted unit cost. The $5,400 figure is not broken down further as such information is not pertinent to Refining Department operations. However, the amount is listed separately in the cost of production report because it is part of the Refining Department's closing work in process inventory.

Materials (if any), labor, and factory overhead added by the department are costed separately to arrive at total work in process. In the case of the Refining Department, no materials were added to the units received; thus, the closing inventory shows no materials in process. However, labor and factory overhead costs were incurred. The work in process analysis stated that labor and factory overhead used on the units in process were sufficient to complete 1,000 units. The cost of labor in process is $910 (1,000 × $.91) and factory overhead in process is $800 (1,000 × $.80). The total cost of the 3,000 units in process is $7,110 ($5,400 + $910 + $800). This cost, added to that transferred to the Finishing Department, $140,400, accounts for the total cost of $147,510 charged to the Refining Department.

Finishing Department.   The cost of production report of the Finishing Department, the third department of The Carson Chemical Company, is illustrated on the next page. Total and unit cost figures were derived using procedures discussed for the cost of production report of the Refining Department. The work completed is transferred to the finished goods storeroom; thus, the title "Transferred to fiinished goods storeroom" is

THE CARSON CHEMICAL COMPANY

FINISHING DEPARTMENT

COST OF PRODUCTION REPORT

FOR THE MONTH OF JANUARY, 19—

QUANTITY SCHEDULE:

Units received from preceding department......................		40,000
Units transferred to finished goods storeroom....................	35,000	
Units still in process ($\frac{1}{4}$ labor and factory overhead).............	4,000	
Units lost in process..	1,000	40,000

COST CHARGED TO THE DEPARTMENT:	Total Cost	Unit Cost
Cost from preceding department:		
Transferred in during the month (40,000)......................	$140,400	$3.51
Cost added by department:		
Labor..	$ 32,400	$ .90
Factory overhead..	19,800	.55
Total cost added...	$ 52,200	$1.45
Adjustment for lost units....................................		.09
Total cost to be accounted for..............................	$192,600	$5.05

COST ACCOUNTED FOR AS FOLLOWS:

Transferred to finished goods storeroom (35,000 × $5.05).........		$176,750
Work in process — closing inventory:		
Adjusted cost from preceding department [4,000× ($3.51 + $.09)]	$ 14,400	
Labor....... (4,000 × $\frac{1}{4}$ × $.90).........................	900	
Fac. overhead (4,000 × $\frac{1}{4}$ × $.55).........................	550	15,850
Total cost accounted for.................................		$192,600

ADDITIONAL COMPUTATIONS:

Equivalent production — Labor and Factory Overhead = $35,000 + \frac{4,000}{4} = 36,000$ units

Unit costs:

$$\text{Labor} = \frac{\$32,400}{36,000} = \$.90 \qquad\qquad \text{Factory overhead} = \frac{\$19,800}{36,000} = \$.55$$

Adjustment for lost units:

Method No. 1 $= \frac{\$140,400}{39,000} = \$3.60$.................$3.60 − $3.51 = $.09 per unit

Method No. 2 $= 1,000$ units × $3.51 = $3,510..............$\frac{\$3,510}{39,000} = \$.09$ per unit

used in place of the title "Transferred to next department." Costs charged to this department come from the payroll distribution and the department's expense analysis sheet. The journal entry transferring costs from the Refining Department follows:

Work in Process — Finishing Department................	140,400	
Work in Process — Refining Department.............		140,400

The entry to transfer finished units to the finished goods storeroom is presented on the next page.

THE CARSON CHEMICAL COMPANY

Cost of Production Report

For the Month of January, 19—

	Mixing Department		Refining Department		Finishing Department	
Quantity Schedule:						
Units started in process.............	50,000					
Units received from preceding dept....			45,000		40,000	
Units transferred to next department...	45,000		40,000			
Units transferred to finished goods storeroom.......................					35,000	
Units still in process................	4,000		3,000		4,000	
Units lost in process...............	1,000	50,000	2,000	45,000	1,000	40,000

	Total Cost	Unit Cost	Total Cost	Unit Cost	Total Cost	Unit Cost
Cost Charged to the Department:						
Cost from preceding department:						
Transferred in during the month....			$ 77,400	$1.72	$140,400	$3.51
Cost added by department:						
Materials........................	$24,500	$ .50				
Labor...........................	29,140	.62	$ 37,310	$ .91	$ 32,400	$ .90
Factory overhead.................	28,200	.60	32,800	.80	19,800	.55
Total cost added....................	$81,840	$1.72	$ 70,110	$1.71	$ 52,200	$1.45
Adjustment for lost units............				.08		.09
Total cost to be accounted for.....	$81,840	$1.72	$147,510	$3.51	$192,600	$5.05

Costs Accounted for as Follows:						
Transferred to next department.......	$77,400		$140,400			
Transferred to finished goods storeroom.					$176,750	
Work in process — closing inventory:						
Adjusted cost from preceding department.........................			$ 5,400		$ 14,400	
Materials........................	$ 2,000					
Labor...........................	1,240		910		900	
Factory overhead.................	1,200	4,440	800	7,110	550	15,850
Total cost accounted for.........		$81,840		$147,510		$192,600

Finished Goods....................................   176,750

Work in Process — Finishing Department...........   176,750

The cost of production reports for The Carson Chemical Company's Mixing, Refining, and Finishing Departments have been discussed and computed separately. It is most likely that these reports would be consolidated in a single report summarizing manufacturing operations of the firm for a specified period. Such a report, as it is illustrated above, should be reviewed to observe the interrelationship of the various departmental reports.

DISCUSSION QUESTIONS

1. What is the primary objective in process costing?
2. A firm has a choice of using either a job order or process cost system. Discuss the relative merits of each.
3. What are the distinguishing features of a process cost system?
4. For the following products indicate whether a job order or a process cost system would be required:

   a. Gasoline
   b. Sewing machines
   c. Chocolate syrup
   d. Textbooks

   e. Dacron yarn
   f. Cigarettes
   g. Space capsules
   h. Men's suits

5. State and discuss three product flow formats.
6. Compare the cost accumulation and summarizing procedures of a job order cost system and a process cost system.
7. Can predetermined overhead rates be used in a process cost system?
8. Would one expect to find service departments in a firm using a process cost system? If so, how would they be handled? Would cost of production reports be used for service departments?
9. What is the purpose of a cost of production report?
10. What are the various sections of a cost of production report? How are they used?
11. Separate cost of production reports are prepared for each production department. Why is this method used in preference to one report for the entire firm?
12. Are month-to-month fluctuations in average unit costs computed in a cost of production report meaningful data in attempting to control costs?
13. What is equivalent production? Explain in terms of its effect on computed unit costs.
14. In a process cost system, physical inventories of work in process must be taken at the end of each accounting period. Ordinarily, each department head is responsible for his own inventory, and the methods he uses to determine such data are crude by comparison with procedures used for determining year-end physical inventory. It is not unusual for a department head to estimate rather than count his inventory in process. Consequently, his figures are bound to have errors. Is this good practice or should more accurate methods, such as having inventory teams determine inventories, be used?
15. What is the justification of spreading the cost of lost units over remaining good units? Should the cost of these units ever be charged to overhead? Will the answer be different if units are lost (a) at the beginning of operations, (b) during operations, (c) at the end of operations, or (d) in the originating department?
16. Select the answer which best completes the following statement. The type of spoilage that should *not* affect the recorded cost of inventories is (a) abnormal spoilage, (b) normal spoilage, (c) seasonal spoilage, or (d) standard spoilage.   (AICPA adapted)

EXERCISES

In solving these exercises round off all amounts, except unit costs, to the nearest dollar. Carry unit costs to five decimal places unless stated otherwise.

1. Computation of Per Unit Manufacturing Cost and Inventory Costing. The Forbes Company, Inc. manufactures electric irons. The costs of production for the year 19— were:

Materials..	$140,000
Labor...	148,000
Factory overhead	103,000

The inventory of finished goods on January 1, 19— consisted of 3,000 electric irons, valued at $15 each. During the year the company sold 23,400 electric irons and had 2,600 units finished and on hand at the end of the year.

Required: The cost of the finished goods inventory, assuming finished units to be costed on the first-in, first-out basis.

2. Total and Per Unit Manufacturing Costs. In October the Acro Company put into process $50,000 of raw materials. The Milling Department used 12,000 labor hours at a cost of $30,000, and the Machining Department used 9,200 labor hours at a cost of $2.25 per hour. Factory overhead is applied at a rate of $3 per labor hour in the Milling Department and $4 per labor hour in the Machining Department. October 1 inventories were: materials, $16,000; materials in process, $6,000; labor in process, $6,500; factory overhead in process, $7,200; and finished goods, $12,400. October 31 inventories were: materials, $18,000; materials in process, $5,000; labor in process, $6,000; factory overhead in process, $7,000; and finished goods, $14,000. The company produced 25,000 units of product during the month.

Required: (1) A schedule showing the cost of work put in process, the cost of goods manufactured, and the cost of goods sold.

(2) The unit cost of materials, labor, and factory overhead for the October production.

3. Quantity Schedule. A spinning mill had the following inventories, measured in kilograms (kg.):

	Opening	*Final*
Raw materials	400,000 kg.	500,000 kg.
Work in process.....................	100,000 kg.	150,000 kg.
Finished goods	100,000 kg.	110,000 kg.

Additional data:

Raw materials purchased	1,600,000 kg.
Finished goods sold................................	1,240,000 kg.

Losses occur uniformly during the manufacturing process.

Required: A quantity schedule for raw materials, work in process, and finished goods.

4. Cost of Production Report; No Inventories; Three Departments. The Haddonfield Company manufactures a rayon product which is processed in three departments known respectively as: Spinning, Twisting, and Winding. There were no inventories of unfinished work at either the beginning or end of October, and 15,000 units of product were finished during October.

Materials used during the month cost $7,200, of which 5/6 were used in the Spinning Department and the remainder in the Winding Department. Wages amounted to $16,800; and an analysis of the payroll shows the amount applicable to each department to be: Spinning, $9,000; Twisting, $4,200; and Winding, $3,600.

Factory overhead incurred directly by each department and general factory overhead apportioned to each department were:

	Spinning	Twisting	Winding
Factory overhead incurred by department....	$3,200	$2,250	$3,100
General factory overhead apportioned........	2,800	4,200	2,900

Required: A cost statement showing the cost per unit in each department and at the end of each stage of production.

5. Cost of Production Report. For December the Production Control Department of Faro Chemical, Inc. reported these production data for Department 2:

Transferred in from Department 1..........................	55,000 liters
Transferred out to Department 3..........................	39,500 liters
In process at end of December............................	10,500 liters

    (with ⅓ labor and factory overhead)

All materials were put into process in Department 1.

The Cost Department collected these figures for Department 2:

Unit cost for units transferred in from Department 1..............	$1.80
Labor costs, in Department 2...................................	$27,520
Factory overhead applied......................................	15,480

Required: A cost of production report for Department 2 for December.

6. Cost of Production Report. Melograno, Inc. uses a process cost system. The costs of Department 2 for the month of April were:

Cost from preceding department.......................		$20,000
Cost added by department:		
Materials...	$21,816	
Labor...	7,776	
Factory overhead..................................	4,104	$33,696

The following information was obtained from the department's quantity schedule:

Units received..	5,000
Units transferred out......................................	4,000
Units still in process......................................	1,000

The degree of completion of the work in process was: 50% of the units were 40% complete; 20% of the units were 30% complete; and the balance of the units were 20% complete.

Required: The cost of production report of Department 2 for April.

7. Cost of Production Report for Two Departments; No Inventory; Normal and Abnormal Lost Units in Department 2. The Miramar Company, Inc. has two production departments and maintains a process cost accounting system.

The following is a summary of the costs for November:

	Materials	*Labor*	*Applied Fac. Ovh.*
Department 1............	$72,000	$ 8,400	$15,600
Department 2............	3,267	54,292	26,255

Reports from the Production Control Department showed that 600 units were started in process, with no inventories at the beginning or end of the month. In Department 2, 10 units were spoiled, of which 4 units were spoiled because of defective materials. The good units, 590, were transferred to finished goods inventory. The company's practice is to distribute all normal spoilage costs among the units remaining in process and completed on the basis of actual number of units, regardless of stage of completion. Units spoiled because of defective materials (considered abnormal spoilage) are classified and costed as completed units; their costs are transferred to a lost unit expense account.

Required: A cost of production report for Departments 1 and 2. Carry all computations to two significant decimal places.

8. Computation of Equivalent Production. Jorcano Manufacturing Company uses a process cost system to account for the costs of its only product, Product D. Production takes place in three departments: Fabrication, Assembly, and Packaging.

At the end of the fiscal year, June 30, 19—, the following inventory of Product D is on hand:

(a) No unused raw materials or packaging materials.

(b) Fabrication Department: 300 units, ⅓ complete as to raw materials and ½ complete as to direct labor.

(c) Assembly Department: 1,000 units, ⅔ complete as to direct labor.

(d) Packaging Department: 100 units, ¾ complete as to packaging materials and ¼ complete as to direct labor.

(e) Shipping or finished goods area: 400 units.

Required: (1) The number of equivalent units of raw materials in all inventories at June 30, 19—.

(2) The number of equivalent units of Fabrication Department's direct labor in all inventories at June 30, 19—.

(3) The number of equivalent units of packaging materials in all inventories at June 30, 19—.

(AICPA adapted)

PROBLEMS

In solving these problems round off all amounts, except unit costs, to the nearest dollar. Carry unit costs to five decimal places unless stated otherwise.

6-1. Cost of Production Report; Three Departments. The cost data of the Batalha Manufacturing Company for August are given on the next page.

Department	Materials	Labor	Factory Overhead
Mixing..........................	$18,000	$11,880	$ 5,940
Refining.......................		11,520	8,640
Finishing......................		11,440	8,580

No beginning inventory. Units started in process, 300,000.

Units in process, August 31:

　　6,000 — in the Mixing Department, with all materials added and estimated
　　　　to be 50% converted.
　　6,000 — just completed by the Mixing Department, and transferred to the
　　　　Refining Department.
　　8,000 — in the Finishing Department, estimated to be 75% converted.

Required: A cost of production report for the three departments for August.

6-2. Cost of Production Report; Three Departments; Income Statement. The
income statement shown below was submitted by the accountant of the North
Dakota Company to the directors of the company. After a careful study of the
results, the directors were of the opinion that the loss shown was incorrect.
It is necessary to prepare another income statement showing unit and departmental costs at each stage of production, with the knowledge that the raw materials put in process are used at the beginning of operations in Department A.

THE NORTH DAKOTA COMPANY
INCOME STATEMENT
FOR YEAR ENDED DECEMBER 31, 19—

Sales (10,000 units @ $3.50)..................			$35,000
Cost of goods sold:			
Materials purchased......................	$8,600		
Direct labor — Dept. A...................	5,160		
Direct labor — Dept. B...................	4,760		
Direct labor — Dept. C...................	3,270		
Factory overhead:			
Department A......................	6,450		
Department B......................	4,760		
Department C......................	1,635	$34,635	
Deduct:			
Raw materials inventory 12/31.........	$ 560		
Work in process, 12/31 (1,000 units in			
each department — all materials, 50%			
labor and overhead; 3,000 units).....	3,750		
Finished goods, 12/31 (400 units @ $2.50)	1,000	5,310	29,325
Gross profit................................			$ 5,675
Commercial expenses:			
Marketing costs..........................	$ 3,000		
Administrative costs......................	5,000		8,000
Net loss....................................			$(2,325)

Required: A corrected income statement and a cost of production report
with quantity schedule and computation of equivalent production.

6-3. Cost of Production Report; Three Departments; Lost Units in All Departments. The Globe Products Company makes a single product in three producing departments. Cost and production data for September are:

	Dept. No. 1001	Dept. No. 1002	Dept. No. 1003
Cost data:			
Materials..................................	$12,250	......	......
Labor.....................................	14,570	$18,655	$ 8,100
Factory overhead..........................	14,100	16,400	19,800
Production data:			
Units started or received from preceding dept..	100,000	90,000	80,000
Units completed and transferred or shipped....	90,000	80,000	70,000
Units in process 9/30......................	8,000	6,000	8,000
Stage of completion of closing inventory:			
Materials.................................	100%	...	...
Labor + factory overhead..................	50%	33⅓%	25%

Required: (1) A schedule of equivalent production for each department.
(2) A cost of production report with quantity schedule.

6-4. Quantity and Equivalent Production Schedules; Adjustment for Lost Units. The Fort Washington Pharma Corporation produces an antibiotic product in three producing departments: the Mixing Department, the Culture Department, and the Purifying and Packing Department. The following quantitative and cost data have been made available:

	Department		
	Mixing	Culture	Purifying and Packing
Production data:			
Started into production..........	8,000 kg.	5,400 kg.	3,200 kg.
Transferred to next department....	5,400	3,200	
Transferred to finished goods storeroom.......................			2,100
In process: 100% materials 1/3 labor and overhead........	2,400		
In process: 100% materials 1/3 labor and overhead........		1,800	
In process: 100% materials 2/3 labor and overhead......			900
Cost data:			
Direct materials.................	$20,670	$ 7,980	$14,400
Direct labor....................	11,160	5,016	11,520
Factory overhead...............	5,580	2,280	5,040
Total........................	$37,410	$15,276	$30,960

Required: (1) A quantity schedule for each of the three departments.
(2) An equivalent production schedule for each of the three departments.
(3) The unit cost of factory overhead in the Mixing Department.
(4) The lost unit cost in the Culture Department if the unit cost transferred in from the Mixing Department amounted to $5.35.

6-5. Equivalent Production and Cost Computations; Report Evaluation. The Moderna Company employs departmental budgets and performance reports in planning and controlling its operations. Department A's budget for January was for the production of 1,000 units of equivalent production, a normal month's volume.

The following performance report was prepared for January by the company's accountant:

Variable costs:	Budget	Actual	Variance
Direct materials......................	$20,000	$23,100	$3,100 (unfavorable)
Direct labor.........................	10,000	10,500	500 (unfavorable)
Indirect labor.......................	1,650	1,790	140 (unfavorable)
Power...............................	210	220	10 (unfavorable)
Supplies............................	320	330	10 (unfavorable)
Total............................	$32,180	$35,940	$3,760
Fixed costs:			
Rent................................	$ 400	$ 400	——
Supervision..........................	1,000	1,000	——
Depreciation.........................	500	500	——
Other...............................	100	100	——
Total............................	$ 2,000	$ 2,000	——
Grand total.....................	$34,180	$37,940	$3,760

Direct materials are introduced at various stages of the process. All conversion costs are incurred uniformly throughout the process. Because production fluctuates from month to month, the fixed overhead is applied at the rate of $2 per equivalent unit as to conversion costs.

Actual variable costs are applied monthly as incurred.

There was no opening inventory at January 1. Of the 1,100 new units started during January, 900 were completed and shipped. There was no finished goods inventory at January 31. Units in process at January 31 were estimated to be 75% complete as to direct materials and 80% complete as to conversion costs. There was no shrinkage, spoilage, or waste of materials during January.

Required: (1) A schedule of equivalent production for January.
(2) A schedule computing the amount of under- or overapplied overhead at January 31.
(3) A schedule computing the cost of goods shipped and the cost of the work in process inventory at January 31 at *actual* cost.
(4) Comments on the performance report. Specific conclusions, if any, to be drawn from the report.

(AICPA adapted)

6-6. Cost of Production Calculations and Report. The Anderson Company manufactures a mechanical device known as "Klebo." The company uses a process cost system.

The manufacturing operations take place in one department and are given at the top of the next page.

Material K, a metal, is stamped to form a part which is assembled with one of the purchased parts "X." The unit is then machined and cleaned after which it is assembled with two units of part "Y" to form the finished device known as a "Klebo." Spray priming and enameling is the final operation.

Time-and-motion studies indicate that of the total time required for the manufacture of a unit, the first operation required 25% of the labor cost, the first assembly an additional 25%, machining and cleaning 12.5%, the second assembly 25%, and painting 12.5%. Factory overhead is considered to follow the same pattern of operations as does labor.

The following data apply to October, the first month of operation:

Material K purchased — 100,000 kilograms......................	$25,000
Part X purchased — 80,000 units.............................	16,000
Part Y purchased — 150,000 units............................	15,000
Primer and enamel used......................................	1,072
Direct labor...	45,415
Factory overhead...	24,905

	Unit Quantity
Units finished and sent to finished goods warehouse...............	67,000
Units assembled but not painted	5,000
Units ready for the second assembly...........................	3,000
Inventories at the end of the month:	
Material K (kg.)..	5,800
Part X (units of part X)...................................	5,000
Part Y (units of part Y)...................................	6,000
Klebos in process (units)..................................	8,000
Units in finished goods inventory...........................	7,500

Required: A cost of production report showing total costs, equivalent production, unit cost, cost of goods finished, and work in process inventories.

(AICPA adapted)

CASES

A. Accounting for Lost Units. The Household Aids Company assembles clip clothespins in three sections; a process cost system is used by the company. Under normal operating conditions, each section has a spoilage rate of 2%. However, spoilage can go as high as 5% and is usually discovered when a faulty pin enters process or on final completion by a section.

The spring mechanism is the only material which can be saved from a spoiled unit. The production foreman assigns a man once or twice a week to remove the springs from spoiled units. The salvaged springs are placed in bins at the assembly tables in Section No. 1 to be used again. No accounting entry is made of this salvage operation.

In the past the controller has made no attempt to account for spoilage separately. Lost unit costs have been absorbed by the units transferred out of the section and those remaining in process. However, because spoilage is increasing, a different method is needed.

Required: What should be recommended?

B. Inventory Costing for Financial Statements. The United Fiber Corporation mines and sells a fibrous mineral. On December 31, 19D, the inventory amounted to 25,000 tons of fiber; all this inventory was produced during 19D and is costed at $19.88 per ton, the average cost per ton produced in 19D. Production and costs in other years were as follows:

Tons Produced and Average Costs

Year	Tons Produced	Cost per Ton
19A...	170,000	$14.65
19B...	180,000	14.85
19C...	175,000	15.06
19D...	110,000	19.88

Production Costs

	Amounts		Per Ton	
	19C	19D	19C	19D
Tons produced..................	175,000	110,000		
Direct labor....................	$ 472,500	$ 401,500	$ 2.70	$ 3.65
Indirect labor..................	346,500	286,000	1.98	2.60
Supplies and other production				
expenses	708,750	479,600	4.05	4.36
Depletion......................	262,500	165,000	1.50	1.50
Salaries (superintendents, plant				
clerks, watchmen, etc.)........	217,000	233,200	1.24	2.12
Depreciation...................	227,500	247,500	1.30	2.25
Other fixed expenses............	400,750	374,000	2.29	3.40
Total.........................	$2,635,500	$2,186,800	$15.06	$19.88

Indirect labor, supplies, and other production expenses are considered variable costs. There are no semivariable costs. Depletion is computed at $1.50 per ton mined, and depreciation on machinery and equipment is computed on a straight-line basis. Due to an extended strike in 19D, much less of the fibrous mineral was mined than during the three preceding years in which production was considered normal. The management explained that the rise in 19D unit labor costs was caused by general increases of from 33% to 40% in hourly wage rates. The increase in the unit cost of supplies and other production expenses is accounted for by an increase in prices of about 10%. All increases took place at the beginning of the year.

Required: (1) Is the pricing of the closing inventory on December 31, 19D, at $19.88 per ton acceptable for financial statement purposes? Discuss fully.

(2) Assuming that the closing inventory of $19.88 per ton is not acceptable for financial statement purposes, how should it be adjusted? Present calculations in full and state how the adjustment should be dealt with in the statements.

(3) Discuss briefly the classification of fixed and variable costs.

(AICPA adapted)

CHAPTER 7

PROCESS COSTING
(Concluded)

In numerous industries all materials needed for the product are put in process in the first department. However, additional materials might also be required in subsequent departments in order to complete the units. The addition of such materials has two possible effects on units and costs in process:

1. The additional materials merely increase the unit cost since these materials become a part of the product manufactured and do not increase the number of final units. For example, in a finishing plant of a textile company, the material added is often a bleach; in a wire company, a plating mixture; in an automobile assembly plant, additional parts. These materials are needed to give the product certain specified qualities, characteristics, or completeness.

2. The added materials increase the number of units and also cause a change in unit cost. In processing a chemical, water is often added to the mixture causing an increase in the number of units and a spreading of costs over a greater number of units.

INCREASE IN UNIT COST DUE TO ADDITION OF MATERIALS

The cost of production report of the Finishing Department (Chapter 6, page 136) is used to illustrate the different effects of the addition of materials on total and unit costs of a department.

In the simplest case, added materials, such as parts of an automobile, do not increase the number of units but increase total costs and unit costs. A materials unit cost must be computed for the department, and a materials cost must be included in the work in process inventory.

Assume that additional materials costing $17,020 are placed in process and charged to the Finishing Department. Assume further that the materials in work in process are sufficient to complete 2,000 of the 4,000 units; that is, units are 50 percent complete as to materials cost. The effect of the additional materials cost is shown in the cost report on page 149.

The only differences in the cost report on page 149 and the cost report on page 136 are the $17,020 materials cost charged to the department and the $.46 materials unit cost ($\frac{\$17,020}{37,000}$). The additional materials cost is also reflected in the total cost to be accounted for, in the cost of units transferred to Finished Goods, and in the closing work in process inventory.

INCREASE IN UNITS AND CHANGE IN UNIT COST DUE TO ADDITION OF MATERIALS

When additional materials result in additional units, different computations are necessary. The greater number of units causes a decrease in unit cost which necessitates an adjustment of the preceding department's unit cost, for the increased number of units will absorb the same total cost transferred from the preceding department.

To illustrate the situation of additional units resulting from the addition of materials, assume the same Finishing Department costs for departmental labor ($32,400) and factory overhead ($19,800), an additional materials cost of $17,020, and an increase of 8,000 units as the result of added materials. The effect of these assumptions on the Finishing Department's cost of production report is shown on page 150.

The additional 8,000 units are first entered in the department's quantity schedule as "Additional units put into process." Departmental unit costs for materials, labor, and overhead are computed by dividing each cost by equivalent production figures. The quantity schedule reports that 44,000 units were completed and transferred to the finished goods storeroom and that 4,000 units are still in process, 50 percent complete as to materials and 25 percent complete as to labor and factory overhead. Therefore, equivalent production is 46,000 units for materials and 45,000 for labor and factory overhead. Dividing departmental materials, labor, and factory overhead costs for the period by these production figures results in a unit cost of $.37 ($\frac{\$17,020}{46,000}$) for materials, $.72 ($\frac{\$32,400}{45,000}$) for labor, and $.44 ($\frac{\$19,800}{45,000}$) for factory overhead, a departmental unit cost of $1.53, and a total departmental cost of $69,220.

THE CARSON CHEMICAL COMPANY
Finishing Department
Cost of Production Report
For the Month of January, 19—

QUANTITY SCHEDULE:

Units received from preceding department......................		40,000
Units transferred to finished goods storeroom...................	35,000	
Units still in process (½ materials — ¼ labor and factory overhead).	4,000	
Units lost in process.......................................	1,000	40,000

COST CHARGED TO THE DEPARTMENT:	Total Cost	Unit Cost
Cost from preceding department:		
Transferred in during the month (40,000).....................	$140,400	$3.51
Cost added by department:		
Materials..	$ 17,020	$ .46
Labor...	32,400	.90
Factory overhead.......................................	19,800	.55
Total cost added......................................	$ 69,220	$1.91
Adjustment for lost units...............................		.09
Total cost to be accounted for	$209,620	$5.51

COST ACCOUNTED FOR AS FOLLOWS:

Transferred to finished goods storeroom (35,000 × $5.51)........		$192,850
Work in process — closing inventory:		
Adjusted cost from preceding department (4,000 × $3.60)......	$ 14,400	
Materials (4,000 × ½ × $.46)............................	920	
Labor (4,000 × ¼ × $.90)...............................	900	
Factory overhead (4,000 × ¼ × $.55).....................	550	16,770
Total cost accounted for		$209,620

ADDITIONAL COMPUTATIONS:

Equivalent production:

$$\text{Materials} = 35,000 + \frac{4,000}{2} = 37,000 \text{ units}$$

$$\text{Labor and factory overhead} = 35,000 + \frac{4,000}{4} = 36,000 \text{ units}$$

Unit costs:

$$\text{Materials} = \frac{\$17,020}{37,000} = \$.46 \qquad \text{Labor} = \frac{\$32,400}{36,000} = \$.90$$

$$\text{Factory overhead} = \frac{\$19,800}{36,000} = \$.55$$

Adjustment for lost units:

$$\text{Method No. 1} = \frac{\$140,400}{39,000} = \$3.60 .... \$3.60 - \$3.51 = \$.09 \text{ per unit}$$

$$\text{Method No. 2} = 1,000 \text{ units} \times \$3.51 = \$3,510 .... \frac{\$ 3,510}{39,000} = \$.09 \text{ per unit}$$

These computations do not differ from those already discussed. Peculiar to this situation is the adjustment of the preceding department's unit cost. Total cost charged to the Finishing Department as cost transferred in from the preceding department must now be allocated over a greater number of units, thereby reducing the unit cost of work done in the preceding department.

THE CARSON CHEMICAL COMPANY
FINISHING DEPARTMENT
COST OF PRODUCTION REPORT
FOR THE MONTH OF JANUARY, 19—

QUANTITY SCHEDULE:

Units received from preceding department.....................	40,000	
Additional units put into process............................	8,000	48,000
Units transferred to finished goods storeroom..................	44,000	
Units still in process (½ materials—¼ labor and factory overhead).	4,000	48,000

COST CHARGED TO THE DEPARTMENT:	Total Cost	Unit Cost
Cost from preceding department:		
Transferred in during the month (40,000).....................	$140,400	$3.51
Cost added by department:		
Materials..	$ 17,020	$ .37
Labor..	32,400	.72
Factory overhead.......................................	19,800	.44
Total cost added.......................................	$ 69,220	$1.53
Adjusted unit cost of units transferred in during the month		2.925
Total cost to be accounted for...........................	$209,620	$4.455

COST ACCOUNTED FOR AS FOLLOWS:

Transferred to finished goods storeroom (44,000 × $4.455)......		$196,020
Work in process — closing inventory:		
Adjusted cost from preceding department (4,000 × $2.925)....	$ 11,700	
Materials (4,000 × ½ × $.37).............................	740	
Labor (4,000 × ¼ × $.72)................................	720	
Factory overhead (4,000 × ¼ × $.44).....................	440	13,600
Total cost accounted for.................................		$209,620

ADDITIONAL COMPUTATIONS:

Equivalent production:

$$\text{Materials} = 44,000 + \frac{4,000}{2} = 46,000 \text{ units}$$

$$\text{Labor and factory overhead} = 44,000 + \frac{4,000}{4} = 45,000 \text{ units}$$

Unit costs:

$$\text{Materials} = \frac{\$17,020}{46,000} = \$.37 \qquad \text{Labor} = \frac{\$32,400}{45,000} = \$.72$$

$$\text{Factory overhead} = \frac{\$19,800}{45,000} = \$.44$$

Adjustment for additional units:

$$\frac{\$140,400}{48,000} = \$2.925$$

In the illustration on page 149, the $140,400 cost transferred to the Finishing Department was absorbed by 40,000 units, resulting in a unit cost of $3.51 ($\frac{\$140,400}{40,000}$). Total cost transferred in remains the same; but because of the 8,000 increase in units, the cost must now be spread over 48,000 units, resulting in a unit cost for the preceding department of $2.925 ($\frac{\$140,400}{48,000}$). The adjusted cost is inserted in the production report above as "Adjusted unit cost of units transferred in during the month" and is added to departmental unit costs to arrive at the cumulative unit cost to the end of operations in the Finishing Department.

When additional materials increase the number of units being processed, it is still possible to have lost units. However, should increased and lost units occur, no separate calculation need be made for the lost units; only net units added are to be used. In the last illustration, 8,000 additional units resulted from added materials. It is quite possible, though, that the materials added should have yielded 10,000 additional units. The difference between the 8,000 units and the anticipated 10,000 units could be due to the loss of 2,000 units. If this is the case, the effect of the lost units is similar to that of units lost in the first department; that is, the cost is absorbed within the department as an increase in unit costs. However, if desired, it is also possible to report the effect of these lost units separately. If 10,000 additional units should have resulted, the effect of losing 2,000 units can be determined as follows: (1) compute the unit cost of work done in preceding departments and in this department as if no loss had occurred; (2) compute the loss by multiplying the unit cost obtained in the above computation by the 2,000 lost units.

OPENING WORK IN PROCESS INVENTORIES

The cost of production reports illustrated in Chapter 6 list closing work in process inventories. These inventories become opening inventories of the next period.

Several methods are used in accounting for these opening inventory costs. In this discussion, two methods are illustrated:

1. *Average costing.* Opening inventory costs are added to the costs of the new period.

2. *First-in, first-out costing.* Opening inventory costs are kept separate and the new costs necessary to complete the work in process inventory are computed.

Average Costing. When opening work in process inventory costs are merged with costs of the new period, the problem is essentially one of securing representative average unit costs. Ordinarily, the averaging process is quite simple.

The February cost reports of the three departments reviewed in the previous chapter are used to illustrate the treatment of opening work in process inventory and to show the relationship of costs from one period to the next. Closing inventories in January departmental cost reports become opening work in process inventories for the month of February.

Computations begin with this January work in process inventory data:

	Department		
	Mixing	*Refining*	*Finishing*
Units.........................	4,000	3,000	4,000
Cost from preceding department....		$5,400	$14,400
Materials in process..............	$2,000		
Labor in process.................	1,240	910	900
Factory overhead in process........	1,200	800	550

Mixing Department. The opening work in process inventory of the Mixing Department shows $2,000 of materials cost, $1,240 of labor cost, $1,200 of factory overhead, and 4,000 units in process. During the month of February additional charges to the department are: materials, $19,840; labor, $24,180; and factory overhead, $22,580. The additional materials put into process are for the production of 40,000 units. Therefore, units to be accounted for total 44,000 (4,000 + 40,000). Of the total units put into process, 39,000 are completed; 38,000 of the completed units were transferred to the Refining Department; and the other 1,000, although completed, are still on hand awaiting transfer. At month-end, 3,000 units are in process, 100 percent complete as to materials but only 66⅔ percent complete as to labor and overhead. During the month, 2,000 units were lost. The above facts are illustrated in the cost of production report of the Mixing Department on page 153.

The unit cost of work done in the Mixing Department is $1.72, consisting of $.52 for materials, $.62 for labor, and $.58 for factory overhead. The $.52 unit cost for materials is computed by adding the materials cost in the opening work in process to the materials cost of the month ($2,000 + $19,840 = $21,840) and dividing the $21,840 total by an equivalent production figure of 42,000 units. The 42,000 figure consists of 38,000 units completed and transferred, 1,000 units completed but still on hand, and 3,000 units in process entirely complete as to materials. It is important to note that the cost of materials already in process is added to the materials cost of the month, before dividing by the equivalent production figure. This method results in an average unit cost for work done in the current and preceding period.

The same principle is followed in computing unit costs for labor and factory overhead. The $.62 unit cost for labor is the result of dividing equivalent production of 41,000 units (work in process only ⅔ complete for labor and factory overhead) into the sum of the opening work in process labor cost of $1,240 and the departmental labor cost for the month of $24,180. The factory overhead unit cost is $.58 ($1,200 + $22,580 ÷ 41,000). The departmental unit cost of $1.72 is the sum of these three individual unit cost figures.

THE CARSON CHEMICAL COMPANY
MIXING DEPARTMENT
COST OF PRODUCTION REPORT
FOR THE MONTH OF FEBRUARY, 19—

QUANTITY SCHEDULE:

Units in process at beginning (all materials — ½ labor and factory overhead).......	4,000	
Units started in process.....................................	40,000	44,000
Units transferred to next department.......................	38,000	
Units completed and on hand.............................	1,000	
Units still in process (all materials — ⅔ labor and factory overhead).	3,000	
Units lost in process.....................................	2,000	44,000

COST CHARGED TO THE DEPARTMENT:	Total Cost	Unit Cost
Cost added by department:		
Work in process — opening inventory:		
Materials..	$ 2,000	
Labor..	1,240	
Factory overhead.......................................	1,200	
Cost added during period:		
Materials..	19,840	$ .52
Labor..	24,180	.62
Factory overhead.......................................	22,580	.58
Total cost to be accounted for.........................	$71,040	$1.72

COST ACCOUNTED FOR AS FOLLOWS:		
Transferred to next department (38,000 × $1.72)...............		$65,360
Work in process — closing inventory:		
Completed and on hand (1,000 × $1.72).....................	$ 1,720	
Materials (3,000 × $.52)...................................	1,560	
Labor (3,000 × ⅔ × $.62)..................................	1,240	
Factory overhead (3,000 × ⅔ × $.58).......................	1,160	5,680
Total cost accounted for................................		$71,040

ADDITIONAL COMPUTATIONS:

Equivalent production:

Materials $= 38,000 + 1,000 + 3,000 = 42,000$ units

Labor and factory overhead $= 38,000 + 1,000 + (⅔ × 3,000) = 41,000$ units

Unit costs:

Materials $= \$2,000 + \$19,840 = \dfrac{\$21,840}{42,000} = \$.52$

Labor $= \$1,240 + \$24,180 = \dfrac{\$25,420}{41,000} = \$.62$

Factory overhead $= \$1,200 + \$22,580 = \dfrac{\$23,780}{41,000} = \$.58$

Total cost charged to the department is disposed of as follows: $65,360 is transferred to the Refining Department and $5,680 is the cost assigned to the closing work in process. The work in process inventory consists of $1,720 (1,000 units × $1.72) for units completed but on hand; $1,560 (3,000 units × $.52) for materials; $1,240 (2,000 units × $.62) for labor; and $1,160 (2,000 units × $.58) for factory overhead.

The units completed but on hand are listed as work in process in the Mixing Department although all operations in that department have been performed on these units. The units remain in the work in process inventory of the Mixing Department to assign it *responsibility* for this part of total work in process. The cost assigned these units is obtained by multiplying the 1,000 completed units by $1.72, the cost of one completed unit. The cost transfer entry for the 38,000 units transferred to the next department is:

> Work in Process — Refining Department............... 65,360
> Work in Process — Mixing Department..............   65,360

Refining Department. Accounting for opening work in process inventory costs in departments other than the first requires additional calculations because part of the cost assigned to the work in process inventory is classified as cost from a preceding department. When the closing work in process inventory was computed, part of the cost of this inventory came from costs added by the preceding department. It is this part of the inventory which now requires separate treatment.

Because costs assigned to the opening work in process inventory are added to costs incurred during the period and these totals are divided by equivalent production figures to secure average unit cost figures, the opening work in process inventory of departments other than the first must be split into two parts:

1. That part of the opening inventory that consists of work which was done in preceding departments.

2. That part of the opening inventory which represents costs added by the department itself.

The portion of the work in process inventory representing the cost of work done in preceding departments is entered in the section of the cost report titled "Cost from preceding department." It is added to the cost of transfers received during the current period from the preceding department. An average unit cost for work done in preceding departments is then computed. The other portion of the inventory which represents costs added by the Refining Department is entered as a departmental cost to be added to other departmental costs incurred during the period. Average unit costs are then computed.

The cost of production report of the Refining Department presented on page 155 illustrates both of the above-mentioned procedures. The analysis of the opening work in process of this department (page 152) lists 3,000 units in process with a cost of $5,400 from the preceding department, a labor cost of $910, and $800 for factory overhead. The following costs are assumed for the month of February: labor, $34,050; and factory overhead, $30,018. Thirty-six thousand units were completed and transferred

THE CARSON CHEMICAL COMPANY
REFINING DEPARTMENT
COST OF PRODUCTION REPORT
FOR THE MONTH OF FEBRUARY, 19—

QUANTITY SCHEDULE:

Units in process at beginning (⅓ labor and factory overhead)......	3,000	
Units received from preceding department......................	38,000	41,000
Units transferred to next department.........................	36,000	
Units still in process (½ labor and factory overhead)............	4,000	
Units lost in process..	1,000	41,000

COST CHARGED TO THE DEPARTMENT:	Total Cost	Unit Cost
Cost from preceding department:		
Work in process — opening inventory (3,000)................	$ 5,400	$1.80
Transferred in during this period.... (38,000).................	65,360	1.72
Total....................... (41,000)................	$ 70,760	$1.726
Cost added by department:		
Work in process — opening inventory:		
Labor...	$ 910	
Factory overhead.....................................	800	
Cost added during period:		
Labor...	34,050	$ .920
Factory overhead.....................................	30,018	.811
Total cost added.......................................	$ 65,778	$ 1.731
Adjustment for lost units................................		.043
Total cost to be accounted for.........................	$136,538	$ 3.500

COST ACCOUNTED FOR AS FOLLOWS:		
Transferred to next department (36,000 × $3.500)...............		$126,000
Work in process — closing inventory:		
Adjusted cost from preceding department [4,000 × ($1.726 + $.043)]	$ 7,076	
Labor (4,000 × ½ × $.920)...............................	1,840	
Factory overhead (4,000 × ½ × $.811).....................	1,622	10,538
Total cost accounted for.................................		$136,538

ADDITIONAL COMPUTATIONS:

$$\text{Unit cost from preceding department} = \frac{\$70,760}{41,000} = \$1.726$$

Equivalent production:

$$\text{Labor and factory overhead} = 36,000 + \frac{4,000}{2} = 38,000 \text{ units}$$

Unit costs:

$$\text{Labor} = \$910 + \$34,050 = \frac{\$34,960}{38,000} = \$.920$$

$$\text{Factory overhead} = \$800 + \$30,018 = \frac{\$30,818}{38,000} = \$.811$$

Adjustment for lost units:

$$\text{Method No. 1} = \frac{\$70,760}{40,000} = \$1.769 ....\$1.769 - \$1.726 = \$.043$$

$$\text{Method No. 2} = 1,000 \text{ units} \times \$1.726 = \$1,726 ....\frac{\$ 1,726}{40,000} = \$.043$$

to the Finishing Department; 4,000 units are in process, 50 percent complete as to labor and factory overhead; 1,000 units were lost in process.

The $5,400 portion of the opening work in process inventory which is cost from the preceding department is entered in the current month's cost report as work in process — opening inventory. It is added to the $65,360 of cost transferred during the month to the Refining Department from the Mixing Department. The average unit cost for work done in the preceding department is computed next by dividing total cost received from the Mixing Department, $70,760, ($5,400 + $65,360) by 41,000 units. The 41,000 figure consists of 3,000 units in the opening work in process inventory and 38,000 units received during the month. The average unit cost for work done in the preceding department is $1.726 $(\frac{\$70,760}{41,000})$. This is a *weighted average* since it considers all units and costs received from the preceding department. It is not the average of the two unit costs, $1.80 and $1.72. Such an average would be inaccurate since there are more units with a unit cost of $1.72 (38,000 units) than with a unit cost of $1.80 (3,000 units). Instead, the total cost is divided by the total units.

Departmental unit costs for labor ($.920) and factory overhead ($.811) are computed as explained in discussing the cost report of the Mixing Department. The $910 of labor in process at the beginning is added to labor put in process during the month, $34,050; and the total of these two labor costs, $34,960, is divided by an equivalent production figure of 38,000 units $(36,000 + \frac{4,000}{2})$ to arrive at the $.920 $(\frac{\$34,960}{38,000})$ unit cost. The factory overhead unit cost of $.811 is the result of dividing total factory overhead used, $30,818, ($800 + $30,018) by equivalent production of 38,000 units. The departmental unit cost is the sum of these two unit costs, $1.731.

The lost unit cost adjustment figure of $.043 is computed on the assumption that units lost cannot be identified as coming from units in process at the beginning or from units received during the period; units are assumed to have been lost from both sources. The lost unit cost is computed by dividing total preceding department cost, $70,760, by remaining good units, 40,000, and subtracting from this adjusted unit cost of $1.769 $(\frac{\$70,760}{40,000})$ the previous average unit cost figure of $1.726. The adjustment because of lost units is $.043 ($1.769 − $1.726). The lost unit adjustment can also be determined by multiplying the 1,000 units lost by the preceding department's average unit cost, $1.726, for a total cost of $1,726 (1,000 × $1.726) which must be absorbed by remaining good units. The lost unit cost adjustment computed in this manner is also $.043 $(\frac{\$1,726}{40,000})$. This lost unit cost adjustment is added to the $1.731 departmental unit cost and to the unadjusted average preceding department unit cost of $1.726 to give a cumulative unit cost figure of $3.50.

THE CARSON CHEMICAL COMPANY
FINISHING DEPARTMENT
COST OF PRODUCTION REPORT
FOR THE MONTH OF FEBRUARY, 19—

QUANTITY SCHEDULE:

Units in process at beginning (¼ labor and factory overhead)......	4,000	
Units received from preceding department......................	36,000	40,000
Units transferred to finished goods storeroom...................	36,000	
Units still in process (⅓ labor and factory overhead)............	3,000	
Units lost in process.......................................	1,000	40,000

	Total Cost	Unit Cost
COST CHARGED TO THE DEPARTMENT:		
Cost from preceding department:		
Work in process — opening inventory (4,000)................	$ 14,400	$ 3.60
Transferred in during this period..... (36,000)................	126,000	3.50
Total........................... (40,000)................	$140,400	$ 3.51
Cost added by department:		
Work in process — opening inventory:		
Labor..	$ 900	
Factory overhead...	550	
Costs added during period:		
Labor..	33,140	$ .92
Factory overhead...	19,430	.54
Total cost added..	$ 54,020	$ 1.46
Adjustment for lost units..................................		.09
Total cost to be accounted for............................	$194,420	$ 5.06

COST ACCOUNTED FOR AS FOLLOWS:		
Transferred to finished goods storeroom (36,000 × $5.06).........		$182,160
Work in process — closing inventory:		
Adjusted cost from preceding department [3,000 × ($3.51+$.09)]	$ 10,800	
Labor (3,000 × ⅓ × $.92)...................................	920	
Factory overhead (3,000 × ⅓ × $.54).......................	540	12,260
Total cost accounted for...................................		$194,420

ADDITIONAL COMPUTATIONS:

$$\text{Unit cost from preceding department} = \frac{\$140,400}{40,000} = \$3.51$$

$$\text{Equivalent production} - \text{Labor and factory overhead} = 36,000 + \frac{3,000}{3} = 37,000 \text{ units}$$

$$\text{Unit costs} - \text{Labor} = \$900 + \$33,140 = \frac{\$34,040}{37,000} = \$.92$$

$$\text{Factory overhead} = \$550 + \$19,430 = \frac{\$19,980}{37,000} = \$.54$$

Adjustment for lost units:

$$\text{Method No. 1} = \frac{\$140,400}{39,000} = \$3.60 ....\$3.60 - \$3.51 = \$.09$$

$$\text{Method No. 2} = 1,000 \text{ units} \times \$3.51 = \$3,510 .... \frac{\$3,510}{39,000} = \$.09$$

THE CARSON CHEMICAL COMPANY
COST OF PRODUCTION REPORT
FOR THE MONTH OF FEBRUARY, 19—

QUANTITY SCHEDULE:	Mixing Department		Refining Department		Finishing Department	
Units in process at beginning...........	4,000		3,000		4,000	
Units started in process................	40,000	44,000				
Units received from preceding department.			38,000	41,000	36,000	40,000
Units transferred to next department.....	38,000		36,000			
Units transferred to finished goods store-room................................					36,000	
Units completed and on hand...........	1,000					
Units still in process..................	3,000		4,000		3,000	
Units lost in process..................	2,000	44,000	1,000	41,000	1,000	40,000

COST CHARGED TO THE DEPARTMENT:	Total Cost	Unit Cost	Total Cost	Unit Cost	Total Cost	Unit Cost
Cost from preceding department:						
Work in process — opening inventory...			$ 5,400	$1.800	$ 14,400	$3.60
Transferred in during this period........			65,360	1.720	126,000	3.50
Total..............................			$ 70,760	$1.726	$140,400	$3.51
Cost added by department:						
Work in process — opening inventory:						
Materials.........................	$ 2,000					
Labor............................	1,240		$ 910		$ 900	
Factory overhead..................	1,200		800		550	
Cost added during period:						
Materials.........................	19,840	$ .52				
Labor............................	24,180	.62	34,050	$ .920	33,140	$ .92
Factory overhead..................	22,580	.58	30,018	.811	19,430	.54
Total cost added....................	$71,040	$1.72	$ 65,778	$1.731	$ 54,020	$1.46
Adjustment for lost units.............				.043		.09
Total cost to be accounted for......	$71,040	$1.72	$136,538	$3.500	$194,420	$5.06

COST ACCOUNTED FOR AS FOLLOWS:						
Transferred to next department.........			$65,360		$126,000	
Transferred to finished goods storeroom...						$182,160
Work in process — closing inventory:						
Completed and on hand.............	$ 1,720					
Adjusted cost from preceding department			$ 7,076		$ 10,800	
Materials.........................	1,560					
Labor............................	1,240		1,840		920	
Factory overhead..................	1,160	5,680	1,622	10,538	540	12,260
Total cost accounted for..........		$71,040		$136,538		$194,420

Total cost to be accounted for is $136,538. Of this total, $126,000 is the cost of the 36,000 units completed and transferred. The balance is cost assigned to the work in process inventory. The entry for the cost of the 36,000 units transferred to the next department is:

Work in Process — Finishing Department.............   126,000
      Work in Process — Refining Department...........   126,000

Finishing Department. To complete this discussion of operations for the month of February, the cost of production report of the Finishing

Department is shown on page 157. The entry to transfer the cost of the 36,000 finished units is:

Finished Goods....................................	182,160	
Work in Process — Finishing Department..........		182,160

Although the cost reports of each department are presented separately, operations of the firm for the month would also be combined in a single cost report as illustrated on page 158.

First-In, First-Out Costing. The preceding discussion describes the average costing method of accounting for opening work in process inventory costs in a process cost system. It is also possible to keep opening work in process costs separate rather than average them in with the additional new costs incurred in the next period. This procedure gives separate unit costs (1) for opening work in process units completed and (2) for units started and finished in the same period.

Some accountants believe the opening work in process cost should be kept intact, adding only that portion of additional costs required to complete units in the opening work in process. Under the first-in, first-out costing method, the cost of completing units in process at the beginning of the period is computed first, followed by the computation of the cost of units started and finished within the period. Use of this procedure leads to at least two different unit costs for work completed within a specific period. The averaging process produces only one completed unit cost.

In order to permit the comparison of the two costing procedures, figures in the cost of production reports illustrated previously are used to explain the details of the fifo method. The illustrations indicate that the two methods of costing do not result in significantly different unit costs; for, in general, manufacturing operations in process cost type industries are more or less uniform from period to period. Each firm will select that costing method which can be applied easily and conveniently and which, at the same time, offers reliable figures for management's guidance.

Mixing Department. The cost of production report of the Mixing Department for the month of February, page 160, uses the fifo method and should be compared with the cost of production report on page 153 which illustrates the average costing method. Four thousand units are in process at the beginning of operations which are 100 percent complete as to materials and 50 percent complete as to labor and factory overhead.

The cost report form remains the same, but the following differences exist in the methods of computing unit costs and of determining costs to be transferred:

1. Opening work in process cost of $4,440 is kept separate and is not broken down into its component parts as in average costing.

THE CARSON CHEMICAL COMPANY
MIXING DEPARTMENT
COST OF PRODUCTION REPORT
FOR THE MONTH OF FEBRUARY, 19 —

QUANTITY SCHEDULE:

Units in process at beginning (all materials — ½ labor and factory overhead)..	4,000	
Units started in process......................................	40,000	44,000
Units transferred to next department...........................	38,000	
Units completed and on hand..................................	1,000	
Units still in process (all materials — ⅔ labor and factory overhead).	3,000	
Units lost in process...	2,000	44,000

	Total Cost	Unit Cost
COST CHARGED TO THE DEPARTMENT:		
Work in process — opening inventory..........................	$ 4,440	
Cost added by department:		
Materials..	$ 19,840	$ .522
Labor...	24,180	.620
Factory overhead..	22,580	.579
Total cost added.......................................	$ 66,600	$ 1.721
Total cost to be accounted for..........................	$ 71,040	

COST ACCOUNTED FOR AS FOLLOWS:

Transferred to next department—
From opening inventory:

Inventory cost..	$4,440		
Labor added (4,000 × ½ × $.620)...................	1,240		
Factory overhead added (4,000 × ½ × $.579).........	1,158	$ 6,838	
From current production:			
Units started and finished (34,000 × $1.721)*.................		58,517	$ 65,355
Work in process — closing inventory:			
Completed and on hand (1,000 × $1.721).....................		$ 1,721	
Materials (3,000 × $.522)...................................		1,566	
Labor (3,000 × ⅔ × $.620)................................		1,240	
Factory overhead (3,000 × ⅔ × $.579).....................		1,158	5,685
Total cost accounted for.................................			$ 71,040

ADDITIONAL COMPUTATIONS:

Equivalent production:

	Materials	Labor and Factory Overhead
Transferred out.......................................	38,000	38,000
Less opening inventory (all units).......................	4,000	4,000
Started and finished this period...........................	34,000	34,000
Add opening inventory (work this period).................	—0—	2,000
Add closing inventory:		
Completed and on hand.............................	1,000	1,000
Still in process.....................................	3,000	2,000
	38,000 units	39,000 units

Unit costs: Materials $= \dfrac{\$19,840}{38,000} = \$.522$

Labor $= \dfrac{\$24,180}{39,000} = \$.620$ Factory overhead $= \dfrac{\$22,580}{39,000} = \$.579$

---

*34,000 units × $1.721 = $58,514. To avoid a decimal discrepancy, the cost transferred from current production is computed as follows: $71,040 − ($6,838 + $5,685) = $58,517.

2. The degree of completion of the opening work in process must be stated in order to compute completed unit costs; average costing does not require the degree of completion of the opening work in process.

Under fifo costing, the cost of completing the 4,000 units in process at the beginning must be computed first. No additional materials were needed; but since the units in process at the beginning were only 50 percent complete as to labor and factory overhead, more labor and overhead cost must be added to complete these units. To determine costs expended in completing opening work in process units and to arrive at the cost of units started and finished within this period, unit costs for materials, labor, and factory overhead added during the period are computed. Materials added during February cost $19,840, sufficient to complete an equivalent production of 38,000 units (34,000 of the 38,000 units transferred were started and completed during the period, 3,000 units were in process at month-end with all the necessary materials, and 1,000 units were entirely complete but still on hand). Therefore, the unit cost for materials is $.522 ($\frac{\$19,840}{38,000}$).

Labor cost for February is $24,180. The labor unit cost is computed after determining the number of units that could have been completed from this total labor cost. The labor cost was sufficient to complete: (1) 50 percent or 2,000 units of the 4,000 units in the opening inventory; (2) 34,000 units started and completed this period; (3) 1,000 units still on hand; and (4) 2/3 or 2,000 units of the 3,000 units still in work in process. Therefore, the equivalent production for labor is 39,000 units [2,000 + (38,000 − 4,000) + 1,000 + 2,000 = 39,000], and the unit cost for labor is $.620 ($\frac{\$24,180}{39,000}$). The same analysis gives a unit cost for factory overhead of $.579 ($\frac{\$22,580}{39,000}$). The unit cost to the end of operations by the department is $1.721, and total cost to be accounted for is $71,040.

In average costing, the cost of the units transferred to the next department was computed by multiplying the number of units transferred by the final unit cost. This procedure cannot be followed under fifo costing. Units in process at the beginning must be completed first and will usually have a completed unit cost different from the unit cost for work started and finished during the period. In any event, two separate computations must be made to determine total cost transferred to the next department. The completed cost pertaining to units in the opening work in process is computed separately from the cost of the units started, finished, and transferred during the period.

To determine the cost of completing the opening work in process, the cost of labor and factory overhead used during the period in completing opening work in process units is added to the $4,440 already included as a cost of such units. Labor and overhead were added at unit costs of $.620

for labor and $.579 for factory overhead to complete the equivalent of 2,000 of the 4,000 units in process. Labor added amounted to $1,240 (2,000 × $.620) and factory overhead $1,158 (2,000 × $.579). Therefore, the total cost of the 4,000 units completed and transferred was $6,838 ($4,440 + $1,240 + $1,158). The other 34,000 units were transferred at a unit cost of $1.721, or at a total of $58,517 (see illustration footnote, page 160). The balance of the cost to be accounted for is in work in process at the end of the period and is computed as shown on the cost of production report, page 160.

Refining Department. The cost report of the Refining Department is illustrated on page 163. Although two separate computations were made to calculate cost transferred out of the Mixing Department, the total cost transferred into the Refining Department is shown as only one amount in its cost report; and the unit cost of $1.72 is obtained by merely dividing the 38,000 total units received into the total cost received of $65,355 ($6,838 + $58,517). This procedure seems to cancel out all the apparent advantages of the fifo method and has been criticized by some writers. It is certain that the method has little to recommend it; however, as long as CPA examination problems continue to require a knowledge of the fifo method, it is advisable to study this procedure. The entry to transfer this cost is:

Work in Process — Refining Department................. 65,355
    Work in Process — Mixing Department...............   65,355

The balance of the report is consistent with the fifo method of costing. The opening work in process inventory, valued at $7,110, is shown in total and is not broken down into its component parts. Labor and factory overhead costs needed to complete the opening in-process units are added to this figure to determine the completed cost of these units to be transferred to the next department. The $.920 unit cost for labor and the $.811 unit cost for factory overhead are found by dividing the equivalent production figure of 37,000 units for labor and factory overhead into the labor cost of $34,050 and factory overhead of $30,018, respectively. The equivalent production figure of 37,000 units consists of: (1) 2,000 units of opening inventory completed; (2) 33,000 units started and finished this period; and (3) 2,000 of the 4,000 units in the closing work in process inventory, or 2,000 + (36,000 − 3,000) + 2,000 = 37,000. The labor cost added to the opening work in process was $1,840 (2,000 × $.920) and factory overhead added was $1,622 (2,000 × $.811). These two amounts are added to the opening work in process cost of $7,110 to give a total cost of $10,572. This is the completed cost of the 3,000 units in opening work in process transferred to the Finishing Department.

THE CARSON CHEMICAL COMPANY
REFINING DEPARTMENT
COST OF PRODUCTION REPORT
FOR THE MONTH OF FEBRUARY, 19—

QUANTITY SCHEDULE:

Units in process at beginning (⅓ labor and factory overhead)......	3,000	
Units received from preceding department......................	38,000	41,000
Units transferred to next department..........................	36,000	
Units still in process (½ labor and factory overhead)............	4,000	
Units lost in process...	1,000	41,000

	Total Cost	Unit Cost
COST CHARGED TO THE DEPARTMENT:		
Work in process — opening inventory........................	$ 7,110	
Cost from preceding department:		
Transferred in during the month (38,000).....................	$ 65,355	$ 1.720
Cost added by department:		
Labor...	$ 34,050	$ .920
Factory overhead...	30,018	.811
Total cost added.....................................	$ 64,068	$ 1.731
Adjustment for lost units...................................		.046
Total cost to be accounted for............................	$136,533	$ 3.497

COST ACCOUNTED FOR AS FOLLOWS:

Transferred to next department —
From opening inventory:

Inventory cost..	$7,110	
Labor added (3,000 × ⅔ × $.920)....................	1,840	
Factory overhead added (3,000 × ⅔ × $.811).........	1,622	$ 10,572

From current production:

Units started and finished (33,000 × $3.497)*................	115,435	$126,007

Work in process — closing inventory:

Adjusted cost from preceding department [4,000×($1.72+$.046)]	$ 7,064	
Labor (4,000 × ½ × $.920).................................	1,840	
Factory overhead (4,000 × ½ × $.811).....................	1,622	10,526
Total cost accounted for.................................		$136,533

ADDITIONAL COMPUTATIONS:

Equivalent production:

	Labor and Factory Overhead
Transferred out...	36,000
Less opening inventory (all units)...........................	3,000
Started and finished this period............................	33,000
Add opening inventory (work this period).....................	2,000
Add closing inventory.......................................	2,000
	37,000 units

Unit costs: Labor $= \dfrac{\$34,050}{37,000} = \$.920$ Factory overhead $= \dfrac{\$30,018}{37,000} = \$.811$

Adjustment for lost units:

Method No. 1 $= \dfrac{\$65,355}{38,000 - 1,000} = \$1.766$ ....$1.766 - \$1.720 = \$.046$

Method No. 2 $= 1,000$ units $\times \$1.720 = \$1,720$ ....$\dfrac{\$ 1,720}{37,000} = \$.046$

---

*33,000 units × $3.497 = $115,401. To avoid a decimal discrepancy, the cost transferred from current production is computed as follows: $136,533 − ($10,572 + $10,526) = $115,435.

The departmental unit cost is $1.731. Because 1,000 units were lost during February, computation of the cumulative cost to the end of operations in the Refining Department requires an adjustment of $.046 for lost units. This lost unit cost adjustment is determined by dividing the total previous department cost of $65,355 by the good units (37,000) of the period, and subtracting from this new unit cost of $1.766 the old unit cost of $1.720 ($1.766 − $1.720 − $.046). It is important to note that for fifo costing, the lost units must be identified as either opening work in process units or new units started during the period. The identification is needed to determine which unit cost should be adjusted. In either case it means that because units were lost, total costs incurred must be spread over a smaller number of units. In the case of the Refining Department, it is assumed that units lost came from those placed in process during the period; that is, from units received in the department in February.

A total of 36,000 units is transferred out of the department, of which 3,000 units came from units in process at the beginning of the period. The cost of the 3,000 units was $10,572. The remaining 33,000 units came from units started and finished during the month. These units were transferred at a cumulative unit cost of $3.497 each and a total cost of $115,435 (see footnote explanation, page 163). The entry to transfer the cost of the 36,000 units to the next department is:

| Work in Process — Finishing Department............ | 126,007 | |
| Work in Process — Refining Department........... | | 126,007 |

The balance of the cost to be accounted for is the closing work in process inventory which is computed in the conventional manner.

Finishing Department. To make this discussion of fifo costing complete, the cost of production report of the Finishing Department is reproduced on page 165.

The entry to transfer the cost of the 36,000 finished units is:

| Finished Goods................................. | 182,166 | |
| Work in Process — Finishing Department.......... | | 182,166 |

The illustration on page 166 is a combined cost of production report for the month of February using fifo costing. In order to observe the differences between the two costing methods discussed, this report should be compared with the cost of production report on page 158 in which average costing is used.

Average Costing versus Fifo Costing. Both average costing and fifo costing have certain advantages. It would be arbitrary to state that one method is either simpler or more accurate than the other. The selection

THE CARSON CHEMICAL COMPANY
FINISHING DEPARTMENT
COST OF PRODUCTION REPORT
FOR THE MONTH OF FEBRUARY, 19—

QUANTITY SCHEDULE:

Units in process at beginning (¼ labor and factory overhead)	4,000	
Units received from preceding department................	36,000	40,000
Units transferred to finished goods storeroom..............	36,000	
Units still in process (⅓ labor and factory overhead)	3,000	
Units lost in process...................................	1,000	40,000

	Total Cost	Unit Cost
COST CHARGED TO THE DEPARTMENT:		
Work in process — opening inventory.....................	$ 15,850	
Cost from preceding department:		
Transferred in during the month (36,000)	$126,007	$ 3.500
Cost added by department:		
Labor...	$ 33,140	$ .921
Factory overhead.....................................	19,430	.540
Total cost added.................................	$ 52,570	$ 1.461
Adjustment for lost units............................		.100
Total cost to be accounted for	$194,427	$ 5.061

COST ACCOUNTED FOR AS FOLLOWS:

Transferred to next department —
From opening inventory:

Inventory cost..........................	$ 15,850		
Labor added (4,000 × ¾ × $.921)............	2,763		
Factory overhead added (4,000 × ¾ × $.540)..	1,620	$ 20,233	
From current production:			
Units started and finished (32,000 × $5.061)*.............		161,933	$182,166

Work in process — closing inventory:

Adjusted cost from preceding department			
[3,000 × ($3.50 + $.10)].........................	$ 10,800		
Labor (3,000 × ⅓ × $.921).................	921		
Factory overhead (3,000 × ⅓ × $.540).................	540	12,261	
Total cost accounted for			$194,427

ADDITIONAL COMPUTATIONS:

Equivalent production:

	Labor and Factory Overhead
Transferred out...	36,000
Less opening inventory (all units)....................................	4,000
Started and finished this period....................................	32,000
Add opening inventory (work this period).............................	3,000
Add closing inventory..	1,000
	36,000 units

Unit costs: $\text{Labor} = \dfrac{\$33,140}{36,000} = \$.921$ $\text{Factory Overhead} = \dfrac{\$19,430}{36,000} = \$.540$

Adjustment for lost units:

Method No. 1 $= \dfrac{\$126,007}{36,000 - 1,000} = \$3.60$.............. $3.60 - \$3.50 = \$.10$

Method No. 2 $= 1,000 \text{ units} \times \$3.50 = \$3,500$............... $\dfrac{\$ 3,500}{35,000} = \$.10$

---

*32,000 × $5.061 = $161,952. To avoid a decimal discrepancy, the cost transferred from current production is computed as follows: $194,427 − ($20,233 + $12,261) = $161,933.

THE CARSON CHEMICAL COMPANY
COST OF PRODUCTION REPORT
FOR THE MONTH OF FEBRUARY, 19—

QUANTITY SCHEDULE:	Mixing Department		Refining Department		Finishing Department	
Units in process at beginning....	4,000		3,000		4,000	
Units started in process........	40,000	44,000				
Units received from preceding department.................			38,000	41,000	36,000	40,000
Units transferred to next dept....	38,000		36,000			
Units transferred to finished goods storeroom.................					36,000	
Units completed and on hand....	1,000					
Units still in process...........	3,000		4,000		3,000	
Units lost in process...........	2,000	44,000	1,000	41,000	1,000	40,000

COST CHARGED TO THE DEPARTMENT:	Total Cost	Unit Cost	Total Cost	Unit Cost	Total Cost	Unit Cost
Work in process — opening inventory....................	$ 4,440		$ 7,110		$ 15,850	
Cost from preceding department:						
Transferred in during the month..			$ 65,355	$ 1.72	$126,007	$ 3.500
Cost added by department:						
Materials....................	$19,840	$ .522				
Labor......................	24,180	.620	$ 34,050	$ .920	$ 33,140	$ .921
Factory overhead...........	22,580	.579	30,018	.811	19,430	.540
Total cost added..........	$66,600	$ 1.721	$ 64,068	$ 1.731	$ 52,570	$ 1.461
Adjustment for lost units......				.046		.100
Total cost to be accounted for	$71,040	$ 1.721	$136,533	$ 3.497	$194,427	$ 5.061

COST ACCOUNTED FOR AS FOLLOWS:

	Total	Unit	Total	Unit	Total	Unit
Transferred to next department —						
From opening inventory:						
Inventory cost...............	$ 4,440		$ 7,110		$ 15,850	
Labor added.................	1,240		1,840		2,763	
Factory overhead added.......	1,158	$ 6,838	1,622	$ 10,572	1,620	$ 20,233
From current production:						
Units started and finished.....		58,517		115,435		161,933
		$65,355		$126,007		$182,166
Work in process — closing inventory:						
Completed and on hand.......	$ 1,721					
Adjusted cost from preceding department...............			$ 7,064		$ 10,800	
Materials....................	1,566					
Labor......................	1,240		1,840		921	
Factory overhead...........	1,158	5,685	1,622	10,526	540	12,261
Total cost accounted for.....		$71,040		$136,533		$194,427

of one or the other method depends entirely upon the opinion of a company's management regarding the most appropriate and practical cost determination procedures.

The basic difference between the two methods concerns the treatment of opening work in process inventory. The averaging method adds opening work in process inventory costs to materials, labor, and factory overhead costs incurred during a period. Unit costs are determined by dividing these costs by equivalent production figures. Units and costs are transferred to the next department as one cumulative figure.

The fifo method retains opening work in process inventory cost as a separate figure. Costs necessary to complete the opening work in process units are added to this total cost. The sum of these two cost totals is the figure at which these units are transferred to the next department. Units started and finished during the period have their own unit cost which is usually different from the completed unit cost of units in process at the beginning of the period. Unfortunately, the true costs are averaged out in the next department, resulting in a loss of much of the value associated with the use of the fifo method.

If the fifo method is used, units lost during a period must be identified as to whether they came from units in process at the beginning or from units received during the period. Also, in computing equivalent production figures in fifo costing, the degree of completion of both opening and closing work in process inventories must be considered.

The disadvantage of fifo costing is that if several unit cost figures are used at the same time, extensive detail is required within the cost of production report which can lead to complex procedures and even inaccuracy. Whether the extra details yield more representative unit costs than the average costing method is debatable, especially in a firm using a process cost system where production is continuous and more or less uniform, and appreciable fluctuations in unit costs are not expected to develop. Under such conditions, the average costing method leads to more satisfactory cost computations.

DIFFICULTIES ENCOUNTERED IN PROCESS COST ACCOUNTING PROCEDURES

Certain difficulties likely to be encountered in actual practice should be mentioned before leaving the subject of process cost accounting procedures:

1. The determination of production quantities and their stages of completion present problems. Every computation is influenced by these figures. Since the data generally come to the cost department from an operating foreman often working under circumstances that make a precise count difficult, a certain amount of doubtful counts and unreliable estimates are bound to exist. Yet, the data submitted form the basis for the determination of inventory costs.

2. Materials cost computations frequently require careful analysis. In the illustrations, materials cost is generally part of the first department's cost. In companies of certain industries, materials costs are not even entered on production reports. When raw materials prices are influenced by fluctuating market quotations, the materials cost may be recorded in a separate report designed to facilitate management decisions in relation to the fluctuating raw materials market.

3. The discussion of lost units caused by shrinkage, spoilage, or evaporation indicates that the time when the loss occurs influences the final cost calculation. Different assumptions concerning the loss would result in different costs of the unit in a department which, in turn, affects inventory costs, the cost of units transferred, and the completed unit cost. Another consideration involves the possibility of treating cost attributable to avoidable loss as an expense of the current period.

4. Industries using process cost procedures are generally of the multiple product type. Joint processing costs must be allocated to the several or many products resulting from the processes. Weighted unit averages or other bases are used to prorate these joint costs to the several products. If units manufactured are used as a basis for cost allocation, considerable difficulties arise in determining accurate unit costs. Additional clerical expenses are necessary if the labor-hour or machine-hour basis for charging overhead to process is used. Management must decide whether economy and low operational cost are compatible with increased information based on additional cost computations and procedures.

It should be noted that some companies use both job order and process costing procedures for various purposes in different departments. This is particularly true when a parallel or selective cost flow format is required. Each system or method employed by a company must be based on reliable production and performance data which when combined with output, budget, or standard cost data will provide the foundation for effective cost control and analysis.

DISCUSSION QUESTIONS

1. State the possible effects on a department's unit costs when materials are added to work in process.
2. When materials added to work in process cause an increase in units, an adjustment must be made to unit costs. This adjustment is computed in a manner comparable to the lost unit calculation. Explain.
3. How is opening work in process accounted for using average costing?
4. Units completed and on hand in a processing department are included in the department's work in process. Why?

5. Why do firms use the first-in, first-out method of computing unit costs?
6. How is opening work in process accounted for when fifo costing is used? Why must the completion stage of opening work in process be known?
7. How are equivalent production figures computed when fifo costing is used?
8. A certain factory transferred out 8,800 completed units during its second period of operation. The period was begun with 400 units 75% completed and ended with 800 units 50% completed. What was the equivalent production for the period? Assume the fifo costing method is used.
9. In another factory, the equivalent production (using the fifo costing method) was 7,000 units during a period which saw 500 units 60% complete on hand at the start and 600 units 75% complete at the end of the period. How many units were completed?
10. What are some of the disadvantages of the fifo costing method?
11. Enumerate several of the basic difficulties frequently encountered in a process cost system.
12. Express an opinion as to the usefulness of data derived from a process cost system for the control of costs.
13. Select the answer which best completes the following statement. During 19B, Marconi Company had total manufacturing costs of $180,000. The business completed 14,000 units of product, of which 4,000 units were half completed in 19A, and started production on an additional 6,000 units that were half completed at the end of 19B. For 19B the production cost per unit was (a) $18; (b) $16.36; (c) $12; or (d) $9.

(AICPA adapted)

EXERCISES

In solving exercises round off all amounts, except unit costs, to the nearest dollar. Carry unit costs to five decimal places unless stated otherwise.

1. Computation of Equivalent Production. Factories A and B each turn out 6,000 units of completed product during April. The following work in process statistics are for the month of April:

	Beginning Inventory			Ending Inventory		
	Units	% Complete		Units	% Complete	
		Materials	Labor and Overhead		Materials	Labor and Overhead
Factory A..............	2,000	100	80	1,200	100	90
Factory B..............	1,200	100	90	2,000	100	80

Required: The equivalent production figures for the two factories using (a) the average method and (b) the fifo method.

2. Computation of Equivalent Production. The Production Control Department of a plant that operates a process cost system sent the following production data for one of the four production departments to the Cost Department:

Product received from previous department:	100,000 kilograms
Product finished and sent to next department:	71,840 kilograms
Product finished and remaining in this department:	4,160 kilograms
Product unfinished in this department:	24,000 kilograms

In this department additional material is added to the work received from the preceding department. Three distinctly different types of materials are used at three separate stages of production in this department:

Material A is added at the start of the process.
Material B is added when the process is ¼ completed.
Material C is added when the process is ¾ completed.

Labor and factory overhead are incurred at a uniform rate throughout the manufacturing process in this department.

Examination of the unfinished work discloses that: ¼ was ⅞ completed; ½ was ½ completed; ¼ was ⅙ completed.

There was no beginning work in process inventory.

Required: (1) The equivalent production figures for each of the materials.
(2) The equivalent production figures for labor and factory overhead.

3. Computation of Equivalent Production. (1) Compute the equivalent production figures for costing from the following data, using the fifo method.

(a) Started in process 40,000 units; transferred 32,000 units; in process end of period, 8,000 units, one half completed.

(b) Started in process 50,000 units; completed and transferred 36,000 units; completed and on hand 6,000 units; in process end of period, 8,000 units, three fourths completed.

(c) Started in process 15,000 units; completed and transferred 12,000 units; in process end of period, 2,000 units, three fourths completed, and 1,000 units, two fifths completed.

(d) Opening inventory 16,000 units, three eighths completed; started in process 40,000 units; transferred 36,000 units; closing inventory, 10,000 units, one half completed, and 10,000 units, three fourths completed.

(e) Opening inventory 12,000 units, one third completed, and 18,000 units, one half completed; started in process 120,000 units; transferred 128,000 units; closing inventory, 6,000 units, one fifth completed and 16,000 units, three fourths completed.

(2) Compute the equivalent production figures for costing, using the average cost method, for parts (d) and (e) above.

4. Cost Assigned to Work in Process Inventory. The manager of a company whose manufacturing process lends itself quite readily to process costing methods approached the accountant with the request to compute, for his study and consideration, the work in process inventory on (a) the average cost basis and (b) the first-in, first-out basis.

The following data are available:

Units in opening inventory, 8,000; all materials, 50% labor and overhead.

Cost of opening inventory: Materials, $3,984; Labor, $2,148; Overhead, $1,692.

Placed in process, 40,000 units. Cost: Materials, $24,000; Labor, $19,968; Overhead, $19,968.

Units completed and transferred, 42,000.

Units in process at the end, 6,000; all materials, 60% labor and overhead.

Required: The costs assigned to the work in process inventory.

5. Cost of Production Report with Materials Added. The Caldwell Company produces a chemical, Caldmetral, which requires processing in three departments. In the third department materials are added, doubling the number of units. The following data pertain to the operations of Department 3 for March:

Units received from Department 2.............................	20,000
Units transferred to finished storeroom.........................	32,000

The balance of the units were still in process—100% complete as to material, 50% complete as to labor and overhead.

Cost transferred from Department 2............................	$30,000

Cost added by the department:

Materials...	$8,800	
Labor..	9,000	
Factory overhead...................................	7,200	$25,000

Required: A cost of production report for Department 3 for March.

6. Cost of Production Report with Average Method. The Shawnee Supply Company manufactures a single product on a continuous plan in three departments.

On November 1 the work in process inventory in Department 2 was:

Cost in preceding department...........................	$13,130
Materials — Department 2................................	None
Labor — Department 2...................................	$ 500
Factory overhead — Department 2........................	$ 50
Units in process......................................	5,000

Costs in Department 2 during November were:

Labor..	$14,200
Factory overhead.....................................	$ 3,450

During November 70,000 units were received from Department 1 at a unit cost of $2.641. There were 68,000 units completed in Department 2, of which 60,000 were transferred to Department 3, and 8,000 were on hand in Department 2 at the end of the month. There were 4,000 units still in process, estimated to be one half complete as to labor and factory overhead. The balance was lost within the department, and its cost is to be absorbed by all the finished and unfinished production of the department.

Required: A November cost of production report for Department 2, using the average costing method for opening work in process inventories.

7. Cost of Production Report — Fifo Method. Syracuse Ceramics, Inc. operates three departments in the production of its product — Molding, Painting, and Firing. During the month of August, the Painting Department transferred 12,400 units to the Firing Department, lost 500 units, and had 800 units in process at the end of August. There were 2,400 units in process on August 1 in the Painting Department. The remaining units started in the Painting Department during August were received from the Molding Department. The costs incurred during the month of August in the Painting Department were: Materials — $5,886; Labor — $7,830; and Factory Overhead — $1,134. The work in process inventory on August 1 was $6,656, and the costs transferred to the Painting Department from the Molding Department amounted to $23,797.80. The Painting Department work in process inventory was three fourths complete on August 1 and one fourth complete on August 31.

Required: A cost of production report for the Painting Department for the month of August, using the first-in, first-out method of accounting for beginning inventories. All computations are to be carried to four decimal places where necessary.

PROBLEMS

In solving these problems round off all amounts, except unit costs, to the nearest dollar. Carry unit costs to five decimal places unless stated otherwise.

7-1. Cost of Production Report with Materials Added. Sanderson, Inc. manufactures Product L in two departments, No. 1 and No. 2. Materials are added in each department increasing the number of units manufactured.

A summary of the cost information for the company's first month of operations (January) is as follows:

	Department No. 1	Department No. 2
Materials.....................................	$ 90,000	$ 67,500
Labor...	39,000	41,400
Factory overhead.............................	7,800	20,700
Total..	$136,800	$129,600

The production foreman reports that 300,000 units were put into production in Department 1. Of this quantity, 75,000, a normal number, were lost in production; and 180,000 were completed and transferred to Department 2. For the balance in process at the end of the month, all materials had been added, but only one third of the labor and factory overhead had been applied.

In Department 2, 45,000 units were purchased outside and added to the units received from Department 1; 195,000 units were completed and transferred to finished goods inventory. The remainder were in process at the end of the month with all materials added, but only 40% complete for labor and factory overhead.

Required: A cost of production report for January.

7-2. Cost of Production Report — Average Method. The Bay City Chemical Company produces a chemical compound subsequently sold to oil refineries for use in the production of high-octane gasoline. Operations take place in two departments, Mixing and Blending.

On March 1, 19—, the work in process inventories in the manufacturing departments showed:

	Mixing	Blending
Cost in preceding department................		$10,620
Materials costs.............................	$3,300	
Labor costs.................................	750	1,550
Factory overhead............................	375	430
Number of units in process.................	1,500 liters	1,800 liters

In the Mixing Department in addition to the work in process inventory, 11,500 liters were placed in production. Of this amount 10,200 liters were completed and transferred to the Blending Department; 2,200 liters were partially complete (all materials had been added, but only one half of the labor and factory overhead had been applied); 600 liters were lost.

In the Blending Department 9,000 liters were completed and transferred to finished stock; 2,700 liters were still in process on which 40% of the labor and overhead had been applied; 300 liters were lost.

The departmental reports showed the following costs for March:

	Mixing	*Blending*
Materials...............................	$52,500	
Labor.....................................	11,680	$16,090
Factory overhead........................	7,535	4,610

Required: A cost of production report for the month of March, using the average costing method.

7-3. Cost of Production Report — Fifo Method. The Freeman Manufacturing Company uses a process cost system. The following information for the month of January was obtained from the books of the company and from the production reports submitted by the foremen:

Production	Department A	Department B
Opening inventory.........................	5,000	3,000
Stage of completion*......................	60%	66⅔%
Started in process........................	25,000	
Received from prior department.............		26,000
Finished and transferred...................	26,000	20,000
Finished and on hand......................		1,000
Closing inventory.........................	4,000	8,000
Stage of completion*......................	25%	37.5%

*For materials, labor, and factory overhead.

Cost Summary		
Work in process — beginning.................	$ 4,970	$ 8,840
Cost for month:		
Materials..............................	30,000	4,840
Labor...................................	9,600	15,400
Factory overhead.......................	10,560	11,880

Required: (1) The company's cost of production report for January, using the fifo method of accounting for opening work in process inventories.

(2) Suppose the company uses the average costing method:
  (a) What are the equivalent production figures for each of the two departments?
  (b) If a cost of production report were required, what additional information would be needed? What information would not be needed?

7-4. Cost of Production Report — Fifo Method; Spoiled Units Cost Charged to Factory Overhead. At the beginning of the month of October the accountant of the Tulsa Processing Company drew up a new form to be used for the cost of production statement for the month. He inserted in the form the ending work in process inventory figure for the month of September in the amount of $3,144. This inventory consisted of 160 units with all materials included but only 50% of the labor and overhead.

During the month of October the Cost Department gathered and recorded the following production and cost data and other information:

Purchases of materials:

Invoice cost...............	$82,600
Freight in.................	13,444
Total materials cost......	$96,044

Materials used for:

Production................	$84,868
Equipment maintenance....	1,940
Factory supplies...........	8,636
Total cost of materials used	$95,444

Payroll:

Direct labor...............	$56,760
Supervision...............	5,800
Indirect labor.............	6,048
Equipment maintenance....	1,360
Total payroll............	$69,968

Other factory overhead:

Heat......................	$ 480
Payroll taxes..............	2,800
Rent of building...........	2,400
Power.....................	3,224
Tools.....................	4,000
Equipment depreciation.....	8,000
Total factory overhead...	$20,904

Production data for the month of October:

In process October 31: 168 units, all materials, $3/7$ labor and overhead.

Started: 6,928 units, all materials placed in production.

Spoiled: 128 units, all materials, $\frac{3}{4}$ labor and overhead; these spoiled units have no salvage value. The material and labor cost spent on these spoiled units is added to the factory overhead.

Finished: 6,792 good units.

Inventories are costed by the fifo method.

20% of the building is occupied by and charged to the Sales Department as heat and rent expense.

Required: (1) Equivalent production figures.

(2) A cost of production report.

(3) The unit cost for the three elements of cost. Carry unit cost computations to two decimal places.

(4) The cost of the work transferred out and the ending work in process inventory.

7-5. Cost of Production Report — Fifo Method. Jersey-Schell, Inc. uses three departments to produce a hair spray. The Finishing Department is the third and last step before the product is transferred to storage vats for bottling or wholesale distribution.

All materials needed to give the hair spray its final composition are added at the beginning of the process in the Finishing Department. Any lost units occur only at this point.

The company uses the fifo method in its cost system. The following data for the Finishing Department for October have been made available:

Production data:

In process, October 1....................................	10,000 gals.
(Labor and factory overhead, $\frac{3}{4}$ complete)	
Transferred in from preceding department.................	40,000 gals.
Finished and transferred to storage......................	35,000 gals.
In process, October 31...................................	10,000 gals.
(Labor and factory overhead, $\frac{1}{2}$ complete)	

Additional data:

Inventory work in process — October 1:

Cost from preceding department......................	$ 38,000
Cost from this department:	
Materials......................................	21,500
Labor...	39,000
Factory overhead................................	42,000
Total inventory work in process, October 1..............	$140,500
Transferred in during October..........................	$140,000
Cost added in this department:	
Materials......................................	$ 70,000
Labor...	162,500
Factory overhead................................	130,000
Total cost added....................................	$362,500
Total cost to be accounted for.........................	$643,000

Required: A cost of production report for October.

(AICPA adapted)

7-6. Average Costing Method; Normal Spoilage During Production. Ballinger Paper Products manufactures a high-quality paper box. The Box Department applies two separate operations—cutting and folding. The paper is first cut and trimmed to the dimensions of a box form by one machine group. One square foot of paper is equivalent to four box forms. The trimmings from this process have no scrap value. Box forms are then creased and folded (i.e., completed) by a second machine group. Any partially processed boxes in the Box Department are cut box forms that are ready for creasing and folding. These partly processed boxes are considered 50% complete as to labor and factory overhead. The Materials Department maintains an inventory of paper in sufficient quantities to permit continuous processing, and transfers to the Box Department are made as needed. Immediately after folding, all satisfactory boxes are transferred to the Finished Goods Department.

During June, 19--, the Materials Department purchased 1,210,000 square feet of unprocessed paper for $244,000. Conversion costs for June were $226,000. A quantity equal to 30,000 boxes was spoiled during paper cutting, and 70,000 boxes were spoiled during folding. All spoilage has a zero salvage value, is considered normal, and cannot be reprocessed. All spoilage loss is allocated between the completed units and partially processed boxes. Ballinger applies the weighted average costing method to all inventories.

Inventory data for June, 19--, are:

Inventory	Physical Unit	June 30, 19-- Units on Hand	June 1, 19-- Units on Hand	Cost
Materials Department:				
Paper...................	square feet	200,000	390,000	$76,000
Box Department:				
Boxes cut (not folded)....	number	300,000	800,000	55,000*
Finished Goods Department:				
Completed boxes on hand.	number	50,000	250,000	18,000

*Materials.................	$35,000
Conversion cost..........	20,000
	$55,000

Required: For the month of June, 19--, prepare:

(1) A report of cost of paper used for the Materials Department.

(2) A schedule showing the physical flow of units (including beginning and ending inventories) in the Materials Department, in the Box Department, and in the Finished Goods Department.

(3) A schedule showing the computation of equivalent units produced in June for materials and conversion costs in the Box Department.

(4) A schedule of the computation of unit costs for the Box Department.

(5) A report of inventory cost and cost of completed units for the Box Department.

(6) A schedule showing the computation of unit costs for the Finished Goods Department.

(7) A report of inventory cost and cost of units sold for the Finished Goods Department.

(AICPA adapted)

7-7. Firm Using Fifo Method of Treating Initial Work in Process Inventory. The cost of production report appearing below shows production and cost data for the Finishing Department of the Powlenko Processing Company. The company uses the fifo costing method in its process cost system. All production and cost data have been placed in the cost of production report.

COST OF PRODUCTION REPORT—FINISHING DEPARTMENT

Quantity Schedule:

Units in process, April 1 (all materials, ¾ labor and overhead).............	10,000
Transferred in during April...	40,000
Total to be accounted for.......................................	50,000
Transferred to finished goods..	35,000
Units lost..	5,000
Units in process, April 30 (all materials, ½ labor and overhead)...........	10,000
Total accounted for...	50,000

Costs Charged to Finishing Department:

Work in process, April 1:		
From preceding department....................................		$ 38,000
From this department:		
Materials (all).....................................	$21,500	
Labor (¾)...	39,000	
Overhead (¾)....................................	42,000	102,500
Total......................................		$140,500
Transferred in during April (40,000).............................		$140,000

Costs added during April:

Materials..	$ 70,000
Labor...	162,500
Overhead..	130,000
Total departmental cost this month..............................	$362,500
Total cost..	$643,000

Required: (1) The unit cost adjustment for lost units.

(2) The equivalent production for labor and overhead.

(3) The total cost of the units transferred to finished goods inventory.

(4) The cost of the final work in process inventory.

(AICPA adapted)

7-8. Computation of Fifo and Average Costing Methods. The King Process Company manufactures one product through two processes — No. 1 and No. 2.

For each unit of Process No. 1 output, 2 units of Raw Material X are put in at the start of processing. For each unit of Process No. 2 output, 3 cans of Raw Material Y are put in at the end of processing. Two pounds of Process No. 1 output are placed in at the start of Process No. 2 for each unit of finished goods started.

Spoilage generally occurs in Process No. 2 when processing is approximately 50% complete.

Work in process accounts are maintained for raw materials, conversion costs, and prior department costs.

The company uses fifo for inventory costing for Process No. 1 and average cost for inventory costing for Process No. 2.

Data for March:

(a) Units transferred:
    From Process No. 1 to Process No. 2................ 2,200 pounds
    From Process No. 2 to finished goods................   900 gallons
    From finished goods to cost of goods sold............   600 gallons
(b) Units spoiled in Process No. 2, 100 gallons.
(c) Raw materials unit costs: X, $1.51 per unit; Y, $2 per can.
(d) Conversion costs: Process No. 1, $3,344; Process No. 2, $4,010.
(e) Spoilage recovery: $100 (treated in Process No. 2 as cost reduction which came from Process No. 1).

(f) Inventory data:

	Process No. 1		Process No. 2	
	Initial	*Final*	*Initial*	*Final*
Units......................	200	300	200	300
Fraction complete, conversion costs...........	1/2	1/3	1/2	2/3
Costs:				
Materials................	$560			
Conversion costs..........	108		$ 390	
Prior department costs.....			2,200	

Required: A cost of production report with a quantity schedule for March.

(AICPA adapted)

7-9. Cost of Production Report for Firm Using Average Costing Method; Units Lost at End of a Process. Ward, Inc. manufactures a single product that passes through two departments: Extruding and Finishing-Packing. The product is shipped at the end of the day in which it is packed. The production in the Extruding and Finishing-Packing Departments does not increase the number of units started.

The cost and production data for the month of October are as follows:

Production Data	*Extruding Department*	*Finishing-Packing Department*
October production statistics:		
Units in process, 10/1.............................	10,000	29,000
Units in process, 10/31............................	8,000	6,000
Units started or received from preceding department..	20,000	22,000
Units completed and transferred or shipped..........	22,000	44,000

	10/1	10/31	10/1	10/31
Percentage of completion of work in process:				
Materials......................................	70%	50%	0%	0%
Labor...	50	40	30	35
Factory overhead...............................	50	40	30	35

Cost Data

Work in process, October 1:		
Cost from preceding department....................		$60,200
Materials......................................	$ 5,900	
Labor...	1,900	1,500
Factory overhead...............................	1,400	2,000
Costs added during October:		
Materials......................................	20,100	4,400
Labor...	10,700	7,720
Factory overhead...............................	8,680	11,830

In the Extruding Department materials are added at various stages throughout the process.

In the Finishing-Packing Department the materials added consist only of packing supplies. These materials are added at the midpoint of the process when the packing operation begins. Cost studies have disclosed that one half of the labor and overhead costs apply to the finishing operation and one half to the packing operation. All lost units occur at the end of the finishing operation when the product is inspected. All of the work in process in this department at October 1 and 31 was in the finishing operation stage of the manufacturing process. The company uses the average costing method.

Required: (1) Units lost, if any, for each department during October.

(2) The equivalent production for the calculation of unit costs for each department for October.

(3) A cost of production report for both departments for October. The report should disclose the departmental total cost and cost per unit (for materials, labor, and overhead) of the units (a) transferred to the Finishing-Packing Department and (b) shipped. Carry unit costs to three decimal places.

(AICPA adapted)

7-10. Fifo Method of Accounting for Initial Work in Process Inventory. Englehard, Inc. produces a chemical agent for commercial use. The company accounts for production in two cost centers: (1) Cooking and (2) Mix-Pack. In the first cost center liquid substances are combined in large cookers and boiled, which causes a normal decrease in volume from evaporation. After cooking, the chemical is transferred to Mix-Pack, the second cost center. It then has an equal quantity of alcohol added before being mixed and bottled in one-liter containers.

Materials are added at the beginning of production in each cost center, and labor is added equally during production in each cost center. The process is "in control" as long as the yield ratio for the Cooking Department is not less than 78%.

The fifo method is used to cost work in process inventories, and transfers are at an average unit cost; i.e., the total cost transferred divided by the total number of units transferred.

The following information is available for the month of October:

Cost Information	Cooking Department	Mix-Pack Department
Work in process, October:		
Materials......................................	$ 990	$ 120
Labor...	100	60
Overhead......................................	80	48
Prior department cost.........................		426
Month of October:		
Materials......................................	39,600	15,276
Labor...	10,050	16,000
Overhead......................................	8,040	12,800

Inventory and production records show that the Cooking Department had 1,000 liters 40% processed on October 1 and 800 liters 50% processed on October 31; the Mix-Pack Department had 600 liters 50% processed on October 1 and 1,000 liters 30% processed on October 31.

Production reports for October show that the Cooking Department started 50,000 liters into production and completed and transferred 40,200 liters to Mix-Pack, and Mix-Pack completed and transferred 80,000 one-liter containers of the finished product to the distribution warehouse.

Required: (1) A quantity report for the Cooking and the Mix-Pack cost centers which accounts for both actual units and equivalent unit production.

(2) A cost of production report for each of the two cost centers which computes total cost and cost per unit for each element of cost in inventories and October production. Compute the total cost and cost per unit for transfers.

(3) The yield ratio for Cooking, indicating whether or not the process was "in control" during October.

(AICPA adapted)

7-11. Calculation of Unit Costs—Fifo Method. The Choate Corporation employs a process cost system to accumulate costs for its Product CHOA. Inventories, costs, and production data for the month of October are shown below.

	Sept. 30	Oct. 31
Raw materials............................	100,000 lbs.	80,000 lbs.
Raw materials cost........................	$100,000	
Work in process inventories:		
All materials, 40% complete as to labor and overhead............................	20,000 units	
Cost.....................................	$ 84,000	
All materials, 33⅓% complete as to labor and overhead...............................		30,000 units
Finished goods inventory..................	40,000 units	24,000 units
Cost	$448,000	
Purchases of raw materials.................		440,000 lbs. @ $1.10 per lb.
Transferred to production..................		460,000 lbs.
Production ratio: 2 lbs:1 unit of CHOA		
Completed during the month...............		220,000 units
Materials and units are costed on the fifo method		
Direct labor..............................	$1,198,800	
Factory overhead..........................	421,800	

Required: (1) Equivalent production units for materials, labor, and factory overhead.

(2) Unit costs for the three cost elements.

(3) Cost of units transferred to finished goods inventory, using the fifo method.

(4) Cost of ending inventory work in process, in detail.

(5) Number of units sold and the cost of the finished goods inventory on October 31 using the: (a) fifo method; (b) average cost method; (c) cost difference per unit and in total.

(AICPA adapted)

7-12. Fifo Method of Treating Initial Work in Process Inventory; Units Lost at End of Process. In the process of verifying the pricing of the company's inventory of work in process and finished goods recorded on the company's books, the auditor finds:

Finished goods inventory, 110,000 units $504,900
Work in process inventory, 90,000 units, 50% completed   330,480

The company follows the practice of pricing the above inventories at the lower of cost or market on a first-in, first-out method. Materials are added to the production line at the start of the process, and overhead is applied to the product at the rate of 75% based on direct labor dollars. The auditor also learns that the market value of the finished goods inventory and the work in process inventory is greater than the amounts shown above, with the exception of the defective units in the ending inventory of finished goods, the market value of which amounts to $1.00 per unit. The difference between the market value and the assigned cost is expensed.

A review of the company's cost record shows:

	Units	Materials	Labor
		Amounts	
Opening inventory, January 1, 19—, 80% completed.	100,000	$100,000	$160,000
Additional units started in 19—	500,000		
Materials costs incurred		550,000	
Labor costs incurred			997,500

	Units	Materials	Labor
		Amounts	
Units completed in 19—:			
Good units	500,000		
Defective units.	10,000		

Finished goods inventory at December 31, 19—, includes 10,000 defective units.

Defective units occur at the end of the process; i.e., units are found to be defective at the point of final inspection.

Required: (1) Schedules indicating:

(a) Effective or equivalent production.

(b) Unit costs of materials, labor, and factory overhead of current period production.

(c) Costing of inventories of finished goods, defective units, and work in process.

(2) The necessary journal entry(ies), if any, to state correctly inventory of finished goods and work in process.

(AICPA adapted)

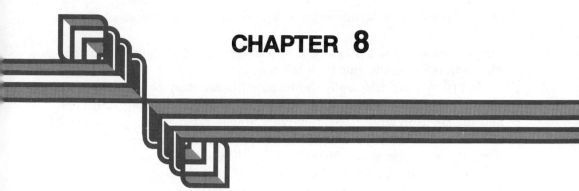

CHAPTER 8

BY-PRODUCTS AND
JOINT PRODUCTS COSTING

Many industrial concerns are confronted with the difficult and often rather complicated problem of assigning costs to their by-products and/or joint products. Chemical companies, coke manufacturers, refineries, flour mills, coal mines, lumber mills, gas companies, dairies, canners, meat packers, and many others produce in their manufacturing or conversion processes a multitude of products to which some costs must be assigned. Assignment of costs to these various products enhances equitable inventory costing for income determination and financial statement purposes. Another and even more important aspect of by- and joint products costing is that it furnishes management with data for use in planning maximum profit potentials and subsequently evaluating the actual profit performance.

DIFFICULTIES IN COSTING BY-PRODUCTS AND JOINT PRODUCTS

By-products and joint products are difficult to cost because true joint costs are indivisible. For example, an ore might contain both lead and zinc. In the raw state these minerals are joint products; and until they become separated by reduction of the ore, the costs of finding, mining, and processing are joint costs. With an ore which contains both lead and zinc, neither lead nor zinc can be produced without the other prior to the split-off stage. The total costs to the split-off stage must be borne by the margins between the selling prices of lead and zinc and the costs to complete and sell lead and zinc after the split-off point.

Joint costs are frequently confused with common costs. However, there is a significant difference between the two, the former being indivisible and the latter divisible. Common costs are allocable among products or services performed because each of the products or services could have been obtained separately. Therefore, any shared costs of obtaining them can be meaningfully allocated on the basis of relative usage of the common facilities. For example, the cost of fuel or power may be allocated to products based on production volumes or metered usage. The indivisibility characteristic of joint costs is not always easy to comprehend, for in some cases joint costs can be divided among joint products in accordance with a common cost-causing characteristic. However, the result of such a division is of limited use to management for decision making.

Because of the indivisibility of joint costs, cost allocation and apportionment procedures used for establishing the unit cost of a product are far from perfect. The costing of joint products and by-products highlights the problem of assigning costs to products whose origin, use of equipment, share of raw materials, share of labor costs, and share of other facilities cannot truly be determined. Whatever methods of allocation are employed, the total profit or loss figure is not affected — provided there are no beginning or ending inventories — by allocating costs to the joint products or by-products, for these costs are recombined in the final income statement. However, joint costs are ordinarily allocated to the products on some acceptable basis to determine product costs needed for inventory carrying costs. For this reason there is an effect on periodic income because different amounts may be allocated to inventories of the numerous joint or by-products under various allocation methods. In addition, product costs may be required for such special purposes as justifying product prices before governmental regulatory bodies. However, the validity of splitting joint costs to determine a fair regulated price for one joint product has been questioned by both accountants and economists.

JOINT COSTS AND SEPARABLE COSTS

Joint costs are costs incurred prior to the point at which separately identifiable products emerge from the same process. The flowchart shown on page 183 depicts products resulting during the production of coke in which coal is the original raw material. In addition to coke as its major product, the process produces sulphate of ammonia, light oil, crude tar, and gas of which the greater quantity is not sold but is used to fire the coke ovens as well as the boilers in the power plant. The coke ovens are the split-off point for cost assignments. The cost of each product consists of

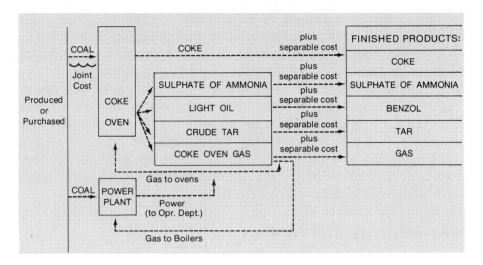

Flowchart — Coke and Its Associated Products

a pro-rata share of the joint costs plus any separable or subsequent costs incurred in order to put the products into salable condition.

BY-PRODUCTS DEFINED

The term "by-product" is generally used by businessmen and accountants to denote the one or more products of relatively small value that are produced simultaneously with a product of greater value. The product with the greater value, commonly called the "main product," is usually produced in greater quantities than the by-products. Ordinarily, the manufacturer has only limited control over the quantity of the by-product that comes into existence. However, the introduction of more advanced engineering methods, such as in the oil industry, has permitted greater control over the quantity of residual products. In fact, one company which formerly paid a trucker to haul away and dump certain waste materials discovered that they were valuable as fertilizer, and this by-product is now an additional source of income for the entire industry.

BY-PRODUCT CHARACTERISTICS

By-products can be classified into two groups according to their marketable condition at the split-off point: (1) those sold in their original form without need of further processing and (2) those which require further processing in order to be salable.

The accounting treatment of by-products necessitates a reasonably complete knowledge of the technological factors underlying their manufacture, for the origin of by-products is not always the same. By-products arising from the cleansing of the main product, such as gas and tar from coke manufacture, generally have a residual value. In some cases, the by-product is leftover scrap or waste such as sawdust in lumber mills. In other cases, the by-product may not be the result of any manufacturing process but may arise from preparing raw materials before they are used in the manufacture of the main product. The separation of cotton seed from cotton, cores and seeds from apples, and shells from cocoa beans are examples of this type of by-product.

METHODS OF COSTING BY-PRODUCTS

The several accepted methods used in industry for costing by-products fall into two categories: (1) Specific costs are not allocated to the by-products for costing purposes. Any income resulting from the sales of the by-product is credited either to income or to the main product. For inventory costing, some independent value may be assigned to the by-product. (Methods 1, 2, and 3 explained below are examples of Category 1.) (2) Some portion of the joint costs is allocated to the by-product. Inventory costs are based on this allocated cost plus any subsequent processing costs (see Method 4). The methods most commonly employed are:

Method 1. Revenues from sales of by-products are listed on the income statement as:
a. Other income.
b. Additional sales revenue.
c. A deduction from the cost of goods sold of the main product.
d. A deduction from total production costs of the main product.

Method 2. Revenues from sales of by-products less the cost of placing the by-products on the market (marketing and administrative expenses) and less any additional processing cost of the by-products are shown on the income statement in a manner similar to that indicated in Method 1.

Method 3. The replacement cost method.

Method 4. The market value (reversal cost) method.

The accounting steps and procedures used with each of these methods are:

Method 1. Method 1 leads to the following possible income statement presentation.

By-Product Revenue as Other Income.

Sales (main product, 10,000 units @ $2)		$20,000
Cost of goods sold:		
Total production costs (12,000 units @ $1.50).........	$18,000	
Ending inventory (2,000 units @ $1.50)	3,000	15,000
Gross profit		$ 5,000
Marketing and administrative expenses		2,000
Profit from operations		$ 3,000
Other income:		
Revenue from sales of by-product		1,500
Net profit for period		$ 4,500

By-Product Revenue as Additional Sales Revenue.   In this case the $1,500 would be shown below the revenue from the main product, making a total sales revenue of $21,500. All other figures, except the resultant gross profit and profit from operations, remain the same.

By-Product Revenue as a Deduction from the Cost of Goods Sold.   In this case the $1,500 income from by-products would be deducted from the $15,000 cost of goods sold figure, thereby reducing the cost and increasing the gross profit figure. The net profit remains at $4,500.

By-Product Revenue Deducted from Production Costs.   In this case the $1,500 revenue from by-product sales is deducted from the $18,000, giving a production cost of $16,500. This revised cost results in a new unit cost of $1.375 for the main product. The final inventory will consequently be $2,750 instead of $3,000. The income statement would appear as follows:

Sales (main product, 10,000 units @ $2)		$20,000
Cost of goods sold:		
Total production costs (12,000 units @ $1.50)	$18,000	
Revenue from sales of by-product	1,500	
Net production costs (12,000 units @ $1.375).........	$16,500	
Ending inventory (2,000 units @ $1.375)	2,750	13,750
Gross profit		$ 6,250
Marketing and administrative expenses........................		2,000
Net profit for period...		$ 4,250

The above illustrations require no complicated journal entries. In all four cases the revenue received from by-product sales is debited to Cash (or Accounts Receivable) and is credited to Income from Sales of By-Product.

With the exception of the last technique illustrated, Method 1 is a typical noncost procedure. In fact, it is merely a reporting device. Using the techniques illustrated, the final inventory cost of the main product is overstated to the extent that some of the cost belongs to the by-products produced. This shortcoming is somewhat removed in the last technique illustrated where the production costs are reduced by the revenue received from the by-product. However, even in this case a sales value rather than a cost is deducted.

Method 2. Method 2 recognizes the need of assigning some cost to the by-product. It does not attempt, however, to allocate any main product costs to the by-product. It strives to set up separate accounts for any expense involved in further processing or marketing the by-product. All figures are shown on the income statement as in Method 1.

Journal entries in Method 2 would involve charges to by-product revenue from accounts such as Payroll for the additional work required and perhaps charges for factory overhead. Marketing and administrative expenses might also be allocated to the by-product on some predetermined basis. Some firms carry an account called By-Product to which all additional expenses are debited and all income is credited. The balance is carried to the income statement where it can be presented as in Method 1, except that accumulated manufacturing costs applicable to any by-product inventory should be reported on the balance sheet.

Method 3. The replacement cost method is used, ordinarily, by firms whose by-products resulting from the manufacturing processes are used within the plant, thereby avoiding the necessity of purchasing certain materials and supplies from outside suppliers. Production costs of the main product, however, receive credit for furnishing such materials. The cost assigned to the by-product is the purchase or replacement cost existing in the market. This method is particularly common in the steel manufacturing industry. Although a number of by-products are sold in the open market, other products such as blast furnace gas and coke oven gas are mixed and used further for heating in open hearth furnaces. The waste heat from open hearths is again used in the generation of steam needed by the various producing departments. The resourceful use of these by-products and their accounting treatment is indicated by the following procedure used by a steel company:

1. Coke oven by-products are credited to cost of coke at average sales price per unit for the month.
2. Coke oven and blast furnace gas are credited respectively to cost of coke and cost of pig iron at computed value based on cost of fuel oil yielding equivalent heat units.
3. Tar and pitch used as fuel are credited respectively to cost of coke at computed value based on cost of fuel oil yielding equivalent heat units.
4. Scrap steel remelted is credited to cost of finished steel at market cost of equivalent grades purchased.

5. Waste heat from furnaces used to generate steam is credited to steel ingot cost at computed value based on cost of coal yielding equivalent heat units.[1]

Method 4. The market value (reversal cost) method is basically similar to the last technique illustrated in Method 1. However, it reduces the manufacturing cost of the main product, not by the actual revenue received, but by an estimated market value of the by-product prevailing at the time the by-product is recovered or sold. Dollar recognition depends on the stability of the market as to price and salability of the by-product. In either case, however, control over quantities is important. The by-product account is charged with the amount credited to the manufacturing cost of the main product. Any additional costs of materials, labor, or factory overhead incurred after the by-product is separated from the main product are charged directly to the by-product. Any proceeds from subsequent sales of the by-product are credited to the by-product account. The balance in this account can be presented on the income statement in the manner outlined for Method 1, except that manufacturing costs applicable to any by-product inventory should be reported in the balance sheet.

The market value (reversal cost) method of ascertaining main product and by-product costs may be illustrated as shown below.

ITEM	MAIN PRODUCT	BY-PRODUCT	
Materials..............................	$ 50,000		
Labor.................................	70,000		
Factory overhead.......................	40,000		
Total production costs (40,000 units)........	$160,000		
Market value (5,000 units @ $2).............			$10,000
Estimated gross profit consisting of:			
(20% of selling price, assumed)...........		$2,000	
Marketing and adm. exp. (5% of			
selling price).......................		500	2,500
			$ 7,500
Estimated costs after split-off:			
Materials.............................		$1,000	
Labor.................................		1,200	
Factory overhead.......................		300	2,500
Value of by-product to be credited			
to main product......................	5,000		$ 5,000
Net cost of main product.................	$155,000		
Add back *actual* costs after split-off.........			2,300
Total.................................			$ 7,300
Total number of units.....................	40,000		5,000
Unit cost..............................	$ 3.875		$ 1.46

[1]Howard C. Greer, "Accounting for By-products and Joint Products," *NACA Bulletin*, Vol. XVII, No. 24, Section 1, p. 1413.

This method accepts the theory that the cost of a by-product is proportional to its sales value. It is a step toward the recognition of a by-product cost prior to its split-off from the main product. It is also the nearest approach to methods employed in joint product costing.

JOINT PRODUCTS AND COSTS DEFINED

Joint products are produced simultaneously by a common process or series of processes with each product possessing more than a nominal value in the form in which it is produced. The definition emphasizes the point that the manufacturing process creates products in a definite quantitative relationship. An increase in one product's output will bring about an increase in the quantity of the other products, or vice versa, but not necessarily in the same proportion.

Joint product costs may be defined as those costs which arise from the common processing or manufacturing of products produced from a common raw material. Whenever two or more distinguishably different products are created from a single cost factor, joint product costs result.

CHARACTERISTICS OF JOINT PRODUCTS

A great number of products or services are linked together by physical relationships which necessitate simultaneous production. To the point of split-off or to the point where these several products emerge as individual units, the costs of the products form a homogeneous whole.

The classic example of joint products is found in the meat-packing industry where various cuts of meat and numerous by-products are processed from one original carcass with one lump sum cost.[2] Another example of joint product manufacturing is found in the production of gasoline where the derivation of gasoline inevitably results in the production of such items as naptha, kerosene, and distillate fuel oils. The simultaneous production of various grades of glue during a manufacturing operation and the processing of soybeans into oil and meal are other examples of joint products. Joint product costing is also found in industries that must grade raw material before it is processed. Tobacco manufacturers (except in cases where graded tobacco is purchased) and virtually all fruit and vegetable canners face the problem of grading. In fact, such manufacturers have a dual problem of joint cost allocation: first, material cost is applicable to all grades and second, subsequent manufacturing costs are incurred simultaneously for all the different grades.

The chief characteristic of the joint product cost is the fact that the cost of these several different products is incurred in a total, indivisible sum for all products and not for each product individually. Total produc-

---

[2]*Financial Planning and Control in the Meat Industry*, prepared by Price Waterhouse & Co. in cooperation with the Accounting Committee, American Meat Institute, Chicago, Ill., 1967.

tion costs of multiple products involve both joint costs and separate, individual product costs.   These separable product costs are identifiable
with the individual product and, generally, need no allocation.

The total sum of production costs consists not only of direct costs, such
as direct materials and direct labor, but also of those indirect factory overhead costs such as plant and machinery depreciation and service facilities
necessary to produce the products. The indirect costs are generally applied
to the product on the basis of the estimated factory overhead rates under
the assumption that there is a functional relationship between the basis
chosen and the cost applicable to the products or segments. The joint
production costs require allocation or assignment to the individual products, and these methods are discussed below. However, while allocation
is possible and even desirable, "the concepts of joint and separable costs
cut across the concepts of direct and indirect costs. It is not always realized
that costs accounted for as direct charges to segments may, in reality,
be joint."[3]

METHODS OF ALLOCATING JOINT COSTS

The allocation of joint materials and manufacturing costs incurred up
to the split-off point can be made by:

1. The market or sales value method based on the relative market values of
   the individual product.
2. The quantitative or physical unit method based on some physical measurement unit such as weight, linear measure, or volume.
3. The average unit cost method.
4. The weighted average method based on predetermined standards or index
   of production.

Market or Sales Value Method. This method enjoys great popularity
because of the argument that the market value of any product is a mani-
festation of the costs incurred in its production. The contention is that if
one product sells for more than another, it is because more cost was
expended to produce it. Therefore, the only logical way to prorate joint
costs is on the basis of the respective market values of the items produced.
The method is really a weighted market value basis using the total market
or sales value of each unit (quantity sold times the unit sales price). The
procedure can be illustrated as follows:

Joint products A, B, C, and D are produced at a total manufacturing
cost of $120,000; quantities produced are: A, 20,000 units; B, 15,000 units;
C, 10,000 units; and D, 15,000 units. Product A sells for $.25; B, for $3;

[3]Walter B. McFarland, *Concepts for Management Accounting* (New York: National Association of Accountants, 1966), p. 45.

C, for $3.50; and D, for $5. These prices are market or sales values for the products at split-off point; i.e., it is assumed that they can be sold in their present state at that point. Management may have decided, however, that it is more profitable to process certain products further before they are sold. Nevertheless, this condition does not destroy the usefulness of the sales value at the split-off point for allocation and decision-making purposes. The proration of joint costs is made in the following manner:

Joint Products	No. of Units Produced	Market Value per Unit	Total Market Value	Ratio of Product Value to Total Market Value	Apportionment of Manufacturing Cost
A	20,000	$ .25	$ 5,000	3.125%	$ 3,750
B	15,000	3.00	45,000	28.125	33,750
C	10,000	3.50	35,000	21.875	26,250
D	15,000	5.00	75,000	46.875	56,250
Total...	60,000	.....	$160,000	100.0%	$120,000

The same results can be obtained if total costs ($120,000) are divided by the total market value of the four products ($160,000). The resulting 75 percent is the percentage of cost in each individual market value. By multiplying each market value by this percentage, the joint cost will be proportioned as shown above.

Proponents of the market or sales value method state that joint costs should be assigned to products in accordance with their sales value because, were it not for such costs, a sales value would not exist. Under this method each joint product yields the same unit gross profit percentage. This can be illustrated by assuming that the units are sold without further processing and that the following sales are made: A — 18,000 units; B — 12,000 units; C — 8,000 units; D — 14,000 units.

	Total	A	B	C	D
Sales — units................	52,000	18,000	12,000	8,000	14,000
Sales — dollars..............	$138,500	$ 4,500	$36,000	$28,000	$70,000
Production costs.............	$120,000	$ 3,750	$33,750	$26,250	$56,250
Less ending inventory........	16,125	375	6,750	5,250	3,750
Cost of goods sold...........	$103,875	$ 3,375	$27,000	$21,000	$52,500
Gross profit.................	$ 34,625	$ 1,125	$ 9,000	$ 7,000	$17,500
Gross profit percentage.......	25%	25%	25%	25%	25%

Considerations Given to Costs After Split-Off. Products not salable in their stage of completion at the split-off point and therefore without any market value require additional processing to place them in marketable condition. In such cases, the basis for allocation of joint costs is a hypothetical market value at the split-off point. To illustrate the procedure, the assumptions listed below are added to the preceding example:

Product	Units Produced	Ultimate Market Value Per Unit	Processing Costs After Split-Off
A	20,000	$0.50	$ 2,000
B	15,000	5.00	10,000
C	10,000	4.50	10,000
D	15,000	8.00	28,000

To arrive at the basis for the apportionment, it is necessary to use a working-back procedure whereby the after split-off processing costs are subtracted from the ultimate sales values to find a hypothetical market value. The following exhibit indicates the steps to be taken:

Product	Ultimate Market Value per Unit	Units Produced	Ultimate Market Value	Processing Costs After Split-Off	Hypothetical Market Value*	60% Cost Allocation**	Total Cost	Cost Percentage***
A	$0.50	20,000	$ 10,000	$ 2,000	$ 8,000	$ 4,800	$ 6,800	68.0
B	5.00	15,000	75,000	10,000	65,000	39,000	49,000	65.3
C	4.50	10,000	45,000	10,000	35,000	21,000	31,000	68.8
D	8.00	15,000	120,000	28,000	92,000	55,200	83,200	69.3
Total................			$250,000	$50,000	$200,000	$120,000	$170,000	68%

---

*at the split-off point
**Percentage to allocate joint costs (using the joint costs total determined on page 190):

$$\frac{\text{Joint Costs}}{\text{Hypothetical Market Value}} = \frac{\$120,000}{\$200,000} = .60 = 60\%$$

***The cost percentage is calculated by dividing total cost by the ultimate market value; e.g., $\frac{\$49,000}{\$75,000} = .653 = 65.3\%$ for Product B, and $\frac{\$170,000}{\$250,000} = .68 = 68\%$ for all products combined.

A new product-line income statement with the same ending inventory units as used above is reproduced on page 192. The ending inventory is calculated by multiplying the sales value of the ending inventory by the cost percentage calculated in the previous exhibit; e.g., Product B — ending inventory = 3,000 units × $5 = $15,000 × 65.3% = $9,795.

PRODUCT-LINE INCOME STATEMENT

	Total	A	B	C	D
Sales — units...............	52,000	18,000	12,000	8,000	14,000
Sales — dollars..............	$217,000	$9,000	$60,000	$36,000	$112,000
Cost of goods sold:					
Joint costs................	$120,000	$4,800	$39,000	$21,000	$55,200
Further processing costs......	50,000	2,000	10,000	10,000	28,000
Total.....................	$170,000	$6,800	$49,000	$31,000	$83,200
Less ending inventory..........	22,211	680	9,795	6,192	5,544
Cost of goods sold...........	$147,789	$6,120	$39,205	$24,808	$ 77,656
Gross profit.................	$ 69,211	$2,880	$20,795	$11,192	$ 34,344
Gross profit percentage........	32%	32%	34%	31%	30%

Since the statement has often been made that every joint product should be equally profitable, the following modification of the sales value technique has been suggested. The overall gross profit percentage (32 percent) is used to (1) determine the gross profit for each product, (2) deduct the gross profit from sales value to find the total cost, and (3) reduce total cost by each product's further processing costs to find the joint costs' share for each product.

	Total	A	B	C	D
Ultimate sales value..........	$250,000	$10,000	$75,000	$45,000	$120,000
Less 32% gross profit					
percentage	80,000	3,200	24,000	14,400	38,400
Total costs.................	$170,000	$ 6,800	$51,000	$30,600	$ 81,600
Further processing costs......	50,000	2,000	10,000	10,000	28,000
Joint costs.................	$120,000	$ 4,800	$41,000	$20,600	$ 53,600

Observe that if sales value, gross profit percentage, or further processing costs are *estimated*, the balance labeled "Joint costs" would serve as the basis for allocating *actual* joint costs to the four products.

Quantitative Unit Method. This method attempts to distribute total joint costs on the basis of some unit of measurement, such as units, pounds, gallons, tons, or board feet. Of course, the joint products must be measurable by the basic measurement unit. If this is not possible, the joint units must be converted to a denominator common to all units produced. For instance, in the manufacture of coke, products such as coke, coal tar, benzol, and sulphate of ammonia are measured in different units. The yield of these recovered units is measured on the basis of the quantity of product extracted per ton of coal.

This table illustrates the weight method of joint cost allocation:

Product	Yield in Pounds of Recovered Product per Ton of Coal	Distribution of Waste to Recovered Products	Revised Weight of Recovered Products	Materials Cost of Each Product per Ton of Coal
Coke	1,320.0	69.474	1,389.474	$2.779
Coal tar.	120.0	6.316	126.316	.253
Benzol.	21.9	1.153	23.053	.046
Sulphate of ammonia.	26.0	1.368	27.368	.055
Gas.	412.1	21.689	433.789	.867
Waste (water). . .	100.0			
Total.	2,000.0	100.000	2,000.000	$4.000

Average Unit Cost Method.   This method attempts to apportion total manufacturing costs to the various products by using an average unit cost obtained by dividing the total number of units produced into the total manufacturing cost. As long as all units produced are measured in terms of the same unit and do not differ greatly, the method can be used without too much misgiving. Where the units produced are not measured in like terms, the method cannot be applied. Using the figures in the market value example, the procedure can be illustrated as follows:

$$\frac{\text{Total Manufacturing Costs}}{\text{Total Number of Units Produced}} = \frac{\$120,000}{60,000} = \$2 \text{ per unit}$$

The cost would be allocated as follows:

To A with 20,000 units.	$ 40,000
To B with 15,000 units.	30,000
To C with 10,000 units.	20,000
To D with 15,000 units.	30,000
	$120,000

Companies using this method argue that all products turned out by the same process should receive a proportionate share of the total costs based on the number of units produced.

Weighted Average Method.   In many industries the above described methods do not give a satisfactory answer to the cost apportionment problem. For this reason, weight factors are often assigned to each unit based upon size of the unit, difficulty of manufacture, time consumed in making the unit, difference in type of labor employed, amount of materials used, etc. Finished production of every kind is multiplied by weight factors to apportion total costs to individual units.

Using figures from the previous example, weight factors assigned to the four products might be as follows:

$$
\begin{aligned}
&\text{Product A} - 3 \quad \text{points}\\
&\text{Product B} - 12 \quad \text{points}\\
&\text{Product C} - 13.5 \quad \text{points}\\
&\text{Product D} - 15 \quad \text{points}
\end{aligned}
$$

The cost allocation would result in these values:

Product	Units	×	Points	=	Weighted Units	×	Cost per Unit*	=	Total Manufacturing Cost
A	20,000		3		60,000		$.20		$ 12,000
B	15,000		12		180,000		.20		36,000
C	10,000		13.5		135,000		.20		27,000
D	15,000		15		225,000		.20		45,000
					600,000				$120,000

$$
\text{*}\frac{\text{Total Manufacturing Cost}}{\text{Total Number of Weighted Units}} = \frac{\$120,000}{600,000} = \$.20 \text{ per unit.}
$$

FEDERAL INCOME TAX LAWS AND JOINT PRODUCTS AND BY-PRODUCTS COSTING

Federal income tax laws concerning the costing of joint products and by-products are not numerous. Legislators recognize the impossibility of establishing a specific code of law for every conceivable situation that involves this type of cost problem. Consequently, the written pronouncement of the law does not establish the boundaries of acceptable procedures too precisely. A digest of legal viewpoint is given in the Federal Income Tax Regulations which state the following:

> *Inventories of miners and manufacturers.* A taxpayer engaged in mining or manufacturing who by a single process or uniform series of processes derives a product of two or more kinds, sizes, or grades the unit cost of which is substantially alike, and who in conformity to a recognized trade practice allocates an amount of cost to each kind, size, or grade of product, which in the aggregate will absorb the total cost of production, may, with the consent of the tax director, use such allocated cost as a basis for pricing inventories, provided such allocation bears a reasonable relation to the respective selling values of the different kinds, sizes, or grades of product.

The above quotation does not fully and unequivocally authorize the utilization of the market value theory of costing joint products and by-products. The words "in conformity to a recognized trade practice" and "with the consent of the tax director" clearly imply that the multiplicity of conceivable situations is far too great to be covered by definite rules that allow or prohibit a particular costing procedure. Thus, in every case (where the size of the business warrants the trouble and expense) before any joint and by-product inventories are assigned costs for income tax purposes, the tax director must study the proposed costing program and inform the producer whether it will be allowed. It is a genuine problem for the tax director to decide whether or not a cost policy conforms closely enough to the accepted standards of the industry, or whether or not the alleged cost of a joint product or a by-product is reasonably related to the market values. So much depends upon the judgment of the tax director that one might justifiably claim that in joint product and by-product costing disputes, the tax director is virtually the enactor of the law. Of course, decisions may be appealed, but the higher tribunals find themselves beset by the same vague, general statute; and thus they, too, must rely almost entirely upon their own independent discretion and practically *make* the law.

Clearly, tax laws have not solved the problem of costing joint products and by-products for the accountant and manufacturer. Tax officials find themselves in exactly the same predicament as any coke producer, oil refiner, or chemical manufacturer even though their immediate objective may be limited to collecting a proper tax. The necessity of defining and interpreting accepted practices in a given industry proves, at least partially, that if the present tax law on joint product and by-product costing — with its implication that the market value method is desirable — is unfair or manifestly inaccurate and illogical, it can and will be changed if industry and the accounting profession can offer better reasons for the use of other procedures.

JOINT COST ALLOCATION IN THE PETROLEUM INDUSTRY

Joint cost allocation plays a significant role in connection with the federal regulation of prices in the petroleum industry. Oil and gas are often joint products. The wildcatter drilling a well generally cannot know whether he will discover oil and/or gas, or nothing. One third of all gas is produced by oil wells. Obviously, there are substantial joint costs, and these costs relate to both crude oil and natural gas. Traditionally, accounting in the oil industry looked upon gas as a by-product; and no serious effort was made to separate gas costs from total joint costs. With the dramatic increase in natural gas demand, coupled with long-distance pipe lines, natural gas has emerged as a full joint product.

In recent years the problem of allocating joint costs between crude oil and natural gas has been intensified due to the Federal Power Commission's role in attempting to establish just and reasonable prices for natural gas. A landmark court decision required the FPC to consider gas costs, at least as a basis of comparison with other regulatory methods. Accordingly, accountants representing the FPC, the gas producers, and the gas distributors have searched for a solution to a problem which theoretically is incapable of other than an arbitrary solution; i.e., splitting joint costs for the purpose of setting a selling price for one of the products, based on actual costs. Despite the best efforts of accountants and economists, the basic problem remains.

The following methods have been used or suggested in order to arrive at some answer to this vexing problem of joint costing:

1. The sales realization method often referred to as the sales allocation or the Federal Trade Commission method
2. The BTU (British Thermal Units) allocation method
3. The relative cost method

Sales Realization Method. The sales realization method divides the joint costs between oil and gas by recognizing first the existence of two types of costs: (1) annual costs and (2) return on investment. Annual costs which include operating costs, depreciation, depletion, exploration, and development are allocated according to the revenues received from the products during a recent test year. The return on investment (a percentage of total net plant and working capital) is allocated between oil and gas according to the "actual average remaining reserve realization ratio." This ratio takes into account the value of the reserves remaining in the ground in the test year, using prices realized by the company in the test year. In short, annual costs (including exploration) are allocated in proportion to the value of annual sales and return on investment in proportion to the value of the remaining reserves.

The sales realization method which uses prices to determine prices has been criticized both by the Federal Power Commission and the gas producers as being a circular method. Cost depends on sales value which depends on prices set on the basis of cost. When the method is applied the first time, the cost is based on the present sales prices whose just and reasonable character is the subject of the regulatory process. Even if the present sales prices are accepted for this purpose, in subsequent price determinations the new cost will be determined in part by the prices set in previous hearings.

BTU Method. The BTU method uses the relative heat content of oil and gas, expressed in British Thermal Units. Equivalent BTU content ratios of gas to oil used range from 4.8 to 6 mcf to 1 bbl. of oil. Joint costs are allocated in proportion to BTU content of the products and can be applied to the output of the test year as well as to the average remaining reserves. The rationale of the method is that the consumer is interested in energy, not in gas, oil, or coal. The BTU method allocates joint costs based on readily ascertainable physical data and can be applied to all the products connected with gas and oil.

The BTU method has been criticized for not properly reflecting the value of all the joint products produced. Only a part of the products resulting from crude oil are valuable for BTU content alone. Gasoline is valuable because of its form. Various modifications of the basic BTU formula have been suggested to give proper weighting to energy form.

Relative Cost Method. Under this method which has been accepted by the Federal Power Commission, production costs from joint product leases are allocated to the oil and gas produced on the basis of the relationship between costs actually incurred in producing the same products from single product leases (i.e., leases from which only oil or only gas is produced).

This method has considerable appeal where the company has sufficient single product leases for computing representative single product costs. In addition, the company should be large enough to assume an averaging of economic and geological lease characteristics. Of course, this method does not provide for allocation of exploration expenditures which represent a significant portion of total costs and are incurred on a company-wide basis.

JOINT PRODUCT COST ANALYSIS FOR MANAGERIAL DECISIONS AND PROFITABILITY ANALYSIS

Joint cost allocation methods indicate only too forcefully that the amount of the cost to be apportioned to the numerous products emerging at the point of split-off is difficult to establish for any purpose. Furthermore, the acceptance of an allocation method for the assignment of joint costs does not solve the problem. The thought has been advanced that no attempt should be made to determine the cost of individual products up to the split-off point; rather, it seems important to calculate the profit margin in terms of total combined units. Of course, costs incurred after the split-off point will provide management with information needed for decisions relating to the desirability of further processing to maximize profits.

Manufacturing of joint products is greatly influenced by both the technological characteristics of the processes and by the markets available for the products. This establishment of a product mix which is in harmony with customer demands appears profitable but is often physically impossible. It is interesting to note that cost accounting in the meat-packing industry serves primarily as a guide to buying, for *aggregate* sales realization values of the various products that will be obtained from cutting operations are considered in determining the price that a packer is willing to pay for livestock. Sales realization values are also considered when deciding to sell hams or other cuts in a particular stage or to process them further.

Joint costs are often incurred for products that are either interchangeable or not associated with each other at all. Increasing the output of one will in most joint cost situations unavoidably increase to some extent the output of the other. These situations fall into the category of the cost-volume-profit relationship and differential cost analysis (see Chapters 24 and 25). Evaluation of many alternative combinations of output can lead to time-consuming computations. Generally, such evaluations are carried out on a computer using sophisticated simulation techniques. Developments in operations research procedures have already provided techniques helpful in solving such problems (see Chapter 28 on linear programming).

For profit planning, and perhaps as its only reliable measure of profitability, management should consider the contribution margin a product makes to joint costs after separable or individual costs are deducted from sales. The contribution margin allows management to predict the amount that a segment or product line will add or subtract from company profits. This margin is not the product's net profit figure. It only indicates relative profitability in comparison with other products. "Net profit determined by allocating to segments an 'equitable' share of all costs, both separable and joint, associated with the group of segments is not a reliable guide to profit-planning decisions because these data cannot be used for predicting the outcome of decisions in terms of the change in aggregate net profit. For these reasons, attempts to allocate joint marketing costs to products and customers by time studies of salespersons' activities often yield results which are unreliable for appraising segment profitability."[4]

The Federal Trade Commission recently required that certain businesses furnish cost-and-profit data for a wide range of specific product categories. In 1974 the Securities and Exchange Commission began requiring that annual reports to stockholders include revenue and profit by lines of business. The Financial Accounting Standards Board is researching possible segment reporting requirements for external financial statements. Businessmen resist such requirements. One of their main arguments is that cost allocation today with multiple products and product lines is wrought with great danger of improper interpretation caused by arbitrarily allocated joint costs. Of course, as this chapter indicates, there are acceptable ways of allocating joint product costs and even separable costs. Yet, it makes a difference which method is chosen. The decision determines the degree of profitability of the various products.

---

[4]*Ibid.*, p. 49.

DISCUSSION QUESTIONS

1. (a) Distinguish between the meanings of a joint product and a by-product.
   (b) Describe and briefly discuss the appropriateness of two acceptable methods of accounting for the by-product in the determination of the cost of the main products.
   (c) Assuming proper treatment of the by-product costs, describe two acceptable methods of allocating to joint products the cost of the initial producing department.
   (AICPA adapted)

2. How may the income from the sale of by-products be shown on the income statement?

3. Does the showing of income from by-products on the income statement influence the unit cost of the main product?

4. By what method can production cost be relieved of the value of a by-product that can be further utilized in production processes? Explain and illustrate.

5. Are by-products ever charged with any cost? Explain.

6. Name four methods for apportioning total production costs to joint products.

7. Why is the market value method for joint cost allocation so often used by industry?

8. What is the chief difference between the quantitative unit method and the average unit cost method?

9. Does the Internal Revenue Service prescribe any definite allocation method for tax purposes? Explain.

10. By-products which require no additional processing after the point of separation are often accounted for by assigning to them a cost of zero at the point of separation and crediting cost of production as sales are made.
    (a) Justify the above method of treating by-products.
    (b) Discuss the possible shortcomings of the treatment.
    (AICPA adapted)

11. Select the answer which best completes the following statement. A joint cost should be allocated (a) to by-products; (b) on the basis of costs after separation; (c) on an authoritatively selected and consistently applied basis; (d) on the basis of selling price of all products.
    (AICPA adapted)

12. Select the answer which best completes the following statement. The method of accounting for joint product costs that will produce the same gross profit rate for all products is the (a) relative sales method; (b) physical measure method; (c) actual costing method; (d) split-off costing method.
    (AICPA adapted)

13. Select the answer which best completes the following statement. The primary purpose for allocating joint costs of a processing center to the various products produced is (a) to develop accurate processing cost variances by product; (b) to report more correct standard product costs for comparative analysis; (c) to establish inventory cost assigned to unsold units; (d) to record accurate cost of sales by product line; or (e) none of the above.
    (NAA adapted)

EXERCISES

In solving these exercises, round off all amounts, except unit costs, to the nearest dollar. Carry unit costs to five decimal places unless stated otherwise.

1. By-Product Costing and Entries. The Owens Chemical Company produces a product known as Ole. In manufacturing this chemical, a by-product results which can be sold as is for $.20 a kilogram or processed further and sold at $.50 a kilogram. The additional processing requires materials of $3,000, labor of $2,000, and factory overhead of $1,000.

The manufacturing costs of the main product and by-product up to the point of separation for the month of February were:

Materials...	$100,000
Labor..	80,000
Factory overhead.....................................	68,000

These costs were sufficient to produce 150,000 kilograms of Ole and 20,000 kilograms of the by-product.

Required: Entries for the by-product when it is:

(a) Stored, without assigning it any cost, and later sold. No additional costs have been added.

(b) Not further processed but stored and priced, using market price to secure its value and reducing the cost of the main product by the amount allocated to the by-product.

(c) Further processed and stored, no costs prior to separation being allocated to it.

(d) Further processed and stored, the cost prior to separation being allocated to it, using the market values at the point of separation for allocating costs prior to separation. The main product sells at $2 per kilogram.

2. Reversal Cost Method for By-Products. The Marksberry Manufacturing Company manufactures one main product and two by-products.

Data for the month of July are:

	Main Product	By-Product A	By-Product B
Sales............................	$150,000	$12,000	$7,000
Manufacturing costs before separation	75,000		
Manufacturing costs after separation.	23,000	2,200	1,800
Marketing and administrative			
expenses	12,000	1,500	1,100

Required: An income statement assuming no beginning or ending inventories and using the reversal cost method for the by-products, allowing 15% net profit for By-Product A and 12% net profit for By-Product B.

3. By-Product Costing. The Taft Corporation, manufacturer of paper from wood pulp, sells its products to converters for processing into bags, boxes, etc. Logs are hauled up from the wood yard and are barked in large drums. The bark saved is dried and used as fuel for the steam boilers. The company estimates that 20% of the steam produced comes from bark. Even though this fuel seems to cost nothing, the cost accountant credits that proportion of the total cost of steam distributed in the period to the cost of paper.

In the process of cooking or digesting the chipped wood, in addition to the pulp, a fatty soap is produced which is siphoned off and refined into a by-product known as tall oil which is sold and used in the making of solvents, paint, soap, etc. For every 20 tons of paper, one ton of tall oil is produced.

Actual data:

(a) 2,000,000 MBTU's of steam were distributed from the boiler during the period at a cost of $0.250 per MBTU.

(b) 60,000 tons of paper were sold at a selling price of $75 per ton. Costs for the period were:

Materials..	$2,700,000
Labor...	264,000
Factory overhead...............................	876,000

(c) The selling price for tall oil was $40 per ton. Costs after separation were:

Additional materials............................	$12,000
Labor...	7,000
Factory overhead...............................	6,500

Required: An income statement for the month for paper using the market value (reversal cost) method for costing the paper and tall oil. Include a credit to the cost of paper for steam.

4. Cost Allocation for By-Products and Joint Products. The cost accountant of the Reinhart Processing Company, Inc. prepared the income statement reproduced below on the assumptions that Mirex is the main product and Vitex is the by-product, and that by-product revenue be treated as other income:

REINHART PROCESSING COMPANY, INC.
INCOME STATEMENT
YEAR ENDED SEPTEMBER 30, 19—

Sales (85,000 lbs. @ $5.20)......................			$442,000
Cost of goods sold:			
Total manufacturing cost*: Mirex..........................		$221,400	
Mirex finishing................		101,700	
		$323,100	
Less inventory of finished Mirex**......................		17,950	305,150
Gross profit on sales...............................			$136,850
Marketing and administrative expenses......................			113,000
Net operating income..........................			$ 23,850
Other income: Sales of Vitex (48,000 @ $.85)................		$ 40,800	
Less: Vitex finishing cost*.......................	$11,440		
Inventory of finished Vitex***.............	1,456		
	$ 9,984		
Vitex marketing expenses..................	9,000	18,984	21,816
Net income for the year.........................			$ 45,666

_____

* Includes beginning inventory
**Inventory of finished Mirex: ***Inventory of finished Vitex:

$$\frac{\$323,100}{90,000} \times 5,000 = \$17,950 \qquad \frac{\$11,440}{55,000} \times 7,000 = \$1,456$$

Required: (1) Characteristics of Vitex which, if any, justify its treatment as a by-product.

(2) Characteristics of Vitex which, if any, justify its treatment as a joint product.

(3) If Vitex is treated as a by-product, the cost, if any, to be associated with the inventory of finished Vitex at September 30, 19—.

(4) Both products are manufactured in part simultaneously from the same raw material. Separation occurs at the end of Process I (or Department I). Compute the Process I cost allocation to Mirex and Vitex as joint products on the sales value basis if Process I — Mirex sells for $3 per lb. and Process I — Vitex sells for $.45 per lb. Production at the end of Process I was 108,000 lbs., of which 5/9 became Mirex and 4/9 Vitex.

5. Joint Products Profit Realization. The Virginia Manufacturing Company produces joint products A and B in a continuous process industry in five producing departments. Materials enter the process in the Cleaning Department, then pass to the Mixing Department. Upon completion of work in the Mixing Department there is a separation of Products A and B. Three fourths of the material started in process becomes Product A and subsequently goes through the Grinding and Packing Departments, after which it is ready for sale. The remaining quarter is sent to the Finishing Department where it is completed as Product B. In the Finishing Department there is a loss of one half of the materials entering the department. Joint costs are allocated at the same cost per ton to Products A and B.

Materials entering the Cleaning Department cost $80 per ton.

Product A sells for $600 per ton and is charged with marketing and administrative expense at 20% of the sales price. Product B sells for $700 per ton and is charged with marketing and administrative expense at 10% of the sales price.

Labor and factory overhead per ton of product manufactured are as follows:

Department	Labor	Factory Overhead
Cleaning..	$50	$30
Mixing...	20	60
Grinding.......................................	20	48
Packing..	80	72
Finishing......................................	15	10

Required: Statements showing net profit per ton on each product.

6. Joint Products Cost Determination. The Fiberglas Corporation manufactures a variety of different products from a single raw material — clear glass marbles. The marbles are melted at a high temperature in the Forming Room, drawn through an opening in the furnace, and wound onto spindles in threadlike form. From the Forming Room, the spindles are sent to either the Insulating Department or the Twisting Department. For the purpose of this problem, two products are made in the Insulating Department and two in the Twisting Department along with a by-product which is waste and which is sold when there is a market or dumped when no market exists. Costs are charged out of the Forming Room by the average unit cost method to either the Insulating or Twisting Department. In these latter two departments, the costs are charged to the individual products by the market value method, with the costs before separation in the Twisting Department being credited with the value of the by-product less its marketing costs, normal profit of 10%, and additional costs before it can be sold.

Data for one month of operation are:

Department	Materials	Labor	Factory Overhead	Market Value	Units Produced
Forming room.........	$10,000	$5,000	$5,000	0	25,000 spindles
Insulating products.....	0	500	500	0	10,000 (from Forming)
Furnace filters.......	2,000	500	500	$50.00	200 filters
Air conditioners.....	1,000	250	250	25.00	200 filters
Twisting	0	5,000	5,000	0	15,000 (from Forming)
Yarn	2,000	4,000	4,000	3.00	10,000 bobbins
Electrical...........	0	1,000	1,000	2.00	5,000 bobbins
Waste materials.......	0	500	250	1.00	1,500 lbs.

Marketing and administrative expense of waste, $150.

Required: Unit costs for the four products.

7. Cost Allocation — Weighted Average Method. The product engineering staff of the Bockhorst Company prepared the following analysis of relative weights for cost elements in the manufacture of joint products A, B, and C in Department 10:

Product	Output for Each Unit of Raw Materials Input	Output for Each Hour of Labor Crew Time	Factory Overhead
A	3	1	The engineers determined that twice as much weight should be given to time spent in production as is given to size; that products A and B are the same total weight and shape, but product C is in total twice as heavy and twice their bulk.
B	4	1–1/6	
C	2	1–1/6	

Joint costs incurred in Department 10 in the month of March:

Materials.....................................	$220,000
Labor..	190,000
Factory overhead.............................	170,000
Total costs incurred.........................	$580,000

Required: Joint costs allocation to the three products by the weighted average method.

(Based on an NAA article)

8. Market Value at the Split-Off Point for Joint Cost Allocation. Miller Manufacturing Company buys Zeon for $.80 a gallon. At the end of processing in Department 1, Zeon splits off into Products A, B, and C. Product A is sold at the split-off point with no further processing; Products B and C require further processing before they can be sold; Product B is processed in Department 2; and Product C is processed in Department 3. The following data is a summary of costs and other related data for the year ended June 30, 19B:

	Department		
	1	*2*	*3*
Cost of Zeon................................	$96,000	....	....
Direct labor................................	14,000	$45,000	$65,000
Factory overhead..........................	10,000	21,000	49,000

	Product		
	A	*B*	*C*
Gallons sold................................	20,000	30,000	45,000
Gallons on hand at June 30, 19B.............	10,000	....	15,000
Sales (in dollars)...........................	$30,000	$96,000	$141,750

There were no inventories on hand at July 1, 19A, and there was no Zeon on hand at June 30, 19B. All gallons on hand at June 30, 19B, were complete as to processing. There were no factory overhead variances. Miller uses the market value at split-off point method of allocating joint costs.

Required: (1) The market value at the split-off point for Product A total units produced for the year.

(2) The total joint costs for the year ended June 30, 19B, to be allocated.

(3) The cost of Product B sold for the year ended June 30, 19B.

(4) The cost assigned to the Product A ending inventory.

(AICPA adapted)

PROBLEMS

In solving these problems, round off all amounts, except unit costs, to the nearest dollar. Carry unit costs to five decimal places unless stated otherwise.

8-1. Main Product Profit Determination. The Neoplastic Company manufactures one main product known only as "Isplastic" and a by-product known as "Notplastic."

Isplastic sells for $1,000 per ton. Marketing and administrative costs are 25% of the selling price. This product is made from three ingredients, P, L, and A, in the following proportions and at the following costs:

P 50%, costs $150.00 per ton of P
L 20%, costs   75.00 per ton of L
A 30%, costs   45.00 per ton of A

Handling and storage charges amount to 12% of the cost of each ingredient.

The plant is divided into five manufacturing departments, of which 1, 2, 3, and 4 are engaged in the manufacture of Isplastic, and 5 in the recovery of the by-product, Notplastic.

The data show the cost of direct labor per ton of ingredients handled and the percentage of departmental factory expense to the direct labor:

Dept. No.	Manufacturing Department	Direct Labor per Ton	Percentage of Departmental Factory Expense to Direct Labor
1	Mixing..............................	$35.00	70%
2	Furnace............................	17.50	280
3	Washing and drying.................	24.00	110
4	Grinding and packing..............	80.00	40

Materials P, L, and A are put in process in the Mixing Department. General factory expenses that cannot be charged to any one department amount to 50% of the departmental direct labor cost for each department.

In Department 2 there is a yield of only 80% of Isplastic from the tonnage of the ingredients mixed. The other 20% is treated in Department 5, two thirds of this 20% being recovered as the by-product, Notplastic, and the other third being entirely waste.

A net profit of $50 per ton is made on the sale of Notplastic after all expenses of every kind are charged against it. This profit is credited to the main product. No charge is made against Notplastic for the raw materials from which it is recovered.

Required: The profit on every ton of Isplastic sold.

(CICA adapted)

8-2. Joint Products Cost Allocation. The Sweet Briar Brick Company resumed operations July 1. The operations of the company consist of mining clay and manufacturing machine-pressed brick and hand-molded brick. The cost of each class of product is determined separately. The company has two service departments: General Plant Expense and Power Plant; and three production departments: Clay Mining, Brick Molding, and Kiln Burning. The cost of Kiln Burning is afterward distributed between Machine-made Brick Firing and Hand-made Brick Firing. As handmade brick requires more careful handling and setting, the cost of burning in kilns is considered one fourth more per 1,000 than that of machine-made brick. Four and one half tons of clay are required per 1,000 bricks. Broken bricks are valued at their weight as clay. Bricks remaining in the kilns at the end of the month are assumed to be one half processed.

The foremen of the various departments make daily reports, which are summarized for the month as follows:

Clay mined.............   8,000 tons
Machine-made brick .....   850,000 9-inch brick molded
Handmade brick and tile 350,000 9-inch brick molded
Kilns..................   800,000 Machine-made brick set
                         620,000 Machine-made brick drawn of which
                                 20,000 are broken
                         300,000 Handmade brick set
                         285,000 Handmade brick drawn of which
                                 10,000 are broken

Operating expenses for the month are analyzed as follows:

	Supplies, Repairs, etc.	Payroll
Clay mining........................	$2,404.00	$1,200.00
Machine-made brick	800.00	1,300.00
Handmade brick.....................	522.00	2,040.00
Kilns..............................	1,850.75	1,660.00
Power house	485.00	325.00
General plant expenses	165.00	455.00

Depletion and depreciation must be provided as follows: Clay lands estimated to contain 2,000,000 tons; cost $60,000. Depreciation: Power Plant, $100; Kilns, $250; Machine Molding, $175; Hand Molding, $75.

A reserve for extraordinary kiln repairs is to be provided, at $.30 per 1,000 brick set in kilns, which is charged to Kiln Burning.

The power is used at the clay mines and at the Machine-made Brick Plant and is distributed in proportion to the horsepower ratings of the motors used, viz.: Clay Mines, 30 hp.; Brick Plant, 50 hp.

The general plant expense is absorbed by the production departments in proportion to the direct labor cost in each.

Required: A statement apportioning the joint costs equitably between the two joint products.

8-3. Inventory Cost Determination; Management Processing Decision.   The Laverock Company's joint cost of producing 1,000 units of Product A, 500 units of Product B, and 500 units of Product C is $100,000. The unit sales values of the three products at the split-off point are Product A — $20; Product B — $200; Product C — $160. Ending inventories include 100 units of Product A, 300 units of Product B, and 200 units of Product C.

Required: (1) The amount of joint cost that would be included in the ending inventory of the three products (a) on the basis of their relative sales value and (b) on the basis of physical units.

(2) The relative merits of each of these two bases of joint cost allocation (a) for financial statement purposes and (b) for decisions about the desirability of selling joint products at the split-off point or processing them further.

(AICPA adapted)

8-4. Joint Product Costs Allocation; Combined Income Statement (Three Products). Colorado Chemical Co. produces one principal product designated "Colossal." Incidental to its production, two additional products, Formidable and Petite, result.

Material is started in Process 1, and the three products emerge from this first process. Colossal is processed further in Process 2; Formidable is processed further in Process 3; Petite is sold without further processing.

For the month of September the following data are available:

Materials put in Process 1   = $12,000

Conversion costs: Process 1 =   8,000
                   Process 2 =   4,000
                   Process 3 =   300

There are no beginning or ending work in process inventories.

Production and sales data:

	Quantity Produced	Quantity Sold	September Sales Price	Market Price End of September
Colossal........	5,000	4,000	$6.00	$6.00
Formidable	3,000	2,000	1.00	.90
Petite.........	1,000	900	.50	.55

Marketing and administrative expenses are related to the quantity sold. It is estimated that next period marketing and administrative expenses will be the same as the actual marketing and administrative expenses for September which were: Colossal, $2,000; Formidable, $800; Petite, $36.

Standard net profit on Formidable is 10% of sales. No profit is realized on Petite sales.

Required: (1) The costs assigned to the Petite inventory and the costs transferred from Process 1 to Petite units during the period.

(2) The costs assigned to the Formidable inventory and the costs transferred from Process 1 to Formidable units during the period.

(3) A combined income statement for the three products.

(AICPA adapted)

8-5. Cost of Production Report for Joint and By-Products. The Constantine Chemical Company produces two principal products known as XO and MO. Incidental to the production of these products, it produces a by-product known as Bypo. The company has three producing departments which it identifies as Departments 101, 201, and 301. Raw materials A and B are started in process in Department 101. Upon completion of processing in that department, one fifth of the material is by-product and is transferred directly to stock. One third of the remaining output of Department 101 goes to Department 201 where it is made into XO, and the other two thirds goes to Department 301 where it becomes MO. The processing of XO in Department 201 results in a 50% gain in weight of materials transferred into the department due to the addition of water at the start of the processing. There is no gain or loss of weight in the other processes.

The company considers the income from Bypo, after allowing $.05 per pound for estimated selling and delivery costs, to be a reduction of the cost of the two principal products. The company assigns Department 101 costs to the two principal products in proportion to their net sales value at point of separation, computed by deducting costs to be incurred in subsequent processes from the sales value of the products.

The following information concerns the operations during April, 19—:

Inventories:

	March 31 Quantity (Pounds)	Cost	April 30 Quantity (Pounds)
Department 101..........................	....	....	....
Department 201..........................	800	$17,160	1,000
Department 301..........................	200	2,340	360
Finished stock — XO.....................	300	7,260	80
Finished stock — MO.....................	1,200	18,550	700
Finished stock — Bypo...................	....	....	....

Inventories in process are estimated to be one half complete in Departments 201 and 301, both at the beginning and the end of the month. The company uses the fifo method for inventory costing.

Costs:	Materials Used	Labor and Factory Overhead
Department 101.....................	$134,090	$87,418
Department 201.....................		31,950
Department 301.....................		61,880

The materials used in Department 101 weighed 18,000 pounds.

Sales Prices:

XO   — $29.50 per pound
MO   —   17.50 per pound
Bypo —   .50 per pound

Prices as of April 30th are unchanged from those in effect during the month.

Required: A departmental cost of production report for the month of April.

(AICPA adapted)

8-6. Joint and By-Products Cost Allocation. Amaco Chemical Company manufactures several products in its three departments:

(a) In Department 1 the raw materials amanic acid and bonyl hydroxide are used to produce Amanyl, Bonanyl, and Am-Salt. Amanyl is sold to others who use it as a raw material in the manufacture of stimulants. Bonanyl is not salable without further processing. Although Am-Salt is a commercial product for which there is a ready market, Amaco Chemical Company does not sell this product, preferring to submit it to further processing.

(b) In Department 2 Bonanyl is processed into the marketable product, Bonanyl-X. The relationship between Bonanyl used and Bonanyl-X produced has remained constant for several months.

(c) In Department 3 Am-Salt and the raw material colb are used to produce Colbanyl, a liquid propellant that is in great demand. As an inevitable part of this process, Demanyl is also produced. Demanyl was discarded as scrap until discovery of its usefulness as a catalyst in the manufacture of glue. For two years Amaco Chemical Company has been able to sell all of its Demanyl production.

In its financial statements Amaco Chemical Company states inventory at the lower of cost (on the first-in, first-out basis) or market. Unit costs of the items most recently produced must therefore be computed. Costs allocated to Demanyl are computed so that after allowing for packaging and selling costs of $.04 per pound, no profit or loss will be recognized on sales of this product.
Certain data for October, 19—, follow:

Raw Materials:

	Pounds Used	Total Cost
Amanic acid.................	6,300	$5,670
Bonyl hydroxide.............	9,100	6,370
Colb.......................	5,600	2,240

Conversion Costs (Labor and Factory Overhead):

	Total Cost
Department 1	$33,600
Department 2	3,306
Department 3	22,400

Products:

	Pounds Produced	Inventories, Pounds September 30	October 31	Sales Price per Pound
Amanyl	3,600			$ 6.65
Bonanyl	2,800	210	110	
Am-Salt	7,600	400	600	6.30
Bonanyl-X	2,755			4.20
Colbanyl	1,400			43.00
Demanyl	9,800			.54

Required: Schedules for the items listed below for October, 19—. Supporting computations should be prepared in good form with answers rounded to the nearest cent.

(a) Cost per pound of Amanyl, Bonanyl, and Am-Salt produced, using the market or sales value method.

(b) Cost per pound of Amanyl, Bonanyl, and Am-Salt produced, using the average unit cost method.

(c) Cost per pound of Colbanyl produced, assuming that the cost per pound of Am-Salt produced was $3.40 in September, 19—, and $3.50 in October, 19—.

(AICPA adapted)

CASES

A. Theoretical Discussion Concerning By-Product Costing. Jamieson Sawmill, located in Angelina County near Lufkin, Texas, recently solved to some extent its problem of disposal of accumulated sawdust. Previously, it was necessary to burn all the sawdust material. In March, 19—, Mr. Jamieson negotiated an agreement with Scoggins Vacuum Co. of Lufkin, Texas, to sell sawdust at $4 per cubic yard, f.o.b. the Scoggins Vacuum Co. plant.

During the first month of the agreement, Scoggins Vacuum Co. purchased twelve dump truck loads with each truck load estimated at 4 cubic yards. The accountant for Jamieson Sawmill was uncertain as to how this transaction should be recorded.

At the close of March, 19—, there were approximately 75 yards of sawdust on hand that Mr. Jamieson felt he would be able to sell to Scoggins Vacuum Co. in the future. Jamieson Sawmill's accountant was again concerned as to how the value of this material should be reflected in the balance sheet.

Required: Theoretical arguments and alternatives concerning (a) when, (b) how, and (c) for how much "value" the events described above should be reflected in the accounts of Jamieson Sawmill.

B. Theory of Joint Product Cost Allocation Methods; Product Mix and Gross Profit Analysis. Kimel, Inc. manufactures two plate glass sizes that are produced simultaneously in the same manufacturing process. Since the small sheets of plate glass are cut from large sheets with flaws, the joint costs are allocated equally to each good sheet, large and small, produced. The difference in after split-off costs for large and small sheets is considerable.

Last year the company decided to increase its efforts to sell the large sheets because they produced a larger gross profit than the small sheets, Accordingly, the amount of the fixed advertising budget devoted to large sheets was increased; and the amount devoted to small sheets was decreased. However, no changes in sales prices were made.

By midyear the Production Scheduling Department had increased the monthly production of large sheets in order to stay above the minimum inventory level. However, it also had cut back the monthly production of small sheets because the inventory ceiling had been reached.

At the end of last year the net result of the change in product mix was a decrease of $112,000 in gross profit. Although sales of large sheets had increased 34,500 units, sales of small sheets had decreased 40,200 units.

Required: (1) Difference between joint product costs and
  (a) After split-off costs
  (b) Fixed costs
  (c) Prime costs

(2) The propriety of allocating joint product costs for general purpose financial statements on the basis of:
  (a) Physical measures, such as weight or units
  (b) Relative sales or market value

(3) In the development of weights for allocating joint costs to joint products, advantages in reducing the relative sales value of each joint product by its after split-off costs.

(4) The mistake made by Kimel, Inc. in deciding to change its product mix, explaining why it caused a smaller gross profit last year.

(AICPA adapted)

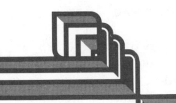

CHAPTER **9**

PLANNED, APPLIED, AND ACTUAL FACTORY OVERHEAD WITH VARIANCE ANALYSIS

The use of a predetermined factory overhead rate for the purpose of charging a fair share of factory expenses to products was introduced briefly in earlier chapters. The discussion is continued, expanded, and analyzed further in this and the next two chapters.

This chapter will: (1) discuss the methods, procedures, and bases available for applying factory overhead, (2) describe methods and procedures for classifying and accumulating actual factory overhead, (3) show computations for over- or underapplied factory overhead, and then (4) analyze the total variance into the spending and idle capacity variances. The next chapter will: (1) cover the departmentalization of factory overhead, (2) explain the creation and use of separate departmental overhead rates, and (3) discuss departmentalization in nonmanufacturing businesses and nonprofit institutions and organizations. Chapter 11 will: (1) describe the relationship of product costing to responsibility accounting, (2) explain this relationship using the maintenance department and its cost as an example, and (3) present monthly overhead variance analysis for use in responsibility accounting and reporting, both for production and service departments.

Factory overhead is generally defined as the cost of indirect materials, indirect labor, and all other factory expenses that cannot conveniently be identified with nor charged directly to specific jobs or products. The assignment of factory overhead to departments and, ultimately, to specific jobs and products is discussed in the next chapter. Factory overhead consists of all production costs other than direct materials and direct labor. Other terms used for factory overhead are factory burden, manufacturing expenses, manufacturing overhead, factory expenses, and indirect manufacturing cost.

Factory overhead possesses two characteristics that require specific recognition and consideration if products are to be charged with a fair share of these expenses. These characteristics deal with the particular relationship of factory overhead to (1) the product itself and (2) the volume of production. Unlike direct materials and direct labor, factory overhead is an invisible part of the finished product. No materials requisition or labor time ticket can indicate the amount of overhead, such as factory supplies or indirect labor, that enters into a job or product. Yet factory overhead is as much a part of a product's manufacturing cost as direct materials and direct labor. Because of the impossibility of tracing factory overhead to specific jobs or specific products, some more or less arbitrary overhead allocation must be made. A properly predetermined factory overhead rate permits an equitable and logical allocation, therewith abandoning the use of actual cost for costing purposes.

The second characteristic deals with the change that many items of overhead undergo with a change in production volume. First, the total amount of fixed overhead remains relatively constant regardless of changes in production volume, yet the fixed overhead per unit of output varies with production volume; second, semivariable costs vary but not in proportion to units produced; and finally, only the variable costs vary proportionately with production output (see chart on page 213). Therefore, as production volume changes, the combined effect of these different overhead patterns can cause unit manufacturing cost to fluctuate considerably unless some method is provided to stabilize overhead costs charged to the units produced.

FACTORY OVERHEAD — PREDETERMINED

A predetermined overhead rate provides the only feasible method of computing product overhead costs promptly enough to serve management needs, identify inefficiencies, and smooth out uncontrollable and somewhat illogical month-to-month fluctuations in unit costs. For example, the various overhead expenses must be charged to all work done during any period. How can such a charge be made? It is possible to allocate actual overhead to all work completed during the month, using a base such as actual direct labor dollars, direct labor hours, machine hours, or some other base. As long as the volume of work completed each month is the same, and costs are within control limits, this method might be accurate. As variations occur, work completed during different months would receive a greater or a smaller charge — an inequitable situation.

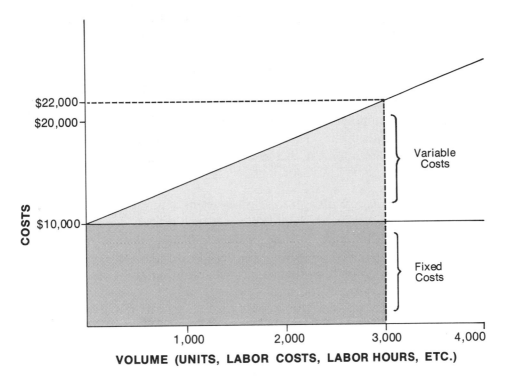

Fixed-Variable Cost Relationship to Volume

For example, costing problems would result if actual costs incurred for repairs and maintenance were charged directly to a job or product. What work should be charged with the expense of these repairs? Should work processed during the month when repairs are made be charged therewith? This procedure is again unreasonable. Ordinarily, repairs are necessary because of wear and tear over a much longer period than one month and are made to permit continuous operations in any month. Furthermore, overhead costs need to be assigned to production promptly, and inefficiencies need to be identified. Therefore, factory overhead is usually charged to work done on an estimated basis. However, the use of estimates can cause certain difficulties because underlying data are the result of opinions and judgments. Consequently, estimates must be the outcome of careful studies.

The Use of a Predetermined Factory Overhead Rate. Predetermined overhead rates are used for both job order and process cost accumulation procedures.

Job Order Costing. Actual costs of direct materials and direct labor used on a job are determined from materials requisitions and time cards and are entered on job order cost sheets. Overhead costs have been pre-determined from cost data to arrive at the total amount of overhead esti-mated for the activity level to be used in computing the rate. This total cost is then related to estimated direct labor hours, machine hours, direct labor dollars, or some other base for the same activity level, ultimately to be expressed in a rate. For example, overhead applicable to a job may be calculated by multiplying actual direct labor hours incurred on the job by the predetermined rate. The amount of overhead is then entered on the job order cost sheet, and the cost of a job is known at the time the job is completed.

Process Costing. With a process cost system, unit costs are computed by dividing total weekly or monthly costs of each process by the output of that process. While a process cost system could produce product costs without the use of overhead rates, predetermined rates are recommended since they speed up unit product cost calculations and offer other distinct advantages when cost or production levels are subject to wide fluctuations. The use of overhead rates for process costing is similar to that for job order costing.

Factors to Be Considered in Selection of Overhead Rates. The types of overhead rates used differ not only from company to company but also from department to department within the same company. The type, significance, and use of factory overhead items must be considered when deciding upon applicable rates. At least five main factors influence the selection of overhead rates:

FACTORS INFLUENCING SELECTION OF OVERHEAD RATES

I. Base to be used

  a. Units of production
  b. Materials cost
  c. Direct labor cost
  d. Direct labor hours
  e. Machine hours

II. Activity level to be used

  a. Normal capacity
  b. Expected actual capacity

III. Inclusion or exclusion of fixed overhead

  a. Absorption costing
  b. Direct costing

IV. Use of a single rate or several rates

  a. Plant-wide or blanket rate
  b. Departmental rates
  c. Cost center rates
  d. Operational rates

V. Use of separate rates for service activities

Base to Be Used. The primary objective in selecting a base is to insure the most accurate application of overhead cost to the work performed. Ordinarily, the base selected should be closely related to functions represented by the overhead cost being applied. If, for example, factory overhead is predominately labor-oriented, such as supervision and indirect labor, the proper base is probably direct labor cost or direct labor hours. If overhead items are predominately investment-oriented, related to the ownership and operation of machinery, then a machine-hour basis is probably most appropriate.   If overhead relates mainly to materials-oriented overhead such as the purchasing and handling of materials, then the materials cost might be considered as the base.

A secondary objective in selecting a base is to minimize clerical costs and effort.   When two or more bases provide approximately the same applied overhead cost to specific units of production, the simplest base should be used. Although the cost of administering the various methods differs from one company to another, the direct labor cost basis or the materials cost basis seems to cause the least clerical effort and cost. The labor and machine hour bases generally require additional clerical work and expense.

Factory overhead rates are stated as percentages or as an amount per hour, unit, pound, product, etc. The following bases are used for applying factory overhead: (1) units of production, (2) materials cost, (3) direct labor cost, (4) direct labor hours, and (5) machine hours.

Units of Production Basis. The units of production basis, the simplest and most direct method of applying factory overhead, is computed as follows:

$$\frac{\text{Estimated Factory Overhead}}{\text{Estimated Units of Production}} = \text{Overhead per Unit}$$

If estimated expenses are $300,000 and the company intends to produce 250,000 units during the next period, each completed unit would be charged with $1.20 ($300,000 ÷ 250,000 units) as its share of factory overhead. An order with 1,000 completed units would be charged with $1,200 (1,000 units × $1.20) of factory overhead.

The units of production basis is satisfactory when a company manufactures only one product; otherwise, the method is either unsatisfactory or subject to arbitrary allocation procedures. However, if the several products manufactured are alike or closely related (their difference being merely one of weight or volume), application of factory overhead can be made on a weight or a point basis. The weight basis applies overhead on the basis of the weight of each unit of product. An example is illustrated at the top of the next page.

	A	B	C
Products manufactured...........................	A	B	C
Estimated number of units manufactured...........	20,000	15,000	20,000
Unit weight of product...........................	5 lbs.	2 lbs.	1 lb.
Estimated total weight produced..................	100,000	30,000	20,000
Estimated factory overhead per pound ($300,000/ 150,000)......................................	$2	$2	$2
Estimated factory overhead for each product........	$200,000	$60,000	$40,000
Estimated factory overhead per unit...............	$10	$4	$2

If the weight basis does not seem to yield a just apportionment of over-head, the method can be improved by assigning a certain number of points to each unit to compensate for differences. For example, a company manu-facturing Products L, S, M, and F computes an overhead rate per product as follows:

Products	Estimated Quantities	Points Assigned	Estimated Total Points	Estimated Factory Overhead per Point	Estimated Factory Overhead for Each Product	Estimated Factory Overhead Cost per Unit
L	2,000	5	10,000	$3	$ 30,000	$15
S	5,000	10	50,000	3	150,000	30
M	3,000	8	24,000	3	72,000	24
F	4,000	4	16,000	3	48,000	12
			100,000		$300,000	

If products are different in any respect such as size, time to produce, or method of production, a uniform charge such as the unit of production method may result in incorrect costing. Other methods must be adopted in such instances.

Materials Cost Basis. In some companies a study of past costs will reveal a correlation between direct materials cost and factory overhead. The study might show that factory overhead has remained approximately the same percentage of direct materials cost. Therefore, a rate based on materials cost might be applicable. In such instances the charge is com-puted by dividing total estimated factory overhead by total direct materials cost expected to be used in the manufacturing processes:

$$\frac{\text{Estimated Factory Overhead}}{\text{Estimated Materials Cost}} \times 100 = \frac{\text{Percentage of Overhead}}{\text{per Direct Materials Dollar}}$$

If estimated expenses are $300,000 and estimated materials cost is $250,000, each job or product completed would be charged with an additional 120 percent ($\frac{\$300,000}{\$250,000} \times 100$) of its materials cost as its share of factory overhead. For example, if the materials cost of an order is $5,000, the order would receive an additional charge of $6,000 ($5,000 × 120%) for overhead.

This method has only limited use because in most cases no logical relationship exists between the direct materials cost of a product and factory overhead used in its production. One product might be made from high-priced materials, while another requires less expensive materials. However, both products might require the same manufacturing process and thus incur approximately the same amount of factory overhead. If the materials cost basis is used to charge overhead, the product using expensive materials will, in this case, be charged with more than its share. To overcome this unfairness, two overhead rates might be calculated: one for items that are materials-oriented, such as purchasing, receiving, inspecting, handling, and storage; the remaining overhead costs would be charged to production using a different base.

Direct Labor Cost Basis. The direct labor cost basis is the most widely used method of applying overhead to jobs or products. Estimated factory overhead is divided by estimated direct labor cost to compute a percentage:

$$\frac{\text{Estimated Factory Overhead}}{\text{Estimated Direct Labor Cost}} \times 100 - \text{Percentage of Direct Labor Cost}$$

If estimated factory overhead is $300,000 and total direct labor cost for the next period is also estimated at $300,000, the overhead rate would be 100 percent ($\frac{\$300,000}{\$300,000} \times 100$). A job or product with a direct labor cost of $3,000 would be charged with $3,000 ($3,000 × 100%) for factory overhead.

Analysis of this method of applying factory overhead indicates that it is a step in the direction of charging overhead equitably to products manufactured. Factory overhead items such as supplies, overtime, and power are used over a period of time. Any method of applying factory overhead must take this time factor into consideration. The direct labor cost basis does so in that labor cost is computed by multiplying number of hours spent on work by an hourly wage rate; the more hours worked, the higher the labor cost and the greater the use and therefore the charge for factory overhead.

The direct labor cost basis is relatively easy to use since information needed to apply overhead is readily available. Its use is particularly favored when (1) a direct relationship between direct labor cost and factory overhead exists and (2) the rates of pay per hour for similar work are comparable. The weekly payroll provides the direct labor cost without any additional record keeping. As long as economy in securing underlying information remains a main prerequisite, the direct labor cost basis can be accepted as the best and quickest of the available methods for applying overhead.

On the other hand, this method can be objected to for two reasons:

1. Factory overhead must be looked upon as adding to the value of a job or product. The added value often comes about through depreciation charges of high-cost machinery which might not bear any relationship to direct labor payroll.

2. Total direct labor cost represents the sum of high- and low-wage production workers. By applying overhead on the basis of direct labor cost, a job or product is charged with more overhead when a high-rate operator performs work instead of a low-rate worker. Such a method can lead to incorrect distribution of factory overhead particularly when numerous operators, with different hourly rates in the same department, perform like operations on different jobs or products.

The next method, the direct labor hours basis, is designed to overcome the latter disadvantage.

Direct Labor Hours Basis. Computation of this rate is as follows:

$$\frac{\text{Estimated Factory Overhead}}{\text{Estimated Direct Labor Hours}} = \text{Rate per Direct Labor Hour}$$

If estimated factory overhead is $300,000 and total direct labor hours are estimated to be 200,000 hours, an overhead rate based on direct labor hours would be $1.50 per hour of direct labor ($300,000 ÷ 200,000 hours). A job that required 400 direct labor hours would be charged with $600 (400 hours × $1.50) for factory overhead.

The use of this method requires accumulation of direct labor hours by job or product. Timekeeping routines with their forms and records must be organized to provide the additional data. The use of the direct labor hours basis requires first a direct relationship between direct labor hours and factory overhead and, second, a difference in the rates of pay per hour for like work, caused by seniority rather than increased output. As long as labor operations are the chief factor in production processes, the direct labor hours method is acceptable as the most equitable basis for applying overhead. However, if shop or factory departments use machines extensively, the direct labor hours method might lead to an inaccurate costing. This disadvantage is overcome through the use of the machine hours method.

Machine Hours Basis. This method is based on time required by a machine or group of machines performing identical operations. Machine hours expected to be used are estimated and a machine hour rate determined as follows:

$$\frac{\text{Estimated Factory Overhead}}{\text{Estimated Machine Hours}} = \text{Rate per Machine Hour}$$

If factory overhead is estimated to be $300,000 and assuming that 300,000 machine hours will be used, the machine hour rate is $1 per machine hour ($300,000 ÷ 300,000 machine hours). Work that required 120 machine hours would be charged with $120 (120 hours × $1) for factory overhead.

This method requires additional clerical work. Shopmen, foremen, or timekeepers will have to collect machine hour data needed to charge overhead to jobs or products. In many instances, the machine hours method is considered the most accurate method of applying overhead. A system must be designed to assure correct accumulation of all required data for proper overhead accounting.

Another application of overhead rates is their use for estimating purposes. When materials and labor costs have been estimated, knowledge of the overhead distribution base quantity needed can be translated easily and efficiently into a factory overhead cost to arrive at total estimated cost. Selection of the correct basis for applying overhead is of utmost importance if a cost system is to provide proper and accurate costs and if management is to receive meaningful and valuable data.

Activity Level to Be Used. In calculating an overhead rate, a great deal depends on the activity level selected. The greater the assumed activity, the lower the fixed portion of the overhead rate because fixed overhead will be spread over a greater number of direct labor dollars, hours, etc. The variable portion of the rate will tend to remain constant at various activity levels. Determination of estimates used in deriving a factory overhead rate depends on whether a long- or a short-range viewpoint is adopted; i.e., whether the activity level used is: (1) normal capacity or (2) expected actual capacity. Other capacity levels are discussed in Chapter 18.

Normal Capacity. The long-range or long-term planning and control approach, or normal capacity concept, advocates an overhead rate in which expenses and production are based on average utilization of the physical plant over a time period long enough to level out the highs and lows that occur in every business venture. A rate based on normal capacity will not change because of changes in actual production; therefore, it results in a more useful unit cost. The rate will be changed when prices of certain expense items change or when fixed costs increase or decrease. A normal capacity rate concept assumes that the rate should not be changed because existing plant facilities are used to a greater or lesser degree. A job or product should not cost more to produce in any one accounting period just because production was lower and fixed charges were spread over a fewer number of units. The calculation of a normal capacity rate follows procedures described above. Factory overhead and bases used are estimated in terms of normal production figures.

In most instances, the use of a normal rate causes applied expenses to differ from actual expenses incurred. The possibility of such a difference or variance must be recognized, but this should not serve to discourage the use of an overhead rate or encourage the change of this rate. In fact, when this variance, generally called over- or underapplied factory overhead, is further analyzed, it reveals much useful management information (see pages 228–235).

Expected Actual Capacity. The short-range or short-term planning and control approach, or expected actual capacity concept, advocates a rate in which overhead and production are based on the expected actual output for the next production period. The method usually results in the use of a different predetermined rate for each period depending on increases or decreases in estimated factory overhead and production figures. The use of a predetermined rate based on expected actual production is often due to the difficulty of judging current performance on a long-range or normal capacity level. The fact that at times the factory overhead charged to production approaches the expenses actually incurred often makes the use of the expected actual factory overhead rate seem logical and acceptable even though the expenses are not representative of normal operations.

The following example of product costing uses overhead rates based on both activity levels. Assume the normal capacity for a company is 150,000 direct labor hours. For the past year the actual capacity attained was 116,000 hours. The management believes that 120,000 hours will be worked during the coming year. Fixed expenses for either capacity level are $120,000, and variable expenses are $.50 per direct labor hour.

The predetermined factory overhead rate based on normal capacity is $1.30 per direct labor hour, and the overhead rate based on expected actual capacity is $1.50 per direct labor hour calculated as follows:

	Normal Capacity	Expected Actual Capacity
Fixed expenses.............................	$120,000	$120,000
Variable expenses:		
150,000 hours × $.50......................	75,000	
120,000 hours × .50......................		60,000
Total estimated overhead....................	$195,000	$180,000
Estimated direct labor hours.................	150,000	120,000
Factory overhead rate.......................	$1.30	$1.50
Fixed overhead rate........................	$ .80	$1.00

The difference in the two rates lies in the fixed overhead rate. The expected actual capacity method increases the rate by $.20 per hour resulting in a greater product cost than with the normal capacity rate. Since fixed expenses are the same for both levels, it must be assumed that management anticipated a volume of business requiring such an amount of fixed costs. It is executive management's task to reach that level of operation which will assure a profitable and competitive position.

Inclusion or Exclusion of Fixed Overhead Items. Ordinarily, cost accounting procedures apply all factory costs to the output of a period. Under these procedures, called "absorption costing," "conventional costing," or "full costing," both fixed and variable expenses are included in overhead rates. Another method of costing, termed "direct costing," is sometimes used, chiefly for internal management purposes. Under this method of costing, only variable overhead is included in overhead rates. Fixed expenses do not become product costs but are treated as period costs meaning that they are charged off in total each period as are marketing and administrative expenses. They are not included in either work in process or finished goods inventories.

Absorption and direct costing are the result of two entirely different cost concepts with respect to product cost, period cost, gross income, and net income. The two methods result in different inventory costs and different period profits. Direct costing is discussed in detail in Chapter 22.

Each of the various bases discussed for applying overhead may be used with absorption or direct costing, with rates based on normal or expected actual capacity.

Of the five main factors influencing the selection of overhead rates outlined at the beginning of this section, two have not been discussed; namely, the use of a single rate or several rates and the use of separate rates for service activities. These methods are discussed in the next two chapters.

The Calculation of a Factory Overhead Rate. Calculating a factory overhead rate involves the following procedure:

Estimating the Activity Level and Expenses. The first step in calculating the overhead rate is to determine the activity level to be used for the base selected and then estimate or budget each individual expense at the estimated activity level in order to arrive at the total estimated overhead.

The list on page 222 shows the estimated factory overhead for Proctor Products, Inc. for a normal capacity activity level estimated at 200,000 direct labor hours.

Classifying Expenses as Fixed or Variable. The classification of expenses according to changes in volume attempts to establish a variability pattern for each expense item. This classification must, in turn, consider certain

PROCTOR PRODUCTS, INC.

ESTIMATED FACTORY OVERHEAD FOR 19—

Expenses	Amount
Supervisors and foremen..................................	$ 70,000
Indirect labor...	75,000
Overtime premium......................................	9,000
Supplies..	23,000
Repairs and maintenance................................	12,000
Electric power..	20,000
Fuel..	6,000
Water..	1,000
FICA taxes...	18,000
Unemployment taxes....................................	5,000
Workmen's compensation................................	3,000
Hospitalization insurance...............................	2,000
Pensions...	15,000
Vacations and holidays..................................	12,000
Group insurance..	4,000
Depreciation — building................................	5,000
Depreciation — equipment..............................	13,000
Taxes (property).......................................	4,000
Insurance (fire)..	3,000
Total estimated factory overhead........................	$300,000

specific assumptions regarding plant facilities, prices, managerial policy, and the state of technology. Once the classification has been decided, the expense may remain in this category for a limited period of time. Should underlying conditions change, the original classification must be reviewed and expenses reclassified as necessary.

Variable expenses change with production volume and are considered a function of volume; that is, the amount of variable expense per unit is constant. Fixed expenses, on the other hand, are just the opposite. The total amount is fixed, but the expense per unit is different for each production level. Increased production causes a decrease in fixed expense per unit. Knowledge of the effect of fixed and variable expenses on the product unit cost is highly important in any study of factory overhead. A knowledge of the behavior of all costs is fundamental to the planning and analytical processes for decision-making purposes.

An examination of fixed and variable expenses indicates the difficulty of segregating all expenses as either fixed or variable. Some expenses are partly fixed and partly variable; some are fixed to a certain production level and then increase as production increases. Furthermore, costs may change in steplike fashion at various production levels. Such expenses are classified as semivariable expenses.

Because expenses are to be classified as either fixed or variable, the fixed portion of any semivariable expense and the degree of change in the

PROCTOR PRODUCTS, INC.

ESTIMATED FACTORY OVERHEAD FOR 19—

Expenses	Fixed	Variable	Total
Supervisors and foremen.................	$ 70,000		$ 70,000
Indirect labor...........................	9,000	$ 66,000	75,000
Overtime premium.......................		9,000	9,000
Supplies................................	4,000	19,000	23,000
Repairs and maintenance................	3,000	9,000	12,000
Electric power..........................	2,000	18,000	20,000
Fuel....................................	1,000	5,000	6,000
Water..................................	500	500	1,000
FICA taxes.............................	3,000	15,000	18,000
Unemployment taxes....................	1,500	3,500	5,000
Workmen's compensation................	500	2,500	3,000
Hospitalization insurance...............	500	1,500	2,000
Pensions...............................	2,000	13,000	15,000
Vacations and holidays.................	2,000	10,000	12,000
Group insurance........................	1,000	3,000	4,000
Depreciation — building.................	5,000		5,000
Depreciation — equipment...............	13,000		13,000
Taxes (property)........................	4,000		4,000
Insurance (fire)........................	3,000		3,000
Total estimated factory overhead.......	$125,000	$175,000	$300,000

variable part must be determined. Several methods are available to aid in finding the constant portion and the degree of variability in the variable portion. These procedures determine the relationship between increases in production and increases in total and individual expenses. For example, when production is expected to increase 10 percent, it is possible to determine the corresponding increase in total expense as well as the increase in individual expenses such as supplies, power, indirect labor, etc. A detailed illustration and discussion of such procedures are presented in Chapter 18.

Total expenses as illustrated on page 222 amount to $300,000; in the illustration above, they are classified as either fixed or variable.

Establishing the Factory Overhead Rate. After the activity level for the selected base and the factory overhead have been estimated, the overhead rates can be computed. Assuming the direct labor hours base is used and direct labor hours for the coming year are estimated to be 200,000 (normal capacity level), the factory overhead rate at this selected activity level would be:

$$\text{Factory Overhead Rate} = \frac{\text{Estimated Expenses}}{\text{Estimated Direct Labor Hours}} = \frac{\$300,000}{200,000} = \begin{array}{l}\$1.50 \text{ per}\\ \text{Direct Labor}\\ \text{Hour}\end{array}$$

This overhead rate can be further broken down into its fixed and variable components:

$$\frac{\$125,000 \text{ Estimated Fixed Overhead}}{200,000 \text{ Estimated Direct Labor Hours}} = \$ .625 \text{ Fixed Portion of the Factory Overhead Rate}$$

$$\frac{\$175,000 \text{ Estimated Variable Overhead}}{200,000 \text{ Estimated Direct Labor Hours}} = \$ .875 \text{ Variable Portion of the Factory Overhead Rate}$$

$$\text{Total Factory Overhead Rate} = \underline{\$1.500} \text{ per Direct Labor Hour}$$

This rate is used to charge overhead to jobs or products. Amounts applied are first entered in subsidiary ledgers such as job order cost sheets and cost of production reports. Direct labor hours, direct labor cost, or other similar data already recorded determine the amount of overhead chargeable to each job or product.

FACTORY OVERHEAD — ACTUAL

Estimating the factory overhead, deciding upon the base and activity level to be utilized, and calculating the overhead rate take place prior to the incurrence or recording of the actual expenses. Factory overhead is applied as soon as the necessary data, in this case direct labor hours, have been made available. Each day, however, as actual overhead items are purchased, requisitioned, or used, the actual transactions are recorded in general and subsidiary ledgers independent of the application of factory overhead based on the predetermined overhead rate.

Accumulation of Actual Factory Overhead for Control. Factory overhead includes numerous items which can be classified in many different ways. Every firm because of its own manufacturing peculiarities will devise its own particular accounts and methods of classifying them. However, regardless of these possible variations, expenses are usually summarized in a factory overhead control account kept in the general ledger. Details of this general ledger account are kept in a subsidiary overhead ledger. This subsidiary ledger also can take many forms, and it may be difficult to recognize it as such, particularly when tabulating or electronic equipment is in use. A subsidiary ledger will group various expense items together under significant selective titles as to kinds of expenses and will also detail the expenses chargeable to individual producing and service departments, thereby permitting stricter control over factory overhead.

The accumulation of factory overhead in accounting records presents several distinct problems. Due to the many varied potential requests and uses of factory overhead data for managerial decision-making purposes, it is almost impossible to set up an all-purpose system for accumulating factory overhead.

A basic objective for accumulating factory overhead is the gathering of information for purposes of control. Control, in turn, requires (1) reporting costs to individual department heads responsible for them and (2) making comparisons with amounts budgeted for the level of operations achieved. The mechanics for collecting overhead items are based on the chart of accounts which indicates the accounts to which various factory overhead items are to be charged.

Overhead items are ultimately identified with specific producing departments. At the end of the month or year, factory overhead applied and actual factory overhead incurred are analyzed. The comparison between actual and applied figures might lead to computation of the spending and the idle capacity variances (see pages 230–232).

Steps in Accounting for Actual Factory Overhead. In small or medium-sized businesses factory overhead accounts have usually been kept in a subsidiary ledger. Punched cards, tapes, or magnetic disks in data processing systems constitute the methods used in large-scale industries with an up-to-date information system. The company's chart of accounts will define the accounts to be used. The overhead accounts shown below comprise a partial list of accounts used:

Supervisors and Foremen	Fuel	Vacations and Holidays
Indirect Labor	Water	Group Insurance
Overtime Premium	FICA Taxes	Depreciation — Building
Supplies	Unemployment Taxes	Depreciation — Equipment
Repairs and Maintenance	Workmen's Compensation	Taxes (Property)
Electric Power	Hospitalization Insurance	Insurance (Fire)
	Pensions	

Each of the above expenses may be departmentalized as discussed in the next chapter.

The steps involved in accounting for factory overhead are:

1. Analysis of overhead transactions

2. Journalization of overhead transactions

3. Posting overhead transactions to the factory overhead subsidiary ledger and the factory overhead general ledger control account

Principal Original Records. Some overhead items are vouchered and paid for during the month; others are the result of current journal entries for supplies and indirect labor used; still others are adjustments made at the end of a fiscal period. The principal source documents used for recording overhead in the journals are: (1) purchase vouchers, (2) materials requisitions, (3) labor job time tickets, and (4) general journal vouchers.

Underlying source documents provide a record of the overhead information which must be analyzed and accumulated in proper accounts. To obtain accurate and useful information, each transaction must be properly classified at its inception. Those responsible for this identification must be thoroughly familiar with names and code numbers of cost accounts as well as with the purpose and function of each account.

Purchase Vouchers. Factory overhead items recorded on purchase vouchers are those charged off in total each period. These transactions are supported by vendors' invoices which are analyzed and classified in accordance with the chart of accounts. The specific account charged is indicated by an account number.

Materials Requisitions. Materials requisitions contain all charges for indirect materials and supply items drawn from storerooms. Requisitions specify the account, code number, and department to which the cost is to be charged. Accounts affected by transactions involving materials requisitions are Indirect Materials, Supplies, Fuel, Lubricants, Shop Supplies, and Sundry Operating Supplies.

Labor Job Time Tickets. Labor job time tickets are used for indirect labor. Foremen, timekeepers, or the workmen themselves enter pertinent data on the time ticket so that proper factory overhead accounts can be charged. The data to be included are: indirect labor operational code, worker's name and code number, and department to which indirect labor is to be charged.

General Journal Vouchers. A general journal voucher is used for making entries in the general journal. Journal entries are principally used for end-of-month adjustments. Typical overhead items involved in such transactions are depreciation, fire insurance, and property taxes.

Books of Original Entry. The books of original entry used to accumulate factory overhead costs are: (1) the accounts payable register and/or the cash payments journal, (2) the general journal, and (3) the factory journal. The format for the books of original entry depends on the basic plan for accumulation of factory overhead items in the accounts.

Accounts Payable Register and/or Cash Payments Journal. Transactions with outsiders are usually recorded in the accounts payable register and/or cash payments journal. Items are journalized from prepared vouchers based on the original source documents (as discussed in

Chapter 4). The entry is usually a debit to Factory Overhead Control. Detailed postings are made to individual expense accounts in the factory overhead subsidiary ledger.

General Journal. Factory overhead transactions are also accumulated in the general journal with perhaps a special column for factory overhead. To avoid the recording of too many items in a general journal, special journals, such as materials requisition and payroll journals, are used.

Factory Journal. The factory journal facilitates the posting process when cost accounts are kept in a separate ledger rather than in the general ledger. In such instances, all cost transactions involving factory cost accounts are entered in the factory journal using factory journal vouchers. The factory journal is posted to the factory ledger. To avoid duplication and to provide self-balancing, reciprocal accounts are used. Use of these reciprocal accounts was described in Chapter 4.

Ledgers Used for Summarizing Factory Overhead. Ledgers used for summarizing factory overhead are: (1) the general ledger and (2) the factory ledger.

General Ledger. The general ledger used in accounting for overhead items is the same as that used in accounting for other transactions. It is a collection of accounts used to summarize various amounts for an accounting period and to reflect certain balances at the end of a period.

Factory Ledger. A factory ledger is often used along with a general ledger. Cost accounts as well as any other accounts pertaining to factory operations are removed from the general ledger and placed in a separate factory ledger as was described in Chapter 4.

Factory Overhead Control Account. Overhead accounts are kept in the general ledger only when accounts are not too numerous; otherwise, the system becomes unwieldy. Because the number of expense accounts is ordinarily quite large, it is customary to have a factory overhead control account in the general ledger and individual overhead accounts in a factory overhead subsidiary ledger. The relationship between the factory overhead control account and its subsidiary ledger is the same as that between the accounts receivable control account and its subsidiary ledger.

When all postings have been made to the factory overhead control account from the various journals, the debit side represents total actual factory overhead incurred during the period. The credit side of the account represents the overhead applied during the period. The illustration on page 228 indicates that actual factory overhead for the period was

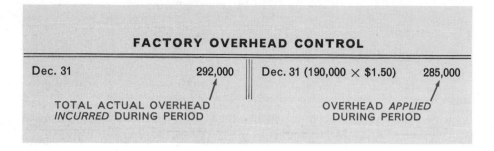

$292,000. (The total of the factory overhead subsidiary ledger equals the amount of the debit to Factory Overhead Control.) Factory overhead applied was $285,000 based on 190,000 actual direct labor hours worked during the period (capacity utilized) and a predetermined factory overhead of $1.50 per direct labor hour.

FACTORY OVERHEAD — APPLIED, OVER- OR UNDERAPPLIED, AND VARIANCE ANALYSIS

This section discusses the meaning of the difference between debits and credits as mentioned above and analyzes the difference to determine the spending and idle capacity variances.

The Mechanics of Applying Factory Overhead. Factory overhead is applied to the work done after the direct materials and the direct labor costs have been recorded. If direct labor hours or machine hours arc the basis for overhead charges, these data must also be available to the cost department. The job order cost sheets or the departmental cost of production reports receive postings as soon as materials or labor data become available. A special section of a job order cost sheet is used for factory overhead, as shown below. This is a reproduction of part of the illustration on page 104 of Chapter 5.

APPLIED FACTORY OVERHEAD

DATE	DEPARTMENT	BASIS OF APPLICATION	HOURS	RATE	COST
11/15	Cutting	$3 per direct labor hour	120	$3.00	$ 360.00
11/15	Planing	$4 per direct labor hour	50	4.00	200.00
11/22	Assembly	$2 per direct labor hour	200	2.00	400.00
11/29	Upholstery	100% of direct labor cost	--	--	1,500.00
		Total Factory Overhead Applied			$ 2,460.00

Section of Job Order Cost Sheet Showing Applied Factory Overhead

The journal entry for summarizing overhead charges to job order cost sheets or departmental cost of production reports is:

Work in Process.................................... 285,000
       Factory Overhead Applied.........................   285,000

Charges made to subsidiary records (the job order cost sheets or departmental cost of production reports) list in detail applied factory overhead charged to jobs or departments. The debit to the work in process control account brings total overhead applied into the general ledger or into the factory ledger if factory cost accounts are kept there. The factory overhead applied account is subsequently closed out to the factory overhead control account by the entry:

Factory Overhead Applied........................... 285,000
       Factory Overhead Control........................   285,000

It is common practice to use a factory overhead applied account because it keeps applied costs and actual costs in separate accounts. However, some companies do not use Factory Overhead Applied but post the credit directly to Factory Overhead Control.

Debits to the factory overhead control account are for actual expenses incurred during the period. There may, of course, be credit adjustments to actual factory overhead in the control account (e.g., the return of supplies to the storeroom). Such credits would reduce total actual factory overhead.

The factory overhead control account collects net actual expenses as debits and applied expenses as credits. It is seldom that the two are equal. There is usually a debit or a credit balance. A debit balance indicates that overhead has been underapplied; a credit balance means that overhead has been overapplied. These over- or underapplied balances must be analyzed carefully for they are the source of much information needed by management for judging the efficiency of the operations and the use of available capacity during a particular period.

Overapplied and Underapplied Factory Overhead. In the factory overhead control account (page 228), actual factory overhead incurred during the period exceeds total factory overhead applied by $7,000. Therefore, factory overhead for the period was $7,000 underapplied. If applied overhead had exceeded actual overhead, overhead would have been overapplied. In either case, the difference must be analyzed to determine the reason or reasons for the over- or underapplied factory overhead. Two separate variances are computed in making the analysis:

1. *Spending variance* — a variance due to budget or expense factors
2. *Idle capacity variance* — a variance due to volume or activity factors

The analysis can be made in the following manner (the factory overhead rates used are those given on pages 223 and 224):

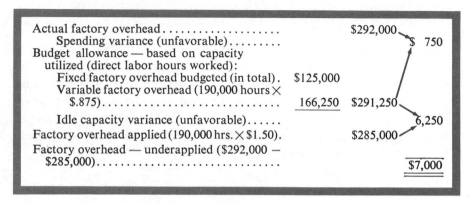

Actual factory overhead.....................		$292,000
Spending variance (unfavorable).........		$ 750
Budget allowance — based on capacity		
utilized (direct labor hours worked):		
Fixed factory overhead budgeted (in total).	$125,000	
Variable factory overhead (190,000 hours ×		
$.875)............................	166,250	$291,250
Idle capacity variance (unfavorable)......		6,250
Factory overhead applied (190,000 hrs. × $1.50).		$285,000
Factory overhead — underapplied ($292,000 −		
$285,000)...............................		$7,000

The analysis can also be made in columnar form as follows:

(1) Actual Factory Overhead	(2) Budget Allowance (Based on Capacity Utilized)	(3) Applied Factory Overhead	(1 − 3) Total Overhead Variance	(1 − 2) Spending Variance	(2 − 3) Idle Capacity Variance
$292,000	Fixed $125,000 Variable 166,250* Total $291,250	$285,000**	$7,000 Debit *or* Unfavorable	$750 Debit *or* Unfavorable	$6,250*** Debit *or* Unfavorable

    *190,000 direct labor hours × variable overhead rate of $.875 per direct labor hour.
   **190,000 direct labor hours × total overhead rate of $1.50 per direct labor hour.
  ***Proof: Idle hours of 10,000 × fixed overhead rate of $.625 per direct labor hour.

Spending Variance. The $750 spending variance is the difference between the actual factory overhead incurred and the budget allowance estimated for capacity utilized; i.e., for the actual activity of 190,000 direct labor hours worked.

The spending variance can also be computed as follows:

Actual factory overhead incurred during the period....................	$292,000
Less budgeted fixed overhead	125,000
Actual variable expenses incurred during the period...................	$167,000
Variable overhead applied during the period (190,000 hours × $.875)..	166,250
Spending variance — unfavorable..................................	$ 750

If actual overhead had been less than budgeted, the spending variance would have been favorable.

A breakdown of the $750 spending variance and comparison of each actual expense with its budgeted figure are useful. Details of the actual

PROCTOR PRODUCTS, INC.

COMPARISON OF ACTUAL AND BUDGETED FACTORY OVERHEAD FOR 19—

(Capacity Utilized: 190,000 Direct Labor Hours = 95% of Normal)

	Budgeted	Actual	Over	Under
Variable and Semivariable Overhead:				
Indirect labor.....................	$ 71,700	$ 72,550	$ 850	
Overtime premium................	8,550	8,700	150	
Supplies........................	22,050	22,720	670	
Repairs and maintenance..........	11,550	10,200		$ 1,350
Electric power...................	19,100	19,650	550	
Fuel...........................	5,750	5,300		450
Water..........................	975	1,000	25	
FICA taxes......................	17,250	17,450	200	
Unemployment taxes..............	4,825	4,925	100	
Workmen's compensation..........	2,875	2,900	25	
Hospitalization insurance.........	1,925	1,935	10	
Pensions.......................	14,350	14,550	200	
Vacations and holidays............	11,500	11,300		200
Group insurance.................	3,850	3,820		30
Total........................	$196,250	$197,000	$ 2,780	$ 2,030
Fixed Overhead:				
Supervisors and foremen...........	$ 70,000	$ 70,000		
Depreciation — buildings..........	5,000	5,000		
Depreciation — equipment.........	13,000	13,000		
Taxes (property).................	4,000	4,000		
Insurance (fire)..................	3,000	3,000		
Total........................	$ 95,000	$ 95,000		
Total overhead.....................	$291,250	$292,000	$ 2,780	$ 2,030
Spending variance — unfavorable.......			$ 750	

expenses are recorded in the factory overhead subsidiary ledger. Comparison of actual with budgeted overhead for capacity worked (190,000 direct labor hours) is illustrated above.

The budgeted figures utilize the concept of the flexible budget discussed in Chapter 18. Basically, the budget figures represent the budget for the level of activity attained (e.g., for indirect labor) from the estimates on page 223; fixed overhead is $9,000; and the variable part of this overhead cost is $.33 $\left(\frac{\$66,000 \text{ Estimated Variable Indirect Labor}}{200,000 \text{ Estimated Direct Labor Hours}}\right)$. The budgeted indirect labor for the activity level attained is $9,000 plus 190,000 direct labor hours × $.33, or $71,700. The same answer can be calculated by multiplying 95 percent $\left(\frac{190,000 \text{ Actual Direct Labor Hours}}{200,000 \text{ Estimated Direct Labor Hours}}\right)$ of $66,000 = $62,700 + $9,000 = $71,700.

Certain of the expenses that are itemized above exceed the budgeted figures; others are below. Each difference must be analyzed; the reason for the difference must be determined; and discussion must be initiated with the individual responsible for its incurrence.

Corrective action should be taken where called for; likewise, effective and efficient performance should be recognized and rewarded. Observe that even underexpenditures may be undesirable. For example, the $1,350 underspent repairs and maintenance amount may suggest insufficient attention to preventive maintenance.

Idle Capacity Variance. The rate used for applying factory overhead is $1.50 per direct labor hour which is based on 200,000 normal capacity hours. However, direct labor hours worked during the period totaled only 190,000 hours; capacity not used, 10,000 direct labor hours. The capacity attained was 95 percent (190,000 ÷ 200,000) of normal.

The $1.50 overhead rate is considered the proper costing price for each direct labor hour used. The fact that operations were at a level below normal should not increase the factory overhead cost of each unit. The cost of idle capacity should be recorded separately and considered a part of total manufacturing cost. The $6,250 idle capacity variance arises because 10,000 available hours were not used, and is computed as follows:

```
Budget allowance (based on capacity utilized)........................  $291,250
Factory overhead applied..........................................   285,000
  Idle capacity variance — unfavorable.............................  $  6,250
```

The idle capacity variance can also be computed by multiplying the 10,000 idle hours by the $.625 fixed expense rate or by multiplying total budgeted fixed expenses of $125,000 by 5 percent (100% − 95%).

Responsibility for the idle capacity variance rests with executive management, inasmuch as this variance indicates the under- or overutilization portion of plant and equipment. The cause of a capacity variance, whether favorable or unfavorable, should always be determined and possible reasons for the variance discovered. One cause may be a lack of proper balance between production facilities and sales. On the other hand, it might be due to a favorable sales price that recovers fixed overhead at an unusually low volume level.

Disposition of Over- or Underapplied Overhead. Because of its importance, the analysis of the over- or underapplied overhead figure is presented in detail. Disposition of this figure is generally quite simple. Although total over- or underapplied overhead is analyzed into spending and idle capacity variances, it need not be journalized and posted in two parts. At the end of the fiscal period, overhead variances may be (1) treated as a period cost, (2) divided between inventories and cost of goods sold, especially if the rate appears to have been in error, or (3) treated as period cost but divided between inventory and cost of goods sold if a gain or favorable depending on the nature of the variance.

Current Internal Revenue Service regulations require inclusion in inventories of an allocated portion of *significant* annual overhead variances. Where the amount involved is *not significant*, in relation to total actual factory overhead, an allocation is not required unless such allocation is made for financial reporting purposes. Also the taxpayer must treat both over- and underapplied overhead consistently. The regulations, however, do permit expensing of the idle capacity variance.

For financial reporting purposes, two procedures that are used for closing over- or underapplied overhead are: (1) close to Cost of Goods Sold or (2) close directly to Income Summary, thereby treating the over- or underapplied overhead as a period cost. The entries are:

```
Cost of Goods Sold....................................   7,000
    Factory Overhead Control.............................        7,000
                               or
Income Summary......................................   7,000
    Factory Overhead Control.............................        7,000
```

The over- or underapplied figure is closed to the cost of goods sold account or to the income summary account depending on whether management considers such a variation a manufacturing or managerial cost. If the variance is closed to the cost of goods sold account, it will appear in the cost of goods sold statement. If it is closed to the income summary account, it will appear in the income statement. The results of both procedures are shown in the statements illustrated on page 234. Regardless of the disposition made of the over- or underapplied figure, the computation, analysis, and reporting of both the spending and idle capacity variances are significant and important.

Interim balance sheets might show over- or underapplied factory overhead as a deferred item until the end of the fiscal period when a decision regarding its disposition must be made.

Further discussion of disposition of variances is reserved for the standard cost chapter (Chapter 20).

INCORRECT OVERHEAD RATES

An overhead rate may turn out to be incorrect because of misjudgments regarding estimated overhead or anticipated activity. A large over- or underapplied overhead figure does not necessarily mean that the overhead rate was wrong. As mentioned, use of a normal overhead rate is purposely designed to show the extent to which normal capacity is or is not used. Likewise, when an overhead rate based on expected actual conditions is used, seasonal variations may lead to large over- or underabsorbed

PROCTOR PRODUCTS, INC.
INCOME STATEMENT FOR 19—

Sales..		$1,600,000
Less: Cost of goods sold at normal.................	$1,195,000	
Underapplied factory overhead.................	7,000	1,202,000
Gross profit..		$ 398,000
Less: Marketing expenses...........................	$ 150,000	
Administrative expenses.......................	100,000	250,000
Net income...		$ 148,000

PROCTOR PRODUCTS, INC.
COST OF GOODS SOLD STATEMENT
FOR YEAR ENDED DECEMBER 19—

Direct materials used..	$ 400,000
Direct labor used..	500,000
Factory overhead applied (See Schedule B-1)........................	285,000
Total manufacturing costs.....................................	$1,185,000
Less work in process inventory change...........................	20,000
Cost of goods manufactured at normal............................	$1,165,000
Plus finished goods inventory change...........................	30,000
Cost of goods sold at normal....................................	$1,195,000
Plus underapplied factory overhead............................	7,000
Cost of goods sold at actual....................................	$1,202,000

SCHEDULE B-1   PROCTOR PRODUCTS, INC.
FACTORY OVERHEAD FOR 19—

Supervisors and foremen.....................................	$ 70,000
Indirect labor..	72,550
Overtime premium..	8,700
Supplies...	22,720
Repairs and maintenance....................................	10,200
Electric power...	19,650
Fuel...	5,300
Water..	1,000
FICA taxes...	17,450
Unemployment taxes..	4,925
Workmen's compensation....................................	2,900
Hospitalization insurance..................................	1,935
Pensions...	14,550
Vacations and holidays.....................................	11,300
Group insurance...	3,820
Depreciation — buildings...................................	5,000
Depreciation — equipment..................................	13,000
Taxes (property)...	4,000
Insurance (fire)...	3,000
Total actual factory overhead...............................	$292,000
Less underapplied factory overhead.........................	7,000
Factory overhead applied....................................	$285,000

overhead which will tend to even itself out during a full year. The best way to detect an incorrect overhead rate is to analyze the factors used in its predetermination. Since a rate is an estimate, small errors should be expected; and the rate need not be changed for such errors.

CHANGING OVERHEAD RATES

Overhead rates are usually reviewed annually. This procedure helps level out costing through the year and ties overhead control in with budget control. If rates are changed during a fiscal or budget period, meaningful comparisons will be difficult. Changes in production methods, prices, efficiencies, and sales expectancy make review and, possibly, revision of overhead rates a necessity at least annually. Revisions should be based on a complete review of all factors involved. The extent to which a company revises its overhead rates depends on frequency of changes, on factors which affect overhead rates, and on management's need and desire for current costs and realistic overhead variance information.

GRAPHIC PRESENTATION OF FACTORY OVERHEAD

This chapter's discussion of estimating, accounting for, and analyzing factory overhead is presented diagrammatically below.

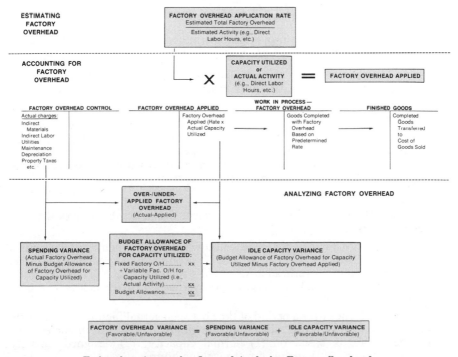

Estimating, Accounting for, and Analyzing Factory Overhead

DISCUSSION QUESTIONS

1. Factory overhead constitutes a much larger proportion of total manufacturing costs today than in the past. This trend is expected to continue. Why?

2. Why will a department's factory overhead vary from month to month?

3. What are the steps involved in accounting for factory overhead?

4. State some of the main expenses that are considered to be factory overhead?

5. Should the wages of an apprentice or trainee be charged to a job or considered as overhead?

6. When and why must predetermined factory overhead rates be used? Indicate the impracticalities and inaccuracies of charging actual overhead to jobs and products.

7. Are predetermined factory overhead rates required in a process cost system? Explain.

8. What is the purpose of each of the following items in job order costing? How do they relate to each other?

   (a) Factory overhead control account
   (b) Job order cost sheet
   (c) Work in process — factory overhead
   (d) Applied factory overhead

9. Why is the selection of a proper predetermined rate so essential to accurate costing? Explain.

10. Name five bases used for applying factory overhead. What factors must be considered in selecting a particular basis?

11. If a company uses a predetermined rate for application of factory overhead, the idle capacity variance is the (a) under- or overapplied fixed cost element of overhead; (b) under- or overapplied variable cost element of overhead; (c) difference in budgeted costs and actual costs of fixed overhead items; (d) difference in budgeted costs and actual costs of variable overhead items; (e) none of the above. Which of these is correct?

   (AICPA adapted)

12. For each of the following statements, select the item which gives the most adequate answer.

    (a) Overapplied factory overhead will always result when a predetermined factory overhead rate is employed and (1) production is greater than defined capacity; (2) actual overhead costs are less than expected; (3) defined capacity is less than normal capacity; or (4) overhead incurred is less than overhead applied.

    (b) The difference over a period of time between actual factory overhead and applied factory overhead will usually be minimal when the predetermined overhead rate is based on (1) normal capacity; (2) designed capacity; (3) direct labor hours; or (4) direct machine hours.

(c) If a predetermined factory overhead rate is not employed and the volume of production is reduced from the level planned, the cost per unit would be expected to (1) remain unchanged for fixed costs and increase for variable costs; (2) increase for fixed costs and remain unchanged for variable costs; (3) increase for fixed costs and decrease for variable costs; or (4) decrease for fixed costs and decrease for variable costs.

(d) A spending variance for factory overhead is the difference between actual factory overhead cost and factory overhead cost that should have been incurred for the actual hours worked and results from (1) price differences for factory overhead costs; (2) quantity differences for factory overhead costs; (3) price and quantity differences for factory overhead costs; or (4) differences caused by production volume variation.

(e) Factory overhead should be allocated on the basis of (1) an activity basis which relates to cost incurrence; (2) direct labor hours; (3) direct labor cost; or (4) direct machine hours.

(AICPA adapted)

13. The factory overhead control account has a credit balance at the end of the period. Was overhead over- or underapplied?

14. If large underabsorbed (underapplied) factory overhead variances occur month after month, the factory overhead rate should be revised to make unit costs more accurate. Comment.

15. Over- or underapplied overhead can be analyzed into two parts called variances. What are these variances, why are they so titled, and how are they computed?

16. Production for Lemona Beverages, Inc., shows a pronounced seasonal fluctuation. Should factory overhead variances be shown as adjustments to the cost of goods sold on the company's monthly income statements? If not, what alternative is possible?

17. The Valley View Manufacturing Company applies factory overhead to production on the basis of direct labor dollars. At the end of the year factory overhead has been overabsorbed to the extent of $60,000. Name at least five factors which would cause this situation and explain what should be done with the credit balance.

18. Select the answer that best completes each of the following statements:

(a) If over- or underapplied factory overhead is interpreted as an error in allocating actual costs against the production for the year, this suggests to an accountant that the over- or underapplied factory overhead for the year should be (1) carried forward in the factory overhead account from year to year; (2) eliminated by changing the predetermined factory overhead rate in subsequent years; (3) apportioned among the work in process inventory, the finished goods inventory, and the cost of goods sold; (4) treated as a special gain or loss occurring during the year.

(AICPA adapted)

(b) Underapplied factory overhead costs are (1) fixed factory costs not allocated to units produced; (2) factory overhead costs not allocated to units produced; (3) excess variable factory overhead costs; (4) costs that cannot be controlled; (5) none of the above.

(NAA adapted)

(c) A company found that the differences in product costs resulting from the application of predetermined factory overhead rates rather than actual factory overhead rates were immaterial even though actual production was substantially less than planned production. The most likely explanation is that (1) factory overhead was composed chiefly of variable costs; (2) several products were produced simultaneously; (3) fixed factory overhead was a significant cost; (4) costs of factory overhead items were substantially larger than anticipated.

(AICPA adapted)

EXERCISES

1. Classification of Expenses.   *Required:* (1) Classification of the following expenses as either (a) indirect labor, (b) indirect materials or supplies, or (c) other factory overhead.

(2) Classification of each expense as fixed, variable, or semivariable.

(a) Building repairs
(b) Coal
(c) Depreciation — machinery and equipment
(d) Fuel oil
(e) Insurance on machinery and equipment
(f) Telephone and telegraph
(g) Workmen's compensation insurance
(h) Small tools
(i) Repairs to machinery and equipment
(j) Power
(k) Rent
(l) Freight-in
(m) Inspectors' wages
(n) Shop supplies
(o) Payroll taxes
(p) Superintendent
(q) Storekeepers' salaries

2. Calculation of Estimated Labor Hours.   The Millan Manufacturing Company employs 200 men who work 8 hours a day, 5 days a week. Normal capacity for the firm is based on the assumption that the equivalent of 46 weeks of work can be expected from an employee.

Required: (1) The number of direct labor hours to be used in setting up the firm's factory overhead rate based on normal capacity.

(2) The number of direct labor hours if the management and the workers agree on a 10-hour, 4-day workweek.

3. Various Overhead Rates.   The Montessori Company estimated its factory overhead for the next period at $320,000. It is estimated that 80,000 units will be produced at a materials cost of $400,000. Production will require 80,000 man-hours at an estimated wage cost of $320,000. The machines will run approximately 50,000 hours.

Required: The factory overhead rate that may be used in applying factory overhead to production on each of the following bases:

(a) Materials cost
(b) Direct labor cost
(c) Direct labor hours
(d) Machine hours

4. Factory Overhead Variance Analysis. Normal capacity of the Ziff Company is set at 80,000 direct labor hours. The expected operating level for the period just completed was 64,000 hours. At this expected capacity, variable expenses were estimated to be $44,800 and fixed expenses, $64,000. Actual results show 70,000 hours were worked during the period.

Required: The following information from the data given:

(a) The predetermined overhead rate based on normal capacity.
(b) The predetermined overhead rate based on expected actual capacity.
(c) The amount of factory overhead charged to production if the company used the normal overhead rate.
(d) The amount of factory overhead charged to production if the company used the expected actual overhead rate.
(e) Would there be a favorable idle capacity variance if the normal capacity rate were used? Illustrate by variance computations.
(f) Would there be a favorable idle capacity variance if the expected actual rate were used? Illustrate by variance computations.

5. Factory Overhead Rates and Variances on Various Capacity Levels. The accountant of the Cordell Manufacturing Company is asked by his management to compute factory overhead rates based on (a) normal capacity, (b) expected actual capacity, (c) practical capacity, and (d) average sales for the previous three years. The accountant prepared the following summary:

	Expected Actual	Average Sales	Normal Capacity	Practical Capacity
Capacity levels..................	80%	85%	90%	100%
Direct labor hours...............	27,200	28,900	30,600	34,000
Factory overhead:				
Fixed factory overhead..........	$102,000	$102,000	$102,000	$102,000
Variable factory overhead.......	136,000	144,500	153,000	170,000
Total	$238,000	$246,500	$255,000	$272,000

Required: (1) Factory overhead rates for each of the four capacity levels. (Make calculations to two decimal places only.)

(2) The amount of over- or underabsorbed factory overhead for the other three levels if actual hours worked and actual factory overhead incurred were identical with the estimated hours and the estimated overhead of the expected actual capacity level.

6. Types of Factory Overhead Rates. Minelli, Inc. engages the services of a CPA firm for the installation of a cost system. Preliminary investigation of the manufacturing operations discloses these facts:

(a) The company makes a line of light fixtures and lamps. The materials cost of any particular item ranges from 15% to 60% of total factory cost, depending on the kind of metal and fabric used in making it.
(b) The business is subject to wide cyclical fluctuations since the sales volume follows new housing construction.

(c) About 60% of the manufacturing is normally done during the first quarter of the year.

(d) For the whole plant, the wage rates range from $2.25 to $5.75 an hour. However, within each of the eight individual departments, the spread between the high and low wage rate is less than 5%.

(e) Each product requires the use of all eight of the manufacturing departments, but not proportionately.

(f) Within the individual manufacturing departments, factory overhead ranges from 30% to 80% of conversion cost.

Required: A letter to the president of Minelli, Inc. explaining whether its cost system should use:

(a) A predetermined overhead rate or an actual overhead rate — departmental or plantwide.

(b) A method of factory overhead distribution based on direct labor hours, direct labor cost, or prime cost

Include the reasons supporting each of these recommendations.

(AICPA adapted)

7. Entries for Factory Overhead. Whirl, Inc. assembles and sells electric mixers. All parts are purchased and labor is paid on the basis of $22 per mixer assembled. The cost of the parts per mixer totals $20. As the company handles only this one product, the unit cost basis for applying factory overhead is used. Estimated factory overhead for the coming period, based on a production of 40,000 mixers, is as follows:

Indirect materials	$22,000
Indirect labor	24,000
Light and power	10,000
Depreciation	10,000
Miscellaneous	14,000

During the period, 39,000 mixers were assembled and actual factory overhead was $82,300. These units were completed but not yet transferred to the finished goods storeroom.

Required: (1) Journal entries to record the above information.
(2) The amount of over- or underapplied factory overhead.

8. Entries and Analysis of Factory Overhead. The following factory overhead estimate for actual direct labor hours worked in the month of April applies to the Farro Company:

Estimated factory overhead	$16,750

Overhead is applied on the basis of direct labor hours. On April 30 the following account balances appeared on the books of the company:

Factory Overhead Control	$18,250
Factory Overhead Applied	17,500

Required: (1) The entry or entries to close out the two factory overhead balances and to set up the over- or underapplied factory overhead account.

(2) The spending and idle capacity variances. Explain why they are favorable or unfavorable.

9. Variance Analysis. Factory overhead for the Deckler Company has been estimated as follows:

Fixed factory overhead................................	$15,000
Variable factory overhead............................	45,000
Estimated direct labor hours........................	20,000

Production for the month reached 75% of the budget, and actual factory overhead totaled $43,000.

Required: (1) Over- or underapplied factory overhead.
(2) Spending and idle capacity variances.

10. Level of Activity; Variance Analysis. The Conley Company estimates its normal factory overhead to be $10,000 per month. During the past four months, overhead applied was:

January...............	$9,000	March................	$ 9,500
February..............	8,500	April................	10,500

Required: (1) The level of operations reached in each of these months.
(2) The over- or underapplied overhead each month when actual expenses were as follows: $9,200 in January; $8,900 in February; $8,800 in March; and $10,650 in April.

11. Rate and Variance Analysis. Annual estimated factory overhead of the Van Den Noort Company for an expected volume of 180,000 kilograms of a product was as follows:

Fixed factory overhead............................	$ 72,000
Variable factory overhead.........................	216,000

Output was 10,000 kilograms in June, and actual factory overhead was $15,400.

Required: (1) The total factory overhead rate per unit and the variable factory overhead rate per unit.
(2) The factory overhead variances, in total and in detail.

12. Variance Analysis. A company's budgeted fixed overhead costs are $50,000 per month plus a variable rate of $4 per direct labor hour. The total factory overhead rate is $6. Actual factory overhead in January is $115,000 and 18,000 direct labor hours were reported.

Required: (1) The total amount of budgeted overhead.
(2) The spending variance.
(3) The idle capacity variance.

13. Variance Analysis. The Ludwig-Wallace Products Corporation uses a job order cost system. Factory overhead is applied on a normal capacity basis using direct labor hours. The annual predetermined (or budgeted) factory overhead rate is $2 per hour based on 50,000 normal capacity hours with variable factory overhead at $70,000 and fixed factory overhead at $30,000. Four job cost sheets show the following data for the month of August:

	Job 301	Job 302	Job 303	Job 304
On August 1:				
Materials.	$3,000	$4,800	Started	Started
Labor....	4,500	6,200	during	during
Overhead.	3,000	3,100	August	August
During August:				
Materials.	$1,800	$2,100	$2,900	$ 600
Labor....	3,300 (1,100 hrs.)	1,600 (400 hrs.)	1,200 (400 hrs.)	1,400 (350 hrs.)
Overhead.	?	?	?	?
On August 31:				
	Completed	Completed	In process	In process

Required: (1) The amount of factory overhead applicable to each job for the month of August.

(2) The total amount of over- or underapplied factory overhead for the month of August. Actual factory overhead amounted to $4,725.

(3) An overhead variance analysis, assuming that the monthly fixed overhead is 1/12 of the annual estimate.

PROBLEMS

9-1. Journal Entries; Job Order System. The Connors Manufacturing Company uses a job order cost system. The following data were obtained from the company's cost records as of June 30, 19—:

Job Order No.	Direct Materials	Direct Labor Hours	Direct Labor Cost
1001	$ 6,300	1,300	$ 2,900
1002	13,600	3,700	7,700
1003	14,500	8,200	18,300
1004	5,400	1,500	3,200
1005	8,200	3,200	6,600
1006	3,700	980	2,100

Factory overhead is charged to jobs on the basis of $3 per direct labor hour. Actual overhead for the month totaled $58,000.

During the month of June, the company's first month of operations, Jobs 1001, 1002, 1003, 1004, and 1005 were completed. Jobs 1001 and 1002 were shipped out, and the customers were billed in the amounts of $18,000 and $42,000 respectively.

Required: General journal entries to summarize the transactions for June. Over- or underapplied factory overhead is not closed out until the end of the year.

9-2. Journal Entries for Monthly Transactions.   McDonald, Inc. uses a job order cost system and applies factory overhead on the basis of direct labor hours. The trial balance as of July 1, 19— is:

McDONALD, INC.
Trial Balance, July 1, 19—

Cash...	$ 20,000	
Notes Receivable..............................	10,000	
Accounts Receivable..........................	28,000	
Allowance for Doubtful Accounts..............		$ 2,800
Materials.....................................	15,000	
Work in Process..............................	10,000	
Finished Goods...............................	5,000	
Prepaid Insurance on Machinery...............	500	
Factory Overhead Control.....................	8,500	
Machinery and Equipment......................	75,000	
Accumulated Depreciation—Machinery and Equipment		25,000
Accounts Payable.............................		10,000
Federal Income Tax Payable...................		2,000
Accrued Payroll Taxes........................		900
Capital Stock.................................		100,000
Retained Earnings............................		31,300
Total..	$172,000	$172,000

Transactions for the month of July, 19— were:

(a) Materials purchased on account, $10,000.

(b) Shop supplies purchased on account, $5,000.

(c) Materials requisitioned, $10,000, of which $7,000 was direct materials.

(d) Paid and distributed payroll: direct labor, $15,000; indirect labor, $5,000; federal income tax withheld, $2,000; FICA tax, $600.

(e) Employer factory payroll taxes for the month, $700.

(f) Factory overhead paid: repairs, $75; rent, $300; power and light, $400.

(g) Depreciation of machinery and equipment, $625.

(h) Expired insurance on machinery, $50.

(i) Paid marketing and administrative expenses, $1,100.

(j) Factory overhead applied to production, $9,800.

(k) Inventories at the end of the month: work in process, $9,000; finished goods, $6,000.

(l) Sales on account, $50,000.

Required: General journal entries to record the above transactions using a factory overhead control account to record both actual and applied overhead. This account is not closed until the end of the year.

9-3. Factory Overhead Application to Jobs. The Tucker Company has been in business for only one month. During this month the firm had the following costs, as shown by its books and records:

Materials used..	$10,000
Direct labor...	15,000
Indirect materials used in plant...............................	3,000
Indirect plant labor...	4,000
Supervisors' salaries, plant...................................	3,000
Labor fringe costs, plant......................................	1,500
Depreciation of plant..	1,000
Depreciation of factory machinery	3,000
Taxes on plant...	300
Marketing and administrative expenses..........................	3,500
Insurance on plant...	200
Miscellaneous factory overhead.................................	1,500
Power and light for plant	500
Advertising..	1,500

During the month the company worked on four orders, three of which were completed. Costs and other pertinent data in connection with these orders are:

	Job 501	Job 502	Job 503	Job 504
Materials cost	$2,000	$3,500	$3,000	$1,500
Direct labor hours	4,000	3,000	1,000	1,000
Machine hours...................	1,900	1,500	800	300
Direct labor cost	$6,000	$4,000	$3,000	$2,000

The company has not set up a predetermined rate for applying factory overhead. It intends to wait until the end of each month to charge actual overhead incurred during the month to jobs worked on during that month. Labor pay rates vary considerably among the various labor skills employed in the plant. There is also a wide variation in the proportionate use made of labor skills on each job order.

Required: (1) The cost of each job using as the basis for charging factory overhead: (a) direct labor cost, (b) direct labor hours, (c) machine hours.

(2) The recommended method of applying factory overhead, assuming that costs will remain in the same proportions.

9-4. Factory Overhead Rates and Application. The Cost Department of the Ronde Company made the following estimates for the coming year: factory overhead, $425,000; materials cost, $850,000; production, 20,800 cases; labor cost, $250,000; labor hours, 106,250.

Required: (1) The factory overhead rate based on (a) labor cost, (b) labor hours, and (c) materials cost.

(2) The amount of overhead to be charged to Lot Order 465 by each rate in (1) above. (Lot Order 465: materials cost, $21,000; labor cost, $14,800 for 3,700 hours.)

9-5. Factory Overhead Analysis. The Moser Company's factory overhead rate is $2 per hour. Budgeted overhead for 3,000 hours per month is $8,000 and at 7,000 hours is $12,000. Actual factory overhead for the month is $9,000, and actual volume is 5,000 hours.

Required: (1) Variable overhead in overhead rate.

(2) Budgeted fixed overhead.

(3) Normal volume or normal capacity hours.

(4) Applied factory overhead.

(5) Over- or underabsorbed factory overhead.

(6) Idle capacity variance.

(7) Spending variance.

9-6. Budgeted Overhead and Variance Analysis. In June the idle capacity variance of Carr Processing, Inc. was zero, and the spending variance showed a debit of $6,000. In July the idle capacity variance was a debit of $8,000, but the spending variance was zero. In June, actual overhead expense was $70,000 for an output of 8,000 tons. July's expense was $56,000, and output was 6,000 tons. In August output was 9,000 tons, and actual overhead expense was $71,000.

Required: (1) Factory overhead budgeted (estimated) for 9,000 tons.

(2) Factory overhead applied in August.

(3) Variances for August.

9-7. Variance Analysis. The Dennis Manufacturing Company's factory overhead for the month of May is summarized below.

Normal capacity is used as the activity level for computing the predetermined factory overhead rate.

FACTORY OVERHEAD — MAY
(Actual Activity — 75% of normal)

Expense	Estimated Factory Overhead at 100% (Normal)	Estimated Factory Overhead at 75% of Normal	Actual Factory Overhead
Superintendence.....	$ 415	$ 415	$ 415
Depreciation........	375	375	375
Taxes............ ...	200	200	200
Rent..............	300	300	300
Power.............	100	75	95
Maintenance labor...	200	150	115
Insurance..........	50	50	50
Idle labor.........	100	75	90
Supplies...........	120	90	95
Indirect labor.......	400	300	270
Payroll taxes........	100	75	95
Total.............	$2,360	$2,105	$2,100

Required: (1) The over- or underapplied overhead.

(2) The idle capacity variance.

(3) The spending variance, in total and by individual expenses.

9-8. Inventory Valuation; Overhead Analysis; Statement of Cost of Goods Sold.
The Cost Department of the Mahle Manufacturing Company received the following monthly data, pertaining solely to manufacturing activities, from the general ledger clerk:

Work in process inventory, January 1	$ 32,500
Raw materials inventory, January 1	21,000
Direct labor	130,000
Raw materials purchased	106,000
Raw materials returned to suppliers	5,050
Supervision	18,500
Indirect labor	29,050
Heat, light, and power	8,700
Depreciation — factory buildings	7,500
Property taxes	4,000
Insurance on factory buildings	3,000
Research and development costs (factory overhead)	14,100
Transportation-in (factory overhead)	6,500
Repairs and maintenance — factory equipment	8,250
Depreciation — factory equipment	7,500
Miscellaneous factory overhead	9,900
Finished goods inventory, January 1	18,000
Factory overhead applied	115,200

Additional data:

(a) Physical inventory taken January 31 shows $9,000 of raw materials on hand.

(b) The January 31 work in process inventory and finished goods inventory show the following raw materials and direct labor contents:

	Direct Materials	Direct Labor
Work in process	$ 9,000	$ 8,000 (= 2,000 hrs.)
Finished goods	10,000	20,000 (= 5,000 hrs.)

(c) Factory overhead is applied to these two ending inventories on the basis of a factory overhead rate of $3.60 per direct labor hour.

Required: (1) The cost assigned to the ending work in process and finished goods inventories, including factory overhead.

(2) A schedule of the total actual factory overhead for the month.

(3) An analysis of the over- or underapplied factory overhead, assuming that the predetermined factory overhead rate was based on the following data:

Variable factory overhead	$70,875
Fixed factory overhead	$42,525
Direct labor hours	31,500

(4) A detailed cost of goods sold statement, assuming over- or underapplied overhead is closed to the cost of goods sold account.

CHAPTER **10**

DEPARTMENTALIZATION OF FACTORY OVERHEAD FOR PRODUCT COSTING AND COST CONTROL

The preceding chapter discussed the establishment and use of one factory-wide predetermined overhead rate, the accumulation of actual factory overhead in books and records, and the analysis of the over- or underapplied factory overhead. These phases are now expanded through the use of predetermined *departmental* factory overhead rates to improve the charging of overhead to jobs and products, to lead to cost control via responsibility accounting, and to provide data useful for analytical and decision-making processes. Methods for the control of materials and labor costs are discussed in other chapters. However, because each product manufactured requires a certain minimum amount of materials and labor, there is a limit to the amount of cost reduction for materials and labor which can be realized through the use of such controls. The situation is different for factory overhead; the tighter the control over such expenses, the better the possibility for reducing them. The departmentalization of factory overhead facilitates this responsibility control which is so necessary if unit and total costs are to stay within predetermined or budgeted ranges.

The departmentalization of overhead costs in nonmanufacturing businesses and in nonprofit organizations is also discussed in this chapter.

THE CONCEPT OF DEPARTMENTALIZATION

Departmentalization of factory overhead means dividing the plant into segments called "departments" or "cost centers" to which expenses are charged. Accountingwise, the main reasons for dividing a plant into separate departments are: (1) more accurate costing of jobs and products and (2) responsible control of overhead costs.

More accurate costing of jobs and products is possible because departmentalization uses different departmental overhead rates for applying factory overhead. A job or product going through a department is charged with factory overhead for work done in that department, using the department's predetermined rate. Therefore, jobs or products are charged with varying amounts of factory overhead depending on the type and number of departments through which they pass rather than being charged with a single plant-wide overhead rate.

Responsible control of overhead costs is possible because departmentalization makes the incurrence of expenses the responsibility of a foreman or supervisor. Expenses which originate directly and completely in a department are identified with the foreman responsible for the supervision of the department.

Computation of predetermined overhead rates requires a series of departmental allocation processes with respect to estimated expenses. These allocations are limited to those necessary for computing overhead rates prior to the beginning of the fiscal period. Actual overhead accumulated during the month or year should remain with the individual department until the end of the accounting period.

Computing complete product costs for pricing purposes involves recognizing all manufacturing costs regardless of their direct or indirect relationship to a given department or product. In addition to its direct costs, each product must bear an equitable share of indirect costs such as utilities, materials handling, inspection, storage, general factory, etc. The selection of the best overhead allocation methods is important in determining equitable product costs.

The entire process of departmentalizing factory overhead is an extension of methods previously discussed. Estimating or budgeting expenses and selecting a proper basis for applying them is still necessary; but, in addition, departmentalizing overhead requires separate estimates or budgets for each department. Actual expenses of a period must still be collected through use of a factory overhead control account and a factory overhead subsidiary ledger, but by departments, as well as by the nature of the expense, to permit comparison with departmentally applied factory overhead. Over- or underapplied factory overhead is computed departmentally and analyzed separately to determine departmental spending and idle capacity variances.

PRODUCING AND SERVICE DEPARTMENTS

Departments are classified as either producing or service departments. For example:

PRODUCING		**SERVICE**	
Cutting	Mill Room	Utilities	Shipping
Planing	Plating	Materials Handling	Medical
Assembly	Knitting	Inspection	Production Control
Upholstery	Mixing	Storage	Personnel
Finishing	Refining	Plant Protection	Maintenance
Machining		Purchasing	Cafeteria
		Receiving	General Factory

A *producing department* is one that engages in the actual manufacture of the product by changing the shape, form, or nature of the material worked upon, or by assembling the parts into a finished article. A *service department* is one rendering a service that contributes in an indirect manner to the manufacture of the product but which does not itself change the shape, form, or nature of the material that is converted into the finished product.

SELECTION OF PRODUCING DEPARTMENTS

A manufacturing company is usually organized along departmental lines for production purposes. Manufacturing processes dictate the type of organization needed: (1) to handle the different operations efficiently, (2) to obtain the best production flow, and (3) to establish responsibility for physical control of production.

The cost information system is designed to fit the departmentalization required for production purposes. The system accumulates manufacturing costs according to such departmentalization whether operations are of the job type or continuous process type. Factors to be considered in deciding the kinds of departments required to control costs and to establish accurate departmental overhead rates are:

1. Similarity of operations, processes, and machinery in each department
2. Location of operations, processes, and machinery
3. Responsibilities for production and costs
4. Relationship of operations to flow of product
5. Number of departments or cost centers

The establishment of producing departments for the purpose of costing and controlling expenses is a problem for the management of every company. No hard and fast rules can be given. The approach most commonly taken divides the factory along lines of functional activities with each activity or group of activities constituting a department. Division of the factory into separate, interrelated, and independently governed units is important for the proper control of factory overhead and the accurate costing of jobs and products.

The number of producing departments used depends on the emphasis the cost system puts on cost control and the development of overhead rates. If the emphasis is on cost control, separate departments might be established for the plant manager and for each superintendent, supervisor, and foreman. When the development of departmental overhead rates emphasizes accurate costing, fewer departments might be used. Sometimes the number of departments needed for cost control is larger than that needed for overhead rates. In such cases, the cost control system can be adapted to proper overhead rates by combining departments, thus reducing the number of rates used without sacrificing control of costs.

In certain instances, particularly when different types of machines are used, departments are further subdivided for cost control and overhead rate purposes, resulting in a refinement in overhead control and in application to the jobs or products passing through a department.

SELECTION OF SERVICE DEPARTMENTS

The selection and designation of service departments has considerable bearing on effective costing and control. Services available for the benefit of producing departments and other service departments can be organized in several ways by (1) establishing a separate service department for each function, (2) combining several functions into one department, and (3) placing service costs in a department called "general factory." The specific service is not identified if service costs applicable to producing and service functions are accumulated in a general factory department.

Determination of the kinds and number of service departments should consider: (1) number of employees needed for each service function, (2) cost of providing the service, (3) importance of the service, and (4) assignment of supervisory responsibility. Establishing a separate department for every service function is rarely done even in large companies. When relatively few employees are involved and activities are closely related, service functions are generally combined for the sake of economy and expediency. Decision with respect to combining service functions is governed by the individual circumstances existing in each company. Since factory overhead rates for job and product costing are calculated for producing departments only, service department expenses are transferred to producing departments for rate-setting and variance analysis.

DIRECT DEPARTMENTAL OVERHEAD IN PRODUCING AND SERVICE DEPARTMENTS

The majority of direct departmental overhead costs can be categorized as follows:

1. Supervision, indirect labor, and overtime
2. Labor fringe benefits
3. Indirect materials and factory supplies
4. Repairs and maintenance
5. Equipment depreciation

These expense categories are generally readily identified with the originating department, whether producing or service. In the discussion that follows, detailed attention is given to each of the categories of direct departmental overhead costs.

Supervision, Indirect Labor, and Overtime. These factory labor categories, in contrast to direct labor, do not alter the shape or content of a product; they are auxiliary to its manufacture. It is important to realize that any factory labor not classified as direct labor is automatically classified as factory overhead.

Inasmuch as overhead is allocated to all products, a lax or incorrect classification results in direct labor applying to only one product being allocated as indirect labor in the form of overhead to other products, thereby understating the one product cost and overstating the others. Thus, decisions on whether or not to classify costs as direct labor can have an important effect on overhead rates. Direct labor cost is often used as the base for determining overhead rates. In such a case, a decision to classify certain labor as "indirect" reduces the denominator and increases the numerator of the ratio $\left(\frac{\text{Factory Overhead}}{\text{Direct Labor Cost}}\right)$ used to compute overhead rates. The following illustration points out the possible effect of incorrect identification of $1,000 of direct labor as indirect labor:

	Correctly Identified as Direct Labor	*Incorrectly Identified as Indirect Labor*
Direct labor..........................	$6,000	$5,000
Factory overhead:		
Indirect labor.......................	$5,000	$6,000
Other overhead......................	1,000	1,000
Total factory overhead.................	$6,000	$7,000
Factory Overhead Rates $= \dfrac{\text{Factory Overhead}}{\text{Direct Labor Cost}} =$	$\dfrac{\$6,000}{\$6,000}$	$\dfrac{\$7,000}{\$5,000}$
	= 100%	= 140%

The premium portion of overtime paid should generally be charged as overhead to the departments in which the overtime occurred. This method should be followed for all labor except for special cases discussed in the labor chapters. However, the straight-time portion of overtime paid to direct labor employees should be charged to direct labor.

Labor Fringe Benefits. Labor fringe benefits include such costs as: vacation and holiday pay, FICA taxes, state and federal unemployment taxes, workmen's compensation insurance, pension costs, hospitalization benefits, and group insurance. In theory, these labor fringe benefits are additional labor costs and should — when they pertain to direct labor employees — be added to the direct labor cost. In practice, such a procedure is usually impractical; therefore, these costs that pertain to direct factory workers are generally included in factory overhead and thereby become part of the factory overhead rate.

Indirect Materials and Factory Supplies. Distinguishing incorrectly between direct and indirect materials (the latter being part of overhead) has the same adverse effects on product costing as failure to make proper distinction between direct and indirect labor. However, distinguishing between direct and indirect materials is usually not so difficult. In a manufacturing operation, direct materials are those which are changed in form through processing, machining, etc., and become an integral part of the end product. Indirect materials, often referred to as factory supplies, are auxiliary to the processing or machining operations and do not become an essential part of the end product.

There are two basic methods of accounting for the cost of supplies: (1) as a direct departmental charge or (2) as a charge to inventories.

Direct Departmental Charge. An easy, though not the most efficient, way to account for factory supplies is to charge the expense to the department that originated the purchase request. This procedure assumes that (1) the department supervisor has the authority to purchase and (2) the cost of the purchase stays within departmental budget limits.

Charge to Inventories. When closer control of supplies is required or when more than one department uses certain supplies, it is not practical or correct to charge only one department at the time of purchase. In such cases, supplies purchased are charged to an inventory account at the time of purchase; and departments using the supplies are charged when supplies are issued.

When an inventory account is used, consumption may be determined by one of two methods. First, if the supply is used only in one department, it is possible to determine the amount to be charged to that department by

(1) taking a physical inventory at the end of each month, (2) adding purchases for the month to the cost of the beginning inventory, and (3) subtracting the final cost assigned to physical inventory at month-end from this total to determine the usage for the month.

A second method of accounting for the cost of supplies through an inventory account involves the use of materials requisitions. Requisitions approved by authorized employees permit charging a department with the proper cost and thereby provide better control over the use of materials than the physical inventory method. However, additional clerical work is required since requisitions must be prepared, priced, and summarized.

Repairs and Maintenance. With respect to repairs and maintenance costs, it is essential (1) to establish control over the total cost incurred by the repairs and maintenance department and (2) to devise effective means for charging maintenance costs to departments receiving the service.

As a rule, the work of repair and maintenance crews is supervised by a maintenance superintendent. If possible and practical, all actual maintenance costs should be charged to a maintenance department so that the total cost is controlled by the maintenance superintendent and kept within a maintenance budget. However, since maintenance is a service function, its costs must be distributed to departments that receive the service.

Maintenance work performed for most departments is generally of a recurring nature, and charges are incurred evenly throughout the year. However, certain types of maintenance work, such as breakdowns and overhauls, occur at irregular intervals and often involve large expenditures. In such cases, companies using departmental budgets may spread the cost of major repairs over the year by making monthly charges to operations based on a predetermined rate. These rates are commonly derived from previous years' experience. Monthly provisions are charged to Maintenance Expense and credited to a reserve account. Actual repair costs are charged to the reserve account. In this manner, large maintenance costs are charged to operations in direct proportion to the operating rate and presumably approximate actual deterioration of the equipment.

Equipment Depreciation. Depreciation is usually a cost not controllable by departmental foremen. However, their use of equipment influences maintenance and depreciation costs. This is true with respect to all types of depreciable assets — machinery and equipment, buildings, vehicles, furniture and fixtures, etc. Some firms show depreciation as a noncontrollable cost on departmental cost statements. For effective costing and controlling, depreciation is usually identified with the departments using the assets; and the cost is charged directly to departments. The recommended method is to compute depreciation by departments based on the cost of equipment in the departments as recorded on detailed fixed asset records. When no records are available or equipment is not specifically used by only one department, depreciation is frequently charged to general plant expense.

INDIRECT DEPARTMENTAL CHARGES

Expenses such as power, light, rent, and depreciation of factory, when shared by all departments, can understandably not be charged directly to a department, be it producing or service. These expenses do not originate with any specific departments. They are incurred for all to use and must, therefore, be prorated to any or all departments using them. The selection of fair bases for such distributions requires careful study.

Selecting appropriate bases for the distribution of these general factory costs is difficult and, in some instances, rests on an arbitrary decision. To charge every department with its fair share of an expense, like rent, a basis using some factor common to all departments must be found. Square footage is such a basis, and in many cases is used for prorating rent expense. In plants with departments occupying parts of the factory with ceilings of unequal height, cubic measurement rather than square footage might be used. Areas occupied by stairways, elevators, escalators, corridors, aisles, and so forth must also be considered. Some of the general factory expenses that require prorating, together with the bases most commonly used, are:

GENERAL FACTORY EXPENSES	DISTRIBUTION BASIS
Factory rent	Square footage
Depreciation — buildings	Square footage
Building repairs	Square footage
Heat	Square footage
Superintendence	Number of employees
Telephone and telegraph	Number of employees or number of telephones
Workmen's compensation insurance	Department payroll
Light	Kilowatt-hours
Freight-in	Materials used
Power	Horsepower-hours

After the distribution bases have been selected, a survey of the factory must be made to secure the information needed to permit the distribution. Information such as total square footage and its breakdown by departments, number of employees in each department, investment in machinery by departments, and estimates of kilowatt-hours (kwh) and horsepower-hours (hph) to be used are items listed in the survey.

PRORATION OF SERVICE DEPARTMENTS' OVERHEAD TO BENEFITING DEPARTMENTS

The expenses of service departments must ultimately be transferred to producing departments to establish predetermined factory overhead rates and to analyze variances. Effective expense control dictates that each service department be first charged with its direct overhead. Service departments may also be charged with general factory expenses as well as with costs from other service departments. Most of the overhead items discussed for producing departments will naturally also be found in service departments. The number and types of service departments in a company depend on its operations and the degree of expense control desired. Service departments used for illustrative purposes are: (1) materials handling, (2) inspection, (3) utilities, and (4) general plant services.

Materials Handling. Materials handling involves the operation of cranes, trucks, fork lifts, loaders, etc. Since many departments are served by this function, a preferred method of organization establishes a separate service department for materials handling activities. All handling costs are charged to this department, and a foreman is made responsible for their control. Costs charged to such a service department are the same as those charged to any department and include wages and labor fringe costs of crane and truck operators; supplies, such as batteries, gasoline, etc.; and repairs and maintenance of the equipment. In addition to centralizing responsibility for materials handling operations, departmentalization has the advantage of collecting all materials handling costs in one place — thus permitting quick measurement of results and reduction of costs through modern materials handling techniques and equipment, changes in routing or production, etc.

Inspection. For cost control, inspection costs are treated in the same manner as other service department costs. However, in certain instances, a special work order may require additional inspection or testing. This type of inspection cost is chargeable to the order and must be so identified. To accumulate these specific charges, separate cost centers may be established for the purpose of charging time and materials for special inspections.

Utilities. Power and fuel are consumed for two major purposes: for operating manufacturing facilities such as machines, electric welding, and cranes, and for what might be termed "working condition" purposes — lighting, cooling, and heating. In most instances, a single billing is received for electric power or natural gas. It is not possible to determine directly the consumption for each of the above purposes — to say nothing of the consumption by specific departments, cost centers, or functions.

However, a direct departmental allocation is often desirable and also possible. A common method used is to install separate meters to measure power or fuel consumed by specific types of equipment. In other instances separate power sources (fuel, natural gas, coal, or electricity) may be used for different facilities or equipment making it possible to determine an individual utility cost by department.

For purposes of departmental and product costing, two methods of accounting for costs of utilities are recommended:

1. Charge all power and fuel costs to a separate utilities department; then allocate to benefiting departments.
2. Charge specific departments with power or fuel cost if separate meters are provided, and charge the remaining power and fuel costs to a separate utilities department or to general plant; this remainder is then allocated to benefiting departments.

Allocation of utilities costs to specific departments is based on special studies that determine each department's horsepower of machines, number of machines, etc.

General Plant Services. Certain expenses other than those discussed above come under the category "general plant" because they cannot be identified directly with any specific producing or service department. Therefore, a separate general plant cost center or department is established to accumulate and control such expenses. Such a department is usually the direct responsibility of the plant superintendent. Salaries of management personnel directly concerned with production are charged to this department if they cannot be charged to specific departments except by arbitrary allocations. Janitor labor and supplies may be charged to general plant unless charged to maintenance or to a department called "building occupancy." Unless separate service departments for plant protection and yard operation are established, these costs are also charged to general plant expense. Real estate and personal property taxes, liability, fire, and use and occupancy insurance might be charged to general plant when they cannot be traced directly to a department.

ESTABLISHING DEPARTMENTAL OVERHEAD RATES

Factory overhead is usually applied on the basis of direct labor dollars or hours when one factory overhead rate is used for the entire plant, since this procedure is considered most convenient and acceptable. The use of department rates requires a distinct consideration of each producing department's overhead which often results in the use of different bases for applying overhead for different departments. For example, it is possible to use a direct labor hour rate for one department and a machine hour rate for another. A further refinement might possibly lead to different bases and rates for cost centers within the same producing department.

In establishing departmental overhead rates for producing departments, all factory overhead, whether of general nature or of service departments, must eventually find its way into the producing departments. Overhead chargeable directly to a producing or service department can be obtained from past records or from new or revised estimates prepared by the budget or cost department in consultation with the department head. General factory expenses, such as heat, power, water, rent, etc., must first be allocated to either producing and service departments or perhaps merely to producing departments. The method depends upon management's decision. Service departments costs should then be distributed equitably to either producing departments and service departments or just to producing departments. The distribution might be based on number of employees, kwh consumption, hph consumption, floor space, asset value, cost of materials to be requisitioned, etc. After service department expenses have been distributed, producing department overhead rates can be calculated in terms of direct labor hours, direct labor costs, machine hours, or some other appropriate basis.

At the end of the fiscal period actual costs of producing and service departments as well as those of general indirect nature are again assembled in the same manner as for estimated factory overhead at the beginning of the year. When all overhead has been assembled in the producing departments, it is then possible to compare actual with applied overhead and to determine the over- or underapplied factory overhead.

ILLUSTRATION FOR ESTABLISHING DEPARTMENTAL OVERHEAD RATES

The illustration uses four producing departments: Cutting, Planing, Assembly, and Upholstery; and four service departments: Materials Handling, Inspection, Utilities, and General Plant. The total estimated factory overhead prepared in Chapter 9, page 223, has now been departmentalized, but under the account classification described above and with a slight modification of figures for ease in calculating departmental rates. The fixed-variable cost classification has been retained. Its purpose will be explained on pages 268 and 269.

The establishment of predetermined factory overhead rates for departmentalized factory operations proceeds in the following manner:

1. Estimate or budget total direct factory overhead of producing and service departments at the selected activity levels. Determine, if possible, the fixed (F) and variable (V) nature of each expense category. (See Exhibit 1.)

PROCTOR PRODUCTS, INC.
Estimated Departmental Factory Overhead
For the Year 19—

COST ACCOUNTS	F or V	TOTAL	PRODUCING DEPARTMENTS				SERVICE DEPARTMENTS			
			Cutting	Planing	Assembly	Upholstery	Materials Handling	Inspection	Utilities	General Plant
Direct departmental expenses:										
Supervisors and foremen	F	$70,000	$9,000	$8,000	$8,000	$8,000	$10,000	$6,000	$9,000	$12,000
Indirect labor	F	9,000	1,000	2,000	1,000	1,500	1,000	500	1,000	1,000
	V	66,000	9,000	3,000	5,000	5,500	11,000	8,500	10,000	14,000
Labor fringe costs	F	10,000	1,500	1,000	1,000	1,000	2,000	1,000	1,500	1,000
	V	47,000	10,500	11,800	9,400	8,200	1,800	1,400	1,900	2,000
Indirect materials	F	4,000	500	500	800	1,200	300	200	200	300
	V	19,000	2,500	2,500	3,200	4,800	1,700	800	1,800	1,700
Repairs and maintenance	F	3,000	600	500	700	600			300	300
	V	9,000	1,400	1,500	1,300	1,800	500	200	1,700	600
Depreciation — equipment	F	13,000	1,500	3,500	1,000	3,000				4,000
Total direct departmental expenses		$250,000	$37,500	$34,300	$31,400	$35,600	$28,300	$18,600	$27,400	$36,900
Indirect departmental expenses:										
Electric power	F	$ 2,000							$ 2,000	
	V	20,000							20,000	
Fuel	F	1,000							1,000	
	V	10,000							10,000	
Water	F	1,000							1,000	
	V	4,000							4,000	
Depreciation — buildings	F	5,000	$ 1,250	$ 1,000	$ 1,500	$ 1,250				
Taxes — property	F	4,000	1,000	800	1,200	1,000				
Insurance — fire	F	3,000	750	600	900	750				
Total indirect departmental expenses		$ 50,000	$ 3,000	$ 2,400	$ 3,600	$ 3,000			$38,000	
Total departmental factory overhead		$300,000	$40,500	$36,700	$35,000	$38,600	$28,300	$18,600	$65,400	$36,900
Total fixed factory overhead		$125,000	$17,100	$17,900	$16,100	$18,300	$13,300	$ 7,700	$16,000	$18,600
Total variable factory overhead		$175,000	$23,400	$18,800	$18,900	$20,300	$15,000	$10,900	$49,400	$18,300

Exhibit 1

PROCTOR PRODUCTS, INC.

FACTORY SURVEY PREPARED AT THE BEGINNING OF THE YEAR

Producing Departments	Number of Employees	%	Kilo-watt-Hours	%	Horse-power-Hours	%	Floor Area (sq. ft.)	%	Cost of Materials Requisitioned	%
Cutting......	30	20	12,800	20	200,000	40	5,250	25	$180,000	45
Planing......	25	17	6,400	10	120,000	24	4,200	20	40,000	10
Assembly....	45	30	19,200	30	80,000	16	6,300	30	40,000	10
Upholstery...	50	33	25,600	40	100,000	20	5,250	25	140,000	35
Total.......	150	100	64,000	100	500,000	100	21,000	100	$400,000	100

Schedule A

2. Prepare a factory survey for the purpose of distributing indirect factory overhead and service department costs. (See Schedule A above.)
3. Estimate or budget total indirect factory overhead such as electric power, fuel, water, building depreciation, property taxes, and fire insurance at the selected activity levels. Decide upon appropriate allocation methods and allocate. (See Exhibit 1 and Schedule A.)
4. Distribute service department costs. (See Exhibit 2 on page 260.)
5. Calculate departmental factory overhead rates. (See Exhibit 2.)

Estimating or budgeting the direct expenses of producing and service departments is a joint undertaking of department heads, supervisors, or foremen and members of the budget or cost department of the company. Labor fringe costs are calculated by the office personnel since the individual supervisor has little influence or knowledge with respect to the underlying rates and figures. Costs of indirect labor and indirect materials are of greater interest to the foreman. Repairs and maintenance costs are often disputed items unless a definite maintenance program has been agreed upon. Departmental depreciation charges are based on management's decision regarding depreciation methods and rates. In the illustration, depreciation of equipment is charged directly to the departments on the basis of asset values and rates set by the controller. Overhead costs not directly chargeable to a department are collected in General Plant. The plant manager, working with budget personnel, estimates and supervises these costs.

Before service department expenses can be prorated to benefiting and ultimately to producing departments, certain underlying data must be obtained. A survey of factory facilities and records usually produces the information needed, such as rated horsepower of equipment in each department, estimated kwh consumption, number of employees in each department, estimated payroll costs, square footage, estimated materials

PROCTOR PRODUCTS, INC.

DISTRIBUTION OF ESTIMATED SERVICE DEPARTMENT COSTS

AND

CALCULATION OF DEPARTMENTAL FACTORY OVERHEAD RATES

FOR THE YEAR 19—

COST ACCOUNTS	TOTAL	PRODUCING DEPARTMENTS				SERVICE DEPARTMENTS			
		Cutting	Planing	Assembly	Upholstery	Materials Handling	Inspection	Utilities	General Plant
Total departmental factory overhead before distribution of service depts......	$300,000	$40,500	$36,700	$35,000	$38,600	$28,300	$18,600	$65,400	$36,900
Distribution of service departments costs:									
Materials handling........... (Base: estimated cost of materials requisitioned)		$12,735	$ 2,830	$ 2,830	$ 9,905	(28,300)			
Inspection................. (Base: equally to assembly and upholstery departments)				9,300	9,300		(18,600)		
Utilities:									
(Bases: 20% on kwh.......		2,616	1,308	3,924	5,232			(13,080)	
50% on hph.........		13,080	7,848	5,232	6,540			(32,700)	
30% on floor area).......		4,905	3,924	5,886	4,905			(19,620)	
General plant............. (Base: number of employees)		7,380	6,273	11,070	12,177				(36,900)
Total service depts. costs distributed....		$40,716	$22,183	$ 38,242	$48,059				
Total departmental factory overhead after distribution of service depts.........	$300,000	$81,216	$58,883	$ 73,242	$86,659				
Bases:									
Direct labor hours.........		40,608		48,140					
Machine hours...........			18,400						
Direct labor cost.........				$122,000					
Rates.................		$2.00 per direct labor hour	$3.20 per machine hour	60% of direct labor cost	$1.80 per direct labor hour				

Exhibit 2

consumption, asset values, etc. Functions performed by each service department must be studied carefully to determine the most equitable basis for distributing the expenses of each.

Indirect departmental expenses are prorated in two ways: electric power, fuel, and water are charged to Utilities from where a distribution is made; depreciation of building, property taxes, and fire insurance are prorated only to producing departments on the basis of floor area as shown in the Factory Survey (Schedule A); i.e., 25 percent of $5,000 = $1,250 charged to the Cutting Department for building depreciation. However, as an alternative, these costs could also be allocated to service departments as well as to producing departments.

Certain rules are followed for the transfer of service department overhead to benefiting departments. One rule states that service department expenses should be transferred on the basis of the use made by producing and other service departments of the respective services. In order to use this rule, a decision must be made with respect to the service department which should be closed first, for service from a service department is received not only by producing departments but also by other service departments. Thus, instead of closing all service department overhead directly to producing departments, some overhead may first be charged to other service departments or to general factory overhead. In some companies (as illustrated in Exhibit 2), service department expenses are transferred only to producing departments. This procedure avoids much clerical work. It can be justified if no material difference in the final costs of a producing department results when the expenses of a service department are not prorated to other service departments or to general plant. However, this procedure fails to measure the *total* cost for individual service departments.

When following the rule stating that service department expenses should be transferred on the basis of the use made of the respective services by all benefiting departments, both producing and service, the usual procedure is to transfer expenses of service departments in the order of the amount of service rendered by the departments; i.e., expenses of the department rendering the greatest amount of service are transferred first.

When service rendered by a department cannot be determined accurately, it is possible to distribute first the expenses of the service department which has the largest total overhead. This rule assumes that the department with the largest amount of expense rendered the greatest amount of service. Whether the amount of service or the amount of expense determines the order of distribution, once costs for a service department are distributed, that department is considered closed and no further distributions are made to it.

Since the illustration shows no transfer of service department costs to other service departments, the order of distribution does not matter. The distribution is made by starting with Materials Handling. The overhead of this department is distributed on the basis of the estimated cost of materials requisitioned per Schedule A; i.e., 45 percent of $28,300 = $12,735 to the Cutting Department.

Inspection costs are transferred to the producing departments Assembly and Upholstery only, on a 50-50 basis, because these two departments are the only ones receiving this type of service in equal amounts.

Utilities costs are transferred in a threefold manner: 20 percent of the costs based on kilowatt-hours, 50 percent on horsepower-hours, and 30 percent on floor area. The amount of $13,080 represents 20 percent of $65,400, the total costs of the department. According to Schedule A, 20 percent of $13,080 = $2,616 is distributed to the Cutting Department. The same method is followed for the other costs and departments. General Plant is distributed on the basis of number of employees; i.e., 20 percent of $36,900 = $7,380 to the Cutting Department.

The distribution of these service department costs is based on percentages in the Factory Survey, page 259. Some accountants proceed in a different manner; they calculate a rate per square foot, or per kwh, or per employee. In connection with General Plant, the method can be illustrated as follows:

$$\frac{\$36,900 \text{ General Plant Costs}}{150 \text{ Employees}} = \$246 \text{ per Employee}$$

Then $246 × 30 employees in the Cutting Department = $7,380.

With all service department costs distributed to the producing departments, the departmental factory overhead rates can be calculated. In Exhibit 2, three different bases are used: direct labor hours, machine hours, and direct labor cost.

ALGEBRAIC METHOD FOR OVERHEAD DISTRIBUTION

The proration of service department expenses to other service departments may be incomplete if a department provides service to a department from which it receives service. Consider a case in which Service Department Y provides service to Service Department Z and, in turn, Z renders service to Y. The incompleteness in proration arises because, using the rules discussed earlier, one department would be closed out before the other and therefore before receiving any expense proration from the other.

If greater exactness is desired, the technique illustrated below can be followed.[1]

Department	Departmental Overhead Before Distribution of Service Departments	Services Provided	
		Dept. Y	Dept. Z
Producing — A	$ 6,000	40%	20%
Producing — B	8,000	40	50
Service — Y	3,630	—	30
Service — Z	2,000	20	—
Total departmental overhead..........	$19,630	100%	100%

Cost allocation by algebra:

Let: $Y = \$3,630 + .30\ Z$
            $Z = \$2,000 + .20\ Y$

Substituting: $Y = \$3,630 + .30\ (\$2,000 + .20Y)$

Solving: $Y = \$3,630 + \$600 + .06Y$
            $.94Y = \$4,230$
            $Y = \$4,500$

Substituting: $Z - \$2,000 + .20\ (\$4,500) - \$2,000 + \$900 = \$2,900$

Distribution of Factory Overhead	Producing Departments		Service Departments		Total
	A	B	Y	Z	
Departmental overhead before distribution of service departments	$ 6,000	$ 8,000	$3,630	$2,000	$19,630
Distribution of:					
Department Y...............	1,800	1,800	(4,500)	900	
Department Z...............	580	1,450	870	(2,900)	
Total departmental overhead.....	$ 8,380	$11,250			$19,630

ACTUAL FACTORY OVERHEAD—DEPARTMENTALIZED

Actual factory overhead is summarized in the factory overhead control account in the general ledger. Details are entered in the factory overhead subsidiary ledger. Departmentalization of actual factory overhead involves the detailed adaptation of previously outlined procedures for handling actual factory overhead. The extra detail can become quite extensive and unduly burdensome unless care is taken to organize the flow of work efficiently.

---

[1]This illustration uses an algebraic method.   Matrix algebra can also be used.   See Thomas H. Williams and Charles H. Griffin, "Matrix Theory and Cost Allocation," *The Accounting Review*, Vol. XXXIX, No. 3, pp. 671–678 and John L. Livingstone, "Matrix Algebra and Cost Allocation," *The Accounting Review*, Vol. XLIII, No. 3, pp. 503–508.

PROCTOR PRODUCTS, INC.
Actual Departmental Factory Overhead
For the Year 19—

COST ACCOUNTS	F or V	TOTAL	PRODUCING DEPARTMENTS				SERVICE DEPARTMENTS			
			Cutting	Planing	Assembly	Upholstery	Materials Handling	Inspection	Utilities	General Plant
Direct departmental expenses:										
Supervisors and foremen	F	$ 70,000	$ 9,000	$ 8,000	$ 8,000	$ 8,000	$10,000	$ 6,000	$ 9,000	$12,000
		9,000	1,000	2,000	1,000	1,500	1,000	500	1,000	1,000
Indirect labor	F	63,000	9,800	2,800	4,200	6,000	10,000	7,300	9,000	13,900
		10,000	1,500	1,000	1,000	1,000	2,000	1,000	1,500	1,000
Labor fringe costs	V	45,000	10,000	11,400	9,700	8,000	1,700	1,300	1,600	1,300
		4,000	500	500	800	1,200	300	200	200	300
Indirect materials	F	23,000	4,300	3,600	2,900	5,400	1,800	1,200	2,100	1,700
		3,000	600	500	700	600			300	300
Repairs and maintenance	V	12,000	1,700	1,800	2,000	2,100	600	300	2,500	1,000
Depreciation — equipment	F	13,000	1,500	3,500	1,000	3,000				4,000
Total direct departmental expenses		$252,000	$39,900	$35,100	$31,300	$36,800	$27,400	$17,800	$27,200	$36,500
Indirect departmental expenses:										
Electric power	F	$ 2,000							$ 2,000	
	V	14,000							14,000	
Fuel	F	1,000							1,000	
	V	7,000							7,000	
Water	F	1,000							1,000	
	V	3,000							3,000	
Depreciation — buildings	F	5,000	$ 1,250	$ 1,000	$ 1,500	$ 1,250				
Taxes — property	F	4,000	1,000	800	1,200	1,000				
Insurance — fire	F	3,000	750	600	900	750				
Total indirect departmental expenses		$ 40,000	$ 3,000	$ 2,400	$ 3,600	$ 3,000			$28,000	
Total *actual* departmental factory overhead before distribution of service departments		$292,000	$42,900	$37,500	$34,900	$39,800	$27,400	$17,800	$55,200	$36,500

Exhibit 3

DEPARTMENTAL EXPENSE ANALYSIS SHEET

Department No.   1--Cutting   For   March, 19--

Explanation	Date	411	412	413	421	433	451	453	Summary

Departmental Expense Analysis Sheet

Departmental Expense Analysis Sheets. Departmentalization of factory overhead requires that each expense be charged to a department as well as to a specific expense account. Such charges are collected on departmental expense analysis sheets. This form, used for both producing and service departments, is partially reproduced above.

In this form, each column represents a certain class of factory overhead that will be charged to the department. For example, the column coded 411 represents supervisors and foremen, 412 represents indirect labor, and so forth. Entries to departmental expense analysis sheets are facilitated by combining department numbers and expense codes. A code such as 1412 indicates that Department No. 1 (Cutting) is charged with indirect labor (Code 412). Similar combinations are used for other departments. The chart of accounts establishes the codes.

The subsidiary ledger must also include a sheet for each indirect factory expense not originally charged to a department so that the total of the subsidiary overhead ledger will equal the total in the factory overhead control account.

Steps and Procedures at End of Fiscal Period. The steps and procedures at the end of the fiscal period are:

1. Prepare a summary of the actual direct departmental factory overhead of producing and service departments. (See Exhibit 3.)
2. Prepare a second factory survey based on the actual data experienced during the year. (See Schedule B.)
3. Allocate actual indirect factory overhead to producing and service departments based on the results of the factory survey at the end of the year. (See Exhibit 3 and Schedule B.)
4. Distribute actual service department costs on the basis of the end-of-the-year factory survey. (See Schedule B and Exhibit 4 on the following pages.)
5. Compare actual total and departmental factory overhead with the total and departmental factory overhead applied to jobs and products during the year, and determine the total and departmental over- or underapplied factory overhead. (See Exhibit 4.)

PROCTOR PRODUCTS, INC.

DISTRIBUTION OF ACTUAL SERVICE DEPARTMENT COSTS
AND
COMPUTATION OF DEPARTMENTAL OVER- OR UNDERAPPLIED FACTORY OVERHEAD
FOR THE YEAR 19—

COST ACCOUNTS	TOTAL	PRODUCING DEPARTMENTS				SERVICE DEPARTMENTS			
		Cutting	Planing	Assembly	Upholstery	Materials Handling	Inspection	Utilities	General Plant
Total actual departmental factory overhead before distribution of service departments.........	$292,000	$42,900	$37,500	$34,900	$39,800	$27,400	$17,800	$55,200	$36,500
Distribution of service department costs:									
Materials handling........... (Base: actual cost of materials requisitioned)		$12,330	$ 2,740	$ 3,014	$ 9,316	(27,400)			
Inspection............... (Base: equally to assembly and upholstery departments)				8,900	8,900		(17,800)		
Utilities: (Bases: 20% on kwh........ 50% on hph........ 30% on floor area)......		2,870 11,592 4,140	883 6,072 3,312	2,760 4,968 4,968	4,527 4,968 4,140			(11,040) (27,600) (16,560)	
General plant............ (Base: number of employees)		8,760	6,205	10,220	11,315				(36,500)
Total service departments costs distributed...........		$39,692	$19,212	$34,830	$43,166				
Total actual departmental factory overhead after distribution of the service departments..........	$292,000	$82,592	$56,712	$69,730	$82,966				
Total *applied* factory overhead.........	285,000	84,020	54,400	67,020	79,560				
(Over-) or underapplied factory overhead..	$ 7,000	$(1,428)	$ 2,312	$ 2,710	$ 3,406				

Exhibit 4

PROCTOR PRODUCTS, INC.

FACTORY SURVEY — DECEMBER 31, 19—

Producing Departments	Number of Employees	%	Kilo-watt-Hours	%	Horse-power-Hours	%	Floor Area (sq. ft.)	%	Cost of Materials Requisitioned	%
Cutting......	35	24	16,978	26	210,000	42	5,250	25	$193,500	45
Planing.....	25	17	5,224	8	110,000	22	4,200	20	43,000	10
Assembly....	40	28	16,325	25	90,000	18	6,300	30	47,300	11
Upholstery...	45	31	26,773	41	90,000	18	5,250	25	146,200	34
Total.......	145	100	65,300	100	500,000	100	21,000	100	$430,000	100

Schedule B

USE OF DEPARTMENTAL FACTORY OVERHEAD RATES

During the fiscal year, as information becomes available at the end of each week or month, factory overhead is applied to a job or product by inserting the computed overhead applied figure in the overhead section of a job sheet or production report. Amounts applied must be summarized periodically for entry in the general journal. The summary entry applicable to the preceding illustration would appear as follows:

Work in Process.................................	285,000	
Factory Overhead Applied — Cutting Department (42,010 direct labor hours x $2)................		84,020
Factory Overhead Applied — Planing Department (17,000 machine hours x $3.20)................		54,400
Factory Overhead Applied — Assembly Department ($111,700 direct labor cost x 60%).............		67,020
Factory Overhead Applied—Upholstery Department (44,200 direct labor hours x $1.80).............		79,560

Separate factory overhead applied accounts have been used here. Entries could also have been made directly to each departmental factory overhead control account.

OVER- OR UNDERAPPLIED FACTORY OVERHEAD

With the year-end overhead distribution sheet completed, total actual departmental factory overhead can now be transferred to the individual departmental factory overhead control accounts. Using the figures provided by the overhead distribution sheet (Exhibit 4), the following entry can be made:

Factory Overhead — Cutting Department	82,592	
Factory Overhead — Planing Department	56,712	
Factory Overhead — Assembly Department	69,730	
Factory Overhead — Upholstery Department	82,966	
Factory Overhead Control		292,000

A comparison of actual and applied overhead of each producing department as well as of the total overhead of the company results in the following over- or underapplied factory overhead:

Total	Cutting	Planing	Assembly	Upholstery
$7,000	$(1,428)	$2,312	$2,710	$3,406

The $7,000 underapplied factory overhead would seem identical with that calculated in Chapter 9. However, this $7,000 figure is the composite sum of the variances of the four producing departments.

SPENDING AND IDLE CAPACITY VARIANCE ANALYSIS

In the previous chapter, page 230, the $7,000 underapplied factory overhead had been analyzed into a $750 unfavorable spending variance and a $6,250 unfavorable idle capacity variance. The $1.50 overhead rate used there and based on 200,000 direct labor hours is not applicable for the departmentalized illustration. New rates with different bases have been created. However, it should be possible to analyze each departmental over- or underapplied figure and determine a departmental spending and idle capacity variance. What is particularly needed is the amount of overhead budgeted for the level of operation attained (capacity utilized) which, in turn, requires a knowledge of the fixed and variable overhead in each producing department. To develop the budget allowance, the estimates shown in the summaries of the departmental factory overhead (Exhibit 1) and the distribution of service department costs (Exhibit 2) are examined. The summary of the departmental factory overhead indicates the fixed and variable departmental costs at the bottom line of the estimates. The service department costs distributed to the producing department as shown in the distribution of service departments costs summary are considered variable costs for the producing departments. The fixed-variable classification does not apply after the distribution.

The *spending and idle capacity variance analysis* reproduced on the next page is prepared for executive management on the basis of the actual

CALCULATION OF ESTIMATED FIXED AND VARIABLE OVERHEAD RATES

	Producing Departments			
	Cutting	*Planing*	*Assembly*	*Upholstery*
Fixed departmental overhead.........	$17,100	$17,900	$ 16,100	$18,300
Variable departmental overhead......	$23,400	$18,800	$ 18,900	$20,300
Variable service department costs.....	40,716	22,183	38,242	48,059
Total variable overhead.............	$64,116	$40,983	$ 57,142	$68,359
Bases:				
Direct labor hours...............	40,608			48,140
Machine hours...................		18,400		
Direct labor cost.................			$122,000	
Fixed overhead rate................	$0.42	$0.98	13%	$0.38
Variable overhead rate.............	1.58	2.22	47%	1.42
Total overhead rate:				
Per direct labor hour.............	$2.00			
Per machine hour................		$3.20		
Of direct labor cost..............			60%	
Per direct labor hour.............				$1.80

CALCULATION OF BUDGET ALLOWANCES*

	Producing Departments			
	Cutting	*Planing*	*Assembly*	*Upholstery*
Fixed overhead....................	$17,100	$17,900	$ 16,100	$18,300
Variable overhead:				
42,010 direct labor hours × $1.58...	66,376			
17,000 machine hours × $2.22.....		37,740		
$111,700 direct labor cost × 47%...			52,499	
44,200 direct labor hours × $1.42...				62,764
Total budget allowance.............	$83,476	$55,640	$ 68,599	$81,064

*Based on capacity utilized; i.e., actual activity.

SPENDING AND IDLE CAPACITY VARIANCE ANALYSIS

Producing Departments	*(1)* *Actual Overhead*	*(2)* *Budget Allowance*	*(3)* *Applied Overhead*	*(1 − 3)* *Total Variance*	*(1 − 2)* *Spending Variance*	*(2 − 3)* *Idle Capacity Variance*
Cutting.....	$ 82,592	$ 83,476	$ 84,020	$(1,428)	$ (884)	$ (544)
Planing.....	56,712	55,640	54,400	2,312	1,072	1,240
Assembly...	69,730	68,599	67,020	2,710	1,131	1,579
Upholstery..	82,966	81,064	79,560	3,406	1,902	1,504
Total.......	$292,000	$288,779	$285,000	$ 7,000	$3,221	$3,779

annual data after the books have been closed. However, the middle- and operating-management levels require cost control information currently at least once a month. With ever greater emphasis placed upon the control of costs by the responsible supervisory personnel, a procedure must be found which communicates to all levels of management the control information in a manner that permits the charging and discharging of responsibility of cost incurrence. This approach is discussed in the next chapter.

OVERHEAD DEPARTMENTALIZATION IN NONMANUFACTURING BUSINESS ACTIVITIES AND NONPROFIT INSTITUTIONS AND ORGANIZATIONS

The responsible control of departmental expenses is equally essential in other than manufacturing activities. The following have or should have divided their large complex entities into administrative and supervisory departments, sections, or service units for cost planning and control:

Nonmanufacturing segments of manufacturing concerns (e.g., marketing departments — see Chapter 23)	Insurance companies
	Educational institutions (public school systems, colleges, and universities)
Retail or department stores	Service organizations (hotels, motels, hospitals, and nursing homes)
Financial institutions (banks, savings and loan associations, and brokerage houses)	Federal, state, and municipal governments (and their agencies)

Retail or department stores have practiced departmentalization for many years by grouping their organizations under the following typical headings: administration, occupancy, sales promotion and advertising, purchasing, selling, and delivery. These groups receive costs similar to those in manufacturing businesses. The group "Occupancy" is almost identical with General Factory, for expenses like building repairs, rent and taxes, insurance on buildings and fixtures, light, heat, power, and depreciation on buildings and fixtures are collected in this group. Again, similar to factory procedures, group costs are prorated to revenue-producing sales departments via a charging or billing rate.

Financial institutions (banks, savings and loan associations, and brokerage houses) should departmentalize their organizations in order to control expenses and establish a profitability rating of individual activities. The size of the institution and the types of services offered will lead to different numbers of departments. The accumulation of departmental costs again follows factory procedure: (1) direct expenses, such as salaries, supplies, and depreciation of equipment are charged directly; (2) general expenses, such as light, heat, and air conditioning are prorated to the departments on appropriate bases. As income and expenses are ascertained, it is possible to create a work cost unit that permits the charging of accounts for services rendered and the analysis of an account's profitability.

The work of *insurance companies* is facilitated by dividing the office into departments. Some departments have several hundred clerks, and the work is highly organized. Insurance companies were almost the first businesses to install large-scale digital computers to (1) reduce the clerical costs connected with the insurance business and (2) calculate new insurance rates and coverage on a more expanded basis for greater profitability. This quite detailed departmentalization might include actuarial, premium collection, group insurance, policyholders' service, registrar, medical, legal, etc. While some costs are unique to the individual group, most are identical with expenses experienced in any office department.

Educational institutions (such as public school systems, colleges, and universities) and *service organizations* (such as hotels, motels, hospitals, and nursing homes) find it increasingly necessary to budget their expenses on a departmental basis in order to control and be able to charge an adequate cost recovering fee for their services. The extended services of social security via Medicare have made a knowledge of costs mandatory in hospitals and nursing homes. Departmentalization will assist management in creating a costing or charging rate for short- or long-term care, for special services, for nurses' instruction, etc., and for professional services (surgical, medical, X rays, laboratory examinations, filling of prescriptions, etc.).

It is generally conceded that the *federal government* employs the greatest number of people in a vast number of departments and agencies. A similar situation exists in *state and local community governments*. This discussion uses the municipality as an example, for its varied services are better known to the public. Common services or departments are: street cleaning, street repairing and paving, public work projects, police and fire departments, city hospitals, sewage disposal plants, trash and garbage collection, etc. These services should be budgeted and their costs controlled on a responsibility accounting basis. Since the costs incurred are not revenue but service-benefit-oriented, an attempt should be made to measure the operating efficiency of an activity based on some unit of measurement such as: police (per capita), street paving and cleaning (per mile), trash and garbage collection (per ton), etc. Ever-increasing costs require additional revenues; this means additional taxes. Taxpayers, however, are looking for efficient service in return for their tax money.

The state and federal governments must be made equally aware of the need for responsible cost control methods so that services will be rendered at a low cost with greatest efficiency. The federal government with its many departments and agencies and a huge sum budgeted for all of these units must particularly make certain that these activities are being administered by cost-conscious and service-minded people. The departmentalization process helps to assure the achievement of such a goal in any governmental unit.

DISCUSSION QUESTIONS

1. For effective control of overhead, a foreman, superintendent, manager, or department head can be held accountable for more than one cost center; but responsibility for a single cost center should not be divided between two or more foremen. Discuss.

2. Why will a department's factory overhead vary from month to month?

3. Even though most companies keep fixed asset records to identify equipment and its original cost by location or department, charges for depreciation, property taxes, and fire insurance are often accumulated in general factory accounts and charged to departments on the basis of equipment values. Is this the best method for controlling such costs? If not, suggest possible improvements.

4. Justify classifying the following items as factory overhead: overtime premiums, rework labor, and day-rate differentials in piece-rate payrolls. List some of the difficulties in estimating these items in the computation of predetermined overhead rates.

5. State reasons for the use of departmental overhead rates instead of a single plantwide rate.

6. The statement has been made that the entire process of departmentalizing factory overhead is an extension of methods used when a single overhead rate is used. Explain.

7. What are some of the factors that must be considered in deciding the kinds and number of departments required to control costs and establish accurate departmental overhead rates?

8. What is a producing department? a service department? Give illustrations of each.

9. What are important reasons for using a general factory overhead category for certain types of overhead instead of allocating it directly to production and other service departments?

10. What are the several steps followed in establishing departmental factory overhead rates?

11. What are some of the practices with respect to the sequence used in transferring service department overhead to producing departments? What bases should be used to transfer the overhead of the service departments listed below:

Production control	Maintenance
Purchasing	Utilities
Medical	Cafeteria
Payroll	Accounting
Storeroom	Personnel

12. What are the important factors involved in selecting the base to be used for applying the factory overhead of a producing department?

13. Procedures followed in computing departmental factory overhead rates determine the accounting for actual factory overhead. Explain. What are departmental expense analysis sheets, and how are they used? Trace a requisition for indirect materials through the departmentalization of factory overhead process.

14. The Sanchez Chemical Company uses departmental factory overhead rates. The rates are based on direct labor hours. Would the sum of departmental over- or underapplied overhead amounts be any different if a plantwide or blanket rate were used? Would the costs of goods sold and inventory values be different?

15. Describe how departmental over- and underapplied overhead is determined, and explain the computations of departmental spending and idle capacity variances.

16. Overhead control in a nonmanufacturing business can be achieved through departmentalization. Explain.

17. Federal, state, and local governments should practice cost control via responsibility accounting. Discuss.

EXERCISES

1. Cost Classification. Products of Mahler Company, Inc. are produced by a series of continuous operations. The company believes that it can keep costs as low as possible by assigning cost responsibility to specific individuals.

Required: Classification of the following items according to specific departments (cost centers):

(a) Factory wages
(b) Depreciation of machinery
(c) Purchasing of raw materials
(d) Factory supplies used

(e) Plant manager's salary
(f) Sales manager's salary
(g) Cost of operating power plant which serves entire plant

2. Entries with Overhead Subsidiary Ledger. The general ledger of the Dole-Johnson Company contains a factory overhead control account supported by a subsidiary ledger showing the details by departments. The plant is departmentalized with one service and three producing departments.

The following table shows details with respect to these departments:

	Machining Dept.	Painting Dept.	Assembly Dept.	General Factory
Building space (sq. ft.)	10,000	4,000	4,000	2,000
Value of machinery	$30,000	$10,000	$6,000	$2,000
Horsepower rating	100	—0—	10	15
Compensation insurance rate (per $100)	$1.50	$1.50	$1.00	$1.00

During January, certain assets expired and some liabilities accrued as outlined below:

(a) Depreciation on buildings, 3% per year; cost, $60,000.
(b) Depreciation on machinery based on 10-year life; machinery cost, $48,000.

(c) Taxes for the year ending December 31 are estimated to be $1,200, of which 60% is on buildings and 40% on machinery.

(d) Fire insurance in the amount of $100,000 is carried on buildings and machinery, and the rate is $.60 per $100 of coverage. Sixty percent of this insurance applies to buildings. The prepaid fire insurance account shows a balance of $300 at January 31 before adjustment.

(e) Compensation insurance is based on the following earnings of factory employees for the month of January: Machining Department, $3,000; Painting Department, $1,200; Assembly Department, $1,600; and General Factory, $600.

(f) Power meter reading at January 31 shows 12,500 kilowatt-hours consumed. Rate is $.03 per kilowatt-hour.

(g) Heat and light bill for the month of January is $300.

(h) Supplies requisitions show $180 used in the Machining Department, $230 in the Assembly Department, and $410 in the General Factory Department.

Required: Journal entries with details entered in the factory overhead subsidiary ledger.

3. Overhead Distribution and Rates. The Bloomfield Products Company has four producing departments: 11, 15, 21, and 25; and three service departments: M, F, and T. The direct departmental overhead has been estimated for the producing departments: No. 11 — $100,000; No. 15 — $140,000; No. 21 — $40,000; No. 25 — $80,000; for the service departments: M — $30,000; F — $50,000; T — $60,000. Service department overhead is to be distributed to producing and service departments in the order of T, F, and M using the following bases: T — floor area; F — number of employees; M — value of equipment investment. It is the company's policy that once a service department's costs have been allocated, no costs from other service departments are to be allocated to it.

Factory survey and production data:

Department	Floor Area (sq. ft.)	Number of Employees	Value of Equipment	Production Data
11	15,000	50	$250,000	72,750 direct labor hours
15	30,000	70	100,000	$161,000 direct labor cost
21	25,000	40	100,000	18,425 machine hours
25	10,000	20	50,000	59,750 direct labor hours
M	20,000	20	50,000	
F	20,000	10	26,000	
T	5,000	10	24,000	
Total	125,000	220	$600,000	

Required: (1) Distribution of service department overhead.

(2) Departmental factory overhead rates.

4. Transfer Entries and Variance Analysis. A distribution of the actual factory overhead of the Columbus Manufacturing Company for the past year is given on page 275. Budgeted factory overhead for the four producing departments (including apportioned service department overhead) is also given for two levels of activity. The company uses a predetermined rate for each producing department based on labor hours at the normal capacity level. Actual hours worked last year were 17,000 for each of the four producing departments.

Actual Factory Overhead

	A	B	C	D	X	Y	Z	Total
Actual expenses..	$10,000	$14,000	$4,000	$8,000	$3,000	$5,000	$6,000	$50,000
Z's expenses......	1,500	750	1,250	500	1,000	1,000	6,000	
Y's expenses.....	1,800	1,200	1,800	600	600	$6,000		
X's expenses.....	2,000	1,000	1,200	400	$4,600			
Total..........	$15,300	$16,950	$8,250	$9,500				$50,000

Budgeted Factory Overhead

	20,000 Hours (Normal)	16,000 Hours
Department A....................................	$17,800	$15,000
Department B....................................	20,200	17,800
Department C....................................	10,600	9,400
Department D....................................	10,600	9,400
Total.......................................	$59,200	$51,600

Required: (1) Assuming that the actual factory overhead incurred was charged to a single factory overhead control account, prepare entries to record (a) the transfer of the actual factory overhead to producing departments and (b) the applied factory overhead of Departments A and B only.

(2) Compute the spending and idle capacity variances for Departments A and B only.

5. Overhead Distribution and Rate Calculation. The Torrence Manufacturing Company has four producing departments and three service departments: Maintenance, Toolroom, and Storeroom. The estimated annual overhead for these seven departments is as follows:

Estimated Expenses	Departments						
	Producing				Service		
	01	02	03	04	Maintenance	Toolroom	Storeroom
Fixed factory overhead......	$36,000	$48,000	$45,000	$30,000	$15,000	$10,500	$12,000
Variable factory overhead......	24,000	22,000	20,000	20,000	10,800	10,500	3,000
Total..........	$60,000	$70,000	$65,000	$50,000	$25,800	$21,000	$15,000

The management decided to distribute the service departments' costs on a dual basis: (a) fixed overhead on a standby or ready-to-serve basis and (b) variable overhead on a billing or charging rate basis. The fixed overhead of the three service departments is to be distributed as shown on page 276.

Allocation of *Fixed Overhead* *of Service Departments*	*Total*	*01*	*02*	*03*	*04*
Maintenance..........	$15,000	$5,000	$4,000	$3,000	$3,000
Toolroom............	10,500	3,500	2,500	2,500	2,000
Storeroom...........	12,000	6,000	3,000	2,000	1,000

The variable overhead of the service departments is distributed on the basis of charging rates based on the following plant survey and other pertinent data:

Department	*Maintenance* *(Area in* *Square Feet)*	*Toolroom* *(Number of* *Employees)*	*Storeroom* *(Number of* *Materials* *Requisitions)*
No. 01.............	12,000	50	30,000
No. 02.............	10,000	40	30,000
No. 03.............	9,000	30	28,000
No. 04.............	5,000	30	12,000
Maintenance.......	5,000	10	
Toolroom.........	3,000	5	
Storeroom.........	1,000	5	

No service department's cost is to be prorated to other service departments.

Required: (1) A factory overhead distribution sheet on the basis of the data and instructions stated above.

(2) Factory overhead rates for the four producing departments based on the following predetermined labor hours, machine hours, and direct labor cost:

Department No.	
01	33,000 machine hours
02	32,000 machine hours
03	39,070 labor hours
04	$59,960 labor cost

6. Overhead Analysis and Causes for Variances. The Lowell Manufacturing Company uses predetermined departmental overhead rates. The rate for the Fabricating Department is $4 per direct labor hour. Direct labor employees are paid $4.50 an hour. A total of 15,000 direct labor hours were worked in the department during the year. Total overhead charged to the department for supervisors' salaries, indirect labor, labor fringe benefit costs, indirect materials, service department costs, etc. was $65,000.

Required: (1) The over- or underapplied factory overhead.

(2) An analysis of factors affecting actual and applied overhead revealed the following situations. For each situation, indicate the effect on the amount of over- or underapplied overhead. Discuss each item separately as though the other factors had not occurred:

(a) One hundred overtime hours were worked by direct laborers for which time-and-a-half was paid. Overtime premium, the amount in excess of the regular rate, is charged as overhead to the department in which the overtime is worked.

(b) A $.15 per hour wage increase was granted November 1. Direct labor hours worked in November and December totaled 2,500.

(c) The company cafeteria incurred a $1,500 loss which was distributed to producing departments on the basis of number of employees. Nine of the 120 employees work in the Fabricating Department. No loss was anticipated when predetermined overhead rates were computed.

7. Algebraic Distribution of Factory Overhead. A company's two service departments serve not only the two producing departments but also one another. The relationships between the four departments can be expressed as follows:

Service Departments	Percentages of Services Consumed by Departments				Service Costs To Be Distributed
	Producing		Service		
	A	B	Y	Z	
Y	50%	40%		10%	$10,000
Z	40%	40%	20%		8,800

Required: (1) The amount of service costs applicable to each department.

(2) The total factory overhead in each producing department if primary overhead amounts to $22,000 in Department A and $29,000 in Department B.

8. Algebraic Distribution of Factory Overhead.   The estimated departmental factory overhead for Producing Departments S and T and Service Departments E, F, and G (before any service department allocations) are:

Producing Departments	*Service Departments*
S............$60,000	E.........$20,000
T............ 90,000	F......... 20,000
	G......... 10,000

The interdependence of the departments is tabulated as follows:

	Services Provided		
Departments	*E*	*F*	*G*
Producing — S......................	—	30%	40%
Producing — T......................	50%	40	30
Service — E......................	—	20	—
Service — F......................	20	—	—
Service — G......................	30	10	—
Marketing.........................	—	—	20
General Office.....................	—	—	10
	100%	100%	100%

Required: (1) The final amount of estimated overhead of each service department after reciprocal transfer costs have been calculated algebraically.

(2) The total factory overhead of each producing department and the amount of Department G cost assigned to the Marketing Department and to General Office.

9. Overhead Distribution. Parker Manufacturing Company has two producing departments, Fabrication and Assembly, and three service departments, General Factory Administration, Factory Maintenance, and Factory Cafeteria. A summary of costs and other data for each department prior to allocation of service department costs for the year ended June 30, 19––, shows:

	Producing Departments		Service Departments		
	Fabrication	Assembly	General Factory Administration	Factory Maintenance	Factory Cafeteria
Direct labor costs........	$1,950,000	$2,050,000	$90,000	$82,100	$87,000
Direct materials costs....	3,130,000	950,000	––––	65,000	91,000
Factory overhead costs...	1,650,000	1,850,000	70,000	56,100	62,000
Direct labor hours.......	562,500	437,500	31,000	27,000	42,000
Number of employees....	280	200	12	8	20
Square footage occupied..	88,000	72,000	1,750	2,000	4,800

The costs of General Factory Administration, Factory Maintenance, and Factory Cafeteria are allocated on the basis of direct labor hours, square footage occupied, and number of employees, respectively. There are no factory overhead variances. Round all final calculations to the nearest dollar.

Required: (1) Assuming that Parker Manufacturing Company elects to distribute service department costs directly to the producing departments without inter-service department cost allocation, compute the amount of Factory Maintenance costs that would be allocated to Fabrication.

(2) Assuming the same policy of allocating service departments to producing departments only, compute the amount of General Factory Administration costs that would be allocated to Assembly.

(3) Assuming that Parker Manufacturing Company elects to distribute service department costs to other service departments (starting with the service department with the greatest total costs) as well as to the producing departments and that once a service department's costs have been allocated, no subsequent service department costs are recirculated back to it, compute:

   (a) The amount of Factory Cafeteria costs that would be allocated to Factory Maintenance.
   (b) The amount of Factory Maintenance costs that would be allocated to Factory Cafeteria.

(AICPA adapted)

PROBLEMS

10-1. Overhead Distribution Sheet. Montag Manufacturing Company applies factory overhead on the following bases:

	Producing Depts.	
	A	B
Materials costs	25%	
Direct labor hours...		$2.50

At the end of the fiscal period the following accounts and their balances have been taken from the books and records:

Work in Process — Materials....................................	$46,000
— Direct Labor................................	29,450
— Factory Overhead (Applied).................	23,250
Indirect Labor...	17,400
Factory Office..	3,200
Building Charges (including depreciation, insurance, etc.)..........	4,000
Powerhouse Expenses (coal, labor, etc.).......................	2,800

Additional information:

	Producing Departments		
	A	*B*	*Powerhouse*
Direct materials..........................	$33,000	$13,000	
Direct labor.............................	11,780	17,670	
Direct labor hours........................	3,500	6,000	
Power used..............................	60%	40%	
Floor space occupied.....................	750 sq. ft.	750 sq. ft.	500 sq. ft.

Indirect labor and factory office are apportioned in direct ratio to the cost of direct labor.

Required: (1) A distribution sheet showing the distribution of factory overhead costs to producing departments and the powerhouse.

(2) The total and departmental over- or underapplied factory overhead after the powerhouse expenses have been allocated to the producing departments.

10-2. Overhead Rates. The Hilsinger Manufacturing Company has three producing departments: A, B, and C. Departmental estimates for the coming year are as follows:

Producing Departments	Factory Over-head	Direct Labor Hours	Direct Labor Costs	Machine Hours
A.......................	$10,000	15,000	$ 24,000	9,000
B.......................	12,000	50,000	75,000	5,000
C.......................	16,000	40,000	60,000	2,000
Total....................	$38,000	105,000	$159,000	16,000

Cost figures for Job Order No. 2235 are:

	Department A	Department B	Department C
Direct materials	$300	$200	—0—
Direct labor costs....................	200	500	$400
Direct labor hours	125	300	250

Required: (1) Plantwide overhead rates for the company using three different bases.

(2) Three different overhead rates for each department.

(3) The cost of Job Order No. 2235 using (a) a plantwide rate based on direct labor hours and (b) separate direct labor hour overhead rates for each department.

10-3. Overhead Distribution Sheet and Rate Calculation. The president of the Luciano Products Company has been critical of the product costing methods whereby factory overhead had always been charged to products on a factory-wide overhead rate. The chief accountant suggested a departmentalization of the factory for the purpose of calculating departmental factory overhead rates. He accumulated the following estimated direct departmental overhead data on an annual basis:

| Overhead Items | Departments | | | | | |
| | Producing | | | Service | | |
	Dept. 10	Dept. 12	Dept. 14	Store-room	Repair Shop	General Factory
Supervision..........	$12,500	$16,000	$14,000	$ 7,200	$ 8,000	$24,000
Indirect labor.........	5,400	6,000	8,000	6,133	7,200	18,000
Indirect supplies.......	4,850	5,600	5,430	1,400	3,651	1,070
Labor fringe benefits...	6,872	9,349	10,145	640	760	2,100
Equipment depreciation.	6,000	8,000	10,000	560	1,740	1,100
Taxes, depreciation of buildings, etc........						20,000
Total...............	$35,622	$44,949	$47,575	$15,933	$21,351	$66,270

The annual light and power bill is estimated at $9,300, to be distributed to the departments on the following usage percentage:

| | Departments | | | | | |
| | Producing | | | Service | | |
	Dept. 10	Dept. 12	Dept. 14	Store-room	Repair Shop	General Factory
	20%	25%	30%	3%	12%	10%

General Factory is closed out first on the basis of area (sq. ft.) occupied:

21,000	25,200	29,400	3,360	5,040	

Storeroom expenses are prorated next, based on estimated requisitions to be handled for the departments:

124,200	81,000	40,500		24,300	

Repair Shop is closed out last, based on the number of estimated maintenance hours to be spent in departments:

4,800	4,200	6,000			

Estimated direct labor hours:

80,000	90,000	80,000			

Required: A factory overhead distribution sheet with calculation of overhead rates for the producing departments based on direct labor hours.

10-4. Overhead Distribution Sheet and Rate Calculation. Dunlap Chemical Co., Inc. consists of three producing departments: Preparation, Mixing, and Packaging; and four service departments: Utilities, Maintenance, Materials Handling, and Factory Office. For the purpose of creating factory overhead rates, the accountant prepared the cost distribution sheet shown below. It contains (a) operational data gathered by the accountant and (b) the expenses of the individual departments.

Data	Totals	Producing Departments			Service Departments			
		Prepara-tion	Mixing	Packag-ing	Utilities	Main-tenance	Ma-terials Han-dling	Factory Office
Operational data:								
Floor space— sq. ft......	53,000	10,000	12,000	16,000	3,000	3,000	5,000	4,000
Maintenance hours.....	6,820	1,860	2,480	930	620		620	310
Metered hours in hundreds..	4,000	1,400	1,600	320		200	320	160
Expenses:								
Indirect labor	$22,000	$ 3,800	$ 2,600	$2,400	$3,500	$4,000	$ 3,300	$2,400
Payroll taxes.	2,522	440	532	420	230	355	320	225
Indirect materials..	5,703	700	938	2,300	920	150	150	545
Depreciation.	850	100	150	50	100	200	200	50
Total.........	$31,075	$ 5,040	$ 4,220	$5,170	$4,750	$4,705	$ 3,970	$3,220

For the distribution of the expenses of the service departments, the following procedures had been decided upon:

(a) Utilities: 80% on metered hours — power
                             20% on floor square footage
(b) Maintenance: Maintenance hours excluding utilities
(c) Materials Handling: 48% to Preparation, 32% to Mixing, and 20% to Packaging
    Pounds Handled: 395,300 in Preparation
                             262,850 in Mixing
(d) Factory Office: Preparation, 40%; Mixing, 30%; Packaging, 30%

Required: (1) Complete the cost distribution sheet. No reciprocal charging should take place.

(2) Factory overhead rates based on pounds handled in Preparation and Mixing and on direct labor cost of $86,000 in Packaging.

10-5. Overhead Distribution Sheet and Rate Calculation. At the end of September the factory ledger trial balance of the Wellinghoff Products Company contained the following factory overhead items and amounts for the past three months:

Indirect Labor................	$30,600	Fuel........................	$ 2,100
Factory Rent.................	1,400	Electricity...................	1,600
Insurance — Machinery and		Factory Supplies Used.........	3,600
Equipment.................	3,200	Social Security Taxes..........	5,130
Compensation Insurance.......	1,400	Maintenance and Repairs —	
Superintendent..............	5,000	Machinery and Equipment...	21,000
Clerical Help — Factory.......	3,900	Depreciation — Machinery and	
		Equipment.................	12,453

No attempt had been made (a) to charge these costs directly to departments or (b) to create departmental overhead rates. The accountant believes that departmentalization is desirable for meaningful product costing and efficient responsibility reporting. He gathered the information shown below concerning the three producing departments, called A, B, and C, and the two service departments, Maintenance and Repairs (other than machinery and equipment) and General Factory.

Data	Totals	Departments				
		Producing			Service	
		A	B	C	Maint.and Repairs	General Factory
Floor space..........	40,000 sq. ft.	15,000	12,000	6,000	4,000	3,000
Number of employees.	100	35	30	15	10	10
Number of direct labor hours.............	38,400	16,800	14,400	7,200		
Cost of machinery and equipment.........	$436,000	$152,600	$130,800	$65,400	$76,300	$10,900
Annual depreciation rate..............		10%	12%	8%	15%	20%

He decided to distribute the factory overhead items on the following bases:

Floor space: factory rent; fuel; 1/4 of electricity.

Number of employees: compensation insurance; superintendent; factory supplies used; social security taxes.

Cost of machinery and equipment: insurance—machinery and equipment; maintenance and repairs — machinery and equipment; 3/4 of electricity.

Indirect labor: 80% to producing departments in the ratio of 3:2:1; the balance to maintenance and repairs.

Clerical help — factory: all to general factory.

Depreciation: on basis of established depreciation rates.

The service departments are to be prorated as follows: 1/10 of Maintenance and Repairs to General Factory; the balance to the producing departments based on direct labor hours. General Factory overhead is distributed to the producing departments based on number of employees.

Required: (1) Distribute factory overhead to the producing and service departments based on the data given; prorate service departments as indicated. (2) Calculate departmental overhead rates based on direct labor hours.

10-6. Cost Center Rates and Variance Analysis. The cost department of the Venus Manufacturing Co. applies factory overhead to jobs and products on the basis of predetermined cost center overhead rates; i.e., in each of the two producing departments, two cost centers have been set up. For the coming year, the following estimates and other data have been made available:

Department 10:	Estimated Annual Factory Overhead			Estimated Annual Machine Hours
	Fixed	Variable	Total	
Cost Center 10-1...........	$14,040	$23,400	$37,440	15,600
Cost Center 10-2...........	26,910	43,290	70,200	23,400

Department 20:				Estimated Annual Direct Labor Hours
Cost Center 20-1...........	$ 8,320	$21,580	$29,900	26,000
Cost Center 20-2..........	6,240	19,760	26,000	20,800

Required: (1) The annual normal cost center overhead rates based on the estimated machine hours in Department 10 and the direct labor hours in Department 20.

(2) Application of factory overhead to the four cost centers on the basis of these actual machine or labor hours used or worked during the month of February:

Cost Centers	10-1	10-2	20-1	20-2
Machine hours....	1,220	2,000		
Labor hours			2,250	1,650

(3) The spending and the idle capacity variances for the two producing departments. Actual factory overhead in Department 10 amounted to $9,630 and in Department 20 to $4,205.

(4) Analysis of the total idle capacity variance of Department 10 into the idle capacity variances of the two cost centers. Use 1/12 of the total annual estimated hours as normal monthly hours.

10-7. Algebraic Distribution of Factory Overhead. The controller of the Haynes Corporation instructs his cost supervisor to initiate a shift from the traditional successive iteration type of cost allocation of service departments to producing departments to a mathematical procedure using algebra to recognize more effectively interdepartmental relationships. The corporation's three producing departments are served by three service departments, each of which consumes part of the services of the other two. After primary but before reciprocal distribution, the account balances of the service departments and the interdependence of the departments were tabulated as shown on the next page.

Department	Departmental Overhead Before Distribution of Service Departments	Services Provided		
		Powerhouse	Personnel	General Factory
Mixing............	$125,000	25%	35%	25%
Refining...........	90,000	25	30	20
Finishing..........	105,000	20	20	20
Powerhouse........	16,000	—	10	20
Personnel.........	29,500	10	—	15
General Factory.....	42,000	20	5	—
	$407,500	100%	100%	100%

Required: (1) The final amount of overhead of each service department after reciprocal transfer costs have been calculated algebraically.

(2) The total factory overhead of each producing department.

10-8. Hospital Costs Allocation Methods.　Providence Hospital completed its first year of operation as a qualified institutional provider under the health insurance (HI) program for the aged and wishes to receive maximum reimbursement for its allowable costs from the government. The hospital compiled the following financial, statistical, and other information:

(a) The hospital's charges and allowable costs for departmental inpatient services were as follows:

Department	Charges for HI Program Beneficiaries	Total Charges	Total Allowable Costs
Inpatient routine services (room, board, nursing)...............	$ 425,000	$1,275,000	$1,350,000
Inpatient ancillary service departments:			
X-ray...............................	$ 56,000	$ 200,000	$ 150,000
Operating room......................	57,000	190,000	220,000
Laboratory..........................	59,000	236,000	96,000
Pharmacy...........................	98,000	294,000	207,000
Other...............................	10,000	80,000	88,000
Total ancillary.....................	$ 280,000	$1,000,000	$ 761,000
Total.............................	$ 705,000	$2,275,000	$2,111,000

(b) For the first year the reimbursement settlement for inpatient services may be calculated at the option of the provider under either of the following apportionment methods:

(1) *Departmental RCC (Ratio of Cost Centers) Method* — provides for listing on a departmental basis the ratios of beneficiary inpatient charges to total inpatient charges with each departmental beneficiary inpatient charge ratio applied to the allowable total cost of the respective department.

(2) *Combination Method (With Cost Finding)* — provides that the cost of routine services be apportioned on the basis of the average allowable cost per day for all inpatients applied to total inpatient days of beneficiaries. The residual

part of the provider's total allowable cost attributable to ancillary (non-routine) services is to be apportioned in the ratio of the beneficiaries' share of charges for ancillary services to the total charges for all patients for such services.

(c) Statistical and other information:

(1) Total inpatient days for all patients........................... 40,000

(2) Total inpatient days applicable to HI beneficiaries (1,200 aged patients with average stay of 12.5 days)........................ 15,000

(3) A fiscal intermediary acting on behalf of the government's Medicare program negotiated a fixed allowance rate of $45 per inpatient day subject to retroactive adjustment as a reasonable cost basis for reimbursement of covered services to the hospital under the HI program. Interim payments based on an estimated 1,000 inpatient days per month were received during the 12-month period subject to an adjustment for the provider's actual cost experience.

Required: (1) Schedules computing the total allowable cost of inpatient services for which the provider should receive payment under the HI program, and the remaining balance due for reimbursement under (a) the Departmental RCC Method and (b) the Combination Method (With Cost Finding).

(2) The method under which Providence Hospital should elect to be reimbursed for its first year under the HI program, assuming the election can be changed for the following year with the approval of the fiscal intermediary. Explain.

(3) Providence Hospital wishes to compare its charges to HI program beneficiaries with published information on national averages for charges for hospital services. Determine with computations (a) the average total hospital charge for an HI inpatient and (b) the average charge per inpatient day for HI inpatients.

(AICPA adapted)

CASES

A. Deciding on Depreciation for Old and New Building. The Rossmoyne Manufacturing Company owned one factory building with a net depreciated cost of $90,000. Machinery and equipment was carried at $120,000. Because of expanding business, it built a new building at a cost of $150,000 and installed $210,000 of equipment therein. During the next several years it put some new equipment into the old building and continued to operate both plants. Depreciation has been computed on a straight-line basis.

Recently the company shut down the old plant because of lack of orders. The sales manager proposes that the company should no longer take depreciation on the old building and machinery. He suggests that while the old plant is useful, it is not in use and is not wearing out. He also suggests that to take depreciation on it increases cost, overvalues inventory, and places the company in a poor competitive position to bid for business since its costs are high.

Required: A full discussion of this proposal.

(AICPA adapted)

| | | | | | Work in Process | | | |
| | | | | | Service Depts. | | Producing Depts. | |
Sources of Information	General Ledger Control	Raw Materials	Store Supplies	Total	Power Plant	General Plant	Pattern Foundry	Machine Shop
From cash payments journal:								
Purchases........	$(27,150)*	$20,000	$7,150					
Direct labor......	(6,150)			$6,150	$300	$350	$2,200	$3,300
Direct factory overhead......	(2,300)			2,300	50	175	730	1,345
Assets acquired......	(9,400)							
Prepaid insurance......	(3,000)							
From general ledger entries:								
Depreciation......	(1,100)			1,100	140	80	**	**
Property taxes......	(250)			250	40	20	**	**
Expired insurance......	(500)			500	100	25	**	**
Repairs to power plant......	(320)			320	320			
From requisitions:								
Raw materials......	150	(27,000)		27,000	500	1,000	15,500	10,000
Store supplies......			(15,150)	15,000	150	1,350	9,000	4,500
From cost of finished jobs report:								
Shipped to customers......	45,000			(45,000)				
For company's own use......	2,460			(2,460)				
Bases for distribution of costs:								
Power plant......							50%	50%
General plant on the basis of store supplies issued to producing departments.								
Indirect costs of producing departments on the basis of the direct labor costs of each department.								

*( ) denotes credit balance.

**Balance on the basis of direct labor costs.

B. Comparing Cost System for Inventory Costing and Income Determination. The Hallahan Manufacturing Company is engaged in manufacturing items to fill specific orders received from its customers. While at any given time it may have substantial inventories of work in process and finished goods, all such amounts are assignable to firm sales orders which it has received.

The company's operations, including the administrative and sales functions, are completely departmentalized. Its cost system is on a job order basis. Direct materials and direct labor are identified with jobs by the use of materials issue tickets and daily time cards. Overhead costs are accumulated for each factory service, administrative, and marketing department. These overhead costs, including administrative and marketing expenses, are then allocated to producing departments and an overhead rate computed for each producing department. This rate is used to apply overhead to jobs on the basis of direct labor hours. The result is that all costs and expenses incurred during any month are charged to the work in process accounts for the jobs.

Required: (1) Comparison of this system, as it affects inventory costing, with the usual system for manufacturing businesses.

(2) Criticism of the system as it affects inventory costing and income determination.

(3) Justifications for the use of the company's system.

(AICPA adapted)

C. Cost Accounting Records; Overhead Distribution; Ledger Accounts. The LaVelle Manufacturing Company uses a job order cost system that has been kept rather inadequately by the former accountant who left in the middle of September. The company's president asks for assistance in getting the books and records in an acceptable order. The company's cost system includes a general ledger and a factory ledger with reciprocal control accounts. A trial balance of the factory ledger at September 1, 19— showed the following:

	Debits	Credits
Raw Materials...................................	$30,000	
Store Supplies..................................	10,000	
Work in Process.................................	20,000	
General Ledger Control..........................		$60,000
	$60,000	$60,000

After reviewing the work done up to September 1, information is gathered for the month of September from the sources indicated on page 286.

Required: On a worksheet using the same headings as those appearing on the sources of information material on the opposite page:

(a) The direct, indirect, and total costs that should be debited to the work in process account for the month of September.

(b) Distribution of service departments' costs to the producing departments as per instructions.

(c) The September 30 balances of the following factory ledger accounts: General Ledger Control; Raw Materials; Store Supplies; Work in Process.

(AICPA adapted)

CHAPTER 11

RESPONSIBILITY ACCOUNTING AND RESPONSIBILITY REPORTING

Direct materials and direct labor are generally directly identifiable with specific products, jobs, or processes. Factory overhead, however, consisting of indirect supplies, indirect labor, and numerous factory expense items such as power, water, utilities, repairs and maintenance, taxes, insurance, and depreciation, creates two distinct problems:

1. Its allocation to products for the purpose of inventory costing and profit determination, and

2. Control of factory overhead with the aid of responsibility accounting.

The well-designed information system yields product costs for inventory costing and profit determination. However, it should also provide a control mechanism encompassing responsibility accounting and make available meaningful cost data useful in setting policies and making decisions. The predetermined or budgeted revenue and expense items form the foundation for comparison with actual results leading to the variance analysis or *management by exception* principle.

The establishment of such a system would allow and maintain the most efficient and profitable balance between manufacturing and marketing. On the one hand, management needs to decide the kinds and costs of its products; on the other hand, management must decide the kinds and prices of its products. The best profit results from the proper balance of these considerations. For these reasons, product costs must be fairly accurate, include all relevant costs, and recognize cost differentials among products.

CONTROL OF FACTORY OVERHEAD AND RESPONSIBILITY ACCOUNTING

Responsibility — Defined. Webster's dictionary defines *responsibility* or *being responsible* as "liable to respond; likely to be called upon to answer; accountable; able to respond or answer for one's conduct and obligations."

Kohler's *A Dictionary of Accountants* defines *responsibility* as "the obligation prudently to exercise assigned or imputed authority attaching to the assigned or imputed role of an individual or group participating in organizational activities or decisions."

The N.A.(C.)A. Research Series No. 22, says: "A responsibility may be defined as an organizational unit having a single head accountable for activities of the unit."

Responsibility Accounting — Basic Concepts. The concepts enumerated below are prerequisites to the initiation and maintenance of a responsibility accounting system.

1. Responsibility accounting is based on a classification of managerial responsibilities (departments) at every level in the organization for the purpose of establishing a budget for each. The individual in charge or with the authority for each responsibility classification should be made responsible and held accountable for the expenses of his activity. This concept introduces the need for the classification of costs into controllable and those not controllable by a department head. Generally, variable costs are charged to a department and are controllable by its manager; fixed costs, though charged to a department, generally are not controllable by its manager.

2. The starting point for a responsibility accounting information system rests with the organization chart in which the spheres of jurisdiction have been determined. Authority leads to the responsibility for certain costs and expenses which are forecast or present in the budget established with the knowledge and cooperation of the supervisor, department head, or manager.

3. Each individual's budget should clearly identify the costs controllable by him. The chart of accounts should be adapted to permit recording of controllable or accountable expenses within the jurisdictional framework.

Personal Factors in Responsibility Accounting. A program to develop management accounting controls must be considered a prime responsibility of top management with the accounting department providing the technical assistance. To assure the follow-through and therewith the ultimate success of the program, management must provide a complete clarification of the objectives and responsibilities of all levels of the organization. This prerequisite requires an understanding by middle and operating management of executive management's goals. The acceptance of responsibility for certain costs and expenses does not always follow the mere issuance of directives and orders. Supervisory personnel, particularly at the foreman level, need guidance and training to achieve the control and/or profit results expected from them. Control responsibility requires a certain fundamental attitude or frame of mind for the task. It just does not happen naturally. One of the most beneficial influences is executive management's own exemplary adherence to the cost-and-profit responsibility it created.

Of equal importance is the motivation for corrective action by the responsible individual. The issuance of reports based on the organization's responsibility concept is not sufficient. The successful achievement of effective management control depends upon the lines of communication between the accounting department, the responsible supervisors, and their superiors. Responsibility accounting requires teamwork in the truest sense of the word.

Responsibility for Overhead Costs. As the preceding overhead chapters indicate, many overhead items are directly chargeable to a given department and become the direct responsibility of the departmental supervisor. Allocated or distributed overhead causes problems in assigning cost responsibility. To calculate a departmental factory overhead rate, these costs must be allocated so that all costs can be charged to the job or product. The allocation procedure, however, is not necessary for cost control; that is, for responsibility accounting. If allocated charges are to be shown on the report furnished to the supervisor, they should be limited to those expenses for which he has assumed control and responsibility. The procedure depends a great deal upon the methods of cost accumulation and allocation employed by a firm. Certain expenses (e.g., electricity) could, when metered for a department, be considered a direct departmental overhead. When these expenses together with others are collected first in an account or in a department such as General Factory or Utilities, the allocation takes place on a preestablished basis. Differences between actual and allocated or charged-out costs in these accounts or departments should not be shown on the reports for the departments served; rather the control or responsibility phase stays with the originating department.

The "Billing" or "Sold-Hour" Rate of a Service Department. The cost system provides for a normal volume distribution of service hours, use hours, and/or maintenance hours to producing or other service departments. The distribution can be looked upon as a purchase by the recipient center or a sale by the servicing center. The distribution to the recipient center is based on what is termed a "billing rate," a "sold-hour rate," a "charging rate," or a "transfer rate." The method is based on the idea that these departments or centers purchase the services in the same manner as direct materials and direct labor. For these cost elements, quantities and cost are controlled and differences noted. The producing or service department foreman is responsible for the number of hours worked, or kw-hours purchased, and the cost incurred in his department.

The determination of the rate follows the procedures discussed in the previous factory overhead chapters:

1. Costs of any service or maintenance department are estimated or budgeted according to their nature (supervision, supplies, electricity, etc.).

2. Costs are classified as fixed or variable. This classification often leads to the realization that many service departmental costs are fixed over fairly wide ranges of service volume.

3. A rate is determined by dividing total departmental cost by the number of hours the service is expected to be needed. The establishment of the use hours, i.e., for the power house, is as important here as it is in factory overhead rate determination. The hours can be based either on past experience in a representative period or on future activity or volume as expressed in the budget. A refinement of the rate is the apportionment of fixed costs to cost centers on a *readiness-to-serve* basis. As some departments would require more service than others, the initial cost proration is made on that basis. The cost remaining is then divided by the budgeted hours of the recipient departments.

4. Actual service department costs incurred in the department are compared with the predetermined or budgeted costs. This comparison is made (1) in the service department to which the expenses are originally charged — actual costs are compared with charged-out or sold-out amounts; (2) in the benefiting (recipient) departments in which the charges for service departments' services are linked with the predetermined budget allowances. This step is the control phase of the service department's charging-out procedure. The foreman of the service department is responsible for the actual cost against the cost or hours charged for service. The benefiting department foreman is responsible for the number of hours or the cost charged for service. Comparison will also lead to the calculation of variances for service and producing departments.

Maintenance Costs and Responsibility Accounting. Maintenance expenses like any other indirect factory cost must find their way into the producing departments to be included in the total departmental cost for the calculation of overhead rates for product costing purposes. Still unsolved is the problem of cost responsibility. The maintenance engineer often believes that his department really incurs no cost at all, for any cost incurrence is for the benefit and at the request of other departments. The factory foreman, on the other hand, may argue that he has no influence upon costs, either personnel or machinery, of the maintenance department. However, a solution must be found not only for product costing purposes, but also for the control of these expenses. The control is in reality twofold: the factory foreman controls the amount of maintenance work, while the maintenance engineer or foreman controls the quantity of men and materials required to serve the various departments. As maintenance work is done at the request of the production foreman, the problem arises as to whether control should be exercised at the *source level* or the *recipient level*.

At the *source level*, service and maintenance labor is organized and supervised. Control at this point requires the predetermination of man-hour requirements in each of the producing and service departments for each service or maintenance function. At the *recipient level*, the cost system establishes predetermined budget allowances for this indirect cost. Budget allowances activated against planned levels of production permit determining the man-hour budgets for each shop service or maintenance unit for advance scheduling of its labor force. Preplanning is the heart of the control, providing an opportunity for corrective action before the hours are worked. Maintenance supervisors and service department foremen are apprised of the budgeted service or maintenance allowance by individual recipient cost centers while the distribution or scheduling of the work itself is left to their discretion.

One major problem, however, rests with the question of how much maintenance or repair work is needed in a department. The answer thereto may reach the executive management group for either a decision or perhaps even the original responsibility for the type and amount of maintenance work required. For at the time the factory was laid out and the machinery installed, a maintenance program should have been planned. The size of the maintenance department, the type or class of workers (carpenters, plumbers, electricians, pipefitters, masons, millwrights, machinists, etc.), and the kind of equipment and tools are greatly influenced by the early decision. On the other hand, experience indicates that such maintenance objectives are lacking in many companies due to management's own lack of interest as well as alleged difficulties encountered in planning, measuring, and controlling the maintenance function.

Many organizations engage the services of outside firms for part or all of their maintenance. This practice does not negate the need for careful planning and control of maintenance cost.

Preventive Maintenance. A plan for the cost determination and the control responsibility of maintenance is both needed and possible. It is suggested that management, the supervisors of producing and service departments, and the maintenance engineering department reach an agreement on the overall maintenance policy to be followed by the plant. This approach constitutes a preventive maintenance program with the objective of keeping equipment in such condition that breakdowns and the need for emergency repairs are at a minimum. Preventive maintenance facilitates the scheduling of maintenance work and helps to obtain better utilization of the maintenance work force and the productive equipment. It also reduces operating losses due to machine breakdowns, extensive damage, or serious injuries to personnel.

A preventive maintenance program can work automatically so that inspection, minor repairs, adjustments, and lubrication are completed as a matter of course. The method further provides for a check on the effectiveness of the maintenance work by the foreman of the serviced or buying unit. The maintenance foreman, in turn, is responsible for the inspection and the upkeep of the facilities.

The discussion has intentionally dealt with factory overhead items only, since their assignment and control occupies the attention of many executives, department heads, supervisors, and foremen. Not only are production people made responsible for the costs of their departments, but other departments and functions in administration and marketing require the same kind of responsibility accounting. Besides factory overhead, the other cost elements also need watching and controlling by responsible managers.

Responsibility for Direct Materials and Direct Labor. Basically, the best approach to assigning responsibility for any cost element is a study of those individuals who are in the most favored position to keep the costs under control. The assignment of responsibility for overhead expenses to foremen, supervisors, and department heads allows a conceivable amount of control. It is admitted, however, that certain expenses are often troublesome; e.g., maintenance expenses. In the direct materials and direct labor areas, the assignment of responsibility for cost incurrences falls upon many shoulders and often becomes very obscure and nearly impossible to identify. Of course, it seems advisable to insist upon the assignment on the basis of *relative* control rather than *absolute* control.

In the direct materials area, the variances or deviations from a predetermined norm or standard will result in: (1) materials price variances, (2) materials quantity, or mix and yield variances, and/or (3) excessive defective work, rejects, or scrap costs. In the direct labor area, the variances or deviations from a predetermined norm or standard will result in: (1) pay rate variations, (2) efficiency variations, (3) and/or overtime costs.

However, these cost elements are not the only ones subject to change for which an executive may be held responsible. In later chapters the deviations from budgeted gross or net profit figures require explanation. The changes in sales prices, in sales volume, and in sales mix are the responsibility of the marketing department. Yet the gross profit figure contains elements of costs as well, so that a further investigation is warranted.

Variance Analysis for Responsibility Accounting. Today with the emphasis on responsible control of financial results via the return-on-capital-employed concept, assets, liabilities, net worth, revenue, and costs form a vast area in which the entire management spectrum from the top executive to the lowest foreman holds some share of responsibility. Like blocks in a pyramid (see page 302), the responsibility travels from the lowest to the highest level of supervision. Each supervisory level is responsible for costs incurred by its supervisor and his subordinates.

To be able to exercise this control, the cost and/or budget department must issue monthly reports that compare the actual results with predetermined amounts or budget allowances. An analysis prepared at the end of the annual fiscal period, as shown in the previous chapter, is not very helpful for immediate control actions. Reports on a monthly or more frequent basis are advisable to allow short-range comparisons of those costs for which operating management is being held responsible.

The illustrative problem beginning on page 295 assumes that variable expenses are controllable at the departmental level while fixed expenses are not. These assumptions apply to almost all costs in most situations. In some circumstances certain variable expenses may be controlled at a higher level in the organization; e.g., employee fringe benefits may be determined by negotiations between executive management and the labor union or by government regulations. Such costs should be analyzed and separately identified to relieve a department manager of this responsibility. Conversely, a department manager may have some control over certain fixed costs — those that involve a long-term commitment (sometimes called "committed fixed expenses") such as equipment depreciation or lease expense and those that can be readily changed in the short run (sometimes called "programmed fixed expenses") such as the number of foremen in the department. These costs should be individually identified as controllable by the manager of the department; and whether fixed or variable, some costs may be joint with respect to two or more departments and thus require arbitrary allocation. Accordingly, their controllability by a single department manager is restricted.

Attention must be called to the fact that in the long run all costs are controllable. Variable costs are generally controllable over short time periods. Some fixed costs, such as supervisory labor or equipment rental, can also be terminated on short notice while other fixed costs, depreciation of fixed assets or a long-term lease agreement, involve a fixed commitment over a longer period of time. Finally, some costs possess a dual short- and long-run controllability characteristic. For example, a five-year contract as to the price of a raw material, representing a long-run commitment, is not immediately controllable and the contract may be negotiable only at a higher management level. However, waste and spoilage of the same material is immediately controllable by the department. Generally, a department manager should be well enough informed to be able to explain cost variances even though the control or certain aspects of the control do not fall within his or her scope of authority and responsibility.

Variance Analysis on a Responsibility Basis — Illustrated. The data, steps, and methods presented below are based on the illustration in the previous chapter. There the annual factory overhead of four producing departments and four service departments was estimated, and product costing rates (factory overhead rates) were calculated after the indirect departmental expenses and service department costs had been apportioned and distributed. At the end of the year annual actual factory overhead was compared with applied factory overhead, and departmental spending and idle capacity variances were determined.

At this point the analysis moves into a monthly comparison. In order to keep the illustration compact, the four producing departments and only one service department, Utilities, are used. Some of the data previously presented must now be modified to serve this control responsibility phase. For product costing purposes, four departmental factory overhead rates have been computed and are listed below.

Cutting department.......	$2.00 per direct labor hour
Planing department.......	$3.20 per machine hour
Assembly department.....	60% of direct labor cost
Upholstery department....	$1.80 per direct labor hour

At the end of January the following actual data are assembled:

Departments	Actual Hours (Labor or Machine) or Labor Cost	Actual Consumption for the Month kwh	hph	Actual Departmental Overhead Before Billing Out Utilities
Cutting..........	3,046 direct labor hours	1,180	19,000	$3,575
Planing..........	1,620 machine hours	700	10,800	3,125
Assembly........	$11,400 direct labor cost	1,700	7,000	2,900
Upholstery.......	4,100 direct labor hours	1,980	8,000	3,570
		5,560	44,800	
Utilities..........				5,860

Floor space data remain the same as shown on page 259 of the previous chapter. Based on the actual production and cost data, the cost department would apply the following amounts of factory overhead to the products passing through the four departments:

Cutting department	=	3,046 direct labor hours × $2.00	=	$6,092
Planing department	=	1,620 machine hours	× $3.20	=	$5,184
Assembly department	=	$11,400 direct labor cost	× 60%	=	$6,840
Upholstery department	=	4,100 direct labor hours × $1.80	=	$7,380

If it is planned to determine the amount of over- or underapplied factory overhead, service department costs would have to be added to the actual direct and indirect departmental overhead to put actual and applied figures on a comparable basis. Such procedures were presented in Chapter 10.

Spending Variance on a Departmental Basis. In responsibility accounting, the emphasis rests upon the comparison of actual departmental expenses with budgeted or estimated costs exclusive of service department costs. In fact, many accountants believe that only the variable overhead (i.e., the controllable expenses for which management holds the department head responsible) should be compared and not the total overhead. Naturally, the procedure varies between different organizations.

In this example, both procedures will be illustrated for the four producing departments and for the one service department: (1) total actual departmental overhead, both fixed and variable, is compared with budgeted or predetermined departmental overhead; (2) only variable or controllable actual departmental overhead is compared with its budgeted or predetermined amount. Service department costs are excluded in both situations.

1.

		Departments			
	Cutting	*Planing*	*Assembly*	*Upholstery*	*Utilities*
Actual departmental overhead............	$3,575	$3,125	$2,900	$3,570	$5,860
Budget allowances: Fixed expenses (1/12 annual fixed costs; e.g., $17,100 ÷ 12 = $1,425)	$1,425	$1,492	$1,342	$1,525	$1,333
Variable expenses: 3,046 hours × $.5762*	1,755				
1,620 hours × $1.0217*		1,655			
$11,400 × 15.5%*			1,767		
4,100 hours × $.4217*				1,731	
5,560 kwh × $.1544*					858
44,800 hph × $.0494*					2,213
1,750 sq. ft.** × $.7057*					1,235
Budget allowances...	$3,180	$3,147	$3,109	$3,256	$5,639
Spending variances..	$ 395	$ (22)	$ (209)	$ 314	$ 221
	unfavorable	favorable	favorable	unfavorable	unfavorable

*Variable cost rate
**1,750 sq. ft. is 1/12 of 21,000 sq. ft. and $1,235 is 1,750 sq. ft. × the annual rate of $.7057.

or 2.

Actual variable depart- mental overhead (e.g., $3,575 — $1,425 fixed	Departments				
	Cutting	*Planing*	*Assembly*	*Upholstery*	*Utilities*
costs)................	$2,150	$1,633	$1,558	$2,045	$4,527
Budgeted variable expenses............	1,755	1,655	1,767	1,731	4,306
Spending variances......	$ 395	$ (22)	$ (209)	$ 314	$ 221
	unfavorable	favorable	favorable	unfavorable	unfavorable

The variable cost rates for the producing departments are calculated by dividing the variable departmental overhead, before service department distribution, by the predetermined or estimated direct labor hours, direct labor cost, or machine hours. This is illustrated in the example below (using data from pages 258 and 260):

$$\frac{\$23,400 \text{ Variable Cost — Cutting Department}}{40,608 \text{ Estimated Direct Labor Hours}} = \$.5762 \text{ per Direct Labor Hour}$$

In the producing departments actual hours or actual costs for the month are multiplied by the variable cost rate to arrive at the budgeted or estimated figure of the variable cost. The variable rates for Utilities (using data from pages 258 and 260) are calculated as follows:

Total departmental cost................	$ 65,400
Less fixed expenses.....................	16,000
Total variable expenses.................	$ 49,400

$49,400 × 20% = $ 9,880 ÷ 64,000 kwh = $.1544 variable rate per kwh
$49,400 × 50% = 24,700 ÷ 500,000 hph = $.0494 variable rate per hph
          $34,580
$49,400 — $34,580 = $14,820 ÷ 21,000 sq. ft. = $.7057 variable rate per sq. ft.

The estimated allowance for Utilities is based on the actual monthly consumption figures, except for the unchanged floor area, multiplied by the corresponding variable rates.

Idle Capacity Variance on a Departmental Basis. Responsibility accounting stresses the control of the variable expenses and the calculation of the departmental spending variance. It is, however, possible to continue the analysis and calculate an idle capacity variance based entirely on departmental costs without any allocation of service department costs or charges. To illustrate, the Cutting Department's total estimated overhead costs are $40,500 with $17,100 fixed and $23,400 variable. The variable overhead rate is $.5762 and the fixed rate $.4211 ($17,100 ÷ 40,608 estimated hours), providing a total of $.9973. A factory overhead rate of $2 per direct labor hour is used in the Cutting Department for product costing purposes; the difference of $1.0027 ($2.00 — $.9973) is accounted for by service department costs assigned to this department.

The analysis is as follows:

(1) Actual Overhead	(2) Budget Allowance	(3) Applied Overhead	(4) Total Variance (1–3)	(5) Spending Variance (1–2)	(6) Idle Capacity Variance (2–3)
$3,575	$3,180	$3,038*	$537 unfavorable	$395 unfavorable	$142** unfavorable

*3,046 actual hours × $.9973
**3,384 (40,608 hours ÷ 12 months) predetermined hours − 3,046 actual hours = 338 idle hours × $.4211

A similar analysis can be made for the service department, Utilities, as follows:

(1) Actual Overhead	(2) Budget Allowance	(3) Utilities' Cost Charged Out	(4) Total Variance (1–3)	(5) Spending Variance (1–2)	(6) Idle Capacity Variance (2–3)
$5,860	$5,639	$5,701*	$159 unfavorable	$221 unfavorable	$(62) favorable

*The amount of cost charged out is based on the total predetermined cost of $65,400 which was to be distributed: 20% or $13,080 based on kwh; 50% or $32,700 on hph; and 30% or $19,620 on floor area, resulting in these charging rates: $.2044 ($13,080 ÷ 64,000 kwh); $.0654 ($32,700 ÷ 500,000 hph); and $.9343 ($19,620 ÷ 21,000 sq. ft.).

The $5,701 is the result of: 5,560 actual kwh × $.2044 = $1,136
                                    44,800 actual hph × $.0654 = 2,930
1,750 sq. ft. (one month, i.e., 1/12 of 21,000 sq. ft.) × $.9343 = 1,635 $5,701

While the responsibility for the cost incurred is, generally speaking, easily identifiable in the producing departments, a service department's cost variances need a great deal of additional investigation. With a service department such as Utilities, the analysis is not so easy because:

1. Utilities can be charged accurately to consuming departments only when departmental or cost center meters are used.

2. Even with meters the quantity used might differ from the quantity produced due to line losses. The pinpointing of the responsibility for these losses is often impossible.

3. Since any utility can often be either purchased from outside or manufactured inside, it could be possible that the interchangeable use of one source with another will give rise to variances for which the cause is also difficult to detect.

Similar difficulties regarding the placing or pinpointing of responsibility for the cost incurrence and the resulting variance are experienced with any service department. The maintenance department has already been cited as an example. In many instances service department costs are largely fixed, at least over a relevant range of activity or volume. For this reason, responsibility is difficult to establish. The idle capacity variance is particularly bothersome when calculated on a monthly basis. The spending variance is somewhat more meaningful since actual and budgeted costs can be compared with their increases and decreases.

As a rule, the manager of the service department is responsible for the variance between the actual cost and the cost based on the number of hours or service units charged out or sold. The manager of the producing or *services received* department is responsible, with the service department foreman, for the number of hours or service units consumed in the department. This statement indicates that a kind of dual responsibility exists between the charges to the *services received* departments and the credits to the *services rendered* departments. The consuming department's cost must be compared with the allowed or budgeted service cost to determine the cost increase or decrease in that department, while the service department must examine its cost on the basis of the quantity consumed or sold.

RESPONSIBILITY REPORTING

Responsibility accounting is a program engulfing all operating management for which the accounting, cost, or budget divisions provide technical assistance in the form of daily, weekly, or monthly control reports. *Responsibility reporting* encompasses the reporting phase of responsibility accounting. In fact, the terms "responsibility accounting" and "responsibility reporting" are generally considered synonymous in that accounting should imply reporting and vice versa.

Reporting to the various levels of management can be divided into responsibility-performance reporting and information reporting. A clear distinction between the two is important; each serves different goals or objectives. *Responsibility-performance reports* are accountability reports with two purposes:

1. To inform the manager and his superior how he has done in the areas for which he is directly responsible for performance.

2. To motivate the manager and his superior to generate the direct action necessary to improve performance.

Information reports are issued for the purpose of providing the manager with information relevant to his areas of interest, although not necessarily directly associated with his specific responsibility for performance.

Information reports serve a broader and different set of goals than performance reports. In the short view, responsibility-performance reports are more important than information reports because of the immediate and pressing needs to keep the business on course. However, from the long view, information reports bearing on the progress and growth of the business are also important.

FUNDAMENTALS OF RESPONSIBILITY-PERFORMANCE REPORTS

Responsibility-performance reports should be based on certain fundamental qualities and characteristics:

1. Reports should fit the organization chart; that is, the report should be addressed to the individual responsible for the items covered by it and who, in turn, will be able to control those costs under his jurisdiction. Managers must be educated to use the results of the reporting system.
2. Reports should be prompt and timely. Prompt issuance of a report requires that cost records be organized so that information is available when it is needed.
3. Reports should be issued with regularity. Promptness and regularity are closely tied in with the mechanical aids used to assemble and issue reports.
4. Reports should be easy to understand. Often they contain accounting terminology that managers with little or no accounting training find difficult to understand, and vital information may be incorrectly communicated. Therefore, accounting terms should be explained or modified to fit the user. Top management should have some knowledge of the kind of items chargeable to an account as well as the methods used to compute overhead rates, make cost allocations, and analyze variances.
5. Reports should convey sufficient but not excessive detail. The amount and nature of the detail depend largely on the management level receiving the report. Reports to management should neither be flooded with immaterial facts nor so condensed that management lacks vital information essential to carrying out its responsibilities.
6. Reports should give comparative figures; i.e., a comparison of actual with budgeted figures or of predetermined standards with actual results and the isolation of variances.
7. Reports should be analytical. Analysis of underlying papers, such as time tickets, scrap tickets, work orders, and materials requisitions, provides reasons for poor performance which might have been due to power failure, machine breakdown, an inefficient operator, poor quality of materials, or many other similar factors.
8. Reports for operating management should, if possible, be stated in physical units as well as in dollars since dollar information may give a foreman not trained in the language of the accountant a certain amount of difficulty.

9. Reports may tend to highlight supposed departmental efficiencies and inefficiencies. Care should be exercised to see that such reports do not encourage departmental activities aimed at "making a good showing" regardless of the effect on the entire organization.

RESPONSIBILITY-REPORTING SYSTEMS — ILLUSTRATED

The illustrations presented on pages 302 and 303 depict the pyramid structure or the reporting procedure for responsibility accounting. The first system is employed in a manufacturing concern while the second system is employed in a bank.

The first step in a responsibility-reporting system is the establishment of lines of responsibility and responsibility areas. Each block in a company's organization chart represents a segment (cost center, division, department, etc.) that is reported upon and that receives reports on the functions responsible to it. Any report prepared according to this concept easily fits into one of these blocks as is illustrated in the organization chart below.

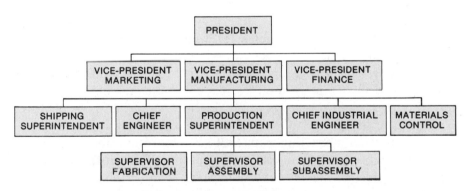

Organization Chart for a Manufacturing Concern

The reports appearing on page 302[1] illustrate the factory overhead reporting structure for each level of responsibility and the relationship of each report to the next higher echelon of responsibility. Starting with Report D (bottom of the pyramid), the Subassembly Department Supervisor is provided with the factory overhead expenses for his area. The supervisors for the Fabrication and Assembly Departments also receive similar reports. The supervisors of these three departments are responsible to the Production Superintendent. Report C summarizes the overhead

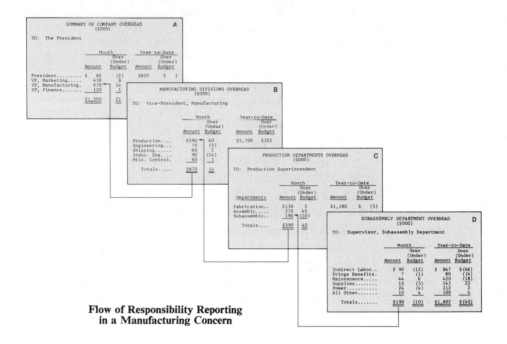

**Flow of Responsibility Reporting
in a Manufacturing Concern**

expenses for the three departments for which the Production Superintendent is held accountable. Report B provides the Vice-President of Manufacturing with performance figures for the five responsibility areas within his division. Finally, the President receives a summary, Report A, indicating overhead expenses not only for his area but also for the three divisions (Marketing, Manufacturing, Finance) reporting to him.

The illustration[2] appearing on page 303 depicts responsibility reporting in a bank utilizing a reporting system that permits effective expense control by accurately identifying and reporting expenses along the bank's organizational lines for enabling proper assignment of responsibility and control at each management level. In Exhibit A, expenses at each management level are identified by area responsibility as well as by natural classification. Exhibit B shows a typical report for an intermediate (middle) level of management while Exhibit C shows a report of a cost center.

REVIEWING THE REPORTING STRUCTURE

To provide all levels of management with all the facts when needed, the reporting system should be kept geared to the requirements of all managerial personnel. Each report should be so arranged that exceptions are

[2]William E. Ellington, Edward T. Kennedy, and Paul W. Landgren, Jr., "Computer-Based Bank Financial Information Systems," *The Arthur Andersen Chronicle*, Vol. 29, No. 2, p. 28.

RESPONSIBILITY EXPENSE SYSTEM: REPORTING FLOW — EXHIBIT A

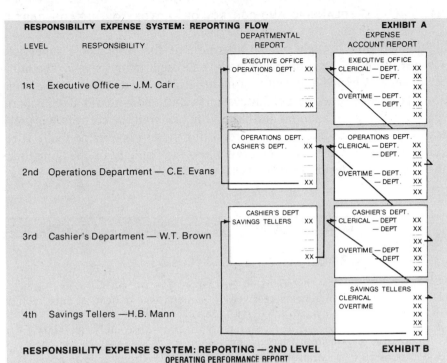

LEVEL	RESPONSIBILITY	DEPARTMENTAL REPORT	EXPENSE ACCOUNT REPORT
1st	Executive Office — J.M. Carr	EXECUTIVE OFFICE — OPERATIONS DEPT. XX ... XX	EXECUTIVE OFFICE — CLERICAL — DEPT. XX / — DEPT. XX / XX / OVERTIME — DEPT. XX / — DEPT. XX / XX
2nd	Operations Department — C.E. Evans	OPERATIONS DEPT. — CASHIER'S DEPT. XX ... XX	OPERATIONS DEPT. — CLERICAL — DEPT. XX / — DEPT. XX / XX / OVERTIME — DEPT. XX / — DEPT. XX / XX
3rd	Cashier's Department — W.T. Brown	CASHIER'S DEPT — SAVINGS TELLERS XX ... XX	CASHIER'S DEPT. — CLERICAL — DEPT XX / — DEPT XX / XX / OVERTIME — DEPT XX / DEPT XX / XX
4th	Savings Tellers — H.B. Mann		SAVINGS TELLERS — CLERICAL XX / OVERTIME XX / XX / XX / XX

RESPONSIBILITY EXPENSE SYSTEM: REPORTING — 2ND LEVEL — EXHIBIT B

OPERATING PERFORMANCE REPORT

DEPARTMENT NAME: OPERATIONS DEPARTMENT				RESPONSIBILITY OF: C. E. EVANS	FOR PERIOD ENDING: APRIL 30, 19XX			
CURRENT PERIOD				**RESPONSIBILITY AREA**	**YEAR TO DATE**			
TOTAL	VARIABLE	FIXED	UNFAVORABLE* VS PLAN		TOTAL	VARIABLE	FIXED	UNFAVORABLE* VS PLAN
$ 35,000	$ 10,000	$ 25,000	$2,000*	OPERATIONS ADMINISTRATION	$ 140,000	$ 40,000	$ 100,000	$ 8,000*
130,000	120,000	10,000	5,000*	CASHIER'S DEPARTMENT	520,000	480,000	40,000	20,000*
120,000	105,000	15,000	4,000	DATA PROCESSING	480,000	420,000	40,000	16,000
55,000	45,000	10,000	1,000	DEPOSIT ACCOUNTING	220,000	180,000	40,000	4,000
•	•	•	•	• • •	•	•	•	•
$375,000	$305,000	$ 70,000	$3,000*	TOTAL PERSONNEL EXPENSE	$1,500,000	$1,220,000	$ 280,000	$12,000*
$ 25,000	$ 10,000	$ 15,000	$3,000	OPERATIONS ADMINISTRATION	$ 100,000	$ 40,000	$ 60,000	$12,000
20,000	5,000	15,000	4,000	CASHIER'S DEPARTMENT	80,000	20,000	60,000	16,000
210,000	35,000	175,000	5,000*	DATA PROCESSING	840,000	140,000	700,000	20,000*
15,000	5,000	10,000	3,000*	DEPOSIT ACCOUNTING	60,000	20,000	40,000	12,000*
•	•	•	•	• • •	•	•	•	•
$290,000	$ 60,000	$230,000	$2,000*	TOTAL NON-PERSONNEL EXPENSE	$1,160,000	$ 240,000	$ 920,000	$ 8,000*
$665,000	$365,000	$300,000	$5,000	TOTAL DEPARTMENTAL EXPENSES	$2,660,000	$1,460,000	$1,200,000	$20,000*

RESPONSIBILITY EXPENSE SYSTEM: REPORTING — 4TH LEVEL — EXHIBIT C

OPERATING PERFORMANCE REPORT

DEPARTMENT NAME: SAVINGS TELLERS				RESPONSIBILITY OF: H. B. MANN	FOR PERIOD ENDING: APRIL 30, 19XX			
CURRENT PERIOD				**RESPONSIBILITY ACCOUNT**	**YEAR TO DATE**			
TOTAL	VARIABLE	FIXED	UNFAVORABLE* VS PLAN		TOTAL	VARIABLE	FIXED	UNFAVORABLE* VS PLAN
$ 3,200		$3,200	$ 200	ADMINISTRATION	$ 12,800		$12,800	$ 800*
900		900	100*	STAFF	3,600		3,600	400*
30,000	$30,000		2,000*	CLERICAL	120,000	$120,000		8,000*
300	300		200*	OVERTIME PREMIUM	1,200	1,200		800*
$34,400	$30,300	$4,100	$2,100*	TOTAL PERSONNEL EXPENSE	$137,600	$121,200	$16,400	$8,400*
$ 4,800		$4,800	$ 200	EQUIPMENT RENTALS	$ 19,200		$19,200	$ 800
200	$ 200		100*	SUPPLIES	800	$ 800		400*
300		300	100	TELEPHONE	1,200		1,200	400
700	700		400	OTHER MISC. EXPENSES	2,800	2,800		1,600*
$ 6,000	$ 900	$5,100	$ 200*	TOTAL NON-PERSONNEL EXPENSE	$ 24,000	$ 3,600	$20,400	$ 800*
$40,400	$31,200	$9,200	$2,300*	TOTAL DEPARTMENTAL EXPENSES	$161,600	$124,800	$36,800	$9,200*

highlighted and brought to the attention of the responsible supervisor without too much searching and reading through many pages. The number of reports issued and sent to a manager also needs constant examination. Too many times a reporting system is cluttered with old, detailed, and voluminous reports; and no one has ever considered the cost of their preparation or their justification. No reporting system is ever perfect. It requires continuous checking and examination in the light of changing times and the vicissitudes of business itself.

DISCUSSION QUESTIONS

1. Overhead control reports received by a department head should include only those items over which he has control. Explain.
2. Enumerate a few general requirements that are absolutely necessary for a successful responsibility accounting system.
3. Responsibility accounting does not involve a drastic change in accounting theory or principles. Discuss.
4. Enumerate some of the benefits that should result from responsibility accounting.   (NAA adapted)
5. The electric bill of the Emmons Company increased from $5,000 to $7,500 between January and February. As a bill is received, its cost is allocated to various departments on the basis of actual usage.
   (a) What factors may have caused the increase?
   (b) Is this an effective way of handling this cost? If not, suggest a better procedure.
6. The departmentalization of factory overhead is essential for maximum control of overhead. Explain in terms of responsibility reporting.
7. Why must service department overhead be included in the overhead rates? Why should actual service department overhead be accumulated in service department accounts instead of being charged directly to production department accounts?
8. Although service department overhead must be included in departmental overhead rates, actual overhead of these departments need not be distributed to departments serviced each period. Explain.
9. Usefulness of the figures is the primary reason for all accounting. Discuss.
10. On what fundamentals should the method of presenting cost data to management be based?
11. Discuss the information which a well-designed cost report should give to the management from the point of view of production and of control. Is there any other information with which the cost figures should be amplified? How should such information be given?
12. Which of the following should not be on a monthly cost control report of a department manager? (1) department labor cost; (2) department supplies cost; (3) depreciation cost on department equipment; (4) cost of materials used in the department.   (NAA adapted)

13. A frequent complaint made by management is that cost reports arrive too late to be of any value to the executives. What are the main contributing causes of this condition, and how can it be remedied?

14. Explain responsibility accounting and the classification of revenues and expenses under this concept.   (AICPA adapted)

15. Periodic internal performance reports based upon a responsibility accounting system should not (a) distinguish between controllable and uncontrollable costs; (b) be related to the organization chart; (c) include allocated fixed overhead in determining performance evaluation; (d) include variances between actual and controllable costs. Which of the above is correct?
                    (AICPA adapted)

16. Select the best answer for the following statement. The concept of "management by exception" refers to management's (1) lack of a predetermined plan; (2) consideration of only rare events; (3) consideration of items selected at random; or (4) consideration of only those items which vary materially from plans.   (AICPA adapted)

17. Select the best answer for each of the following statements.
    (a) Of most relevance in deciding how or which costs should be assigned to a responsibility center is the degree of (1) avoidability; (2) causality; (3) controllability; (4) variability.
    (b) Of most relevance in deciding how indirect costs should be assigned to product is the degree of (1) avoidability; (2) causability; (3) controllability; (4) linearity.
    (c) The most desirable measure of departmental performance for evaluating the performance of the departmental manager is departmental (1) revenue less controllable departmental expenses; (2) net income; (3) contribution to indirect expenses; (4) revenue less departmental expenses.
                    (AICPA adapted)

18. The three charges listed below are found on the monthly report of a division which manufactures and sells products primarily to outside companies. State which, if any, of these charges are consistent with the "responsibility accounting" concept. Support each answer with a brief explanation.
    (a) A charge for general corporation administration at 10% of division sales.
    (b) A charge for the use of the corporate computer facility. The charge is determined by taking actual annual Computer Department costs and allocating an amount to each user on the ratio of its use to total corporation use.
    (c) A charge for goods purchased from another division. (The charge is based upon the competitive market price for the goods.)
                    (NAA adapted)

EXERCISES

1. Maintenance Charging Rate. A *charging rate* is frequently used to charge Maintenance Department overhead to departments using its services. The charge is determined by multiplying the number of man-hours of service provided by the charging rate which is computed by the following formula:

$$\frac{\text{Total Actual Maintenance Department Overhead}}{\text{Total Man-Hours Worked}}$$

The superintendent of the Stamping Department of a company using this system was upset when he received a $15,000 maintenance charge for work that involved approximately the same number of man-hours as work done in a previous month when the charge was $12,000.

Required: (1) Factors which might have caused the increased charge.

(2) What improvements can be made for the distribution of this company's Maintenance Department overhead?

2. Transfer Rates and Variance Analysis. The Haiger Company uses predetermined departmental overhead rates to apply factory overhead. In computing these rates, every attempt is made to transfer service department overhead to producing departments on the most equitable bases. Budgeted overhead and other data for the Maintenance Department and General Factory are:

	Maintenance Dept.	*General Factory*
Monthly fixed overhead.....	$7,500	$30,000
Variable overhead.........	$1.00 per maintenance labor hour	$20.00 per employee (producing departments only)
Average hourly wage rate....	$4.50	
Normal level of activity......	15,000 maintenance hours per month	1,000 producing department employees

Required: (1) Charging or billing rates to be used to transfer estimated maintenance and general factory overhead to producing departments together with a description of the method used to charge actual maintenance and general factory costs to benefiting departments.

(2) Spending and idle capacity variances for the service departments using the following actual November results:

Maintenance overhead.........................	$27,000
General factory overhead......................	$55,000
Maintenance labor hours......................	16,000
Producing department employees..............	1,100

3. Billing Rate and Variance Analysis. The LeClerc Company operates its own power-generating plant. Power cost is distributed to the producing departments by charging the fixed cost according to the standby capacity provided and the variable cost on the basis of a predetermined rate multiplied by actual consumption. The rated standby capacity of the three departments A, B, and C is 50,000, 37,500, and 12,500 kwh respectively per month.

The following information relative to the producing departments and the power plant for the months of January through May is available:

	Consumption in Kilowatt-Hours			Power Plant	
	Dept. A	*Dept. B*	*Dept. C*	*Fixed*	*Variable*
January..............	45,000	40,000	10,000	$10,000	$ 9,800
February.............	55,000	35,000	11,000	10,000	10,000
March..............	47,500	38,000	11,000	10,000	9,900
April................	53,800	37,000	12,500	10,000	10,900
May	44,000	33,000	13,000	10,000	9,500

Predetermined variable power costs are based on $.10 per kwh.

Required: (1) Power cost chargeable to each department for each of the five months.

(2) The over- or underdistributed variable costs of the power plant for each of the five months.

4. Power Plant Charging Rate. During the month of November the actual expenses of operating a power plant amounted to $9,300, of which $2,500 was considered a fixed cost.

	Producing Departments		Service Departments	
Schedule of Horsepower-Hours:	*A*	*B*	*X*	*Y*
Needed at capacity production.....................	10,000	20,000	12,000	8,000
Used during the month of November...............	8,000	13,000	7,000	6,000

Required: (1) The dollar amounts of the power plant expenses to be allocated to each producing and service department. Fixed costs are assigned based on the power plant's readiness to serve.

(2) Reasons for allocating the costs of one service department to other service departments as well as to producing departments.

(AICPA adapted)

5. Service Departments Sold-Hour Rates; Variance Analysis. A company's two service departments provide the following data:

Service Center	*Monthly Budget*	*Service-Hours Available*	*Actual Monthly Expense*
Carpenter Shop..........	$20,000	4,000	$19,300
Electricians.............	30,000	5,000	23,400

The two service departments serve three producing departments that show the following budgeted and actual cost and service-hours data:

	Estimated Services Required		Actual Services Used	
Department No.	*Carpenter Shop*	*Electricians*	*Carpenter Shop*	*Electricians*
1........	1,200 hrs.	1,800 hrs.	800 hrs.	2,000 hrs.
2........	1,500 hrs.	2,000 hrs.	1,600 hrs.	1,700 hrs.
3........	1,300 hrs.	1,200 hrs.	900 hrs.	1,100 hrs.

Required: (1) The sold-hour rates for the two service departments.

(2) The amounts charged to the producing departments for services rendered.

(3) The spending variance for the two service departments, assuming that 60% of the budgeted expenses are fixed in both departments.

6. Billing Rates; Variance Analysis. The management of the Hollander Manufacturing Company wishes to secure greater control over service departments and decides to create a billing rate for the Maintenance and Payroll Departments. For the month of September the following predetermined and actual operating and cost data have been made available:

Maintenance Department:

Predetermined data (beginning of the month):

Normal level of maintenance hours per month...................... 3,200

Average hourly rate for maintenance worker...................... $5.50

Other maintenance costs:

	Fixed Costs per Month	Variable Costs per Maintenance Labor Hour
Supervision........................	$9,800	$.50
Tools and supplies..................	2,300	.75
Other miscellaneous items...........	700	.05

Actual data (end of the month):

Maintenance hours worked................................. 3,455

Maintenance workers earnings............................. $19,610

Other costs (supervision, etc.)............................. 16,390

Payroll Department:

Predetermined data (beginning of the month):

Average number of employees in factory and office................ 1,200

Budgeted fixed costs for department............................ $12,000
  plus $2 for each employee in factory and office

Actual data (end of the month):

Number of employees in factory and office...................... 1,165

Total costs in the payroll department......................... $14,375

Required: (1) The billing rate for the two departments.
(2) A variance analysis for the two departments for the month of September.

7. Overhead Analysis; Report to Supervisor. For the month of April, the cost and operating data on factory overhead for Department 10 were as shown at the top of the next page.

Required: (1) A variance analysis of the factory overhead for Department 10.
(2) A departmental report for the supervisor of Department 10 with explanations regarding the format used.

	Budgeted Factory Overhead Month of April	*Actual Factory Overhead Month of April*
Variable departmental overhead:		
Supplies................................	$ 2,000	$ 1,700
Repairs and maintenance.................	800	600
Indirect labor..........................	4,000	3,600
Power and light.........................	1,200	1,150
Heat....................................	400	350
Total..............................	$ 8,400	$ 7,400
Fixed departmental overhead:		
Building expenses........................	$ 800	$ 840
Depreciation — machinery................	2,400	2,400
Taxes and insurance.....................	400	420
Total..............................	$ 3,600	$ 3,660
Total departmental overhead................	$12,000	$11,060
Operating data:		
Normal capacity hours....................	8,000	
Factory overhead rate per hour...........	$1.50	
Actual hours — April....................		6,400

PROBLEMS

11-1. Overhead Rates; Variance Analysis in Producing and Service Departments.
Management control of the Santel Products Co. prepared the budgeted and actual data shown below.

	Budgeted Data — 19—				*Actual Data — March, 19—*		
Departments	*Direct Labor Cost*	*Direct Labor Hours*	*Factory Overhead Fixed*	*Variable*	*Direct Labor Cost*	*Direct Labor Hours*	*Factory Overhead Costs*
Machining........	$72,000	22,000	$12,840	$14,400	$6,780	2,130	$3,186*
Assembling.......	84,000	28,000	14,100	18,300	6,220	2,310	3,741*
Tools and Supplies.	–0–	–0–	3,600	5,600	–0–	–0–	919
Materials Handling.	–0–	–0–	5,700	6,000	–0–	–0–	1,080

*Includes service departments

The fixed overhead of the service departments is apportioned to the producing departments on a 60:40 percent basis and the variable overhead on the basis of direct labor hours. Budgeted direct labor hours are based on normal capacity utilization. Factory overhead is applied on the basis of direct labor hours.

Required: (1) Departmental factory overhead rates for producing departments based on (a) direct labor cost and (b) direct labor hours.

(2) (a) Departmental over- or underabsorbed factory overhead and (b) spending and idle capacity variances of producing and service departments. (Round off calculations to two decimal places.)

11-2. Variance Analysis in Producing and Service Departments Based on Responsibility Reporting. Production in the Milstein Linoleum Company, Inc. moves through four producing departments assisted by three service departments. Departmental overhead rates are established at the beginning of the fiscal year to aid in costing products completed. Actual factory overhead is accumulated and monthly budget reports are sent to each department supervisor for the purpose of responsibility accounting. On the basis of predetermined departmental expenses and after the allocation of the three service departments' costs, the following overhead rates for the four producing departments for product costing purposes were calculated:

| | Producing Departments | | | |
	Forming	Molding	Finishing	Packing and Shipping
Departmental expenses:				
Variable expenses...............	$19,500	$120,000	$22,400	$16,000
Fixed expenses..................	19,500	77,000	15,820	7,000
Total direct departmental expenses...	$39,000	$197,000	$38,220	$23,000
Distributed service departments' costs:				
Machine shop...................	6,200	14,800		
Hydraulic power................	1,400	15,600		
General plant..................	5,400	28,600	5,780	7,000
Total departmental overhead........	$52,000	$256,000	$44,000	$30,000
Factory overhead rates............	$4 per direct labor hour	$8 per machine hour	275% per direct labor cost	$2 per 100 units

Actual departmental production and cost data at the end of the budget period are as follows:

| | Producing Departments | | | | Service Departments | | |
	Forming	Molding	Finishing	Packing and Shipping	Machine Shop	Hydraulic Power	General Plant
Departmental expenses:							
Variable expenses..	$21,800	$116,000	$20,780	$19,300	$ 8,100	$ 5,000	$12,880
Fixed expenses....	19,500	77,000	15,820	7,000	14,000	12,000	36,000
Total actual expenses.	$41,300	$193,000	$36,600	$26,300	$22,100	$17,000	$48,880

| | Producing Departments | | | |
	Forming	Molding	Finishing	Packing and Shipping
Production data:				
Direct labor hours.	13,150			
Machine hours....		30,900		
Direct labor cost...			$18,100	
Units shipped.....				1,588,000

Required: (1) The amount of factory overhead applied in each of the four producing departments.

(2) The spending and idle capacity variances for the Forming and Molding Departments before service departments' costs are allocated.

(3) The amount of departmental overhead variance for which each departmental supervisor is being held responsible considering only variable costs for *all* departments. Assume that the use of service department facilities was exactly the same as the amount budgeted when the producing departments' overhead rates were calculated.

11-3. Variance Analysis of Producing and Service Departments Overhead. Rehn Products, Inc., decided to push for a greater amount of cost consciousness and cost responsibility among its departmental supervisors. The allocation of service departments' costs to the producing departments for the calculation of factory overhead rates has been in use for some time. Now the management asks the Cost Department, with the cooperation of the departmental supervisors, to prepare not only departmental budgets but also to give the supervisors monthly reports for cost control information.

The company operates with three producing departments, A, B, and C, and two service departments, Repairs and Maintenance, and Utilities. For the year 19—, the Cost Department had prepared the departmental factory overhead budgets and determined the following factory overhead rates based on direct labor hours:

DEPARTMENTAL FACTORY OVERHEAD BUDGETS

	Producing Departments			Service Departments	
				Repairs and	
Expenses	*A*	*B*	*C*	*Maintenance*	*Utilities*
Total budgeted expenses*....	$52,000	$52,450	$41,900	$56,000	$49,000
Allocation of service depts.:					
Utilities:					
Based on kilowatt hours...	40,000	45,000	35,000	20,000	
Costs..................	$14,000	$15,750	$12,250	$ 7,000	$49,000
					($.35 per kilowatt hour)
Repairs and maintenance:					
Based on direct labor hours	20,000	31,000	19,000		
Costs..................	$18,000	$27,900	$17,100	$63,000	
Total..................	$84,000	$96,100	$71,250	($.90 per direct labor hour)	
Departmental overhead rates:					
Based on direct labor hours	$4.20	$3.10	$3.75		

*The expenses and their amounts used to arrive at these figures have been omitted.

Actual cost and operating data *before* allocation of service departments' costs at the end of the budget period are:

| | Producing Departments | | | Service Departments | |
| | A | B | C | Repairs and Maintenance | Utilities |
Expenses	A	B	C	Maintenance	Utilities
Total actual expenses*.......	$56,220	$52,850	$42,580	$55,320	$49,240
Operating data:					
Direct labor hours.........	20,480	29,850	20,100		
Kilowatt hours............	39,300	46,200	35,800	18,950	

*The expenses and their amounts used to arrive at these figures have been omitted.

Predetermined rates are used to allocate service departments' costs.

Required: (1) The amount of factory overhead applied for each of the three producing departments.

(2) The amount of over- or underapplied factory overhead for each of the three producing departments, charging them with service department costs on the basis of actual kilowatt hours or labor hours multiplied by the billing rate.

(3) The total variance for each of the two service departments.

11-4. Billing Rate; Variance Analysis. The Croesus Corporation has three producing departments: Assembling, Painting, Finishing and Packing; and one service department: General Factory. Overhead is applied to the product via departmental overhead rates that include a share of the service department's expenses. The following monthly predetermined and actual costs and production data are available:

| | Departments | | | |
| | Producing | | | Service |
	Assembling	Painting	Finishing and Packing	General Factory
Variable expenses per direct labor hour...............	$ .50	$ .25	$ .30	$1.00
Fixed expenses.............	$2,800	$4,000	$2,320	$6,000
Normal monthly activity (direct labor hours).......	2,000	1,600	2,400	
Actual monthly results:				
Expenses.................	$4,400	$4,100	$3,300	$12,600
Hours worked............	2,050	1,500	2,200	

The service department's expenses are distributed to the producing departments on the basis of direct labor hours.

Required: (1) The charging or billing rate of the service department.

(2) The factory overhead rate for each of the three producing departments with the service department's expenses being prorated on the basis of the billing rate calculated in (1).

(3) The spending and idle capacity variances for each of the three producing departments.

(4) The spending variance of the service department.

11-5. Billing Rates; Estimated Factory Overhead and Variance Analysis. The Riehle Machine Tool Co. has two producing departments, Planers and Radial Drills, and two service departments, Maintenance and Utilities. The Cost Department collected the following data and information:

ESTIMATED DATA FOR THE YEAR 19—

| | Producing Departments | | Service Departments | |
	Planers	Radial Drills	Maintenance	Utilities
Factory overhead:				
Fixed overhead..........	$18,000	$15,000	$ 6,000	$4,800
Variable overhead.......	15,000	9,000	4,500	3,600
Total.................	$33,000	$24,000	$10,500	$8,400
Direct labor hours.......	12,000	7,500		
Maintenance hours......	2,500	1,000	3,500	
Kilowatt hours..........	45,000	25,000		70,000

ACTUAL DATA FOR THE MONTH OF JANUARY 19—

| | Producing Departments | | Service Departments | |
	Planers	Radial Drills	Maintenance	Utilities
Factory overhead:				
Fixed overhead..........	$ 1,500	$ 1,250	$ 500	$ 400
Variable overhead.......	1,620	1,050	670	310
Total.................	$ 3,120	$ 2,300	$ 1,170	$ 710
Direct labor hours.......	1,020	680		
Maintenance hours......	320	80	400	
Kilowatt hours..........	4,000	2,000		6,000

  Required: (1) The billing (or charging) rate for each of the two service departments, Maintenance and Utilities.

  (2) The total predetermined factory overhead for each of the two producing departments, Planers and Radial Drills, and their departmental factory overhead rates based on direct labor hours. Service departments' expenses are to be distributed on the basis of the billing rates calculated in (1) above.

  (3) An analysis of the over- or underapplied factory overhead of each of the two producing departments for the month of January, isolating the spending and idle capacity variances. Service departments' expenses are to be charged on the basis of actual hours (maintenance or kilowatt) multiplied by the billing rate. This method treats these expenses as being wholly variable.

  (4) A calculation and analysis of the over- or underdistributed factory overhead in each of the two service departments, isolating the spending and idle capacity variances.

11-6. Budget Allowance; Variance Analysis Based on Responsibility Reporting. The controller of the Kowalski Corporation prepared the following forecast income statement for the year 19—:

FORECAST INCOME STATEMENT — YEAR 19—

	Amount	Unit
Sales (60,000 units)	$600,000	$10.00
Cost of goods sold: (see Schedule I)	384,000	6.40
Gross profit	$216,000	$ 3.60
Operating expenses:		
Marketing expenses $80,000		
Administrative expenses 70,000	150,000	2.50
Net profit	$ 66,000	$ 1.10

Schedule I — Estimated cost of goods sold:

	Amount	Unit
Direct materials	$102,000	$ 1.70
Direct labor	162,000	2.70
Factory overhead	120,000	2.00
Total	$384,000	$ 6.40

  The product's manufacturing processes require two producing departments that make use of the services of Department 76 — Maintenance and Department 95 — Janitorial. To charge the products moving through the two departments, the cost accountant has prepared an overhead distribution sheet and calculated factory overhead rates for product costing as reproduced at the top of the next page.

PREDETERMINED DEPARTMENTAL OVERHEAD AND PRODUCTION DATA

	Producing Departments		Service Departments	
Data	Dept. 10	Dept. 12	Dept. 76 Maintenance	Dept. 95 Janitorial
Production units.............	60,000	60,000		
Direct labor hours............	30,000	24,000		
Direct labor cost.............	$90,000	$72,000		
Factory overhead:				
Variable overhead..........	$27,000	$22,800	$ 5,100	$2,700
Fixed overhead............	17,520	34,230	8,400	7,200
Share of Department 76....	7,500	6,000	$13,500	$9,900
Share of Department 95....	1,980	2,970		50% 4,950
Total factory overhead........	$54,000	$66,000		
To marketing and administrative expenses				$4,950
Factory overhead rate........ (based on direct labor hours)	$1.80	$2.75		

Department 76 costs were allocated to the two producing departments on the basis of the direct labor hours. Department 95 costs were prorated 50% to the factory and 50% to the general offices. The two producing departments shared the 50% on a ⅖–⅗ basis respectively.

For the month of January the Planning Department scheduled 5,000 units. At the end of the month, sales and production showed the following results:

Sales... 4,900 units
Production — completed in both departments................ 5,200 units

Actual hours and costs at the end of the month:

	Dept. 10	Dept. 12	Dept. 76	Dept. 95
Hours worked........................	2,680	2,060		
Actual factory overhead:				
Variable overhead....................	$2,700	$2,240	$495	$340
Fixed overhead......................	1,500	3,000	700	600

Required: (1) The budget allowance for each of the two producing departments for the month of January based on: (a) scheduled production hours, (b) actual production hours.

(2)   The spending and idle capacity variances for each of the two producing departments based on actual production hours.

(3) The spending variance for each of the two service departments.

CASE

Critique of Departmental Cost Report. The supervisor of the Welding Department of the Abilene Fabricating Company received the following budget report for the month of May, 19—:

	Budget	Actual	Variance Over (Under)
Labor — spot welding..........	$13,200	$13,280	$ 80
Labor — arc welding...........	22,900	22,700	(200)
Labor — materials handling.....	1,400	4,800	3,400
Welding supplies..............	3,500	3,520	20
Machinery repairs.............	7,900	9,850	1,950
Power costs...................	4,300	5,400	1,100
Heat, light...................	900	870	(30)
Depreciation — equipment......	2,700	2,700	——
Insurance....................	600	585	(15)
Property taxes................	500	490	(10)
Total.....................	$57,900	$64,195	$6,295

The welding supervisor, a conscientious employee, had never experienced such an unusually large, unfavorable variance. He consulted the manager of the Budget Department and was told that:

(a) Total costs of operating the company's power plant are accumulated and prorated to each department based on total labor costs. With labor costs being high in May in the Welding Department and low in other departments, a large portion of the power costs were charged to the Welding Department.

(b) Employees of the Repair Department keep time records on each repair job. The total costs of the Repair Department are prorated to each benefiting department based on the time spent in each department.

(c) The Budget Department manager could not explain the large variance in materials handling labor. Time tickets prepared by the timekeepers indicated the validity of the charge. The supervisor went to the timekeeper for an explanation. He reminded him of Job 705 which required 1,000 heavy parts to be returned from the Assembly Department, reworked, and sent back one at a time. The materials handling cost had been charged to the Welding Department. The supervisor remembered that the units had to be reworked because the blueprints he used for the original welding had been incorrect.

The supervisor returned to the Welding Department disillusioned with the budget program. He felt that his efforts to keep expenses in line with the budget were useless in view of the way expenses were charged to him. Do you agree with the supervisor? How should these costs for power, machinery repairs, and materials handling be treated?

Required: A statement indicating possible improvements or changes in the present methods.

CHAPTER **12**

MATERIALS CONTROL
PROCEDURES
AND COSTING METHODS

Effective materials management is essential and important in order to (1) provide the best type of service to customers, (2) produce at maximum efficiency, and (3) manage inventories at predetermined levels to stabilize investments in inventories. To succeed in effectively managing materials requires the development of a highly integrated and coordinated system involving sales forecasting, purchasing, receiving, storage, production, shipping, and actual sales. Materials management must consider both the theory of costing materials and inventories and the practical mechanics of cost calculations and record keeping.

Costing materials presents some important, often complex, and sometimes highly controversial questions concerning the costing of materials used in production and the cost of inventory remaining to be consumed in a future period. In financial accounting, the subject is usually presented as a problem of inventory valuation; in cost accounting, the primary problem is a determination of the cost of various materials consumed in production and a proper charge to cost of goods sold. The discussion of materials management in this chapter deals with:

1. Procedures for materials procurement and use
2. Materials costing methods
3. Cost of materials in inventory at the end of a period
4. Costing procedures for scrap, spoiled goods, and defective work

PROCEDURES FOR MATERIALS PROCUREMENT AND USE

Although production processes and materials requirements vary, the cycle of procurement and use of materials usually involves the following steps:

1. *Engineering, planning*, and *routing* determine the design of the product, the materials specifications, and the requirements at each stage of operations. Engineering and planning not only determine the maximum and the minimum quantities to run and the bill of materials for given products and quantities but also cooperate in developing standards where applicable.

2. The *production budget* provides the master plan from which details concerning materials requirements are eventually developed.

3. The *purchasing requisition* informs the purchasing agent concerning the quantity and the type of materials needed.

4. The *purchase order* contracts for appropriate quantities to be delivered at specified dates to assure uninterrupted operations.

5. The *receiving report* certifies quantities received and may report results of inspection and testing for quality.

6. The *materials requisition* notifies the storeroom or warehouse to deliver specified types and quantities of materials to a given department at a specified time or is the authorization for the storeroom to issue materials to departments.

7. The *materials ledger cards* record the receipt and the issuance of each class of materials and provide a perpetual inventory.

Accounting procedures for materials procurement and use involve forms and records necessary for general ledger financial accounting as well as those necessary for costing a job, process, or department, and for maintaining perpetual inventories and other statistical summaries. The purchase requisition, purchase order, receiving report, materials requisition, bill of materials, scrap report, returned materials report, materials ledger cards, and summary of materials used are some of the forms used for materials control under a cost system. The purchases journal, the cash payments journal, the general journal, and the general ledger control accounts are also used.

The discussion in this section is not based on any particular type or size of industry. it is, rather, a general description of the accounting and controlling procedures involved in the procurement and use of materials. The flowchart on page 319 shows procedures for purchasing, receiving, recording, and paying materials; i.e., the procurement phase.

Purchases of Productive Materials. The actual purchase of all materials is usually made by the purchasing department headed by a general purchasing agent. In small and medium-size companies, department heads

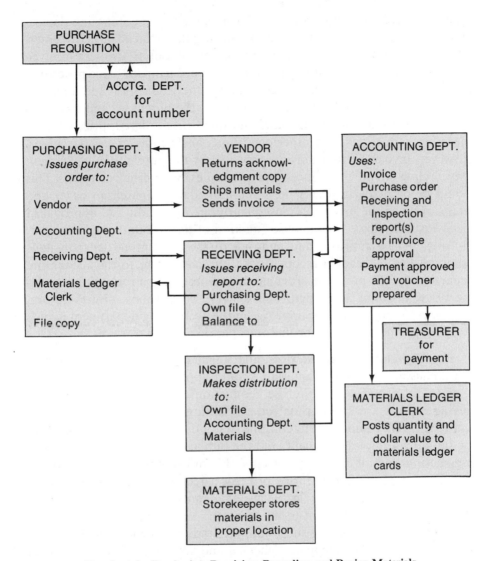

Flowchart for Purchasing, Receiving, Recording, and Paying Materials

or foremen have authority to purchase materials as the need arises. In any case, systematic procedures should be written up in order to fix responsibility and to provide full information regarding the ultimate use of materials ordered and received.

The purchasing department should: (1) receive purchase requisitions for materials, supplies, and equipment; (2) keep informed concerning sources of supply, prices, and shipping and delivery schedules; (3) prepare and place purchase orders; and (4) arrange for adequate and systematic reports between the purchasing, the receiving, and the accounting departments. A further function of the purchasing department in many enterprises is the verification and approval for payment of all invoices received in response to purchase orders placed by the department. This procedure is said to have the advantage of centralizing the verification and approval of invoices in the department that originates the purchases and has complete information concerning items and quantities ordered, prices, terms, shipping instructions, and other conditions and details of the purchases. However, invoice verification and approval by the purchasing department may violate sound procedures and principles of internal control. This would be particularly true if the same individual prepared an order and later approved the invoice. Consequently, invoice audit and approval in many instances have been made a function of the accounting department. Shifting invoice approval and auditing to the accounting department is accomplished by sending a copy of the purchase order to the accounting department. The purchase order carries all necessary information regarding price, discount agreement, and delivery stipulations. Furthermore, the centralization of invoice approval in the accounting department avoids delaying payments within the discount period.

Purchases of Supplies, Services, and Repairs. The procedure followed in purchasing productive materials should apply to all departments and divisions of a business. Purchase requisitions, purchase orders, and receiving reports are appropriate for accounting department supplies and equipment, the company cafeteria, the first aid unit, the treasurer's office, the building service department, and the public relations, personnel, sales, engineering, and all other departments. If, for example, the cost accounting department needs new forms printed, a requisition should be sent to the purchasing department in the usual manner; and a purchase order should be prepared and sent to the printer.

In the case of magazine subscriptions, trade and professional association memberships for company officials, and similar services, the official or department head may send in a requisition in the usual manner. A requisition, an order, and an invoice for all goods and services purchased are a necessity in controlling all purchases properly.

Repair contracts on an annual basis for typewriters, calculators, duplicating equipment, and some types of factory equipment may be requisitioned and ordered in the usual manner. In other cases, a department head or other employee may telephone for service and in a matter of minutes may have a machine repaired and back in operation. In such cases, the purchasing agent issues a so-called blanket purchase order that amounts to approval of all repair and service costs of a specific type without knowing the actual amount charged. When the repair bill is received, the invoice clerk checks the amount of the bill with the department head where the repairs took place and then approves the invoice for payment.

Purchasing Forms.   The principal forms required in purchasing are the purchase requisition and the purchase order.

The Purchase Requisition.   The *purchase requisition* originates with a stores or warehouse clerk who observes that the quantity on hand is at a set ordering minimum, or with a materials ledger clerk who may be responsible for notifying the purchasing agent when to buy, or with a works manager who foresees the need for special materials or unusual quantities, or with a research or engineering department employee who needs materials or supplies of a special nature, or with a computer that has been programmed to produce automatically replenishment advice to the purchasing department.   For standard materials, the purchasing agent may need little information other than the stock number and uses judgment concerning where to buy and the quantity to order.   For other purchase requests, it may be necessary to give meticulous descriptions, catalog numbers, weights, standards, brand names, exact quantities to order, and suggested prices.

A purchase requisition is illustrated below.   One carbon copy remains with the originating employee, and the original is sent to the purchasing department for execution of the request.

PURCHASE REQUISITION (This is not a Purchase Order.)			No. **07615**		
TO: Purchasing Department			Mo.	Day	Yr.
DELIVER TO: _____		DATE REQUIRED: _____			
		FOR: _____			
SUGGESTED SUPPLIER: _____					

PLEASE ORDER THE ITEMS LISTED BELOW:

Quantity	Item No.	Description	Unit Price	Amount

BUDGET CONTROL		
Allowance For Period $_____	Balance Available $_____ Amt. This Purchase $_____ Remaining Balance $_____	Ordered By Approved By

Purchase Requisition

The Purchase Order. The *purchase order*, signed by the purchasing agent or other official, is a written authorization to a vendor to supply specified quantities of described goods at agreed terms and at a designated time and place. As a matter of convenience, the vendor's order forms may be used; but in typical practice, the order forms are prepared by the purchasing company, and the form is adapted to the particular needs of the purchaser. As a matter of record and for accounting control, a purchase order should be issued for every purchase of materials, supplies, or equipment, whether the purchase is made by mail, telephone, telegraph, or from a salesman. Where a purchase commitment is made by wire or in an interview with a sales representative, the purchase order serves as confirmation to the vendor and places the required documents in the hands of those concerned in the purchasing company.

The purchase order gives the vendor a complete description of the goods and services desired, the terms, the prices, and the shipping instructions. Where necessary, the description may refer to attached blueprints and specification pages. The original and one carbon copy, the latter being labeled "Acknowledgment Copy," are sent to the vendor. The vendor is asked to return the carbon copy with his signature which indicates to the purchasing agent that the order was received and will be delivered according to the specifications enumerated in the purchase order. The acknowledgment copy is a necessary form for contract procedure. Other carbon copies are distributed as shown in the flowchart on page 319.

Receiving. The function of the receiving department is to unload and unpack incoming materials; to check quantities received against the shipper's packing list; to identify goods received with descriptions on the purchase order; to prepare a receiving report; to notify the purchasing department of discrepancies discovered; to arrange for inspection when necessary; to notify the traffic department and the purchasing department of any damage in transit; and to route accepted materials to the appropriate factory location.

The *receiving report* will show purchase order number, account number to be charged, name of the vendor, details relating to transportation, and quantity and type of goods received. The form also provides a space for the inspection department to note either the complete approval of the shipment or the quantity rejected and reason for the rejection. If inspection does not take place immediately after receipt of the material, the receiving report is distributed as follows: (1) the receiving department keeps one copy and sends another copy to the purchasing department as an advance notice of the arrival of the material and as a means of avoiding further follow-up by the purchasing agent; (2) all other copies go to the inspection department, and distribution of them is not made until inspection is completed. After inspection, one copy of the receiving report, with the inspection result noted thereon, is sent for payment to the accounting department where it is matched with the purchase order and the vendor's invoice. Other copies go to various departments such as materials and production planning. The copy to the storekeeper accompanies the materials so that he knows the quantity and the kind of materials he is receiving.

Approval and Data Processing. By the time materials reach the receiving department via parcel post, express, truck, rail, air, or water transportation, the company usually will have received the invoice from the vendor. This invoice is then routed to the accounting department and is filed with the copy of the purchase order until the receiving report arrives. When the receiving report with its inspection report is in, the receiving report and the invoice are examined to see that materials received meet purchase order specifications as to items, quantities, prices, price extensions, discount and credit terms, shipping instructions, and other possible conditions. Inasmuch as the purchase order and the receiving report contain the account number that was originally placed on the purchase requisition, the invoice clerks need no further assistance in this respect; and speedy approval is assured. When the invoice is found correct in all respects or has been adjusted because of rejects as noted by the inspection department, the invoice clerk approves it, attaches it to the purchase order and the receiving report, and sends these papers to another clerk for the preparation of the voucher.

Invoice approval is an important step in materials control procedure since it certifies that the goods have been received as ordered and that payment can be made. The invoice approval information is often built into a rubber stamp, and each invoice is stamped. The verification procedure is handled by responsible invoice clerks, thus assuring systematic examination and handling of the paper work necessary for adequate control of materials purchases. The preparation of the voucher is based on the information taken from the invoice approval stamp.

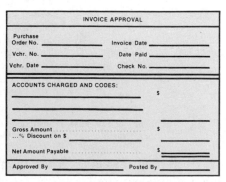

Invoice Approval Stamp

The voucher data are entered first in the purchases journal and then in the cash payments journal according to the due date for payment. The original voucher and two carbon copies are sent to the treasurer for issuance of the check.   The treasurer mails the check with the original voucher to the vendor, files a voucher copy, and returns one voucher copy to the accounting department for the vendor's file.   Purchase transactions entered in the purchases journal affect the control accounts and the subsidiary records as shown in the chart below.

TRANSACTION	GENERAL LEDGER CONTROL		SUBSIDIARY RECORDS
	Debit	Credit	
Materials purchased for stock	Materials	Accounts Payable	Entry in the Received section of the materials ledger card
Materials purchased for a particular job or department	Work in process	Accounts Payable	Entry in the Direct Materials section of the production or job order
Materials and supplies purchased for factory overhead purposes	Materials	Accounts Payable	Entry in the Received section of the materials ledger card
Supplies purchased for marketing and administrative offices	Materials, Marketing, or Adm. Expense Control	Accounts Payable	Entry in the Received section of the materials ledger card *or* in the proper columns of the marketing or administrative expense analysis sheets
Purchases of services or repairs	Factory Overhead, Marketing, *or* Adm. Expense Control	Accounts Payable	Entry in the proper account columns of the expense analysis sheets
Purchases of equipment	Equipment	Accounts Payable	Entry on the equipment ledger card

**Summary of Purchase Transactions of Materials, Services, and Equipment
with Accounting Records**

Correcting Invoices.   When the purchase order, receiving report, and invoice are compared, various errors and omissions such as those listed below may be revealed:

1. Some of the materials ordered may not be received. If the invoice covers only the goods actually shipped and received, no adjustment is necessary; and the invoice may be approved for immediate payment.   On the

purchase order the invoice clerk will make a notation of the quantity received in place of the quantity ordered. The vendor may explain that he is out of stock or otherwise unable to deliver specified merchandise. In such a case an immediate ordering from other sources may be necessary.

2. Items ordered may not be received but may be entered on the invoice. In this situation the shortage is noted on the invoice and is deducted from the total before payment is approved. A letter to the vendor explaining the shortage is usually in order.

3. The seller may ship a quantity larger than called for on the purchase order. The purchaser may keep the entire shipment and add the excess to the invoice, if not already invoiced; or the excess may be returned or held, pending instructions from the seller. Some companies issue a supplementary purchase order that authorizes the invoice clerk to pay the overshipment.

4. Materials of a wrong size or quality, defective parts, and damaged items may be received. If the items are returned, a correction on the invoice should be made before payment is approved. It may be advantageous to keep damaged or defective shipments if the seller makes adequate price concessions, or the items may be held subject to his instructions.

5. When delivered prices are quoted and purchases are made on this basis, it may be expedient for a purchaser to pay transportation charges. The amount paid by the purchaser is deducted on the invoice, and the paid freight bill is attached to the invoice as evidence of payment.

Electronic Data Processing for Materials Received and Issued. The preceding description of invoice approval and payment was for a manual operation performed by an accounts payable clerk or an invoice clerk. In an electronic data processing (EDP) system, the computer — to a great extent — replaces the clerk. Upon receipt of the invoice (the source document), the accounts payable clerk enters the account distribution on the invoice. The data are then directly inputted from the invoice to the computer data bank via a terminal device. The data are edited, audited, and merged with the purchase order and the receiving order data, both of which have been stored in the computer data bank. The common matching criterion on all documents is the purchase order number. Quantities, dollar values, due dates, terms, and unit prices are matched. When in agreement, the cost data will be entered in the accounts payable computer file with a date for later payment or a printout of a check will be transmitted for payment.

The above procedure deals with the accounts payable phase of a purchase transaction. Yet, of equal importance is the need for posting the data in quantities and dollar values to the materials inventory file in the EDP system. The information would then enter the EDP system from either the invoice (the source document) or the invoice approval form, which would have to include all computer-necessary data. The internal computer program would update the materials inventory file. The program

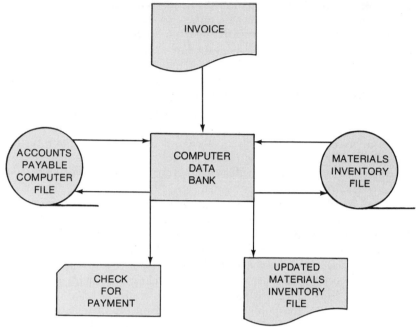

Integration of a Purchase Transaction for Materials into the Accounts Payable Phase of an EDP System

applicable to the accounts payable phase of a purchase transaction for materials can be depicted in the flowchart above.

A second program would also have been designed for the withdrawal of the materials that would eliminate the manual postings to the materials inventory file.

Cost of Acquiring Materials. A guiding principle in accounting for the cost of materials is that all costs incurred in entering a unit of raw materials into factory production should be included. Acquisition costs such as the vendor's invoice price and transportation charges are visible costs of the purchased goods. Less obvious costs of materials entering factory operations are costs of purchasing, receiving, unpacking, inspecting, insuring, storing, and general and cost accounting.

Controversial concepts and certain practical limitations result in variations in implementing the principles of costing for materials even with respect to easily identified acquisition costs. Calculating a number of cost additions and adjustments to each invoice involves clerical expenses which may be greater than benefits derived from the increased accuracy. Therefore, materials are commonly carried at the invoice price paid the vendor, although all acquisition costs and price adjustments affect the materials

costs. As a result, acquisition costs are generally charged to factory overhead when it is not practical to follow a more accurate costing procedure.

Purchase Discount. The handling of discounts on purchases is one
major problem in accounting for materials costs. Trade discounts and
quantity discounts normally are not on the accounting records but are
treated as price reductions. Cash discounts should be handled as price
adjustments but often are accounted for as *other income.* Income is not
produced by buying. A lower purchase cost may well widen the margin
between sales price and cost, but it takes the sale to produce income.
When the vendor quotes terms such as 2/10, n/30 or 3/10, n/30 on a $100
invoice, is he trying to sell the goods for $100 or is he determined to get
$98 or $97 as the case may be? The purchaser has two dates to make
payment: on the tenth day, which allows time to receive, unpack, inspect,
verify, voucher, and pay for the goods; or twenty days later. For the additional twenty days an additional charge or penalty of 2 percent is assessed
if the terms are 2/10, or 3 percent if the terms are 3/10. If regarded as
interest, the extra charge is $\frac{360 \text{ days}}{20 \text{ days}}$ = 18 periods × 2 percent = 36 percent
per year, or $\frac{360 \text{ days}}{20 \text{ days}}$ = 18 periods × 3 percent = 54 percent per year. On
these terms the seller is pricing on essentially a cash basis, and the pur-
chaser has no reasonable choice except to buy on the cash basis.

Although the nature of a purchase discount is readily understood, for
practical reasons the gross materials unit cost of the invoice is commonly
recorded in the materials account; the cash discount is recorded as a credit
account item. Otherwise it would be necessary to compute the discount on
each item with four or more decimal place unit costs.

Freight-In. Freight or other transportation charges on incoming shipments are obviously costs of materials, but differences occur in the cost
allocation of these charges. A vendor's invoice for $600 may show 25
items weighing 1,700 pounds shipped in five crates, with the attached freight
bill showing a payment of $48. The delivered cost is $648. But how much
of the freight belongs to each of the invoice items, and what unit price
should go on the materials ledger card? When the purchased units are not
numerous and are large in size and unit cost, computation of actual
amounts of freight may be feasible; otherwise, some logical, systematic,
and expedient procedure is necessary.

If freight charges are debited to Materials, the total amount should be
added proportionately to each materials card affected. This might be done
by assuming that each dollar of materials cost carries an equal portion of
the freight. $\frac{\text{Freight Cost } \$48}{\text{Materials Cost } \$600}$ would add $.08 to each dollar on the invoice.
The relative weight of each item on the invoice might be determined and

used as a basis for calculating the applicable freight. If invoice item No. 4 is estimated to weigh 300 pounds, then $\frac{300}{1,700} \times \$48$ or $8.47 would be added for freight. This procedure is also likely to result in four or more decimal place unit costs on the materials ledger cards. In order to simplify procedures, all freight costs on incoming materials and supplies may be charged to Freight-In. As materials are issued for production, an applied rate for freight-in (and other handling costs) might be added to the unit price kept on the ledger cards. Such an amount is thus added to the Work in Process debit, or to Factory Overhead for indirect materials, with a credit to Freight-In. Any balance in Freight-In at the end of a period is closed to Cost of Goods Sold or prorated to Cost of Goods Sold and inventories.

Another often advocated method of accounting for incoming freight costs on materials is to estimate the total for an accounting period and include this amount in computing the factory overhead charge rate. Freight-In would then become one of the accounts controlled by Factory Overhead.

For materials or supplies used in marketing and administrative departments, freight, transportation, or delivery costs should be charged to the appropriate nonmanufacturing account.

Applied Acquisition Costs. If it is decided that materials cost should be the net price paid the vendor plus incoming freight charges plus other acquisition costs, such as those of the purchasing department, receiving department, testing, insurance, and applicable accounting functions, an applied rate might be added to each invoice and to each item. When this procedure is impractical, a single amount can be added to the total materials cost for a given lot, order, or department. A single rate for these combined costs can be used, or a more accurate method of using separate rates for each class of costs can be computed as follows:

$$\frac{\text{Estimated Purchasing Dept. Cost for Month or Budget Period}}{\text{Estimated Number of Purchases or Estimated Amount of Purchases}} = \begin{array}{l}\text{Rate per Purchase,}\\ \text{or Rate per Dollar}\\ \text{Purchased}\end{array}$$

$$\frac{\text{Estimated Receiving Dept. Cost for Month or Budget Period}}{\text{Estimated Number of Items to Be Received During Period}} = \text{Rate per Item}$$

$$\frac{\text{Estimated Materials Department Cost for Month or Budget Period}}{\text{Estimated Number of Items, Feet of Space, Dollar Value, etc.}} = \begin{array}{l}\text{Rate per Item, Cubic}\\ \text{Feet, Dollar Stored, etc.}\end{array}$$

$$\frac{\text{Estimated Accounting Dept. Cost for Month or Budget Period}}{\text{Estimated Number of Transactions}} = \text{Rate per Transaction}$$

This procedure results in the accounting treatment shown below:

```
Materials.................................    xxx
      Purchasing Dept. Expenses Applied......         xxx
      Receiving Dept. Expenses Applied........        xxx
      Materials Dept. Expenses Applied........        xxx
      Accounting Dept. Expenses Applied......         xxx
```

Actual expenses incurred by each of the departments for which applied rates are used will be debited to the applied accounts. Differences between the expenses incurred by the departments during the period and the expenses applied to materials cost would represent over- or underapplied expenses and would be closed to Cost of Goods Sold or prorated to Cost of Goods Sold and inventories.

Storage and Use of Materials. Materials, together with a copy of the receiving report, are forwarded to storerooms from the receiving or inspection department. The storekeeper and his assistants are responsible for safeguarding the materials, which means that materials and supplies are placed in proper bins or other storage spaces, that they are kept safely until required in production, and that all materials taken from the storeroom are properly requisitioned. It is good policy to restrict admittance to the storeroom to employees of that department only and to have these employees work behind locked doors, issuing materials through cage windows somewhat as a bank teller operates.

Since the cost of storing and handling materials may be a substantial amount, careful design and arrangement of storerooms can result in significant cost savings. Materials can be stored according to: (1) the materials account number; (2) the frequency of use of the item; (3) the factory area where the item is used; or (4) the nature, size, and shape of the item. In practice no single one of these bases is likely to be suitable, but size and shape of materials usually dictate the basic storeroom arrangement. Variations can then be introduced, such as placing most frequently used items nearest the point of issue and locating materials used primarily in one factory area nearest that area.

Bin Cards. Stock or *bin cards* are effective ready references that may be attached to storage bins, shelves, racks, or other containers. Bin cards usually show quantities of each type of material received, issued, and on hand. They are not a part of the accounting records as such, but they show the quantities on hand in the storeroom at all times and should agree with the quantities on the materials ledger cards in the accounting department. The design of a bin card is not limited to the size or shape illustrated at the right.

Bin Card

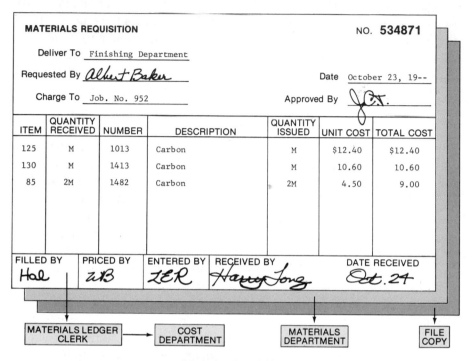

MATERIALS REQUISITION					NO. **534871**	

Deliver To Finishing Department

Requested By *Albert Baker*   Date October 23, 19--

Charge To Job. No. 952   Approved By *J.T.*

ITEM	QUANTITY RECEIVED	NUMBER	DESCRIPTION	QUANTITY ISSUED	UNIT COST	TOTAL COST
125	M	1013	Carbon	M	$12.40	$12.40
130	M	1413	Carbon	M	10.60	10.60
85	2M	1482	Carbon	2M	4.50	9.00

FILLED BY	PRICED BY	ENTERED BY	RECEIVED BY	DATE RECEIVED
Hal	*WB*	*LER*	*Harry Jong*	*Oct. 24*

MATERIALS LEDGER CLERK	COST DEPARTMENT	MATERIALS DEPARTMENT	FILE COPY

Materials Requisition

Issuing and Costing Materials into Production. To control the quantity and cost of materials, supplies, and services requires a systematic and efficient system of purchasing, recording, and storing. Equally necessary and important is a systematic and efficient procedure for issuing materials and supplies.

Materials Requisition. The *materials requisition* (see illustration on this page) is a written order to the storekeeper to deliver materials or supplies to the place and the department designated or to give the materials to the person presenting a properly executed requisition. It is drawn by someone who has the authority to requisition materials for use in the department. The authorized employee may be a production control clerk, a department head, a foreman, a group leader, an expediter, or a materials release analyst. In a computerized system, the computer program will often prepare the requisition in the form of a tabulating card.

The materials requisition constitutes the basic form for materials withdrawn from the storeroom. Its preparation results in entries in the Issued section of the materials ledger cards and in postings to the job order cost sheets, production reports, or the various expense analysis sheets for individual departments. All withdrawals result in debits to Work in Process or to expense control accounts for factory overhead, marketing, or administrative expenses, and in credits to Materials.

Materials Requisition Journal. With the posting to the materials ledger cards, the job order cost sheets, the production reports, and the expense analysis sheets completed, it is still necessary to post the materials withdrawals to the proper ledger control accounts. This task is greatly facilitated by the use of a *materials requisition journal*, which acts as a form of materials summary. A materials requisition journal might take the following form:

MATERIALS REQUISITION JOURNAL

Date	Credits Mtls.	Description	Req. No.	Job or Acct. No.	Debits Work in Process	Fac. Ovh. Control	Marketing Exp. Control	Adm. Exp. Control	Sundries Acct. No.	L F	Amount
19--Oct.											
1	600 00	Direct materials.....	4101	5317	600 00						
1	225 00	Indirect materials ...	4102	411		225 00					
3	1,800 75	Direct materials......	4103	5318	1,800 75						
3	195 50	For installation	4104						135	✓	195 50
4	75 00	Supplies...........	4105	630				75 00			
4	112 80	Supplies..........	4106	530		112 80					
	41,160 90				36,400 00	2,280 00	1,525 40	760 00			195 50

Materials Requisition Journal

At the end of the month the totals of the various columns are posted directly to the ledger accounts.

Tabulating Cards as Materials Requisitions. Tabulating cards are convenient input or output devices for computer operations. To produce the card, the computer is asked via the console operator to perform certain materials issuance transactions for jobs or products. The card serves as authority for the storekeeper to issue the materials. Internal computer operations will perform the issuance, update the materials data bank, and eventually produce output reports including totals that will be entered in the general ledger accounts unless those accounts are also part of the EDP system.

Indirect materials or supplies for factory or office will also be stored in the inventory data bank of the computer. When such materials are needed, a request will inform the computer as to type, quantity, and requesting department. Supplies requisitioned for marketing and administrative departments would be charged to their respective departments.

Bill of Materials. The *bill of materials*, a kind of master requisition, is a printed or duplicated form that lists all the materials and parts necessary for a typical job or production run. Time is saved, and efficiency is promoted through the use of a bill of materials. When a job or production run is started, all the materials listed on the bill of materials are sent to the factory or are issued on a prearranged time schedule. As the bill of materials is a rather cumbersome medium for posting purposes, data processing improves the procedure by preparing simultaneously tabulating cards for materials requisitions. While the storekeeper issues the materials as stated on the bill of materials, the tabulating cards can be processed in the materials ledger section and in the cost department at almost the same time as the materials are used in the factory. A computer program will provide the printouts of the bill of materials and process the information internally to update the accounting records.

Materials (or Stores) Ledger Card — Perpetual Inventory Record. As purchased materials go through the systematic verification of quantities, prices, physical condition, and other checks, the crux of the accounting procedure is to establish a perpetual inventory — maintaining for each type of material a record showing quantities and prices of materials received, issued, and on hand. Materials ledger cards or stock ledger sheets constitute a subsidiary materials ledger controlled by the materials or inventory accounts in the general ledger or in the factory ledger if inventory accounts are kept at the factory.

Materials ledger cards commonly show the account number, description or type of material, location, unit measurement, and maximum and minimum quantities to carry. These cards constitute the *materials ledger*, new cards being prepared and old ones discarded as changes occur in the types of materials carried in stock. The ledger card arrangement is basically the familiar debit, credit, and balance ruling columns under the description of Received, Issued, and Balance. A materials ledger card is illustrated below.

Piece or Part No. _____   Reorder Point _____

Description _____   Reorder Quantity _____

Materials Ledger Card	RECEIVED				ISSUED				BALANCE		
	Date	Rec. No.	Qty.	Amount	Date	Req. No.	Qty.	Amount	Quantity	Unit Cost	Amount

In some businesses, the approved invoice with supporting documents, such as the purchase order and receiving report, goes to the materials ledger clerk. These documents enable the clerk to make the necessary entries in the Received section of the materials ledger card. Each receipt increases the balance on hand, and the new balance is extended upon entry of the receipt.

Unsatisfactory goods or defective units should be detected by the inspection department before being stored or even paid for. The receiving report should show materials actually accepted, and the ledger entries are made after all adjustments. However, goods accepted in the storeroom may be found unsatisfactory after part of a shipment has been used in the factory; and the balance may then be returned to the vendor. Since these units were entered in the Received and Balance sections of the materials ledger card when they were placed in the storeroom, an adjustment must be made. The recommended procedure is to enter the quantity and the value of the returned shipment *in red* in the *Received* section and to reduce the balance accordingly.

When the storekeeper issues materials, a copy of the requisition is sent to the materials ledger clerk who then makes an entry in the Issued section of the materials ledger card showing the date, the requisition number, the job, lot, or department number, the quantity, and the cost of the issued materials. The new balance is computed and entered in the Balance column. As already explained, these manual operations will be performed in an EDP system based on the computer program designed for any or all materials transactions.

MATERIALS COSTING METHODS

The ultimate objective in accounting is to produce accurate and meaningful cost figures that can be used for purposes of control and analysis and eventually matched against revenues produced in order to determine net operating income.

After the unit cost and total cost of incoming materials are entered in the Received section of a materials ledger card, the next step is to cost these materials as they move either from storeroom to factory as direct or indirect materials or from storeroom to marketing and administrative expense accounts as supplies. The more common methods of costing materials issued and inventories are:

1. First-in, first-out (fifo)
2. Average cost
3. Last-in, first-out (lifo)
4. Other methods — such as month-end average cost, last purchase price or market price at date of issue, and standard cost

These methods relate to assumptions as to flow of costs. The *physical flow* of *units* may coincide with the method of cost flow in use, though such a condition is not a necessary requirement. This discussion deals with raw materials inventory; however, the same costing methods are also applicable to work in process and finished goods inventories.

The illustrations discussed below assume a perpetual inventory system; i.e., an entry is made each time the inventory is reduced. Such a procedure is a desirable characteristic of most cost accounting systems. The alternative to a perpetual inventory system is the physical inventory system whereby purchases are added to the beginning inventory, the ending (remaining) inventory is counted and costed, and the difference is considered the cost of materials issued.

First-In, First-Out (fifo) Method of Costing. The first-in, first-out (fifo) method of costing is used to introduce the subject of materials costing. This illustration, as well as those for the average and lifo costing methods, is based on the following transactions:

Feb. 1. Beginning balance: 800 units @ $6 per unit.
　　　 4. Received 200 units @ $7 per unit.
　　　 10. Received 200 units @ $8 per unit.
　　　 11. Issued 800 units on a fifo basis.
　　　 12. Received 400 units @ $8 per unit.
　　　 20. Issued 500 units on a fifo basis.
　　　 25. Returned 100 excess units from the factory to the storeroom to be recoded at the latest issued price of $8.
　　　 28. Received 600 units @ $9 per unit.

The above transactions would be calculated as follows:

Fifo Costing Method — Illustrated:

Feb. 1. Beginning balance..............	800 units @ $6 = $4,800		
4. Received......................	200 units @ $7 = 1,400		
10. Received......................	200 units @ $8 = 1,600	$7,800	
11. Issued........................	800 units @ $6 =	4,800	
Balance....................	$\begin{cases}200 \text{ units @ } \$7 = 1,400 \\ 200 \text{ units @ } \$8 = 1,600\end{cases}$	3,000	
12. Received......................	400 units @ $8 = 3,200	6,200	
20. Issued........................	$\begin{cases}200 \text{ units @ } \$7 = 1,400 \\ 300 \text{ units @ } \$8 = 2,400\end{cases}$	3,800	
Balance....................	300 units @ $8 = 2,400		
25. Returned to storeroom...........	100 units @ $8 = 800		
28. Received......................	600 units @ $9 = 5,400	8,600	
Balance....................	$\begin{cases}400 \text{ units @ } \$8 = \$3,200 \\ 600 \text{ units @ } \$9 = 5,400\end{cases}$	$8,600	

The fifo method of costing issued materials follows the principle that materials used should carry the actual experienced cost of the specific materials units used. The method assumes that materials are issued from the oldest supply in stock and that the cost of those units when placed in stock is the cost of those same units when issued. However, fifo costing may be used even though physical withdrawal is in a different order. Advantages claimed for the fifo costing method are:

1. The materials used are drawn from the cost records in a logical and systematic manner.

2. The assumed movement of materials in a continuous, orderly, single-file manner represents a condition necessary to and consistent with efficient materials control, particularly where materials are subject to deterioration, decay, and quality or style changes.

The fifo method is recommended whenever (1) the size and cost of raw materials units are large, (2) materials are easily identified as belonging to a particular purchased lot, and (3) not more than two or three different receipts of the materials are on a materials card at one time. Fifo costing is definitely awkward if frequent purchases are made at different prices and if units from several purchases are on hand at the same time. Added costing difficulties arise when returns to vendors and returns to stores occur.

Average Costing Method. Issuing materials at an average cost assumes that each batch taken from the storeroom is composed of uniform quantities from each shipment in stock at the date of issue. Often it is not feasible to mark or label materials items piece by piece with invoice prices and thus to identify the used unit with its acquisition cost. It may be reasoned that units are issued more or less at random as far as the specific units and the specific costs are concerned and that an average cost of all units in stock at the time of issue is a satisfactory measure of materials cost. However, average costing may be used even though the physical withdrawal is in an identifiable order. If raw materials tend to be made up of numerous small items low in unit cost and especially if prices are subject to frequent change, average costing is practical and commendable. Average costing is advantageous because:

1. It is a realistic costing method useful to management in analyzing operating results and appraising future production.

2. Average costs minimize the effect of unusually high and unusually low raw materials prices, thereby making possible more stable cost estimates for future work.

3. It is a practical and less expensive perpetual inventory system.

The average costing method divides the total cost of all materials of a particular class by the number of units on hand to find the average price. The cost of new invoices is added to the total in the Balance column; the units are added to the existing quantity; and the new total cost is divided by the new quantity to arrive at the new average price. Materials are issued at the established average cost until a new purchase is recorded. Although a new average price may be computed when materials are returned to vendors and when excess issues are returned to stores, for practical purposes it seems sufficient to reduce or increase the total quantity and cost, allowing the unit price to remain unchanged. When a new purchase is made and a new average is computed, the discrepancy created by the returns will be absorbed.

Using the data of the fifo illustration (page 334), the transactions can be summarized in this manner:

Average Costing Method — Illustrated:

			Average Cost
Feb. 1. Beginning balance..........	800 units @ $6	= $4,800	
4. Received.................	200 units @ $7	= 1,400	
Balance..............	1,000 units	6,200	$6.20
10. Received.................	200 units @ $8	= 1,600	
Balance..............	1,200 units	7,800	6.50
11. Issued....................	800 units @ $6.50 =	5,200	
Balance..............	400 units	2,600	6.50
12. Received.................	400 units @ $8	= 3,200	
Balance..............	800 units	5,800	7.25
20. Issued....................	500 units @ $7.25 =	3,625	
Balance..............	300 units	2,175	7.25
25. Returned to storeroom......	100 units	725	
Balance..............	400 units	2,900	7.25
28. Received.................	600 units @ $9	= 5,400	
Balance..............	1,000 units	$8,300	8.30

Last-In First-Out (lifo) Method of Costing. The last-in, first-out (lifo) method of costing materials issued is based on the premise that materials units issued should carry the cost of the most recent purchase. The physical flow may actually be in a different order. The method assumes that most recent cost (approximately the cost to replace the consumed units) is most significant in matching cost with revenue in the income determination procedure.

To illustrate lifo costing, the transactions for the fifo illustration on page 334 are also used at the top of page 337.

Under lifo procedures, the objective is to charge the cost of current purchases to work in process or other operating expenses and to leave the oldest and presumably also the lowest costs in the inventory. Several alternative ways of applying the lifo method can be used. Each procedure will result in different costs for materials issued, for the ending inventory,

Lifo Costing Method — Illustrated:

Feb. 1. Beginning balance..............	800 units @ $6 = $4,800	
4. Received......................	200 units @ $7 = 1,400	
10. Received......................	200 units @ $8 = 1,600	$7,800
11. Issued........................	⎰ 200 units @ $8 = 1,600 ⎱ 200 units @ $7 = 1,400 ⎰ 400 units @ $6 = 2,400 ⎱	5,400
Balance....................	400 units @ $6 = 2,400	
12. Received.....................	400 units @ $8 = 3,200	5,600
20. Issued........................	⎰ 400 units @ $8 = 3,200 ⎱ 100 units @ $6 = 600	3,800
Balance....................	300 units @ $6 = 1,800	
25. Returned to storeroom...........	100 units @ $6 = 600	
28. Received.....................	600 units @ $9 = 5,400	7,800
Balance....................	⎰ 400 units @ $6 = 2,400 ⎱ 600 units @ $9 = 5,400	$7,800

and consequently in a different net profit. It is mandatory, therefore, to follow the chosen procedure consistently.

The basic difference between the various applications of the lifo method is the time interval between inventory computations. In the above illustration of lifo costing, a new inventory balance is computed after each receipt and each issue of materials, with the ending inventory consisting of 1,000 units valued at $7,800. If, however, a physical rather than a perpetual costing procedure is used whereby the issues are determined at the end of the period by ignoring day-to-day issues and by subtracting total ending inventory from the total of the opening balance plus the receipts, the ending inventory would consist of:

800 units, on hand in the beginning inventory @ $6	= $4,800
200 units, from the oldest purchase made, Feb. 4 @ $7	= 1,400
1,000 units, lifo inventory at the end of February.......	$6,200

Both procedures are appropriate applications of the lifo method, even though the cost of materials used and the ending inventory figures differ. Such a difference does not occur in fifo costing.

This later procedure, whatever cost flow assumption is in use, is particularly appropriate in process costing where individual materials requisitions are seldom used and the materials move into process in bulk lots as in flour mills, spinning mills, oil refineries, and sugar refineries. The procedure also functions smoothly for a company that charges materials to work in process from month-end consumption sheets which provide the cost department with quantities used.

Lifo Costing Method — Advantages and Disadvantages. The advantages of the lifo costing method are:

1. Materials consumed are priced in a systematic and realistic manner.

2. Unrealized inventory gains and losses are minimized, and reported operating profits are stabilized in industries subject to sharp materials price fluctuations.

3. Inflationary prices of recent purchases are charged to operations in periods of rising prices, thus reducing profits, resulting in a tax saving, and therewith providing a cash advantage through deferral of income tax payments. The tax deferral creates additional working capital as long as the economy continues to experience an annual inflation rate increase.

The disadvantages of the lifo costing method are:

1. The election of lifo for tax purposes is binding for all subsequent years unless a change is authorized or required by the Internal Revenue Service (IRS).

2. Lifo is a "cost only" method with no write-down allowed for tax purposes to the lower of cost or market. Should the market decline below lifo cost in subsequent years, the business would be at a tax disadvantage. When prices drop, the only option may be to liquidate the inventory by charging off the older (higher) costs, However, liquidation for tax purposes must take place at the end of the year. According to IRS regulations, liquidation during the fiscal year is not acceptable if the inventory returns to its original level at the end of the year.

3. Lifo must be used in financial statements if it is elected for tax purposes.

4. The record-keeping requirements under lifo are substantially greater than those under alternative costing and pricing methods.

5. Inventories may be depleted due to unavailability of raw materials to the point of consuming inventories costed at older or perhaps the oldest (lowest) prices. This situation will create a mismatching of current revenues and costs.

The decision to adopt the lifo method has great appeal in a period of inflation, but it should not be automatic. Long-range effects as well as short-term benefits must be considered.

Other Materials Costing Methods. Although fifo, average cost, and lifo are commonly used methods of costing materials units into work in process, various other methods exist. Briefly, some of the other methods are described on the next page.

CH. 12   MATERIALS CONTROL PROCEDURES & COSTING METHODS   **339**

Month-End Average Cost. To insure quick costing and early reporting of completed jobs or products, some companies establish at the close of each month an average cost for each kind of material on hand and use this cost for all issues during the following month. A variation of this method, when perpetual inventory costing procedures are not used, is mentioned in process costing; namely, to wait until the end of a costing period to compute costs for raw materials consumed. The cost used is obtained by adding both quantity and dollars of purchases to opening inventory figures, thus deriving an average cost.

Market Price at Date of Issue. Raw materials precisely standardized and traded on commodity exchanges, such as cotton, wheat, copper, or crude oil, are sometimes costed into production at the quoted price at date of issue. In effect, this procedure substitutes replacement cost for experienced or consumed cost but has the virtue of charging materials into production at a current and significant price. This method of materials costing and that of using the last purchase price are often used, especially for small, low-priced items.

Standard Cost. This method charges materials units issued at a predetermined or estimated price reflecting a normal or an expected future price. Receipts and issues of materials are recorded in quantities only on the materials ledger cards or in the computer data bank, thereby simplifying the record keeping and reducing clerical or data processing costs.

In recording materials purchases, the difference between actual and standard cost is recorded in a purchase price variance account. The variance account enables management to observe the extent to which actual materials costs differ from planned objectives or predetermined estimates. Materials are charged into production at the standard price, thereby eliminating the erratic costing inherent in the actual cost methods. Standard quantities for normal production runs at standard prices enable management to detect trouble areas and take corrective action immediately. Materials pricing under standard costs is discussed in Chapters 19 and 20.

Analysis and Comparison of Costing Methods. The several methods of materials costing represent industry's intense study and effort to measure costs. Undoubtedly, there is no one best method applicable to all situations; methods may vary even within the same company. The same method need not be used for the entire inventory of a business. Whatever the method of costing, it should be followed consistently from period to period.

The various costing methods represent different views of the cost concept. The best method to use is the one that most clearly reflects the periodic net income; consumed cost must be subtracted from current revenue produced. Perhaps no materials costing method will reflect consumed materials cost with complete accuracy at all times in all situations. The most appropriate method of costing materials will as nearly as possible: (1) relate current costs to current sales; (2) reflect the procurement, manufacturing, and sales policies of a particular company; and (3) carry forward to the new fiscal period a previously incurred residual cost which will be consumed in subsequent periods.

Adequate comparison of the various methods of costing is difficult and involved. The ending inventory figures of the three previous illustrations indicate:

Fifo costing..................... $8,600
Average costing.................. 8,300
Lifo costing..................... 7,800 (*or* $6,200, depending upon the timing of the costing procedure)

Certain generalizations can be made relative to the use of fifo, average cost, and lifo. In periods of rising prices, fifo costing will result in materials being charged out at lowest costs; lifo will result in materials being charged out at highest costs; and average costing will result in a figure between the two. In a period of falling prices, the reverse situation will develop — with fifo showing the highest cost of materials consumed, lifo showing the lowest cost of materials used, and average cost showing a result between the other two methods.

COST OF MATERIALS IN INVENTORY AT THE END OF A PERIOD

When the cost basis is used in costing inventories for financial statements and income tax returns, the sum total of the materials ledger cards must agree with the general ledger materials control account which, in turn, is the materials inventory figure on the balance sheet. Unless a shift from the cost basis is made in valuing the year-end inventory, the method used for costing materials issued is the method used for assigning dollars to inventory.

Inventory Valuation at Cost or Market, Whichever is Lower. American accounting tradition follows the practice of pricing year-end inventories at *cost or market, whichever is lower.* This departure from any experienced cost basis is generally defended on the grounds of conservatism. A more logical justification for cost or market inventory valuation can be made if the position is taken that a full stock is necessary to expedite production and sales. If physical deterioration, obsolescence, and price declines occur, or if stock when finally utilized cannot be expected to realize its stated cost plus a normal profit margin, the reduction in inventory value constitutes an additional cost of the goods produced and sold during the period when the decline in value occurred.

AICPA Cost or Market Rules.   The American Institute of Certified Public Accountants (AICPA) decided on a move away from the traditional *cost or market, whichever is lower* principle of valuing inventories.   After defining inventory and reiterating that the major objective of accounting for inventories is the proper determination of income through the process of matching appropriate costs against revenues, the AICPA states:

> The primary basis of accounting for inventories is cost, which has been defined generally as the price paid or consideration given to acquire an asset. As applied to inventories, cost means in principle the sum of the applicable expenditures and charges directly or indirectly incurred in bringing an article to its existing condition and location.[1]

In this Bulletin the AICPA takes the position that cost may properly be determined by any of the common methods of costing already discussed in this chapter.   The position of the AICPA is clearly stated in the following sentence: "In keeping with the principle that accounting is primarily based on cost, there is a presumption that inventories should be stated at cost."   Having advocated the basic cost principle, the Bulletin then reverts at least part way to the traditional cost or market rule.

The AICPA in effect says it is mandatory that cost be abandoned in valuing inventory when the usefulness of goods is no longer as great as its cost. This, then, becomes a principle of *cost, or residual useful cost, whichever is lower:*

> A departure from the cost basis of pricing the inventory is required when the utility of the goods is no longer as great as its cost. Where there is evidence that the utility of goods, in their disposal in the ordinary course of business, will be less than cost, whether due to physical deterioration, obsolescence, change in price levels, or other causes, the difference should be recognized as a loss of the current period. This is generally accomplished by stating such goods at a lower level commonly designated as *market*.[2]

The last sentence returns to the traditional meaning of *cost or market, whichever is lower* by saying that the residual useful cost is *market*, which in turn is defined as replacement cost.   In the AICPA's *cost or market* approach to inventory valuation, it is clear that the Institute does not hold

---

[1]*Accounting Research and Terminology Bulletin — Final Edition*, AICPA (New York: 1961), p. 28.
[2]*Ibid.*, p. 30.

that a replacement cost should be used for inventory value merely because it is lower than the acquisition cost figure. The real test is the usefulness of the inventory (whether it will sell for its cost). The AICPA is more precise in stating what figure should be used in case the inventory cost cannot be recovered:

> As used in the phrase *lower of cost or market*, the term *market* means current replacement cost (by purchase or by reproduction, as the case may be) except that:
>
> 1. Market should not exceed the net realizable value (i.e., estimated selling price in the ordinary course of business less reasonably predictable costs of completion and disposal); and
>
> 2. Market should not be less than net realizable value reduced by an allowance for an approximately normal profit margin.[3]

The position of the American Institute of Certified Public Accountants in regard to inventory valuation may be interpreted as follows:

1. In principle, inventories are to be priced at cost.

2. Where cost cannot be recovered upon sale in the ordinary course of business, a lower figure is to be used.

3. This lower figure is normally *market* replacement cost, except that the amount should not exceed the expected sales price less a deduction for costs yet to be incurred in making the sale. On the other hand, this lower *market* figure should not be less than the expected amount to be realized in the sale of the goods, reduced by a normal profit margin.

To illustrate the preceding narrative, assume that a certain commodity sells for $1; marketing expenses are 20 cents; the normal profit is 25 cents. The lower of cost or market as limited by the foregoing concepts is developed in each case as illustrated at the top of page 343.[4]

The lower of cost or market procedure may be applied to each inventory item, or it may be applied to major inventory groupings or to the inventory as a whole. Application of this procedure to the individual inventory items will result in the lowest inventory value. However, application to inventory groups or to the inventory as a whole may provide a sufficiently conservative valuation with less effort.

Adjustments for Departures from the Costing Method Used. The problem of year-end inventory valuation is primarily a question of the materials

---

[3]*Ibid.*, p. 31.

[4]Adapted from Harry Simons, *Intermediate Accounting*, 5th ed. (Cincinnati: South-Western Publishing Co., 1972), pp. 287–288.

			MARKET			
Case	Cost	Replace-ment Cost	Floor (Estimated Sales Price Less Costs of Completion and Disposal and Normal Profit)	Ceiling (Estimated Sales Price Less Costs of Completion and Disposal)	Market (Limited by Floor and Ceiling Values)	Lower of Cost or Market
A	$.65	$ .70	$.55	$.80	$.70	$.65
B	.65	.60	.55	.80	.60	.60
C	.65	.50	.55	.80	.55	.55
D	.50	.45	.55	.80	.55	.50
E	.75	.85	.55	.80	.80	.75
F	.90	1.00	.55	.80	.80	.80

A: Market is not limited by floor or ceiling; cost is less than market.
B: Market is not limited by floor or ceiling; market is less than cost.
C: Market is limited to floor; market is less than cost.
D: Market is limited to floor; cost is less than market.
E: Market is limited to ceiling; cost is less than market.
F: Market is limited to ceiling; market is less than cost.

cost consumed in products produced and sold to customers and the cost assignable to goods in inventory ready to move into production and available for sales the next fiscal period. This question is important, because the materials ledger cards would have to be adjusted for any change in unit prices if there is a departure from the commonly used costing method. As the new unit price could not be made available to the materials ledger clerk for some time after the year-end inventory was taken and priced, and the detailed task of changing hundreds and even thousands of cards would be overwhelming and not very useful, companies create an inventory valuation account to overcome this difficulty. Instead of adjusting the ledger cards, a general journal entry is made as follows:

	Subsidiary Record	Debit	Credit
Cost of Goods Sold (or Factory Overhead Control)...		5,000	
Inventory Adjustment—Lower of Cost or Market.	5,000		
Materials—Allowance for Inventory Price Decline..			5,000

In the subsequent fiscal period, Materials — Allowance for Inventory Price Decline is closed out to Cost of Goods Sold (or Factory Overhead Control) to the extent necessary to bring the materials consumed that are still carried at a higher cost to the desirable lower cost level.

Use of the valuation account retains the cost of the inventory and at the same time reduces the materials inventory for statement purposes to the desired cost or market, whichever is lower valuation without disturbing the materials ledger cards. On the balance sheet the entry on page 343 should result in this presentation:

Materials [at cost]......................................	$100,000	
Less: Allowance for Inventory Price Decline..............	5,000	
Materials [at cost *or* market, whichever is lower]...........		$95,000

The price decline may be shown as a factory overhead item in the statement of cost of goods sold; or it may be deducted from the ending inventory at cost, thus increasing the cost of materials used.

Whenever the task of adjusting materials ledger cards to a lower cost or market figure is not burdensome and the data are available early in the next year, it should be accomplished by dating the entry with the first day of the new fiscal period and entering in the Balance section the units on hand at the unit price determined for inventory purposes. In such a case, the credit portion of the adjusting entry would be to the materials account.

Transfer of Materials Cost to Finished Production. The ultimate and intended destination of all raw materials units is to finished products sold and delivered to customers. Cost of materials used on each job or in each department are transferred from the materials requisition to the job order cost sheet or to the cost of production report. When the job, order, or process is completed, the effect of materials used is expressed in this entry:

Finished Goods.....................................	xxxx	
Work in Process...................................		xxxx

In production devoted to filling specific orders, cost sheets should provide sufficient information relative to cost of goods sold. Should a considerable portion of production be for a stock of goods to fill incoming orders, a finished goods ledger is very advantageous in maintaining adequate and proper control over the inventory. The finished goods ledger, controlled by the finished goods account in the general ledger, is similar in form and use to materials ledger cards. The finished goods may also be costed out on a fifo, average cost, or lifo basis as well as consideration being given to the concept of lower of cost or market.

Some production may consist of components manufactured for use in subsequent manufacturing operations. If the units move directly into these operations, the transfer is simply from one departmental work in process account to the next. However, if the components must be held in inventory, their cost should be debited to Materials and credited to Work in Process.

Physical Inventory. Even with a perpetual inventory system, periodic physical counts are necessary to discover and eliminate discrepancies between actual count and balances on the materials ledger cards due to: errors in transferring invoice data to the cards; mistakes in costing requisitions; unrecorded invoices or requisitions; or spoilage, breakage, and theft. In some enterprises, plant operations are suspended periodically during a seasonal low period or near the end of the fiscal year while a physical inventory is taken. In others, an inventory crew or members of the internal audit department make a count of one or more stock classes every day throughout the year, presumably on a well-planned schedule where every materials item will be inventoried at least once during the year.

Adjusting Materials Ledger Cards and Accounts to Conform with Inventory Count. When the inventory count differs from the balance on the materials ledger card, the ledger card is adjusted to conform to the actual count. If the ledger card balance shows more materials units than the inventory card, an entry is made in the Issued section; and the Balance section is reduced to equal the verified count. In case the materials ledger card balance is less than the physical count, the quantity difference may be entered in the Received section or may be entered in red in the Issued section with the Balance section being increased to agree with the actual count.

In addition to the corrections on the materials ledger cards, the materials account must be adjusted for the increase or decrease by means of a general journal entry. If the inventory count is less than that shown on the materials ledger card, the entry would be:

	Subsidiary Record	Debit	Credit
Factory Overhead Control.....................		xxxx	
Inventory Adjustment to Physical Count....	xxxx		
Materials................................			xxxx

COSTING PROCEDURES FOR SCRAP, SPOILED GOODS, AND DEFECTIVE WORK

Generally, manufacturing operations cannot escape the occurrence of certain losses or output reduction due to scrap, spoilage, or defective work. Management and the entire personnel of an organization should cooperate to reduce such losses to a minimum. As long as they occur, however, they require the attention of the accounting system for the purpose of reporting and controlling.

Scrap and Waste. In many manufacturing processes the nature of the raw material (metal, wood, plastic, fiber, etc.) results in waste and scrap due to: (1) the processing of materials, (2) defective and broken parts, (3) obsolete stock, (4) revisions or abandonment of experimental projects, and (5) the scrapping of worn out or obsolete machinery. This scrap should be collected and placed in storage for sale to scrap dealers. At the time of sale, the following entry is usually made:

```
Cash (or Accounts Receivable).......................   xxxx
    Income from Sale of Scrap (or Factory Overhead
    Control).......................................          xxxx
```

The amount realized from the sale of scrap and waste can be treated in two ways with respect to the income statement:

1. The amount accumulated in Income from Sale of Scrap may be closed directly to Income Summary and shown on the income statement under Other Income.

2. The amount may be credited to Factory Overhead Control, thus reducing the total factory overhead expense and thereby the cost of goods manufactured.

When scrap is collected from a job or department, the amount realized from the sale of scrap is often treated as a reduction in the materials cost charged to the individual job or product. The entry to record this method would be:

```
Cash (or Accounts Receivable).......................   xxxx
    Work in Process................................          xxxx
```

When the quantity and value of scrap material is relatively high, it should be stored in a designated place under the supervision of a storekeeper. A scrap report is generally prepared in duplicate to authorize transfer and receipt of the scrap. The original is forwarded to the materials ledger clerk, and the carbon copy remains as a file copy in the department in which the scrap originated. The materials ledger clerk can follow two procedures:

1. *Open a materials ledger card, filling in the quantity only.* The dollar value would not be needed. When the scrap is sold, any of the previous entries and treatment of the income item might be made.

2. *Record not only the quantity but also the dollar value of the scrap delivered to the storekeeper.* The value would be based on scrap prices quoted on the market at the time of entry. The entry would be:

Scrap Inventory...................................... xxxx
    Income from Sale of Scrap (*or* Work in Process *or* Factory
       Overhead Control)................................ xxxx

When the scrap is sold, the entry would be:

Cash (*or* Accounts Receivable)........................ xxxx
    Scrap Inventory.................................... xxxx

Any difference between the price at the time the inventory is recorded and the price realized at the time of sale would be a plus or minus adjustment in the income from sale of scrap account, the work in process account, or the factory overhead control account, consistent with the account credited in the first entry.

To reduce accounting for scrap to a minimum, often no entry is made until the scrap is actually sold. At that time, Cash or Accounts Receivable is debited while Income from Sale of Scrap is credited. This is an expedient method of handling the problem and is justified where a more accurate accounting becomes expensive and burdensome.

Proceeds from the sale of scrap are in reality a reduction in production cost. As long as the amounts are relatively small, the accounting treatment is not a major consideration. What *is* important is an effective scrap control system based on periodic reporting to responsible supervisory personnel. Timely scrap reports for each producing department call attention to unexpected items and unusual amounts and should induce prompt corrective action.

DEPARTMENT Fabricating

FOR WEEK ENDING November 10, 19--

WEEKLY SCRAP REPORT

PART NO.	DESCRIPTION	UNITS USED	SCRAPPED	% SCRAP	COST	REASON
115b	Joints	7,200	108	1.50	$ 7.00	
115e	Fins	9,400	305	3.23	30.50	
115s	Guides	15,600	520	3.33	41.40	}Defective
115k	Supports	8,500	42	.50	5.30	}parts

TOTAL FOR WEEK... $ 104.20

SCRAP COST — YEAR TO DATE .... $ 4,533.75

PREDETERMINED SCRAP ALLOWANCE FOR THE YEAR... $ 5,000.00

Weekly Scrap Report

Spoiled Goods. Cost accounting should provide product costs and cost control information. In the case of spoilage, the first requirement is to know the nature and cause of the spoiled units. The second requirement, the accounting problem, is to record the cost of spoiled units and to accumulate spoilage costs and report them to responsible personnel for corrective action.

If spoilage is normal in the manufacturing process, its cost should be treated as factory overhead, included in the predetermined factory overhead rate, and prorated over all production of a period. The degree of materials and machine precision and the perfection of labor performance necessary to eliminate spoiled units entirely would involve costs far in excess of some normal or tolerable level of spoilage. Spoilage may happen at any time at any stage of the productive process. Because spoilage in a particular job or lot in process is unpredictable, it is immaterial to cost allocation. Therefore, normal spoilage is spread over the entire production of a period via the factory overhead rate.

If, on the other hand, spoilage is caused by an order's exacting specifications, difficult processing, or other unusual and unexpected factors, the spoilage cost should be charged directly to that order.

Accounting for Spoiled Materials — Charged to Total Production. The Nevada Products Company has a monthly capacity to manufacture 125,000 three-inch coil springs for use in mechanical brakes. Production is scheduled in response to orders received. Spoilage, which is caused by a variety of unpredictable factors, averages $.05 per spring. During November, 25,000 springs were produced each week with materials cost of $.40 per unit, labor cost $.50 per unit, and factory overhead was charged to production at a rate of 150% of the direct labor cost which included the estimated $.05 per spring for spoilage. The entry to record work put into production each week is:

```
Work in Process — Materials..........................    10,000
Work in Process — Labor..............................    12,500
Work in Process — Factory Overhead...................    18,750
    Materials........................................             10,000
    Payroll..........................................             12,500
    Factory Overhead Applied.........................             18,750
```

On the last working day of the month, the entire day's production of 4,000 units is spoiled due to improper heat treatment; however, these units can be sold for $.50 each in the secondhand market.

In order to record the loss on spoiled goods and the possible resale value, the entry that charges all production during the period with a proportionate share of the spoilage is:

	Subsidiary Record	Debit	Credit
Spoiled Goods.....................................		2,000	
Factory Overhead Control.........................		4,600	
Loss on Spoiled Goods.........................	4,600		
Work in Process — Materials....................			1,600
Work in Process — Labor.......................			2,000
Work in Process — Factory Overhead............			3,000

It should be noted that the 25,000 units completed each week without spoiled units occurring that week carry a unit cost of $.40 for materials, $.50 for labor, and $.75 for overhead; total, $1.65. During the period or on the order when spoilage does occur, the cost of materials, labor, and factory overhead in the spoiled units reduced by the recovery or sales value of these units ($1,600 materials plus $2,000 labor plus $3,000 factory overhead = $6,600 cost minus $2,000 cost recovery = $4,600 spoilage loss) is *relocated* or *transferred* from Work in Process to Factory Overhead Control. Each of the 96,000 good units produced during the month has a charged-in cost of $.05 for spoilage (96,000 × $.05 = $4,800), and the "actual" spoilage during the period is $4,600. The good units produced during the week or on the order where spoilage did occur carry a cost of $.40 for materials, $.50 for labor, and $.75 for overhead because spoilage is charged to all production — not to the lot or order which happens to be in process at the time of spoilage.

In other words, the weekly $41,250 production costs ($165,000 for four weeks) less the $6,600 credit resulting from spoiled units leaves $158,400 to be divided by the 96,000 good units manufactured during the month at a cost of $1.65 per good unit.

The factory overhead charged to Factory Overhead Control during the month represents the depreciation, insurance, taxes, indirect materials, and labor, etc., actually experienced during the month, along with the $4,600 spoilage cost which occurred. All production during the month is charged with $.75 overhead per unit and credited to the factory overhead applied account. Factory Overhead Applied is an adjunct account tied to Factory Overhead Control; therefore, a closing entry is made transferring the factory overhead applied account to the factory overhead control account. Overhead variance analysis is then in order.

For effective cost control, normal spoilage rates and amounts need to be established for each department and for each type or class of materials. Weekly or monthly spoilage reports similar to the scrap report illustrated on page 347 should be reviewed by an individual who has the responsibility and authority to initiate corrective action where needed.

This discussion has assumed spoilage to be at normal or acceptable levels. If abnormal, avoidable spoilage occurs, the loss may be charged to a current period expense account rather than to Factory Overhead Control and should be reported as a separate item in the cost of goods sold statement.

Accounting for Spoiled Materials — Charged to a Particular Job Order. The Nevada Products Company has a contract to manufacture 10,000 heavy-duty coil springs for the Swenson Supply Company. This order requires a steel wire that is harder and slightly heavier than stock normally used, but the production process as well as labor time and overhead factors are identical with the standard product. Materials cost for each of these springs is $.60. This special order requires exacting specifications, and spoilage is to be charged to the order. The $.05 per unit spoilage factor is now eliminated from the overhead rate, and 140% of direct labor cost, or $.70 per unit, is the rate used on this job. The order is put into production the first day of December, and sampling during the first hour of production indicates that eleven units of production are required to secure ten good springs. Entries to record costs placed into production for 11,000 units are:

```
Work in Process — Materials...........................    6,600
Work in Process — Labor..............................    5,500
Work in Process — Factory Overhead...................    7,700
    Materials.........................................           6,600
    Payroll...........................................           5,500
    Factory Overhead Applied..........................           7,700
```

One thousand units did not meet specifications and are spoiled but can be sold as seconds for $.45 per unit. The entry to record the spoilage is:

```
Spoiled Goods........................................     450
    Work in Process — Materials.......................            150
    Work in Process — Labor...........................            125
    Work in Process — Factory Overhead................            175
```

$$\frac{\text{Sales recovery} \quad \$\ 450}{\text{Cost of 1,000 units \$1,800}} = 25\% \times \begin{cases} \$600 \text{ Materials cost} & = \$150 \\ \$500 \text{ Labor cost} & = \$125 \\ \$700 \text{ Factory overhead} & = \$175 \end{cases}$$

or

$$\frac{\text{Materials cost \$ 6,600}}{\text{Total job cost \$19,800}} \times \$450 \text{ sales recovery} = \$150$$

$$\frac{\text{Labor cost} \quad \$\ 5,500}{\text{Total job cost \$19,800}} \times \$450 \text{ sales recovery} = \$125$$

$$\frac{\text{Factory overhead \$ 7,700}}{\text{Total job cost} \quad \$19,800} \times \$450 \text{ sales recovery} = \$175$$

The entry transferring the completed order to Finished Goods would be:

Finished Goods..	19,350	
Work in Process — Materials...........................		6,450
Work in Process — Labor...............................		5,375
Work in Process — Factory Overhead...................		7,525

The net result of this treatment is to charge the spoilage loss of $1,350 ($1,800 − $450 cost recovery) to the 10,000 good units that are delivered at the original contract price. The unit cost of completed springs is $1.935 ($19,350 ÷ 10,000 units).

Defective Work.   In the manufacturing process, imperfections may arise because of faults in materials, labor, or machines. If the unit can be reprocessed in one or more stages and made into a standard salable product, it is often profitable to rework the defective unit. Although spoiled work cannot usually be made into a first-class finished unit without uneconomical expenditures, defective work can be corrected to meet specified standards with additional materials, labor, and factory overhead.

Two methods of accounting for the added cost to upgrade the defective work are appropriate, depending upon circumstances. If defective work is experienced on regular manufacturing, the additional costs to correct defective units (based on previous experience) are included in the predetermined factory overhead and in the resulting factory overhead rate.

To illustrate, assume a company has an order for 500 units of a product that has direct production costs of $5 for materials and $3 for labor with factory overhead charged to production at 200% of labor cost. Fifty units are found to be defective and will have to be reworked. The production costs are: $30 for materials, $60 for labor, and overhead at 200% of direct labor cost (all of which are charged to all of the production). The entries are:

	Subsidiary Record	Debit	Credit
Work in Process — Materials......................		2,500	
Work in Process — Labor.........................		1,500	
Work in Process — Factory Overhead..............		3,000	
Materials.....................................			2,500
Payroll..			1,500
Factory Overhead Applied......................			3,000
Factory Overhead Control........................		210	
Defective Work.........................(Dr.)	210		
Materials......................................			30
Payroll..			60
Factory Overhead Applied......................			120
Finished Goods.................................		7,000	
Work in Process — Materials...................			2,500
Work in Process — Labor.......................			1,500
Work in Process — Factory Overhead...........			3,000

The unit cost of the completed units is $14.00 ($7,000 ÷ 500 units).

Suppose, however, that the same company received a special order for 500 units with the agreement stating that any defective work is chargeable to the contract. During production, 50 units are found to be improperly assembled. Cost to correct these defective units is $30 for materials, $60 for labor, and 200% of the direct labor cost for factory overhead. The entries in this case are:

	Debit	Credit
Work in Process — Materials...........................	2,500	
Work in Process — Labor..............................	1,500	
Work in Process — Factory Overhead..................	3,000	
Materials...		2,500
Payroll...		1,500
Factory Overhead Applied...........................		3,000
Work in Process — Materials...........................	30	
Work in Process — Labor..............................	60	
Work in Process — Factory Overhead..................	120	
Materials...		30
Payroll...		60
Factory Overhead Applied...........................		120
Finished Goods......................................	7,210	
Work in Process — Materials.........................		2,530
Work in Process — Labor.............................		1,560
Work in Process — Factory Overhead.................		3,120

The unit cost in this case is $14.42 instead of $14.

Whenever the defective work cost is charged directly to the job, a slight overcharge of factory overhead results because of the inclusion of rework cost in the factory overhead rate. One remedy to correct this discrepancy would be to create a new independent overhead rate or separate costs for the special job.

SUMMARY OF MATERIALS MANAGEMENT

Materials managers are almost constantly confronted with these problems and requirements:

1. Inventories account for a large portion of the working capital requirements of most businesses. This fact makes materials and/or inventory management a major problem of significant importance requiring constant attention by all three management levels.

2. At present, the problem has become even more acute due to market conditions and the inflationary costs of materials.

3. Materials management and materials control need an organization in which individuals have been vested with responsibility for, and authority over, the various details of procuring, maintaining, and disposing of inventory. Such a person or persons must have the ability to obtain, coordinate, and evaluate the necessary facts and to take and obtain action where it is needed.

DISCUSSION QUESTIONS

1. List the more frequently used forms incident to the procurement and use of materials.

2. Should formal purchase requisitions and purchase orders be prepared for the purchase of incidental supplies, services, and repairs? Why?

3. How is an invoice approved for payment?

4. In an electronic data processing system, the computer — to a great extent — replaces the accounting clerk. Explain.

5. Does the method of inventory costing have its principal effect on the balance sheet or on the income statement?

6. In costing materials received and placed in stock, should the cost of transportation, receiving, inspecting, and storing be added to the purchase price? State reasons.

7. An invoice for materials shows a total of $5,400; terms: 3/10, n/30. If the purchaser elects to pay the invoice at the end of 30 days, what is the effective interest cost resulting from failure to take the discount?

8. During periods of rapid increase or decrease in materials prices, which costing method might result in a more desirable figure for cost of goods manufactured and sold?

9. Discuss the advantages and disadvantages of the lifo costing method.

10. A company maintains a perpetual inventory control system. Is it also necessary to take an annual year-end inventory?

11. At times physical quantities of materials as determined by actual count and inspection do not agree with the figures in materials ledger cards. What may cause such discrepancies? What accounting steps are taken to adjust the differences?

12. Several methods of accounting for scrap materials are discussed in this chapter. Which method do you regard as most accurate?

13. An item of inventory purchased this period for $15 has been written down to its current replacement cost of $10. It sells for $30 with disposal costs of $3 and normal profit of $12. Which of the following statements is *not* true?
    (a) The cost of goods sold of the following year will be understated.
    (b) The current year's income is understated.
    (c) The ending inventory of the current year is understated.
    (d) Income of the following year will be understated.
                                                                (AICPA adapted)

14. What procedures would you adopt in order to deal with the following items listed in the materials ledger cards:

    (a) Scrap delivered to the storeroom
    (b) Return of materials to storage in excess of production requirements
    (c) Gain or loss in weight through climatic conditions while in storage
    (d) Short lengths of material cut to waste during the productive operations
    (e) Breakage in the storeroom

15. In charging out materials, how would you account for the cost of the following forms of waste:

    (a) Sawdust; split, broken, and short ends of boards; and shavings from planing machines in lumber mills
    (b) Off-cuts in cutting paper linings and wrappers
    (c) Off-cuts and broken pieces in foil wrapping
    (d) Scraps in suit and dress factories
    (e) Turnings from engine lathes

16. In the control of materials costs, why is the knowledge that excessive waste is occurring likely to be of greater value than the income derived from sales of scrap?

17. In some situations labor and materials costs incurred on spoiled or defective work are treated as factory overhead. In other cases the cost of perfecting defective work is charged directly to the job. Explain the appropriate use of each accounting treatment.

18. Which of the following statements is true in applying the *lower-of-cost-or-market* rule to work in process inventory?

    (a) This category of inventory is an exception, and the rule does not apply.
    (b) Costs of completing the inventory are added to costs of disposal, and both are deducted from estimated selling price when computing realizable value.
    (c) Market value *cannot* ordinarily be determined.
    (d) Equivalent production is multiplied by the selling price.

                                                        (AICPA adapted)

19. A client who wishes to include as a part of the cost of raw materials all of the cost of acquiring and handling incoming materials wants to know:

    (a) The principal items that may enter into the cost of materials acquisition and handling.
    (b) The arguments favoring the inclusion of these items as a part of raw materials in storage.
    (c) The arguments against inclusion of these items as a part of the cost of raw materials in storage.

                                                        (AICPA adapted)

20. In order to effect an approximate matching of current costs with related sales revenue, the last-in, first-out (lifo) method of pricing inventories has been developed.

    (a) Describe the establishment of and subsequent pricing procedures when lifo is applied to units of product with a periodic inventory system in use.
    (b) Discuss the general advantages and disadvantages claimed for the lifo method.

                                                        (AICPA adapted)

EXERCISES

1. Materials Costing Methods. The Mellan Company began using a new raw material during May, 19—, with these transactions:

May 2. Received 100 units @ $5.40 per unit; total cost, $540.00.
     8. Received 30 units @ $8.00 per unit; total cost, $240.00.
   15. Issued 50 units.
   22. Received 120 units @ $9.00 per unit; total cost, $1,080.00.
   29. Issued 100 units.

Required: With a perpetual inventory control system in use, state the cost of materials consumed and the cost assigned to the inventory at the end of May using: (a) first-in, first-out costing; (b) last-in, first-out costing; and (c) average costing. Present computations using materials ledger cards.

2. Allocation of Freight. An invoice for the raw materials A, B, and C is received from the Lawson Manufacturing Company. The invoice totals are A, $15,000; B, $8,000; and C, $22,000. The freight charges on this shipment weighing 9,000 kilograms are $990. Shipping weights for the respective materials are 2,900, 2,400, and 3,700 kilograms.

Required: (1) The cost per kilogram to be entered on the materials ledger cards for A, B, and C if each dollar of invoice cost is assigned an equal portion of the freight charge.

(2) The cost per kilogram to be entered on the materials ledger cards for each material if the freight cost is assigned on a basis of shipping weight for each material.

3. Ledger Accounts for Materials Cost Flow. The Littner Company produces a product from one basic raw material. During one week of operations, the materials ledger card reflected the following transactions:

1st weekday   Beginning balance: 1,400 pounds @ $4.60 per lb.
2d   "   Received 1,000 pounds @ $4.80 per lb.
3d   "   Issued 800 pounds.
4th   "   Issued 800 pounds.
5th   "   Received 1,200 pounds @ $5.00 per lb.
6th   "   Issued 800 pounds.

Other costs for the week were direct labor, $4,800, and factory overhead, $4,360; 1,700 units of product were completed, and 1,500 were sold. There was no beginning inventory of finished goods, and no work is left in process over the weekend.

Required: (1) Ledger accounts for Materials, Work in Process, Finished Goods, and Cost of Goods Sold, using (a) fifo costing and (b) lifo costing. Assume a perpetual inventory system is used.

(2) The final inventory by the lifo costing method if inventory is taken at the end of the week and if day-to-day receipts and issues are ignored.

4. Correcting Perpetual Inventory Cards. The following differences were reported in reconciling the physical inventories of materials with the materials ledger cards. The physical inventory has been verified and is correct in each case.

Material	Physical Inventory	Materials Ledger Balance	Differences Reported
1	2,000 units	2,100 units	The accountant neglected to record an issue of direct materials to production. Average cost per unit, $2.
2	500 units	400 units	An invoice and receiving report for 100 units purchased at $3 per unit has not been recorded.
3	1,000 gals.	1,030 gals.	The shrinkage is a normal condition of storage and issue of this material. Average cost per gallon, $.30.
4	900 lbs.	930 lbs.	Shortage due to theft. Average cost per pound, $10.

Required: (1) A separate correcting entry in general journal form for each transaction.

(2) The procedure necessary to correct or adjust the materials ledger card for each difference.

5. Materials Costing Methods. The following information is to be used in costing inventory on October 31:

October 1. Beginning balance: 800 units @ $6 each.
       5. Purchased 200 units @ $7 each.
       9. Purchased 200 units @ $8 each.
      16. Issued 400 units.
      24. Purchased 300 units @ $9 each.
      27. Issued 500 units.

Required: The cost of materials used and the cost assigned to the October 31 inventory by each of these perpetual inventory costing methods: (a) first-in, first-out (fifo); (b) last-in, first-out (lifo); (c) moving average, using a materials ledger card; (d) most recent purchase price.

6. Physical Inventory. A company's own power plant uses coal as the principal fuel. The coal is delivered by rail and stored in an open field close to the powerhouse from which it is fed into furnaces by conveyor belt.

Required: Method(s) to determine coal consumption during a time period and the coal on hand at the end of the period.

7. Inventory Valuation — AICPA Rule. The AICPA's position regarding inventory valuation was under discussion in an accounting seminar. The members were asked to decide on the proper valuation for the following situations with these pertinent factors and simplified figures:

	Situation				
	1	*2*	*3*	*4*	*5*
Cost..	$100	$100	$100	$40	$100
Net realizable value*.......................	80	80	80	80	80
Net realizable value less normal profit**......	50	50	50	50	50
Market (replacement cost)..................	60	90	40	30	110

*Market is not to exceed this amount (upper limit of market).
**Market is not to be less than this amount (lower limit of market).

Required: The inventory value for each situation based on the AICPA rule.

8. Journal Entries to Correct Materials Accounts. The following transactions were completed by the Patterson Company:

(a) The inventory of raw materials on the average costing basis was $4,200 and represented a book quantity of 8,000 units. An actual count showed 7,780 units.
(b) $150 of materials issued to Job Order No. 182 should have been charged to the Repair Department.
(c) Materials returned from the factory as excess on requisitions for Job Order No. 257 amounted to $382.
(d) Materials returned to vendor amounted to $165. Freight-out on this shipment, to be borne by the Patterson Company, was $14, paid in cash.
(e) Finished goods returned by customers: cost, $1,500; selling price, $2,100.
(f) Summary of materials requisitions totaled $4,814.50, of which $214.50 represented supplies used.
(g) Materials purchased and placed in stockroom, $6,150, of which $500 represented supplies. Freight-in paid, all applicable to direct materials, amounted to $70.
(h) Supplies returned to the storeroom, $150.
(i) Scrap materials sent to the storeroom valued at selling price (debit Scrap Materials):

   From direct materials...... $190
   From supplies...........   10

(j) Spoiled work received in storeroom: original cost, $60; salable value, $20. Loss is charged to total production.
(k) Scrap was sold for $250 cash; the book value of the scrap was $200 (see transaction (i) above).

Required: The entries or adjustments, if any, affecting the general ledger that should be made for each of the above transactions.

9. Effect of Costing Methods on Reported Earnings. The Halikulani Corporation reported the following earnings for two succeeding years based on the fifo costing method: 19B, a profit of $117,345; 19C, a loss of $30,070. The management has been discussing changing to the lifo costing method. The controller prepared these comparative data:

Inventory	*Liters*	*fifo*	*lifo*
December 31, 19A.........................	250,000	$112,500	$112,500
December 31, 19B.........................	237,500	201,500	105,000
December 31, 19C.........................	256,500	169,000	117,500

Required: The profit or loss for 19B and 19C if the Halikulani Corporation had used the lifo method of costing inventories.

10. Fifo-Lifo and Cash Flow. Due to rising prices for materials, the problem of using the most appropriate inventory costing method has become very acute. With the wide variety of methods available for accounting of inventories, it is important to select one that will be the most beneficial for a company. To illustrate, assume that two companies are almost identical except that one uses fifo costing and the other uses lifo costing. Both companies have a beginning inventory of 200 units @ $2 per unit. The ending inventory is 240 units, for which the current cost per unit is $2.40. Sales during the fiscal period totaled 180 items @ a selling price of $3.60. The income tax rate is 50% for both companies.

Required: (1) The amount of total materials available for sale.

(2) Income statements showing after-tax earnings for both companies.

(3) Cost assigned to the ending inventory based on the fifo and lifo costing methods.

(4) The cash position at the end of the fiscal year, assuming that all transactions, materials purchases, sales, and income taxes were paid for in cash.

(5) A brief evaluation of the results.

(Based on a Haskins & Sells Newsletter)

11. Journal Entries to Correct Defective Work. The Spurrier Products Company manufactures, among other items, a unique nutcracker. One order from the San Diego Specialty Company for 1,000 nutcrackers showed the following costs per unit:

Materials....................................... $3.00
Labor.......................................   2.00
Factory overhead applied at rate of 125% of labor cost.

Final inspection revealed that 120 units were improperly machined. These units were broken down, properly machined, and reassembled. Cost of correcting the defective nutcrackers consists of $1.20 per unit labor plus overhead at the normal rate, which includes an allowance for defective work.

Required: Entries to record *all* costs related to the completion of the order when the:

(a) Job is charged with the cost of defective work.

(b) Cost of correcting defective work is not charged to a specific order.

12. Journal Entries for Spoiled Work. Dino Fashions, Inc., in producing Lot No. 647, which called for 500 dresses, Style No. 34, incurred costs as follows:

Materials.................................... $24 per dress
Labor....................................... 20 per dress
Factory overhead............................ 17 per dress*

---

*Includes an allowance for spoiled work of $1.

When the lot was completed, inspection rejected 20 spoiled dresses which were sold for $30 each.

Required: (1) Entries if the loss is to be charged to Lot No. 647.

(2) Entries if the loss is to be charged to all production of the fiscal period.

PROBLEMS

12-1. Analyzing a Company's Future Plant Expansion Based on Its Costing Methods. The board of directors of the Windham Corporation is considering the possibility of a plant expansion. After some research and a review of the company's materials costing methods, the president presents the controller with the proposition of using the lifo method instead of the present fifo method because of its apparent tax advantages. A reduction of the company's income tax liability might provide additional capital for the planned expansion. The president requests the controller to make a further study on the proposal. The controller's analysis regarding the inventory is based on these transactions for June, 19—:

> June 1. Beginning balance: 200 units @ $3.00 per unit.
>   2. Purchased 500 units @ $3.20 per unit.
>   7. Issued 400 units.
>   11. Purchased 300 units @ $3.30 per unit.
>   14. Issued 400 units.
>   17. Purchased 400 units @ $3.20 per unit.
>   21. Issued 200 units.
>   24. Purchased 300 units @ $3.40 per unit.
>   26. Purchased 400 units @ $3.50 per unit.
>   29. Issued 600 units.

Sales were 1,600 units @ $7 per unit; marketing and administrative expenses were $2,100.

Required: (1) Comparative income statements based on the transactions for June, 19—, using the lifo and fifo methods and a 50% income tax rate.

(2) The cash position of the Windham Corporation at the end of June, 19—, assuming that all transactions, purchases, sales, and nonmanufacturing expenses were paid in cash.

12-2. Ledger Cards for Materials. Records of the Summit Company show the following purchases and issues of materials during October:

> October 1. Beginning balance: 2,800 units @ $12.00 per unit.
>   4. Issued 1,200 units.
>   6. Received 1,000 units @ $13.30 per unit.
>   8. Issued 1,000 units.
>   14. Received 400 units @ $14.00 per unit.
>   17. Issued 800 units.
>   20. Received 500 units @ $14.16 per unit.
>   25. Issued 900 units.
>   27. Received 1,200 units @ $13.00 per unit.

Required: (1) A materials ledger card using fifo costing.

(2) A materials ledger card using lifo costing.

(3) A materials ledger card using average costing.

(4) Cost of materials issued during October for the three methods.

(5) Cost of ending inventories.

(6) The October 31 inventory if the market price of the materials on that date is $11 per unit.

12-3. Applied Acquisition Costs. Zeks Industries, Inc. records incoming materials at invoice price less cash discounts plus applied receiving and handling cost. For product Zeno, the following data are available:

	Budgeted for the Month	Actual Costs for the Month
Freight-in and cartage-in................	$ 1,500	$ 1,580
Purchasing Department cost.............	4,800	4,500
Receiving Department cost.............	3,900	4,200
Storage and handling....................	4,200	3,800
Testing, spoilage, and rejects...........	2,600	3,120
Totals............................	$17,000	$17,200

The purchasing budget shows estimated net purchases of $136,000 for the month; actual invoices net of discounts total $141,500 for the month.

Required: (1) The applied acquisition costing rate for the month.

(2) The amount of applied costs added to materials purchased during the month.

(3) The possible disposition to be made of the variance.

12-4. Ledger Account and Materials Ledger Cards. The Carroza Company is engaged in manufacturing a product designated as Carro. Information concerning the purchase and use of materials during April is as follows:

Materials Requirements: To manufacture one unit of Carro requires:

Material A — one unit; Material B — one unit; Material C — two units

All materials are issued when an order is placed in production.

Orders Placed in Process During April:

Date Started	Quantity
April 2	100
5	500
14	300
18	800
20	200
28	500

Materials on Hand April 1:

Material	Quantity	Cost
A	700	$700
B	700	350
C	1,400	140

Materials Purchased During April:

Material	Date	Quantity	Cost
A	April 6	1,000	$ 900
A	16	1,000	950
B	6	1,000	450
B	16	1,000	475
C*	6	5,000	400
		Total.......	$3,175

*1,000 units of Material C were unsuitable and were returned to the vendor April 12.

Required: Set up the balances as of April 1 in the materials account and in the materials ledger cards, and record the April transactions assuming fifo costing.

12-5. Inventory Valuation. In January the materials ledger card for metal castings of a certain kind and weight showed the following data:

Received				Issued		
	Units	*Cost Per Unit*			*Requisition Number*	*Units*
Jan. 1. Balance	100	$1.00		Jan. 4.	107	80
10. Purchase	100	.95		11.	216	70
20. Purchase	200	.90		23.	461	60
28. Purchase	100	.88		29.	515	120

Required: (1) The ending inventory cost, assuming that a perpetual inventory system is used with the lifo costing method.

(2) The ending inventory cost, assuming that a periodic inventory system is used and that the physical inventory is priced by the lifo costing method.

(3) Using an assumed fifo cost value for this ending inventory of $165 and a replacement cost of $160, determine the value to be used in the balance sheet if: the lower of cost or market is to be used, the estimated selling price is $1.25 per unit, the estimated costs of disposal are $.25 per unit, and the normal profit is $.05 per unit.

(4) The journal entry necessary to reflect the decline in inventory value computed in (3) above if this cost is considered to be a normal cost of the manufacturing operation.

12-6. Inventory Valuation at Other Than Cost. In some instances accounting principles require a departure from valuing inventory exclusively at cost.

Required: (1) The proper inventory price per unit for these cases:

	Case				
	1	*2*	*3*	*4*	*5*
Cost.....................................	$2.00	$2.00	$2.00	$2.00	$2.00
Net realizable value*...................	1.30	2.05	1.80	2.40	1.90
Net realizable value less normal profit**...	1.10	1.85	1.60	2.20	1.70
Market (replacement cost)...............	1.20	2.10	1.85	2.15	1.60

*Market is not to exceed this amount (upper limit of market).
**Market is not to be less than this amount (lower limit of market).

(2) The proper price per unit, assuming that the item in Case 5 is also in stock at the end of the next fiscal period and that the four values are $2, $1.90, $1.70, and $2.05, respectively.

(*Continued*)

(3) Normally, inventory amounts include the costs of Freight-In. Under certain circumstances, however, these costs are excluded from the determination of inventory cost.

(a) The circumstances under which this exclusion might be practiced with comments on the propriety of the exclusions.

(b) Without discussion, other materials-related costs that might similarly be excluded from inventory cost.

12-7. Journal Entries for Spoiled and Defective Work; Revising an Invoice. Masten Manufacturing, Inc. produces small motors on special orders. In February a U.S. Air Force contract for the production of 120 motors at cost plus a fixed fee of $1,145 was completed. This invoice was mailed to the contracting officer of the U.S. Air Force:

INVOICE

Materials Cost.	$11,786.25
Labor Cost.	7,811.25
Factory Overhead.	5,207.50
Total Cost.	$24,805.00
Fixed Fee.	1,145.00
Total (for 120 motors).	$25,950.00

The Air Force Cost Inspector objected to this billing, stating that the spoilage of 5 motors and additional costs for 1 defective motor had been charged directly to the Air Force job, whereas the procedure previously had been to spread such costs over all the jobs.

The spoiled motors had been sold as scrap for $50 each (the original scrap value assigned to them). The defective motor had required $30 of additional materials and 5 labor hours to correct its defects. Men working on the contract were paid $3 per hour and had worked a total of 7,200 hours, of which 2,630 hours had been spent on the Air Force contract. Masten Manufacturing, Inc. uses a predetermined factory overhead rate of $2 per labor hour. Each motor requires $95 of direct materials. Spoiled and defective work is discovered during final inspection after all normal labor costs have been incurred.

Required: Assuming that the company's work in process account has *not* been credited for any work completed during February:

(a) All journal entries that Masten Manufacturing, Inc. has made in connection with this contract.

(b) The journal entries the company should have made for the spoiled and defective work.

(c) The journal entries to correct the books and complete the contract.

(d) A revised invoice for the U.S. Air Force.

12-8. Accounting for Spoiled Work. The Galarde Manufacturing Co. produces a variety of products, each requiring several parts. The parts are manufactured and placed in stock for assembly as needed. The following cost sheet for Part No. 105 indicates the present costing method.

COST SHEET

For Part No. 105	Job Order No. 6-5574
Quantity started 2,000	Date started 2/5/—
Quantity finished	Date wanted 2/28/—
Quantity spoiled	Date finished 2/26/—

Materials:

2,000 pieces Material Stock No. 81 (all material issued
at beginning of job)......................... $4,000

Labor Cost:

Dept.	Operator	Pieces Started	Pieces Finished	Labor Cost	
21	3	2,000	1,990	$ 400	
21	7	1,990	1,975	597	
21	9	1,975	1,960	395	$1,392
23	14	1,960	1,955	784	
23	17	1,955	1,940	1,173	1,957

Total labor cost............................... 3,349

Factory Overhead:

Dept.	Rate	
21	100%	1,392
23	200%	3,914

Total factory overhead......................... 5,306

Total cost.. $12,655

Unit price of 1,940 pieces............................. $6.52

The spoiled parts are placed in a pile, and at intervals the parts are sold. At the time of sale an entry is made debiting Cash and crediting Sale of Spoiled Parts. On the income statement, the sale of spoiled parts is shown as Miscellaneous Income.

Required: (1) Recalculation of the cost of the good parts and the spoiled work cost for each department, assuming each spoiled part has a scrap value of $1.

(2) The journal entries to be made at the time Job Order No. 6-5574 is completed. Assume the spoilage is to be charged to total production.

(3) The information contained in a monthly spoilage report that is sent to the department foremen.

12-9. Journal Entries for Spoiled Units. The Hayes Company manufactures Product C at a cost per unit of $6 that consists of $1 for material, $2 for labor, and $3 for factory overhead costs. During May, 1,000 units were spoiled that could have been sold for $.60 each. The accountant said that the entry for these 1,000 spoiled units could be one of these four:

Entry		*Debit*	*Credit*
1	Spoiled Goods...............................	600	
	Work in Process — Materials..................		100
	Work in Process — Labor.....................		200
	Work in Process — Factory Overhead..........		300
2	Spoiled Goods...............................	600	
	Factory Overhead Control....................	5,400	
	Work in Process — Materials..................		1,000
	Work in Process — Labor.....................		2,000
	Work in Process — Factory Overhead..........		3,000
3	Spoiled Goods...............................	600	
	Loss on Spoiled Goods.......................	5,400	
	Work in Process — Materials..................		1,000
	Work in Process — Labor.....................		2,000
	Work in Process — Factory Overhead..........		3,000
4	Spoiled Goods...............................	600	
	Accounts Receivable.........................	5,400	
	Work in Process — Materials..................		1,000
	Work in Process — Labor.....................		2,000
	Work in Process — Factory Overhead..........		3,000

Required: The circumstances under which each of the above entries would be appropriate.

(AICPA adapted)

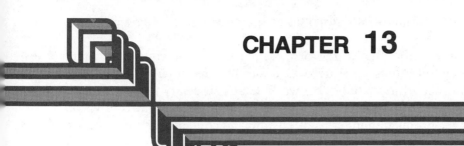

CHAPTER 13

QUANTITATIVE MODELS
FOR MATERIALS PLANNING
AND CONTROL

The planning and control of inventory from product design to final delivery are of considerable strategic significance to management. Inventories serving as a cushion between the production and consumption of goods exist in various forms: raw materials awaiting processing; inventories of partially completed products or components; finished goods at the factory, in transit, in warehouse distribution points, and in retail outlets available for customers and consumers. At each of these stages a sound economic justification for the inventory should exist. Size of inventory at production sites reflects the economics inherent in large production runs, or in economic ordering, handling, and shipping lots, or the need for flexibility in the face of uncertain future demand. Each additional unit carried in inventory generates some additional costs. Inventory investment varies with the type of industry and characteristics of a company; on the average, inventory accounts for about one third of total assets, and for many manufacturers the cost of materials represents about one half of total product cost.

Any inventory planning and control method should have but one goal that might be expressed in two ways: (1) to minimize total costs or (2) to maximize profit within specified time and resource allocations.

PLANNING MATERIALS REQUIREMENTS

Materials planning begins with the design of a product. Whether it is a regular product or a special contract, a series of planning stages is necessary to get raw materials into production. In the preliminary stages the engineering division studies the proposal, design, blueprints, and other available specifications and prepares a product requirement statement. The tooling department studies the work details necessary to manufacture the product in the particular plant. The manufacturing control division examines the production in terms of existing and contemplated production schedules. The materials planning and cost estimating departments study the cumulative information and submit a cost estimate for the production proposal. The long-range or economic planning section suggests a product price based on considerations of present product lines, economic conditions and expectations, company policies, and expansion plans. Executive management must finally decide whether to proceed with, reject, or modify the proposal.

To plan manufacturing requirements, every **stock** item or class of items must be analyzed periodically to:

1. Forecast demand for the next month, quarter, or year.
2. Determine acquisition lead time.
3. Plan usage during the lead time.
4. Establish quantity on hand.
5. Place units on order.
6. Determine reserve or safety stock requirements.

Using these six steps, the quantity to order in September for November delivery, with a lead time to order and receive delivery of two months and approximately a two weeks' supply as the desired safety stock, is as follows:

Planned or forecast usage from review date:

September production...........................		2,500 units
October production............................		2,000 units
November production...........................		2,500 units
Desired inventory, November 30.................		1,000 units
Total to be provided.......................		8,000 units
Quantity on hand, September 1..................	1,600 units	
On order for September delivery................	2,000 units	
On order for October delivery.................	2,000 units	5,600 units
Quantity to order for November delivery...........		2,400 units

Future requirements for each purchased or produced item play a central role in materials control. If usage requirements are not accurately planned, even the most elaborate control system will result in the wrong level of inventory during and at the end of a future period.

Materials planning deals with two fundamental factors: (1) the quantity to purchase and (2) the time to purchase — or simply, *how much* and *when* to buy. Determination of how much and when to buy involves two conflicting kinds of cost — the cost of holding or carrying and the cost of inadequate carrying. The nature of these conflicting costs is indicated in this comparison:

COST OF HOLDING OR CARRYING	ESTI-MATES	COST OF INADEQUATE CARRYING
Interest *or* investment		Extra purchasing, handling, and
of working capital......	10.00%	transportation costs
Taxes and insurance.....	1.25	Higher price due to small order quantities
Warehousing or storage..	1.80	Frequent stockouts resulting in
Handling................	4.25	disruptions of production schedules,
Deterioration and		overtime, and extra setup time
shrinkage of stocks....	2.60	Lost sales and loss of customer
Obsolescence of stocks..	5.20	goodwill
Total..................	25.10%	

INVENTORY CARRYING AND ORDERING COSTS FOR ECONOMIC ORDER QUANTITY CALCULATIONS

The *economic order quantity* is the amount of inventory to be ordered at one time for purposes of minimizing annual inventory costs. If a company buys in large quantities, the cost of holding or carrying the inventory is high because of the high investment. If purchases are made in small quantities, frequent orders with correspondingly high ordering costs will result. Therefore, the quantity to order at a given time must be determined by balancing two factors: (1) the cost of possessing (carrying) materials and (2) the cost of acquiring (ordering) materials. Buying in larger quantities may decrease the unit cost of acquisition, but this saving may be more than offset by the cost of carrying materials in stock for a longer period of time.

The above listed six cost factors of holding or carrying an inventory, expressed as a percentage of the average inventory investment, can be estimated and measured. The product or item inventory costs to which these cost factors are applied should include only those costs that vary with the level of inventory. For example, in the case of warehousing or storage, only those costs should be included that will vary with changes in the number of units ordered. The cost of labor and equipment used in the storeroom is normally a fixed cost and should not be considered a part of the carrying charge. Similarly, insurance costs are included only when the company has a monthly reporting type of policy with premiums being charged on the fluctuating inventory value. A standard insurance policy for one year or more should be considered a fixed cost that is irrelevant to the decision.

However, it is difficult, if not impossible, to determine costs of not carrying enough inventory; yet they must be considered in deciding upon order quantities and order points. Ordering costs are very difficult to measure, yet they are needed in computing the economic order quantity. For any order, the fixed costs of order placing are not relevant; only the variable or out-of-pocket costs of procuring an order should be included. The costs of processing an order include preparing the requisition and the purchase order, handling the incoming shipment and preparing a receiving report, communicating in case of quantity/quality errors or delays in receipt of materials, and accounting for the shipment including the payment. Costs of inadequate carrying, other than ordering costs, relate to such questions as savings in freight and quantity discounts as well as to the question of when to order, including appropriate allowance for *safety stock* (discussed later in this chapter).

Depending upon many factors, it may cost from $2 to $20 or more to process an order and from 10 to 35 percent of the average inventory investment to hold materials. Techniques for analyzing cost behavior, described and illustrated in Chapter 18, should facilitate the determination of realistic carrying and ordering cost estimates. Mathematical and statistical techniques permit improved planning and control in an endeavor to maximize profits and minimize costs.

Tabular Determination of the Economic Order Quantity. A tabular arrangement of data relative to a materials item allows the determination of an approximate economic order quantity, and thereby the number of orders that need to be placed monthly, quarterly, or yearly.

Illustration:

Estimated requirements for next year.............................	2,400 units
Cost of the item per unit..	$1.50
Ordering cost (per order)...	$6.00
Inventory carrying cost (% of average inventory value).............	10%

Based on these data, various possible order sizes can be evaluated:

Quantitative Data

Order size in units..................	200	400	800	1,200	2,400
Number of orders....................	12	6	3	2	1
Average inventory (order size ÷ 2)....	100	200	400	600	1,200

Cost Data

Average inventory cost...............	$150	$300	$600	$900	$1,800
Total carrying cost (10% of average inventory).........	$15	$30	$60	$ 90	$180
Total ordering cost..................	72	36	18	12	6
Cost to order and carry.............	$87	$66	$78	$102	$186

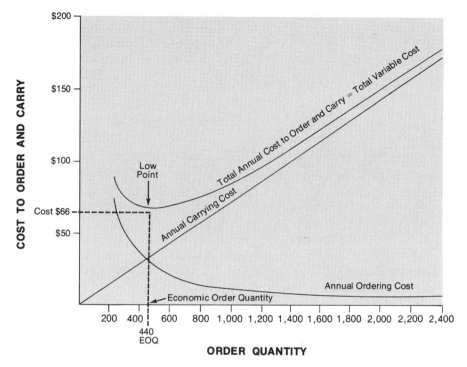

Graphic Determination of the Economic Order Quantity

Of the order sizes calculated, 400 is the most economical; thus, an order should be placed every 60 days. However, the most economical order size may not have been calculated; there may be some unit quantity between 200/400 or 400/800 with a cost to order and carry that is lower than $66.

Graphic Determination of the Economic Order Quantity. The graphic illustration above shows the lowest point of the total cost to order and carry curve, about $66, and the most economic order quantity of about 440 units. The ideal order size is the point when the sum of both costs is at a minimum; i.e., the total cost curve is at its lowest. This point occurs when the annual carrying charges equal the ordering charges; i.e., where these two cost lines intersect.

The Economic Order Quantity Formula. To determine the economic order quantity by a tabular or graphic method is lengthy and may not provide the most accurate answer. Companies using order-point calculations based upon economic order quantities usually prefer to use a formula. With information such as quantity required, unit price, inventory carrying cost, and cost per order, differential calculus makes it possible to compute economic order quantity by formula. One formula variation is on page 370.

$$\text{Economic Order Quantity} = \sqrt{\frac{2 \times \text{Annual Required Units} \times \text{Cost per Order}}{\text{Cost per Unit of Material} \times \text{Carrying Cost Percentage}}}$$

$$\text{or} \qquad \text{EOQ} = \sqrt{\frac{2 \times \text{RU} \times \text{CO}}{\text{CU} \times \text{CC}\%}}$$

This formula for the economic order quantity, or least-cost order quantity in units, is the square root of a fraction whose numerator is twice the product of the annual unit demands and the cost per order and whose denominator is the product of the unit price and the annual carrying rate. Using this formula and the data from page 368 results in:

$$\text{EOQ} = \sqrt{\frac{2 \times 2{,}400 \times \$6}{\$1.50 \times 10\%}} = \sqrt{\frac{28{,}800}{.15}} = \sqrt{192{,}000} = 438 \text{ units}$$

Given the terms EOQ, RU, CO, CU, and CC as specified, the formula is derived as follows:

$$\frac{\text{RU}}{\text{EOQ}} = \text{Number of orders placed annually}$$

$$\frac{\text{RU} \times \text{CO}}{\text{EOQ}} = \text{Annual ordering cost}$$

$$\frac{\text{EOQ}}{2} = \text{Average number of units in inventory at any point in time}$$

$$\frac{\text{CU} \times \text{CC} \times \text{EOQ}}{2} = \text{Annual carrying cost}$$

$$\frac{\text{RU} \times \text{CO}}{\text{EOQ}} + \frac{\text{CU} \times \text{CC} \times \text{EOQ}}{2} = \begin{array}{l}\text{Total annual cost of inventory,} \\ \text{designated as AC[1]}\end{array}$$

---

[1]This latter equation is then solved utilizing differential calculus to determine minimum total annual cost of inventory, AC, represented by the EOQ formula:

$$\text{AC} = \frac{\text{RU} \times \text{CO}}{\text{EOQ}} + \frac{\text{CU} \times \text{CC} \times \text{EOQ}}{2}$$

$$\text{AC} = \text{RU} \times \text{CO} \times \text{EOQ}^{-1} + \frac{\text{CU} \times \text{CC} \times \text{EOQ}}{2}$$

$$\frac{d\text{AC}}{d\text{EOQ}} = -\text{RU} \times \text{CO} \times \text{EOQ}^{-2} + \frac{\text{CU} \times \text{CC}}{2}$$

$$\frac{d\text{AC}}{d\text{EOQ}} = \frac{-\text{RU} \times \text{CO}}{\text{EOQ}^2} + \frac{\text{CU} \times \text{CC}}{2}$$

$$\text{Set } \frac{d\text{AC}}{d\text{EOQ}} = 0 ; \frac{-\text{RU} \times \text{CO}}{\text{EOQ}^2} + \frac{\text{CU} \times \text{CC}}{2} = 0$$

$$\frac{\text{CU} \times \text{CC}}{2} = \frac{\text{RU} \times \text{CO}}{\text{EOQ}^2}$$

$$\text{EOQ}^2 \times \text{CU} \times \text{CC} = 2 \times \text{RU} \times \text{CO}$$

$$\text{EOQ}^2 = \frac{2 \times \text{RU} \times \text{CO}}{\text{CU} \times \text{CC}}$$

$$\text{EOQ} = \sqrt{\frac{2 \times \text{RU} \times \text{CO}}{\text{CU} \times \text{CC}\%}}$$

It is also possible to express EOQ in dollars rather than in units. The following formula is usually employed:

$$EOQ = \sqrt{\frac{2 \times AB}{1}} \quad where \quad \begin{aligned} A &= \text{Annual requirements in dollars} \\ B &= \text{Ordering costs (per order)} \\ I &= \text{Inventory carrying cost (\% of average} \\ & \quad \text{inventory value)} \end{aligned}$$

Example. Using this formula and the following data from the earlier illustration:

$$
\begin{aligned}
A &= \$3{,}600 \; (or \; 2{,}400 \text{ units @ } \$1.50) \\
B &= \$6 \\
I &= 10\% \text{ per year}
\end{aligned}
$$

$$EOQ = \sqrt{\frac{2 \times \$3{,}600 \times \$6}{.10}} = \$657 \text{ total costs, } or$$

$$438 \text{ units} \left(\frac{\$657}{\$1.50}\right)$$

A second example is given to indicate the results when new cost data enter the formula. Any shift in cost data by either increasing the carrying rate or lowering the ordering cost will affect the answer. Of course, only those cost components that vary directly with order or production quantities should be used; i.e., the variable costs.

Example:

$$
\begin{aligned}
RU &= \text{6,000 units of material No. 60,841 used per year (500 units per month)} \\
CO &= \$15 \text{ ordering cost per order} \\
CU &= \$2.50 \text{ cost per unit of material} \\
CC &= 20\% \text{ carrying cost as a percent of inventory}
\end{aligned}
$$

The calculation is:

$$EOQ = \sqrt{\frac{2 \times 6{,}000 \times \$15}{\$2.50 \times 20\%}} = \sqrt{\frac{180{,}000}{.50}} = \sqrt{360{,}000} = 600 \text{ units}$$

The economic order quantity for the stock item is 600 units, or ten orders per year. Other order quantities resulting in more or less than ten orders per year are not so economical, as proven by the tabular arrangement illustrated at the top of the next page.

Annual Usage	Orders per Year	Units per Order	Value per Order	Ordering Costs	Carrying Costs	Total Costs
$15,000	1	6,000	$15,000	$ 15	$1,500	$1,515
	2	3,000	7,500	30	750	780
	3	2,000	5,000	45	500	545
	4	1,500	3,750	60	375	435
	5	1,200	3,000	75	300	375
	6	1,000	2,500	90	250	340
	7	857	2,142	105	214	319
	8	750	1,875	120	188	308
	9	667	1,668	135	167	302
	10	600	1,500	150 ←——→ 150		300
	11	545	1,363	165	136	301
	12	500	1,250	180	125	305

Table Showing Order Quantity vs. Ordering and Carrying and Total Costs

Purchase Order Tables. While determination of economical order quantities requires extensive study and computation, careful control at the order stage is the most effective method for obtaining maximum use of inventory investment and for minimizing surplus stock and obsolete materials. For the purpose of determining economical order quantities, relatively few materials classes can be established. Preparation of purchase order tables for each class of materials may also be an effective aid in maintaining balance between cost of ordering and cost of carrying materials.

The purchase order table below also considers the effect of quantity price discounts, using a cost-comparison approach. The quantity discount may alter the optimum answer. By purchasing in quantities larger

COST OF MATERIALS WITH VARYING SIZES OF PURCHASE ORDERS								
Number of Orders per Year	1	2	3	4	5	6	8	12
Size of Order	$12,000	$ 6,000	$ 4,000	$ 3,000	$ 2,400	$ 2,000	$ 1,500	$ 1,000
Average Inventory	6,000	3,000	2,000	1,500	1,200	1,000	750	500
Quantity Discount	8%	6%	5%	5%	4½%	4%	4%	4%
Cost of Materials	$11,040	$11,280	$11,400	$11,400	$11,460	$11,520	$11,520	$11,520
Carrying Cost (10% of average)	600	300	200	150	120	100	75	50
Cost to Order ($6 per order)	6	12	18	24	30	36	48	72
Total Cost per Year	$11,646	$11,592	$11,618	$11,574	$11,610	$11,656	$11,643	$11,642

Purchase Order Table

than the minimum, quantity price discounts and/or freight savings may be made, enabling the purchase to be made at a lower cost per unit. However, buying in larger quantities involves a larger investment in inventories. Therefore, larger quantities should only be purchased if an added return on the average added investment is adequate.[2]

The EOQ Formula and Production Runs. The EOQ formula is equally appropriate in computing the optimum size of a production run, in which case CO represents an estimate of setup costs and CU the variable manufacturing cost per unit.

Illustration: Assume that stock item No. 841967 is manufactured rather than purchased, that setup costs such as labor cost of rearranging and adjusting machines (CO) are \$62, and that the variable manufacturing cost (CU) is \$2 per unit.

$$\sqrt{\frac{2 \times 6,000 \text{ units} \times \$62 \text{ setup cost}}{\$2 \text{ variable manufacturing cost} \times 20\%}} = \sqrt{\frac{744,000}{.4}} = \sqrt{1,860,000} = 1,364 \text{ units},$$

the optimum size of a production run

Determining the Time to Order. The economic order formula answers quite satisfactorily the quantity problem of inventory control. However, the *time to order* question is just as important.

The problem of *when to order* is controlled by three factors: (1) time needed for delivery, (2) rate of inventory usage, and (3) safety stock. Unlike the generally accepted solution to the economic order quantity, the order point has no generally applicable and acceptable solution. Determining the order point would be relatively simple if lead time — the interval between placing an order and having materials on the factory floor ready for production — and the usage pattern for a given item were definitely predictable. For most stock items there is a variation in either or both of these factors which almost always causes one of three results: (1) if lead time or usage is below expectation during an order period, the new materials will arrive before the existing stock is consumed, thereby adding to the cost of carrying inventory; (2) if lead time or usage is greater than expected, a *stockout* will occur with the resultant incurrence of costs associated with not carrying enough inventory; (3) if *average* lead time and figures are used to determine an order point, a stockout could be expected on every other order.

---

[2]For further discussion of consideration of quantity discounts in EOQ computations, see: Richard I. Levin and Charles A. Kirkpatrick, *Quantitative Approaches to Management*, (2d Edition, New York: McGraw-Hill Book Company, 1971), pp. 134–139.

Forecasting materials usage requires the expenditure of time and money. In materials management, forecasts are an expense as well as an aid to balancing the cost to acquire and the cost to carry inventory. Since perfect forecasts are rarely possible, an inventory cushion or safety stock is often the least costly device for protecting against a stockout. The basic problem is to determine the safety stock quantity. If the safety stock is greater than needed, carrying costs will be too high; if too small, frequent stockouts will occur resulting in inconveniences, disruptions, and additional costs. The optimum safety stock is that quantity which results in minimal total annual cost of stockouts and carrying costs. Carrying costs are determined in the same manner as in calculating economic ordering quantity. The annual cost of stockouts depends upon their probability and the actual cost of each stockout.

Example: If a safety stock of 20 units would cause a 20 percent probability of running out of stock during an order period, and if an order was processed ten times a year, two stockouts per year on the average would occur. If each stockout costs $50 and if the carrying costs per 20 units of safety stock are $15, the total stockout and carrying costs would be $115. If by increasing the safety stock to 40 units the probability of a stockout is reduced to 10 percent or once a year, stockout cost would be $50 and carrying cost $30, a total of $80. If increasing the safety stock to 80 units reduces the stockout probability to 5 percent or once every two years, the annual stockout cost would be $25 with carrying costs of $60, a total of $85. Analysis of this type covering important stock items leads to smooth operations and effective materials management.

Order Point Formula. Order points and/or reorder points are based on usage during the time necessary to requisition, order, and receive delivery of materials plus an allowance for protection against stockout. The order point is reached when inventory on hand and quantities due in are equal to the lead time usage quantity plus the safety stock quantity. In equation form the order point may be expressed as:

$$I + QD = LTQ + SSQ, \text{ when:}$$

$I = $ *Inventory* balance on hand

$QD = $ *Quantities due in* from orders previously placed, materials transfers, and returns to stock

$LTQ = $ *Lead time quantity* equals average lead time in months, weeks, or days multiplied by average month's, week's, or day's use

$SSQ = $ *Safety stock quantity*

Two approaches are illustrated:

1. Usage and lead time are known with certainty; and, therefore, no safety stock is provided.
2. Based on the same figures, a safety stock is injected into the calculation. Both examples are solved mathematically and graphically.

First Illustration. Assume the use of 175 units per week of a stock item (35 units each Monday through Friday, or 25 units seven days a week) and a lead time of four weeks which establishes an order point at 700 units (175 units × 4 weeks). Assuming that unit cost is $.50, carrying cost 20%, order cost $24, and annual usage 175 units per week for 52 weeks, then the EOQ is computed at 2,090 units.

$$EOQ = \sqrt{\frac{2 \times 9,100 \times \$24}{\$.50 \times 20\%}} = \sqrt{\frac{436,800}{.10}} = \sqrt{4,368,000} = 2,090 \text{ units}$$

Each order provides a 12 weeks' supply (2,090 ÷ 175 = 12). Figure 1 shows the control pattern of this item if usage and lead time are definitely known. It is apparent that (1) if lead time is more than four weeks, a stockout will result; and (2) if usage exceeds 700 units in any four-week period following an order point, a stockout is inevitable. Since perfect prediction of usage and lead time is unrealistic, a safety stock allowance is needed.

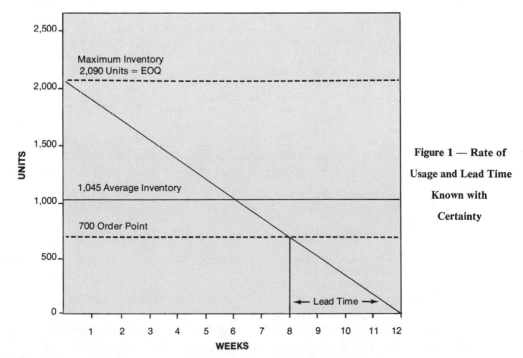

Figure 1 — Rate of Usage and Lead Time Known with Certainty

Second Illustration. Assuming the same usage of 175 units per week shown in Figure 1, with a lead time of normally four weeks but possibly as long as nine weeks, the reorder point would be 175 units × 4 weeks = 700 units usage during normal lead time plus 875 safety stock (175 units × 5 weeks) = 1,575 order point. Assuming a beginning inventory of 2,800 units and no orders outstanding, the usage, order schedule, and inventory levels would be:

```
2,800  units beginning inventory
1,225  usage to order point (1,225 ÷ 175 weekly usage = 7 weeks)
1,575  order point
  700  usage during normal lead time (700 ÷ 175 weekly usage = 4 weeks)
  875  maximum inventory or safety stock at date of delivery
2,090  EOQ units received
2,965  maximum inventory
1,920  average inventory assuming normal lead time and usage (2,090 EOQ ÷
         2 = 1,045 plus 875 safety stock)
```

Figure 2 depicts materials planning under the above assumptions and shows that a stockout would not occur unless lead time exceeds nine weeks, assuming normal usage.

In most businesses a constant normal usage is not likely to occur because it depends upon production schedules, and production depends upon sales. For instance, should the usage rate be as high as 210 units per week, with lead time normally four weeks or possibly as long as nine weeks, the safety stock would have to be 1,190 units and the order point 1,890 units, calculated as follows:

```
Normal usage for normal lead time of four weeks: 700 units (175 units×4 weeks)
Safety stock:
  Normal usage for five weeks' delay.. 875
      (175 units × 5 weeks)
  Usage variation.................... 315
      (210 − 175 = 35 × 9 weeks)            1,190 units
  Order point......................          1,890 units
```

Assuming a beginning inventory of 2,800 units with no orders outstanding, the usage, order schedule, and inventory levels would be:

```
2,800  units beginning inventory
  910  usage to order point (910 ÷ 210 maximum weekly usage = 4.3 weeks)
1,890  order point
  700  normal usage for normal lead time (700 ÷ 175 normal weekly usage =
         4 weeks
1,190  maximum inventory or safety stock at date of delivery
2,090  EOQ units received
3,280  maximum inventory
2,235  average inventory assuming normal lead time and usage (2,090 EOQ ÷
         2 = 1,045 plus 1,190 safety stock)
```

Figure 3 shows materials planning under the above assumptions that the rate of usage and the lead time are known but variable.

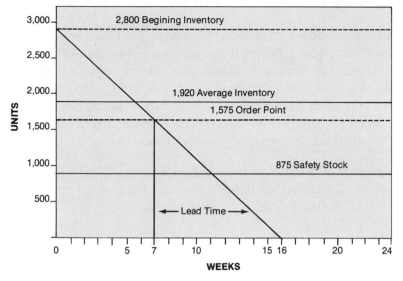

Figure 2 — Rate of Usage Known with Certainty and Lead Time Known but Variable

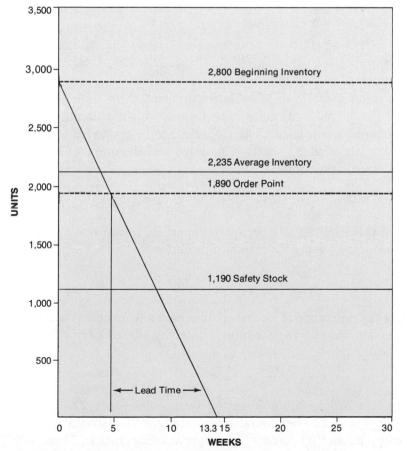

Figure 3 — Rate of Usage and Lead Time Known but Variable

377

Safety Stock Calculations by Statistical Methods. The preceding situations tend to provide a safety stock for the *extreme* boundaries of usage and lead time variability. In other situations, the amount of safety stock is often calculated by traditional rules of thumb, such as a two weeks' supply. These approaches have given way to statistical techniques for a reasonable degree of protection at lower costs. With any increasing complexity of calculations, computer application is inevitable.

Statistical Method Illustrated. The tabulation of an eight months' actual consumption of Material No. 925 together with the forecast monthly usage form the basis for the following statistical approach:

	Forecast (Col. 1)	Units Consumed (Col. 2)	Forecast Minus Units Consumed (Col. 3)	Column 3 Squared (Col. 4)
January.........	260	250	10	100
February........	218	225	− 7	49
March..........	260	275	−15	225
April..........	230	240	−10	100
May............	275	280	− 5	25
June...........	270	260	10	100
July...........	245	240	5	25
August.........	270	280	−10	100
			−22	724

In Column 3, the differences of forecast requirements from actual usage are arithmetically derived and totaled. In Column 4, the Column 3 differences are squared and totaled. The Column 3 total is squared and divided by the number of time periods (8 months) and the quotient is subtracted from the Column 4 total:

$$724 - \frac{(-22)^2}{8} = 724 - \frac{484}{8} = 724 - 60.5 = 663.5$$

The result is divided by the number of time periods minus one and the square root computed, giving the standard deviation:

$$\sqrt{\frac{663.5}{8-1}} = \sqrt{94.786} = 9.74$$

The average of the difference of forecast requirements from actual usage is computed next by dividing the Column 3 total by the number of time periods (months):

$$\frac{-22}{8} = -2.75$$

Two times the standard deviation minus the average difference, 22.23 units [2(9.74) − (−2.75)], or 22 when rounded to the nearest unit, would protect against a *stockout* about 97.5 percent of the time (a safety stock of 22 units).

Here the average difference of -2.75 increases the safety stock because the actual usage is, on the average, greater than the forecast usage. A positive average difference would indicate that the actual usage is on the average less than the forecast, thus reducing the safety stock figure.

Three times the standard deviation minus the average difference, approximately 32 units $[3(9.74) - (-2.75)]$ of safety stock, would result in about 99.5 percent protection against stockouts due to variation in usage based upon experience of eight months.

With a usage forecast of 260 units for a needed lead time of one month and a safety stock of 22 units, the order point is 282 units for Material No. 925. Of course, an additional safety stock allowance may be needed if lead time varies, again giving consideration to the degree of protection desired by management. When the stock reaches the order point level, it should trigger an order for the most economical order quantity.

Lead time units must be the same time period units of measure as those used in computing the standard deviation; e.g., days, weeks, or months. The above illustration uses months as time period units and assumes a lead time of one month. When the lead time is not one month, proper computation of the safety stock requires that the desired number of standard deviations times the standard deviation times the square root of the number of time period units be computed; and from this product the average difference multiplied by the number of time period units is subtracted. Assuming the same standard deviation and average difference as computed above, two standard deviations and a lead time of four months, the safety stock would be computed as follows:

$$\text{Safety Stock} = (2 \times 9.74 \times \sqrt{4}) - (-2.75 \times 4)$$
$$= (19.48 \times 2) + 11$$
$$= 38.96 + 11$$
$$= 49.96 = \text{approximately 50 units for safety stock}$$

Forecasting Usage. The number of units needed during the lead time, and the lead time itself are the two variables which influence the *when to order* decision. It is usually possible to estimate fairly accurately the time required to receive materials. It is seldom possible to forecast exactly the materials needed even for a short future period; and when thousands of items are involved, the task becomes prodigious even with the aid of a computer. Some forecasting techniques are briefly mentioned in order to indicate the scope and complexity of the task:

1. Factor listing or barometric methods
2. Statistical methods
3. Forcasting surveys

Factor listing involves enumerating the favorable and unfavorable conditions likely to influence sales of the various divisions or products of a company and relies upon the forecaster's judgment to evaluate the degree of the influence factor. *Barometric methods* result in systematized factor listing.

Statistical methods describe historical patterns in time series. The methods may be simple or complex, but the purpose is to reveal patterns that have occurred in the past and project them into the future. The usual procedure results in plotting time series data on a graph (such as total sales, sales of specific lines or products, inventory units or dollars, man hours or machine hours operated), thus revealing a trend, a seasonal or cyclical pattern. A moving average may be used to smooth a series and remove irregular fluctuations, but the intent is to describe mathematically the growth or decline over a period of time. Regression analysis usually employs the least-squares method (see Chapter 18) to determine economic relationships between a dependent variable and one or more independent variables, such as sales territory, family incomes, advertising expenditures, and price of product.

Forecasting surveys are used to avoid complete dependence on historical data. They are commonly made to determine consumer buying intentions, opinions, or feelings about the business outlook, and capital investment intentions.

General Observations. The key to good inventory planning rests primarily in sufficient knowledge of the fundamental techniques to develop enough self-confidence to permit their practical adaption to the specific needs of the company. Basically, economic order quantity and computed order points assume:

1. Relatively uniform average demand.
2. Gradual usage of inventory.
3. Normal distribution of demand forecast errors.
4. Constant purchase price per unit regardless of order size.
5. Available funds when the order point is reached.
6. Statistical independence of demand for all inventory items.

Circular slide rules made expressly for computing EOQ are available, easy to use, and sufficiently accurate for all practical purposes. The formula can be translated into a logarithmic chart or nomograph which makes its use mechanical, requiring no mathematical knowledge.

Aside from all the technical and mathematical steps, it is important to remember that the following fundamentals largely determine the success of the inventory planning procedures:

1. The order point is singularly the most significant factor affecting inventory planning inasmuch as it establishes the inventory level. It determines the investment in inventories and the ability to provide satisfactory customer service. The order point is primarily dependent on the accuracy of the sales or usage forecast.

2. Of equal importance is the establishment of unit costs, carrying and ordering costs, and the investment factor. They are involved in determining the economic order quantity.

MATERIALS CONTROL

Materials control is accomplished through functional organization, assignment of responsibility, and documentary evidence obtained at various stages of operations from the approval of sales and production budgets to the completion of products which are ready for sale and shipment to warehouse stocks or to customers.

Two levels of inventory control exist: unit control and dollar control. Purchasing and production managers are primarily interested in unit control; they think, order, and requisition in terms of units instead of dollars. Executive management is primarily interested in the financial control of inventories. These executives think in terms of an adequate return on capital employed, meaning dollars invested in inventory must be utilized efficiently and effectively. Inventory control is operating successfully when inventory increases or decreases, both in amount and time, follow a predetermined and predictable pattern related to sales requirements and production schedules.

The control of materials must meet two opposing needs: (1) maintenance of an inventory of sufficient size and diversity for efficient operations and (2) maintenance of a financially favorable inventory. A basic objective of good materials control is the ability to place an order at the right time with the right source to acquire the right quantity at the right price and quality. Effective inventory control should:

1. Provide a supply of required materials and parts for efficient and uninterrupted operations.
2. Provide ample stocks in periods of short supply (seasonal, cyclical, or strike), and anticipate price changes.
3. Store materials with a minimum of handling time and cost and protect them from loss by fire, theft, elements, and damage through handling.
4. Keep inactive, surplus, and obsolete items to a minimum by systematic reporting of product changes which affect materials and parts.
5. Assure adequate inventory for prompt delivery to customers.
6. Maintain the amount of capital invested in inventories at a level consistent with operating requirements and management's plans.

Control Principles. Inventory control systems and techniques should be based on these fundamental principles:

1. Inventory is created by (a) spending money for raw materials and parts and (b) additional labor and overhead costs to process the materials into finished goods.

2. Inventory is reduced through sales and scrapping.

3. Accurate sales and production schedule forecasts are essential for efficient purchasing, handling, and investment in materials.

4. Management policies, which attempt to balance size and diversity of inventory for efficient operations and cost of maintaining that inventory, are the greatest factor in determining inventory investment.

5. Ordering materials is a response to forecasts; scheduling production controls inventory.

6. Inventory records alone do not achieve inventory control.

7. Control is comparative and relative, not absolute. It is exercised through people with varying experiences and judgment. Rules and procedures guide these individuals in making evaluations and decisions.

Organizing for Materials Control. Effective control of the large investment in raw materials, work in process, semifinished components, and finished goods inventories may be achieved by various organizational patterns. Materials control is commonly centralized in one department called the materials management or materials control department with a responsible executive heading the organization. Size of company, number of purchased items in a finished product, physical size, weight, and unit value of items, and time required to manufacture a product are factors that influence the organization and personnel required for effective materials control. A materials management organization may include some or all of the following sections:

Planning and Scheduling	Warehousing
Purchasing	Packing
Receiving	Traffic
Inspection	Shipping
Stores	Statistical Analysis
Materials Handling	Value Analysis
Finished Goods	New Product Planning

Materials Control Methods. Materials control methods differ primarily in (1) frequency of review of the status of materials and (2) care and cost expended in making the review, especially estimating future usage of an item. In the case of critical items and high-value materials, it is necessary to make a weekly or even daily review with experienced supervisory personnel (responsible for control). For low-value items a quarterly, semiannual, or annual review may be adequate. On low-cost items, large orders of three to six months' supply and large safety stocks are appropriate since carrying costs are usually low and risk of obsolescence is often negligible.   Control methods include: (1) order cycling, (2) min-max method, (3) two-bin system, and (4) automatic order system.

The *order cycling* or *cycle review method* examines periodically (each 30, 60, or 90 days) the status of quantities on hand of each item or class. Different companies use different time periods between reviews and may use different cycles for different types of materials. High-value items and items that would tie up normal operations if out of stock usually require a short review cycle. On low-cost and noncritical items a longer review cycle is common since these materials would be ordered in larger quantities, and a stockout would not be as costly. In the order cycling system, at each review period orders are placed to bring quantities up to some determined and desired level. This quantity is often expressed as a number of days' or weeks' supply.

For low-cost items the system is called the 90-60-30-day technique, a rather simple method. When a quantity on hand drops to 60 days' supply, a replenishment order is placed for a 30 days' supply. The days of supply for order point or order quantity can be adjusted to projected sales for seasonal items.

The *min-max method* is based on the premise that the quantities of most stock items are subject to definable limits. A maximum quantity for each item is established. A minimum level provides the margin of safety necessary to prevent stockouts during a reorder cycle. The minimum level sets the order point, and the quantity to order will usually bring inventory to the maximum level.

The *two-bin system* of inventory control separates each stock item into two piles, bundles, or bins. The first bin contains enough stock to satisfy usage which occurs between receipt of an order and the placing of the next order; the second bin contains the normal amount used from order to delivery date plus the safety stock. When the first bin is empty and the second bin is tapped, a requisition for a new supply is prepared. The second bin or reserve quantity is determined originally by estimating usage requirements and adding a safety stock adequate to cover the time required for replenishing the materials. For example, if monthly usage of an item is ten dozen, a one-month safety stock is desired; and if 30 days are required to place an order and receive delivery, the second bin or segregated reserve should contain 20-dozen units. A purchase order must be written when the reserve stock is tapped; otherwise, a stockout is likely to occur. The two-bin or "last bag" system requires little paper work and is particularly appropriate for control of "C" items under the ABC proportional value system, in which "C" items are not on perpetual inventory records. Reordering takes place when the "last bag" is opened.

The *automatic order* or *order point system* is "automatic" in the sense that ordering an economic order quantity is triggered when a materials ledger card shows that the balance on hand has dropped to the order point. The system is especially advantageous in companies employing electronic data processing equipment. The materials control department reviews materials items, forecasts usage and lead time, establishes safety stock requirements, and determines economic order quantities. Thereafter, subject to quarterly or semiannual review, receipts and issues are machine-recorded on the materials cards. When the quantity on hand drops to the established order point, the materials cards are automatically machine-sorted and are routed to order clerks who activate orders for the quantity specified. Companies with computers go even further in their use of the automatic order system. The computer reviews and updates order points, recalculates economic order quantities, and even writes purchase orders.

Selective Control — The ABC Plan. Segregation of materials for *selective control*, called the *ABC plan*, is an analytical approach based upon statistical averages. The ABC plan measures the cost significance of each materials item. "A" or high-value items would be under the tightest control and the responsibility of the most experienced personnel. 'C" items would be under simple physical controls such as the two-bin system with safety stocks. The plan provides impressive savings in materials costs.

The procedure for segregating materials for selective control consists of six steps:

1. Determine future use in units over the review forecast period — month, quarter, or year.

2. Determine the price per unit for each item.

3. Multiply the projected price per unit by the projected unit requirement to determine the total cost of that item during the period.

4. Arrange the items in terms of total cost, listing first the item with the highest total cost.

5. Compute for each item its percentage of the total for: (a) units — number of units of each item divided by total units of all items and (b) total cost — total cost of each item divided by total cost of all materials.

6. Plot the percentages on a graph.

The table and graph on page 385 demonstrate ABC inventory classification.

Item	Units	% of Total		Unit Cost	Total Cost	% of Total	
1	800	8 } 12%		$20.00	$16,000	32.0 } 56% = A	
2	400	4		30.00	12,000	24.0	
3	1,600	16		4.50	7,200	14.4	
4	1,400	14 } 42%		5.00	7,000	14.0 } 38% = B	
5	1,200	12		4.00	4,800	9.6	
6	2,000	20		1.00	2,000	4.0	
7	1,600	16 } 46%		.50	800	1.6 } 6% = C	
8	1,000	10		.20	200	.4	
Totals	10,000	100			$50,000	100.0 100%	

Distribution of Inventory Usage Values (Cumulative Percentages)

The ABC plan concentrates on important items and is also known as "control by importance and exception" (CIE). Because it is impractical to give equal attention to all items in inventory, stock items are classified and ranked on the basis of their descending importance based upon annual dollar value of each item, thus providing a *proportional value analysis.* In most situations an arbitrary number of items can be selected on a percentage basis to approximate:

10% of the items to equal 70% of the dollar cost of materials used
30% of the items to equal 25% of the dollar cost of materials used
60% of the items to equal 5% of the dollar cost of materials used

The following table suggests the handling of high-, middle-, and low-value items to achieve effective control:

	High-Value Items (A)	Middle-Value Items (B)	Low-Value Items (C)
Quality of personnel .	Very best available	Average	Low
Records needed	Very complete	Simple	Not essential
Order point and quantity use	As guides, frequent changes	Infrequent review	Strictly used
Number of orders per year	Generally high	Two to six	One or two
Replacement time . . .	As short as possible	Normal	Can be long
Amount of safety stock	Low	Moderate	High
Inventory turnover . . .	High	Moderate	Low

Physical Control of Materials in the Storeroom. The receiving or inspection department forwards materials to storerooms together with a copy of the receiving report. The storekeeper and his assistants are responsible for safeguarding the materials. Materials and supplies are placed in proper bins or other storage spaces to be kept there safely until required in production. Materials taken from the storeroom must be properly requisitioned. Admittance to the storeroom should be restricted to employees of that department. These employees often work behind locked doors, issuing materials through cage windows.

Since the cost of storing and handling materials may be a very substantial amount, careful design and arrangement of storerooms can result in significant cost savings. Materials can be stored according to: (1) materials account number; (2) frequency of use; (3) factory area where used; or (4) nature, size, and shape. In practice no single one of these bases is likely to be suitable, but size and shape of materials usually dictate the basic storeroom arrangement. Variations can then be introduced, such as placing most frequently used items nearest the point of issue and locating materials used primarily in one area nearest that location.

Controlling Materials in Process. The materials cost control responsibility is not ended when materials are requisitioned for production. Until goods are finished, packed, sold, and shipped, inventory control problems and cost savings potentials exist. This is particularly true of in-process inventories which are intimately related to production processes and schedules. Generally, the objective is to maintain inventory levels based either on maximum production or the lowest unit cost. The in-process inventory control is often neglected. The computation of turnover rates permits identifying such inventory problems and measuring the effectiveness of control procedures. A computation is usually made for each manufacturing department, cost center, or process by dividing the cost of units transferred to the next department by the average inventory cost of the transferring department. Turnover rates vary from one department to another; hence the focus is upon turnover rate changes. Scheduling or production problems are often indicated by a declining turnover rate. For cost control purposes the downtrend in turnover rates should suggest analysis and induce corrective action.

Controlling Finished Goods. Accurate sales forecasting is the key to effective management of finished goods inventories and the ability to meet delivery dates to customers. This must be communicated to production control departments for the development of production schedules to meet delivery commitments and in turn provide sales managers with the goods to meet customers' requirements.

In order to meet customer preferences and competition, many product lines feature a growing array of colors, sizes, and optional equipment. This results in added inventory items, more work in process inventory and finished subassemblies, and the need for tighter control.

Control of Obsolete and Surplus Inventory. Almost every organization is faced with the problem of surplus and obsolete inventory at one time or other. Whatever the many possible reasons for such conditions may be, some action is required to reduce or eliminate these items from inventory and free the related capital. To accomplish a reduction, management should first make certain that the buildup will not continue due to present ordering policies and, second, take steps to dispose of stock. Accurate perpetual inventory records showing acquisition and issue quantities and dates, as well as periodic review of the records are necessary to identify obsolete and surplus items. Obsolete inventory usually results from changing a design or dropping a product. Prompt sale of the inventory for the first reasonable offer is usually the best policy.

DISCUSSION QUESTIONS

1. An inventory planning and control system is designed to minimize the total cost of ordering and carrying inventory. Therefore, inventory control is good as long as the investment in inventory is declining. Discuss.

2. Is general management concerned primarily with unit control or financial control of inventory?

3. What data is needed in order to exercise effective management of materials costs and inventories?

4. What are some of the costs of not carrying enough inventory? How can these costs be measured?

5. What factors are used to determine the inventory level at which an order should be placed?

6. It is generally true that production and inventory management can be no better than the sales forecast. Name some techniques used to forecast sales.

7. In what situation are selective control, automatic control, and bin control of materials effective?

8. What are the principal differences in commonly used control plans?

9. The control of materials must meet two opposing needs. What are they?

10. The principle of *exception* should be utilized fully for effective materials control. Explain.

11. What difference does it make whether an annual requirement of 720 units costing $50 each is ordered weekly, monthly, quarterly, twice a year, or once a year?

12. Several factors influence the location and arrangement of materials in a storeroom or warehouse. What factor(s) are regarded as most important?

13. What is the key to controlling finished goods inventory in a manufacturing company?

14. Expected annual usage of a particular raw material is 2,000,000 units, and the economic order quantity is 10,000 units. The invoice cost of each unit is $500, and the cost to place one purchase order is $80. For each of the following sentences, select the correct answer based on the above data:

    (a) The average inventory is (1) 1,000,000 units; (2) 5,000 units; (3) 10,000 units: (4) 7,500 units.

    (b) The estimated annual order cost is (1) $16,000; (2) $100,000; (3) $32,000; (4) $50,000.

    (AICPA adapted)

15. A sales office of Helms, Inc. has developed the following probabilities for daily sales of a perishable product.

Daily Sales Units	Probabilities
100	.2
150	.5
200	.2
250	.1
Total......	1.0

The product is restocked at the start of each day. If the company desires a 90% probability of satisfying sales demand, the initial stock balance for each day should be (a) 250; (b) 160; (c) 200; (d) 150.

(AICPA adapted)

16. Leslie Company has developed an inventory model for Product A and needs a solution for minimizing total annual inventory costs. Included in Product A's inventory costs are the costs of holding, ordering and receiving, and incurring stockouts. Select the answer that would best complete the following sentence: The solution for minimizing inventory costs would state (a) at what inventory level to reorder and how many units to reorder; (b) either at what inventory level to reorder or how many units to reorder; (c) how many units to reorder but not at what inventory level to reorder; (d) at what inventory level to reorder but not how many units to reorder.

(AICPA adapted)

17. Inventories usually are an important asset for both manufacturing and merchandising firms. A proper balance of inventory quantities is desirable from several standpoints. Maintaining such a balance is dependent upon a number of factors including ordering at the proper time and in the correct lot size. Serious penalties may attend both overstocking and stockout situations.

   (a) In connection with inventory ordering and control, certain terms are basic. Explain each of the following: (1) economic order quantity, (2) order point, (3) lead time, and (4) safety stock.
   (b) (1) What are the costs of carrying inventories? Explain.
       (2) How does overstocking add to the cost of carrying inventories?
   (c) (1) What are the consequences of maintaining minimal or inadequate inventory levels?
       (2) What are the difficulties of measuring precisely the costs associated with understocking?
   (d) Discuss the propriety of including carrying costs (of normal inventory, overstocking, and understocking) in the inventory cost: (1) for external reporting and (2) for internal decision making.

(AICPA adapted)

EXERCISES

1. Usage Forecast and Inventory Balances. On October 5, the materials analyst of Endicott Corp. is asked to determine the number of units of Material No. 1776 to purchase for December delivery. She has reviewed production schedules and calculates 360 units of the material will be needed for October production, 320 units in November, and 300 units for December production. The lead time to process an order and receive delivery on this material is two months, and a safety stock of approximately two weeks' supply is maintained based on an average monthly usage of 320 units. The inventory card shows an October 5 balance of 180 units with 300 units on order for October delivery and 340 units on order for November delivery.

Required: (1) A schedule showing the quantity to order for delivery during December.

(2) If the planned usage between October 5 and December 31 occurs as scheduled and outstanding orders are received on expected delivery dates, the number of units on hand on (a) November 1; (b) December 1; (c) December 31.

2. Use of EOQ Formula. Shields, Inc. has an annual usage of 100 units of Item M with a purchase price of $55 per unit. The following data are applicable to Item M:

Ordering costs..................... $5 per order
Carrying cost percentage........... 15%

Required: The economic order quantity (EOQ).

3. Cost Saving Using EOQ Table. The Branden Company estimates that 36,000 ring binders will be needed next year to service clients. Heretofore, binders have been ordered as needed, a procedure which has not proved satisfactory. The cost of binders ordered in 100-unit lots or more is $1.25 each. The Cost Department estimates a cost of $5.60 to place and process an order. Further calculations indicate that it costs about 12% of average inventory cost to carry the inventory. The Purchasing Department believes that the practical limits for ordering binders would be a maximum of 45 and a minimum of 10 orders a year.

Required: (1) A table indicating the most economical order quantity.

(2) The difference in the most economical order quantity if the carrying cost is 20% of average inventory.

4. Use of EOQ Formula. From the tabular presentation made in solving Exercise 3, management of the Branden Company concedes that order quantities should be somewhere in the range of 1,500 to 1,800 binders, thus requiring some 20 to 24 orders per year. However, the feeling is expressed that there should be a more direct and accurate way to determine the most economical order quantity.

Required: (1) The economic order quantity and the frequency of orders, using the EOQ formula.

(2) Explain whether the increased accuracy through use of the formula seems justified.

5. Determining Optimum Size of Production Run. A customer has been ordering 5,000 special design metal columns at the rate of 1,000 per order during the past year. The production cost is $12 a unit — $8 for materials and labor and $4 overhead cost. It costs $1,500 to set up for one run of 1,000 columns, and inventory carrying cost is 20%. Since this customer may buy at least 5,000 columns this year, the company would like to avoid making five different production runs.

Required: The most economic production run.

6. Cost Resulting from Inability to Use EOQ. The Electro Company manufactures some of its product lines from raw materials to finished units, and for other products assembles purchased parts. For one product annual purchase of 10,000 subassembled parts at $100 each is being experienced. Per order and receiving cost is $200, and the carrying cost is 25%.

This is only one of many inventory items the firm must carry, and a capital rationing decision has been made to spend only $10,000 at a time on these sub-assemblies. Units must be ordered in multiples of 100.

Required: (1) Computation of the EOQ.

(2) By changing the EOQ and inventory level to the availability of capital, the "opportunity loss" expressed as carrying cost.

(American Production and Inventory Control Society adapted)

7. ABC Plan of Control. Manitoba Industries, Inc. is considering a system of selective control of materials using the following data:

Materials Stock No.	Quarterly Usage in Units	Unit Cost	Total Cost
115.24	2,000	$20.00	$ 40,000
115.25	20,400	.25	5,100
115.26	5,600	10.50	58,800
115.27	1,000	30.00	30,000
115.28	18,600	1.00	18,600
115.29	7,560	2.50	18,900
115.30	8,880	3.25	28,860
115.31	4,920	2.00	9,840
115.32	6,840	2.00	13,680
115.33	30,000	.50	15,000
115.34	9,980	1.50	14,970
115.35	8,220	2.50	20,550
Totals	124,000		$274,300

Required: (1) Assuming the ABC plan of selective control is indicated, arrange the data for presentation to management.

(2) A chart to depict the situation.

8. Charting ABC Inventory Items. The Inventory Management Group of the Landon Company decided to classify and group the items in an inventory by ranking them according to their revenue-producing potentials since a major portion of sales dollar volume is contributed by a relatively small percentage of items. Based on the ABC plan of selective control, the Inventory Management Group established this inventory pattern:

VOLUME-COST DISTRIBUTION OF INVENTORY

Volume-Cost Group	Number of Items	Percent of Total Number of Items	Percent of Sales Volume Contributed
A	480	23%	78%
B	250	12	12
C	1,370	65	10
Total	2,100	100%	100%

Required: A chart based on the above analysis.

(Based on an NAA article)

PROBLEMS

13-1. EOQ Formula and Safety Stock. Robney Company sells a number of products to many restaurants in the area. One product is a special meat cutter with a disposable blade. Blades are sold in a package of 12 blades at $20 per package. It has been determined that the demand for the replacement blades is at a constant rate of 2,000 packages per month. The packages cost the Robney Company $10 each from the manufacturer and require a three-day lead time from date of order to date of delivery. The ordering cost is $1.20 per order, and the carrying cost is 10% per annum. The Robney Company uses the economic order quantity formula.

Required: (1) The economic order quantity.

(2) The number of orders needed per year.

(3) The total cost of buying and carrying blades for the year.

(4) Assuming there is no reserve (e.g., safety stock) and that the present inventory level is 200 packages, when should the next order be placed? (Use 360 days = 1 year.)

(5) Discuss the problems that most firms would have in attempting to apply the EOQ formula to their inventory problems.

(NAA adapted)

13-2. Cost Saving by Use of EOQ. The Howe Construction Company has been buying a given item in lots of 1,200 units which is a six months' supply. The cost per unit is $12; order cost is $8 per order; and carrying cost is 25%.

Required: The savings per year by buying in economical lot quantities.

13-3. Establishing Safety Stock. The Arrow Products Company has been experiencing stockouts on one of its important materials, even though deliveries are dependable within one month from the date of an order. Management asks that a safety stock for this item be established and provides the following record of actual and forecast usage during the past nine months.

Month	Usage	Forecast	Month	Usage	Forecast
January	475	490	June	520	510
February	480	490	July	500	510
March	490	475	August	490	510
April	500	485	September	485	500
May	510	500			

It is believed that a 97.5 percent protection against a stockout is adequate.

Required: (1) A schedule showing the safety stock required.

(2) The safety stock required if the normal lead time is two months.

13-4. Economic Lot Size — EOQ Formula. The Production Control Department of the Texas Manufacturing Company wishes to establish economic lot sizes in units for different items of materials. The Cost Department has determined the unit cost, ordering cost, and carrying cost and has made the data available in this form:

Item	Annual Requirements (Units)	Unit Cost	Ordering Cost per Order	Carrying Cost Percentages
1	10,000	$10.00	$ 4	10%
2	4,000	0.80	5	25
3	1,000	1.00	16	20
4	10,000	5.00	18	10
5	20,000	8.00	20	5

Required: Compute economic order size for the five items.

13-5. Comparison of Order Quantity Methods. Verdon Electronics, Inc., a small manufacturer of electronic instruments, has found that 20% of its inventory items account for 76% of total annual dollar usage and that 50% of its inventory items account for only 6% of total annual dollar usage.

Its major competitor applies the "ABC" item-dollar value concept in determining order quantities in the following manner:

Inventory Category	Percentage of Inventory Items	Order Quantity
A	20	1 month's usage
B	30	2 months' usage
C	50	6 months' usage

Verdon Electronics' industrial engineers contend that such rules-of-thumb are quite arbitrary and that more precise techniques are warranted. Their case is supported by the application of the EOQ formula to the following two sets of assumptions:

	High-Dollar Usage Item	Low-Dollar Usage Item
Replenishment cost (dollars per order).....	$5	$5
Inventory holding cost (dollars cost per year per dollar of inventory)...............	$.20	$.20
Total yearly usage (units per year)........	1,200	1,200
Purchase cost per unit of the item........	$20	$.05

Required: The economic order quantity for the high-dollar and low-dollar usage item and comparison with the order quantities used by the company's competitor.

(Based on an article in *The Price Waterhouse Review*)

13-6. EOQ; Order Point; Graphic Illustration of Materials Management. The new financial vice-president of Titan Products Corporation is directing an intensive analysis of working capital management. The objective is to attain more efficient resource allocation and higher earnings from each dollar of assets.

Materials cost of one important manufactured product is $12 per unit; sales average 100 units per month; and one month from order date to receipt of materials can be expected. Calculations show that variable costs of placing an order and handling the incoming shipment total $50, and the cost of holding units in stock is 25% of the average inventory.

Required: (1) The most economic order quantity.

(2) The order point.

(3) A graphic presentation of materials management.

13-7. Establishing Safety Stock. With the knowledge of Titan's "average" usage of 100 units per month and the expected lead time of one month, additional information reveals that lead time has begun to vary between one and two months, and the Marketing Department provides the following schedule of forecast and actual sales for the past eight months:

Month	Forecast	Actual
May......................	100	80
June......................	110	100
July......................	90	90
August....................	90	70
September.................	100	120
October..................	90	110
November.................	120	100
December.................	100	130

A stockout would close the production line for this product, and failure to make delivery on schedule would result in dissatisfied customers. 99.5% protection against a stockout seems justified.

Required: (1) The safety stock in units.

(2) The reorder point.

13-8. Economic Order Quantity; Stock Reorder Point. The management services division of a firm of certified public accountants has been engaged to install an accounting system for the Komtron Corporation. Among the inventory control features Komtron desires as a part of the system are indicators of "how much" to order "when." The following information is furnished for one item, called a Komtronic, which is carried in inventory:

(a) Komtronics are sold by the gross (twelve dozen) at a list price of $800 per gross, f.o.b. shipper. Komtron receives a 40% trade discount off list price on purchases in gross lots.

(b) Freight cost is $20 per gross from the shipping point to Komtron's plant.

(c) Komtron uses about 5,000 Komtronics during a 259-day production year and must purchase a total of 36 gross per year to allow for usage and normal breakage. Minimum and maximum usages are 12 and 28 Komtronics per day, respectively.

(d) Normal delivery time to receive an order is 20 working days from the date a purchase request is initiated. A rush order in full gross lots can be received by air freight in five working days at an extra cost of $52 per gross. A stockout (complete exhaustion of the inventory) of Komtronics would stop production, and Komtron would purchase Komtronics locally at list price rather than shut down the plant.

(e) The cost of placing an order is $10; the cost of receiving an order is $20.

(f) Space storage cost, insurance, and taxes are approximately 16.8% of the net delivered cost of average inventory; and Komtron expects a return of at least 8% on its average inventory investment. (Ignore rate of return on investment in order and carrying cost, for simplicity.)

Required: (1) A schedule computing the total annual cost of Komtronics based on uniform order lot sizes of one, two, three, four, five, and six gross of Komtronics. The schedule should show the total annual cost according to each lot size. From the schedule, indicate the economic order quantity (economic lot size to order).

(2) The economic order quantity by use of the EOQ formula.

(3) A schedule computing the minimum stock reorder point for Komtronics. This is the point below which the Komtronics inventory should not fall without reordering so as to guard against a stockout. Factors to be considered include average lead-period usage and safety stock requirements.

(4) A schedule computing the cost of a stockout of Komtronics. Factors to be considered include the excess costs for local purchases and for rush orders. Assume no komtronics are on order at the time the stockout occurs, and that rush orders are one gross per order.

(AICPA adapted)

CASES

A. Improving Materials Control Procedures. A small company manufacturing various commodities for stock, and to a lesser extent for special orders, is faced with difficulties in its control of raw materials.

Under the present system materials are requested from the storekeeper by production foremen according to their work needs. Materials requisitions signed by a foreman and identifying the production or lot number to which they relate are used. The purchasing agent, who is also office manager, orders regular stock items upon notice of the materials ledger clerk that a particular item has reached the reorder point. Incoming materials are checked in by the storekeeper who prepares a daily report of materials received.

One of the major difficulties has been coordinating purchasing with accounting. In addition to the purchasing agent, the plant superintendent and some of the foremen are free to order, especially when supplies and parts are needed which are not regularly carried in the storeroom. As a result of purchases being made by the superintendent and foremen, frequently no document for the order is available when a vendor's invoice is received. When goods do not meet specifications, the person upon whose request the goods were ordered proceeds to return the goods to the vendor; and, generally, the Accounting Department is not notified. Sometimes a remittance in payment for a vendor's bill is made for goods which have been returned.

Required: Comments on the basic difficulties in the company's control procedures, and recommended corrective measures.

B. Inventory Control. Kutlery Knives, Inc. produces various types of kitchen knives. The blades and handles are purchased already processed, and Kutlery Knives, Inc. merely assembles the two parts by riveting the handles. Customers of the business are large retail stores ordering large quantities of specific types of knives.

While there is always a quantity of finished knives on hand, production is scheduled to fill orders received rather than for stock.

In addition to supplies of handles, blades, and rivets, the company maintains at all times a small inventory of supplies and parts necessary for the upkeep of the machinery. Continuous inventory records are not maintained.

At the end of every month the foreman of the factory supervises the counting of blades, handles, and rivets. A listing of these items is given to the accountant who, by comparison with the inventory at the end of the previous month and purchases during the month, calculates the quantities of blades, handles, and rivets used during the month.

The blades, rivets, and handles on hand are valued at the last purchase price; and an entry is put through the books debiting Work in Process and crediting Materials with the amount required to reduce the materials account to the value of inventory on hand.

The management is suspicious that the workers are either being very wasteful or are pilfering substantial quantities of blades and handles. They also feel that too much time is lost each month taking inventory and that some better method of determining cost of materials used can be developed.

Required: A system of accounting for inventories and for the quantities and costs of materials used which will satisfy the objections of management, explaining how the new system would eliminate the weaknesses of the present system.

(CICA adapted)

C. Economic Order Quantity; Inventory Control. LASI Automobile Supply, Inc. is both a retail and wholesale auto supply business, selling engine repair parts and a line of accessories. The company also operates a paint and body shop and installs mufflers, shock absorbers, and tail pipes.

Six months ago LASI was contacted by a national manufacturer of automotive glass about the possibility of becoming an area wholesale distributor of curved windshields. The distributorship was accepted primarily to supply area garages, but soon windshield replacement became a feature of the body shop.

Deciding between weekly and monthly ordering of windshields, the company's CPA obtained the following information:

(a) Insurance, storage, and handling costs of the windshields are estimated at $432 per year.
(b) LASI should sell about 300 windshields per month, combining installations in their own shop and sales to repair shops.
(c) Delivered price of the windshields to LASI is $45 each.
(d) An agreement between the manufacturer and LASI requires an average inventory of 60 units.
(e) Cost of placing an order is $15.

Required: (1) Advice on the quantity and frequency of orders.

(2) Recommended procedure for controlling the inventory to assure ordering only those windshields needed to replace the models sold.

CHAPTER **14**

CONTROLLING AND
ACCOUNTING FOR
LABOR COSTS

Labor cost represents the human contribution to production and is an important cost factor requiring constant measurement, control, and analysis. The economic advantage of increased production at lower unit costs, along with rising wage rates and ever-increasing fringe benefits, have accelerated the trend toward greater use of automatic equipment to produce more goods in fewer labor hours. Changes in the utilization of a labor force often require changes in methods of compensating labor, followed by changes in accounting for labor costs.

All wage payments are, in the last analysis, directly or indirectly based on and limited by the productivity and skill of the worker. Therefore, proper motivation, control, and accounting for this human cost factor is one of the most influential problems in the management of an enterprise. A cooperative and enthusiastic labor force, loyal to the company and its policies, can contribute greatly toward efficient, low-cost operations. Labor costing is only one element in good employer-employee relations. Adequate records, easily understood and readily available, constitute an important factor in harmonious relations between management, employees, labor unions, government agencies, and the general public.

BASIS FOR LABOR COST CONTROL

Labor cost control is based on pertinent and timely information transmitted to management. Top executives are often primarily interested in the ratio of labor costs to total costs and in changes in the labor cost ratio. A plant superintendent needs to know details of labor costs by departments, product lines, by direct and indirect workers, and by jobs or processes. Shop foremen need similar detailed information applicable to their jurisdiction.

Cost control is often described as an attitude or state of mind as much as an activity. Labor cost control begins with an adequate production planning schedule supported by man-hour requirements and accompanying labor costs, determined well in advance of production runs. In most manufacturing plants it is usually possible to establish a reasonably accurate ratio of direct labor hours and number of employees to dollar sales by product lines, and, by relating this ratio to the sales forecast, to predict future labor requirements. The relationship between sales volume and personnel needs is perhaps more direct and predictable in wholesale, retail, financial, and service enterprises. Effective labor cost control is achieved through (1) production planning, (2) use of labor budgets and labor time and wage standards, (3) labor performance reports, and (4) appropriate payment for labor performance including wage incentive systems.

PRODUCTIVITY AND EFFICIENCY MEASUREMENT AND LABOR COSTS

Control of labor costs requires a *standard of performance* to measure the productivity and efficiency of the work performed and to appraise the differences between expectation and accomplishment.

Productivity may be defined as the measurement of production performance using the expenditure of human effort as a yardstick. Perhaps productivity could also be described as the efficiency with which resources are converted into commodities and/or services that people want. Or one could ask: "How productive (in units) and how efficient (cost-wise) were plant operations during the past period?"[1] Greater productivity can be achieved by better processes, improved or modern equipment, or any other factor that improves the utilization of manpower. The objective of productivity measurement is to provide management with a concise and accurate index for the comparison of actual results with a standard of performance. Productivity measurement should recognize the individual contribution of factors such as men (including management), plant and equipment used in production, products and services utilized in production, capital invested, and government services utilized (as indicated by

---

[1]Frank W. Kolmin and Michael J. Cerullo, "Measuring Productivity and Efficiency," *Management Accounting*, Vol. LV, No. 5, p. 32.

taxes). However, in many productivity statistics, particularly those developed by the Bureau of Labor Statistics of the U. S. Department of Labor, the measurement takes into account only one element of input — labor. It ignores such essential factors as capital and land, thereby assigning the credit or cause of changes in productive efficiency solely to the labor input factor.

At their best, productivity measurement ratios are crude statistical devices. The most generally utilized measurement has been physical output per man-hour — a term considered more descriptive than labor productivity.

The Importance of Measuring Productivity and Efficiency. In today's economy the need for more and better goods at the lowest possible cost requires greater productivity per man-hour. This does not mean that workers will have to work harder physically, but that management and labor should employ ingenuity and inventive ability to develop methods, machines, and products that will reduce the number of man-hours required to make a product. This requirement leads to an answer to the question: "What is a fair day's (or a standard day's) work?"

In many organizations time studies conducted by industrial engineers provide the answer to the above question. A "fair day's work" is the amount of work expected of an individual in return for his base rate or his guaranteed hourly wage. With an incentive wage system, a worker is paid in proportion to his output beyond the standard of performance. Setting a standard of performance is not an easy task, for it is often accompanied by serious disputes between management and labor unions. The pace or speed at which the observed person is working is noted and referred to as *rating* or *performance rating*. The rating factor is applied to the selected time to obtain a *normal time*; e.g., the time it should take a person working at a normal pace to do the job. Allowances are added for personal time, rest periods, and possible delays. The final result is the *standard time* for the job, expressed in minutes per piece or in units to be produced per hour.

Productivity-Efficiency Ratio. The *productivity-efficiency ratio* is employed in connection with the productivity and performance standard to measure the operating achievement of a machine, an operation, an individual, a department, or an entire organization.

Departmental ratios, such as the labor efficiency ratio discussed below, assist in judging the efficiency of department heads and foremen. A *labor efficiency ratio* usually expresses the difference between actual hours worked and standard hours allowed for the work performed. For example, if 4,000 hours at $5 an hour is standard and if 4,400 hours are used, then there is an unfavorable labor efficiency ratio: $\dfrac{\text{Actual labor hours} \quad 4,400}{\text{Standard labor hours } 4,000} =$ 110%, which indicates that actual labor hours exceeded the standard hours by 10%. If the standard cost for 4,000 hours is \$20,000, then 10% × \$20,000 = \$2,000, the dollar amount of the labor efficiency variance. The relationship can also be expressed as a ratio of standard labor hours to actual labor hours: $\dfrac{\text{Standard labor hours } 4,000}{\text{Actual labor hours} \quad 4,400} = 90.9\%$ efficiency compared with the standard which means that labor productivity was 91% efficient. If 4,400 actual labor hours at the \$5 standard rate per hour cost \$22,000, then 9.1% of \$22,000 = \$2,000 (approximate due to rounding) which is the dollar amount of the unfavorable labor efficiency variance.

The calculation of labor cost variances is discussed in greater detail in Chapter 19, the first standard cost chapter. At this point it is sufficient to indicate that, based on the above data and an assumed actual labor rate of \$5.25 per hour, the variance analysis would be:

4,400 actual labor hours at \$5.25 per hour.........................	\$23,100
4,400 actual labor hours at \$5 per hour...........................	22,000
Labor rate variance (unfavorable).................................	\$ 1,100

4,400 actual labor hours at \$5 per hour...........................	\$22,000
4,000 standard labor hours at \$5 per hour........................	20,000
Labor efficiency variance (unfavorable)...........................	\$ 2,000

Base Rate (or Job Rate). The basic payment for work performed is called the *base rate* or *job rate*. A base rate should be established for each operation in a plant or office and grouped by class of operation. The establishment of equitable compensation for the performance of each occupation and operation in a plant or office is not a simple task. An equitable wage rate or *salary structure* requires an analysis, description, and evaluation of each job within the plant or office. The value of all jobs must relate to wages and salaries paid for like work in the community and in the industry or business as a whole. Maintaining competitive wage rates and salaries facilitates the acquisition and retention of quality personnel.

Fringe Costs (or Fringes). Base wages or salaries do not comprise the entire labor cost picture. Besides the base rate, supplements, sometimes called fringe costs (or fringes), form a substantial element of labor cost. Fringe costs — such as FICA tax, unemployment taxes, holiday pay, vacation pay, overtime premium pay, pension costs, costs of living adjustments, etc. — must be added to the base rate in order to arrive at the full labor cost. While these fringe costs are generally included in the factory overhead rate, they should not and cannot be overlooked in management's planning and control responsibilities, in decision-making analyses, or as a more specific example in labor-management wage or salary arbitration sessions. Workers' demands for a 10¢ per hour increase in pay may result in far greater expenditures by the company when related fringe costs are considered.

LABOR PERFORMANCE REPORTS

Production schedules, performance standards, and labor budgets represent plans and expectations; but effective control of labor efficiency and costs depends upon meaningful and timely performance reports sent to foremen and supervisors who are directly responsible for departmental production. Labor performance reports are designed to compare budgets and standards with actual results attained, thereby pointing to variances from planned and expected performance. The departmental direct labor cost report below and the plant-wide labor cost report, issued weekly or monthly (page 402), and the daily performance and idle time reports (page 402) illustrate media used to provide foremen and plant managers with information needed for effective cost control.

The expected direct labor cost for the week is computed from the October labor budget for the Cooler Assembly Department on page 407. For example, in motor assembling the Cooler Assembly Department produced 600 units of Model No. 625 requiring 1.5 hours of budgeted labor per unit, 800 units of Model No. 500 with 1.5 hours of budgeted labor per unit, and 500 units of Model No. 600 with 1.3 hours of budgeted labor per unit; a total of 2,750 budgeted labor hours @ $6 per hour for a total of $16,500.

DEPARTMENTAL DIRECT LABOR COST REPORT

Department   Cooler Assembly   Foreman   H. Stevenson

Production   No. 625--600 units   Week Ending   October 12, 19--

             No. 500--800 units

             No. 600--500 units

Operation	Actual Cost	Expected Cost	Expected		Reasons
Motor.........	$16,925.00	$16,500.00	$425 over	2.6%	Reboring hangers
Fan...........	3,000.00	3,060.00	60 under	2.0%	Good group
Freon........	5,675.00	5,220.00	455 over	8.7%	Overtime and reweld
Total...	$25,600.00	$24,780.00	$820 over		

LABOR COST REPORT		Plant Midville			Week Ending October 12, 19--		
Department	Labor Class	Actual Labor Cost			Estimated Labor Cost		
		This Week	Last Week	Year to Date	This Week	Last Week	Year to Date
Cutting	Direct.... Indirect..	$28,500 2,200	$28,200 2,250	$1,174,380 81,640	$28,200 2,240	$28,000 2,200	$1,172,500 81,800
	Total..	$30,700	$30,450	$1,256,020	$30,440	$30,200	$1,254,300
Forming	Direct.... Indirect..	$13,600 1,600	$13,400 1,600	$ 430,525 65,600	$13,750 1,600	$13,450 1,620	$ 431,000 65,700
	Total..	$15,200	$15,000	$ 496,125	$15,350	$15,070	$ 496,700
Cooler Assembly	Direct.... Indirect..	$25,600 2,825	$26,100 2,800	$1,152,250 117,880	$24,780 2,750	$24,000 2,750	$1,150,000 117,000
	Total..	$28,425	$28,900	$1,270,130	$27,530	$26,750	$1,267,000

The above labor cost report is sent to executive and plant management to indicate (1) the trend of direct and indirect labor cost in the three departments and (2) the actual cost compared with the estimated cost figures.

The Physical Reports for Labor and the Daily Idle Time Report[2] below combine three types of daily labor reports: (1) employee performance,

PHYSICAL REPORTS FOR LABOR

Daily Performance Report by Employees				Daily Performance Report by Departments			
Employee No.	Actual Producing Hours	Standard Hours of Output	Percent Performance	Department	Actual Producing Hours	Standard Hours of Output	Percent Performance
105	8	10	125.0	1	110	90	81.8
110	6	7	116.7	2	280	300	107.1
112	5	4	80.0	3	150	145	96.7

DAILY IDLE TIME REPORT

Depart- ment	Total Direct Labor Hours	Productive Direct Labor Hours		Idle Time Due To							
				Maintenance		No Materials		Other		Total	
		Amount	%	Amount	%	Amount	%	Amount	%	Amount	%
1	3,200	$2,900	90.6	$200	6.2	$ 50	1.6	$ 50	1.6	$300	9.4
2	1,300	1,200	92.3	25	1.9	25	1.9	50	3.9	100	7.7
3	600	550	91.7	20	3.3	30	5.0			50	8.3
4	200	180	90.0	10	5.0			10	5.0	20	10.0
Total	5,300	$4,830	91.1	$255	4.8	$105	2.0	$110	2.1	$470	8.9

[2]William L. Ferrara, "An Integrated Approach to Control of Production Costs," *NAA Bulletin*, Vol. XLI, No. 9, p. 65.

(2) departmental performance, and (3) idle time. Physical factors such as hours are coupled with percentages to improve the effectiveness of these reports.

The Daily Efficiency Report as illustrated below is designed for and issued to shop superintendents to help maintain schedules that depend greatly upon the utmost efficiency of shop personnel. The report shows actual hours, standard hours, and the percent of efficiency of each group.

		Daily Hours		Cumulative Hours		Efficiency %*		
Group	Group Name	Actual	Standard	Actual	Standard	Daily	Cumulative	Remarks
0501	Handling Labor & Mat.	153.1	172.6	752.3	811.9	112.7	107.9	
1001	Shipping	133.6	174.3	1883.2	2604.6	125.8	138.3	
	Totals--Todd Division	291.7	346.9	2635.5	3416.5	118.9	129.6	
5001	Dimension Mill #1	75.6	270.6	1028.7	1044.2	357.9	101.5	
5101	Machine Room #1	16.1	17.1	305.6	341.0	106.2	111.6	
5102	Dimension Mill #2	55.1	72.0	449.5	560.7	130.6	124.7	
5103	Machine Room #2	155.1	174.5	988.7	906.2	112.5	91.7	
5201	Wood Subassembly	148.1	210.8	1153.7	1106.7	142.3	95.9	
5701	Insulation	50.0	44.9	625.9	702.3	89.8	112.2	
8407	Door Frame Paint	11.0	2.4	96.7	47.0	21.8	48.6	

DAILY EFFICIENCY REPORT   Date: 5/17/--   Issued: 5/18/--

*Standard ÷ Actual

THE COMPUTER'S CONTRIBUTION TO LABOR COST CONTROL

Wherever large numbers of hourly workers perform standardized labor tasks, a computer program can calculate and report each worker's daily earnings and efficiency. Because such a report is too voluminous and impractical for a plant manager or foreman to use, one procedure is to program for significant unfavorable shifts in performance from one day to the next. This type of report provides for management by exception, whereby the supervisor can direct effort to correcting problems of a very few workers and prevent chronic difficulties. From a work force of five hundred employees, a daily report from the computer might appear as shown below.

MANPOWER PERFORMANCE REPORT
(Significant Adverse Change)   May 19, 19--

Employee	% Efficiency Last Month			% Efficiency Yesterday	Previous Five Days % Efficiency					Number Of Times Reported This Month
	Low	High	Average							
BOWEN, T.	72%	84%	78%	64%	76	79	83	81	78	1
DURHAM, L.	75	91	83	69	71	73	85	90	90	2
GORDON, E.	70	78	74	31	76	71	75	78	74	1
HOESL, A.	62	88	75	56	80	84	76	65	87	3
PEREZ, G.	86	98	92	81	85	93	97	94	92	1

The report is focused on adverse change in performance from the workers' historical pattern. For example, G. Perez is a highly efficient performer, but the 81% efficiency rate is out of character for this worker; and management has an opportunity to take early corrective action if needed.

With daily efficiency performances in computer storage, management can be provided with monthly or quarterly reports on chronically low efficiency workers. The following illustration is indicative of the information needed to increase effectiveness in manpower utilization and labor cost control. Even with no knowledge of the situation, a reading of the illustration suggests that Asbury, Clarke, and probably Varney are not likely to be satisfactory workers in this department if 75% of the standard rate is considered minimal. Dettmer and Mayes appear to be new employees and seem to be improving, while Shaw appears capable of attaining the desired productivity level but may have difficulty in doing so.

MANPOWER PERFORMANCE REPORT
(Chronically Low Performance)   November 30, 19--

Employee	% Efficiency Last 12 Months			% Efficiency This Month	Previous Five Months % Efficiency	Number Of Times Reported This Year
	Low	High	Average			
ASBURY, M.	33%	43%	38%	40%	42 49 43 51 46	6
CLARKE, G.	42	58	50	52	56 45 51 45 51	7
DETTMER, C.	58	74	66	71	70 68 66 58 63	3
MAYES, W.	60	66	63	66	64 60 56 54 50	2
SHAW, T.	70	84	77	68	70 75 68 75 80	5
VARNEY, M.	45	73	59	64	60 65 68 66 64	4

Effective control is best achieved by careful use of comparisons between actual performance and predetermined standards of performance. Daily or weekly comparisons may be in aggregate (i.e., by department or division), or they may be made for each employee.

Departmental labor cost reports can be combined to form a plant summary of operating performance, most useful to the plant superintendent and other production officials.

PRODUCTIVITY, INFLATION, AND PRICES

In recent years the topic of inflation has received ever-increasing coverage from TV and news publications, leading to a mounting public and political interest. Why the interest? Inflation erodes the value of savings, reduces purchasing power, and creates serious disparities between individuals on fixed incomes and workers receiving steady pay increases. Some wage earners, whose wages rise faster than prices, are less affected by this inflationary spiral. Individuals whose incomes do not rise as fast as prices are forced to curb their spending habits because the prices of goods and services rise so rapidly.

While production has generally been increasing, resulting in more available goods and services, costs have risen even faster. Whenever output does not keep pace with costs, unit costs — and, therefore, prices — go up. Wage increases, often excessive, have been a significant factor in this wage-price spiral because labor costs form such a large part of total costs. If prices are to be kept from rising, then wage increases should not exceed an amount that will cause further increases in unit costs. In recent years, employment costs — wages, salaries, and fringes — have risen more than output or production per man-hour, leading to higher prices to meet higher unit labor costs. In some cases, labor costs increased when output per man-hour actually dropped.

To offset or curtail the wage-price spiral requires (1) increased productivity reflected in lower prices rather than higher wages, so that everyone may benefit; (2) wages held at a level that will not cause higher labor cost per unit of product; and (3) governmental reduction in deficit financing.

ORGANIZATION FOR LABOR COST CONTROL

To achieve labor cost control, other departments and functions besides the accounting department are involved, such as personnel, time and motion study, production planning, budgeting, and timekeeping. In fact, the entire control process begins with the design of the product and continues as a cooperative activity until the product is sold.

Personnel Department. The chief function of a personnel department is to provide an efficient labor force. In a general way, this department is responsible for seeing that an entire organization follows good personnel policies; but very little of the real personnel work is done by employees of the personnel department. Personnel relations are personal relations — between department heads and their subordinates, between foremen and workers, and among all employees.

Personnel functions, dealing with the human resources of the organization, involve recruiting and employment procedures, training programs, job descriptions, job evaluations, and time and motion studies. Hiring of employees may be for replacement or for expansion. Replacement hiring starts with a labor requisition sent to the personnel department by a department head or foreman. If the original vacancy is for one of the better jobs, that job will usually be filled by promotion; and the replacement requisition will be for the job which is finally vacant. Expansion hiring requires authorization by executive management. Authority to hire results from approval of the manpower requirements of a production schedule rather than from separate requisitions to fill individual jobs. The personnel department, in conjunction with department heads concerned, plans the expansion requirements and agrees upon promotions and promotional transfers to be made, the number and kind of workers to be hired, and the dates at which new recruits will report for work. Recruitment, interviewing, testing, physical examinations, induction procedures, and assignment to jobs are carried out by the personnel department.

Employment practices must not only comply with regulations set forth at the federal level (i.e., the Equal Employment Opportunity Commission; the Department of Health, Education, and Welfare; and the Department of Labor) but also with regulations of a Human Rights Commission in several of the states.

Production Planning Department. A production planning department is responsible for the scheduling of work, the release of job orders to the producing departments, and the dispatching of work in the factory. The release of orders is generally accompanied by materials requisitions and labor time tickets that indicate the operations to be performed on the product. Specific and understandable listing of detailed operations is important if work is to be performed within the time allowed and with the materials provided. Delays caused by lack of materials, machine breakdowns, or need for additional instructions give rise to complaints by the workers and lead to additional labor costs. Production schedules prepared several weeks in advance, utilizing labor time standards for each producing department, lead to cost control through the use of departmental labor budgets similar to the illustration on the next page.

PROCEDURES FOR LABOR COSTING

The above-mentioned activities lay the groundwork necessary to account for and control labor costs. The accounting for wages and salaries requires the work of the:

1. *Timekeeping department* — gathers and collects total and specific time worked on a job, product, process, or in a department.
2. *Payroll department* — determines the gross and net amount of earnings of each worker, computes the total payroll, and keeps earnings records for each employee.
3. *Cost department* — charges jobs, products, processes, or departments with the cost applicable as evidenced by the payroll distribution.

In detail, labor costing procedures involve:

1. The employment history of each worker — date hired, wage rate, initial assignment, promotions, tardiness, sickness, and vacations.

LABOR BUDGET

Department   Cooler Assembly   For   October, 19--

Prepared   September 10, 19--

Model No. or Job No.	Units Scheduled	Expected Assembly Hours Per Unit			Total Expected Direct Labor Hours
		Motor	Fan	Freon	
625	2,000	1.5	.25	.5	4,500
748	1,000	1.5	.30	.6	2,400
500	3,000	1.5	.20	.4	6,300
600	1,500	1.3	.40	.5	3,300
	7,500				16,500

Variable and Fixed Costs	Total Costs	Cost per Unit	No. of Employees*
Variable costs:			
Direct labor--16,500 hrs. @ $6......	$ 99,000	$13.200	94
Indirect labor--1,000 hrs. @ $3.....	3,000	.400	6
Total variable labor budget......	$102,000	$13.600	
Fixed costs:			
Supervision--700 hrs. @ $7..........	$ 4,900	$ .653	4
Clerical & Packing--350 hrs. @ $3.60	1,260	.168	2
Total fixed labor budget.........	$ 6,160	$ .821	___
Total for October....................	$106,160	$14.421	106

*No. of hrs. ÷ 1/6 (22 days x 8 hrs.)

Departmental Labor Budget

2. Adequate information for compliance with union contracts, social security laws, wages and hours legislation, income tax withholdings, and other federal, state, and local government requirements.

3. The time required for each basic manufacturing operation in order to develop efficient methods.

4. The establishment of labor cost standards for comparative purposes.

5. Productivity in relation to type of wage payment creating the best system of compensation for each kind of work.

6. The time worked by each employee, his wage rate, and his total earnings for each payroll period.

7. The output or accomplishment of each employee.

8. The amount of direct labor cost and hours to be charged to each job, lot, process, or department, and the amount of indirect labor cost. The direct labor cost or hours information may be used as a basis for factory overhead allocation.

9. Total labor cost in each department for each payroll period.

The accounting principles, procedures, and objectives in labor costing are relatively simple, although considerable difficulty in their application may be experienced with large numbers of workers or where workers shift from one type of work to another under various factory conditions. Basically, two sets of underlying detailed records are kept, one for financial accounting and the other for cost accounting. The procedures for labor accounting are outlined in the parallel presentation below. The journal entries associated with these procedures, as well as those pertaining to labor-related costs, are discussed and illustrated in the next chapter.

FINANCIAL ACCOUNTING	COST ACCOUNTING
A record is kept of the total time worked and the total amount earned by each worker.	A record is kept of the time worked on each job, process, or department by each worker and the cost thereof.
The daily or weekly amount earned by each worker is entered on the payroll book.	The direct labor hours and cost are entered on the respective job sheets or production reports; the indirect labor cost is entered in the proper column of the departmental expense analysis sheets or standing orders.

Each payroll period the total amount of wages paid to workers results in the following entry:
Payroll..................................... xxx
    Income Tax Withheld......... xxx
    FICA Tax Payable............... xxx
    Accounts Payable
      or Cash............................. xxx
	The weekly or month-end entry for labor distribution is:
	Work in Process.................. xxx
	Factory Overhead Control.. xxx
	    Indirect Labor............... xxx
	    Payroll.............................. xxx

Labor Accounting Procedures

Timekeeping Department. Securing an accurate record of the time purchased from each employee is the first step in labor costing. To do so, it is necessary to provide by means of a:

1. *Clock card* unquestionable evidence of the employee's presence in the plant from the time of entry to departure.

2. *Job ticket* (or *time ticket*) information as to the type of work performed while the employee is in the plant.

Both forms are supervised, controlled, and collected by the time-keeping department. As the earnings of the employee depend mainly upon these two forms and as the timekeeper processes them in the first step toward final payment, the timekeeping department forms a most valuable link in harmonious labor-management relationships. In fact, to many a worker, the timekeeper is management. Frequently it is the time-keeper's performance of his duties that is the basis for a worker's first opinion of the company.

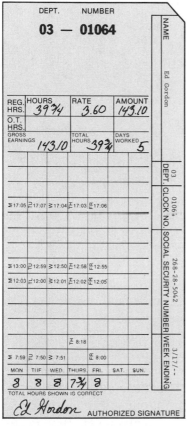

Clock Card

Clock Card. A *clock card* provides space for the name and number of the employee and usually covers an entire payroll period. When completed, the clock card shows the time a worker started and stopped work each day or shift of the payroll period, with overtime and other premium hours clearly indicated.

The *time clock* (or *time recorder*) is a modern mechanical instrument for recording employee time in and out of the office and the factory. Under a typical procedure, each employee is assigned a clock number that identifies the department and the employee. The clock number is used for identification on the payroll and in charging labor time to departments and production orders. Usually time-keepers are stationed near the clocks during change of shifts to expedite smooth and rapid movement in and out of the plant and to insure proper clock card procedures.

In small plants a time clock may not be used. In such cases it is customary to provide a board or rack near the entrance where each worker has a card, or in some cases a metal disk, that carries his name and identification number. Upon entering the plant, the worker removes his card or disk from the rack or board and places it on a smaller rack or board in the department where he works. Time-keepers, or in many cases the foremen, check each department, record the names of those present on a payroll sheet, and return the cards or disks to the entrance way to be available for the next work period. While such a method of labor cost recording seems less exact than the clock card procedure, reliance must be placed on the timekeeper or the foreman to secure accurate records.

Time Ticket (or Job Ticket). In accounting for materials, the receiving sheet and the invoice are evidence that the goods have been received and payment therefore is in order. In accounting for labor, the clock card is evidence that time has been purchased

DATE _5/27/ —_		JOB TICKET	
EMPLOYEE'S NAME _Warren Mayes_ SHIFT _A_			
TIME STARTED	TIME STOPPED	CHARGE ACCOUNT NUMBER	
8:00	12:00	361	
HRS. WORKED	EARNINGS	DESCRIPTION OF WORK	
4	15.40	*Finishing*	
OVERTIME HRS.	OVERTIME EARN.	PIECE NO. OR JOB NO.	
—	—	748	
RATE	TOTAL EARNINGS	PIECES COMPLETED	OPERATION NO.
3.85	15.40	14	27
		FOREMAN'S APPROVAL *EDV*	

Job Ticket

and is comparable to the receiving sheet. The *time ticket* (or *job ticket*) shows the specific use that has been made of the time purchased and is comparable to the materials requisition.

When the individual time ticket is used, a new ticket must be made out for each job worked on during the day. As this procedure leads to many tickets per employee, some plants use a *daily time report* on which the worker lists his jobs.

The best procedure for filling in the time or job tickets depends upon many factors peculiar to shop operations. In some factories, where little time is consumed and the work permits ready access to the forms, the workers prepare their own time tickets. In other factories, timekeepers, dispatch clerks, and foremen have desks near the work stations. Employees report to the timekeeper when changing jobs, get a new assignment from the dispatch clerk, secure instructions at the foreman's desk, get the required tools at the tool crib, and thus shift from one job to another with a minimum of time and effort. Under a wage incentive plan, time tickets form the basis for calculating bonuses. When wages are based on hours worked, the time tickets provide a means of auditing the clock cards and a source of data concerning efficient utilization of labor.

Each day, usually after the morning shift has clocked in, the time-keeper collects all the time tickets or the daily time reports of the previous day together with the clock cards. The total time reported on the time tickets for each employee is compared with the total hours of his clock card. If there is any difference, an adjustment is made as follows: If the clock card shows more hours than the time tickets, the difference is reported as idle time. If the time tickets show more hours than the clock card, the error is corrected in consultation with the foreman and the worker. The time tickets are sent daily to the payroll department.

The degree of accuracy in reporting time varies from plant to plant, but in most situations a report to the exact minute is neither necessary nor practical. Many companies find it advantageous to use a decimal system, measuring the hour in ten periods of six minutes each rather than the regular clock interval of five-minute periods and twelve periods per hour. Computation of time in terms of tenths of an hour is much faster than computation of time in minutes or in twelfths of an hour. On a decimal system, a job started at 9:23 a.m. and finished at 11:38 a.m. would be reported as 9.4 and 11.6 with an elapsed time of 2.2 hours.

Payroll Department. Preparation of the company's payroll from clock cards, time tickets, or time sheets is done by the payroll department. The work, procedures, and functions of this department depend upon the size and complexity of a company. Some companies require only a simple payroll department staffed by one or two payroll clerks who perform the work manually; others require an elaborate payroll department with many employees and computerized procedures. In any case, the payroll department is responsible for the important task of recording the job classification, department, and wage rate for each employee. It records hours worked and wages earned, makes payroll deductions, determines the net amount due each employee, maintains a permanent earnings record for each employee, and prepares the paycheck, or provides the cashier's or treasurer's office with the necessary records to make the payments.

The work of the payroll department follows two basic steps: (1) computation of the payroll and (2) distribution of the payroll to jobs, processes, and departments.

The final computed payroll may be recorded in a payroll journal, payroll record, payroll report, or payroll sheet. The record may be a bound book with sheets ruled for the special needs of a company; it may be a loose-leaf book, cards, or sheets for filing; or it may be produced on sheets or rolls through the use of payroll machines or computerized methods. A record of individual employee earnings and deductions must also be maintained. Practically all large enterprises and many smaller ones use a computerized system for payroll preparation.

Payroll Payments. If the number of employees is not large, all workers are usually paid on the same day, which may be weekly, semimonthly, or monthly. Some companies stagger the payroll during the week in order to give an even flow to the work of the payroll department. If workers are paid in cash, it is necessary to transport the payroll cash from a bank to the payroll office, to prepare pay envelopes for each worker, and to arrange them alphabetically or by clock number for distribution to the employees.

In most instances employees are paid by check. Payroll checks may be drawn against the regular checking account, or a special payroll deposit may be used. The special payroll bank account is especially advantageous with large numbers of workers. If a payroll fund is deposited in the bank, the payroll department certifies the amount required for a particular payment date, a voucher is drawn for the specified amount, and a check is drawn against the regular deposit account and is deposited in the payroll fund. By utilizing this procedure, only one check, drawn on the general bank account, appears in the cash payments journal each payroll period. The paymaster prepares checks for each employee — each drawn against the special payroll account. When machine methods are used for payroll accounting, the payroll journal, the checks, the check register, and the employee's earnings record are commonly prepared in one simultaneous operation.

Payroll Distribution. The individual job ticket or daily time report show the use made of the time purchased from each factory employee. The tickets for each employee must agree with his total earnings for the week. Time tickets are sorted by jobs, departments, and types of indirect labor to permit the distribution of the total payroll to Work in Process and to the various indirect labor accounts or to the departmental expense analysis sheets controlled by Factory Overhead Control. Distribution of the payroll is speeded up when automated methods are used. If the payroll department does not prepare the distribution summary, the job tickets are sent to the cost department, which must perform this task. Labor costs distributed to jobs, processes, or departments must agree with the total amount recorded in the payroll account. Often the distribution summary also shows the labor hours when they are the basis for the application of factory overhead.

Cost Department. On the basis of the labor distribution summary or the time tickets, the cost department records the direct labor cost on the appropriate cost sheets or production reports, and indirect costs on the departmental expense analysis sheets. In some factories cost accounting activities are decentralized, and cost work becomes largely a matter of organization and direction in carrying out a system for recording payroll information and labor costs. In such a supervisory capacity, cost clerks may be stationed in producing departments to assist in accumulating and classifying labor costs, using the summarized time tickets to compute production costs and services by job orders, units of output, departmental operations, and product types. In other factories the cost department may be highly centralized and may not direct and control any timekeeping or payroll preparation.

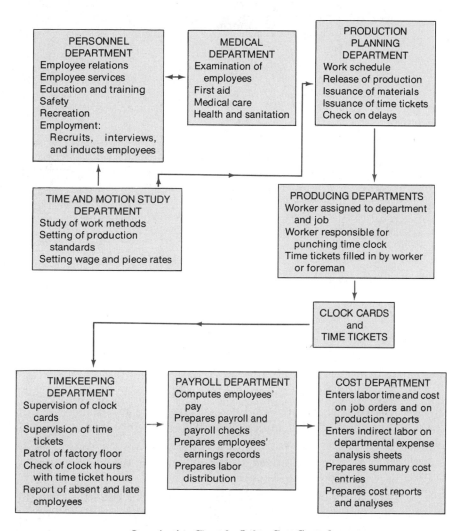

Organization Chart for Labor Cost Control

The above organization chart summarizes the departmental interrelationships required for effective labor cost control and accounting.

The preceding labor costing procedures have emphasized manufacturing labor. Labor costing of nonmanufacturing labor, such as marketing and administrative employees, also requires the same detailed cost accumulation and distribution procedures.

COMPUTERIZED PAYROLL PROCEDURES

The preceding discussion of labor and payroll procedures was based on manual and/or semimechanical operations. Yet almost from the very

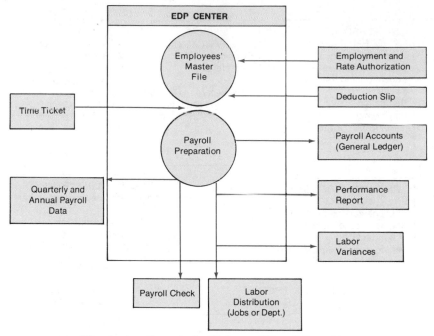

Flowchart — Computerized Labor and Payroll Procedures

moment that electronic computers were invented and employed in business, payroll procedures were generally the first to be programmed for these new machines. The reason for this immediate acceptance lay in the fact that businesses had definitive payroll accounting procedures which lent themselves to computer adaptation. Consequently, payroll accounting procedures can be computerized to the extent that the need for manual processing is virtually eliminated.

The preparation of labor performance reports was discussed and illustrated earlier in this chapter. However, their presentation is made possible because computerized labor accounting begins the day an employee is hired and the data for the employee's name, number, job classification, shift, department, direct/indirect pay rate, deductions, etc., are entered in the employee's master file. From that moment on, the employee's activities and those of every other employee are inputted for payroll data, labor distribution, and a permanent employment data bank.

Computerized labor and payroll procedures are depicted in the flowchart above.

INCENTIVE WAGE PLANS

In the modern industrial enterprise of mass production and many employees, a worker's wage is based on negotiated labor contracts, productivity studies, job evaluation, profit sharing, incentive wage plans, and guaranteed annual wages. Because all wages are paid for work performed, an element of incentive is present in all wage plans. In contrast with pay by the hour, week, or month, an incentive wage plan should reward a worker in direct proportion to his increased output. As stated earlier, a fair day's work standard should be established so that the worker can meet and even exceed it, thereby receiving the full benefits from the incentive wage plan. At one time incentive wage plans for factory workers were widely used. Recent studies now show that about half of all large companies use incentive wage plans for at least some of their work centers. Union attitudes toward incentive wage plans vary. Some unions oppose incentive plans while others — such as those in the textile, shoe, and steel industries — support them.

Requirements of an Incentive Wage Plan. To be successful, an incentive wage plan must meet certain requirements: (1) applicability to situations in which a worker can increase output, (2) provision for proportionately more pay for output above standard, (3) setting fair standards so that extra effort will result in bonus pay, and (4) immediate reward every payday. Along with these essentials, the plan needs to be reasonably simple and understandable to workers as well as to managers.

Purpose of an Incentive Wage Plan. The primary purpose of an incentive wage plan is to induce a worker to produce more, to earn a higher wage, and at the same time to reduce unit costs. The plan seeks to insure greater output, to increase control over labor cost by insuring more uniform unit costs, and to change the basis for reward from hours served to work accomplished. Naturally, producing more in the same period of time should result in higher pay for the worker. Because of the greater number of units produced, it should also result in a lower cost per unit for fixed factory overhead and labor cost combined.

For example, suppose that a factory operation takes place in a building that is rented for $1,200 per month (or $40 per day) and that insurance, taxes, and depreciation amount to $64 per day. Assume further that 10 workers on an 8-hour day are paid $3 per hour and that each worker produces 40 units of product per day (an individual production rate of 5 units per hour). Now suppose that the workers and the management agree that a rate of $3.30 per hour will be paid if a worker produces 48 units per day, thereby increasing the hourly output from 5 to 6 units.

The illustration at the top of the next page, reduced to cost per hour and cost per unit to produce the product, shows how a wage incentive can reduce unit costs and at the same time provide the worker with a higher income.

ORIGINAL SYSTEM, $3 PER HOUR (10 workers)				NEW SYSTEM, $3.30 PER HOUR (10 workers)			
Cost Factor	Amount per Hour	Units per Hour	Unit Cost	Cost Factor	Amount per Hour	Units per Hour	Unit Cost
Labor.....................	$30	50	$.60	Labor.....................	$33	60	$.5500
Rent.......................	5	50	.10	Rent.......................	5	60	.0833
Depreciation, insurance, and taxes..................	8	50	.16	Depreciation, insurance, and taxes..................	8	60	.1333
Total	$43	50	$.86	Total	$46	60	$.7666

Effect of an Incentive Wage Plan on Unit Costs

Although the hourly labor cost of the ten-man crew increases from $30 to $33, the cost of a complete unit of product is reduced from $.86 to $.7666. The unit cost decrease is caused by two factors: (1) unit output per worker is increased 20 percent with a 10 percent increase in wages and (2) the same amount of fixed factory overhead is spread over 60 units instead of 50 units of product an hour. For greater precision, such an analysis should also include labor-related costs such as employer's payroll taxes, etc.

These general principles have been applied to most discussions on incentive wage plans. However, the lowering of conversion or manufacturing costs as the significant desirable consequence of an increase in production resulting from an incentive wage plan, here illustrated on a cost per unit basis, could be explained in terms of a total differential (marginal or incremental) cost analysis (see Chapter 25).

If the introduction of an incentive wage system results in greater labor productivity, the desirability of achieving this increased productivity may be evaluated by the net incremental change in *total* revenues and/or costs. Since total fixed costs, by definition, are not expected to change in response to (small) changes in production volume, these cost elements should be ignored in the analysis, and attention directed to the other items sensitive to volume changes.

If the market will absorb additional output, the marginal revenue [and costs] of this output becomes important in the evaluation. If the market is saturated, or if other capacity restrictions preclude an increase in volume, the revenue side may be ignored and then the increased productivity anticipated would provide benefits to the extent that the labor formerly devoted to production could be eliminated or used in some alternative way, i.e., the appropriate benefit is the labor's opportunity cost, and any concurrent reduction in time-related variable costs. The benefits derived from these items must, of course, be reduced by any increases resulting from extra incentive payments to employees and the extra costs involved in administering a more complex compensation plan.[3]

---

[3]Werner G. Frank, "Evaluation of Wage Incentives: Fixed Costs, Revisited," *The Accounting Review*, Vol. XLVII, No. 1, p. 156.

Types of Incentive Wage Plans.   In actual practice, time wages and output wages are not clear-cut and distinct.   Incentive plans typically involve wage rates based upon various combinations of output and time. Many wage incentive systems retain the names of industrial engineers and efficiency experts who originated the plans — the Taylor Differential Piece Rate Plan, the Halsey Premium Plan, the Bedaux Point System, the Gantt Task and Bonus Plan, and the Emerson Efficiency System.   Most of these plans — like obsolete machinery — are no longer used, but many adaptations are still in use.

An employee's earnings are determined by the (1) ratio of a worker's production to standard production, (2) hourly base rate for the job classification, and (3) incentive wage plan in use.   In order to demonstrate the operation of incentive wage plans, the straight piecework plan, the 100 percent bonus plan, and the group bonus plan are discussed as representative examples.

Straight Piecework Plan.   The *straight piecework plan*, one of the simplest incentive wage plans, pays wages above the base rate for production above the standard.   The production standard is computed in minutes per piece and is then translated into money per piece.   If time studies determine that five minutes is to be the standard time required for producing one unit, the standard rate is 12 pieces per hour.   If a worker's base pay rate is $3.72 per hour, the piece rate is $.31.   A worker is generally guaranteed a base pay rate, even if he fails to earn that amount in terms of output.   If a worker's production exceeds 12 pieces per hour, the $.31 per unit still applies.   In the table below, with standard production of 12 pieces per hour and with a guaranteed hourly rate, the labor cost per unit of output declines until the standard is reached and then remains constant at any level of output above standard.

Units per Hour	Guaranteed Hourly Rate	Piece Rate	Earned per Hour	Labor Cost per Unit	Overhead per Hour	Overhead per Unit	Conversion Cost per Unit
10	$3.72	0	$3.72	$.372	$2.40	$.240	$.612
11	3.72	0	3.72	.338	2.40	.218	.556
12	3.72	$.31	3.72	.310	2.40	.200	.510
13	3.72	.31	4.03	.310	2.40	.185	.495
14	3.72	.31	4.34	.310	2.40	.171	.481
15	3.72	.31	4.65	.310	2.40	.160	.470
16	3.72	.31	4.96	.310	2.40	.150	.460

Table Illustrating the Straight Piecework Plan

While piece rates reflect an obvious cause-effect relationship between output and pay, the incentive is effective only when workers can control their rates of output. Piece rates would not, of course, be effective where output is machine-paced. As previously stated, modification of production standards and labor rates becomes necessary when increases in output are the result of the installation of new and better machines.

100 Percent Bonus Plan. The *100 percent bonus plan* is a variation of the straight piecework plan. It differs in that standards are never stated in terms of money, but in time per unit of output. Instead of a price per piece, a *standard time* is allowed to complete a job or unit; and the worker is paid for the standard time at his hourly rate if the job or unit is completed in standard time or less. Thus if a worker produces 100 units in an 8-hour shift and the standard time is 80 units per shift (or 10 units per hour), he would be paid his hourly rate for 10 hours. In other variations of the 100 percent bonus plan, savings are shared with the foreman and/or the company.

A *production indicator* must be figured for every worker each payroll period before earnings can be computed. Production standards in units of output per hour are set by industrial engineers. Hours of work and units produced are reported to the payroll department where the reported hours worked are multiplied by the hourly production standard to determine the standard units. The worker's hourly production is then divided by the standard quantity resulting in the production indicator, or *efficiency ratio*. The efficiency ratio multiplied by the worker's base rate results in the hourly earnings for the period. The table below illustrates how earnings are computed, assuming standard production to be 15 units per hour.

Worker	Hours Worked	Output Units	Standard Units	Efficiency Ratio	Base Rate	Base × Efficiency Ratio	Total Earned	Labor Cost per Unit	Overhead per Hour	Overhead per Unit	Conversion Cost per Unit
Abrames	40	540	600	90	$2.75	$0.0000	$110.00	$.2037	$2.40	$.1778	$.3815
Gordon	40	660	600	110	2.75	3.0250	121.00	.1833	2.40	.1455	.3288
Hanson	40	800	600	133	2.75	3.6575	146.30	.1829	2.40	.1200	.3029
Jonson	38	650	570	114	2.80	3.1920	121.30	.1866	2.40	.1404	.3270
Stowell	40	750	600	125	3.00	3.7500	150.00	.2000	2.40	.1280	.3280
Wiebold	40	810	600	135	2.86	3.8610	154.44	.1906	2.40	.1185	.3091

Table Illustrating the 100 Percent Bonus Plan

The standard time plan has gained in popularity because of the frequency of wage increases. The standards, stated in terms of time and output quantity, need no adjustment when wage rates change. Since the system emphasizes time rather than money, the plan lends itself to the development of controls and efficiency standards.

Group Bonus Plan. Today industry employs a great variety of incentive wage plans, some of which depend upon superior productive performance of a whole department or an entire factory. Factory operations often require workers to work as groups or crews using large machines. Although the work of each employee is essential to the machine operation, it is frequently impossible to separate the work of one individual member of a crew for incentive purposes. It is impossible for a worker on an assembly line to increase his output without the cooperation of the entire group. Group bonus plans have proven successful in such situations. Usually, the bonus earned by the group for production in excess of a quota or standard is divided among the group members in accordance with their respective base rates. Group plans reduce the amount of clerical work necessary to compute labor cost and payrolls and the amount of supervision necessary to operate the incentive system. Group plans may also contribute to better cooperation among workers, and good workers are likely to bring pressure to bear upon poor workers who might jeopardize the earning of the group bonus.

Group bonus plans, like those designed for individual incentive, are intended to encourage production at rates above a minimum standard. Each worker in the group receives his hourly rate for production up to the standard output. Units produced in excess of the standard are regarded as time saved by the group, and each worker is in effect paid a bonus for time saved as well as being paid for time worked. Group plans quite often lead to the *absence of* something, such as accidents, spoilage, waste, and absenteeism. For example, a bonus may be paid to a crew or department which has not had an accident for a specified period of time, or which has a reject rate in units of output below a specified ratio.

The following table illustrates the operation of a 100 percent group bonus plan. A crew of 10 men uses costly equipment, and each man is paid $5 an hour for a regular 8-hour shift. Standard production is 50 units per hour, or 400 units per shift; overhead is $320 per 8-hour shift, or $40 per hour.

Units Produced	Std. Hrs. for Units Produced	Actual Hours	Regular Group Wage	Bonus (Hrs. Saved @ $5)	Total Group Earnings	Labor Cost per Unit	Over-head Cost per Unit	Conversion Cost per Unit
350	70	80	$400	$ 0	$400	$1.143	$.914	$2.057
400	80	80	400	0	400	1.000	.800	1.800
425	85	80	400	25	425	1.000	.753	1.753
450	90	80	400	50	450	1.000	.711	1.711
475	95	80	400	75	475	1.000	.674	1.674
500	100	80	400	100	500	1.000	.640	1.640

Table Illustrating the 100 Percent Group Bonus Plan
(Standard rate, 400 units per shift)

General Observations Regarding Incentive Wage Plans. The installation and successful operation of incentive wage plans require not only the combined efforts of the personnel department, labor unions, factory engineers, and accountants but also the cooperation and willingness of each worker. The discussion on wage incentives is:

> . . .based on the premise that monetary bonuses will, in fact, motivate workers to achieve higher production rates. While this seems a reasonable assumption, the writing of behavioral scientists and the empirical research that has been carried out suggest that the relationship between monetary incentives and increased production is not a simple or unambiguous one. William F. Whyte, a behavioral scientist, notes in a study of the effect of piecework on productivity, 'It is only in a fraction of the jobs. . .that the piecework proves an incentive to tap the full productive capacities of workers.'[4] After describing in detail a number of case situations, he concludes, 'Management should recognize that financial incentives are both a technical engineering and a human relations problem.'[5] This suggests that management should approach the design, evaluation, and implementation of such plans with the awareness of their possible behavioral, as well as economic, implications.[6]

WAGE INCENTIVE TIME STANDARDS VIA LEARNING CURVE THEORY

Incentive wage plans assume that monetary bonuses will motivate workers to achieve higher productivity rates. In turn, the greater the output, the lower the conversion cost per unit. Yet, the previous discussion also stresses the fact that motivation is not always based on financial rewards. Furthermore, an incentive wage plan, based on fixed time standards — no matter how scientifically engineered — often does not appear to motivate workers. A fixed time standard is best explained by referring to the 100 percent bonus plan (page 418), in which the standard is fixed at 80 units per day (or 10 units per hour during an 8-hour shift). Even with such drawbacks, many current incentive wage plans still use fixed time standards for rewarding individual performance through bonus payments. The deficiencies existing in fixed time standards of wage incentives have been remedied by means of the learning curve theory.

The *learning curve theory* stipulates that every time the cumulative quantity of units produced is doubled, the cumulative average time per unit is reduced by a given percentage; that is, "the last unit will cost (in time, hours, or dollars) a given percentage less than the last unit produced prior to doubling the quantity. If it is assumed that this reduction is 20 percent, it means that the second unit requires 80 percent of the time required for the first unit; the fourth unit, 80 percent of the second; the eighth unit, 80 percent of the fourth; and so on. With this theory, the

---

[4]William F. Whyte, *Money and Motivation* (Harper & Bros., 1955), p. 28.
[5]*Ibid.*, p. 262.
[6]Frank, *op. cit.*, pp. 159–160.

following table of values for an 80 percent learning curve can be computed, assuming that 10 direct labor hours are required to produce the first unit:[7]

Unit Number	×	Cumulative Average Required Man-Hours per Unit	=	Estimated Total Time Needed To Perform the Task
1		10.0		10.0 hours
2		8.0 (10.0 hours × 80%)		16.0 hours
4		6.4 (8.0 hours × 80%)		25.6 hours
8		5.1 (6.4 hours × 80%)		40.8 hours
16		4.1 (5.1 hours × 80%)		65.6 hours
32		3.3 (4.1 hours × 80%)		105.6 hours
64		2.6 (3.3 hours × 80%)		166.4 hours

Computations for a Typical 80 Percent Learning Curve

The results indicate that the rate is constant at each *doubling* of the accumulated number of times the task is performed. The figures in the second column are the *cumulative average* times *per unit*. To estimate the total time needed to perform the task the first 32 times, the calculation would be $32 \times 3.3 = 105.6$ hours; for the first 64 times, $64 \times 2.6 = 166.4$ hours; etc.

The 80 percent learning curve is used here for illustrative purposes. The actual percentage will, of course, depend on the particular situation. At the extremes, the actual percentage could range from 100 percent (if no learning occurs; i.e., 100 minutes × 100% = 100 minutes), to 50 percent. At the latter extreme, if the average accumulated time for the first unit is 100 minutes, then the time for the second unit must equal zero (i.e., 100 minutes × 50% = 50 minutes — accumulated average time per task unit at the 2 task units level, or a total of 100 minutes for the 2 accumulated units). Inasmuch as the first unit required 100 minutes, this would mean that the time for the second unit must be equal to zero:

$$\frac{100 + 0}{2} = 50 \text{ minutes, average time per task unit}$$

Thus, the 50 percent rate is an upper limit of learning — one that can never be reached.[8]

By means of the learning curve, the time standard or unit standard used for determining a worker's earnings has now changed to a variable time instead of the fixed time standard. The variable time standard is said to meet more equitably the needs of an incentive wage system. "The improvement phenomenon, as well as its mathematical model, the learning

---

[7]James A. Broadston, "Learning Curve Wage Incentives," *Management Accounting*, Vol. XLIX, No. 12, pp. 15–23.

[8]For further discussion of learning curves, see Leonard W. Hein, *The Quantitative Approach to Managerial Decisions* (Englewood Cliffs, N. J.: Prentice-Hall, Inc., 1967), pp. 90–113.

curve, provides an insight into human capabilities that bears directly up-on the ability of workers to do work and the time required for them to learn new skills. An actual learning curve may show small irregularities; yet it will eventually follow an underlying natural characteristic of group or individual human activity."[9]

As soon as a worker has passed the learning stage and begins to pro-duce the expected number of units (i.e., reaches the "standard" profi-ciency), he will begin to draw bonus pay for doing the operation in less than standard time. Then the worker may even slow down a little and yet perform the operation in "standard" time or better, drawing the bonus pay but working less hard for it.

Government procurement agencies have used the learning curve theory as a tool for cost evaluation in negotiating prices for contracts. When a bid on a contract is entered, the unit labor costs are usually esti-mated. The learning curve theory permits the determination of lot costs for various stages of production. As production progresses, the average unit labor cost should decrease.

By comparing the budgeted costs with the experienced labor costs in the initial stages of production, the trend of the labor costs can be deter-mined. If, for example, an average labor cost of $20 per unit is to be achieved, the following output and cost table with 80, 85 and 90 percent learning curves can be predetermined:[10]

| *Cumulative* | Learning Curve | | |
Quantity	80%	85%	90%
25.............................	$61.02	$45.36	$33.22
50.............................	48.82	38.56	30.47
100............................	39.06	32.78	27.43
200............................	31.25	27.68	24.69
400............................	25.00	23.53	22.22
800............................	20.00	20.00	20.00

Output and Cost Table for 80%, 85%, and 90% Learning Curve

The learning curve theory allows projection of the final average unit cost at any stage of production. The learning curve also predicts man-hours with accuracy and reliability, establishes manpower load, and al-lows production control to take advantage of reducing time per unit by increasing lot sizes, thereby maintaining a level work force. It further provides a basis for standard cost variances calculations (see Chapter 19),

---

[9]Broadston, *op. cit.*, p. 15.
[10]William H. Boren, "Some Applications of the Learning Curve to Government Contracts," *NAA Bulletin*, Vol. XLVI, No. 2, pp. 21–22.

allows judgment of a manager's performance relative to the department's target, and finally provides a basis for cost control by analyzing upward swings of the learning curve.

UNION CONTRACTS

Many possible provisions relative to wages, hours, and working conditions are always present when a labor contract is negotiated. The employer and employee have a mutual interest in the terms of a contract and a mutual responsibility for carrying out the agreement.

Inasmuch as the union serves as the employees' representative and the agreement is signed by both union and company officials, the contract is likely to be printed for distribution to all interested parties. Provisions of a typical contract involve the personnel department in the hiring, promotion, and dismissal of employees; the payroll department in the determination of regular wages, premium pay for overtime, holidays, vacations, night shifts, and premium rates or bonus payments under incentive wage plans; and the cost department, since a contract represents the terms and price of labor to be purchased during the life of a contract. It is important that managers of these departments become thoroughly familiar with provisions of the contract and that all procedures in connection with labor accounting be designed and executed in harmony with its provisions. Grievances leading to stoppages and strikes can be caused by poorly understood or poorly executed union agreements. The accounting function is a vital link in harmonious labor-management relations.

DISCUSSION QUESTIONS

1. Define *productivity*.

2. What is meant by *performance rating*?

3. The subject of inflation has been receiving ever-increasing attention throughout the nation and the world? Why?

4. All wage payments are ultimately limited by and are usually based, directly or indirectly, on the productivity of the worker. Is this statement generally true?

5. The basis for labor cost control is the provision of pertinent and timely information to management. What kind of information is needed by executive management as compared with that needed by departmental managers?

6. How can labor efficiency be determined or measured?

7. In a highly mechanized or automated plant, direct labor tends to become a fixed cost. Discuss the validity of this statement.

8. In controlling labor cost, is the primary objective to control labor cost per hour of work or per unit of output?

9. In what way are the creation and maintenance of an efficient labor force a cooperative effort?

10. In accounting for and controlling labor costs, what is the function of: (a) the timekeeping department, (b) the payroll department, and (c) the cost accounting department?

11. What purpose is served by: (a) the clock card; (b) the time ticket?

12. If an employee's clock card shows more time than his time tickets, how is the difference reconciled?

13. Accounting for labor has a twofold aspect: financial accounting and cost accounting. Differentiate between the two.

14. What is the purpose of determining the labor hours: (a) worked by each employee; (b) worked on each job, or in each department?

15. What is the purpose of an incentive wage plan?

16. Do you consider it necessary to record the time spent by pieceworkers on their various jobs or operations? Give reasons.

17. Wage incentive plans are successful in plants operating near full capacity.
   (a) Discuss the desirability of using these plans during periods of curtailed production.
   (b) Would you advise the installation of an incentive wage plan in a plant operating at 60% of capacity? Discuss.

18. In most incentive wage plans, does production above standard reduce the labor cost per unit of output? Discuss.

19. Differentiate between wages based on the straight piecework plan, the 100 percent bonus plan, and the group bonus plan.

20. Because of faulty determination of piecework rates, workers' earnings in a particular plant have been unduly high. Sales volume and prices are declining, and it is necessary to reduce production costs. What solution would you suggest?

21. State the basic concept underlying the relationship involved in the learning curve theory.

22. Name some situations for the application of the learning curve theory.

23. It is frequently stated that accurate cost accounting is of great value in wage negotiations. How may cost records contribute to settlement of wage disputes?

24. The management of the Marquette Manufacturing Company established a key man bonus plan in which a bonus is paid to the foreman, assistant foreman, or any other supervisor within a specific department based on net savings made in the department. The company does not pay out the entire bonus but pays part in cash and places the remainder in a fund. The fund acts as a reserve against which negative variances are charged during the year. At the end of February, the net savings in a certain department for the month amount to $680. Of these savings, 20% are distributed to the supervisory staff. The department employs a foreman and an assistant. The method of sharing the bonus is on a point scale basis with 100 points assigned to the foreman and 60 points to his assistant. How much bonus is each supervisor entitled to receive?

25. A factory foreman at Steblecki Corporation discharged an hourly worker but did not notify the Payroll Department. The foreman then forged the worker's signature on time cards and work tickets and, when giving out the payroll checks, diverted the checks drawn for the discharged worker to his own use. Select the statement that would be the most effective procedure for preventing this activity:
    (a) Require a written authorization for each employee added to or removed from the payroll.
    (b) Have a paymaster with no other payroll responsibility than that of distributing payroll checks.
    (c) Have someone other than persons who prepare or distribute the payroll obtain custody of unclaimed payroll checks.
    (d) From time to time, rotate persons distributing the payroll.

(AICPA adapted)

EXERCISES

1. Production Planning and Control Reports. Ferguson Fabricators, Inc., a supplier of bulk metals and alloys, recently negotiated to supply 3,000 sections of aluminum air conditioning ductwork for an office building under construction. The order requires fabricating, cutting, and assembly. Based on experience, the foreman prepared the following daily budget:

Department	Sections Scheduled	Hours Budgeted
Fabricating..........	100	50
Cutting.............	100	30
Assembly...........	100	25

Realizing the need for up-to-the-minute production information, the foreman obtained these results of the first day's activity:

Department	Sections Produced	Hours Required
Fabricating..........	112	48
Cutting.............	81	30
Assembly...........	77	22

The second day's report showed:

Department	Sections Produced	Hours Required
Fabricating..........	120	49
Cutting.............	96	30
Assembly...........	96	23

Required: (1) Action to be taken by the foreman, based on the first day's report.

(2) Action needed according to the results on the second day's report.

2. Labor Performance Variances.   Ellsworth-Trevor, Inc. prepares monthly production budgets for its largest selling product, Elsby, which is manufactured through three departments: Mixing, Processing, and Packaging. Budgeted and actual amounts for April were as shown on the next page.

Department	Budgeted Hours	Actual Labor Cost	Units Produced
Mixing...........	1,100	$ 4,312	740
Processing........	3,320	12,700	615
Packaging........	580	1,744	800

The following standards have been adopted for this product:

Department	Standard Hours per Unit	Standard Labor Cost per Hour
Mixing...........	1.5	$4.10
Processing........	5.0	4.50
Packaging........	0.5	4.00

Required: A labor cost control report for April.

3. 100 Percent Bonus Plan. Mary Mullin, employed by the Barnegat Bay Canning Company, submitted the following labor data for the first week in June:

Monday..........	270 units	8 hours
Tuesday..........	210 units	8 hours
Wednesday.......	300 units	8 hours
Thursday........	240 units	8 hours
Friday...........	260 units	8 hours

Required: A schedule showing Mary's daily earnings, the effective hourly rate, and the labor cost per unit, assuming a 100 percent bonus plan with a base wage of $4 per hour and a standard production rate of 30 units per hour.

4. 100 Percent Bonus Plan. Tronicircuit Corporation produces printed circuits for the electronics industry. The firm has recently initiated a 100 percent bonus plan with standard production set at 50 units per hour.

The company employs 10 workers on an 8-hour shift at $5 per hour. Depreciation on plant equipment is $4.50 per hour, and other overhead is applied at $3.50 per hour.

Production for the first week under the 100 percent bonus plan was:

Monday...............	3,800 units
Tuesday..............	4,500 units
Wednesday............	4,600 units
Thursday.............	4,500 units
Friday...............	4,400 units

Management is interested in appraising the results of the new incentive wage plan.

Required: A schedule showing employee earnings, unit labor cost, unit overhead cost, and conversion cost per unit.

5. Incentive Wage Plan. Memorizon Electronics Company, a relatively small supplier of computer-oriented parts, is currently engaged in producing a new component for the computer sensory unit.

The company has been producing 150 units per week; fixed factory overhead was estimated to be $600 per week. The following is a schedule of the pay rates of three workers properly classified as direct labor:

Employee	Hourly Rate
Clancy, D..........	$3.00
Luken, T..........	4.00
Schott, J..........	3.50

Customers have been calling in for additional units, but management does not want to work more than 40 hours per week. In order to motivate its workers to produce more, the company decided to institute an incentive wage plan. The following schedule describes the plan formulated and started on a trial basis:

Employee	Base Rate	Incentive Premium
Clancy, D..........	$1.75	$.50 per unit
Luken, T..........	2.75	$.50 per unit
Schott, J..........	2.25	$.50 per unit

The first week the plan was put into operation production increased to 165 units. The shop superintendent studied the results and believed the plan too costly; production had increased 10%, but labor costs had increased by approximately 23.2%. He requested permission to redesign the plan to make the labor cost increases proportionate to the productivity increase.

Required: (1) The approximate dollar value of the 23.2% labor cost increase.
(2) An opinion, supported by figures, as to whether the shop superintendent was correct in assuming that the incentive wage plan was too costly. Discuss other factor(s) to be considered.

6. Piece Rates with Increased Productivity. Employees of Duwel Power Tools are paid $4.20 per hour for an 8-hour shift. Currently, production has been 3 units per hour per worker. A management consultant team has proposed the following piece rate incentive plan.

(a) $1.40 per unit up to 27 units per 8-hour day
(b) $1.44 per unit from 27 through 29 units per day, for all units
(c) $1.48 per unit from 30 through 32 units per day, for all units
(d) $1.51 per unit from 33 through 36 units per day, for all units
(e) $1.535 per unit for 37 units and above, for all units

Overhead consists almost entirely of depreciation, taxes, and insurance. Consequently, it is assumed that the current overhead rate of $5.50 per labor hour will remain constant.

Required: (1) An analysis of the proposal showing unit conversion cost for production of 24, 27, 30, 33, and 37 units.
(2) An opinion as to whether or not (a) management and (b) employees would be receptive to such a plan.

7. Cost of Training Program to Upgrade Workers' Productivity. Pocahontas Products, Inc. employs 40 machine operators for the same type of work. The average output per employee is 48 good units per hour with two rejects per hour per worker. The last efficiency report shows 50% of the operators averaged only 40 good units an hour with three rejects, while the other 50% averaged 55 good units per hour with one reject. The piece rate is $.15 each for good units. Repairing rejects costs $.25 each.

The job is a one-man, one-machine operation. The depreciation cost of each machine is $1,000 a year, and the variable cost of operating one machine is $.20 an hour. Fixed factory overhead other than depreciation is $4 per machine hour. The plant operates 2,000 hours a year, or 250 days.

Required: Assuming that product demand increases, the amount the company can afford to pay for a training program which would upgrade the 20 poorer workers to equal the average production of the better operators.

8. Learning Curves and Production Costs. A company's new process will be carried out in one department. The production process has an expected learning curve of 80 percent. The costs subject to the learning effect for the first batch produced by the process were $10,000.

Required: Using the simplest form of learning function, the cumulative average cost per batch subject to the learning effect after the 16th batch has been produced.

(AICPA adapted)

PROBLEMS

14-1. Planning Manpower and Labor Costs. Virontrol, Inc. is a relatively new company in the environmental control industry and is experiencing tremendous growth in product demand. To meet customers' increasing demands, the management is considering the addition of a nighttime operation production shift beginning October 1.

Production takes place in three departments: Assembly, Molding, and Finishing. Standard time in the Molding Department is 10 minutes per unit produced, while the Finishing Department averages 12½ items per hour. Employees in these two departments are paid $5 per hour. Two people are needed in the Assembly Department, each with a monthly salary of $850, to serve the extra shift. One foreman for each 19 workers is needed in the Molding and Finishing Departments, and 5 cleanup employees are required. Foremen are paid $1,200 per month, and each member of the cleanup crew is paid $3.50 per hour.

Under normal conditions, the company schedules 20 work days per month with standard monthly production of 120,000 units.

Required: A monthly labor budget for the extra shift, showing the time required in each department, the labor cost for each department and service, unit labor cost, and the number of employees required.

14-2. Labor Performance Report; Efficiency Variances. The DeLeone Company is interested in improving its control over labor costs. The Accounting Department assembled the following data for September:

Labor Activity	Actual Hours	Actual Expenses
Productive labor time...................	8,000	$46,900
Setup time............................	200	1,254
Cleanup time..........................	110	462
Down time............................	350	1,776

A predetermined standard of 7,700 hours of productive labor has been provided. Statistical analysis has established that setup time, cleanup time, and down time should be 3%, 1%, and 4%, respectively, of standard production time allowed. The standard labor rate is $6 per hour.

Required: (1) A labor performance report for September to be sent to the plant manager. For control purposes, it should include total variances and labor efficiency variances.

(2) An explanation and analysis for any difference between the labor efficiency variance and the total labor variance.

14-3. Incentive Wage Plans. Different departments of the Winkle Chocolate Company use different incentive wage plans. For instance, Irving Dunn of the Mixing Department is covered by a 100 percent bonus plan, while his wife Peggy of the Wrapping Department participates in a straight piecework arrangement. Both employees receive a guaranteed base rate of $3.50 per hour.

Irving produced 15 units per hour every day of the first week in May. Standard production under his plan is only 12 units.

Peggy, whose straight piecework plan has designated 18 units per hour as the standard, produced 20 units per hour Monday through Thursday and 21 units per hour on Friday of the same week.

Required: The weekly gross earnings of both employees, assuming that both work 5 days a week and 8 hours each day and that the $3.50 base rate forms the basis applicable to both incentive wage plans.

14-4. Group Bonus Plan. Employees of Chianti Enterprises work in groups of five, plus a group leader. Standard production for a group is 400 units for a 40-hour week. The workers are paid $4 an hour until production reaches 400 units; then a bonus of $1.20 per unit is paid, with $1 being divided equally among the five workers and with the remainder passing to the group leader (who is also paid a weekly salary of $150). Factory overhead is $3 per direct labor hour and includes the group leader's earnings.

The production record of a group for one week shows:

	Hours Worked	Units Produced
Monday..................	40	72
Tuesday..................	40	81
Wednesday..............	40	95
Thursday................	40	102
Friday..................	40	102

Required: (1) Based upon the above data, show the week's earnings of the group (excluding the leader), the labor cost per unit, the overhead cost per unit, and the conversion cost per unit (carrying figures to three decimal places).

(2) Assuming Chianti Enterprises uses the group bonus plan, a schedule showing *daily* earnings of the group (excluding the leader), unit labor cost, unit overhead cost, and the conversion cost per unit.

14-5. Group Bonus Plan. Ten-man crews work as teams in a Processing Department. Each crew member is paid a bonus if his group exceeds the standard production of 200 kilograms per hour.

The amount of the bonus is computed by first determining the percentage by which the group's production exceeds the standard; one half of this percentage is then applied to a wage rate of $4.80 to determine the hourly bonus rate. Each man in the group is paid a bonus for his group's excess production in addition to his wages at hourly rates.

	Production Record for the Week	
	Hours Worked	*Production (in Kilograms)*
Monday....................................	79	16,040
Tuesday...................................	80	17,599
Wednesday...............................	74	16,200
Thursday..................................	78	17,429
Friday.....................................	80	18,036

Required: On the basis of the production record:

(1) The group's bonus for each day and for the week.

(2) The week's earnings for each employee, assuming that each worker earned $4.80 per hour and that each worked the same number of hours during the week.

14-6. Quarterly Bonus Allotment. Aquapipes, Inc. is a manufacturer of standard pipe fittings for water and sewage lines. A bonus is paid to its employees based upon the production recorded each calendar quarter. Normal production is set at 240,000 units per quarter. A bonus of $.10 per unit is paid for any units in excess of the normal output for each quarter. Distribution of the bonus is made on the following point basis:

Employees Participating	*Points Allowed for Each Employee*
1 Works manager..............................	250
2 Production engineers.........................	200
5 Shop foremen...............................	200
1 Storeskeeper................................	100
5 Factory office clerks.........................	10
150 Factory workers.............................	20

The employees' earnings are not penalized for any month in which the actual output falls below the monthly average of the normal quarterly production. In such a case, the deficiency is deducted from any excess in subsequent months before any bonus is earned by and paid to the employees.

At the end of March, cumulative actual production amounted to 270,000 units.

Required: (1) A calculation showing the amount of bonus payable to the employees in the different classifications.

(2) Journal entries at the end of each month on the basis of the production figures: January, 75,000 units; February, 94,000 units; March, 101,000 units.

(3) A statement as to whether this bonus is considered a direct labor cost or a factory overhead item and its position on the income statement.

14-7. Incentive Wage Plans. The company's union steward complained to the Payroll Department that several union members' wages had been miscalculated in the previous week. The schedule below indicates the wages and conditions of the earnings of the workers involved:

Worker	Incentive Wage Plan	Total Hours	Down Time Hours	Units Pro- duced	Stan- dard Units	Base Rate	Gross Wages per Books
Dodd	Straight piecework	40	5	400	——	$3.00	$142.00
Hare	Straight piecework	46	——	455*	——	3.00	138.60
Lowe	Straight piecework	44	4	420**		3.00	151.10
Ober	Percentage bonus plan	40	——	250	200	3.00	140.00
Rupp	Percentage bonus plan	40	——	180	200	2.50	85.50
Suggs	Emerson Efficiency	40	——	240	300	2.80	116.60
Ward	Emerson Efficiency	40	2	590	600***	2.80	140.00

*Includes 45 pieces produced during the 6 overtime hours.

**Includes 50 pieces produced during the 4 overtime hours. The overtime, brought about by the "down time," was necessary to meet a production deadline.

***Standard units for 40 hours production.

The company's union contract contains the following description of the systems for computing wages in various departments of the company. The minimum wage for a worker is his base rate, which is also paid for any down time when the worker's machine is under repair or he is without work. The standard work week is 40 hours. Workers are paid 150% of base rates for overtime production.

(a) *Straight Piecework.* The worker is paid at the rate of $.33 per piece produced.

(b) *Percentage Bonus Plan.* Standard quantities of production per hour are established by the Engineering Department. The worker's average hourly production, determined from his total hours worked and his production, is divided by the standard quantity of production to determine his efficiency ratio. The efficiency ratio is then applied to his base rate to determine his hourly earnings for the period.

(c) *Emerson Efficiency System.* A minimum wage is paid for production up to $66\frac{2}{3}\%$ of standard output or "efficiency." When the worker's production exceeds $66\frac{2}{3}\%$ of the standard output, he is paid at a bonus rate. The bonus rate is determined from the following table:

Efficiency	Bonus
Up to $66\frac{2}{3}\%$	0%
$66\frac{2}{3}\%$ – 79%	10%
80% – 99%	20%
100% – 125%	45%

Required: A schedule comparing each individual's gross wages per books with the gross wages calculated.

(AICPA adapted)

14-8. Computation of "Learning Curve" and Other Program Costs Deferred. A company in the business of producing large special-purpose computers has introduced a new model of an existing product. The new machine represents a significant technological advancement, and substantial learning curve costs are expected. Based on extensive studies, the company has determined that it is reasonable to forecast a market of at least 200 units for the new computer. Accordingly, the company has calculated its estimated average cost of sales per machine of $100,000, as follows:

Initial tooling and other production costs....................	$ 2,000,000
Estimated production costs (200 units $\times$ $90,000).............	18,000,000
Total estimated production costs...........................	$20,000,000
Number of units to be produced and sold....................	200
Average cost per unit ($10,000 initial costs + $90,000 production costs)...	$100,000

At the balance sheet date, the company has received firm orders for 150 computers. As of this same date, the company has delivered and installed 45 computers; 35 additional units are in production and are estimated to represent 15 equivalent completed units. Total costs incurred at the balance sheet date, including initial tooling and other production costs amounted to $9,350,000.

Required: The amount to be reported as production "learning curve" and other program costs deferred.

(Based on an Ernst & Ernst publication)

CASES

A. Computerized Payroll Procedures. In connection with her examination of the financial statements of the Olympia Manufacturing Company, a CPA is reviewing procedures for accumulating direct labor hours. She learns that all production is by job order and that all employees are paid hourly wages, with time-and-one-half for overtime hours.

Olympia's direct labor hour input process for payroll and job-cost determination is summarized in the following flowchart:

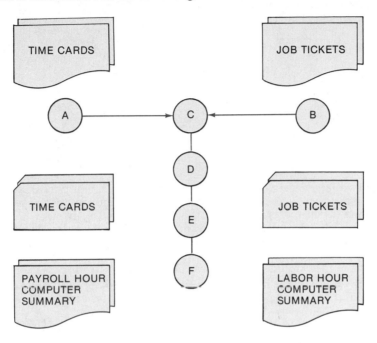

Steps A and C are performed in the Timekeeping Department; Step B in the factory operating departments; Step D in the Payroll Audit and Control Department; Step E in the Data Preparation (Keypunch) Department; and Step F in the Computer Operations Department.

Required: For each input processing Step A through F:

(a) List the possible errors or discrepancies that may occur.

(b) Cite the corresponding control procedure that should be in effect for each error or discrepancy.

NOTE: Limit the discussion of Olympia's procedures to the input process for direct labor hours (as shown in Steps A through F in the flowchart). Do not discuss personnel procedures for hiring, promotion, termination, and pay rate authorization. In Step F, do not discuss equipment, computer program, and general computer operational controls.

Organize your answer for each input-processing step as follows:

Step	*Possible Errors or Discrepancies*	*Control Procedures*

(AICPA adapted)

B. Setting Productivity Standards. The Alton Company intends to expand its Punch Press Department with the purchase of three new presses from Presco, Inc. Mechanical studies indicate that for Alton's intended use, the output rate for one press should be 1,000 pieces per hour. The Alton Company has similar presses now in operation that average 600 pieces per hour. This average is derived from these individual outputs:

Worker	Daily Output (in Pieces)
ALFERS, L.............................	750
BROWN, J.............................	750
GREEN, R.............................	600
HOAG, H.............................	500
JONES, R.............................	550
SMITH, G.............................	450
Total........................	3,600
Average daily output..............	600

Alton's management also plans to institute a standard cost accounting system in the very near future. Alton's engineers are supporting a standard based upon 1,000 pieces per hour; the Accounting Department, a standard based upon 750 pieces per hour; and the Punch Press Department foreman, a standard based upon 600 pieces per hour.

Required: (1) Arguments used by each proponent to support his case.

(2) The alternative which best reconciles the needs of cost control and the motivation of improved performance. Explain the choice made.

(NAA adapted)

C. Controlling Hiring Practices and Payroll Procedures. The Besco Corporation employs about fifty production workers and has these payroll procedures:

The factory foreman interviews applicants and on the basis of the interview either hires or rejects them. When hired, the applicant prepares a W-4 form (Employee's Withholding Exemption Certificate) and gives it to the foreman, who writes the hourly rate of pay for the new employee in the corner of the W-4 form. He then gives the form to a payroll clerk as notice that the worker has been employed. The foreman verbally advises the Payroll Department of rate adjustments.

A supply of blank time cards is kept in a box near the entrance to the factory. Each worker takes a time card on Monday morning, fills in his name, and notes in pencil on the time card his daily arrival and departure times. At the end of the week the worker drops the time card in a box near the factory door.

The completed time cards are taken from the box on Monday morning by a payroll clerk. Two payroll clerks divide the time cards alphabetically, one taking the A to L section of the payroll and the other taking the M to Z section. Each clerk is fully responsible for his section of the payroll. He computes the gross pay, deductions, and net pay, posts the details to the employees' earnings records, and prepares and numbers the payroll checks. Employees are automatically removed from the payroll when they fail to turn in a time card.

The payroll checks are manually signed by the chief accountant and given to the foreman. The foreman distributes the checks to the workers in the factory and arranges for the delivery of the checks to absent workers. The payroll bank account is reconciled by the chief accountant who also prepares the various quarterly and annual payroll tax reports.

Required: Suggestions for improving the Besco Corporation's system of internal control for factory hiring practices and payroll procedures.

D. Timesaving vs. Cost Saving. Laurel, Inc., manufacturers of a large variety of women's garments, employs one thousand female workers in its production departments.

Some time ago the management engaged the services of a CPA firm for the purpose of making a complete analysis of the methods of production. Its findings and recommendations were given to a committee for the purpose of studying them before instituting any changes in the existing production setup.

The committee is presently discussing a suggestion aimed at reduction of the time required for a particular operation. The operation is performed on all products and takes ten minutes or approximately 30% of total productive labor. It is claimed that, by applying a new method, twenty seconds per item could be saved.

One committee member, although recognizing that no investment would be necessary, believes that the proposed timesaving method is too insignificant to be worth considering.

Required: Comments on the committee member's attitude, explaining your agreement or disagreement considering the fact that the pay rate is $2.50 per hour and the standard work week is 40 hours.

E. Labor Budget and Performance Variances. The Devon Co.'s contract with the labor union guarantees a minimum wage of $500 per month to each direct labor employee having at least ten years of service. One hundred employees currently qualify. All direct labor employees are paid $5 per hour.

The direct labor budget for the current year, 19—, was based on the annual usage of 400,000 hours of direct labor at $5 or a total of $2,000,000. Of this amount, $50,000 (100 employees × $500 a month) or $600,000 for the year was regarded as fixed. The budget for any given month was determined by the formula $50,000 plus $3.50 × direct labor hours worked. Data on performance for the first three months of 19— show:

	January	February	March
Direct labor hours worked............	22,000	32,000	42,000
Direct labor costs budgeted...........	$127,000	$162,000	$197,000
Direct labor costs incurred...........	$110,000	$160,000	$210,000
Variances (F — favorable;			
U — unfavorable).........	$ 17,000F	$ 2,000F	$ 13,000U

The factory manager is perplexed by the results, which show favorable variances when production is low and unfavorable variances when production is high. He believes control over labor costs is consistently good.

Required: (1) Explanation of causes of variances and an illustration, using amounts and diagrams as appropriate.

(2) Explanation of this direct labor budget as a basis for controlling direct labor cost, indicating changes that might improve control over direct labor cost and facilitate performance evaluation of direct labor employees.

(AICPA adapted)

CHAPTER 15

ACCOUNTING FOR
LABOR-RELATED COSTS

Fundamentally, a labor cost consists of the hourly rate, the daily or weekly wage, or the monthly salary paid to an employee. Yet, in addition to the basic earnings computed on hours worked or units produced, many other cost elements enter into labor cost, such as overtime earnings; premium pay for work on holidays, Saturdays, and Sundays where overtime is not involved; shift bonuses or differentials; production incentives such as an attendance bonus, length of service bonus, nonaccident bonus, and Christmas or year–end bonus; paid vacations; apprenticeship or trainee costs and training programs for the hard core unemployed; dismissal or severance pay; and retirement pensions. In addition to these elements, labor cost usually includes paid holidays; unemployment compensation; Federal Insurance Contributions Act benefits; other insurance such as life, accident, health, and workmen's compensation; hospital and surgical benefits for employees and their dependents; and in some companies pay for jury service, and even free lunches. The total cost to keep an employee at work for an hour or a full day will include some or all of these fringe benefits. For factory workers the labor and the labor-related costs may be classified as direct labor, indirect labor, or factory overhead; for sales personnel, as marketing expenses; and for office and administrative personnel, as administrative expenses.

OVERTIME EARNINGS

The Fair Labor Standards Act of 1938, commonly referred to as the Wages and Hours Law, established a minimum wage per hour with time

436

and a half for hours worked in excess of 40 in one week. Subsequently the Act has been amended, broadening the coverage and raising the minimum to a level of $2.30 an hour in 1976. Some types of organizations and workers are exempt from the provisions of the Act and its amendments, or have lower minimums.

A number of payroll practices are mandatory to comply with the Wages and Hours Law. For each employee, records must show:

1. Hours worked each working day and the total hours worked during each work week
2. Basis on which wages are paid
3. Total daily or weekly earnings at straight time
4. Total wages paid during each pay period, the date of payment, and the work period covered by the payment
5. Regular rate of pay and total extra pay for overtime worked each week

Overtime earnings consist of two elements: (1) the regular pay due for the employee's work and (2) the overtime premium pay, which is an additional cost due to work done beyond the regular work day (as specified in some labor union contracts) or 40-hour work week. For most workers, an employer must pay as a minimum the regular rate plus one half the rate for overtime employment. For example, if an employee is paid $4 per hour for a regular work week of 40 hours yet works 45 hours, his gross earnings are:

Regular work week.	40 hours @ $4 =	$160
Overtime..........	5 hours @ 4 =	20
Overtime premium.	5 hours @ 2 =	10
Gross earnings.....		$190

Even though these details are not required by the Wages and Hours Law, it is good payroll practice to separate regular wages and overtime premium wages.

Charging overtime premium pay to a specific job or department, or to factory overhead depends primarily upon the reason for the overtime work. The contract price of a particular job, taken as a rush order with the foreknowledge that overtime will be necessary, may include the premium wage factor, which should be charged to the specific job. For example, if a lawyer brings a brief to a printing plant on Friday afternoon and wants it set in type and printed by Monday morning, all of the premium pay should be charged to that job. In another situation, Job No. 205 may be due for delivery on a particular date; but delays, slow production, or inadequate plant capacity in finishing up numerous other jobs may make it necessary to work overtime on Job No. 205. Neither this job nor any one of the other jobs is responsible for the overtime. When a plant is working overtime because it has more orders than it can complete in the regular time, the overtime premium pay should be included in the predetermined factory overhead rate as factory overhead because it cannot properly be allocated to work that happens to be in process during overtime hours.

BONUS PAYMENTS

Bonus payments may be a fixed amount per employee or job classification, a percentage of profits, a fraction of one month's wages, or some other calculated amount. The amount of bonus for each employee may be a fixed and long-established tradition of a company, or the amount may vary from year to year. Bonus payments are production costs, marketing expenses, or administrative expenses as the case may be; but when and how should they be charged to operations? If a factory worker's average weekly earnings amount to $260 and the company intends to pay him two weeks' pay as a bonus at the end of the year, his earnings actually amount to $270 per week with $260 paid for each week and with the additional $10 per week paid in a lump sum of $520 ($10 × 52 weeks) at the end of the year. In order to spread the bonus cost over production throughout the year via the predetermined factory overhead rate, the weekly entry would be:

	Subsidiary Record	Debit	Credit
Work in Process...............................		260.00	
Factory Overhead Control......................		10.00	
Bonus Pay..........................	10.00		
Payroll......................................			260.00
Liability for Bonus.........................			10.00

When the bonus is paid, the liability account is debited and Cash and the withholding accounts are credited.

In theory, this and other labor-related or fringe benefit costs are additional labor costs and for direct labor should be charged to Work in Process the same as the employees' gross wages. In practice, such a procedure usually is impractical; and these costs are generally included in the predetermined factory overhead rate.

VACATION PAY

Vacation pay presents cost problems similar to those of bonus payments. When a shop employee is entitled to a paid vacation of 2 weeks, the total wages earned during 50 weeks of productive labor are paid over a period of 52 weeks. For example, assume that an employee has a base wage of $200 per week and is entitled to a paid vacation of 2 weeks. The cost of his labor is $200, plus $8 per week. In 50 weeks at $8 per week, the deferred payment of $400 will equal the expected vacation pay. The entry to set up the weekly labor cost including the provision for vacation pay would be:

	Subsidiary Record	Debit	Credit
Work in Process..............................		200.00	
Factory Overhead Control......................		8.00	
Vacation Pay........................	8.00		
Payroll.....................................			200.00
Liability for Vacation Pay.................			8.00

When the vacation is taken, the liability account is debited and Cash and the withholding accounts are credited. Similarly, accrual should be made for employer liability pertaining to sick leave, holidays, jury duty, military training, or other personal activities for which the employer pays compensation.[1]

Salaried employees usually receive two or more weeks of vacation. Pay of a salaried worker, as well as payment for other absences, is generally considered a cost of the period in which the absence occurs. The rationale for this treatment is that the salaried employee's work either continues to a large extent during the absence with associates performing the duties or it is performed at the time of the employee's return.

Should it become necessary to hire temporary employees to perform the duties of salaried personnel while on vacation or absent for some other reason, this additional expense is rightfully charged to the departmental salary accounts. In some instances, the wages of salaried personnel should be accrued as described earlier.

GUARANTEED ANNUAL WAGE PLANS

While a guaranteed annual wage plan for all industrial workers is far from realization, a step in that direction has been taken in the labor contracts that provide for the company to pay employees who are laid off. In one industry's plan, for example, the unemployed worker is guaranteed 60 to 65 percent of his normal take-home pay, beginning the second week of layoff and continuing for as long as 26 weeks. The company pay is a supplement to the state unemployment insurance. In order to provide funds from which payments can be made during unemployment periods, a specified amount such as $.10 an hour for each worker is paid into a fund by the company for financing layoff payments.

---

[1]The accrual of employer obligations for labor-related costs for personal absence is required in accounting for government contracts to which Cost Accounting Standards Board (CASB) regulations apply. See CASB Standard No. 408, "Accounting for Costs of Compensated Personal Absence," *Federal Register*, Vol. 39, No. 183, pp. 33681-33686.

In principle, if it is assumed that layoffs will eventually occur, it is clear that the employee while working is earning $.10 an hour — an amount that is not included in the payroll check at the end of the payroll period. This amount is held in reserve by the company in order to make payments during unemployment periods. For a factory worker whose base pay rate is $5 an hour, the cost effect of unemployment pay for a 40-hour week is illustrated by this entry:

	Subsidiary Record	Debit	Credit
Work in Process...............................		200.00	
Factory Overhead Control......................		4.00	
Unemployment Pay..................	4.00		
Payroll................................			200.00
Liability for Unemployment Pay...........			4.00

Another version of the above plan is one which not only guarantees that the weekly payroll check will not fall below a minimum figure but also sets no limit on how high earnings may rise during other weeks of the pay period. This plan amounts to a "floor" placed under weekly earnings to keep them above a predetermined minimum. Employees are paid their actual earnings each pay period; the guarantee comes into effect only when earnings drop below the minimum.

APPRENTICESHIP AND TRAINING PROGRAMS

In many plants new workers receive some preliminary training before they become economically productive. The portion of the wages paid in excess of the average or standard paid for the productive output, plus the cost of instruction, is an indirect labor cost to be charged to the total annual output through inclusion in the factory overhead rates. In case of unusual training programs due to the opening of a new plant or the activating of a second or third shift, a case can be made for treating the training cost as development or starting load cost and deferring a portion of the cost over a considerable period of time.

HUMAN RESOURCE ACCOUNTING

In annual reports management often speaks in glowing terms of its employees as the company's most valuable asset. Yet management makes little effort to assess the value of this asset, and the company's accounting system does little to provide any assistance. *Human resource accounting* is the process of developing financial assessments of people or groups of people within organizations and society and the monitoring of these assessments over time. It deals with investments in people and with the related economic results. Managers are being asked to give more serious consideration to human resource investment decisions and to the human resource impact of all their decisions. Thus, the personnel function within an organization may serve more efficiently its role of acquisition, development, and utilization of human resource potential.

Human resource accounting attempts to evaluate investments in human assets. Many firms invest heavily in personnel training programs without evaluating the expected payoff or the return on such investments. A firm is apt to send its managers to a variety of executive development programs whose value is essentially taken on faith and which are discontinued when profits cannot afford them.

A human resource accounting system needs first to identify incurred human resource costs that are to be separated from the firm's other costs. The techniques and procedures used should distinguish between the asset and expense components of human resource costs. The resulting human resource assets would then be classified into functional categories such as recruiting, hiring, training, development, and familiarization. Such information would purportedly enable management to make decisions based on a realistic cost/benefit analysis and cost amortization and would further provide investors with an improved basis to assess the value of an enterprise for purposes of making better investment decisions.

The quantification of human resources appears to be the first stumbling block for the creation of human resource accounting. All companies have methods of measuring sales, profits, investments in plant and equipment, investments in inventories, etc. Similarly, incurred human resource costs such as training programs can be measured although determining the time period for amortization may be difficult. But beyond the possibility of capitalizing certain incurred human resource costs, how does a company set a quantitative value for such attributes as loyalty, skills, morale, decision-making ability, intelligence, etc.? Since it seems difficult to quantify these human factors, it seems equally difficult to assign asset status to human resources except where measured incurred costs can be identified. The justification for measuring an asset value is based on the economic concept that an asset is capable of providing future benefits to the firm. Therefore, the employee group is important to the future success of the company and, as such, has value that should be reported as assets on the balance sheet. Asset determination for human resources is particularly meaningful for professional sports franchises where a "superstar" is essentially *the* asset that creates gate receipts. As is the case with any other asset, the professional athlete can be sold or traded; thus, the increasing litigation involving current player contracts.

In spite of the difficulties, a number of proposals have been expounded that attempt to utilize human resource accounting. Some proposals focus on incurred costs only while others encompass estimated values. These proposals, reviewed in a *Management Accounting*[2] article, are:

1. *Capitalizing salaries* — whereby a firm merely capitalizes salaries paid its employees, assuming that what the employees are doing will be of some future benefit to the firm and that appropriate rates of capitalization can be determined.

2. *Capitalizing the cost of "acquiring" an employee* — envisions capitalizing the cost of "acquiring" an employee, a plan that would require collecting the costs of acquiring, hiring, and training. (A precedent for this method exists in professional sports.)

3. *Capitalizing startup costs* — involves not only capitalizing startup costs but goes one step further by considering the synergistic components of cost and time required for members of a firm to establish effective co-operative working relationships.

4. *Behavioral variables approach* — whose foundations are even more tenuous than startup costs. Here, periodic measurements would be made of the key causal and intervening variables for the corporation as a whole. Statistical variation in leadership styles, technical proficiency levels, etc. (causal variables), and the resulting changes in subordinate attitudes, motivations, and behavior (intervening variables) can establish relationships among such variables. These changes would produce changes in the end result variables such as productivity, innovation, and manpower developments; and trends in earnings can then be predicted. These forecasts are discounted to find the present value of the human resources.

5. *Opportunity costs* — suggest that investment center managers are encouraged to bid for any scarce employee they desire. The winning manager includes his bid in his investment base. The division's benefit is the increased profit produced by the new employee.

6. *Economic value approach* — compares differences in present and future earnings of similar firms in the same industry. Ostensibly, the differences are due to their human organization. Future earnings are forecast and discounted to find their present value. A portion thereof is allocated to human resources based on their contribution.

7. *Present value method* — involves a determination of wage payments over a five-year period, and then a discounting of these payments at the rate of return of owned assets in the economy for the most recent year. This calculation yields the present value of the future five-years' wage payments based on this year's return.

8. *Stochastic rewards valuation model (designed by Eric Flamholtz)* — involves a stochastic process defined as a natural system that changes in time in accordance with the law of probability. To measure an individual's value to an organization requires:

---

[2]Roger Jauch and Michael Skigen, "Human Resources Accounting: A Critical Evaluation," *Management Accounting*, Vol. LV, No. 11, pp. 33–36.

(a) An estimate of the time interval during which an individual is expected to render services to the organization, and

(b) A measure of the services expected to be derived from the individual during this interval.

The resource's expected value is then multiplied by a discount factor to arrive at the present value of expected future services.

At present, as theory and techniques for human resource accounting have become known and established, the problem must turn to models and methods subjected to empirical testing. Research is required to demonstrate both its feasibility and its effects on attitude and behavior. Unless empirical data from organizations using human resource accounting systems are collected, analyzed, and published, the attractiveness of current theoretical arguments may soon lose its glamour.[3]

PENSION PLANS

A *pension plan* is an arrangement whereby a company provides retirement benefit payments for each employee in recognition of his or her work contribution to the company. This arrangement may be an *informal* pension plan calling for voluntary payments to the retired employee in amounts and under conditions more or less at the descretion of the employer, or it may be a *formal* plan with the benefit payments and other features explicitly stated or readily computed or otherwise determined. A formal plan is usually set forth in a written document, but an established unwritten policy with regard to pension payments may be sufficiently definitive to constitute a formal plan.

A pension plan is probably the most important, as well as the most complicated, factor associated with labor and labor costs. A pension plan is also important in that it influences personnel relations, company financing, income determination, income tax considerations, and general economic conditions.

Pension Cost Factors. The ultimate cost of a company pension plan depends upon several related factors:

1. The number of employees reaching retirement age each year
2. The average benefit to be paid to each retired employee
3. The average period over which benefits will be paid
4. Income from pension fund investments
5. Income tax allowances
6. Expense of administration
7. Treatment of benefits to employees who leave the company before reaching the pension age

---

[3]"American Accounting Association Report of the Committee on Accounting for Human Resources," *The Accounting Review,* Supplement to Vol. XLIX, pp. 114–124.

Pension Cost Estimate. When a pension plan is initiated, the amount necessary to provide pensions for all the present employees who are expected to stay until retirement is the product of (1) the number of employees eventually to retire, (2) the average benefit, and (3) the average period of payment.

Example: Assume a company has 100 employees who are each to be paid $1,200 per year for an average of 10 years to equal an estimated eventual cost of $1,200,000. If each employee who retires has worked an average of 30 years, the average annual cost is $40,000 ($1,200,000 ÷ 30 years). The annual cost per employee would then be $400 ($40,000 ÷ 100 employees). If each employee works 40 hours per week and 50 weeks per year, the pension cost for each of the 2,000 hours worked is $.20. While this procedure ignores administrative costs and possible earnings from funds invested, it is indicative of a method that may be used to convert the pension cost to an hourly basis.

Pension Cost Allocation. In the case of bonuses and paid vacations, part of the total earnings of an employee is withheld or accrued for a period of months and then paid in a lump sum. In the case of pension payments, the wage is earned; and the labor cost is incurred many years before the payment is made. As a matter of principle, if an employee is paid a base wage of $160 for a 40-hour week and if the retirement payments to be made will amount to $.20 an hour for all the hours purchase from this employee, the pension cost incurred is $8 per week chargeable to factory overhead, marketing, or administrative costs as the case may be.[4]

Employee Retirement Income Security Act of 1974. On September 2, 1974, the Employee Retirement Income Security Act of 1974[5] (more commonly known as the Pension Reform Act of 1974) was enacted. This Act makes certain that promised pensions are actually paid at retirement age and sets minimum government standards for pension vesting, participation, funding, management, and a variety of other matters. The Act also covers a wide range of employee welfare plans in addition to pension or retirement plans and establishes both "labor" standards (administered by the Secretary of Labor) and "tax" standards (administered by the Secretary of the Treasury). The labor and tax standards taken together bring under a common body of legislation practically all employee benefit plans not specifically exempted from the Act.

---

[4]For an extensive study of accounting for pension plans, refer to: AICPA *Research Study No. 8* (1965) by E. L. Hicks; AICPA *APB Opinion No. 8* (1966); FASB *Interpretation No. 3*, 1974.

[5]*Explanation of Pension Reform Act of 1974.* (P. L. 93–406), Commerce Clearing House, Inc., Pamphlet No. 4891, pp. 1–96.

Virtually every private pension, profit-sharing, thrift, or savings plan will have to be amended within the next few years in order to comply with the Pension Reform Act of 1974. All plans will have to contend with increased record keeping, compliance, and reporting. Many plans will be burdened with increased costs and/or funding obligations. Plans most likely to be affected are those that (1) have not provided for a substantial degree of vesting prior to retirement, (2) have not been funding past service costs or have operated on a "pay-as-you-go" basis, and (3) have had restrictive criteria as to age and years of service as a condition for participation.

The Pension Reform Act of 1974, a vast and momentous piece of legislation, should be studied by every accounting student. The presentation here enumerates only a few matters that are relevant to labor-related costs. Among the more important changes and new requirements affecting employers and employees are:

1. New employees cannot be denied participation for more than one year unless an employee is under twenty-five years of age or benefits are fully vested at the end of a three-year waiting period.

2. Minimum funding standards require that an employer's minimum annual contribution generally must include the normal cost for the year plus level amortization of initial past service liabilities over forty years for existing plans and over thirty years for new plans, and liabilities resulting from plan amendments and experience gains and losses over thirty years and fifteen years, respectively.

3. In case the assets of a terminated plan are not sufficient to pay the insured benefits, the Pension Benefit Guaranty Corporation (PBGC) guarantees vested benefits of terminated plans up to $750 per month for each participant or beneficiary. To finance this insurance program, the PBGC will collect a premium from all covered plans. The annual premiums are $1 per participant for single-employer plans and 50 cents per participant for multi-employer plans. For many existing plans, this benefit coverage is retroactive to July 1, 1974; and the obligation to pay the premiums began on the date of enactment.

4. Descriptions of the plan and annual financial, actuarial, and other information must be provided to participants and beneficiaries and to the Secretaries of Labor and the Treasury.

Vesting. A participant of a pension plan is assured of receiving future benefits under a plan when his rights to the benefits become vested. *Vesting* is a kind of guarantee that enough money has been set aside by a company to enable the payment of an employee's pension at retirement age and that his benefits cannot be forefeited even in the event of dismissal or discontinuance of company operations. An employee who resigns before retirement age will still be entitled upon retirement to receive the benefits in which his rights were vested before his resignation. The Pension Reform

Act of 1974 sets minimum standards for vesting of employee benefits that must be met by all plans subject to the participation standards. To protect participants and beneficiaries against a possible loss of pension benefits arising from plan termination, the Act created the aforementioned Pension Benefit Guaranty Corporation (PBGC) within the Department of Labor.

Funding. The Pension Reform Act of 1974 established minimum funding standards for certain defined benefit plans. The effect of these standards is to impose time limitations for accumulating sufficient assets to pay retirement benefits to participants. Generally, employers must contribute currently the normal cost of the plan for the plan year plus a level funding, including interest, of past service costs and certain other costs. Each plan must establish and maintain a funding standard account. A plan satisfies the minimum funding deficiency at the end of the year, as reflected in its funding standard account. An accumulated funding deficiency is the excess of the total charges over the total credits to the funding standard account. The law will not permit the use of the so-called "pay-as-you-go" method, whereby employers would make periodic pension payments directly to retired employees.

Present Value (PV). Basic to all funding methods is the concept of *present value (PV)*, sometimes referred to as *capitalized value.* The present value principle permits the value at any given point of time under a set of future conditions to be expressed as the equivalent value at a different point of time. The principle is particularly useful in dealing with financial transactions involving a time series, such as periodic contributions, retirement annuities, etc. It permits the computation of an entire series of financial transactions over a period of time to be expressed as a single value at any point of time.

The Role of the Actuary. Computations relating to pension plan costs, contributions, and benefits are made by an *actuary* — an expert in pension, life insurance, and related matters involving life contingencies. An actuary employs mathematical, statistical, financial, and other techniques to compute costs or benefits, to equate costs with benefits, and to evaluate and project actuarial experience under a plan. Membership in the American Academy of Actuaries, or one of the other recognized actuarial organizations, identifies a person as a member of the actuarial profession.

Administrative Problems. The Pension Reform Act of 1974 mandates sweeping changes in the structure and administration of all types of qualified employee benefit plans. For many businesses, the new and more rigid tax requirements for eligibility, vesting, and funding means dramatically increased pension costs.

Pension costs (excluding social security costs) are now running from 5 percent to 10 percent of a company's annual payroll — a level often equivalent to 25 percent or more of its annual profit. It may only be a matter of time before pension costs rise to 20 percent of a company's annual payroll, or higher. This increase will in turn be translated into price increases that will fuel further wage increases and lead to even higher pension costs. In addition, the Pension Reform Act of 1974 creates a staggering number of complicated, nontax requirements in such areas as disclosure, reporting, investments, and insurance.

ADDITIONAL LEGISLATION AFFECTING LABOR-RELATED COSTS

Costing labor and keeping payroll records were relatively simple prior to the first social security act. This legislation made it necessary for many employers to initiate or redesign payroll procedures in order to make an accurate accounting for payroll deductions. Later, other state and federal legislation imposed additional requirements affecting the accounting for wages and salaries.[6]

Federal Insurance Contributions Act (FICA). This legislation is administered and operated entirely by the federal government. Originally enacted in August of 1935 and operative January 1, 1936, the Act provided that employers in a covered industry must withhold 1 percent of the wages paid to each employee up to $3,000 of earnings in any one year, which amounted to a maximum of $30 of FICA tax. The employer was required to contribute an equal amount. Employees in several types of work, such as agricultural workers, domestic services, federal, state, and municipal employees, nonprofit organizations, self-employed persons, and a variety of others, were specifically excluded in the 1935 Act.

The Federal Insurance Contributions Act has been amended several times since 1935, the amendments tending to bring more employees under the Act, and to increase the benefits, the tax rate, and the wage base upon which the tax is levied. Under the 1965 amendments to FICA, the long debated Federal Hospital Insurance Program (Medicare) was enacted.[7]

---

[6]These pages summarize the major provisions. U. S. Treasury Department Internal Revenue Service Circular E entitled "Employer's Tax Guide" is an excellent source for a more comprehensive coverage of these regulations. A free copy of the current edition can be obtained by writing to the nearest District Director, Internal Revenue Service.

[7]Although 6 percent for FICA tax was not the current rate at publication date, it is used in the illustrations and in the end-of-chapter material because it facilitates calculation of the tax. The actual rate changes from time to time. The wage base to which the tax applies, assumed in this textbook to be on annual wages up to $15,000 paid each employee, is also subject to change.

Records Necessitated by the FICA. The Federal Insurance Contributions Act requires that employers who are subject to its provisions keep records providing:

1. The name, address, and social security account number of each employee.
2. The total amount and the date of each remuneration payment and the period of service covered by such payment.
3. The amount of such remuneration payment that constitutes taxable wages.
4. The amount of tax withheld or collected.

Although the legislation does not order, suggest, or recommend forms or details for securing the required information, the employer must keep records that will enable a government agency to ascertain whether the taxes for which the employer is liable are correctly computed and paid. These records must be kept for at least four years after the date the tax becomes due or the date the tax is paid, whichever is later. Employees are not required to keep records, but the Act recommends that each employee keep accurate and permanent records showing the name and address of each employer, dates for beginning and termination of employment, wages earned, and tax withheld during employment.

Collection and Payment of the FICA Tax.   All employers, except in excluded classes of employment, are required to pay a tax on wages paid equal to the amount paid by the employees; and the employer is further required to collect the FICA tax from the employees by deducting the current percent from the wages paid each payday up to the current annual limit or base to which the tax applies.

In general, federal income tax withheld and employee and employer FICA taxes must be deposited with either an authorized commercial bank depository or a Federal Reserve Bank on a quarter-monthly, monthly, or quarterly basis, depending on the amount of taxes to be remitted. On or before the last day of the month following each calendar quarter — April 30, July 31, October 31, and January 31 — the employer is required to file a quarterly return, remitting the FICA and withheld federal income taxes applicable to the expired quarter reduced by any deposits made. Ten additional days are allowed for filing the quarterly report if all deposits are made on time.

Federal Unemployment Tax Act (FUTA). Unemployment compensation insurance is another phase of social security legislation affecting labor costs and payroll records. Unlike FICA, which is strictly a federal program, FUTA provides for cooperation between state and federal governments in the establishment and administration of unemployment insurance. When the initial legislation was enacted in August, 1935 by the federal government, provisions of FUTA forced various states to pass adequate unemployment laws.

Under the Federal Unemployment Tax Act, an employer in covered employment must pay an unemployment insurance tax to the federal government. The federal annual earnings base is $4,200 of each employee's annual wages paid with .5 percent or $21 a year payable to the federal government for the cost of administering the federal-state unemployment compensation program.

While the federal legislation provides for a 3.2 percent employer payroll tax (.5 percent to the federal government and 2.7 percent to the state), most states provide a merit rating plan under which an employer who stabilizes employment may pay less than 2.7 percent to the state agency with zero as a possible payment. A few states use an earnings base of more than $4,200 in determining the state tax.[8] Most states provide for maximum unemployment insurance rates above 2.7 percent with rates tending toward a maximum of 4 to 5 percent.

Records Necessitated by the FUTA. Every employer subject to unemployment taxes must keep records providing:

1. The total amount of remuneration paid to each employee during the calendar year.
2. The total amount of such remuneration that constitutes taxable wages.
3. The amount of contributions paid into each state unemployment compensation fund, showing separately (a) payments made and not deducted from the remuneration of his employees and (b) payments made and deducted from the remuneration of his employees.
4. All information required to be shown on the prescribed tax return.

As with the FICA tax, the Federal Unemployment Tax Act does not prescribe or recommend forms or procedures for securing the required information. Each employer is expected to use accounting procedures and to prepare accounting records that will enable the Internal Revenue Service to determine whether the tax is correctly computed and paid.

Payment of the FUTA Tax. The federal portion of the unemployment tax is payable quarterly. However, if the employer's tax liability (plus any accumulated tax liability for previous quarters) is $100 or less for the fiscal year, only one payment is required by January 31 of the following year. The related tax return, due January 31, is sent to the IRS regional service center of the employer's principal place of business.

---

[8]The $4,200 base and the rates of .5 percent (federal) and 2.7 percent (state) were current at the time of publication and are used in the illustrations and in the end-of-chapter material.

State Unemployment Reports and Payments. The various state unemployment compensation laws require reports from employers to determine their liability to make contributions, the amount of taxes to be paid, and the amount of benefit to which each employee is entitled if he becomes unemployed. While the reports and report forms vary from state to state, the more important requirements are:

1. *Status Report.* The status report determines whether an employer is required to make contributions to the state unemployment insurance fund.

2. *Contribution Report.* All employers covered by the state unemployment compensation laws are required to file quarterly tax returns, commonly called Contribution and Wage Reports. The report provides a summary statement of wages paid during the quarter, a computation of the tax, names of employees, and wages paid to each during the quarter.

3. *Separation Report.* When it becomes necessary to lay off workers, printed materials prepared by the State Employment Commission are provided informing employees how to secure new employment and how to make an application for unemployment benefits. An employee quitting without good cause or discharged for ample reason may be ineligible for unemployment payments. In these cases, an employer files a separation notice with the State Employment Commission. Since any unemployment benefits paid to a former employee may increase the employer's state rate, the separation notice is filed (when justified) in order to prevent the charge-back that the State Employment Commission would otherwise make.

Workmen's Compensation Insurance. Workmen's compensation insurance laws provide insurance benefits for workers or their survivors for losses caused by accidents and occupational diseases suffered in the course of employment. These are all state laws and in most states have been in effect for many years. While the benefits, premium costs (usually less than 1 percent of the payroll), and various other details vary from state to state, the total insurance cost is borne by the employer. The employer may have the option of insuring with an approved insurance company or through a state insurance fund. In some cases, if the size and the financial resources are sufficient, the enterprise may carry its own risk.

Withholding of Federal Income Tax, State Income Tax, and City Wage Tax. The employer is required to withhold federal income tax — and state income and city wage tax, if applicable — from salary and wage payments to employees and to furnish information to the Internal Revenue Service showing the amount of remuneration paid each employee and the amount of federal income tax withheld. The collection of income taxes from employees and the remittance of these taxes obviously affect payroll accounting. Before a new employee begins work, he or she is required to fill out a withholding exemption certificate (W-4 form).

Income taxes are withheld from each wage payment in accordance with the amount of the employee's earnings and the exemptions claimed on the W-4 form. Employers are required to furnish a written statement or receipt to each employee from whom taxes have been withheld showing the total wages earned and the amount of taxes withheld (income taxes and FICA) during a calendar year. This withholding statement (W-2 form) must be delivered to the employee on or before January 31 of the following year. If employment is terminated before December 31, the W-2 form must be furnished within 30 days from the last payment of wages. Each employer must deposit federal income taxes withheld and file a quarterly return in the manner described in the discussion of collection and payment of the FICA tax on page 448.

A reconciliation of the quarterly returns with duplicate copies of the W-2 forms furnished employees must accompany the fourth-quarter return each year. Therefore, payroll records must show the names of persons employed during the year, the periods of employment, the amounts and dates of payment, and the taxes withheld each payroll date.

The state may also levy an income tax that must be withheld from employees' wages. The tax withheld must be remitted to the taxing authorities along with required reports.

A city or municipality may levy a wage earnings tax on an employee working within its boundaries even though the employee is not a resident. Here, too, reports and payments must not only be made to the local taxing authority, but information must also be supplied to the employee.

The Fair Labor Standards Act, FICA tax, federal and state taxes for unemployment compensation insurance, workmen's compensation laws, and other governmental regulations require a multiplicity of forms for their monthly, quarterly, and annual reports. Competent personnel in a company's payroll department are needed to comply with all regulations.

LABOR-RELATED DEDUCTIONS

In addition to compulsory payroll deductions, a variety of other deductions are withheld from the take-home pay with the consent of the employee.

Insurance.   Many companies provide various benefits for their employees, such as health, accident, hospital, and life insurance. It is common for the company and the employee to share the cost, with the employee's share being deducted from wages each payroll period or at regular intervals. If the company has paid insurance premiums in advance, including the employee's share, an asset account such as Prepaid Health and Accident Insurance will be debited at the time that the payments are made; and the account will be credited for the employees' share of the premiums when the payroll deductions are made. In this payroll deduction, as in all similar cases, a subsidiary ledger showing the contributions of each employee is necessary; and one or more general ledger accounts are maintained.

Union Dues.   Many enterprises employing union labor agree to a union shop and to a deduction of initiation fees and regular membership dues from the wages of each employee. To account for these deductions, a column is provided in the payroll journal; and a general ledger account entitled Liability for Union Dues Collected is carried to show the liability for amounts withheld from the employees. At regular intervals, the company prepares a report and remits the dues collected to the union treasurer.

U.S. Savings Bonds.   In order to cooperate with the federal government, an employer and an employee frequently agree to some systematic plan of withholding from wages each payroll period a fixed amount for the purpose of purchasing U.S. Savings Bonds. A deduction column is provided in the payroll journal for the detailed record with each employee, and a general ledger account entitled Employee U. S. Savings Bond Deposits is set up to show the liability for wages withheld for this purpose. When the accumulated amount withheld from a given employee is sufficient to purchase a bond, an entry is made debiting Employee U. S. Savings Bond Deposits and crediting Cash.

Payroll Advances.   For a variety of reasons, payroll advances may be made to officers, salesmen, and factory workers. The advances may be in the form of cash or in the form of raw materials or finished goods. To provide control, an advance authorization form should be executed by a responsible official and should be sent to the payroll department. The asset account debited for all advances, representing a receivable to the company, might be entitled Salary and Wage Advances.

When the advances take the form of merchandise, the credit would be to Materials or to Finished Goods. If the merchandise is charged to the employee at a figure above cost, the credit may be to Sales. When the price is above cost but substantially less than the regular sales price, an account entitled Sales to Employees might be maintained. At the regular payroll date, the employee's earnings are entered in the payroll journal as usual; and the advance is deducted from wages to be paid. The amount of the advance being deducted is credited to Salary and Wage Advances.

SUMMARY OF LABOR-RELATED COSTS

The hourly wage or monthly salary which an employer agrees to pay is only a portion of the total wage cost involved. One recent survey shows that by including overtime and holiday premium pay, shift differential, production bonus, and other sundry payroll items as employee benefits, the benefits average 37.8 percent of straight-time earnings. Some of the labor-related costs not included in the basic wages are:

FICA tax for employees' old-age and survivors' and disability insurance and the hospital insurance program................	6.0%
Federal unemployment insurance tax (FUTA)...................	.5
State unemployment insurance (representing a typical rate with most companies paying less than the 2.7% maximum)...........	2.0
State workmen's compensation insurance (rates vary with the hazards — a fraction of 1% to 3% and over)..............	1.0
Vacation pay and paid holidays (two weeks of vacation and 7 to 10 holidays in relation to 52 weeks of 40 hours)..............	8.0
Total fringe benefits for practically any employer...........	17.5%

Other labor-related costs commonly experienced:

Contributions to pension fund (probable average)..............	10.0%
Recreation, health services, life insurance, medical care.........	4.0
Contributions to unemployment pay funds....................	3.5
Time off for voting, jury duty, grievance meetings, etc...........	1.3
Services related to parking lots, income tax, legal advice, supper money, uniforms, etc.....................................	1.5
Total other labor-related costs.............................	20.3%
Typical total labor-related costs expressed as a percentage of straight-time earnings....................................	37.8%

RECORDING LABOR COSTS

Many methods of recording wage transactions exist, depending in part upon the entries (if any) that are posted from the payroll journal itself. Details of payroll accounting and some of the problems incident to labor costing have been presented in the preceding pages. It is worth repeating that the basic principle of labor costing is simple and straightforward.

A record of the labor time "purchased" is made through use of the clock card; a record of the performance received is made through the use of time tickets or the daily time report.   The accounting entries required, therefore, are:

1. To record wage payments due employees and the liability for all amounts withheld from wages.
2. To charge the total labor cost to appropriate jobs, processes, and departments.

Weekly, semimonthly, monthly, or as often as a payroll is met — the total amount earned by workers is debited to Payroll with credits to Accrued Payroll and to the withholding accounts. The cost of labor purchased is summarized and recorded as debits to Work in Process, Factory Overhead Control, Marketing Expense Control, and Administrative Expense Control and as a credit to Payroll. When the payroll is paid, Accrued Payroll is debited, thereby discharging the liability for the labor purchased. Employer payroll taxes must also be recorded.

The accounting for labor costs and payroll liabilities is illustrated in general journal form on pages 455 and 456 based upon these assumptions:

1. The payroll period is for the month of January, 19B.

January, 19B

Sun	Mon	Tue	Wed	Thu	Fri	Sat
		1	2	3	4	5
6	7	8	9	10	11	12
13	14	15	16	17	18	19
20	21	22	23	24	25	26
27	28	29	30	31		

2. The payroll is paid on January 9, 19B, and on January 23, 19B, covering wages earned through the preceding Saturday. Note that the wages of the last week of December, 19A, would be paid on January 9 and that the payment of January 23 would cover work done through January 19.

3. Payroll figures for labor cost earned during January are:

Direct factory labor.........................	$38,500
Indirect factory labor.......................	18,000
Sales salaries...............................	20,000
Office and administrative salaries.............	12,000
Total payroll...............................	$88,500

4. Wages paid during January, 19B: $50,000 on January 9, and $40,000 on January 23. Of the income tax withheld, $4,800 is on the payroll of January 9 and $3,700 on that of January 23.

5. Wages earned and unpaid on December 31, 19A, total $26,000. On January 31, the amount is $24,500.

(continued)

	Subsidiary Record	Debit	Credit

Reversing entry for wages payable as of December 31:

| Jan. 2 | Accrued Payroll...................... | | 26,000.00 | |
| | Payroll............................. | | | 26,000.00 |

Jan. 9	Payroll..............................		50,000.00	
	Accrued Payroll......................			37,550.00
	Federal Income Tax Withheld..........			4,800.00
	FICA Tax Payable.....................			3,000.00
	Salary and Wage Advances.............			2,200.00
	Liability for Union Dues Collected.......			1,000.00
	Employee U.S. Savings Bond Deposits...			1,200.00
	Prepaid Health and Accident Insurance...			250.00
	Accrued Payroll......................		37,550.00	
	Cash................................			37,550.00

Jan. 23	Payroll..............................		40,000.00	
	Accrued Payroll......................			31,800.00
	Federal Income Tax Withheld..........			3,700.00
	FICA Tax Payable.....................			2,400.00
	Liability for Union Dues Collected.......			1,000.00
	Employee U.S. Savings Bond Deposits...			900.00
	Prepaid Health and Accident Insurance...			200.00
	Accrued Payroll......................		31,800.00	
	Cash................................			31,800.00

Jan. 31	Payroll..............................		24,500.00	
	Accrued Payroll......................			24,500.00
	Work in Process — Labor...............		38,500.00	
	Factory Overhead Control..............		6,429.50	
	FICA Tax......................	2,310.00		
	Unemployment Insurance Taxes....	1,232.00		
	Workmen's Compens. Insurance....	385.00		
	Pension Cost....................	1,540.00		
	Health and Accident Insurance.....	192.50		
	Estimated Unemployment Cost.....	770.00		
	Payroll.............................			38,500.00
	FICA Tax Payable....................			2,310.00
	Federal Unemployment Tax Payable......			192.50
	State Unemployment Tax Payable........			1,039.50
	Prepaid Workmen's Compensation Ins....			385.00
	Liability for Pensions..................			1,540.00
	Prepaid Health and Accident Insurance...			192.50
	Liability for Unemployment Pay........			770.00

(continued)

		Subsidiary Record	Debit	Credit
Jan. 31 (cont.)	Factory Overhead Control................		21,186.00	
	Indirect Labor...................	18,000.00		
	FICA Tax......................	1,080.00		
	Unemployment Insurance Taxes....	576.00		
	Workmen's Compensation Ins......	180.00		
	Pension Cost...................	900.00		
	Health and Accident Insurance.....	90.00		
	Estimated Unemployment Cost.....	360.00		
	Payroll.............................			18,000.00
	FICA Tax Payable....................			1,080.00
	Federal Unemployment Tax Payable......			90.00
	State Unemployment Tax Payable........			486.00
	Prepaid Workmen's Compensation Ins....			180.00
	Liability for Pensions..................			900.00
	Prepaid Health and Accident Insurance...			90.00
	Liability for Unemployment Pay.........			360.00
	Marketing Expense Control..............		22,940.00	
	Sales Salaries...................	20,000.00		
	FICA Tax......................	1,200.00		
	Unemployment Insurance Taxes ...	640.00		
	Pension Cost...................	1,000.00		
	Health and Accident Insurance.....	100.00		
	Payroll.............................			20,000.00
	FICA Tax Payable....................			1,200.00
	Federal Unemployment Tax Payable......			100.00
	State Unemployment Tax Payable........			540.00
	Liability for Pensions..................			1,000.00
	Prepaid Health and Accident Insurance...			100.00
	Administrative Expense Control..........		13,724.00	
	Office and Administrative Salaries...	12,000.00		
	FICA Tax......................	720.00		
	Unemployment Insurance Taxes ...	384.00		
	Pension Cost...................	560.00		
	Health and Accident Insurance.....	60.00		
	Payroll.............................			12,000.00
	FICA Tax Payable....................			720.00
	Federal Unemployment Tax Payable......			60.00
	State Unemployment Tax Payable........			324.00
	Liability for Pensions.................			560.00
	Prepaid Health and Accident Insurance...			60.00

6. The cost of the employer's payroll taxes is recorded when the month-end labor cost distribution entry is made, with separate liability accounts for federal and state agencies. Employees' FICA taxes are recorded as a liability when they are withheld at the payroll date, in compliance with the regulations.

Added assumptions:
Unemployment insurance: .5% federal; 2.7% state.
Workmen's compensation insurance: 1% of factory payroll earned.

Added assumptions (*continued*):

> Pension cost estimated to be $4,000 per month, divided as follows: direct factory labor, $1,540; indirect factory labor, $900; sales salaries, $1,000; office and administrative salaries, $560.
> Payroll advances, $2,200 deducted on Jan. 9 payroll.
> Union dues collected, $1,000 each payroll period.
> Savings bonds deductions, $1,200 on Jan. 9 and $900 on Jan. 23.
> Health and accident insurance, 1% of payroll, shared equally.
> Cost for estimated unemployment payments under guaranteed annual wage plan, 2% of factory labor earned.

This illustration records the *employer's* payroll taxes as a liability when the wages are *earned*, following the accrual concept of account. As a practical matter, many employers do not accrue payroll taxes at the end of each fiscal period because the legal liability does not occur until the next period when the wages are paid. This latter practice may be considered acceptable if it is consistently applied or if the amounts are not material.

DISCUSSION QUESTIONS

1. The hourly wage of an employee is $5.50, but the labor cost of the employee is considerably more than $5.50 an hour. Explain.

2. An employee, who is paid $4 per hour for a 40-hour week with time and a half for overtime and double time for Sundays and holidays, works 40 hours Monday through Friday, 8 hours on Saturday, and 4 hours on Sunday. Figure the employee's regular pay, overtime pay, overtime premium, and total earnings for the week. How should the overtime premium wages be accounted for?

3. For many years a company has paid all employees with 1 to 10 years of service one month's wages as a Christmas bonus and employees with more than 10 years' service two months' wages. It is company policy to give 2-week paid vacations to those with 1 to 10 years' service and 4-week paid vacations to those with more than 10 years' service. What accounting procedures should be followed with respect to the bonus and vacation pay?

4. An important function of cost accounting is accounting for labor costs and related fringe benefits.
   (a) Define *direct labor* and *indirect labor*.
   (b) Discuss reasons for distinguishing between direct and indirect labor.
   (c) Give three costing methods of accounting for the premium costs of overtime direct labor. State circumstances under which each method would be appropriate.
   (d) The Northgate Company has expensed vacation pay on the cash basis in prior years and is considering changing to the accrual basis in the next fiscal period. What would be the effects of this change upon the next fiscal period's annual financial statements?

(AICPA adapted)

5. The productive efficiency of the Brighton Company depends upon superior group leaders and foremen. The company management suggests that group leaders, foremen, and selected workmen organize a class in personnel administration and group leadership. The class is set up at a nearby university with one of the regular professors in charge. The employees attend the class at night on their own time, but the company pays the tuition charges. How should the company account for this cost?

6. In recent years the concept of human resource accounting has been theorized in management and accounting literature.
   (a) How could this theory be defined?
   (b) What are the objectives of the concept?
   (c) State the theoretical proposals that have been made in favor of human resource accounting.
   (d) What are some of the more serious drawbacks of this new accounting concept?

7. A certain company employs approximately 100 factory workers for a 40-hour week and on the average operates 48 weeks each year. Under the provisions of the pension plan, it is estimated that 40 of the employees will be pensioned after an average of 25 years of employment. It is further estimated that, on the average, pension payments will be $200 a month for a period of 10 years. Set up a schedule estimating the pension cost per hour of labor purchased.

8. The Spangler Company has just entered into a pension plan for the first time as a result of union contract negotiations. The plan became effective as of January 1, 19—. On December 31, 19—, only two entries have been made on the books of the company. The first entry (a debit to Retained Earnings and a credit to Cash in the amount of $5,000) was the first of a series of five equal annual payments required to be made to an insurance company to cover the cost of pensions based on past services. The second entry was a debit to Factory Overhead Control and a credit to Cash in the amount of $3,000 to cover the current year's contribution to the insurance company for pension costs based on the current year's factory wages. Did the two entries reflect properly the facts relative to the pension plan? Present your reasoning and describe any changes which you conclude are needed.

(AICPA adapted)

9. The term "pension plan" has been referred to as a formal arrangement for employee retirement benefits, whether established unilaterally or through negotiation, by which commitments, specific or implied, have been made that can be used as the basis for estimating costs. What is the preferable procedure for computing and accruing the costs under a pension plan? Explain.

(AICPA adapted)

10. Choose the correct procedure in completing the following sentence.
    Past service benefit costs incurred upon the adoption of a pension plan should be charged (debited) to (a) the current period; (b) retained earnings; (c) current and future periods benefited; (d) future periods benefited.

(AICPA adapted)

11. The increasing amount of fringe benefits has focused the attention of accountants on these costs. One of the principal costs is that of pension plans.
    (a) Distinguish between "pay-as-you-go" and funded pension plans.
    (b) The total cost of contributions that must be paid ultimately to provide pensions for the present participants in a plan cannot be determined precisely in advance; however, reasonably accurate estimates can be made by the use of actuarial techniques. List the factors entering into the determination of the ultimate cost of a funded pension plan.

                                                             (AICPA adapted)

12. When a funded pension plan is adopted, its total cost to the employer for the first year may be apportioned to past-service cost and current-service cost.
    (a) Distinguish between these two costs.
    (b) How should these costs be charged to accounting periods?
    (c) What should be the balance sheet treatment of these costs if the employer must (by contract) accumulate in a trusted fund enough equity to guarantee employees their benefits upon retirement?

                                                             (AICPA adapted)

13. Explain these terms as they apply to accounting for pension plans: (a) actuarial valuation; (b) vested benefits.

14. Enumerate the social security taxes by indicating (a) whether they are federal or state taxes and (b) whether they are paid by the employer, the employee, or both.

15. What is meant by the merit-rating provisions of the unemployment compensation laws of various states?

16. The Glencoe Company has a straight hourly wage rate system with the hourly rates ranging from $2.75 to $4.25 depending solely on the length of the employee's service with the company. Sometimes, unusually high or unusually low labor cost occurs on a job or in a department depending upon the seniority of the workers who draw the production assignment. The company does not wish to change its wage policy but also does not want per-unit labor cost to depend on the seniority of workers on a particular job or in a particular department. How might the company accomplish both of these objectives?

Unless otherwise directed, use these rates in the exercises, problems, and cases that follow: FICA tax, 6%; federal unemployment insurance tax, .5%; state unemployment insurance tax, 2.7%.

EXERCISES

1. Distribution of Labor Cost. The general ledger of the Alvarez Products Company showed these balances at the end of November: direct labor, $24,000; indirect labor, $5,500; sales salaries, $6,000; and office salaries, $4,500. FICA tax is applicable to 60% of the payroll in each department; unemployment insurance rates apply to only 20%. Income taxes to be withheld are $5,350, and there is a city payroll tax of 1% on employee gross earnings. Due to an excellent employment record, the company pays 1% state unemployment insurance tax.

Required: (1) The entry to record payroll liability.

(2) The entry to distribute the payroll cost.

(3) The entry to record the employer's payroll taxes.

2. Payroll Taxes. It is the policy of the Tager Company to recognize employer payroll taxes as wages are incurred; employee payroll deductions, however, are not recorded until after the payment of the wages to which the deductions apply.

On December 31, the accrued factory payroll of the Tager Company had a $2,000 balance, of which $500 represented indirect labor. During January, factory wages amounting to $15,200 were earned, of which $11,400 was direct labor. There was no accrued payroll at the end of January.

Deductions on wages paid in January were:

Advances to Employees.....................................	$525
Employees' Life Insurance Premiums.........................	325
Employees' Stock Subscriptions..............................	400
Union Dues...	185
Income Taxes...	1,720
Employees' FICA Tax......................................	6%

Required: The entries to record the payroll, payment of wages, distribution of labor cost, and employer's payroll taxes.

3. Payroll Taxes. The following information, taken from daily time tickets, summarizes time and piecework for the week ended April 30 for a producing department.

Employee	Clock No.	Job Order No.	Hours Worked	Production Pieces	Hourly Rate	Piece Rate
Busam, J..........	90	641	40	960	.....	$.24
Garner, M.........	91	...	46	...	$5.00	....
Stange, B.........	92	638	40	...	4.80	....
Wolf, T...........	93	...	40	...	5.20	....

The company operates on a 40-hour week and pays time and a half for overtime. Additional information is as follows:

(a) A FICA tax deduction should be made for each employee.

(b) An advance of $20 was made to Busam on April 26.

(c) A 2% deduction is to be made from each employee's wage for the company's employee health and hospital benefit plan.

(d) Garner works in the storeroom issuing materials; Wolf is the foreman; all others work directly on special orders as noted.

(e) Use 10% in computing income taxes withheld. State unemployment insurance is 2%.

Required: (1) The calculation of each employee's gross pay, deductions, and net pay.

(2) Journal entries (a) to set up the accrued payroll and other liabilities, (b) to pay the payroll, and (c) to distribute the payroll and to record the employer's payroll taxes.

4. Fringe Benefits. Mary Murphy works for the Colorado Land Development Corporation at a monthly salary of $1,380. The company contributes $368 a year into a pension fund in her behalf and grants her a two-week paid vacation annually. The state unemployment insurance rate is 1.3%. All labor-related costs are considered part of Mary's salary as a sales representative.

Required: (1) The entry to record Mary's employment cost in March.
(2) The entry for December.

5. Payroll Entries. Pasceri Products, Inc. operates on a six-day work week, Monday through Saturday, with paychecks being distributed on the following Wednesday. Examination of the firm's books indicates the following entry made on January 2:

```
Accrued Payroll.......................................  5,000
     Payroll..........................................         5,000
```

On January 31, an analysis of payroll records reveals that $27,000 of direct labor (including $730 overtime premium) and $3,500 of indirect labor (including $380 overtime premium) were incurred during January. Ten percent of the employees' earnings are withheld for income taxes.

During January the following payrolls were paid:

January 7 (December 29–January 3).......................	$7,500
January 14 (January 5–10)...............................	7,800
January 21 (January 12–17).............................	7,600
January 28 (January 19–24).............................	6,900

Required: (1) The entries to record each of the payrolls met during January.
(2) The entries to record accrued labor at the end of January, to distribute payroll, and to record employer's taxes on wages *earned* in January.
(3) Ledger accounts for Accrued Payroll and Payroll.

6. Pension Costs. The Mathis Company employs 125 factory workers for a 40-hour week and, on the average, operates 50 weeks each year. Under the provisions of a pension plan, it is estimated that 70 of the employees will be pensioned after an average of 25 years of employment. It is further estimated that, on the average, pension payments will be $250 a month for a period of 10 years. For the payroll period of March 15, factory labor totaled 5,000 hours.

Required: (1) The pension cost.
(2) The entry to record the pension cost in the March 15 payroll.

7. Cost Principles and Cost Determination. A company operating a machine shop undertook to produce, as a subcontractor under a prime contract with a government agency, certain parts on a cost-plus-a-fixed-fee basis. The hours of operation were about evenly divided between the above contract and the regular business of the company.

Each day the work required for the regular company business was completed first. The remainder of the day, with whatever overtime was necessary, was given over to production under the contract. During the contract period, overtime hours represented a substantial proportion of the total hours worked. Under an agreement with the employees, time and a half was paid for all hours over eight worked each day.

Job sheets recorded the actual cost of materials and direct labor, including any overtime premium paid. Factory overhead was applied on the basis of the labor cost so recorded, and the job sheets were adjusted each month to eliminate any balance in the overhead variance account.

Required: (1) Objections to the cost accounting principles applied.

(2) Incorrectness of the client's statements.

(3) Procedure for making a revised cost determination.

(AICPA adapted)

PROBLEMS

15-1. Entries for Payroll and Payroll Taxes. The general ledger accounts of the Rundo Company contained these credit balances for the period October 1 through November 30:

Federal Income Tax Withheld.............................	$8,500
FICA Tax Payable...	940
Federal Unemployment Tax Payable.......................	90
State Unemployment Tax Payable.........................	408

For the December 1–15 payroll, which totaled $28,000, employees' FICA deductions amounted to only $730 since some of the employees had already earned the maximum applicable during the year. For the same period, income taxes withheld totaled $2,372.

The company apportions employer payroll taxes as follows: 60% to Factory Overhead, 30% to Marketing Expenses, and 10% to General Office Expenses. The state unemployment insurance tax rate is 2%, and only $5,000 of the payroll is subject to this tax since all other employees had earned more than $4,200 by December 1. The company closed for the year on December 15 and had no more payroll expenses.

Required: (1) The entry to record the payroll for the period December 1–15.

(2) The entry to pay the payroll of December 1–15.

(3) The entry to record the employer's payroll taxes for the period December 1–15.

(4) The entry to record payment of all taxes due governmental agencies for the period October 1 through December 31.

15-2. Payroll Entries — General and Factory Office. Airpol, Inc. manufactures air pollution control devices. The firm maintains factory records at each plant location. At the St. Louis factory, a payroll journal is maintained as a book of original entry for the factory employees, even though salaries of personnel in the Shipping Department and Finished Goods Stockroom are charged to marketing expenses. Payroll checks are prepared at the home office and sent to the factory for delivery to the factory employees. Overtime premium wages are treated as factory overhead. The liability for payroll taxes is kept on the general office books. Factory payroll taxes are charged to factory overhead.

For the week ending May 30, the following factory payroll summary was prepared:

FACTORY PAYROLL SUMMARY

For Week Ending May 30, 19--

Department	Labor Hours	Payroll (Earned Hours)	Overtime Premium	Income Tax Withholding (10%)	FICA Tax (6%)	Net Pay
Casting.........	240	$1,134	$ 54	$118.80	$ 71.28	$ 997.92
Forging........	410	1,720	80	180.00	108.00	1,512.00
Machining......	560	2,860	60	292.00	175.20	2,452.80
Assembly.......	160	640		64.00	38.40	537.60
Toolroom.......	84	344	8	32.20	21.12	295.68
Storeroom......	82	322	4	33.60	20.16	282.24
Stockroom......	40	140		14.00	8.40	117.60
Shipping........	40	152		15.20	9.12	127.68
Total........	1,616	$7,322	$206	$752.80	$451.68	$6,323.52
Sales Office......	....	$1,600	...	$160.00	$ 96.00	$1,344.00
General Office....	....	$ 750	$ 50	$ 80.00	$ 48.00	$ 672.00

A recapitulation of the time tickets for direct labor showed:

RECAPITULATION OF TIME TICKETS

For Week Ending May 30, 19--

Job No.	Casting Department	Forging Department	Machining Department	Assembly Department
682	$ 253	$ 315	$ 650	$120
683	218	359	530	80
684	166	194	310	60
685	209	380	500	120
686	145	124	330	80
687	143	166	280	100
688	...	182	260	80
Totals..........	$1,134	$1,720	$2,860	$640

Required: Entries in journal form for the factory office and general office books to record:

(a) Preparation of the payroll.

(b) Payment of the payroll.

(c) Distribution of the payroll.

(d) Recording of the employer's payroll taxes. (State unemployment insurance, 1.6% of the payroll.)

15-3. Distribution of Labor Cost.   Kinsel Development Company is a home building concern that currently has four houses under construction.   Labor costs are assembled with the use of clock cards and time tickets.   From these records the payroll clerk compiled the following data for the week ended August 3:

| Employees' Names | Total Weekly Clock Hours | Job Time Tickets | | | |
| | | Job Numbers and Hours | | | |
		222	223	224	225
Evans........................	40	35		5	
Hurst (Supervisor)...............	42				
Lindstrom.....................	45	20	15		10
Norton.......................	40			30	6
Wesson (Indirect labor)..........	40				

Construction employees are paid $7.90 per hour; Hurst receives $10.10 per hour, and Wesson receives $5.80 per hour.   The customer who is having House No. 222 constructed wanted construction completed two months ahead of its scheduled completion date.   The company agreed to the rush arrangement but required the customer to bear the overtime charges.   The only overtime spent on No. 222 this week was 3 hours of Lindstrom's time.   All other overtime was due to previous job slowdowns on account of the weather.

Required: (1) The total payroll and the total amount of "take home" pay, assuming a 15% deduction for federal income tax, a 3% state income tax, and a 1% city wage tax.

(2) A journal entry for the calculations in (1).

(3) A distribution of the payroll to the various jobs and other appropriate accounts as determined by the analysis.   Omit employer's payroll tax accounts.

15-4. Payroll Taxes, Vacation Pay, and Payroll.   The normal work week at Helton Publishing, Inc. is five days—Monday through Friday, with payday being the following Tuesday.   On November 1, after the reversing entry was posted, the payroll account showed a $230 credit balance, representing labor purchased during the last two days of October.

November

Sun	Mon	Tue	Wed	Thu	Fri	Sat
			1	2	3	4
5	6	7	8	9	10	11
12	13	14	15	16	17	18
19	20	21	22	23	24	25
26	27	28	29	30		

Deductions for FICA tax and 10% for income taxes are withheld from each payroll check.

The labor summary for November shows a purchase of $8,200 of direct labor and $2,600 of indirect labor.   Vacation pay is charged to current production at a rate of 4% of total payroll.

Payrolls for November were: Nov. 7, $2,890; Nov. 14, $2,920; Nov. 21, $1,900; Nov. 28, $2,880.

Required: (1) Entries to record each payroll.

(2) The labor cost entry on November 30, treating the employer's payroll taxes and vacation pay as factory overhead. The state unemployment tax rate is 2%.

(3) Ledger accounts for Payroll and Accrued Payroll and the entry to record accrued wages at the end of November.

15-5. Overtime Premium. The Jernigan Clothing Company produces several lines of women's fashions and has had exceptional success in selling its products to leading department stores across the nation. Jernigan employs 20 production workers, paying $4 per hour for a 5-day, 40-hour work week; 20% of wages are withheld for income taxes, and state unemployment insurance is 1.4%.

Currently, production reports indicate that the workers average 320 dresses per day. Since customer demand is considerably greater than that, the firm's management decided to work overtime for the first week in May to increase daily output to 440 dresses.

By May 23 production had met customer orders, and no additional overtime was needed. On the following day, May 24, however, an accident caused five employees to halt work for one hour while repairs were made. The five-man crew was forced to work one hour overtime that evening to maintain regular production schedules.

On May 27 a salesman called in a rush order for 280 dresses which needed to be ready for delivery by the following Monday. It was decided to work the entire work force on Sunday, May 29, at 200% wages to fill this order.

Required: (1) Entries to record the payroll liability and labor cost for the first week in May.

(2) The entry to record labor cost for May 24.

(3) The entry to record the labor cost for the rush order.

15-6. Pension Plans. The DiMario Corporation adopted a pension plan for its employees on January 1, 19E. A trial balance of the records of the plan at December 31, 19F, follows:

	Debit	Credit
Cash...	$ 400	
Investments (at cost)...................................	3,400	
Bone, Equity...		$1,590
Cohan, Equity..		1,060
Dohler, Equity...		850
Income from Investments — Received in 19F............		300
	$3,800	$3,800

The following data pertain to the corporation's employees for 19F:

	Date Employed	Date Terminated	Salary Paid in 19F
Bone........................	Dec. 8, 19A	—	$17,900
Cohan.......................	Feb. 1, 19C	—	14,100
Dohler......................	Dec. 8, 19C	April 9, 19F	3,500
Kolman......................	Sept. 15, 19D	—	8,000
Jones.......................	Sept. 21, 19F	Dec. 22, 19F	3,000
Lohman	May 6, 19F	—	5,500
Total.......................			$52,000

The provisions of the plan include the following:

(a) The corporation shall contribute 10% of its net income before deducting income taxes and the contribution, but not in excess of 15% of the total salaries paid to the participants in the plan who are in the employ of the corporation at year end. The employees make no contributions to the plan.

(b) An employee shall be eligible to participate in the plan on January 1 following the completion of one full year of employment.

(c) The corporation's contribution shall be allocated to the participants' equities on the following point system:
  (1) For each full year of employment — 2 points.
  (2) For each $100 of salary paid in the current year — 1 point.

(d) A participant shall have a vested interest of 10% of his total equity for each full year of employment. Forfeitures shall be distributed to the remaining participants in proportion to their equities in the plan at the beginning of the year. Terminated employees shall receive their vested interests at year end.

(e) Income from the plan's investments shall be allocated to the equities of the remaining participants in proportion to their equities at the beginning of the year.

The DiMario Corporation's net income in 19F before income taxes and contribution to the plan was $73,250.

Required: (1) A schedule computing the corporation's contribution to the plan for 19F.

(2) A schedule computing the vested interests of the participants terminating their employment during 19F.

(3) A schedule showing the allocation of the corporation's 19F contribution to each participant.

(4) A schedule showing the allocation of the plan's 19F income on investments and forfeitures by terminated participants.

(AICPA adapted)

15-7. Pension Plans. The Hercules Tire Company is planning a pension system for some of its employees and wishes to provide funds for meeting the payments under the pension plan.

The company does not contemplate making any pension payments under the plan until January, 1982. Payments in 1982 and thereafter to the present group of covered employees are expected to be as follows:

January 1, 1982	$ 5,000	January 1, 1989	$22,000
January 1, 1983	7,000	January 1, 1990	17,000
January 1, 1984	10,000	January 1, 1991	12,000
January 1, 1985	14,000	January 1, 1992	8,000
January 1, 1986	16,000	January 1, 1993	5,000
January 1, 1987	20,000	January 1, 1994	2,000
January 1, 1988	25,000	January 1, 1995	2,000

Starting January 1, 1977, and continuing for five years, the company will deposit $20,000 a year in a special fund. On January 1, 1976, the company wishes to make a lump sum deposit of an amount sufficient to provide the remaining funds needed for meeting the pensions. Taking a conservative stand, the company's management expects that all of the above funds will earn 3.5% interest compounded annually during the entire life of the fund.

Periods	Amount of $1 at Compound Interest	Present Value of $1 at Compound Interest	Amount of Annuity of $1 at End of Each Period	Present Value of Annuity of $1 at End of Each Period
1	1.0350	.9662	1.0000	0.9662
2	1.0712	.9335	2.0350	1.8997
3	1.1087	.9019	3.1062	2.8016
4	1.1475	.8714	4.2149	3.6731
5	1.1877	.8420	5.3625	4.5151
6	1.2293	.8135	6.5502	5.3286
7	1.2723	.7860	7.7794	6.1145
8	1.3168	.7594	9.0517	6.8740
9	1.3629	.7337	10.3685	7.6077
10	1.4106	.7089	11.7314	8.3166
11	1.4600	.6849	13.1420	9.0016
12	1.5111	.6618	14.6020	9.6633
13	1.5640	.6394	16.1130	10.3027
14	1.6187	.6178	17.6770	10.9205
15	1.6753	.5969	19.2957	11.5174

Required: The amount of payment which should be made on January 1, 1976, with all supporting computations in good form. The table of values at 3.5% interest shown above may be used as needed.

(AICPA adapted)

15-8. Definitions and Pension Costs. The Caldwell Manufacturing Corporation — in operation for the past 23 years — decided late in 19A to adopt, beginning on January 1, 19B, a funded pension plan for its employees. The pension plan was to be noncontributory and would provide for vesting after five years of service by each eligible employee. A trust agreement was entered into whereby a large national insurance company would receive the yearly pension fund contributions and administer the fund.

Management through extended consultation with the fund trustee, internal accountants, and independent actuaries, arrived at these conclusions:

(a) The normal pension cost for 19B would be $30,000.
(b) The present value of the past service cost at the date of inception of the pension plan (January 1, 19B) is $200,000.
(c) Because of the large sum of money involved, the past service costs would be funded at a rate of $23,365 per year for the next fifteen years. The first payment is not due until January 1, 19C.
(d) In accordance with Accounting Principles Board Opinion No. 8, the "unit credit method" of accounting for the pension costs would be followed. Pension costs would be amortized over a ten-year period. The ten-year accrual factor is $29,805 per year. Neither the maximum nor minimum amortization amounts as prescribed by Accounting Principles Board Opinion No. 8 would be violated.
(e) Where applicable, an 8% interest rate would be assumed.

Required: (1) Definition of: (a) normal pension cost; (b) past service cost.
(2) The amounts that would be reported in the company's: (a) 19B income statement for *Pension Expense*; (b) balance sheet as of December 31, 19B, for *Deferred Past Service Costs* and *Due to Pension Trustee*; (c) notes for both of these financial statements. [If the amount cannot be calculated, use *$xxx*.]
(3) The amounts that would be reported in the company's: (a) 19C income statement for *Pension Expense* and *Interest on Unfunded Past Service Costs*;

(b) balance sheet as of December 31, 19C, for *Deferred Past Service Costs* and *Due to Pension Trustee*; (c) notes for both of these financial statements. [If the amount cannot be calculated, use *$xxx*.]

(NAA adapted)

CASES

A. Payroll Taxes.   In January, 19C, the financial statements of the Grabill Company for the year ended December 31, 19B, were examined. The company filed the necessary payroll tax returns for the first three quarters of 19B and had prepared drafts of the returns scheduled to be filed by January 31, 19C.

The following information was available from the general ledger, copies and drafts of payroll tax returns, and other sources:

General Ledger:

Account	Balance as of December 31, 19B	Composition of Balance
Wages (various expense accounts)...	$121,800.00	12 monthly entries from the payroll summaries
Payroll Taxes Expense............	8,458.00	FICA (6% of $102,000), $6,120; state unemployment tax (2.7% of $59,000), $1,593; federal unemployment tax (.5% of $59,000), $295; amounts withheld from employees for FICA tax in October and November and paid to depositary, $450
Employees' Payroll Taxes Withheld.....	3,122.50	December income tax, $1,530; October through December FICA tax, $1,592.50
Employer's Payroll Taxes Payable......	956.50	December FICA tax, $462.50; October through December state unemployment tax, $199; 19B federal unemployment tax, $295

Additional information:

(a) In August 19B, six laborers were hired to tear down an old warehouse building located on the site where a new warehouse would soon be constructed. The laborers' 19B wages totaling $1,000 were charged to the land and buildings account. Payroll taxes were not withheld.

(b) Included in a 19B wages expense account is one month's salary of $1,400 paid to the president on December 30, 19B, for his 19A vacation allowance.

(c) A gross factory payroll of $1,200 through December 31, 19B, and the related FICA taxes (employer and employee) were accrued on the general ledger at the year end for a portion of the week ending January 4, 19C. Each of the employees included in this payroll earned between $4,000 and $6,000 as a Grabill employee in 19B.

(d) In December, 19B, a contractor was paid $2,300 for making repairs to machinery usually made by company employees and the amount was charged to Wages Expense. No payroll taxes were withheld.

(e) Copies of 19B tax returns:

	Totals for Year	First Three Quarters (Duplicate Copies of Returns)	Last Quarter (Pencil Draft)
Gross wages.............................	$121,800	$95,870	$25,930
Wages taxable for FICA...................	102,000	88,500	13,500
FICA tax................................	12,240	9,735	2,505
Income tax withheld.....................	15,740	11,490	4,250
Wages taxable for state unemployment tax....	59,000	51,640	7,360
Total state unemployment tax (employer only)....................	1,593	1,394	199
Total federal unemployment tax — employer only (pencil draft of return for full year).......	295		

Required: (1) A schedule presenting the computation of total taxable wages to be reported on the 19B payroll tax returns for FICA tax and for state unemployment tax.

(2) A schedule presenting the computation of the amounts (to the nearest dollar) which should be paid with each of the year-end payroll tax returns to be filed in January, 19C, for (a) FICA tax and income tax withheld, (b) state unemployment tax, and (c) federal unemployment tax.

(3) A schedule to reconcile the differences between the amounts which should be paid with payroll tax returns to be filed in January, 19C [as computed for (2) above], and the balances shown at December 31, 19B, in the related general ledger liability accounts.

(AICPA adapted)

B. Costs of Pension Plans and Financial Statements.   Casey and Lewis Printers, Inc. was organized in 1955 and fifteen years later established a formal pension plan to provide retirement benefits for all employees.   The plan is noncontributory and is funded through a trustee, the First National Bank, which invests all benefits as they become due.   Original past service cost of $110,000 is being amortized over 15 years and funded over 10 years on a present-value basis at 5%.   The company also funds an amount equal to current normal cost net of actuarial gains and losses.   There have been no amendments to the plan since inception.

The independent actuary's report is shown on page 470.

Required: (1) On the basis of accounting requirements for the cost of pension plans, an evaluation of the (a) treatment of actuarial gains and losses and (b) computation of pension cost for financial-statement purposes.   (Ignore income tax considerations.)

(2) A footnote for the company's financial statements for the year ended June 30, 19A, in accordance with Accounting Principles Board Opinion No. 8. [Independent of the answer to (1), assume that the total amount to be funded is $32,663; the total pension cost for financial-statement purposes is $29,015; all amounts presented in Parts II, III, and IV of the actuary's report are correct.]

(AICPA adapted)

CASEY & LEWIS PRINTERS, INC.

Basic Noncontributory Pension Plan

Actuarial Report as of June 30, 19A

I. Current Year's Funding and Pension Cost:

Normal cost (before adjustment for actuarial gains) computed under the entry-age-normal method............		$ 34,150
Actuarial gains:		
Investment gains (losses):		
Excess of expected dividend income over actual dividend income..... $ (350)		
Gain on sale of investments........ 4,050		
Gains in actuarial assumptions for:		
Mortality...................... 3,400		
Employer turnover............... 5,050		
Reduction in pension cost from closing of plant........................ 8,000		
Net actuarial gains..................		20,150
		14,000
Normal cost (funded currently)......... $ 14,000		
Past service costs:		
Funding.......................... 14,245		
Amortization.....................		10,597
Total funded.................. $ 28,245		
Total pension cost for financial-statement purposes.........................		$ 24,597

II. Fund Assets:

Cash...............................	$ 4,200	
Dividends receivable..................	1,525	
Investment in common stocks, at cost (market value, $177,800)............	162,750	$168,475

III. Actuarial Liabilities:

Number of employees.................	46
Number of employees retired...........	0
Yearly earnings of employees...........	$598,000
Actuarial liability....................	$145,000

IV. Actuarial Assumptions:

Interest..............................	5%
Mortality............................	1951 Group Annuity Tables
Retirement...........................	Age 65

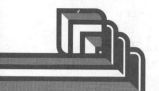

CHAPTER **16**

PLANNING AND BUDGETING
OF PROFITS, SALES,
COSTS, AND EXPENSES

Cost accounting is a "tool of management," and as such serves as a means for planning and control. General or financial accounting is primarily concerned with the preparation and issuance of monthly and annual financial statements. Cost accounting, however, provides management with total and detailed costs of products, thereby enabling executives to formulate intelligent production plans and sales policies. Detailed statements furnished to management at short intervals compare and analyze actual costs of materials, labor, factory overhead, marketing, and administrative expenses with estimates and standards prepared in advance of production. This permits responsible management levels to exercise effective control over the operations of divisions and departments. A standard cost system combined with budgets constitutes the most logical foundation for the achievement of these multiple tasks and goals.

PROFIT PLANNING

Sound and intelligent planning of profits, sales, and costs and expenses is both more important and more difficult than ever before in this age of rapid technological change and heightened recognition of the need to consider social and political parameters. Modern profit planning encourages desirable action and recognizes the divisional and departmental autonomy and responsibility of managers, motivating them to strive for attainment of their personal objectives in congruence with the organiza-tion's objectives. Profit planning is directed to the final objectives of the organization and generally includes all of its important elements. Bud-geting, employed as a tool of both planning and control, offers manage-ment one of its best means for placing an organization on a definite course and keeping it there. A *budget* is simply a plan expressed in financial and other quantitative terms. The terms "budgeting" and "profit planning" can be viewed as synonymous.

Profit planning is a well thought-out operational plan with its financial implications expressed as both long- and short-range profit plans or bud-gets in the form of financial statements, including balance sheets, income statements, and cash and working capital projections. Profit planning is especially effective in enabling middle management to help plan profit and control costs. It is management's primary tool to accomplish its objectives.

Long-Range Profit Planning.   In recent years business has become aware of a need to introduce long-range profit planning or forecasts. These long-range plans are not stated in precise terms, nor are they expected to be completely coordinated future plans. They deal rather with specific areas such as future sales, long-term capital expenditures, extensive re-search and development activities, and financial requirements. Long-range profit planning intends to find the most probable course of events or range of probabilities. It deals with the futurity of present decisions. To find the best short-range plans and make the wisest decisions, manage-ment must look to the future. Long-range planning does not eliminate risk, for risk-taking is the essence of economic activity. The end result of successful long-range profit planning is a capacity to take a greater risk, for this is the only way to improve entrepreneurial performance. Long-range planning has been defined as "the continuous process of making present decisions systematically and, with the best possible knowledge of their futurity, organizing systematically the efforts needed to carry out these decisions and measuring the results of these decisions against the expectations through organized, systematic feedback."[1] Long- and short-range planning should be merged into integrated strategic planning.

Market trends and economic factors, growth of population, personal consumption expenditures, and indices of industrial production form the background for long-range planning. Quantitative sales estimates for a three- to five-year forecast are developed, followed by a dollar evaluation of the combined plans. The financial section might culminate in a pro-spective income statement showing by years anticipated sales, variable costs, contribution margin, fixed factory overhead, fixed marketing and

---

[1]Peter F. Drucker, "Long-Range Planning," *Management Science*, Vol. 5, No. 3, p. 240.

administrative expenses, and net operating income. A balance sheet by years can be prepared to indicate anticipated cash balances, inventory levels, accounts receivable balances, liabilities, etc. This financial long-range plan might also be supported by a cash flow statement.

Setting Profit Objectives. A management's long-range plans can only be achieved through successful long-run profit performance where the basic requirements are growth and a reasonably high and stable level of profit.

In setting profit objectives, management needs to consider the following factors:

1. Profit or loss resulting from a given volume of sales
2. Sales volume required to recover all consumed costs, to produce a profit adequate to pay dividends on preferred and common stock, and to retain sufficient earnings in the business for future needs
3. Break-even point
4. Sales volume that the present operating capacity can produce
5. Operating capacity necessary to attain the profit objectives
6. Return on capital employed

Most companies operate with some kind of profit expectancy which motivates their planning. Fundamentally, three different procedures can be followed to set the profit objectives.

1. The *a priori* method in which the profit objectives take precedence over the planning process. At the outset, management specifies a given rate of return to be achieved in the long run which it seeks to realize by means of planning directed toward that end.

2. The *a posteriori* method in which the determination of profit objectives is subordinated to the planning, and the objectives emerge as the product of the planning itself.

3. The *pragmatic* method in which management uses a profit standard that has been tested empirically and sanctioned by experience. By using a target rate of profit derived from experience, expectations, or comparisons, management establishes a more or less definite profit level which is considered satisfactory for the company; and this constitutes a relative profit standard. The rate of return on capital (total assets) employed, introduced in Chapter 2, is generally considered the most important statistic in long-range profit planning and setting profit objectives. The usual practice is to compute rates of return for each individual year covered in the long-range plan in order to show whether planned increases in total net income will keep pace with increases in assets and to measure the effectiveness with which management is likely to use the assets. This comparative analysis is prepared at both corporate as well as divisional

and/or operating levels. Though return on capital employed is the basic measure of profit performance (discussed in detail in Chapter 27), companies typically use several other measures such as the ratio of net income to sales, the ratio of sales to shareholders' capital, and earnings per common share.[2]

Heightened public expectations with regard to social responsibilities compel companies to consider the social consequences when formulating plans to achieve profit objectives. Increasingly, important actions must be evaluated in a context that includes social as well as economic impacts. Potential social impacts specifically pertain to ". . . environmental pollution, the consumption of nonrenewable resources, and other ecological factors; the rights of individuals and groups; the maintenance of public service; public safety; health and education; and many other such social concerns."[3] Such social factors are likely necessary considerations in the framework of corporate thinking.

Short-Range Plans or Budgets. Long-range plans with their future expectancy of profits and growth must, however, be placed on a shorter range for both planning and more importantly control of the contemplated course of action. The short-range budget may cover periods of three, six, or twelve months depending upon the nature of the business. One year, however, is the usual planning period. For efficient planning, the annual budget should be expanded into an eighteen-month budget, allowing for a three-month period at the end of the old year, twelve months for the regular budget period and an additional three months into the third year. These overlapping months are needed in order to allow transition from year to year and to make adjustments based on prior months' experience. The budget period should be divided into months. It should:

1. Be long enough to complete production of the various products.
2. Cover at least one entire seasonal cycle for a business of a seasonal nature.
3. Be long enough to allow for the financing of production well in advance of actual needs.
4. Coincide with the financial accounting period to compare actual results with budget estimates.

Some organizations use a *continuous budget* by which a month or quarter in the future is added as the month or quarter just ended is dropped, and the budget for the entire period is revised and updated as

[2]"Long-Range Profit Planning," *Research Report No. 42* (New York: National Association of Accountants, 1964), pp. 60–65.
[3]Robert K. Elliott, "Social Accounting and Corporate Decision-Making," *Management Controls*, Vol. XXI, No. 1, p. 2.

needed. This procedure forces management to think continuously about its short-range plans.

Advantages of Profit Planning. Profit planning or budgeting has the advantages of:

1. Providing a disciplined approach to the solution of problems.

2. Obliging management to make an early study of its problems and instilling into an organization the habit of careful study before making decisions.

3. Developing throughout the organization an atmosphere of profit-mindedness, encouraging an attitude of cost-consciousness and maximum resource utilization.

4. Enlisting the aid and coordinating the operating plans of the diverse organizational segments of the entire management organization so that the final decisions and contingency plans represent the total organization in the form of an integrated, comprehensive plan.

5. Affording the opportunity of appraising systematically every facet of the organization as well as examining and restating periodically its basic policies and guiding principles.

6. Coordinating and correlating all efforts, for no management activity reveals weaknesses in organization so quickly as the orderly procedure necessary for systematic budgeting.

7. Aiding in directing capital and effort into the most profitable channels.

8. Encouraging a high standard of performance by stimulating competition, providing a sense of purpose, and serving as an incentive to perform more effectively.

9. Providing yardsticks or standards for measuring performance and gauging the managerial judgment and ability of the individual executive.[4]

Limitations of Profit Planning. While the advantages of profit planning or budgeting are unquestionably impressive and far-reaching, certain limitations and pitfalls need to be mentioned:

1. Planning, budgeting, or forecasting is not an exact science; a certain amount of judgment is present in any budgetary plan. A revision or modification of estimates should be made when variations from the estimates warrant a change of plans.

2. A profit planning program needs the cooperation and participation of all members of management. Basic for success is executive management's

---

[4]Adapted from Peter A. Noll and Edward A. Radetsky, "Values of Profit Planning," *NAA Bulletin*, Vol. XLV, No. 6, p. 36.

absolute adherence to and enthusiasm for the budget plan. Too often a budgetary plan has failed because executive management has paid only lip service to its execution.

3. Profit planning does not eliminate nor take over the role of administration. Executives should not feel "hemmed-in." Rather, the budgetary plan is designed to provide detailed information that allows the executives to operate with strength and vision toward achievement of the organization's objectives.

4. Installation takes time. Often, a management becomes impatient and loses interest because it expects too much too soon. The budget plan must first be sold to the responsible people; and they, in turn, must then be guided, trained, and educated in the fundamental steps, methods, and purposes of a budgetary system.

PREREQUISITES OF A BUDGET PLAN

A company's organization chart and its chart of accounts form the two basic frameworks on which to build a coordinated, cooperative, and efficient system of managerial planning and budgetary control. The organization chart defines the functional responsibilities of each executive whose activities justify a budget. Final responsibility for the budget rests with top management. However, each executive is responsible for the preparation and execution of his departmental budget. If a budgetary control system is to be successful, it is necessary to have the full cooperation of each company official, and each official must understand the budget system and his role in making the system successful.

THE BUDGET COMMITTEE

The budget committee is composed of executives in charge of major functions of the business and includes the sales manager, the production manager, the chief engineer, the treasurer, and the controller.

The principal functions of the budget committee are to:
1. Decide on general policies.
2. Request, receive, and review individual budget estimates.
3. Suggest revisions.
4. Approve budgets and later revisions.
5. Receive and analyze budget reports.
6. Recommend action designed to improve efficiency where necessary.

In performing these functions, the budget committee becomes a management committee. It is a powerful force in knitting together the various activities of the business and enforcing real control over operations.

DETAILS OF THE TOTAL PERIODIC BUDGET

The budget committee's initial function is to request, receive, and review individual budget estimates. A complete set of budgets generally consists of:

1. Sales estimates by:
   a. Territory and product, or
   b. Territory, customer group, and product
2. Estimates of inventory, production, and purchase requirements
3. Estimates of materials, labor, and factory overhead combined into a cost of goods sold schedule
4. Detailed expense budgets for marketing and administrative expenses
5. A budget of major repairs, replacements, and improvements of plant and machinery, and research and development expenditures
6. A cash budget showing cash receipts and disbursements
7. A forecast income statement
8. A forecast balance sheet showing the estimated financial position of the company at the end of the budget period

SALES BUDGET

The most important single element in a budgetary control system is a sound and accurate sales forecast. This forecast must consider past sales and be based on market and sales analyses. The task of preparing the sales budget is usually approached from two different angles: (1) judging and evaluating external influences and (2) considering internal influences. These two influences are brought together in an intelligent and workable sales budget. External influences are the general trend of industrial activity, governmental policies, cyclical phases of the nation's economy, purchasing power of the population, population shift, and changes in buying habits and modes of living. Internal influences are sales trends, factory capacities, new products, plant expansion, seasonal products, sales force estimates, and establishment of quotas for salesmen and sales territories. Last but not least, the profit desired by the company plays a significant part.

Forecasting Sales. The preparation of sales estimates is usually the responsibility of the marketing manager assisted by individual salesmen and market research personnel. Because of the many dissimilarities in the marketing of products, actual methods used to forecast sales vary widely in various companies. One method of forecasting sales still used by many companies is the preparation of sales estimates by individual salesmen. Each salesman supplies his district manager with estimates of what he thinks he can sell in his territory during the coming period. These estimates are consolidated and perhaps adjusted by the district marketing manager before he forwards them to the general marketing manager where further adjustments are made. These adjustments make allowances for expected economic conditions and competitive conditions of which salesmen are unaware, as well as allowances for expected canceled orders and sales returns that ordinarily would be disregarded by salesmen who base their estimates on the orders they expect to procure.

In many firms the method described above has been either supplemented or superseded by the establishment of market research or market analysis divisions which assist the marketing manager and the salesmen in arriving at more accurate estimates.

In larger organizations the forecasting procedure starts with known factors; namely, (1) the company's sales of past years broken down by product groups and profit margins, (2) industry or trade sales volume and perhaps profits, and (3) unusual factors influencing sales in the past. The company's past sales figures often require a restudy or reclassification due to changes in products, profit margins, competition, sales areas, distribution methods, or changes within the industry. Industry or trade volume of sales and profits are secured from trade associations, trade publications, and various business magazines. For some industries the U. S. Department of Commerce publishes information that is useful as background data. Unusual factors influencing past sales are inventory conditions, public economic sentiment, competition, and customer reactions. Charting a company's physical volume in units of various products for a three- to five-year period and comparing it with the industry's volume will disclose the company's sales trend and permit pinpointing factors that affected past sales.

With such known facts assembled, the sales forecast turns toward prediction of the future. Although the feeling frequently exists that this is the crystal-ball area, a good sound basis for determining future sales can be established by considering:

1. General business conditions.
2. The industry's prospects and the company's potential share of the total industry market.
3. The plans of other and particularly competitive companies.

Seasonal Variations. When the annual sales forecast has finally been approved, it must be placed on an operating period basis. Experience will show that each product manufactured has its own seasonal sales pattern. Records are examined to determine the trend a product has followed during past years. Consideration should be given to the causes of the fluctuations. They might be due to customs or habits based on local or national traits, climate, holidays, or even influences caused by companies in the firm's own industry. All this information is used in preparing a monthly sales budget.

The seasonal or operating sales budget is of great help in judging the records of individual salesmen. Averaging sales over a budget period is not sufficient to assure success of a sales program. Too many times low sales in one month have been excused with the optimistic statement that sales in the following month will make up the difference. When this does not happen, the sales budget and the entire budget plan suffer.

Sales Budget on a Territory and Customer Basis. A sales budget should not only be placed on a monthly basis for each product but should also be prepared by territories or districts and classified as to types of customers. (See illustration below.) The customer classification will show sales to jobbers, wholesalers, retailers, institutions, governmental agencies, schools and colleges, foreign businesses, etc. Such a breakdown indicates the contribution each class of trade makes to total sales and profits. An analysis of this type will often reveal that certain classes of customers or trades are not given sufficient attention by sales managers and salesmen. A customer budget can thus become a strong means for analyzing possible new trade outlets. It also assists in locating reasons for a drop in sales to various customer classes so that such a decrease can be investigated quickly and remedial steps taken.

PRODUCT X
SALES BUDGET
(BY TERRITORY AND BY CUSTOMER GROUP)
FOR YEAR ENDING DECEMBER, 19—

Territory	Customer Group	January Qty.	January Value	February Qty.	February Value	December Qty.	December Value	Total Qty.	Total Value
North	A	1,440	$ 86,400	1,620	$ 97,200	1,260	$ 75,600	21,600	$1,296,000
	B	960	57,600	1,080	64,800	840	50,400	14,400	864,000
	Total	2,400	$144,000	2,700	$162,000	2,100	$126,000	36,000	$2,160,000
East	A	400	$ 24,000	450	$ 27,000	350	$ 21,000	6,000	$ 360,000
	B	400	24,000	450	27,000	350	21,000	6,000	360,000
	Total	800	$ 48,000	900	$ 54,000	700	$ 42,000	12,000	$ 720,000
South	A	1,440	$ 86,400	1,620	$ 97,200	1,260	$ 75,600	21,600	$1,296,000
	B	1,760	105,600	1,980	118,800	1,540	92,400	26,400	1,584,000
	Total	3,200	$192,000	3,600	$216,000	2,800	$168,000	48,000	$2,880,000
West	A	640	$ 38,400	720	$ 43,200	560	$ 33,600	9,600	$ 576,000
	B	960	57,600	1,080	64,800	840	50,400	14,400	864,000
	Total	1,600	$ 96,000	1,800	$108,000	1,400	$ 84,000	24,000	$1,440,000
Total		8,000	$480,000	9,000	$540,000	7,000	$420,000	120,000	$7,200,000

Estimating Production and Inventory Requirements. Prior to the final acceptance of a sales budget, the ability of the factory to produce the quantities estimated must be determined. This step is determined primarily by the production capacity of the plant. When reliable records of past experiences are available, coordination of the sales budget with the production budget is not too difficult.

However, production planning must realize that the best possible level of production keeps men and machinery operating all year with a sufficient but economic inventory on hand. If, for example, the sales budget should indicate that in certain months factory employment would fall seriously below a desirable level, it would be necessary to attempt to increase sales volume or increase inventories. Should estimated sales be higher than available capacity, the possibility of increasing plant capacity through purchase or rental of new machinery and factory space must be considered.

If factory capacity is available, an efficient rate of production should be established to avoid serious fluctuations in employment. To hire and lay off workers is always expensive. Stabilization of employment is desirable and should become a definite company policy. An even flow of production will make for better labor relations.

When scheduling production, beginning and ending inventories of finished stock on hand at the end of each month are important. It is necessary to have inventories on hand which permit fulfillment of the month's sales requirements. At the same time, the investment in inventories should be held to a level consistent with sound financial policy.

PRODUCTION BUDGET

A production budget is stated in physical units and frequently is merely the sales budget adjusted for any inventory changes (as shown below). Seasonal fluctuations of sales are usually leveled out in production planning in order to stabilize employment without causing a shortage of finished products, inefficient service to customers, or large inventories.

The production budget, like other budgets, will be detailed by months or quarters along with a tentative annual budget. Uncertainty of estimated

PRODUCT X
PRODUCTION BUDGET
FOR YEAR ENDING DECEMBER, 19—

	January	February	December	Year, 19––
Units required to meet sales budget....	8,000	9,000	7,000	120,000
Add desired ending inventory..........	6,400	7,400	4,400	4,400
Total units required...............	14,400	16,400	11,400	124,400
Less estimated beginning inventory.....	4,400	6,400	1,400	4,400
Planned production...............	10,000	10,000	10,000	120,000

sales makes this desirable in many concerns. The detailed budget should be broken down by work stations for comparison with actual production. The nature of the breakdown will be determined by plant layout, type of production, and other factors.

For a company that does not manufacture a standard product but produces only on orders, plans cannot be too detailed. The problem here is to be prepared for production when orders are received. However, if there are standardized parts, production can often be budgeted in a manner similar to that used by a company producing a standard product. In special-order work, the routing and scheduling of work through the factory is of prime importance to prevent delays and to utilize production facilities fully.

Coordination of the production budget with the sales budget is of extreme importance, otherwise production may become unbalanced. The sales department may emphasize volume and overlook balance. Sales personnel may concentrate on selling what they think are the most profitable lines and overlook products that the company has facilities to produce and which cannot be used for other products. Such a condition may result in idle capacity with resultant losses greater than if sales effort had been concentrated otherwise.

No division of a manufacturing business has made so much progress in scientific management as the production department. When competition becomes keen and pressure for price cutting increases, management looks for reduced production costs. With labor resisting decreases or pressing for increases in wages, reduction must take the form of labor-saving devices and careful planning, routing, and scheduling. Constant effort is always directed toward devising new ways and short cuts that will lead to more efficient production and cost savings. Any gains in production efficiency will be reflected in earnings.

The production budget deals with the scheduling of operations, the determination of volume, and the establishment of maximum and minimum quantities of raw materials and finished goods inventories. Its summaries and details provide the basis for preparing the budgets of materials, labor, and factory overhead. These three elements of cost constitute the cost of goods sold section of the income statement, and their totals are estimated in the manufacturing budget.

MANUFACTURING BUDGET

With the forecasted sales volume translated into physical units in the production budget, the future costs of materials, labor, and factory overhead essential to the sales and production program can be computed. These costs, often based on standard costs, are usually summarized in a manufacturing budget which, in effect, is made up of three budgets: materials, labor, and factory overhead. The costs are further classified into fixed and variable costs and budgeted accordingly: variable costs as a constant dollar amount per unit; fixed costs only in total. A fundamental axiom of the relationship of fixed and variable costs to the product must never be forgotten: fixed costs are fixed in total, but variable per unit; variable costs are variable in total, but fixed per unit. Example:

LOPEZ COMPANY
MANUFACTURING BUDGET ESTIMATES
FOR YEAR ENDING DECEMBER 31, 19—

Production	20,000 Units	25,000 Units
Direct materials cost, $5 per unit.............	$100,000	$125,000
Direct labor cost, $3 per unit................	60,000	75,000
Variable factory overhead, $1 per unit........	20,000	25,000
Fixed factory overhead......................	40,000	40,000
Fixed factory overhead per unit..............	($2)	($1.60)

The factory overhead is budgeted in greater detail by responsibility centers or departments with the strong probability that flexible budgets would be prepared for each center. The budget information thus developed becomes part of the master budget to be used as a standard or target against which the performance of the individual department is judged and evaluated. Detailed budgets are also prepared for direct materials and direct labor.

Direct Materials Budget. A materials budget indicating the quantity and cost of materials required to produce the predetermined units of finished goods is usually the first cost budget prepared. A materials budget:

1. Permits the purchasing department to set up a purchasing schedule that assures delivery of materials when needed.
2. Leads to the determination of minimum and maximum quantities of raw materials and finished parts that must be on hand.
3. Establishes a means by which the treasurer can gauge the financial requirements of the purchasing department.

The materials budget usually deals with direct materials only. Supplies and indirect materials are generally included in the factory overhead budget; however, the necessary factors discussed below are also applicable to supplies and indirect materials.

Purchase Requirements. The production planning department determines the quantity and type of materials required for the various products manufactured by a company. Most companies have standard parts lists and bills of materials which detail all materials requirements. The requirements are given to the purchasing department which sets up a buying schedule making certain that sufficient materials are always available without overstocking or creating a shortage. (See schedule below.) In preparing the schedules, the purchasing department must consider: (1) changes in possible delivery promises by the supplier and (2) changes in the rate of materials consumption because of unforeseen circumstances.

RAW MATERIAL A
PRODUCTION, INVENTORY, AND PURCHASE REQUIREMENTS SCHEDULE
FOR YEAR ENDING DECEMBER 31, 19—

Raw Material A	January	February	December	Total
Beginning inventory...	80,000	80,000	80,000	80,000
Purchases..........	45,000	45,000	50,000	600,000
Materials available....	125,000	125,000	130,000	680,000
Ending inventory.....	80,000	80,000	80,000	80,000
Materials used.......	45,000	45,000	50,000	600,000

Minimum and Maximum Quantities. The materials ledger cards of many companies carry a section in which the minimum and maximum quantities to be stored are shown. These figures indicate to the stock record clerk quantities that should not be exceeded and below which stocks should not drop. When either condition develops, the clerk will inform the purchasing department — or in some companies the production planning department. Coordination of materials records with purchasing department data acts as a check on both overstocking materials and the danger of a possible shortage.

Data for Cash Budget. The completed direct materials budget broken down by types and quantities is priced to arrive at the dollar value of materials needed for the year. Funds needed for monthly purchases are included in the cash budget (see Chapter 17). An increase or decrease in expenditures for materials must be known to the treasurer so that necessary funds will be available at the proper time.

Direct Labor Budget. The labor budget must tie in with the general program laid out by the production planning department. It is generally preferable to prepare a separate direct labor budget and to include indirect labor in the factory overhead budget. Direct labor is based on specifications drawn up by product engineers. Indirect labor is included in the factory overhead budget and consists of those employees who work in producing departments as helpers as well as the large contingent of indirect workers engaged in maintenance work, in hauling, or of those who work as crane operators, materials clerks, receiving clerks, and so forth.

The labor budget for direct and indirect labor guides the personnel department in determining the number and types of workers needed. If the labor force has been with the firm for several years and if the production schedule does not call for additional workers, the task of the personnel department is rather easy. It is the increase or decrease of the labor force that requires the personnel department to make plans in advance to assure availability of workers. Frequently the personnel department must provide a training program which must be so timed that the production department can rely on receiving workers at the proper time. When workers are to be laid off, the personnel department must prepare a list of the workers affected, giving due recognition to skill and seniority rights. In many companies this schedule is prepared in collaboration with union representatives to protect employees from any injustice or hardship.

The hours or the number of men must be translated into dollar values. Established labor rates as agreed upon in union contracts are generally used. Should conditions indicate that labor rates might change, the new rates should be used so that the financial budget reflects the most recent figures available.

Factory Overhead Budget. The factory overhead budget is prepared on the basis of the chart of accounts, which properly classifies expense accounts and details the various cost centers. As discussed previously, expenses can be grouped in several ways:

1. Natural expense classification, such as indirect materials and supplies, indirect labor, freight, light, power, etc.

2. Departmental or functional classification, which divides or determines the expense in terms of the department or cost center that incurred or originated the expense

3. Division of expenses according to variability, i.e., variable and fixed

The natural expense classification alone is not too useful for budget purposes. Expenses are usually incurred by various departments. It is by dealing with individual departments that the value and importance of budgetary control for expenses becomes significant. The departmental expense classification falls into two main categories: producing departments and service departments.

Preparation of any expense budget should be guided by the underlying principle that every expense is chargeable to a department supervised by an executive, department head, or foreman who should be held accountable and responsible for expenses incurred.   Those expenses for which the department supervisor can be held directly responsible should be included and clearly identified in his budget.   If additional expenses for which he has little or no direct responsibility are allocated to his department, these expenses should be separately identified.

The department supervisor should be asked to submit an estimate of his departmental expenses based on the projected activity of his department for the budget period.   Past costs are tempered by estimates about the future.   These estimates are reviewed in the light of other budgets, and all estimates are coordinated.   Any revision is submitted to the department supervisor for review before incorporation in the overall budget. This procedure is of great value psychologically.   If the individual department supervisor responsible for expenses incurred feels that the budget figures are his estimates, he will cooperate more willingly in executing the budget.

The factory overhead budget of a department is generally prepared as a report which enables executive management and individual department supervisors to make monthly comparisons of budgeted and actual expenses.   The report illustrated below presents end-of-month analysis.

MOLDING DEPARTMENT
FACTORY OVERHEAD BUDGET
FOR JULY, 19—

	Budgeted	Actual	Over	Under
Indirect labor............	$ 930	$ 900		$ 30
Oil.....................	10	10		
Fuel....................	30	35	$ 5	
Tools...................	50	25		25
Heat....................	50	20		30
Power and light.........	180	180		
Repairs to machinery.....	100	50		50
Supervisor..............	900	900		
Depreciation............	100	100		
Spoiled work............	50	20		30
	$2,400	$2,240	$ 5	$165

The Budgeted column indicates expenses allowed for the month of July.   The Actual column shows amounts actually spent during the month. The last two columns indicate amounts by which actual expenses are above or below budgeted figures.

The factory overhead budget illustrated is for the month of July.   It represents a subdivision of the annual budget.   This type of monthly or seasonal budget is highly valuable if expenses are to be analyzed for a period shorter than twelve months. Each item of expense, such as heat, light, repairs, or power, must be considered on a volume-of-activity basis to make the monthly budget as nearly accurate as possible. Such a comparision is accomplished through the use of flexible budgeting (Chapter 18).

Budget of the Maintenance Department. Among the expenses commonly included in a departmental overhead budget is the item "Repairs to machinery," which is based on the budget of the maintenance department — a service department (see Chapter 11). The cost of repairs and maintenance is an important item in most companies. Because of the nature of repairs and maintenance work, control of these costs is quite frustrating. Disturbing factors are the irregularity of repair jobs, their unpredictability, the impossibility of measuring their cost in advance, and the difficulty of determining their causes. Economical use of plant and equipment is the joint responsibility of production and maintenance personnel, such as the department supervisor who uses the equipment and the maintenance force who repair and keep it in good condition.

BUDGETING COMMERCIAL EXPENSES

The company's chart of accounts is also the basis for cost ascertainment and budgetary control of commercial expenses which include both marketing (often referred to as selling or distribution expenses) and administrative expenses. These expenses may be classified by primary accounts and by functions. Classification by primary accounts stresses the nature or the type of expenditure, such as salaries, commissions, repairs, light and heat, rent, telephone and telegraph, postage, advertising, travel expenses, sales promotion, entertainment, delivery expenses, freight-out, insurance, donations, depreciation, taxes, and interest. Classification by function emphasizes departmental activities, such as selling, advertising, warehousing, billing, credit and collection, transportation, accounting, purchasing, engineering, and financing, and is consistent with the concept of responsibility accounting.

Budgeting and Analyzing Commercial Expenses by Primary Accounts.
Budgeting and analyzing commercial expenses by primary accounts is the simplest method of classification. Expenses are recorded on the books in primary expense accounts and appear in the income statement in this manner:

COMMERCIAL EXPENSES:

Marketing expenses:

Advertising..........................	$ 4,200	
Sales salaries........................	16,760	
Store supplies.......................	3,740	
Depreciation — store equipment..........	5,400	
Depreciation — delivery equipment........	6,600	
Depreciation — building (store area)......	3,300	
Total marketing expenses		$40,000

Administrative expenses:

Office salaries.......................	$18,450	
Depreciation — building (office area)......	2,200	
Bad debts expense....................	1,590	
Insurance...........................	1,660	
Miscellaneous general expenses..........	6,100	
Total administrative expenses...........	30,000	
Total commercial expenses..............		$70,000

As expenses are incurred, they are coded according to the chart of accounts, posted to ledger accounts, and then taken directly to the income
statement. No further allocation is made or even attempted. At the end of
a period actual expenses are compared either with budgeted expenses or
with expenses of the previous month or year.

Budgeting and Analyzing Commercial Expenses by Functions. To control
commercial expenses, it is necessary to group them by functional activities
or operating units. Such a classification of commercial expenses, often
referred to as a departmental classification, can be compared to collecting
factory overhead by departments or cost centers. A departmental classification of commercial expenses adds to rather than replaces the process
of classifying expenses by primary accounts, because primary account
classifications are maintained within each department. When a departmental classification system is used, it is important that the classification
conforms to the company's organization chart.

Since organizational structures vary so much in different types of business organizations, it is impossible to suggest with exactness the division
that should exist for marketing and administrative expenses. In the first
place, departments known by the same name will perform widely different functions. Also, requests by management for cost information vary
from one company to the next depending upon the size and complexity of
the sales organization and the experience, ability, and training of the executive staff. However, departmentalization should be carried out so that
every item of expense is appropriately charged to a department.

Direct and indirect departmental expenses also exist as used in
factory cost procedures. Direct expenses are those charged directly to a

department, such as salaries, wages, supplies, travel expenses, and entertainment expenses. Indirect expenses are general or service department expenses that are prorated to benefiting departments. Expenses such as rent, insurance, and utilities, when shared by several departments, constitute this type of expense.

To identify an outlay of cash or the incurrence of a liability with a function requires considerably more work than is required by the primary account method. However, the chart of accounts will normally provide the initial breakdown of expenses. Usually the allocation of expenses to departments and the identification of the primary account classification within each department can be made at the time the voucher is prepared. This procedure requires coding the expenditure at the time it is requistioned for purchase. An increased expense caused by the use of this functional method is more than offset by the advantages of improved cost control.

Marketing Expenses Budget. A company's marketing activities can be divided into two broad categories:

1. *Obtaining the order* — involving the functions of selling, advertising, and market analysis
2. *Filling the order* — involving the functions of order assembly, packing, warehousing, shipping, transportation, billing, and credit and collection

The supervisors or department heads of functions connected with marketing activities prepare budget estimates for the coming year. Some estimates are based on individual judgment; others on the cost experienced in previous years, modified by expected sales volume. Expenses such as depreciation and insurance depend upon the policy established by management. With all departmental budgets completed, the total estimated marketing costs become part of the master budget. At the end of a month or other period, budgeted expenses of all marketing functions are compared with actual expenses to determine favorable or unfavorable trends, and to take steps to remedy them.

Administrative Expenses Budget. Estimating administrative expenses is often quite difficult. One difficulty deals with the problem of classifying certain expenses as either production or administrative expenses. Expenses such as purchasing, engineering, personnel, and research can be found in either category, or in some cases allocated between the two as well as to marketing costs. Management must decide how these expenses should be classified so that they may be budgeted and properly controlled. Another difficulty for expense items, such as donations, cafeteria, and patents, lies in determining the persons responsible for the incurrence and control of these costs. However, an attempt should be made to place every item of expense under the jurisdiction and control of some executive who estimates the administrative expenses for his section or division.

Administrative expenses include the same items as outlined previously. Additional expenses peculiar to the administrative activity are those often listed as corporate expenses; namely, directors' fees, franchise taxes, capital stock taxes, donations, as well as professional services by accountants, lawyers, and engineers. In order to make these expenses the responsibility of a department head, administrative functions may be divided as follows: company executive, treasurer, controller, general accounting, and general office. Each function will incur certain expenses common to all of them, such as salaries, depreciation of office equipment, telephone and telegraph, etc., while other expenses are peculiar to a particular department.

The above departmentalization lists the section "general office." The establishment of such a function is a recent development in office organization. The office manager is in charge and supervises all employees classified as filing clerks, mail clerks, librarians, stenographers, secretaries, receptionists, and switchboard operators. This permits better control and more intense utilization of manpower in clerical jobs where overlapping and overexpansion are common.

Expenses, such as donations to the Red Cross or United Fund, occur at definite times during the year and can be budgeted accordingly. Donations may be pledged and paid in equal installments throughout the year. Gifts to educational and charitable institutions should be budgeted over a period of three to five years to create effective and well-planned budgets.

DISCUSSION QUESTIONS

1. Profit planning includes a complete financial and operational plan for all phases and facets of the business. Discuss.

2. Differentiate between long-range profit planning and short-range budgeting.

3. Discuss the three different procedures that a company's management might follow to set profit objectives.

4. The classical economic model of competition assumes that the objective of the entrepreneur is to maximize profits. The fundamental elements of accounting theory are based on the objective of measuring the ownership interest and changes in the amount of the ownership interest (e.g., profits)

in the financial resources of the firm. How does this view relate to that of current organization theorists with respect to (a) the nature of organization objectives and (b) the establishment of such objectives?

(NAA adapted)

5. The development of a budgetary control program requires specific systems and procedures needed in carrying out management's functions of planning, organizing, and controlling. Enumerate these steps.

6. How is management's function of control executed through a budgetary control system?

7. State the fundamental axiom of fixed and variable costs to the product.

8. Commercial expenses are generally identified as marketing and administrative expenses. How are these expenses grouped for budgetary purposes?

EXERCISES

1. **Profit Planning.** Next year's budget of a company shows:

Cost of goods sold	$1,050,000
Administrative expenses	90,000
Sales	1,600,000
Financial expenses	31,000

The ratio of sales to invested capital is 2 to 1. A satisfactory profit for the enterprise would be 15% on invested capital.

Required: The amount available for marketing expenses, not included in the above estimates, if the required profit is to be attained.

2. **Forecast Cost of Goods Sold Statement.** Mendez, Inc. with $8,000,000 of par stock outstanding, plans to budget net earnings of 6%, before income taxes, on this stock.

The Marketing Department budgets sales at $12,000,000.

The budget director approves the sales budget and expenses as follows:

Marketing	15% of sales
Administrative	5% of sales
Financial	1% of sales

Labor is expected to be 50% of total manufacturing costs; raw materials for the budgeted production will cost $2,500,000; therefore, any savings on manufacturing costs will have to be in factory overhead.

Inventories are to be as follows:

	Beginning of Year	End of Year
Finished goods	$200,000	$500,000
Work in process	50,000	150,000
Raw materials	400,000	300,000

Required: The projected cost of goods sold statement, showing therein the budgeted purchases of materials and the adjustments for inventories of raw materials, work in process, and finished goods.

3. Quarterly Sales Budget by Districts; Inventory Schedule. Estimated sales for the first three-month period of the coming year of the Swartz Company are:

District	Jan.	Feb.	March	Total
	%	%	%	%
Maine................	50	30	20	100
New Hampshire........	55	30	15	100
Vermont..............	50	25	25	100
Massachusetts.........	50	25	25	100

Estimated unit sales by districts for the three months are:

District	Unit Sales
Maine..	20,000
New Hampshire...	30,000
Vermont...	10,000
Massachusetts...	40,000
Total...	100,000

The unit sales price is $2.

Company policy expects an inventory of 10,000 units at the beginning and the end of each three-month period. The production schedule is:

January..	55%
February...	30%
March..	15%

Required: (1) An estimate of sales by units and dollars for each of the first three months for each district and in total.

(2) A schedule of the end-of-month inventories by units. The beginning inventory is 10,000 units.

4. Sales Budget by District and Products. The Lambertson Wholesale Company completed a survey of its prospective sales during the year 19B based on 19A results. Summarized by product and by district, these estimates in units for the year are:

	Pennsylvania	New Jersey	Total
Product A................	990	594	1,584
Product B.	1,540	880	2,420
			4,004

It has been the experience of the company that the sales estimates have normally been 10% in excess of actual sales, disregarding other influencing factors.

After adjusting for salesmen's variations in estimating, it is necessary to adjust for normal growth of product. It is expected that sales of Product A will be 10% more than in 19A, and sales of Product B will be 5% less.

In the past, when general business was 20% under normal, the corporation's business was 30% under normal; when general business was above normal, the reverse was true. In 19B, business in general was expected to be 10% below normal according to reliable estimates.

The budget executive's estimate of sales after correction for normal growth but before considering business trends is 4,000 units.

Required: An estimated sales budget by district and by product.

5. Sales Budgets by Territories and Product Lines. Javierolon Electronics Corporation has two product lines, high-speed printers and electronic typewriters. The company's market research department prepared the following sales forecast for the coming year:

	High-Speed Printers	Electronic Typewriters
Industry's total sales forecast.................	25,000	75,000
Company's share of the market...............	20%	10%
Sales price per unit.........................	$1,800	$450

The sales force submitted these territorial sales estimates:

	High-Speed Printers	Electronic Typewriters
New England Area.........................	1,200	1,800
Middle Atlantic............................	3,000	4,200
Southern States...........................	1,800	2,000
Total....................................	6,000	8,000

To establish an acceptable forecast, the budget director averages the two estimates. The resulting forecast is then broken down by territories in the same ratio as reflected in the estimates of the sales force.

Required: A sales forecast showing unit sales and total sales revenue by sales territory and by product lines.

6. Production Budget. The Penscot Company's sales forecast for the next quarter, ending June 30, indicates the following:

Product	Expected Unit Sales
Ceno..	14,000
Nepo..	37,500
Teno..	54,300

Inventories at the beginning and desired quantities at the end of the quarter are as follows:

Product	Units	
	March 31	June 30
Ceno...	5,800	6,200
Nepo...	10,600	10,500
Teno...	13,000	12,200

Required: A production budget for the second quarter.

7. Production Budget. The Metamora Canning Company produces frozen and condensed soup products. Frozen soups come in three principal varieties: snapper, shrimp, and pea. The condensed soups come in two principal varieties: tomato and chicken noodle. The sales division prepared the following tentative sales budget for the first six months of the coming year:

Product	Number of Cans Budgeted for Sales
Frozen soups:	
Snapper.............................	250,000
Shrimp	150,000
Pea	350,000
Condensed soups:	
Tomato	1,000,000
Chicken noodle......................	750,000

The following inventory levels have been decided upon:

	Work in Process				Finished Goods	
	Beginning		Ending		Beginning	Ending
	Units	% Processed	Units	% Processed	Units	Units
Frozen soups:						
Snapper.......	5,000	80	4,000	75	15,000	20,000
Shrimp	3,000	70	3,000	75	8,000	5,000
Pea	4,000	75	5,000	80	20,000	20,000
Condensed soups:						
Tomato.......	25,000	80	40,000	75	75,000	60,000
Chicken noodle.	15,000	60	25,000	80	30,000	20,000

Required: A production budget for the six-month period.

8. Production, Inventory, and Purchase Requirements. The following estimates and information have been gathered as part of the budget preparation of the Hobbynook Co. The company manufactures a hobbyshop sales item, consisting of two types of material which the company precuts and preshapes for sale to hobbyists. The sales for the second and third quarter of the coming year have been estimated as follows:

	Second Quarter	Third Quarter
Philadelphia and suburban areas.......................	10,000 kits	35,000 kits
Western Pennsylvania................................	8,000 kits	25,000 kits
State of Maryland....................................	5,000 kits	20,000 kits
Total..	23,000 kits	80,000 kits

It is decided that finished kits inventories are to be: 25,000 at the end of the second quarter, and 5,000 at the end of the third quarter. The inventory at the start of the second quarter will consist of 8,000 finished kits.

Each kit is packaged in a colorful cardboard box and contains 2 units of Material A and 5 units of Material B.

The inventory of materials at the beginning of the second quarter will be:

Boxes...........	125,000
Material A......	15,000 units
Material B.......	45,000 units

There are sufficient boxes on hand for both quarters; none will be purchased during the two periods.

Material A can be bought whenever needed and in any quantity desired. The starting inventory of 15,000 units is considered to be an ideal quantity.

Material B must be purchased in quantities of 10,000, or multiples of 10,000. It is desired that, at the end of both the second and third quarters, a minimum quantity of 30,000 units be on hand, or as close thereto as the standard purchase quantity will permit.

Required: (1) Schedule of ending inventories and budgeted production of kits for each quarter.

(2) Schedule of production requirements and purchase requirements for each quarter for each of the three types of materials.

9. Labor Cost Budget. The Satzger Manufacturing Company produces numerous related small parts. The Cost Department has always prepared a labor budget in dollars only since no information regarding the number of parts manufactured is available. During the past year direct labor costs by quarters were reported as follows:

Quarters	Machining Department	%	Finishing Department	%	Total
First...............	$15,813	21%	$ 4,416	23%	$20,229
Second.............	18,072	24	4,608	24	22,680
Third..............	20,331	27	4,992	26	25,323
Fourth.............	21,084	28	5,184	27	26,268
Total..........	$75,300	100%	$19,200	100%	$94,500

The ratios of direct labor to total manufacturing costs during the past year averaged:

Machining Department... 23.75%
Finishing Department.. 20.00%

These ratios are expected to remain the same for the coming year. Manufacturing costs excluding direct labor costs have been budgeted for the coming year with $244,000 for the Machining Department and $86,000 for the Finishing Department. The percentage distribution of labor requirements for each quarter will be the same for the coming year.

Required: The direct labor cost requirements for each quarter of the coming budget period.

10. Manufacturing Budget; Overhead Rate. The initial survey of the budget committee of Techni-Toy, Inc. indicates a sales forecast of 95,000 plastic dolls. Management also plans to produce 5,000 dolls for stock. The purchasing agent indicates that economic lot purchases of 3,500 kilograms of plastic @ $.60 per kg. and 2,000 liters of paint @ $3 per liter are required to produce the 100,000 units.

Budgeted factory overhead expenses for this production schedule amount to:

Fixed factory overhead:

Depreciation — buildings........................ $ 500
Depreciation — equipment....................... 800
Supervision.................................... 3,200
Insurance...................................... 220

Variable factory overhead:

Indirect labor................................. $ .250 per direct labor hour
Indirect supplies.............................. .004 per unit
General factory................................ .050 per direct labor hour

Labor hours and rates for the two operations are:

Plastic Molder........2,000 hours @ $3.20 per hour
Painter.............1,200 hours @   3.00 per hour

Required: (1) A manufacturing budget.
(2) The factory overhead rate based on direct labor hours.

11. Budgeted Cost of Goods Sold and Merchandise Purchases. The Zel Company, a wholesaler, budgeted these sales for June, July, and August of 19—:

	June, 19--	July, 19--	August, 19--
Sales on account..........	$1,500,000	$1,600,000	$1,700,000
Cash sales................	200,000	210,000	220,000
Total sales.............	$1,700,000	$1,810,000	$1,920,000

All merchandise is marked up to sell at its invoice cost plus 25%. Merchandise inventories at the beginning of each month are at 30% of that month's projected cost of goods sold.

Required: (1) The cost of goods sold for June, 19—.
(2) Merchandise purchases for July, 19—.

(AICPA adapted)

12. Critique of Performance Report. The Kristina Company uses a fixed or forecast budget to measure its performance against the objectives set by the forecast and to help in controlling costs. At the end of a month, management received the report below which compares actual performance with budgeted figures:

Items of Cost	Actual	Budget
Units produced.....................................	73,500	75,000
Direct materials....................................	$37,020	$39,000
Direct labor..	5,950	6,000
Factory supplies....................................	1,550	1,500
Indirect labor......................................	710	726
Repairs and maintenance...........................	2,300	2,250
Insurance and taxes................................	350	355
Rent...	2,000	2,000
Depreciation.......................................	2,200	2,200
Total..	$52,080	$54,031

Required: Conclusions to be drawn from this report indicating weaknesses, if any, of this type of budget.

PROBLEMS

16-1. Sales, Materials, Labor, and Inventory Budgets. A budget department gathered the following data concerning future sales and budget requirements:

Anticipated Sales for 19--			Expected Inventories January 1, 19--	Desired Inventories December 31, 19--
Product	Units	Price		
A	20,000	$55	8,000 units	10,000 units
B	50,000	50	15,000 units	15,000 units
C	30,000	80	6,000 units	6,000 units

Materials used in manufacture:

		Amount Used per Unit of Product		
Stock No.	Unit	A	B	C
110	Each	3		5
50	Each	2	1	3
41	Kilograms		2	
30	Kilograms		3	
40	Meters	5		4

Anticipated Purchase Price for Raw Materials		Expected Inventories January 1, 19––	Desired Inventories December 31, 19––
110	$3.00 each	21,000 each	25,000 each
50	2.00 each	17,000 each	23,000 each
41	2.50 per kilogram	10,000 kilograms	15,000 kilograms
30	4.00 per kilogram	18,000 kilograms	18,000 kilograms
40	3.25 per meter	25,000 meters	30,000 meters

Labor requirements and rates (direct labor):

Product	Hours per Unit	Rate Per Hour
A.................	4	$4.00
B.................	5	3.00
C.................	5	4.20

Overhead is applied at the rate of $2 per direct labor hour.

Required: (1) Sales budget (in dollars).

(2) Production budget (in quantities).

(3) Direct materials budget (in quantities).

(4) Direct materials purchase budget (in dollars).

(5) Direct labor budget (in dollars).

(6) Finished goods inventory, December 31, 19–– (in dollars).

16-2. Materials Purchases, Production, and Inventory Budgets. The purchasing agent and the cost accountant of Animations, Inc. are trying to solve the problem of scheduling purchases in connection with a planned expansion in the production of rocking horses. All lumber used is procured in a standard size, of which the following amounts, which include a due allowance for waste, are used in one complete rocking horse:

Oak　　—　　2 board feet
Pine　　—　　5 board feet
Maple　—　10 board feet

A sales budget has been approved, and the following production schedule has been drawn up for 19A:

Quarter	Rocking Horses
1st	75
2d	150
3d	175
4th	200

The production schedule for the first quarter of 19B calls for approximately 220 rocking horses.

Delivery of lumber is slow and uncertain; but by ordering early, delivery can be assured during the quarter desired. Lumber must be purchased in quantities that are multiples of 300 board feet of each kind of lumber; but since there is a very good discount for purchases of 1,500 board feet lots for all kinds of lumber combined, such purchases are made whenever possible. Otherwise, the minimum requirements are always purchased. In determining minimum requirements, it is necessary to have on hand at the beginning of a quarter sufficient materials to take care of production for that quarter.

Purchases of 1,500 board feet lots are restricted because of limited storage facilities. At the present time there is sufficient space to store 3,000 board feet of all types of lumber combined. During the early part of the year it is anticipated that a new shed will be constructed to store an additional 1,200 board feet. It is expected that the total storage space of 4,200 board feet will be available prior to the end of the second quarter.

Inventory of lumber on January 1, 19A is as follows:

> Oak   — 150 board feet
> Pine — 600 board feet
> Maple — 900 board feet

Required: Schedule, or schedules, indicating the materials production requirements, materials purchases, and materials inventories for each type of lumber, by quarter, expressed in board feet.

16-3. Materials Requirements and Purchases Budget. The Budget Department of the Mifer-Jifson Manufacturing Company prepares an annual production and materials requirement budget in which the first quarter of the year is on a monthly basis and the balance of the year in totals by quarters. In the third month of a quarter, detailed budgets are again prepared for the next quarter.

The company produces two products, Miff and Jiff, which require three raw materials, XLO, YO, and ZMO, in the following quantities (kilograms):

	Materials Requirement and Costs		
Product	*XLO*	*YO*	*ZMO*
Miff............	1 kg.	2½ kg.	1½ kg.
Cost.....	$1.50 per kg	$1 per kg.	$2 per kg.
Jiff............	1 kg.	2 kg.	½ kg.

Production schedule:

	First Quarter			*Remaining Three Quarters*		
Product	*January*	*February*	*March*	*2d*	*3d*	*4th*
Miff......	3,000	3,500	3,800	10,000	11,000	12,000
Jiff.......	5,000	5,500	6,000	17,000	18,000	18,000

At the beginning of the budget year, raw materials inventories are expected to have reached the following levels: XLO — 6,000 kg.; YO — 14,000 kg.; ZMO — 8,000 kg. The ending raw materials inventories should be about 10% higher than the consumption of the last month of the year. For budget purposes the last month's production is considered to be one third of that of the quarter's.

Required: (1) A materials requirement budget showing: type and quantity of raw materials required per product, units (kilograms) of raw materials required, and a summary of the materials required per product.

(2) A purchases budget (on an annual basis — not broken down into the first three months and the remaining three quarters) showing: quantity required for production, ending inventories, beginning inventories, purchases, and cost of purchases.

16-4. Sales Forecasts; Purchases and Materials Requirements. The management of Soyar Food Products, Inc. decided to install a budgetary control system under the supervision of a budget director and her committee. The company manufactures, together with many other food articles, a patented breakfast food that is sold in packages of two sizes — 1 lb. and 2 lb. The cereal is made from two types of grain, called R (rye) and S (soy) for this purpose. There are two operations: (a) processing and blending and (b) packaging. The grains are purchased by the bushel measure, a bushel of R containing 70 lbs. and a bushel of S containing 80 lbs. Three bushels of grain mixed in the proportion of 2R:1S produce 198 lbs. of finished product; the entire loss occurs in the first department.

To prepare estimated sales figures for the first six months of the coming year, the budget committee first asked the salesmen to prepare sales estimates on which the committee might base its own next six-month sales forecast. The salesmen's budget in condensed form showed:

Salesmen's Estimates of Sales in Units

	I	*II*	*III*	*Other*	*6 Months' Total*
			TERRITORIES		
1-lb. package.....	10,000	15,000	12,000	613,000	650,000
2-lb. package.....	12,000	18,000	12,000	783,000	825,000
Total..........	22,000	33,000	24,000	1,396,000	1,475,000

The figures submitted by the salesmen are analyzed by the budget committee in the light of general business conditions. The company uses the Federal Reserve Board Index together with its own trade index to prepare a trend percentage that exists in the business. The trend percentage indicates that a .91 general index figure should be applied to the salesmen's estimates in order to arrive at the final sales figures. The monthly sales figure is to be set up as one sixth of the total figure finally computed. The finished goods inventory is to be kept at zero if possible; the work in process inventory near the present level, which is about 160,000 lbs. of blended material.

Factory facilities permit processing sales requirements as stated in the sales budget. The production manager decided to accept the monthly sales figures for his production budget.

Purchases of grains in bushels have been arranged for delivery as follows:

	Type R		*Type S*	
	Quantity (bu.)	*Price*	*Quantity (bu.)*	*Price*
January................	5,000	$1.30	2,000	$1.20
February...............	2,000	1.40	1,000	1.20
March.................	—0—	—0—	3,000	1.25
April..................	8,000	1.50	3,000	1.00
May...................	3,000	1.50	—0—	—0—
June..................	4,000	1.60	4,000	1.00
Beginning Inventory, January 1.............	10,000	1.20	3,000	1.00

Raw materials are charged into production on the fifo basis.

Required: (1) A revised sales forecast based on the index.
(2) A sales forecast on a dollar basis; the 1-lb. package sells for $.25 and the 2-lb. package for $.50.
(3) A schedule of raw materials purchases.
(4) A computation of raw materials requirements for production.
(5) A schedule of the raw materials account (fifo basis), indicating beginning inventory, purchases, usage, and ending inventory for the six-month period taken as a whole.

CHAPTER **17**

BUDGETING EXPENDITURES AND CASH, FORECAST STATEMENTS, BUDGETING FOR NONMANUFACTURING BUSINESSES AND NONPROFIT ORGANIZATIONS, PERT/COST, HUMAN BEHAVIOR

This second budget chapter discusses specific budgets such as capital expenditures and research and development costs which play a most significant and fundamental part in the long- and short-range plans of any management. Closely related thereto is the cash budget that reveals excesses and/or shortages of funds. The forecast annual statements serve as a master budget and final check on the ultimate results expected from the combined sales-cost-profit plan. Financial forecasts for external users, budgeting for nonmanufacturing businesses and nonprofit organizations, zero-base budgeting, the modern planning and control systems (PERT and PERT/Cost), probabilistic budgets, and a discussion of human behavior in budget building conclude the presentation.

CAPITAL EXPENDITURES BUDGET

Capital expenditures include long-term commitments of resources to realize future benefits. Budgeting capital expenditures is one of the most important areas of managerial decision. The magnitude of funds involved and the length of time required to recover the investment call for penetrating analysis and capable judgment. Decisions regarding current manufacturing operations can always be changed if a change is considered the best course of action. Capital expenditures, however, represent long-term commitments. Because the benefits of a capital expenditure will be reaped over a fairly extended length of time, managerial errors could become quite costly for many years.

In order to minimize the number of capital expenditure errors, management of many firms has established definite procedures and methods for evaluating the merits of a project before funds are released (see Chapter 26). Funds available for capital expenditures are normally limited. Management must gear any facility improvements and plant expansion programs to funds supplied by internal operations and external sources.

True control of capital expenditures is exercised in advance by requiring that each request be based on evaluation analyses. Managerial control requires facts regarding engineering estimates, expected sales volumes, production costs, and marketing costs. Management usually has a firm conviction as to what is consistent with long-range objectives of the business. It is fundamentally interested in making certain that the project will contribute to the earnings position of the company.

Short- and Long-Range Capital Expenditures. Capital expenditure programs involve both short- and long-range projects. Provisions must be made in the current budget for short-range capital expenditures. These short-range projects must be examined in the light of their economic worth as compared with other projects seeking final approval. The process of budgeting provides the only opportunity to examine projects side by side and to evaluate the contribution of each to future periods.

Long-range projects which will not be implemented in the current budget period need only be stated in general terms, for the exchange and addition of capital assets are only significant in the current budget period. In the main, long-range capital expenditure plans remain as a management responsibility and are translated into budget commitments only as the opportune time for their implementation approaches. Timing is most important to the achievement of the most profitable results in planning and budgeting capital expenditures.

RESEARCH AND DEVELOPMENT BUDGET

The *research and development budget* involves identifying program components and estimating their costs. In recent years the management of many firms has been acutely aware of the increased necessity for and rapid growth of research and development activities. Management must consider the cost of research and development activities from both the long- and short-range points of view. From the long-range viewpoint, management must assure itself that the program is in line with future market trends and demands and that the future cost of the program is not at odds with forecasted economic and financial conditions. From the short-range viewpoint, management must be assured that experimental efforts are being expended on programs which promise a satisfactory margin of return on the dollars invested.

The research and development staff must present its ideas to management along with the data needed for making decisions. The controller's staff will assist in the preparation of budgets with clearly defined goals and properly evaluated cost data.[1]

Research and Development — Defined.   Research and development projects compete with other projects for available financial resources. The value of the research and development program must be shown as clearly as possible so that management can compare it with similar programs and with other investment opportunities. Therefore, the motivation and intent of the experimental activities must be carefully identified.

Definitions of these activities aid in their delineation for planning and control.

1. *Research* is planned search or critical investigation aimed at discovery of new knowledge with the hope that such knowledge will be useful in developing a new product or service (hereinafter "product") or a new process or technique (hereinafter "process") or in bringing about a significant improvement to an existing product or process.

2. *Development* is the translation of research findings or other knowledge into a plan or design for a new product or process or for a significant improvement to an existing product or process whether intended for sale or use. It includes the conceptual formulation, design, and testing of product alternatives, construction of prototypes, and operation of pilot plants. It does not include routine or periodic alterations to existing products, production lines, manufacturing processes, and other on-going operations even though those alterations may represent improvements and it does not include market research or market testing activities.[2]

The Research and Development Budget as a Planning Device. The budget is still the most useful tool for planning research and development programs. Other planning devices are used at times, but the budget is considered best for (1) balancing the research and development program, (2) coordinating the program with the company's other plans and projects, and (3)

---

[1]For a comprehensive treatment of the research and development subject, examine:

Raymond Villers, *Research and Development: Planning and Control*, a research study and report prepared for the Financial Executives Research Foundation (New York, 1964).

Robert E. Seiler, *Improving the Effectiveness of Research and Development* (New York: McGraw-Hill, Inc., 1965).

[2]Statement of Financial Accounting Standards No. 2, "Accounting for Research and Development Costs," Financial Accounting Standards Board (Stamford, Connecticut: 1974), pp. 2–3.

checking certain phases of nonfinancial planning. The budget forces management to think in advance about planned expenditures, both in total amounts
and in each sphere of effort. It helps achieve coordination, for it presents
an overall picture of proposed research and development activities which
can be reviewed and criticized by other operating managers. Exchange of
opinions and information at planning meetings constitutes management's
best control over the program.

Another important purpose of research and development budgeting is
to coordinate these plans with the immediate and long-term financial plans
of the company. Finally, the budget forces the research and development
director and his staff to think in advance about major aspects of the
program: personnel requirements must be examined, individual or group
work loads assessed, equipment requirements studied, special materials
procured, and necessary facilities provided. These phases of the research and development program are often overlooked or duplicated.

**Methods and Forms of a Research and Development Budget and/or
Project Requests.** Management expects the executive in charge of research
and development to submit a complete and detailed budget which can be
evaluated as part of the entire planning program. Submission of data
takes many forms. Information regarding segmentation and allocation of
time and effort to various phases of the program is of particular interest to
executive management, as well as to divisional managers. The following
research and development balance sheet has been proposed:[3]

RESEARCH AND DEVELOPMENT BALANCE SHEET
PROGRAM PLANNED FOR 19—

(Percentages of Total Effort by Area of Inquiry and by Phase)

Phase	Cost Reduction			Improved Products			New Products			Total
	A*	B	C	A	B	C	A	B	C	
Applied research.	4%	3%	3%	2%	4%	4%	1%	1%	3%	25%
Development....	5%	12%	3%	4%	1%		2%		3%	30%
Basic research...	7%	6%	2%	5%			10%		15%	45%
Total by product lines.........	16%	21%	8%	11%	5%	4%	13%	1%	21%	100%
Total by area of inquiry.......		45%			20%			35%		

*A, B, and C refer to product lines.

[3] J. B. Quinn, "Study of the Usefulness of Research and Development Budgets," *NAA Bulletin*, Vol. XL, No. 1, pp. 79–90.

The overall research and development program is supported by a specific budget request which indicates the jobs or steps within each project, the necessary man hours, the service department time required, and required direct departmental funds. Each active project is reviewed monthly, comparing projected plans with results attained.

Accounting for Research and Development Costs. Accounting treatment of research and development costs generally requires expensing in the period incurred because of the uncertainty of the extent or length of future benefit to the company. Exception to the expensing requirement applies to costs of research and development expenditures that are (1) conducted for others, (2) unique to extractive industries, or (3) incurred by a government-regulated enterprise such as a public utility which often defers research and development costs because of the rate-regulated aspects of its business. Equipment and purchased intangibles having *alternative future uses* should be recorded as assets and expensed through depreciation or amortization. Research and development costs, when expensed, should be reported as one item in the operating expenses part of the income statement.[4]

CASH BUDGET

A *cash budget* involves detailed estimates of anticipated cash receipts and disbursements for the budget period or some other specific period. It has generally been recognized not only as an extremely useful but also absolutely essential management tool. Planning cash requirements is basic to good business management. Even if a company does not prepare extensive budgets for sales and production, it should set up a budget or estimate of cash receipts and disbursements.

Purpose and Nature of a Cash Budget. More specifically, a cash budget:

1. Indicates the effect on the cash position of seasonal requirements, large inventories, unusual receipts, and slowness in collecting receivables.
2. Indicates the cash requirements needed for a plant or equipment expansion program.
3. Points up the need for additional funds from sources such as bank loans or sales of securities and the time factors involved. In this connection it might also exert a cautionary influence on plans for plant expansion leading to a modification of capital expenditures decisions.
4. Indicates the availability of cash for taking advantage of discounts.
5. Assists in planning the financial requirements of bond retirements, income tax installments, and payments to pension and retirement funds.
6. Shows the availability of excess funds for short-term or long-term investments.

---

[4]Statement of Financial Accounting Standards No. 2, *op. cit.*, pp. 1–2, 6.

The period of time covered by a cash budget varies with the type of business and its cash position. Generally, a cash budget should be prepared by months for a year with changes made at the end of each month in order to (1) incorporate deviations from the previous forecast and (2) add a month to replace the month just passed so that a *rolling* cash budget covering the next twelve months is always available. As the coming month or week moves closer, weekly or even daily cash receipts and disbursements schedules are considered necessary for prudent and efficient cash management.

A cash budget includes no accrual items. For instance, payroll may be accrued at the beginning and end of each month. If at the beginning and end of a month accrued payroll amounts to $4,800 and $3,300 respectively, and the budget shows that $18,000 in wages and salaries will be earned by employees, the treasurer computes the monthly cash requirement for the payroll as follows:

Accrued payroll at beginning of month...........................	$ 4,800
Add payroll earned as per budget...............................	18,000
	$22,800
Deduct accrued payroll at end of month.........................	3,300
Amount of cash to be paid out..................................	$19,500

Additional adjustments are necessary for deductions from employees' earnings when these deductions are not remitted in the month withheld.

Preparation of a Cash Budget. Preparation of a cash budget may follow either of two generally accepted procedures:

1. The cash receipts and disbursements method
2. The adjusted profit and loss or income method

In the first method, all anticipated cash receipts, such as cash sales, cash collections on accounts receivable, dividends, interest on notes and bonds, proceeds from sales of assets, royalties, bank loans, stock sales, etc., are carefully estimated. Likewise, cash requirements for materials purchases, supplies, payroll, repayment of loans, dividends, taxes, purchases of plant or equipment, etc., must be determined.

Data required to prepare a cash budget by the receipts and disbursements method come from the:

1. Sales budget.
2. Materials budget, which shows planned purchases.
3. Labor budget, which indicates wages earned.
4. Various types of expense budgets, both manufacturing and commercial, which indicate expenses expected to be incurred. Noncash expenses such as depreciation are excluded.

5. Plant and equipment budget, which details cash needed for the purchase of new equipment or replacements.

6. Treasurer's or executive's budget, which indicates requirements for dividends, loans, donations, income taxes, etc.

These data sources are used in estimating cash receipts and disbursements for each budgeted time period segment.

The primary sources of cash receipts are cash sales and collections of accounts receivable. Estimates of collections of accounts receivable are based on the sales budget and on the company's collection experience. A study is made of a representative period to determine how customers pay their accounts, how many take the discount offered, and how many pay within 10 days, 30 days, and so forth. These experiences are set up in a schedule of anticipated collections from sales. Collections during a month will be the result of: (1) this month's sales, and (2) accounts receivable of prior months' sales. To illustrate, assume that during each month collections on accounts receivable showed the following pattern:

From this month's sales.....................................	10.8%
From prior months' accounts receivable:	
Last month's sales..	78.2
2 months old...	6.3
3 months old...	2.1
4 months old...	1.2
Cash discounts taken.......................................	1.2
Doubtful accounts...	.2
	100.0%

On the basis of these percentages, collections for the month of July are computed as follows:

Month	Credit Sales	%	Collections
July..............	$160,000	10.8	$ 17,280
June..............	200,000	78.2	156,400
May..............	175,000	6.3	11,025
April.............	180,000	2.1	3,780
March............	178,000	1.2	2,136
Total collections for July.............			$190,621

Seasonal variations should also be considered if they affect the collections pattern.

Estimated cash disbursements are computed from the materials budget, the labor budget, various expense budgets for manufacturing and commercial costs, the equipment budget, and the treasurer's budget for items such as dividends, interest and payments on bonds and loans, donations, or taxes as they relate to the timing of payments.

In the second method of preparing the cash budget — the adjusted profit and loss or income method — cash estimates come from the forecasted profit of the period adjusted for noncash transactions and for expected cash-oriented changes in asset and liability accounts not affected by profit calculations. Using the forecasted profit for the month or fiscal period as a starting point, various noncash transactions are added back to net profit for the period. Noncash items are depreciation, doubtful accounts receivable, expired insurance premiums, accruals for warranties or guarantees, and income tax accruals. The next step is to add anticipated decreases in assets or increases in liabilities and to deduct anticipated increases in assets or decreases in liabilities. The expected cash position at the end of a period is the cash balance at the beginning of the period plus or minus the net cash increase or decrease as indicated by the analysis of the forecast profit. This method is not as effective a planning and control technique as is the cash receipts and disbursements method because it is usually in terms of aggregate cash flows rather than in terms of detailed cash receipt and disbursement components.

A cash budget is generally quite accurate when it covers a short period of one or two months, but it requires constant attention. Most firms recheck their cash budget at the end of each day, week, or month to make allowances for new conditions.

PROJECTED OR FORECAST INCOME STATEMENT

A *projected income statement* (see page 507) contains summaries of the sales, manufacturing, and expense budgets. Its purpose is to project net income, the goal toward which all efforts are directed. No new estimates are actually made; figures taken from various budgets are merely arranged in the form of an income statement. The sales budget gives expected sales revenue; the manufacturing budget furnishes manufacturing costs and cost of goods sold which, when deducted from sales, give the estimated gross profit. Estimates from the marketing and administrative expense budgets are subtracted from estimated gross profit to arrive at the net operating income. Other income and expense items are either added or deducted to determine net income before taxes. Finally, the provision for income taxes is deducted to determine net income after taxes. Preparation of a forecast income statement offers management the opportunity to judge the accuracy of the budget work and investigate causes for variances.

PROJECTED INCOME STATEMENT

BY MONTHS FOR YEAR ENDING DECEMBER, 19—

	January	February	December	Totals
Sales........................	$ 480,000	$ 540,000	$420,000	$ 7,200,000
Cost of goods sold:				
Raw materials used..........	$ 180,000	$ 180,000	$200,000	$ 2,400,000
Direct labor................	90,000	90,000	100,000	1,200,000
Factory overhead:				
Fixed....................	49,500	49,500	49,500	594,000
Variable.................	54,000	54,000	60,000	720,000
Cost of goods manufactured..	$ 373,500	$ 373,500	$409,500	$ 4,914,000
Add beginning finished goods inventory (fifo)..........	630,000	667,500	491,400	630,000
	$1,003,500	$1,041,000	$900,900	$ 5,544,000
Less ending finished goods inventory	667,500	664,000	614,250	614,250
Cost of goods sold..........	$ 336,000	$ 377,000	$286,650	$ 4,929,750
Gross profit..................	$ 144,000	$ 163,000	$133,350	$ 2,270,250
Commercial expenses:				
Marketing expenses:				
Fixed	$ 25,000	$ 25,000	$ 25,000	$ 300,000
Variable.................	12,000	13,500	10,500	180,000
Administrative expenses:				
Fixed....................	20,000	20,000	20,000	240,000
Variable.................	8,000	9,000	7,000	120,000
Total commercial expenses...	$ 65,000	$ 67,500	$ 62,500	$ 840,000
Net income from operations....	$ 79,000	$ 95,500	$ 70,850	$ 1,430,250
Other expenses:				
Bad debts expense..........	$ 4,800	$ 5,400	$ 4,200	$ 72,000
Interest on notes payable.....	500	500	500	6,000
Sales discount..............	9,600	10,800	8,400	144,000
Total....................	$ 14,900	$ 16,700	$ 13,100	$ 222,000
Other income:				
Interest income.............	– –	– –	1,250	7,500
Purchases discount..........	3,600	3,600	4,000	48,000
Other expenses (net).......	$ 11,300	$ 13,100	$ 7,850	$ 166,500
Net income before taxes........	$ 67,700	$ 82,400	$ 63,000	$ 1,263,750
Less provision for income taxes (50%)....................	33,850	41,200	31,500	631,875
Net income after taxes.........	$ 33,850	$ 41,200	$ 31,500	$ 631,875

PROJECTED OR FORECAST BALANCE SHEET

A *projected balance sheet* (see page 508) estimated for the beginning of the budget period is the starting point for the preparation of a forecast balance sheet for the end of the budget period. It incorporates all changes in assets, liabilities, and capital predicted in the budgets submitted by the various departments.

PROJECTED BALANCE SHEET

BY MONTHS FOR YEAR ENDING DECEMBER, 19—

ASSETS	January 1	January 31	February 28	December 31
Cash......................	$ 400,000	$ 173,000	$ 99,300	$ 245,675
Accounts receivable.........	250,000	153,400	180,100	149,500
Less allowance for doubtful accounts...............	(2,500)	(1,300)	(700)	(2,500)
Inventories:				
Raw materials............	320,000	320,000	320,000	320,000
Finished goods...........	630,000	667,500	664,000	614,250
Plant and equipment........	3,000,000	3,000,000	3,000,000	3,000,000
Less accum. depreciation..	(600,000)	(616,850)	(633,950)	(815,400)
Other assets................	202,500	200,650	198,550	167,100
U. S. Government bonds.....				500,000
Interest receivable...........				7,500
Total assets..............	$4,200,000	$3,896,400	$3,827,300	$4,186,125
LIABILITIES AND CAPITAL				
Current liabilities...........	$ 770,000	$ 231,000	$ 77,000	
Accounts payable (purchases).		32,400	32,400	$ 36,000
Accounts payable (factory overhead and marketing and administrative expenses)....		134,800	136,800	137,600
Interest payable.............		500	1,000	
Income taxes payable........		33,850	75,050	118,650
Long-term debt.............	120,000	120,000	120,000	
Capital stock...............	960,000	960,000	960,000	960,000
Retained earnings and surplus reserves.................	2,350,000	2,383,850	2,425,050	2,933,875
Total liabilities and capital..	$4,200,000	$3,896,400	$3,827,300	$4,186,125

Numerous advantages result from the preparation of a forecast balance sheet. One advantage is that a forecast balance sheet discloses unfavorable ratios which management may wish to change for various reasons. Unfavorable ratios can lower credit ratings or cause a drop in the value of the corporation's securities. A second advantage of a projected balance sheet is that it serves as a check on the accuracy of all other budgets. Still another advantage is that the projected balance sheet makes possible the computation of a return-on-investment ratio by relating net income to capital employed. An inadequate return on investment would suggest a need for budget changes.

FINANCIAL FORECASTS FOR EXTERNAL USERS

The extensive use of budgets in the internal management of organizations is well recognized. Recent years have seen increasing recognition of the importance of financial forecasts for external users as well, because investors and potential investors seek to enhance the process of predicting the future.

What has happened in the past, as reported in the financial statements, may be looked to as an indicator of the future. Often, however, past results may not be indicative of future expectations and may need to be tempered accordingly.

The question of whether or not forecasts should be included in external financial statements is controversial. Opponents point out the uncertainty of forecasts and the potential dangers of undue reliance upon them. On the positive side, it has been argued that the inclusion of forecasts in external financial statements "should be provided when they will enhance the reliability of users' predictions."[5] Furthermore, the assertion has been made that:

1. Forecasts . . . should be presented with their significant underlying assumptions, so that each user can evaluate them in the context of his own needs. The underlying assumptions supporting forecasts, however, should not be presented in such detail that they affect adversely the enterprise's competitive position.

2. The use of ranges to supplement single numbers may be appropriate . . . The limits of the range would indicate the uncertainty inherent in the forecast.

3. Forecasts . . . should be updated periodically and ultimately compared with actual accomplishments. . . . The preparer should explain . . . significant differences between the original and revised forecasts and between forecasts and actual results.[6]

Securities and Exchange Commission regulations presently permit but do not require inclusion of financial forecasts in external financial reporting.

PLANNING AND BUDGETING FOR NONMANUFACTURING BUSINESSES AND NONPROFIT ORGANIZATIONS

Nonmanufacturing Businesses. Many industrial concerns still pay only lip service to these suggested steps, methods, and procedures. To an even greater extent, nonmanufacturing businesses — and especially nonprofit organizations — generally lack an effective planning and control mechanism. However, under the guidance of the National Retail Merchants Association, department stores have followed merchandise budget procedures that have a long and quite successful history.

---

[5]AICPA, Study Group on the Objectives of Financial Statements, *Objectives of Financial Statements* (1973), p. 46.
[6]*Ibid.*, p. 47.

A budget plan for a retail store is considered a necessity inasmuch as the profit per dollar of sales is generally low — usually from 1 to 3 percent. Planning, budgeting, and control administration are strongly oriented toward profit control on a total store as well as on a departmental basis. The merchandise budget is set up on predetermined sales and profits, generally on a six-month basis following the two merchandising seasons: spring-summer and fall-winter. The merchandise budget includes sales, purchases, expenses, capital expenditures, cash, and annual statements.

It might seem quite logical for a department store or a wholesaler to plan and budget its activities. What about banks, savings and loan associations, insurance companies, etc.? The functional classification for the purpose of expense or responsibility control within these institutions is discussed in Chapter 10. However, these types of businesses should also create a long-range profit plan coordinating long-term goals and objectives of the institution. Forecasting would deal with deposit size and mix, number of insured and mix of policies, capital requirements, types of earning assets, physical facilities, new, additional, or changed depositor or client services, personnel requirements, and operational changes. The long-range goal should be translated into short-range budgets, starting at the lowest level of responsibility, building and combining the various organizational units into one whole.

Nonprofit Organizations. Each January the President of the United States sends his budget message to Congress. The total sum requested for the fiscal year 1976 amounted to more than $350 billion — an enormous sum of money. Yet, in spite of the many decades in which governmental budgeting has been practiced, the planning, control, and benefits received have been severely criticized by the general public, responsible for the money via payment of taxes. While the federal government might be under more obvious attack, state, county, and municipal governments are equally criticized not only for the lack of a satisfactory control system, but also for the ill-conceived procedure for planning the costs and revenues needed to govern.

The concept of a planning, programming, budgeting system, commonly referred to as PPBS, has received attention and acceptance in governmental budgeting and accounting. *PPBS* might be defined as an analytical tool to assist management: (1) in the analysis of alternatives as the basis for rational decision making and (2) in allocating resources to accomplish stated goals and objectives over a designated time period. As an analytical tool, the analysis is focused upon the outputs or final results, rather than the inputs, or the initial dollars expended. The outputs are directly relatable to the planned goals or objectives through use of performance budgets.   The analysis technique is therewith closely related to a cost-benefit analysis.

The system had its origin in the Defense Department's attempt to quantify huge expenditures in terms of benefits derived from activities and programs of the public sector.   A private enterprise measures its benefits in terms of increased revenues or decreased costs.   The public sector might provide some benefits that are measurable; in general, however, the social problem complicates this measurement.   The idea that governmental programs should be undertaken in the light of final benefits has caused agencies active in the field of health, education, and welfare services to examine the application of PPBS to their activities and programs.   Throughout federal, state, and local governments, PPBS is still in a developmental stage.   The system needs a great deal of refinement and innovation, an understanding of its aims and methods at many government levels, and active participation of executive and middle management.

It is difficult to measure the benefits or outputs of any governmental program.   Yet the nation's citizens are ever more critical of services received for money spent.   A plan and budget program assuring them of a managerial approach to any government's spending plan will go a long way to pacify the taxpayer.

In the same way that governmental units have become budget and cost conscious, nonprofit or not-for-profit organizations like hospitals, churches, school districts, colleges, universities, fraternal orders, libraries, labor unions, etc. have been ever-increasingly compelled to put their financial houses in order by adopting strong measures of budgetary control. In the past, efforts to control costs were generally exercised through pressure to reduce budget increases rather than through methods improvements or program changes.   Real long-range planning has seldom been practiced.   Management techniques should be adapted to fill the needs of these nonprofit organizations.   Personnel practices, such as programs to train and improve the performance of the administrative personnel, must be made effective within these institutions.

Basically, the objectives of nonprofit organizations are directed toward the economic, social, educational, or spiritual benefit of individuals or groups who have no vested interest in such organizations in the form of ownership or investment.   The presidents, boards of directors, trustees, or administrative officers are charged with the stewardship of economic resources like their counterparts in profit-seeking enterprises, except that here their job is primarily to use or spend these resources instead of trying to derive monetary gain.   It is expressly for this nonprofit objective that these organizations should install adequate and effective methods and procedures in planning, budgeting, and cost control.

ZERO-BASE BUDGETING

Customarily, those in charge of an established budgetary program are required to justify only the *increase* sought above last year's appropriation. What they are already spending is usually accepted as necessary, with little or no examination.

Beginning in the early 1970s, the concept of zero-base budgeting was introduced in some governmental and business organizations. *Zero-base budgeting* is a budget-planning procedure for the reevaluation of an organization's programs and expenditures. It requires each manager to justify his *entire* budget request in detail and places the burden of proof on him to justify why he should be authorized to spend any money at all. It starts with the assumption that zero will be spent on each activity — thus, the term "zero-base." What a manager is already spending is not accepted as a starting point.

Each manager is asked to prepare for each activity or operation under his control a "decision package" that includes an analysis of cost, purpose, alternative courses of action, measures of performance, consequences of not performing the activity, and benefits. The zero-base budgeting approach asserts that in building the budget from zero, two types of alternatives should be considered by managers: (1) different ways of performing the same activity and (2) different levels of effort of performing the activity.[7]

Sound budgeting procedures should always require a careful evaluation of all operating facts each time the budget is prepared. Therefore, the zero-base budgeting procedure is new and unique mainly in approach rather than in basic planning and control philosophy.

PERT AND PERT/COST — SYSTEMS FOR PLANNING AND CONTROL

The accountant's ever-increasing involvement in management planning and control has in recent years led to the use of systems which use network analysis and critical path methods for planning, measuring progress to schedule, evaluating changes to schedule, forecasting future progress, and predicting and controlling costs. These systems are variously referred to as PERT (Program Evaluation and Review Technique) or CPM (Critical Path Method). The origin of PERT is military; it was introduced in connection with the Navy Polaris program. CPM's origin is industrial. Many companies have been using these methods in planning, scheduling, and costing such diverse projects as construction of buildings, installation of equipment, and research and development activities. Yet there is also an

---

[7]For a comprehensive treatment of zero-base budgeting, see Peter A. Pyhrr, *Zero-Base Budgeting* (New York: John Wiley & Sons, Inc., 1973).

opportunity for using PERT in the field of business administration for tasks such as scheduling the closing of books, revising standard cost data, scheduling the time elements for the preparation of departmental budgets, cash flows, and preparing the annual profit plan.[8]

The PERT System. Whether a military, industrial, or business administration task, *time* is the fundamental element of any of the projects cited. The major burden of the method is the determination of the longest time duration for the completion of the entire project. This calculation is based on the length of time required for the longest sequence of activities. All of the individual tasks to complete a given job or program must be visualized in a *network* which points out interrelationships and is comprised of events and activities. An *event* represents a specified accomplishment at a particular instant in time, such as B or E in the network chart (page 514). An *activity* represents the time and resources necessary to move from one event to another; e.g., B⟶E in the chart.

Time estimates for PERT are made for each activity on a three-way basis; i.e., optimistic (t_o), most likely (t_m), and pessimistic (t_p). From these estimates an expected time (t_e) is calculated for each activity based on the formula:

$$t_e = \frac{t_o + 4t_m + t_p}{6} \; ,$$

expressed in time periods and often in units of one week. The three-way basis appears on the network with three numbers on each activity line.

The formula is derived from the Beta distribution. Referring to the flowchart, the activity D-F has a value of $t_e = 7$ determined as follows:

$$\text{If } t_o = 5; t_m = 6; t_p = 13;$$

$$t_e = \frac{5 + 4\,(6) + 13}{6} = \frac{42}{6} = 7$$

---

[8]For discussion of such uses of PERT, see:

Robert L. Shultis, "Applying PERT to Standard Cost Revisions," *NAA Bulletin*, Vol. XLIV, No. 3, pp. 35–43.

James G. Case, "PERT — A Dynamic Approach to Systems Analysis," *NAA Bulletin*, Vol. XLIV, No. 9, pp. 27–38.

Gordon B. Davis, "Network Techniques and Accounting — With an Illustration," *NAA Bulletin*, Vol. XLIV, No. 11, pp. 11–18.

A. H. Russell, "Cash Flows in Networks," *Management Science*, Vol. 16, No. 5, pp. 357–373.

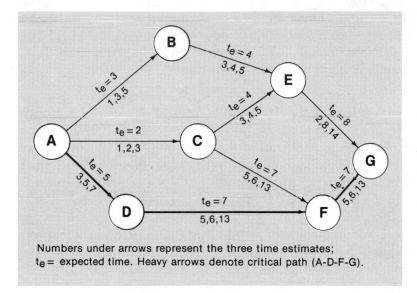

Numbers under arrows represent the three time estimates;
t_e = expected time. Heavy arrows denote critical path (A-D-F-G).

PERT
Network
with Time
Estimates
in Weeks

The longest path through the network is known as the *critical path*
and is denoted on the flowchart by the line connecting A-D-F-G. All
other paths on the network are called *slack paths*. Shortening of total
time can be accomplished only by shortening the critical path rather than
a slack path. However, should the critical path A-D-F-G which totals
nineteen weeks be shortened to fifteen weeks, A-C-F-G (assuming F-G
remains unchanged) would then become the critical path because it is
then the longest.

The PERT/Cost System. The PERT/Cost System is really an expansion of PERT. It seems advisable to assign cost to time and activities,
thereby providing total financial planning and control by functional
responsibility. The predetermination of cost is in harmony with the accountant's budgeting task and follows the organizational and procedural
steps used in responsibility accounting. The PERT/Cost estimates are
activity- or project-oriented.

The association of actual time and costs with the selected plan is im-
portant for control purposes. In the network chart (page 515), the activi-
ties noted by solid nodes represent completed events. The dollar figures
in the white blocks represent estimated costs; e.g., $30,000 for activity F-G.
Figures in the tinted blocks to the right of the estimates are actual costs.
Letters t_e represent estimated time while t_a indicates actual time figures.
Dollars are expressed in thousands and time in weeks. Activities A-B,
A-C, and A-D have been completed. A-B required one half week more

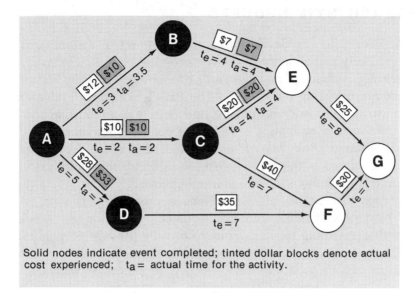

Solid nodes indicate event completed; tinted dollar blocks denote actual
cost experienced; t_a = actual time for the activity.

**PERT/Cost Network with Time (in Weeks)
and Cost (in Thousands of Dollars)**

time than planned; however, it is on a slack path and will not affect total
project duration. If excess time were such that a slack path became long
enough to be the critical path, then total time would be involved. The
actual activity cost of $10,000 for A-B compared to a budget of $12,000
indicates an underrun of $2,000. Activity A-C budget and actual figures
coincide for time and cost. A-D had an overrun of $5,000 and a two-week
slippage. The slippage requires immediate attention because A-D is on the
critical path. Immediate investigation and corrective action seem needed
for B-E and C-E. According to the present status report both activities
have consumed the budgeted time and cost and still have not been completed.

Each activity is defined at a level of detail necessary for individual job
assignments and supervisory control. Control is on scheduled tasks, with
time and cost as the common control factors. New cost accumulation methods must be devised to be compatible with PERT/Cost control concepts.

PERT/Cost is an integrated management information system designed
to furnish management with timely information useful in planning and
controlling schedules and costs of projects to blend with existing management information systems and to provide additional important data. In
conjunction with PERT and critical path techniques, computer systems are
providing top management with far better means for directing large-scaled,
complex projects. Management can now measure cost, time, and technical
performance on an integrated basis.

PROBABILISTIC BUDGETS

The budget may be developed based on one set of assumptions as to the most likely performance in the forthcoming period. However, there is increasing evidence of management's evaluating several sets of assumptions before finalizing the budget. The PERT-like three-level estimates, referred to as optimistic, most likely, and pessimistic, offer one possibility and would involve estimating each budget component assuming the three conditions stated. *Probability trees* can be used in which several variables can be considered in the analysis; e.g., number of units sold, sales price, and variable manufacturing and marketing costs.

To each discrete set of assumptions a probability can be assigned based on past experience and management's best judgment about the future, thus revealing to management not only a range of possible outcomes but also a probability associated with each. Further statistical techniques can then be applied, including an expected (weighted, composite) value, the range, and the standard deviation for the various budget elements, such as sales, manufacturing, and marketing costs. For example, the expected value for sales may be $960,000 with a range from a low of $780,000 to a high of $1,200,000 and a standard deviation of $114,600.

The computational capability of the computer facilitates the consideration of complex sets of assumptions and permits the use of simulation programs, making it possible to develop more objectively determined probabilities.[9]

BUDGET BUILDING AND HUMAN BEHAVIOR

In several instances the statement has been made that the assembling, receiving, and approving of budget data is a cooperative effort. While budgeting requires the participation of executive management, it is even more important to secure the participation and wholehearted cooperation and understanding of the middle and lower management echelons. Anyone who has ever been charged with the task of creating a budget and establishing budget figures, particularly of departmental overhead, must have

---

[9]An exhaustive treatment of these techniques is beyond the scope of this discussion. For expanded discussion and illustrations, see:

William L. Ferrara and Jack C. Hayya, "Toward Probabilistic Profit Budgets," *Management Accounting*, Vol. LII, No. 3, pp. 23–28.

Belverd E. Needles, Jr., "Budgeting Techniques: Subjective to Probabilistic," *Management Accounting*, Vol. LIII, No. 6, pp. 39–45.

Hugh J. Watson, "Financial Planning and Control," *Management Adviser*, Vol. IX, No. 6, pp. 43–48.

been aware of the irrational and often obstinate behavior of certain supervisors with respect to the contemplated budget program.[10] In some firms budgeting is perhaps the most unpopular management and/or accounting device for planning and control.

In recent years considerable attention has been paid to the behavioral implications[11] of accounting which are related to providing managers with the data required for planning, coordinating, and controlling activities. Cost accounting and budgeting play an important role in influencing behavior at all of the various stages of the management process including: (1) setting goals; (2) informing individuals what they must do to contribute to the accomplishment of these goals; (3) motivating desirable performance; (4) evaluating performance; and (5) suggesting when corrective action must be taken. In short, accountants cannot ignore the behavioral sciences (psychology, social-psychology, and sociology) because the "information for decision making" function of accounting is essentially a behavioral function.

The individual manager's attitude toward the budget will depend greatly upon the existing good relationship within the management group. By looking to the future, guided by the company plan, with an opportunity for increased compensation, greater satisfaction, and eventually promotion, the middle and lower management group might achieve remarkable results. A discordant management group, unwilling to accept the budget's underlying figures, might show such poor accomplishment that it "compels the administration to defer trying the planning and control idea until it has put its house in order."[12] For budget building, Peirce suggests:

> In the field of cost control, use the budget as a tool to be placed in the foremen's hand — not as a club to be held over their heads. To implement this rule, it may be a good idea to design an educational program. Meetings attended by line and staff supervisors may prove an effective vehicle. Cost reduction must be placed on the basis of mutual effort toward a common aim. The creation of this atmosphere is an essential, definite step in budget practice.[13]

---

[10]Chris Argyris, *The Impact of Budgets on People* (New York: Financial Executives Research Foundation; formerly, Controllership Foundation, Inc., 1952).

[11]For references explaining behavioral implications of accounting in some detail, see:

William J. Bruns, Jr., and Don T. DeCoster, *Accounting and Its Behavioral Implications* (New York: McGraw-Hill, Inc., 1969).

Edwin H. Caplan, *Management Accounting and Behavioral Science* (Reading, Mass.: Addison-Wesley Publishing Co., Inc., 1971).

[12]James L. Peirce, "The Budget Comes of Age," *The Harvard Business Review*, Vol. 32, No. 3, pp. 58–67.

[13]*Ibid.*, p. 65.

Budget building means building people first.

The symptoms of budget irritations may point to deeper meanings in the spiritual emancipation of mankind. We are beginning to learn that no tool can be used effectively unless the hand that guides it is rightly motivated. Like all other techniques of business, the budget should be a door open to more satisfying and profitable work — not an instrument of torture.

Then it will be known that what you can do without a budget you can do better with one. It will be seen that the entire planning and control procedure is a device for freeing men to do their best work — not a machine of restriction and condemnation.

Planning is but another word for the vision that sees a creative achievement before it is manifest. Control is but a name for direction. The genius of management cannot fail to turn the budget idea finally into positive channels, so that people individually as well as business leadership generally will reap the harvest that it promises.[14]

DISCUSSION QUESTIONS

1. What is meant by a *capital expenditure*? How does a capital expenditure differ from a revenue expenditure?
2. Research and development expenditures form a major element of cost in many firms. These costs are controlled largely by management decision as to their contribution to the overall, long-term benefit to the company. These research and development expenditures are not necessarily governed by current operating requirements or business volume but can be expanded or contracted as management sees fit. Companies have now begun to establish budgetary procedures that are to provide control and accounting systems for research and development expenditures. What are such procedures specifically designed to achieve?
3. Name (a) some purposes of and (b) some reasons for a research and development program.
4. Name the two methods used for the preparation of a cash budget.
5. Managers of large or small industrial or commercial enterprises consider a cash budget an extremely useful management tool. Why?
6. The forecast income statement may be viewed as the apex of budgeting. Explain this statement.
7. The projected balance sheet may indicate an unsatisfactory financial condition. Discuss.
8. What governing criterion has been suggested for determining whether or not to include forecasts in external financial statements?
9. Discuss the need for planning and budgeting in (a) nonmanufacturing businesses and (b) nonprofit organizations.
10. What is the objective of the control concept generally referred to as PPBS?

---

[14]*Ibid.*, p. 66.

11. Select the answer that best completes the following statement: A perfor-mance budget used in PPBS relates a governmental unit's expenditures to (a) objects of expenditure; (b) expenditures of the preceding fiscal year; (c) individual months within the fiscal year; (d) activities and programs.

(AICPA adapted)

12. What is the basic idea involved in zero-base budgeting?

13. PERT, Program Evaluation and Review Technique, is a method of planning, replanning, and progress evaluation in order to exercise greater control over any major program, project, job, or task in government or in business. (a) What is one of the major advantages of PERT? (b) What common denominator is used by this technique? (c) What is the purpose of a PERT network? (d) What are the three time estimates used?

14. State the relationship between PERT and PERT/Cost systems.

15. Contrast the probabilistic budget and the traditional budget in terms of information provided to management.

16. Discuss the manner in which budget building and human behavior are related to each other.

17. Select the answer that best completes the following statement: The measure of employee attitude toward objectives which is most relevant in participa-tive budgeting is the level of (a) absorption; (b) appreciation; (c) arbitrari-ness; (d) aspiration.

(AICPA adapted)

18. The budget is a very common instrument used by many businesses. While it usually is thought to be an important and necessary tool for management, it has been subject to some criticism from managers and researchers studying organizations and human behavior. (a) Describe and discuss the benefits of budgeting from the behavioral point of view. (b) Describe and discuss the criticisms leveled at the budgeting processes from the behavioral point of view. (c) What solutions are recommended to overcome the criticisms described in (b)?

(NAA adapted)

EXERCISES

1. Cash Budget. A treasurer gathered the following data related to the com-pany's cash position for the next six months:

Cash balance, January 1....................................	$ 5,000
Monthly payroll — estimated................................	40,000
Payroll accrued at end of year as well as at the end of each month..	4,000
Interest payable in June....................................	500
Taxes payable in March....................................	10,000

Other data:

	January	February	March	April	May	June
Cash sales...........	$15,000	$14,000	$12,000	$16,000	$14,500	$18,000
Purchases...........	12,000	16,500	14,000	18,000	25,000	12,500
Accounts payable.....	11,000	30,000	25,000	30,000	24,000	30,000
Credit sales.........	65,000	80,000	72,000	60,000	75,000	68,000

(November, $60,000) (December, $70,000)

Credit sales are collected 50% in the month sales are made, 45% in the month following, and 5% in the second month. Purchases and accounts payable are paid in the month incurred.

Required: A cash budget, by months, for the period January through June.

2. Cash Requirements for Manufacturing Operations. Based on the sales forecast for the season, the Planning Department has prepared the following production schedule for the coming month: 25,000 units of Product A and 24,000 units of Product B. The manufacturing specifications for the products are:

Product A	*Product B*
2 kilograms (kg.) material X @ $.30	3 kg. material W @ $.80
½ kilogram (kg.) material Y @ $.20	¾ kg. material Y @ $.20
2 man-hours of labor @ $6	1.5 man-hours of labor @ $6

To the direct labor man-hours, a 5% allowance for idleness should be added. The indirect labor is estimated to be 5% of direct labor man-hours (excluding idleness), and the wage rate is $5. The factory overhead estimate is based on the flexible budget that is representative of expected actual costs, as follows:

Fixed Costs		*Variable Costs*
Depreciation...............	$ 6,900	$1.80 per direct labor hour (includes idle
Insurance (one year prepaid).	800	time and indirect labor costs)
Superintendence............	3,000	
Total for a month.........	$10,700	

It is planned to increase the inventory of material X 4,000 kg. and to decrease the inventory of material W 2,000 kg. as of the beginning of next month.

Required: An estimate of the amount of cash necessary for the manufacturing operations of the month.

3. Cash Receipts and Disbursements Schedule. On April 1, Tuscon Office Supplies has a cash balance of $18,400. Sales for the previous four months were: December, $60,000; January, $55,000; February, $50,000; March, $65,000; and forecast sales for April are $55,000. Collections from customers conform to the following pattern: 60% in the month of sale; 30% in the month following the sale; 8% in the second month following the sale; and 2% uncollectible.

Materials purchases were: December, $35,000; January, $40,000; February, $30,000; March, $45,000. Purchases for April are budgeted to be $50,000. All purchases are paid within the terms of the discount period followed in the industry of a 2% cash discount if paid 15 days from the end of the month purchased.

Payroll and other cash expenditures for the month of April are expected to require $12,000.

Required: (1) Expected cash disbursements during April.
(2) Expected cash collections during April.
(3) Expected cash balance, April 30.

4. Cash and Purchases Budget. Tomlinson Retail seeks assistance in developing cash and other budget information for May, June, and July of 19—. On April 30, 19—, the company had cash of $5,500, accounts receivable of $437,000, inventories of $309,400, and accounts payable of $133,055. The budget is to be based on the following assumptions:

Sales:

(a) Each month's sales are billed on the last day of the month.

(b) Customers are allowed a 3% discount if payment is made within 10 days after the billing date. Receivables are recorded at the gross selling price.

(c) Sixty percent of the billings are collected within the discount period; 25% are collected by the end of the month; 9% are collected by the end of the second month; and 6% prove uncollectible.

Purchases:

(a) Fifty-four percent of all purchases of material and a like percentage of marketing, general, and administrative expenses are paid in the month purchased with the remainder paid in the following month.

(b) Each month's units of ending inventory are equal to 130% of the next month's units of sales.

(c) The cost of each unit of inventory is $20.

(d) Marketing, general, and administrative expenses (of which $2,000 is depreciation) are equal to 15% of the current month's sales.

Actual and projected sales are as follows:

19—	Dollars	Units
March.................	$354,000	11,800
April.................	363,000	12,100
May.................	357,000	11,900
June.................	342,000	11,400
July.................	360,000	12,000
August.................	366,000	12,200

Required: (1) Budgeted cash disbursements during June, 19—.
(2) Budgeted cash collections during May, 19—.
(3) Budgeted units of inventory to be purchased during July, 19—.

(AICPA adapted)

5. Production Budget; Forecast Income Statement. The Budget Department of the Glencoe Manufacturing Company prepared these estimates for the coming year:

	Beginning	Ending
Inventories (annual):		
Raw materials (in units).......................	5,000	6,000
Finished goods (in units).......................	10,000	7,000
Sales (gross)......................................	100,000 (units)	
Average sales price per unit.........................	$4.00	
Raw materials, unit usage rate and cost..............	2 units of material for each finished unit, @ $.25 each	
Direct labor, per unit of finished product.............	$1.00	
Factory overhead rate per unit of finished product.....	150% of direct labor cost	

Marketing and administrative expenses are budgeted at 16% of gross sales.

Required: (1) A production budget (annual basis) indicating *units* to be manufactured.
(2) A forecast income statement. (Present the cost of goods sold section of the income statement in detail, including the beginning and ending inventories.)

6. Projected Income Statement. The Budget Department of the Crompton Machine Co. accumulates the following data for the coming year:

The Sales Budget shows expected revenue of $125,000.

The Production Budget reveals the following pertinent data:
Materials issued to work in process, $35,000
Labor, $30,000
Fixed factory overhead, $10,000

Variable factory overhead can be computed from the data given in the exercise.

Marketing and administrative expenses are estimated to be 25% of the cost of goods sold.

Inventories:	Planned January 1	Planned December 31
Raw materials	$5,000	$6,000
Work in process.............................	6,000	8,000
Finished goods	6,000	5,000

The company's aim is a net income before taxes equal to 10% of sales.

Required: A projected income statement for the coming year with a schedule showing in detail the computation of the cost of goods sold.

7. Departmental Forecast Budget. The plant manager of a company requests advice about a department manufacturing machine tools of varying sizes. The figures shown below are the actual results for the years indicated. He is concerned with the recent decline in output and profit and the recent increases in factory overhead. It has been company practice to use the actual factory overhead to direct labor percentages of each year for costing products made in the following year. Production for the next year will be 180,000 units.

		Last Year	Previous Year	Best Year	Normal Year
Materials used	(1)...............	$ 30,000	$ 45,000	$40,000	$ 36,000
Direct labor	(2)...............	60,000	90,000	80,000	72,000
Factory overhead	(3)...............	50,000	67,500	52,000	48,000
Total......		$140,000	$202,500	$172,000	$156,000
Departmental profit for year...........		2,500	7,500	28,000	15,000
Sales value of output.................		$142,500	$210,000	$200,000	$171,000
Output......		200,000	300,000	400,000	360,000
Rate of factory overhead (3) to direct labor cost (2)..		83.3%	75%	65%	66.6%
Estimated amount of fixed overhead included in above factory overhead...		$ 15,000	$ 15,000	$ 12,000	$ 12,000

Required: (1) A departmental budget for the coming year with the estimated profit.
(2) An opinion on the factory overhead rate to be used.
(3) Any other comments of interest to the manager.
(The unit sales price, raw materials prices, and wage rates are expected to remain the same as for last year.)

8. Forecast Income Statement; Departmental Budget Allowances. The Kelso Company annually prepares a budget for the coming year, a portion of which is given below.

FORECAST INCOME STATEMENT
FOR YEAR ENDING DECEMBER 31, 19—

		Total	Standards per Unit
Sales (300,000 units).....................		$900,000	$3.00
Cost of goods sold (see Schedule 1)........		600,000	2.00
Gross profit on sales....................		$300,000	$1.00
Commercial expenses:			
Marketing expenses....................	$150,000		$ .50
Administrative expenses...............	75,000	225,000	.25
Net operating profit....................		$ 75,000	$ .25

SCHEDULE 1
COST OF GOODS SOLD (300,000 UNITS)

	Total	Standards per Unit
Direct materials.................................	$240,000	$ .80
Direct labor.....................................	180,000	.60
Factory overhead (see Schedule 2)	180,000	.60
	$600,000	$2.00

SCHEDULE 2
DEPARTMENTAL ANALYSIS OF FACTORY OVERHEAD

Item	Producing #4	Producing #6	Service A	Total
Production (units).................	300,000	300,000		300,000
Direct labor hours.................	60,000	30,000		90,000
Direct labor cost..................	$120,000	$ 60,000		$180,000
Factory overhead:				
Fixed factory overhead...........	$ 36,000	$ 30,000	$ 9,000	$ 75,000
Variable factory overhead........	54,000	33,000	18,000	105,000
	$ 90,000	$ 63,000	$ 27,000	$180,000
Service department prorated on direct labor hour basis............	18,000	9,000	27,000	
	$108,000	$ 72,000		$180,000
Factory overhead rate per direct labor hour.........................	$1.80	$2.40		

Required: (1) A forecast income statement for October assuming that production for the month is scheduled to be 26,000 units and that 22,000 units will be sold. The over- or underabsorbed fixed factory overhead should appear on the statement. Marketing expenses are 50% fixed, and all administrative expenses are fixed.

(2) The forecast budget allowances of the two producing departments and the service department for the month of October. Budgeted service department cost for October is distributed on the basis of the forecast direct labor hours for the month.

9. PERT Network. A budget department prepared the following time estimates for a contemplated project with 36 days as the target date:

Event	Activity	t_o	t_m	t_p
2	1–2	1	2	3
3	1–3	8	9	10
4	1–4	4	6	20
5	2–5	4	7	10
6	3–6	3	6	45
6	4–6	2	3	10
8	5–8	4	8	24
5	6–5	1	3	5
7	6–7	3	4	5
8	7–8	6	10	14

Required: (1) A calculation of t_e (expected time) for each activity.

(2) The PERT network for the above data.

(3) Total t_e for each path and identification of the critical path for the project.

10. PERT Network and Critical Path for Construction Project. The DeAngelis Construction Company of Chillicothe, Ohio, is planning the construction of a modern type home in a new residential area. If this venture proves successful, it will serve as the model plan for the construction of a large number of homes.

Mr. DeAngelis has identified in random order the activities and units of time (in days) required to construct the home.

Activity	Units of Time Required (Days)	Activity	Units of Time Required (Days)
Perform plumbing work..	5	Brick outside...........	6
Perform electrical work..	6	Sheetrock and panel rooms	6
Excavate...............	2	Shingle roof...........	5
Install wall framework...	7	Complete house exterior..	4
Perform preliminary plumbing work and pour foundation..........	3	Complete house interior..	6
		Inspect completed home..	1
Install ceiling joists and rafters...............	5		

Required: (1) A network of the activities and events necessary to accomplish the construction project.

(2) Identification and length of critical path.

11. PERT Critical Path. A construction company has contracted to complete a new building and has asked for assistance in analyzing the project. Using the

Program Evaluation Review
Technique (PERT), the network illustrated at the
right, has been developed.

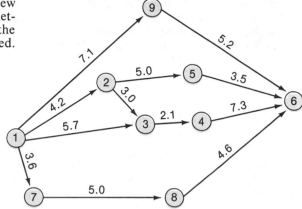

All paths from the start point, Event 1, to the finish point, Event 6, represent activities or processes that must be completed before the entire project
(the building) will be completed. The numbers above the line segments represent expected completion times for the activities. The expected time is based
upon the commonly used three-estimate method, 1-4-1. For example, the three-
estimate method gives an estimated time of 4.2 to complete Activity 1-2.

Required: (1) The critical path.

(2) The effect on the critical path resulting from an unfavorable time
variance of 1.9 for Activity 7-8. Explain.

(AICPA adapted)

12. PERT/Cost Network; Critical Path; Departmental Cost. The Rio Bravo
Company recently initiated a new product development project estimated to
cost $31,500. The list of activities constituting this project, together with esti-
mates of the number of weeks each activity would take and the cost to carry it
out, is illustrated in the table below. In this table each activity is identified by
a two-digit number, the first digit denoting the preceding event and the second
digit indicating the event that signals the end of the activity.

Activity	Department	Estimated Time (Weeks)	Estimated Cost
01	A	2	$ 1,100
12	A	1	500
23	B	3	2,500
24	D	7	3,500
25	F	2	2,200
34	C	3	3,300
35	G	1	400
45	B	5	4,000
49	A	3	1,600
56	D	2	900
67	C	1	1,200
68	E	6	4,200
78	G	2	700
79	F	4	4,100
89	G	3	1,300
		Total...	$31,500

Required: (1) A PERT/Cost network to represent the project.

(2) Events through which the critical path passes and the number of weeks which the project is expected to take.

(3) The cost assignable to each department.

PROBLEMS

17-1. Cash Budget. The Standard Mercantile Corporation ends its fiscal year on December 31. In early January, 19B, the company's CPA was asked to assist in the preparation of a cash forecast. This information is available regarding the company's operations:

(a) Management believes the 19A sales pattern is a reasonable estimate of 19B sales. Sales in 19A were:

January.....................................	$ 360,000
February....................................	420,000
March......................................	600,000
April.......................................	540,000
May..	480,000
June..	400,000
July..	350,000
August......................................	550,000
September...................................	500,000
October.....................................	400,000
November...................................	600,000
December....................................	800,000
Total..................................	$6,000,000

(b) On December 31, accounts receivable totaled $380,000. Sales collections are generally made as follows:

During month of sale......................	60%
In first subsequent month..................	30%
In second subsequent month...............	9%
Uncollectible accounts.....................	1%

(c) The purchase cost of goods averages 60% of the selling price; on December 31, the cost of the inventory on hand is $840,000 of which $30,000 is obsolete. Arrangements have been made to sell the obsolete inventory in January at half of the normal selling price on a COD basis.

The company wants to maintain the inventory as of the 1st of each month at a level of three months' sales as determined by the sales forecast for the next three months. All purchases are paid for on the 10th of the following month. On December 31, accounts payable for purchases totaled $370,000.

(d) Recurring fixed expenses amount to $120,000 per month including depreciation of $20,000. For accounting purposes the company apportions the recurring fixed expenses to the various months in the same proportion as that month's estimated sales bears to the estimated total annual sales. Variable expenses amount to 10% of sales.

Payments for expenses are made as follows:

	During Month Incurred	Following Month
Fixed expenses...........	55%	45%
Variable expenses........	70%	30%

(e) Annual property taxes amount to $50,000 and are paid in equal installments on December 31 and March 31. The property taxes are in addition to the expenses in (d) above.

(f) It is anticipated that cash dividends of $20,000 will be paid each quarter on the 15th day of the third month of the quarter.

(g) During the winter, unusual advertising costs will be incurred that require cash payments of $10,000 in February and $15,000 in March. These advertising costs are in addition to the expenses in (d) above.

(h) Equipment replacements are paid for at the rate of $3,000 per month. The equipment has an average estimated life of six years.

(i) The company must make a federal income tax payment of $60,000 in March.

(j) On December 31, 19A, the company had a bank loan with an unpaid balance of $280,000. The loan requires a principal payment of $20,000 on the last day of each month plus interest at $\frac{1}{2}\%$ per month on the unpaid balance at the first of the month. The entire balance is due on March 31, 19B.

(k) On December 31, 19A, the cash balance was $100,000.

Required: A cash forecast statement by months for the first three months of 19B, showing the cash on hand (or deficiency of cash) at the end of each month. Present all computations and supporting schedules in good form.

(AICPA adapted)

17-2. Estimated Operating Statement; Cash Receipts and Disbursements Statement; Estimated Balance Sheet. About three weeks before the end of each year the Budget Department of the Tonkens Company prepares an operating budget for the coming year. The budget for the year 19B showed the following figures:

Depreciation — buildings.....................................	$ 5,625
Depreciation — machinery and equipment.....................	23,750
Direct labor...	121,875
General and administrative expenses.........................	36,875
Factory insurance expense...................................	12,000
Interest expense...	9,000
Direct materials purchases..................................	123,750
Provision for bad debts.....................................	9,750
Sales...	462,500
Marketing expenses...	71,500

The trial balance of the company as of December 31, 19A is:

TRIAL BALANCE
DECEMBER 31, 19A

Cash in Bank...............................	$ 10,000.00	
Accounts Receivable........................	145,000.00	
Allowance for Uncollectible Accounts.........		$ 22,500.00
Inventories of Raw Materials, Work in Process, and Finished Goods at December 31, 19A....	195,000.00	
Prepaid Insurance..........................	1,875.00	
Prepaid Interest...........................	1,250.00	
Land......................................	50,000.00	
Buildings..................................	187,500.00	
Accumulated Depreciation — Buildings........		30,000.00
Machinery and Equipment...................	120,000.00	
Accumulated Depreciation — Machinery and Equipment..............................		65,000.00
Accounts Payable..........................		70,000.00
Notes Payable.............................		162,500.00
Accrued Payroll...........................		3,750.00
Capital Stock.............................		250,000.00
Retained Earnings.........................		94,125.00
Sales.....................................		420,000.00
Cost of Goods Sold........................	323,330.00	
General and Administrative Expenses.........	67,800.00	
Bad Debts Expense........................	8,300.00	
Interest Expense..........................	7,820.00	
Total.................................	$1,117,875.00	$1,117,875.00

It is expected that on December 31, 19B accounts receivable will amount to 35% of the sales budget. Bad debts amounting to $7,000 will be charged to Allowance for Uncollectible Accounts during the budget year and it is estimated that $3,000 will be collected from accounts previously written off (to be treated as income).

The inventories on December 31, 19B will amount to $172,500. Prepaid interest on December 31, 19B will amount to $1,625 and prepaid insurance will be $1,440.

It is expected that additions to fixed assets will be:

Buildings......................................	$ 8,750
Machinery and equipment......................	10,500

Accounts payable on December 31, 19B are estimated at $77,500 and the accrued payroll will be $2,190. A cash dividend of $15,000 will be paid during the budget year.

Required: (1) An estimated operating statement as of December 31, 19B.

(2) A statement of estimated cash receipts and disbursements for the year ending December 31, 19B. Do not provide for any payments on notes payable but show the amount available, if any, to reduce notes payable and yet maintain the same bank balance as of December 31, 19A. Income tax considerations are to be ignored.

(3) An estimated balance sheet as of December 31, 19B.

17-3. Projected Income Statement; Cash Budget. The management of Moplacon Products Corporation, a molded plastic container manufacturer, determined in October, 19A, that additional cash was needed to continue operations. The company began negotiating for a one-month bank loan of $100,000 that would be discounted at 6% per annum on November 1. In considering the loan, the bank requested a projected income statement and a cash budget for November.

The following information is available:

(a) Sales were budgeted at 120,000 units per month in October 19A, December 19A, and January 19B and at 100,000 units in November 19A. The selling price is $2 per unit. Sales are billed on the 15th and last day of each month on terms of 2/10, net 30. Past experience indicates sales are evenly spread through the month and 50% of the customers pay the billed amount within the discount period. The remainder pay at the end of thirty days; bad debts average ½% of gross sales. The estimated amounts for cash discounts on sales and losses on bad debts are deducted from sales.

(b) The inventory of finished goods on October 1 was 30,000 units. The finished goods inventory at the end of each month is to be maintained at 25% of sales anticipated for the following month. There is no work in process.

(c) The inventory of raw materials on October 1 was 22,800 pounds. At the end of each month the raw materials inventory is to be maintained at not less than 40% of production requirements for the following month. Materials are purchased as needed in quantities of 25,000 pounds per shipment. Raw materials purchases of each month are paid in the next succeeding month on terms of net 30 days.

(d) All salaries and wages are paid on the 15th and last day of each month for the period ending on the date of payment.

(e) All factory overhead and marketing and administrative expenses are paid on the 10th of the month following the month in which incurred. Marketing expenses are 10% of gross sales. Administrative expenses, which include depreciation of $500 per month on office furniture and fixtures, total $33,000 per month.

(f) The standard cost of a molded plastic container, based on *normal* production of 100,000 units per month, is as follows:

Materials — ½ pound.............	$ .50
Labor..........................	.40
Variable factory overhead.........	.20
Fixed factory overhead............	.10
Total.........................	$1.20

Fixed overhead includes depreciation on factory equipment of $4,000 per month. Over- or underabsorbed factory overhead is included in cost of goods sold.

(g) The cash balance on November 1 is expected to be $10,000.

Required: Assuming the bank loan is granted, prepare:

(a) Schedules computing inventory budgets by months for (1) finished goods production in units for October, November, and December and (2) raw materials purchases in pounds for October and November.

(b) A projected income statement for the month of November. Ignore income taxes.

(c) A cash budget for the month of November, showing the opening balance, receipts (itemized by dates of collection), disbursements, and balance at the end of the month.

(AICPA adapted)

17-4. Forecast Income Statement. Blackrock Mining Company mines and processes rock and gravel. The management is presently engaged in planning and projecting operations for the coming year. The company's officers have available the following information:

From books and records:

Mining properties...	$ 60,000
Accumulated depletion (one year)................................	3,000
Equipment..	150,000
Accumulated depreciation (one year)...........................	10,000
Sales...	300,000
Production cost (including depreciation and depletion)...............	184,000
Administrative expenses..	60,000

From market studies and cost analyses:

(a) The total yards of material sold are expected to increase 15% next year, and the average sales price per cubic yard will be increased from $1.50 to $1.60.

(b) When the mining properties were purchased, the recoverable rock and gravel deposits were estimated at 4,000,000 cubic yards.

(c) The $184,000 production costs include direct labor of $110,000 of which $10,000 was due to labor inefficiencies experienced in the early stages of operation. Beginning next year, the union contract calls for a 6% increase in hourly rates. Other production costs except depreciation, depletion, and direct labor will increase 5% in the next fiscal period.

(d) New equipment costing $75,000 will be placed in operation during the second half of the coming year. It is expected to result in a direct labor hour savings of 10%. The new equipment will have a twenty-year life. All depreciation is computed on the straight-line method. The old equipment will continue in use.

(e) Depletion allowable on rock and gravel is to be calculated on the same basis as for the previous year with consideration for the increase in materials sold.

(f) Administrative expenses will increase $8,000.

Required: A forecast income statement for the coming year. Show computations to support the figures in the income statement.

(AICPA adapted)

17-5. Projected Gross Profit Statement. Chromalloy, Inc. manufactures and markets a product under the trade name "Alchrome." The basic characteristics of the company's operations and accounting are:

(a) Production is scheduled to maintain finished goods inventory at a constant ratio (10%) to current sales.

(b) Production is spaced evenly during each period.

(c) Finished goods inventory at the end of the period is valued at the average cost of manufacturing for the period.

(d) Inventories of work in process and raw materials are small and may be ignored.

Production and sales data and the manufacturing cost of goods sold for the two preceding periods are:

	Period	
Units	*1*	*2*
Beginning inventory......................	1,000	2,000
Production............................	21,000	31,000
	22,000	33,000
Sales.................................	20,000	30,000
Ending inventory........................	2,000	3,000

Sales and Costs	Period 1		Period 2	
	Amount	Per Unit	Amount	Per Unit
Sales..............................	$361,520		$552,000	
Cost of goods sold:				
Direct materials..................	$ 44,078	$2.10	$ 68,508	$2.21
Direct labor.....................	80,220	3.82	130,200	4.20
Factory overhead.................	49,713	2.37	62,213	2.01
Inventory variation...............	(7,510)		(8,680)	
Total cost of goods sold........	$166,501		$252,241	
Gross profit......................	$195,019		$299,759	

Other pertinent data are as follows:

(a) The product is made by mixing materials A and B. The relative quantity of each of the two materials entering production and in finished units can be varied, but it was kept constant during Periods 1 and 2. In Period 3, the quantity of raw material A used in a unit of product will be decreased 8%, and the quantity of raw material B used in a unit of product will be increased 12%. The price of material A is expected to continue the trend of the past two periods, and the price of material B is expected to increase 5% in Period 3. The cost of each raw material used in production has been as follows:

Materials	Period 1		Period 2	
	Amount	%	Amount	%
A.................................	$23,141	52.5	$37,542	54.8
B.................................	20,937	47.5	30,966	45.2
Total.........................	$44,078	100.0	$68,508	100.0

(b) Direct labor hours per unit have been approximately constant during Periods 1 and 2 and are expected to remain at the same figure in Period 3. Effective at the middle of each of Periods 1 and 2, wage increases of 10% per man hour have been granted. A similar increase is expected at the middle of Period 3.

(c) The amount of fixed factory overhead was $23,463 during Periods 1 and 2 and is expected to continue at the same amount during Period 3. The variable portion of factory overhead is expected to remain at the same amount per unit of production as in Periods 1 and 2.

(d) Sales in Period 3 are expected to be 25,000 units at $19 per unit.

Required: A projected statement of sales, cost of goods sold, and gross profit for Period 3, based on the preceding data. The statement should be supported with schedules of:

(a) Production data for Period 3.

(b) Materials costs.

(c) Direct labor costs.

(d) Factory overhead, showing the fixed and variable elements.

(e) Inventory variation (increase or decrease).

(AICPA adapted)

17-6. PERT/Cost Network. Late in 19A, the Pyote Instrument Company was the successful bidder on a contract to design and produce the instrument panel for a new fighter plane. The price agreed upon on the bid was $475,000, and the work was to be completed by June 30, 19B.

Work on the contract was scheduled to begin on February 27, 19B, and management decided to utilize PERT/Cost techniques to control production time and costs. Analysis of the contract showed the following tasks with estimates of cost and time:

Task	Time Estimates (Weeks)			Cost Estimates	
	Optimistic	Most Likely	Pessimistic	Variable per Week	Fixed Cost
Design instrumentation (DI)..	6	7	8	$ 7,500	$18,500
Design panel (DP)...........	2	3	10	8,000	8,000
Design power system (DPS)..	3	4	5	28,000	4,000
Build instrumentation (BI)....	4	5	12	18,000	12,000
Build panel (BP).............	3	5	7	4,500	2,500
Build power system (BPS)....	4	6	8	4,800	1,200
Assemble and ship (A&S)....	1	2	3	4,000	2,000

Three special considerations applied to the sequence of the scheduling:
- (a) The designing of the instrumentation and the panel had to be completed before the designing of the power system could begin.
- (b) The designing of the panel had to be completed before the building of the instrumentation could begin.
- (c) The building of the panel had to be completed before the building of the power system could begin.

At the end of the week beginning April 3, 19B, the following data were assembled concerning the status of the work on the contract as of that date:

Task	Weeks	Cost	% of Work Completed
Design instrumentation.........	6	$63,000	100
Design panel..................	4	41,000	100
Build instrumentation..........	1	13,000 ⎫ Variable	16⅔
Design power system...........	1	30,000 ⎬ Cost	25
Build panel...................	1	3,000 ⎭ Only	20

Required: (1) The PERT/Cost network as of the beginning of the contract February 27, 19B, showing the critical path.
(2) An updated PERT/Cost network at the end of the week of April 3, 19B.
(3) A report for management as of the end of the week of April 3, 19B showing the schedule status and the cost status of the contract.

17-7. Sales and Production Schedules; Income Statement. Otmar Tables, Inc. manufactures coffee tables in three styles: Spanish, Modern, and Early American. Sales take place in the North Central area: Missouri, Nebraska, Kansas, and Iowa; and in the South Central area: Oklahoma, Arkansas, and Texas. Manufacturing requires three departments. The table top is started in the Cutting and Sanding Department; the legs, costing $2.00 a set, are added in the Assembling Department; and a special finishing compound is added in the Finishing Department. This compound costs $1.25 a pint, with one pint used for each table.

The management and department heads agreed on these estimates for the first quarter of 19—:

Sales Forecast	South Central	North Central	Sales Price Per Unit
Spanish style...............	8,000	5,000	$20.
Modern style...............	5,000	5,000	15.
Early American style.......	7,000	7,500	18.

Inventories (fifo system):

Raw Materials	Beginning Inventories		Ending Inventories	
	Units	Unit Cost	Units	Unit Cost
Lumber (board feet)........	22,000	$ .25	40,000	$ .25
Legs (sets)...............	1,500	2.00	2,000	2.00
Finishing compound (pints)..	1,600	1.25	2,000	1.25

Work in process: None at beginning or end of any month or quarter.

Finished goods:	Beginning Inventories		Ending Inventories	
Tables	Units	Unit Cost	Units	Unit Cost
Spanish style.............	500	$12.75	1,500	$14.25
Modern style.............	500	12.20	500	13.50
Early American style.......	1,000	12.50	500	13.75

The factory overhead includes ten supervisors, each earning $800 per month, and building, supplies, and utility expenses of $30,000 a month. Total factory overhead is equally distributed to the three departments and also shared equally by the tables produced. The factory overhead rate in each department is $1 per table.

Marketing expenses: $25,000 per month.

Administrative expenses: $20,000 per month.

Income tax rate: 30% based on net income before taxes.

Lumber requirements per style: Spanish, 8 board feet; Modern, 5 board feet; and Early American, 6 board feet. Lumber cost is $.25 per board foot.

Labor cost is $4.00 per hour for all workers.

Labor time requirements per table are:
   Cutting and Sanding Department, ¾ hour
   Assembling Department, ½ hour
   Finishing Department, ¼ hour

Required: For the first quarter ending March 31, 19—, prepare:

(a) A sales budget — by styles and by sales areas.
(b) A production budget — by styles (in units).
(c) A direct raw materials budget — by materials and by styles (in units).
(d) A purchases budget — by materials (in units and costs).
(e) The cost of raw materials required for the quarter's production — by materials and by styles.
(f) A schedule of beginning and ending inventories — by materials for raw materials and by styles for finished goods.
(g) A direct labor budget — by styles and by departments.
(h) A factory overhead budget (overhead applied) — totals to be broken into costs by styles and by departments.
(i) A combined cost of goods manufactured and sold statement.
(j) A combined income statement.

17-8. Hospital Budget. The administrator of Wright Hospital presents the accountant with a number of service projections for the year ending June 30, 19—. Estimated room requirements for inpatients by type of service are:

Type of Patient	Total Patients Expected	Average Number of Days in Hospital		Percent of Regular Patients Selecting Types of Service		
		Regular	Medicare	Private	Semiprivate	Ward
Medical....	2,100	7	17	10%	60%	30%
Surgical....	2,400	10	15	15	75	10

Of the patients served by Wright Hospital, 10% are expected to be under Medicare — all of whom are expected to select semiprivate rooms. Both the number and proportion of Medicare inpatients have increased over the past five years. Daily rentals per inpatient are: $40 for a private room, $35 for a semiprivate room, and $25 for a ward.

Operating-room charges are based on *man-minutes* (number of minutes the operating room is in use multiplied by the number of personnel assisting in the operation). The per man-minute charges are $.13 for inpatients and $.22 for outpatients. Studies for the current year show that operations on inpatients are divided as follows:

Type of Operation	Number of Operations	Average Number of Minutes Per Operation	Average Number of Personnel Required
A............	800	30	4
B............	700	45	5
C............	300	90	6
D............	200	120	8
Total......	2,000		

The same proportion of inpatient operations is expected for the next fiscal year, and 180 outpatients are expected to use the operating room. Outpatient operations average 20 minutes and require the assistance of three persons.

The budget for the year ending June 30, 19—, by departments, is:

General services:

Maintenance of plant.....................................	$ 50,000
Operation of plant.......................................	27,500
Administration..	97,500
All others..	192,000

Revenue-producing services:

Operating room...	68,440
All others..	700,000
Total...	$1,135,440

The following information is provided for cost allocation purposes:

General services:	Square Feet	Salaries
Maintenance of plant............................	12,000	$ 40,000
Operation of plant..............................	28,000	25,000
Administration.................................	10,000	55,000
All others.....................................	36,250	102,500
Revenue-producing services:		
Operating room...............................	17,500	15,000
All others.....................................	86,250	302,500
Total......................................	190,000	$540,000

Basis of allocations:

Maintenance of plant — salaries	Administration — salaries
Operation of plant — square feet	All others — 8% to operating room

Required: For the year ending June 30, 19—, prepare schedules to show the:
(a) Projected number of patient days (number of patients X average hospital stay) by types of patients and types of service.
(b) Projected operating-room man-minutes for inpatients and outpatients. (For inpatients, show the breakdown of total operating-room man-minutes by types of operations.)
(c) Projected gross revenue from routine services.
(d) Projected gross revenue from operating-room services.
(e) Projected cost per man-minute for operating-room services. (Assume that the total man-minutes figured in (b) is $800,000 and that the step-down method of cost allocation is used (i.e., costs of the general services departments are allocated *in sequence* as listed in the problem data — to the general services departments served by Wright Hospital and to the revenue-producing departments. Once a department is allocated, no costs are subsequently allocated to it.)

(AICPA adapted)

17-9. Revenue Projection for a School System. The Wood County School Board bases its revenues budget for the fiscal year ending July 31, 19B, on projections of receipts for the fiscal year ending July 31, 19A. The receipts are summarized by type and source as follows:

WOOD COUNTY SCHOOL BOARD
ACTUAL REVENUES RECEIVED
FOR FISCAL YEAR ENDING JULY 31, 19B

Type and Source	Sales Tax	State Grants	Federal Grants	Allocation of Federal Revenue Sharing
City A..............	$ 300,000			$ 250,000
City B.............	450,000			300,000
All other cities........	210,000			200,000
Unincorporated areas..	150,000			
Federal government...			$750,000	
State government.....	300,000	$200,000		1,000,000
Total...........	$1,410,000	$200,000	$750,000	$1,750,000

These "actual revenues" represent receipts as of March 31, 19A. Projected receipts for the remainder of the fiscal year ending July 31, 19A, are: (1) sales tax collections should continue at the same rate; (2) additional state grants are expected to amount to $50,000; (3) no more federal funds of any kind are forthcoming until after July 31, 19A.

Revenues for 19B are expected to change as follows: (1) sales tax collections are projected to increase by 10%; (2) state grants will remain the same; (3) federal grants will be cut by two thirds; (4) federal revenue-sharing allocations should increase by 10%.

Required: (1) A schedule of actual and projected revenues (by type and source) for the fiscal year ending July 31, 19A.
(2) A schedule of projected revenues (by type and source) for the fiscal year ending July 31, 19B.

CASE

Analysis of Budgeted Performance. Mr. George Johnson was hired on July 1, 19A, as assistant general manager of the Botel Division of Staple, Inc. It was understood that he would be elevated to general manager of the division on January 1, 19C, when the then current general manager retired; and this was duly done. In addition to becoming acquainted with the division and his new duties, George was specifically charged with the responsibility for development of the 19B and 19C budgets. As general manager in 19C, he was obviously responsible for the 19D budget.

Staple, Inc. is a highly decentralized multiproduct company. Each division is quite autonomous. The corporate staff approves division-prepared operating budgets but seldom makes major changes in them. The corporate staff actively participates in decisions requiring capital investment (for expansion or replacement) and makes the final decisions. The division management is responsible for implementing the capital program. The major method used by Staple, Inc. to measure division performance is "contribution return on division net investment." The budgets presented below were approved by the corporate staff. Revision of the 19D budget is not considered necessary even though 19C actual departed from the approved 19C budget.

BOTEL DIVISION (000 OMITTED)

	Actual			Budget	
Accounts	19A	19B	19C	19C	19D
Sales..................................	$1,000	$1,500	$1,800	$2,000	$2,400
Less division variable costs:					
Material and labor................	$ 250	$ 375	$ 450	$ 500	$ 600
Repairs.........................	50	75	50	100	120
Supplies........................	20	30	36	40	48
Less division programmed fixed costs:					
Employee training................	30	35	25	40	45
Maintenance.....................	50	55	40	60	70
Less division committed fixed costs:					
Depreciation.....................	120	160	160	200	200
Rent............................	80	100	110	140	140
Total........................	$ 600	$ 830	$ 871	$1,080	$1,223
Division net contribution................	$ 400	$ 670	$ 929	$ 920	$1,177
Division investment:					
Accounts receivable.................	$ 100	$ 150	$ 180	$ 200	$ 240
Inventory........................	200	300	270	400	480
Fixed assets......................	1,590	2,565	2,800	3,380	4,000
Less accounts payable and wages payable	(150)	(225)	(350)	(300)	(360)
Net investment.................	$1,740	$2,790	$2,900	$3,680	$4,360
Contribution return on net investment.....	23%	24%	32%	25%	27%

Required: (1) Identification of George Johnson's responsibilities under the management and measurement program described above.

(2) Appraisal of George Johnson's performance in 19C.

(3) Recommendation to the president of Staple, Inc. of any changes in the responsibilities assigned to managers or in the measurement methods used to evaluate division management, based on this analysis.   (NAA adapted)

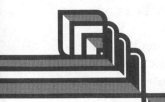

CHAPTER 18

THE FLEXIBLE BUDGET, COST BEHAVIOR ANALYSIS, STATISTICAL CORRELATION ANALYSIS

The budgets discussed and illustrated in the two previous chapters are known as fixed or forecast budgets. Sales and costs estimated for the coming year are compared with actual results. When a company's activities can be estimated within close limits, the fixed budget seems satisfactory. The term "fixed" budget is actually misleading, since it is also subject to revision. *Fixed* merely denotes that the budget is not adjusted to actual volume attained. It represents a prefixed point with which actual results are compared. Budgets are based on certain definite assumed conditions and results. However, completely predictable situations exist in only a few cases. If business conditions change radically, causing actual operations to differ widely from fixed budget plans, this management tool cannot be expected to be reliable or effective. The fact that costs and expenses are affected by fluctuations in volume limits the use of the fixed budget and leads to the use of the flexible budget.

THE FLEXIBLE BUDGET

The need for a flexible budget can be simply illustrated as follows. The owner of an automobile knows that the more he uses his car per year the more it costs him to operate it; he also knows that the more he uses his car the less it costs per mile. The reason for this lies in the nature of the expenses, some of which are fixed while others are variable or semivariable. Insurance, taxes, registration, and garaging are fixed costs which remain the same whether the car is operated 1,000 or 20,000 miles. The costs of tires, gas, oil, and repairs are variable costs and depend largely upon the miles driven. Obsolescence and depreciation result in a combined type of semivariable cost which fluctuates to some degree but does not vary directly with the usage of the car. The cost of operating the automobile per mile depends on the number of miles driven. Mileage constitutes the basis for judging the activity of the automobile. If the owner prepares an estimate of total costs and compares his actual expenses with the budget at year end, he cannot tell how successful he has been in keeping his expenses within the allowed limits without accounting for the mileage factor.

The underlying principle of a flexible budget is the need for some norm of expenditures for any given volume of business, which norm should be known beforehand to provide a guide to actual expenditures. To recognize this principle is to accept the fact that every business is dynamic, ever-changing, and never static. It is erroneous, if not futile, to expect a business to conform to a fixed, preconceived pattern.

Preparation of flexible budgets results in the construction of a series of formulas, one for each department. Each series, in turn, has a formula for each account in the department or cost center. The formula for each account indicates the fixed amount and/or a variable rate. The fixed amount and variable rate remain constant within prescribed ranges of activity. The variable portion of the formula is a variable rate expressed in relation to a base such as direct labor hours, direct labor cost, or machine hours.

Predetermination of the fixed expense total and the variable rate, as well as the subsequent application of the rate to the level of activity actually experienced, permits calculation of allowable expenditures for the volume of activity attained. These budget figures are compared with actual costs making possible a closer control of the performance by the department head than is the case with allowances based on a fixed budget. The end-of-period comparison is used to measure the performance of each department head. It is this ready-made comparison that makes the flexible budget a valuable instrument for cost control. The flexible budget assists in evaluating the effects of varying volumes of activity on profits and on the cash position.

Originally, the flexible budget idea was applied principally to the control of departmental factory overhead. In recent years, however, the idea has been applied to the entire budget so that production as well as marketing and administrative budgets are prepared on a flexible budget basis.

OBJECTIVES OF BUDGETARY CONTROL

Both the fixed and flexible budget provide management with information necessary to attain the major objectives of budgetary control:

1. An organized procedure for planning
2. A means for coordinating the activities of the various divisions of a business
3. A basis for cost control

Planning is one of the primary functions of management. The fixed budget provides an organized method of planning and a procedure for measuring the nature and the extent of deviations from the preconceived plan. It is the organized means for formalizing and coordinating plans of the many individuals whose decisions influence the conduct of a business.

A budget plan requires and results in coordination between all management levels of a business. Production must be planned in relation to expected sales, materials must be acquired in line with expected production requirements, facilities must be expanded as foreseeable future needs justify, and finances must be planned in relation to the funds needed for the expected volume of sales and production.

Cost control is predicated on the idea that actual costs will be compared with budgeted costs, relating what did happen with what should have happened. To accomplish this, an acceptable measure of what costs should be under any given set of conditions must be available. The most important factor affecting costs is volume or rate of activity. By predetermining the expense allowable for any given rate of activity and then comparing such allowances with actual expenses, a better measurement of the performance of an individual department is achieved and control of costs is more readily accomplished.

CAPACITY AND VOLUME (ACTIVITY)

The discussion of the actual preparation of a flexible budget must be preceded by some basic understanding of the term "capacity." The terms "capacity" and "volume" (or activity) are used in connection with the construction and use of both fixed and flexible budgets. *Capacity* constitutes that fixed amount of plant and machinery and, as will be discussed later, of personnel to whom management has committed itself and with whom it expects to conduct the business. *Volume* is the variable factor in business. It is related to capacity by the fact that volume (activity) attempts to make the best use of existing capacity.

Any budget is a forecast of expected sales, costs, and expenses. Materials, labor, factory overhead, marketing, and administrative expenses must be brought into harmony with the sales volume. In discussing the sales budget it was pointed out that sales volume is measured not only by sales the market could absorb, but also by plant capacity and machinery available to produce the goods. A plant or a department may produce 1,000 units or work 10,000 hours, but the questions arise: Is this volume (or activity) compatible with the capacity of the plant or department? Is the production of 1,000 units or the working of 10,000 hours greater or smaller than the amount of sales the company can safely expect to achieve in a given market during a given period? Answers to these questions depend upon decisions made regarding the capacity available for each department.

CAPACITY LEVELS

The following capacity levels require attention: theoretical, practical, expected actual, and normal.

Theoretical Capacity. The theoretical capacity of a department is its capacity to produce at full speed without interruptions. It is achieved if the plant or department produces at 100 percent of its rated capacity.

Practical Capacity. It is highly improbable that any company can operate at theoretical capacity. Allowances must be made for unavoidable interruptions, such as time lost for repairs, inefficiencies, breakdowns, setups, failures, unsatisfactory materials, delay in delivery of raw materials or supplies, labor shortages and absences, Sundays, holidays, vacations, inventory taking, and pattern and model changes. The number of work shifts must also be considered. These allowances reduce theoretical capacity to the practical capacity level. This reduction is caused by internal influences and does not consider the chief external cause, lack of customers' orders. Reduction from theoretical to practical capacity typically ranges from 15 percent to 25 percent, which results in a practical capacity level of 75 percent to 85 percent of theoretical capacity.

Expected Actual Capacity. The use of expected actual capacity for each period is often advocated, a concept that makes for a short-range outlook. It is feasible with firms whose products are of a seasonal nature, and market and style changes allow price adjustments according to competitive conditions and customer demands.

Normal Capacity. Firms may modify the above capacity levels by considering the utilization of the plant or various departments in the light of meeting average commercial demands or sales over a period long enough to level out the peaks and valleys which come with seasonal and cyclical variations. Finding a satisfactory and logical balance between plant capacity and sales volume constitutes one of the important problems of business management.

Once the normal (or average) capacity level has been agreed upon, overhead costs can be estimated and factory overhead rates computed. Use of these rates will cause all overhead of the period to be absorbed, provided normal capacity and normal expenses prevail during the period. Any deviation from normal capacity and/or normal overhead will result in variances as already discussed in the factory overhead chapters. It is the ease and speed with which the actual results may be compared with budgeted figures that make the flexible budget of inestimable value in analyzing end-of-period deviations.

Current Internal Revenue Service regulations permit the use of practical, expected actual, or normal capacity in assigning factory overhead costs to inventories.

The effect of the various capacity levels on predetermined factory overhead rates used is illustrated below. If the 75 percent capacity level is considered to be the normal operating level, the overhead rate is $2.40 per direct labor hour. At higher capacity levels the rate is lower due to fixed overhead.

EFFECT OF VARIOUS CAPACITY LEVELS ON PREDETERMINED FACTORY OVERHEAD RATES

Item	Normal Capacity	Practical Capacity	Theoretical Capacity
Percentage of production capacity....	75%	85%	100%
Direct labor hours..................	7,500 hrs.	8,500 hrs.	10,000 hrs.
Budgeted factory overhead:			
Fixed............................	$12,000	$12,000	$12,000
Variable.........................	6,000	6,800	8,000
Total............................	$18,000	$18,800	$20,000
Fixed factory overhead rate per direct labor hour..............	$1.60	$1.41	$1.20
Variable factory overhead rate per direct labor hour..............	.80	.80	.80
Total factory overhead rate per direct labor hour...........	$2.40	$2.21	$2.00

Importance of Determining Normal Capacity. The starting point in establishing budgets is the determination of a plant's normal capacity. Although there may be some differences between a normal long-run volume and the sales volume expected in the next period, normal capacity is useful in establishing sales prices and controlling costs. Thus determining a plant's normal capacity level is all-important. It is the basis for

(1) the entire budget system, (2) calculating factory overhead rates and product standard costs, and (3) operating plans. However, other capacity assumptions are sometimes used due to existing circumstances.

Factors Involved in Determining Normal Capacity. In determining the normal capacity of a plant, both its physical capacity and average sales expectancy must be considered; neither plant capacity nor sales potential alone is sufficient. As previously mentioned, sales expectancy should be determined for a period long enough to level out cyclical variations rather than on the sales expectancy for a short period of time. It should also be noted that machinery bought for future use and outmoded machinery must be excluded from the considerations which lead to the determination of the normal capacity level.

Calculation of the normal capacity of a plant is not a simple matter, for it requires many different judgment factors. Normal capacity should be determined first for the business as a whole and then broken down by plants and departments. Determination of a departmental capacity figure might indicate that for a certain department the planned program is an overload while in another it will result in excess capacity. The capacities of several departments will seldom be in such perfect balance as to produce an unhampered flow of production. For the department with the overload, often termed the "bottle-neck" department, actions such as the following might have to be taken:

1. Working overtime
2. Introducing an additional shift
3. Temporarily transferring operations from the department to another where spare capacity is available
4. Subcontracting the excess load
5. Purchasing additional equipment

On the other hand, the department with excess facilities might have to reduce them; or the sales department might be asked to search for additional orders to utilize the spare capacity.

Idle Capacity vs. Excess Capacity. A distinction must be made between idle and excess capacity. *Idle capacity* results from the temporary idleness of production or distribution facilities due to a slowdown in production because of a temporary lack of orders. Idle facilities are restored to full use as soon as the need arises. Their cost is usually part of the expense total used in setting up the overhead rate and is at all times a part of the product cost. However, as explained in the factory overhead and standard cost chapters, the cost of idle capacity can be isolated both for control purposes and for the guidance of management.

Excess capacity, on the other hand, results either from greater productive capacity than the company could ever hope to use, or from unbalanced equipment or machinery within departments.   Unbalanced machinery involves excess capacity of one machine in contrast with output of other machines with which it must be sychronized.   Any expense arising from excess capacity should be excluded from the factory overhead rate and from the product cost. The expense should be treated as a deduction in the income statement. In many instances, it seems wise to dispose of excess plant and equipment.

Purposes of Establishing Normal Capacity. Once normal capacity has been determined, it can be used for these purposes and aims:

1. Preparation of departmental flexible budgets and computation of predetermined factory overhead rates
2. Compilation of the standard cost of each product
3. Establishment of sales prices
4. Establishment of a plant-wide budget
5. Scheduling production
6. Assigning cost to inventories
7. Measurement of the effects of changing volumes of production
8. Determination of the break-even point
9. Control and possible reduction of costs

The normal capacity level fulfills both long- and short-term purposes. The long-term utilization of the normal capacity level relates the marketing phase and therewith the pricing policy of the business to the production phase over a long period of time, leveling out fluctuations that are of short duration and of comparatively minor significance. The short-term utilization relates to the use made by management of the normal capacity level in analyzing changes or fluctuations that occur during an operating year. This short-term utilization measures temporary idleness and aids in an analysis of its causes.

ANALYSIS OF COST BEHAVIOR

The success of a flexible budget depends upon careful study and analysis of the relationship of expenses to volume of activity or production and results in classifying expenses as (1) fixed, (2) variable, and (3) semivariable.

Fixed Expenses. A *fixed expense* remains the same in total as activity increases or decreases. Fixed factory overhead includes the conventional items such as depreciation (straight-line basis), property insurance, and real estate taxes. These and many other expenses not inherently fixed acquire the *fixed* characteristic through the dictates of management policy.

Yet, just as management decisions create fixed costs, other decisions can alter the circumstances and change a fixed item both as to its classification and amount. In other words, there is really nothing irrevocably fixed with respect to any expense classified as fixed. The amounts of fixed expenses remain valid only on the assumption that the underlying conditions remain unchanged. In the long run, all expenses are variable. Some fixed expenses, however, can be changed in the short run because of changes in the volume of activity or for other reasons (e.g., the number and salaries of the management groups, advertising, and research expenses) and are sometimes called "programmed fixed expenses." Other fixed expenses (e.g., depreciation or a long-term lease agreement) may commit management for a much longer period of time; they have therefore been labeled "committed fixed expenses."

Variable Expenses. A *variable expense* is expected to increase proportionately with an increase in activity and decrease proportionately with a decrease in activity. Variable expenses include: supplies, indirect factory labor, receiving, storing, rework, perishable tools, and maintenance of machinery and tools. A measure of activity — such as direct labor hours or dollars, or machine hours — must be selected as an independent variable for use in estimating the variable expense (the dependent variable) at specified levels of activity. A rate of variability per unit of activity is thus determined.

Variable expenses are subject to certain fundamental assumptions if they are to remain so classified. For instance, it is assumed that prices of supplies or indirect labor do not change, that manufacturing methods and procedures do not vary, and that efficiencies do not fluctuate. If conditions change, the need for and use of variable expense items also change. For these reasons, variable expenses require constant attention so that revisions can be instigated from time to time.

Semivariable Expenses. A *semivariable expense* displays both fixed and variable characteristics, as in: salaries of supervisors, accountants, buyers, typists, clerks, janitors, employees' insurances, pension plans, maintenance of buildings and grounds, purchased power, water, gas, telephone and telegraph, office machine rentals, coal, fuel oil, some supplies, and even membership dues in trade, professional, and recreational organizations and clubs.

Three reasons for this semivariable characteristic of some expenses are:

1. The need to have a minimum organization, or to consume a minimum quantity of supplies or services in order to maintain readiness to operate. Beyond this minimum cost which is fixed, additional cost varies with volume.

2. Accounting classifications based upon object of expenditure or function commonly group fixed and variable items together. As an example, the cost of steam may be charged to one account although the cost of steam used for heating is dependent upon weather and not production volume, while the cost of steam used in the manufacturing process varies closely with volume of production in the factory.

3. Production factors are divisible into infinitely small units. When such costs are charted against their volume, their movements appear as a series of steps rather than as a continuous straight line. This situation is quite noticeable in moving from a one-shift to a two-shift or from a two-shift to a three-shift operation. Such moves result in definite steps in the cost line because a complete set of foremen, clerks, etc., must be added at one point.[1]

The cost-line of a semivariable expense is depicted graphically below. The chart illustrates that the fixed portion of this semivariable expense is at $200 (Line A). The variable portion increases in a straight line (Line B), indicating that for each increase in volume (the independent variable), there is a corresponding increase in the variable portion of the expense (the dependent variable).

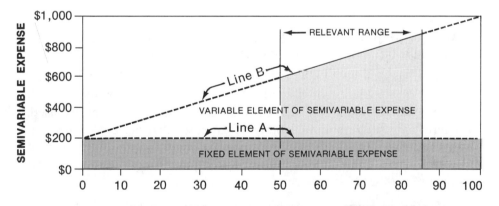

BASE EXPRESSED AS A REALISTIC MEASURE OF ACTIVITY
(e.g., in sales dollars, units produced, labor dollars, or labor hours)

Fixed and Variable Elements of a Semivariable Expense

This straight line (Line B) is often stated as being in linear or proportional relationship to the base. This linearity is used and accepted in most cost studies even though many semivariable and variable expenses do not fluctuate in this manner. Thus, it must be understood that the rate of variability in relation to volume does not necessarily take place indiscriminately from zero to 100 percent. But the degree of error is negligible as long as activity remains within a reasonably relevant range,

---

[1] *NA(C)A Bulletin*, Vol. 30, No. 20, pp. 1224–1225.

as illustrated on the chart. *Relevant range* is defined as the range of activity over which the amount of fixed expense and the rate of variability remain unchanged and applies to expenses that are either all fixed or all variable as well as to those that are of the semivariable type.

Further, the expense at zero activity, calculated using the various statistical methods discussed below, is a fixed expense only if the linear relationship found in the range of observations extends back to zero activity. Otherwise, the expense figure calculated at the zero activity level is merely the value resulting from finding the point at which the regression line computed from the available data intersects the vertical expense line. In such a case, a given expense may be more accurately described, for example, as fixed at $1,000 *up to* an activity level of say 2,000 direct labor hours, with *additional* activity within a relevant range having a variable rate of say $.60 per direct labor hour.

Thus, fixed and variable expenses are related to volume (activity) within appropriate or *relevant* ranges of operations; and the fixed expense and rate of variability will depend upon the particular range of operations under consideration.

DETERMINING THE FIXED AND VARIABLE ELEMENTS OF A SEMIVARIABLE EXPENSE

Two approaches can be used to determine the fixed portion and the degree of variability of a semivariable expense: (1) historical and (2) analytical. It should be observed that these same procedures are used in determining the rate of variability of expenses that are entirely variable. In such cases, a variable rate is found; and the computed fixed portion is simply zero. Moreover, an entirely fixed expense would yield a fixed portion, with a zero variable rate.

Historical Approach. The historical approach makes use of the following statistical methods: (1) high and low points method, (2) statistical scattergraph method, (3) method of least squares, and (4) method of least squares for multiple independent variables. These methods are used in determining the fixed and variable elements of a semivariable expense.

High and Low Points Method. This technique can best be explained by using an example. To establish the fixed and variable elements of machine repair costs for a producing department, actual expenses incurred during two different periods are listed on page 547. Periods (data points) selected are the high and low periods as to *activity level* from the array of historical data being analyzed. These periods are usually, but not necessarily, also the highest and lowest figures for the *expense* being analyzed.

MACHINE REPAIR EXPENSES FOR A PRODUCING DEPARTMENT

	Activity Level— Direct Labor Hours		Expenses
High......................	6,840 hours	100%	$2,776
Low	2,736 hours	40%	1,750
Difference................	4,104 hours	60%	$1,026

Variable rate = $1,026 ÷ 4,104 hours = $.25 per direct labor hour

	High	Low
Total expense.............................	$2,776	$1,750
Variable expense ($.25 per direct labor hour)..	1,710	684
Fixed element.............................	$1,066	$1,066

If the periods having the highest or lowest activity levels are not the same as those having the highest or lowest expense being analyzed, the activity level should govern in making the selection. These two periods are selected because they represent conditions at two different activity levels. Care must be taken not to select data points distorted by abnormal conditions.

The 60 percent difference between the activity levels selected is 4,104 hours with a cost variation of $1,026. The variable rate is determined by dividing $1,026 by the 4,104 hours, arriving at a variable costing rate per direct labor hour of $.25. The fixed portion in the total expense is found by subtracting the figure obtained by multiplying high activity hours (6,840) times the variable hourly rate ($.25) from the high activity cost ($2,776). The same answer is obtained when low activity hours and cost are used.

With variable and fixed elements established, it is easy to calculate expense totals for various levels of activity, an important factor in the construction of the flexible budget and in the determination of the budget allowance in standard cost accounting.

Expense levels may also be determined by the use of graphs such as the one shown on page 548.

The graph shows not only the total expense and its fixed and variable elements, but it also permits the quick calculation of any budget allowance within the relevant range of activity; i.e., for 4,000 hours, the total expense is $2,066 composed of $1,066 fixed cost and $1,000 variable cost. The budget allowance could also be computed as follows: 4,000 hours × $.25 (the variable rate per hour) + $1,066 (fixed cost) = $2,066.

The calculations are simple, but the method's disadvantage is that it determines cost behavior based on only two data points and assumes that

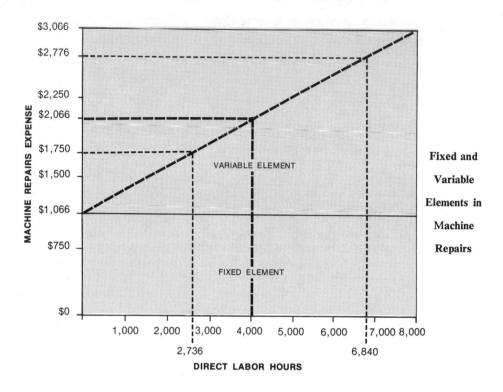

Fixed and Variable Elements in Machine Repairs

the other data points lie on a straight line between the high and low points. Because the high and low points method uses *only* two data points, it *may not* yield answers that are as accurate as those derived when a larger number of points are considered as is done in the statistical scattergraph method and the method of least squares.

Statistical Scattergraph Method. A technique widely used for analyzing semi-variable expenses is the statistical scatter-graph method. In this method various costs are plotted on a vertical line — the *y-axis*; and measurement figures (direct labor dollars, direct labor hours, units of output, or percentage of capacity) are plotted along a horizontal line — the *x-axis*. The data used for preparing the statistical scattergraph on page 549 are given at the right.

Each point on the statistical scatter-graph represents the electricity expense for a particular month. For instance, the

Month	Direct Labor Hours	Electricity Expense
January.....	34,000	$ 640
February...	30,000	620
March.....	34,000	620
April........	39,000	590
May........	42,000	500
June........	32,000	530
July.........	26,000	500
August.....	26,000	500
September..	31,000	530
October....	35,000	550
November..	43,000	580
December ..	48,000	680
Total....	420,000	$6,840
Monthly average .	35,000	$ 570

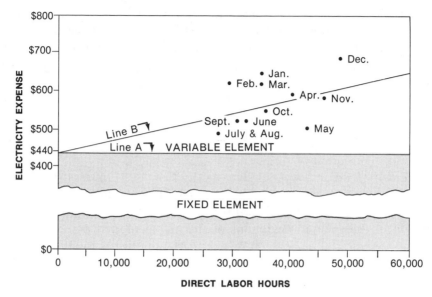

**Statistical Scattergraph Representing the Fixed and Variable
Elements for Electricity Expense**

point labeled "Nov." represents the electricity expense for November
when 43,000 direct labor hours were worked.   The x-axis shows the direct
labor hours, and the y-axis shows the electricity expense. In the scattergraph, Line B is plotted by visual inspection. The line represents the
trend shown by the majority of data points. Generally, there should be
as many data points above as below the line. Another line is drawn
parallel to the base line from the point of intersection on the y-axis, which
is read from the scattergraph as approximately $440. This Line A
represents the fixed element of the electricity expense for all activity
levels within the relevant range. The triangle formed by Lines A and B
shows the increase in electricity expense as direct labor hours increase.

The increase for electricity expense, based on direct labor hours, is
computed as follows:

Fixed Expense per Month* = $440

$$\underset{\text{Expense}}{\text{Average Monthly}} - \underset{\text{Element}}{\text{Fixed}} = \underset{\text{Element of Expense}}{\text{Average Monthly Variable}}$$

$$\$570 \quad - \quad \$440 \quad = \quad \$130$$

$$\frac{\text{Average Monthly Variable Element of Expense}}{\text{Average Monthly Direct Labor Hours}} = \frac{\text{Variable Cost Per}}{\text{Direct Labor Hour}}$$

$$\frac{\$130}{35,000 \text{ Hours}} = \$.0037 \text{ per Direct Labor Hour}$$

---

*As read approximately from the scattergraph.

It is now possible to state that the electricity expense consists of $440 fixed expense per month and of a variable factor of $.0037 per direct hour.

Line B is drawn as a straight line even though the points do not follow a perfect linear pattern. In most analyses, a straight line is adequate, because it is a reasonable approximation of cost behavior within the relevant range. Mathematicians have worked out a technique, the "method of least squares," for computing a more exact straight line called a "regression line."

Method of Least Squares. The method of least squares (sometimes called "simple regression analysis") determines mathematically a line of best fit or a regression line drawn through a set of plotted points so that the sum of the squared deviations of the actual plotted points from the point directly above or below it on the regression line is a minimum.

The following steps are required to arrive at the desired answer using the method of least squares. (Data from page 548 are used for this illustration.)

1. First, determine the average direct labor hours and electricity expense. Total direct labor hours are 420,000 which, when divided by 12, result in an average of 35,000 hours per month. Total expense is $6,840, or an average of $570 per month ($6,840 ÷ 12).

2. Differences between actual monthly figures and the average monthly figure computed in (1) above are tabulated in Columns 1 to 4 below.

Month	Column 1 Direct Labor Hours	Column 2 Difference from Average of 35,000 hrs.	Column 3 Electricity Expense	Column 4 Difference from Average of $570 Electricity Exp.	Column 5 Column 2 Squared	Column 6 Column 2 × Column 4
January.....	34,000	− 1,000	$640	+ 70	1,000,000	− 70,000
February....	30,000	− 5,000	620	+ 50	25,000,000	− 250,000
March......	34,000	− 1,000	620	+ 50	1,000,000	− 50,000
April.......	39,000	+ 4,000	590	+ 20	16,000,000	+ 80,000
May........	42,000	+ 7,000	500	− 70	49,000,000	− 490,000
June........	32,000	− 3,000	530	− 40	9,000,000	+ 120,000
July........	26,000	− 9,000	500	− 70	81,000,000	+ 630,000
August......	26,000	− 9,000	500	− 70	81,000,000	+ 630,000
September...	31,000	− 4,000	530	− 40	16,000,000	+ 160,000
October.....	35,000	0	550	− 20	0	0
November...	43,000	+ 8,000	580	+ 10	64,000,000	+ 80,000
December...	48,000	+ 13,000	680	+ 110	169,000,000	+ 1,430,000
					512,000,000	2,270,000

3. Two multiplications must be made: (1) differences computed in Column 2 are squared and entered in Column 5 and (2) the same differences are multiplied by differences in Column 4 and entered in Column 6.

4. It is now possible to compute a variable rate for electricity expense:

$$\frac{\text{Column 6}}{\text{Column 5}} = \frac{2,270,000}{512,000,000} = .0044 \text{ } or \text{ } 44\% \text{ } or \text{ } \$.44 \text{ per 100 Direct Labor Hours}$$

5. Using the equation for a straight line, y = a + bx, where "y" is the total expense at an activity level "x," "a" is the "y" intercept (or fixed expense), and "b" is the slope of the line (degree of variability, or variable rate), the fixed expense computation is:

$$y = a + bx$$
Where: y = $570 Average Electricity Expense

$$b = \frac{2,270,000}{512,000,000} = \$.0044 \text{ Variable Rate of Electricity Expense per Direct Labor Hour}$$

$$x = 35,000 \text{ Average Direct Labor Hours}$$
Thus: $570 = a + \$.0044 \text{ } (35,000)$
$$\$570 = a + \$154$$
$$\$570 - \$154 = a$$

$$a = \$416 \text{ Fixed Element of Electricity Expense per Month}$$

The above answer differs somewhat from the figure determined by the scattergraph method because visual inspection does not offer so accurate an answer as this mathematical procedure. This preciseness injects a higher degree of objectivity and lack of bias into the figures. Many accountants and industrial engineers responsible for budget preparations prefer this more scientific technique. However, it is still useful to plot the data first, as illustrated on page 549, in order to verify visually the existence of a reasonable degree of correlation. Whatever method is used, abnormal data should be excluded.

Method of Least Squares for Multiple Independent Variables. Typically, cost behavior is shown as dependent on a single measure of volume or on some other independent variable (e.g., the behavior of the dependent variable, electricity expense, was described by the independent variable, direct labor hours). However, a cost may vary because of more than one factor.

In the method of least squares discussion above (simple regression analysis), only one independent variable was considered. Multiple regression analysis is a further application and expansion of the method of least squares, permitting the consideration of more than one independent variable. With multiple independent variables, the cost relationship can no longer be shown on a two-dimensional graph.

The simple least-squares equation for a straight line, $y = a + bx$, with "a" as the fixed element and "b" as the degree of variability for the independent variable "x," can be expanded to include more than one independent variable. For example, two independent variables are given in the equation $y = a + bx + cz$ with "c" as the degree of variability for an additional independent variable "z."

The least-squares concept is fundamentally the same for several independent variables as it is for only one. The arithmetical computations become more complex, but the widespread availability of computer programs makes its use more feasible insofar as the numerical manipulations are concerned.

If the cost behavior of a group of expenses in one or more expense accounts is being described, an alternate to multiple variables (and hence to the considerations necessitated by multiple variables when applying the least squares method) may be possible. That is, expenses may be grouped and classified in sufficient detail so that expenses in a particular group are all largely related to only one independent variable. This would allow the use of the method of least squares as earlier illustrated; i.e., simple regression analysis. If this approach is not feasible (i.e., if the final classification or grouping still finds more than one independent variable required to describe the cost behavior), then multiple regression analysis should be employed.[2]

Statistical Correlation Analysis. Application of the statistical scattergraph method accomplishes *visual* verification of a reasonable degree of correlation. Perfect correlation would exist if all plotted points fell on the regression line. Mathematical measurements may be used to quantify correlation. *Correlation* means establishing the relation between the values of two attributes; i.e., the relationship of the independent variable (x, or direct labor hours in the illustration) and the dependent variable (y, or electricity expense in the illustration), before arriving at the fixed cost and the variable rate for semivariable expenses, or the variable rate for entirely variable expenses.

In statistical theory the *coefficient of correlation*, known as a number "r," is a measure of the extent to which two variables are related linearly. When $r = 0$, there is no correlation; and when $r = \pm 1$, the correlation is perfect. As r approaches $+1$, the correlation is positive, meaning the dependent variable (y) increases as the independent variable (x) increases; and the regression line would slope upward to the right. As r approaches -1, the correlation is negative or inverse, meaning the dependent variable

---

[2]For a comprehensive treatment, see Chapter 17, "Regression and Correlation: Multivariate Analysis," Charles T. Clark and Lawrence L. Schkade, *Statistical Analysis for Administrative Decisions* (Cincinnati: South-Western Publishing Co., 1974).

(y) decreases as the independent variable (x) increases; and the regression would slope downward to the right.

The *coefficient of determination,* known as the number "r^2," is found by squaring the coefficient of correlation. The coefficient of determination is considered easier to interpret than the coefficient of correlation (r) because it represents the percentage of explained variance. The larger the coefficient of determination, the closer it comes to the coefficient of correlation until both coefficients equal 1. The word "explained" does not mean that the variation in the dependent variable was caused by the variations in the independent variable but that the fluctuations are related to the fluctuations in the independent variable.

Applying the correlation analysis technique to the data on page 550, a coefficient of determination of less than .25 results (see page 554). This means that less than 25% of the change in electricity expense is related to the change in direct labor hours. The conclusion is that the cost is related not solely to direct labor hours but to other factors as well, such as the time of day for production or the season of the year. Furthermore, some other independent variable such as machine hours may afford better correlation.

The illustrative data, formula, and the calculation of the coefficient of correlation (r) and the coefficient of determination (r^2) are presented below.

	Direct Labor Hours (x)	Electricity Expense (y)	(xy)	(x^2)	(y^2)
January.....	34,000	640	21,760,000	1,156,000,000	409,600
February....	30,000	620	18,600,000	900,000,000	384,400
March......	34,000	620	21,080,000	1,156,000,000	384,400
April.......	39,000	590	23,010,000	1,521,000,000	348,100
May........	42,000	500	21,000,000	1,764,000,000	250,000
June........	32,000	530	16,960,000	1,024,000,000	280,900
July........	26,000	500	13,000,000	676,000,000	250,000
August......	26,000	500	13,000,000	676,000,000	250,000
September...	31,000	530	16,430,000	961,000,000	280,900
October.....	35,000	550	19,250,000	1,225,000,000	302,500
November...	43,000	580	24,940,000	1,849,000,000	336,400
December...	48,000	680	32,640,000	2,304,000,000	462,400
Total.......	420,000	6,840	241,670,000	15,212,000,000	3,939,600

In the third column, each independent variable (x) is multiplied by each corresponding dependent variable (y). Next, each x value and each y value is squared. All columns are then totaled and along with the number of observations (months in this illustration and designated in the formula as "n"), provide the figures required by the formula.

$$r = \frac{n\,\Sigma xy - (\Sigma x)(\Sigma y)}{\sqrt{\left[n\Sigma x^2 - (\Sigma x)^2\right]\left[n\Sigma y^2 - (\Sigma y)^2\right]}}$$

$$= \frac{(12)\,(241,670,000) - (420,000)\,(6,840)}{\sqrt{\left[(12)\,(15,212,000,000) - (420,000)\,(420,000)\right]\left[(12)\,(3,939,600) - (6,840)\,(6,840)\right]}}$$

$$= \frac{2,900,040,000 - 2,872,800,000}{\sqrt{\left(182,544,000,000 - 176,400,000,000\right)\left(47,275,200 - 46,785,600\right)}}$$

$$= \frac{27,240,000}{\sqrt{(6,144,000,000)\,(489,600)}} = \frac{27,240,000}{\sqrt{3,008,102,400,000,000}}$$

$$= \frac{27,240,000}{54,846,170} = +.49666 \; ; \; r^2 = .24667$$

To illustrate a case in which a high degree of correlation exists, the cost of electricity (y) from the previous example has been slightly altered with direct labor hours remaining on the same level. The solution below indicates an almost perfect correlation between the two attributes which would argue for accepting this relationship for the calculation of the factory overhead rate and the construction of the flexible budget.

Illustration of a better correlation:

	Direct Labor Hours (x)	Electricity Expense (y)	(xy)	(x²)	(y²)
January.....	34,000	660	22,440,000	1,156,000,000	435,600
February....	30,000	590	17,700,000	900,000,000	348,100
March......	34,000	660	22,440,000	1,156,000,000	435,600
April.......	39,000	680	26,520,000	1,521,000,000	462,400
May........	42,000	740	31,080,000	1,764,000,000	547,600
June........	32,000	610	19,520,000	1,024,000,000	372,100
July........	26,000	580	15,080,000	676,000,000	336,400
August......	26,000	550	14,300,000	676,000,000	302,500
September...	31,000	630	19,530,000	961,000,000	396,900
October.....	35,000	640	22,400,000	1,225,000,000	409,600
November...	43,000	750	32,250,000	1,849,000,000	562,500
December...	48,000	770	36,960,000	2,304,000,000	592,900
Total.......	420,000	7,860	280,220,000	15,212,000,000	5,202,200

$$r = \frac{n\Sigma xy - (\Sigma x)(\Sigma y)}{\sqrt{\left[n\Sigma x^2 - (\Sigma x)^2\right]\left[n\Sigma y^2 - (\Sigma y)^2\right]}}$$

$$= \frac{(12)(280,220,000) - (420,000)(7,860)}{\sqrt{\left[(12)(15,212,000,000) - (420,000)(420,000)\right]\left[(12)(5,202,200) - (7,860)(7,860)\right]}}$$

$$= \frac{3,362,640,000 - 3,301,200,000}{\sqrt{\left(182,544,000,000 - 176,400,000,000\right)\left(62,426,400 - 61,779,600\right)}}$$

$$= \frac{61,440,000}{\sqrt{(6,144,000,000)(646,800)}}$$

$$= \frac{61,440,000}{\sqrt{3,973,939,200,000,000}}$$

$$= \frac{61,440,000}{63,039,188} = +\underline{.97463}; \; r^2 = \underline{.94990}$$

Analytical Approach. Historical procedures deal primarily with past costs; thus, unusual conditions should have been eliminated to assure working with reliable and comparable data. Yet, in spite of all caution, values determined by any of the techniques illustrated might not fit the situation expected to exist in the coming month or year. For this reason, the analytical approach should be used in conjunction with the above techniques in determining the variability of expenses.

Industrial engineers and operating personnel working with the controller's staff study each function (activity, job) to determine (1) the necessity of the function, (2) the most efficient method to do the job, and (3) the proper cost of performing the work at various levels of production. This approach is particularly appropriate for indirect labor as well as for all expenses, for close scrutiny of every expense item will frequently reveal conditions allowed to exist in the past without being known or questioned. Therefore, findings based on historical data should be adjusted when future conditions point to a change.

Value of Determining Cost Behavior. The determination of fixed and variable elements of a semivariable expense and the creation of itemized as well as total fixed and total variable costs is necessary in order to plan, analyze, control, measure, or evaluate:

1. Departmental expenses allowed at various levels of activity.
2. Operating efficiency of a department.
3. Contribution margin and direct costing.
4. Utilization of facilities.
5. Break-even point and cost-volume-profit situations.
6. Marketing profitability of territories, products, and customers.
7. Company profit structure.
8. Differential and comparative cost decisions.
9. Proposed capital expenditures.
10. Effect of alternative courses management might wish to follow.

The fixed-variable cost classification plays a major role in all subsequent chapters dealing with profit planning, cost control, and decision making.

PREPARING A FLEXIBLE BUDGET

Considerable discussion has been devoted to the development of the underlying details necessary for the preparation of a flexible budget. It is not intended to convey the idea that the factory overhead budget on a flexible basis outranks the budgets for other functions of the business, because these other functions can also utilize the flexible budget concept. Any increase or decrease in business activity must be reflected throughout the enterprise. However, in some activities or departments changes will be greater or smaller than in others. Certain departments have the ability to produce more without much additional cost, while in others costs increase or decrease in more or less direct proportion to production increases or decreases. The flexible budget attempts to deal with this problem.

When the fixed dollar amount and the variable rate of an expense have been determined, budget allowances for any level within a relevant range of activity can be computed without difficulty. Illustrated on page 557 is a budget allowances schedule for normal capacity that becomes the basis for preparing a flexible budget for the Machining Department.

In the flexible budget on page 558, the factory overhead rate declines steadily as production moves to the 100 percent operating level; then it increases because items such as rework operations and supervision increase faster than at lower levels and because overtime premiums and night premiums are introduced. While such cost increases are revealed through the flexible budget, the situation indicates a possible departure from the use of the equations for a straight line, $y = a + bx$; in this case, $6,000 fixed expenses $+ 1.00(x)$, for all levels of activity. However, it must be emphasized that *one* definite level must be agreed upon and used for setting the predetermined factory overhead rate for applying overhead cost to production. Costs and base selected and the resulting rate will lead to spending and idle capacity variances that might warrant a rate change in the next period for the sake of more meaningful cost control and pricing procedures. In any case, the effective use of cost data for planning, control, and decision-making purposes requires reasonably accurate knowledge of cost behavior.

The flexible budget for the Machining Department with its fixed expenses and its variable rate per direct labor hour for each variable or semivariable expense item requires additional comment. The factory overhead rate based on direct labor hours means that all variable expenses are

BUDGET ALLOWANCES FOR MACHINING DEPARTMENT

Activity Base: Normal capacity, 4,000 direct labor hours per month = 80% rated capacity

Acct. No.	Account Title	Fixed Expense	Variable Rate per Direct Labor Hour
01	Indirect Labor.............................	$ 600	$.175
02	Clerical Help.............................	100	.050
10	Setup Men................................	800	.070
14	Rework Operations.......................	100	
28	Supervision...............................	1,200	
41	Factory Supplies.........................	200	.055
	Total Controllable by Department Head......	$3,000	.35
55	Insurance — Fire, etc.....................	80	
57	Taxes — State and Local..................	50	
63	Depreciation.............................	500	
	Total Noncontrollable.....................	$ 630	
71	Maintenance..............................	$ 600	.20
74	Building Occupancy.......................	780	.10
77	Gas, Water, Steam, and Air	540	.30
79	General Expenses.........................	450	.05
	Total Service Departments (apportioned)......	$2,370	.65
	Total......................................	$6,000	$1.00

Summary:

Fixed expenses............................... $ 6,000
Variable expenses:
    4,000 direct labor hours @ $1 per hour....... 4,000
Total cost at normal capacity................. $10,000

Factory overhead rate of Machining Department
    at normal capacity ($10,000 ÷ 4,000 hours).....$2.50 per direct labor hour

FLEXIBLE BUDGET FOR MACHINING DEPARTMENT

Operating Level		Monthly Allowances				
Based on direct labor hours.........		3,500	4,000*	4,500	5,000	5,500
Percentage of capacity..............		70%	80%	90%	100%	110%
Acct. No.	Account Title					
01	Indirect Labor..............	$ 1,212.50	$ 1,300.00	$ 1,387.50	$ 1,475.00	$ 1,562.50
02	Clerical Help................	275.00	300.00	325.00	350.00	375.00
10	Setup Men..................	1,045.00	1,080.00	1,115.00	1,150.00	1,185.00
14	Rework Operations..........	100.00	100.00	100.00	135.00	160.00
28	Supervision.................	1,200.00	1,200.00	1,200.00	1,400.00	1,800.00
41	Factory Supplies............	392.50	420.00	447.50	475.00	502.50
44	Overtime Premium..........	....	....	....	500.00	600.00
46	Night Premium..............	....	....	....	....	120.00
	Total Controllable by Department Head...............	$ 4,225.00	$ 4,400.00	$ 4,575.00	$ 5,485.00	$ 6,305.00
55	Insurance — Fire, etc.........	$ 80.00	$ 80.00	$ 80.00	$ 80.00	$ 80.00
57	Taxes — State and Local.....	50.00	50.00	50.00	50.00	50.00
63	Depreciation................	500.00	500.00	500.00	500.00	500.00
	Total Noncontrollable.......	$ 630.00	$ 630.00	$ 630.00	$ 630.00	$ 630.00
71	Maintenance................	$ 1,300.00	$ 1,400.00	$1,500.00	$ 1,600.00	$ 1,865.00
74	Building Occupancy.........	1,130.00	1,180.00	1,230.00	1,280.00	1,330.00
77	Gas, Water, Steam, and Air..	1,590.00	1,740.00	1,890.00	2,040.00	2,190.00
79	General Expenses...........	625.00	650.00	675.00	700.00	725.00
	Total Service Departments....	$ 4,645.00	$ 4,970.00	$ 5,295.00	$ 5,620.00	$ 6,110.00
	Total Factory Overhead.....	$ 9,500.00	$10,000.00	$10,500.00	$11,735.00	$13,045.00
	Factory Overhead Rate per Direct Labor Hour........	$2.714	$2.500	$2.333	$2.347	$2.372

*Normal capacity.

related to this type of activity base. In many instances the activity base is never uniform for all overhead items. Certain departments within a firm may have different bases, and a single department may require different bases and rates for different groups of expenses. Within a department only, a low correlation or none at all may exist between some of the expenses and the activity base selected. It is therefore essential to study the correlation of volume in physical terms, such as units produced, labor hours worked, or machine hours used, with the dollar cost for each item or for a group of items. Such studies indicate quite often that a new base must be chosen for some or all of the expenses to arrive at the most acceptable separation of fixed and variable expenses. The use of statistical correlation analysis is suggested to discover the correct volume base to be used before attempting to separate the fixed and variable elements of the many expense items that are semivariable in nature and before describing the rate of variability of entirely variable expenses.

FLEXIBLE BUDGETING THROUGH ELECTRONIC DATA PROCESSING AND STEP CHARTS

The determination of the fixed and variable elements in each departmental expense is a time-consuming task, particularly when computations, calculations, and analyses are performed either manually or by a desk calculator. The application of data processing techniques can eliminate this tedious chore and at the same time provide the necessary tool for budgetary control and responsibility reporting throughout the year.

Whenever increases or decreases in certain expenses due to change in product or change in processing, etc., are anticipated, the projected overhead amounts are adjusted accordingly; otherwise, the predetermined rates are used. Some expenses are budgeted on a step-chart basis which is in harmony with the relevant range idea mentioned previously.[3]

The step charts indicate the allowance for nonproduction personnel at various levels of production activity. Each bisected square is an indication as to the number of nonproduction personnel (upper left-hand corner) and salary levels allowable (lower right-hand corner) at each step. In the step chart for service departments (below), the levels are based on the

Department __Production Control__   Service Departments Only

DEPARTMENTAL ALLOWANCE FOR NONPRODUCTION PERSONNEL

ALL   a/o 00   MONTHLY ALLOWANCE FOR NONPRODUCTION PERSONNEL

NUMBER OF PRODUCTION HOURS (From – To)	PRODUCTION CONTROL MANAGER	SUPERVISOR MATERIAL	ASSISTANT SUPERVISOR	PRODUCTION EXPEDITOR	DEPARTMENT SCHEDULER LEVEL B	ORDER ANALYST LEVEL 7	ENGINEERING CHG COORDINATOR	VERIFICATION CLERK	PRODUCTION SCHEDULER LEVEL 9	CLERK LEVEL 3	SECRETARY	STOCK CHASER LEVEL 8
10M – 10.9M	1 / 926	2 / 1586	1 / 600	1 / 430	3 / 1200	4 / 1600	1 / 517		1 / 432	1 / 369	1 / 303	5 / 1750
11 – 11.9	1 / 926	2 / 1586	1 / 600	1 / 430	3 / 1200	5 / 2000	1 / 517		1 / 432	2 / 738	1 / 303	6 / 2100
12 – 12.9	1 / 926	3 / 2257	1 / 600	1 / 430	3 / 1200	5 / 2000	1 / 517	1 / 387	1 / 432	2 / 738	1 / 303	6 / 2100
13 – 13.9	1 / 926	3 / 2257	1 / 600	1 / 430	3 / 1200	5 / 2000	1 / 517	1 / 387	1 / 432	3 / 1107	1 / 303	6 / 2100
14 – 14.9	1 / 926	4 / 2839	1 / 600	1 / 430	3 / 1200	5 / 2000	1 / 517	1 / 387	1 / 432	3 / 1107	1 / 303	7 / 2450
15 – 15.9	1 / 926	4 / 2839	1 / 600	1 / 430	3 / 1200	5 / 2000	1 / 517	1 / 387	1 / 432	3 / 1107	1 / 303	7 / 2450
16 – 16.9	1 / 926	4 / 2839	1 / 600	1 / 430	4 / 1600	5 / 2000	1 / 517	1 / 387	1 / 432	4 / 1476	1 / 303	7 / 2450
17 – 18	1 / 926	4 / 2839	1 / 600	1 / 430	4 / 1600	5 / 2000	1 / 517	1 / 387	1 / 432	5 / 1845	1 / 303	7 / 2450

Step Chart for a Service Department

---

[3]Eugene J. McNaboe, "Flexible Budgeting Through Electronic Data Processing, "*Management Accounting*, Section 1, Vol. XLVII, No. 7, pp. 9–17.

Department Metal Cutting

Producing Departments Only

DEPARTMENTAL ALLOWANCE FOR NONPRODUCTION PERSONNEL

MONTHLY ALLOWANCE FOR NONPRODUCTION PERSONNEL

NUMBER OF PRODUCTION PERSONNEL		FOREMAN a/c 06	SUPERVISOR a/c 06	ASSISTANT FOREMAN a/c 06	MFG. QUALITY ANALYST a/c 06								
From	To												
0	10	1 / 837											
11	20	1 / 837	1 / 500		1 / 525								
21	30	1 / 837	2 / 1000		1 / 525								
31	40	1 / 837	4 / 2000		2 / 1050								
41	50	1 / 837	5 / 2500	1 / 600	2 / 1050								
51	60	1 / 837	5 / 2500	1 / 600	3 / 1575								
61	70	1 / 837	6 / 3000	1 / 600	3 / 1575								
71	80	1 / 837	6 / 3000	1 / 600	4 / 2100								
81	90	1 / 837	7 / 3500	1 / 600	4 / 2100								
91	100												

Step Chart for a Producing Department

total number of production hours in all producing departments; for producing departments, the levels are based on the number of production workers (as shown above). The availability of such detailed data enhances the development of monthly departmental budgets by subexpense classifications.

FLEXIBLE BUDGET OF A SERVICE DEPARTMENT

Service department expenses in a budget allowance schedule and in a flexible budget require additional explanation. The expenses of the Maintenance Department are estimated at a fixed amount of $4,200 with a variable charging rate of $9.50 per maintenance hour. The Department's flexible budget may be set up in the manner illustrated on page 561.

At 80 percent capacity, total expenses amount to $27,000. Assuming that the company has two producing departments and two service departments to which a fixed cost of $1,200, $2,000, $600, and $400, respectively,

FLEXIBLE BUDGET FOR MAINTENANCE DEPARTMENT

Operating Level		Monthly Allowances				
Maintenance hours.........		2,100	2,400	2,700	3,000	3,300
Percentage of plant capacity.		70%	80%	90%	100%	110%
Acct. No.	Account Title					
01	Craftsmen...........	$12,600	$14,400	$16,200	$18,000	$23,000
28	Supervison..........	2,000	2,000	2,000	2,000	2,000
41	Factory Supplies.....	5,950	6,800	7,650	8,500	9,350
61	Tools...............	1,400	1,600	1,800	2,000	2,300
63	Depreciation........	1,400	1,400	1,400	1,400	1,400
74	Building Occupancy...	800	800	800	800	800
	Total Expenses.......	$24,150	$27,000	$29,850	$32,700	$38,850
Fixed Expenses.............		$ 4,200	$ 4,200	$ 4,200	$ 4,200	$ 4,200
Variable Expenses..........		19,950	22,800	25,650	28,500	34,650
Variable Charging Rate per Maintenance Hour.......		$9.50	$9.50	$9.50	$9.50	$10.50

is charged as the readiness-to-serve cost of the Maintenance Department, the remaining balance of $22,800 is divided by the total number of maintenance hours (2,400) to arrive at a variable rate of $9.50 per hour.

Note that the variable rate increases at the 110 percent level due to sharper increases in some expenses. Flexible budgets are prepared for service departments to permit (1) comparison of actual expenses with allowed expenses at the prevailing level of operations and (2) establishment of a fairer use rate or sold-hour rate by charging operating departments with fixed expenses regardless of activity and with a variable cost based on departmental activity. (See the discussion in Chapter 11.)

FLEXIBLE MARKETING AND ADMINISTRATIVE BUDGETS

To complete this discussion, a flexible marketing and administrative budget is illustrated on the next page.

In contrast to the factory overhead budget which bases its expense levels in most cases on direct labor hours, machine hours, or direct labor dollars, the budget for commercial expenses is often based on net sales. This practice has been criticized in recent years, and other methods are suggested in Chapter 23.

The preceding flexible budget discussion indicates that the establishment of such budgets is of prime importance to business management and a basic requirement of any cost information system. Management is interested in knowing ahead of time what it should cost to make and sell products at varying levels of output and what the expected profits are to be.

FLEXIBLE MARKETING AND ADMINISTRATIVE BUDGET						
Item		**Monthly Allowances**				
Net Sales....................		$600,000	$700,000	$800,000	$900,000	$1,000,000
Marketing	**Based on Sales**					
Sales Salaries.........	5%	$30,000	$35,000	$40,000	$45,000	$50,000
Advertising...........	1%	6,000	7,000	8,000	9,000	10,000
Sales Expenses........	2%	12,000	14,000	16,000	18,000	20,000
Misc. Expenses.......	.5%	3,000	3,500	4,000	4,500	5,000
Depreciation.........	Fixed	10,000	10,000	10,000	10,000	10,000
Total Marketing..............		$61,000	$69,500	$78,000	$86,500	$95,000
Administrative	**Based on Sales**					
Executives' Salaries....	Fixed	$20,000	$20,000	$20,000	$30,000	$50,000
General Expenses.....	3%	18,000	21,000	24,000	27,000	30,000
Depreciation.........	Fixed	5,000	5,000	5,000	5,000	5,000
Insurance............	Fixed	3,000	3,000	3,000	3,000	3,000
Taxes................	Fixed	4,000	4,000	4,000	4,000	4,000
Total Administrative.........		$50,000	$53,000	$56,000	$69,000	$92,000

DISCUSSION QUESTIONS

1. Name some relative advantages in the use of a flexible budget over a fixed budget.

2. What is the underlying principle of a flexible budget?

3. Differentiate among (a) theoretical capacity, (b) practical capacity, (c) expected actual capacity, and (d) normal capacity.

     (AICPA adapted)

4. A company has been operating a budget system for a number of years. Production volume fluctuates widely. It reaches its peak in the fall but is quite low during the rest of the year. Manufacturing for stock during the dull period as a means of smoothing out the volume fluctuations is impractical because of frequent and sudden changes in specifications prescribed by the customers. Actual annual volume has been substantially below normal volume. The budget produces large unfavorable capacity variances since overhead rates are computed from normal volume and are inadequate to absorb the overhead which should be charged into production during the low-volume periods. This fixed type of budget based on an unrealistic normal production volume fails to serve its planning and control purpose. As a consultant you are asked to diagnose the situation and offer advice.

5. (a) What situations give rise to idle capacity costs? (b) How and why should such costs be accounted for? (c) What is excess capacity cost?

6. Why is it important to classify factory overhead as variable, fixed, and semi-variable?

7. Why should a semivariable expense be separated into its fixed expense total and its variable percentage?

8. What methods are available to separate semivariable expenses?

9. In analyzing the relationship of total factory overhead with changes in direct labor hours, this relationship was found to exist: $y = \$1,000 + \$2x$.

   Select the answer which best completes each of the following statements:
   (a) The above equation was probably found through the use of the mathematical technique known as (1) linear programming; (2) multiple regression analysis; (3) the method of least squares (simple regression analysis); (4) dynamic programming; (5) none of these.
   (b) The relationship shown above is (1) parabolic; (2) curvilinear; (3) linear; (4) probabilistic; (5) none of these.
   (c) The "y" in the above equation is an estimate of (1) total variable costs; (2) total factory overhead; (3) total fixed costs; (4) total direct labor hours; (5) none of these.
   (d) The $2 in the above equation is an estimate of (1) total fixed costs; (2) variable costs per direct labor hour; (3) total variable costs; (4) fixed costs per direct labor hour; (5) none of these.

   (NAA adapted)

10. Explain the meaning of "multiple regression analysis."

11. What is the purpose of a statistical correlation analysis in cost behavior analysis?

12. The fixed-variable expense analysis is not valuable just for the preparation of flexible budgets. It has received and should deserve major attention in connection with many analytical processes. Name some.

13. Can service departments' expenses also be set up using flexible budget procedures? What makes the situation difficult? How are the expenses allocated to producing departments?

14. Select the answer which best completes each of the following statements:
   (a) Flexible budgeting is a reporting system wherein the (1) budget standards may be adjusted at will; (2) reporting dates vary according to the activity levels reported upon; (3) statements included in the budget report vary from period to period; (4) planned activity level is adjusted to the actual activity level before the budget comparison report is prepared.
   (b) If a company wishes to establish a factory overhead budget system in which estimated costs can be derived directly from estimates of activity levels, it should prepare a (1) capital budget; (2) flexible budget; (3) cash budget; (4) discretionary budget; (5) fixed budget.
   (c) The budget for a specific cost during a fiscal period was $80,000 while the actual cost for the same period was $72,000. Considering these facts, it can be stated that the plant manager has done a *better* than expected job in controlling the cost if (1) the cost is variable and actual production was 90% of budgeted production; (2) the cost is variable and actual production equaled budgeted production; (3) the cost is variable and actual production was 80% of budgeted production.

(d) The primary difference between a fixed budget and a flexible budget is that a fixed budget (1) includes only fixed costs while a flexible budget includes only variable costs; (2) is concerned only with future acquisitions of fixed assets while a flexible budget is concerned with expenses that vary with sales; (3) cannot be changed after a fiscal period begins while a flexible budget can be changed after a fiscal period begins; (4) is a budget for a single level of some measure of activity while a flexible budget consists of several budgets or a range of budgets based on some measure of activity.

(e) Of little or no relevance in evaluating the performance of an activity would be (1) flexible budgets; (2) fixed budgets; (3) the difference between planned and actual results; (4) the planning and control of future activities.

(f) The concept of "the ideal capacity of a plant" as used in cost accounting is its (1) theoretical maximum capacity; (2) best capacity for normal production; (3) capacity used for standard costing; (4) capacity below which production should not fall.

(g) The variable factory overhead rate under the practical capacity, expected actual capacity, and normal capacity levels would be the (1) same except for normal capacity; (2) same except for practical capacity; (3) same except for expected actual capacity; (4) same for all three levels.

(h) The term "relevant range" as used in cost accounting means the range (1) over which costs may fluctuate; (2) over which cost relationships are valid; (3) of probable production; (4) over which relevant costs are incurred.

(i) The effect of changes in volume on semivariable costs may be approximated by means of a statistical technique employing (1) linear programming; (2) calculation of expected value; (3) the method of least squares; (4) matrix algebra.

(j) Given actual amounts of a semivariable expense for various levels of output, the method that gives the most precise measure of the fixed and variable elements is (1) the use of Bayesian statistics; (2) linear programming; (3) the statistical scattergraph method; (4) the method of least squares.

(AICPA adapted)

EXERCISES

1. Factory Overhead Rates; Unabsorbed Fixed Overhead. The Frisco Company's management is considering the use of a flexible budget for variable factory overhead and wishes a study of its operations based on the following data made available by the Cost Department:

Capacity (in percentages).........	80%	90%	100%	110%
Direct labor hours...............	48,000	54,000	60,000	66,000
Variable factory overhead.........	$96,000	$108,000	$120,000	$132,000

Fixed factory overhead is budgeted at $250,000 for each of the four levels of activity.

Required: (1) The total factory overhead rate at the 80%, 100%, and 110% capacity levels based on direct labor hours.

(2) The variable factory overhead rate for the same three capacity levels.
(3) The amount of unabsorbed fixed overhead if the company operates at 80% of capacity, yet applies a rate based on the 100% capacity level.

2. Determining Variable and Fixed Budget Allowances. The supplies expense of a department is budgeted with $5,000 at a level of 15,000 direct labor hours and with $4,000 at a level of 10,000 direct labor hours.

Required: (1) The variable budget allowance per 100 direct labor hours.
(2) The fixed budget allowance for this expense.

3. Separating Fixed and Variable Costs; Statistical Correlation Analysis. A controller is interested in an analysis of the fixed and variable costs of electricity as related to direct labor hours. The following data have been accumulated:

Month	Electricity Cost	Direct Labor Hours
November...................	$1,548	297
December...................	1,667	350
January....................	1,405	241
February...................	1,534	280
March.....................	1,600	274
April......................	1,600	266
May.......................	1,613	285
June......................	1,635	301

Required: (1) The amount of fixed overhead and the variable cost ratio using (a) the high and low points method, (b) a scattergraph with trend line fitted by inspection, and (c) the method of least squares.
(2) The coefficient of correlation (r) and the coefficient of determination (r²).

4. Fixed and Variable Costs Analysis; Correlation Analysis. The management of the Monterrey Hotel is interested in an analysis of the fixed and variable costs in the electricity used in its relationship to hotel occupancy. The data shown below have been gathered from books and records for the year 19--.

	Guest Days	Electricity Cost
January....................	1,000	$ 400
February...................	1,500	500
March.....................	2,500	500
April......................	3,000	700
May.......................	2,500	600
June......................	4,500	800
July.......................	6,500	1,000
August....................	6,000	900
September.................	5,500	900
October...................	3,000	700
November.................	2,500	600
December.................	3,500	800
Year total...............	42,000	$8,400

Required: (1) The fixed and variable elements of electricity costs by (a) the method of least squares, (b) the high and low points method, and (c) a scattergraph with trend line fitted by inspection. Compute the variable rate to four decimal places.

(2) The other element besides occupancy which might affect the amount of electricity used in any one month.

(3) The coefficient of correlation (r) and the coefficient of determination (r²).

5. Determining Cost Variability; Correlation Analysis. At present, the establishment of factory overhead rates with a flexible budget is under discussion at the Montag Company. Factory overhead (exclusive of power) has been set at $3,000 per month plus $.125 per unit manufactured. Power costs and production data are as follows:

	Power Costs	Units Produced
May........................	$620	85,000
June.......................	660	105,000
July.......................	560	85,000
August.....................	535	80,000
September..................	710	110,000
October....................	700	105,000

Required: (1) The fixed and variable cost elements included in the cost of power using the high and low points method.

(2) The total budgeted factory overhead for 100,000 units.

(3) The coefficient of correlation (r) and the coefficient of determination (r²).

6. Method of Least Squares. The 19-- financial statements of the MacKenzie Park Co., a manufacturer of Trivets, require an analysis of selected aspects of the company's operations.

Representative labor hours and production costs for the last four months of 19-- were:

Month	Labor Hours	Production Costs
September................	2,500	$ 20,000
October..................	3,500	25,000
November.................	4,500	30,000
December.................	3,500	25,000
Total..................	14,000	$100,000

Required: The fixed monthly production costs of Trivets and the variable production costs per labor hour using the method of least squares.

(AICPA adapted)

7. Fixed-Variable Cost Analysis; Correlation Analysis. A company making aluminum tubing from aluminum billets uses a process in which the billets are heated by induction to a very high temperature before being put through an extruding machine that shapes the tubing from the billets. The inducer, a very large coil into which the billet is placed, must sustain a great flow of current to heat the billets to the desired temperature. Regardless of the number of billets to be processed, the coil is kept on during the entire operating day because of the time involved in starting it up. The Cost Department wants to charge the variable (i.e., the direct cost) directly to each billet and the fixed portion to factory overhead. For the analysis, the following data have been assembled:

Month	No. of Billets	Cost of Electricity	Month	No. of Billets	Cost of Electricity
January.....	2,000	$400	July.......	1,400	$340
February....	1,800	380	August.....	1,900	390
March......	1,900	390	September..	1,800	380
April.......	2,200	420	October....	2,400	440
May........	2,100	410	November..	2,300	430
June........	2,000	400	December..	2,200	420

Required: (1) A fixed-variable expense analysis using the method of least squares.

(2) A graph indicating the results calculated.

(3) The coefficient of correlation (r) and the coefficient of determination (r²).

8. Cost Variability and Correlation Analysis. Clovis Hospital is interested in an analysis of the fixed and variable costs of supplies as related to patient days of occupancy. The following data have been accumulated:

Month	Cost of Supplies	Patient Days of Occupancy
November..................	$2,153	1,164
December..................	2,201	1,405
January...................	2,060	885
February..................	2,009	910
March....................	2,040	995
April.....................	2,015	927
May.....................	1,997	874
June.....................	2,098	1,140

Required: (1) The fixed and variable cost elements included in the cost of supplies by (a) the high and low points method, (b) a scattergraph with trend line fitted by inspection, and (c) the method of least squares.

(2) The coefficient of correlation (r) and the coefficient of determination (r²).

9. Flexible Budget Construction. The Montgomery Products Company produced and shipped 10,000 units of Product L-BO during the month of October. The product and its raw materials are highly perishable; therefore, no inventories are carried. Materials prices for the month of October were 30% below normal due to a depressed market. Due to administrative errors the 2% cash discount for prompt payment was not taken. The monthly labor costs were 10% higher than normal because a number of new workers were receiving on-the-job training. Factory overhead was 15% lower than it will be in the future; 40% of the overhead is considered fixed. Marketing and administrative expenses are fixed at $5,000 per month with a variable factor of $500 for each 1,000 units produced.

The actual costs for October were:

Direct materials...............................	$ 9,100
Direct labor...................................	14,740
Factory overhead..............................	17,000
Marketing and administrative expenses...........	11,000

Required: A flexible budget at volumes of 8,000, 12,000, and 14,000 units showing (a) the cost per unit at the various levels and (b) the selling price per unit at each level if the company wishes to earn a net income of 20% of sales before taxes.

10. Flexible Budget. The Ontario Corporation operates its producing departments under a flexible budget with monthly allowances established for 20% intervals. Capacity is based on direct labor hours with 2,500 direct labor hours representing 100% normal capacity.

In the month of October the Shelving Department operated at the 87% level. The exhibit shows budget allowances at the 80% and 100% levels.

FLEXIBLE BUDGET FOR SHELVING DEPARTMENT

FOR OCTOBER, 19--

Percentage of Capacity	80%	100%
Direct labor hours......................	2,000	2,500
Direct labor costs......................	$4,000	$5,000
Foreman's salary.......................	$ 500	$ 500
Indirect labor.........................	1,350	1,500
Clerical salaries.......................	700	750
Factory supplies.......................	430	500
Depreciation..........................	500	500
Taxes.................................	250	250
Insurance.............................	200	200
Maintenance..........................	380	400
Power.................................	360	400
Total indirect expenses................	$4,670	$5,000
Factory overhead rate..................	$2.335	$2.00

Required: (1) A detailed flexible budget for the 87% level.
(2) The amount of underabsorbed fixed factory overhead.

11. Flexible Budget. A division manager is interested in obtaining the fixed and variable costs relationship applicable to activity levels. Costs definitely fixed in the amount of $60,000 are depreciation of plant, property, and equipment. Marketing and administrative expenses of $125,000 are also of a relatively fixed nature. Materials costs are $7 per unit with spoilage averaging 2% of total materials costs. Labor costs are $2.25 per hour with 15 hours required to produce 10 units.

Other expenses which generally were considered wholly variable yet seem to possess a fixed component are:

Expenses	At 30,000 Units of Production	At 80,000 Units of Production
Supervision................	$12,500	$20,000
Indirect labor...............	9,600	15,600
Payroll taxes................	3,000	7,500
Heat, light, and power.......	8,000	18,000
Indirect materials...........	2,500	5,000
Maintenance of machinery ...	6,000	9,000
Miscellaneous factory costs...	2,500	4,500
Total....................	$44,100	$79,600

Total production has never exceeded 100,000 units in any one year.

Required: (1) A schedule indicating all fixed expenses in detail.

(2) A flexible budget for all expenses when the company is operating at both the 30,000 and the 80,000 units of production levels.

PROBLEMS

18-1. Statistical Correlation Analysis. The Cost Department of the Elco Electric Company attempts to establish a flexible budget to assist in the control of marketing expenses each month. An examination of individual expenses shows:

Item	Fixed Portion	+	Variable Portion
Salesmen's salaries.....................	$1,200		none
Salesmen — retainers.................	2,000		none
Salesmen — commissions.............	none		4% on sales values
Advertising........................	5,000		none
Travel expenses......................	?		?

Observations or a management decision cannot split the travel expenses satisfactorily into their fixed and variable portions. Statistical analysis is needed. Before beginning such an analysis, it is thought that the variable portion of travel expenses might vary in accordance either with the number of calls made on customers each month or the value of orders received each month. Records reveal the following details over the past twelve months:

Month	Calls Made	Orders Received	Travel Expenses
January................	410	$53,000	$3,000
February..............	420	65,000	3,200
March................	380	48,000	2,800
April.................	460	73,000	3,400
May..................	430	62,000	3,100
June.................	450	67,000	3,200
July..................	390	60,000	2,900
August...............	470	76,000	3,300
September............	480	82,000	3,500
October..............	490	62,000	3,400
November............	440	64,000	3,200
December.............	460	80,000	3,400

Required: (1) The coefficient of correlation and coefficient of determination between (a) travel expenses and the number of calls made and (b) travel expenses and orders received.

(2) A comparison between the answers obtained in (1a) and (1b).

(Based on an article in the *NAA Bulletin*)

18-2. Flexible Budget; Overhead Rate. The controller of the Mexicali Corporation decided to prepare a flexible factory overhead budget ranging from 80% to 110% of capacity for the next year with 50,000 hours as the 100% level. The

data used in the construction of this budget were based on either past experiences, shop supervisors' figures, or management's decisions. For expenses of a
semivariable nature, it was necessary to determine the fixed amount and the
variable rate via the high and low points method. The direct labor rate was
$2.50 per hour. Additional data are:

Factory overhead data available:

Annual fixed expenses:

Depreciation..............................	$ 9,000 per year
Insurance.................................	1,500 per year
Maintenance costs (including payroll taxes and fringe benefits).........................	12,000 per year
Property taxes.............................	1,500 per year
Supervisory staff (including payroll taxes and fringe benefits).........................	18,000 per year

Variable expenses:

Shop supplies.............................	$.10 per direct labor hour
Indirect labor (excluding inspection)..........	$.15 per direct labor hour
Payroll taxes..............................	5% of labor cost, direct and indirect
Fringe benefits............................	11% of labor cost, direct and indirect

Semivariable expenses:
(Figures constitute previous six years' experience)

Year	Direct Labor Hours	Power and Light	Inspection (Including Payroll Taxes and Fringe Benefits)	Other Semi-variable Expenses
19A	44,000	$1,500	$9,200	$8,000
19B	40,000	1,400	9,000	7,500
19C	45,000	1,600	9,200	8,200
19D	49,000	1,750	10,000	8,800
19E	52,000	1,800	10,400	9,400
19F	55,000	1,850	10,800	9,600

Required: (1) A flexible factory overhead budget ranging from 80% to
110% of capacity, with 10% intervals.
(2) The total factory overhead rate, variable cost rate, and fixed cost rate
for 100% of capacity.

18-3. Factory Overhead Budget. The Shawanoe Company is divided into three
departments: Mixing, Processing, and Finishing. To manufacture one unit of
its product, direct labor and materials costs are:

Departments	Hours	Labor Cost Rate	Total	Materials Cost Total
Mixing.....................	3	$1.50	$4.50	$5.00
Processing..................	2	2.00	4.00	1.00
Finishing...................	2	2.10	4.20	2.00

The monthly sales forecast predicts sales of 1,000 units for the coming month
which the company plans to sell at $47 per unit.

For the preparation of the factory overhead budget, the company intends to
use the following data:

Variable Expenses	*Applicable to Each Department*
Indirect labor..................	1/3 of direct labor cost
Indirect materials...............	1/4 of materials cost
Heat..........................	$.10 per direct labor hour
Light.........................	$.20 per direct labor hour
Power........................	$.30 per direct labor hour
Miscellaneous..................	5% of total direct labor and direct materials cost

Fixed Expenses		*Apportioned to Each Department*
Superintendent.......	$2,000	1/5 Mixing, 2/5 Processing, 2/5 Finishing
Rent.................	1,500	1/3 each
Insurance...........	600	1/3 each

Required: (1) A factory overhead budget for each department.

(2) A manufacturing budget showing total costs as well as departmental costs of the three cost elements.

(3) The total product unit cost.

(4) A brief description of the procedure the company should follow if demand drops to 600 units.

18-4. Flexible Budget; Cost Variability Analysis. The Cleves Chemical Company is a small firm which manufactures cleaning fluid. Its management realizes that, as a small company, it must strive constantly to control and reduce costs in order to meet the competition by both large and small chemical firms. The president is interested in a budget system which the company can use effectively during the coming year, 19F, to help achieve some degree of control over costs.

The Accounting Department provided the following information:

Plant capacity: 2,250,000 liters of cleaning fluid per year.
Selling price will average an expected $.52 per liter next year.

Operation results for the past five years were as follows:

	19A	*19B*	*19C*	*19D*	*19E*
Liters of product sold (thousands).........	1,200	1,400	1,750	2,000	1,800
Revenue from sales....	$600,000	$650,000	$750,000	$900,000	$850,000
Cost of goods sold:					
Materials...........	$300,000	$340,000	$375,000	$500,000	$495,000
Labor..............	120,000	154,000	200,000	250,000	240,000
Factory overhead....	17,000	19,000	22,500	25,000	23,000
Total..............	$437,000	$513,000	$597,500	$775,000	$758,000
Gross profit..........	$163,000	$137,000	$152,500	$125,000	$ 92,000
Marketing expenses....	$ 16,000	$ 16,000	$ 18,000	$ 20,000	$ 20,000
Administrative expenses.	30,000	30,000	30,000	30,000	30,000
Total..............	$ 46,000	$ 46,000	$ 48,000	$ 50,000	$ 50,000
Net operating profit....	$117,000	$ 91,000	$104,500	$ 75,000	$ 42,000

No budgets had ever been used by the company because it was felt that budgeting was not feasible for such a small company where most of the operations were directly under the president and two assistants. Prior to his resignation, the former chief accountant had devised a standard labor cost for 19D at $.10909 per liter for the entire process. An examination of the figures indicates that they are quite adequate except for an expected rise of about 10% in wage rates since 19D. Materials costs are expected to rise by 4% for the coming year over 19E prices. The average cost of the mix of materials was $.25 per liter of fluid. Materials usage seldom varies; the differences in materials costs over the years represent changes in the cost of materials.

Required: A flexible budget in income statement form for the year 19F. The statements should cover a range from 1,250,000 to 2,250,000 liters, with increments of 250,000 liters. Use the high and low points method in segregating the fixed and variable elements of any semivariable expenses.

18-5. Budget Planning and Performance Comparison. At the end of 19A, the management of the Lukasek Manufacturing Company received the following condensed income statement:

INCOME STATEMENT — 19A

Sales...			$4,000,000
Cost of goods sold:			
Direct materials.............................	$800,000		
Direct labor................................	600,000		
Variable factory overhead.....................	240,000		
Fixed factory overhead.......................	400,000	2,040,000	
Gross profit on sales............................			$1,960,000
Less commercial expenses:			
Marketing expenses:			
Variable......................	$240,000		
Fixed.........................	360,000	$600,000	
Administrative expenses:			
Variable......................	$320,000		
Fixed.........................	480,000	800,000	1,400,000
Net operating profit............................			$ 560,000

The company's budget committee decided on the following changes for the year 19B:

A 20% sales volume increase; no price changes
Fixed administrative expenses to increase $40,000

There are no other cost changes; all costs classified as variable are completely variable.

At the end of the year 19B, the actual results were as follows:

Sales..	$4,600,000
Direct materials.............................	940,000
Direct labor.................................	700,000
Variable factory overhead.....................	270,000
Fixed factory overhead.......................	410,000
Variable marketing expenses...................	276,000
Fixed marketing expenses.....................	364,000
Variable administrative expenses...............	380,000
Fixed administrative expenses.................	510,000

Required: (1) A budget report comparing 19B's forecast data with 19B's actual results.

(2) A budget report which would adequately portray and appraise the performance of those individuals charged with the responsibility of providing satisfactory earnings and effective cost control. Sales prices did not change. This report should make use of flexible budget procedures.

18-6. Budget Planning and Performance Comparison. The Melcher Co. produces farm equipment at several plants. The business is seasonal and cyclical in nature. The company has attempted to use budgeting for planning and controlling activities, but the variable nature of the business has caused some company officials to be skeptical of its usefulness. The accountant for the Adrian Plant has been using a system she calls "flexible budgeting" to help her plant management control operations.

The president asks her to explain what the term means, how she applies the system at the Adrian Plant, and how it can be applied to the company as a whole. The accountant presents the following data as part of her explanation.

Budget data for 19--:

Normal monthly capacity of the plant in direct labor hours....	10,000 hours
Materials cost (6 lbs, @ $1.50).........................	$9 per unit
Labor cost (2 hours @ $3)...........................	$6 per unit

Factory overhead estimate at normal monthly capacity:

Variable factory overhead:

Indirect labor.........................	$ 6,650
Indirect materials......................	600
Repairs.............................	750
Total variable factory overhead........	$ 8,000

Fixed factory overhead:

Depreciation.........................	$	3,250
Supervision..........................		3,000
Total fixed factory overhead..........		$ 6,250

Total fixed and variable factory overhead....	$14,250
Planned units for January, 19--............	4,000
Planned units for February, 19--...........	6,000

Actual data for January, 19--:

Hours worked..........................	8,400
Units produced........................	3,800

Costs incurred:

Materials (24,000 lbs.)..................	$36,000
Direct labor.........................	25,200
Indirect labor........................	6,000
Indirect materials.....................	600
Repairs.............................	1,800
Depreciation.........................	3,250
Supervision..........................	3,000
Total............................	$75,850

Required: (1) A manufacturing budget for January, 19--.

(2) A report for January, 19--, comparing actual and budgeted costs for the month's actual activity, assuming that the units produced are to be the measurement of activity used in preparing the "flexible budget."

(3) Can flexible budgeting be applied to the nonmanufacturing activities of the Melcher Co.? Explain.

(NAA adapted)

18-7. Flexible Budget. Department A, one of 15 departments in the manufacturing plant, is involved in the production of all of the six products manufactured by Augustin Products, Inc. Because Department A is highly mechanized, its output is measured in direct machine hours. Flexible budgets are utilized throughout the plant in planning and controlling costs, but here the focus is upon the application of flexible budgets only in Department A. The following data covering a time span of approximately six months were taken from the various budgets, accounting records, and performance reports (only representative items and amounts are utilized here).

On March 15, 19A, the following flexible budget was approved for Department A to be used throughout the fiscal year 19A-B, beginning on July 1, 19A. This flexible budget was developed through the cooperative efforts of Department A's manager, his supervisor, and certain staff members from the Budget Department.

FLEXIBLE BUDGET FOR DEPARTMENT A

FOR FISCAL YEAR 19A-B

Controllable Costs	Fixed Amount Per Month	Variable Rate Per Direct Machine Hour
Employees' salaries....................	$ 9,000	
Indirect wages.......................	18,000	$.07
Indirect materials....................		.09
Other costs.........................	6,000	.03
Total............................	$33,000	$.19

On May 5, 19A, the annual sales plan and the production budget were completed. In order to continue preparation of the annual profit plan (which was detailed by month), the production budget was translated to planned activity for each of the 15 departments. The planned activity for Department A was:

	For Twelve Months Ending June 30, 19B				
	Year	July	August	Sept.	Oct.–June
Planned output in direct machine hours.........	325,000	22,000	25,000	29,000	249,000

On August 31, 19A, Department A's manager was informed that the planned September output had been revised to 34,000 direct machine hours. He expressed some doubt as to whether this volume could be attained.

On September 30, 19A, Department A's accounting records showed the following actual data for September:

Actual output in direct machine hours......................... 33,000

Actual controllable costs incurred:

Employees' salaries......................................	$ 9,300
Indirect wages..	20,500
Indirect materials.......................................	2,850
Other costs..	7,510
Total...	$40,160

Required: The requirements below relate primarily to the potential uses of the flexible budget for the period March through September, 19A.

(a) What activity base is utilized as a measure of volume in the budget for Department A? Explain how the range of the activity base to which the variable rates per direct machine hour are relevant should be determined.

(b) The high and low points method was utilized in developing this flexible budget. Using indirect wage costs as an example, illustrate how this method would be applied in determining the fixed and variable components of indirect wage costs for Department A. Assume that the high and low values for indirect wages are $19,400 at 20,000 direct machine hours and $20,100 at 30,000 direct machine hours.

(c) Explain and illustrate how the flexible budget should be utilized:

(1) In budgeting costs when the annual sales plan and production budget are completed (about May 5, 19A, or shortly thereafter).

(2) In budgeting a cost revision based upon a revised production budget (about August 31, 19A, or shortly thereafter).

(3) In preparing a cost performance report for September, 19A.

(AICPA adapted)

CASES

A. Setting Up a Budgetary Program. Jim Thomas was appointed budget officer of the Washington Laundry Equipment Company in 19--. He had no previous budgeting background, and the president asked him to sct up a budgetary program that worked effectively. The president also told Jim that it was his responsibility to see that actual expenses stayed within the amounts specified in the budget.

Jim requested the Accounting Department to supply him with weekly budget reports showing the budgeted amount of each expense for the week (computed by dividing the annual budgeted amount by 52), actual expenses incurred during the week, and the variance for each expense. He also informed all supervisors that any continued excess of actual expenses over budgeted amounts would be cause for dismissal.

The first week's budget report for the Sales Department was as follows:

	Actual	Budget (1/52 of Annual Total)	Variance Over/(Under)
Sales...........................	$217,000	$188,000	$29,000
Depreciation....................	$ 2,000	$ 2,010	$ (10)
Salespersons' travel..............	3,170	2,700	470
Telephone and telegraph..........	861	740	121
Office supplies...................	419	390	29

Jim was highly disturbed over the unfavorable expense variances and told the sales manager that continued unfavorable variances would be sufficient cause for his dismissal. The sales manager then discussed the situation with the president, stating that "either the new budget officer leaves or I'm quitting."

Required: (1) Are the expenses for the Sales Department "unfavorable?"

(2) Assuming you were president of the Washington Laundry Equipment Company, which of the two men would you support? Explain your choice.

(3) Suggest means for improving the budgetary program.

B. Cost Behavior and the Flexible Budget. The Clark Company has a contract with a labor union guaranteeing a minimum wage of $500 per month to each direct labor employee with at least twelve years of service. At present, 100 employees qualify for this coverage. All direct labor employees are paid $5 per hour.

The direct labor budget for 19–– was based on the annual usage of 400,000 direct labor hours $\times$ $5, or a total of $2,000,000. Of this amount, $50,000 (100 employees $\times$ $500) per month (or $600,000 for 19––) was regarded as fixed expenses. Thus, the budget for any specific month was determined by the formula: $50,000 + $3.50 $\times$ direct labor hours worked.

Data on the performance for the first three months of 19–– are:

	January	*February*	*March*
Direct labor hours worked............	22,000	32,000	42,000
Direct labor costs — flexible budget....	$127,000	$162,000	$197,000
Direct labor costs incurred............	110,000	160,000	210,000
Variance (U — unfavorable; F — favorable)........	17,000F	2,000F	13,000U

The factory manager was perplexed by the results that showed favorable variances when production was low and unfavorable variances when production was high, because he believed that his control over labor costs was consistently good.

Required: (1) Explanation and illustration of variances, using amounts and diagrams as necessary.

(2) Explanation of this direct labor flexible budget as a basis for controlling direct labor cost, indicating changes that might be made to improve control over direct labor cost and to facilitate performance evaluation of direct labor employees.

(AICPA adapted)

CHAPTER 19

STANDARD COSTING: SETTING STANDARDS AND ANALYZING VARIANCES

Standard cost systems — having usefully served management since their introduction many years ago as a method of uniting accounting and industrial engineering — aid in planning operations, motivating employees, controlling costs, detecting above- or below-standard performance, and in gaining an insight into the probable impact of managerial decisions on cost levels and profits.

COMPARISON OF BUDGETS AND STANDARDS

The budget is considered one method of securing reliable and prompt information regarding the operation and control of the enterprise. When manufacturing budgets are based on standards for materials, labor, and factory overhead, the strongest team for control and reduction of costs is created.

Standards are almost indispensable in establishing a budget. Because both aim at the same objective — managerial control — it is often felt that the two are one and the same and cannot function independently. This opinion is supported by the fact that both methods use predetermined costs for the coming period. Both budget and standard costs make it possible to prepare reports which compare actual costs and predetermined costs for management.

Building budgets without the use of standard cost figures can never lead to a real budgetary control system. The figures used in the illustrations in the budget chapters are only fair estimates even though they have been set with the greatest care and with the cooperation of those involved. Under such conditions the budget is in a vulnerable position and can hardly be considered as the basis against which actual results are to be measured. This shortcoming is recognized within the budget area itself; thus, the flexible budget is added as a refinement.

With the use of standard costs, a budget becomes a summary of standards for all items of revenue and costs. When actual costs are superseded by standard costs, the preparation of budgets for any volume and mixture of products is more reliably and speedily accomplished.

The principal difference between budgets and standard costs lies in their scope. The budget, as a statement of expected costs, acts as a guidepost which keeps the business on a charted course. Standards, on the other hand, do not tell what costs are expected to be, but rather what they will be if certain performances are achieved. A budget emphasizes the volume of business and the cost level which should be maintained if the firm is to operate as desired. Standards stress the level to which costs should be reduced. If costs reach this level, profits will be increased.

STANDARD COSTS DEFINED

A *standard cost* has two components: a standard and a cost. A standard is like a norm and whatever is considered normal can generally be accepted as standard. For example: if a score of 72 is the standard for a golf course, a golfer's score is judged on the basis of this standard. In industry the standards for making a desk, assembling a radio, refining crude oil, or manufacturing railway cars are based on carefully determined quantitative and qualitative measurements and engineering methods. A standard must be thought of as a norm in terms of specific items, such as pounds of materials, hours[1] of labor required, and hours of plant capacity to be used. In many firms a standard can be operative for a long time. A change is needed only when production methods or products themselves have become obsolete or undesirable.

Calculation of a standard cost is based on physical standards. Standard costs are the predetermined costs of manufacturing a single unit or a number of product units during a specific period in the immediate future. They are the planned costs of a product under current and/or anticipated operating conditions. Materials and labor costs are generally

---

[1]The term "hours" in this chapter and in Chapter 20 means "direct labor hours."

based on normal, current conditions allowing for alterations of prices and rates and tempered by the desired efficiency level. Factory overhead is based on normal conditions of efficiency and volume.

STANDARDS — BASIC AND CURRENT

Two types of standards are often discussed: basic and current. A basic standard is a yardstick against which both expected and actual performances are compared. It is similar to an index number against which all later results are measured. Current standards are of three types:

1. The expected actual standard set for a level of operations and costs expected for the coming year. It is to be a reasonably close estimate of hoped-for actual results.

2. The normal standard set for a level of operations regarded as normal and representing an average figure intended to smooth out the absorption of fixed factory overhead over the firm's economic or seasonal cycle. Advocates of direct costing avoid this problem by treating fixed costs as period costs to be written off at the end of the current fiscal period.

3. The theoretical standard set for a level of operations regarded as the ideal or maximum level of efficiency. Such standards constitute goals to be aimed for rather than performances that can be currently achieved.

PURPOSES OF STANDARD COSTS

Standard costs are used for:
1. Establishing budgets.
2. Controlling costs and motivating and measuring efficiencies.
3. Promoting possible cost reduction.
4. Simplifying costing procedures and expediting cost reports.
5. Assigning costs to materials, work in process, and finished goods inventories.
6. Forming the basis for establishing bids and contracts and for setting selling prices.

These six purposes should be considered fundamental to the use of standard costs. The effectiveness of controlling costs depends greatly upon a knowledge of expected costs. Standards serve as a measurement which calls attention to cost variations. Executives and supervisors become cost-conscious as they become aware of results. This cost-consciousness tends to reduce costs and encourages economies in all phases of the business.

The use of standard costs for accounting purposes simplifies costing procedures through the reduction of clerical labor and expense. A complete standard cost system is usually accompanied by standardization of productive operations. Standard production or manufacturing orders, calling for standard quantities of product and specific labor operations, can be prepared in advance of actual production. Materials requisitions, labor time tickets, and operation cards can be prepared in advance of production, and standard costs can be compiled. As orders for a part are placed in the shop, previously established requirements, processes, and costs will apply. The more standardized the production, the simpler the clerical effort. Reports can be systematized to present complete information regarding standards, actual costs, and variances. Reports are integrated and tie in with the financial accounts.

A complete standard cost file by parts and operations simplifies assigning costs to raw materials, work in process, and finished goods inventories. The use of standard costs stabilizes the influence of materials costs. Placing bids, securing contracts, and establishing selling prices are greatly enhanced by the availability of reliable standards and the continuous review of standard costs.

The standard cost system may be used in connection with either the process or job order cost accumulation method. However, it is more often used in process cost accumulation because of the greater practicality of setting standards for a continuous flow of like units than for unique job orders.

SETTING STANDARDS

The success of a standard cost system depends on the reliability, accuracy, and acceptance of the standards. Extreme care must be taken to be sure that all factors have been considered in the establishment of standards. In certain cases, averages of past experience taken from the accounting records of previous periods are used as standards. However, the most effective standards are set by the industrial engineering department on the basis of a careful study of all products and operations and genuine participation by those individuals whose performance is to be measured by the standards.

Often standards are set after a more or less intensive study of past costs. Time studies determine the time required to perform various direct labor operations. Engineering studies should also be made of quantities and types of materials needed.

Whatever method is used, standards must be established for a definite period of time to be effective in the control and analysis of costs. Standards are usually computed for a six- or twelve-month period; a longer period is sometimes used, but rarely a shorter period.

Above all, standards must be set, and the system implemented, in an atmosphere that gives full consideration to human behavior characteristics of managers and workers.

STANDARD COST CARDS

Standard materials, labor, and factory overhead costs are kept on a standard cost card that shows the itemized cost of each materials part and labor operation as well as the overhead cost. A standard cost card, illustrated below, gives the standard unit cost of a product.

The master standard cost card is supported by individual cards that indicate how the standard cost was compiled and computed. Each subcost card represents a form of standard cost card.

Date of Standard July 1, 19--			STANDARD COST CARD FOR PRODUCT Alpac						
MATERIALS	ITEM CODE	QUAN- TITY	STANDARD UNIT PRICE	DEPARTMENT					TOTALS
				1	2	3	4	5	
	2-234	4	$3.00/pc.		$12.00				
	3-671	24	1.00/doz.			$2.00			
	5-489	2	2.50/pc.					$ 5.00	
	5-361	8	1.50/pc.					12.00	
	TOTAL MATERIALS COST								$ 31.00
DIRECT LABOR	OPERA- TION NUMBER	STANDARD HOURS	STANDARD RATE PER HOUR	DEPARTMENT					
				1	2	3	4	5	
	2-476	3	$6.00		$18.00				
	2-581	11½	6.40		73.60				
	3-218	4	6.30			$25.20			
	5-420	2½	6.20					$15.50	
	TOTAL DIRECT LABOR COST								132.30
FACTORY OVERHEAD	STANDARD HOURS	RATE PER DIRECT LABOR HOUR		DEPARTMENT					
				1	2	3	4	5	
	14½	$1.80			$26.10				
	4	2.00				$8.00			
	2½	1.50						$3.75	
	TOTAL FACTORY OVERHEAD........................								37.85
	TOTAL MANUFACTURING COST PER UNIT								$201.15

Standard Cost Card

MATERIALS COST STANDARDS

Two standards must be developed for materials costs:

1. A materials price standard
2. A materials quantity (or usage) standard

Materials Price Standard and Variance. Determining the price or cost to be used as standard cost is often difficult because the prices used are controlled more by external factors than by a company's management. Prices selected should reflect current market prices and are generally used throughout the forthcoming fiscal period.

If the actual price paid for an item is more or less than the standard price, a price variance occurs. Price increases or decreases occurring during the year are recorded in the price variance accounts. Prices will be revised at inventory dates or whenever an important change in the market price of any of the principal raw materials or parts takes place. Price standards permit (1) checking the performance of the purchasing department and (2) measuring the effect of price increases or decreases on the company's profits.

Materials Quantity Standard and Variance. Quantity or usage standards are generally developed from materials specifications prepared by the departments of engineering (mechanical, electrical, or chemical) or product design. In a small or medium-sized company the superintendent or even the foremen will state basic specifications regarding type, quantity, and quality of materials needed and operations to be performed.

If the product to be manufactured has never been made or if past records are not considered a reliable basis on which to predict future costs, quantity standards may be set through an analysis of the most economical size, shape, and quality of the product and the results expected from the use of various kinds and grades of materials. The standard quantity should also take into consideration allowances for acceptable levels of waste, spoilage, shrinkage, seepage, evaporation, leakage, etc. In such cases the standard quantity is increased to include these factors. The determination of the percentage of spoilage or waste should be based on figures that prevail after experimental and developmental stages of the product have been passed.

The materials quantity variance is computed by comparing the actual quantity of materials used, priced at standard cost, with the standard quantity allowed, priced at standard cost. The *standard quantity allowed* is found by multiplying the quantity of materials that should be required to produce one unit (the standard quantity per unit) times the *actual* number of units produced during the period for which the variances are being computed. The *units produced* are the equivalent units of production for the materials cost being analyzed.

Illustration. These data will be used for computing the materials variances:

Standard unit price of Item Code 5-489 of
   the standard cost card (page 581)........ $2.50
Purchased............................. 5,000 pieces @ $2.47
Requisitioned......................... 3,550 pieces
Standard quantity allowed for actual pro-
   duction........................... 3,500 pieces*

*1,750 units produced × 2 standard pieces of Item Code 5-489 per unit of production.

The materials purchase price variance is computed as follows:

	Pieces ×	Unit Cost	= Amount
Actual quantity purchased...	5,000	$2.47 actual	$12,350
Actual quantity purchased...	5,000	2.50 standard	12,500
Materials purchase price variance.............	5,000	$(.03)	$ (150) Credit *or* favorable

The $150 credit is a favorable materials purchase price variance, and $.03 expresses the unit cost difference. As an alternative, the materials purchase price variance can be recognized when the materials are used rather than when they are purchased and is then called the "materials price usage variance" (see Chapter 20).

The materials quantity (or usage) variance is computed as follows:

	Pieces ×	Unit Cost	= Amount
Actual quantity used......	3,550	$2.50 standard	$8,875
Standard quantity allowed..	3,500	2.50 "	8,750
Materials quantity variance.	50	2.50 standard	$ 125 Debit *or* unfavorable

The $125 debit is the dollar value of the unfavorable materials quantity (or usage) variance. The 50-pieces figure is the physical amount variance.

LABOR COST STANDARDS

Two standards must also be developed for labor costs:

1. A rate (wage or cost) standard
2. An efficiency (time or usage) standard

Rate Standard and Variance. In many plants the standard is based on rates established in collective bargaining agreements that define hourly wages, piece rates, and bonus differentials. Without a union contract rates are based on the agreed-upon earnings rate as determined between the employee and the personnel department at the time of hiring. Since rates are generally based on definite *a priori* agreements, labor rate variances are not too frequent. If they occur, they are generally due to unusual short-term conditions existing in the factory. Setting standards for labor is a problem which requires a detailed study of conditions under which standards are to be used. Generalizations are impossible. Each situation requires special attention with regard to all factors involved.

To assure fairness in rates paid for each operation performed, job rating has become a recognized procedure in industry. When a rate is revised or a change is authorized temporarily, it must be reported promptly to the payroll department to avoid delays, incorrect pay, and faulty reporting. Any difference between standard and actual rates gives rise to labor rate (wage or cost) variances.

Efficiency Standard and Variance. Determination of labor efficiency standards is a specialized function; therefore, they are usually established by industrial engineers using time and motion studies. Standards are set in accordance with scientific methods and accepted practices. They are based on actual performance of a worker or group of workers possessing average skill and using average effort while performing manual operations or working on machines operating under normal conditions. Time factors for acceptable levels of fatigue, personal needs, and delays beyond the control of the worker are studied and included in the standard. Such allowances are an integral part of the labor standard.

Establishment of time standards requires a detailed study of manufacturing operations. Standards based on operations (1) are understood by the foreman, (2) can be used by the foreman as he knows the time allowed, and (3) permit translation of individual operations into products, styles, patterns, or parts. While personal factors are considered a part of direct labor cost in most plants, time required for setting up machines, waiting, or breakdown are included in factory overhead instead of the direct labor standard.

At the end of any agreed upon reporting period (day, week, or month) actual hours worked are compared with standard hours allowed to arrive at a labor efficiency (or time) variance. The *standard hours allowed* figure is found by multiplying the direct labor hours established or predetermined to produce one unit (the standard labor hours per unit) times the *actual* number of units produced during the period for which the variances are being computed. The *units produced* are the equivalent units of production for the labor cost being analyzed.

Illustration. The data used to compute the labor variances are based on Operation 2-476 of the standard cost card (page 581).

Actual hours worked.....................................	1,880 hours
Actual rate paid.......................................	$6.50 per hour
Standard hours allowed for actual production..............	1,590 hours*
Standard rate...	$6 per hour

       *530 units produced × 3 standard Operation 2-476 direct labor hours per unit of production.

The labor rate variance is computed as follows:

	Time × *Rate*	=	*Amount*	
Actual hours worked........	1,880	$6.50 actual	$12,220	
Actual hours worked........	1,880	6.00 standard	11,280	
Labor rate variance........	1,880	$ .50	$ 940	Debit *or* unfavorable

The labor rate (wage) variance amounts to $940 and is unfavorable. The difference in terms of the rate is $.50 per hour.

The labor efficiency variance is computed as follows:

	Time × Rate		=	Amount	
Actual hours worked........	1,880	$6	standard	$11,280	
Standard hours allowed......	1,590	$6	"	9,540	
Labor efficiency variance....	290	$6	"	$1,740	Debit or unfavorable

The unfavorable labor efficiency variance is $1,740 due to the use of 290 hours in excess of standard hours allowed.

The recapitulation of the two labor variances is:

Actual labor cost.................................	$12,220	
Standard labor cost...............................	9,540	
Net labor variance...............................	$ 2,680	Debit or unfavorable

This unfavorable labor cost variance was the result of:

Labor rate variance.........................	$ 940	Debit (unfavorable)
Labor efficiency variance.....................	1,740	Debit (unfavorable)
Net labor variance..........................	$2,680	Debit or unfavorable

The Learning Curve. When a new product or process is started, the labor efficiency standard used for standard costing and budget development should consider the learning curve phenomenon (see Chapter 14). The learning curve may well be at least in part an explanation of the labor efficiency variance associated with employees assigned to existing tasks that are new to them. Labor-related factory overhead costs and perhaps material usage might also be affected.

FACTORY OVERHEAD COST STANDARDS

Procedures used for establishing and using standard factory overhead rates resemble the methods discussed in Chapters 9 and 10 dealing with the estimated factory overhead and its application to jobs and products. It will be recalled that an overhead budget provides budget allowances for a specific anticipated level of activity, while a flexible budget provides allowances that vary with activity. Both types of budgets aim for the control of variable overhead. Control is achieved by keeping actual expenses within ranges established by the budget. The maximum limit of a range is the amount set up in the flexible budget. However, for costing jobs or products it is necessary to establish a normal overhead rate based on total factory overhead at normal capacity volume. Total overhead includes fixed and variable expenses. The effect of volume on overhead cost per unit is illustrated on the next page.

FACTORY OVERHEAD BEHAVIOR PER UNIT OF PRODUCT

Production volume (units)..........	80,000	90,000	100,000	110,000
Factory overhead:				
Variable................................	$112,000	$126,000	$140,000	$154,000
Fixed..	60,000	60,000	60,000	60,000
Total...................................	$172,000	$186,000	$200.000	$214,000
Factory overhead per unit:				
Variable..................................	$1.40	$1.400	$1.40	$1.400
Fixed......................................	.75	.666	.60	.545
Total unit overhead cost...................	$2.15	$2.066	$2.00	$1.945

The illustration indicates the basic pattern of overhead behavior. Fixed expenses remain fixed, within a normal range of activity as volume (output) changes, but vary per unit. The greater the number of units, the smaller the amount of fixed overhead expense per unit. Variable expenses, on the other hand, increase proportionately with each increase of volume (output) and remain fixed per unit.

This characteristic of overhead behavior is important in establishing a standard factory overhead rate. Overhead absorption is accomplished by selecting some plant capacity as the base for charging overhead to jobs or products. This rate charges each unit produced with (1) variable expenses and (2) fixed expenses.

Variable expenses can be measured and controlled at any volume by the foremen with the aid of a flexible budget. The variable expenses in the flexible budget correspond to applied variable overhead, and variable overhead variances result from a comparison of actual variable costs with the flexible budget (applied) variable factory overhead.

Fixed expenses can be absorbed fully only by operating at the volume on which the rate is based. If the base set for overhead absorption is reached, budgeted and absorbed cost figures will be identical. Because this is highly improbable, a difference occurs between budgeted fixed expenses and absorbed fixed overhead; and fixed overhead variances result from an analysis of this difference. For purposes of analysis, budgeted fixed overhead is used. Any difference that might occur between budgeted and actual fixed overhead would become a part of the variable overhead variances. Differences, called "variances," become the yardstick by which management measures the success or failure of its control of overhead and utilization of facilities.

The Standard Factory Overhead Rate. The *standard factory overhead rate* is a predetermined rate that uses direct labor hours as the basis for computing the rate itself and for applying factory overhead. Other bases may also be used; e.g., direct labor dollars or machine hours (see Chapter 9). However, direct labor hours is the basis generally used in standard costing.

The data from Department 3's flexible budget (shown below) is used to illustrate the computation of the standard factory overhead rate and the overhead variances. Assuming that the 100% column represents normal capacity, the standard factory overhead rate is computed as follows:

$$\frac{\text{Total Factory Overhead}}{\text{Direct Labor Hours}} = \frac{\$8,000}{\$4,000} = \$2 \text{ per Standard Direct Labor Hour}$$

At the 100% capacity level, the rate consists of:

$$\frac{\text{Total } \textit{Variable} \text{ Factory Overhead}}{\text{Direct Labor Hours}} = \frac{\$4,800}{\$4,000} = \begin{array}{l} \$1.20 \text{ Variable Factory} \\ \text{Overhead Rate} \end{array}$$

$$\frac{\text{Total } \textit{Fixed} \text{ Factory Overhead}}{\text{Direct Labor Hours}} = \frac{\$3,200}{\$4,000} = \begin{array}{l} .80 \text{ Fixed Factory} \\ \text{Overhead Rate} \end{array}$$

Total Factory Overhead Rate at Normal Capacity. $2.00 per Standard Direct Labor Hour

---

DEPARTMENT 3
MONTHLY FLEXIBLE BUDGET

	80%	100%	120%	Per Direct Labor Hour
Capacity (expressed as a percentage of normal.....				
Standard production........	800	1,000	1,200	
Direct labor hours.........	3,200	4,000	4,800	
Variable factory overhead:				
Indirect labor.............	$1,600	$2,000	$2,400	$ .50
Indirect materials.........	960	1,200	1,440	.30
Supplies..................	640	800	960	.20
Repairs...................	480	600	720	.15
Power and light...........	160	200	240	.05
Total variable factory overhead..............	$3,840	$4,800	$5,760	$1.20
Fixed factory overhead:				
Supervisor................	$1,200	$1,200	$1,200	
Depreciation of machinery.	700	700	700	
Insurance.................	250	250	250	
Property taxes............	250	250	250	
Power and light...........	400	400	400	
Maintenance..............	400	400	400	
Total fixed factory overhead..................	$3,200	$3,200	$3,200	$3,200 per month
Total factory overhead.......	$7,040	$8,000	$8,960	$3,200 per month + $1.20 per D.L.H.

Overall (or Net) Factory Overhead Variance. Jobs or processes are charged with costs applicable to them on the basis of standard hours allowed multiplied by the standard factory overhead rate. The *standard hours allowed* figure is found by multiplying the labor hours required to produce one unit (the standard labor hours per unit) times the *actual* number of units produced during the period. The *units produced* are the equivalent units of production for the factory overhead cost being analyzed. At the end of each month, overhead actually incurred is compared with the expenses charged into process using the standard factory overhead rate. The difference between these two figures is called the overall (or net) factory overhead variance.

Illustration. At the end of a month, the data for Department 3 are as follows:

Actual overhead..	$7,384
Standard hours allowed for actual production.............	3,400 hours*
Actual hours used......................................	3,475 hours
Overall factory overhead variance.......................	$584

*850 units produced × 4 standard Department 3 direct labor hours per unit of production.

The overall factory overhead variance — the difference between actual overhead incurred and overhead costed into production — is computed and shown below.

Actual departmental overhead.......................	$7,384
Overhead charged to production (3,400 standard hours allowed × $2 standard overhead rate).............	6,800
Overall (or net) overhead variance....................	$ 584 Debit *or* unfavorable

This unfavorable overall overhead variance needs further analysis to reveal detailed causes for the variance and to guide management toward remedial action. Analysis of the net overhead variance may be made by:

1. The two-variance method.
2. The three-variance method.
3. The four-variance method.

Two-Variance Method. The two variances are: (1) controllable variance and (2) volume variance. The controllable variance is the difference between actual expenses incurred and the budget allowance based on standard hours allowed for work performed. The volume variance represents the difference between the budget allowance and the standard expenses charged to work in process (standard hours allowed × standard overhead rate).

(1) *Controllable Variance:*

Actual factory overhead.....................		$7,384
Budget allowance based on standard hours allowed:		
Fixed expenses budgeted..................	$3,200	
Variable expenses (3,400 standard hours allowed × $1.20 variable overhead rate).......	4,080	7,280
Controllable variance......................		$ 104 Debit *or* unfavorable

The controllable variance consists of variable expenses only and can also be computed as follows:

Actual variable expense ($7,384 actual factory overhead − $3,200 of fixed expenses budgeted)...............	$4,184
Variable expenses for standard hours allowed..........	4,080
Controllable variance.............................	$ 104 Debit *or* unfavorable

The controllable variance is the responsibility of the department manager to the extent that he can indeed exercise control over the costs to which the variances relate.

(2) *Volume Variance:*

Budget allowance based on standard hours allowed.....	$7,280
Overhead charged to production....................	6,800
Volume variance.....................................	$ 480 Debit *or* unfavorable

This variance consists of fixed expenses only and can also be computed as follows:

Normal capacity hours.........................	4,000
Standard hours allowed for actual production.....	3,400
Capacity hours not utilized, or not utilized efficiently.....................................	600
Volume variance (600 hours × $.80*).................	$480 Debit *or* unfavorable

---

*Fixed expense rate at normal capacity.

The volume variance indicates the cost of capacity available but not utilized or not utilized efficiently and is considered the responsibility of executive and departmental management.

Three-Variance Method. The three variances are: (1) spending variance, (2) idle capacity variance, and (3) efficiency variance. The spending variance is the difference between actual expenses incurred and the budget allowance based on actual hours worked. The idle capacity variance is the difference between the budget allowance based on actual hours and actual hours worked multiplied by the standard overhead rate. These two variances are identical with the spending and idle capacity variances discussed in the factory overhead Chapters 9 and 10. The efficiency variance is the difference between actual hours worked multiplied by the standard overhead rate and the standard hours allowed times the standard overhead rate.

(1) *Spending Variance:*

Actual factory overhead......................		$7,384
Budget allowance based on actual hours worked:		
Fixed expenses budgeted....................	$3,200	
Variable expenses (3,475 actual hours × $1.20		
variable overhead rate)....................	4,170	7,370
Spending variance...........................		$ 14 Debit *or*
		unfavorable

The spending variance consists of variable expenses only and can also be computed as follows:

Actual variable expenses ($7,384 actual factory overhead	
— $3,200 fixed expenses budgeted).................	$4,184
Allowed variable expenses for actual hours...........	4,170
Spending variance.................................	$ 14 Debit *or*
	unfavorable

The spending variance is the responsibility of the department manager who is expected to keep his actual expenses within the budget. By basing the budget allowance on actual hours instead of on standard hours allowed as shown in the controllable variance, the foreman receives a more favorable budget allowance which reduces his variance from $104 to $14.

(2) *Idle Capacity Variance:*

Budget allowance based on actual hours worked.......	$7,370
Actual hours (3,475) × standard overhead rate ($2)....	6,950
Idle capacity variance.............................	$ 420 Debit *or*
	unfavorable

This variance consists of fixed expenses only and can also be computed as follows: 4,000 hours − 3,475 hours = 525 hours × $.80 (fixed expense rate) = $420.

An idle capacity variance indicates the amount of overhead that is either under- or overabsorbed because actual hours are either less or more than the hours on which the overhead rate was based. Department 3 operated at 86.875% of normal capacity based on actual hours. The variance is the responsibility of executive management.

(3) *Efficiency Variance:*

Actual hours (3,475) × standard overhead rate ($2).....	$6,950
Overhead charged to production.....................	6,800
Efficiency variance.....................................	$ 150 Debit *or*
	unfavorable

This variance can also be computed as follows: 3,475 hours − 3,400 hours = 75 hours × $2 = $150.

The efficiency variance consists of fixed and variable expenses and results because actual hours used are more or less than standard hours allowed. Causes for this variance are inefficiencies, inexperienced labor, changes in operations, new tools, different types of materials, etc. This variance and its cause reflect the effect of the labor efficiency variance on factory overhead, when labor dollars or labor hours are the basis for applying factory overhead; if machine hours are the basis, the variance relates to efficiency of machine usage, and so forth for other overhead application bases.

Four-Variance Method. The four variances are: (1) spending variance, (2) variable efficiency variance, (3) fixed efficiency variance, and (4) idle capacity variance. Actually, these four variances merely add to the three-variance method an analysis of the efficiency variance into its fixed and variable components.

(1) *Spending Variance:*

Actual factory overhead.............................	$7,384
Budget allowance based on actual hours worked........	7,370
Spending variance....................................	$ 14 Debit *or*
	unfavorable

This spending variance is identical with that of the three-variance method.

(2) *Variable Efficiency Variance:*

Budget allowance based on actual hours worked........	$7,370
Budget allowance based on standard hours allowed.....	7,280
Variable efficiency variance.........................	$ 90 Debit *or*
	unfavorable

This variance recognizes the difference between the 3,475 actual hours worked and the 3,400 standard (or allowed) hours for the work performed. Multiplying the difference of 75 hours times $1.20 (variable expense rate) results in $90. The sum of the spending and variable efficiency variances equals the controllable variance, $104, of the two-variance method.

SUMMARY OF FACTORY OVERHEAD VARIANCE ANALYSIS METHODS

Method	Column 1 Actual Factory Overhead	Column 2 Budget Allowance for Factory Overhead (Actual Hours Worked)	Column 3 Budget Allowance for Factory Overhead (Standard Hours Allowed)	Column 4 Actual Hours x Standard Overhead Rate*	Column 5 Factory Overhead Costed to Production**	Variances for Each Method	Overall (or Net) Factory Overhead Variance (Unfavorable)
Two-Variance Method	$7,384	....	$7,280	....	$6,800	Controllable variance (Col. 1 − Col. 3)............$104 Volume variance (Col. 3 − Col. 5)............$480	$584
Three-Variance Method	$7,384	$7,370	....	$6,950	$6,800	Spending variance (Col. 1 − Col. 2)............$14 Idle capacity variance (Col. 2 − Col. 4)............$420 Efficiency variance (Col. 4 − Col. 5).....$150	$584
Four-Variance Method	$7,384	$7,370	$7,280	$6,950	$6,800	Spending variance (Col. 1 − Col. 2)............$14 Variable efficiency variance (Col. 2 − Col. 3)............$90 Fixed efficiency variance***............$60 Idle capacity variance (Col. 2 − Col. 4)............$420	$584

*3,475 actual hours worked × $2 standard factory overhead rate.
**3,400 standard hours allowed × $2 standard factory overhead rate.
***(3,475 actual hours worked − 3,400 standard hours allowed) × $.80 fixed factory overhead rate.

(3) *Fixed Efficiency Variance:*

3,475 actual hours × \$.80 fixed overhead rate \$2,780
3,400 standard hours allowed × \$.80 fixed overhead
  rate   2,720

Fixed efficiency variance (75 hours × \$.80) . . . .   \$ 60 Debit *or*
                                                                    unfavorable

The fixed efficiency variance and the idle capacity variance, shown below, are split-offs of the \$480 unfavorable volume variance of the two-variance method which was computed by multiplying the 600 hours not utilized by the \$.80 fixed overhead rate. The fixed efficiency variance indicates how effectively or ineffectively a foreman has employed available capacity.

(4) *Idle Capacity Variance:*

4,000 normal capacity hours × \$.80 fixed overhead rate . . .   \$3,200
3,475 actual hours worked × \$.80 fixed overhead rate . . .   2,780

Idle capacity variance (525 hours × \$.80) . . . .   \$ 420 Debit *or*
                                                                 unfavorable

This variance is identical with the idle capacity variance of the three-variance method and represents the idle or unused capacity; i.e., the difference between budgeted (normal) capacity and actual capacity utilized. It informs management that 525 hours otherwise available and expected to be used, costing \$420 in terms of fixed expenses, remained idle during the month.

The question might arise as to which factory overhead variance analysis method is most frequently used in industry. Although all methods are commonly used, the two-variance method seems to be favored. It should be noted that at times the methods are intermingled, are given different titles, and involve additional analyses. A summary of the three methods described in this chapter is given on page 592.

MIX AND YIELD VARIANCES

Basically, the establishment of a standard product cost requires the determination of price and quantity standards. In a number of industries, particularly of the process type, materials mix and materials yield play significant parts in setting the final product cost and in effecting cost reduction and profit improvement.

Materials specification standards are generally set up for various grades of raw materials and types of secondary materials. In most cases specifications are based on laboratory or engineering tests. Comparative costs of various grades of materials are used in the process of arriving at a satisfactory product mix, and changes are often made when it seems possible to use less costly grades of raw materials or substitute materials.

In addition, a substantial cost reduction can be achieved through the improvement of the yield of good products in the factory. A variance analysis program pointing out and evaluating causes of low yield aids operating management in this endeavor.

Mix Variance. After the establishment of the standard specification, a variance representing the difference between the standard of formula materials and the standard cost of the materials actually used can be calculated. This variance is generally recognized as a mix (or blend) variance. The *mix (or blend) variance* is the result of mixing basic raw materials in a ratio different from standard materials specifications.

In a woolen mill, for instance, the standard proportions of the grades of wool for each yarn number are reflected in the standard blend cost. Any differences between the actual wool used and the standard blend results in a blend or mix variance. Industries like textiles, rubber, and chemicals whose products must possess certain chemical or physical qualities find it quite feasible and economical to apply different combinations of basic raw materials and still achieve a perfect product. In cotton fabrics it is common to mix cotton from many parts of the world with the hope that the new mix and its cost will contribute to improved cost and profit. In many cases the new mix is accompanied by either a favorable or unfavorable yield of the final product. Such a situation makes it difficult at times to judge correctly the origin of the variances. A favorable mix variance, for instance, may be offset by an unfavorable yield variance, or vice versa. Thus, any apparent advantage created by one may be canceled out by the other.

Yield Variance. *Yield* can be defined as the amount of prime product produced from a given amount of materials. The *yield variance* is the result of obtaining a yield different from the one expected on the basis of input. In a gray iron foundry the materials charged into the cupola include raw materials, coke, flux material, and all alloy materials and innoculants used as ladle additions. Cupola operation involves the application of heat to melt the metal as well as a complex thermochemical reaction. This process results in yield, meaning good castings made from the melted metal expressed as a percent of total metal charged.

It is important to recognize raw materials cost differences due to differences in yield when costing or pricing individual castings or patterns. In most instances the total cost of melted metal is divided by the yield percentage to arrive at a cost which is to be charged to the next operation. If, for example, the cost of melted pounds is $18 per 1,000 lbs. and the yield is 90 percent, then dividing $18 by 900 lbs. (90 percent of 1,000 lbs.) results in a cost of $20 to be charged to the next operation.

In sugar refining a normal loss of yield develops when 96 pounds of sucrose available in the standard 100 pounds of raw sugar is processed into refined sugars. Part of this sucrose emerges as blackstrap molasses, and a small percentage is completely lost. On the average it takes approximately 102.5 pounds of sucrose in raw sugar form to produce 100 pounds of sucrose in finished sugars.

In the canning industry it is customary to estimate the expected yield of grades per ton of fruit purchased or delivered to the plant. Should actual yields deviate from predetermined percentages, cost and profit of the grade will differ.   The difference may be due to a shift of the raw materials into a different grade which has a lower selling value.

Since the final product cost contains not only materials but also labor and factory overhead, the emergence of a yield gain or loss when the finished product is transferred to the finished goods inventory also requires the recognition of a yield variance for labor and factory overhead. The actual quantities resulting from the processes are multiplied by the standard cost which includes all three cost elements. A labor yield variance must be looked upon as the result of the quality and/or quantity of the materials handled, while the factory overhead yield variance is due to the greater or smaller number of hours worked. It should be noted that the overhead yield variance may have a significant effect on the amount of under- or overabsorbed factory overhead.

Illustrative Problem Involving Mix and Yield Variances. The illustrative problem presented shows the calculation of mix and yield variances in connection with manufacturing chewing gum. It should be noted that actual output is placed into finished goods inventory at the total standard cost per unit. This method leads to yield variances not only for materials but also for labor and factory overhead.

The Springmint Company, a manufacturer of chewing gum, uses a standard cost system.   Standard product and cost specifications for 1,000 lbs. of chewing gum are as follows:

	Quantity ×	Price	= Cost		
Gum base....	800 lbs.	$.25 per lb.	$200		
Corn syrup...	200 lbs.	.40 per lb.	80		
Sugar........	200 lbs.	.10 per lb.	20		
Input......	1,200 lbs.		$300	$\dfrac{\$300}{1{,}200 \text{ lbs.}}$	= $.25 per lb.*
Output....	1,000 lbs.		$300	$\dfrac{\$300}{1{,}000 \text{ lbs.}}$	= $.30 per lb.*

*Weighted averages.

The production of 1,000 lbs. of chewing gum requires 1,200 lbs. of raw materials. Hence, the expected yield is 1,000 lbs. ÷ 1,200 lbs., or 5/6ths.

Materials records indicate:

	Beginning Inventory	Purchases in January	Ending Inventory
Gum base........	10,000 lbs.	162,000 lbs. @ $.24	15,000 lbs.
Corn syrup.......	12,000 lbs.	30,000 lbs. @ .42	4,000 lbs.
Sugar...........	15,000 lbs.	32,000 lbs. @ .11	11,000 lbs.

The company recognizes the materials price variances at the time materials are purchased.

To convert 1,200 lbs. of raw materials into 1,000 lbs. of finished product requires 20 hours at $6 per hour, or $.12 per lb. Actual direct labor hours and cost for January are 3,800 hours at $23,104.

Factory overhead is applied on a direct labor hour basis at a rate of $5 per hour ($3 fixed, $2 variable), or $.10 per lb. Normal overhead is $20,000 with 4,000 direct labor hours. Actual overhead for the month is $22,000. Actual finished production for the month of January is 200,000 lbs.

The standard cost per pound of finished chewing gum is:

Materials...	$.30
Labor...	.12
Factory overhead......................................	.10
	$.52 per lb.

ANALYSIS OF VARIANCES FOR JANUARY

Materials Variances:

Materials	Quantity	Actual Price	Standard Price	Unit Price Variance	Price Variance
Gum base..	162,000 lbs.	$.24	$.25	$(.01)	$(1,620)
Corn syrup.	30,000 lbs.	.42	.40	.02	600
Sugar......	32,000 lbs.	.11	.10	.01	320
Net materials purchase price variance.....................					$ (700) Credit *or* favorable

Actual quantities at standard prices:

Gum base (157,000 lbs. @ $.25)...............	$39,250	
Corn syrup (38,000 lbs. @ $.40)...............	15,200	
Sugar (36,000 lbs. @ $.10)...............	3,600	$58,050
231,000 lbs.		

Actual quantity at standard materials cost:

Actual input (231,000 lbs. × $.25*).............	$57,750	
or		
Standard (expected) output from actual input [192,500 lbs. (1,000/1,200 or 5/6 of 231,000 lbs.) × $.30*].....................................	$57,750	57,750
Materials mix variance.............................		$ 300 Debit *or* unfavorable

*Weighted average cost computed on page 595.

Actual quantity at standard materials cost (see previous page)............................. $57,750

Actual output quantity at standard materials cost:

Actual output (200,000 lbs. × $.30)........... $60,000

or

Input needed to produce 200,000 lbs. (240,000 lbs. × $.25)............................. $60,000   60,000

Materials yield variance...................... $ (2,250) Credit *or* favorable

The materials purchase price variance is computed as shown on page 583. The materials quantity variance, also illustrated on page 583, can be computed for each material as follows:

Gum base:

	Unit	×	Unit Cost	=	Amount
Actual quantity used....	157,000 lbs.		$.25		$39,250
Standard quantity allowed............	160,000 lbs.*		.25		40,000
Materials quantity variance.........................					$ (750) Credit *or* favorable

*An output of 200,000 lbs. should require an input of 240,000 lbs., with a standard yield of 1,000 lbs. output for each 1,200 lbs. input. Then the

$240,000$ lbs. × $\frac{800 \text{ lbs.}}{1,200 \text{ lbs.}}$ gum base portion of the

formula = 160,000 lbs.

Corn syrup:

	Unit	×	Unit Cost	=	Amount
Actual quantity used....	38,000 lbs.		$.40		$15,200
Standard quantity allowed............	40,000 lbs.*		.40		16,000
Materials quantity variance.........................					$ (800) Credit *or* favorable

*The 240,000 lbs. × $\frac{200 \text{ lbs.}}{1,200 \text{ lbs.}}$ corn syrup portion

of the formula = 40,000 lbs.

Sugar:

	Unit	×	Unit Cost	=	Amount
Actual quantity used....	36,000 lbs.		$.10		$3,600
Standard quantity allowed............	40,000 lbs.*		.10		4,000
Materials quantity variance.........................					$ (400) Credit *or* favorable

*The 240,000 lbs. × $\frac{200 \text{ lbs.}}{1,200 \text{ lbs.}}$ sugar portion of

formula = 40,000 lbs.

Total materials quantity variance...................... $ (1,950) Credit *or* favorable

The total materials quantity variance can also be found by comparing actual quantities at standard prices, $58,050 ($39,250+$15,200+$3,600), to actual output quantity at standard materials cost, $60,000 (200,000 lbs. × $.30) for a total favorable variance of $1,950. The mix and yield variances separate the materials quantity variance into two parts:

Materials mix variance......................	$ 300 Debit *or* unfavorable
Materials yield variance....................	(2,250) Credit *or* favorable
Materials quantity variance.................	$(1,950) Credit *or* favorable

The materials mix variance can be viewed in the following manner:

	Actual Quantity (Lbs.)	Standard Formula (Lbs.) ×	Total Actual Quantity (Lbs.) =	Actual Quantity Using Standard Formula (Lbs.)	Quantity Variation (Lbs.) ×	Standard Unit Price =	Materials Mix Variance
Gum base.	157,000	$\frac{800}{1,200}$	231,000	154,000	3,000	$.25	$750
Corn syrup	38,000	$\frac{200}{1,200}$	231,000	38,500	(500)	.40	(200)
Sugar.....	36,000	$\frac{200}{1,200}$	231,000	38,500	(2,500)	.10	(250)
	231,000 lbs.			231,000 lbs.			$300

The yield variance occurred because the actual production of 200,000 lbs. exceeded the expected yield or output of 192,500 lbs. (5/6ths of 231,000 lbs.) by 7,500 lbs.; and the yield difference multiplied by the standard weighted materials cost per output pound of $.30 equals the favorable yield variance of $2,250.

Labor Variances:

The expected output (yield) of 192,500 lbs. of chewing gum (231,000 lbs. of raw materials issued multiplied by the expected yield of 5/6ths equals 192,500 lbs.) should require 3,850 standard labor hours (20 hours per thousand pounds of chewing gum produced; and, similarly, the actual output (yield) of 200,000 lbs. of chewing gum should require 4,000 standard labor hours. The computation of labor variances is as follows:

Actual payroll..................................	$23,104
Actual hours (3,800) × standard labor rate ($6)......	22,800
Labor rate variance..............................	$ 304 Debit *or* unfavorable
Actual hours × standard labor rate................	$22,800
Standard hours allowed for expected output (3,850) × standard labor rate ($6).........................	23,100
Labor efficiency variance.........................	$ (300) Credit *or* favorable

Standard hours allowed for expected output × standard labor rate..................................... $23,100
Standard hours allowed for actual output (4,000) × standard labor rate ($6)......................... 24,000
Labor efficiency variance......................... $ (900) Credit *or* favorable

The labor rate variance is computed as shown on page 584. The traditional labor efficiency variance, illustrated on page 585, is computed as follows:

	Time ×	Rate =	Amount
Actual hours worked.............	3,800	$ 6	$22,800
Standard hours allowed...........	4,000	6	24,000
Labor efficiency variance...........	(200)	$ 6	$ (1,200) Credit *or* favorable

The labor yield variance calculation identifies the portion of the labor efficiency variance attributable to obtaining an unfavorable or, as in this illustration, a favorable yield (3,850 standard hours allowed for expected output − 4,000 standard hours allowed for actual output = 150 hours × $6 standard labor rate = $900). The favorable labor efficiency variance of $300 is the portion of the traditional labor efficiency variance that is attributable to factors other than yield; and the sum of the two, $900 plus $300, equals the $1,200 traditional labor efficiency variance.

Factory Overhead Variances:

Three-Variance Method (Adapted To Compute a Yield Variance)

Actual factory overhead................... $22,000
Budget allowance (based on actual hours):
    Fixed expenses budgeted............... $12,000
    Variable expenses (3,800 hours × $2)..... 7,600   19,600
Spending variance...................... $ 2,400 Debit *or* unfavorable

Budget allowance (based on actual hours)............ $19,600
Actual hours (3,800) × standard overhead rate ($5)..... 19,000
Idle capacity variance......................... $ 600 Debit *or* unfavorable

Actual hours × standard overhead rate............... $19,000
Standard hours allowed for expected output (3,850) × standard overhead rate ($5)...................... 19,250
Overhead efficiency variance..................... $ (250) Credit *or* favorable

Standard hours allowed for expected output × standard overhead rate..................................... $19,250
Standard hours allowed for actual output (4,000) × standard overhead rate ($5)....................... 20,000
Overhead yield variance......................... $ (750) Credit *or* favorable

The spending and idle capacity variances are computed in the same manner as discussed on page 590. The overhead efficiency variance and the overhead yield variance, when combined, equal the efficiency variance discussed earlier in this chapter on page 591. The overhead yield variance measures that portion of the total overhead variances resulting from a favorable yield (3,850 hours − 4,000 hours = 150 × $5 = $750).

Two-Variance Method (Adapted To Compute a Yield Variance)

Actual factory overhead.........................		$22,000
Budget allowance (based on standard hours allowed for expected output):		
Fixed expenses budgeted..............	$12,000	
Variable expenses (3,850 hours × $2)...	7,700	19,700
Controllable variance....................		$ 2,300 Debit *or* unfavorable

Budget allowance (based on standard hours for expected output).......................................		$19,700
Standard hours allowed for expected output (3,850) × standard overhead rate ($5)...................		19,250
Overhead volume variance........................		$ 450 Debit *or* unfavorable

Standard hours allowed for expected output × standard overhead rate...........................		$19,250
Standard hours allowed for actual output (4,000) × standard overhead rate ($5).....................		20,000
Overhead yield variance.........................		$ (750) Credit *or* favorable

The unfavorable spending variance, $2,400, combined with the variable part of the overhead efficiency variance (3,800 hours − 3,850 hours) × $2 = $100 favorable, both from the three-variance method above, equals $2,300 unfavorable, the controllable variance. The idle capacity variance, $600 unfavorable, combined with the fixed part of the overhead efficiency variance (3,800 hours − 3,850 hours) × $3 = $150 favorable, both from the three-variance method shown above, equals $450 unfavorable, the overhead volume variance. The favorable overhead yield variance is the same as for the three-variance method and can be viewed as consisting of $300 variable cost (3,850 standard hours allowed for expected output − 4,000 standard hours allowed for actual output) × $2, and $450 fixed cost, (3,850 − 4,000) × $3.

The journal entries for the variances discussed on the previous pages are illustrated in the next chapter.

MANAGERIAL USEFULNESS OF VARIANCE ANALYSIS

Costs of production are affected by internal factors over which management has a large degree of control. An important job of executive management is to make the members of various management levels understand that all of them are part and parcel of the management team. The task of imparting this cost control consciousness falls, in part, upon standard costs with their variances. With their aid, management is informed of the effectiveness of production effort as well as that of the supervisory personnel.

Supervisors who often handle two thirds to three fourths of the dollar cost of the product are made directly responsible for the variances which, as the chapter discussion indicates, show up as materials variances (price, quantity, yield, and scrap) or as direct labor variances (rate and efficiency). Materials and labor variances can be computed for each materials item, for each labor operation, and for each workman.

Factory overhead variances (spending, controllable, idle capacity, volume, and efficiency) indicate the failures or successes of the control of variable and fixed overhead expenses in each department.

Variances are not ends in themselves but, rather, springboards for further analysis, investigation, and action. However, variances will also permit the supervisory personnel to defend itself and its employees against failures that were not their fault. A variance provides the yardstick to measure the fairness of the standard, allowing management to redirect its effort and to make reasonable adjustments. Action to eliminate the causes of undesirable variances and to encourage and reward desired performance lies in the field of management, but supervisory and operating personnel rely on the accounting information system for facts which make possible intelligent action toward the control of costs.

DISCUSSION QUESTIONS

1. Recently a conference speaker discussing budgeted and standard costs made the following statement: "Budgets and standards are not the same thing. They have different purposes and are set up and used in different ways, yet a specific relationship exists between them."
   (a) Identify distinctions or differences between budgets and standards.
   (b) Identify similarities between budgets and standards.

2. A team of management consultants and company executives concluded that a standard cost installation was a desirable vehicle for accomplishing the objectives of a progressive management. State a few uses of standard costs that can be associated with the above decision.

3. Is a standard cost system equally applicable to job order costing and process costing?

4. The problem of setting a standard cost generally leads to a discussion of what should be included in and what should be excluded from standard costs. What determines the final decision?

5. Does a standard cost system increase or decrease the amount of accounting and clerical effort and expense required to prepare cost reports and financial statements?

6. What types of variances are computed for materials, labor, and factory overhead?

7. In a paper mill, materials specification standards are set up for various grades of pulp and secondary furnish (waste paper) for each grade and kind of paper produced. Yet at regular intervals the cost accountant is able to determine a materials mix variance. Why?

8. How does the calculation of a mix variance differ from that of a quantity variance?

9. Yield is often expressed as the percentage actually obtained of the amount theoretically possible. The yield figure is a useful managerial control of materials consumption. Explain.

10. A cost standard in a process industry is often based on an assumed yield rate. Any difference in actual yield from standard yield will produce a yield variance. Express this variance in formula form.

11. The isolation of a yield variance results in yield variances not only for materials but also for labor and factory overhead. Why?

12. Select the correct answer for each of the following statements.

(a) The product cost determined in a standard cost accounting system is a (1) direct cost; (2) fixed cost; (3) joint cost; (4) expected cost.

(b) A company employing very tight (theoretical) standards in a standard cost system should expect that (1) a large incentive bonus will be paid; (2) most variances will be unfavorable; (3) employees will be strongly motivated to attain the standards; (4) costs will be controlled better than if lower standards were used.

(c) A company controls its production costs by comparing its actual monthly production costs with the expected levels. Any significant deviations from these expected levels are investigated and evaluated as a basis for corrective actions. The quantitative technique that most probably is being used is (1) correlation analysis; (2) differential calculus; (3) risk analysis; (4) standard cost variance analysis; (5) time series or trend regression analysis.

(d) One purpose of standard costs may be described as (1) promoting and measuring performance; (2) controlling and reducing costs; (3) simplifying production operations; (4) setting cost to manufacture; (5) all of the above; (6) none of the above.

(e) In a standard cost system the materials purchase price variance is obtained by multiplying the (1) actual price by the difference between actual quantity purchased and standard quantity allowed; (2) actual quantity purchased by the difference between actual price and standard price; (3) standard price by the difference between standard quantity purchased and standard quantity allowed; (4) standard quantity purchased by the difference between actual price and standard price.

(f) If the current standard calls for the use of 1,000 units @ $1 each and the actual usage is 1,050 units @ $.90 each, the materials price variance is (1) $100; (2) $55; (3) $105; (4) $50, and the materials quantity variance is (1) $100; (2) $55; (3) $105; (4) $50.

(g) A company has set its normal capacity at 24,000 hours for the current year. Fixed overhead was budgeted for $18,000 while variable overhead was budgeted for $24,000. Actual hours worked for the current year were 22,000. The idle capacity variance for the current year is (1) $1,750; (2) $2,000; (3) $3,500; (4) $1,500.

(AICPA adapted)

EXERCISES

Wherever variances are required in the following exercises, indicate whether they are favorable or unfavorable.

1. Materials Variance Analysis. The Abrahamson Container Company uses five pieces of metal, 2 meters by 1 meter, at $12 per piece as the standard for its production of nonrust vats. During one month's operations, 4,900 vats were produced at a cost of $11.75 per piece for 25,000 actual pieces of material.

Required: The materials price and quantity variances.

2. Labor Variance Analysis. Hidalgo County Rural Electric Cooperative has determined that when ditch-digging equipment is used, the labor time per foot of underground line installed should be 5 minutes and that the average hourly labor pay rate should be $4.

In June two ditch-digging units installed 4,800 feet of line at a labor cost of $1,435 and at an average hourly rate of $4.10.

Required: The labor rate and efficiency variances.

3. Factory Overhead Variance Analysis. The Tejas Manufacturing Company employs a standard cost accounting system. The standard factory overhead rate was computed based on normal capacity:

Budgeted variable expenses..........	$12,000
Budgeted fixed expenses.............	8,000
Total........................	$20,000

$$\text{Factory overhead rate:} \frac{\$20,000}{20,000 \text{ hours}} = \$1.00 \text{ per direct labor hour}$$

Two labor hours are required to manufacture each finished unit. During the month, 8,750 units were completed. There were no beginning or ending work in process inventories. 18,400 labor hours were worked and actual factory overhead was $18,250.

Required: An analysis of factory overhead using the two-, three-, and four-variance methods.

4. Factory Overhead Variance Analysis. The accountant for the McGee Company prepared the following flexible monthly factory overhead budget:

Direct Labor Hours	Budgeted Factory Overhead
10,400	$21,600
9,600	20,400
8,800	19,200
8,000 (normal capacity)	18,000
7,200	16,800

In August the actual factory overhead was $21,200. The company operated at 125% of normal capacity. Standard hours allowed for actual production were 10,200.

Required: An analysis of factory overhead by (a) the two-variance method and (b) the three-variance method.

5. Labor and Overhead Analyses. The Glenmore Company prepares a flexible factory overhead budget and applies these budgeted expenses to production by means of a normal capacity rate.

FLEXIBLE BUDGET — GLENMORE COMPANY			
Capacity	**90%**	**100%** (normal)	**110%**
Direct labor hours.........	360,000	400,000	440,000
Fixed expenses............	$234,000	$234,000	$240,000
Variable expenses.........	113,400	126,000	138,600
Total factory overhead.....	$347,400	$360,000	$378,600

The following data pertain to the operations of the company for the year just ended:

Actual payroll for the year..................................	$544,640
Actual labor hours worked.................................	368,000
Standard labor cost for the year...........................	$540,000
Standard labor rate per hour..............................	1.50
Actual factory overhead...................................	325,000

Required: (1) Rate and efficiency variances for direct labor.
(2) Overhead variances on the basis of the three-variance method.
(3) Overhead variances on the basis of the two-variance method.
(4) Further analysis of the controllable and volume variances.

6. Variance Analysis for a Hospital: Materials, Labor, and Overhead. At the Enid Municipal Hospital one of the departments, the Laboratory, has standard costs for each of its activities.

The Laboratory has developed the following standards for performing routine blood tests:

Materials (1 packet of chemicals @ $.50).......................... $ .50
Labor (10 minutes @ $6 per direct labor hour).................... 1.00
Overhead ($12 per direct labor hour)*............................ 2.00

Standard cost per blood test..................................... $3.50

*Based on 5,000 tests (or 833.3 direct labor
hours per month; fixed, $4.80; variable, $7.20
per direct labor hour).

During April, 4,800 blood tests were made; and the following costs were incurred:

Materials (5,000 packets @ $.52).............................. $ 2,600
Labor (850 hours @ $6 per direct labor hour)................... 5,100
Overhead.. 9,200

Total.. $16,900

$$\frac{\$16,900}{4,800 \text{ blood tests}} = \$3.52 \text{ average cost per blood test}$$

Required: Two-variance analysis for materials, labor, and overhead.

7. Variance Analysis: Materials, Labor, and Overhead. The Highway Repair Fund of the State of Ohio employs a standard cost system in accounting for its expenditures. The standards were established by the engineers of the Capital Improvements Department of the state on the basis of "per cubic yard" of materials used.

Based on normal highway repair of 30,000 cubic yards per month, the standards are:

Materials ($5 per cubic yard)................................. $5.00
Labor (½ hour at $2)... 1.00

Overhead:
Fixed ($1 per direct labor dollar)........................ 1.00*
Variable ($1 per direct labor dollar)..................... 1.00

Standard cost per cubic yard................................. $8.00

*Total fixed overhead, $30,000.

The actual expenditures incurred for January were:

Materials (33,000 cubic yards)................................ $168,300
Labor (17,000 hours).. 33,150
Overhead.. 66,000

Required: An analysis of the materials, labor, and overhead variances, using the two-variance method for overhead.

8. Factory Overhead Variance Analysis. The Cherokee Corporation uses a standard cost system. The following overhead costs and production data are available for one of the producing departments:

Factory overhead in process at beginning
     (6,000 standard direct labor hours)............... $13,200
Actual overhead for the month.................... $90,230

Overhead budgeted for the month:
     Fixed overhead....................... $8,000
     Variable overhead.................... $2 per direct labor hour

Normal monthly direct labor hours...............   40,000
Actual direct labor hours worked................   40,300
Standard (or allowed) direct labor hours
     for the work completed and transferred out......   39,500
Factory overhead in process at end of month.......   5,500 standard direct
                                               labor hours

Required: (1) The standard factory overhead rate.
(2) The standard direct labor hours worked.
(3) The work in process factory overhead account showing the appropriate debit and credit postings and the final inventory.
(4) The amount of the volume variance.

9. Variance Analyses: Materials, Labor, and Factory Overhead; Process Cost Procedure. The Redman Company manufactures a product whose standard product cost is as follows:

Direct materials   — 24 kilograms (kg.) @ $3.00 per kg........... $72.00
Direct labor   —   6 hours @   3.25 per hour........   19.50
Factory overhead —   6 hours @   .75 per hour........   4.50
     Total unit standard cost.................................... $96.00

The factory overhead was based on the following flexible budget:

	80%	*90%*	*100%*	*110%*
Hours (direct labor)...........	36,000	40,500	45,000	49,500
Variable expenses.............	$18,000	$20,250	$22,500	$24,750
Fixed expenses................	11,250	11,250	11,250	11,250
Total factory overhead........	$29,250	$31,500	$33,750	$36,000

Actual data for the month of November:

Planned production, 7,500 units.
Materials put into production, 192,410 kg. @ $3.04 per kg. (average cost).
Direct labor, 46,830 hours @ $3.30 average labor cost.
Actual factory overhead, $36,340.

Other data:

Opening inventory, work in process,   80 units, all materials, 50% converted.
Closing inventory, work in process, 100 units, all materials, 50% converted.
Started in process during November, 7,850 units.

Required: A variance analysis of (a) the direct materials, (b) the direct labor cost, and (c) the factory overhead (two-variance method).

10. Variance Analyses — Materials, Labor, and Factory Overhead. The Brad-town Furniture Company uses a standard cost system in accounting for its production costs.

The standard cost of a unit of furniture follows:

Lumber, 100 feet @ $150 per 1,000 feet.....................		$15.00
Direct labor, 4 hours @ $2.50 per hour.....................		10.00
Factory overhead:		
Fixed (30% of direct labor)........................	$3.00	
Variable (60% of direct labor)....................	6.00	9.00
Total unit cost.......................................		$34.00

The following flexible monthly overhead budget is in effect:

Direct Labor Hours	*Budgeted Overhead*
5,200..	$10,800
4,800..	10,200
4,400..	9,600
4,000 (normal capacity).........................	9,000
3,600	8,400

The actual unit costs for the month of December were as follows:

Lumber used (110 feet @ $120 per 1,000 feet).................	$13.20
Direct labor (4¼ hours @ $2.60 per hour)....................	11.05
Factory overhead ($10,560 ÷ 1,200 units)....................	8.80
Total actual unit cost.....................................	$33.05

Required: An analysis of each element of the total variance from standard cost for the month of December. Use the two- and the three-variance method for factory overhead.

(AICPA adapted)

11. Quantity and Equivalent Production Schedules; Cost Variance Analyses. The Rudell Corporation operates a machine shop and employs a standard cost system. In September the firm was the low bidder on a contract to deliver 600 kartz by November 15 at a contract price of $200 each. Rudell's estimate of the costs to manufacture each kartz was:

40 lbs. of materials @ $1.50 per lb..............................	$ 60
20 hours of direct labor @ $2 per hour...........................	40
Factory overhead (40% variable)................................	30
Total cost...	$130

On September 1 when the contract was obtained, 30 completed kartz were still in work in process; 70 kartz were in process with 2,800 lbs. of materials at a cost of $4,200 and 60% processed; and 2,000 pounds of materials at a cost of $3,000 were in raw materials inventory. All costs were at standard. In September, 500 kartz were started in production; 480 kartz were transferred to finished goods inventory. The work in process inventory at September 30 was 10% processed with all materials added at the start of production. The materials inventory is priced under the fifo method at actual cost.

The following information is available for the month of September:

Materials purchased:

Pounds	Amount
8,000	$12,000
8,000	12,000
4,000	5,600

Materials requisitioned and put into production: 21,000 lbs.

Direct labor payroll amounted to $18,648 for 8,880 hours.

Factory overhead was applied on the basis of allowed standard hours. Actual factory overhead incurred was $13,140. Standard normal capacity was estimated at 400 kartz per month.

Required: (1) A quantity schedule.
(2) An equivalent production schedule.
(3) Variance analysis of (a) direct materials, (b) direct labor, and (c) factory overhead using the two-variance method.

(AICPA adapted)

12. Price, Mix, and Yield Variances. The Zorba Manufacturing Company uses a standard cost system. The standard cost card for one of its products shows the following materials standards:

Material	Pounds	×	Standard Price Per Pound	=	Amount
A	20		.70		$ 14
B	5		.40		2
C	25		.20		5
Total materials cost per unit.........................					$ 21

The standard 50 lb. mix cost per lb. is $ .42 ($21 ÷ 50 lbs.). The standard mix should produce 40 lbs of finished product, and the standard cost of finished product per lb. is $.525 ($21 ÷ 40 lbs.).

Actual results for the period were:

Raw materials of 500,000 lbs. were used as follows:

Material A.................................230,000 lbs. @ $.80 per lb.
Material B................................. 50,000 lbs. @ $.35 per lb.
Material C.................................220,000 lbs. @ $.25 per lb.

The output of the finished product was 390,000 lbs.

Required: Product analysis showing materials price, mix, and yield variances from standards.

13. Price Mix, and Yield Variances. The Hampton Chemical Company produces Petrocloronal using the following standard proportions and costs of materials:

	Kilograms (kg.)	Cost per Kilogram	Amount
Material A...........................	50	$5.00	$250.00
Material B...........................	40	6.00	240.00
Material C...........................	60	3.00	180.00
	150	4.4667	$670.00
Standard shrinkage (33-⅓%)..........	50		
Net weight and costs.................	100	6.70	$670.00

A recent production run yielding 100 output kilograms required an input of:

	Kilograms (kg.)	Cost per Kilogram
Material A................................	40	$5.15
Material B................................	50	6.00
Material C................................	65	2.80

Required: Materials price, mix, and yield variances.

(Based on an article in *Management Accounting*)

14. Price, Mix, and Yield Variances. Soda ash, a commercial anhydrous sodium carbonate, is made artificially by the Solvay process. The following raw materials data are the standard costs for the January production of 100 tons:

Salt........................	160	tons @ $14.00 per ton	$2,240
Limestone...................	130	tons @ 18.00 per ton	2,340
Coke........................	10	tons @ 21.00 per ton	210
Coal........................	6¼ tons @	8.00 per ton	50
Total input quantity and cost.....	306¼ tons		$4,840
Average input cost.......................................			$15.80

The following data are available regarding the raw materials:

	Inventory Beginning	Purchases	Inventory Ending
Salt	15 tons @ $12 per ton	180 tons @ $14.50 per ton	25 tons
Limestone	10 tons @ 19 per ton	135 tons @ 17.50 per ton	15 tons
Coke	½ ton @ 20 per ton	20 tons @ 18.00 per ton	8½ tons
Coal	¾ ton @ 8 per ton	10 tons @ 8.50 per ton	4 tons

Materials are charged into production by the lifo method.

Required: An analysis of the January materials variances: price, mix, and yield.

15. Price, Mix, and Yield Variances. Trexamatic, Inc. produces a product called Datrex, a fluid used in the operation of its computers and business machines. Each month it manufactures and bottles 6,000 quarts of this product to fill the needs of its dealers and customers, the production being in five separate runs of 1,200 quarts each. The standard product mix for making 1,200 quarts of Datrex is:

> Material R: 700 quarts @ $.25 per quart
> Material S: 600 quarts @ .20 per quart
> Material T: 200 quarts @ .45 per quart

December's production of 6,000 quarts was as follows:

Material	Actually Used	Actual Price
R	3,400 quarts	$.26 per quart
S	2,900 quarts	.22 per quart
T	1,300 quarts	.40 per quart

Required: The materials price, mix, and yield variances for Trexamatic's December production run.

PROBLEMS

Wherever variances are required in the following problems, indicate whether they are favorable or unfavorable.

19-1. Standard Cost Statement; Final Bid Price. The Arkansas Packaging Corporation proposes to manufacture a standard box. Operations will be: (a) cutting the plywood in Department 1, (b) assembling in Department 2, and (c) attaching a purchased mechanism in Department 3.

Specifications and Standards

Dimensions of box with cover: 2' x 3' x 1½'
Plywood to be purchased in panels 4' x 6' (In setting standard quantities of plywood, allow for unavoidable waste.)
Quantity to be manufactured: 20,000 boxes
Bid price to be cost plus 10% profit

Price of plywood: $256 per M (thousand) square feet

Other materials required:
Corner angles, hinges, and handles in Department 2 ....$6.30 per set
Mechanism in Department 3........................ 9.20 each
Screws, rivets, and glue:
    Used in Department 2........................... .34
    Used in Department 3........................... .10

Labor and factory overhead:

	Time	Rate per Hour	Factory Overhead
Department 1	.085 hour	$2.40	100% direct labor cost
Department 2	1.100 hour	2.20	150% direct labor cost
Department 3	.250 hour	1.60	75% direct labor cost

Actual Performance

Purchased: 25,500 spruce plywood panels, 4' x 6' @ $256 per M sq. ft.
              20,250 sets hardware.............$131,625
              20,300 mechanisms.............. 183,512

Issued from stock: 18,928 ply panels
                      12,130 sets hardware
                      10,064 mechanisms
                      $5,280 screws, etc.

Analysis of labor and factory overhead:

	Time	Labor Cost	Factory Overhead
Department 1	1,512 hours	$ 3,689	$ 4,180
Department 2	12,100 hours	25,652	41,360
Department 3	3,012 hours	4,880	3,740

Production report:

Department 1	15,120 boxes, cut
Department 2	12,100 boxes, assembled
Department 3	10,040 boxes, complete

Required: Statement showing standard cost in itemized and departmentalized form, and final bid price.

19-2. Standard Cost Sheet; Labor Variance Analysis. Olano, Inc. plans to sell its new skin care lotion, Lanosof, in a 4-ounce bottle at a suggested retail price of $1. Cost and production studies show these costs:

Container:

Item No.	Description	Cost	Comments
2147	4 oz. bottle	$5.75 per gross	Allow 2% for waste and breakage
315	Label	3.30 per 1,000	Allow 4% for waste and breakage

Raw Materials:

Item No.	Description	Cost	Quantity Used per 125 Gallon Batch
4247	Compound 34A	$40 per 100 lbs.	70 lbs.
3126	Alcohol and glycerin	40 per 100 lbs.	68 lbs.
4136B	Perfume oil*		4 lbs.

*Perfume oil is mixed by the company according to its secret formula.

Standard costs of a 90 lb. batch of perfume oil are as follows:

Ingredients... $2,169.95
Direct labor — 4.4 hours @ $2.28 per hour................   10.03
Factory overhead — $7.50 per batch plus $1.95 per standard labor hour.

(Note: A gallon contains 128 oz.)

Allowance for Lost Materials:

Allow 5% of standard materials cost for overfilling, waste, and breakage.

Direct Labor per Gross:

Compounding......................... 0.15 hours @ $1.90 per hour
Filling and packing..................... 1.00 hours @ $1.75 per hour

Factory Overhead:

Compounding.........................	$3.00 per standard labor hour
Filling and packing.....................	$1.75 per standard labor hour
	plus $.95 per gross

Required: (1) A standard cost sheet for one gross bottles of this product, arranging the data under the five subheadings listed above. Calculations should be made to the nearest cent per gross.

(2) The company expected to produce 1,000 gross of Lanosof Lotion in its first week of production, but actually produced only 850 gross. Its direct labor cost of filling and packing was: 825 hours — $1,467.75. Prepare an analysis of the labor variance from standard.

(AICPA adapted)

19-3. Materials and Labor Variance Analysis. The Emmerich Manufacturing Company uses a standard cost system in accounting for the cost of its single product. The standard was set as follows:

Standard output per month, 10,000 units
Standard direct labor per unit, 8 hours @ $1.30 per hour

Standard direct materials per unit:

Material P — 10 kilograms @ $.275 per kilogram
Material Q —   5 units   @ $.64   per unit

Total standard cost per unit including overhead on a direct labor hour basis, $23.55.

The following operating data were taken from the records for March:

In process first of month, none
Completed during month, 8,000 units

In process end of month, 1,000 units, which are one-half complete as to labor and overhead and have had all of Material P issued for them and sufficient Material Q for one half of them.

Direct labor was $88,440, which was at a rate of $1.32 per hour.

Materials issued to production:

94,000 kilograms of P @ $.26 per kilogram
42,600 units of Q   @ $.65 per unit

Overhead for the month amounted to $61,640.

Required: A schedule showing the variance of actual cost from standard cost and an analysis of variances for labor and materials, separating each into the factors that caused them. Compute two variances for *each* material and two variances for labor. Show all computations.

(AICPA adapted)

19-4. Materials, Labor, and Overhead Variance Analysis. St. Paul Foundry, Inc. produces gray iron castings for customers on a job-shop basis.

Raw materials necessary for production at standard costs are:

Materials	*Standard Cost*
Scrap iron...........	$56.00 per gross ton (2,240 lbs.)
Pig iron.............	67.20 per gross ton
Coke...............	70.00 per ton (2,000 lbs.)
Flux................	20.00 per ton

Raw materials are loaded into the cupola in 500-lb. "charges" consisting of:

Materials	Quantities
Scrap iron...............................	425 lbs.
Pig iron..................................	20 lbs.
Coke......................................	45 lbs.
Flux......................................	10 lbs.
	500 lbs.

A "charge" is a load of materials dumped into the cupola. The standard yield of good iron per charge is 430 lbs.

During the month, 600 charges were melted and yielded the standard amount of good castings. The following amounts of raw materials were requisitioned and used during the month:

Raw Materials	Quantities	Actual Cost
Scrap iron......................	256,800 lbs.	$ 7,704.00
Pig iron........................	12,600 lbs.	315.00
Coke............................	26,400 lbs.	1,056.00
Flux............................	6,000 lbs.	60.00

The standard labor rate was $2.50 per hour, and 3,200 hours should have been worked based on the production for this month. Actual direct labor cost was $7,824 for an actual average labor rate of $2.40 per hour.

Total annual factory overhead including fixed overhead is $200,000 to be applied on the basis of estimated 40,000 direct labor hours. The variable overhead rate is $2.60 per direct labor hour. Actual overhead during January was $15,800.

Required: (1) Materials price and quantity variances for each material.
(2) Labor rate and efficiency variances.
(3) Overhead variances (two-variance method).
(4) Standard materials cost per pound of iron (materials cost only) carried to three decimal places.

19-5. Standard Cost Variances Analysis. The Tryon Manufacturing Company manufactures the product TRYAD in standard batches of 100 units. A standard cost system is used. The standard costs for a batch are:

Raw materials (70 lbs. @ $.50 per lb.).............................	$ 35
Direct labor (40 hours @ $2.75 per hour)........................	110
Factory overhead (40 hours @ $1.75 per hour).....................	70
Total standard cost per batch of 100 units.....................	$215

Production for November amounted to 210 batches. Relevant statistics are:

Normal capacity per month.............................	24,000 units
Raw materials used......................................	14,500 lbs.
Cost of raw materials used.............................	$ 8,000
Direct labor cost (8,600 hrs.).........................	23,000
Actual factory overhead.................................	15,000
Fixed factory overhead at normal capacity..................	7,200

The management has noted that actual costs per batch deviate from standard costs per batch.

Required: A variance analysis for materials, labor, and factory overhead using the two- and three-variance methods for overhead.

(AICPA adapted)

19-6. Total, Labor, and Factory Overhead Spending Variance Analysis. The Groomer Company manufactures two products, Florimene and Glyoxide, that are used in the plastics industry. The company uses a standard cost system. Selected data follow:

	Florimene	*Glyoxide*
Data on standard costs:		
Raw materials per unit...	3 lbs. @ $1 per lb.	4 lbs. @ $1.10 per lb.
Direct labor per unit.....	5 hrs. @ $2 per hr.	6 hrs. @ $2.50 per hr.
Variable factory overhead per unit.............	$3.20 per direct labor hr.	$3.50 per direct labor hr.
Fixed factory overhead per month...........	$20,700	$26,520
Normal activity per month.	5,750 direct labor hrs.	7,800 direct labor hrs.
Units produced in September:	1,000 units	1,200 units
Costs incurred in September:		
Raw materials...........	3,100 lbs. @ $.90 per lb.	4,700 lbs. @ $1.15 per lb.
Direct labor..............	4,900 hrs. @ $1.95 per hr.	7,400 hrs. @ $2.55 per hr.
Variable factory overhead.	$16,170	$25,234
Fixed factory overhead...	$20,930	$26,400

Required: Select the correct answer for each of the following statements. Support each answer with computations that are clearly labeled.

(a) The total variances to be explained for both products in September are:
(1) Florimene, $255 (favorable); Glyoxide, $909 (unfavorable).
(2) Florimene, $7,050 (favorable); Glyoxide, $6,080 (favorable).
(3) Florimene, $4,605 (favorable); Glyoxide, $3,131 (favorable).
(4) Florimene, $2,445 (unfavorable); Glyoxide, $2,949 (unfavorable).
(5) none of the above.

(b) The labor efficiency variances for both products in September are:
(1) Florimene, $195 (favorable); Glyoxide, $510 (unfavorable).
(2) Florimene, $1,700 (favorable); Glyoxide, $1,000 (favorable).
(3) Florimene, $200 (favorable); Glyoxide, $500 (unfavorable).
(4) Florimene, $195 (favorable); Glyoxide, $510 (favorable).
(5) none of the above.

(c) The labor rate variances for both products in September are:
(1) Florimene, $245 (favorable); Glyoxide, $370 (unfavorable).
(2) Florimene, $200 (favorable); Glyoxide, $500 (unfavorable).
(3) Florimene, $1,945 (favorable); Glyoxide, $630 (favorable).
(4) Florimene, $245 (unfavorable); Glyoxide, $370 (favorable).
(5) none of the above.

(d) The spending variances for variable factory overhead for both products in September are:

(1) Florimene, $720 (unfavorable); Glyoxide, $786 (favorable).
(2) Florimene, $167 (unfavorable); Glyoxide, $35 (unfavorable).
(3) Florimene, $170 (unfavorable); Glyoxide, $34 (unfavorable).
(4) Florimene, $1,900 (favorable); Glyoxide, $1,960 (favorable).
(5) none of the above.

(AICPA adapted)

19-7. Variance Analyses; Unit Manufacturing Cost. Bronson Company manufactures a fuel additive with a stable selling price of $40 per drum. Since the company lost a government contract, it has been producing and selling 80,000 drums per month (50% of normal capacity). For the coming fiscal year, management expects to increase production to 140,000 drums per month.

The following facts about the company's operations are available:

(a) Standard costs per drum of product manufactured:

Materials:

8 gallons of Miracle Mix...............................	$16
1 empty drum..	1
	$17

Direct labor — 1 hour.................................	$5
Factory overhead.....................................	$6

(b) Costs and expenses during September, 19--:

Miracle Mix:

500,000 gallons purchased @ $950,000; 650,000 gallons used

Empty drums:

94,000 purchased @ $94,000; 80,000 used

Direct labor:

82,000 hours worked @ $414,100

Factory overhead:

Depreciation of building and machinery (fixed).........	$210,000
Supervision and indirect labor (semivariable)..........	460,000
Other factory overhead (variable)....................	98,000
Total factory overhead........................	$768,000

(c) Other factory overhead was the only actual factory overhead cost that varied from the overhead budget allowance for the September, 19--, level of actual production; other actual factory overhead was $98,000, and the budgeted amount was $90,000.

(d) At a normal capacity of 160,000 drums per month, supervision and indirect labor costs are expected to be $570,000. All cost functions are linear.

(e) None of the September, 19--, cost variances is expected to occur proportionally in future months. For the coming fiscal year, the Cost Standards Department expects the same standard usage of materials and direct labor hours. The average prices expected are: $2.10 per gallon of Miracle Mix, $1 per empty drum, and $5.70 per direct labor hour. The current flexible budget of factory overhead costs is considered applicable to future periods without revision.

(f) September, 19––, production was 80,000 drums.

Required: (1) Variance analyses for September, 19––: (a) materials purchase price variance, (b) materials quantity (or usage) variance, (c) labor rate variance, (d) labor efficiency (time or usage) variance, (e) controllable variance and volume variance for factory overhead.

(2) The actual manufacturing cost per drum of product expected at production of 140,000 drums per month, using these cost categories: materials, direct labor, fixed factory overhead, and variable factory overhead.

(AICPA adapted)

19-8. Reconstruction of Records; Variance Analysis; Standard Cost Sheet. The Sharpstown Company lost most of its factory cost records early in February, 19B, due to a fire.

The trial balance of the factory ledger at December 31, 19A follows:

		Debit	Credit
Inventories:	Raw Materials....................	$ 54,000	
	Finished Goods...................	65,900	
	Work in Process.................	—0—	
General Ledger...............................			$119,900
		$119,900	$119,900

All payments on behalf of the factory are made by the home office.

A copy of the January 19B standard cost variance report was found showing the following data:

		Unfavorable	Favorable
Raw materials	— price variance............		$2,000
	— quantity variance.........	$ 480	
Direct labor	— rate variance.............	3,000	
	— efficiency variance........		1,250
Factory overhead	— spending variance........		1,000
	— idle capacity variance.....	3,000	
	— efficiency variance........		1,000

The executive to whom the variance report had been sent noted beside the spending variance "Budget Allowance for January, $26,000" and wrote on the top of the report "January Production, 25,000 units."

The following additional facts are made available:

(a) Standard costs are revised annually at the beginning of each fiscal year. The figures in the trial balance reflect 19B standards.

(b) The actual direct labor costs for January 19B were $33,000 based on 12,000 actual hours worked. This information as well as the fact that actual hours or production represent 80% of normal hours or production was obtained from the Payroll Department of the home office.

(c) The supplier of the single raw material used mailed copies of the January invoices indicating that 25,000 units had been purchased at a cost of $38,000. One unit of production requires two units of raw materials.

(d) Raw materials are carried at standard cost. No change was made at January 1, 19B.

(e) Overhead is applied to production on the basis of standard direct labor hours.

(f) Sales in January 19B were 28,000 units.

(g) All production was completed in January 19B and forwarded to the finished goods warehouse.

Required: (1) A detailed variance analysis of the three cost elements.

(2) The budget allowance if the two-variance analysis method for factory overhead had been used.

(3) The 19B product standard cost sheet.

19-9. Standard Costs for Lots; Variance Analysis of Cost Elements. Vincenti Shirts, Inc. manufactures short- and long-sleeve men's shirts for large stores. Vincenti produces a single quality shirt in lots to each customer's order and attaches the store's label to each. The standard costs for a dozen long-sleeve shirts are:

Direct materials..........................	24 meters @ $ .55	$13.20
Direct labor.............................	3 hours @ $2.50	7.50
Factory overhead.........................	3 hours @ $2.25	6.75
Standard cost per dozen.................		$27.45

During October, 19—, Vincenti worked on three orders for long-sleeve shirts. Job cost records for the month disclose the following:

Lot	Units in Lot	Materials Used	Hours Worked
30	1,000 dozen	24,100 meters	3,000 hours
31	1,650 "	40,440 "	5,130 "
32	1,200 "	28,750 "	2,870 "

The following information is also available:

(a) Vincenti purchased 96,000 meters of materials during October at a cost of $53,200. The materials price variance is recorded when goods are purchased and all inventories are carried at standard cost.

(b) Direct labor incurred amounted to $28,600 during October. According to payroll records, production employees were paid $2.60 per hour.

(c) Overhead is applied on the basis of direct labor hours. Factory overhead totaling $25,500 was incurred during October.

(d) A total of $324,000 was budgeted for factory overhead for the year 19—, based on estimated production at the plant's normal capacity of 48,000 dozen shirts per year. Overhead is 40% fixed and 60% variable at this level of production.

(e) There was no work in process at October 1. During October Lots 30 and 31 were completed; all materials were issued for Lot 32, and it was 80% completed as to labor.

Required: (1) A schedule computing the standard cost for October, 19—, of Lots 30, 31, and 32.

(2) A schedule computing the materials price variance for October, 19—.

(3) For each lot produced during October, 19—, schedules computing the (a) materials quantity variance in meters; (b) labor efficiency variance in hours; and (c) labor rate variance in dollars.

(4) A schedule computing the total controllable and volume overhead variances for October, 19—.

(AICPA adapted)

19-10. Materials Price, Quantity, Mix, and Yield Variance Analysis. Sudsall Corporation manufactures a laundry detergent that requires three major components — A, B, and C.

A standard unit of input of 125 kilograms (kg.) consists of:

Material A............	50 kilograms	@	$ .80 per kg.	$ 40.00
Material B............	50	"	@	.70	"	35.00
Material C............	25	"	@	1.00	"	25.00
	125 kilograms					$100.00

A 20% shrinkage of the material put in process has been experienced. Shrinkage takes place in the early stages of the process, so that any work in process inventory will be considered completely shrunk.

The following data are available for the month of November:

Work in process inventory, November 1........................ 3,000 kg.

Input during the month:

Material A............	4,800 kilograms	@	$.84 actual cost
Material B............	5,400	"	@	.71	"
Material C............	2,500	"	@	.99	"

Output:

Finished product.. 9,900 kg.
Work in process inventory, November 30..................... 3,200 kg.

Required: All materials variances, including the total quantity variance analyzed as to mix and yield components, for November.

19-11. Price, Mix, and Yield Variances. Chocolate manufacturing operations require close control of the daily production and cost data. The computer printout for a batch of one ton of cocoa powder indicates the following materials standards:

Ingredients	Quantities (Pounds)	Unit Cost	Mix Cost
Cocoa beans........	800	$.45	$ 360
Milk..............	3,700	.50	1,850
Sugar.............	500	.25	125
Total batch........	5,000	$.467 (weighted average)	$2,335

On December 7, the company's Commodity Accounting and Analysis Section reported the following production and cost data for the December 6 operations.

Ingredients put in process:

Cocoa beans..........	225,000 lbs. @ $.425 per lb.	$ 95,625
Milk.................	1,400,000 lbs. @ .533 per lb.	746,200
Sugar...............	250,000 lbs. @ .240 per lb.	60,000
	1,875,000 lbs.	$901,825

Transferred to cocoa powder inventory: 387 tons
No work in process inventory

Required: Materials price, mix, and yield variances.

19-12. Materials, Mix and Yield, Labor, and Overhead Variances. The Brandon Cement Manufacturing Company uses a standard cost system for its production of cement. Cement is produced by mixing two major raw material components, A (lime) and B (clay), with water and by adding a third raw material component C, quantitatively insignificant.

Materials standards and cost for the production of 100 tons output are:

Components	Tons	Cost	Percent of Input Quantity	Amount
Material A	55	$43.00	50%	$2,365
Material B	44	35.00	40%	1,540
Material C	11	25.00	10%	275
Input	110		100%	$4,180 = $38.00 per ton
Output	100			4,180 = $41.80 per ton

The monthly factory overhead budget for a normal capacity level of 16,500 direct labor hours is as follows:

	Fixed Overhead	Variable Overhead
Plant manager....................	$ 2,000	
Supervisors.....................	1,800	
Indirect labor....................	2,220	$ 810
Indirect supplies.................	850	2,040
Power and light..................	300	2,200
Water..........................	480	2,000
Repairs and maintenance.........	500	1,200
Insurance......................	450	
Depreciation—production facilities.	3,775	
Total........................	$12,375	$8,250

To convert 110 tons of raw materials into 100 tons of finished cement requires 500 direct labor hours at $2.50 per direct labor hour or $12.50 per ton. Factory overhead is applied on a direct labor hour basis.

Actual data for the month of April:

Production of 3,234 tons of finished cement, with costs as follows:

Direct labor............................	15,800 hrs. @ $2.65 per hr.	
Fixed factory overhead....................	$11,075	
Variable factory overhead.................	$ 8,490	

	Materials Purchased		Materials Requisitioned
	Quantity	Price per Ton	Quantity
Material A...............	2,000 tons	$44	1,870 tons
Material B...............	1,200 tons	37	1,100 tons
Material C...............	500 tons	24	440 tons

No inventories of raw materials or work in process at the beginning of the month of April existed. The materials price variance is assumed to be realized at time of purchase.

Required: (1) Materials price, mix, and yield variances.
(2) Direct labor rate, efficiency, and yield variances.
(3) Factory overhead spending, idle capacity, efficiency, and yield variances.

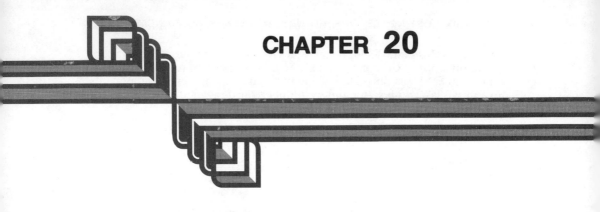

CHAPTER 20

STANDARD COSTING: ACCUMULATING, REPORTING, AND EVALUATING COSTS AND VARIANCES

Standard costs should be incorporated into the regular accounting system. The incorporation of standard costs into the records gives full recognition to the true meaning of standard cost accounting. It permits the most efficient use of a standard cost system and leads to a tie-in with the accounting system as a whole, thereby making for savings and increased accuracy in clerical work. Some companies prefer to keep standard costs for statistical purposes only. In either case, however, variances can be analyzed for cost control; and standard costs can be used in developing budgets, bidding on contracts, and setting prices.

STANDARD COSTING METHODS

Standard costs should be viewed as costs which pass through the data processing system into financial statements. Variations exist in the data accumulation methods adopted for standard costs. Some systems employ the partial plan, others the single plan. Both plans center around the entries to the work in process account and under both the work in process account can be broken down either by individual cost elements (materials, labor, and factory overhead) and/or by departments.

The Partial Plan. In the *partial plan* the work in process account is debited for the actual cost of materials, labor, and factory overhead and

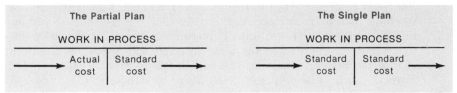

Standard Costing Methods

is credited at standard cost when goods are completed and transferred to finished goods inventory.

Any balance remaining in the work in process account consists of two elements: (1) the standard cost of work still in process and (2) the variances caused by differences between actual and standard costs. Additional analysis is needed to isolate variances.

The Single Plan. The *single plan* debits and credits the work in process account at standard costs only.

This plan (discussed in detail in the following pages) forms the basis for all standard cost exercises and problems found at the end of this chapter, unless a statement to the contrary is made.

The entries described in this chapter are periodic (often monthly) summaries of standard costs, actual costs, and resulting variances. Timely identification and reporting are major control features of standard cost accounting and may require prompt communication for very short time frames.

STANDARD COST ACCOUNTING PROCEDURES FOR MATERIALS

The recording of materials purchased can be handled by three different methods:

1. Record the price variance at the time materials are received and placed in stores. This means that the general ledger control account Materials is debited at standard cost and that the materials ledger cards are kept in quantities only. A standard price is noted on the card at the time the standards are set. As purchases are made, no prices are recorded on these cards. This procedure results in clerical savings and speedier postings.
2. Record the materials at actual cost when received, and determine the price variance at the time materials are requisitioned for production. This means that the general ledger control account Materials is debited at actual cost and that the materials ledger cards show quantities and dollar values as in a historical cost system. Certain advantages of a standard cost system are lost by this method. Furthermore, when materials are requisitioned for production, the problem of deciding which actual cost is applicable is again present.

3. Use a combination of the two methods in (1) and (2). Calculate variances when the materials are received, but defer charging variances to production until the materials are actually placed in process. At that time only the variance applicable to the quantity used will appear as a current charge, the balance remaining as a part of the materials inventory. This method results in two types of materials price variances: (1) a materials purchase price variance originating at the time materials purchases are first recorded and (2) a materials price usage variance arising at the time materials are used; the occurrence of the materials price usage variance is a reduction of the materials purchase price variance.

For control purposes the price variance should be determined at the time the materials are received. If it is not computed and reported until the materials are requisitioned for production, then remedial action is difficult because the time of computation is so far removed from the time of purchase.

Illustrations. These different methods for recording materials purchased are illustrated below. The data used for these methods are identical with that used in the previous chapter:

Standard unit price as per standard cost card........	$2.50
Purchased......................................	5,000 pieces @ $2.47
Requisitioned...................................	3,550 pieces
Standard quantity allowed for actual production......	3,500 pieces

Method 1. The journal entry at the time materials are received is:

Materials...	12,500	
Accounts Payable....................................		12,350
Materials Purchase Price Variance.....................		150

When materials are issued to the factory, the entry is:

Work in Process.....................................	8,750	
Materials Quantity Variance...........................	125	
Materials...		8,875

Method 2. At the time materials are received, the entry is:

Materials...	12,350	
Accounts Payable....................................		12,350

No variance is computed. However, when materials are issued, the journal entry is:

Work in Process.....................................	8,750.00	
Materials Quantity Variance...........................	125.00	
Materials...		8,768.50
Materials Price Usage Variance........................		106.50

Computations for this entry are:

	Pieces ×	Unit Cost	=	Amount	
Actual quantity used............	3,550	$2.47 actual		$8,768.50	
Actual quantity used............	3,550	2.50 standard		8,875.00	
Materials price usage variance.....	3,550	$(.03)		$ (106.50)	Credit or favorable

	Pieces ×	Unit Cost	=	Amount	
Actual quantity used...........	3,550	$2.50 standard		$8,875.00	
Standard quantity allowed.......	3,500	2.50 standard		8,750.00	
Materials quantity variance.......	50	$2.50 standard		$ 125.00	Debit or unfavorable

In this method the materials price usage variance account appears on the books *after* the materials are issued, and then only for the quantity issued — not for the entire purchase. For this computation, the actual cost used is $2.47 per piece. As no other cost is available and no other purchases were made, this cost is correct. In practice, the actual cost used would depend upon the type of inventory costing method employed, such as fifo, lifo, or average costing.

The price variance occurred because the materials were purchased at $.03 less than the standard price; the quantity variance because 50 pieces were used in excess of the standard quantity allowed.

Method 3. This entry, identical with the first entry in Method 1, would be made when the materials are received:

Materials..	12,500	
Accounts Payable.................................		12,350
Materials Purchase Price Variance....................		150

When the materials are issued, two entries are made:

Work in Process....................................	8,750	
Materials Quantity Variance.........................	125	
Materials......................................		8,875

This entry recognizes the 50 pieces used beyond the standard quantity.

Materials Purchase Price Variance......................	106.50	
Materials Price Usage Variance......................		106.50

This entry transfers $106.50 from the purchase price variance account to the materials price usage variance account. Any balance remaining in the materials purchase price variance account at the end of the accounting period is used to adjust the inventory valued at standard cost to actual cost. This balance takes on the aspect of a valuation account. The balance sheet would show:

Materials (at standard cost).....................................	$3,625.00
Less materials purchase price variance......................	43.50
Materials (adjusted to actual)................................	$3,581.50

STANDARD COST ACCOUNTING PROCEDURES FOR LABOR

As stated in the labor chapters, the payroll is computed on the basis of clock cards, job tickets, and other labor time information furnished to the payroll department. These basic records supply the data for the computation of the labor variances in connection with standard costs.

The necessary journal entries are illustrated with the data used in the previous chapter; i.e.:

Actual hours worked.................................	1,880 hours
Actual rate paid......................................	$6.50 per hour
Standard hours allowed for actual production........... .	1,590 hours
Standard rate..	$6 per hour

The following journal entry is made to set up the total actual direct labor payroll, assuming there were no payroll deductions:

Payroll..	12,220	
Accrued Payroll...................................		12,220

To distribute the payroll and to set up the variance accounts, the journal entry is:

Work in Process....................................	9,540	
Labor Rate Variance.................................	940	
Labor Efficiency Variance............................	1,740	
Payroll..		12,220

STANDARD COST ACCOUNTING PROCEDURES FOR FACTORY OVERHEAD

As explained in the previous chapter, factory overhead variances can be computed by employing the two-variance, three-variance, or four-variance methods.

Standard costs and budgetary control methods are closely related, a relationship that is particularly important for the analysis of factory overhead. Actual factory overhead is measured not only against the applied overhead cost, but also against a budget prepared at the beginning of the fiscal period and based on the capacity at which the company expects to operate during the period as well as against actual and standard activity allowed for actual production.

Again, the data in Chapter 19 are used to illustrate the journal entries:

	Direct Labor Hours	Total Overhead	Overhead Rate per Hour
Normal capacity............................	4,000	$8,000	$ 2.00
Consists of: Fixed overhead................		$3,200	$ .80
Variable overhead.............		4,800	1.20
Actual direct labor hours and actual overhead ..	3,475	$7,384	
Standard hours allowed for actual production..	3,400		

Two-Variance Method. The entries are :

1. For actual factory overhead:

Factory Overhead Control........................	7,384	
Various Credits.................................		7,384

2. When overhead is applied to work in process:

Work in Process..................................	6,800	
Factory Overhead Control.......................		6,800

(If the factory overhead applied account is used, it is subsequently transferred to the factory overhead control account.)

3. The factory overhead control account now has a debit balance of $584 which can be analyzed and closed out as follows:

Controllable Variance............................	104	
Volume Variance.................................	480	
Factory Overhead Control.......................		584

Three-Variance Method. The entries are:

1. For actual factory overhead:

Factory Overhead Control........................	7,384	
Various Credits.................................		7,384

2. When overhead is applied to work in process:

Work in Process..................................	6,800	
Efficiency Variance..............................	150	
Factory Overhead Control.......................		6,950

3. The factory overhead control account now has a debit balance of $434 which can be analyzed as spending and idle capacity variances and closed as follows:

Spending Variance................................	14	
Idle Capacity Variance...........................	420	
Factory Overhead Control.......................		434

As an alternative, Entry 2 may be recorded as a debit to Work in Process and as a credit to Factory Overhead Control for $6,800. The balance in Factory Overhead Control of $584 would then be closed as follows:

Spending Variance................................	14	
Efficiency Variance..............................	150	
Idle Capacity Variance...........................	420	
Factory Overhead Control.......................		584

Four-Variance Method. The entries are:

1. For actual factory overhead:

Factory Overhead Control........................	7,384	
Various Credits.................................		7,384

2. When overhead is applied to work in process:

Work in Process..	6,800	
Variable Efficiency Variance..........................	90	
Fixed Efficiency Variance.............................	60	
Factory Overhead Control..........................		6,950

3. The factory overhead control account now has a debit balance of $434, which can be analyzed as spending and idle capacity variances and closed as follows:

Spending Variance...................................	14	
Idle Capacity Variance..............................	420	
Factory Overhead Control........................		434

As an alternative, Entry 2 may be recorded as a debit to Work in Process and as a credit to Factory Overhead Control for $6,800. The balance in Factory Overhead Control of $584 would then be closed as follows:

Spending Variance...................................	14	
Variable Efficiency Variance..........................	90	
Fixed Efficiency Variance.............................	60	
Idle Capacity Variance..............................	420	
Factory Overhead Control........................		584

STANDARD COST ACCOUNTING PROCEDURES FOR COMPLETED PRODUCTS

Completion of production requires the transfer of costs from the work in process account to the work in process account of another department; or, in the case of the last department, to the finished goods account. Transfers are at standard costs.

The journal entry for the transfer of finished products is as follows:

Finished Goods (at standard cost).........................	xxxx	
Work in Process (at standard cost)......................		xxxx

The finished goods ledger card will show quantities only because the standard costs of the units remain the same during a period unless severe cost changes occur. When goods are shipped to customers, the entry is:

Cost of Goods Sold (at standard cost).....................	xxxx	
Finished Goods (at standard cost)......................		xxxx

JOURNAL ENTRIES FOR MIX AND YIELD VARIANCES

The journal entries for the mix and yield variances computed in the previous chapter are:

Entries for Direct Materials.

1. To record materials purchases:

Materials...	55,700	
Accounts Payable.................................		55,000
Materials Purchase Price Variance................		700

2. To charge materials into production:

Work in Process..................................	57,750	
Materials Mix Variance...........................	300	
Materials......................................		58,050

3. To transfer materials cost to finished goods:

Finished Goods...................................	60,000	
Materials Yield Variance.......................		2,250
Work in Process................................		57,750

Entries for Direct Labor Cost.

1. To set up payroll liability:

Payroll..	23,104	
Accrued Payroll................................		23,104

2. To transfer payroll to work in process and to isolate variances:

Work in Process..................................	23,100	
Labor Rate Variance.............................	304	
Labor Efficiency Variance.......................		300
Payroll..		23,104

3. To transfer labor cost to finished goods:

Finished Goods...................................	24,000	
Labor Yield Variance...........................		900
Work in Process................................		23,100

Entries for Factory Overhead (Two-Variance Method).

1. To record actual overhead:

Factory Overhead Control.........................	22,000	
Various Credits................................		22,000

2. To apply factory overhead to products:

Work in Process..................................	19,250	
Factory Overhead Control.......................		19,250

3. To set up controllable and volume variances:

Controllable Variance............................	2,300	
Overhead Volume Variance.......................	450	
Factory Overhead Control.......................		2,750

4. To transfer factory overhead to finished goods:

Finished Goods...................................	20,000	
Overhead Yield Variance.......................		750
Work in Process................................		19,250

It should be noted that Work in Process is debited for the standard production (yield) that should be attained from the input into the system and not for the standard for the amount of actual production (output).

The resulting difference is the yield variance for each cost element. When the transfer of the finished products to the warehouse or stockroom is reported to the cost department, one compound journal entry in place of the three individual entries for each element, as shown above, could be made:

Finished Goods (200,000 lbs. × $.52)...............	104,000	
Work in Process (192,500 lbs. expected yield × $.52)...		100,100
Yield Variance (7,500 lbs. gain × $.52).............		3,900

The $3,900 favorable yield variance is comprised of:

Materials yield variance...........................	$2,250	favorable
Labor yield variance..............................	900	"
Overhead yield variance...........................	750	"

Expressed as a percentage, the yield gain is 3.89 percent.

$$\frac{200,000 \text{ lbs.}}{192,500 \text{ lbs.}} = 103.89 \text{ or } \frac{7,500 \text{ lbs.}}{192,500 \text{ lbs.}} \times 100 = 3.89\%$$

VARIANCE CONTROL AND RESPONSIBILITY

Variances are not ends in themselves. Rather, management scrutinizes variances in an attempt to answer questions such as "Why did the variances occur?" And, if variances are unfavorable, "What corrective actions can be taken?" Questions such as these must be answered if management is to carry out an effective control process. The extent of variance investigation should be based on the estimated cost of making the investigation versus the value of the anticipated benefits. To be of greatest value, variances should be identified quickly and reported as frequently as possible (in some instances, daily), for the closer the reporting to the point of incurrence, the greater the chance for control and remedial action. Of course, there is no substitute for competent supervision, but variance reporting should be an aid to the supervisor in carrying out his control responsibilities.

Variances must be identified with the manager responsible for the costs incurred. Reasons for the variances should be ascertained and plans for necessary corrective action made either by discussing possible causes with the supervisor or by examining underlying data and records. Likewise, efficient and effective performance should be recognized and rewarded. One explanation of variances may be out-of-date physical and monetary standards, a possibility that should be considered here.

The purchasing department carries the primary responsibility for materials price variances, and control is obtained by getting several quotations, buying in economical lots, taking advantage of cash discounts, and selecting the most economical means of delivery. However, economic conditions and unexpected price changes by suppliers may be outside the limits of its control. Internal factors such as costly rush orders necessitated by sudden changes in production plans requiring materials at special prices would not be the fault of the purchasing department.

Materials quantity variances may result from many causes.   If the materials are of poor quality, the fault may be with the individual who prepared the purchase requisition which informed the purchasing department concerning the quality of materials to be purchased. If the purchasing department varied from the purchase requisition specifications, the fault may lie with that department.   Or perhaps the faulty materials resulted from a poor job of inspection when they were received.   Other causes include inexperienced or inefficient workers, faulty equipment, changes in production methods, or faulty blueprints. The reasons must be identified if the variances are to have meaning.

Labor rate variances tend to be fairly minor because labor rates are usually based on union agreements. Rate variances may occur, however, because of the use of a single average rate for a department, operation, or craft, while several different rates exist for the individual workers. Then, too, a worker may be assigned to a task that normally pays a different rate. In this case the responsibility might be found within the planning or scheduling of work assignments.

Labor efficiency variances may occur for a multitude of reasons: faulty materials, inexperienced workers, faulty or poor equipment, equipment breakdowns, changes in production methods, incorrect scheduling, lack of materials, faulty blueprints. These and many other reasons can be observed in factories.

Factory overhead variances are of two kinds: variable factory overhead and fixed factory overhead. The spending or controllable variance is basically the responsibility of the department head. Differences between actual cost and the allowed budget figure, in turn, may be caused by higher prices, different labor rates, etc.   The idle capacity or volume variance is generally ascribed to top management levels.   The decision with regard to the utilization of plant capacity and the setting of the predetermined overhead rate's volume base rests with the planning group. However, changes within the range of fixed costs occur due to changes in depreciation rates, increase in insurance premiums, increases in salaries of top-level managers, etc. The managerial significance and use of the spending and idle capacity variances are discussed in more detail in Chapter 9, pages 229–233. Responsibility for overhead efficiency variances (both the fixed and variable components) is generally attributed to the department manager.

No significant variance, whether favorable or unfavorable, should be without some kind of investigation and critical analysis.   An unusual favorable variance also signals the need for investigation. Perhaps standards are out-of-date or the favorable variance is more than offset by a related unfavorable variance (e.g., low cost materials of poor quality) or necessary activities such as maintenance of equipment are being neglected, causing lower expenditures and a favorable variance. Of course, management should use the occurrence of desirable favorable variances as an opportunity to recognize and reward efficient and effective performance of responsible managers and workers.

Analysis is necessary to highlight the significance of each variance in terms of explaining the origin, the responsibility, and the cause of the variance. Explanations of the reasons for the variances have limited usefulness in improving future control of costs because the explanations seldom suggest corrective action. Variance analysis is not complete until a decision is made as to necessary corrective action. The results of implemented corrective action must then be measured and reported.

TOLERANCE LIMITS FOR VARIANCE CONTROL

The control of standard cost variances and their incurrence is expected to be the responsibility of a designated manager. However, some variance in cost measurements can be expected, due to the factors employed in creating the basic physical and economic standard and the nature of the variance. With an expected variance in mind, the question must be asked, "How large a variance from standard should be tolerated before it is considered abnormal?" In other words, some tolerance limit or range should be established so that if the cost variance falls within this range, it can be considered acceptable; if the variance exceeds the range, an investigation should be made, provided the cost of conducting it is reasonable.

A decision to investigate is based on cost reports indicating incurred costs and deviations (variances) therefrom. The search for the reasons for the variance follows the pattern described above whereby a manager investigates the possible causes of the variance(s). This type of investigation concentrates on the control of processes and individual performances. What is needed now is the calculation of control limits for the variances from the standard. Past data on established operations, tempered by estimated changes in the future, usually furnish reliable bases for estimating expected costs and calculating control limits that serve to indicate good as well as poor periods of operation.

Illustration I. Assume that $10,000 is the value to appear in the factory overhead budget for maintenance expenses. A significant range should then be established, based on the assumption that actual maintenance costs will be larger or smaller than the budget figure. The question is "By how much?" Assume the answer, again based on past experience and future expectations, to be $\pm$ $2,000; i.e., the figure needed to judge the significance of the cost variance.

At the end of the month actual maintenance expenses are $14,000 indicating a variance of $4,000 ($14,000 − $10,000). Such an answer might call for further investigation into the causes of the variance. Suppose, however, actual expenses are only $10,900. Then the variance is $900. This is an acceptable deviation requiring no further investigation, at least at this time. Should the unfavorable variance persist in the next and other report periods, the causes, which in the cumulative may be judged significant, should be looked into.

The cost classification, maintenance expenses, is used in the above example as a fixed cost which assumes that no deviation from the basic amount is expected as a result of a change in the level of activity. However, this cost is generally classified as a semivariable expense; i.e., a fixed amount plus a variable rate which depends, in this case, on direct labor hours as the source of activity or volume. Then, a relationship between the variance and volume must be established.

Illustration II. Assume a tolerance limit of $3,000 when activity is 10,000 direct labor hours. When direct labor hours increase or decrease, the tolerance limit is $3,000 $\pm$ $.05 per hour for any difference in 10,000 direct labor hours and standard hours allowed for actual production. Assuming that $10,000 is the budget allowance for 12,700 direct labor hours and the actual cost of $14,000 was incurred when standard direct labor hours allowed were 12,700, the tolerance limit would be $3,000 + $.05(2,700) = $3,135. The $3,135 would be used to evaluate the $4,000 ($14,000 − $10,000) variance.

Control and investigation limits should be established in order to present cost and variance information so that each variance is highlighted in a manner indicating whether or not the variance is above the upper control limit, within the control limit, or below the lower control limit. Such information enables the responsible manager or supervisor to accept the deviations from the standard as a valuable tool for the control of costs in his department and lessens the dangers of their being more averse to risk than upper-level managers prefer. A manager, unduly concerned about the penalty for even small variances, may perform in a manner that hampers rather than enhances profitable operations.

DISPOSITION OF VARIANCES

Variances may be disposed of in either of the following ways: (1) they may be closed to Income Summary or (2) they may be treated as adjustments to Cost of Goods Sold and to inventories.

Decisions with respect to the most acceptable treatment of variances require considerations beyond the mere argument that only actual costs should be admitted to the financial statements. The determination of an actual cost is almost impossible. The use of a factory overhead rate as practiced in many companies indicates that management has accepted this procedure and finds it workable. To argue that charging off variances in the period in which they arise might distort the net income figure reveals a misunderstanding of standard costs. The treatment of variances depends upon: (1) type of variance — materials, labor, or factory overhead, (2) size of variance, (3) experience with standard costs, (4) cause of variance (e.g., incorrect standards), and (5) timing of the variance, (e.g., an unusual variance caused by seasonal fluctuations).

The disposition of variances can be summarized as follows:

1. Any variances which are caused by inactivity, waste, or extravagance should be written off as they represent losses. They should not be deferred by capitalizing them in the inventory accounts. This would include quantity variances on materials and labor as well as idle time (capacity) and efficiency variances on overhead.

2. An inventory reserve account should be established and charged with part of the price (spending and rate) variances to an extent which would bring the work in process and finished goods inventories up to, but not in excess of, current market values. The rest of the price (spending and rate) variance amounts should be written off, as they represent excess costs. In this way, the inventory accounts themselves will be valued at standard cost while the inventories on the balance sheet will, as a whole, be shown at reasonable values through the use of the inventory reserve account. In addition, losses caused by excessive costs and inefficiencies will be shown in the operating statement for the period in which they occur.[1]

First Method: Closed to Income Summary. Stating the work in process and finished goods inventories and the cost of goods sold at standard costs allows comparison of sales revenue and standard cost by product class. In these circumstances, the accepted procedure for handling cost variances at the end of the month or year is to consider them as profit or loss items. Unfavorable (or debit) manufacturing cost variances are deducted from the gross profit calculated at standard cost. Favorable (or credit) variances are added to the gross profit computed at standard cost. All variances shown on the income statement should be supported by a variance analysis report. Variances, in effect, represent differences between the actual and standard costs of operations for the month or year.

---

[1]W. Wesley Miller, "Standard Costs and Their Relation to Cost Control," *NA(C)A Bulletin*, Vol. XXVII, No. 15, p. 692.

INCOME STATEMENT
FOR YEAR ENDED DECEMBER 31, 19—

Sales...		$52,000
Cost of goods sold (at standard) — see Schedule 1...............		24,000
Gross profit (at standard).....................................		$28,000

Adjustments for standard cost variances:

	Debit Balances	
Materials purchase price variance.................	$ 1,200	
Labor efficiency variance.........................	600	
Controllable variance.............................	720	
Volume variance.................................	1,200	
	$ 3,720	
Total debit variances.............................		3,720
Gross profit (adjusted)...........................		$24,280
Less: Marketing expenses..........................	$12,000	
Administrative expenses........................	6,000	18,000
Net operating profit.............................		$ 6,280

Schedule 1
COST OF GOODS SOLD
FOR YEAR ENDED DECEMBER 31, 19—

Materials purchased................................	$20,000	
Less inventory (ending)............................	4,000	
Materials used....................................		$16,000
Direct labor......................................		10,000
Factory overhead..................................		20,000
		$46,000
Less work in process (ending)......................		16,000
Cost of goods manufactured.........................		$30,000
Less finished goods inventory (ending)...............		6,000
Cost of goods sold.................................		$24,000

The treatment of manufacturing cost variances using this method is depicted in the income statement illustrated above.

Variance accounts are closed at the end of the period to the income summary account by the following entry:

Income Summary.......................................	3,720	
Materials Purchase Price Variance......................		1,200
Labor Efficiency Variance.............................		600
Controllable Variance.................................		720
Volume Variance......................................		1,200

As an alternative, all variances may be closed to the cost of goods sold account rather than directly to the income summary account. The *total* amount in Cost of Goods Sold (units sold at standard costs plus the variances) would then be closed to Income Summary.

Accountants who use the above procedures believe that only standard costs should be considered true costs. No variance is treated as an increase or decrease in manufacturing costs but as a deviation from contemplated costs due to abnormal inactivity, extravagance, inefficiencies or efficiencies, or other changes of business conditions. This viewpoint leads to debiting or crediting all variances to the income summary account at the end of the month or at the end of the fiscal period. However, some proponents of the above procedure suggest that the unused portion of the materials purchase price variance should be linked with materials still on hand and shown on the balance sheet as part of the cost of the ending materials inventory.

If an adjustment is made for the materials purchase price variance whereby a part of the variance is attached to the materials inventory to place it on an actual cost basis, the following computation would be made:

Balance in materials inventory = $4,000 or 20% of purchases made
Materials purchase price variance = $1,200

20% of $1,200 or $240 of the variance would be transferred to the materials account.

This method would increase the materials account and lower the cost of goods sold, increasing the net operating profit from $6,280 to $6,520. The journal entry would be:

Income Summary..	3,480	
Materials..	240	
Materials Purchase Price Variance.........................		1,200
Labor Efficiency Variance.................................		600
Controllable Variance.....................................		720
Volume Variance..		1,200

The treatment of variances illustrated in this section is considered acceptable by independent auditors as long as standards are reasonably representative of what costs ought to be.

Second Method: Adjustments to Cost of Goods Sold and Inventories. A second method used for the distribution of variances distributes them to inventories and Cost of Goods Sold. *Accounting Research Bulletin No. 43* states with respect to the costing of inventories that:

> Standard costs are acceptable if adjusted at reasonable intervals to reflect current conditions so that at the balance sheet date standard costs reasonably approximate costs computed under one of the recognized bases. In such cases descriptive language should be used which will express this relationship, as, for instance, "approximate costs determined on the first-in, first-out basis," or, if it is desired to mention standard costs, "standard costs, approximating average costs."[2]

---

[2]AICPA Committee on Accounting Procedures, "Inventory Pricing," *Accounting Research Bulletin No. 43*, p. 30.

Current Internal Revenue Service regulations require inclusion in inventories of an allocated portion of significant annual standard cost variances. Where the amount involved is not significant in relation to total actual factory overhead for the year, an allocation is not required unless such allocation is made for financial reporting purposes. Also, the taxpayer must treat both favorable and unfavorable variances consistently. Regulations, however, do permit expensing of the idle capacity variance. Cost Accounting Standards Board regulations also require inclusion of significant standard cost variances in inventories.

Using the previous figures and other data, the following computations and prorations would be made when variances are distributed to inventories and Cost of Goods Sold:

1

PERCENTAGE OF COST ELEMENTS IN INVENTORIES AND COST OF GOODS SOLD

Account	Materials		Labor		Factory Overhead	
	Amount	%	Amount	%	Amount	%
Work in Process..............	$ 6,000	37.5	$ 2,000	20	$ 8,000	40
Finished Goods..............	2,000	12.5	2,000	20	2,000	10
Cost of Goods Sold.........	8,000	50.0	6,000	60	10,000	50
Total.......................	$16,000	100.0	$10,000	100	$20,000	100

2

ALLOCATION OF VARIANCES

Account	Total Amount	Work in Process	Finished Goods	Cost of Goods Sold
Materials Purchase Price Variance*.........	$ 960	$ 360	$120	$ 480
Labor Efficiency Variance...................	600	120	120	360
Controllable Variance......................	720	288	72	360
Volume Variance..........................	1,200	480	120	600
Total.......................................	$3,480	$1,248	$432	$1,800

*Original variance of $1,200 − $240 allocated to Materials = $960.

Proration of these variances to Work in Process, Finished Goods, and Cost of Goods Sold results in the income statement illustrated on the next page. The adjusted net operating profit is $8,200 compared to the net operating profit of $6,280 shown in the previous income statement (page 633). The difference of $1,920 is summarized as follows:

Cost added to: Materials......................................		$ 240
Work in Process....................................		1,248
Finished Goods.....................................		432
Difference......................................		$1,920

INCOME STATEMENT

FOR YEAR ENDED DECEMBER 31, 19—

Sales...		$52,000
Cost of goods sold (standard adjusted to actual) — see Schedule 1.........		25,800
Gross profit (actual)...		$26,200
Less: Marketing expenses..................................	$12,000	
Administrative expenses	6,000	18,000
Net operating profit..		$ 8,200

Schedule 1

COST OF GOODS SOLD

FOR YEAR ENDED DECEMBER 31, 19—

	Standard	Variance	Actual
Materials available	$20,000		$21,200
Materials purchase price variance.............		$1,200	
Less materials inventory (ending)...............	4,000		4,240
Materials purchase price variance.............		240	
Materials used..............................	$16,000		$16,960
Materials purchase price variance.............		$ 960	
Direct labor	10,000		10,600
Efficiency variance..........................		600	
Factory overhead............................	20,000		21,920
Controllable variance.......................		720	
Volume variance............................		1,200	
Total manufacturing cost.....................	$46,000	$3,480	$49,480
Less work in process (ending).................	16,000	1,248	17,248
Cost of goods manufactured...................	$30,000	$2,232	$32,232
Less finished goods inventory (ending)...........	6,000	432	6,432
Cost of goods sold...........................	$24,000	$1,800	$25,800

Entries transfer the prorated amounts to the respective accounts in the general ledger only. Subsidiary inventory accounts and records are not adjusted. The various adjustment accounts could be shown on the balance sheet as valuation or contra accounts against standard inventory values or combined with them to form one amount. At the beginning of the next period, the portion of these proration entries that affects inventory accounts is reversed in order to return opening inventories to standard costs.

In connection with closing variances, a problem arises with respect to the allocation of variances to product or commodity groups. Usually, standard cost variances are shown as deductions in total and not allocated to major commodity groups to determine the profit and loss per commodity. Experience has shown that it is almost impossible to do otherwise. The basic idea of variance analysis is misconstrued when such prorations are attempted. The isolation of variances is for the purpose of controlling costs and determining what the variances are, where they occurred, and what caused them.

REVISION OF STANDARD COSTS

Standards should be changed only when underlying conditions change or when they no longer reflect the original concept. In fact, the idea that standards should be changed more than once a year can only weaken their effectiveness and increase operational details. However, standard costs require continuous review and, at times, frequent change. Events, rather than time, determine whether standard costs should be revised. Conditions necessitating revision may be classified as internal or external. Technological advances, design revisions, method changes, labor rate adjustments, and changes in physical facilities are among the internal conditions. External conditions include materials price changes, market trends, customer special requirements, and changes in the competitive situation. Sometimes changes have already been incorporated in the standard costs being used in order to reflect the new conditions. New materials prices and new labor rates also affect indirect materials prices and indirect labor rates which, in turn, influence the standard overhead rate. Other overhead costs, too, may change.

If standard costs are changed at the end of the fiscal period, the change-over is comparatively easy. When such changes are made, any adjustment to the next period's beginning inventory should be made with care so that inventories are not "written up or down" arbitrarily. The National Association of Accountants offers the following answers to the question as to whether or not the ending inventory should be adjusted for such changes:

1. If the new standard costs reflect conditions which affected the actual cost of the goods in the ending inventory, most firms adjust inventory to the new standard cost and carry the contra side of the adjusting entry to cost of sales by way of the variance accounts. In effect, this procedure assumes that the standard costs used to cost goods in the inventory have been incorrect and that restatement of inventory cost is needed to bring inventories to a correct figure on the books. Since the use of incorrect standards has affected the variance accounts as well as the inventory, the adjustment is carried to the variance accounts.

2. If the standard costs represent conditions which are expected to prevail in the coming period but which have not affected costs in the past period, ending inventories are costed at the old standards. It appears to be common practice to adjust the detailed inventory records to new standard costs.
   In order to maintain the control relationship which the inventory accounts have over subsidiary records, the same adjustment is entered in the inventory control accounts; and the contra entry is carried to an inventory valuation account. Thus, the net effect is to state the inventory in the closing balance sheet at old standard costs. In the

next period the inventory valuation account is closed to cost of sales when the goods to which the reserve relates move out of inventories. By use of this technique, the detailed records can be adjusted to new standards before the beginning of the year while at the same time the net charge to cost of sales in the new period is for old standard cost since the latter cost was correct at the time the goods were acquired.[3]

BROAD APPLICABILITY OF STANDARD COSTING

The use of standard costing is not limited to manufacturing situations. This powerful working tool for planning and control can be used in other aspects of business organizations (as discussed in Chapter 23, "Marketing Cost and Profitability Analysis").

The nonprofit organization sector also affords many opportunities to utilize standard costing concepts and techniques in hospitals, governmental agencies, etc., in harmony with the Chapter 17 discussion of budgets for nonprofit organizations.

Though standard costs may not be formally recorded in the accounts, many relatively small organizations such as automotive repair shops and construction contractors can utilize the comparison of actual to standard quantities, times, and costs for bidding, pricing of jobs or projects, planning of work, including staffing needs, and the planning and control of routine operating activities.

DISCUSSION QUESTIONS

1. Some firms incorporate standard costs into their accounts; others maintain them only for statistical comparisons without incorporation into the double-entry system of cost records. Discuss.

2. The use of standard costs for costing finished goods and sales is considered to have several advantages. What are these advantages?

3. The charging of overhead into work in process may be applied on the basis of standard hours or standard labor dollars allowed for actual production. At times a company might apply overhead on the basis of actual hours or actual labor dollars. Discuss.

4. Differences between actual costs and standard costs are found in the variance accounts of which a great number are discussed in the chapter. What considerations might determine the number of variance accounts?

5. Discuss the meaning of variance control and responsibility by various levels of management.

---

[3]"How Standard Costs Are Being Used Currently," *NA(C)A Standard Cost Research Series*, p. 64.

6. The determination of periodic net income depends greatly upon the cost assigned to raw materials, work in process, and finished goods inventories. What considerations determine the costing of inventories at standard or at approximately actual cost by companies using standard costs?

7. According to field studies, overhead variances are generally treated as period costs. Why would this procedure exist?

8. The use of standard costs in pricing and budgeting is quite valuable since decisions in the fields of pricing and budgetary planning are made before the costs under consideration are incurred. Discuss.

9. Standard costing procedures are widely used in manufacturing operations and, more recently, have become common in many nonmanufacturing operations.

   (a) Define standard costs.

   (b) What are the advantages of a standard cost system?

   (c) Present arguments in support of each of the following three methods of treating standard cost variances for purposes of financial reporting:

      (1) They may be carried as deferred charges or credits on the balance sheet.

      (2) They may appear as charges or credits on the income statement.

      (3) They may be allocated between inventories and cost of goods sold.

                                              (AICPA adapted)

10. Select the correct answer for each of the following statements.

   (a) Which of these variances is least significant for cost control? (1) labor rate variance; (2) materials quantity variance; (3) factory overhead spending variance; (4) factory overhead volume variance; (5) labor efficiency variance.

   (b) At the end of the fiscal year, the Graham Company had several substantial variances from standard variable manufacturing costs. The one for which there is the strongest justification for allocation between inventories and cost of goods sold is the one attributable to (1) additional costs of raw material acquired under a speculative purchase contract; (2) a breakdown of equipment; (3) overestimates of production activity for the period, resulting from failure to predict an unusual decline in the market for the company's product; (4) increased labor rates won by the union as a result of a strike during the year.

   (c) Standard costing will produce the same financial statement results as actual or conventional costing when standard cost variances are distributed to (1) cost of goods sold; (2) an income or expense account; (3) cost of goods sold and inventory; (4) a balance sheet account.

                                        (AICPA and NAA adapted)

EXERCISES

Wherever variances are required in the following exercises, indicate whether they are favorable or unfavorable.

1. Factory Overhead Analysis. The management of a company learned of the possibility of computing overhead variances by isolating two or three variances.

The following data are provided:

Flexible Budget:	100%	90%	Actual Costs
Fixed costs.........................	$1,160	$1,160	$1,160.00
Power..............................	740	666	710.00
Maintenance and repairs.............	50	45	48.00
Indirect labor......................	400	360	393.90
Supplies...........................	150	135	144.00
Total...........................	$2,500	$2,366	$2,455.90
Standard hours.....................	2,000 (100%)		
Actual hours.......................	1,950		
Allowed hours......................	1,900		

Required: (1) The variances resulting when the two- or the three-variance procedure is used.

(2) An additional analysis of the controllable and volume variances in order to convince the management of the value of a standard cost system. Explain the meaning of these variances.

2. Journalizing Standard Cost Transactions. The Alexander Products Co. uses a standard cost system and a flexible budget. Normal capacity for the month of September was 2,400 direct labor hours. Based on 2,400 hours, factory overhead was estimated to be $1.80 per direct labor hour. Based on 2,200 direct labor hours, factory overhead was estimated to be $4,160. The standard labor cost was $3.20 per direct labor hour; each direct worker was scheduled to complete 5 units per hour. The standard materials cost was $1.50 per kilogram; each unit requires 2 kilograms of materials.

During September, 11,500 units were manufactured. On September 1, 25,000 kilograms of materials were purchased for $1.52 per kilogram; subsequently, 1,000 kilograms were returned to the supplier. Payroll records for September showed wages paid for 2,320 direct labor hours at an average rate of $3.25 per hour. Materials requisitions showed that 23,400 kilograms of materials had been consumed during September. Actual factory overhead for September totaled $4,160. During September, 10,000 units were sold on open account for $6 per unit.

There was no inventory of work in process at the beginning or at the end of September. All units sold were taken from current production. Alexander Products records only quantities on the materials ledger cards. Seven variance accounts are in the chart of accounts: two for materials, two for labor, and three for factory overhead.

Required: General journal entries to record the above transactions.

3. Journal Entries; Variance Analysis. Students Manufacturing, Inc. produces custom-made tie-dyed sweatshirts for distribution on college campuses. The following standards have been established:

Materials: Cotton cloth (2 yds. @ $1 per yd.)......................	$2.00
Dyes (1 pint @ $.50).................................	.50
Labor (½ hour @ $2 per hour)...........................	1.00
Factory overhead (½ hour @ $1 per hour).......................	.50
	$4.00

Yearly production budget is based upon normal plant operations of 20,000 hours with fixed factory overhead of $8,000. Inventories at January 1, 19—, were:

Cotton cloth (2,000 yds. @ $1 per yd.).......................... $2,000
Dye (1,000 pints @ $.50).......................................   500
Work in process (1,000 units; ¼th finished as to conversion; all materials issued)..   2,875
Finished goods (500 @ $4 each)................................   2,000

Production for January:

3,000 units completed
   750 units ⅓d converted, all materials added

Transactions for January:

Cotton cloth purchased................   5,000 yds. @ $1.10 per yd.
Dyes purchased.......................   2,500 pints @ $.49
Cotton cloth to factory...............   5,600 yards
Dyes issued to factory................   2,700 pints
Direct labor payroll..................   1,550 hours @ $1.90 per hour
Actual factory overhead............... $1,700
Sales................................   3,100 sweatshirts @ $8 on account

Transferred completed Work in Process to Finished Goods.

Required: General journal entries to record the January transactions, accounting for work in process at standard cost and recognizing variances in the proper accounts. Use the two-variance method in computing materials, labor, and factory overhead variances; recognize the materials price variance at the time of purchase. Use separate inventory and variance accounts for each raw material. Close all variances into Cost of Goods Sold.

4. Materials Variance Analysis and Journal Entries. Toronto Plastics Corporation produces kitchen utensils. The company uses a standard cost system for controlling manufacturing costs. One of its finished products is a small salad bowl. This product is manufactured from three distinct raw plastics — Rexo, Zyco, and Durel. The Raw Materials section of the standard cost card for this product, for use during this cost period, indicated the following standards for the raw materials necessary to manufacture each job of 1,000 salad bowls.

Material	Standard Quantity and Price	Total
Rexo...............	150 lbs. @ $1	$150
Zyco...............	250 lbs. @ $2	500
Durel..............	100 lbs. @ $3	300
Total standard materials cost per job.........................		$950

During the current cost period, the completed job orders included ten jobs of 1,000 salad bowls each.
Cost data relative to materials for these ten jobs were:

Material	Purchased	Consumed
Rexo.............	1,800 lbs. @ $1.10	1,400 lbs. @ $1.10
Zyco.............	1,000 lbs. @ $1.80	1,000 lbs. @ $1.80
"	2,000 lbs. @ $2.00	1,600 lbs. @ $2.00
Durel.............	1,200 lbs. @ $3.20	850 lbs. @ $3.20

Required: (1) The amount of variations from standard, both price and quantity, for each item of raw material under each of the following assumptions: (a) price variations are computed on materials purchased and (b) price variations are computed on materials issued to production, using the fifo costing method.

(2) General journal entries for the purchase and issue of materials under the various assumptions given in (1).

5. Factory Overhead Variance Analysis; Journal Entries. The following overhead data of the Ponca Company are presented for analysis of the variances from standard:

Budget Data: (normal capacity)
Direct labor hours............................... 20,000
Estimated overhead:
　Fixed... $ 8,000
　Variable...................................... 15,000

Actual Results:
Direct labor hours............................... 18,700
Overhead:
　Fixed... $ 8,060
　Variable...................................... 14,100
Standard hours allowed for actual production: 18,500

Required: (1) Overhead variances using the three-variance method.
(2) Overhead variances using the two-variance method.
(3) All journal entries based on the two-variance method.

6. Standard Cost Cycle with Entries. Pemberton Manufacturing Company operates a cost accounting system based on standard costs which are incorporated in the manufacturing cost accounts. The differences between standard costs and actual costs are reflected in appropriate variance accounts; namely, Materials Purchase Price Variance, Materials Quantity Variance, Labor Rate Variance, Labor Efficiency Variance, and three variances for factory overhead. The company follows the plan of realizing the materials price variance at the time of purchase, regardless of the time of usage. All variances are closed to the cost of goods sold account.

Budgets are prepared to furnish production managers information as to expected capacity. Normal capacity for a month is 60 job lots consisting of 100 widgets per lot.

Pemberton Manufacturing Company, using engineering standards, determined the following standard costs for the production of each lot (100 widgets):

Materials (300 lbs. of materials @ $3) .... $ 900
Labor (75 hours of direct labor @ $2.20)....................... 165
Overhead (75 hours of factory overhead @ $2) 150

Total standard cost per 100 widgets......................... $1,215

(Budgeted fixed overhead, $4,500)

During the period direct materials were purchased in the following quantities, at the prevailing market prices, in economical lot sizes:

7,300 lbs. @ $2.90
7,000 lbs. @ $3.10
8,000 lbs. @ $3.00

At the completion of the period the production and cost records showed the following results:

(a) Direct labor payroll costs were:

$$
\begin{aligned}
2{,}000 \text{ hours } @ \, \$2.20 \\
1{,}200 \text{ hours } @ \, \$2.15 \\
850 \text{ hours } @ \, \$2.40 \\
700 \text{ hours } @ \, \$1.90
\end{aligned}
$$

(b) Actual factory overhead costs incurred were $10,440.

(c) Materials requisitioned and used in the production process were tallied and found to represent 17,870 lbs.

(d) There was no work in process inventory at the beginning or end of the accounting period.

(e) 58 lots were completed during the period.

(f) The sales manager stated that 5,700 widgets had been sold during the period at a unit price of $21.

(g) Marketing expenses were $15,700.

(h) General and administrative expenses were $11,700.

Required: All entries associated with the information given.

7. Price, Mix, and Yield Variances; Journal Entries. Medicus, Inc. produces an antiseptic powder which is sold in bulk to institutions such as schools, hospitals, etc. The product's mixture is tested at intervals during the production process. Materials are added as needed to give the mixture the desired drying and medicating properties.   The standard mixture with standard prices for a 100-lb. batch is as follows:

10 lbs. of hexachlorophene @ $.45 per lb.
10 lbs. of para-chlor-meta-xylenol @ $.30 per lb.
30 lbs. of bentonite @ $.08 per lb.
20 lbs. of kaolin @ $.10 per lb.
50 lbs. of talc @ $.05 per lb.

During the month of January the following materials were purchased:

1,500 lbs. of hexachlorophene @ $.47 per lb.
1,100 lbs. of para-chlor-meta-xylenol @ $.33 per lb.
4,000 lbs. of bentonite @ $.07 per lb.
2,500 lbs. of kaolin @ $.11 per lb.
6,000 lbs. of talc @ $.04 per lb.

The materials price variance is recorded when materials are purchased.

Production for the month consisted of 10,700 lbs. of finished product. There were no beginning or ending inventories of work in process.
The following actual materials quantities were put into production:

1,050 lbs. of hexachlorophene
1,125 lbs. of para-chlor-meta-xylenol
3,080 lbs. of bentonite
2,200 lbs. of kaolin
5,300 lbs. of talc

Required: (1) Calculation of all materials variances (price, mix, and yield).
(2) Journal entries for (a) purchase, (b) usage, (c) completion of materials, and (d) disposition of variances, assuming all completed units were sold.

8. Disposition of Variances by Adjustments to Cost of Goods Sold and Inventories.
Dona Manufacturing Corporation uses a standard cost system which records
raw materials at actual cost, records the materials price variance at the time
that raw materials are issued to work in process, and prorates all variances at
the end of the year. Variances associated with direct materials are prorated,
based on the direct materials balances in the appropriate accounts; and variances associated with direct labor and factory overhead are prorated, based on
the direct labor balances in the appropriate accounts.

The following information is available for the year ended December 31,
19—:

Raw materials inventory at December 31, 19—.................	$ 65,000
Finished goods inventory at December 31, 19—:	
Direct materials...	87,000
Direct labor...	130,500
Applied factory overhead..................................	104,400
Cost of goods sold for year ended December 31, 19—:	
Direct materials...	348,000
Direct labor...	739,500
Applied factory overhead..................................	591,600
Direct materials price variance (unfavorable)...................	10,000
Direct materials quantity variance (favorable)..................	15,000
Direct labor rate variance (unfavorable)......................	20,000
Direct labor efficiency variance (favorable)....................	5,000
Factory overhead incurred.................................	690,000

There were no beginning inventories and no ending work in process inventory. Factory overhead is applied at 80% of standard direct labor.

Required: (1) The amount of direct materials price variance to be prorated
to finished goods inventory at December 31, 19—.

(2) The total amount of direct materials in the finished goods inventory at
December 31, 19—, after all variances have been prorated.

(3) The total amount of direct labor in the finished goods inventory at
December 31, 19—, after all variances have been prorated.

(4) The total cost of goods sold for the year ended December 31, 19—,
after all variances have been prorated.

(AICPA adapted)

9. Standard Cost Card; Income Statement. The Duncan-Geiler Company manufactures a product based on standard specifications and costs. At the end of the
month the following information is available:

Inventories, April 1, 19—:	*Quantity*	*Standard Cost*
Materials.....................................	6,000 units	$12,000
Finished goods...............................	4,000 units	84,000

Actual and standard quantities and costs for the month are summarized
as follows:

	Quantities		*Costs*	
	Actual	*Standard*	*Actual*	*Standard*
Materials purchases (units)...........	100,000		$193,500	$200,000
Materials requisitions (units).........	95,000	94,000		
Direct labor (hours)................	46,800	47,000	164,970	164,500
Factory overhead — actual...........			143,800	

The company's standard factory overhead rate is based on:

Variable factory overhead: $2 per direct labor hour

Fixed factory overhead: $50,000 for 50,000 direct labor hours, considered normal capacity

During the month the company planned 24,000 units, yet only 23,500 units were produced and placed into finished goods inventory. There was no work in process at the beginning or the end of the period. 21,000 units were sold for $35 per unit. Marketing and administrative expenses amounted to $185,000.

Required: (1) The standard manufacturing cost card for the product.
(2) An income statement for the month. Variances for materials, labor, and factory overhead are closed out into Cost of Goods Sold. Use the two-variance method for factory overhead.

10. Comparative Income Statement. The Budget Department of the Cardinal Products Company prepares a forecast income statement for each month's operations. At the end of the month a comparative income statement is sent to management. For November, the following comparison was received:

COMPARATIVE INCOME STATEMENT

MONTH OF NOVEMBER

	Budget	Actual
Sales (10,000 units)	$120,000	$120,000
Cost of goods sold	80,000	88,388
Gross profit	$ 40,000	$ 31,612
Marketing and administrative expenses	25,000	28,000
Net operating profit	$ 15,000	$ 3,612

The standard cost of a unit of product is as follows:

Direct materials (8 items @ $.55 per item)	$4.40
Direct labor (¾ hour @ $2.80 per hour)	2.10
Factory overhead (¾ hour @ $2 per hour)	1.50
Total standard product cost per unit	$8.00

The factory overhead rate, for a total of 10,000 units of normal production, was based on:

Variable expenses	$ 6,000
Fixed expenses	9,000
	$15,000

Actual results for the month show:

Materials used: 2% above standard requirements; average cost $.58 per item.
Payroll: $24,960 for 7,800 hours worked.
Factory overhead: $16,100.
Assume all marketing and administrative expenses are variable.
Assume 10,000 units were produced and sold.

Required: A comparative income statement for November, accounting for the difference between the budgeted and the actual net operating profit.

11. Overhead Variance Analysis; Budget Report. The Cost Department of Sumner Products, Inc. prepared the following flexible budget for November:

Production based on standard....................	9,938	11,180	12,422	13,664
Labor hours......................................	4,000	4,500	5,000	5,500
Capacity percentage..............................	80%	90%	100%	110%

Factory overhead:

Fixed:

Superintendence...............................	$ 6,510	$ 6,510	$ 6,510	$ 7,100
Indirect labor....................................	5,750	5,750	5,750	5,750
Manufacturing supplies.........................	3,490	3,490	3,490	3,510
Maintenance.....................................	1,680	1,680	1,680	1,680
Heat, power, and light..........................	110	110	110	110
Depreciation....................................	675	675	675	675
Insurance.......................................	352	352	352	352
Total fixed overhead.........................	$18,567	$18,567	$18,567	$19,177

Variable:

Indirect labor....................................	$ 1,928	$ 2,169	$ 2,410	$ 2,651
Manufacturing supplies.........................	1,720	1,935	2,150	2,365
Maintenance.....................................	628	707	785	864
Heat, power, and light..........................	61	68	76	84
Total variable overhead......................	$ 4,337	$ 4,879	$ 5,421	$ 5,964
Total factory overhead.......................	$22,904	$23,446	$23,988	$25,141

At the end of the month of November, cost accounting tabulation showed 9,689 items manufactured, 4,150 labor hours worked, and actual factory overhead as follows:

Superintendence............................	$ 6,605
Indirect labor...............................	7,512
Manufacturing supplies......................	5,450
Maintenance.................................	2,317
Heat, power, and light.......................	195
Depreciation................................	675
Insurance...................................	352
Total factory overhead....................	$23,106

Required: (1) Overhead variances using (a) the three-variance and (b) the two-variance methods.

(2) An itemized budget report for the spending variance, including actual factory overhead, budgeted factory overhead, and variances.

12. Monthly Income Statement; Variance Analysis. The Princeton King Pin Company buys boards, one inch thick, of seasoned maple to manufacture wooden pins that are sold in sets of 10 pins each at $45 per set. The maple board is glued together under pressure and heat, then cut to appropriate size for turning on a lathe. After turning, the pin is dipped into white lacquer, hung up to dry, and finally painted with two red stripes around the neck of the pin. The business is small and rather seasonal. For the month of August, in preparation for the fall orders, the owner estimates costs and sales of 800 sets as follows:

Sales (800 sets @ $45).............................		$36,000
Cost of goods sold:		
Materials (maple and others): $5 per set..............	$ 4,000	
Labor: 8 hours × $3 per hour × 22 days × 20 workers..	10,560	
Overhead: Fixed......................................	8,800	
Variable: $6 per set.....................	4,800	
Total cost of goods sold.............................		28,160
Gross profit for August.........................		$ 7,840

Cost per set: $28,160 ÷ 800 sets = $35.20 per set

At the end of August, these costs and other information are available:

Actual production.............................	760 sets (no inventory)
Actual sales..................................	720 sets @ $45
" "	40 sets @ $43
Actual labor hours............................	3,360 hours
Average rate per hour.........................	$ 3.05
Overhead, fixed...............................	$8,800
Overhead, variable............................	$4,680

Price of maple wood increased $.40 per set. Overhead is applied on the unit of production basis.

Required: A statement of gross profit for August, including significant variances from predetermined production and sales.

PROBLEMS

Wherever variances are required in the following problems, indicate whether they are favorable or unfavorable.

20-1. Conversion to Standard Cost; Entries; Variance Analysis. On May 1, 19—, the trial balance of the factory ledger accounts of the Albany Company appeared as follows:

Raw Materials (1,000 kilograms)...................	$ 620.00	
Finished Goods (100 units).......................	3,100.00	
General Ledger Control...........................		$3,720.00
	$3,720.00	$3,720.00

The company desires to install and maintain a system of standard costs in which all inventories will be carried at standard cost. It has made the necessary materials and labor studies which reveal for its only product:

Direct Materials: One raw material is used in the manufacturing process; 20 kg. should be used for each unit of finished product and should cost $.60 per kg.

Direct Labor: Time studies indicate an allowance of 5 hours of direct labor at an hourly rate of $2.50 for each unit of finished product.

The only data possessed by the company concerning factory overhead is the following data for the first four months of 19—:

	Direct Labor Hours	Total Factory Overhead
January	5,000	$ 8,100
February	9,500	9,990
March	13,000	11,460
April	8,000	9,360

The plant had been constructed to provide a normal productive capacity for 2,500 units of finished product per month.

The controller suggested that a standard overhead rate be calculated at normal capacity, using a flexible budget based on the data for the first four months of 19—, as determined by the high and low points method.

Operating data for May:

Raw materials purchases: 60,000 kg. at a unit cost of $.58
Raw materials used: 48,000 kg.

Payroll:

Direct labor: 12,000 hours at $2.40
Indirect labor: 2,000 hours at $2

Factory overhead charges transferred from the home office: $7,000
Units produced: 2,300
Units sold: 2,200
No work in process inventory at the end of May

Required: (1) A standard cost card for the product.

(2) Entries to record the above data using two materials variances, two labor variances, and three factory overhead variances, including an entry to adjust all opening inventories to standard cost.

(3) Factory overhead analysis using the two- and four-variance methods.

20-2. Ledger Accounts; Work in Process and Finished Goods Inventories Adjusted to Actual Cost. The Chapelle Company began operations on January 1, 19—. It manufactures a single product. The company installed a standard cost system but will adjust all inventories to actual cost for financial statement purposes at the end of the year.

The following accounts are used in the company's standard cost system:

Raw Materials	Materials Quantity Variance
Direct Labor	Labor Rate Variance
Factory Overhead	Labor Efficiency Variance
Work in Process	Factory Overhead Efficiency Variance
Finished Goods	Factory Overhead Idle Capacity Variance
Materials Price Usage Variance	Factory Overhead Spending Variance

Under the cost system, raw materials are maintained at actual cost. Charges made to Work in Process are all made at standard prices. Variance accounts are used into which all variances are entered as they are identified.

One half of the cost of raw materials for each unit is put into production at the beginning of the process and the balance when the processing is about one-third completed.

Standard costs were based on 256,000 direct labor hours with a production of 1,600 units. The standards are as follows:

Materials (100 lbs. @ $2).....................................	$200
Direct labor (160 hrs. @ $2.25)...............................	360
Factory overhead (160 direct labor hours @ $1)................	160
(The fixed portion of the overhead rate is $.40.)	
Total standard cost per unit...............................	$720

A summary of the transactions for the year ended December 31, 19—, shows the following:

Materials purchased (180,000 lbs. @ $2.20)...............	$396,000
Direct labor (247,925 hrs. @ $2.40).....................	595,020
Factory overhead.......................................	248,640
Materials issued to production.........................	177,600 lbs.
Units processed:	
Units completed......................................	1,500
Units one-half complete..............................	150
Units one-fourth complete............................	30

Required: (1) Ledger accounts with the above transactions recorded therein.

(2) Entries to adjust Finished Goods to actual cost for materials. No adjustment is needed for labor and factory overhead. No other accounts should be used.

(3) A statement showing details of the materials cost included in Work in Process as adjusted to actual cost.

(AICPA adapted)

20-3. Journal Entries; Income Statement with Variances. The Gomez Company makes unit M. The manufacturing of unit M is based on three successive and continuous operations, namely, operations M-10 to M-12, inclusive, in which the manufacturing cost of each unit is developed as shown by the following tabulation of percentages of cost to manufacture:

PERCENTAGE OF COST TO MANUFACTURE UNIT M

Operation	Materials	Labor	Overhead
M-10..	20%	20%	40%
M-11..		35	40
M-12..	80	45	20
Total....................................	100%	100%	100%

(Gomez does not record the actual labor charges applicable to each operation.)

The Gomez Company operates a cost accounting system based on standard costs which are incorporated in the manufacturing cost accounts. The differences between standard costs and actual costs are reflected in appropriate variance accounts; namely, materials purchase price, materials usage, direct labor rate, direct labor time, and overall factory overhead. The materials purchase price variance is assumed to be realized at the time of purchase, irrespective of time of usage. Three work in process accounts are maintained: materials, labor, and factory overhead.

The inventories applicable to unit M as of December 31, 19A, stated in accordance with the foregoing schedule of standard costs, are as follows:

> Materials: Item M-a — 100 units; Item M-b — 100 units
> Work in process: 50 units complete through operation M-10
> Finished goods: none

The standard manufacturing costs used for unit M, based on a planned monthly production ranging between 8,000 and 12,000 units, are as follows:

	Per Unit M	
	Quantity	*Amount*
Materials:		
Item M-a (issued in operation M-10)................	1	$ .50
Item M-b (issued in operation M-12)................	1	2.00
Direct labor (total for all operations at uniform rate of $5 per		
hour)...	¼ hour	1.25
Factory overhead (applicable to operations as a whole):		
Variable expenses.................................		.60
Fixed expenses...................................		.90
		$5.25

Transactions and other facts during January, 19B, are:

Transactions:

	Amount
Materials purchases:	
Item M-a — 12,000 units @ $ .55 per unit......................	$ 6,600
Item M-b — 12,000 units @ $2.10 per unit.....................	25,200
Payroll for all operations:	
Direct labor — 3,100 hours @ $1.2625 per ¼ hour...............	15,655
Indirect labor	1,500
Factory overhead, other than indirect labor......................	15,000
Marketing, administrative, and general expenses...................	31,600

Other facts:

During January, 19B, 11,000 units of M were transferred to the finished goods warehouse and 10,500 units were sold at $10 per unit M.

As of January 31, 19B, 100 units of work in process are complete through operation M-11, but all materials are in process.

Materials requisitions indicate issuances of materials items M-a and M-b in the quantities required for the production through the respective operations indicated. A supplementary materials requisition, however, indicates that item M-a actually used was 2% in excess of standard quantity.

Required: (1) Journal entries of transactions for the month.
(2) An income statement showing appropriate manufacturing cost variances.

(AICPA adapted)

20-4. Standard Costing in the Accounts; Variance Disposition. Tolbert Manufacturing Company uses a standard cost system in accounting for the cost of production of its only product, Product A. The standards for the production of one unit of Product A are:

Direct materials: 10 feet of Item 1 at $.75 per foot; and 3 feet of Item 2 at $1 per foot
Direct labor: 4 hours at $3.50 per hour
Factory overhead: applied at 150% of standard direct labor costs

There was no inventory on hand at July 1, 19A. A summary of costs and related data for the production of Product A during the year ended June 30, 19B, showed that:

(a) 100,000 feet of Item 1 were purchased at $.78 per foot.
(b) 30,000 feet of Item 2 were purchased at $.90 per foot.
(c) 8,000 units of Product A were produced which required 78,000 feet of Item 1, 26,000 feet of Item 2, and 31,000 hours of direct labor at $3.60 per hour.
(d) 6,000 units of Product A were sold.
(e) At June 30, 19B, 22,000 feet of Item 1, 4,000 feet of Item 2, and 2,000 completed units of Product A were on hand. (All purchases and transfers are recorded at standard.)

Required: (1) The total debits to the raw materials account for the purchase of Item 1, for the year ended June 30, 19B.

(2) The total debits to the work in process account for direct labor, for the year ended June 30, 19B.

(3) The balance in the materials quantity variance account for Item 2, before allocation of standard variances.

(4) Assuming that all standard variances are prorated to inventories and Cost of Goods Sold, the amount of: (a) the materials quantity variance for Item 2 to be prorated to raw materials inventory and (b) the materials purchase price variance for Item 1 to be prorated to raw materials inventory.

(AICPA adapted)

20-5. Allocating Variances; Computing Standard and Actual Manufacturing Costs; Inventory Schedules. The Calvin Corporation commenced doing business on December 1, 19—. The corporation uses a standard cost system for the manufacturing costs of its only product, Haemex. The standard costs for a unit of Haemex are:

Raw materials.....................	10 kilograms @ $.70 per kg.	$ 7
Direct labor......................	1 hr. @ $2 per hr.	2
Factory overhead (applied on the basis of $2 per direct labor hour)		2
Total......		$11

Additional information:

(a) The following data were extracted from the corporation's books for the month of December:

	Units	Debit	Credit
Budgeted production.......................	3,000		
Units sold...............................	1,500		
Sales.......................................			$30,000
Sales discounts.............................		$ 500	
Materials price usage variance...............		1,500	
Materials quantity variance..................		660	
Direct labor rate variance....................		250	
Factory overhead spending variance..........			300
Purchases discounts lost.....................		120	

The company records purchases of raw materials net of discounts. The amounts shown above for purchases discounts lost and materials price usage variance are applicable to raw materials used in manufacturing operations during the month of December.

(b) Inventory data at December 31, 19—, indicate the following inventories were on hand:

Raw materials............................ None
Work in process.......................... 1,200 units
Finished goods........................... 900 units

The work in process inventory was 100% complete as to materials and 50% as to direct labor and factory overhead. The corporation's policy is to allocate variances over the cost of goods sold and ending inventories; i.e., work in process and finished goods.

Required: (1) A schedule allocating the variances and purchases discounts lost to the ending inventories and to cost of goods sold.

(2) A schedule computing the cost of goods manufactured at standard cost and at actual cost for December, 19—. Amounts for materials, labor, and factory overhead should be shown separately.

(3) A schedule computing the actual cost of materials, labor, and factory overhead included in the work in process inventory and in the finished goods inventory at December 31, 19—.

(AICPA adapted)

20-6. Equivalent Production Schedules; Analyzing Differences of Actual and Standard Materials Costs. Dexon Pharmaceutical Company processes a single product, Mudexin, and uses a standard cost accounting system. The process requires preparation and blending of three materials in large batches with a variation from the standard mixture sometimes necessary to maintain quality. The following information is available for the Blending Department.

The standard cost card for a 500-pound batch shows the following standard costs:

	Quantity	Unit Price	Total Cost	
Materials:				
Mucilloid...........................	250 pounds	$ .14	$35	
Dextrose..........................	200 pounds	.09	18	
Other ingredients...................	50 pounds	.08	4	
Total per batch..................	500 pounds			$ 57
Labor:				
Blending.......................	10 hours	$3.00		30
Factory overhead:				
Variable...........................	10 hours	$1.00	$10	
Fixed.............................	10 hours	.30	3	13
Total standard cost per 500-pound batch.........................				$100

During October 410 batches of 500 pounds each of the finished compound were completed and transferred to the Packaging Department.

Blending Department inventories totaled 6,000 pounds at the beginning of the month and 9,000 pounds at the end of the month. Both inventories were completely processed but not transferred and consisted of materials in their standard proportions. Inventories are carried in the accounts at standard cost prices.

During the month of October the following materials were purchased and put into production:

	Pounds	Unit Price	Total Cost
Mucilloid.................................	114,400	$ .17	$19,448
Dextrose..................................	85,800	.11	9,438
Other ingredients.........................	19,800	.07	1,386
Totals.................................	220,000		$30,272

Wages paid for 4,212 hours of direct labor at $3.25 per hour were $13,689. Actual factory overhead costs for the month totaled $5,519.

The standards were established for a normal production volume of 200,000 pounds (400 batches) of Mudexin per month. At this level of production variable factory overhead was budgeted at $4,000; and fixed factory overhead was budgeted at $1,200.

Required: (1) A schedule presenting:
   (a) The equivalent production computation for the Blending Department for October production in both pounds and batches.
   (b) The standard cost of October production itemized by components of materials, labor, and factory overhead.

(2) Schedules computing the differences between actual and standard costs, and analyzing the differences as materials variances (for each material) caused by (a) price differences and (b) quantity differences.

(3) Explain how materials variances arising from quantity differences could be further analyzed and prepare schedules presenting such an analysis.

(Note: No labor or overhead variances are to be calculated.)

(AICPA adapted)

20-7.   Income Statement; Standard Process Costing; Variance Analysis. The Belkraft Corporation manufactures Product G which is sold for $20 per unit. Raw Material M is added before processing starts, and labor and overhead are added evenly during the manufacturing process. Production capacity is budgeted at 110,000 units of G annually. The standard costs per unit of G are:

Direct materials:		
M, 2 pounds @ $1.50 per pound.......................		$ 3.00
Direct labor (1.5 hours per unit).........................		6.00
Factory overhead:		
Variable...	$1.50	
Fixed..	1.10	2.60
Total standard cost per unit...........................		$11.60

A process cost system is used employing standard costs. Inventories are valued at standard cost. All variances from standard costs are charged or credited to Cost of Goods Sold in the year incurred.

Inventory data for the year 19—:

	Units	
	January 1	December 31
Raw materials: M (pounds).................	50,000	60,000
Work in process:		
All materials, ⅔ processed.................	10,000	
All materials, ⅓ processed.................		15,000
Inventory, finished goods....................	20,000	12,000

During 19—, 250,000 pounds of M were purchased at an average cost of $1.485 per pound; and 240,000 pounds were transferred to work in process inventory. Direct labor costs amounted to $656,880 at an average labor cost of $4.08.

Actual factory overhead for 19—:

Variable...	$181,500
Fixed...	114,000

110,000 units of G were completed and transferred to finished goods inventory. Marketing and administrative expenses were $651,000.

Required: An income statement for the year 19—, including all manufacturing cost variances. (Use the two-variance method for factory overhead.)

(AICPA adapted)

20-8. Schedules Comparing Actual with Standard Costs; Adjusting Finished Goods to Cost or Market Values, Whichever is Lower. The Deakin Corporation manufactures a single product which passes through several departments. The company has a standard cost system. On December 31, 19—, inventories at standard cost are as follows:

	Work in Process	Finished Goods
Direct materials......................	$75,000	$ 60,000
Direct labor.........................	7,500	20,000
Factory overhead.....................	15,000	40,000
Total..............................	$97,500	$120,000

No raw materials inventory existed.

Prior to any year-end inventory adjustments, the controller prepared the preliminary income statement shown at the top of page 655 for the year ended December 31, 19—.

All purchases discounts were earned on the purchase of raw materials. The company has included a scrap allowance in the cost standards; the scrap sold cannot be traced to any particular operation or department.

Required: (1) A schedule computing the actual cost of goods manufactured. The schedule should provide for a separation of costs into direct materials, direct labor, and factory overhead.

(2) A schedule comparing the computation of ending inventories at standard cost and at actual cost. The schedule should provide for a separation of costs into direct materials, direct labor, and factory overhead.

(3) A schedule to adjust the finished goods inventory to the lower of cost or market. Without prejudice to the solution to (2), assume that the finished

INCOME STATEMENT (PRELIMINARY)

Sales..		$900,000
Cost of goods sold:		
Standard cost of goods sold:		
Direct materials.............................	$300,000	
Direct labor.................................	100,000	
Factory overhead............................	200,000	
Total....................................	$600,000	
Variances:		
Direct materials.............................	$ 25,400	
Direct labor.................................	25,500	
Overabsorbed factory overhead..................	(16,500)	
Total....................................	$ 34,400	634,400
Gross profit.......................................		$265,600
Marketing expenses:		
Sales salaries.................................	$ 28,000	
Sales commissions.............................	72,000	
Shipping expenses.............................	18,000	
Other marketing expenses.......................	7,000	
Total....................................	$125,000	
General and administrative expenses................	50,000	175,000
Net income from operations........................		$ 90,600
Other income:		
Purchases discounts............................	$ 8,000	
Scrap sales...................................	9,000	17,000
Net income before taxes..........................		$107,600

goods inventory was composed of 1,000 units with a cost of $180 each. The current market price for the product is $250. The company, however, has an old contract to sell 200 units at $175 each. The normal gross profit rate is $33\frac{1}{3}\%$ of cost. The shipping expenses for the old contract will be $5 per unit; the sales commission is 8% of the sale.

(AICPA adapted)

20-9. Revision of Standard Costs; New Standard Costs Applied to Inventory. The standard cost of Product MSY-2, manufactured by the New Orleans Manufacturing Company, is as follows:

	Prime Cost	Factory Overhead 50%	Total
Material A.............................	$10.00		$10.00
Material B.............................	5.00		5.00
Material C.............................	2.00		2.00
Direct labor — Cutting.................	8.00	$4.00	12.00
Direct labor — Shaping.................	4.00	2.00	6.00
Direct labor — Assembling	2.00	1.00	3.00
Direct labor — Boxing..................	1.00	.50	1.50
Total.............................	$32.00	$7.50	$39.50

The company manufactured 10,000 units of Product MSY-2 at a total cost of $395,000 for the period under review. Materials A, B, and C are issued in the Cutting Department.

The following variance accounts relating to this product appear on the books for the period:

	Debit	Credit
Materials price variance:		
Due to a favorable purchase of total requirements of Material A.....................................		$19,500
Materials usage variance:		
Excessive waste during period.....................	$ 6,000	
Labor rate variance:		
5% wage increase to direct workers...............	7,500	
Labor efficiency variance:		
Due to shutdown caused by strike...................	17,000	
Factory overhead variance — fixed overhead:		
Due to shutdown caused by strike..................	8,000	
Factory overhead variance — variable overhead:		
Due to permanent savings in costs of certain services...		18,000

The inventory at the end of the period is as follows:

		Unit Cost	Total
100 units Material A.............................	@	$10.00	$ 1,000
100 units Material B.............................	@	5.00	500
100 units Material C.............................	@	2.00	200
200 units Product MSY-2 in process — Cutting... ...	@	29.00	5,800
200 units Product MSY-2 in process — Shaping......	@	35.00	7,000
200 units Product MSY-2 in process — Assembling...	@	38.00	7,600
200 units Product MSY-2 finished and boxed........	@	39.50	7,900
Total...			$30,000

Required: (1) A schedule of revised standard costs which will clearly indicate the cumulative standard for each successive operation.

(2) A schedule applying the revised standard costs to the ending inventory.

(AICPA adapted)

CASES

A. Variance Control and Responsibility. The Fillep Co. utilizes a standard cost system. The variances for each department are calculated and reported to the department manager. It is expected that the managers will use the information to improve their operations and recognize that it is used by their superiors for performance evaluation.

Joan Daley was recently appointed manager of the Assembly Department of the company. She has complained that the system as designed is disadvantageous to her department. Included among the variances charged to the departments is one for rejected units. The inspection occurs at the end of the Assembly Department. The inspectors attempt to identify the cause of the rejection so that the department where the error occurred can be charged with it. Not all errors can be easily identified with a department. These are totaled and apportioned to the departments according to the number of identified errors. The variance for rejected units in each department is a combination of the errors caused by the department plus a portion of the unidentified causes of rejects.

Required: (1) Is Joan Daley's claim valid? Explain the reason(s) for your answer.

(2) What would you recommend the company do to solve its problem with Joan Daley and her complaint?

(NAA adapted)

B. Variance Analysis; Variance Control Responsibility. The Carberg Corporation manufactures and sells a single product. The company uses a standard cost system, and the standard cost per unit of product is as follows:

Material (one pound plastic @ $2).............................	$ 2.00
Direct labor (1.6 hours @ $4).................................	6.40
Variable factory overhead cost per unit.........................	3.00
Fixed factory overhead cost per unit...........................	1.45
	$12.85

The factory overhead cost per unit was calculated from the following annual overhead cost budget for a 60,000 unit volume:

Variable factory overhead cost:

Indirect labor (30,000 hours @ $4).........................	$120,000
Supplies (Oil — 60,000 gallons @ $.50).....................	30,000
Allocated variable service department costs...................	30,000
Total variable factory overhead cost.........................	$180,000

Fixed factory overhead cost:

Supervision...	$ 27,000
Depreciation..	45,000
Other fixed costs..	15,000
Total fixed factory overhead cost............................	$ 87,000
Total budgeted annual factory overhead cost for 60,000 units.....	$267,000

The charges to the Manufacturing Department for November, when 5,000 units were produced, are:

Materials (5,300 pounds @ $2)...............................	$10,600
Direct labor (8,200 hours @ $4.10)..........................	33,620
Indirect labor (2,400 hours @ $4.10)........................	9,840
Supplies (Oil — 6,000 gallons @ $.55).......................	3,300
Allocated variable service department costs....................	3,200
Supervision..	2,475
Depreciation...	3,750
Other fixed costs...	1,250
Total..	$68,035

The Purchasing Department normally buys about the same quantity as is used in production during a month. In November 5,200 pounds were purchased at a price of $2.10 per pound.

Required: (1) Calculate these variances from standard costs for the data given:

(a) materials purchase price variance; (b) materials quantity variance; (c) direct labor rate variance; (d) direct labor efficiency variance; (e) total factory overhead variance for 5,000 units of production, analyzed for *each* expense classification.

(2) The company has divided its responsibilities so that the Purchasing Department is responsible for the price at which materials and supplies are purchased, while the Manufacturing Department is responsible for the quantities

of materials used. Does this division of responsibilities solve the conflict between price and quantity variances? Explain.

(3) Prepare a report which details the factory overhead budget variance. The report, which will be given to the Manufacturing Department manager, should display only that part of the variance that is the manager's responsibility and should highlight the information in ways that would be useful to that manager in evaluating departmental performance and in considering corrective action.

(4) Assume that the department manager performs the timekeeping function and that, at various times, an analysis of factory overhead and direct labor variances has shown that he has deliberately misclassified labor hours (e.g., listed direct labor hours as indirect labor hours and vice versa) so that only one of the two labor variances is unfavorable. It is not economically feasible to hire a separate timekeeper. What should the company do, if anything, to resolve this problem?

(NAA adapted)

C. Theoretical Discussion of Standard Costs Variances, Capacity, and Variance Allocation. Last year Mafco Corporation adopted a standard cost system. Labor standards were set on the basis of time studies and prevailing wage rates. Materials standards were determined from materials specifications and prices then in effect. In determining its standard for overhead, Mafco estimated that a total of 6,000,000 finished units would be produced during the next five years to satisfy demand for its product. The five-year period was selected to average out seasonal and cyclical fluctuations and allow for sales trends. By dividing the annual average of 1,200,000 units into the total annual budgeted overhead, a standard cost was developed for factory overhead.

At June 30, 19—, the end of the current fiscal year, a partial trial balance revealed the following:

	Debit	Credit
Materials purchase price variance........................		$25,000
Materials quantity variance...........................	$ 9,000	
Labor rate variance................................	30,000	
Labor efficiency variance............................	7,500	
Controllable variance...............................	2,000	
Volume variance....................................	75,000	

Standards were set at the beginning of the year and have remained unchanged. All inventories are priced at standard cost.

Required: (1) Conclusions to be drawn from each of the six variances shown in the Mafco Corporation's trial balance.

(2) The amount of fixed factory overhead cost to be included in product cost depends on whether or not the allocation is based on (a) ideal (or theoretical) capacity, (b) practical capacity, (c) normal capacity, or (d) expected annual capacity. Describe each of these allocation bases and give a theoretical argument for each.

(3) A theoretical justification for each of the following methods of accounting for the net amount of all standard cost variances for year-end financial reporting:

(a) Presenting the net variance as an income or expense on the income statement.

(b) Allocating the net variance among inventories and cost of goods sold.

(AICPA adapted)

CHAPTER 21

CONVENTIONAL GROSS PROFIT ANALYSIS

The standard cost discussion deals with the determination and analysis of variances for each of the cost elements, materials, labor, and factory overhead, which constitute the major portion of the cost of goods sold section of the income statement. Subtracting the cost of goods sold figure from sales results in the gross profit. Any deviation from the predetermined standard cost is normally shown as an increase or decrease in the gross profit. The adherence of the actual to the budgeted or standard gross profit figure is highly desirable. Therefore, a careful analysis of unexpected changes in gross profit is advantageous to a company's management. Not only do the individual cost elements influence the gross profit figure, but the sales figure itself must be held accountable for any change occurring in the gross profit.

CAUSES OF GROSS PROFIT CHANGES

A change in the gross profit is due to one or a combination of the following:

1. Changes in selling prices of products

2. Changes in volume sold

3. Changes in cost elements

The second of the above three causes — changes in volume sold — may be further divided into two parts:

1. Changes in volume
2. Changes in types of products sold, often called *product mix* or *sales mix*

Volume refers to the number of physical units, while product mix considers the change in the composition of goods sold.

GROSS PROFIT ANALYSIS

The determination of the various causes for an increase or decrease in the gross profit can be made in a manner similar to that illustrated in connection with the computation of standard cost variances. It should be understood, however, that gross profit analysis is often possible without the use of standard costs or budgets. In such a case, prices and costs of the previous year, or any year selected as the basis for the comparison, serve as the basis for the computation of the variances. When standard costs and budgetary methods are employed, a greater degree of accuracy and more effective results are achieved. Both methods are illustrated below.

Illustration I. This first illustration shows an analysis of gross profit based on the previous year's figures.

The Silcon Manufacturing Company presents the following gross profit sections of its operating statements for the years 19A and 19B:

	19A	*19B*	*Changes*
Sales (net).....................	$120,000	$140,000	+$20,000
Cost of goods sold.............	100,000	110,000	+ 10,000
Gross profit on sales..........	$ 20,000	$ 30,000	+$10,000 net increase

Additional data taken from various records indicate that the sales and the cost of goods sold figures can be broken down as shown below and on page 661.

		19A Sales		*19A Cost of Goods Sold*	
Quantity		*Unit Price*	*Total*	*Unit Price*	*Total*
Product X = 8,000 units @		$5.00	$ 40,000	$4.00	$ 32,000
Product Y = 7,000 units @		4.00	28,000	3.50	24,500
Product Z = 20,000 units @		2.60	52,000	2.175	43,500
Total sales..............			$120,000	Total cost	$100,000

		19B Sales		19B Cost of Goods Sold	
Quantity	Unit Price	Total		Unit Price	Total
Product X = 10,000 units @	$6.60	$ 66,000		$4.00	$ 40,000
Product Y = 4,000 units @	3.50	14,000		3.50	14,000
Product Z = 20,000 units @	3.00	60,000		2.80	56,000
Total sales.............		$140,000		Total cost	$110,000

The illustration indicates that, in comparison with the year 19A, sales in 19B increased $20,000 and costs increased $10,000, resulting in an increase in gross profit of $10,000. What caused this increase?

The method shown below follows a procedure similar to the one employed in connection with the computation of standard cost variances. Sales and costs of 19A are accepted as the basis (or standard) for all comparisons. A sales price and a sales volume variance are computed first; a cost price and cost volume variance are computed next. The sales volume variance and the cost volume variance are analyzed further as a third step to compute a sales mix and a final sales volume variance.

First Step. Computation of sales price and sales volume variances:

Actual sales 19B.. $140,000

Actual 19B sales at 19A prices:
  X = 10,000 units × $5.00 = $50,000
  Y = 4,000 units × 4.00 = 16,000
  Z = 20,000 units × 2.60 = 52,000....................... 118,000

Favorable sales price variance............................. $ 22,000

Actual 19B sales at 19A prices............................. $118,000

Total sales 19A (used as standard)......................... 120,000

Unfavorable sales volume variance.......................... $ 2,000

Second Step. Computation of cost price and cost volume variances:

Actual cost of goods sold 19B.............................. $110,000

Actual 19B sales at 19A costs:
  X = 10,000 units × $4.00 = $40,000
  Y = 4,000 units × 3.50 = 14,000
  Z = 20,000 units × 2.175 = 43,500....................... 97,500

Unfavorable cost price variance............................ $ 12,500

Actual 19B sales at 19A costs.............................. $ 97,500
Cost of goods sold 19A (used as standard)................. 100,000

Favorable cost volume variance............................. $ 2,500

At this point the above analysis shows the following results which might explain the reason for the $10,000 increase in gross profit:

Favorable sales price variance.............................. $22,000

Favorable volume variance (net) consisting of:
        $2,500 favorable cost volume variance
Less   2,000 unfavorable sales volume variance
Net $ 500 favorable volume variance......................   500

                                                                   $22,500
Less unfavorable cost price variance..........................   12,500
Increase in gross profit....................................... $10,000

Third Step. Computation of the sales mix and the final sales volume variances:

The net $500 favorable volume variance is a composite of sales volume and cost volume variances and as such is rather meaningless. It can and should be further analyzed into the more significant and valuable sales mix and final sales volume variances. To accomplish this analysis, one additional figure must be determined — the average gross profit realized on the units sold in the base (or standard) year. The computation is as follows:

$$\frac{\text{Total Gross Profit of 19A Sales}}{\text{Total Number of Units Sold 19A}} = \frac{\$20,000}{35,000} = \$.5714$$

The $.5714 represents the average gross profit realized on all units sold in 19A. This gross profit per unit is multiplied by the total number of units sold in 19B (34,000 units) resulting in $19,427, which is the total gross profit that would have been achieved in 19B if all units had been sold at 19A's average gross profit per unit.

The calculation of the sales mix and the final sales volume variances can now be made:

19B sales at 19A prices....................................... $118,000
19B sales at 19A costs..   97,500

Difference.. $ 20,500
19B sales at 19A average gross profit.........................   19,427

Favorable sales mix variance.................................. $ 1,073

19B sales at 19A average gross profit......................... $ 19,427
Total sales 19A (used as standard).................... $120,000
Cost of goods sold 19A (used as standard)...........   100,000

Difference..   20,000
Unfavorable final sales volume variance............... $ 573

Check: Favorable sales mix variance.......................... $ 1,073
        Unfavorable final sales volume variance................   573
        Net increase (favorable)............................. $ 500

The sales mix variance can be viewed in the following manner:

Product	*19B Sales Units*	*19A Sales Units*	*%*	*19B Sales (In 19A Proportions)*	*Col. 1 − Col. 2*	*19A Unit Gross Profit*	*Col. 3 × Col. 4*
	Column 1			**Column 2**	**Column 3**	**Column 4**	
X	10,000	8,000	22.86	7,772*	2,228	$1.000**	$2,228
Y	4,000	7,000	20.00	6,800	(2,800)	.500	(1,400)
Z	20,000	20,000	57.14	19,428	572	.425	243
Total....	34,000	35,000	100.00	34,000	-0-		

Rounding error..............   2

Favorable sales mix variance.. $1,073

*34,000 × 22.86% = 7,772.
**$5 sales price − $4 cost of goods sold = $1.

The final sales volume variance is the difference in sales units for the two years multiplied by the 19A average gross profit per unit.

19B sales units.....................................	34,000
19A sales units.....................................	35,000
Unit sales difference................................	1,000
Average gross profit per unit........................	× $.5714
Unfavorable sales volume variance....................	$571.40
Rounding error......................................	1.60
Unfavorable final sales volume variance..............	$573.00

Recapitulation:

	Gains	Losses
Gain due to increased sales price....................	$22,000	
Loss due to increased cost...........................		$12,500
Gain due to shift in sales mix.......................	1,073	
Loss due to decrease in units sold...................		573
Total..	$23,073	$13,073
Less...	13,073	
Net increase in gross profit.........................	$10,000	

Illustration II. The gross profit analysis shown on pages 664–667 uses budgets and standard costs. The analysis is based on three statements:

1. The budgeted income statement prepared at the beginning of the period

2. The actual income statement prepared at the end of the period

3. An income statement prepared at the end of the period on the basis of actual sales priced at budgeted sales prices and standard costs

Statement 1

VITT MANUFACTURING, INC.
BUDGETED INCOME STATEMENT

Product	Units	Sales		Cost		Gross Profit	
		Price	Amount	Price	Amount	Price	Amount
A	6,000	$15.00	$ 90,000	$12.00	$ 72,000	$3.00	$18,000
B	3,500	12.00	42,000	10.00	35,000	2.00	7,000
C	1,000	10.00	10,000	8.75	8,750	1.25	1,250
	10,500	$13.52*	$142,000	$11.02*	$115,750	$2.50*	$26,250

*Weighted averages.

Statement 2

VITT MANUFACTURING, INC.
INCOME STATEMENT (ACTUAL)

Product	Units	Sales		Cost		Gross Profit	
		Price	Amount	Price	Amount	Price	Amount
A	5,112	$16.00	$ 81,792	$13.98	$ 71,465	$2.02	$10,327
B	4,208	12.00	50,496	9.72	40,901	2.28	9,595
C	1,105	9.00	9,945	8.83	9,757	.17	188
	10,425	$13.64*	$142,233	$11.71*	$122,123	$1.93*	$20,110

*Weighted averages.

Statement 3

VITT MANUFACTURING, INC.
INCOME STATEMENT (ACTUAL AT BUDGETED PRICES)

Product	Units	Sales		Cost		Gross Profit	
		Price	Amount	Price	Amount	Price	Amount
A	5,112	$15.00	$ 76,680	$12.00	$ 61,344	$3.00	$15,336
B	4,208	12.00	50,496	10.00	42,080	2.00	8,416
C	1,105	10.00	11,050	8.75	9,669	1.25	1,381
	10,425	$13.26*	$138,226	$10.85*	$113,093	$2.41*	$25,133

*Weighted averages.

According to Statement 1, Vitt Manufacturing expected to make a gross profit of $26,250 based on an estimated production of 10,500 units and an average gross profit of $2.50 per unit. The company actually made a gross profit of only $1.93 per unit because budgeted gross profit of $26,250 exceeded actual gross profit of $20,110 by $6,140 (see Statement 2). On the basis of the budget, Product A is the most profitable product while Product C is the least profitable per unit. Actually due to variations in sales price and cost, Product B is the most profitable while Product C is the least profitable per unit.

Statement 3 indicates that the average gross profit would have been $2.41 per unit if the sales price and cost per unit had been according to the budget. Changes in sales prices, sales volume, sales mix, and costs resulted in a gross profit of only $1.93 per unit.

Had prices, costs, and units sold prevailed as budgeted, the gross profit would have been $26,250. Actual gross profit was only $20,110. What caused this decrease of $6,140 in gross profit?

In the three steps shown, all figures are taken directly from the basic statements mentioned with the exception of $26,062.50, which is computed by multiplying the actual units sold by the average gross profit as per Statement 1; i.e., 10,425 units $\times$ $2.50 = $26,062.50.

First Step. Computation of sales price and sales volume variances:

Actual sales..	$142,233
Actual sales at budgeted prices......................	138,226
Favorable sales price variance.......................	$ 4,007

Actual sales at budgeted prices......................	$138,226
Budgeted sales.......................................	142,000
Unfavorable sales volume variance....................	$ 3,774

Second Step. Computation of cost price and cost volume variances:

Cost of goods sold — actual..........................	$122,123
Budgeted costs of actual goods sold..................	113,093
Unfavorable cost price variance......................	$ 9,030

Budgeted costs of actual goods sold..................	$113,093
Budgeted costs of budgeted goods sold................	115,750
Favorable cost volume variance.......................	$ 2,657

Third Step. Computation of the sales mix and the final sales volume variances:

In the above calculations two volume variances appear:

Unfavorable sales volume variance....................	$3,774
Favorable cost volume variance.......................	2,657
Net unfavorable volume variance......................	$1,117

As stated previously, the net volume variance figure should be further analyzed into the sales mix and the final sales volume variance as follows:

Actual sales at budgeted prices.........................	$138,226.00
Budgeted costs of actual goods sold.....................	113,093.00
Difference...	$ 25,133.00
Budgeted gross profit of actual goods sold (10,425 × $2.50).....................................	26,062.50
Unfavorable sales mix variance.........................	$ 929.50

Budgeted gross profit of actual goods sold......		$ 26,062.50
Budgeted sales...............................	$142,000	
Budgeted costs of budgeted goods sold.........	115,750	
Budgeted gross profit.........................		26,250.00
Unfavorable final sales volume variance........		$ 187.50

Check: Unfavorable sales mix variance...................	$ 929.50
Unfavorable final sales volume variance...........	187.50
Unfavorable volume variance....................	$ 1,117.00

Again, the sales mix variance can be viewed in the following manner:

	Column 1			Column 2	Column 3	Column 4	
	Actual Sales	Budgeted Sales		Actual Sales (In Budgeted	Col. 1 −	Budgeted Unit Gross	Col. 3 ×
Product	Units	Units	%	Proportions)	Col. 2	Profit	Col. 4
A	5,112	6,000	57.14	5,957*	(845)	$3.00	$(2,535.00)
B	4,208	3,500	33.33	3,475	733	2.00	1,466.00
C	1,105	1,000	9.53	993	112	1.25	140.00
Total..	10,425	10,500	100.00	10,425	-0-		

Rounding error.....................	(.50)
Unfavorable sales mix variance......	$ (929.50)

*10,425 × 57.14% = 5,957.

The final sales volume variance is the difference in actual and budgeted sales units multiplied by the budgeted average gross profit per unit.

Actual sales units.....................................	10,425
Budgeted sales units...................................	10,500
Unit sales difference..................................	75
Budgeted average gross profit per unit.................	×$2.50
Unfavorable final sales volume variance................	$187.50

Recapitulation: *Gains*   *Losses*

Gain due to increased sales prices....................	$4,007	
Loss due to increased cost..........................		$ 9,030.00
Loss due to shift in sales mix.......................		929.50
Loss due to decrease in units sold................		187.50
Total...	$4,007	$10,147.00
Less..		4,007.00
Net decrease in gross profit........................		$ 6,140.00

FURTHER REFINEMENT OF SALES VOLUME ANALYSIS

In the above computation sales mix and final sales volume variances were determined with the aid of an average gross profit figure and total figures only. However, it is often necessary to trace the causes for a change to the individual product lines. Using the figures from the income statements of Vitt Manufacturing, Inc., an analysis by products can be made in the manner shown below.

VITT MANUFACTURING, INC. ANALYSIS BY PRODUCT						
Amounts Based On	Product A		Product B		Product C	
	Sales	Cost	Sales	Cost	Sales	Cost
Statement 3...	$76,680	$61,344	$50,496	$42,080	$11,050	$9,669
Statement 1...	90,000	72,000	42,000	35,000	10,000	8,750
Difference....	−$13,320	+$10,656	+$ 8,496	−$ 7,080	+$ 1,050	−$ 919
Net..........	−$2,664		+$1,416		+$131	

Recapitulation: *Sales Volume*

	Gains	*Losses*
On Product A...		$2,664
On Product B...	$1,416	
On Product C...	131	
Total...	$1,547	$2,664
Less gain...		1,547
Net loss due to sales mix variance and final sales volume variance...		$1,117

USES OF GROSS PROFIT ANALYSIS

The analysis based on budgets and standard costs forcefully depicts the weak spots in the year's performance. Management is now able to outline the remedies that should be taken to correct the situation.[1] In Illustration II the gain due to higher prices is more than offset by the increase in cost, the shift to less profitable products, and the decrease in units sold. As the planned gross profit is the responsibility of the marketing as well as the manufacturing departments, the gross profit analysis brings together these two major functional areas of the firm and points to the need for further study by both of these departments. The marketing department must explain the changes in sales prices, the shift in the sales mix, and the decrease in units sold while the production department must account for the increase in cost. To be of real value, the cost price variance should be further analyzed into variances for materials, labor, and factory overhead as explained in the two preceding standard cost chapters.

DISCUSSION QUESTIONS

1. Why is the gross profit figure significant?
2. What causes changes in the gross profit?
3. Explain the term "product mix" or "sales mix."
4. By what methods can a change in the gross profit figure be analyzed?
5. Illustrate how the sales price variance is determined. If the sales price variance were to be journalized in the books, how would such a journal entry vary from an entry made for the materials purchase price variance?
6. How are the sales mix and the final sales volume variances computed?
7. What is the significance of the average gross profit figure of the base or standard?
8. The gross profit analysis based on budgets and standards makes use of three basic statements. Name them.
9. What important information is revealed by a gross profit analysis on a product basis?
10. Whose task is it to see that the planned gross profit is met?

EXERCISES

1. Price — Gross Profit Relationship. How much must be added to the cost price to realize a gross profit on sales of: 50%, 40%, 35%, 30%, 25%, 20%, 15%, 12½%, 10%, 8%, 5%?

2. Deciding on Correct Method. The accountant for Kyle, Inc. observed the following change in sales revenue between two years:

---

[1]See Raymond L. Kelso and Robert R. Elliot, "Bridging Communications Gap Between Accountants and Managers," *Management Accounting*, Vol. LI, No. 5, pp. 41–44.

19A   100 articles @ $3 = $300
19B   120 articles @ $4 = 480
                          —————
                          $180 difference (increase)

Wishing to analyze the $180, he used the following method, with this result:

Method 1:
Changes because of quantity increase 20 × $4 = $ 80
Changes because of price increase   100 × $1 = 100
                                                —————
                                                $180

Somewhat doubtful of his answer, he tried another method, with this result:

Method 2:
Changes because of quantity increase 20 × $3 = $ 60
Changes because of price increase   120 × $1 = 120
                                                —————
                                                $180

Required: Selection and justification of the correct method.

3. Gross Profit Analysis.   Actual and budget data for 19— for the Carver Distributing Company are:

	Product A	*Product B*	*Total*
Actual sales...............	60,000 units × $1.00	20,000 units × $2.00	$100,000
Actual cost of goods sold...	60,000 units × .80	20,000 units × 1.85	85,000
Budgeted sales............	50,000 units × 1.25	35,000 units × 2.50	150,000
Budgeted cost of goods sold	50,000 units × 1.00	35,000 units × 2.00	120,000

Required: (1) The computations of the following variances: (a) sales price; (b) sales volume; (c) cost price; (d) cost volume.
(2) An analysis of the total volume variance into the sales mix and final sales volume variances.

4. Gross Profit Analysis.   Bates Brothers Clothiers handles two lines of men's suits — The Bostonian and The Varsity.   For the years 19A and 19B, Sam Bates, the store owner and manager, realized a gross profit of $159,300 and $159,570, respectively.   He was puzzled because the dollar sales volume and number of suits sold was higher for 19B than for 19A yet the gross profit had remained about the same.
The firm's accounting records provided the following detailed information:

Year	*The Bostonian*			*The Varsity*		
	Suits	*Cost*	*Sales Price*	*Suits*	*Cost*	*Sales Price*
19A............	1,650	$105	$175	1,460	$70	$100
19B............	1,320	114	190	1,975	80	110

Required: (1) The price and volume variances for sales and cost.
(2) An analysis of the total volume variance into the sales mix and final sales volume variances. (Compute the 19A average gross profit to 1/10th of 1¢.)

5. Gross Profit Analysis. The controller of Lowell Municipal Hospital prepared the following statement of operations, comparing the years 19B to 19A.

	19B	19A
Inpatient service days........................	330,000	300,000
Patient service revenues......................	$13,860,000	$12,000,000
Cost of services rendered:		
Medicinals, linens, & other supplies...........	$ 1,400,000	$ 1,000,000
Salaries — nurses, interns, residents, staff......	9,000,000	7,500,000
Patient service overhead....................	1,500,000	1,500,000
Total cost of services rendered.............	$11,900,000	$10,000,000
Gross profit................................	$ 1,960,000	$ 2,000,000
Administrative expenses....................	2,013,000	1,800,000
Excess of revenues over expenditures...........	$ (53,000)	$ 200,000

Required: An analysis of the comparative statement of operations, listing the causes of the 19B excess of expenditures over revenues and the causes of the decline since 19A.

6. Gross Profit Analysis. Operating profits of the Volrath Manufacturing Company for the years ending December 31, 19A and 19B, were as follows:

	Year Ending December 31	
Particulars	19A	19B
Net sales..	$482,961	$679,241
Cost of goods sold	434,665	503,645
Gross profit	$ 48,296	$175,596
General expenses............................	76,258	89,533
Net operating profit (loss)......................	$(27,962)	$ 86,063

At the end of 19A the management became convinced that an increase in the selling price of the product was necessary if future losses were to be avoided. Accordingly, a general increase of 15% was made on all selling prices, effective January 1, 19B. At the same time a new plant manager was installed who gave much of his attention during the year to reducing plant costs.

When the results for the year 19B became available, a dispute arose between the plant manager and the vice-president in charge of sales. Both believed that the increase in profits during 19B was due principally to the increase of 15% in selling prices, but the plant manager insisted that savings in factory costs were greater in amount than the increase in gross profits due to the increased volume of sales (i.e., increased quantity of goods sold as distinct from the increase in selling prices) while the vice-president was equally insistent that the opposite was the case.

Required: An analysis accounting for the real reasons for the increase in gross profit.

7. Gross Profit Analysis. The 19A income statement of the Royer Corporation showed:

Sales (90,500 units)................	$760,200
Cost of goods sold.................	452,500
Gross profit.......................	$307,700

For 19B the management forecasts a sales volume of 100,000 units at a sales price of $8.20 per unit. For this range of activity, variable costs are estimated to be $4.80 per unit. No fixed costs are included in the cost of goods sold.

Required: An analysis of the variation in gross profit between the two years indicating the effects of changes in sales prices, sales volume, and unit costs.

(AICPA adapted)

PROBLEMS

21-1. Gross Profit Analysis. The Chapeau Company manufactures both men's and women's hats. The traditional selling price for men's hats has been $8 per hat, whereas women's hats have sold for $7. The president was very pleased with the performance of his company in 19A which, summarized, was as follows:

Gross sales (43,000 hats)............	$325,000	
Cost of goods sold.................	200,000	
Gross profit.......................	$125,000	(38%)

The president felt that 38% gross profit was satisfactory; and, since the 43,000 hats sold was an increase of 8,000 over the previous year, he felt that the company was enjoying a healthy growth.

The sales manager happily informed the president that expected sales for 19B were 45,000 hats. Based on this estimate, the controller submitted the following budget for 19B to the president:

	Sales Units	Sales Amount	Cost	Gross Profit
Men's hats...........	30,000	$240,000	$132,000	$108,000
Women's hats........	15,000	105,000	84,000	21,000
Total.............	45,000	$345,000	$216,000	$129,000

The president noted that this was an increase of $4,000 gross profit over last year with the gross profit percentage remaining virtually unchanged.

At the end of 19B, actual results revealed that the expected 45,000 hats were sold, but gross profit declined $35,000 instead of increasing $4,000. The results were as follows:

	Sales Units	Sales Amount	Cost	Gross Profit
Men's hats...........	25,000	$187,500	$112,500	$75,000
Women's hats........	20,000	135,000	120,000	15,000
Total.............	45,000	$322,500	$232,500	$90,000

The president, furious with the results and the apparently erroneous forecast, summoned his staff for a conference and demanded an explanation. The sales manager was quick to defend his position, pointing out that his department met the sales quota of 45,000 hats and therefore was not to blame. He accused the controller of allowing costs to get out of hand.

The controller, realizing he was not entirely to blame, explained that he was not responsible for forecasting price changes when such changes are brought about by competition. He also pointed out that a substantial portion of the error was due to the sales manager's inability to maintain sales of the more profitable men's hat line at the level estimated.

In order to settle the dispute, the president asked the controller to prepare a complete analysis of the $39,000 variance from budgeted gross profit, along with suggestions to correct the situation.

Required: The information requested in the preceding paragraph.

21-2. Gross Profit Analysis.   The Shell-Macke Mining Company mines SLEMAC, a commonly used mineral. For the years 19A and 19B the company's comparative report of operations showed:

	19A	19B	Increase (Decrease)
Net sales..........................	$ 840,000	$ 891,000	$ 51,000
Cost of goods sold................	945,000	688,500	(256,500)
Gross profit (loss).................	$(105,000)	$ 202,500	$ 307,500

Additional information:
  (a) On January 1, 19B SLEMAC's sales price was increased from $8 to $11 per ton.
  (b) On the same day, new machinery was placed in operation which reduced the cost of mining from $9 to $8.50 per ton.
  (c) Ending inventories, costed on the lifo basis, did not change.

Required: A gross profit analysis accounting for the effects of the changes in price, volume, and price-volume factors upon (1) sales and (2) cost of goods sold.

(AICPA adapted)

21-3. Gross Profit Analysis.   The president of the Normolle Manufacturing Company, which manufactures only one product, requests an analysis of the causes of change in gross profit.

An investigation reveals the following information:

	19B		19A	
	Amount	Per Unit	Amount	Per Unit
Sales..............	$122,400	$10.20	$100,000	$10.00
Cost of goods sold..	70,080	5.84	60,000	6.00
Gross profit........	$ 52,320	$ 4.36	$ 40,000	$ 4.00

Required: A detailed analysis of the causes for the change in gross profit.

(AICPA adapted)

21-4. Final Sales Volume and Sales Mix Variances Using Contribution Margin. The Arsco Co. makes three grades of indoor-outdoor carpets. The sales volume for the annual budget is determined by estimating the total market volume for indoor-outdoor carpet and then by applying the company's prior year market share, adjusted for planned changes due to company programs for the coming year.   The volume is apportioned between the three grades based upon the prior year's product mix, again adjusted for planned changes due to company programs for the coming year.

Given below are the company's budgeted income statement for 19— and the results of operations for 19—.

19— INCOME STATEMENT (BUDGETED)

	Grade 1	Grade 2	Grade 3	Total
Sales units............	1,000 rolls	1,000 rolls	2,000 rolls	4,000 rolls
Sales dollars				
(000 omitted).......	$1,000	$2,000	$3,000	$6,000
Variable expenses.....	700	1,600	2,300	4,600
Contribution margin..	$ 300	$ 400	$ 700	$1,400
Traceable fixed				
expenses..........	200	200	300	700
Traceable margin.....	$ 100	$ 200	$ 400	$ 700
Marketing and administrative				
expenses...				250
Net operating profit..				$ 450

19— INCOME STATEMENT (ACTUAL)

	Grade 1	Grade 2	Grade 3	Total
Sales units...........	800 rolls	1,000 rolls	2,100 rolls	3,900 rolls
Sales dollars				
(000 omitted).......	$810	$2,000	$3,000	$5,810
Variable expenses.....	560	1,610	2,320	4,490
Contribution margin..	$250	$ 390	$ 680	$1,320
Traceable fixed				
expenses..........	210	220	315	745
Traceable margin.....	$ 40	$ 170	$ 365	$ 575
Marketing and administrative				
expenses...				275
Net operating profit..				$ 300

Industry volume was estimated at 40,000 rolls for budgeting purposes. Actual industry volume for 19— was 38,000 rolls.

Required: (1) The profit impact of the final sales volume variance for 19—, using budgeted contribution margins.

(2) The portion of the variance, if any, to be attributed to the present condition of the carpet industry.

(3) The dollar impact on profits (using budgeted contribution margins) of the shift in product mix from the budgeted mix.

(NAA adapted)

21-5. Estimated Gross Profit. Kelco Co. produces one principal product. The income from sales of this product for the year 19A is expected to be $200,000. Cost of goods sold will be as follows:

Materials used..........................	$40,000
Direct labor.............................	60,000
Fixed overhead..........................	20,000
Variable overhead.......................	30,000

The company realizes that it faces rising costs and in December is attempting to plan its operations for the year 19B. It is believed that if the product is not redesigned, the following changes in operations will result: materials prices will average 5% higher; rates for direct labor will average 10% higher; variable overhead will vary in proportion to direct labor costs; if sales price is increased to produce the same rate of gross profit as the 19A rate, there will be a 10% decrease in the number of units sold in 19B.

If the product is redesigned according to suggestions offered by the sales manager, it is expected that a 10% increase can be obtained in the number of units sold with a 15% increase in sales price per unit. However, change in the product would involve several changes in cost; i.e., a different grade of material would be used, and 10% more of it would be required for each unit. The price of this proposed grade of material has averaged 5% below the price of the material now being used, and that 5% difference in price is expected to continue for the year 19B. Redesign would permit a change in processing methods enabling the company to use fewer skilled workers. It is believed that the average pay rate for 19B would be 10% below the average for 19A due to that change. However, about 20% more labor per unit would be required than was needed in 19A. Variable overhead is incurred directly in relation to production. It is expected to increase 10% because of price changes and to increase an additional amount in proportion to the change in labor hours.

Required: (1) A statement showing the estimated gross profit if the same product is continued for 19B.

(2) A statement showing the estimated gross profit if the product is redesigned for 19B.

(AICPA adapted)

CASES

A. Gross Profit Analysis of Time-Sharing Computer Programs. The senior systems analyst of Sweetenall, Inc., Bob Canedy, developed in his spare time three unique packages of computer programs: Package 1, Inventory Control; Package 2, Sales Analysis; Package 3, Report Preparation. After realizing their marketability, he struck out on his own, forming Data-Pack Co., a computer time-sharing service bureau. He rented an adequate computer and leased some data communication lines and terminals, then placed his packages on-line. Once operational, he planned to sell the use of his packages to industrial customers by the system-connect-hour; i.e., total time elapsing while customer's terminal is directly connected to the central computer.

In the process of establishing profitable selling prices, Bob decided to project his costs for the first year. Using processing information provided by the computer salesman, Bob allocated total costs to the packages as follows:

| Package | Computer Rental ($56,000) | | Other Common Costs ($14,000) | | Weighted Average [4 × Col. (1)] + Col. (2) ÷ 5 | Common Costs Allocation | Trace-able Costs | Total Costs |
	Core Requisitions (000 Bits)	% of Total Core Requisitions (1)	CPU* Hrs. ÷ System Connect Hrs.	% of Total CPU to System Connect Hrs. (2)				
1	80	60	.18	10	50%	$35,000	$10,000	$ 45,000
2	33	25	.90	50	30%	21,000	14,000	35,000
3	20	15	.72	40	20%	14,000	6,000	20,000
Total	133	100	1.80	100	100%	$70,000	$30,000	$100,000

*CPU denotes Central Processing Unit.

Working from his expected costs, Bob computed his desired markup for each of the packages. Since he knew that the useful lives of the programs were only a few years, he decided to recoup the investment in time that he had spent on developing the programs by using that criterion in computing a selling price, as follows:

Package	Man-Days Spent in Developing Programs	% of Total Development (3)	Projected Sales (Hrs.)	Hourly Costs (per Unit) (4)	Unit Markup [Col. (3) × Col. (4)]	Unit Sales Price	Total Sales (Hrs. × Sales Price)
1	27	15	900	$50	$ 7.50	$57.50	$ 51,750
2	108	60	1,000	35	21.00	56.00	56,000
3	45	25	500	40	10.00	50.00	25,000
Total	180	100	2,400				$132,750

After the first year of operation, Data-Pack's income statement appeared as follows:

Sales:

```
Package 1: 1,200 hrs. @ $53.....................  $63,600
Package 2:   900 hrs. @ $58.....................   52,200
Package 3:   700 hrs. @ $46.....................   32,200    $148,000
```

Less cost of goods sold:

	Common Costs	Traceable Costs	Total Costs	
Package 1......	$40,000	$14,000	$54,000	
Package 2......	24,000	12,000	36,000	
Package 3......	16,000	5,000	21,000	111,000

Net operating profit. . . . . $ 37,000

Bob was pleased that his new firm had exceeded planned profits by $4,250. However, it was evident that changes in demand for the packages and changes in costs and selling prices had made this "gain" only coincidental.

Required: A gross profit analysis to determine the effects of demand and fluctuating prices on sales revenue so that a new price for the really profitable package can be established.

B. Comparative Income Statement and Profit Analysis. The Navasota Manufacturing Company wishes an analysis of the comparative income statements for 19A and 19B shown below:

	19B	*19A*
Gross sales.....................................	$12,000,000	$8,750,000
Less allowances and adjustments..............	1,500,000	500,000
Net sales.....................................	$10,500,000	$8,250,000
Cost of goods sold:		
Raw materials (special)......................	$ 4,000,000	$2,100,000
Materials (other)............................	800,000	300,000
Direct labor.................................	4,800,000	2,700,000
Indirect factory overhead....................	400,000	150,000
Depreciation.................................	1,200,000	1,200,000
	$11,200,000	$6,450,000
Add beginning finished goods inventory.........	2,200,000	1,000,000
	$13,400,000	$7,450,000
Less ending finished goods inventory...........	6,000,000	2,200,000
Cost of goods sold...........................	$ 7,400,000	$5,250,000
Gross profit.................................	$ 3,100,000	$3,000,000
General, administrative, and marketing expenses...	400,000	250,000
Net operating profit.........................	$ 2,700,000	$2,750,000

The company manufactures one single uniform product for sale in a competitive market.

The management knows that wages have risen in its industry and in its plant by an overall average of about 50% from 19A to 19B. Special raw materials used in the manufacturing process increased approximately 50%, and other costs have risen in varying degrees. However, unit selling prices did not increase in proportion to the costs. Although the number of units sold increased 20% from 250,000 in 19A to 300,000 in 19B, the company did not expect the profit for 19B to be as favorable as the statements indicate because of the adverse conditions stated. However, the operating departments claimed large savings due to technological manufacturing improvements and the shifting of supervisors and personnel.

The management is faced with the necessity of making important decisions with respect to the payment of dividends, the adjustment of executives' compensation, and a program of plant expansion. Although the income statement indicates a favorable profit before taxes, the company's cash position is not strong. The management, being at a loss to understand the apparent contradictions presented by the increased costs and the results shown by the statements, has requested an analysis of the statements and an examination of the factors for the profit of 19B, assuming for the purpose of comparison that the year 19A was a normal one for the company. It is requested that the analysis indicate to what extent each factor influences the profit.

In addition to the above, the following information is available:

	19B	*19A*
Beginning finished goods inventory.......	100,000 units	50,000 units
Ending finished goods inventory.........	200,000 units	100,000 units
Production............................	400,000 units	300,000 units
Direct labor man hours.................	2,845,000 hours	2,400,000 hours

Special raw materials used:	*Net Tons*	*Amount*
19A Gross weight...................	2,000	$2,600,000
Scrap recovered...............	500	500,000
Net weight used...............	1,500	$2,100,000
19B Gross weight...................	2,300	$4,450,000
Scrap recovered...............	300	450,000
Net weight used...............	2,000	$4,000,000

Depreciation was computed on a straight-line basis.

The company maintains a simple process cost system. Inventories are priced at moving average costs computed monthly; that is, the cost used for inventory pricing at the end of any month is computed at the average of the beginning inventory and the cost of production for the month. It was noted that costs for the latter months of 19B were considerably higher than for the early months of the year as increased labor and materials costs became effective.

In-process inventories are not a factor in the foregoing statements.

Required: (1) An analysis showing the factors responsible for the 19B gross and net profits as compared with the 19A gross and net profits.

(2) An analysis of the extent to which the operating department has effected savings in labor and raw materials costs.

CHAPTER 22

DIRECT COSTING AND
THE CONTRIBUTION MARGIN

The factory overhead chapters presented the use of the factory overhead rate for product costing and pricing. The method combined all factory overhead costs, fixed and variable, into a composite rate. At the time the rate is constructed, a capacity, volume, or activity level must be decided upon so that all costs and expenses can be expected to be recovered over a certain period of time. This type of costing, known as *absorption*, *full*, or *conventional costing*, assigns direct materials and direct labor costs and a share of both fixed and variable factory overhead to units of production.

At the end of each month or year, differences between actual and applied overhead resulting from the use of a predetermined overhead rate are considered to be the over- or underapplied factory overhead and when expensed cause fluctuations in the unit product costs. Fixed costs included in over- or underapplied factory overhead contribute to the unit product cost fluctuations. Realizing the influence of fixed expenses upon production costs, inventory values, and operating income, factory overhead is divided into fixed and variable elements.

THE NATURE OF ABSORPTION COSTING

In *responsibility accounting* this division permits management to place cost accountability on those individuals responsible for the incurrence of these costs. The factory overhead rate used for product costing still includes both variable and fixed elements.

In *standard cost accounting* a dual factory overhead rate, one for variable cost and one for fixed cost, can be employed. The rate is still on the absorption costing basis; however, the unit standard as to fixed cost with its overhead based on standard volume will remain stable, and the *standard* cost of goods sold will generally be proportional to sales volume.

When a short-run standard volume is compared with the long-run or normal capacity concept of the standard cost system, a difference is calculated: (1) volume variance or (2) idle capacity and fixed efficiency variances. If it could be expected that such favorable or unfavorable variances would balance out in the long run, they could be deferred and the fixed costs included in the periodic cost of goods sold would vary directly and proportionately with sales volume. In the above cases, the fixed overhead in its *long-run*, normal capacity concept behaves like the unit variable cost. However, if variances are expensed each period, fluctuations in the unit product cost occur. The unit product cost will also fluctuate in cases in which the capacity level used to calculate the factory overhead rate is different from one period to the next, because the fixed part of the rate will be higher when a lower capacity level is used and lower when a higher level is used. Failure to use a predetermined factory overhead rate also causes even wider unit product cost fluctuations because fixed factory overhead is then allocated to production based on the actual activity level for the accounting period.

Information accumulated in NAA research studies over a period of years indicates that the concept of long-range normal or standard unit cost for costing production, sales, and inventory is not often applied in practice. The reasons given for the failure to carry out theory based on the long-run concept of cost are:

1. Long-range normal or standard volume cannot be reliably determined. First, this is a consequence of the fact that long-range volume for a growing company with indefinite future life cannot be defined in concrete terms capable of being implemented by measurement techniques. Second, long-range forecasts of future volume have, at best, a wide and unknown margin of error.

2. The services of manufacturing facilities and organization tend to expire with the passage of time whether or not utilized to produce salable goods. Consequently, the period costs of these services also expire with time. To carry such costs forward to future periods results in mismatching of costs with revenues because no benefits from such costs will be received in the future and nothing is contributed by the costs toward production of future revenues. Thus, the practice of charging unabsorbed period cost against revenues of the current period has been justified by reasoning that this charge measures cost of idle capacity and not cost of production. Similarly, apportionment of large over-absorbed balances reflects the opinion that unit production costs based on standard volume have been overstated.[1]

---

[1]"Current Applications of Direct Costing," *NAA Research Report No. 37*, pp. 72–73.

The foregoing examination, the NAA study concludes, indicates that "the concept of long-run unit cost of production is unsatisfactory in measuring short-period income. The fault in this case is that the wrong cost concept was chosen for the purpose — i.e., the long-run concept of cost was used to measure short-run operations."[2]

It has been pointed out repeatedly that the normal capacity concept used for establishing overhead rates is long-range in nature. Business-persons, on the other hand, want monthly — and even weekly — earnings reports. They want to know what was earned last month. They do not ask for a profit figure covering the firm's entire production and sales cycle. Although the usefulness of costing methods for managerial purposes has been aided immeasurably through the use of factory overhead rates and flexible budgets, management always asks for more direct and understandable answers. Direct costing seeks to satisfy these demands.

DIRECT COSTING DEFINED

Direct costing charges the products with only those costs that vary directly with volume. Only prime costs (direct materials and direct labor) plus variable factory overhead expenses are used to assign costs to inventories — both work in process and finished goods — and to determine the cost of goods sold. Variable or direct costs such as direct materials, direct labor, and variable factory overhead are examples of costs chargeable to the product. Costs such as straight-line or accelerated depreciation, insurance, and factory and property taxes that are a function of time rather than of production are excluded from the cost of the product. Also excluded are salaries of the executive and managerial staff, as well as those of supervisors, foremen, and office and sales employees. Wages of certain factory employees, such as maintenance crews, guards, etc., are also considered period costs rather than product costs.

FACETS OF DIRECT COSTING

Direct costing focuses attention upon the product and its costs. This interest moves in two directions: (1) to external financial reporting, costing of inventories, income determination, and financial reporting and (2) to internal uses of the fixed-variable cost relationship and the contribution margin concept. The internal uses deal with the application of direct costing in profit planning, pricing decisions, in other phases of decision making, and in cost control. Diagrammatically, direct costing can be presented as illustrated on page 681.

---

[2]*Ibid.*, p. 73.

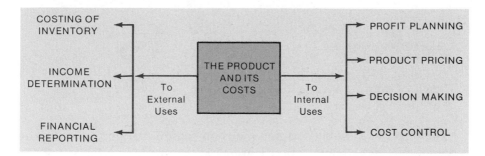

Facets of Direct Costing

INTERNAL USES OF DIRECT COSTING

Top management, marketing executives, production managers, and cost analysts have generally praised the planning, control, and analytical potentialities of the direct costing method. Absorption costing obscures the true relationship between prices, costs, and volume due to the behavior of fixed costs when calculated on a unit cost basis. Direct unit costs remain constant for various volumes of production and sales as does contribution margin per unit. A net income per unit is not calculated; only a net income on total sales of all products is determined.

Direct Costing as a Profit-Planning Tool. *Profit planning*, often called planning budget or plan of operations, is a management plan covering all phases of future operations to attain a stated profit goal. Such a plan includes long- and short-range planning. Direct costing is quite useful in planning for short periods, in pricing special orders, or in making current operating decisions. With its separation of variable (product) and fixed (period) costs and the calculation of the contribution margin figure, direct costing facilitates any analysis of the cost-volume-profit relationship.

The break-even analysis, the rate of return on investment, the contribution margin by a segment of total sales, and the total profit from all operations based on a given volume are planning problems that can be solved with the aid of a direct costing structure. It should be noted that a company's accounting staff should, and most likely will, have used these analytical tools even before the upsurge of direct costing; but direct costing facilitates the identification of relevant analytical data.

The profit-planning potential of direct costing is illustrated in the summary on page 682. These figures are based on the assumption that total variable costs are perfectly variable, with the unit variable cost remaining at the $42 figure, and that fixed costs are perfectly fixed in total. Such assumptions make for quick profit approximations as distinguished from detailed budget calculations.

Item	Per Unit	Total	Percentage of Sales
Sales (10,000 units).................	$70	$700,000	100
Less variable costs.................	42	420,000	60
Contribution margin................	$28	$280,000	40
Less fixed costs.....................		175,000	25
Net operating income...............		$105,000	15

The direct or variable cost and the contribution margin (sales revenue — variable costs = contribution margin) allow quick and fairly reliable decisions in short-run profit planning. In such situations, it is assumed that the change or shift of a small segment within the total volume does not require major changes in capacity, which means in fixed costs. Generally, total period costs are subtracted from the contribution margin figure to arrive at net operating income. Period costs that are specific or relevant to a product, a product line, or any segment of the business should be isolated and attached to the product in order to increase the usefulness of these costs for decision-making purposes.

Direct costing's variable and fixed costs aid management further in planning and evaluating the profit resulting from a change of volume, a change in the sales mix, in make-or-buy situations, and in the acquisition of new equipment. A knowledge of the variable or out-of-pocket costs, fixed costs, and the contribution margin provides guidelines for the selection of the most profitable products, customers, territories, and other segments of the entire business. These uses are discussed in later chapters.

Direct Costing as a Guide to Product Pricing. The contribution margin approach to costing, pricing, and planning receives increased attention by economists, business managers, and accountants. The economist uses the term "monopolistic competition," a hybrid of pure competition and monopoly. This monopolistic competition creates a market which has certain characteristics: (1) many firms sell the same or similar products, differentiated only by name, by real or alleged quality, or by service, rather than by price; (2) a firm cannot change the price without considering the reactions of its competitors; and (3) a firm has little difficulty entering or leaving the market. These characteristics are typical for most company situations. How do these features of monopolistic competition affect pricing and costing methods?

Contribution margin, or as the economist calls it, "marginal income," is the result of subtracting variable costs from sales revenues. The best or optimum price is that which will yield the maximum excess of total revenues over total cost. The volume at which the increase in total cost due to the addition of one more unit of volume is just equal to the increase in total revenue, or a zero increase in total profit, is the optimum volume.

The price at which this volume can be obtained is the optimum price. A higher price will lower the quantity demanded and decrease total profit. A lower price may increase the quantity sold and lead, conceivably, to abnormal manufacturing costs because of production inefficiencies by requiring production during overtime, again decreasing total profit.

Management's thinking is generally in terms of the contribution margin, or the direct costing approach. In a highly competitive market, prices might be regulated through supply and demand, but to what extent? Management, it is contended, has little or no influence on demand which rests with the consumer. However, it can certainly regulate supply; and, indeed, the stimulation of demand is not always beyond management's influence.

In multiproduct pricing, management needs to know whether each product can be priced competitively in the industry and still contribute sufficiently to the contribution margin for fixed cost recovery and profit. The useful part of a unit cost is the direct cost segment, for it consists of those cost elements that are comparable among firms in the same industry.

A long-run pricing policy should, however, make use of a full product cost; i.e., a product cost which includes that portion of fixed (capacity) costs instrumental in the manufacturing process. (Other pricing methods are presented in Chapter 27.)

Acceptance of direct costing by each business manager should be on the basis of simplicity and better presentation of relevant cost information for managerial uses rather than on defects of absorption costing or allegations as to its failures.

Direct Costing for Managerial Decision Making. Installation of a direct costing system requires a study of cost trends and a segregation of fixed and variable costs. The identification and classification of costs as either fixed or variable, with semivariable expenses properly subdivided into their fixed and variable components, provide a framework for the accumulation and analysis of costs. This also provides a basis for the study of contemplated changes in production levels or proposed actions concerning new markets, plant expansion or contraction, or special promotional activities. Of course, it is important to recognize that a study of cost behavior which identifies fixed and variable costs can be accomplished without the use of a formal direct costing system.

The NAA Research Report No. 37 summarizes its findings on this phase of direct costing as follows:

> Companies participating in this study generally feel that direct costing's major field of usefulness is in forecasting and reporting income for internal management purposes. The distinctive feature of direct costing which makes it useful for this purpose is the manner in which costs are matched with revenues.

The marginal income (contribution margin) figure, which results from the first step in matching costs and revenues in the direct costing income statement, is reported to be a particularly useful figure to management because it can be readily projected to measure increments in net income which accompany increments in sales. The theory underlying this observed usefulness of the marginal income figure in decision making rests upon the fact that, within a limited volume range, period costs tend to remain constant in total when volume changes occur. Under such conditions, only the direct costs are relevant in costing increments in volume.

The tendency of net income to fluctuate directly with sales volume was reported to be an important practical advantage possessed by the direct costing approach to income determination because it enables management to trace changes in sales to their consequence in net income. Another advantage attributed to the direct costing income statement was that management has a better understanding of the impact that period costs have on profits when such costs are brought together in a single group.[3]

Direct Costing as a Control Tool. The direct costing procedure is said to be the product of an allegedly incomprehensible income statement prepared for management. The possible inverse fluctuations of production costs and sales figures due to over- or underabsorbed factory overhead require a different type of costing procedure. By adopting direct costing, management and marketing management in particular believe that a more meaningful and understandable income statement can be furnished by the accountant. But is the new type of income statement merely to serve the marketing department? Reports issued should serve all divisions of an enterprise. It seems appropriate, therefore, also to prepare reports for all departments or responsibility centers based on standard costs, flexible budgets, and a division of all costs into their fixed and variable components, the latter being considered fundamental in direct costing.

The marketing manager would receive a statement that places sales and production costs in direct relationship to one another. Differences between intended sales and actual sales caused by changes in sales price, sales volume, or sales mix, which are the direct responsibility of the marketing manager and his organization, are detailed for their analysis (as discussed in Chapter 21).

Other managers can examine and interpret their reports with respect to the cost variances originating in their respective areas of responsibility. The production manager is able to study the materials quantity variance, the labor efficiency variance, and the controllable overhead variance. Variable expenses actually incurred can be analyzed by comparing them with the allowable budget figure for work performed. The purchasing agent or manager evaluates the purchase price variance. The personnel manager can be held accountable for labor rate variances. General management which originally authorized and approved plant capacity

---

[3]*Ibid.*, pp. 84–85.

in the form of men and machines is primarily responsible for any fixed overhead variances arising because of lower or higher utilization of existing facilities.   No variances should result in direct costing with respect to fixed expenses, since all fixed costs are charged against revenue instead of to the product; i.e., to inventories.

Reports constructed on the direct costing basis and augmented by the additional information described become valuable control tools. A profit-responsible management group is continually reminded of the original profit objective for the period. Subsequent approved deviations from the objective are revaluated in light of the current performance. Accounting by organizational lines makes it possible to direct attention to the appropriate responsibility. Performance is no longer evaluated on the basis of last month or last year, for now each period has its own standard.

EXTERNAL USES OF DIRECT COSTING

The proponents of direct costing believe that the separation of fixed and variable expenses, and the accounting for each according to some direct costing plan, will simplify both the understanding of the income statement and the assignment of costs to inventories.

The Chart of Accounts Modified for Recording and Reporting Purposes. To keep fixed overhead out of the product costs, variable and fixed expenses should be channeled into separate accounts. For this reason, it is suggested that the chart of accounts be expanded so that every natural expense classification has two accounts — one for the variable and one for the fixed portion of the expense. Also, instead of one overhead control account, two have to be used: Factory Overhead Control — Variable Expenses and Factory Overhead Control — Fixed Expenses.   When variable expenses are charged to work in process using an overhead rate, the credit is to an applied overhead account now labeled Variable Factory Overhead Applied. Differences between actual and applied variable overhead constitute (1) controllable or (2) the spending and variable efficiency variances when a standard cost system is used and a spending variance when standard costing is not used. Because fixed expenses are not charged to work in process, they are excluded from the predetermined overhead rate. The total fixed expenses accumulated in the account Factory Overhead Control — Fixed Expenses are charged directly to Income Summary.

Effects of Direct Costing and Absorption Costing on Inventories and Operating Profits. The following information is used to illustrate and compare the effects of absorption costing and direct costing on gross profit, inventory costing, and net operating income.

The normal capacity of a plant is 20,000 units per month, or 240,000 units a year.   Variable costs per unit are: direct materials, $3; direct labor, $2.25; and variable factory overhead, $.75 — a total of $6.   Fixed factory overhead is $300,000 per year, $25,000 per month, or $1.25 per unit at normal capacity.   The units of production basis is used for applying overhead.   Fixed marketing and administrative expenses are $5,000 per month, or $60,000 a year; and variable marketing and administrative expenses are $3,400, $3,600, $4,000, and $3,000 for the first, second, third, and fourth months, respectively.

Actual variable factory overhead is not given. The assumption is made that actual and applied variable overhead are the same; otherwise, variable overhead variances could be computed. Likewise, no materials or labor variances are assumed. All these variances would be the same in either the absorption costing method or the direct costing method.

Actual production, sales, and finished goods inventories in units are:

	First Month	Second Month	Third Month	Fourth Month
Units in beginning inventory.......			3,000	1,000
Units produced...................	17,500	21,000	19,000	20,000
Units sold.......................	17,500	18,000	21,000	16,500
Units in ending inventory..........		3,000	1,000	4,500

Sales price per unit: $10

The illustrations assume no work in process inventory.

Illustration I — Absorption Costing.   In absorption costing fixed factory overhead is included in the unit cost and also in the costs assigned to inventory.

	First Month	Second Month	Third Month	Fourth Month
Sales..............................	$175,000	$180,000	$210,000	$165,000
Direct materials......................	$ 52,500	$ 63,000	$ 57,000	$ 60,000
Direct labor.........................	39,375	47,250	42,750	45,000
Variable factory overhead..............	13,125	15,750	14,250	15,000
Fixed factory overhead................	21,875	26,250	23,750	25,000
Cost of goods manufactured...........	$126,875	$152,250	$137,750	$145,000
Beginning inventory...................			21,750	7,250
Cost of goods available for sale.........	$126,875	$152,250	$159,500	$152,250
Ending inventory.....................		21,750	7,250	32,625
Cost of goods sold....................	$126,875	$130,500	$152,250	$119,625
Fixed (over-) or underapplied factory overhead	3,125	(1,250)	1,250	
Cost of goods sold at actual...........	$130,000	$129,250	$153,500	$119,625
Gross profit on sales.................	$ 45,000	$ 50,750	$ 56,500	$ 45,375
Marketing and administrative expenses..	8,400	8,600	9,000	8,000
Net operating income for the month....	$ 36,600	$ 42,150	$ 47,500	$ 37,375

Illustration II—Direct Costing. In direct costing fixed factory overhead is excluded from the unit cost and from the costs assigned to inventory.

	First Month	*Second Month*	*Third Month*	*Fourth Month*
Sales.................................	$175,000	$180,000	$210,000	$165,000
Direct materials.......................	$ 52,500	$ 63,000	$ 57,000	$ 60,000
Direct labor..........................	39,375	47,250	42,750	45,000
Variable factory overhead..............	13,125	15,750	14,250	15,000
Variable cost of goods manufactured....	$105,000	$126,000	$114,000	$120,000
Beginning inventory....................			18,000	6,000
Variable cost of goods available for sale.	$105,000	$126,000	$132,000	$126,000
Ending inventory......................		18,000	6,000	27,000
Variable cost of goods sold............	$105,000	$108,000	$126,000	$ 99,000
Gross contribution margin.............	$ 70,000	$ 72,000	$ 84,000	$ 66,000
Variable marketing and administrative expenses..........................	3,400	3,600	4,000	3,000
Contribution margin...................	$ 66,600	$ 68,400	$ 80,000	$ 63,000
Less fixed expenses:				
Factory overhead....................	$ 25,000	$ 25,000	$ 25,000	$ 25,000
Marketing and administrative expenses.	5,000	5,000	5,000	5,000
Total fixed expenses...................	$ 30,000	$ 30,000	$ 30,000	$ 30,000
Net operating income for the month......	$ 36,600	$ 38,400	$ 50,000	$ 33,000

The above example assigned standard costs to inventory — in this case to finished goods only. Should work in process inventories be present, they would be treated in the same manner. If standard costs are not used, then an assumption as to flow of costs must be followed; e.g., average, fifo, lifo, etc.

COMPARISON OF ABSORPTION COSTING WITH DIRECT COSTING

The illustrations show three specific differences between absorption costing and direct costing: (1) gross profit vs. gross contribution margin, (2) costs assigned to inventory, and (3) net operating income.

Gross Profit vs. Gross Contribution Margin. The inclusion or exclusion of fixed expenses from inventories and cost of goods sold causes the gross profit to vary considerably from the gross contribution margin. The gross contribution margin (sales revenue — variable manufacturing costs) in direct costing is greater than the gross profit in absorption costing. This difference has resulted in some criticism of direct costing. It is argued that a greater gross contribution margin might mislead the marketing department into asking for lower prices or demanding higher bonuses or benefits. In defense of direct costing, it is well to recognize the fact that selling prices and bonuses are in most cases not based on gross profit but on net income. This net income will be the same in each method when no inventories exist or when no change in total cost assigned to inventory occurs from the beginning to the end of the period. Although the two illustrations were on a monthly basis, they could just as well have been quarterly or annual. The shorter period is chosen to indicate more forcefully the effects of each method.

As explained previously, managers favor direct costing because sales figures guide cost figures. Variable cost of goods sold varies directly with sales volume. The influence of production on profit is eliminated. The idea of "selling overhead to inventories" might sound plausible and appear pleasing at first; but when the prior month's inventories become this month's opening inventories, the apparent advantages cancel out. The results of the second month with absorption costing offer a good example of the effects of large production with cost being deferred in inventories into the next period. Illustration I (absorption costing) also demonstrates the effect of expensing the fixed over- or underapplied factory overhead resulting from production fluctuations.

Costs Assigned to Inventory. Changes brought about in inventory costing have been the main point of attack by opponents of direct costing. The illustrations show the following ending inventories:

	First Month	Second Month	Third Month	Fourth Month
Absorption costing..................	$ -0-	$21,750	$7,250	$32,625
Direct costing.....................	-0-	18,000	6,000	27,000
Differences.......................	$ -0-	$ 3,750	$1,250	$ 5,625

Differences are caused by the elimination of fixed manufacturing expenses from inventories in direct costing. In absorption costing, these fixed expenses are included as they form part of the predetermined factory overhead rate. The exclusion of this overhead from inventories and its offsetting effect on periodic income determination has been particularly criticized.

The Position of the American Institute of Certified Public Accountants (AICPA). The AICPA's position toward direct costing for external reporting is almost wholly unfavorable. The basis for this position is Accounting Research Bulletin No. 43, issued by the AICPA. Its "Inventory Pricing" chapter begins by stressing that "a major objective of accounting for inventories is the proper determination of income through the process of matching appropriate costs against revenues."

The Bulletin continues by stating that "the primary basis of accounting for inventories is cost, which has been defined generally as the price paid or consideration given to acquire an asset. As applied to inventories, cost means in principle the sum of the applicable expenditures and charges directly or indirectly incurred in bringing an article to its existing condition and location." In discussing the second point, the Bulletin states quite emphatically that "it should also be recognized that the exclusion of all overheads from inventory costs does not constitute an accepted accounting procedure." This last statement seems to apply to direct costing. Proponents of direct costing might, however, argue that while the exclusion of all overhead is not acceptable, by inference the exclusion of some is acceptable. This argument might sound true, but it does not seem to have any bearing on the Institute's acceptance of direct costing since in an earlier discussion of *cost* the Bulletin states that "under some circumstances, items such as idle facility expense, excessive spoilage, double freight, and rehandling costs may be so abnormal as to require treatment as current period charges rather than as a portion of the inventory cost." This appears to be the type of overhead that the AICPA recognizes as excludable from inventories.

There is nothing to date indicating that the Financial Accounting Standards Board (an independent private sector body, which in 1973 began its work of promulgating accounting standards) will take a position on direct costing contrary to that of the AICPA.

Research studies conducted by the National Association of Accountants and the Financial Executives Research Foundation indicate that an ever-increasing number of companies use direct costing for internal responsibility reporting while others use it for profit planning, short-range price setting, and management control. It should be noted that the management services divisions of CPA firms have been extremely active in installing direct costing systems for internal management purposes. The auditors of these firms adjust the year-end figures for income tax returns and external reporting in harmony with the requirements of the Internal Revenue Service (IRS) and the Securities and Exchange Commission (SEC).

Internal Revenue Service (IRS) Regulations. The IRS refuses to accept annual financial reports prepared on the basis of the direct costing method. Section 471 of the Internal Revenue Code provides two tests to which "each inventory must conform: (1) it must conform as nearly as possible to the best accounting practice in the trade or business and (2) it must clearly reflect income." The regulations, however, also provide that consistency in inventory practice be given greater weight than is given to any particular method of inventory costing so long as the method used is in accord with the regulations. The regulations define inventory cost in the case of merchandise produced to be "(1) the cost of raw materials and supplies entering into or consumed in connection with the product, (2) expenditures for direct labor, and (3) indirect expenses incident to and necessary for the production of the particular article, including in such indirect production costs an appropriate portion of management expenses." A 1973 amendment to Section 471 specifically identifies the direct costing method as "not in accord with the regulations."

The Position of the Securities and Exchange Commission (SEC). The SEC, like the IRS, refuses to accept annual financial reports prepared on the basis of the direct costing method. This refusal on the part of the SEC is generally the result of (1) its policy to favor consistency among reporting companies as far as possible and (2) its attitude that direct costing is not generally accepted accounting procedure. In filing reports with the SEC, a firm that uses direct costing must adjust its inventories and reported net income to what they would have been had absorption costing been used.

Net Operating Income. The difference in net operating income between absorption costing and direct costing is attributable to the fixed cost charged to inventory as illustrated below. The data are from Illustrations I and II on pages 686 and 687.

	First Month	Second Month	Third Month	Fourth Month
Illustration I — Absorption Costing:				
Net operating income for the month.....	$36,600	$42,150	$47,500	$37,375
Illustration II — Direct Costing:				
Net operating income for the month.....	36,600	38,400	50,000	33,000
Difference............................	$ -0-	$ 3,750	$(2,500)	$ 4,375
Illustration I — Absorption Costing:				
Inventory change (ending less beginning inventory) increase (decrease)..........	$ -0-	$21,750	$(14,500)	$25,375
Illustration II — Direct Costing:				
Inventory change (ending less beginning inventory) increase (decrease)..........	-0-	18,000	(12,000)	21,000
Difference (inventory change in units × fixed portion of overhead rate $1.25)..........	$ -0-	$ 3,750	$(2,500)	$ 4,375

The inventory change in this illustration is for finished goods only; however, if there were work in process inventories, they too would be included in inventory change in order to reconcile the difference in net operating income. Also, any over- or underapplied fixed factory overhead deferred on the balance sheet rather than being currently expensed would be a reconciling item in explaining the difference in net operating income.

It has been observed that the amount of fixed cost charged to inventory is affected not only by the quantities produced but by the inventory costing method employed — a fact which is largely overlooked. The authors believe that a statement like "When production exceeds sales (i.e., in-process and finished inventories increasing), absorption costing shows a higher profit than does direct costing; or when sales exceed production (i.e., in-process and finished inventories decreasing), absorption costing shows a lower profit than does direct costing"[4] is, although often correct, not universally valid. The authors' analysis presents the differences in net operating income under absorption costing and direct costing in relation to four methods of inventory costing — average costing, fifo, lifo, and standard costing. They show that the usual generalizations about full and direct costing hold only under the lifo and the standard costing methods; however, under the fifo and the average costing methods, the results are more complex than those considered by the usual generalizations which therefore do not apply.

ADJUSTMENT OF DIRECT COSTING FIGURES FOR EXTERNAL REPORTING

As long as the AICPA, the IRS, and the SEC do not accept the direct costing procedure for external reporting purposes, some reconciliation to results obtained by the absorption costing method seems to be the only solution for a company using direct costing. The differences between the net operating income figures of each method are reconciled on page 690. As previously noted, net operating income differences are identical with the differences in costs assigned to inventory caused by the inclusion or exclusion of fixed expenses.

Company practice indicates that comparatively simple procedures are employed to determine the amount of periodic adjustment. According to the NAA Research Report No. 37, one company reports that at the end of each year period manufacturing costs are divided by actual production to create a costing rate which is applied to the units on hand. Another company expresses period expenses as a rate per dollar of direct labor and direct expenses at normal volume. The dollar amount of direct labor and direct expenses in the year-end inventory is then multiplied by the foregoing rate to arrive at the period expense component of the closing inventory.

---

[4]Yuji Ijiri, Robert K. Jaedicke, and John L. Livingstone, "The Effect of Inventory Costing Methods on Full and Direct Costing," *Journal of Accounting Research*, Vol. 3, No. 1, pp. 63–74.

A third company allocates all manufacturing overhead to production departments with the result that period manufacturing cost is collected in seven major pools corresponding to the company's major product lines. However, the period costs are not allocated to individual products within product lines. At the end of each month, period cost is transferred from inventory to cost of sales on the basis of the relative amounts of direct cost in production and sales. Since the amount of period cost associated with the several product lines varies widely, it is thought desirable to make the segregation by product lines for external reporting purposes.[5]

DISCUSSION QUESTIONS

1. Differentiate between direct costs or expenses and direct costing.

2. Differentiate between differential costs and direct costing.

3. How does underapplied factory overhead come into existence?

4. Distinguish between period costs and product costs.

5. Why does the direct costing theorist state that fixed manufacturing costs are not to be included in inventories?

6. Why should the chart of accounts be expanded when direct costing is used?

7. Has the Internal Revenue Service approved direct costing for tax purposes? Explain.

8. A manufacturing concern follows the practice of charging the cost of direct materials and direct labor to Work in Process but charges off all indirect costs (factory overhead) directly to Income Summary. State the effects of this procedure on the concern's financial statements and comment on the acceptability of the procedure for use in preparing financial statements.

(AICPA adapted)

9. Why is it said that an income statement prepared by the direct costing procedure is more helpful to management than an income statement prepared by the absorption costing method?

10. In the process of determining a proper sales price, what kind of cost figures are likely to be most helpful?

11. A speaker remarked recently that even though direct costing has attractive merits, there are certain items that should be considered before converting the present system. What hidden dangers are present in direct costing?

12. Supporters of direct costing have contended that it provides management with more useful accounting information. Critics of direct costing believe that its negative features outweigh its positive attributes.

(a) Describe direct costing. How does it differ from conventional absorption costing?

---

[5]"Current Applications of Direct Costing," *NAA Research Report No. 37*, pp. 94-95.

(b) List the arguments for and against the use of direct costing.

(c) Indicate how each of the following conditions would affect the amounts of net income reported under conventional absorption costing and direct costing, assuming a standard costing system is used.

(1) Sales and production are in balance at standard volume.
(2) Sales exceed production.
(3) Production exceeds sales.

(AICPA adapted)

13. Select the correct answer for each of the following statements.

(a) A basic cost accounting method in which the fixed factory overhead is added to inventory is (1) absorption costing; (2) direct costing; (3) variable costing; (4) process costing.

(b) Reporting under the direct costing concept is accomplished by (1) including only direct costs in the income statement; (2) matching variable costs against revenues and treating fixed costs as period costs; (3) treating all costs as period costs; (4) eliminating the work in process inventory account.

(c) Income computed by the absorption costing method will tend to exceed income computed by the direct costing method if (1) units produced exceed units sold; (2) variable manufacturing costs decrease; (3) units sold exceed units produced; (4) fixed manufacturing costs decrease.

(d) When a firm uses direct costing, (1) the cost of a unit of product changes because of changes in number of units manufactured; (2) profits fluctuate with sales; (3) an idle capacity variation is calculated by a direct costing system; (4) product costs include variable administrative costs; (5) none of the above.

(e) When a firm prepares financial reports by using absorption costing, it may find that (1) profits will always increase with increases in sales; (2) profits will always decrease with decreases in sales; (3) profits may decrease with increased sales even if there is no change in selling prices and costs; (4) decreased output and constant sales result in increased profits; (5) none of the above.

(f) Under the direct costing concept, unit product cost would most likely be increased by (1) a decrease in the remaining useful life of factory machinery depreciated on the units-of-production method; (2) a decrease in the number of units produced; (3) an increase in the remaining useful life of factory machinery depreciated on the sum-of-the-years'-digits method; (4) an increase in the commission paid to salesmen for each unit sold.

(g) Absorption costing differs from direct costing in the (1) fact that standard costs can be used with absorption costing but not with direct costing; (2) kinds of activities for which each can be used to report; (3) amount of costs assigned to individual units of product; (4) amount of fixed costs that will be incurred.

(AICPA and NAA adapted)

EXERCISES

1. Inventory Costs — Absorption Costing vs. Direct Costing. As part of its investigation regarding the possible adoption of direct costing, the management of the Garcia Company asks the controller what effect the adoption of such procedures would have on inventories. In developing the answer to this question, the following figures, representing operations for the past year, are used:

> Units produced — 50,000, of which 15,000 were not sold
> Direct materials.......................... $200,000
> Direct labor............................   260,000
>
> Factory overhead:
>   Variable expenses......................   150,000
>   Fixed expenses........................   75,000

Required: (1) The cost to be assigned the 15,000 units in inventory using absorption costing.

(2) The cost to be assigned the 15,000 units in inventory using direct costing.

2. Income Statements — Absorption Costing vs. Direct Costing. The Levine Corporation produced 24,000 units (normal capacity) of product during the first quarter of 19—. 20,000 units were sold @ $22 per unit. Cost of this production was:

> Materials................................ $ 60,000
> Direct labor............................   60,000
>
> Factory overhead:
>   Variable costs........................   120,000
>   Fixed costs...........................   96,000

Marketing and administrative expenses for the quarter total $70,000; all are fixed expenses.

Required: (1) An income statement using absorption costing.

(2) An income statement using direct costing.

3. Comparative Income Statement — Absorption Costing vs. Direct Costing. On April 1 Evergreen Lawn Sprinklers, Inc. began production of a new model. During April and May the company produced 7,000 units each month; 6,000 units were sold in April and 7,500 units in May. The sales price is $10 per sprinkler. Direct materials cost is $3 per unit, and direct labor cost is $4 per unit. At the 7,000 unit operating level variable factory overhead is charged to production at $1 per unit and the fixed factory overhead at $.60 per unit. There was no over- or underapplied factory overhead in either month. Marketing and administrative expenses were $5,000 each month. There were no work in process inventories.

Required: Comparative income statements for April and May using (a) the absorption costing method and (b) the direct costing method.

4. Direct Costing Statements; Gross Profit Analysis. The Duro-Auto Seat Cover Corporation manufactures one style of automobile seat covers for mail order houses.

The following information was received by management covering the past three months:

	January	February	March
Sales (at $10 per unit).....................	$5,000	$2,000	$20,000
Beginning inventory......................	—0—	$2,500	$ 6,500
Cost of goods manufactured in month.....	$5,000	5,000	5,000
Cost of goods available for sale...........	$5,000	$7,500	$11,500
Ending inventory........................	2,500	6,500	1,500
Cost of goods sold......................	$2,500	$1,000	$10,000
Gross profit............................	$2,500	$1,000	$10,000

Supplementary information:

Sales price per unit: $10
Units manufactured per month: 1,000
Standard cost per unit at normal volume: $5

Total manufacturing costs:
Variable................$3,000
Fixed.................. 2,000

The Cost Department believes that perhaps a direct standard costing system may be more helpful for management purposes than the standard absorption system presently in use.

Required: (1) Income statements for each of the three months on the direct standard cost basis.

(2) Computations explaining the differences in gross profit for each month.

5. Comparison of Absorption Costing with Direct Costing. Landon, Inc. produced 15,000 units of its product in 19— and sold 10,000 of these units. Actual production costs were:

Direct labor........................... $90,000
Direct materials....................... 60,000
Variable factory overhead............... 30,000
Fixed factory overhead................. 50,000

Assume the following:

(a) Anticipated labor cost is $6 per unit; direct labor cost is used as a basis for applying overhead.
(b) $120,000 direct labor is used in determining the factory overhead rate. At that level the fixed cost is estimated to be $50,000 and the variable cost $40,000.
(c) Under- or overabsorbed factory overhead is closed to Cost of Goods Sold at the end of the year.

Required: (1) Assuming that the company uses a predetermined factory overhead rate based on absorption costing, compute the (a) factory overhead rate, (b) factory overhead applied to production for the period, (c) total cost of goods sold, and (d) ending inventory.

(2) Assuming that the company had used direct costing, compute the (a) ending inventory and (b) cost of goods sold. Fixed factory overhead is not closed to the cost of goods sold account.

6. Absorption Costing vs. Direct Costing; Income Statements. The following data pertain to the operations of the McGreevey Manufacturing Company for the year 19—:

> Sales in kilograms: 75,000
> Finished goods inventory, January 1, 19—: 12,000 kilograms
> Finished goods inventory, December 31, 19—: 17,000 kilograms
> Sales price: $10
>
> Manufacturing costs:
>   Variable costs per kilogram of production: $4
>   Fixed factory overhead: $160,000 (normal capacity: 80,000 kilograms)
>
> Marketing and administrative expenses:
>   Variable cost per kilogram of sales: $1
>   Fixed marketing and administrative expenses: $150,000

A standard costing system is used.

Required: (1) Income statement for 19— under the (a) absorption costing method and (b) direct costing method.
(2) An accounting for the difference in net operating income under the two concepts.

7. Direct Costing Statements; Analysis of Profit Differences. The Travis Manufacturing Company's Cost Department prepares quarterly income statements based on absorption costing. For the last two quarters of last year and the first quarter of this year, the following income statements were sent to management:

INCOME STATEMENTS

	3rd quarter	4th quarter	1st quarter
Sales ($20 per unit).................	$1,600,000	$1,600,000	$1,600,000
Cost of goods sold (at standard).......	$1,200,000	$1,200,000	$1,200,000
Fixed marketing and administrative expenses.....................	250,000	250,000	250,000
Factory overhead volume variance.....	100,000	250,000	(50,000)
Total costs........................	$1,550,000	$1,700,000	$1,400,000
Net operating income (loss)...........	$ 50,000	$ (100,000)	$ 200,000

Other cost, sales, and production data are:

(a) Beginning inventory, 3rd quarter.............   40,000 units
(b) Standard variable manufacturing costs........   50% of sales price
(c) Normal sales demand......................   100,000 units per quarter
(d) Standard productive capacity utilization.......   100,000 units per quarter
(e) Actual sales and production in the three quarters:

Quarters	Sales	Production
Third	80% of normal	80% of normal
Fourth	80% of normal	50% of normal
First	80% of normal	110% of normal

Required: (1) Income statements for the three quarters based on direct costing procedures.

(2) An explanation for the differences in net operating income for each quarter.

8. Income Statements — Absorption Costing vs. Direct Costing; Analysis of Profit Differences. The following annual flexible budget has been prepared by Accuro, Inc. for use in making decisions relating to its Product X.

FLEXIBLE BUDGET — PRODUCT X

	100,000 Units	*150,000 Units*	*200,000 Units*
Sales volume......................	$800,000	$1,200,000	$1,600,000
Manufacturing costs:			
Variable.........................	$300,000	$ 450,000	$ 600,000
Fixed............................	200,000	200,000	200,000
Total manufacturing costs..........	$500,000	$ 650,000	$ 800,000
Marketing and other expenses:			
Variable.........................	$200,000	$ 300,000	$ 400,000
Fixed............................	160,000	160,000	160,000
Total marketing and other expenses.	$360,000	$ 460,000	$ 560,000
Net operating income (loss)...........	$ (60,000)	$ 90,000	$ 240,000

The 200,000 unit budget has been adopted and will be used for allocating fixed manufacturing costs to units of Product X. At the end of the first six months, the following information is available:

	Units
Production completed.....................................	120,000
Sales (at $8 per unit).....................................	60,000

All fixed costs are budgeted and incurred uniformly throughout the year, and all costs incurred coincide with the budget.

Over- and underapplied fixed manufacturing costs are deferred on the balance sheet until the end of the year.

Required: (1) The amount of fixed manufacturing costs applied to production during the first six months under absorption costing.

(2) In income statement format (including ending inventory), (a) the net operating income (loss) for the first six months under absorption costing; (b) the net operating income (loss) for the first six months under direct costing.

(3) Computations explaining the difference in net operating income (loss).

(AICPA adapted)

PROBLEMS

22-1. Income Statements — Absorption Costing vs. Direct Costing. The controller of the Shriver Manufacturing Company has been encountering considerable difficulties explaining to management the fluctuations in profits resulting from differences between the volume of sales and the volume of production within an accounting period. Management tends to think of profits as being directly related to the volume of sales and therefore finds it confusing when this month's sales are higher than last month's, yet profits are lower because of underabsorbed fixed overhead.

To demonstrate the results more forcefully, the controller prepared the following data applicable to each four-month period:

Standard production volume.......................... 50,000 units
Selling price....................................... $2.50 per unit
Standard variable costs at standard volume.............. $50,000
Standard fixed overhead............................. 25,000

Results:

	Jan. 1 — April 30	May 1 — Aug. 31	Sept. 1 — Dec. 31
Actual sales.............	40,000 units	50,000 units	60,000 units
Actual production........	60,000 units	40,000 units	50,000 units

Actual costs equal standard costs in all situations.

Required: Income statements using direct costing and absorption costing for each of the three periods.

22-2. Unit Product Costs and Comparative Gross Profit Statements Based on Absorption Costing and Direct Costing.

The Accounting Department of the Hinckley Corporation gathered the following cost and other data:

Plant's normal annual activity: 40,000 direct labor hours
Annual total fixed manufacturing costs: $60,000
Hours required to produce a unit of product: 5
Direct materials and direct labor cost per unit of product: $28
Variable factory overhead per unit of product: $5 (5 hrs. @ $1 per hour)
Selling price per unit of product: $45

Required: (1) Using the plant's normal activity level as the base, the total manufacturing costs per unit of product based on (a) absorption costing and (b) direct costing.

(2) Comparative gross profit statements using (a) absorption costing and (b) direct costing, based on the following four situations:

Year	Produced	Sold
1st	8,000 units	7,000 units
2nd	10,000 units	6,000 units
3rd	7,000 units	7,000 units
4th	4,000 units	9,000 units

22-3. Absorption Costing vs. Direct Costing.

The management of the Topping Co. has been investigating the use of direct costing procedures in lieu of its present conventional system. Instructions have been issued to the controller to advise management regarding the results of such a change. The controller's personnel assigned to this task gathered the following information:

Normal plant capacity.......... 150,000 units or 300,000 direct labor hours
Direct materials cost at standard........................... $ 4 per unit
Direct labor cost, $3 per hour, 2 hours per unit.............. 6 per unit
Variable factory overhead, $2 per hour...................... 4 per unit
Total variable manufacturing cost........................... $14 per unit

Fixed factory overhead........................ $300,000 per year
Variable marketing and administrative expenses..... $2.80 per unit sold
Fixed marketing and administrative expenses........ $180,000 per year
Unit sales price..................................... $24

Actual sales and production results are:

Sales.......................	160,000 units
Production..................	140,000 units
Opening inventory...........	25,000 units (priced at standard costs based on absorption costing)

Unfavorable variances:

Labor efficiency variance.....................................	$13,500
Controllable variance..	9,200

Favorable variance:

Direct materials price variance.............................	8,800

All variances are written off to Cost of Goods Sold.

Required: (1) Income statements using (a) absorption costing and (b) direct costing.

(2) An explanation of the difference in net income under the two methods.

(3) The effect on retained earnings if the company decides to convert to direct costing as of the beginning of the year covered by the above data.

22-4. Direct Costing Statement with Variance Analysis. The Holland Manufacturing Company operates a direct costing system. For the month of March the following costs, sales, and other data are available:

Production and sales data:

Units started...	1,000
Units completed.......................................	900
Units in process, all materials, 50% labor and overhead.....	100
Units sold..	800
Sales price per unit.....................................	$150

Standard variable unit product cost:

Direct materials..	$10
Direct labor (5 hrs. × $4)...............................	20
Variable factory overhead (5 hrs. × $1)....................	5
Total variable manufacturing cost.........................	$35
Variable product marketing expenses (10% of sales price).....	15
Total direct variable cost................................	$50

Cost data for the month of March:

	Standard	Actual
Variable factory overhead.....................	$ 5,000*	$ 5,400
Fixed factory overhead........................	15,000	15,000
Fixed marketing expenses.....................	20,000	20,000
Fixed administrative expenses.................	30,000	30,000
Labor hours in operations completed...........		5,075 hrs.
Direct labor used............................		$20,550
Direct materials used.........................		9,600

*For normal capacity of 1,000 units.

Required: (1) An income statement based on direct costing, including *net* variances for the direct costs of manufacturing and marketing.

(2) The cost of the ending inventories for work in process and finished goods, based on absorption costing in a standard cost system.

22-5. Comparative Statement of Cost of Goods Sold; Variance Analysis. The standard cost card of the product MOLEN of the Molenger Manufacturing Company shows the following details:

Direct materials, 4 units of OLME @ $2 unit......................	$ 8
Direct labor, 2 hours per finished product...........................	9
Factory overhead, $3 per direct labor hour.........................	6
Total manufacturing cost..	$23

The $3 factory overhead rate is based on $120,000 fixed cost and a $2 variable rate per direct labor hour.

Molenger's Cost Department reports that a process cost system with the fifo method for work in process inventory is used and that the following inventory, cost, and production data were experienced during the year:

Units in process:

> January 1:   2,000 units, all materials, 50% processed
> December 31: 1,000 units, all materials, 50% processed

Other data:

> Finished goods, January 1, 1,000 units; December 31, 1,500 units
> Materials put in process: 260,000 units of OLME
> Actual factory overhead: $398,700, including an increase of $15,000 in fixed overhead during the year. 66,000 units of MOLEN were transferred to the warehouse.

The company's management stated that the present absorption standard cost system should be changed to a direct standard cost system. Variable cost variances are to be charged or credited to Cost of Goods Sold.

Required: A comparative cost of goods sold statement, using absorption standard costing and direct standard costing.

22-6. Entries Based on Absorption Costing and Direct Costing. Ono Company uses a standard cost accounting system based on the absorption costing theory. The company manufactures one product, the standard cost of which is:

Direct materials gross weight allowed.......	4 1/6 lbs.	@ $1.92 =	$ 8.00
Allowance for inherent loss (4%).........	1/6 lb.		
Weight of finished product...............	4 lbs.		
Direct labor...........................	3 hours	@ $1.80 =	5.40
Factory overhead......................	3 hours	@ $2.00 =	6.00
Total standard cost per unit of product......................			$19.40

In developing the 19— budget and standards, company officials planned to produce 41,000 units of product requiring 123,000 standard direct labor hours in 246 operating days. The annual factory overhead was analyzed as follows:

		Per Hour
Nonvariable with production.....................	$110,700	$ .90
Variable directly with production in labor hours......	135,300	1.10
Total factory overhead for 19—anticipated.........	$246,000	$2.00

The following account balances, among others, are in the general ledger at May 31, 19—. All of the external transactions for May have been journalized and posted as have all accruals, deferrals, and other internal transactions except those relating to Work in Process, Finished Goods, variances, and Cost of Goods Sold.

	Debit	*Credit*
Finished Goods.....................................	$ 48,500	
Work in Process...................................	13,240	
Materials...	74,310	
Sales ($26 per unit)..............................		$421,200
Cost of Goods Sold...............................	238,620	
Direct Labor.....................................	20,160	
Factory Overhead.................................	22,375	
Materials Price Variance..........................	476	
Materials Quantity Variance.......................		960
Direct Labor Rate Variance........................		30
Direct Labor Efficiency Variance...................	180	
Factory Overhead Spending Variance.................	50	
Factory Overhead Efficiency Variance................	200	
Factory Overhead Idle Capacity Variance.............		450

The company carries materials inventory at actual cost and records the variances when charging Work in Process.

Production plans for May called for 11,000 direct labor hours in 22 working days. On this basis, a flexible budget for factory overhead for the month had been drawn as follows:

Fixed overhead (22 days @ $450 per day)*.......................	$ 9,900
Variable overhead (11,000 hours @ $1.10 per hour)...............	12,100
	$22,000

---

*The company divides the total fixed costs by the number of working days in the year and charges overhead each month on the basis of the budgeted number of working days rather than on the basis of $1/12$ of the annual amount.

May production obtained, in terms of complete units, was:

Units in process May 1 (materials complete, 3/4 converted)........	800
Units finished...	3,800
Units in process May 31 (materials complete, 1/2 converted).......	1,000

Direct materials put into production weighed 16,580 lbs. and cost $32,082. Actual direct labor hours totaled 11,200.

Required: (1) Journal entries to complete the general ledger record at May 31, 19—.

(2) Journal entries to complete the general ledger record assuming that the company had been using direct costing instead of absorption costing.

22-7. Income Statements — Absorption and Direct Costing; Profit and Break-Even Analysis. Seiler, Inc. has a maximum productive capacity of 210,000 units per year. Normal capacity is regarded as 180,000 units per year. Standard variable manufacturing costs are $11 per unit. Fixed factory overhead is $360,000 per year. Variable marketing expenses are $3 per unit sold, and fixed marketing expenses are $252,000 per year. The unit sales price is $20.

The operating results for 19— are: sales, 150,000 units; production, 160,000 units; beginning inventory, 10,000 units; and net unfavorable variance for standard variable manufacturing costs, $40,000. All variances are written off as additions to (or deductions from) standard cost of goods sold.

Required: (1) Income statements for 19— under (a) absorption costing and (b) direct costing.

(2) A brief account of the difference in net operating income between the two income statements in (1).

(3) The break-even point expressed in sales dollars.

(4) Units to be sold to earn a net operating income of $60,000 per year.

(5) Units to be sold to earn a net operating income of 10% on sales.

For (3), (4), and (5), assume there are no variances from standards for manufacturing costs. (See Chapters 2 and 24 for a discussion of break-even analysis.)

(AICPA adapted)

22-8. Absorption Costing vs. Direct Costing. Norwood Corporation is considering changing its method of inventory costing from absorption costing to direct costing and wants to determine the effect of the proposed change on its 19— financial statements.

The firm manufactures Gink, which is sold for $20 per unit. A raw material, Marsh, is added before processing starts; and labor and factory overhead are added evenly during the manufacturing process. Production capacity is budgeted at 110,000 units of Gink annually. The standard costs per unit of Gink are:

	Unit Cost
Marsh (2 lbs. @ $1.50 per lb.).........................	$ 3.00
Labor...	6.00
Variable factory overhead..................................	1.00
Fixed factory overhead..................................	1.10
Total unit cost..	$11.10

A process cost system is used employing standard costs. Variances from standard costs are now debited or credited to Cost of Goods Sold. If direct costing were adopted, only variances resulting from variable costs would be debited or credited to Cost of Goods Sold.

Inventory data for 19— are as follows:

	Units	
	January 1	*December 31*
Marsh (lbs.).............................	50,000	40,000
Work in process:		
2/5ths processed.......................	10,000	
1/3d processed.........................		15,000
Finished goods..........................	20,000	12,000

During 19— 220,000 lbs. of Marsh were purchased, and 230,000 lbs. were transferred to work in process inventory. Also, 110,000 units of Gink were transferred to finished goods inventory. Annual fixed factory overhead, budgeted and actual, was $121,000. There were no variances between standard and actual variable costs during the year.

Required: (1) Schedules for the computation of (a) equivalent units of production for materials, labor, and factory overhead for the year 19—; (b) number of units sold during 19—; (c) standard unit costs under direct costing and absorption costing; (d) over- or underapplied fixed factory overhead, if any, for 19—.

(2) A comparative cost of goods sold statement for 19—, using standard direct costing and standard absorption costing.

(AICPA adapted)

22-9. Comparative Income Statements; Income Reconciliation; Direct Costing Advantages and Disadvantages. S. T. Shire Company uses direct costing for its internal management purposes and absorption costing for its external reporting purposes. Thus, at the end of each year, financial data must be converted from direct costing to absorption costing in order to satisfy external requirements.

At the end of 19A, the company anticipated that sales would rise 20% the next year. Therefore, production was increased from 20,000 units to 24,000 units to meet this expected demand. However, economic conditions kept the sales level at 20,000 units for each year.

The following data pertain to 19A and 19B:

	19A	19B
Selling price per unit.................................	$30	$30
Sales (units)..	20,000	20,000
Beginning inventory (units)..........................	2,000	2,000
Production (units)....................................	20,000	24,000
Ending inventory (units).............................	2,000	6,000
Total unfavorable materials, labor, and variable factory overhead variances......................................	$5,000	$4,000

Standard variable costs per unit for 19A and 19B are:

Materials...	$ 4.50
Labor..	7.50
Variable factory overhead.............................	3.00
Total...	$15.00

Annual fixed costs for 19A and 19B (budgeted and actual) are:

Production...	$ 90,000
Marketing and administrative..........................	100,000
Total..	$190,000

The factory overhead rate under absorption costing is based upon practical plant capacity, which is 30,000 units per year. All variances and over- or underabsorbed factory overhead are closed to Cost of Goods Sold. Income taxes are to be ignored.

Required: (1) Income statements for 19B based on (a) direct costing and (b) absorption costing. (The beginning and ending inventories need not be shown on the income statements; i.e., show Cost of Goods Sold as one figure.)

(2) An explanation of the difference, if any, in the net operating income figures and the entry, if necessary, to adjust the book figures to the financial statement figures.

(3) The advantages and disadvantages attributed to direct costing for internal purposes, if the company develops its internal financial data on a direct costing basis.

(4) The arguments for and against the use of direct costing in external reporting. (Many businesspersons believe direct costing is appropriate for external reporting while others oppose its use for this purpose.)

(NAA adapted)

CHAPTER 23

MARKETING COST
AND PROFITABILITY ANALYSIS

.The concept of *marketing* means the matching of a company's products with markets for the satisfaction of customers at a reasonable profit for the firm. Marketing managers, in turn, must decide the (1) product selection, design, color, size, packaging, etc., (2) price(s) to be charged, (3) advertising and promotion needed, and (4) physical distribution to be followed. These numerous decisions require organization, planning, and control. Marketing activities are usually organized by product or brand lines or by territories or districts. The planning and control phases should be based on a well-structured marketing cost and profitability analysis system.

The preparation of and need for budgeting in planning and controlling the marketing activity of a firm is discussed in Chapter 16. At the end of each month, budget reports are issued that indicate the success or failure of holding expenses within budgetary boundaries.

The problems associated with marketing costs do not end with these budgetary procedures. Cost control at the departmental level is the important feature of any cost improvement program. In marketing, which includes selling as well as other marketing-oriented phases of a company, emphasis ordinarily rests on selling rather than on costs. To limit marketing costs unreasonably might lead to a curtailment of sales activities, which in turn could mean the gradual deterioration or elimination of certain types of sales; conversely, indiscriminate and wasteful spending should not be sanctioned.

SCOPE OF MARKETING COSTS

The control and analysis of marketing costs must extend beyond the scope of a departmental budget. This phase of cost accounting calls for the determination of marketing costs for managerial decisions, thereby making it an integral part of business planning and policy formulation.

Management requires meaningful marketing cost information in order to determine and analyze the profitability of (1) a territory or territories; (2) certain classes of customers, such as wholesalers, retailers, institutions, and governmental units; (3) products, product lines, or brands; and (4) promotional efforts by salespersons' calls, telephone, mail, television, radio, etc.

Control and analysis of marketing costs complement each other. Control begins with the assignment of marketing expenses to various costing groups such as territories, customers, and products. However, assigned costs must be controlled through analysis within the jurisdictional function in order to hold each marketing activity to the predetermined profitability level.

Control and analysis are enhanced by (1) predetermining costs allowed for marketing efforts and (2) establishing functional costing rates based on standards and budgets designed to aid in achieving marketing objectives.

Until recently, marketing activities were restricted largely to fulfilling existing demands; today, the scope of marketing has been broadened and expanded in its search for the creation and discovery of new demands for a company's products and services. This new outlook requires the best available working tools for management's use; yet, in many organizations the marketing activity has not always received the management and accounting attention rendered to other business operations. In today's economy, the strategic importance and magnitude of marketing costs are great enough to merit increased attention in every company.

The subject of marketing cost and profitability analysis will be presented under the following topics:

1. Comparison of manufacturing and marketing costs
2. Marketing cost control
3. Control of functional activity by the flexible budget and standards
4. Marketing profitability analysis
5. The contribution margin approach
6. Robinson-Patman Act and marketing cost analysis
7. Illustrative marketing cost and profitability analysis problem

It is important to note that general and administrative expenses and research and development costs for manufacturing as well as other business enterprises should also be planned, analyzed, and controlled. Department stores and other merchandising businesses recognized the functional cost control concept many years ago. The financial success of these firms is in no small measure due to extreme care in controlling and reducing costs on a departmental-functional line basis. In fact, the same concepts and techniques are applicable to these other nonmanufacturing costs experienced in municipal, state, and federal units and agencies and other nonbusiness organizations where functional cost control and analysis are not only possible but, in many instances, positively necessary. For example, municipal functions such as trash collection or street cleaning should be placed on a departmental budget basis with a supervisor responsible for the efficient operation of the function and accountable for the cost control phase within the limits of the budget.

COMPARISON OF MANUFACTURING AND MARKETING COSTS

The control and analysis of marketing costs present certain complexities. First of all, logistic systems are many and varied. Manufacturers of certain products use basically the same raw materials and machinery. However, in marketing a product, the same companies may use vastly different channels of distribution ranging from a direct simplex distribution to a complex marketing system. Promotional efforts may be directed to narrow or broad customer groups. Every phase of the distribution process may differ. Therefore, a meaningful comparison of the marketing costs of one company with another is almost impossible.

Not only do distribution methods vary, but they are also extremely flexible. A company may find that a change in market conditions necessitates a change in its channels of distribution. Its tactics may change several times before the best method is found. Even then, methods are constantly on trial for quick revision or drastic changes. Such changes would be disastrous in production. Once a factory is set up, management is not likely to change its manufacturing techniques to any great extent; therefore, standards once set for a particular machine do not require much revision. However, distribution standards must be revised with every change in the method of distribution.

The psychological factors present in selling a product are perhaps the main reasons for differences between manufacturing and marketing costing. Management can control cost of labor, hours of operation, and number of machines operated; but management cannot tell what the customer will do. Various salespersons may have different effects on the same customer who responds to varying appeals. Customer resistance is the enigma in the problem of marketing cost analysis. The customer is a controlling rather than controllable factor; his wishes and his peculiarities govern the method of doing business.

There is also the attitude of management itself. Although factory managers are eager to measure their accomplishments in terms of reduced cost per unit, most sales managers consider increased sales the yardstick for measuring their efficiency, although they do not always mean greater profits.

Cause and effect, generally obvious in the factory, are not so readily discernible in the marketing processes. For example, many promotional costs are incurred for future results, creating a time lag between cause and effect. Conversely, the effects of manufacturing changes are usually felt quickly; and matching between effort and result usually can be determined. Furthermore, manufacturing results are more readily quantified than are marketing costs. For marketing costs, it is often not so easy to identify quantities or units of activity with the cost incurred and results achieved.

Generally accepted accounting practice does not charge Cost of Goods Sold and ending inventories with marketing and administrative expenses. These and other nonmanufacturing expenses usually fall into the category of period costs, even if variable, and as such are charged off in total at the end of the accounting period. Thus, marketing costs are generally charged against the operations of the accounting period in which they are incurred while production costs are held in inventory until the units are sold. This practice is followed because it is felt that too much uncertainty exists as to the probable results in future periods arising from incurred marketing expenses. Marketing assets (such as delivery trucks) should, of course, be expensed over their useful lives — not when acquired.

In the field of marketing costs, it is more common to speak of marketing cost analysis rather than of marketing cost accounting. A tie-in of marketing costing with the general accounts, desirable as it is, is often not necessary. A rate for charging marketing expenses to operations similar to the factory overhead rate is sometimes employed, but this procedure is not widely used.

Marketing cost control and analysis deals primarily with historical or past costs, dealing chiefly with the evaluation of past performances as related to standards and budgets. In connection with future policies, forecast or predetermined figures are employed. In either case, whether judging past performances or deciding on future activities, the possibility of reducing costs and increasing profits through modern methods applied to the marketing area presents a real challenge to management and the accountant.

The control and analysis of marketing costs should follow these cost control methods that serve factory management so well:

1. Departmentalization of activities or functions
2. Assignment of responsibility for operations
3. Recognition of direct and indirect departmental expenses
4. Separation into fixed and variable expenses
5. Determination and establishment of bases such as direct labor cost, direct labor hours, or machine hours used to apply factory overhead to jobs, products, or processes
6. Comparison of actual with budgeted expenses for a continuous control by responsible department supervisors and foremen
7. Flexible budgets and standard costs

MARKETING COST CONTROL

Functional Classification.   The first step in the control of marketing costs is the classification of natural expenses according to functions or activities. It is essential that each function and its associated expenses be made the responsibility of an individual department head. Marketing functions are of many types, depending on the nature of the business, and its organization, size, and method of operation.

Each function should be a homogeneous unit whose activity can be related to specific items of cost. A function might incur its particular pattern of natural expenses, but most functions will have similar expenses such as salaries, insurance, taxes, heat, light, power, supplies, etc. The chart of accounts should be so designed that each function receives as many of its charges as possible directly instead of through allocations.

Functional classifications of marketing costs might be structured in the following manner:

1. Selling
2. Warehousing
3. Packing and shipping
4. Advertising
5. Credit and collection
6. General accounting (for marketing)

Direct and Indirect Expenses.   Direct expenses are those expenses that can be identified directly with a department, function, or activity, such as the salary of the branch office manager or the depreciation of a delivery truck. Expenses which can be identified with a territory, customer, product, or definite type of sales outlet may also be considered direct costs.

The charging of these direct expenses to various marketing classifications is highly desirable. The chart of accounts with its coding system should be designed to permit the direct assignment of a marketing expense to its point of incurrence.

Marketing expenses have been coded in the 500 series (500–599) in the chart of accounts illustrated in Chapter 4. However, a three-digit number is ordinarily not sufficient to permit the proper assignment of an expense. For this reason, the original number might be expanded as follows:

DIGITS	CODE	CLASSIFICATION
First two digits............	05	Marketing expenses
Third and fourth digits.....	-01-	Primary or natural expense (e.g., Salaries — Sales Supervision)
Fifth and sixth digits.......	-10-	Function or department
Seventh and eighth digits..	-20-	Territories or districts
Ninth and tenth digits......	-30-	Product or product line

The use of a ten-digit code number indicates the great amount of detail required for a meaningful analysis. Electronic data processing equipment permits the use of these and additional code numbers and classifications. Whenever possible or feasible, direct charging of expenses to the various classifications is desirable. Because this method still requires considerable clerical expense, a company may use one of these methods for allocating marketing costs: (1) assigning them to territories, customers, or products as a percentage based on sales, manufacturing cost, or some other basis or (2) creating a standard unit cost for each activity — similar to factory costs.

The assignment of marketing expenses as percentages of sales or manufacturing costs, or on some other basis, does not offer reliable results. The procedure has been used in the past for want of more satisfactory methods. The determination of a functional unit costing rate is a more dependable solution. The charging of marketing expense activities on the basis of a costing rate is a logical extension of widely adopted factory standard costing procedures. Furthermore, the availability of such a rate permits quick and decisive analysis. Actual expenses would be collected in the customary manner, charging them to their departmental and natural expense classifications in a subsidiary ledger controlled by a marketing expenses control account in the general ledger.

Indirect costs are those expenses incurred for the benefit of more than one marketing activity which must be allocated by appropriate bases to the various functions. Expenses of this type include items such as heat, light, maintenance, and sales manager's salary. Because these expenses cannot be assigned directly, they are recorded in total and then allocated to various activities. The apportionment process poses two basic questions:

(1) what bases should be used for the allocation and (2) how far should the allocations be carried out? As a solution to the first, statements and opinions stress the fact that the bases used should be fair and equitable; they should be an ideal combination of efforts expended and benefits reaped. The second question occurs because of doubts raised as to the advantages of full allocation of all indirect expenses. Suggestions have been made that certain expenses should be omitted from the allocation procedure when they are not measurable in relation to the function or activity. This is especially true when benefits are so widely dispersed over many functions that any allocation is a mere guess.

Fixed and Variable Expenses. Representative fixed expenses are salaries of executive and administrative sales staffs; salaries of warehousing, advertising, shipping, billing, and collection departments; and costs of associated permanent facilities, such as rent and depreciation. These fixed costs have also been called capacity costs.

Variable marketing costs include the expenses of handling, warehousing, and shipping that tend to vary with sales volume. They have been referred to as volume costs or as expenses connected with the filling of an order. Another type of variable marketing cost originates in connection with promotional expenses such as salespersons' salaries, travel, and entertainment and some advertising expenses. These expenses are variable — not so much because of a change in sales volume but because of management decisions. In fact, once agreed to by management, these expenses may be fixed — at least for the budget period under consideration.

Management must examine these costs carefully in the planning stage, for sales volume may have little influence upon their behavior. Proper recognition of the fixed-variable cost classification is valuable in connection with managerial decisions dealing with the possible opening or closing of a territory, new methods of packaging goods, servicing different types of outlets, or adding or dropping a product line.

Selection of Bases for the Allocation of Functional Costs. The selection of bases or units of measurement for allocation purposes can be compared with the computation of overhead rates for factory expenses. Factory overhead rates use a base which most definitely expresses the effort connected with the work of the department, such as labor hours, machine hours, or labor dollars. A similar procedure is to divide the total cost of each marketing function by the units of functional service (the base) to obtain the cost per unit.

The selection of bases or units of measurement requires careful thought and analysis, for the degree to which the final rates represent acceptable costs is greatly dependent upon the adequacy of the bases selected. Each function must be examined with respect to that factor which most influences the volume of its work. Because of the varied services rendered by the numerous functions, different bases are used. It is possible, however, to use one basis for two or more functions. Some of the bases are:

FUNCTION	COST ALLOCATION BASES
Selling.....................	Gross sales dollar value of products sold or number of salespersons' calls on customers (based on salespersons' time reports)
Warehousing.............	Size, weight, or number of products shipped or handled
Packing and shipping.....	Number of shipping units, weight, or size of units
Advertising...............	Quantity of product units sold, relative media circulation, cost of space directly assignable, or not related to orders
Credit and collection......	Number of customers' orders, transactions, or invoice lines
General accounting........	Number of customers' orders, transactions, or invoice lines

Determination of Functional Unit Cost. The final step in the entire process is the calculation of the unit cost of the activity by dividing the total cost of the function by the measurement unit or base selected. A vast amount of information must be collected in order to establish a functional unit costing rate. The tedious and voluminous assembly of such underlying information is often the reason for the lack of a marketing cost system. When, as suggested, the system is based on standards, the initial work might be more elaborate. However, once the procedure is established, its actual operation should not only be less expensive, but the value derived should far outweigh any previous expenses incurred in establishing the system.

CONTROLLING FUNCTIONAL ACTIVITY BY USING A FLEXIBLE BUDGET AND STANDARDS

Sales estimates are basically the most important figures in any budget. The accuracy and usefulness of practically all other estimates depend on them. Methods used in determining sales budget estimates are discussed in Chapter 16. Total sales are ordinarily broken down into the various kinds of products to be sold, into monthly or weekly sales, and into sales by salespersons, territories, classes of customers, and methods of distribution. Divisional quotas are useful guides for determining the desirability of cultivating various outlets and for judging the efficiency of sales methods and policies. Budgets are set up to anticipate the amount of functional expenses for the coming period and to compare them with the actual expense. Because of the influence of volume and capacity, a comparison of actual costs with predetermined fixed budget figures does not always give a fair evaluation of the activities of a function; and the use of flexible budgets should be considered for the control of marketing costs.

The flexible budget for a distributive function such as billing might take this form:

FLEXIBLE BUDGET FOR BILLING DEPARTMENT
FOR JULY, 19—

Expenses	Functional Unit — Invoice Line			
	50,000	55,000	60,000	65,000
Clerical salaries................	$ 400	$ 400	$ 400	$ 400
Supervision.....................	300	300	300	300
Depreciation—building..........	75	75	75	75
Depreciation—equipment........	125	125	125	125
Supplies.......................	250	275	300	325
Total........................	$1,150	$1,175	$1,200	$1,225

A standard functional unit cost is then established for each activity or function on the basis of normal capacity. These standard unit costs will furnish bases for comparisons with actual costs, and spending and idle capacity variances can be isolated.

Assuming that 60,000 invoice lines represent normal capacity, the following standard billing rate per invoice line would be computed:

$$\frac{\$1,200}{60,000 \text{ Invoice Lines}} = \$.02 \text{ per Invoice Line}$$

Assuming $900 fixed expenses and $300 variable expenses, the variable portion of the rate is:

$$\frac{\$300}{60,000 \text{ Invoice Lines}} = \$.005 \text{ per Invoice Line}$$

If actual sales required 63,000 invoice lines for a month at a total of $1,250, the computation of the cost variances for billing expenses can be made in a manner similar to that discussed in connection with factory overhead (Chapter 9) and consistent with the basic idea of flexible budgeting.

The computation of the variance for the Billing Department is as follows:

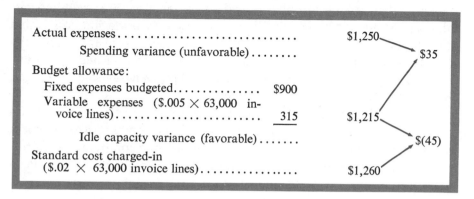

Actual expenses...........................		$1,250
Spending variance (unfavorable)........		$35
Budget allowance:		
Fixed expenses budgeted..............	$900	
Variable expenses ($.005 × 63,000 invoice lines).......................	315	$1,215
Idle capacity variance (favorable).......		$(45)
Standard cost charged-in		
($.02 × 63,000 invoice lines)...............		$1,260

The increased volume leads to a favorable idle capacity variance due to overabsorption of fixed expenses. On the other hand, the supervisor overspent his $1,215 budget allowance by $35.

Journal entries could be made as for factory overhead:

```
Billing Expenses Charged-In............................     1,260
    Applied Billing Expenses...............................          1,260

Actual Billing Expenses..................................     1,250
    Sundry Credits.........................................          1,250

Applied Billing Expenses.................................     1,260
Billing Expenses — Spending Variance.....................        35
    Billing Expenses — Idle Capacity Variance.................              45
    Actual Billing Expenses................................          1,250
```

Accountants usually do not favor carrying this type of variance analysis through ledger accounts. The analysis is usually statistical and is presented to management in report form.

MARKETING PROFITABILITY ANALYSIS

The functional unit costs are used to analyze costs and determine the profitability of territories, customers, products, and salespersons. In most cases a continuous reshuffling or rearranging of expense items is needed to find the required costs and profits. The possibility of improving marketing cost and profitability analysis has been enhanced by the availability of electronic data processing equipment capable of processing the great amount of quantitative detail so characteristic of these analyses.

Analysis by Territories. Analysis by territories is perhaps the simplest. When marketing activities are organized on a territorial basis, each identifiable geographical unit can be charged directly with the expenses incurred within its area — thereby minimizing the proration of expenses. Expenses that can be assigned directly to a territory are: salespersons' salaries, commissions, and traveling expenses; transportation cost within the delivery area; packing and shipping costs; and advertising specifically identified with the territory. Expenses that must be prorated to the territory are: general management, general office, general sales manager, credit and collection, and general accounting.

The identification of expenses by territories can lead to the preparation of the income statement shown below. This comparative statement permits control and analysis of expenses as well as the computation of profit margins. When sales and/or expenses seem to be out of line, management can take corrective action.

INCOME STATEMENT BY TERRITORIES

	Territory		
	No. 1	No. 2	No. 3
Net sales..............................	$210,000	$80,000	$175,000
Cost of goods sold.....................	160,000	60,000	140,000
Gross profit..........................	$ 50,000	$20,000	$ 35,000
Marketing expenses:			
Selling...............................	$ 15,000	$ 8,600	$ 23,900
Warehousing.........................	3,600	1,400	3,100
Packing and shipping.................	1,500	400	1,900
Advertising..........................	2,000	1,000	500
Credit and collection.................	800	250	1,200
General accounting...................	1,200	1,400	1,800
Total marketing expenses..............	$ 24,100	$13,050	$ 32,400
Administrative expenses (equally).......	5,000	5,000	5,000
Total marketing and administrative expenses.........................	$ 29,100	$18,050	$ 37,400
Net income (loss) per territory...........	$ 20,900	$ 1,950	$ (2,400)

Analysis by Customers. Although most marketing costs can be assigned directly to territories, the analysis by customers offers no such easy solution. Relatively few costs can be traced directly to customers. Perhaps transportation and sales discounts can be considered direct, but all other expenses are allocated on the basis of functional unit costing rates.

Allocation and analysis of these costs by customers is normally not made for individual customers. The large number of customers makes such a procedure rather cumbersome if not impossible. For this reason, customers are grouped according to certain characteristics to make the

analysis meaningful. An analysis of customers can be made (1) by territories, (2) by size of average order, (3) by customer-volume groups, or
(4) by kinds of customers.

Analysis of Customers by Territories.   This type of analysis reflects
territorial cost differences due to the customer's proximity to warehouses,
volume of purchases, service requirements, and the kinds of merchandise
bought. These factors can make certain sales profitable or unprofitable.
The analysis would proceed in the same manner outlined for territories
except that the costs would be broken down by customers or kinds of
customers within each territory.

Analysis of Customers by Size of Average Order. The size of a customer's
order is closely related to his profitability or nonprofitability. The analysis
might indicate that a considerable portion of orders comes from customers
who cost the company more in selling to them than the orders are worth
in terms of gross profit. Companies have therefore resorted to setting
minimum dollar values or minimum quantities for orders, thereby reducing the number of transactions and increasing profits. Selective selling
has found much favor among many executives. It requires changing
habits and routines, something which is often difficult to bring about.

In order to present management with a quick view of the situation
regarding size of average order in relation to number of customers, time
spent, and total dollar sales, the chart illustrated below might be helpful.

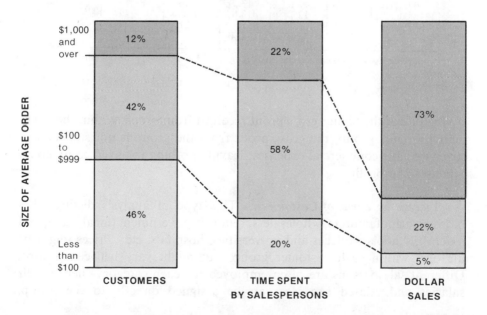

Analysis of Customers by Size of Average Order

Analysis by Customer-Volume Groups. An analysis of customers by customer-volume groups is like that of the size-of-average-order analysis with this exception. Instead of classifying customers by an order's dollar value, the customer-volume group analysis is based on an order's quantity or volume. This type of analysis yields information as to (1) the profitability of various customer-volume groups and (2) the establishment of price differentials. The analysis shown below indicates that only those customers who buy more than 150 units during a week are profitable. Though they represent about 46 percent of the customers, they purchase over 95 percent of the units sold. Sales to these customers provide the profits.

ANALYSIS BY CUSTOMER-VOLUME GROUPS[1]

Customer-Volume Group (Number of Units Purchased During Week)	Customers (% of Total)	Volume (% of Total)	Gross Profit per 100 Units (Dollars)	Variable Commercial Expenses per 100 Units (Dollars)	Net Income* per 100 Units (Dollars)
Customers unsuccessfully solicited......	17.1	....	....	....	....
1–25...............	7.6	0.2	$1.66	$4.01	†$2.35
26–50..............	8.3	0.7	1.38	2.55	† 1.17
51–100.............	12.0	1.9	1.25	1.78	† .53
101–150...........	9.3	2.4	1.26	1.32	† .06
151–200...........	7.8	2.9	1.14	1.13	.01
201–250...........	6.4	3.0	1.12	.95	.17
251–500...........	17.1	13.2	1.06	.75	.31
501–1,000..........	12.7	18.6	1.02	.49	.53
1,001–10,000.......	1.7	57.1	.81	.24	.57
Total............	100.0	100.0	....	....	....

*Gross profit less variable commercial (marketing and administrative) expenses only.
†Loss.

In spite of the higher gross profit received from orders within the lower than 150 units group, the gross profit from the group is not sufficient to cover variable commercial expenses, leaving nothing for fixed commercial expenses and profit.

Analysis by Kinds of Customers. This type of analysis distinguishes between manufacturers, wholesalers, retailers, government (local, state, and federal), schools, colleges and universities, hospitals, etc. Prices might be uniform within each customer group, but might vary between groups. Different salespersons are often employed for each category; hence their salaries and related expenses can be assigned directly to the group.

---

[1]U. S. Department of Commerce, *Economic Series No. 72*, p. 25.

Delivery to such groups might be different; some delivery might be contracted with outside truckers; another might be made by the firm's own trucks. For analytical purposes, revenues and costs should be related to each kind of customer.

Analysis by Products.   Just as customers are grouped by territories, order size, quantity of order, and kinds for purposes of analysis, products sold can be grouped according to product lines possessing common characteristics. The grouping can also be by brands.

With the aid of functional costing rates, a product line (or brand line) income statement can be prepared for the evaluation of profitable and unprofitable product lines.   The statement illustrated below relates the actual contribution of each product line to total profits for the year.

PRODUCT LINE INCOME STATEMENT

(CONTRIBUTION MARGIN APPROACH)

	Total	Product Line 1	Product Line 2	Product Line 3
Net sales......................	$3,100,000	$1,540,000	$1,070,000	$490,000
Less cost of goods sold (variable costs).............	1,927,000	925,000	590,000	412,000
Gross contribution margin........	$1,173,000	$ 615,000	$ 480,000	$ 78,000
Less variable marketing expenses:				
Selling.....................	$ 243,300	$ 112,300	$ 89,000	$ 42,000
Warehousing................	87,100	48,000	27,500	11,600
Packing and shipping.........	66,000	39,000	17,800	9,200
Advertising.................	38,000	20,000	12,000	6,000
Credit and collection.........	19,700	12,300	4,200	3,200
General accounting..........	52,200	23,000	16,800	12,400
Total variable marketing expenses..	$ 506,300	$ 254,600	$ 167,300	$ 84,400
Margin available for fixed expenses and net income (contribution margin)......................	$ 666,700	$ 360,400	$ 312,700	$ (6,400)
Less fixed expenses (manufacturing and nonmanufacturing) directly related to individual product lines...............	120,000	40,000	60,000	20,000
Margin available for common fixed expenses and net income.......	$ 546,700	$ 320,400	$ 252,700	$(26,400)
Less common fixed expenses (manufacturing and nonmanufacturing.................	230,000	N o t	a l l o c a	t e d
Net income before taxes.........	$ 316,700			

Analysis by Salespersons. The selling function in each analysis includes costs such as salespersons' salaries, travel, and other expenses connected with their work. In many instances salespersons' expenses form a substantial part of the total expenses incurred in selling in a territory or to a customer class or product group. The control and analysis of these expenses should, therefore, receive management's closest attention. To achieve this control, performance standards and standard costs should be established. These standards are used not only for the control of costs but also for determining the profitability of sales made by salespersons. Therefore, the discussion is presented in two parts: (1) cost control; (2) profitability analysis.

Cost Control. In the allocation table on page 711, selling expenses are assumed to be allocated on the basis of calls made. A call or visit by a salesperson is usually made for two reasons: to sell and to promote the merchandise or products. The problem is to determine the cost of doing each of these types of work and to compare the actual cost with the standard cost allowed for a call.

A salesperson's call often involves several kinds of work. He not only calls on the customer, but also helps the merchant with the display in the store or window. This practice is common in cosmetic, pharmaceutical, and fast-food businesses. Because the salesperson's time is consumed by such activities, a standard time allowed per call is often very difficult to establish. To obtain the necessary statistics for establishing such standards, and to make comparisons, the salesperson might have to prepare a customer or town report providing information regarding the type of calls made as well as the quantity, type, and dollar value of products sold. This information is the basis for much of the analysis discussed previously.

Profitability Analysis. Having obtained the means of controlling salespersons' activities, it is also possible to analyze sales in relation to profitability. Sales volume alone does not tell the complete story. High volume does not always insure high profit. Sales-mix plays an important part in the final profit. Although a salesperson might wish to follow the line of least resistance, management must strive to sell the merchandise of all product groups, particularly those with the highest profit margins. As sales territories are often planned for sales by product groups, it is necessary that such anticipation be followed up by analyzing the salespersons' efforts. The table on page 719 indicates how such an analysis can be made.

THE CONTRIBUTION MARGIN APPROACH

Generally, the income statement shows a profit figure after all marketing and administrative expenses have been deducted. This total cost and profit approach assigns all the expenses, direct or indirect, fixed or variable, to each segment analyzed. The procedure is commonly used

SALES, COSTS, AND PROFITS BY INDIVIDUAL SALESPERSONS[2]
FOR APRIL, 19—

Col. 1	Col. 2	Col. 3	Col. 4	Col. 5	Col. 6	Col. 7	Col. 8	Col. 9	Col. 10	Col. 11	Col. 12
Sales-person	Ship-ments	% of Quota	Salary and Com-mis-sion	Travel Ex-penses	Cost of Hand-ling	Total Cost (4+5+6)	Gross Profit	Net Income (8−7)	Net Income, % of Sales (9÷2)	Ship-ments, % of Total*	Poten-tial, % of Total*
A	$26,000	80	$2,000	$3,000	$2,340	$ 7,340	$ 7,540	$ 200	0.8	6.7	9.0
B	26,000	122	1,900	1,800	2,340	6,040	7,800	1,760	6.8	6.7	5.5
C	39,000	100	2,800	2,100	3,500	8,400	11,700	3,300	8.5	10.1	10.5
D	22,000	108	1,800	2,000	1,980	5,780	7,050	1,270	5.8	5.8	5.5
E	21,000	110	1,700	1,700	1,890	5,290	6,720	1,430	6.8	5.4	5.0
F	54,000	125	3,500	3,100	5,700	12,300	14,600	2,300	4.3	14.0	10.0
G	21,000	98	1,600	1,200	1,700	4,500	6,720	2,220	10.6	5.5	5.5
H	46,000	101	3,400	1,000	4,100	8,500	13,800	5,300	11.5	12.0	12.0

*For 8 salespersons out of a total of 15 salespersons.

since management is familiar with it and believes that no profit is realized until all expenses, manufacturing and nonmanufacturing, have been recovered.

Marketing cost analysis thus attempts to allocate marketing expenses to territories, customers, products, or salespersons. However, because these marketing costs contain direct and indirect, fixed and variable amounts, allocations are extremely difficult and the end results very doubtful. It has been suggested that only variable manufacturing costs be subtracted from each segment's sales, thus arriving at a figure described as "gross contribution margin." (The conventional income statement deducts *all* manufacturing costs, in arriving at a figure described as "gross profit.") Furthermore, only variable nonmanufacturing expenses would be subtracted from the gross contribution margin of a territory, customer class, product, or salesperson. Fixed expenses would be shown separately and not allocated unless specifically attributable to a segment. Should a territory, customer class, or product group contribute nothing to the recovery of fixed expenses, the situation should be examined and remedial steps taken. The product line income statement on page 717 illustrates this approach. Moreover, in the case of joint costs, variable as well as fixed costs are best viewed as they relate to the contribution made by the group of products or territories rather than based on arbitrary allocations; e.g., to individual products or territories (see "Joint Product Cost Analysis for Managerial Decisions and Profitability Analysis," pages 197–198). The arbitrary nature of joint cost allocations is also a fundamental reason for criticism of proposals to report segment or product-line revenues, costs, and profits in published financial statements.

---

[2]U. S. Department of Commerce, *Economic Series No. 72*, p. 106.

Although sales volume remains the ultimate goal of most sales managers, the trend has been toward a greater recognition of contribution margin as the basis for judging the success and profitability of marketing activities. The increased use of standard production costs has aided the analysis of gross profit as discussed in Chapter 21. Even though a manufacturer might know the production costs, the question remains: "How much can the company afford for marketing costs?" The problem of determining allowable marketing expenses is intensified because once a sales program gets under way, the majority of expenses become fixed costs, at least in the short run.

The analysis discussed here combines the fixed and variable costs of each functional group to arrive at a functional unit costing rate per activity. But the allocation of joint expenses in any type of analysis is often difficult and uncertain. Proponents of the contribution margin approach point out that *only* specific and direct costs, whether variable or fixed, should be assigned to territories, customers, product groups, or salespersons with a clear distinction as to their fixed and variable characteristics. Moreover, for the purpose of identifying costs with responsible managers, it is desirable to identify each reported cost with its controllability by the manager in charge of the reported activity.

The contribution margin approach has influenced the thinking of the volume-minded sales manager or salesperson who must recognize that profit is more beneficial than volume. The contribution margin is a better indicator than sales as to the amount available for recovery of fixed manufacturing costs, fixed marketing and administrative expenses, and a profit.

EFFECT OF THE ROBINSON-PATMAN ACT ON MARKETING COST ANALYSIS

The Robinson-Patman Act of June, 1936 amended Section 2 of the Clayton Act, which was enacted to prevent large buyers from securing excessive advantages over their smaller competitors by virtue of their size and purchasing power. As the Clayton Act prohibited discrimination only where it had a serious effect on competition in general, and as it contained no other provisions for the control of price discrimination, it was felt that an amendment to the Act was needed in order to insure competitive equality of the individual enterprise in face of the threat of bigness to a competitive society. The following clause of the Robinson-Patman Act is of special interest in connection with marketing costs:

To make it unlawful for any person engaged in commerce to discriminate in price or terms of sale between purchasers of commodities of like grades and quality; to prohibit the payment of brokerage or commissions under certain conditions; to suppress pseudo-advertising allowances; to provide a presumptive measure of damages in certain cases; and to protect the independent merchant, the public whom he serves, and the manufacturer who sells him his goods from exploitation by unfair competitors.

The amendment does not imply that price discriminations in the sense of price differentials are entirely prohibited or that a seller is compelled or required to grant any price differential whatever. A vendor may sell to all customers at the same price regardless of differences in the cost of serving them. At the core of the amendment are the provisions that deal with charging different prices to different customers. Differentials granted must not exceed differences in the cost of serving different customers. Cost of serving includes cost of manufacturing, selling, and delivering, which may differ according to methods of selling and quantities sold. The burden of proof is on both the buyer and the seller and requires a definite justification for the discounts granted and received. It is necessary to prove that no discrimination took place with respect to:

1. Price differences
2. Discounts
3. Delivery service
4. Allowances for service

5. Advertising appropriations
6. Brokerage or commissions
7. Consignment policies

These discriminating possibilities fall chiefly into the field of marketing costs. Many interesting problems have arisen and will continue to arise because of the nature of these costs and the numerous variations and combinations in the manner of sale and delivery. As indicated, it is difficult to apply many marketing costs to particular products. Therefore, it is important for concerns performing distribution functions to accumulate cost statistics regarding their marketing costs because the Act makes allowances for differences in costs. The Act has increased the interest in marketing cost analysis and its part in the determination of prices. The cost justification study on the next page serves to illustrate this point.

If a competitor believes that discrimination exists, he must make a complaint substantiated by evidence acquired from published price lists or from other persuasive evidence of this kind. The complaint is valid if all of the following violations have been committed:

1. There must be a price discrimination.
2. The discrimination must be between competitors.
3. The discrimination must be on products of like grades and quality.
4. The discrimination must be in interstate commerce.
5. There must be an injurious effect on competition.

The most effective method for a firm to answer any such complaint is to have a functional unit cost system for marketing costs. In fact, no firm should be placed in a situation of having to make a cost study after the

COST JUSTIFICATION STUDY

A producer of a heavy bulk chemical, which sells f.o.b. point of manufacture at $25 a ton in minimum quantities of a full rail carload (approximately 40 tons), is offered a contract for 500 to 1,000 carloads a year if it will reduce its f.o.b. shipping point price by 6 percent. The producer does not want to reduce the selling price to other customers, to whom annual shipments range from 10 to 200 carloads. The only source of cost differences is sales solicitation and service expense.

The sales manager estimates (since exact records are not available) that salespersons typically pursue the following call schedule:

Customer Size (in Carloads)	Annual Number of Sales Calls
10–40	12
41–80	24
81–150	36
151 and up	50

The sales manager further estimates that each sales call costs approximately $50–$70 regardless of customer size. After questioning, he agrees that study would probably show that calls on large customers (more than 100 carloads) are longer in duration than calls on smaller customers. For study and testing purposes, it was assumed that a call on a small customer costs $60 and a call on a large customer costs $90. The cost-sales relationship illustrated in Exhibit 1 can now be developed.

DIFFERENTIAL COST

LARGE VS. SMALL CUSTOMERS

	Annual Carloads per Customer				
	25	50	100	200	500
Sales value............................	$25,000	$50,000	$100,000	$200,000	$500,000
Number of sales calls................	12	24	36	50	50
Assumed cost per call................	$ 60	$ 60	$ 90	$ 90	$ 90
Assumed cost of call per customer.....	720	1,440	3,240	4,500	4,500
Assumed cost of call as a percent of sales	2.9%	2.9%	3.2%	2.25%	0.9%

Exhibit 1

Since the assumed differential costs are less than the 6 percent proposed discount, it appears obvious that a discount of that magnitude is not susceptible to cost justification. Indeed, it is possible that even a one percent discount to a 500-carload customer might be hard to justify since it is probable that more exact costing would narrow the spread in the percentages among the various classes.[3]

citation. Experience has proven that such belated cost justification studies seldom are successful. Therefore, the firm should (1) establish records

---

[3]Herbert G. Whiting, "Cost Justification of Price Differences," *Management Services*, Vol. 3, No. 4, pp. 31–32.

that show that price differentials are extended only to the extent justified by maximum allowable cost savings and (2) maintain the cost data currently through spot checks conducted periodically to insure that the price differentials are in conformance with current cost conditions. In justifying price differentials, it is important to note that marginal costing can not be utilized; i.e., a plant operating at 80 percent capacity and wishing to add an order to increase its capacity to 90 percent cannot restrict its cost considerations to that incremental element of variable costs due to the volume change.[4] (The reduced cost per unit resulting from the greater volume must be spread over all units.)

In general, the Robinson-Patman Act seems to be working toward greater equity between prices, inasmuch as pricing schedules appear to be more carefully attuned to differences in marketing costs than they were before the enactment of this particular type of control.

The accountant must be prepared to study the subject actively and continuously to help management avoid unintentional price discriminations that might be in violation of the law. The marketing manager must also follow the effect of any pricing policy to determine whether it is profitable and produces the kind of business necessary to the wholesome operation of the enterprise. The problem is one of continuous analysis.

ILLUSTRATIVE PROBLEM IN MARKETING COST AND PROFITABILITY ANALYSIS

The Gardner-Michel Manufacturing & Equipment Co. manufactures and sells a variety of small power tools, dies, drills, files, milling cutters, saws, and other miscellaneous hardware. The company's catalog lists the merchandise under sixteen major classifications. Customers fall into five categories: retail hardware stores, manufacturers, public school systems, municipalities, and public utilities. Territories include New Jersey and Pennsylvania. The company's president believes that in certain areas the cost of marketing the products is too high, that certain customers' orders do not contribute enough to cover fixed costs and earn a profit, and that certain products are being sold to customers and in territories on an unprofitable basis. Therefore, the president has instructed the controller to review the firm's marketing costs and to study the steps, methods, and procedures necessary to provide more accurate information about the profitability of territories, products, and customers.

---

[4]John E. Martin, "Use of Costs for Justifying Price Differentials," *Arthur Andersen Chronicle*, Vol. XXIV, No. 4, pp. 33–40.

The controller has designed and operated a standard marketing cost system which gives management the desired information for the control and analysis of marketing and administrative expenses. The preparation and assembling of statistical and cost data were carried out in the following sequence:

1. Total marketing expenses were estimated (or budgeted).
2. Six marketing functions (selling, warehousing, packing and shipping, advertising, credit and collection, general accounting) were established.
3. Direct or functional (departmental) costs were assigned directly to functions; and indirect expenses were allocated via a measurement unit, such as kilowatt-hour, footage, number of employees, etc.
4. Fixed and variable expenses were determined for each function.
5. Functional unit measurement bases were selected for the purpose of assigning costs to the segments to be analyzed; i.e., territory or product.
6. Functional unit measurements or bases applicable to a territory or a product were determined.
7. Unit standard manufacturing costs and standard product selling prices were established.
8. Data regarding the types and number of units sold in the territories were prepared.
9. Income statements by (a) territories and (b) product lines in one territory were prepared for management.

Exhibit 1 summarizes the results of the study prepared by the controller. Column 1 shows the total budgeted expenses per function. Each total is supported by a budget showing the amount for each individual expense of the function. Columns 2 and 3 place total expenses in a variable and fixed expense classification. Column 4 indicates the functional unit measurement selected as being reliably applicable to that function. Column 5 lists the quantity or value of the measurement unit used to determine the functional unit costing rate. Columns 6, 7, and 8 indicate the variable, fixed, and total functional unit costing rates.

Exhibits 2 and 3 list the details necessary for the preparation of (1) Exhibit 1 and (2) the income statements (Exhibits 4 and 5). To simplify the illustration, nonmanufacturing costs, other than marketing costs, have been excluded.

The product-line income statement for the territory of Pennsylvania (Exhibit 5) indicates that the volume and/or price of Product 1 is not sufficient to result in a profit. This analysis is carried further with the aid of a fixed-variable analysis of manufacturing costs and marketing expenses to determine the contribution made by the product line to the total fixed costs and profit (Exhibit 6). This exhibit assumes the nonexistence of unallocated joint costs, fixed or variable. The product-line income statement on page 717 illustrates a presentation with unallocated costs. Next,

DETERMINATION OF FUNCTIONAL UNIT COSTING RATES

Function	Budgeted Expenses			Functional Unit Measurement Base (4)	Quantity (5)	Functional Unit Costing Rates		
	Total (1)	Variable (2)	Fixed (3)			Variable (6)	Fixed (7)	Total (8)
Selling.............	$ 95,500	$ 38,200	$ 57,300	Gross sales dollar value of product sold	$1,910,000	2%	3%	5%
Warehousing.........	75,000	45,000	30,000	Weight of units shipped	375,000	$ .12	$ .08	$ .20
Packing and shipping.	63,000	37,500	25,500	Quantity product units sold	150,000	.25	.17	.42
Advertising.........	54,000		54,000	Quantity product units sold	150,000		.36	.36
Credit and collection..	28,800	18,720	10,080	Number of customers' orders	7,200	2.60	1.40	4.00
General accounting...	49,200	21,300	27,900	Number of times product items appear on customers' invoices	15,000	1.42	1.86	3.28
Total functional distribution expenses.	$365,500	$160,720	$204,780					

Exhibit 1

DATA CONCERNING PRICE, COST, QUANTITY, WEIGHT, AND TRANSACTIONS OF PRODUCTS

Product Class	Product 1	Product 2	Product 3
Standard product selling price............	$10.00	$15.00	$18.00
Unit standard manufacturing cost.........	8.00	11.00	12.00
Quantity of product units sold............	80,000	50,000	20,000
Weight of units shipped (kilograms).......	2.25 kg.	2.5 kg.	3.5 kg.
Number of times product items appear on customers' invoices..................	6,400	5,700	2,900
Number of customers' orders.............	2,400	3,000	1,800

Exhibit 2

DATA CONCERNING TRANSACTIONS IN TERRITORIES

Territory	Quantity of Products Sold			Number of Times Product Items Appear on Customers' Invoices			Number of Customers' Orders		
	Product 1	Product 2	Product 3	Product 1	Product 2	Product 3	Product 1	Product 2	Product 3
Pennsylvania	55,000	30,000	16,000	4,000	2,900	1,000	1,000	1,900	900
New Jersey	25,000	20,000	4,000	2,400	2,800	1,900	1,400	1,100	900

Exhibit 3

INCOME STATEMENT FOR ALL PRODUCT CLASSES IN THE TWO TERRITORIES

	Total	Territory	
		Pennsylvania	New Jersey
Gross sales.............................	$1,910,000	$1,288,000	$622,000
Less cost of goods sold.................	1,430,000	962,000	468,000
Gross profit...........................	$ 480,000	$ 326,000	$154,000
Less marketing expenses:			
Selling.............................	$ 95,500	$ 64,400	$ 31,100
Warehousing.......................	75,000	50,950	24,050
Packing and shipping...............	63,000	42,420	20,580
Advertising........................	54,000	36,360	17,640
Credit and collection................	28,800	15,200	13,600
General accounting.................	49,200	25,912	23,288
Total.........................	$ 365,500	$ 235,242	$130,258
Net income............................	$ 114,500	$ 90,758	$ 23,742

Exhibit 4

INCOME STATEMENT BY PRODUCT CLASSES IN THE PENNSYLVANIA TERRITORY

| | | Product Class | | |
	Total	Product 1	Product 2	Product 3
Gross sales......................	$1,288,000	$550,000	$450,000	$288,000
Less cost of goods sold	962,000	440,000	330,000	192,000
Gross profit....................	$ 326,000	$110,000	$120,000	$ 96,000
Less marketing expenses:				
Selling.....................	$ 64,400	$ 27,500	$ 22,500	$ 14,400
Warehousing................	50,950	24,750	15,000	11,200
Packing and shipping........	42,420	23,100	12,600	6,720
Advertising.................	36,360	19,800	10,800	5,760
Credit and collection..........	15,200	4,000	7,600	3,600
General accounting...........	25,912	13,120	9,512	3,280
Total....................	$ 235,242	$112,270	$ 78,012	$ 44,960
Net income (loss)...............	$ 90,758	$(2,270)	$ 41,988	$ 51,040

Exhibit 5

INCOME STATEMENT OF PRODUCT CLASS WITH FIXED-VARIABLE ANALYSIS OF MANUFACTURING AND MARKETING COSTS IN THE PENNSYLVANIA TERRITORY

		Product 1
Gross sales...		$550,000
Less cost of goods sold (variable unit cost = 60% of $8)....		264,000
Gross contribution margin................................		$286,000
Less variable marketing expenses:		
Selling..	$11,000	
Warehousing......................................	14,850	
Packing and shipping..............................	13,750	
Credit and collection..............................	2,600	
General accounting................................	5,680	47,880
Contribution margin......................................		$238,120
Less fixed costs and expenses:		
Manufacturing costs — fixed...........................	$176,000	
Marketing expenses — fixed:		
Selling..	$16,500	
Warehousing......................................	9,900	
Packing and shipping..............................	9,350	
Advertising......................................	19,800	
Credit and collection..............................	1,400	
General accounting................................	7,440	240,390
Net loss — Product Class 1 — Pennsylvania.................		$ (2,270)

Exhibit 6

the steps required to bring about an improvement in the profitability of this product line should be determined. Functional marketing cost analysis permits this type of analysis which should eventually lead to a selective selling program supported by product break-even analyses and by cost-volume-profit and differential cost analyses (see Chapters 24 and 25).

DISCUSSION QUESTIONS

1. What general principles should be observed in planning a system of control for marketing expenses?

2. On what bases would you assign the following marketing expenses to a number of different types of commodities sold by a company:

   (a) Salespersons' salaries
   (b) Salespersons' commissions
   (c) Storing finished goods
   (d) Warehouse expenses
   (e) Advertising on national scale
   (f) Expenses of company's own delivery trucks
   (g) Sales manager's salary
   (h) Sales office expenses

3. How are marketing expenses to be classified in order to find the cost of selling jobs or products?

4. Outline a procedure for determining the marketing costs for a concern manufacturing two products. This organization uses national advertising and assigns salespersons to definite territories for contact with established dealers and also to secure additional retail outlets.

5. A method still commonly used today in analyzing marketing expenses is to relate them to either the total factory costs or the total sales value. This method is merely a relationship and not a scientific basis. Discuss.

6. The advertising policy of a company includes exhibition of the plant to customers. Visitors are received and guides are supplied from the production staff.

   (a) How should this cost be treated in the records?
   (b) What adequate control of this expenditure can be provided from the point of view of production and sales promotion?

7. A company with a national sales force divides the country into sales territories, which are again divided into districts. The products are nationally advertised and are sold to retail shops. Assuming 1,000 sales per day with an average of four items to each order, what marketing cost system should be installed to build up:

   (a) The necessary sales statistics to control sales by both territories and lines?
   (b) The expenses of such a sales force?
   (c) Records and statistical analyses for use in the preparation of sales budgets and profit margins?

8. What are the objectives of profit analysis by sales territories in income statements?

                                                    (AICPA adapted)

9. A firm employing its own transport service delivers its products up to a distance of 130 miles from home in quantities varying from 1 to 20 cwt. On the return trip empties are collected from certain customers and a quantity of raw materials from suppliers. How would you distribute the cost incurred by this service?

10. (a) On what basis would you propose to analyze sales expenses in order to enable management to judge the effectiveness of this function?
    (b) What cost data should be given to salespersons and for what purpose?

11. When and to what extent is the inclusion of marketing and administrative expenses in inventory values justifiable?

12. Explain briefly the difference between the profit and the contribution margin approach in marketing cost analysis.

13. For what reasons did the Robinson-Patman Act lead to the establishment of marketing cost procedures in business?

EXERCISES

1. Comparative Statement — Applied vs. Actual Expenses. The management of the Eldridge Company has requested the establishment and use of volume-related standards for marketing cost analysis to allow management to know what the marketing costs should have been as well as what they are. With standard costing rates set for various functional costs, charges can be made on the basis of these rates and applied to actual sales volume.

The assistant controller presents the following data supporting the analysis:

Planned sales:

	Number of Orders	Number of Units	Sales Amount
Product A.....	2,000	4,000	$ 80,000
Product B.....	8,000	16,000	160,000
Total.........	10,000	20,000	$240,000

Standards for marketing expenses:

Advertising...................... 4% of sales
Salespersons' salaries and expenses... 5% of sales
Order filling expenses.............. $.30 per order
Order handling — Product A.......$.40 per unit
                   — Product B........$.10 per unit

Actual results for the month:

	Number of Orders	Number of Units	Sales Amount
Product A......	2,800	5,000	$100,000
Product B......	6,000	12,000	120,000
Total	8,800	17,000	$220,000

Expenses for the month:

	Total	Deferred to Next Month	Expenses for Month
Advertising......................	$ 8,700	$700	$ 8,000
Salespersons' salaries and expenses.	12,000		12,000
Order filling......................	2,850		2,850
Order handling..................	4,500	500	4,000

Required: An analysis of marketing expenses, showing applied expenses contrasted with actual expenses and the resulting variances. (Compute only one variance for each expense.)

2. Income Statement by Customer Classes. The Rochester Company assembles a washing machine that is sold to three classes of customers: department stores, retail appliance stores, and wholesalers. The data with respect to these three classes of customers are shown below.

Customer Class	Dollar Sales	Gross Profit	Number of Sales Calls	Number of Orders	Number of Invoice Lines
Department stores........	$180,000	$ 26,000	240	120	2,100
Retail appliance stores........	240,000	80,000	360	580	4,600
Wholesalers....	300,000	71,000	400	300	3,300
Total........	$720,000	$177,000	1,000	1,000	10,000

Actual marketing costs for the year are:

Function	Costs	Measure of Activity
Selling..............	$65,000	Salespersons' calls
Packing and shipping.	12,000	Customers' orders
Advertising.........	10,000	Dollar sales
Credit and collection.	15,000	Invoice lines
General accounting...	18,000	Customers' orders

Required: An income statement by customer classes with functional distribution of marketing expenses. (When allocating the advertising expense, round to the nearest $100.)

3. Territorial Income Statement; Managerial Decision-Making Costs. The Golemme Company manufactures textile equipment. Sales are made by company salespersons directly to textile manufacturers in three sales territories.

The following information concerning territories was obtained from the standard sales and marketing expense budgets for the year:

Item	Territory 1	Territory 2	Territory 3	Total
Net sales......................	$120,000	$100,000	$180,000	$400,000
Salespersons' salaries...........	6,000	5,000	9,000	20,000
Salespersons' traveling expenses.	3,650	2,350	5,000	11,000
Warehouse expenses...........	1,200	1,000	3,300	5,500
Delivery expenses.............	2,000	3,000	6,000	11,000
Supplies......................	500	400	800	1,700

Other standard marketing expenses and methods used to allocate both standard and actual expenses to territories are as follows: advertising, 5% of net sales; credit and collection expenses, 2% of net sales; sales office expenses, $15,000, distributed equally; general sales salaries, $16,000, distributed on basis of net sales; sales commissions paid to salespersons, 8% of net sales. The cost of manufacturing the looms sold is 60% of net sales.

Required: (1) A standard income statement comparing the standard net sales, manufacturing cost, marketing expenses, and net income or loss for the three territories.

(2) An explanation of how the figures developed in (1) aid management in determining:
  (a) Whether a territory should be dropped or whether attempts should be made to further develop such territory by increased advertising, service, etc.
  (b) The responsibility for incurrence of marketing costs.
  (c) Whether salespersons should discontinue calling on a certain class of customer.

4. Profitability Analysis by Channels of Marketing; Variance Analysis. The Litenpower Electric Company manufacturers small electrical home appliances and distributes them via retailers, wholesalers, and department stores. The company's marketing cost system employs functional standard marketing costs that aid in charging and controlling marketing expenses by channels of distribution.

During the month of December the Cost Department calculated the following standard unit costs for the coming year:

Selling.....................	$ 1.75 per salesperson's call
Warehousing.................	12.00 per 1,000 cubic feet of product sold
Packing and shipping..........	47.00 per 1,000 cubic feet of product sold
Advertising..................	1.25 per media circulation
Credit and collection..........	.08 per invoice line
General accounting...........	.35 per customer order

At the end of the year, actual activity and costs were:

			Activity		
Function	Total Actual Costs	Measure of Activity	Retailers	Whole-salers	Depart-ment Stores
Selling.............	$187,500	Salespersons' calls.	75,000	10,000	15,000
Warehousing........	12,100	Cu. ft. of product.	390,000	160,000	250,000
Packing and shipping.	35,900	Cu. ft. of product.	390,000	160,000	250,000
Advertising.........	11,200	Media circulation.	4,000	1,000	5,000
Credit and collection..	23,800	Invoice lines	115,000	75,000	60,000
General accounting...	9,300	Customers' orders.	18,500	2,000	4,500

Other actual data:

Sales..	$670,000	$310,000	$405,000
Gross profit percentage........................	25%	40%	30%

Required: An income statement by channels of marketing with:
(a) Functional marketing expenses at standard.
(b) The variances of actual from standard costs to arrive at actual net income.

5. Salespersons' Performance Reports. A corporate budget director designed a control scheme in order to be able to compare and evaluate the efforts of the company's three salespersons and the results attained. Specifically, each salesperson is to make five calls per day; the budget provides for $20 per day per salesperson for travel and entertainment expenses: each salesperson was assigned a sales quota of $200 a day. The Budget Department collects the data on actual performance from the daily sales reports and the weekly expense vouchers and then prepares a monthly report therefrom. This report includes both variances from standard and performance indexes. For the performance index, standard performance equals 100, 10% greater than standard equals 110, etc.

The records for the month of November with 20 working days show:

Salesperson	Sales Calls	Travel Expenses	Sales
Palmer, K......	70	$500	$7,000
Thompson, J. ..	100	400	4,200
Weatherbil, O...	120	360	3,000

Required: A monthly report comparing the standard and actual performances of the salespersons (including the performance indices) for (a) sales calls, (b) travel expenses, (c) sales, and (d) sales revenue per call.

6. Cost Justification Study. Larson-Manss Distributors, Inc. has been accused of discriminating against its small-order customers (25 to 50 cases) in Territory 1 as compared with the same class of customers in Territories 2, 3, and 4. The company has broken down its marketing costs by territories and now desires to prorate the territorial costs among classes of customers within each territory. A tabulation of the average distribution costs per year in Territory 1 shows:

Expense	Amount
Advertising:	
Direct-to-customer catalog..................	$ 3,600
Radio and newspapers.....................	9,000
Salespersons' salaries.....................	36,000
Salespersons' commissions..................	48,000
Delivery expenses........................	28,800
Traveling costs of salespersons..............	10,800
Collection costs.........................	8,400
	$144,600

The Accounting Department has tabulated the following to assist in prorating costs in Territory 1 between small-, medium-, and large-order customers:

	Small-Order Customers	Medium-Order Customers	Large-Order Customers
Net sales.....................................	$150,000	$220,000	$350,000
Number of sales orders taken.......................	2,500	2,000	1,500
Number of cases of product sold....................	100,000	150,000	250,000
Relative shipping cost (per order)....................	$1	$2	$3
Number of customers.............................	1,500	1,500	2,000
Relative number of miles traveled per day (per sales person).......................................	4	10	16
Number of salespersons...........................	13	6	5

In the Collection Department, bookkeeping costs per order handled are about ten cents. Each customer is mailed a statement of his account at the end of the month, and the customers make single monthly remittances on account.

All salespersons are paid the same salary; each salesperson works with a single class of customer.

Required: A proration of the marketing costs of Territory 1 to the three order-size classes of customers to justify costs. Indicate the base or bases on which each proration is made.

PROBLEMS

23-1. Territorial Profit Contribution Report. The Shamblin Products Company uses a "territorial profit contribution report" as an effective tool for marketing cost analysis. The report is coordinated with the company's semiannual budget by establishing the profit required from each sales territory to meet all branch and head office operating expenses plus expected net income for each month. This procedure gives the sales managers not only a sales budget in both quantity and value but also the estimated profit required from each territory under their supervision.

About two months before the beginning of the semiannual accounting period, the Budget Department prepared the following forecast income statement:

FORECAST INCOME STATEMENT

FOR SIX MONTHS ENDED DECEMBER 31, 19—

Net sales....................................		$10,000,000
Cost of goods sold............................		6,000,000
Gross profit...............................		$ 4,000,000
Sales territorial expenses:		
Freight to customers........................	$ 700,000	
Salaries and commissions....................	1,500,000	
Traveling expenses and miscellaneous...........	300,000	2,500,000
Territorial profit...........................		$ 1,500,000
General marketing and administrative expenses:		
Marketing expenses.........................	$1,000,000	
Administrative expenses.....................	300,000	1,300,000
Net income...............................		$ 200,000

The sales forecast broken down by months and territories is as follows:

			Territories		
Month	75	42	55	Others	Total
July...............	$ 10,000	$ 8,000	$ 8,000	$ 974,000	$ 1,000,000
August............	15,000	11,000	12,000	1,462,000	1,500,000
September.........	15,000	11,000	12,000	1,462,000	1,500,000
October...........	30,000	22,000	24,000	2,924,000	3,000,000
November.........	20,000	15,000	16,000	1,949,000	2,000,000
December.........	10,000	8,000	8,000	974,000	1,000,000
Total............	$100,000	$75,000	$80,000	$9,745,000	$10,000,000

(Territories 75, 42, and 55 are shown in detail; the others are in a total sum to simplify the problem.)

According to the income statement, the territories are expected to contribute $1,500,000 (recovery of marketing expenses, $1,000,000; administrative expenses, $300,000; and net income, $200,000). This profit contribution of $1,500,000 is prorated to each sales territory on the basis of the estimated sales for the same period.

The budget of the territorial profit contribution for the three territories for the three-month period ending September 30, 19—, showed the following costs and expenses:

Territories	Cost of Goods Sold	Freight	Salaries and Commissions	Travel Expenses, Etc.
75	$24,890	$1,820	$6,500	$ 790
42	18,319	1,746	4,250	1,185
55	14,815	3,845	6,200	2,340

Actual results in the three territories for the same period were:

Territories	Sales	Cost of Goods Sold	Freight	Salaries and Commissions	Travel Expenses, Etc.
75	$44,250	$27,878	$2,212	$6,100	$1,437
42	33,465	24,710	2,245	3,900	1,420
55	18,865	11,378	3,329	5,820	1,940

Required: (1) A territorial profit contribution report for the three territories comparing (a) actual profit contribution with the budgeted amount and (b) budgeted contribution to meet marketing and administrative expenses and net income with actual results.

(2) Factors or a combination of factors that might have caused a loss or the failure to fulfill budget requirements in any territory.

(Based on an NAA article)

23-2. Income Statements by Products and Order-Size Classes. The feasibility of allocating marketing and administrative expenses to products or order-size classes for managerial purposes has been considered by the management of the Ard Co. It is apparent that some costs can be assigned equitably to these classifications; others cannot. The company's cost analyst proposed the following bases for apportionment:

APPORTIONMENT BASES (WHERE APPLICABLE) OF MARKETING COSTS
FOR PRODUCT AND ORDER-SIZE ANALYSES

Expense	Type of Analysis	
	By Products	By Order-Size Classes
Sales salaries	Not allocated	Sales dollars times number of customers in class
Sales traveling	Not allocated	Number of customers in class
Sales office	Not allocated	Number of customers in class
Sales commissions	Direct	Direct
Credit management	Volume of sales in dollars	Number of customers in class
Packing and shipping	Weight times number of units	Weight times number of units
Warehousing	Weight times number of units	Weight times number of units
Advertising	Not allocated	Not allocated
Bookkeeping and billing	Volume of sales in dollars	Number of orders
General marketing and administrative	Not allocated	Not allocated

From books, records, and other sources, the following data have been compiled:

Order-Size Class	Number of Customers	Number of Orders	Cost of Goods Sold	Total Sales	Product Sales		
					X	Y	Z
Under $25	1,000	6,000	$ 59,000	$ 100,000	$ 35,000	$ 40,000	$ 25,000
$25–$100	250	4,000	177,000	300,000	105,000	120,000	75,000
$101–$200	100	4,000	354,000	600,000	210,000	240,000	150,000
Over $200	50	1,000	236,000	400,000	140,000	160,000	100,000
Total	1,400	15,000	$826,000	$1,400,000	$490,000	$560,000	$350,000

Other data:

Product	Weight	Cost of Goods Sold	Units Sold
X............	1 kg.	$252,000	98,000
Y...........	3 kg.	294,000	70,000
Z...........	2 kg.	280,000	175,000

Marketing and administrative expenses for the year:

Sales salaries...	$ 38,250
Sales traveling..........	28,000
Sales office (variable).....	15,400
Sales commissions (5%)......................................	70,000
Credit management...	14,000
Packing and shipping.......................................	32,900
Warehousing...	16,450
Advertising...	150,000
Bookkeeping and billing....................................	42,000
General marketing and administrative........................	80,000
Total......................................	$487,000

Required: (1) A product income statement with an analysis of marketing and administrative expenses by product showing the allocation of expenses to each product.

(2) An income statement with an analysis of marketing and administrative expenses by order-size classes.

(Based on an NAA article)

23-3. Profitability Analysis of Order-Size Groups. The management of the Bono Machine Tools Company requests a study of the small-order cost problem by measuring its magnitude and making known its effect on profits. To determine the extent of this problem, the data below have been assembled.

Customers' Order Size	Number of Orders	Dollar Sales	Standard Cost
Under $ 10.00	1,700	$ 6,500	$ 5,037
$ 10 to $ 49.99	1,100	27,000	20,925
50 to 99.99	350	27,000	20,925
100 to 499.99	700	151,000	117,025
500 and over	150	188,500	146,088
Total	4,000	$400,000	$310,000

The marketing expenses to be allocated to the five customers' groups are:

(a) Shipping and warehousing
(b) Order handling
(c) General and administrative expenses
(d) Selling expenses
(e) Commissions

Allocation of shipping and warehousing is worked out on the basis of a ratio which considers both weight of shipments and number of orders handled. The analysis indicates:

	Weight	Number of Orders
Freight shipments...............	387,000 kg.	1,680
Parcel post shipments..............	6,500 kg.	2,320
Total......................	393,500 kg.	4,000

The allocation is:

	% of Shipments by Weight	% of Shipments Handled	Total	% of Total
Freight..........	98	42	140	70
Parcel post.......	2	58	60	30

The detailed data assembled further shows that all orders under $10 and 620 orders in the $10 to $49.99 class are sent via parcel post. Shipping and warehousing costs total $7,000.

Order-handling expenses amount to $9,000 to be allocated on a cost per order basis with each invoice being considered a separate order.

General and administrative expenses........................	$17,000
Marketing expenses.......................................	24,000
Commissions...	27,000

(All distributed on the basis of sales dollars.)

Required: (1) Using the partially completed form below, (a) allocation of the costs to the various groups (b) computation of the percentages as indicated, and (c) determination of the net income (loss) of each order-size group.

ANALYSIS OF PROFITABILITY OF SALES BY ORDER-SIZE GROUPS

Order Size	Number of Orders	% of Orders	Dollar Sales	% of Sales	Standard Cost	Gross Profit
Under $10	1,700		$ 6,500		$ 5,037	
$10 to $49.99	1,100		27,000		20,925	
$50 to $99.99	350		27,000		20,925	
$100 to $499.99	700		151,000		117,025	
$500 and over	150		188,500		146,088	
Total	4,000	%	$400,000	%	$310,000	$

Shipping and Warehousing	Order Handling	General and Adm. Exp.	Selling Expenses	Commis- sions	Net Income (Loss) Contribution
$	$	$	$	$	$

(2) The alternatives, or combination of alternatives, that might be used to make sales more profitable since this industry (machine tools) cannot eliminate small orders by refusing to accept them or by penalizing the small purchaser through higher charges.

(Based on an NAA article)

23-4. Standard Cost Variance Analysis; Revision of Sales Prices. Gibeaut Corporation's actual and standard marketing costs for the month of January are:

	Budget at Standard Cost	Actual Operations
Sales......................................	$750,000	$750,000
Direct marketing costs:		
Selling...............................	$ 12,000	$ 15,000
Shipping salaries......................	7,000	9,450
Indirect marketing costs:		
Order filling.........................	17,250	21,500
Other................................	2,100	2,500
Total costs............................	$ 38,350	$ 48,450

Additional data:

(a) The company sells a single product for $10 per unit.

(b) Shipping salaries and indirect marketing costs — Other are allocated on the basis of shipping hours.

(c) January shipping hours are:

Budgeted hours...............................	3,500
Standard operating level......................	4,400
Actual hours.................................	4,500

(d) Order-filling costs are allocated on the basis of sales and are comprised of freight, packing, and warehousing costs. An analysis of the amount of these standard costs by unit order size follows:

	Order Filling Standard Costs Classified by Unit Order Size			
Unit — Volume Classification	1-15	16-50	Over 50	Total
Freight....................	$ 1,200	$ 1,440	$ 2,250	$ 4,890
Packing...................	2,400	3,240	4,500	10,140
Warehousing..............	600	720	900	2,220
Total..................	$ 4,200	$ 5,400	$ 7,650	$17,250
Units sold...............	12,000	18,000	45,000	75,000

Required: (1) Computation and analysis of variances from standard cost for (a) shipping salaries and (b) indirect marketing costs — other. The analysis should compare actual and standard costs at the standard operating level.

(2) Management realizes that the marketing cost per unit decreases with an increase in the size of the order and, hence, wants to revise its unit sales prices upward or downward on the basis of the quantity ordered in proportion to the allocated freight, packing, and warehousing standard costs. Management assumes that the revised unit prices will require no changes in standards for sales

volume, the number of units sold in each order size classification, and the profit per unit sold.

(a) For each unit volume classification, a schedule computing the standard cost per unit for each order filling cost: freight, packing, and warehousing. Use the format in item (d) above for this schedule.

(b) A schedule computing the revised unit sales prices for each unit-volume classification.

(AICPA adapted)

23-5. Cost Allocations to Individual Stores; Sales Expansion Decision. Excel Foods, Inc., a grocery chain consisting of three stores, operates in a state with legislation that permits each of its municipalities to levy an income tax on corporations operating within their respective municipalities. This legislation establishes a uniform tax rate that may be levied by the municipality. Regulations also provide that the tax is to be computed on income derived within the taxing municipality after a reasonable and consistent allocation of general overhead expenses. General overhead expenses have not been allocated previously to Excel's stores and include warehouse, general office, advertising, and delivery expenses.

Each municipality in which Excel Foods, Inc. operates a store has levied the corporate income tax as provided by state legislation, and management is considering two plans for allocating general overhead expenses to each store. The 19— operating results, before deducting general overhead expenses and taxes for each store, were:

	Store			
	Ashville	Burns	Clinton	Total
Net sales....................	$416,000	$353,600	$270,400	$1,040,000
Less cost of goods sold........	215,700	183,300	140,200	539,200
Gross profit................	$200,300	$170,300	$130,200	$ 500,800
Less local operating expenses:				
Fixed.....................	$ 60,800	$ 48,750	$ 50,200	$ 159,750
Variable..................	54,700	64,220	27,448	146,368
Total.....................	$115,500	$112,970	$ 77,648	$ 306,118
Net income before general overhead and taxes.............	$ 84,800	$ 57,330	$ 52,552	$ 194,682

General overhead expenses in 19— were as follows:

Delivery and warehousing expenses:		
Delivery expenses.................................	$40,000	
Warehouse operations............................	30,000	
Warehouse depreciation..........................	20,000	$ 90,000

Central office expenses:		
Advertising.......................................	18,000	
Central office salaries............................	37,000	
Other central office expenses.....................	28,000	83,000
Total general overhead expenses..................		$173,000

Additional information:

(a) One fifth of the warehouse space is used to house the central office, and depreciation of this space is included in other central office expenses. Warehouse operating expenses vary with the quantity of merchandise sold.

(b) Delivery expenses vary with the distance and the number of deliveries. The distances from the warehouse to each store and the number of deliveries made in 19 — were:

Store	Miles	Number of Deliveries
Ashville............................	120	140
Burns..............................	200	64
Clinton............................	100	104

(c) All advertising is prepared by the central office and is distributed in the areas in which stores are located.

(d) As each store was opened, the fixed portion of central office salaries increased by $7,000 while other central office expenses increased by $2,500. Basic fixed central office salaries amounted to $10,000 and basic fixed other central office expenses amounted to $12,000. The remainder of central office salaries, and the remainder of other central office expenses vary with sales.

Required: (1) The net income for each store that would be subject to the municipal tax levy on corporation income, for each of the following plans to allocate general overhead expenses:

Plan 1..............   Allocate all general overhead expenses on the basis of sales volume.

Plan 2..............   First, allocate central office salaries and other central office expenses evenly to warehouse operations and to each store.

Second, allocate the resulting warehouse operations expense, warehouse depreciation, and advertising to each store on the basis of sales volume.

Third, allocate delivery expenses to each store on the basis of delivery miles × number of deliveries.

(2) A management decision to determine which store should be selected for expansion in order to maximize corporate profits. This expansion will increase Excel's sales by $50,000, its local fixed operating expenses by $7,500, and will require ten additional deliveries from the warehouse.

(AICPA adapted)

CASES

A. Critique of Allocation Methods for Marketing Costs. In recent years marketing costs of the Mele Company have increased more than other expenditures. For more effective control the company plans to provide each local manager with an income statement for his territory showing monthly and year-to-date amounts for the current and the previous year. Each sales office is supervised by a local manager; sales orders are forwarded to the main office and filled from a central warehouse; billing and collections are also centrally processed.   Expenses are first classified by function and then allocated to each territory in the following ways:

Function	*Basis*
Sales salaries......................................	Actual
Other selling expenses.............................	Relative sales dollars
Warehousing expenses.............................	Relative sales dollars
Packing and shipping..............................	Weight of package
Billing and collections............................	Number of billings
General marketing expenses........................	Equally

Required: (1) Discuss the effectiveness of the Mele Company's comparative income statements by sales territories as a tool for planning and control.   The answer should include additional factors that should be considered and changes that might be desirable for effective planning by management and evaluation of the local sales managers.

(2) Compare the degree of control that can be achieved over production costs and marketing costs and explain why the degree of control differs.

(3) Criticize the Mele Company's allocation and/or inclusion of (a) other selling expenses, (b) warehousing expenses, and (c) general marketing expenses.

(AICPA adapted)

B. Evaluating Salespersons' Compensation Plan.   The manager of a wholesale distributorship compiled the following data of marketing costs for two salespersons and wants to know if the firm's compensation plan is working to the detriment of the company:

	Salespersons	
	Dorn	*Tolan*
Gross sales..	$247,000	$142,000
Sales returns...	17,000	2,000
Cost of goods sold....................................	180,000	85,000
Reimbursed expenses (e.g., entertainment).................	5,500	2,100
Other direct charges (e.g., samples distributed).............	4,000	450
Commission rate on gross sales dollars....................	5%	5%

Required: (1) A salesperson's compensation plan should encourage him to work to increase the measure of performance to which his compensation is related.   List any questionable sales practices by a salesperson that might be encouraged by basing commissions on gross sales.

(2) (a) Do the data reveal any evidence that the compensation plan may be working to the detriment of the company?   (b) What other information should the manager obtain before reaching definite conclusions about this particular situation?   Why?

C. Commissions for Sales Force Motivation.   The Parsons Company compensates its field sales force on a commission and year-end bonus basis.   The commission is 20% of standard gross profit (selling price − standard cost of goods sold on a full absorption costing basis), contingent upon collection of the account. The customer's credit is approved by the Credit Department. A year-end bonus of 15% of commissions earned is paid to salespersons who equal or exceed their annual sales target. The annual sales target is usually established by applying approximately a 5% increase to the preceding year's sales.

Required: (1) The features of this compensation plan that would seem to be *effective* in motivating salespersons to accomplish company goals of higher profits and return on investment. Explain.

(2) The features of this compensation plan that would seem to be *counter-effective* in motivating the salespersons to accomplish the company goals of higher profits and return on investment. Explain.

(NAA adapted)

D. Marketing Strategy. Katz Brothers, a department store dominant in its market area, is easily accessible to public and private transportation, has adequate parking facilities, and is near a large permanent military base. The president seeks advice on a recently received proposal.

A local bank in which the department store has an account recently affiliated with a national credit card plan and has extended an invitation to Katz Brothers to participate. Under the plan, affiliated banks mail credit-card applications to persons in the community with excellent credit ratings regardless of whether they are bank customers. A recipient wishing to receive a credit card completes, signs, and returns the application and installment credit agreement. Thus activated, card holders may charge merchandise or services at any participating establishment throughout the nation.

The affiliated banks guarantee payment to all participating merchants on all invoices presented that have been properly completed, signed, and validated with the impression of credit cards that are not expired, reported stolen, or otherwise canceled. Merchants may turn in all card-validated sales tickets or invoices to their affiliated bank at any time and receive immediate credits to their checking accounts of 96.5% of the face value of the invoices. Card users paying the bank in full within 30 days for amounts billed will have no added charges levied against them. If payments are made under a deferred payment plan, the bank adds a service charge amounting to an effective interest rate of 18% per annum on unpaid balances. Only the affiliated banks and the franchiser of the credit card plan share in these revenues.

The 18% service charge approximates what Katz Brothers has been billing its customers who pay their accounts over an extended period on a schedule similar to that offered under the credit card plan. Participation in the plan does not prevent the store from continuing to conduct its credit business as it has in the past.

Required: (1) The *positive* and the *negative* financial- and accounting-related factors to be considered in deciding whether to participate in this credit card plan. Explain.

(2) If the department store does participate, the income statement accounts and the balance sheet accounts that may change materially as the plan becomes fully operative. Explain. (Such factors as market position, sales mix, prices, markup, etc., are expected to remain about the same as in the past.)

(AICPA adapted)

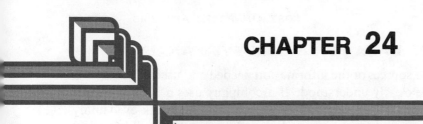

CHAPTER 24

BREAK-EVEN AND COST-VOLUME-PROFIT ANALYSIS

The break-even analysis, the construction of break-even charts, and the related cost-volume-profit analysis constitute another area of cost accounting providing management with cost-and-profit data required for profit planning, policy formulating, and decision making.

The term "break-even" implies that point at which the company neither makes a profit nor suffers a loss. Break-even analysis transmits information to management that would normally require voluminous reports and tables. Break-even analysis is made with the aid of a break-even chart. The chief advantage of a break-even chart lies in its efficiency as a compact, readable reporting device.

Based primarily on accounting data, there are limitations to the use of break-even analysis. The data involved, the assumptions made, the manner in which the information is obtained, and the way the data are expressed must be considered in connection with results indicated in the analysis and on the chart. Although a break-even analysis is not a sure way to profits, it is a valuable aid in uncovering profit potential.

A *break-even analysis* indicates at what level cost and revenue are in equilibrium. The *break-even point*, obtained directly by mathematical computation, is usually presented in graphic form because it not only shows management the point at which neither a profit nor a loss occurs, but also indicates more forcefully the possibilities associated with changes in costs or sales. A *break-even chart* can be defined as a graphic analysis of the relationship of costs and sales to profit.

SOURCES OF DATA FOR BREAK-EVEN ANALYSIS

The source or sources of the information needed and used in break-even analysis must be clearly understood. If a company uses a flexible budget, most of the information required already exists; and the break-even analysis and charts become merely by-products of the current flexible budget.

The relationship between standard costs and budgets is pointed out in the budget chapters. Anticipated sales revenue based on market conditions and tempered by plant capacity is first determined. Existing flexible budgets are reviewed and revised to incorporate expected changes in prices and operating conditions. Forecasted production (in units of product or hours) becomes the basis for establishing standard costing rates for materials, labor, and factory overhead. Values so determined are then incorporated in the budget.

Where possible, standards are also set for marketing and administrative activities and used in budget construction which becomes a summary of standards. The data in the flexible budget can be used directly and without refinement for break-even analysis or can be converted into a break-even chart, which is better understood by management than a voluminous budget report in tabular form. As standard costs are a current, accurate, and readily obtainable source of data for various types of cost reports and analyses, they form a most valuable tool for the preparation of a chart designed to indicate future profit possibilities. In observing the specific uses of break-even analysis, the relationship of standard costs and flexible budgets to break-even analysis will become even more apparent.

Direct costing with its segregation of fixed and variable costs and its contribution margin immediately furnishes the data for determining a company's break-even point. The income statement prepared by direct costing methods provides ready information when management is faced with decisions affected by cost-volume-profit relationships.

DETERMINING THE BREAK-EVEN POINT

Data for break-even analysis cannot be taken directly from the conventional or full cost income statement. The form of the statement and the manner in which data are presented do not permit a convenient and practical analysis for planning, policy making, and profit determination. The conventional income statement must, therefore, be broken down to show the fixed and variable portions of each cost. Of the three classes of expenses: fixed, semivariable, and variable, the semivariable expenses must be separated into their fixed and variable components. The fixed portion is stated as a total figure; the variable portion as a rate or a percentage. This procedure is demonstrated beginning on page 546. If such an analysis has been made, the costs and expenses in a conventional income statement can be restated as follows:

Cost Item*	Total	Variable	Fixed
Materials..........................	$1,000,000	$1,000,000	
Labor.............................	1,400,000	1,400,000	
Factory overhead...................	1,600,000	400,000	$1,200,000
Marketing expenses.................	350,000	150,000	200,000
Administrative expenses.............	250,000	50,000	200,000
	$4,600,000	$3,000,000	$1,600,000
Percentage of net sales..............		60%	

*Sales are assumed to be $5,000,000.

The above figures show that out of every sales dollar $.60, or 60 percent of the total, is required to pay variable costs. The balance, 40 percent, is available to cover all other costs and make a profit and is expressed as a percentage of sales. Each dollar of sales contributes $.40 toward this goal. To find the total sales dollars required to recover the fixed costs of $1,600,000, only the total fixed costs are divided by 40 percent. The 40 percent is referred to as the *contribution margin ratio (C/M)* and is determined by dividing the contribution margin (sales — variable costs) by sales revenue. It is also known as the *marginal income ratio* or the *profit-volume ratio.* The term used most prevalently in this textbook is "contribution margin ratio" to coincide with the term "contribution margin."

$$\frac{\text{Fixed Costs}}{\text{Contribution Margin Ratio}(C/M)} = \frac{\$1,600,000}{.40} = \$4,000,000 \begin{array}{l} \text{Break-Even Sales} \\ \text{Volume in Dollars} \end{array}$$

The resulting $4,000,000, known as the break-even point, represents that sales volume in dollars at which neither a profit is made nor a loss is incurred by the company. This break-even figure can be checked as follows:

Net sales..	$4,000,000
Less variable costs (60% of net sales).....................	2,400,000
Contribution margin....................................	$1,600,000
Less fixed costs.......................................	1,600,000
Net income (loss)......................................	-0-

If a sales volume of $5,000,000 can be regarded as normal, the percentage of normal at which the company must operate in order to break even is computed as shown below.

$$\frac{\text{Break-Even Sales Volume in Dollars}}{\text{Normal Sales Volume in Dollars}} = \frac{\$4,000,000}{\$5,000,000} = 80\% \begin{array}{l} \text{Break-Even Capacity} \\ \text{Percentage} \end{array}$$

The answer indicates the company "breaks even" when operating at 80 percent of normal capacity. If profits are desired, a higher activity level must be reached. For this reason, a businessperson should neither set the break-even point as a goal nor accept the break-even analysis as an easy mechanical substitute for the complex art of managing an enterprise. Analysis is a means to an end — not an end in itself.

The computation of the break-even point can be summarized in the following formula:

$$\text{Break-Even Sales Volume in Dollars} = \frac{\text{Total Fixed Expenses}}{1 - \dfrac{\text{Total Variable Expenses}}{\text{Total Sales Volume in Dollars}}}$$

Substituting the figures previously used:

$$\text{Break-Even Sales Volume in Dollars} = \frac{\$1,600,000}{1 - \dfrac{\$3,000,000}{\$5,000,000}}$$

$$= \frac{\$1,600,000}{1 - .60}$$

$$= \frac{\$1,600,000}{.40}$$

$$= \$4,000,000$$

An alternative formula is:

$$\text{Break-Even Sales Volume in Dollars} = \frac{\text{Total Fixed Expenses}}{\text{Contribution Margin Ratio}}$$

The contribution margin ratio in this alternative formula equals the denominator in the previous formula; i.e.:

$$1 - \frac{\text{Total Variable Expenses}}{\text{Total Sales Volume in Dollars}}$$

The conventional income statement can be replaced by a contribution margin income statement, which emphasizes the margin available for fixed costs and profit.

CONTRIBUTION MARGIN INCOME STATEMENT

Net sales..	$5,000,000
Less variable costs (60% of net sales)........................	3,000,000
Contribution margin..	$2,000,000
Less fixed costs..	1,600,000
Net income..	$ 400,000

The break-even point can also be computed in units. With a unit sales price of $4 and variable costs at 60 percent of sales, or $2.40 (60% of $4) per unit, the contribution margin per unit is $1.60 ($4 − $2.40). Dividing total fixed costs by the contribution margin per unit, the break-even point in units is obtained:

$$\text{Break-Even Sales Volume in Units} = \frac{\text{Total Fixed Expenses}}{\text{Contribution Margin per Unit}} = \frac{\$1,600,000}{\$1.60} = \underline{\underline{1,000,000 \text{ units}}}$$

Should the break-even sales volume in dollars be determined first, break-even units can be found by dividing dollar sales by the unit sales price:

$$\frac{\text{Break-Even Sales Volume in Dollars}}{\text{Unit Sales Price}} = \frac{\$4,000,000}{\$4} = \underline{\underline{1,000,000 \text{ units}}}$$

Conversely, if break-even is first computed in units, break-even sales dollars can be determined by multiplying break-even sales units by the unit sales price:

Break-Even Sales Volume in Units × Unit Sales Price = 1,000,000 Units × $4 = $\underline{\underline{\$4,000,000}}$

The break-even computation and the charts use data from a single operating statement with costs divided into fixed and variable elements. The analysis may be based on historical data, past operations, or future sales and costs. In the latter case, the starting point of the analysis is the determination of estimated costs for various levels of output with the help of the flexible budget. With costs at different levels of activity, analyses can be made for a wide range of sales possibilities. The analysis resolves itself into three major elements: (1) defining volume and sales price, (2) determining fixed and variable costs, and (3) relating cost to volume.

CONSTRUCTING A BREAK-EVEN CHART

The computations just reviewed can be presented in a break-even chart. The chart takes its name from the fact that the point at which the cost line and the sales line intersect is the break-even point. Information needed to construct a break-even chart includes the following:
1. Forecast sales
2. Fixed and variable costs

The break-even chart on the next page is constructed as follows:
1. A horizontal base line, the *x-axis*, is drawn and spaced into equal distances to represent the sales volume in dollars or in number of units.
2. A vertical line, the *y-axis*, is drawn at the extreme left and right sides of the chart. The y-axis at the left is spaced into equal parts and represents sales and costs in dollars.

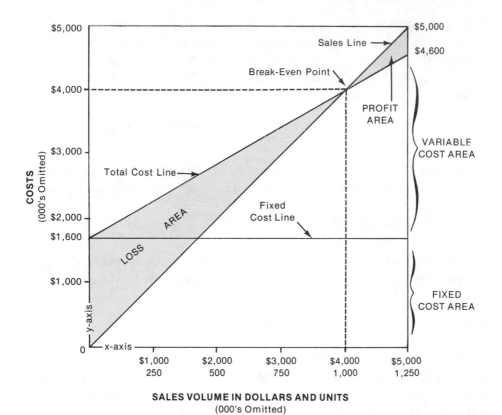

SALES VOLUME IN DOLLARS AND UNITS
(000's Omitted)

3. A *fixed cost line* is drawn parallel to the x-axis at the $1,600,000 point of the y-axis.

4. A *total cost line* is drawn from the $1,600,000 fixed cost point on the y-axis to the $4,600,000 cost point on the right side of the y-axis.

5. The *sales line* is drawn from the 0 point at the left (the intersection of the x-axis and y-axis) to the $5,000,000 point on the right y-axis.

6. The total cost line intersects the sales line at the *break-even point* representing $4,000,000 sales or 1,000,000 units of sales.

7. The shaded area to the left of the break-even point is the *loss area* while the shaded area to the right of the break-even point is the *profit area*.

The notion of relevant range, as stated in the flexible budget discussion (pages 545–546), applies to break-even analysis. That is, the amount of fixed costs and variable costs, as well as the slope of the sales line, are applicable only to a defined range of activity and must be redefined for activity outside the relevant range. Furthermore, *linear* cost and sales behavior are assumed and have general acceptance within the relevant range of activity.[1]

---

[1]Calculus can be employed in dealing with curvilinear functions. See Travis P. Goggans, "Break-even Analysis with Curvilinear Functions," *The Accounting Review*, Vol. XL, No. 4, pp. 867–871.

AN ALTERNATE BREAK-EVEN CHART

In the chart on page 746, the fixed cost line is parallel to the x-axis; and variable costs begin above fixed costs. Such a chart emphasizes fixed costs at a definite amount for various levels of activity. Many analysts prefer an alternate chart in which the variable costs are drawn first, and fixed costs are superimposed on the variable cost line.

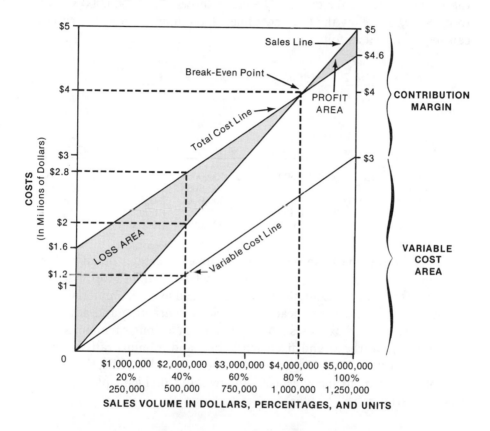

Break-Even Chart with Fixed Costs Superimposed on Variable Costs

The space between the total variable cost and the sales line represents the contribution margin. Where the total cost line intersects the sales line, the break-even point has been reached. The space between the sales line and the total cost line beyond the break-even point represents the net profit for the period at any volume. The space between the total cost line and the sales line to the left of the break-even point indicates the fixed costs not yet recovered by the contribution margin and is the net loss for the period at any volume below the break-even point.

Using the previous data, this alternate break-even chart indicates the recovery of fixed costs at various levels of percentage capacity and at dollar sales or unit sales. Should sales, for example, drop to $2,000,000, variable costs would be $1,200,000 (60 percent of $2,000,000) while fixed costs remain at $1,600,000. The loss at this point would be $800,000 [$2,000,000 − ($1,200,000 + $1,600,000)]. This solution is indicated by the broken lines on the chart. The chart shows the $2,000,000 sales line to be $800,000 below the total cost line. In columnar form, the situation can be illustrated as follows:

Col. 1	Col. 2	Col. 3	Col. 4	Col. 5	Col. 6
			Contri-bution Margin		Net Income (Loss)
Number of Units	Sales	Variable Costs	(Col. 2 − Col. 3)	Fixed Costs	(Col. 4 − Col. 5)
250,000	$1,000,000	$ 600,000	$ 400,000	$1,600,000	$(1,200,000)
500,000	2,000,000	1,200,000	800,000	1,600,000	(800,000)
750,000	3,000,000	1,800,000	1,200,000	1,600,000	(400,000)
1,000,000	4,000,000	2,400,000	1,600,000	1,600,000	None
1,250,000	5,000,000	3,000,000	2,000,000	1,600,000	400,000

A break-even chart can be constructed in even greater detail by breaking down fixed and variable costs into subclassifications (top, page 749). Variable expenses, for example, may be classified as direct materials, direct labor, variable factory overhead, and variable marketing and administrative expenses. Fixed expenses may be divided in a similar manner showing fixed factory overhead and fixed marketing and administrative expenses separately. Even the profit wedge might be subdivided indicating application of the profit to income taxes, interest and dividend payments, and retained earnings.

EFFECT OF CHANGES IN FIXED COSTS ON BREAK-EVEN POINT

If this company's management were able to reduce fixed expenses to $1,450,000, the break-even point would be $3,625,000 ($\frac{\$1,450,000}{.40}$). If sales remained at the $5,000,000 figure, the profit would increase from $400,000 to $550,000; and the break-even point would be 72.5 percent of sales instead of 80 percent. The change in the break-even point resulting from a reduction in fixed costs is shown by the broken lines in the chart illustrated at the bottom of page 749.

The effects of changes in the per unit variable cost or in the unit sales price can also be charted, thus adding a dynamic dimension to the analysis.

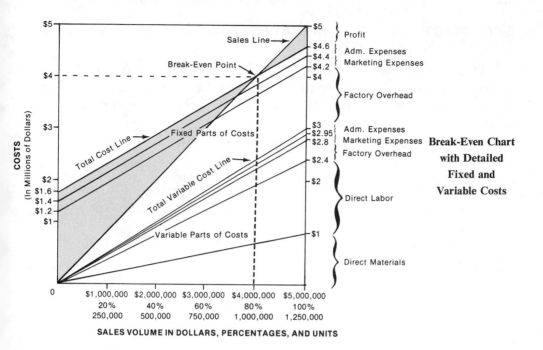

Break-Even Chart with Detailed Fixed and Variable Costs

SALES VOLUME IN DOLLARS, PERCENTAGES, AND UNITS

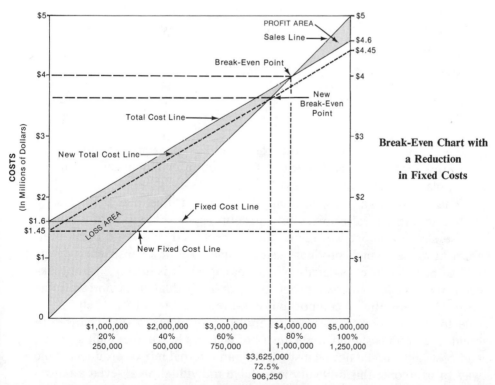

Break-Even Chart with a Reduction in Fixed Costs

SALES VOLUME IN DOLLARS, PERCENTAGES, AND UNITS

EFFECT OF CHANGES IN SALES MIX
ON BREAK-EVEN POINT

When a shift in product sales mix occurs, a change in profit can also be expected unless the same contribution margin ratio is realized on all products. An illustration of such a shift would be the reduction in sales of a high-margin item.

Suppose that a company budgets as follows:

Sales..		$1,500,000
Variable expenses.............................	$900,000	
Fixed expenses................................	400,000	1,300,000
Net income....................................		$ 200,000

The break-even sales volume in dollars would be $1,000,000, computed as follows:

$$\text{Variable Expenses} \quad = \quad \frac{\$900,000}{\$1,500,000} = 60\% \text{ of Sales}$$

$$\begin{array}{c}\text{Break-Even Sales Volume} \\ \text{in Dollars}\end{array} \quad = \quad \frac{\$400,000}{.40} = \$1,000,000$$

At the end of the fiscal period (assuming no change occurred in total fixed expenses or in per unit sales price or variable costs), the company's income statement shows:

Sales..		$1,420,000
Variable expenses.............................	$900,000	
Fixed expenses................................	400,000	1,300,000
Net income....................................		$ 120,000

The break-even volume in this case is now approximately $1,092,000, indicating that the decrease in sales of the high-margin item caused an unfavorable increase of about $92,000 in the break-even point.

This situation can happen in any business. It illustrates the necessity of taking various sales mixes into account in any break-even analysis. It also stresses the inadequacy of the conventional composite break-even chart in which a single product business operation or a consistent average mix of products is considered. When management is interested in break-even analyses for different products, with individual fixed and variable costs, the conventional composite break-even chart is not very helpful. A rule to be followed in the case of multiple products is that changes in break-even points should be the result of changes in volume, selling prices, and costs and should not be distorted by an internal mix of products. One way to overcome this difficulty is to have individual break-even analyses and charts for each product.

The break-even chart is fundamentally a static analysis. Changes in most cases can only be shown by drawing a new chart or a series of charts.

BREAK-EVEN ANALYSIS FOR DECISION MAKING

Break-even charts and analyses offer wide application for testing proposed actions, for considering alternatives, or for other decision-making purposes. For example, the technique permits determination of the effect on profit of a shift in fixed and/or variable expenses when old machinery is replaced by new equipment. In firms with multiple plants, products, and sales territories, charts may be prepared which show the effects of the shift in sales quantities, sales prices, and sales efforts. With such information, management is able to direct the firm's operations into the most profitable channels. For a company with numerous divisions the analysis is particularly valuable in determining the influence on profits of an increase in divisional fixed costs. If, for example, a company's overall contribution margin ratio [1 — (variable costs ÷ sales)] is 25 percent, a division manager must realize that for every $1 of proposed increase in fixed costs, sales revenue must increase by no less than $4 if the existing profit position is to be maintained ($1 ÷ 25% = $4).

The break-even analysis formula is also useful in projecting sales necessary to realize a projected profit or to minimize a calculated loss. Assume that the contribution margin ratio (C/M) is 40 percent, that the fixed costs are $1,600,000, and that the profit objective is $400,000. The sales figure necessary to realize the profit objective is:

$$\frac{\text{Total Fixed Costs} + \text{Profit Objective}}{\text{Contribution Margin Ratio (C/M)}} = \frac{\$1,600,000 + \$400,000}{.40} = \$5,000,000$$

If management wants to determine the sales level that would lead to a precalculated loss of $200,000, then:

$$\frac{\text{Total Fixed Costs} - \text{Estimated Loss}}{\text{Contribution Margin Ratio (C/M)}} = \frac{\$1,600,000 - \$200,000}{.40} = \$3,500,000$$

These projections can also be "read" from the break-even charts on pages 746 and 747.

THE UNIT PROFIT GRAPH

A break-even chart is generally prepared on the basis of total revenue and expenses. These dollar sales and expense figures can be translated into a profit-per-unit graph in order to demonstrate more vividly to management the influence of fixed costs on the product unit cost. As an example,

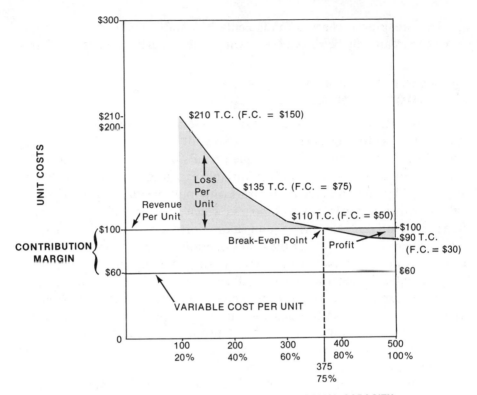

UNITS OF PRODUCT AND PERCENTAGE OF NORMAL CAPACITY

Unit Profit Graph Showing the Influence of Fixed and Variable Costs on Unit Cost

assume the following normal capacity, 100 percent; total sales, $50,000 (500 units @ $100); variable expenses, $30,000; fixed expenses, $15,000; net income, $5,000. The break-even point is $37,500 ($15,000 ÷ .40) or 75 percent of normal capacity ($37,500 ÷ $50,000). The variable cost is $60 per unit, and the fixed cost is $30 if 500 units are made and sold. As volume decreases, the fixed cost per unit increases. This relationship is illustrated in the above graph.

The effect of varying volume on fixed cost per unit can also be expressed in columnar form:

	100 Units	200 Units	300 Units	375 Units	400 Units	500 Units
Variable unit cost.........	$ 60	$ 60	$ 60	$ 60	$ 60.00	$ 60
Fixed cost..............	150	75	50	40	37.50	30
Total unit costs...........	$210	$135	$110	$100	$ 97.50	$ 90
Unit sales price..........	100	100	100	100	100.00	100
Net income (loss) per unit..	$(110)	$ (35)	$ (10)	Break Even	$ 2.50	$ 10

The analyses illustrated in the unit profit graph on page 752 and in the tabular presentation, together with a break-even analysis, are important tools in answering the question: "What unit cost or costs should be used in determining selling prices?" A break-even chart will help in understanding the effect on profits when sales prices increase or decrease with fixed and variable costs remaining constant.

UNIT COST FORMULAS

The unit profit graph and the tabular presentation on page 752 show total unit costs that vary from a high of $210 per unit to a low of $90 per unit. When unit costs of various products are compared, the analyst must observe the production rates of each product, each of which may be at a different level — otherwise the comparison may be misleading. Unit costs must be judged at all levels of activity to obtain a true comparison.

New formulas can be developed which aid in the determination of the effect of changing costs or level of activity upon unit costs. Using figures from the example introduced on page 752, total cost of $45,000 ($15,000 + $30,000) divided by total units (500) gives a unit cost of $90. The formula is: Unit Cost $= \frac{\$15,000 + \$30,000x}{500x}$. At the 100 percent level of activity, x in the equation is 1. Use of this formula facilitates the computation of unit costs under conditions of fluctuating activity levels. The formula would be: Unit Cost $= \frac{a + b_1 x}{b_2 x}$, where a = fixed costs; b_1 = variable expenses at normal capacity level; b_2 = units of production at normal capacity level; and x = level of activity, expressed as a percentage of normal capacity.

To illustrate the formula, assume that fixed expenses increase $2,000 to $17,000 and that variable expenses decrease $3,000 to $27,000 at the 100 percent level of activity. Using these facts, the computations below illustrate the determination of the new break-even point, the unit cost at the new break-even point, and the new unit cost when operating at 90 percent of capacity.

New Break-Even Point

$\qquad$ New Profit $= (sx - b_1 x) - a =$ new profit equation, where a, b_1, and x
$\qquad\qquad$ are as previously defined and s = total sales at normal
$\qquad\qquad$ capacity.
$\qquad$ New Profit $= (\$50,000x - \$27,000x) - \$17,000$
$\qquad$ New Profit $= \$23,000x - \$17,000$

Letting $\quad$ New Profit $= 0$
$\qquad\qquad 0 = \$23,000x - \$17,000$
$\qquad\qquad x = \dfrac{\$17,000}{\$23,000}$
$\qquad\qquad x = \underline{.739 \times 100, \text{ or } 74\% \text{ capacity}}$ (approximate)

(*or*)

Fixed Cost = $17,000

Variable Cost = $27,000, or $54 per unit, or 54% of sales

$$\frac{\$17,000}{1 - .54} = \frac{\$17,000}{.46} = \underline{\underline{\$37,000, \text{ or } 74\% \text{ capacity (approximate), or 370 units}}}$$

Unit Cost at New Break-Even Point

$$\text{Unit Cost} = \frac{a + b_1 x}{b_2 x}$$

$$= \frac{\$17,000 + \$27,000 \,(.74)}{500 \,(.74)}$$

$$= \frac{\$17,000 + \$19,980}{370}$$

$$= \underline{\underline{\$100 \text{ (approximate)}}}$$

Unit Cost at 90 Percent of Capacity

$$\text{Unit Cost} = \frac{\$17,000 + \$27,000 \,(.90)}{500 \,(.90)}$$

$$= \frac{\$17,000 + \$24,300}{450}$$

$$= \underline{\underline{\$92 \text{ (approximate)}}}$$

The above equations permit the development of unit costs using data included in the budget. They further permit quick and easy computations in connection with problems raised by changing conditions. Budget data expressed in equations permit quicker analysis of the effects of a variety of changes in unit costs.

MARGIN OF SAFETY

Information developed from a break-even analysis offers additional useful control data such as the *margin of safety*, which is a selected sales figure less break-even sales. From the data on page 743, where sales are $5,000,000, the margin of safety is $1,000,000 ($5,000,000 − $4,000,000). Expressed as a percentage of sales, the margin of safety is 20 percent and is called the *margin of safety ratio (M/S)*.

$$\text{Margin of Safety Ratio } (M/S) = \frac{\text{Selected Sales Figure} - \text{Break-Even Sales}}{\text{Selected Sales Figure}}$$

$$= \frac{\$5,000,000 - \$4,000,000}{\$5,000,000}$$

$$= \underline{20\%}$$

The margin of safety indicates how much sales may decrease before the company will suffer a loss. The margin of safety is directly related to profit. Using the same data from page 743, with a contribution margin ratio of 40 percent and a margin of safety ratio of 20 percent, then:

$$\text{Profit} = \text{Contribution Margin Ratio} \times \text{Margin of Safety Ratio}$$
$$P = C/M \times M/S$$
$$P = 40\% \times 20\%$$
$$P = \underline{\underline{8\%}}$$

If the contribution margin ratio and the profit percentage are known, the margin of safety ratio is:

$$M/S = \frac{P}{C/M} = \frac{8\%}{40\%} = \underline{\underline{20\%}}$$

DYNAMIC PROFIT CHARTING

Management can employ formulas and/or charts in order to (1) set proper output levels and achieve a profit goal, (2) select the most profitable product lines, (3) examine pricing policies, and (4) decide on new machinery and equipment or on new expansion plans. The better the understanding of charts and analyses, the better the managerial results. Management must understand that:

1. A change in per unit variable costs changes the contribution margin ratio and the break-even point.
2. A change in selling price changes the contribution margin ratio and the break-even point.
3. Contribution margin figures are affected only by changes per unit in variable costs and selling prices.
4. A change in fixed costs changes the break-even point but not the contribution margin figure.
5. A combined change in fixed and variable costs in the same direction causes an extremely sharp change in the break-even point.

APPLYING COST-VOLUME-PROFIT ANALYSIS

A cost-volume-profit analysis is generally prepared from annual budget figures, but figures from monthly statements can also be used. Furthermore, the analysis can also be applied to a specific product class, to distribution outlets, to methods of sale, and for profit determination. The analysis may be based on the results of only two representative months, as shown in the following illustration:

	Sales	Total Costs	Profit
Month of June.............................	$50,000	$40,000	$10,000
Month of May..............................	40,000	36,000	4,000
Net difference.............................	$10,000	$ 4,000	$ 6,000

An increase in sales of $10,000 resulted in an increase in costs of $4,000 and an increase in profit of $6,000. This indicates that each dollar increase in sales covered its variable costs of $.40 and contributed $.60 to profit or fixed expenses and profit.

The variable cost factor is found by subtracting the C/M ratio from 100 percent. As $6,000 ÷ $10,000 = 60 percent (the C/M ratio), the variable cost ratio is 100 percent − 60 percent = 40 percent or, more directly, $4,000 ÷ $10,000 = 40 percent. Knowing the variable cost ratio, the fixed costs in total costs for the month of June may be found as follows:

Total costs..................	$40,000
Variable costs ($50,000 × .40)	20,000
Fixed costs.................	$20,000

For the month of May the fixed costs are also $20,000, computed as follows: $36,000 − $16,000 ($40,000 sales × .40) = $20,000. This fact is in accordance with the generally accepted validity of the linear relationship of the cost-output figures. The correctness of this assumption can be tested by assuming the following data for the month of October:

Sales..........	$60,000
Total costs.....	45,000
Profit.........	$15,000

Previously, the variable cost ratio was 40 percent, and the fixed costs were $20,000. However, a check shows:

Total actual costs.....................................		$45,000
Expected: Variable costs ($60,000 × .40)..............	$24,000	
Fixed costs............................	20,000	44,000
Difference..		$ 1,000

This difference should be investigated. Fixed and variable costs must be checked to discover any shift of these elements. However, the cause may rest in a shift of the product mix or in numerous other factors.

The C/M ratio permits the computations of the profit without the necessity of detailed calculations of variable costs. The formula is: P = (S × C/M) − FC with P representing profit; S, sales; and FC, fixed costs. Again using the figures of the contribution margin income statement on page 744, the profit could be computed as follows:

$$P = (S \times C/M) - FC$$
$$P = (\$5,000,000 \times .40) - \$1,600,000$$
$$P = \$2,000,000 - \$1,600,000$$
$$P = \$400,000$$

The same formula permits the computation of additional data. If, for example, a company has fixed costs of $90,000 with sales at $300,000 and a profit of $60,000, the C/M ratio is:

$$P = (S \times C/M) - FC$$
$$\$60,000 = (\$300,000 \times C/M) - \$90,000$$
$$\$60,000 + \$90,000 = (\$300,000 \times C/M)$$
$$\frac{\$150,000}{\$300,000} = C/M$$
$$50\% = C/M$$

Or suppose the same company with a C/M ratio of 50 percent suffers a $30,000 loss. The volume of sales is:

$$P = (S \times C/M) - FC$$
$$- \$30,000 = (S \times .50) - \$90,000$$
$$- \$30,000 + \$90,000 = (S \times .50)$$
$$\frac{\$60,000}{.50} = S$$
$$\$120,000 = S$$

The answer, $120,000 sales volume, can be checked in this manner:

Sales...		$120,000
Less:		
Variable costs (50% of sales)	$60,000	
Fixed costs......................................	90,000	150,000
Loss..		$ (30,000)

While such quick computations are indeed possible and undoubtedly helpful in many circumstances, the fact still remains that the reasonably accurate separation of semivariable expenses into their fixed and variable elements must precede any subsequent use of such figures, if the figures are to be meaningful.

THE PROFIT-VOLUME ANALYSIS GRAPH

Break-even analysis and cost-volume-profit analysis also employ the *profit-volume (P/V) analysis graph*, which relates profits to volume and is constructed as follows:

1. The graph is divided into two parts by the sales line represented by a horizontal line in the graph on page 758.

2. Total fixed costs are marked off below the sales line on the left-hand vertical line. The computed profit or loss figure is located by moving horizontally to the point representing assumed sales dollars, then moving vertically to the point representing the computed profit or loss.

3. Fixed cost and profit points are joined by a diagonal line which crosses the sales line at the break-even point.

Using the figures from the contribution margin income statement on page 744, the P/V analysis graph shown below can be constructed.

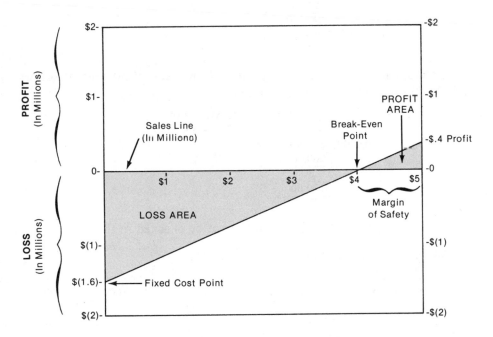

Profit-Volume Analysis Graph

GRAPHIC PRESENTATION OF
PROFIT-VOLUME RELATIONSHIP

A break-even chart presents a more compact picture of a company's profit structure than a tabular report. A P/V analysis graph indicates more forcefully the results of various possible courses that management might consider. Management, contemplating possible price increases and decreases for one of its products, might receive the results of its considerations in a summary similar to the one at the top of page 759.

A 10 percent drop in prices reduces the profit to the break-even point, and a 20 percent drop in prices causes a $40,000 loss. However, the 10 percent and 20 percent price increases cause profits to increase $40,000 and $80,000, respectively. The various price increases or decreases would result in the graph illustrated on page 759.

% Change in Sales Price	Decrease 20%	Decrease 10%	Normal Volume	Increase 10%	Increase 20%
Units...............	200,000	200,000	200,000	200,000	200,000
Sales...............	$320,000	$360,000	$400,000	$440,000	$480,000
Variable costs........	200,000	200,000	200,000	200,000	200,000
Contribution margin..	$120,000	$160,000	$200,000	$240,000	$280,000
Fixed costs..........	160,000	160,000	160,000	160,000	160,000
Net profit...........	....	0	$ 40,000	$ 80,000	$120,000
Net loss.............	$ 40,000	0	....	....	....
Net profit per unit....	....	....	$.20	$.40	$.60
Net loss per unit.....	$.20	....	....	....	....
% change in profit....	−200%	−100%	....	+100%	+300%
Return on investment*	− 20%	0%	20%	40%	60%
Break-even point.....	$426,667	$360,000	$320,000	$293,333	$274,286

*Investment is $200,000.

**Summary Illustrating the Effect of
Price Changes on Profit**

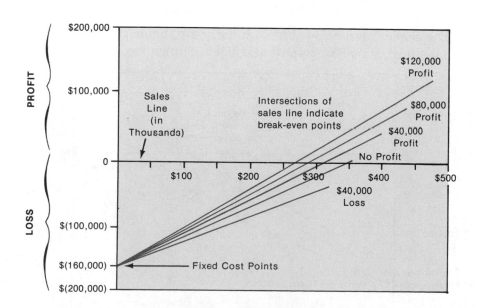

**P/V Analysis Graph Illustrating the Effect of
Price Changes on Profit**

Suppose a company's management wishes to have the following plans regarding sales, costs, volume, and profit depicted in a P/V graph:

Plan 1:		*Plan 2:*	
Decrease in price	10%	Increase in price	10%
Increase in volume	12%	Decrease in volume	12%
Variable costs increase	4%	Variable costs decrease	4%
Fixed costs increase	5%	Fixed costs decrease	5%

The effect of these plans is summarized below:

Composite Changes	Plan 1	Normal Volume	Plan 2
Units.....................	224,000	200,000	176,000
Sales...................	$403,200	$400,000	$387,200
Variable costs	232,960	200,000	168,960
Contribution margin.........	$170,240	$200,000	$218,240
Fixed costs	168,000	160,000	152,000
Net profit.................	$ 2,240	$ 40,000	$ 66,240
Net profit per unit	$.01	$.20	$.3763
% change in profit	−94.4%	....	+65.6%
Return on investment*.......	1.12%	20%	33.1%
Break-even point...........	$397,895	$320,000	$269,677

*Investment is $200,000.

The graph shown below, based on the above summary data illustrates a composite P/V analysis graph that is highly informative.

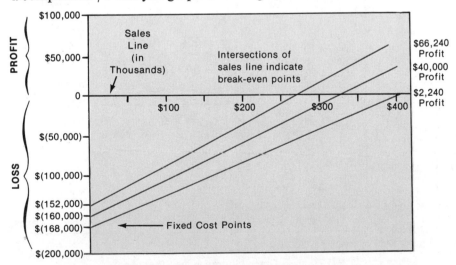

P/V Analysis Graph Illustrating the Effect of All Profit-Volume Factors

PRICE DECREASES AND VOLUME INCREASES

In an analysis of the effect of a price decrease on volume, it is often argued that the price decrease will in most instances be offset by an increase in volume, and, therefore, profits will not be reduced. Such an argument seems very plausible at first. Many businesspersons, however, have found that price reduction does not necessarily lead to the desired increase in volume. If the increase in volume does occur, it is often not large enough to overcome the effect of the price reduction on total profit.

This problem of a possible price reduction's being offset by a volume increase was studied by the U. S. Steel Corporation. The purpose of the study was "to ascertain the increase in volume that would have to take place to offset various decreases in steel prices by the United States Steel Corporation subsidiaries, taking into consideration the effect of increased volume on costs, and to estimate the financial gain or loss which would result from price reductions." The study reached the following conclusion. Because of the low elasticity of demand for steel, the increase in volume resulting from a reduction in price would be less than the increase needed to offset the adverse effects of the lower price on profits. The following data were prepared:

VOLUME INCREASES NEEDED TO COMPENSATE FOR AVERAGE PRICE DECREASES COMPARED TO MAXIMUM PROBABLE RESULTING VOLUME INCREASES

% Reduction in Price	% of Volume Increase Required to Offset Price Decrease	% of Greatest Probable Resulting Volume Increase
1%	3.4%	1.0%
5	19.6	5.3
10	48.8	11.1
15	96.7	17.7
20	190.3	25.0

The data indicate that the increase in steel consumption to be expected from a drop in price is not very great. While offsetting volume increases may be more favorable in other types of businesses and industries, they are, in general, hardly enough to overcome reduced revenues. In most cases a price reduction must be accompanied not only by increased volume but also by a reduction in the costs of the product.

PRODUCT ANALYSIS

The discussion so far has dealt with cost-volume-profit relationships based on total costs and total sales revenue. It is, however, much more desirable to investigate these relationships for individual products. Breakdown of costs and sales by products might appear impractical especially when hundreds of small items are manufactured. In such instances, it is advisable to reduce the large number of products to several major lines. In order to determine a better product cost for purposes of planning and control, many firms have departmentalized or productized their sprawling factory output. With such departmentalization, the contribution that each product or product group makes to the total contribution margin can be gauged more satisfactorily.

Variable costs used in previous illustrations are a composite of the variable costs of the several manufacturing cost centers, the marketing departments, and administrative divisions. However, it is possible to determine the variable cost of each product line because:

1. Direct materials and direct labor costs can be based on standard costs.

2. Variable factory overhead can be based on normal production hours, labor dollars, or machine hours established for the cost centers of the plant. The flexible budget for each cost center serves as an excellent basis for the determination of product factory overhead.

3. Variable marketing and administrative expenses can be charged directly to products or allocated on the basis of the sales value of each product or gross profit return or other bases discussed in Chapter 23. Of course, such allocations are arbitrary; and this limitation should not be overlooked.

Once the sales value and variable costs of each product have been determined, it will be apparent that each product has a different contribution margin and C/M ratio. To illustrate cost-volume-profit analysis by products, the figures of the Normal Volume column of the summary on page 760 are used and separated into four products resulting in the detailed data shown below.

Product	Sales Value of Production	Variable Costs	% of V.C. to Sales	Contribution Margin	C/M Ratio
A	$120,000	$100,000	83%	$ 20,000	17%
B	140,000	60,000	43	80,000	57
C	90,000	30,000	33	60,000	67
D	50,000	10,000	20	40,000	80
Total	$400,000	$200,000	50%	$200,000	50%
			Less fixed costs.	160,000	
			Net profit	$ 40,000	

$$\text{Break-even point} = \frac{\$160,000}{.50} = \underline{\$320,000}$$

The contribution margin and C/M ratio are shown for each product and in total. The C/M ratio in this illustration varies from 17 percent for Product A to 80 percent for Product D. If the present sales mix can be altered or if sales can be expanded, products with higher C/M ratios afford greater relative contributions to profit per dollar of sales. But the product's C/M ratio, related sales dollars, and contribution margin must be related to facility utilization. The product offering the higher C/M ratio is desirable only if the resulting contribution margin (C/M ratio × sales dollars) is greater than could be achieved by some alternate use of the same facilities.

GRAPHIC PRESENTATION OF THE COST-VOLUME-PROFIT RELATIONSHIP FOR INDIVIDUAL PRODUCTS

Previous P/V analysis graphs dealt with total sales and total costs. The P/V analysis graph below indicates the profit path for each product and is constructed as follows:

1. The horizontal line OO represents sales and is marked off from zero to $400,000.

2. The profit path for all products is then drawn, starting at the $(160,000) fixed cost point in the loss area and ending at the $40,000 profit point in the profit area. The break-even point is at the point of crossover from the loss to the profit area.

3. The profit path of each product is plotted next. It starts with the product with the highest C/M ratio — in this case, Product D. The line begins at

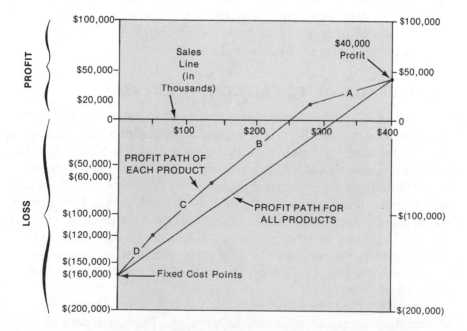

P/V Analysis Graph for Individual Product Analysis

the toal fixed cost point and is drawn to the $(120,000) point in the loss area directly below the $50,000 sales-volume point. The plotting indicates that $40,000 of the $160,000 fixed costs have been recovered.

4. The profit path of Product C starts at the point where D's path ended. The line for Product C ends opposite the loss figure of $(60,000) and below the sales volume figure of $140,000. The $(60,000) figure shows that $60,000 additional fixed costs were recovered. The $140,000 point on the sales line is the accumulated sales total of Products D and C ($50,000 + $90,000).

5. The profit path for Product B begins at the end of C's path and leads across the sales line into the profit area to the $20,000 profit point immediately above the sales volume figure of $280,000.

6. Product A with the lowest C/M ratio is charted last. It adds $20,000 to the profit, and its path ends at the $40,000 profit figure.

The plotting of the profit path of each product provides management with an interesting pictorial report — the steeper the slope, the higher the C/M ratio. If any product does not have a contribution margin, its path or slope would be downward. Also, the dollar amount of each product's contribution margin can be "read" from the graph by measuring the vertical distance from one plotted point to the next. Similar graphs can also be used for the analysis of sales by territories, salespersons, and classes of customers. It is then possible to portray the profitability of territories, the effectiveness of salespersons' selling activities, and the type of customers whose purchases mean greatest profit to the company. In this way, sales effort is measured by marginal contributions toward fixed costs and profit — and not by sales volume.

THE FALLACY OF TOTAL COST ANALYSIS

Product A in the illustration demonstrates an important point in cost-volume-profit analysis. Because this product contributes a lower contribution margin and C/M ratio than the other products, it is often felt that it should be discontinued. This reasoning is particularly prevalent when the profitability of a product is determined by distributing all fixed and variable costs to all products. Depending on methods used to allocate fixed costs, it is likely that certain products will show a profit — others a loss. But individual variable product costs and sales — not total costs — are important in the analysis. To help make this clear, a distribution of the fixed costs to each product on the basis of the variable cost ratios is illustrated on page 765.

The analysis indicates that Product A is a loss item and should be eliminated. Such reasoning is obviously wrong. Product A actually contributes $20,000 to the company's total profit picture. Most methods used

FIXED COSTS DISTRIBUTION TO EACH PRODUCT
BASED ON VARIABLE COST RATIOS

Product	Sales Value of Production	Total Cost*	Profit	Percentage of Profit to Sales
A	$120,000	$180,000	−$60,000	−50%
B	140,000	108,000	32,000	22.8
C	90,000	54,000	36,000	40
D	50,000	18,000	32,000	64
Total	$400,000	$360,000	$40,000	10%

*Computation of Total Cost:

Product	Variable Cost	Variable Cost Ratio		Fixed Cost		Fixed Cost Distribution	Total Cost
A	$100,000	$\dfrac{\$100,000}{\$200,000}$	×	$160,000	=	$80,000	$180,000
B	60,000	$\dfrac{60,000}{200,000}$	×	160,000	=	48,000	108,000
C	30,000	$\dfrac{30,000}{200,000}$	×	160,000	=	24,000	54,000
D	10,000	$\dfrac{10,000}{200,000}$	×	160,000	=	8,000	18,000
Total	$200,000						

to distribute fixed costs to products confuse cost-volume-profit relationships, for they do not recognize the change in costs and profits produced by a change in volume or product mix. Confusion is eliminated by following the contribution margin principle which sets apart not only the fixed costs that must be allocated, but also those that are directly assignable to a specific product and concentrates attention on the margin between sales and variable costs. Products make a favorable contribution as long as the sales revenue exceeds the related variable cost.

An alternate product should replace the existing one only if idle capacity is not available and only if the alternate product will yield a larger total dollar contribution toward recovering fixed costs and profit. Also, since some fixed costs can be changed in the short run, the analysis must consider any change in fixed cost associated with moving from the existing product to an alternate product. It is assumed, of course, that the added product can be marketed without disturbing the market for other products of the company.

In the case of joint products, *variable* as well as *fixed* joint costs are best viewed as they relate to the contribution made by the *group* of joint products rather than based on arbitrary allocation to each product (see "Joint Product Cost Analysis for Managerial Decisions and Profitability Analysis," pages 197–198).

DISCUSSION QUESTIONS

1. Define *break-even point*.
2. How can the break-even point be computed?
3. What is the relationship of budgets and standards to break-even analysis?
4. (a) Why must the conventional income statement be restated for computation of the break-even point? (b) What type of statement is constructed?
5. State the formulas commonly used to determine the break-even point in dollars; in units.
6. The break-even chart is an excellent planning device. Discuss.
7. The break-even chart and the unit profit graph intend to show the same information but seem to differ. How?
8. (a) What is meant by *margin of safety?* (b) How is such a figure determined?
9. The following quotation taken from a company's dividend notice shows an effort on the part of the company to promulgate facts on the subject of break-even points:

   ". . . certain specific steps involving operating economies, made 'the hard way' by elimination of personnel and consolidation of duties, were one factor. Price increases . . . were another. Lowering the cost of distribution was the third. All three of these steps were within the control of the management. Management recognizes the importance of lowering the break-even point . . ."

   (a) By comparative illustrations, show what the management of the company has accomplished.
   (b) To demonstrate your familiarity with computing the break-even point, determine it from the following facts:

      Ratio of variable costs to sales is 30%.
      Aggregate fixed expenses are $63,000.

10. Discuss the weaknesses inherent in the preparation and uses of break-even point analyses.
11. What is meant by the term "cost-volume-profit relationship"? Why is this relationship important in business management?
12. What can cause a change in profits?
13. How does the break-even point move when changes occur in (a) variable expenses? (b) fixed expenses?
14. What is meant by a contribution margin income figure?
15. Why is a graphic form of presentation preferable to a tabular form?
16. A price reduction is always accompanied by a proportionate volume increase. Discuss.
17. Why is a cost-volume-profit analysis by products valuable to management?
18. Illustrate how the contribution of each product to the recovery of fixed expenses and to the total profit of the company can be presented in graphic form.
19. Cost-volume-profit relationships provide management with a simplified framework for organizing its thinking on a number of problems. Discuss.

20. A break-even chart, as illustrated below, is a useful technique for showing relationships between costs, volume, and profits.

    (a) Identify the numbered components of the break-even chart.
    (b) Discuss the significance of the concept of the "relevant range" to break-even analyses.

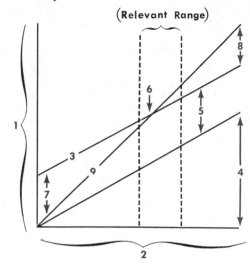

(AICPA adapted)

21. Use the P/V analysis graph at the right to select the correct answers from the sentences given in (a) and (b).

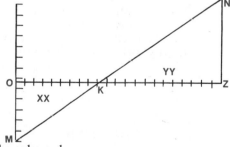

    (a) (1) The areas *XX* and *YY* and the point *K* represent profit, loss, and sales volume at the break-even point, respectively.
        (2) The Line *O-Z* represents the sales volume.
        (3) The line *N-Z* represents fixed costs.
        (4) The line *M-N* represents total costs.
        (5) None of the above.

    (b) The vertical scale represents (1) sales volume; (2) units produced; (3) the profit area above *O* and the loss area below *O*; (4) the contribution margin; (5) none of the above.

(NAA adapted)

22. Select the correct answer for each of the following statements.

    (a) An accountant would typically have the following in mind when referring to the margin of safety: (1) the excess of budgeted or actual sales revenue over the fixed costs; (2) the excess of actual sales over budgeted sales; (3) the excess of sales revenue over the variable costs; (4) the excess of a selected sales figure over break-even sales; (5) none of the above.

(b) The alternative that would decrease the contribution margin per unit the most is a 15% (1) decrease in selling price; (2) increase in variable expenses; (3) increase in selling price; (4) decrease in variable expenses; (5) decrease in fixed expenses.

(c) If fixed costs decrease while variable costs per unit remain constant, the new contribution margin in relation to the old contribution margin will be (1) unchanged; (2) higher; (3) lower; (4) indeterminate; (5) none of the above.

(d) Cost-volume-profit relationships which are curvilinear may be analyzed linearly by considering only (1) a relevant range of activity; (2) relevant fixed costs; (3) relevant variable costs; (4) fixed and semivariable costs.

(e) Cost-volume-profit analysis is most important for the determination of the (1) volume of operation necessary to break even; (2) relationship between revenues and costs at various levels of operations; (3) variable revenues necessary to equal fixed costs; (4) sales revenue necessary to equal variable costs.

(f) In 19A the contribution margin ratio of the Wayne Company was 30%. In 19B fixed costs are expected to be $120,000 — as in 19A. Sales are forecast at $550,000 — a 10% increase over 19A. To increase net income by $15,000 in 19B, the contribution margin ratio must be (1) 20%; (2) 30%; (3) 40%; (4) 70%.

(g) The major assumption as to cost and revenue behavior underlying conventional cost-volume-profit calculations is the (1) constancy of fixed costs; (2) variability of unit prices and efficiency; (3) curvilinearity of relationships; (4) linearity of relationships.

(h) The cost-volume-profit analysis underlying the conventional break-even chart does *not* assume that (1) sales prices per unit will remain fixed; (2) total fixed costs remain the same; (3) some costs vary inversely with activity; (4) costs are linear and continuous over the relevant range.

(NAA and AICPA adapted)

EXERCISES

Exercises 1-14 cover basic cost accounting procedures and mathematical calculations for break-even and cost-volume-profit analyses.

1. The Zimmerman Company's budget for 19— is:

Sales	$1,400,000
Variable costs	560,000
Fixed costs	800,000
Net income	40,000

Required: (1) The break-even sales volume and a proof of the answer. (2) The sales volume needed for a desired net income of $150,000.

2. The Michel Company makes these data available for 19—:

Annual fixed costs	$ 3,000,000
Contribution margin ratio (C/M)	30%
Present sales	$15,000,000

Required: (1) The break-even point.
(2) The margin of safety in dollars and the margin of safety ratio.
(3) The sales required to earn a profit of $2,000,000.

3. The firm of Smith and Thompson, certified public accountants, has been studying the sales requirements of the Frisco Bottling Company. In the course of the study, the managing partner submits the following estimated data:

Sales..	$900,000
Direct materials..	210,000
Direct labor..	165,200
Fixed factory overhead.......................................	169,000
Variable factory overhead....................................	102,600
Fixed marketing expenses.....................................	71,000
Variable marketing expenses..................................	80,000
Fixed administrative expenses................................	9,500
Variable administrative expenses.............................	4,150

Required: The break-even point in dollars.

4. The following data of the Earley Co. are given for May:

Plant capacity................................	2,000 units per month
Fixed costs...................................	$4,000 per month
Variable costs................................	$2.50 per unit
Selling price.................................	$5 per unit

Required: (1) The break-even point in dollars.
(2) The break-even chart. (Use a dollar scale for both the x-axis and y-axis; label and identify each element of the chart.)

5. From the books and records of the Coe Company, the cost analyst extracted the following data:

Costs	Variable Costs	Fixed Costs	Total
Direct materials................	$3,000,000	—	$ 3,000,000
Direct labor....................	3,000,000	—	3,000,000
Factory overhead................	800,000	$500,000	1,300,000
Marketing expenses..............	700,000	300,000	1,000,000
Administrative expenses.........	500,000	200,000	700,000
Sales amounted to..............			$10,000,000

Required: (1) The contribution margin ratio (C/M).
(2) The break-even point.
(3) The proposal has been made to increase fixed costs $100,000, with sales and variable costs remaining the same.
  (a) The new break-even point.
  (b) The new profit.
(4) Another proposal considers a modernization of present equipment at an annual increase of fixed costs of $250,000, with the expectation of saving the same amount in each of the direct materials and the direct labor costs. Refer to the original data in (1). The results of this proposal with respect to (a) the contribution margin ratio (C/M), (b) the break-even point, and (c) the profit of the company.

6. An analysis of past and future costs of the Gonzales Manufacturing Company led to the following information:

Cost Elements	Variable Costs (Percentage of Sales)	Fixed Costs
Direct materials.....................	32.8%	
Direct labor.......................	28.4	
Factory overhead..................	12.6	$284,900
Marketing expenses...............	4.1	68,400
General and administrative expenses.	1.1	66,700

Budgeted sales for the next year are $2,850,000.

Required: (1) The break-even sales volume in dollars.
(2) The profit at the budgeted sales volume.
(3) The profit if actual sales:
    (a) Drop 12% from budgeted sales.
    (b) Increase 3% from budgeted sales.

7. The Dolan Company's variable costs average 60% of its sales volume.

Required: (1) The sales volume in dollars if the Dolan Company is to cover its fixed costs of $600,000 and make a profit (before income taxes) of $200,000. (Compute answer to nearest $1,000.)
(2) The sales volume in dollars to earn the same profit as in (1) above if selling prices are increased by 10% while *total* fixed costs and *unit* variable costs remain unchanged. (Compute answer to nearest $1,000.)

8. Maximum productive capacity of the Leger Corporation has been set at 210,000 units per year. Normal capacity is regarded as 180,000 units per year. Standard variable manufacturing costs are $11 per unit. Fixed factory overhead is $368,000 per year. Variable marketing expenses are $5 per unit, and fixed marketing expenses are $252,000 per year. The unit sales price is $20.

Required: (1) The break-even point expressed in dollar sales.
(2) The units that must be sold to earn a profit of $60,000 per year.
(3) The units that must be sold to earn a profit of 10% on sales.

9. The annual budget of The Eversole Co. shows:

Sales (40,000 units).....................................		$80,000
Fixed production costs...............................	$20,000	
Fixed marketing and administrative costs...............	26,000	
Variable production costs............................	19,000	
Variable marketing and administrative costs.............	5,000	
Total costs...		70,000
Profit from operations.............................		$10,000

Required: With each part independent of all other parts unless so stated:
(1) The company's break-even point in sales dollars.
(2) The company's break-even point in units.
(3) The company proposes to buy equipment to replace workers. If this is done, fixed costs will increase $2,280 and variable costs will decrease $1,000, when sales are $80,000. What is the new break-even point in sales dollars?

(4) Assume fixed costs are increased by $2,000 and variable costs by $1,000 at the $80,000 sales level. How much must sales be increased to make the same $10,000 profit?

(5) The sales manager proposes an increase in unit sales price of 5%, with an expected drop of 15% in volume. Variable costs are expected to bear the same relationship to sales dollars as in the original annual budget. If approved, what would be the budgeted profit? What would be the new break-even point in sales dollars?

10. Operations of the Wadsworth Company in 19— disclosed a margin of safety ratio (M/S) of 20% and a contribution margin ratio (C/M) of 60%.

Required: (1) The net income for 19—, assuming the fixed costs amounted to (a) $60,000 and (b) $24,000.

(2) An income statement to prove answers to (a) and (b).

11. Prince Dog Food Company has budgeted for 19— fixed costs of $50,000, sales of $250,000, and a profit of $80,000.

Required: The contribution margin ratio (C/M).

12. Laurel Mills, Inc., with fixed costs of $100,000, found that when sales jumped from $300,000 to $400,000, the profit increased by $40,000. Both sales levels exceeded the break-even point.

Required: The profit at a sales volume of $650,000.

13. On sales of $2,000,000, the contribution margin ratio of the Taro Manufacturing Company is 40%.

Required: (1) The percent increase in dollar volume required to offset a 10% decrease in price in order to end up with the same dollar profit.

(2) The new sales volume in dollars.

14. The Choctaw Company has sales of $200,000, a margin of safety ratio of 25%, and a contribution margin ratio of 33⅓%. A decrease of fixed costs and a decrease of sales prices have changed the margin of safety ratio to 40% and the contribution margin ratio to 30%.

Required: (1) The amount of sales decrease.

(2) The new break-even point.

(3) The new net income.

(4) The amount of fixed costs decrease.

15. Price Decrease vs. Volume Increase. The Arch-Trenton Zinc Diecasting Co. is one of several suppliers of Part X to an automobile manufacturing firm. Orders are distributed to the various diecasting companies on a fairly even basis. However, the sales manager believes that a 25% increase in units sold is possible through a price reduction.

The following data are available:

	Present	Proposed
Unit price............................	$2.50	$2.25
Unit sales volume..................	200,000	Plus 25%
Variable costs (total)...............	$350,000	Same unit rate
Fixed costs........................	120,000	$120,000
Net income........................	30,000	?

Required: (1) The new net income or loss based on the sales manager's proposal. (2) The unit sales volume required to make the original $30,000 net income.

16. Break-Even Analysis Under Various Situations. The accountant for the Schwenker Corporation is asked to make a break-even analysis for the following situations:

Situation	*Required*
Total fixed costs amount to $1,500,000 while the variable costs to sales ratio is 75%.	(1) The break-even point in dollars.
Forty percent of the above 75% ratio is applicable to direct materials cost while the remaining 35% consists of conversion costs. Materials increased by 10%.	(2) The new materials cost ratio. (3) The new variable cost ratio. (4) The new break-even point.
	Base the answers to (5), (6), and (7) on (1).
Labor strikes for a 10% increase in wage rates. In the present 75% ratio, the labor cost represents 15%.	(5) The new labor cost ratio. (6) The new variable cost ratio. (7) The new break-even point.
	Base the answers to (8) and (9) on (1).
The advertising manager suggests an increase of $250,000 in the advertising budget to be accompanied by a 10% reduction in sales prices.	(8) The new variable cost ratio. (9) The new break-even point.
Take all changes simultaneously into consideration.	(10) The variable cost ratio. (11) The new break-even point. (12) An income statement to prove the answers to (10) and (11).

17. Achieving Management's Profit Goal. The Mark Company's income statement shows:

Sales...........................		$ 80,000
Variable costs..................	$63,420	
Fixed costs.....................	25,150	88,570
Net loss........................		$ (8,570)

Presently total labor costs amount to $30,000. Management believes that (a) if an increase of productivity of labor is possible, labor costs per unit could be reduced by 8% of total labor costs; (b) if sales volume could be increased by a uniform price reduction of 5% on all of the additional business; and (c) if fixed costs were reduced by $1,150, a net income of $4,000 (before income taxes) might be achieved.

Required: The amount of sales needed to reach the desired profit goal.

18. Marketing Strategy via Contribution Margin Analysis. Break-even analyses are planning tools. Management, of course, wants to do more than just break even; it wants to maximize dollar profits. This means that break-even analyses and charts are actually *profit-planning* devices.

For example, Cromex, Inc. is considering the replacement of one item from its product line with another. Present costs and output data are:

Item	Price	Variable Costs per Item	Percent Total of Sales Volume
A	$20	$10	40%
B	25	15	35
C	30	18	25

Total fixed costs per year: $150,000
Total sales last year: $500,000

Item C is to be replaced by Item D. Forecasted costs and output data are:

Item	Price	Variable Costs per Unit	Percent Total of Sales Volume
A	$20	$10	50%
B	25	15	30
D	28	14	20

Total fixed costs per year: $150,000
Total expected sales: $500,000

Required: Analysis of and decision on the proposed change.

19. Break-Even Analysis with Shifting Costs and Profits. The Savannah Company provides the following data:

Normal plant capacity.................	200,000 units
Fixed costs.........................	$120,000
Variable costs......................	$1.35 per unit
Selling price.......................	$2.25 per unit

Required: (1) The break-even point, in dollars, number of units, and per-cent of capacity.

(2) The margin of safety ratio and the margin of safety in dollars, when operating at normal plant capacity.

(3) The new break-even point in dollars, if the selling price is reduced to $2; other data remain the same.

(4) Volume in dollars required to yield a profit of $30,000 if the calculation is based on (a) the data of (1) above; (b) the data of (3) above.

(5) The break-even point in dollar sales if fixed costs are reduced by $20,000; state in sales dollars, number of units, and percent of capacity based on data given in (1) above only.

(6) The expected profit if budgeted sales of $450,000 are realized with costs the same as at the beginning of the problem and when (a) the selling price per unit is $2.25; (b) the selling price per unit is $2.

20. Break-Even Analysis, New Equipment; New Profit Goal. The management of the Kent William Company is presently thinking about (1) buying a machine that will reduce the number of production workers and at the same time (2) cutting the selling price of the product. The new machine will increase costs by $10,000 due to depreciation; variable costs will decrease about 25% due to the reduction of direct workers; finally, the selling price will be reduced by 10%.

Before these changes were under consideration, the company had experienced the following costs and prices:

Selling price per unit........................	$ 100
Variable costs per unit......................	60
Total fixed costs...........................	30,000

Required: (1) Based on the original data:
    (a) The break-even number of units.
    (b) The profit if the company operates at a 900-unit volume.
  (2) Considering the contemplated changes:
    (a) The new break-even number of units.
    (b) The profit if the company wishes to retain the 900-unit volume.
    (c) The profit if the company should experience a sales volume of 1,000 units as the sales manager predicts on the basis of the price reduction.
  (3) The new profit if the company did *not* buy the new machine and laid off no workers, but reduced the price by 10% and increased volume to 950 units.

21. Sales Mix; Contribution Margin. The contribution margin indicates how much each product is contributing to fixed costs and profit in the present sales mix. The contribution margin also informs management as to which products will add more to profit if sales of these units can be increased.

Variable costs can be utilized in this type of analysis when management seeks an answer to the question: "Which product shall we *push*?"

Per Unit Data	*Product A*	*Product B*
Selling price......................	$12.60	$5.50
Variable costs....................	9.62	4.18
Fixed costs.......................	2.07	.65
Units per hour....................	45	70

Required: (1) The amount of profit per unit for each product.

(2) The percentage of profit to selling price for each product.

(3) The amount of contribution per unit toward fixed costs and profit for each product.

(4) The contribution margin ratio for each product.

(5) The contribution per hour toward fixed costs and profit for each product.

(6) The course yielding the greater contribution toward fixed costs and profit if management contemplates the allocation of:
    (a) 200 hours to Product A and 100 hours to Product B, or
    (b) 100 hours to Product A and 200 hours to Product B.

(Based on an NAA article)

22. Break-Even Analysis — Hospital Operations. The controller of St. Paul's Baptist Hospital analyzed its operations and found this information:

Costs	Variable	Fixed
Direct patient supplies.............................	$100,000	
Direct salaries......................................	754,625	
Patient service overhead...........................	25,000	$105,000
Administrative expenses............................	75,000	175,000
Total.......................................	$954,625	$280,000

These costs are based on normal inpatient service days of 27,275 in the eighty-bed hospital and on patient service revenues of $1,227,375. Deficits are financed by contributions from the Southern Baptist Convention.

Required: (1) The contribution margin ratio (C/M). (Compute the answer to 1/100th of 1%.)
(2) The break-even point in revenue volume and inpatient service days.
(3) The margin of safety ratio (M/S). (Compute the answer to 1/100th of 1%.)
(4) Since the hospital is currently operating at its highest practicable capacity, a proposal has been made for the construction of an additional wing of twenty beds. Fixed costs are expected to increase in about the same ratio as the current fixed costs per bed ratio; the variable cost to sales should remain the same. (Compute the new break-even point in revenue volume and in inpatient service days.)

23. Break-Even Analysis. The Carey Company sold 100,000 units of its product at $20 per unit. Variable costs are $14 per unit (manufacturing costs of $11 and marketing costs of $3). Fixed costs are incurred uniformly throughout 19— and amount to $792,000 (manufacturing costs of $500,000 and marketing costs of $292,000).

Required: (1) The break-even point in units and in dollars.
(2) The number of units that must be sold to earn a net income of $60,000 for 19— before income taxes.
(3) The number of units that must be sold to earn an aftertax income of $90,000 if the income tax rate is 40%.
(4) The number of units required to break even if labor costs are 50% of variable costs and 20% of fixed costs and if there is a 10% increase in wages and salaries.

(AICPA adapted)

PROBLEMS

24-1. Selling Price; Forecast Income Statement; Break-Even Analysis. The Vantage Manufacturing Company has recently leased manufacturing facilities for production of a new product. Based on studies made by the cost analyst, the following data have been made available:

	Amount	Per Unit
Estimated costs:		
Direct materials...............................	$ 96,000	$4.00
Direct labor...................................	14,400	.60
Factory overhead..............................	24,000	1.00
Administrative expenses.......................	28,800	1.20
Total......................................	$163,200	$6.80
Estimated annual sales.......................................		24,000 units

Marketing expenses are expected to be 15% of sales, and profit is to amount to $1.02 per unit.

Required: (1) The selling price per unit.
(2) A projected income statement for the year.
(3) The break-even point expressed in dollars and in units, assuming that 50% of the factory overhead and all of the administrative expenses are fixed but that all other costs are fully variable. (Compute the C/M ratio to 1/100th of 1%.)

(AICPA adapted)

24-2. Sales Mix and Break-Even Analysis. Rite-Beverage Bottling Company produces a variety of bottled drinks. The company has classified its products into these three basic categories:

Brand	Selling Price per Case	Variable Cost per Case
Trade-Name Brands.....	$1.50	$1.40
Tru-Ade Brands........	1.20	1.00
Dietary Brands.........	1.00	.40

The fixed costs of the company are $38,000 annually and do not change with any change in product mix nor with total volume changes of less than 50%. During 19A sales of Trade-Name Brands accounted for 50% of the company's total sales in cases. Sales of Tru-Ade Brands were four times that of Dietary Brands. Total sales revenue for the year was $500,000.

Required: (1) The break-even sales in dollars and units of each product group for 19A based on the actually experienced sales mix. (Show answers to nearest $1,000.)
(2) The amount which could be spent for advertising in 19B to increase sales of the more profitable lines so that Tru-Ade sales would account for 50% of sales in cases; Dietary 20%; and Trade-Name 30% with the company still making a profit of one and one-half times that of 19A on the same total sales revenue.

24-3. Break-Even Point and Contribution Margin with a Change of Prices and Costs. The management of Transradio, Inc. was disappointed with the profit experienced on the sale of its 100,000 transistor radios even though this represented a record number of sales with a net profit of $400,000. Competition from other firms in the industry was causing the management to worry about its market position. It was also concerned about the possibility that variable costs would increase in the next year as they had in the previous year. Total fixed costs amounted to $1,800,000; and they, too, were expected to increase. At the moment an average price of $42 was received for the product. A breakdown of fixed and variable costs per unit shows:

Variable Costs	Per Unit	Fixed Costs	Total
Direct materials................	$10	Fixed factory overhead.......	$ 500,000
Direct labor....................	5	Selling and advertising.......	700,000
Variable factory overhead.......	5	Administrative and general...	600,000
Total variable costs...........	$20	Total fixed costs..........	$1,800,000

The income statement of the company for the year under examination appears as follows:

Sales...		$4,200,000
Cost of goods sold:		
Direct materials.............................	$1,000,000	
Direct labor................................	500,000	
Factory overhead............................	1,000,000	2,500,000
Gross profit on sales.............................		$1,700,000
Selling and advertising expenses..................	$ 700,000	
Administrative and general expenses..............	600,000	1,300,000
Net income......................................		$ 400,000

The management faces the problem of finding out what will happen if costs and prices of the product are changed. A 7% decrease in prices and a 7% increase in fixed costs have been considered. An analysis of past conditions indicated that variable costs have been increasing at a rate of 7% each year. The management requests the controller to offer his ideas in the solution of this problem. The management is interested in some knowledge regarding the percentage increase in volume necessary under each of the possible outcomes to maintain the same profit of $400,000.

Required: (1) The current break-even point and the contribution margin.

(2) Taken individually, the break-even point, the contribution margin, and the net income if:

    (a) Prices are reduced 7%.
    (b) Variable costs increase 7%.
    (c) Fixed costs increase 7%.

(3) The increase in volume necessary to offset each of the changes in (a), (b), and (c).

(4) The change which is most influential on the net income.

24-4. Break-Even Analysis When Costs and Sales Mix Change.   The O. J. Jentzen Company, Inc., a small manufacturer of machine tools, is interested in knowing the effect of a change in its sales mix on net income. It has recently become aware of the potential benefits to be derived from separation of costs into fixed and variable components, and the analysis therefrom. The controller has been asked by the vice-president in charge of marketing to consider the potential effects from shifts in sales mix between its two major products, A (original equipment) and B (replacement parts). Expected sales for both products for 19— are identical at $15,000,000. For Product A, the variable cost ratio is 55%; for Product B, 35%. Fixed costs are $4,000,000 and $7,000,000 for Products A and B, respectively.

Required: (1) The expected net income of each product for 19— and the combined net income for both products.

(2) Management has considered increasing sales of either Product A or B by 20% with the total sales of both products remaining the same at $30,000,000. Assuming the variable cost ratios and fixed costs for each product remain constant, the decision that would yield the greater aggregate net income.

(3) Validity of the decision for (2) if total fixed costs decline by 10% for each product.

(4) Validity of the decision for (2) if management believes it can reduce the variable cost ratio of Product A to 45%.

(5) Variable cost ratio which would make no difference whether Product A or B was increased by 20% in volume.

24-5. Product Mix Ratio and Break-Even Analysis. In constructing a break-even chart, analysts have been aware of the difficulty of dealing with the product mix in a multi-product firm. Yet, break-even analysis has been useful in making product mix decisions. To illustrate this usefulness, a cost analyst assumed the following situation for a company's three major products:

	Product		
	A	*B*	*C*
Sales price........................	$10.00	$8.00	$11.00
Variable costs....................	6.00	5.00	9.00
Contribution margin..............	$ 4.00	$3.00	$ 2.00
Total fixed costs, $200,000.			

For (1) and (2) below, compute the C/M ratio to 1/100th of 1%.

Required: (1) The break-even point if the three products are sold in the ratio of 4:3:7 units.

(2) The new break-even point if management decides to concentrate its sales efforts on Product A with its higher contribution margin resulting in a new sales ratio of 6:3:5 units.

24-6. Break-Even Analysis. The R. A. Ro Company, a manufacturer of quality handmade pipes, has experienced a steady growth in its sales for the past five years. Increased competition, however, has led Mr. Ro, the president, to believe that an aggressive advertising campaign will be necessary next year to maintain the company's present growth.

To prepare for next year's advertising campaign, the accountant presents Mr. Ro with the following data for the current year 19A:

COST SCHEDULE

	Per Pipe
Variable costs:	
Direct labor...	$ 8.00
Direct materials..	3.25
Variable factory overhead................................	2.50
Total variable costs....................................	$ 13.75
Fixed costs:	
Manufacturing...	$ 25,000
Marketing...	40,000
Administrative..	70,000
Total fixed costs.......................................	$135,000
Selling price per pipe..................................	$25
Expected sales, 19A (20,000 units)......................	$500,000
Federal income tax rate.................................	40%

Mr. Ro has set the 19B sales target at a level of $550,000, or 22,000 pipes.

Required: (1) The projected aftertax net income for 19A.

(2) The break-even point in units for 19A.

(3) The aftertax net income for 19B if an additional fixed marketing expense of $11,250 is spent for advertising in 19B (with all other costs remaining constant) in order to attain the 19B sales target.

(4) The break-even point in dollar sales for 19B if the additional $11,250 is spent for advertising.

(5) The required sales level in dollar sales to equal 19A's aftertax net income, if the additional $11,250 is spent for advertising in 19B.

(6) The maximum amount that can be spent on additional advertising at a sales level of 22,000 units, if an aftertax net income of $60,000 is desired.

(NAA adapted)

24-7. Break-Even Analysis. The Dooley Co. manufactures two products — Baubles and Trinkets. The following data are projects for the coming year:

	Baubles		Trinkets		Total
	Units	Amount	Units	Amount	Amount
Sales..................	10,000	$10,000	7,500	$10,000	$20,000
Fixed costs..............		$ 2,000		$ 5,600	$ 7,600
Variable costs...........		6,000		3,000	9,000
Total costs............		$ 8,000		8,600	$16,600
Net income before taxes...		$ 2,000		$ 1,400	$ 3,400

Required: (1) Assuming the facilities are not jointly used, the break-even sales in units for Baubles.

(2) Assuming the facilities are not jointly used, the break-even sales in dollars for Trinkets.

(3) Assuming that consumers purchase composite units of four Baubles and three Trinkets, the composite unit contribution margin.

(4) If consumers purchase composite units of four Baubles and three Trinkets, the break-even units for both products.

(5) If Baubles and Trinkets become one-to-one complements and there is no change in the company's cost function, the break-even dollars. (Round the contribution margin ratio to two decimal places.)

(6) If a composite unit is defined as one Bauble and one Trinket, the composite contribution margin ratio. (Round to two decimal places.)

(AICPA adapted)

24-8. Contribution Margin; Break-Even Analysis. The president of the Givens Company wants guidance on the advisability of eliminating Product C, one of the company's three similar products, or investing in new machinery to reduce the cost of Product C in the hope of reversing Product C's operating loss sustained in 19—. The three similar products are manufactured in a single plant in about the same amount of floor space, and the markets in which they are sold are very competitive.

A condensed operating income statement for all three products and for Product C only for the year ending October 31, 19—, is shown on page 780.

GIVENS COMPANY
OPERATING INCOME STATEMENT
FOR YEAR ENDING OCTOBER 31, 19—

	All Three Products	Product C
Sales...	$2,800,150	$350,000
Cost of goods sold:		
Raw materials..............................	$ 565,000	$ 80,000
Labor		
Direct.....................................	1,250,000	150,000
Indirect (fixed)...........................	55,000	18,000
Fringe benefits (15% of labor)...............	195,750	25,200
Royalties (1% of Product C sales)	3,500	3,500
Maintenance and repairs (fixed).................	6,000	2,000
Factory supplies............................	15,000	2,100
Depreciation (straight line).....................	25,200	7,100
Electrical power.............................	25,000	3,000
Scrap and spoilage.........................	4,300	600
Total cost of goods sold....................	$2,144,750	$291,500
Gross profit...................................	$ 655,400	$ 58,500
Marketing, general, and administrative expenses:		
Sales commissions..........................	$ 120,000	$ 15,000
Officers' salaries............................	32,000	10,500
Other wages and salaries (fixed)...............	14,000	5,300
Fringe benefits (15% of wages, salaries, and		
commissions)............................	24,900	4,620
Delivery expenses...........................	79,500	10,000
Advertising expenses (variable)................	195,100	26,000
Miscellaneous fixed expenses...................	31,900	10,630
Total marketing, general, and administrative		
expenses...................................	$ 497,400	$ 82,050
Net operating income (loss).....................	$ 158,000	$ (23,550)

Required: (1) A schedule showing the contribution margin for Product C
for the year ending October 31, 19—. Assume that each element of cost and
expense is entirely fixed or variable within the relevant range and that the change
in inventory levels has been negligible.

(2) A schedule computing the break-even point of Product C in terms of
annual dollar sales volume. Assume that in fiscal 19— the variable costs and
expenses of Product C totaled $297,500 and that its fixed costs and expenses
amounted to $75,100. Sales for 19— amounted to $350,000.

(3) The direct labor costs of Product C could have been reduced by $75,000
and the indirect labor costs by $4,000 by investing an additional $340,000
(financed with 5% bonds) in machinery with a ten-year life and an estimated
salvage value of $30,000 at the end of the period. However, the company would
have been liable for total severance pay costs of $18,000 (to be amortized over
a five-year period), and power costs would have increased $500 annually.

Assuming the information given above in (2), a schedule computing the
break-even point of Product C in terms of annual dollar sales volume if the additional machinery had been purchased and installed at the beginning of the year.

(AICPA adapted)

24-9. Hospital Department Break-Even Analysis. Columbus Hospital operates a general hospital but rents space and beds to separate entities for specialized areas such as pediatrics, maternity, psychiatric, etc. The hospital charges each separate entity for common services to its patients such as meals and laundry and for administrative services such as billings, collections, etc. All uncollectible accounts are charged directly to the entity. Space and bed rentals are fixed for the year.

For the fiscal year ending June 30, 19A, the Pediatrics Department charged each patient an average of $65 per day, had a capacity of 60 beds, operated 24 hours per day for 365 days, and had a revenue of $1,138,800.

Expenses charged by the hospital to the Pediatrics Department for the fiscal year ending June 30, 19A, were:

	Basis of Allocation	
	Patient Days (Variable)	Bed Capacity (Fixed)
Dietary....................................	$ 42,952	
Janitorial.................................		$ 12,800
Laundry...................................	28,000	
Laboratory (other than direct charges to patients).....................	47,800	
Pharmacy.................................	33,800	
Repairs and maintenance...................	5,200	7,140
General administrative services..............		131,760
Rent......................................		275,320
Billings and collections.....................	40,000	
Bad debts expense.........................	47,000	
Other expenses............................	18,048	25,980
	$262,800	$453,000

The only personnel directly employed by the Pediatrics Department are supervising nurses, nurses, and aides. The hospital has minimum departmental personnel requirements based on total annual patient days.

Hospital requirements beginning at the minimum expected level of operation were as follows:

Annual Patient Days	Aides	Nurses	Supervising Nurses
10,000 – 14,000	21	11	4
14,001 – 17,000	22	12	4
17,001 – 23,725	22	13	4
23,726 – 25,550	25	14	5
25,551 – 27,375	26	14	5
27,376 – 29,200	29	16	6

The staffing levels above represent full-time equivalents, and it should be assumed that the Pediatrics Department always employs only the minimum number of required full-time equivalent personnel. Salaries of supervising nurses, nurses, and aides are therefore fixed within ranges of annual patient days.

Annual salaries for each class of employee were: supervising nurses, $18,000; nurses, $13,000; and aides, $5,000.

Required: The minimum number of patient days necessary for the Pediatrics Department to break even for the fiscal year ending June 30, 19B, if the additional 20 beds are not rented. Patient demand is unknown but assume that revenue per patient day, cost per patient day, cost per bed, and employee salary rates will remain the same as for the fiscal year ended June 30, 19A.

(AICPA adapted)

24-10. Break-Even Analysis; Cash Flow Analysis. Nicoletta Calderone began the operation of her pizza parlor in 19A. A building was rented for this purpose at $400 per month. Two men were hired to work full time as waiters at the parlor while six college students were hired to work 30 hours per week delivering pizza. A public accounting service was employed at $300 per month. The necessary pizza parlor equipment and delivery trucks were purchased with cash. Ms. Calderone noticed that expenses for utilities and supplies were reasonably constant.

Ms. Calderone's business increased between 19A and 19D. Since 19A, net income for each year more than doubled. She does not understand why her profits have increased faster than her volume.

A projected income statement for 19E prepared by the accounting service is shown below.

NICOLETTA'S PIZZA PARLOR
PROJECTED INCOME STATEMENT
FOR YEAR ENDING DECEMBER 31, 19E

Sales..		$95,000
Cost of food sold..................................	$28,500	
Wages and fringe benefits — pizza parlor help...........	8,150	
Wages and fringe benefits — delivery help..............	17,300	
Rent..	4,800	
Accounting services................................	3,600	
Depreciation — delivery equipment....................	5,000	
Depreciation — pizza parlor equipment................	3,000	
Utilities..	2,325	
Supplies (soap, floor wax, etc.)......................	1,200	73,875
Net income before taxes............................		$21,125
Income taxes.....................................		6,338
Net income.......................................		$14,787

The average pizza sells for $2.50. Assume that Ms. Calderone pays out 30% of her income in taxes.

Required: (1) The break-even point in number of pizzas that must be sold.
(2) The cash remaining from the 19E income-producing activities if Ms. Calderone withdraws $4,800 for her personal use.
(3) The volume that must be reached in number of pizzas sold in order to obtain a desired aftertax net income of $20,000.
(4) A brief explanation as to why profits have increased at a faster rate than sales.
(5) A brief explanation as to why cash flow for 19E will exceed net income.

(NAA adapted)

24-11. Linear Demand Curve; Profit Maximization; Break-Even Analysis. The Carin Coat Co. manufactures high-quality raincoats. Because of a great fluctuation in the demand for these coats, a market research firm was engaged to investigate the market requirements at different price levels. The research revealed a linear demand curve having the following characteristics:

At a selling price of $80 each, 800 coats can be sold.
At a selling price of $70 each, 1,650 coats can be sold.
At a selling price of $60 each, 2,500 coats can be sold.
At a selling price of $50 each, 3,350 coats can be sold.
At a selling price of $40 each, 4,200 coats can be sold.

The variable expenses amount to $30 per raincoat while the fixed expenses average $40,000 per year.

Required: Assuming that the only feasible selling prices are $80, $70, $60, $50, or $40, diagrammatic expositions of the cost-profit-price relationship within the demand constraint in order to indicate:

(a) The maximum profit per unit and the price and volume at which it will be achieved.

(b) The maximum profit possible, and the price and volume at which it will be achieved.

(c) The contribution margin ratio, the break-even point, and the margin of safety ratio based on the answer computed in (b).

24-12. Product Mix and Contribution Margin Analysis. Product mix has an important effect on costs and profits. It is quite common that some products of a multi-product company are more profitable than others. The greater profit can arise from one or more causes, such as: customer demand, unusual skill or know-how, special equipment, efficient layout, etc. Obviously, the greater the quantity of higher-profits products in the product mix, the greater the total profit. On the other hand, less profitable, or even loss items, are sometimes deliberately pushed for specific reasons such as diversification of product lines, entering into a new field or outlet with the product, a leader item for introducing more profitable products, etc. However, it is especially important to press the more profitable items when feasible.

To consider some of the problems of product mix, the following data have been made available. A company with a plant with 20 machines makes three products. On a one-shift operation 24,000 units — considered 100% capacity — can be produced per day, with production going 8,000 units to Product A, 12,000 units to Product B, and 4,000 units to Product C.

Each unit sells for $1, and a profit of 10% on total sales is earned. On the basis of these data, the operating statement, ignoring nonmanufacturing costs, appears as follows:

		Amount	*Average per Unit*	
Sales (24,000 units)...................		$24,000		$1.00
Cost of units sold:				
Direct materials....................	$6,100		$.254	
Direct labor.......................	8,200		.342	
Variable factory overhead...........	1,780	16,080	.074	.67
Contribution margin................		$ 7,920		$ .33
Fixed factory overhead..............		5,520		.23
Net income........................		$ 2,400		$ .10

Business is good, and management decides to run two-hours-a-day overtime in order to handle additional orders which are readily obtainable. Management has always used the average unit cost in its calculations. Now it studies its variable cost picture on a product basis and finds that costs are as shown below.

	Product A	Product B	Product C
Direct materials........................	$ .200	$ .300	$ .225
Direct labor............................	.300	.400	.250
Variable factory overhead................	.055	.085	.080
Total variable cost......................	$ .555	$ .785	$ .555
Daily production units...................	8,000	12,000	4,000
% of daily production total..............	33%	50%	17%

Management decides to push Product C since it is now marketing the lowest quantity. Orders are received and 4,000 additional units are produced during the two extra hours previously considered. Sales price remains at $1 per unit.

Required: (1) An income statement showing the result of this decision.

(2) After the extra volume order of Product C, the Sales Department reports that additional orders for Product B could be obtained. Management hesitates at first because of the low margin but then decides to go ahead because no fixed costs are to be charged to the additional orders. 12,000 units are produced and sold at $1. An income statement showing the result of this decision.

(3) The not too pleasing result of *pushing* Product B leads to the decision to secure orders for only 4,000 additional units of Product A to sell for $1. An income statement showing the result of selling 4,000 additional units of Product A produced in the overtime hours.

(4) As a result of these three decisions and experiences, management instructs the accountant to prepare a product-income statement (use form below) with actual production mix at full capacity — one shift, no overtime — showing the contribution of each product to the normal profit of $2,400. Originally, management had decided that production be devoted: one-half to Product A; the balance equally to Products B and C.

PRODUCT-INCOME STATEMENT

Actual Product Mix — Full Capacity — One Shift

Normal Day	Total	Product A	Product B	Product C
% of plant devoted....	100%	50%	25%	25%
% of plant produced...	100%	33%	50%	17%
Units of output........	24,000	8,000	12,000	4,000

	$	% of Sales	$	% of Sales	$	% of Sales	$	% of Sales
Sales.................								
Direct materials.......								
Direct labor...........								
Variable factory overhead..............								
Total variable costs....								
Contribution margin...								
Fixed factory overhead.								
Net income...........								

(5) A statement in outline form showing management the reasons for the differences as apparent from the four statements prepared.

(Based on an article in *The Controller*)

24-13. Contribution Margin; Production Increase; Product Mix Shift.   The Cebula Company manufactures a line of dolls and a doll dress sewing kit. The management requests assistance from the Cost Department in determining an economical sales and production mix for the coming year. The Sales Department provides the following data:

Product	Estimated Demand for Next Year (Units)	Established Net Price (Units)
Joanna....................	50,000	$6.00
Trean.....................	42,000	2.90
Sarah	35,000	9.90
Meredith..................	40,000	5.00
Sewing kit................	325,000	3.00

To promote sales of the sewing kit, there is a 15% reduction in the established net price for a kit purchased at the same time that a Cebula doll is purchased. Accounting records indicate the following:

(a) The production standards per unit:

Product	Direct Materials	Direct Labor
Joanna....................	$1.40	$1.60
Trean.....................	.70	1.00
Sarah	2.69	2.80
Meredith..................	1.00	2.00
Sewing kit................	.60	.80

(b) The labor rate of $4 per hour is expected to continue without change in the next year. The plant has an effective capacity of 130,000 labor hours per year on a single-shift basis. Present equipment can produce all of the products.
(c) Next year's total fixed costs will be $100,000. Variable overhead costs will be equivalent to 25% of direct labor cost.
(d) The company's small inventory of its products can be ignored.
(e) Assume that all nonmanufacturing costs are fixed.

Required: (1) A schedule computing the contribution margin of a unit of each product.
(2) A schedule computing the contribution margin of a unit of each product per labor dollar expended on the product.
(3) A schedule computing the total labor hours required to produce the estimated sales units for next year. Indicate the item and number of units to be increased (or decreased) in production to attain the company's effective productive capacity.
(4) Without regard to the answer in (3), assume that the estimated sales units for next year would require 12,000 labor hours in excess of the company's effective productive capacity. Discuss the possible methods of providing the missing capacity. Include in your discussion all factors that must be taken into consideration in evaluating the methods of providing the missing capacity.

(AICPA adapted)

24-14. New Sales Policies; Profit-Volume Analysis. The management of the Weisbach Specialties Co., Inc. has been considering a new sales policy for the coming year. Two different plans have been suggested, either of which — so the management hopes — will increase the volume of sales, reduce the ratio of marketing expenses to sales, decrease unit production costs, and increase net income.

The proposals are as follows:

Plan 1 — Premium Stamp Books:

It is proposed that each package of Product A will contain 8 premium stamps, and each package of Product B will contain 4 premium stamps. Premium stamp books will be distributed to consumers; and when a book is filled with 100 stamps, it will be redeemed by the award of a cash prize in an amount indicated under an unbroken seal attached to the book at the time of distribution. Every 10,000 books distributed will provide for prizes in accordance with the following schedule:

Number of Books	Prize for Each	Total Amount in Prizes
1	$150.00	$ 150
5	50.00	250
14	20.00	280
50	10.00	500
160	5.00	800
1,020	1.00	1,020
8,750	.40	3,500
10,000		$6,500

This schedule is fixed and not subject to alteration or modification. The cost of this plan will be as follows:

Books, including distribution cost.... $ 15 per 1,000 books
Stamps......................... $ 1 per 1,000 stamps
Prizes......................... $650 per 1,000 books

The premium stamp book plan will take the place of all previous advertising, and previously established selling prices will be maintained.

Plan 2 — Reduced Selling Prices:

It is proposed that the selling price of Product A will be reduced by $8\frac{1}{3}\%$ and of Product B by 5% and that the advertising expenditures will be increased over those of the prior year. This plan is an alternative to Plan 1, and only one will be adopted.

The following information regarding the previous year's operations and anticipated changes has been provided:

Marketing expenses were 18% of sales, of which one third was for advertising. Administrative expenses were 5% of sales.

Prior year's operations:

	Product A	Product B
Quantity sold.............................	200,000 units	600,000 units
Production cost per unit......................	$.40	$.30
Selling price per unit........................	.60	.40

Expected changes:

	Product A	Product B
Increase in unit sales volume:		
Plan 1..................................	50%	50%
Plan 2..................................	40%	25%
Decrease in unit production cost:		
Plan 1..................................	5%	10%
Plan 2..................................	7½%	6⅔%
Advertising:		
Plan 1..................................	None	None
Plan 2..................................	8% of sales	7% of sales
Other marketing expenses:		
Plan 1..................................	15% of sales	12% of sales
Plan 2..................................	12% of sales	12% of sales
Premium book expenses:		
Plan 1..................................	As indicated	
Plan 2..................................	None	None
Administrative expenses:		
Plan 1..................................	4% of sales	4% of sales
Plan 2..................................	Same dollar amount as prior year	

Required: A schedule comparing operations of the previous year with those under both proposed plans.

(AICPA adapted)

24-15. Profit-Volume Analysis when One Factory Is Shut Down and a Foreign Subsidiary Is Opened. The Dodson Corporation's home office is located in Trenton, New Jersey. The company leases factory buildings in Pennsylvania, Michigan, and North Carolina. The same single product is manufactured in all three factories. The following information is available for 19A's operations:

	Total	Pennsylvania	Michigan	North Carolina
Sales......................	$900,000	$200,000	$400,000	$300,000
Variable costs..............	$500,000	$100,000	$220,000	$180,000
Fixed costs:				
Factory.................	180,000	50,000	55,000	75,000
Administration...........	59,000	16,000	21,000	22,000
Allocated home office expenses	63,000	14,000	28,000	21,000
Total..................	$802,000	$180,000	$324,000	$298,000
Net income from operations..	$ 98,000	$ 20,000	$ 76,000	$ 2,000

Home office expenses are allocated on the basis of units sold. The sales price per unit is $10.

Management is undecided whether to renew the lease of the North Carolina factory which expires on December 31, 19B, and which will require a rent increase of $15,000 per year if renewed. If the factory is shut down, the amount expected to be realized from the sale of the equipment is greater than its book value and would cover all termination expenses.

If the North Carolina factory is shut down, the company can continue to serve customers of the North Carolina factory by one of the following methods:

(a) Expanding the Pennsylvania factory, which would increase present fixed costs by 15%. Additional shipping expense of $2 per unit will be incurred on the increased production.

(b) Entering into a long-term contract with a competitor who will serve the North Carolina factory customers and who will pay the Dodson Corporation a commission of $1.60 per unit.

Dodson Corporation is also planning to establish a subsidiary in Mexico to produce the same product. Based on estimated annual Mexican sales of 40,000 units, cost studies produced these estimates for the Mexican subsidiary:

	Annual Cost	
	Total	% Variable
Direct materials...............	$193,600	100%
Direct labor...................	90,000	70
Factory overhead..............	80,000	64
Administrative expenses........	30,000	30

The Mexican production will be sold by manufacturer's representatives who will receive a commission of 8% of the sales price. No portion of the United States home office expense will be allocated to the Mexican subsidiary.

Required: (1) A schedule showing the corporation's estimated net income from United States operations under each of the following procedures:
    (a) Expansion of the Pennsylvania factory.
    (b) Negotiation of long-term contract on a commission basis.
    (2) The sales price per unit that would result in an estimated 10% profit on sales if management wants to price its Mexican product to realize a 10% profit on the sales price.
    (3) The break-even point in sales dollars for the Mexican subsidiary if the answer to part (2) is a sales price of $11 per unit.

(AICPA adapted)

24-16. Increase in Labor Cost and Depreciation; New Sales Price. The management of the Besser Corporation anticipates a 10% wage increase on January 1 of next year. Presently, labor comprises $12 of the per unit total variable cost. No other cost changes are expected. The management needs assistance to formulate a reasonable product strategy for next year.

A regression analysis indicates that volume is the primary factor affecting costs. Semivariable costs have been separated into their fixed and variable segments by means of the least-squares criterion. Beginning and ending inventories never differ materially.

The following current year data have been assembled for the analysis:

Current selling price per unit..........................	$80
Variable cost per unit................................	48
Annual volume of sales................................	5,000 units
Fixed costs (no labor cost included)...................	$51,000

Required: (1) The increase in the selling price necessary to cover the 10% wage increase and still maintain the current profit-volume ratio.

(2) The number of units to be sold to maintain the current net income if the sales price remains at $80 and the 10% wage increase goes into effect.

(3) The management believes that an additional $190,000 in machinery (to be depreciated at 10% annually) will increase present capacity (5,300 units) by 30%. If all units produced can be sold at the present price and the wage increase goes into effect, how would the estimated net income, before capacity is increased, compare with the estimated net income after capacity is increased? Computations of estimated net income before and after the expansion.

(AICPA adapted)

24-17. Computer Marketing, Pricing, and Financing Strategy. North Shore Industries, Inc. recently established the South Bend Division to manufacture and market a new type of computer. North Shore's executive committee is considering financing alternatives.

Engineering estimates indicate that the variable cost of manufacturing a unit will be $20,000, and the variable marketing cost of a unit will be $10,000 with a sales price set at $50,000 per unit. State and federal income taxes are estimated at 55% of net income before taxes.

It is further estimated that South Bend will incur fixed costs totaling $4,000,000 per year including depreciation. North Shore must secure an additional $10,000,000 to finance the South Bend Division and for this plans to issue at par either stocks or bonds. South Bend must bear the financing cost in addition to other costs.

Required: (1) The number of units which must be sold annually at $50,000 per unit to pay all costs, meet any dividend requirement, and comply with the stated objective under each of the following alternatives:

(a) 6% nonparticipating, cumulative, preferred stock is issued.

(b) 5% bonds are issued.

(c) 5% bonds are issued and North Shore requires that South Bend contribute 6% of its sales to be credited to North Shore Industries' retained earnings for internal financing and future expansion.

(d) 5% bonds are issued and North Shore requires that South Bend contribute annually both $100,000 to be paid out as dividends to North Shore's common stockholders and 6% of South Bend's sales to be credited to North Shore's retained earnings for internal financing and future expansion.

(2) South Bend will have 72 salespersons. Market surveys indicate that each salesperson must sell an average of one unit every three months if the sales price of the computer is set at $50,000 per unit, and that none is likely to sell more than one unit in any month. North Shore's management requests a computation of:

(a) The probability that any salesperson will sell a computer in any month.

(b) The average number of units that South Bend can expect to sell per month at $50,000.

(3) The market surveys also indicated that each salesperson should be expected to sell one unit every four months if the sales price should be set at

$60,000 per unit. Reduced sales would cause the variable cost of marketing a unit to increase to $12,000. North Shore's management requests:

(a) A recomputation of requirement (1) (d) under this alternative.

(b) Advice whether to set the sales price at $50,000 or $60,000 with an explanation for the recommended sales price.

(AICPA adapted)

24-18. Effect of Product Mix Variation. The officers of the Bradshaw Company reviewed the profitability of the company's four products and the potential effect of several proposals for varying the product mix. An excerpt from the income statement for 19— and other data follows:

	Total	P	Q	R	S
			Product		
Sales..................	$62,600	$10,000	$18,000	$12,600	$22,000
Cost of goods sold.........	44,274	4,750	7,056	13,968	18,500
Gross profit..............	18,326	5,250	10,944	(1,368)	3,500
Operating expenses........	12,012	1,990	2,976	2,826	4,220
Net income before taxes....	$ 6,314	$ 3,260	$ 7,968	$(4,194)	$ (720)
Units sold...............		1,000	1,200	1,800	2,000
Sales price per unit........		$10.00	$15.00	$7.00	$11.00
Variable cost of goods sold per unit...............		$2.50	$3.00	$6.50	$6.00
Variable operating expenses per unit...............		$1.17	$1.25	$1.00	$1.20

Total fixed costs are not expected to fluctuate as a result of changes under consideration.

Required: (1) The effect on net income if Product R is discontinued.

(2) The effect on net income if Product R is discontinued and if a consequent loss of customers causes a decrease of 200 units in sales of Product Q.

(3) The effect on net income if Product R's sale price is increased to $8 with a decrease in the number of units sold to 1,500 with no effect on the other products.

(4) The effect on net income if a new Product T is introduced and Product R is discontinued with no effect on the other products. (The total variable costs per unit of Product T would be $8.05, and 1,600 units can be sold at $9.50 each. The plant in which Product R is produced can be utilized to produce Product T.)

(5) The effect on net income if production of Product P is reduced to 500 units (to be sold at $12 cach) and if production of Product S is increased to 2,500 units (to be sold at $10.50 each). (Part of the plant in which Product P is produced can easily be adapted to produce Product S, but changes in quantities make changes in the sales price advisable.)

(6) The effect on net income if production of Product P is increased by 1,000 units to be sold at $10 each by adding a second shift. (Higher wages must be paid, thus increasing the variable cost of goods sold per unit to $3.50 for each additional unit.)

(AICPA adapted)

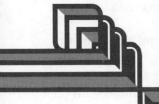

CHAPTER 25

DIFFERENTIAL
COST ANALYSIS

Many management decisions involve problems of alternative choice such as:

1. Taking or refusing certain orders.
2. Increasing, curtailing, or stopping production of certain products.
3. Selecting new sales territories.
4. Spending additional amounts for sales promotion.
5. Reducing the price of a single, special order.
6. Making a price cut in a competitive market.
7. Evaluating make-or-buy alternatives.
8. Replacing present equipment with new machinery (see Chapter 26).

Historical costs drawn from the accounting records do not give management all the information needed to determine alternative courses of action. Many terms, concepts, and classifications must be introduced and incorporated in the system to enable the accountant to provide useful, meaningful, and executive-guiding cost data.

Differential cost is the difference in the cost of alternative choices. It is the cost that must be considered when a decision has to be made involving an increase or decrease of *n-units* of output above a specified output. The differential cost aids in deciding at what price the firm can afford to sell additional goods. As long as the additional output and its differentially-costed price do not influence the existing, traditional units and their prices, and as long as the minimum sales price for these added units exceeds this differential cost, the additional output is desirable because a gain results. Any added revenue above the differential cost results in a gain. If these additional units are to be sold in the same market in competition with the present output and prices, the situation is quite different. A reduction in price to all customers for the sake of utilizing capacity to its full limit might add very little additional revenue to the total amount, while the associated increase in costs and expenses might cause negative results.

The differential cost of added production is the difference between the cost of producing the present smaller output and that of the contemplated, larger output. This differential cost is generally synonymous with the variable costs of producing the *n-units*, assuming fixed costs remain the same. If, however, fixed costs must be increased; e.g., through the addition of a new machine or the rental of additional space, then these costs should be considered differential costs.

Differential cost is often referred to as *marginal* or *incremental cost*. The term "marginal cost" is widely used by economists, but accountants seem to prefer the term "differential." Engineers generally speak of incremental costs as the added cost incurred when a project or an undertaking is extended beyond its originally intended goal. Differential cost analysis provides the costs which the managerial problem of alternative choice demands. The studies are not merely confined to an analysis of adding *n-units* and computing their cost; they also include such problems as the shutdown of a plant, the making or buying of a part, the abandonment of part of a plant or of output, and the expansion of plant capacity.

DIFFERENTIAL COST STUDIES ILLUSTRATED

Several hypothetical cases illustrating the use of differential cost analysis in solving management problems are discussed in the following sections. In order to achieve a better understanding of this method of analysis, a discussion of the importance of variable costs and the relationship of these costs to differential costs is first presented.

The Importance of Variable Costs. Previous chapters stressed the importance of distinguishing between fixed and variable costs. In break-even analysis fixed and variable costs play an all-important part. In differential cost studies variable costs are significant, for they usually represent the differential cost.

Suppose a plant has a maximum capacity of 100,000 units, but normal capacity production is set at 80,000 units, or 80 percent of capacity. At this level the predetermined overhead rate is computed so that fixed expenses are fully absorbed when operating at the 80,000-unit level. If less units are produced, unabsorbed fixed overhead results; if more units are produced, fixed overhead is overabsorbed.

If this company should make only one unit, its cost would be:

Variable cost............	$	5 per unit
Total fixed costs.........		100,000 for this unit
Total...............		$100,005

The fixed cost per unit is reduced to $1.25 ($100,000 ÷ 80,000 units) at normal capacity (80,000 units).

At normal capacity, the cost per unit is:

Variable cost...........	$5.00
Share of fixed cost.......	1.25
Total...............	$6.25

If, however, additional capacity can be utilized, the unit cost of the additional units would be only the variable cost, $5, unless the additional units should require additional fixed expense outlays. This is the differential cost. The term "differential cost" applies only to those costs that will change. A differential cost statement might appear thus:

	Present Business	With Additional Business
Sales.....................................	$100,000	$110,000
Variable costs	60,000	66,000
Contribution margin......................	$ 40,000	$ 44,000
Fixed costs	30,000	30,000
Net income............................	$ 10,000	$ 14,000

The additional business requires variable costs only, inasmuch as capacity costs (i.e., fixed costs) represent adequate unused capacity to handle the additional business. The additional business would yield a positive contribution margin if sold at any price above $6,000, its variable cost.

The illustration above can also be presented in this manner:

	Present Business	Additional Business	Total
Sales.....................	$100,000	$10,000	$110,000
Variable costs	60,000	6,000	66,000
Contribution margin........	$ 40,000	$ 4,000	$ 44,000
Fixed costs	30,000	none	30,000
Net income...............	$ 10,000	$ 4,000	$ 14,000

This statement also shows that the additional business is charged with the variable costs only, the present business absorbing all fixed costs.

Historical Cost Allocation vs. Differential Cost Presentation. The two preceding statements are of importance to subsequent discussion, for they indicate that:

1. Cost computations and cost allocations as commonly employed by cost accountants cannot be used in differential cost studies.

2. Variable costs are differential costs unless the additional business also involves additional fixed cost outlay.

Although variable costs are of primary importance in a differential cost statement, the existence of unused or idle capacity often leads management to think in terms of differential costs. If available capacity is not fully utilized, a differential cost analysis might indicate the possibility of selling additional output at a figure lower than the existing average unit cost. The idea is that the new or additional business can be accepted as long as the variable cost is recovered. Of course any contribution to the recovery of fixed costs and, after full recovery, to profit, is desirable. It is only when additional fixed costs must be incurred that they become part of the differential cost analysis. The term "fixed" is perhaps a misnomer. If they are incurred for the new business only, they are certainly variable expenses. Should they continue, however, they would become permanent costs due to their fixed nature. In the latter case, management must be cautioned against a quick decision in favor of the additional business, for it might find itself with additional fixed costs and a capacity greater than originally contemplated and greater than needed.

Assume a company manufactures 450,000 units, which is 90 percent of normal capacity. Fixed factory overhead amounts to $335,000 which is $.67 $\left(\frac{\$335,000}{500,000 \text{ units}}\right)$ for each unit manufactured when operations are at 100 percent of normal capacity.[1] The variable factory overhead rate is $.50 per unit. Direct materials cost is $1.80, and direct labor cost is $1.40 per unit. Each unit sells for $5. Marketing as well as general and administrative expenses are omitted to simplify the presentation. On the basis of

---

[1] The normal capacity used for the application of factory overhead does not necessarily represent available practical capacity. Normal capacity represents average expected utilization whereas practical capacity represents maximum production potential. If normal capacity is less than practical capacity, the idle capacity variance (the unabsorbed fixed factory overhead) is smaller with the use of normal instead of practical capacity in determining the factory overhead rate. Consequently, normal capacity yields an idle capacity variance that understates the true unused, yet available capacity.

these data and following historical cost accounting procedures, the accountant would prepare the following income statement:

INCOME STATEMENT

Sales (450,000 units @ $5)........................		$2,250,000
Cost of goods sold:		
Direct materials (450,000 units @ $1.80)..........	$810,000	
Direct labor (450,000 units @ $1.40).............	630,000	
Variable factory overhead (450,000 units @ $.50)..	225,000	
Fixed factory overhead (450,000 units @ $.67).....	301,500	1,966,500
Net income from operations.......................		$ 283,500
Unabsorbed fixed factory overhead [$335,000 − $301,500 (450,000 units @ $.67)]................		$ 33,500
Net income from operations (adjusted).............		$ 250,000

The sales department reports that a customer has offered to pay $4.25 per unit for an additional 100,000 units. The accountant is instructed to compute the gain or loss on this order. To make the additional 100,000 units, an annual rental cost of $10,000 for new equipment would be incurred.

COST STATEMENT FOR ADDITIONAL BUSINESS

Sales (100,000 units @ $4.25).......................		$425,000
Cost of goods sold:		
Direct materials (100,000 units @ $1.80)...........	$180,000	
Direct labor (100,000 units @ $1.40)..............	140,000	
Variable factory overhead (100,000 units @ $.50)....	50,000	
Fixed factory overhead (100,000 units @ $.67)......	67,000	437,000
Loss on this order.................................		$ 12,000

In the previous statement all cost elements take the existing unit costs. Fixed overhead is allocated on the basis of the rate established ($.67 per unit.) This cost computation would cause management to reject the offer. A second look, however, reveals the effect of the new order on total factory overhead:

Fixed factory overhead (at present).................		$335,000
Fixed factory overhead (because of additional business)..		10,000
Total fixed factory overhead.......................		$345,000
Fixed factory overhead charged into production:		
For 450,000 units (old business)..................	$301,500	
For 100,000 units (additional business)............	67,000	368,500
Overabsorbed fixed factory overhead.................		$ 23,500

Instead of underabsorbed fixed factory overhead of $33,500, the additional business would result in overabsorbed factory overhead of $23,500 or a net composite gain of $57,000 in absorbed factory overhead. This $57,000 minus the computed $12,000 loss on the order results in a gain of $45,000.

DIFFERENTIAL COST STATEMENT FOR ADDITIONAL BUSINESS

Sales (100,000 units @ $4.25)......................		$425,000
Cost of goods sold:		
Direct materials (100,000 units @ $1.80)............	$180,000	
Direct labor (100,000 units @ $1.40)..............	140,000	
Variable factory overhead (100,000 units @ $.50)....	50,000	
Absorption of additional fixed cost to produce this order.......................................	10,000	380,000
Gain on this order...............................		$ 45,000

The additional business has been charged with differential cost only. The unit cost of the additional units can be computed as follows:

$$\frac{\text{Cost of Goods Sold}}{\text{Additional Units}} = \frac{\$380,000}{100,000} = \$3.80 \text{ Unit Cost per Additional Unit}$$

The Flexible Budget and the Differential Cost Statement. A differential cost statement determines the cost and related revenue of the additional output. A flexible budget with its revised costs for each rise in the capacity level can be linked with differential activity. The flexible budget shows the various expenses at different levels of production. It moves from one capacity level to the next, carrying with it proportionate increases in variable expenses. It indicates that others, the fixed expenses, remain comparatively stationary through various levels of activity.

In the flexible budget illustrated on page 797, the average unit cost at 60 percent of capacity is computed by dividing the total cost at that capacity by the number of units produced ($\frac{\$324,250}{60,000 \text{ units}} = \$5.40$). Total differential cost is arrived at by subtracting total estimated cost for one level of activity from that of another level (total cost at 80 percent, $423,400 − total cost at 60 percent, $324,250 = $99,150, the differential cost between these two levels). Differential unit cost is computed by:

1. Subtracting one level of output from the next higher level (output at 80 percent, 80,000 units minus output at 60 percent, 60,000 units = 20,000 units, the differential output).

2. Dividing the differential cost total between these two levels by the added number of units ($\frac{\$99,150}{20,000 \text{ units}} = \$4.96$, the differential cost per unit).

FLEXIBLE BUDGET WITH COSTS AT DIFFERENT RATES OF OUTPUT
(100,000 Units = 100% Normal Capacity)

Capacity	60%	80%	100%	120%
Variable costs:				
Direct cost of operations:				
Direct materials...........	$102,000	$136,000	$170,000	$204,000
Direct labor..............	93,000	124,000	155,000	186,000
Total.................	$195,000	$260,000	$325,000	$390,000
Indirect cost of operations:				
Heat......................	$ 720	$ 960	$ 1,200	$ 1,440
Light and power..........	1,440	1,920	2,400	2,880
Repairs and maintenance....	2,460	3,280	4,100	4,920
Supplies..................	1,260	1,680	2,100	2,520
Indirect workers...........	9,120	12,160	15,200	18,240
Total................	$ 15,000	$ 20,000	$ 25,000	$ 30,000
Nonoperating expenses:				
Clerical help..............	$ 11,580	$ 15,440	$ 19,300	$ 23,160
Wages, general............	6,960	9,280	11,600	13,920
Supplies..................	1,260	1,680	2,100	2,520
Total.................	$ 19,800	$ 26,400	$ 33,000	$ 39,600
Fixed costs (within ranges):				
Operating expenses:				
Foremen.................	$ 15,250	$ 20,500	$ 20,500	$ 25,750
Superintendent...........	15,000	15,000	15,000	17,750
Set-up men..............	5,000	7,500	7,500	8,500
Depreciation.............	8,000	9,400	9,400	9,400
Insurance................	2,600	2,600	2,600	2,600
Total.................	$ 45,850	$ 55,000	$ 55,000	$ 64,000
Nonoperating expenses:				
Executives................	$ 28,000	$ 35,000	$ 35,000	$ 40,000
Assistants...............	12,500	16,400	16,400	19,200
Taxes....................	2,100	3,400	3,400	4,800
Legal and accounting......	6,000	7,200	7,200	7,200
Total.................	$ 48,600	$ 62,000	$ 62,000	$ 71,200
Total cost....................	$324,250	$423,400	$500,000	$594,800
Units of output......................	60,000	80,000	100,000	120,000
Average unit cost....................	$5.40	$5.29	$5.00	$4.96
Differential cost total.................		$ 99,150	$ 76,600	$ 94,800
Differential cost per unit..............		$4.96	$3.83	$4.74

The illustration also shows that an increase of production from 100,000 to 120,000 units means an increase of $94,800 in total cost and a new unit cost of $4.96 in comparison with a unit cost of $5 at the 100,000 unit level. The reduced unit cost is due to absorption of fixed cost by the greater number of units. It is this type of information that is needed for the solution of managerial problems involving a choice of alternatives. Naturally, the illustration tells only part of the story; many finer details would have to be worked out. However, a flexible budget based on standard costs for the various cost elements considerably facilitates the solution of differential cost problems.

Application of the Flexible Budget for Differential Cost Analysis. In the following pages the practical application of differential cost analysis methods by an oil refinery is presented.[2]

The basic function of refining is the separation, extraction, and chemical conversion of the crude oil's component elements into usable and marketable products by skillful utilization of heat, pressure, and catalytic principles. The basic petroleum products are obtained through a physical change caused by the application of heat through a wide temperature range. These basic products pass off as gaseous vapors when the proper temperatures have been reached. Within a temperature differential of 300° (275° F to 575° F) the different liquid products called fractions, ends, or cuts, pass off as vapors and are then condensed back into liquids. The initial application of heat drives off the lightest fractions — the naphthas and gasoline; the successively heavier fractions, such as kerosene and fuel oil, follow as the temperature rises. This process of vaporizing the crude and condensing the gaseous vapors to obtain the various cuts is commonly referred to as primary distillation.

Certain of these cuts (such as straight-run gasoline) are marketable with but little treating. Other products must undergo further processing in order to make them more valuable and, naturally, more salable. Thus, heavier fractions, such as kerosene and gas oil, may be subjected to cracking and consequently made to yield a more valuable product such as gasoline. Cracking is a process during which, by the use of high temperatures and pressures and perhaps in the presence of a catalyst, a heavy fraction is subjected to destructive distillation and converted to a lighter hydrocarbon possessing different chemical characteristics, among these a lower boiling point. The heaviest of the fractions resulting from primary distillation is known as residuum or heavy bottoms. This residuum, after further processing, treating, and blending, forms lubricating oils and ancillary wax or asphalt products.

The above description is given to indicate that the various operations, such as primary distillation and cracking, yield certain distillates or fractions. The management of a refinery must decide what to do with each

---

[2]Adapted from a study prepared by John L. Fox, later published in *NACA Bulletin*, Vol. XXXI, No. 4, pp. 403–413, under the title, "Cost Analysis Budget to Evaluate Operating Alternatives for Oil Refiners."

fraction. At what stage of refining should each be sold? Or should additional fractions be bought from other refineries to make further use economical and also profitable? What price should be paid for the additional units? Should the company enlarge the plant in order to be able to handle a greater volume? What alternate courses should management take in order to break into the most profitable market at the moment?

The accountant can help management through the preparation of departmental flexible budgets for the secondary operating departments. Secondary operating departments comprise those departments in which further processing might take place. For these flexible budgets a different term is used here: *cost analysis budgets*. They differ from the flexible budget used for control purposes in several respects. All expenses are included in the analysis budget. Budgeted expenses of service departments are allocated to operating departments at corresponding capacity levels. The aim of these analysis budgets is to discover the departmental differential costs.

The amounts stated for each class of expense at each production level are computed on separate work sheets where the various individual expenses are separated into their fixed and variable elements. This separation, previously described, is necessary to arrive at the estimated expenses for each level of production.

Analysis budgets, such as the one shown on page 800, are made up for the following departments:

Treating	Solvent Extraction
Filters and Burners	Wax Specialties
Cracking	Canning
Solvent Dewaxing	Barrel House

Each department represents some secondary processing or finishing operation.

Management problems such as whether to purchase intermediate distillates for further processing or whether to sell intermediate distillates on hand without further processing can be solved with the use of differential cost data, based on the departmental cost analysis budget. The hypothetical cases discussed below illustrate the methods that may be employed in solving such problems.

Application 1: Sell or Process Further. A refiner has on hand 20,000 gallons of fuel oil. He must decide whether to sell it as fuel oil or crack it into gasoline and residual fuel. The following facts are available:

Current prices:
Fuel oil... $.07 per gallon
Gasoline... $.14 per gallon

ANALYSIS BUDGET

Department: Cracking   Period Budgeted:_____ to _____

Supervisor:_____   Normal Capacity (100%) 100,000 gallons through-put

Department and/or Expense Account	Shut-Down	60%	80%	100%	120%
Direct Expenses:	$3,000	$7,000	$8,000	$ 8,500	$11,500
Allocated Expenses:					
Fixed and variable.............	500	1,000	1,500	2,000	3,000
Total costs......................	$3,500	$8,000	$9,500	$10,500	$14,500
Through-put:					
Total gallons.................		60,000	80,000	100,000	120,000
Differential gallons.............		60,000	20,000	20,000	20,000
Differential cost..................		$4,500	$1,500	$ 1,000	$ 4,000
Unit differential cost..............		$ .075	$ .075	$ .05	$ .20
Unit average cost................		$ .133	$ .119	$ .105	$ .1208

Cracking analysis budget:
    Present operations 80% of capacity
    Differential cost (80% to 100%) = $.05 per input gallon
    Cracking yields: 75% gasoline; 15% residual fuel oil; 10% loss

The refiner can then prepare the following analysis:

DIFFERENTIAL INCOME COMPUTATION

Potential revenue — products from cracking:
    Gasoline (15,000 gallons @ $.14)............................... $2,100
    Fuel oil (3,000 gallons @ $.07)................................   210
                                                                    $2,310
    Less potential revenue — fuel oil (20,000 gallons @ $.07)........   1,400
Differential revenue... $ 910
    Less differential cost (20,000 gallons @ $.05)...................   1,000
Loss from cracking of fuel oil................................... $ 90*

_____

*Not an accounting loss, per se, but a loss of profit that would result from an improper choice of alternatives.

Thus, judging from a quantitative standpoint, it would be more profitable to sell the 20,000 gallons of fuel oil as such rather than process them further.

Application 2: Price to Pay for an Intermediate Stock. A refiner has been offered 10,000 gallons of cylinder stock. The usual bargaining process will determine the final price. The would-be purchaser is interested in knowing how high a price he can pay and still make a profit. The stock purchased would be processed into conventional bright stock and sold at that stage, since the blending unit for making finished motor oils is currently working at full capacity. Available information is as follows:

> Cylinder stock is of such a quality and type that it will probably yield:
> 90% Bright stock
> 5% Petrolatum
> 5% Loss
> Current prices: Bright stock $.50 per gallon; Petrolatum — no market

Differential costs associated with processing 10,000 gallons of cylinder stock through several units (from analysis budgets):

Solvent dewaxing............	$.02 per gallon
Solvent extracting...........	.02 per gallon
Filtering....................	.01 per gallon
Total.....................	$.05 per gallon

Using this information, the refiner can analyze his position and determine his bargaining margin:

Revenue — bright stock (9,000 gallons @ $.50).....................	$4,500
Differential costs (10,000 gallons @ $.05).........................	500
Margin...	$4,000

$$\$4,000 \div 10,000 \text{ gallons} = \$.40 \text{ per gallon}$$

The refiner is now ready to bargain for the purchase of the cylinder stock. He knows that a purchase price of $.40 a gallon represents his break-even point — to pay more would produce a loss, to pay less would result in a gain. He then makes his decision as to how much profit is required to justify the purchase. Here the concept of *opportunity costs* also enters into the final decision. If the available capacity could be more profitably used for another purpose, then perhaps the proposed purchase should not be consummated.

Application 3: Choice of Alternate Routings. A refiner is trying to decide whether to treat and sell the kerosene fraction or to crack it for its gasoline content. The current decision involves 10,000 gallons of raw kerosene. Pertinent information available to him is as follows:

Current prices:	
Kerosene................	$.08 per gallon
Gasoline.................	.14 per gallon
Fuel oil.................	.07 per gallon
Cracking yields:	
Gasoline.................	85%
Residual fuel oil.........	5%
Loss....................	10%

Differential costs associated with potential gallons through-put (from analysis budgets):

Cracking....................	$.03 per gallon
Treating....................	.01 per gallon

Using the above amounts, the refiner can prepare the following analysis:

Net potential revenue — products from cracking:

Gasoline (8,500 gallons @ $.14)........................	$1,190	
Fuel oil (500 gallons @ $.07)........................	35	
	$1,225	
Less differential cost (10,000 gallons @ $.03)............	300	$925

Net potential revenue — kerosene:

Total revenue (10,000 gallons @ $.08)....................	$ 800	
Less differential cost (10,000 gallons @ $.01)............	100	700
Gain from cracking rather than treating....................		$225

In this situation, the more profitable alternative is to crack the kerosene fraction.

Application 4: Proposed Construction of Additional Capacity. A refiner discovers that the market for finished neutrals is such that his present capacity does not satisfy the demand. He feels certain that an addition to the solvent dewaxing and solvent extracting units would prove profitable. The additional wax distillate stock required would be purchased on the open market at the current rate. However, before going ahead with the construction, he first consults the chief accountant who presents the analysis illustrated on page 803.

It would appear from the accountant's analysis that the proposed increase in the productive capacity would not be justified under the stated conditions. Furthermore, even a potential profit should yield a satisfactory return on the additional capital investment (see Chapter 26).

LINEAR EQUATIONS FOR DIFFERENTIAL COST STUDIES

Differential costs are the difference in costs between two levels of activity as illustrated on page 797. Linear equations facilitate the determination of such costs. If, for instance, y_1 represents the total cost at one level of activity and y_2 the total cost at another level of activity, then $y_2 - y_1$ equals the differential cost. Using the linear equation $y = a + bx$, where a = costs that do not change, b = the 100 percent capacity level of

ANALYSIS BASED UPON THE ANALYSIS BUDGETS

Unit differential cost:
  Capacity from 100% to 120% (increase of 10,000 gallons through-put)
    Solvent Dewaxing Department — $.10 per gallon through-put
    Solvent Extracting Department — $.10 per gallon through-put

Assumed yield from wax distillate:
  90% Viscous neutral
  1.5% Paraffin (8 pounds per gallon)
  8.5% Loss

Current market prices:
  Viscous neutrals — $.47 per gallon.
  White crude scale wax — $.08 per pound
  Wax distillate stock — $.35 per gallon*

*Not a published market price but the price management believes it will have to pay to acquire the stock.

SCHEDULE OF PROJECTED ACTION

Differential revenue:
  9,000 gallons viscous neutrals @ $.47 . . . . $4,230
  1,200 pounds paraffin @ $.08   96
                                                                              $4,326
    Less cost of wax distillate stock (10,000 gallons @ $.35)   3,500
  Margin to apply against differential costs . . . . $ 826

Differential costs:
  Solvent Dewaxing Department (10,000 gallons @ $.10) . . . $1,000
  Solvent Extracting Department (10,000 gallons @ $.10) . . .   1,000   2,000
  Potential loss from differential production $1,174

costs that change, and x = percent of capacity, a differential cost equation can be written thus:

$$\text{Differential Cost} = y_2 - y_1 = (a + bx_2) - (a + bx_1)$$
$$= a + bx_2 - a - bx_1$$
$$= bx_2 - bx_1$$
$$= b(x_2 - x_1)$$

Using the flexible budget on page 797, the differential cost between operations at 80% and 100% capacity can be determined as follows (b represents the variable costs, $325,000 + $25,000 + $33,000, at the normal capacity level with no change in fixed costs between these two levels):

$$\text{Differential Cost} = \$383,000 \ (1.00 - .8)$$
$$= \$383,000 \ (.2)$$
$$= \$ \ 76,600$$

Often this differential cost does not agree with that shown in the flexible budget due to the fact that there has been a change in fixed costs or the variable costs may have been treated curvilinearly rather than linearly; that is, they may be treated by examination and experience as suggested in Chapter 18. Without a flexible budget, the linear equation method usually offers a quick and reasonably reliable answer.

LINEAR PROGRAMMING FOR DIFFERENTIAL COST STUDIES

A differential cost study deals with determination of incremental revenues, costs, and margins with regard to the alternative use of fixed facilities or available capacity. The differential cost study must often determine the profitability of the short-run use of available capacity. Such incremental analyses might become rather involved due to the multiple constraints on production and number of products possible. The accountant could try numerous combinations to arrive at the incremental revenues and costs associated with each. Today he will find assistance in solving this dilemma by means of mathematical or linear programming which is discussed in Chapter 28. This newer kind of decision model allows the accountant to determine the optimum course of action when the resources allocation problem is complex and its solution neither obvious nor feasible by trial and error, hunch, guess, or intuition.

DIFFERENTIAL COST ANALYSIS AND THE MARKET

Whenever a differential cost analysis leads to a decision by management, it is assumed that the acceptance of an additional order at or above the differential cost is not going to disturb the market of the product or products now offered. Orthodox accounting procedure advocates the distribution of total cost over total output. Fixed factory overhead is supposed to be spread evenly over all old and new units. A previous example illustrated that such orthodox thinking might lead management to incorrect decisions. It appears that as long as the additional units bring in sufficient revenue to cover their differential costs and a profit margin, it is wise to accept the additional business. Any additional business is not necessarily restricted to the same products presently marketed, for it might be one which can be manufactured with existing facilities and personnel.

If a new product or additional units of a product presently marketed by the firm are placed in a competitive market, they might have to be marketed at established prices; otherwise, competitors might retaliate by cutting prices. Any price cutting should be carefully observed by the accountant.

He is in a position to point out to management when a certain price would be unprofitable and therefore undesirable. If sales of the new product vary unfavorably from original intentions, management should take corrective action. If management properly utilizes the accounting information system as a vehicle to supervise and control more efficiently the operations of the business, in this case the sales department, such a trend could be discovered in time to put any needed remedial measures into effect.

LONG-RUN IMPLICATIONS OF DIFFERENTIAL COST ANALYSIS

Care must be taken to avoid action to maximize short-run profits if such action is likely to be detrimental to the overall company profit objective of long-run profit maximization. Walter B. McFarland issued this warning:

> Because overall company profit objectives are usually long-run objectives, it seems advisable to consider long-run implications of decisions which are intended to maximize short-run profits. To illustrate, addition of a product for the purpose of utilizing capacity which is currently excess may preclude more profitable use of the same capacity at a later date. Likewise, at a time when capacity is temporarily inadequate to meet sales demand, actions to maximize short-run profits (e. g., raising profits, dropping low margin products or customers) may be inconsistent with long-run profit objectives.[3]

USE OF PROBABILITY ESTIMATES

The decision-making process is typically based on a single set of assumptions, operating under an assumption of conditions of certainty when generally recognized conditions of certainty do not, in fact, exist. The problem is usually handled by saying that business judgment and a "feel" for risk and uncertainty are used to temper the quantitative analysis of the relevant data. Much of the difficulty is due to the fact that few managers can or are willing to estimate a probability distribution. Instead, the manager estimates the future event as a single figure, his "best guess."

Increasingly, however, attention is being given to estimates of a *range* of possible events and the use of probability estimates to allow for risk and uncertainty in order to indicate the likelihood of the incurrence of these events. (See pages 846–850 in Chapter 26 relating to sensitivity analysis and allowance for risk and uncertainty.) In many decision-making analyses a wealth of reasonably reliable historical data permit the assignment of fairly objective probabilities as, for example, in (1) setting forth probabilities of the rate of material usage and the lead time for

---

[3]Walter B. McFarland, *Concepts for Management Accounting* (New York: National Association of Accountants, 1966), p. 55.

order filling in computing safety stock or (2) determining safe flying weather from a given airport. In other cases, probability estimates may be much more subjective, resulting, for example, in a probability of occurrence for the most probable, pessimistic, and optimistic assumptions.

PROBABILITY DISTRIBUTION ILLUSTRATED

A company's contribution margin per unit sold is $10. A study of a 40-month period indicates highly irregular sales and no specific sales trend:

Unit Sales per Month	Number of Months	Probability
4,000	8	8/40 = .20
5,000	10	10/40 = .25
6,000	12	12/40 = .30
7,000	6	6/40 = .15
8,000	4	4/40 = .10
	40	1.00

These probabilities can then be used to compute a weighted contribution margin or expected value, assuming past experience as a reasonable basis for future prediction:

Unit Sales per Month	Contribution Margin per Unit	Contribution Margin	Probability	Weighted Contribution Margin (Expected Value)
4,000	$10	$40,000	.20	$ 8,000
5,000	10	50,000	.25	12,500
6,000	10	60,000	.30	18,000
7,000	10	70,000	.15	10,500
8,000	10	80,000	.10	8,000
		Expected average monthly contribution margin.....		$57,000

The total weighted contribution margin represents the *average* monthly contribution margin the company should expect, based on past experience. Management is also interested in the range of expected contribution margins — from a low of $40,000 to a high of $80,000 — and the probability associated with each figure in the range.

DIFFERENTIAL COST STUDIES FOR MAKE-OR-BUY DECISIONS

Another phase of alternative actions that a management faces and for whose solution cost data must supply partial answers is the problem of whether to make or buy component parts or tools. This problem arises particularly in connection with the possible use of idle equipment, idle space, and even idle labor. In such situations, a manager is inclined to consider making certain parts instead of buying them in order to utilize existing facilities.   Faced with a make-or-buy decision, the manager should:

1. Consider the quantity and quality of the parts or the tools as well as the technical know-how required, weighing such requirements for both the short-run and long-run period.

2. Compare the cost of making them with the cost (or price) of buying them.

3. Compare to possibly more profitable alternative uses that could be made of the firm's own facilities if the parts are bought.

4. Adopt a course of action related to the firm's overall policies. Customers' and suppliers' reactions often play a part in these decisions. Retaliation or ill will could result. Whether or not it is profitable to make or to buy depends in each case upon the circumstances surrounding the individual situation.

The accountant's statement should present both the differential cost of making the parts and a "full cost" computation that includes not only the cost of the materials, labor, variable overhead, and any new fixed cost but also a share of the already existing fixed costs and even a profit figure. A cost study with only the differential costs and with no allocation of existing fixed overhead or of profit seems in the majority of cases to favor the making of the parts. If management, however, were asked to sell the parts at the differential price, it might be unwilling to do so. The differential cost study is appropriate in a short-run emergency and is also indicative of possible cost savings. If the decision to make or to buy will affect an entire budget year, the accountant should present:

1. A statement that compares the company's cost of making the parts with the price of the vendor. The statement should present the differential costs of the part or tool as well as a share of existing fixed expenses and a profit figure to place the total cost on a comparable basis.

2. A restatement of the budget, indicating the effect that the allocation of existing fixed costs to the manufacture of additional parts or tools will have on total costs and total profit.

A study by the National Association of Accountants makes the following observations about cost considerations:

To evaluate the alternatives properly, costs to make vs. costs to buy must be based on the same underlying assumptions. Thus, costs for each of the alternatives must be based on the identical product specifications, quantities, and quality standards.

Determination of the "cost to buy" cannot be limited to existing costs shown on supplier invoices. The competitive nature of supplier pricing requires that current optimum third-party prices based upon identical specifications and quantities be used for evaluation of this alternative. There are many examples of lower prices being obtained from suppliers for larger quantities, standardization of specifications, etc., as well as from the use of competitive bids and/or the threat of self-manufacture. All direct and indirect costs of functions and facilities which are properly allocable to the "buy" alternative, under the "full cost" concept, must be considered. Cost to buy must also include the "full cost" to bring the product to the same condition and location as if self manufactured — including freight, handling, purchasing, incoming inspection, inventory carrying costs, etc.

Determination of the "cost to make" cannot be limited to those identified as manufacturing costs or used in the valuation of inventories. All direct and indirect costs of functions and facilities which are properly allocable to self-manufacture under the "full cost" concept must be considered.

The long-term nature of most make-or-buy decisions requires that cost determinations not only consider present costs but also projections of future costs resulting from inflationary factors, technological changes, productivity, mechanization, etc. More specifically, the projection of the future cost to make and the cost to buy must give full consideration to what the costs "should be" under obtainable conditions and reflect all possible improvements—not just what may be achieved under existing operating conditions.[4]

An evaluation of make-or-buy alternatives must also consider differences in the required capital investment and the timing of cash flows (see Chapter 26).

DIFFERENTIAL COST STUDIES FOR SHUTDOWN OF FACILITIES

Differential cost analysis is also used when a business is confronted with the possibility of a shutdown of facilities, both manufacturing and marketing. In the short run, a firm seems to be better off operating than not operating, as long as the products or services sold recover their variable costs and make a contribution toward the recovery of fixed costs. If operations are continued, certain expenses connected with the shutting down of the facilities would be saved. Furthermore, costs that would have to be incurred when a closed facility is reopened can also be saved. Management might also consider the fact that it has made an investment in the

---

[4]"Criteria for Make-or-Buy Decisions," *NAA Statement Number 5, Committee on Management Accounting Practice*, pp. 5, 7–8.

training of its active employees which would be lost in the event of a shut-down. Recruiting and training new workers would add to present costs. Another factor is the loss of established markets. To reenter a market later requires a reeducation of the consumers of the company's products. Morale of other employees as well as community goodwill may also be adversely affected.

A shutdown of facilities does not eliminate all costs. Depreciation, interest, property taxes, and insurance continue during complete inactivity. To orientate management regarding the possible steps to be taken, the accountant might again resort to the flexible budget to determine the effects of continuing operations as long as differential costs or any amount above them can be secured. This does not mean, however, that the volume set in the budget should be considered final. In view of probable prices, the most advantageous point can be determined only by considering several dif-ferent volume levels.

OTHER COST CONCEPTS

In addition to differential cost, several other cost concepts are used extensively in the management decision-making process.

Opportunity Costs. *Opportunity costs* are the measurable value of an opportunity bypassed by rejecting an alternative use of resources. In the second application of the refinery illustration (pages 800–801), a decision has to be made as to how much profit is required to justify the purchase of the cylinder stock. Here the concept of opportunity costs also enters into the final decision. If the available capacity could be used more profitably for another purpose, then perhaps the intended purchase should not be made. The decision to employ or not to employ the available capacity in favor of one or the other alternative in the future suggests that opportunity costs are also a type of future costs.

Other examples may aid in better understanding this concept. The opportunity cost of using a machine to produce one product is the sacri-fice of possible earnings from other products that might be produced using the machine. The opportunity cost of the time an owner puts into his own business is the salary he could earn elsewhere. Opportunity costs require the measurement of sacrifices associated with alternatives. If a decision requires no sacrifice, there is no opportunity cost.

Imputed Costs. *Imputed costs* are hypothetical costs representing the cost or value of a resource measured by its use value. Imputed costs do not involve actual cash outlay nor are they recorded in the books. Interest on invested capital, rental value of company-owned properties, and salaries of owner-operators of sole proprietorships or partnerships are types of imputed costs. There are perfectly good reasons for not bringing such costs into a company's regular cost and profit calculations; however, in making comparisons and in reaching a decision, the inclusion of imputed costs is relevant and important.

Out-Of-Pocket Costs. While imputed costs do not lead to cash outlays, *out-of-pocket costs* do so, either immediately or at some future date. These costs are also often identified as variable or direct costs, for they are the costs relevant to any decision when the total product costs have little or no relevance. This cost concept is significant in management's deciding whether or not a particular venture will at least return the cash expenditures caused by the contemplated business undertaking.

Relevant-Irrelevant Costs. In many instances throughout this text the terms "relevant" or "irrelevant" have been used. The dictionary defines *relevant* as "bearing upon, or properly applying to, the case in hand; of a nature tending to prove or disprove the matters in issue; pertinent." Applying the definition of the term to the purposes of cost accounting, it indicates that no single cost figure and concept fits all managerial demands, actions, and decisions. What is necessary is the selection of the appropriate decision model and the kinds of information most useful in implementing the selected model. Differences in the purposes must be recognized and the cost tailored accordingly.

Chapter 22 with its absorption costing vs. direct costing arguments affords an excellent opportunity to observe the need of different costs for different purposes. This chapter's discussion of cost terms in connection with decision making expresses the relevancy or irrelevancy of a certain cost only too forcefully. Every phase and every decision requires close attention to the inclusion or exclusion of *pertinent* costs and revenues. The task is not easy. The term "relevant" is more a statement of the problem rather than a solution to it. Costs must be (1) classified in an appropriate manner in order to allow their immediate application to as many situations as feasible, (2) observed and tested in their applicability to a given situation, and (3) perhaps discarded in favor of future (nonhistorical) costs to permit a comparative analysis for the selection of one alternative in contrast with one or several others.

Not only which but how much information to collect and analyze must be determined. Too much information is an inefficient use of resources; too little may increase the likelihood of a poor decision. Ideally, one should obtain information if the anticipated *value* exceeds its anticipated *cost*. The question centers around obtaining an *additional* amount of information; and, again, the information should be sought as long as the expected differential information value exceeds its differential cost.[5] Of course, management may be forced to make a decision with less information than it would like simply because there is insufficient time to acquire more information. In some cases information may not be available even though cost-and-time constraints would permit its collection.

Sunk Costs. *Sunk costs* are the irrecoverable costs in a given situation. The expenditure having been made in the past, its chances for recovery are almost nil. The meaning of a sunk cost will become particularly apparent when a decision must be reached regarding the exchange of an old asset for a new asset (see Chapter 26 dealing with investment analysis.) As explained there, the undepreciated book balance of the old asset is a sunk cost and entirely irrelevant to the decision-making process except in computing the income tax liability. Sunk costs also play a part in reaching the decision to abandon or continue operations. The essential feature of sunk costs in making managerial decisions is that they may be irrelevant either in whole or in part. Accountants have been reluctant in excluding these costs from their traditional mode of analysis.

DISCUSSION QUESTIONS

1. Differential costs do not correspond to any possible accounting category. Explain.
2. Differential costs have also been termed alternative costs. In what connections are such alternative costs desirable?
3. Suggest a broad definition of the term "differential cost." What other terms are often used and by whom?
4. Distinguish between marginal cost and marginal costing (or direct costing).
5. Why is the variable cost so important in differential cost studies? Which cost is more important in break-even analysis? Why?
6. Discuss explicitly the difference between an analysis based on historical cost data and one based on differential cost procedures. In what respect are they alike? Why is differential cost analysis of greater value to management?
7. How does the flexible budget assist in the preparation of differential cost analyses?
8. What type of questions could be answered for management from the differential cost analysis illustrated in the chapter on pages 798–803?
9. When differentially-costed products are marketed, close watch must be kept on their sales trend. Why?
10. Differential cost studies deal not only with alternatives that mean increased business but also with decreased business or even shutdown conditions. Explain.

---

[5]For further discussion and a quantitative illustration, see "American Accounting Association Report of Committee on Managerial Decision Models," *The Accounting Review*, Supplement to Vol. XLIV, pp. 58–64.

11. For each of the following statements, select the correct answer.

(a) As part of the data presented in support of a proposal to increase the production of clock-radios, the sales manager of Wittman Electronics reported the total additional cost required for the proposed increased production level. The increase in total cost is known as (1) controllable cost; (2) differential cost; (3) opportunity cost; (4) out-of-pocket cost.

(b) An item whose entire amount is usually a differential cost is (1) factory overhead; (2) direct cost; (3) conversion cost; (4) period cost.

(c) In the development of accounting data for decision-making purposes, relevant costs are defined as (1) future costs which will differ under each alternative course of action; (2) the change in prime cost under each alternative course of action; (3) standard costs which are developed by time and motion study techniques because of their relevance to managerial control; (4) historical costs which are the best available basis for estimating future costs.

(d) The effect on a company's net income before income taxes of discontinuing a department with a contribution to overhead of $16,000 and allocated overhead of $32,000, of which $14,000 cannot be eliminated, would be to (1) decrease net income before income taxes by $2,000; (2) decrease net income before income taxes by $18,000; (3) increase net income before income taxes by $2,000; (4) increase net income before income taxes by $16,000.

(e) Costs that do not appear in accounting records and that do not require dollar outlays but do involve a foregone opportunity by the entity whose costs are being measured are (1) conversion costs; (2) differential costs; (3) imputed costs; (4) prime costs.

(f) Pena Company temporarily has unused production capacity. The idle plant facilities can be used to manufacture a low-margin item. The low-margin item should be produced if it can be sold for more than its (1) fixed costs; (2) variable costs; (3) variable costs plus any opportunity cost of the idle facilities; (4) indirect costs plus any opportunity cost of the idle facilities.

(AICPA adapted)

EXERCISES

1. Planning Profit and Cost Potential. Palo Alto Mills, Inc. is considering manufacturing and marketing a new type of hosiery. Market research studies point to a sales price of $12 per dozen. Cost studies show a variable manufacturing cost of $5.50 per dozen with a fixed manufacturing cost at $75,000 per year for every 150,000 dozen produced; i. e., fixed factory overhead would step up in $75,000 increments.

Required: The amount available for marketing and administrative expenses for a planned profit contribution of $5 per dozen at an annual sales level of 150,000 dozen.

2. Differential Cost Statement for Special Order. The Detroit sales manager of Brolin Manufacturing, Inc. called the home office stating that she could secure a special order involving 3,600,000 gross of Product A if it could be sold for 12½% off the list price.

Management contacted the cost analyst who sent the following analysis to the vice-president in charge of sales with a notation that the profit on this order would be $167,400 ($405,000 − $237,600):

SPECIAL ORDER COST ANALYSIS

	19— Forecast 60% of Capacity		Special Order Added to 19— Forecast 80% of Capacity	
	Rate	Amount	Rate	Amount
Sales revenue (10,800,000 gross).....	$.14	$1,512,000	$ .14	$1,512,000
Special order (3,600,000 gross).......			.1225	441,000
Total.........................		$1,512,000		$1,953,000
Standard costs:				
Direct materials..................	$.040	$ 432,000	$ .040	$ 576,000
Direct labor.....................	.021	226,800	.021	302,400
Variable factory overhead.........	.010	108,000	.010	144,000
Fixed factory overhead...........	.020	216,000	.020	288,000
Variable marketing expenses.......	.005	54,000	.005	72,000
Fixed marketing expenses.........	.009	97,200	.009	129,600
Fixed administrative expenses.....	.007	75,600	.007	100,800
Total standard cost...............	$.112	$1,209,600	$ .112	$1,612,800
Profit at standard cost..............	$.028	$ 302,400	$ .0236	$ 340,200
Volume variances:				
Factory overhead................		(36,000)		36,000
Marketing expenses..............		(16,200)		16,200
Administrative expenses..........		(12,600)		12,600
Profit at actual cost...............		$ 237,600		$ 405,000

( )Denotes unfavorable variances.

The vice-president in charge of sales, confused by this statement, asked for an explanation. The cost analyst told him that on the basis of 19— forecast the company would be operating below its factory overhead absorption volume of 70% of capacity. The special order being above this predetermined volume would cause a swing from underabsorbed to overabsorbed fixed expenses.

Required: A statement that could have saved the cost analyst much time and have been more helpful and meaningful to the sales executive.

(Based on an NAA article)

3. Acceptance of Special Foreign Order. Gyro Gear Company produces a special gear used in automatic transmissions. Each gear sells for $28, and the company sells approximately 500,000 gears each year. Unit cost data for 19— are:

Direct materials....................	$6
Direct labor......................	5

	Variable	Fixed
Other costs:		
Manufacturing......................	$2	$7
Marketing.........................	4	3

Required: (1) The unit cost of gears for direct costing inventory purposes.

(2) The relevant unit cost to a pricing decision on an offer from a foreign manufacturer to purchase 25,000 gears. (Domestic sales would be unaffected by this transaction. If the offer is accepted, variable marketing costs will increase $1.50 per gear for insurance, shipping, and import duties.)

(AICPA adapted)

4. Capacity Theory; Special Order Acceptance. Last year the Bradburn Company, manufacturer of a single product, operated at 80% of normal capacity. The company bases its factory overhead rate on normal capacity and had, therefore, a substantial amount of underapplied factory overhead for the period.

Early this year the company received an order for a substantial number of units at 30% off the regular $7 sales price. The controller wants to accept the order because $.80 of the total manufacturing cost of $5 per unit is fixed overhead and because the additional units can be produced within the company's practical capacity.

Required: (1) Definition of (a) theoretical capacity, (b) practical capacity, (c) normal capacity, and (d) expected capacity.

(2) Quantitative discussion of the several financial considerations that the president should review before accepting or rejecting the order.

5. Differential Cost Analysis for New Product. The Research Division of the Maine Corporation, a chemical manufacturer, has developed a new product named Zip. The product will be marketed through the company's regular sales agents. However, at the main office a sales manager will have to be added at a minimum total annual salary of $22,000. Annual advertising and promotion expenditures are expected to be $20,000. Both preliminary and secondary surveys of marketing areas have revealed that a price of $.85 per pound will place Zip in a favorable competitive position. It is estimated that 400,000 pounds of Zip can be sold during the initial year. A long-range sales forecast predicts the same or even better sales in the future.

To accommodate the new product, present plant facilities will have to be altered at an estimated cost of $40,000 (useful life ten years). Property taxes and insurance will increase about $1,000. The addition to the factory will be financed at a rate of 5%. While the present foremen staff can handle the increased output, another foreman's assistant, one maintenance worker, and an additional helper for the warehouse must be employed at a total annual cost of $25,000. It is also anticipated that the additional billing work requires the hiring of an accounts receivable clerk at $6,000 per annum. The Production Department has estimated that prime costs will be $.37 per unit (direct materials, $.20; direct labor, $.17). The factory overhead rate for the plant is $.35 per unit, of which $.10 is considered to be the variable portion. Variable marketing and general and administrative expenses have been set at $.05 per pound of product.

Required: (1) A statement showing anticipated first year results, before income taxes, which could be attained if the new product is added.

(2) The percentage by which the marketing survey could be off without sustaining a loss (the margin of safety ratio).

(Based on a *Management Services* article)

6. New Product Analysis. Amex Company is considering the introduction of a new product which will be manufactured in an existing plant; however, new equipment costing $150,000 with a useful life of five years (no salvage value) will be necessary. The space in the existing plant to be used for the new product is currently used for warehousing. When the new product takes over the warehouse space, on which the actual depreciation is $20,000, Amex Company will rent warehouse space at an annual cost of $25,000. An accounting study produces the following estimates of differential revenue and expense on an average annual basis:

Sales..	$500,000
Cost of merchandise sold (excluding depreciation)...	385,000
Depreciation of equipment (straight-line)...........	30,000
Marketing expense.............................	10,000

The company requires an average annual rate of return of 11% (after income taxes) on the average investment in proposals. The effective income tax rate is 46%. (Ignore the time value of money.)

Required: (1) The average annual differential costs for the first five years (including income taxes) which must be considered in evaluating this decision.
(2) The minimum annual net income needed to meet the company's requirement for this proposal.
(3) The estimated annual residual income (after allowing for return on investment in new equipment) resulting from introduction of the new product.
(4) The estimated differential cash flow during the third year.

(AICPA adapted)

7. Sell or Process Further. From a particular joint process, Watkins Company produces three products — X, Y, and Z. Each product may be sold at the point of split-off or processed further. Additional processing requires no special facilities, and production costs of further processing are entirely variable and traceable to the products involved. In 19—, these products were processed beyond split-off. Joint production costs for the year were $60,000. Sales values and costs needed to evaluate Watkins' 19— production policy follow:

Product	Units Produced	Sales Values at Split-Off	Additional Costs and Sales Values If Processed Further	
			Sales Values	Added Costs
X....................	6,000	$25,000	$42,000	$9,000
Y....................	4,000	41,000	45,000	7,000
Z....................	2,000	24,000	32,000	8,000

Joint costs are allocated to the products in proportion to the relative physical volume of output.

Required: (1) For units of Product Z, the unit production cost most relevant to a sell, or process further, decision.
(2) The products the company should subject to additional processing in order to maximize profits.

(AICPA adapted)

8. Contribution Margin and Probability Analysis. Travis County Simmental, Ltd., a Texas three-year limited partnership, is considering the purchase of 11 first-time bred Simmental heifers at a cost of $10,000 each. The estimated cost of insuring the heifers against disease and theft and of maintaining the herd from date of purchase until they are sold, along with their calves, is $1,000 per heifer.

It is estimated, based on industry experience with three-quarter Simmental heifers bred for the first time, that two of the heifers' calves will be stillborn and these heifers will have a rebred sale value of $10,000 each. The other heifers, having demonstrated both their fertility and ability to give birth, will have an estimated sale value of $16,000. Their calves, which will be seven-eighths Simmentals and which are sold along with the rebred parent heifer, are expected to sell for $20,000 if heifers and $1,250 if bulls.

The probabilities of combinations of heifer and bull calves from nine live births were obtained from the Texas-Oklahoma Simmental Cattlebreeders Association and are as follows:

Heifers	Bulls	Probabilities
9	0	.002
8	1	.018
7	2	.070
6	3	.164
5	4	.246
4	5	.246
3	6	.164
2	7	.070
1	8	.018
0	9	.002
Total.............		1.000

Required: (1) The contribution margin for each combination of heifers and bulls (to the nearest even cent) and the weighted contribution margin for the proposed transaction.

(2) How the answers would differ if, after purchasing the heifers, the Simmental market prices decline (a) by 25% or (b) by 50%.

9. Comparative Cost Study. The Merriman Company, manager of an office building, is considering putting in certain concessions in the main lobby. An accounting study produces the following estimates, on an average annual basis:

Salaries...		$ 7,000
Licenses and payroll taxes............................		200
Cost of merchandise sold:		
Beginning inventory.............................	$ 2,000	
Purchases......................................	40,000	
Available.....................................	$42,000	
Ending inventory................................	2,000	40,000
Share of heat, light, etc...............................		500
Pro rata building depreciation..........................		1,000
Concession advertising................................		100
Share of company administrative expenses...............		400
Sales of merchandise..................................		49,000

The investment in equipment, which would last 10 years, would be $2,000.

As an alternative, a catering company has offered to lease the space for $750 per year, for 10 years, and to put in and operate the same concessions at no cost to the Merriman Company. Heat and light are to be furnished by the office building at no additional charge.

Required: A cost study and statement of other factors to aid the Merriman Company in the decision.

(AICPA adapted)

10. Make-or-Buy Decision. The management of the Petersburg Corporation requests assistance from its economic analyst in arriving at a decision whether to continue manufacturing a certain part of an assembly or to buy it from an outside supplier who has been quoting a price of $9 per unit.

The company's annual requirement is 5,000 units, and the costs accumulated for their special manufacture are:

Materials.....................................	$26,500
Direct labor..................................	28,000*
Indirect labor................................	6,000*
Power..	300
Other costs..................................	640

*Exclusive of 14% labor fringe benefits.

If the parts are purchased outside, present machinery used to make the parts could be sold and its book value would be realized. This step would reduce total machinery depreciation by $2,000 and property taxes and insurance by $1,000.

If the parts were purchased from an outside supplier, the following additional costs would be incurred: freight, $.50 per unit; indirect labor for receiving, materials handling, inspection, etc., $5,000, exclusive of 14% labor fringe benefits generally added to labor costs.

Required: (1) A statement comparing the costs of manufacturing the parts with the costs of purchasing them from the outside supplier.

(2) A brief discussion dealing with matters other than cost factors of which management should be made aware.

(AICPA adapted)

11. Make-or-Buy Decision. Standard costs and other data for two component parts used by Griffon Electronics are presented below:

	Part A4	Part B5
Direct materials...................................	$ .40	$ 8.00
Direct labor......................................	1.00	4.70
Factory overhead.................................	4.00	2.00
Unit standard cost................................	$5.40	$14.70
Units needed per year............................	6,000	8,000
Machine hours per unit...........................	4	2
Unit cost if purchased............................	$5.00	$15.00

In past years, Griffon Electronics has manufactured all of its required components; however, in 19— only 30,000 hours of otherwise idle machine time can be devoted to the production of components. Accordingly, some of the parts must be purchased from outside suppliers. In producing parts, factory overhead is applied at $1 per standard machine hour. Fixed capacity costs, which will not be affected by any make-or-buy decision, represent 60% of the applied factory overhead.

The 30,000 hours of available machine time are to be scheduled so that Griffon realizes maximum potential cost savings.

Required: (1) The relevant unit production costs to be considered in the make-or-buy decision to schedule machine time.

(2) The units of A4 and B5 that Griffon should produce if the allocation of machine time is based on potential cost savings per machine hour.

(AICPA adapted)

12. Deciding to Discontinue a Product. The Zehr Company manufactures and sells three products. Results of operations for the year just ended, by products, are:

	Product A	Product B	Product C	Total
Sales........................	$100,000	$190,000	$250,000	$540,000
Total costs..................	90,000	210,000	210,000	510,000
Profit (loss).................	$ 10,000	$ (20,000)	$ 40,000	$ 30,000
Variable cost rate, expressed as a percentage of sales.........	40%	80%	60%	

Required: Reasons, supported quantitatively, for the pros or cons of the discontinuance of the production and sales of Product B.

13. Continuing Research Project; Sunk Costs. Management of the Sifri Chemical Company is reviewing a research project that was initiated with the purpose of developing a new product. Expenditures to date on the project total $126,000. The Research and Development Department now estimates that an additional $24,000 will be required to produce a marketable product. Current market estimates indicate a lifetime profit potential having a present value of $40,000 for the product, excluding Research and Development expenditures.

Required: Advice to management.

PROBLEMS

25-1. Differential and Opportunity Costs. George Jackson owns and operates a small machine shop manufacturing (1) a standard product available from many other similar businesses and (2) products to customer order. His accountant prepared the 19— income statement shown on page 819.

Depreciation is for machines used in the respective product lines. Power is apportioned on the estimate of power consumed. Rent is for the building space that has been leased for ten years at $7,000 per year. Rent and also heat and light are apportioned to the product lines based on amount of occupied floor space. All other costs are current expenses identified with the product line causing them.

A valued custom-parts customer asks Jackson to manufacture 5,000 special units for her. The machine shop is working at capacity, and Jackson would have to discontinue the manufacture of other orders to take this special order.

INCOME STATEMENT FOR 19--

	Custom Sales	Standard Sales	Total
Sales.....................................	$50,000	$25,000	$75,000
Materials.............................	$10,000	$ 8,000	$18,000
Labor.................................	20,000	9,000	29,000
Depreciation...........................	6,300	3,600	9,900
Power.................................	700	400	1,100
Rent...................................	6,000	1,000	7,000
Heat and light.........................	600	100	700
Other.................................	400	900	1,300
Total costs............................	$44,000	$23,000	$67,000
Net income............................	$ 6,000	$ 2,000	$ 8,000

He cannot renege on custom orders already agreed to but could reduce his standard product output by about one half for one year while producing the specially requested custom part. The customer is willing to pay $7 for each part. The materials cost would be about $2 per unit while the labor would be $3.60 per unit. Jackson will have to spend $2,000 for a special device that will be discarded when the job is completed.

Required: (1) The following costs related to the 5,000 unit custom order: (a) differential cost of the order; (b) full cost of the order; (c) opportunity cost of taking the order.

(2) An explanation as to why Jackson should accept or reject the order.

(NAA adapted)

25-2. Sell or Process Further. The management of the Bay Company is considering a proposal to install a third production department within its existing factory building. With the present production setup, raw material is passed through Department I to produce Materials A and B in equal proportions. The portions of Materials A and B produced are constant due to the inherent nature of the manufacturing process. Material A is then passed through Department II to yield Product C. Material B is presently being sold "as is" at a price of $20.25 per pound. Product C has a selling price of $100 per pound.

The per pound standard costs currently being used by the Bay Company are:

	Department I (Materials A & B)	Department II (Product C)	(Material B)
Prior department costs....		$53.03	$13.47
Direct materials..........	$20.00		
Direct labor.............	7.00	12.00	
Variable factory overhead.	3.00	5.00	
Fixed factory overhead:			
Attributable...........	2.25	2.25	
Allocated common (⅔, ⅓)...	1.00	1.00	
	$33.25	$73.28	$13.47

These per pound standard costs were developed by using an estimated production volume of 200,000 pounds of materials as the normal volume. The Bay Company assigns Department I costs to Materials A and B in proportion to their net sales values at the point of separation, computed by deducting subsequent standard production costs from sales prices except that the $300,000 of common fixed factory overhead costs are allocated to the two producing departments on the basis of the space used by the departments.

The proposed Department III would be used to process Material B into Product D. It is expected that any quantity of Product D can be sold for $30 per pound. Standard costs per pound under this proposal were developed by using 200,000 pounds of material as the normal volume and are:

	Department I (Materials A & B)	Department II (Product C)	Department III (Product D)
Prior department costs.........		$52.80	$13.20
Direct materials..............	$20.00		
Direct labor.................	7.00	12.00	5.50
Variable factory overhead......	3.00	5.00	2.00
Fixed factory overhead:			
Attributable...............	2.25	2.25	1.75
Allocated common (½, ¼, ¼).	.75	.75	.75
	$33.00	$72.80	$23.20

Nonmanufacturing costs are expected to be the same for either alternative.

Required: A decision by management as to whether Bay should install Department III, thereby producing Product D if sales and production levels are expected to remain constant in the foreseeable future and if there are no foreseeable alternative uses for the available factory space. (Show calculations.)

(NAA adapted)

25-3. Make-or-Buy Decision. The Weaver Products Company, Inc. produces a product at $.51 variable cost per unit plus $.21 for overhead expenses when manufacturing 50,000 such units. A supplier offers to furnish the identical unit for $.60 each. An analysis of some of the costs incurred in the past to produce the unit indicates:

Direct materials..............................	$13,000
Direct labor..................................	12,000
Payroll taxes.................................	480
Supervision..................................	4,000
Payroll taxes.................................	160
Other expenses...............................	200

It was further ascertained that the materials unit cost would increase $.03 per unit.

The Weaver Company has projected next year's sales to be 75,000 units.

Required: (1) A decision whether (a) to buy or (b) to make.

(2) Intangible factors to be considered in addition to a cost analysis to arrive at a sound make-or-buy decision.

25-4. Make-or-Buy Decision; Working Capital Analysis. The Mansell Company must decide whether it should continue to manufacture or should purchase Mansers, a component of the company's product. The annual requirement for Mansers is 10,000 units, and the part is available from an outside supplier in any quantity at $5 per unit.

The following information is available:

(a) The Machining Department starts and substantially completes Mansers, and minor finishing is completed by the use of direct labor in the Finishing Department. The Assembly Department places Mansers in the finished product.

(b) Machinery used to produce Mansers could be sold for its book value of $15,000 and the proceeds invested at 6% per year if the Mansers were purchased. Property taxes and insurance would decrease $300 per year if the machinery were sold. The machinery has a remaining life of 10 years with no estimated salvage value.

(c) The Machining Department has devoted about 25% to the production of Mansers, but labor and other costs for Mansers in this department except heat and light and the continuing rent, property taxes, and insurance could be eliminated without affecting other operations. The Finishing Department's costs include direct labor totaling $800 devoted to Mansers. If Mansers were not manufactured, half of the resulting available direct labor would be used as indirect labor and the remaining half would result in paid idle time of the employees.

(d) In 19— when 10,000 Mansers were produced, pertinent Machining Department costs were:

	Total Costs	Costs Allocated to Mansers
Materials..................................	$95,000	$24,200
Direct labor...............................	39,400	12,200
Indirect labor.............................	20,600	7,800
Heat and light.............................	12,000	3,000
Depreciation...............................	6,000	1,500
Property taxes and insurance................	15,000	3,750
Production supplies.........................	4,000	800

(e) In addition, the Machining Department total costs included $18,300 payroll taxes and other benefits.

(f) Overhead allocated on the basis of 200% of direct labor cost was $40,000 for the Finishing Department and $20,000 for the Assembly Department in 19—. Overhead in these departments is 25% fixed and 75% variable.

(g) If the Mansers are purchased, Mansell will incur added costs of $.45 per unit for freight and $3,000 per year for receiving, handling, and inspecting the product.

Required: (1) A schedule comparing Mansell's total annual cost of Mansers if manufactured with their annual cost if purchased. (Ignore income taxes.)

(2) The annual net cash outflow, ignoring income taxes, if Mansers are (a) manufactured and (b) purchased. (Without regard to the solution to (1) above, assume that the total annual cost of Mansers — if manufactured and if purchased — is $60,000.)

(3) The working capital requirements to be considered in deciding whether to manufacture or purchase Mansers.

(AICPA adapted)

25-5. Make-or-Buy Decision. Vernom Corporation, a manufacturer of a highly successful line of summer lotions and insect repellents, has decided to diversify in order to stabilize sales throughout the year. A natural area for the company to consider is the production of winter lotions and creams to prevent dry and chapped skin.

After considerable research, a winter products line has been developed. However, because of the conservative nature of the company's management, Vernom's president has decided to introduce only one new product for the coming winter. If the product is a success, further expansion in future years will be initiated.

The product selected, Chap-Off, is a lip balm that will be sold in a lipstick-type tube. The product will be sold to wholesalers in boxes of 24 tubes at $8 per box. Because of available capacity, no additional fixed costs will be incurred to produce Chap-Off. However, a $100,000 fixed cost will be absorbed by Chap-Off to allocate a fair share of the company's present fixed costs to the new product.

Using the estimated sales and production of 100,000 boxes of Chap-Off as the standard volume, the Accounting Department developed these costs:

Direct labor..	$2.00 per box
Direct materials....................................	$3.00 per box
Total factory overhead.............................	$1.50 per box
Total..	$6.50 per box

The Vernom Corporation has approached a cosmetics manufacturer to discuss the possibility of purchasing empty tubes for Chap-Off at $.90 per 24 tubes. If Vernom accepts this purchase proposal, it is estimated that direct labor and variable factory overhead costs would be reduced by 10% and that direct materials costs would be reduced by 20%.

Required: (1) A decision as to whether the Vernom Corporation should manufacture or purchase the empty tubes. (Show calculations.)

(2) The maximum purchase price acceptable to the Vernom Corporation for the cosmetic manufacturer's empty tubes. (Explain.)

(3) A decision as to whether the Vernom Corporation should manufacture or purchase the empty tubes, assuming that revised estimates show the sales volume at 125,000 boxes instead of at 100,000 boxes. At this new volume, additional equipment — at an annual rental of $10,000 — must be acquired to manufacture the empty tubes. (Show calculations.)

(4) The answer to (3) if the company has the option of manufacturing and purchasing the empty tubes at the same time. Assume that 100,000 boxes are to be manufactured and the remainder purchased. (Show calculations.)

(5) The nonquantifiable factors to be considered in determining whether the Vernom Corporation should manufacture or purchase the empty tubes.

(NAA adapted)

25-6. Make-or-Buy Decision Involving Alternative Use of Facilities. Virginia Manufacturing Company has manufactured Products P and Z at its Richmond Plant for several years. On March 31, 19A, Product P was dropped from the product line. The company manufactures and sells 50,000 units of Product Z annually, and this is not expected to change. Unit direct materials and direct labor costs are $12 and $7, respectively.

The Richmond Plant is in a leased building renting for $75,000 annually and with a lease expiring on June 30, 19E. The lease provides the company with the right of sublet and with all nonremovable leasehold improvements reverting to the lessor. At the termination of the lease, the company intends to close the Richmond Plant scrapping all of the equipment.

Product P has been manufactured on two assembly lines occupying 25% of the Richmond Plant. As of June 30, 19A, the assembly lines will have a book value of $135,000 and a remaining useful life of seven years. This is the only portion of the Richmond Plant available for alternative uses.

The company uses one unit of Product D to produce one unit of Product Z. Product D is purchased under a contract requiring a *minimum* annual purchase of 5,000 units. The contract expires on June 30, 19E. A list of Product D unit costs follows:

Annual Purchases (in Units)	Unit Cost
5,000–7,499	$2.00
7,500–19,999	1.95
20,000–34,999	1.80
35,000–99,999	1.65
100,000–250,000	1.35

Alternatives are available for using the space previously used to manufacture Product P. Some may be used in combination. All can be implemented by June 30, 19A. Should no action be taken, the Richmond Plant is expected to operate profitably, and factory overhead is not expected to differ materially from past years when Product P was manufactured. The alternatives are to:

(a) Sell the two Product P assembly lines for $70,000 to a purchaser who will buy only if the equipment can be acquired from both lines. The purchaser will pay all removal and transportation costs.

(b) Sublet the floor space for an annual rental of $12,100 with a lease requirement that the equipment be removed at a nominal cost and that leasehold improvements costing $38,000 be installed. (Annual indirect costs are expected to increase by $3,500 as a result of the sublease and are to be borne by the Virginia Manufacturing Company.)

(c) Convert one *or* both Product P assembly lines to manufacture Product D at a cost of $45,500 for each line. The converted lines will have a remaining useful life of ten years. Each modified line can manufacture any number of units of Product D up to a maximum of 37,000 units at a unit direct materials and direct labor cost of $.10 and $.25, respectively. Annual factory overhead is expected to increase from $550,000 to $562,000 if one line is converted and to $566,000 if both lines are converted.

Required: A schedule analyzing the best utilization of the following alternatives for the four years ended June 30, 19E (ignore income taxes and the time value of money):

(a) Continue to purchase Product D; sell equipment; rent space.

(b) Continue to purchase Product D; sell equipment.

(c) Manufacture Product D on two assembly lines; purchase Product D as needed.

(d) Manufacture Product D on one assembly line; purchase Product D as needed.

Allow one column for the evaluation of each alternative. Letter the columns *a, b, c,* and *d.*

(AICPA adapted)

25-7. Break-Even Analysis; Plant Shutdown; Stockholders' Return. The management of the SouthernTex Cottonseed Mills, Inc. has requested its cost analysis section to assist in the development of information to be used for managerial decisions. The company's plant has the capacity to process 20,000 tons of cottonseed per year with the following yield per ton of cottonseed:

Product	Average Yield per Ton of Cottonseed	Average Selling Price per Trade Unit
Oil..............	300 lbs.	$ .15 per lb.
Meal............	600 lbs.	50.00 per ton
Hulls...........	800 lbs.	20.00 per ton
Lint............	100 lbs.	3.00 per hundredweight (cwt.)
Waste..........	200 lbs.	

A special marketing study revealed that the company can expect to sell its entire output for the coming year at the average selling prices listed above. The company's costs are as follows:

Materials costs: Average price paid, $35 per ton
Processing costs: Variable costs, $9 per ton of cottonseed put into process
       Fixed costs, $108,000 per year
Marketing costs: All variable, $20 per ton sold
Administrative costs: All fixed, $90,000 per year

Required: (1) A detailed analysis of the company's break-even point.

(2) In view of conditions in the cottonseed market, the management would also like to know the average maximum amount the company can afford to pay for a ton of cottonseed which management has defined as the amount that would result in the company's having losses no greater when operating than when closed down under the existing cost and revenue structure. Management states that the fixed costs shown in the break-even analysis will continue unchanged even when the operations are shut down. Assume that the company is to process 20,000 tons of cottonseed.

(3) A statement to management mentioning and discussing those factors, other than the costs entered into in the computation of (2), that should be considered in deciding whether to shut down the plant.

(4) The stockholders consider 25% before corporate income taxes the minimum satisfactory return on their investment in the business. The stockholders' equity in the company is $968,000. Compute the maximum average amount that the company can pay for a ton of cottonseed to realize the minimum satisfactory return on the stockholders' investment when operating at capacity.

(AICPA adapted)

25-8. Sales Probability and Contribution Margin Analysis.   Krull Products Corporation produces a chemical compound which deteriorates and must be discarded if it is not sold by the end of the month during which it is produced.

The total variable cost of the manufactured compound is $25 per unit, and it is sold for $40 per unit. The compound can be purchased from a competitor at $40 per unit plus $5 freight per unit. It is estimated that failure to fill orders would result in the complete loss of 8 out of 10 customers placing orders for the compound.

The corporation has sold the compound for the past 30 months. Demand has been irregular and there is no sales trend. During this period sales per month have been:

Units Sold per Month	Number of Months
4,000	6
5,000	15
6,000	9

Required: (1) For each of the following, a schedule of the:

(a) Probability of sales of 4,000, 5,000, or 6,000 units in any month.

(b) Contribution margin if sales of 4,000, 5,000, or 6,000 units are made in one month and 4,000, 5,000, or 6,000 units are manufactured for sale in the same month; i.e., nine possible combinations of units sold and units manufactured. Assume all sales orders are filled.

(c) Average monthly contribution margin that the corporation should expect over the long run if 5,000 units are manufactured every month and all sales orders are filled.

(2) The cost of the primary ingredient used to manufacture the compound is $12 per unit of compound. It is estimated that there is a 60% chance that the primary ingredient supplier's plant may be shut down by a strike for an indefinite period.   A substitute ingredient is available at $18 per unit of compound, but the corporation must contract immediately to purchase the substitute or it will be unavailable when needed. A firm purchase contract for either the primary or the substitute ingredient must now be made with one of the suppliers for production next month. If an order were placed for the primary ingredient and a strike should occur, the corporation would be released from the contract and management would purchase the compound from the competitor. Assume that 5,000 units are to be manufactured, and all sales orders are to be filled.

(a) The monthly contribution margin from sales of 4,000, 5,000, and 6,000 units if the substitute ingredient is ordered.

(b) A schedule computing the average monthly contribution margin that the corporation should expect if the primary ingredient is ordered with the existing probability of a strike at the supplier's plant. Assume that the expected average monthly contribution margin from manufacturing will be $65,000 using the primary ingredient, or $35,000 using the substitute, and the expected average monthly loss from purchasing from the competitor will be $25,000.

(c) Should management order the primary or substitute ingredient during the anticipated strike period (under the assumptions stated in (2)(b) above)? Why?

(d) Should management purchase the compound from the competitor to fill sales orders when the orders cannot be filled otherwise? Why?

(AICPA adapted)

25-9. Contribution Margin and Probability Analysis. The Colt-Squeri Company, a wholesale chemical products distributor, ships 10,000 liters of Astrojel per day in an airplane owned by the company. The daily shipment is made to a government-owned military research laboratory in Ohio. The area where the company is located is sometimes fogbound, and shipment can then be made only by rail. Extra costs of preparation for rail shipment reduce the contribution margin of this product from $.40 per liter to $.18 per liter, and there is an additional fixed cost of $3,100 for modification of packaging facilities to convert to rail shipment (incurred only once per conversion).

The fog may last for several days, and Colt-Squeri normally starts shipping by rail only after rail shipments become necessary to meet commitments to the customer, in which case the shipments are still only 10,000 liters per day.

A meteorological report reveals that during the past ten years the area has been fogbound 250 times for at least a day and that of the 250 times fog continued 100 times for a second consecutive day, 40 times for at least a third consecutive day, 20 times for at least a fourth consecutive day, and 10 times for a fifth consecutive day. Occasions and length of fog were both random. Fog never continued for more than five days, and there were never two separate occurrences of fog in any six-day period.

Required: (1) A schedule of the daily contribution margin (ignoring fixed conversion costs) when (a) there is no fog and shipment is made by air and (b) there is fog and shipment is made by rail.

(2) A schedule of the probabilities of the possible combinations of foggy and clear weather on the days following a fogbound day. The schedule should show the probability that if fog first occurs on a particular day, the (a) next four days will be foggy; (b) next three days will be foggy and Day 5 will be clear; (c) next two days will be foggy and Days 4 and 5 will be clear; (d) next day will be foggy and Days 3, 4, and 5 will be clear; (e) next four days will be clear.

(3) Assuming the probability exists that it would be unprofitable to begin shipping 10,000 liters per day by rail on either the fourth or fifth consecutive foggy day, a schedule of the probable weighted three-day contribution (including fixed conversion costs) that should be expected from rail and air shipments if (a) rail shipments were started on the third consecutive foggy day and the probability that the next two days will be foggy is .25; (b) the probability that the next day will be foggy and Day 5 will be clear is .25; and (c) the probability that the next two days will be clear is .50. The company returns immediately to air shipments on the first clear day.

(4) A discussion of the reliability of the data upon which conclusions are based. Include (a) financial data reliability and (b) meteorological data reliability.

(AICPA adapted)

25-10. Probability Analysis. Vendo, Inc. operates the concession stands at the Tecumseh College football stadium. Tecumseh College has had successful football teams for many years; as a result, the stadium is virtually always filled. The college is located in an area with almost no rainfall during its football season. From time to time, Vendo has found that its supply of hot dogs is inadequate while at other times the supply has been a surplus. A review of Vendo's sales records for the past ten seasons reveals the following frequency of hot dogs sold:

VENDO, INC.
HOT DOG SALES FOR PAST TEN SEASONS
(Frequency of Sales)

Hot Dogs	Number of Games
10,000.	5
20,000.	10
30,000.	20
40,000.	15
Total.	50

Hot dogs sell for $.50 each at a cost of $.30 each to Vendo. Unsold hot dogs are donated to a local orphanage.

Required: (1) A table representing the expected value of each of the four possible strategies of ordering 10,000, 20,000, 30,000, or 40,000 hot dogs, assuming that only the four quantities listed were ever sold and that the occurrences were random events. (Ignore income taxes.)

(2) The best strategy of the four strategies in (1), based on the expected value.

(3) The dollar value of perfect information in this problem.

(NAA adapted)

25-11. Alternative Proposals and Break-Even Analysis on Shop, Lodge, and Restaurant Operations. Helga Wedekind, the Austrian ski champion, operates a ski shop, restaurant, and lodge in the Sierra Nevada mountains during the 120-day ski season from November 15 to March 15. She has been thinking of changing her operations and keeping the lodge open all year.

For the year ended March 15, 19D the statement of operations showed:

	Ski Shop		Restaurant		Lodge	
	Amount	Percent	Amount	Percent	Amount	Percent
Revenue.	$27,000	100%	$40,000	100%	$108,000	100%
Costs:						
Cost of goods sold	14,850	55	24,000	60		
Supplies.	1,350	5	4,000	10	7,560	7
Utilities	270	1	1,200	3	2,160	2
Salaries	1,620	6	12,000	30	32,400	30
Insurance	810	3	800	2	9,720	9
Property taxes on building. .	540	2	1,600	4	6,480	6
Depreciation. . . .	1,080	4	2,000	5	28,080	26
Total costs. . .	$20,520	76	$45,600	114	$ 86,400	80
Net income (loss)	$ 6,480	24%	$ (5,600)	(14)%	$ 21,600	20%

Additional Data:

(a) The lodge has 100 rooms, and the rate from November 15 to March 15 is $10 per day for one or two persons. The occupancy rate from November 15 to March 15 is 90%.

(b) Ski shop and restaurant sales vary in direct proportion to room occupancy.

(c) For the ski shop and restaurant, cost of goods sold, supplies, and utilities vary in direct proportion to sales. For the lodge, supplies and utilities vary in direct proportion to room occupancy.

(d) The ski shop, restaurant, and lodge are located in the same building. Depreciation on the building is charged to the lodge. The ski shop and restaurant are charged with depreciation on equipment only. The full cost of the restaurant equipment became fully depreciated on March 15, 19D; but the equipment has a remaining useful life of three years. The equipment can be sold for $1,200 but will be worthless in three years. All depreciation is computed by the straight-line method. The undepreciated cost of the building, ski shop, and lodge equipment equals its present disposable value.

(e) Insurance premiums are for annual coverage for public liability and fire insurance on the building and equipment and are the same whether or not facilities are in use. All building insurance is charged to the lodge.

(f) Salaries are the minimum necessary to keep each facility open and are for the ski season only, except for the lodge security guard who is paid $5,400 per year.

Two alternatives are being considered by Ms. Wedekind for the future operation of the ski lodge:

(a) To close the restaurant during the ski season because "it does not have enough revenue to cover its out-of-pocket costs." If the restaurant were closed during the ski season, lodge occupancy would drop to 80% of capacity. The restaurant space would be used as a lounge for lodge guests.

(b) To keep the lodge open from March 15 to November 15. The ski shop would be converted into a gift shop if the lodge should be operated during this period with conversion costs of $1,000 in March and $1,000 in November each year. Revenues from the gift shop would be the same per room occupied as revenues from the ski shop; variable costs would be in the same ratio to revenues and all other costs would be the same for the gift shop as for the ski shop. The occupancy rate of the lodge at a room rate of $7 per day is estimated at 50% during the period from March 15 to November 15 whether or not the restaurant is operated.

Required: (Ignore income taxes and use 30 days per month for computational purposes.)

(1) A projected income statement for the ski shop and lodge from November 15, 19D to March 15, 19E, assuming the restaurant is closed during this period and all facilities are closed during the remainder of the year.

(2) Assuming all facilities will continue to be operated during the 4-month period of November 15 to March 15 of each year:

(a) An analysis which indicates the projected contribution or loss of operating the gift shop and lodge during the eight-month period from March 15 to November 15. Assume that the restaurant will be closed during this eight-month period.

(b) The minimum room rate that should be charged to allow the lodge to break even during the eight months from March 15 to November 15, assuming the gift shop and restaurant are not operated during this period.

(AICPA adapted)

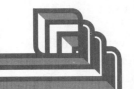

CHAPTER 26

CAPITAL EXPENDITURE
PLANNING, EVALUATING,
AND CONTROL

Capital expenditures involve long-term commitments of resources to realize future benefits. They reflect basic company objectives and have a significant, long-term effect on the economic well-being of the firm.

Considerable attention has been devoted to techniques for evaluating capital expenditure proposals. Indeed, evaluation represents an important segment of the capital expenditure process. In the final analysis, the firm must earn a reasonable return on invested funds to satisfy the profit objective. Yet evaluation is only one essential requirement for the effective administration of a capital expenditure program. Equally important is the effective planning and control of such expenditures because (1) the long-term commitment increases financial risk, (2) the magnitude of expenditures is substantial and the penalties for unwise decisions are usually severe, and (3) the decisions made in this area provide the structure that supports the operating activities of the firm.

This chapter presents capital expenditures in three phases: (1) planning, (2) evaluating, and (3) control.

PLANNING FOR CAPITAL EXPENDITURES

The *planning* phase consists of relating plans to objectives, structuring the framework, searching, budgeting capital expenditures, and requesting authority for expenditure.

Relating Plans to Objectives. Various organizational levels play different roles relative to objectives. Ideally, executive management sets broad objectives; managers of functional activities formulate specific policies and programs for action which, when approved, are executed by operating levels of management. All levels of the organization need to be conscious of objectives. The lower the level at which a decision is authorized, the greater the need for guidelines extending to detailed procedures and standards. Investment projects not conducive to such detail require handling at a higher level. Individual projects must be consistent with objectives and must be capable of being blended into a firm's operations.

Structuring the Framework. An organization's established capital expenditure framework forms the basis for the implementation of the capital expenditure program. The framework is important because the very nature of performing tasks implies a sound frame of reference. Several factors influence the molding and revisions of a firm's framework: the company's organizational structure, its philosophy and applications of principles of organization, its size, the nature of its operations, and the characteristics of individual projects.

A company manual may be used to detail policies and procedures and illustrative forms required for administering the capital expenditure program. Such manuals should be stripped down to helpful levels and should (1) encourage people to submit and work on ideas, (2) focus attention on useful analytical tasks, and (3) facilitate rapid project development and expeditious review.

Searching. A capital investment program yields the best results only when the best available proposals are considered and all reasonable alternatives of each proposal have been brought into the analysis for evaluating and screening. Ideas should come from all segments of the enterprise. Persons in the organization should participate in the search activity within the bounds of their technical knowledge and ability, their authority and responsibility, their awareness of operating problems, and existing management guidelines regarding desirable projects. Care must be taken to create and maintain an incentive to search out and bring good projects into the system. This incentive is strong when there is a genuine feeling that all proposals will be reviewed in a fair and objective manner.

Budgeting Capital Expenditures. The capital expenditures budget is typically prepared for a one-year period. It presents management with the investment plans for the coming period for which approval is sought, as these plans appear at the time the budget is prepared.

Some projects never materialize; others are added through amendments to the budget during the budget year. Thus, the budget must be adaptable to changing needs. The capital expenditures budget is no authorization to commit funds; it merely affords an opportunity to consolidate plans by looking at projects for the total organization, side by side. The capital expenditures budget should be reconciled with the other periodic budgeting activities of the firm; e.g., expense and cash budgets (see Chapters 16 and 17). The annual capital budget should be reconciled with long-range capital investment and operating plans and objectives.

The capital expenditures budget passes through several management levels as it moves toward final approval at the top management level. A clear explanation of the content of the approved budget should be transmitted to the various management levels to avoid misunderstandings.

Requesting Authority for Expenditure. Most companies agree that the periodic budget is an approval of ideas and does not grant automatic approval to commit funds. Authority to commit funds and commence work, other than necessary preliminary administrative costs, should come by means of an Authority for Expenditure (AFE). The AFE procedure is, in effect, a second look at budgeted projects based on an up-to-date set of documents justifying and describing the expenditure. The AFE and supporting detail should be originated at the level at which the expenditure will occur, with staff assistance if needed.

Approval of the AFE should be delegated to the organizational level having the necessary competence to make the decision, as opposed to requesting executive management's approval for each AFE. The philosophy of companies varies as to the extent of decentralization of approval authority. The amount, type, and significance of the expenditure ought to be considered in determining the required level of approval. Required approvals also may be governed by whether or not certain designated evaluation criteria are met.

During the budgeted year, periodic reports should be prepared comparing, by categories, expenditures on approved AFE's to the budget. The reports ought to be prepared for use by the organization levels originating the requests for expenditures as well as those granting approval. Higher echelons find summaries helpful, with out-of-line items reported in detail.

EVALUATING CAPITAL EXPENDITURES

Evaluating refers to the basic theory, techniques, and procedures for the appraisal and reappraisal of projects throughout the course of their development. A number of evaluations of a single proposal may be necessary because of:

1. Changing circumstances that result during the time span from the origin of the project idea to the completion of the project.

2. Varying alternative solutions of the problem for which the project is designed.

3. Varying assumptions as to the amount and time pattern of cash flows.

The best available evaluation tools should be used appropriately, coupled with a profound understanding of the risk and danger existing in over-reliance on quantitative answers based on many assumptions and estimates.

Economic evaluation and related techniques have received prime attention in the literature dealing with capital investment programs. The most advanced methods consider the time value of money in computing an estimated return on investment. Representative evaluation techniques are presented later in this chapter. However, many imponderables may also affect the decision; e.g., competition, legal requirements, social responsibilities, and emergencies. Furthermore, there is a need to select investments that will keep the firm in balance and be consistent with objectives. The circumstances of each expenditure alternative must be considered in passing judgment on the criteria used. Even then there may be justifiable differences of opinion with respect to governing criteria. The mechanics of various techniques are important, but of still greater importance is the relationship of this activity to the overall capital expenditure planning and control process and the need for creative and thoughtful management.

Classification of Capital Expenditures. Capital expenditure projects can be classified as: (1) equipment-replacement expenditures, (2) expansion investments, and (3) improvements of existing products and/or additions of new products.

Equipment-Replacement Expenditures. These include both like-for-like and obsolescence replacements. The basis for decision making is future or prospective cost savings — comparing future costs of old equipment with future costs of new equipment. The analysis of future costs requires the determination of the prospective purchase price less any ultimate resale or salvage value. The most difficult problem is to estimate the probable economic life of the new equipment. This is the core of any capital expenditure decision. For the present equipment, the future decline in disposal value must be estimated. The original cost of the present facility is a sunk and irrecoverable cost totally irrelevant to the decision-making process. The accumulated depreciation allowance is also independent of the company's real future costs. Book values are not significant for the replacement decision except for the treatment of income tax liability related to fixed asset transactions.

Expansion Investments. Expansion investments involving plant enlargement and the invasion of new markets constitute another category of capital investments. In these cases the comparison is made between doing or not doing the job, with the basis for a decision now shifted from cost savings to the expected addition to profits including the consideration of cash inflow. The added profit is estimated by preparing a projected income statement showing additional revenues and expenses over the life of the project. The degree of uncertainty in this type of investment is much greater than in the first category.

Improvements of Existing Products and/or Additions of New Products. The basis for a decision on projects in this category is strategic; that is, the relative competitive market position compels the firm to make investments. Failure to keep abreast of competitors can cause deterioration of the market share. Since no historical basis for making the decision exists and the return of such investments must be based on increased profits, a high degree of sound judgment and business insight is required in making a decision.

A proposal may involve more than one classification. For example, a firm may consider a proposal to replace a job printing press, whose maintenance cost has become excessive, with a new press that will offer an expanded productive capacity. Also, certain expenditures may be required because of tactical or legal requirements rather than purely economic reasons. For example, a manufacturer may be forced into the production of a less profitable product because of competitive pressure; recreation facilities may be installed for employee use; or air and water pollution regulations may necessitate an expenditure for a waste disposal unit. Certain projects are musts to the point that use of an evaluation technique is superfluous; e.g., the washout of a section of a railway trestle. Other projects, though indicating an acceptable economic return, may be rejected because of lack of funds, failure to fit into overall objectives, failure to meet other evaluation criteria, such as corner locations for gasoline service stations, or external circumstances.

Some projects may not be independent of one another and in such cases should be grouped together for evaluation purposes as a compound project. The following quotation illustrates this point:

> Contingent or dependent projects can arise, for instance, when acceptance of one proposal is dependent on acceptance of one or more other proposals. One simple example would be the purchase of an extra-long boom for a crane which would be of little value unless the crane itself were also purchased; the latter, however, may be justified on its own. When contingent projects are combined with their independent prerequisites, the combination may be called a compound project. Thus a compound project may be characterized by the algebraic sum of the payoffs and costs of the component projects plus, perhaps, an interaction term.[1]

[1]H. Martin Weingartner, "Capital Budgeting of Interrelated Projects: Survey and Synthesis," *Management Science*, Vol. XII, No. 7, p. 492.

Representative Evaluation Techniques. Four evaluation techniques are described, illustrated, and their advantages and disadvantages presented. These methods are chosen because they are the representative tools in current usage: (1) the payback (or payout) period method, (2) the average annual return on investment method, (3) the present value method, and (4) the discounting cash flow (DCF) method.

Nonc of these methods serves every purpose or every firm. The circumstances and needs of the situation determine the most appropriate techniques to be used. A company may use more than one technique (e.g., payback period and DCF) in evaluating each project; however, the same method or methods should be used uniformly for every project throughout the firm. Confusion could arise if Division A used the discounted cash flow method while Division B used the average annual return on investment method. These evaluation techniques, if thoroughly understood by the analysts who use them, should aid management — but management must still exercise judgment and make the decisions. Certainly the cost of applying the evaluation techniques should be justified in terms of the value to management. Moreover, inaccurate raw data used in the calculations or lack of uniform procedures may yield harmful and misleading conclusions.

For purposes of discussing and illustrating the evaluation methods listed above, the following situation is assumed: The Shields Company is operating at the limit of the capacity of one of its producing units. Maintenance costs of the existing unit have become excessive. A new unit can be purchased at a cost of $85,796, less trade-in allowance. The old unit has a trade-in value of $3,000, making the net purchase price $82,796. The expected economic life of the new unit is eight years. Straight-line depreciation is to be used, with an estimated salvage value of $8,300. The old unit has a zero book value (that is, the accumulated depreciation in this situation is assumed to equal the capitalized cost) and its trade-in value will therefore reduce the depreciable basis of the new asset. Such treatment is consistent with the income tax requirement of adjusting the depreciable basis of the new asset for any gain or loss resulting from a replacement in kind.[2] However, if the old asset is sold outright rather than being traded-in, then the gain or loss would be recognized at the time of the sale. It is estimated that the utilized capacity of the new unit will yield an aftertax cash flow calculated as shown on page 835.

The company's cost of capital is estimated to be 10 percent. Cost of capital (discussed on pages 845–846) represents the minimum reward that investors demand for investing their money in a firm.

---

[2]If the book value of the old asset is not zero, then the *cash invested* (net of the trade-in allowance) will be less than the adjusted depreciable basis of the new asset by the amount of the old asset's book value.

SHIELDS COMPANY — AFTERTAX CASH FLOW

Col. 1	Col. 2	Col. 3	Col. 4	Col. 5	Col. 6	Col. 7	Col. 8
Year	Estimated Cash Savings Relating to Present Capacity (Primarily Maintenance)*	Estimated Cash Income Relating to Use of Increased Capacity	Total Columns 2 + 3	Depre- ciation**	Taxable Income Columns 4 − 5	Federal and State Income Taxes Column 6 × 48%	Net Increase in Aftertax Cash Inflow Columns 4 − 7
1	$18,388	$15,324	$33,712	$ 9,312	$24,400	$11,712	$ 22,000
2	10,707	15,312	26,019	9,312	16,707	8,019	18,000
3	10,188	21,600	31,788	9,312	22,476	10,788	21,000
4	8,265	21,600	29,865	9,312	20,553	9,865	20,000
5	2,496	21,600	24,096	9,312	14,784	7,096	17,000
6	1,923	26,019	27,942	9,312	18,630	8,942	19,000
7	—	26,019	26,019	9,312	16,707	8,019	18,000
8	—	26,019	26,019	9,312	16,707	8,019	18,000
							$153,000
			Cash inflow from salvage value at end of economic life....				8,300
							$161,300

*The illustration uses uneven numbers in Columns 2 and 3 in order to yield dollars in Column 8 in even thousands for ease in subsequent computations.
**Basis of $82,796 − $8,300 salvage value = $74,496 ÷ 8 years = $9,312 annual depreciation.

In this example, which involves both a replacement and expansion type investment, the cash investment is restricted to the cost of the fixed asset unit. Some projects require the commitment of working capital for inventories, receivables, etc. When such commitments exist, they should be included as a part of the initial investment and, to the extent that they are recoverable, should be shown as cash inflow in the recovery year(s).

Differential aftertax cash flow must be estimated. Cash flow that will remain unchanged is not relevant. The old unit represents a sunk cost and enters into the computations only as a reduction (through trade-in) of the cost of the new unit. The impact of income taxes (both federal and state) is also significant, both as to the amount and timing of cash flow. Management should take cognizance of income taxes in looking at the projected profitability of a proposal including the tax treatment of losses and gains resulting from the sale of any displaced assets. Therefore, the computations that follow are based on aftertax data.[3]

The Payback (or Payout) Period Method. This technique measures the length of time required by the project to recover the initial outlay. The

---

[3]This discussion does not consider the investment tax credit which as a result of federal tax and fiscal policy has been available from time to time in the past as an incentive to stimulate capital investment. The investment tax credit, if available, would simply have the effect of reducing the cash outflow related to the cost of a capital investment but would not reduce the depreciable basis of the new asset.

calculated payback period is compared with the payback period acceptable to management for this particular kind of project. The computation is illustrated as follows:

Year	Cash Flow Total	Cash Flow Needed	Payback Years Required
1	$22,000	$22,000	1.0
2	18,000	18,000	1.0
3	21,000	21,000	1.0
4	20,000	20,000	1.0
5	17,000	1,796	.1
Investment....................		$82,796	

Total payback period in years.........................4.1

If the estimated cash flow is uniform for each year, the payback period can be computed by dividing the investment by the annual cash flow; for example, if cash flow equals $22,000 each year, then $82,796 ÷ $22,000 = 3.8 years.

The Average Annual Return on Investment Method. This method is sometimes referred to as the accounting or the financial statement method. Two variations of this approach are presented on page 837.

These two variations differ in that in the first the denominator is the original investment, $82,796; in the second the denominator is the average investment, $45,548.

The previous methods fail to account for the time value of money. The next two techniques, the present value and the discounted cash flow methods, consider this important factor over the project's estimated economic life.

The Present Value Method. A dollar received a year hence is not the equivalent of a dollar received today, because the use of money has a value. To illustrate, if $500 can be invested at 20 percent, $600 will be received a year later ($500 + 20% of $500). The $600 to be received next year has a present value of $500 if 20 percent can be earned ($600 ÷ 120% = $500). The difference of $100 ($600 − $500) represents the time value of money. In line with this idea, the estimated results of an investment proposal can be stated as a cash equivalent at the present time; i.e., its present value.[4]

---

[4]The basic formula for present value is:

$$PV = S\frac{1}{(1+i)^n} \ or \ \frac{S}{(1+i)^n} \ or \ S(1+i)^{-n} \ when$$

PV = present value of future sum of money
S = future sum of money
i = earnings rate for each compounding period
n = number of periods

AVERAGE ANNUAL RETURN ON <u>ORIGINAL</u> INVESTMENT

$$\frac{\text{Net Profit After Taxes}}{\text{Economic Life}} \div \text{Original Investment}$$

Net profit after taxes but without deduction for depreciation....... $153,000
Less depreciation*... 74,496

Net profit after taxes for economic life....................... $ 78,504

$$\frac{\$78,504}{8 \text{ years}} \div \$82,796 = \$9,813 \div \$82,796 = \underline{11.85\%}$$

---

*The depreciable basis of the new equipment is estimated to be $82,796 and its salvage value to be $8,300. Hence, depreciation is $74,496 ($82,796 − $8,300). In this illustration depreciation is assumed to be the only noncash item and is thus the only adjustment required in converting from cash flow to the accrual basis.

AVERAGE ANNUAL RETURN ON <u>AVERAGE</u> INVESTMENT

$$\frac{\text{Net Profit After Taxes}}{\text{Economic Life}} \div \text{Average Investment}$$

Original investment... $82,796
Investment at end of economic life (salvage value)............... 8,300
                                                                   $91,096

Average investment.................... $$\frac{\$ 91,096}{2} = \$45,548$$

$$\frac{\$78,504}{8 \text{ years}} \div \$45,548 = \$9,813 \div \$45,548 = \underline{21.54\%}$$

**Two Variations of the Average Annual
Return on Investment Method**

Present value tables have been devised to facilitate application of present value theory. The table on page 868 presents computations to three decimal places and shows today's value, or the present value, of each dollar to be received or paid in the future for various rates of interest and periods of time.[5] By multiplying the appropriate factor obtained from the table times an expected future cash flow, the present value of the cash flow is easily determined.

The present value concept can be applied to the Shields Company problem by discounting at the company's 10 percent estimated cost of capital. Some firms may wish to set as their discount rate something in excess of the cost of capital or use different rates depending on risk and other characteristics of a particular project. However, for the sake of uniformity for comparison purposes, it seems preferable to discount all proposals at a constant rate; and, preferably, the rate should be the cost of capital. Management can interject an allowance for risk and other characteristics peculiar to each specific proposal in the raw data or in the net present value answer. An allowance for the effect of inflation may be added as well.

The computation follows (data from aftertax cash flow schedule):

Year	Cash (Outflow) or Inflow	Present Value of $1 10%	Net Present Value of Flow
0	$(82,796)	1.000	$(82,796)
1	22,000	0.909	19,998
2	18,000	0.826	14,868
3	21,000	0.751	15,771
4	20,000	0.683	13,660
5	17,000	0.621	10,557
6	19,000	0.564	10,716
7	18,000	0.513	9,234
8	26,300 ($18,000+$8,300)	0.467	12,282
		Net present value..............	$ 24,290

The net present value of $24,290 indicates that the true rate of return is greater than the cost of capital discount rate. Net present value of zero would indicate a rate of return of exactly 10 percent. When cash flows differ from period to period, the "Present Value of $1" table (page 868) must be used for each individual period. If the cash flow is uniform for each period, then the "Present Value of $1 Received or Paid Annually for Each of the Next N Years" table (page 869) can be used with the advantage of having to multiply only the cumulative factor by the cash flow of one period (discussed on page 841).

---

[5]Ordinary tables, such as those included in this chapter, assume that all cash flows occur at the end of each period and that interest is compounded at the end of each period. Either or both of these assumptions can be varied by use of the calculus so that instead of assuming that the cash flows occur at the end of each period, they can be presumed to occur continuously, and interest can be compounded continuously. Although the continuous assumptions often are more representative of actual conditions, the tables in this chapter are more frequently found in practice.

A project's useful life is one of the uncertainties often associated with capital expenditure evaluations. Equipment obsolescence or shifts in market demands may occur. In project evaluation, management may wish to know the minimum necessary life for a project in order to recover the original investment and earn a desired rate of return on the investment. The *present value payback* calculation focuses on this question and is computed as follows, using the "net present value of flow" figures shown on page 838.

Year	Net Present Value of Flow Total	Needed	Present Value Payback Years Required
1	$19,998	$19,998	1.0
2	14,868	14,868	1.0
3	15,771	15,771	1.0
4	13,660	13,660	1.0
5	10,557	10,557	1.0
6	10,716	7,942	.7
Investment......................		$82,796	
Total present value payback in years......................			5.7

Based on the present value of *estimated* cash flows, 5.7 years will be required to recover the $82,796 original investment and earn a desired 10 percent rate of return on the annual unrecovered investment balance. Additionally, the present value payback will be shortened by the present value of the project's salvage value. Observe that this computation differs from the conventional payback method which determines the time necessary to recover the initial outlay, without regard to present value considerations.

The Discounted Cash Flow Method. Discounted cash flow is another discount measure of project profitability. In the present value method, the discount rate is known or at least predetermined; here it is not. This rate is defined as the rate of discount at which the sum of positive present values equals the sum of negative present values. Present value theory is still used, the analysis being developed a bit further to determine the discounted rate of return before stopping to compare with some standard.

The discounted rate of return for the Shields Company can be determined by trial and error; i.e., by computing net present value at various percentages to find the rate at which the net present value is zero. This computation is illustrated in the table on page 840.

The discounted rate is greater than 16 percent and less than, but close to, 18 percent. The trial-and-error search should continue until *adjacent* rates in the table are found — one rate yielding a positive net present value with another rate yielding a negative net present value.

Year	Cash (Outflow) or Inflow	Present Value of $1 16%	Net Present Value of Flow	Present Value of $1 18%	Net Present Value of Flow
0	$(82,796)	1.000	$(82,796)	1.000	$(82,796)
1	22,000	0.862	18,964	0.847	18,634
2	18,000	0.743	13,374	0.718	12,924
3	21,000	0.641	13,461	0.609	12,789
4	20,000	0.552	11,040	0.516	10,320
5	17,000	0.476	8,092	0.437	7,429
6	19,000	0.410	7,790	0.370	7,030
7	18,000	0.354	6,372	0.314	5,652
8	26,300	0.305	8,022	0.266	6,996
			$ 4,319		$ (1,022)

Expanded tables permit the determination of a net present value nearer zero. However, an approximation is obtainable by interpolation and is accomplished as follows:

$$16\% \text{ plus } 2\% \times \frac{\$4,319}{\$5,341} = 16\% + 2\% \,(.809) = 16\% + 1.62\% = 17.62\%, \text{ say } 18\%$$

The figure $5,341 is a total ($4,319 + $1,022) since the second figure is a negative one and, according to the formula, should be subtracted.[6]

The discounted cash flow method permits management to maximize corporate profits by selecting proposals with the highest rates of return as long as the rates are higher than the company's own cost of capital plus management's allowance for risk and uncertainty. In most circumstances, the use of the discounted cash flow instead of the present value method at a given interest rate will not seriously alter the ranking of projects.

Note that the rate of return, using either the discounted cash flow method or the net present value method, is computed on the basis of the unrecovered capital from period to period, not on the original investment. In the illustration, the DCF rate of return of 18 percent denotes that over the eight years the aftertax cash inflow equals the recovery of the original investment plus a return of 18 percent on the unrecovered investment from period to period. The net present value figure of $24,290 indicates that over the eight years this additional amount, or a total of $107,086 ($82,796 plus $24,290), could have been spent on the machine; and the original investment, plus a return of 10 percent on the unrecovered investment from period to period, could still have been recovered.

Tables for Uniform Cash Flow. Tables are available that afford more rapid calculation when the cash flow is estimated to be the same each period (see table on page 869). Tables of this type are constructed as follows:

---

[6]A short-cut computation of the DCF rate of return, provided the cash flow is the same for each period, is discussed on page 841.

Period	Present Value of $1 (From page 868 table) 10%	Present Value of $1 Received or Paid Annually for Each of the Next N Years (From page 869 table) 10%
1	0.909	0.909
2	0.826	1.736 (.909 + .826)*
3	0.751	2.487 (1.736 + .751)
4	0.683	3.170
5	0.621	3.791
6	0.564	4.355
7	0.513	4.868
8	0.467	5.335

*Difference of .001 results from rounding off.

If the flow is uniform for seven years, for example, one can simply multiply the flow for one period by the cumulative factor of 4.868 and obtain approximately the same answer as by multiplying the individual factors by the flow for each period and totaling the seven products. For example, if a project costing $20,000 is expected to yield a uniform annual cash flow after taxes of $5,000 for seven years, then the present value is $5,000 × 4.868 = $24,340 while the net present value is $4,340 ($24,340 − $20,000).

Another use of this table, assuming uniform cash flow, involves computing the payback period and finding the factor nearest the payback period on the line of the table that represents the stated economic life. The rate of return, thus located by reading the vertical column heading, is an approximation of the discounted cash flow rate of return. For example, if the economic life of a project is 10 years, the payback period 5.186, and the cash flow uniform, the approximate DCF rate of return would be 14 percent (see table on page 869). If desired, a more precise rate of return can be found by interpolation:

Present Value Factor	Present Value Factor
14% = 5.216	14% = 5.216
$\dfrac{15\% = 5.019}{.197}$;	$\dfrac{\text{Payback period} = 5.186}{.030}$;

$\dfrac{.030}{.197} \times 1\% + 14\% = .15 \times 1\% + 14\% = .15\% + 14\% = \underline{\underline{14.15\%}}$, the precise rate of return

Advantages and Disadvantages. The following lists present several advantages and disadvantages of the preceding four evaluation techniques.

The Payback (or Payout) Period Method.

Advantages:

1. Simple to compute.
2. May be used to select those investments yielding a quick return of cash.
3. Permits a company to determine the length of time required to recapture its original investment, thus offering an indicator of the degree of risk of each investment.
4. The reciprocal of the payback period may be used under certain conditions as a rough approximation of the rate of return calculated by the discounted cash flow method. The approximation exists when the project's life is long (approximately double or more) as compared to the length of the payback period and when the annual savings and/or cash inflow are relatively uniform in amount. In the example, the reciprocal is 24 percent (1 ÷ 4.1) and compares to the discounted cash flow computation (page 840) of 18 percent. The lack of uniformity of annual cash flow in this example accounts in large part for the roughness of the approximation. Also, the project's life is only 8 years, compared to a payback period of 4.1 years. If the project's life were longer, the approximation would be closer.
5. It is a widely used, rough-and-ready method that is certainly an improvement over a hunch, rule of thumb, or intuitive method.

Disadvantages:

1. Ignores the time value of money. For the Shields Company, the payback period is 4.1 years. Assume that the "Net Increase in Aftertax Cash Inflow" had been: Year 1, $55,000; Year 2, $12,000; Year 3, $10,000; Year 4, $5,500; and Year 5, $2,960. The computation would be:

Year	Cash Flow Total	Cash Flow Needed	Payback Years Required
1	$55,000	$55,000	1.0
2	12,000	12,000	1.0
3	10,000	10,000	1.0
4	5,500	5,500	1.0
5	2,960	296	.1
Investment....................		$82,796	
Total payback period in years.........................			4.1

In both cases the payback period is 4.1 years; however, in the latter computation $33,000 more ($55,000 − $22,000) was received in the first year. Thus, the latter situation is more desirable from an investment standpoint because money has a time value; that is, a dollar is worth more the earlier it is received.

2. Ignores income which may be produced beyond the payback period. In the example, the payback period is 4.1 years; the economic life, 8 years; and the "Net Increase in Aftertax Cash Inflow," $161,300. Suppose an alternative project indicates a "Net Increase in Aftertax Cash Inflow" of $82,796 in the first three years and an economic life of four years with

"Net Increase in Aftertax Cash Inflow" in the fourth year of $10,000. Although the latter case has a shorter payback period, the original example of a 4.1 year payback and net cash inflow of $161,300 is more desirable where immediate cash problems are not of critical importance.

3. Fails to consider salvage value, if any.

In spite of these apparent shortcomings, the payback method is still widely used in many firms, if only to serve as an initial screening device or to complement the answers of more sophisticated methods.

The Average Annual Return on Investment Method.

Advantages:

1. Facilitates expenditure follow-up due to more readily available data from accounting records.
2. Considers income over the entire life of the project.

Disadvantages:

1. Ignores the time value of money as did the payback method. Two projects might have the same average return yet vary considerably in the pattern of flow of cash. In such a case, the recognition of the time value of money would point up the desirability of the alternative having greater cash flow in the earlier periods.
2. Inapplicable if any of the investment is made after the beginning of the project.

The Present Value Method.

Advantages:

1. Considers the time value of money.
2. Considers income over the entire life of the project.

Disadvantages:

1. Some argue that this method is too difficult to use.
2. Management must determine a discount rate to be used. However, a well-informed management should already be aware of its cost of capital that should represent the benchmark for discount rate purposes.
3. If projects being compared involve different dollar amounts of investment, the project with more profitable dollars, as computed by the present value method, may not be the better project if it also requires a larger investment.

Example: Earning a net present value of $1,000 on an investment of $100,000 is not as economically wise as earning $900 on an investment of $10,000, provided that the $90,000 difference in investments can be used to earn at least $101 in other projects. In this case, a net present value index should be used rather than the net present value dollar figure. This index places all competing projects on a comparable basis for the purpose of ranking them. In the Shields Company, the computation is:

$$\text{Net Present Value Index} = \frac{\text{Net Present Value}}{\text{Required Investment}} = \frac{\$24,290}{\$82,796} = .2934$$

This index simplifies finding the optimum solution for competing projects when the total budget for capital outlays is fixed arbitrarily, because one is able to rank by percentages rather than absolute dollars.

4. May be misleading when dealing with alternative projects or limited funds under the condition of unequal lives in that the alternative with the higher net present value may involve longer economic life to the point that it would be less desirable than an alternative having a shorter life. The problem of dealing with alternatives having unequal lives is discussed on page 845.

The Discounted Cash Flow Method.

Advantages:

1. Considers the time value of money.
2. Considers income over the entire life of the project.
3. The percentage figure may have more meaning for management than the net present value or net present value index computed by the present value method.
4. The percentage figure allows a generally sound, uniform ranking of projects.

Disadvantages:

1. Too difficult to use according to some.
2. Implies that earnings are reinvested at the rate earned by the investment, whereas the present value method implies earnings are reinvested at the rate of discount. It is argued that the latter assumption is more reasonable.

The Error Cushion. A project whose estimated desirability is very near a cut-off point for the type of project being evaluated affords very little cushion for errors. For example, if the management of a chain of automotive muffler shops anticipates that a new location should be expected to yield a minimum discounted cash flow of 12 percent, there is obviously a greater cushion for errors in estimates used in computing the rate of return when the answer is 20 percent as opposed to 13 percent. Similarly, if one alternative is clearly superior to others for a particular project, there is a better cushion against errors than if two or more of the best alternatives indicate approximately the same expected results.

Reasonably accurate estimates are desirable in evaluating any project; however, a higher degree of sophistication and care, at a higher cost of obtaining the data, may be necessary to add confidence when the evaluation is close to a cut-off point or when two or more project alternatives yield about the same "best" answer.

In many cases, the desirability of a project or the selection from alternatives for a particular project will be so obvious that the cost of making sophisticated data estimates and even the task of evaluation techniques is not justified.

Other Situations and Considerations.   The following topics related to evaluating capital expenditure proposals require a brief discussion: alternatives having unequal lives, purchase versus leasing, cost of capital, sensitivity analysis, allowance for risk and uncertainty, computer usage for evaluation analysis, and the particular relevance of each in the study of capital investment evaluation techniques.

Alternatives Having Unequal Lives.   An additional difficulty in capital expenditure evaluation arises when alternatives with different economic lives are compared.   To illustrate, a firm may be faced with the problem of acquiring equipment for a manufacturing operation.   Two alternatives are available: Equipment A, expected to last 18 years, and Equipment B, expected to last 5 years.   There are two ways to deal with this problem:

1. Repeat the investment cycle for Equipment B a sufficient number of times to cover the estimated economic life of Equipment A; in the example, $3\frac{3}{5}$ times.   An estimate of the salvage value of the fourth equipment investment cycle for Equipment B at the end of the life for Equipment A is needed in order to reflect a common terminal date.

2. The period considered can be the life of the shorter-life alternative, Equipment B, coupled with an estimate of the recoverable value of Equipment A at the end of 5 years.   The analysis would then cover only the five-year period, with the recoverable value of Equipment A being treated as a cash inflow at the end of the period.   A serious difficulty rests in the need to estimate a value of the longer-life asset at the end of 5 years.   Such an intermediate recoverable value may not be an adequate measure of the service value of the equipment at that point in its useful life.

Purchase Versus Leasing.   A lease arrangement may be available as an alternative to investing in a capital asset.   If so, this possibility should be evaluated by determining the incremental annual cost of leasing versus purchasing.   The *aftertax savings* should be sufficient to yield the desired rate of return on the anticipated purchase price.

Cost of Capital.   *Cost of capital* represents the expected return for a given level of risk that investors demand for investing their money in a firm.   Cost of capital, as related to capital expenditure planning, evaluating, and control, may refer to a specific cost of capital from a particular financing effort to provide funds for a specific project.   Such use of the concept connotes the marginal cost of capital point of view and implies linkage of the financing and investment decisions.   This view has been challenged as a useful concept for allocating capital; the funds available for one or all projects are more generally considered to be a commingling of more than one source. Therefore, it is not surprising that different costs of capital exist depending upon the sources. A company could obtain funds from (1) bonds, (2) preferred and common stock, (3) use of retained earnings, and (4) loans from banks. If a company obtains funds by some combination of these sources to achieve or maintain a particular capital structure, then the cost of capital (money) is the weighted average cost of each money source. This weighted average considers the joint costs and the desired relative proportions of each type of capital and may be computed as follows:

Funds — Source	Desired Long-Run Proportion of Funds To Be Provided	After-Tax Cost	Weighted Cost
Bonds..................	.20	.03	.006
Preferred stock..........	.20	.08	.016
Common stock and retained earnings......	.60	.13	.078
	1.00	Weighted average cost of capital......	.100 = 10%

The following represent measures of different costs of capital:

1. The cost of bonds is the aftertax rate of interest.
2. The cost of preferred stock is the dividend per share divided by the present market price.
3. The cost of common stock and retained earnings is the expected earnings per share, after taxes and after preferred dividends are paid, divided by the present market price.[7]

Since the subject of cost of capital is rather involved, this presentation serves only as a brief introduction.

Sensitivity Analysis. A comparison of the results of the present value or discounted cash flow evaluation techniques with the rate of the cost of capital is useful in helping management to arrive at a decision. However, a management never feels entirely assured, for too many estimates enter into quantitative analyses. Any element of the project, be it revenue, cost, or the investment itself, is subject to variations or changes. Certain estimates are more sensitive to variations than others. Under these circumstances the analyst must present a variety of possible results using numerous figures so that management can judge the impact of all possibilities. This type of approach, called *sensitivity analysis*, indicates in graphic or tabular form the effect of one project factor on another.

---

[7]Conflicting opinions exist regarding the treatment of the investors' tax effect on the cost of equity acquired through the retention of earnings.

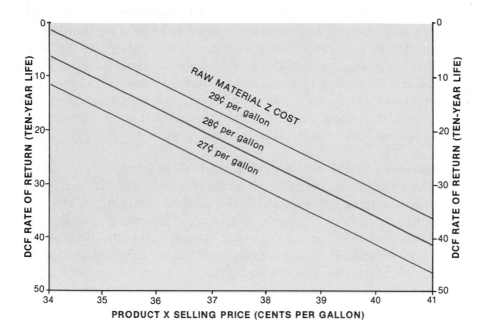

**Sensitivity Analysis Graph Illustrating the
DCF Rate of Return Analysis for Product X
(Plant Capacity, 5 Million Gallons Per Year; Investment, $600,000)**

To illustrate, assume that a project for a new product, X, was developed on the basis of a selling price of $.38 a gallon and at that price the expected DCF rate of return was 26 percent. An expanded analysis showing the rate of return at selling prices ranging from $.34 to $.41 per gallon would be a form of sensitivity analysis. Variations in price, volume, labor cost, materials cost, and project investment are factors usually considered in such calculations. They are varied singly, as above, or in combination. For example, suppose the range of DCF rates of return described above were based on an assumption that the primary raw material, Z, would cost $.28 per gallon. The range of rates of return with the selling price ranging from $.34 to $.41 per gallon could also be computed assuming the primary raw material would cost $.29 and $.27, if these are reasonable possibilities.

The graph shown above presents this illustration in visual form, assuming that a plant having a capacity of five million gallons per year and an economic life of ten years will require a $600,000 investment. Annual sales volume is also assumed to be five million gallons. The DCF rate of return can be read for the various combinations of Product X selling prices and Raw Material Z costs.

Sensitivity analysis thus presents a variety of outcomes so that management can look at the expected impact of a range of possibilities. The

usefulness of data can be further enhanced by injecting probability estimates to allow for risk and uncertainty in order to indicate how likely it
appears that selling price or other factors will vary (see pages 849–850).

These techniques are equally useful in planning and in a variety of
decision-making analyses in which the estimated impact of changed assumptions and their probabilities are relevant, such as in developing long-
range plans, the annual budget, break-even and cost-volume-profit analysis, differential cost analysis, and linear programming.

Allowance for Risk and Uncertainty. Risk and uncertainty must be
considered when estimates are made of future events because ever-present
uncertainty creates a degree of risk in the ultimate occurrence of any set of
assumptions used in computing a unique set of estimated cash flows for
a particular investment project. To assist management in the final decision,
the analyst may resort to a presentation of a three or more level project
estimate to indicate the possible outcomes. This *risk analysis* is basically
an extension of sensitivity analysis.

The following procedure is one possible method for dealing with risk
and uncertainty:

1. Determine the net present value of the net cash flows for three different
   assumptions:
   a. Most probable series of events.
   b. A reasonably pessimistic series of events.
   c. A reasonably optimistic series of events.

2. Weigh the three net present values, using the best information available
   or using standard weights.

3. The sum of the three weighted net present values may be used to represent
   the net present value of the investment, taking risk and uncertainty into
   consideration (to a limited degree).

For example:

	Net Present Value	×	Probability Weights	=	Weighted Net Present Value
Most probable (from page 838)..	$24,290		.50		$12,145
Pessimistic assumptions.........	5,000		.30		1,500
Optimistic assumptions	35,000		.20		7,000
Weighted net present value....					$20,645

Allowing for risk and uncertainty can be further demonstrated by referring to the illustration introduced on page 847 in the discussion of
sensitivity analysis. Assume that probability estimates are made as follows:

Product Selling Price	Probability of Occurrence
$.39	30%
.38	30
.37	40
	100%

Raw Material Z Cost	Probability of Occurrence
$.29	20%
.28	70
.27	10
	100%

The annual sales volume is expected to be five million gallons. In this example, the raw materials cost variation is assumed to be independent of price and volume; hence, it may increase, remain the same, or decrease at any of the three Product X selling prices.[8] Other selling prices and Raw Material Z costs are assumed to have a zero probability of occurrence. The resulting nine possible outcomes for these assumptions and their related probabilities are summarized below:

(1)	(2)	(3)	(4)	(5)	(6)	(7)
Product X		*Raw Material Z*		*Combined Probability*	*DCF Rate of*	*Weighted DCF Rate of Return*
Selling Price	*Probability*	*Cost*	*Probability*	*(2) × (4)*	*Return**	*(5) × (6)*
$.39	.30	$.29	.20	.06	26	.0156
	.30	.28	.70	.21	31	.0651
	.30	.27	.10	.03	36	.0108
.38	.30	.29	.20	.06	21	.0126
	.30	.28	.70	.21	26	.0546
	.30	.27	.10	.03	31	.0093
.37	.40	.29	.20	.08	16	.0128
	.40	.28	.70	.28	21	.0588
	.40	.27	.10	.04	26	.0104
				1.00	Weighted DCF rate of return....	.2500 = 25%

---

*These rates were read from the graph on page 847.

---

[8]Many economic variables are not independent of one another; e.g., the raw material cost may influence the selling price of the finished product. If there is dependence of the variables, computational procedures must be modified by substituting conditional probabilities into Column 4. See Charles T. Clark and Lawrence L. Schkade, *Statistical Analysis for Administrative Decisions* (2d ed.; Cincinnati: South-Western Publishing Co., 1974), pp. 138–142.

Not only is the weighted DCF rate of return of 25 percent of interest to management, but management should also find useful the cumulative probabilities of realizing a rate of return at least equal to each of the various rates. Beginning with the highest rate for the nine possibilities, the following cumulative probabilities can be determined:

DCF Rate of Return	Cumulative Probability
36%	.03
31	.27 (.03 + .21 + .03)
26	.58 (.03 + .21 + .03 + .06 + .21 + .04)
21	.92
16	1.00

Thus, there is a .03 probability that the rate of return will be 36 percent, a .27 probability that the rate will be *at least* 31 percent, a .58 probability that the rate will be *at least* 26 percent, etc.

Computer Usage for Evaluation Analysis. The ever-increasing installation of electronic data processing equipment offers the analyst an opportunity to expand the investment evaluation analysis beyond a mere handful of manual computations. The computer permits the creation of numerous models that simulate various possibilities and probabilities of expected results. The main purpose of the simulation process is to improve the quality of management's decisions by offering new and more reliable information and guidance. Whenever the key factors in a business problem are susceptible to various patterns of variations, the use of models and simulation will be especially helpful. It should be understood that even the most sophisticated and computerized analytical methods do not relieve any management of the all-important task of making the final decision.

CONTROL OF CAPITAL EXPENDITURES

The *control* phase consists of (1) control and review of a project while it is in process and (2) follow-up or post-audit of project results.

Control and Review While in Process. When a project or a series of projects has finally been approved, methods, techniques, and procedures must be set in motion to permit the control and review of all project elements (costs, time, quality, and quantity) until completion. *Control responsibility* needs to be clearly designated, recognizing the necessity of assistance from and coordination with many individuals and groups including those external to the company. Actual results should be compared to approved plans and evaluation results. Variations or trends to deviations from plans should be reported to responsible authorities on time in order to facilitate corrective action as quickly as possible. Day-to-day, on-the-scene observation and up-to-date reports should provide good cost control vehicles. Construction engineers have long used such devices as bar charts for planning and controlling the timing of project activities.

Program Evaluation and Review Technique with Cost (PERT/Cost) (see Chapter 17) utilizes the network scheme to show the interrelationships of the multiple activities required to complete the average to large-scale project. Any project, be it the installation of a single large machine, a complex of machinery and equipment, or the construction of a new factory or office building, will involve many diverse tasks. Some of them can be done simultaneously; others must await the completion of preceding activities. This technique offers a clear and an all-inclusive picture of the operation as a whole in contrast to the bars on the Gantt chart. The use of PERT/Cost is particularly appropriate for those evaluation cases where more than one estimate is needed due to risk and uncertainty and the desire to expedite and increase the reliability of difficult estimates.

The cost of administering the control phase should be commensurate with the value derived. Overcontrol is an inefficient use of administrative resources.

Follow-Up of Project Results.   Follow-up or post-audit means comparing and reporting results as related to the outcome predicted at the time the investment project was evaluated and approved. Follow-up affords a test of the existing planning and control procedure and therewith the possibility of reinforcing of successful projects, salvaging or terminating failing projects, and improving upon future investment proposals and decisions. Generally, there appears to be a need for follow-up, but actual work in this area still lags far behind advances made in other capital expenditure phases. Common hindrances to follow-up procedures are management's unwillingness to incur additional administrative costs, difficulty of quantifying the results of certain types of investments, apparent failure of the accounting or cost system to produce needed information, lack of personnel qualified to perform the follow-up tasks, and last but not least, resentment of those being audited and examined.

Value received as related to the cost of obtaining the follow-up information should determine the extent of any follow-up. For uniformity, efficiency, and independent review, management should designate a centralized group to prescribe procedures and audit the performance of the follow-up activity. The assembled data should be utilized as a control device and be reported to the controlling levels of management. Out-of-line results should then trigger corrective action in harmony with the management by exception principle.

DISCUSSION QUESTIONS

1. Why are effective planning and control of capital expenditures important?
2. How can capital expenditure projects be classified?
3. Differentiate between economic life and physical life of a project.
4. Define the payback (or payout) period method.
5. How do the two average annual return on investment methods discussed in this chapter differ?
6. Modern capital expenditure evaluation uses the present value concept. How can this concept be stated?
7. Discuss the differences in the computations of the present value and the discounted cash flow methods.
8. List the advantages and disadvantages of the following evaluation methods:
   a. The payback (or payout) period method
   b. The average annual return on investment method
   c. The present value method
   d. The discounted cash flow method
9. Define cost of capital.
10. Define sensitivity analysis.
11. After a capital expenditure has been made, what should the company's analysts do in the matter of reporting the results of these decisions?
12. Select the correct answer for each of the following statements.

   (a) In selecting the purchase of one of two machines to replace an old machine, the management of Ashworth Company should consider as relevant (1) historical costs associated with the old machine; (2) future costs that will be classified as variable rather then fixed; (3) future costs that will be different under the two alternatives; (4) future costs that will be classified as fixed rather than variable.

   (b) The payback method measures (1) how quickly investment dollars may be recovered; (2) the cash flow from an investment; (3) the economic life of an investment; (4) the profitability of an investment.

   (c) The method of project evaluation that considers the time value of money is the (1) average annual return on original investment; (2) average annual return on average investment; (3) discounted cash flow; (4) payback.

   (d) A company is considering the purchase of a new conveyor belt system that is to be used for carrying parts and subassemblies from building to building within its plant complex. It is expected that the system will have a useful life of at least ten years and that it will substantially reduce labor and waiting-time costs. If the company's average cost of capital is about 15% and if some evaluation must be made of cost-benefit relationships, including the effects of interest, to determine the desirability of the purchase, the most relevant quantitative technique for evaluating the investment is (1) cost-volume-profit analysis; (2) present value analysis; (3) payback analysis; (4) Program Evaluation and Review Technique with Cost (PERT/Cost).

(e) A planned factory expansion project has an estimated initial cost of $800,000. Using a 20% discount rate, the present value of future cost savings from the expansion is $843,000. To yield exactly a 20% time-adjusted rate of return, the actual investment cost cannot exceed the $800,000 estimate by more than (1) $160,000; (2) $20,000; (3) $43,000; (4) $1,075.

(AICPA adapted)

EXERCISES

1. Investment Analysis. The Weinman Company is considering a capital investment for which the initial outlay is $20,000. Net annual cash receipts, after taxes, are predicted to be $4,000 for ten years. Straight-line depreciation is to be used, with an estimated salvage value of zero.

Required: (1) Payback period.
(2) Average annual return on original investment.
(3) Average annual return on average investment.
(4) Net present value at 10% and present value payback period.
(5) Discounted cash flow rate of return.

2. Investment Analysis. The Grand Prairie Company is considering the purchase of a giant press costing $100,000. The estimated cash benefit is:

Year	Cash Benefit
1	$25,000
2	40,000
3	40,000
4	40,000
5	35,000
6	30,000
7	25,000
8	20,000
9	15,000
10	10,000

The press is to be depreciated on a straight-line basis over a period of ten years. The salvage value is zero. Assume a 50% tax rate and a cost of capital of 10%.

Required: (1) Payback period.
(2) Average annual return on original investment.
(3) Average annual return on average investment.
(4) Net present value.
(5) Discounted cash flow rate of return.

3. Equipment Replacement Analysis. The Timmerman Products Company is considering replacing an existing piece of equipment. The following data have been compiled:

(a) Old equipment: Cost.................................... $45,000
Accumulated depreciation.................. 30,000
Book value.............................. $15,000

Expected remaining life: 3 years

Current salvage value equals cost of removal. Loss on disposal of old equipment is to be recognized in the current year.

(b) New equipment: cost, $26,000; estimated life, 3 years.

(c) Capitalized cost of rearranging production line to utilize new equipment: $4,000

(d) Estimated operating costs per year:

	Old Equipment	New Equipment
Direct labor.....	$30,000	$12,000
Supplies........	14,000	11,500
Maintenance....	8,000	6,000
Supervision.....	6,000	6,000
Power.........	4,000	7,000
Depreciation....	5,000	10,000 [($26,000 + $4,000) ÷ 3]

(e) Assume the income tax rate to be 50%.

Required: Assuming a loss on the sale or disposal of equipment is treated as an ordinary tax deduction, resulting in a tax saving of 50%, should the company purchase the machine if it requires a return of 6% on investment after tax considerations? Calculate (a) the net present value and (b) the discounted cash flow rate of return.

4. Investment Analysis. For a certain project for the city of Toledo, the following data have been made available:

Original investment......................	$93,510
Estimated life of project.................	15 years
Average annual cash savings..............	$20,000

Required: (1) The payback period.

(2) The return on the investment by the discounted cash flow method.

(3) Charts and table showing the constant return on the declining balance of the original investment over the economic life of the project.

5. Equipment Investment Analysis. The Hamblin Manufacturing Company produces a single product. The results of its operations for 19— are summarized in the following condensed income statement:

Sales.................................		$2,000,000
Less cost of goods sold:		
Fixed costs........................	$ 250,000	
Variable costs.....................	1,400,000	1,650,000
Gross profit.........................		$ 350,000
Operating expenses:		
Fixed expenses.....................	$ 66,000	
Variable expenses..................	200,000	266,000
Net income before income tax.........		$ 84,000
Income tax...........................		42,000
Net income...........................		$ 42,000

The company is considering the purchase of equipment to replace an existing manual operation. It is estimated that the equipment will effect annual savings of $1,900 in labor and other direct cash costs. The new equipment is estimated to have an installed cost of $10,000 and an economic life of 10 years with no salvage value at the end of its life. Depreciation is computed on a straight-line basis. Assume that the company expects to pay income taxes of 50%.

Required: (1) Payback period.

(2) Average annual return on original investment.

(3) Average annual return on average investment.

(4) Net present value assuming the company wishes to earn 10% on its investment, after taxes.

(5) Present value payback period.

(6) Net present value index.

(7) Discounted cash flow rate of return.

6. Equipment Replacement Analysis. Ms. Jo Sage, owner of Sage Bottles, is considering the purchase of a new bottling machine which operates at twice the speed of the present equipment, costs $75,000 with an estimated life of 20 years, and will have a salvage value of $10,000 at the end of the period. The cost accountant believes that the only real saving the new machine would bring is the elimination of the present night shift consisting of 2 men, working 8 hours per night, 5 nights per week, and 50 weeks per year at the rate of $6 per hour. The present fully depreciated machine will receive a trade-in allowance of $10,000. The trade-in value will reduce the depreciable basis of the new asset.

The firm's policy has been that any capital expenditure should return at least 16% on the capital invested. The company's present tax rate is 50%. Consider the discounted value of any end-of-life cash value of the new equipment.

Required: An equipment-replacement study, indicating the payback period, the rate of return based on the discounted cash flow method, the net present value (assuming the cost of capital is 10%), and the present value payback period.

7. Feasibility Study. A proposed addition to the Hidden Valley Colorado ski lift facilities requires an investment of $1,300,000, and it is estimated that net income after taxes over the life of the project will total $600,000. The ski resort manager, Ms. Maura Shelton, has prepared these estimates:

Estimated useful life. . . . . 5 years
Estimated salvage value. . . . . —0—
Method of depreciation. . . . . straight-line

ESTIMATED REVENUES AND EXPENSES
(Thousands of Dollars)

			Year			
	1	*2*	*3*	*4*	*5*	*Total*
Revenue.	$ 500	$1,000	$2,000	$2,500	$2,000	$8,000
Expenses: Depreciation. . . .	$ 260	$ 260	$ 260	$ 260	$ 260	$ 1,300
Other (cash).	400	750	1,400	1,750	1,400	5,700
	$ 660	$1,010	$1,660	$2,010	$1,660	$7,000
Income before taxes.	$ (160)	$ (10)	$ 340	$ 490	$ 340	$1,000
Income taxes (40%).	$ 0	$ 0	$ 136	$ 196	$ 136	$ 468
Loss carry forward.	0	0	(68)*	0	0	(68)
Net taxes.	$ 0	$ 0	$ 68	$ 196	$ 136	$ 400
Net income after taxes.	$ (160)	$ (10)	$ 272	$ 294	$ 204	$ 600

*($160+ $10) × .40 = $68.

Required: (1) The average annual return on original investment.

(2) The average annual return on average investment.

(3) The payout period.

(4) The net present value and the net present value index at 8%.

(5) The discounted cash flow rate of return.

(Based on an article in *Managerial Planning*)

8. Equipment Feasibility Study. Ms. Delores Sanchez, president of Sanchez Vending, Inc. is considering a possible change in her purchasing policy covering change-making machines. For several years she has purchased Model A machines at a cost (new) of $4,000 each. These machines are traded in after two years for new ones. The trade-in value is $1,000 each. Operating costs, including $1,500 depreciation, are $5,125 a year for each machine.

The policy she is now considering would involve purchasing the more expensive Model H machines, costing $5,000 each when new, and using them for four years before trading them in for $1,000 each. Model H's operating costs for each machine, including $1,000 depreciation, would be $5,125 a year, and in addition a major overhaul at a cost of $750 would be called for after two years of operation.

Both machines perform essentially the same change-making service but Model H has a capacity exceeding that of Model A by 10%.

The company's cost of capital is 10%. Income tax is to be taken into account at a rate of 50%.

Required: (1) In terms of net present value, the cost for one machine (a) when continuing the use of the Model A machine and (b) when using the Model H machine.

(2) Does the analysis in (1) provide the requisite information for Ms. Sanchez to make her decision? If not, what additional information would be necessary?

9. Purchase vs. Leasing. Sangaman's is considering two alternatives for providing additional warehousing space for its department stores. The purchase price of this facility is assumed to be $330,000 with an economic life of ten years. The estimated salvage value at the end of the economic life is zero, and the straight-line depreciation method is to be used. The irrevocable lease provides that Sangaman's pays an annual rent of $50,000 for ten years, payable at the beginning of each year.

Maintenance costs, insurance, etc., are covered in a separate contract with the lessor whether the asset is purchased or leased. Assume that an income tax rate of 50% is to be paid at the end of each year and that the taxing authorities will permit taxation of the lease-rental agreement as a lease.

Required: The discounted cash flow rate of return of the aftertax cash savings of purchasing rather than leasing.

(Based on an article in *Management Accounting*)

10. Allowing for Risk and Uncertainty in Present Value Calculations. It is generally agreed that the present value of money techniques for evaluating capital expenditures are superior to other criteria such as payback or the average annual return on investment method. Present-value techniques, however, are often presented with an assumption of certainty, which is not entirely applicable to real-world situations.

The administrator of Portland Municipal Hospital is considering the purchase of new operating-room equipment at a cost of $7,500. The surgical staff has furnished the following estimates of useful life and cost savings. Each useful life estimate is independent of each cost savings estimate.

Years of Estimated Useful Life	Probability of Occurrence
4.................	.25
5.................	.50
6.................	.25
	1.00

Estimated Cost Savings	Probability of Occurrence
$1,900.............	.30
2,000.............	.40
2,100.............	.30
	1.00

Required: The weighted net present value, allowing for risk and uncertainty and using a 10% discount rate.

(Based on an article in *Management Adviser*)

11. Equipment Purchase and Follow-Up Analysis. As part of a cost reduction program, the management of Montgomery Products, Inc. is considering the purchase of a new machine tool that has as its purpose an increase in productivity by reason of improved performance due to a speed of two and a half times over the present equipment.

The Engineering Department proposes the following investment for the new machine tool and its related costs:

New equipment...	$91,000
Installation cost.......................................	4,000
Relocation, alteration, and rearrangement costs................	5,000

All of these costs are to be capitalized. The present equipment is fully depreciated and has a zero trade-in value.

Other annual production and cost data of present and new equipment are estimated as follows:

	Present Equipment	Proposed Equipment
Machine hours.............................	10,000 hrs.	4,000 hrs.
Output...................................	10,000 units	10,000 units
Variable costs ($4 per machine hr.)...........	$40,000	$16,000
Tooling (subcontracted)....................	8,000	—0—
Depreciation annual (20-year life)...........		5,000
Other expenses............................		5,000

At the end of the first year, actual results were:

Machine hours..	5,000 hrs.
Output..	11,500 units

New equipment...	$90,000
Installation cost..	6,000
Relocation, alteration, and rearrangement costs..............	6,000

Variable costs..	$20,000
Tooling..	1,000
Depreciation...	5,100
Other expenses...	6,000

The income tax rate is 50%.

Required: (1) For the proposal, the (a) payback period, (b) average annual return on the original investment, and (c) return by the discounted cash flow method.

(2) For the actual results at the end of the first year, assuming these results represent expectations for the life of the project, the (a) payback period, (b) average annual return on the original investment, and (c) return by the discounted cash flow method.

(Based on an article in *Management Accounting*)

PROBLEMS

26-1. Equipment Replacement Study. The Sureseal Gasket & Mfg. Company, which is currently producing wire ring gaskets by hand labor with a minor amount of machinery, is contemplating the purchase of an automatic machine which will cut down the amount of labor needed in the process. The process entails the cutting of the wire by hand, the welding of the gasket by machine, and subsequently the deburring, sanding, and forming of the gaskets by hand.

The materials costs under both methods would be $3,000. Maintenance and repairs for the old process cost $70, and the expected cost applicable to the new machine is $200. Tools and supplies under the old process amounted to $3,250, while the new machine would require only $1,000. These figures represent annual costs.

The company works on a two shift, forty-hour week, fifty weeks of the year, and pays a premium of $.11 an hour for the second shift. The welding of the gaskets is done by one man on each shift; the first shift man receives $5.25 per hour under the old process. The new machine would require only one man on each shift also. He would receive $5.00 per hour for the first shift.

After the gaskets are welded, they have to be deburred, sanded, and formed. Under the old method, this required three men on each shift; the first shift received $4.50 per hour. The new machine would automatically debur the gaskets; therefore, under the new method only two men would be needed on each shift to form and sand the gaskets. They would receive $4.50 per hour.

Electricity under the old method was charged at $.02 per kilowatt hour, and the old machines consumed 2 kilowatt hours per hour of operation. The new machine would consume 8 kilowatt hours of electricity per hour of operation and would cost $.02 per kilowatt hour.

The old machinery has a trade-in value and a book value of $3,000 at the present time. The salvage value for depreciation purposes is $3,000 for both the old and new machines. The new machine would cost $63,000 less trade-in, and have a useful life of 15 years. The estimated cash value of the new machine at the end of 15 years will be negligible.

Required: An equipment replacement study, indicating the net cash savings per year based on a 50% tax rate, the payback period, and the rate of return based on the discounted cash flow method.

26-2. Equipment Economy Study. Several years ago, Suhar Manufacturing Co. began using the discounted cash flow method for the evaluation of the return on investment of capital expenditure proposals. Since the screening of alternatives is often done by operating people, a formal yet rather simple evaluation procedure had to be devised. In each case it is assumed that the investment is completed at the start of the project and that the operating savings or income resulting from the investment will be earned in equal annual installments during the life of the asset. Annual savings are determined by comparing present costs with the estimated costs which will exist if the investment is made, and are adjusted for the increase in income taxes following the savings in order to express the savings in terms of cash flow.

The works manager of the company has been concerned about the possible replacement of a large semiautomatic machine which is ten years old and requires excessive maintenance and down time. Full allowance for depreciation has been taken, book value is zero, and no trade-in allowance will be given. It could be improved by adding new controls and a modern loading device that eliminates one direct operator and reduces materials handling. The improvement would cost $9,000 and would have a 3-year economic life (no salvage value). The other alternative is the purchase of a new machine costing $21,000 with a 10-year life (no salvage value), eliminating two direct operators and reducing materials handling. In summary, the proposals appear as follows:

Annual Operating Costs	Present Machine	Proposal A— Present Machine with Improvements	Proposal B— New Machine
Direct labor	$11,000	$8,700	$3,000
Indirect labor	4,000	2,400	2,400
Fringe benefits	1,200	800	600
Maintenance and repairs	2,000	800	1,200

Company's income tax rate = 40%

Required: (1) The payback period for Proposals A and B.

(2) The rate of return on investment by the discounted cash flow method for Proposals A and B.

(3) Management's best decision.

(Based on an NAA article)

26-3. Projects Profitability Study. The Wassler Manufacturing Company is considering its capital spending program for the next period. Only those projects which meet certain investment criteria will be undertaken. Four projects have been proposed by different department heads. The Cost Analysis Section has prepared the following data concerning the projects:

Project #1	Capital outlay	$15,000
	Net cash savings in cost (per year)	4,000 during the next 5 years; 2,000 during the second 5 years
Project #2	Capital outlay	$25,000
	Net increase in cash income (per year)	4,000 during the next 20 years
Project #3	Capital outlay	$20,000
	Net cash savings in cost (per year)	3,000 during the next 5 years; 5,000 during the second 5 years
Project #4	Capital outlay	$35,000
	Net increase in cash income (per year)	10,000 the first 2 years; 5,000 the next 8 years; 4,000 the next 10 years

The investment criteria established by the company is to invest in only those projects which have a payback period of less than one half the estimated useful life of the project. The payback period is computed on an aftertax basis. The discounted cash flow of the investments must be at a rate greater than 10%, after taxes.

Required: (1) The aftertax payback period for each project. Depreciation is straight-line (no salvage value) and the tax rate is 45%. The economic life of the projects is indicated by the number of years of expected returns.

(2) The rates of return expected for the project using the discounted cash flow method.

(3) The project(s) which meet the criteria for investment.

26-4. New Product Investment Analysis. The Baxter Company manufactures short-lived fad-type items.

The R & D Department has developed an item that would be an interesting promotional gift for office equipment dealers. Aggressive and effective effort by Baxter's sales personnel has resulted in almost firm commitments for this product for the next three years. It is expected that the product's value will be exhausted by that time.

In order to produce the quantity demanded, Baxter will need to buy additional machinery and rent 12,500 square feet of additional space. There is another 12,500 square feet of space adjoining the Baxter facility which Baxter will rent for 3 years at $4 per square foot per year if it decides to make this product.

The equipment will be purchased for about $900,000. It will require $30,000 in modifications, $60,000 for installation, and $90,000 for testing; all of these activities will be done by a firm of engineers hired by Baxter. All of the expenditures will be paid for on January 1, 19A.

The equipment should have a salvage value of about $180,000 at the end of the third year. No additional general overhead costs are expected to be incurred.

The following estimates of revenues and expenses for this product for the three years have been developed:

	19A	*19B*	*19C*
Sales.............................	$1,000,000	$1,600,000	$800,000
Material, labor, and additional			
factory overhead..................	$ 400,000	$ 750,000	$350,000
Assigned general overhead.............	77,500	112,500	72,500
Rent (12,500 square feet of space × $4)....	50,000	50,000	50,000
Depreciation........................	450,000	300,000	150,000
Total expenses......................	$ 977,500	$1,212,500	$622,500
Net income before income tax..........	$ 22,500	$ 387,500	$177,500
Income tax (40%).....................	9,000	155,000	71,000
Net income.........................	$ 13,500	$ 232,500	$106,500

Required: (1) A schedule showing the net increase in aftertax cash inflow for this project.

(2) A decision (with supporting computations) as to whether this project should be undertaken if the Baxter Company requires a two-year payback period for its investment.

(3) The aftertax average annual return on average investment for the project.

(4) A decision (with supporting computations) as to whether the project will be accepted if the company sets a required 20% aftertax rate of return. (A newly hired business school graduate recommends that the Baxter Company consider using the net present value analysis to study this project.)

(NAA adapted)

26-5. Plant Replacement vs. Outside Materials Purchase. The management of the Ellington Manufacturing Company is considering the advisability of either replacing the existing foundry plant with a modern Electric-Arc smelting plant or purchasing semifinished castings from an outside source.

Recent governmental regulations have made the factory area a clean-air zone, and the annual cost of cleaning the exhaust gases emitted by the foundry would amount to $30,000. Management does not consider the old plant worth this additional cost.

The present foundry equipment is old and uneconomical due to the difficulty in controlling the production of castings to the correct materials specifications. The entire present castings production is absorbed by the other production departments within the company.

A price of $320,000 has been quoted for the new Electric-Arc smelting plant including installation expenses and antiatmospheric pollution filters. The new plant is to become obsolete in ten years with negligible scrap value. Depreciation expense will be $32,000 per year. The old plant's account shows a balance of $10,000 (full tax allowance having been taken); this amount is expected to be realized if the plant is sold for scrap within the next year or so. However, the $10,000 will be required to pay dismantling and removal costs. Annual operating costs of the new Electric-Arc smelting plant to produce the budgeted volume of good quality castings would be $600,000. The fixed costs incurred would be $90,000 directly related to the foundry operation, excluding depreciation on the new plant, plus fixed general factory overhead of $100,000. The fixed general factory overhead expense will occur whether or not the plant is replaced.

The Allied Steel Corporation can supply the budgeted volume of good quality castings to the correct materials specifications for $800,000.

A preliminary annual cost computation for castings shows:

Operating costs...........................	$600,000
Foundry fixed overhead.....................	90,000
General plant overhead (fixed)..............	100,000
Depreciation on new plant..................	32,000
Total costs.............................	$822,000
Cost of purchasing........................	$800,000
Savings through purchasing................	$ 22,000

Required: A more thorough investigation of the problem, paying due regard to the company's minimum required rate of return on investment of 15%, and its long-term cash forecast. Assuming a 50% income tax rate, compute the payback period and the discounted cash flow rate of return.

26-6. Project Planning Analysis. The cost analyst of Poinciana Oil Products, Inc. prepared the following data and chart for three possible projects:

	Project A	Project B	Project C
Original investment.....................	$100,000	$100,000	$100,000
Life of investment......................	25 years	25 years	25 years
Total cash flow (after taxes)..............	$350,000	$350,000	$350,000
Average annual cash flow (after taxes).....	14,000	14,000	14,000
Annual depreciation (straight-line)........	4,000	4,000	4,000

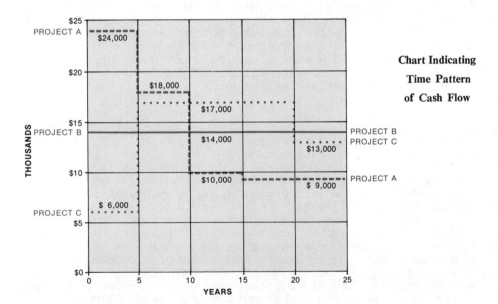

Chart Indicating Time Pattern of Cash Flow

Dollar figures within the chart are for amounts *per year.*

Required: (1) The average annual return on original investment.

(2) The average annual return on average investment.

(3) The payback period.

(4) The return on investment by the discounted cash flow method.

26-7. Purchase vs. Leasing. Madisons, Inc. has decided to acquire a new machine either by an outright cash purchase at $25,000 or by a leasing alternative of $6,000 per year for the life of the machine. Other relevant information is:

Purchase price due at time of purchase.......................	$25,000
Estimated useful life......................................	5 years
Estimated salvage value if purchased.........................	$3,000
Annual cost of maintenance contract to be acquired with either lease or purchase..	$500

Additional information:

(a) Assume a 40% income tax rate and the use of the straight-line method of depreciation.

(b) Assume that the taxing authorities will permit taxation of the lease agreement as a lease.

(c) The company's cost of capital is 10%.

Required: (1) The present value of the purchase price of the new machine.

(2) Under the purchase alternative, the present value of the estimated salvage value.

(3) Under the purchase alternative, the annual tax reduction (cash inflow) related to depreciation.

(4) Under the purchase alternative, the annual aftertax cash outflow for maintenance.

(5) A recommendation to management (with supporting computations), using the net present value evaluation method.

(AICPA adapted)

26-8. Purchase vs. Leasing with Options. A manager is interested in evaluating the relative merits of options available under a proposed lease arrangement. The following facts are available:

Purchase. The purchase price of the facility is assumed to be $330,000; the economic life is assumed to be 10 years; and the salvage value at the end of the economic life is zero. Straight-line depreciation is used.

Leasing: The annual rental of the facility is $80,000 for three years, payable at the beginning of each year — a three-year commitment. Thereafter, year-to-year lease renewals at the option of the lessee are available at the rate of $60,000 per year payable at the beginning of each year.

Purchase Option. A purchase option is available with total purchase price payment due at the end of three years when the estimated purchase price and salvage value is $200,000. If the facility is purchased, it can be sold for this same amount at the end of three years.

Other Facts. The maintenance costs, insurance, etc., are covered in a separate contract with the lessor whether the asset is purchased or leased. The income tax rate is 50% and is paid at the end of each year. Assume the taxing authorities will permit taxation of the lease-rental agreement as a lease.

Required: (1) The discounted cash flow rate of return of the difference between aftertax cash savings of purchasing rather than leasing assuming that (a) the use of the facility is terminated at the end of three years; (b) the facility is leased three years, at which time the purchase option is exercised; (c) the facility is leased for the entire ten years.

(2) A discussion of how the analysis in (1) above can be used in determining whether to purchase or lease the facility.

(Based on an article in *Management Accounting*)

26-9. Equipment Feasibility Study with Allowance for Risk and Uncertainty. The plant manager of the Scahill Corporation, confronted with a need to purchase a machine, is faced with a choice between Machine A and Machine B, both of which have the desired operating characteristics and capabilities.

Each machine has an estimated life of three years, but Machine A will cost $5,000, compared to Machine B's initial cost of $10,000. However, an analysis of the operating costs associated with each of the machines reveals that the cost per unit with Machine A is $1 and with Machine B is $.50, excluding depreciation. The product's selling price is $4.

The manager feels that the number of units required for each of the next three years may be 2,000, 3,000, or 5,000 units. He feels that an annual requirement for 3,000 units is the most probable and that a requirement for either 2,000 or 5,000 units per year is less probable than for 3,000 units. Estimates of probability, based in part upon analysis of the past and in part on the manager's best appraisal of the future, have been quantified as follows:

Annual Requirements	*Probability of Occurrence*
2,000	.2
3,000	.6
5,000	.2

Required: (1) The net present value for each of the three activity levels for Machines A and B using a discount rate of 6%.

(2) The weighted net present value for each machine. (Ignore income tax considerations.)

(Based on an article in *Management Services*)

26-10. New Product Analysis Considering Risk and Uncertainty; Net Present Value. Vernon Enterprises designs and manufactures toys. Past experience indicates that the product life cycle of a toy is three years. Promotional advertising produces large sales in the early years, but there is a substantial sales decline in the final year of a toy's life.

Consumer demand for new toys placed on the market tends to fall into three classes. About 30% of the new toys sell well above expectations; 60% sell as anticipated; and 10% have poor consumer acceptance.

A new toy has been developed, and the following sales projections were made by carefully evaluating its consumer demand:

Consumer Demand for New Toy	Chance of Occurring	Estimated Sales in		
		Year 1	Year 2	Year 3
Above average...	30%	$1,200,000	$2,500,000	$600,000
Average.........	60	700,000	1,700,000	400,000
Below average....	10	200,000	900,000	150,000

Variable costs are estimated at 30% of the selling price. Special machinery must be purchased at a cost of $860,000 and will be installed in an unused portion of the factory which Vernon has unsuccessfully been trying to rent for several years at $50,000 per year and which has no prospects for future utilization. Fixed costs (excluding depreciation) of a cash-flow nature are estimated at $50,000 per year on the new toy. The new machinery is to be depreciated by the sum-of-the-years-digits method with an estimated salvage value of $110,000 and will be sold at the end of the third year. Advertising and promotional expenses will total $100,000 in the first year, $150,000 in the second year, and $50,000 in the third year. These expenses will be deducted as incurred for income tax reporting.

The management of Vernon Enterprises believes that federal and state income taxes will total 60% in the foreseeable future.

Required: (1) A schedule of the new toy's probable sales for each year, assuming the occurrence of (a) above average sales, (b) average sales, and (c) below average sales.

(2) A schedule of the new toy's probable net income for each year of its life, assuming that the probable sales computed in (1) are $900,000 in the first year, $1,800,000 in the second year, and $410,000 in the third year.

(3) A schedule of net cash flows from the new toy's sales for each of the years involved and from disposition of the machinery purchased. [Use the sales data given in (2).]

(4) A schedule of the net present value of net cash flows computed in (3), assuming a minimum desired rate of return of 10%.

(AICPA adapted)

26-11. Equipment Replacement Study. The management of New Brunswick Products, Inc. is considering replacing machinery purchased eight years ago costing $80,000 with new machinery costing $130,000. The old machinery has a remaining useful life of eight years; and its trade-in value is estimated to be $40,000 now, while the trade-in value eight years hence is estimated to be its book value plus removal costs. Equipment manufacturers advise that both the old and new machinery will probably be obsolete in eight years to the point that replacement will be mandatory. The proposed new equipment has an estimated life of eight years; at the end of eight years of use, its market value is assumed to be equal to its book value at that time with no removal costs to be borne by New Brunswick. Incoming freight and installation costs in connection with the new machinery will be $20,000. Removal costs of $1,000 are anticipated in connection with the old machinery.

The annual costs of operating the old and new machinery are presented on page 866.

	Actual for the Old Machinery	*Anticipated for the New Machinery*
Variable costs.......................	$50,000	$15,000
Fixed costs (excluding depreciation)....	11,000	18,500

The desired minimum aftertax rate of return normally required by the company is 12%. The income tax rate applicable throughout is 50%.

Assume, for income tax purposes, that the sum-of-the-years-digits depreciation method is used for the old and new machinery with a 10% provision for residual value. Any gain or loss on the disposal of the old machinery will serve to adjust the depreciable basis of the new replacement machinery.

Required: (1) A decision as to whether or not New Brunswick should replace the existing machinery now.

(2) The net present value, the net present value index, and the rate of return on the investment by the discounted cash flow method.

26-12. Projects Evaluation Analysis. Rowekamp Corporation is beginning its first capital expenditures planning and control program and needs assistance in the evaluation of a project to expand operations designated as Proposed Expansion Project #12 (PEP #12).

(a) The following capital expenditures are under consideration:

> $ 300,000 Fire sprinkler system
> 100,000 Landscaping
> 600,000 Replacement of old machines
> 800,000 Projects to expand operations (including PEP #12)
> _____
> $1,800,000 Total

(b) The corporation requires no minimum return on the sprinkler system or the landscaping. However, it expects a minimum return of 6% on all investments to replace old machinery. It also expects investments in expansion projects to yield a return that will exceed the average cost of the capital required to finance the sprinkler system and the landscaping in addition to the expansion projects.

(c) Under PEP #12, a cash investment of $75,000 will be made one year before operations begin. The investment will be depreciated by the sum-of-the-years-digits method over a three-year period and is expected to have a salvage value of $15,000. Additional financial data for PEP #12 follow:

Time Period	Revenue	Variable Costs	Maintenance, Property Taxes, and Insurance
0–1	$80,000	$35,000	$ 8,000
1–2	95,000	41,000	11,000
2–3	60,000	25,000	12,000

The amount of the investment recovered during each of the three years can be reinvested immediately at a rate of return approximating 15%. Each year's recovery of investment, then, will have been reinvested at 15% for an average of six months at the end of the year.

(d) The capital structure of Rowekamp Corporation follows:

	Amount	Percentage
Bonds at 5% interest........................	$ 3,500,000	10%
4% cumulative preferred stock, $100 par......	1,750,000	5
Common stock and retained earnings.........	29,750,000	85
	$35,000,000	100%

(e) Additional available data are:

	Current Market Price	Expected Earnings per Share After Taxes	Expected Dividends per Share
Preferred stock.............	$120	———	$4.00
Common stock.............	50	$3.20	1.60

(f) Assume that the corporate income tax rate is 50%.

(g) The present value of $1 due at the end of each year and discounted at 15% is:

End of Year	Present Value
2 years before 0	$1.32
1 year before 0	1.15
0	1.00
1 year after 0	.87
2 years after 0	.76
3 years after 0	.66

(h) The present values of $1 earned uniformly throughout the year and discounted at 15% follow:

Year	Present Value
0–1	$ .93
1–2	.80
2–3	.69

Required: (1) Assuming that the cutoff rate for considering expansion projects is 15%, prepare a schedule calculating the (a) annual cash flows from operations for PEP #12 and (b) net present value of the cash flows for PEP #12.

(2) The budget committee has asked for a check of the reasonableness of the cutoff rate. One of the factors to be considered is an estimate of the average cost of capital to this firm. It requests a schedule, supported by computations in good form, to compute the average cost of capital weighted by the percentage of the capital structure which each element represents.

(3) (a) Assuming that the average cost of capital computed in (2) is 9%, prepare a schedule to compute the minimum return (in dollars) required on expansion projects to cover the average cost of capital for financing the sprinkler system and the landscaping in addition to expansion projects. Assume that it is necessary to replace the old machines. (b) Assuming that the minimum return computed in (3) (a) is $150,000, calculate the cutoff rate on expansion projects.

(AICPA adapted)

PRESENT VALUE OF $1

Future Years	1%	2%	4%	6%	8%	10%	12%	14%	15%	16%	18%	20%	22%	24%	25%	26%	28%	30%	35%	40%	45%	50%
1	.990	.980	.962	.943	.926	.909	.893	.877	.870	.862	.847	.833	.820	.806	.800	.794	.781	.769	.741	.714	.690	.667
2	.980	.961	.925	.890	.857	.826	.797	.769	.756	.743	.718	.694	.672	.650	.640	.630	.610	.592	.549	.510	.476	.444
3	.971	.942	.889	.840	.794	.751	.712	.675	.658	.641	.609	.579	.551	.524	.512	.500	.477	.455	.406	.364	.328	.296
4	.961	.924	.855	.792	.735	.683	.636	.592	.572	.552	.516	.482	.451	.423	.410	.397	.373	.350	.301	.260	.226	.198
5	.951	.906	.822	.747	.681	.621	.567	.519	.497	.476	.437	.402	.370	.341	.328	.315	.291	.269	.223	.186	.156	.132
6	.942	.888	.790	.705	.630	.564	.507	.456	.432	.410	.370	.335	.303	.275	.262	.250	.227	.207	.165	.133	.108	.088
7	.933	.871	.760	.665	.583	.513	.452	.400	.376	.354	.314	.279	.249	.222	.210	.198	.178	.159	.122	.095	.074	.059
8	.923	.853	.731	.627	.540	.467	.404	.351	.327	.305	.266	.233	.204	.179	.168	.157	.139	.123	.091	.068	.051	.039
9	.914	.837	.703	.592	.500	.424	.361	.308	.284	.263	.225	.194	.167	.144	.134	.125	.108	.094	.067	.048	.035	.026
10	.905	.820	.676	.558	.463	.386	.322	.270	.247	.227	.191	.162	.137	.116	.107	.099	.085	.073	.050	.035	.024	.017
11	.896	.804	.650	.527	.429	.350	.287	.237	.215	.195	.162	.135	.112	.094	.086	.079	.066	.056	.037	.025	.017	.012
12	.887	.788	.625	.497	.397	.319	.257	.208	.187	.168	.137	.112	.092	.076	.069	.062	.052	.043	.027	.018	.012	.008
13	.879	.773	.601	.469	.368	.290	.229	.182	.163	.145	.116	.093	.075	.061	.055	.050	.040	.033	.020	.013	.008	.005
14	.870	.758	.577	.442	.340	.263	.205	.160	.141	.125	.099	.078	.062	.049	.044	.039	.032	.025	.015	.009	.006	.003
15	.861	.743	.555	.417	.315	.239	.183	.140	.123	.108	.084	.065	.051	.040	.035	.031	.025	.020	.011	.006	.004	.002
16	.853	.728	.534	.394	.292	.218	.163	.123	.107	.093	.071	.054	.042	.032	.028	.025	.019	.015	.008	.005	.003	.002
17	.844	.714	.513	.371	.270	.198	.146	.108	.093	.080	.060	.045	.034	.026	.023	.020	.015	.012	.006	.003	.002	.001
18	.836	.700	.494	.350	.250	.180	.130	.095	.081	.069	.051	.038	.028	.021	.018	.016	.012	.009	.005	.002	.002	.001
19	.828	.686	.475	.331	.232	.164	.116	.083	.070	.060	.043	.031	.023	.017	.014	.012	.009	.007	.003	.002	.001	.001
20	.820	.673	.456	.312	.215	.149	.104	.073	.061	.051	.037	.026	.019	.014	.012	.010	.007	.005	.002	.001	.001	
21	.811	.660	.439	.294	.199	.135	.093	.064	.053	.044	.031	.022	.015	.011	.009	.008	.006	.004	.002	.001		
22	.803	.647	.422	.278	.184	.123	.083	.056	.046	.038	.026	.018	.013	.009	.007	.006	.004	.003	.001			
23	.795	.634	.406	.262	.170	.112	.074	.049	.040	.033	.022	.015	.010	.007	.006	.005	.003	.002	.001			
24	.788	.622	.390	.247	.158	.102	.066	.043	.035	.028	.019	.013	.008	.006	.005	.004	.003	.002	.001			
25	.780	.610	.375	.233	.146	.092	.059	.038	.030	.024	.016	.010	.007	.005	.004	.003	.002	.001	.001			
26	.772	.598	.361	.207	.135	.084	.053	.033	.026	.021	.014	.009	.006	.004	.003	.002	.002	.001				
27	.764	.586	.347	.207	.125	.076	.047	.029	.023	.018	.011	.007	.005	.003	.002	.002	.001	.001				
28	.757	.574	.333	.196	.116	.069	.042	.026	.020	.016	.010	.006	.004	.002	.002	.001	.001	.001				
29	.749	.563	.321	.185	.107	.063	.037	.022	.017	.014	.008	.005	.003	.002	.002	.001	.001	.001				
30	.742	.552	.308	.174	.099	.057	.033	.020	.015	.012	.007	.004	.003	.002	.001	.001	.001					
40	.672	.453	.208	.097	.046	.022	.011	.005	.004	.003	.001	.001										
50	.608	.372	.141	.054	.021	.009	.003	.001	.001	.001												

868

PRESENT VALUE OF $1 RECEIVED OR PAID ANNUALLY FOR EACH OF THE NEXT N YEARS

Future Years	1%	2%	4%	6%	8%	10%	12%	14%	15%	16%	18%	20%	22%	24%	25%	26%	28%	30%	35%	40%	45%	50%
1	.990	.980	.962	.943	.926	.909	.893	.877	.870	.862	.847	.833	.820	.806	.800	.794	.781	.769	.741	.714	.690	.667
2	1.970	1.942	1.886	1.833	1.783	1.736	1.690	1.647	1.626	1.605	1.566	1.528	1.492	1.457	1.440	1.424	1.392	1.361	1.289	1.224	1.165	1.111
3	2.941	2.884	2.775	2.673	2.577	2.487	2.402	2.322	2.283	2.246	2.174	2.106	2.042	1.981	1.952	1.923	1.868	1.816	1.696	1.589	1.493	1.407
4	3.902	3.808	3.630	3.465	3.312	3.170	3.037	2.914	2.855	2.798	2.690	2.589	2.494	2.404	2.362	2.320	2.241	2.166	1.997	1.849	1.720	1.605
5	4.853	4.713	4.452	4.212	3.993	3.791	3.605	3.433	3.352	3.274	3.127	2.991	2.864	2.745	2.689	2.635	2.532	2.436	2.220	2.035	1.876	1.737
6	5.795	5.601	5.242	4.917	4.623	4.355	4.111	3.889	3.784	3.685	3.498	3.326	3.167	3.020	2.951	2.885	2.759	2.643	2.385	2.168	1.983	1.824
7	6.728	6.472	6.002	5.582	5.206	4.868	4.564	4.288	4.160	4.039	3.812	3.605	3.416	3.242	3.161	3.083	2.937	2.802	2.508	2.263	2.057	1.883
8	7.652	7.325	6.733	6.210	5.747	5.335	4.968	4.639	4.487	4.344	4.078	3.837	3.619	3.421	3.329	3.241	3.076	2.925	2.598	2.331	2.108	1.922
9	8.566	8.163	7.435	6.802	6.247	5.759	5.328	4.946	4.772	4.607	4.303	4.031	3.786	3.566	3.463	3.366	3.184	3.019	2.665	2.379	2.144	1.948
10	9.471	8.983	8.111	7.360	6.710	6.145	5.650	5.216	5.019	4.833	4.494	4.192	3.923	3.682	3.571	3.465	3.269	3.092	2.715	2.414	2.168	1.965
11	10.368	9.787	8.760	7.887	7.139	6.495	5.938	5.453	5.234	5.029	4.656	4.327	4.035	3.776	3.656	3.544	3.335	3.147	2.752	2.438	2.185	1.977
12	11.255	10.575	9.385	8.384	7.536	6.814	6.194	5.660	5.421	5.197	4.793	4.439	4.127	3.851	3.725	3.606	3.387	3.190	2.779	2.456	2.196	1.985
13	12.134	11.348	9.986	8.853	7.904	7.103	6.424	5.842	5.583	5.342	4.910	4.533	4.203	3.912	3.780	3.656	3.427	3.223	2.799	2.468	2.204	1.990
14	13.004	12.106	10.563	9.295	8.244	7.367	6.628	6.002	5.724	5.468	5.008	4.611	4.265	3.962	3.824	3.695	3.459	3.249	2.814	2.477	2.210	1.993
15	13.865	12.849	11.118	9.712	8.559	7.606	6.811	6.142	5.847	5.575	5.092	4.675	4.315	4.001	3.859	3.726	3.483	3.268	2.825	2.484	2.214	1.995
16	14.718	13.578	11.652	10.106	8.851	7.824	6.974	6.265	5.954	5.669	5.162	4.730	4.357	4.033	3.887	3.751	3.503	3.283	2.834	2.489	2.216	1.997
17	15.562	14.292	12.166	10.477	9.122	8.022	7.120	6.373	6.047	5.749	5.222	4.775	4.391	4.059	3.910	3.771	3.518	3.295	2.840	2.492	2.218	1.998
18	16.398	14.992	12.659	10.828	9.372	8.201	7.250	6.467	6.128	5.818	5.273	4.812	4.419	4.080	3.928	3.786	3.529	3.304	2.844	2.494	2.219	1.999
19	17.226	15.678	13.134	11.158	9.604	8.365	7.366	6.550	6.198	5.877	5.316	4.844	4.442	4.097	3.942	3.799	3.539	3.311	2.848	2.496	2.220	1.999
20	18.046	16.351	13.590	11.470	9.818	8.514	7.469	6.623	6.259	5.929	5.353	4.870	4.460	4.110	3.954	3.808	3.546	3.316	2.850	2.497	2.221	1.999
21	18.857	17.011	14.029	11.764	10.017	8.649	7.562	6.687	6.312	5.973	5.384	4.891	4.476	4.121	3.963	3.816	3.551	3.320	2.852	2.498	2.221	2.000
22	19.660	17.658	14.451	12.042	10.201	8.772	7.645	6.743	6.359	6.011	5.410	4.909	4.488	4.130	3.970	3.822	3.556	3.323	2.853	2.498	2.222	2.000
23	20.456	18.292	14.857	12.303	10.371	8.883	7.718	6.792	6.399	6.044	5.432	4.925	4.499	4.137	3.976	3.827	3.559	3.325	2.854	2.499	2.222	2.000
24	21.243	18.914	15.247	12.550	10.529	8.985	7.784	6.835	6.434	6.073	5.451	4.937	4.507	4.143	3.981	3.831	3.562	3.327	2.855	2.499	2.222	2.000
25	22.023	19.523	15.622	12.783	10.675	9.077	7.843	6.873	6.464	6.097	5.467	4.948	4.514	4.147	3.985	3.834	3.564	3.329	2.856	2.499	2.222	2.000
26	22.795	20.121	15.983	13.003	10.810	9.161	7.896	6.906	6.491	6.118	5.480	4.956	4.520	4.151	3.988	3.837	3.566	3.330	2.856	2.500	2.222	2.000
27	23.560	20.707	16.330	13.211	10.935	9.237	7.943	6.935	6.514	6.136	5.492	4.964	4.524	4.154	3.990	3.839	3.567	3.331	2.856	2.500	2.222	2.000
28	24.316	21.281	16.663	13.406	11.051	9.307	7.984	6.961	6.534	6.152	5.502	4.970	4.528	4.157	3.992	3.840	3.568	3.331	2.857	2.500	2.222	2.000
29	25.066	21.844	16.984	13.591	11.158	9.370	8.022	6.983	6.551	6.166	5.510	4.975	4.531	4.159	3.994	3.841	3.569	3.332	2.857	2.500	2.222	2.000
30	25.808	22.396	17.292	13.765	11.258	9.427	8.055	7.003	6.566	6.177	5.517	4.979	4.534	4.160	3.995	3.842	3.569	3.332	2.857	2.500	2.222	2.000
40	32.835	27.355	19.793	15.046	11.925	9.779	8.244	7.105	6.642	6.234	5.548	4.997	4.544	4.166	3.999	3.846	3.571	3.333	2.857	2.500	2.222	2.000
50	39.196	31.424	21.482	15.762	12.234	9.915	8.304	7.133	6.661	6.246	5.554	4.999	4.545	4.167	4.000	3.846	3.571	3.333	2.857	2.500	2.222	2.000

CHAPTER **27**

PROFIT PERFORMANCE
MEASUREMENTS,
INTRACOMPANY
TRANSFER PRICING,
PRODUCT PRICING METHODS

The establishment of a profit goal based on budgets and standards, the delegation of authority and the assignment of responsibility to middle and lower management levels, and finally the creation of decentralized, autonomous divisions of a company lead to the need for measuring the operating and profit performance of top as well as subordinate executives. The return-on-capital-employed concept assists management in appraising company-wide as well as divisional operating performance. Appraising profit performance is discussed first, followed by the subject of intracompany transfer pricing which plays a significant role in divisional and departmental result measurement. Finally, the chapter deals with different product pricing methods with which management may establish product prices needed to cover costs and return a profit.

APPRAISING PROFIT PERFORMANCE

The return-on-capital-employed concept for internal profit measurement purposes relates to (1) profit planning and decision making and (2) measuring management's and managers' performance.

The Return-on-Capital-Employed Concept. The rate of return on capital employed may be expressed as the product of two factors: the percentage of profit to sales and the capital-employed turnover rate. In equation form, the concept appears as shown below.

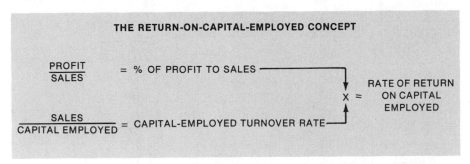

THE RETURN-ON-CAPITAL-EMPLOYED CONCEPT

$$\frac{\text{PROFIT}}{\text{SALES}} = \% \text{ OF PROFIT TO SALES}$$

$$\frac{\text{SALES}}{\text{CAPITAL EMPLOYED}} = \text{CAPITAL-EMPLOYED TURNOVER RATE}$$

X =   RATE OF RETURN ON CAPITAL EMPLOYED

If sales were cancelled out in the two fractions, the end result would still be the same. However, the shortened formula does not express the real objective of the concept which deals with two independent variables — profit on sales and turnover of capital employed. Using the full formula gives management a better comprehension of the elements leading to the final result. The earnings percentage reflects a cost-price relationship; i.e., the success or lack of success of maintaining satisfactory control of costs. The turnover rate reflects the rapidity with which committed assets are employed in the operations. The return on capital is an internal measure of operating management. It is not a guide for shareholders or investors who measure profitability or earning power by relating profits to equity capital.

The elements that produce the final rate and whose result will respond to any change or movement in any of the factors indicate that no factor or element can be disregarded, minimized, or overemphasized without impairing the quality of managerial decisions. Changes in the profit margin can be caused by an increase or decrease in sales or costs. An improved turnover rate with no change in sales prices indicates that the capital employed is worked harder; that is, more sales are coming out of the same investment.

Complete details of the relationships of the capital-employed ratio to the underlying ratios — percentage of profit to sales and capital-employed turnover rate — are portrayed more vividly in the chart on page 872.

Executive management of many companies has shown a growing acceptance of this concept as a tool to aid management in planning for the future, in establishing selling prices, and in measuring operational profitability.

Return-on-Capital-Employed Ratio on a Company Basis. The rate of return on capital employed is the product of two factors, and several combinations can lead to the same result. If a company's management wishes

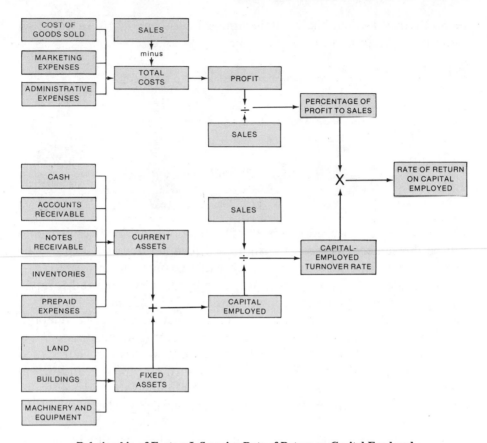

Relationship of Factors Influencing Rate of Return on Capital Employed

to earn 20 percent on capital employed, this rate can be based on any of
the following calculations:

Percentage of Profit to Sales	Capital-Employed Turnover Rate	Rate of Return on Capital Employed
10%	2	20%
8	2.5	20
6	3.333	20
4	5	20
2	10	20

What is a satisfactory return on capital employed? Unfortunately,
there is no rate that will fit all companies. Manufacturing companies will
have a different rate from utilities, banking institutions, merchandising
firms, or service companies. Managerial judgment and experience supported by comparisons with other companies can result in establishing an
objective rate of return on capital employed. Every industry has companies
with high, medium, and low rates of return. Structure and size of the firm

influence the rate considerably. A company with a diversified line of products might have only a fair return rate when all products are pooled in the analysis. In such cases it seems advisable to establish separate objectives for each line and for the total company. Methods for product-line analyses are discussed in a later section of this chapter.

The Formula's Underlying Data. The computation of a rate of return on capital employed is unquestionably very easy. Figures used in the calculation are derived from the balance sheet and income statement. No general agreement exists, however, with respect to the profit, sales, and capital employed figures used in computing the rate.

Consider, for instance, the profit figure. Which profit should be used? The income statement generally reports several profits such as (1) net operating income or profit, which includes cost of goods sold and mar- keting and administrative expenses but excludes nonoperating income and expenses; (2) net income or net profit before taxes, which would in- clude the nonoperating income and expense items, and (3) the net income or net profit after taxes, representing the amount that is transferred to retained earnings. Using net operating income or profit means that only transactions of an operating nature should be considered. This profit figure is preferred in connection with divisional or departmental analyses, for nonoperating items are usually the responsibility of the entire company. The use of net income before or after taxes is significant when judging the enterprise as a whole. Net income after taxes is more defensible because tax money is not available to management, and managerial efficiency should be judged only by the ultimate result.

The profit figure to be used remains a managerial decision. Obvi- ously, different results will be obtained by employing one or the other figure. It seems that the decision depends in large measure upon the type of analysis, whether for a small segment or for the entire organization. The allocation of nonoperating items or income taxes might distort the analysis in the case of a departmental or product analysis.

The sales figure commonly used is net sales — gross sales less sales returns and allowances and sales discounts.

The third element, capital employed, can be equated with the term "total assets," or the sum of current assets and fixed assets. The word "investment" is intentionally avoided because its common use in connec- tion with capital investment (fixed assets) or owner's investment (net worth or equity capital) is misleading and confusing. In this case, though, the entire asset side must be considered, and the term "capital employed" seems to express this element best. However, beyond the term itself, the phrase "capital employed" raises pertinent questions regarding each asset item included.

Current Assets. The three most significant items classified as current assets are cash, receivables, and inventories. The problems of valuation relating to these three current assets are presented below.

Cash. Ordinarily, cash is the amount shown on the balance sheet that is required for the total business operations. However, if cash should include funds set aside for a future expansion or development program, these amounts should be deducted from cash or from whatever account was charged. Funds, such as pension, welfare, or tax funds, should be excluded. Yet, even these items are challenged. Some companies believe that if such items are treated uniformly in relation to total cash or assets, any change of the balance sheet figure is not warranted. On the other hand, certain managers do not accept the stated cash figure but consider a predetermined percentage based on cost — or one related to cost of goods sold, or an amount equal to say one half of the annual operating expenses — as practical for the analysis.

Receivables. Values used for receivables should be either at gross or net of the allowance for uncollectible accounts. The question of deduction of the allowance will be considered in greater detail in connection with fixed assets. At this point one may say that the procedure should be uniform for all receivables allowances. Should the allowance be in excess of actual needs, an adjustment seems appropriate.

Inventories. The several acceptable costing methods, such as fifo, average, or lifo, give rise to some differences when the return ratio is compared with that of other companies in the industry. How such differences should be adjusted or what allowance if any should be made for comparative purposes is difficult to state. Again, if an allowance account is used for lower of cost or market adjustments, the question arises as to whether or not the inventory should be used as net of the allowance. Here, too, uniformity plays a significant role.

Some companies' inventories are costed on a standard cost or direct costing basis. Use of these two bases will, as in the case of lifo, generally depress inventory values on a company's balance sheet. However, for internal comparison the use of either method on a uniform basis should not influence results. The same reasoning applies to other individual company deviations from normal procedures.

The use of capital employed as a base does not consider the sources of the funds. Therefore, liabilities, current or fixed, which provided the money used in the purchase of assets are not deducted from the assets. However, some accountants believe that current liabilities should be deducted from current assets to obtain the figure for working capital to be used in place of the current assets figure.

Fixed Assets.   In dealing with fixed assets, three possible valuation methods have been favored: (1) original cost (original book value), (2) depreciated cost (original cost less the depreciation allowance; i.e., net book value), and (3) estimated replacement value or price level changes. The arguments for the first two bases are summarized below.

Original Cost.   Those accountants favoring the original cost basis argue that:

1. Assets of manufacturing companies, unlike those of mining companies, are considered to be on a continuing rather than on a depleted and abandoned basis.

2. Gross assets of one plant can be compared better with those of another plant where depreciation practices, or the age of the assets, may be different.

3. Accumulated depreciation is not deducted from the gross asset value of property since it represents the retention in business of the funds required to keep intact the stockholders' original investment.   Actually, fixed assets are used to produce net income during their entire life; and, therefore, full cost is considered a sort of investment until the assets are retired from use.

Depreciated Cost.   Those accountants who favor the use of the depreciated cost for fixed assets state the following reasons:

1. While invested capital is conventionally understated at the present time, the wrong method of increasing it cannot be relied on to furnish the right results; and the attempt can only add to the existing confusion in accounting thinking.

2. Cash built up via a depreciation allowance, if added to the gross assets, amounts to overstating the investment.   Fixed assets are shown at net depreciated costs, thus avoiding duplication of assets.

3. An investment is something separate and distinct from the media through which it is made.   The purchase price of a machine should be regarded as the prepaid cost for the number of years of production expected. Each year this number will decline, and the decline should be offset by cash withheld from gross revenues.   The function of depreciation accounting is to maintain the aggregate capital by currently providing substitute assets to replace the aggregate asset consumption (depreciation) of the year.

Replacement Value or Price Level Changes.   Those accountants who state that fixed assets should be included at replacement values, or realizable market values, argue that such values are closest to a realistic approach to the problem.   They believe a company's management receiving a certain and apparently satisfactory return based on book values should face the facts and recognize the situation as being out-of-step with actual conditions.   They further assert that some equalization of facility values

of the different divisions or companies should be provided especially between those with old plants that were built at relatively low cost and those
with new plants that were built at high cost. This method, of course,
poses the serious problem of finding proper values.

Closely allied to any discussion of appropriate fixed asset values, and
particularly the use of current market or replacement values, are considerations as to the effect of price level changes on profits, sales, and, of course,
capital employed. This is neither the time nor place to enter into a lengthy
treatise on the subject. It suffices to state that sales and profits and the
current assets might be measured in current dollar values while the fixed
assets and their expired cost might lag from one to twenty or more years
behind. Perhaps the fixed asset investment, or at least parts of it, should
be translated into current dollars.

General Comments on Determining Capital Employed. Many accountants suggest that the amount of capital employed (total assets) be
averaged over the fiscal period — if possible. Neither the beginning- nor
the end-of-year balance sheet figures, but rather an average figure, might
provide a satisfactory basis of measurement. Such a procedure tends to
equalize unusually high or low year-end asset values or seasonal influences,
particularly in divisional comparisons. Here again, the question of using
gross asset figures or net asset figures poses a problem.

In the last analysis, consistency and uniformity are primary requisites
and their importance cannot be overemphasized. The return on capital
employed, simple as the calculation is, generally deals with a complexity
of operations and/or a great diversity of product lines. Under such
circumstances it seems wise to avoid additional complexity of accounting,
seeking instead clarity in the presentation of operating results without
sacrifice of substance.

Return on Capital Employed as a Divisional Performance Measurement.
The return-on-capital-employed ratio is a valid measure of profitability
for the total company as well as for units and for its products. While a
company's total analysis and comparison with the industry's ratios are
significant for executive management, the real purpose of the return-on-
capital-employed ratio is for internal profit measurement and control.
Trends are more meaningful than percentage ratios. Consistency and
uniformity, mentioned earlier, are of prime importance.

The determination of a rate of return on capital employed at the
departmental or divisional level encounters certain allocation difficulties.
All costs and assets, even those which are not specific to the segment or
product to be measured, must be allocated to it. Unless this is done, the
validity of returns computed for the segments can be questioned. If, for

instance, certain expenses are not allocated, the segments will show a higher return in the aggregate than that of the company. Some users believe that the allocation problem can be solved by simply setting the segment's objectives or desired returns higher than those of the company. This approach might create a psychological dilemma, for it would be difficult to obtain additional effort from the unit supervisory staff when a unit shows a return which is higher or better than the company average. Furthermore, it still does not eliminate the endless arguments against any basis used for cost allocations.

The allocation of sales, costs, and capital employed to segments to be measured is replete with the same fundamental difficulties experienced in the allocation of factory overhead to departments or products. The rationale of overhead expense allocation requires charging costs to the individual who has control over the expenditure. The same reasoning is applicable to this allocation process, for it is necessary to determine the profitability, efficiency, and effectiveness of divisions, departments, or products in terms of return on capital employed.

No one basis of allocation suits every circumstance, but allocation can be expedited by following the method used for overhead distribution. The procedure of overhead allocation for computing overhead rates is threefold: (1) direct departmental expenses are charged to each department, (2) general expenses are prorated to production and service units via certain bases, and (3) service departments' expenses are distributed to the producing departments. This procedure can also be followed with respect to costs applicable to departments or divisions. For product analysis, standard or predetermined costs offer a quick answer to allocation difficulties. This is also true with regard to product sales; however, sales figures usually can be identified directly with specific segments.

The bases of allocation of assets to segments might follow this pattern:

Cash: gross sales billed; cost of goods sold; in ratio to total product cost; a standard percentage of sales or cost of goods sold; manufacturing cost less any noncash items.

Accounts Receivable: direct to segments or products based on gross sales billed; gross sales for the average number of days reflected in receivables.

Raw Materials: direct to segments or products; on the basis of materials consumed; on the basis of annual consumption figures; in ratio to actual or normal usage or standard direct materials cost.

Finished Goods: direct.

Fixed Assets: based on the allocation of depreciation for cost purposes; in ratio to depreciation, preferably first to plant operations and then to product lines based on the use of facilities at either normal, standard, or actual volume. General or service facilities costs, such as the power-house, hospital, machine shop, and plant laboratory, will already have been prorated to products so that the allocation of the investment in these facilities can follow cost. The powerhouse, for instance, producing steam, electricity, and water will be prorated on the basis of pounds of steam used, kilowatts of electricity taken, and gallons of water consumed by each product.

The determination of divisional return on capital is a matter of relating performance to assets placed at the disposal of divisional management. Prevalently, the matter is expressed as the relationship of net operating income to total assets.

Divisional return-on-capital-employed measures have been criticized as a motivational tool because a division may seek to maximize relative profits rather than absolute profits. Assume that a division which is presently earning 30 percent on capital employed is considering a project whose return would be only 25 percent. The divisional management might decline the project because the return on total divisional capital would decrease. Yet, if the acceptance of the project would make the best use of these divisional resources from a total company point of view, then, even with a lower return for the total company, the project should be accepted.

Graphs as Operating Guides. Profits, sales, and capital employed are the three factors in the return-on-capital-employed equation. Sound planning and successful operation must point toward the optimum com-bination of these three factors. As stated earlier, the combination will necessarily vary depending upon the characteristics of the product. The heavy industry with products tailor-made to customers' specifications will have different profit margins and turnover ratios compared to the mass production industries of highly competitive consumer goods. In multiproduct companies the three basic factors cannot be uniform due to different types of operations among products.

However, in order to judge in concrete though flexible terms the per-formance of segments or products in their relationship to a desired overall return on capital employed, a special type of graph can be of immeasurable assistance. The graph on page 879 shows possible combinations of per-centage of profit to sales and capital-employed turnover rate which yield a 20 percent return. It has the advantage of flexibility in appraising profit performance and also offers an approach by which performance can be analyzed for improvement.

A 20 percent return permits numerous combinations of the underlying factors. When individual divisions, departments, or products are plotted on the graph, the segment's data might appear to the left or right of the

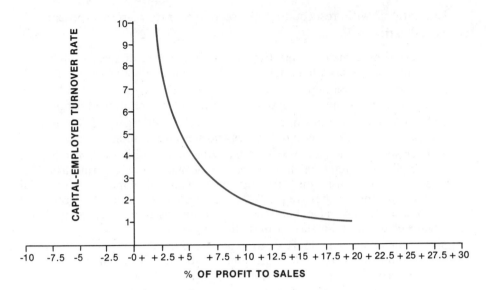

Graph Illustrating the Relationship Between the % of
Profit to Sales and the Capital-Employed Turnover Rate
(Based on a 20% Rate of Return on Capital Employed)

basic curve. If on the left, the unit has a substandard capital-employed-return performance below that expected for the company as a whole. A segment whose ratios appear to the right of the basic curve produces a return in excess of that expected for the entire company. The same interpretation applies when the company's total return is plotted.

Advantages and Limitations of the Use of the Rate of Return on Capital Employed for Internal Profit Measurement. Advantages of the use of the rate of return on capital employed lie in its tendency to:

1. Focus management's attention upon earning the best profit possible on the capital (total assets) available.

2. Serve as a yardstick in measuring management's efficiency and effectiveness in managing the company as a whole and its major divisions or departments.

3. Tie together the many phases of financial planning, sales objectives, cost control, and the profit goal.

4. Afford comparison of managerial results both internally and externally.

5. Develop a keener sense of responsibility and team effort in divisional and departmental managers by enabling them to measure and evaluate their own activities in the light of the results achieved by other managers.

6. Aid in detecting weaknesses with respect to the use or nonuse of individual assets particularly in connection with inventories.

Limitations with respect to the use of the rate-of-return-on-capital-employed ratio are:

1. Lack of agreement on the right or optimum rate of return might discourage managers whose opinion is that the rate is set at an unfair level.
2. Proper allocation requires certain data regarding sales, costs, and assets. The accounting and cost system might not give such needed details.
3. Values and valuations of assets, particularly with regard to jointly used assets, might give rise to difficulties and misunderstandings.
4. Excessive preoccupation with financial factors due to constant attention to ratios and trends might distract management's interest from technical and other responsibilities. Product research and development, managerial development, progressive personnel policies, good employee morale, and good customer and public relations are just as important in earning a greater profit and assuring continuous growth.
5. Managers may be influenced to make decisions that are not the best for the long-run interests of the firm merely for the sake of making the current period rate of return on capital employed "look good."
6. A *single* measure of performance (e.g., return on capital employed) may result in a fixation on improving the components of the one measure to the neglect of needed attention to other desirable activities — both short- and long-run.

Return on Capital Employed as a Tool for Planning and Decision Making. Budgeting is the principal planning and control technique employed by most companies. Among the multiple phases of budgeting, sales forecasting is still considered the most difficult task in profit planning. Assuming that an acceptable sales budget has been established and production, manufacturing, and commercial expense budgets have been prepared, break-even analyses and return-on-capital-employed ratios are useful in evaluating the entire planning procedure.

Management's objectives or goals with respect to the long-range return, as well as the immediate returns for each division, plant, or product, influence and guide budget-building procedures. As sales, costs, and assets employed are placed in the perspective of the rate of return on capital employed as envisioned by management, the attitude of the lower echelon responsible for assembling the figures undergoes a marked change. Divisional or departmental budgets are compared with predetermined goals. If too low, examination and revision can perhaps achieve the desired result unless it is unattainable. If an unusually excellent return is calculated, the reasons for it can be investigated. Management can either accept the situation as is because of one-time favorable circumstances or decide on a temporary modification of its planning goal. At any rate, the return on capital employed offers a most satisfactory foundation for the construction of both annual and long-range planning budgets. When considering long-range plans regarding addition of new products, dropping of old products, expansion of production facilities, or investing additional capital in research and development, application of the return on capital employed on any future projects always has a sobering effect if these projects have been conceived haphazardly or overoptimistically.

A successful technique in planning for profit improvement is to: (1) define quantitatively (for sales, profits, and capital employed) the gap which exists between performance at present and that represented by long-term objectives; (2) fix the problems precisely by examining the details of each factor; (3) formulate a specific scheduled program of action for each; and (4) translate the planned results of each program in terms of its effect upon income and asset accounts.

The effect of planned programs on assets, profit, and return on capital employed is shown below.

EFFECT OF PLANNED PROGRAMS FOR PROFIT IMPROVEMENT

	Present		Change by Volume	Change by Cost Reduction	Asset Curtail-ment	Future	
Assets:							
Inventory......	$ 500,000				$100,000−	$ 400,000	
Other current assets........	200,000		$ 20,000+			220,000	
Fixed assets....	300,000			$80,000+		380,000	
Total assets..	$1,000,000		$ 20,000+	$80,000+	$100,000−	$1,000,000	
Profit:							
Sales billed.....	$1,000,000	100.0%	$200.000+			$1,200,000	100.0%
Manufacturing costs.........	$ 770,000	77.0%	$140,000+	$88,000−		$ 822,000	68.5%
Marketing and administrative expenses.....	130,000	13.0	10,000+	2,000−		138,000	11.5
Total costs and expenses.....	$ 900,000	90.0%	$150,000			$ 960,000	80.0%
Net operating profit.......	$ 100,000	10.0%	$ 50,000+	$90,000+		$ 240,000	20.0%
Return on capital employed:							
% of profit to sales........		10.0%					20.0%
Capital-em-ployed turn-over rate (times).......		1.0					1.2
Return on capital em-ployed (%)...		10.0%					24.0%

Information Value of Return-on-Capital-Employed Concept. Whether it is used for a top executive, plant or product manager, plant engineer, salesperson, or accountant, the return-on-capital-employed concept tends to mesh the interest of the entire organization. This one figure acts not only as a measurement of the cooperative efforts of a company's divisions and segments but also shows the extent to which profitable coordination exists. A company's interlocking efforts are never more effectively demonstrated than by this rate.

Return-on-capital-employed information provides an executive with a brief yet comprehensive picture of the true status of all operations in every plant and for every major product line. The plant manager receives a statement which definitely measures the plant's operating results in the one figure for which he is responsible. The product engineer's opportunities and responsibilities are centered in the creation of a product which can be manufactured at minimum cost and sold in profitable quantities without an abnormal increase in the asset investments. The salesperson realizes that price changes, justified as they seem, are only effective if they contain a profit increment which yields an adequate return. An appreciation of the return-on-capital-employed concept by all employees will build an organization interested in achieving fair profits and an adequate rate of return.

Multiple Performance Measurements. There is danger in undue fixation on a single measure of performance whether for the entire company or for its individual divisions. The result may be emphasis on improving the components of the one measure (e.g., return on capital employed) to the neglect of needed attention to other desirable activities — both in the short- and long-run. Accordingly, many well-managed companies use multiple performance measurements.

One company using multiple measurements for divisional performance rating describes its method as a quantification of progress against agreed-upon standards and feels that it provides good, prudent measures of operating results.[1] Each year common standards are adopted by agreement of divisional managers and corporate management. *Points* are assigned to standards, reflecting those areas determined by management which require special attention in each division.

The measures of performance are in three broad areas:

1. Profits for the current year are compared to the profits for the preceding year in absolute dollars, margins, and return on capital employed.
2. Profits are compared to the budget.

---

[1]Frank J. Tanzola, "Performance Rating for Divisional Control," *Financial Executive*, Vol. XLIII, No. 3, pp. 20–24.

3. Cash and capital management measures are employed. Here, the emphasis is on effective management of inventory and receivables.

The claimed advantages are that:

1. Performance of division managers is more fairly measured than would result from using solely a return-on-capital-employed figure.
2. Management can readily see those divisions which are performing well and those divisions which are not performing so well.
3. Lost points serve as "red flags" by directing management's attention to areas requiring attention and to the reasons and the corrective actions taken or needed.
4. The system has flexibility as to timely, needed shifting of management emphasis.

Company management in this example concludes that it is not enough merely to tabulate performance statistics. The results must be effectively communicated, corrective action must be taken, and good performance must be rewarded. The system must also have the interest and support of division and corporate management.

INTRACOMPANY TRANSFER PRICING

The effectiveness of the use of the return on capital employed as a device for measuring the performance of divisional segments of a company depends considerably on the accuracy of allocating the costs and assets associated with the unit, segment, or product. Decentralized operating divisions become separate financial entities. A shift to and emphasis of the return-on-capital-employed concept for measuring operational performance requires some rather fundamental policy changes. In an effectively decentralized multiplant or multiproduct organization, the unit manager is expected to run his portion of the enterprise as a semiautonomous business. As long as his unit, segment, or product is not entirely independent and separable, goods and services are generally transferred from one unit to another, a situation common to integrated corporations. The finished or semifinished product of one or more divisions or subsidiaries frequently becomes the raw material of one or more other divisions. Besides, some service functions are centralized and might conceivably deal with a number of profit centers. When transfers of goods or services are made, a portion of the *revenue* of one profit center becomes a portion of *cost* of another; and the price at which transfers are made influences the earnings reported by each profit center. Whatever pricing system is used can distort any reported profit and make it a poor guide for operating decisions. In the end the cost or price used for the transfer will find its way into the calculation of the return on capital employed due to the very nature of the formula.

The arbitrary nature of intracompany transfer pricing is one reason for criticism of proposals to report segment or product-line revenues and profits in published financial statements. A steel company may operate a coal mine and sell some of its output on the open market but use the remainder in its own steel mills. The coal's transfer price can control whether the Mining Division shows a large, small, or zero profit.

External factors may influence the transfer price determination. A company with an overseas plant, where tax rates are low, may keep the transfer price high for materials sent to the domestic facility in order to retain profits abroad. Or a company with warehouses in a state with an inventory tax may keep transfer prices low on goods brought into the state in order to reduce its tax bill.[2]

Years ago transfer pricing played only a minor role, chiefly as part of a cost accounting system for the purpose of cost control. Today the technique of transfer pricing has expanded into a complex set of procedures in the administration of the decentralized segments of an enterprise. The existence of multiple management objectives makes it extremely difficult for a company to establish logical and sound intracompany transfer prices. A pricing method can be chosen only after the primary purposes for the use of the information from transfers has been identified.

In a totally centralized firm, executive management basically makes all decisions with respect to the operations of the divisions. This centralized profit responsibility makes cost control responsibility the basis for measuring a manager's performance. A cost-based transfer price is usually sufficient in this situation. This type of pricing or charging is discussed in Chapter 11 ("Responsibility Accounting and Responsibility Reporting") in connection with interplant or intraplant service charges for work of an indirect nature completed for another department or plant.

Service charges may consist of actual materials costs, actual labor costs, and related overhead costs. Even more effectively, a service charging rate should have been established in advance of the work performed so that servicing and benefiting departments or plants know in advance the costs connected with these services. A company without any integration processes (i.e., having only one process, or even more than one process) might have so little volume of intracompany transfers that it would be too time-consuming and costly to price the transfer at any other than cost value.

In a totally decentralized corporation, a division's or profit center's monthly or annual profit is generally used as a basis for evaluating managerial performance, determining managers' bonuses, and calculating profit-sharing percentages. The value of the final profit as a measuring stick

---

[2] "The Numbers Game," *Forbes*, Vol. 114, No. 3, pp. 37–38.

depends not only upon the manager's executive abilities but also upon the transfer prices used. The establishment of proper transfer prices must satisfy these three fundamental criteria: (1) allow central management to judge as accurately as possible the performance of the divisional profit center in terms of its separate contribution to the total corporate profit, (2) motivate the divisional manager to pursue the division's own profit goal in a manner conducive to the success of the company as a whole, and (3) serve as stimuli to increase the manager's efficiency without losing the division's autonomy as a profit center.[3] In their theoretical setting, the three criteria express a very sound approach. As a practical matter, it might not be that simple. Behaviorial considerations are of paramount importance. Accordingly, a transfer price should be a just price to the selling and to the buying party. Any advantage gained by one will be a disadvantage to the other and, at the end, may be detrimental to the corporate profit goal.

In the last analysis, the profit center manager's interest must remain congruent with the firm's interest. For example, assume that Division X offers its Product A to Division Y at a transfer price of $14, which includes a $2 profit, a $9 variable cost, and a $3 fixed cost (which presumably will remain unchanged in total as activity fluctuates). The same product is also available from an outside supplier at $11. Division Y, acting to minimize its costs, will prefer to purchase Product A at the lower external price of $11. However, such a decision would not be congruent with the best interests of the total firm, which would be spending $11 rather than $9, the variable cost (and, in this example, the differential cost since the total fixed cost is assumed not to change). This analysis assumes that from the total firm point of view no more profitable use could be made of the Division X facilities used in supplying Product A to Division Y. If the intracompany transfer is desirable for the firm, there still remains the task of establishing a just transfer price for both divisions for divisional performance measurement.

Therefore, a transfer pricing system must be designed that can be judged in terms of its usefulness for divisional performance evaluation, for decision making that is in the best interest of the *total* firm, for efficient divisional autonomy as well as for its ease of application, and for meeting of legal and external reporting requirements. No one method of transfer pricing can effectively satisfy all of the requirements.

The best transfer price can be defined only as it is best for a particular purpose. Four basic methods of pricing intracompany transfers are reviewed: (1) transfer pricing based on cost, (2) market-based transfer pricing, (3) negotiated transfer pricing, and (4) arbitrary transfer pricing.

[3]Joshua Ronen and George McKinney, III, "Transfer Pricing for Divisional Autonomy," *Journal of Accounting Research*, Vol. 8, No. 1, pp. 99–112.

Transfer Pricing Based on Cost. Cost-based pricing is widely used in strongly centralized companies. The cost figure may be actual, standard, direct, or differential. (The cost figure selected may be quite similar to that described on pages 290–291, "The 'Billing' or 'Sold-Hour' Rate of a Service Department.") The company's cost system should permit the computation of a product's unit cost, even at various stages of production (see process costing Chapters 6 and 7). The cost method's primary advantage is simplicity in that it avoids the elimination of intracompany profits from inventories in consolidated financial statements and tax returns. Differential cost is especially useful in decision-making analyses while actual (absorption) cost is generally used in preparing financial statements for external users. The transferred cost can readily be used to measure production efficiency by comparing actual with budgeted costs. Finally, the method allows simple and adequate end-product costing for profit analysis by product lines.

Considering the disadvantages, a transfer price based on cost is not suited to companies with a decentralized structure which needs to measure the profitability of autonomous units. Also, the producing department may not be sufficiently conscientious in controlling costs that are to be transferred. The use of standard costs for transfer pricing may alleviate this problem. A transfer price based on cost lacks not only utility in the field of divisional planning, motivating, and evaluating to operate efficiently but also the objectivity required of a good performance standard of a market-based transfer price.

Market-Based Transfer Pricing. The market-based transfer price is usually identical with the one charged to outside customers, therby making it the best profitability and performance measurement. Divisional operations are on a competitive basis with the same price charged for external and internal customers. Some companies apply a discount to the market price, reflecting economics resulting from intracompany trading. The method reflects product profitability and division management performance, aids in future planning, and is generally required by foreign tariff laws.

The most serious drawback to this method is the requirement for a well-developed outside competitive market. Unfortunately, a market price is not always determinable for intermediate products. Also, the market-based price adds an element of profit or loss with each transfer of product and therewith complicates the accounting procedures. Thus, the transfer of a product by this method makes a determination of the actual cost of the final product difficult when the product itself has passed through numerous manufacturing stages.

In analyzing a study of practice made by the National Industrial Conference Board on *Interdivisional Transfer Pricing*, Sharav observes that:

> In most cases of vertical transfers (between units at different stages of the manufacturing and marketing process), where the transferring division is viewed as a cost center, its transfer will be priced at cost. However, where the transferer is a profit center, . . . the transfer price may include a profit factor thus approximating outside market prices. [However,] . . . Horizontal transfers (transferer and transferee are situated at the same stage of the production and marketing process) are usually executed at cost, which may, of course, include freight and handling charges.
>
> . . . companies using cost-based transfer prices choose in many cases actual costs which are derived from divisional operating statements and underlying cost records. Often, where available, standard or budgeted costs are employed. In contrast to the preference expressed in the literature, marginal [differential] costs are used by only a few companies.
>
> A modified version of cost is the so-called cost-plus transfer price. It is comprised of cost plus a markup that is meant to provide a return on investment in divisional assets. Much less frequently used, this transfer price may be applied in lieu of the hard-to-establish market price.[4]

Negotiated Transfer Pricing.   The negotiated transfer price is used in the absence of a competitive outside market. It is felt that the setting of the price by negotiation between buying and selling divisions allows unit managers the greatest degree of authority and control over the profit of their units. A serious problem encountered with this method is that negotiation can not only become very time-consuming but can also require frequent reexamination and revision of prices. Often the negotiated price diverts the efforts of the manager from activities promoting company welfare to those affecting divisional results only.

Arbitrary Transfer Pricing.   An arbitrary transfer price has been used quite frequently in the past. The price usually set arbitrarily by executive management is at a level considered best for overall company interests with neither the buying nor selling units having any control over the final decision. The method's disadvantages far outweigh any kind of advantage. It can defeat the most important purpose of decentralizing profit responsibility (namely, making divisional personnel profit conscious) and severely hampers the profit incentive of unit managers.

Dual Transfer Pricing Approach.   The consuming (buying) and producing (selling) divisions may differ in the purpose a transfer price is to serve. For example, a consuming division may rely on a transfer price in make-or-buy decisions or in determining a final product's sales price based on an awareness of total differential costs. A producing division

---

[4]Itzhak Sharav, "Transfer Pricing — Diversity of Goals and Practices," *The Journal of Accountancy*, Vol. 137, No. 4, p. 59.

may use a transfer price to measure its divisional performance and, accordingly, would argue against any price that would not provide a producing division profit.

In such circumstances, a company may find it useful to adopt a dual transfer pricing approach in which the:

1. Producing division uses a market-based, negotiated, or arbitrary transfer price in computing its revenues from intracompany sales.

2. Variable costs of the producing division are transferred to the purchasing division, together with an equitable portion of fixed costs.

3. Total of the divisional profits will be greater than for the company as a whole, and the profit assigned to the producing division would be eliminated in preparing company-wide financial statements.

Under this system, a producing division would continue to have a profit inducement to expand sales and production, both externally and internally. Yet, the consuming divisions would not be misled; their costs would be the firm's actual costs and would not include an artificial profit. Variable costs, as well as fixed costs, should be associated with the purchase to ensure that the consuming division is aware of the total cost implications. Of course, the benefits from a dual transfer pricing approach can be achieved only if the underlying cost data are accurate and reliable.[5]

General Observations on Transfer Pricing. As long as measuring the performance of areas of managerial responsibility remains one of management's primary objectives, intracompany transfer pricing should permit each unit of a company to earn a profit commensurate with the functions it performs.[6] Experience shows that earnings attributable to individual profit responsibilities are best measured by transfer prices based upon values established in a competitive market. However, regardless of what transfer price is used for divisional performance measurement, the differential costs of goods transferred from division to division should be known and used for decision-making purposes.[7]

---

[5]Adapted from Richard B. Troxel, "On Transfer Pricing," *Management Controls*, Vol. XX, No. 7, pp. 160–162.

[6]The transfer pricing methods employed in the meat industry can be studied in the brochure *Financial Planning and Control in the Meat Industry*, prepared by Price Waterhouse & Co. in cooperation with the Accounting Committee, American Meat Institute (Chicago, Illinois, 1967), pp. 142–143.

[7]For further study, the nature and scope of several major transfer pricing models categorized as to (1) the economic theory of the firm, (2) mathematical programming approaches, and (3) other analytical approaches are covered in A. Rashed Abdel-khalik and Edward J. Lusk, "Transfer Pricing — A Synthesis," *The Accounting Review*, Vol. XLIX, No. 1, pp. 8–23.

PRODUCT PRICING METHODS

Product pricing is a complex subject and is neither a one-person nor a one-activity job. Theorists and practitioners differ on various pricing theories. In practice, the solution to a pricing problem becomes a research job that requires the cooperation and coordination of the economist, statistician, market specialist, industrial engineer, and accountant. Since the determination of a sales price requires consideration of many factors, some of which defy measurement or control, prudent and practical judgment is necessary. Accountants can provide executive management and marketing managers with mileposts to be used as guides when traveling the relatively uncharted road toward successful pricing.

The relationship between costs and prices is not only one of the most difficult for a businessperson to determine, but its final determination can have social and even political implications. Price setting is that field of business in which management truly becomes an art. A selling price, generally thought of as the rate of exchange between two commodities, is determined in many industries in a manner that gives individual companies some degree of control over the price. This is particularly true when a company is the sole manufacturer of a particular product. Even companies that experience a great deal of competition have some measure of control, for the products they sell may be different, the quality may vary, or the services rendered may differ. Although a firm may exercise some control over selling prices, the costs incurred in order to do business are usually more within its control.

Prices may be influenced not only by competition but also by what customers are willing to pay and by governmental regulations and controls. The Robinson-Patman Act must be complied with to avoid alleged price discrimination. Even if a company has little or no control over a selling price, it faces the question of whether or not it can operate profitably at the price that can be charged. In order to determine adequate profit expectations, costs must be known and used as building blocks to determine the minimum price required to justify entering or continuing in a given market.

Costs are generally considered to be the starting point in a pricing situation even though a rigid relationship is not expected to exist. Prices and pricing policy vary in relation to costs and volume as well as to the selection of a long- or short-range view. The long-run approach allows change in products, manufacturing methods, plant capacity, and marketing and distribution methods. It aims to obtain prices which will return all or full costs and provide an adequate return on the capital invested. A normal or average product cost is the basis used for long-range pricing. A short-range pricing policy looks toward the recovery of at least part of the total cost to meet changing needs resulting from fluctuating sales volume, sales mix, and prices. In such cases, the differential cost of a product may serve as a guide for the determination of prices. Variable costs are the principal source of cost differentials which must be computed in such pricing problems (see Chapters 22 and 25).

The accountant's assistance to management in the highly important field of pricing products requires a profound knowledge and recognition of all cost items as well as inventory costing methods as they flow through the cost accounting cycle (see Chapter 12).

The development of an imagination that appreciates and understands the economic and political forces at play is required of the accountant. He or she must not only be an economist but also be an investment analyst and must be able to see problems through management's eyes. By doing so, the accountant in reality becomes a vital part of management with cost accounting as a necessary tool.

Methods Used for Determining Selling Prices. Even though price-setting procedures are difficult, methods are available that will assist in the computation and determination of sales prices. The following methods will be discussed: (1) profit maximization — relating total revenues with total costs, (2) pricing based on a return on capital employed, (3) conversion cost pricing, (4) contribution margin and the differential cost approach to pricing, and (5) standard costs for pricing.

Profit Maximization—Relating Total Revenues with Total Costs. The aim and purpose of most business enterprises is to obtain a price that contributes the largest amount to its profit. Economic theorists describe this as *profit maximization.* The profit return on each unit sold is not so important as the total return realized from all units sold. The price that yields the largest profit at a certain volume is the price to be charged to a consumer.

The schedule below shows variable costs at $7 per unit with fixed costs at $300,000 for all ranges of output. The most profitable selling price is $14 per unit with a contribution margin of $560,000 and with a net income of $260,000 after deducting fixed costs.

Selling Price Per Unit	Number of Units To Be Sold	Total Sales Volume	Variable Costs ($7 Per Unit)	Fixed Costs	Net Income (Loss)
$20	20,000	$ 400,000	$140,000	$300,000	$ (40,000)
18	40,000	720,000	280,000	300,000	140,000
16	60,000	960,000	420,000	300,000	240,000
14*	80,000	1,120,000	560,000	300,000	260,000
12	100,000	1,200,000	700,000	300,000	200,000
10	120,000	1,200,000	840,000	300,000	60,000
8	140,000	1,120,000	980,000	300,000	(160,000)

*Most profitable selling price.

Profit maximization is not to be looked upon as the immediate return expected, but rather as a goal to be realized over several months or even years. However, during these months and years sales policies, competition, customers' practices, cost changes, and other economic or even political influences might radically alter all previous presuppositions.

Pricing Based on a Return on Capital Employed. This procedure attempts to develop a price required to yield a predetermined or desired rate of return on capital employed. The method illustrated below, based on a percentage markup on cost, will yield a given rate of return:

$$\text{Percentage Markup on Cost} = \frac{\text{Capital Employed}}{\text{Total Annual Costs}} \times \frac{\text{The Desired Rate of}}{\text{Return on Capital Employed}}$$

$$\text{Percentage Markup on Cost} = \frac{\$20,000,000}{\$ 5,000,000} \times 20\% = \underline{\underline{80\%}}$$

$$\frac{\text{Sales}}{\text{Volume}} = \frac{\text{Total Annual}}{\text{Costs}} + \frac{\text{Percentage Markup}}{\text{on Cost}} \times \frac{\text{Total Annual}}{\text{Costs}}$$

$$\frac{\text{Sales}}{\text{Volume}} = \$5,000,000 + (80\% \times \$5,000,000)$$
$$= \$5,000,000 + \$4,000,000* = \underline{\underline{\$9,000,000}}$$

---

*Or, $\$4,000,000 = 20\%$ (Desired Rate of Return on Capital Employed) $\times \$20,000,000$ (Capital Employed).

A formula[8] that gives specific effect to variations in the amount of capital required to support differing sales volume is:

$$\text{Price} = \frac{\dfrac{\text{Total Costs} + (\% \text{ Desired Return} \times \text{Fixed Assets})}{\text{Sales Volume in Units}}}{1 - (\% \text{ Desired Return} \times \% \text{ Current Assets to Sales})}$$

This formula assumes that the capital employed, particularly cash, accounts receivable, and inventories, varies in direct proportion with sales. The NAA Research Report No. 35 states that "a possible objection to the above method is that a change in selling price, by itself, would have no direct effect on the investment in inventory since the latter is stated at cost. This objection can be avoided by introducing inventory as a ratio to factory cost rather than as a ratio to selling price."

The preceding formula can be stated and illustrated in an equivalent— yet much simpler — form. Assume that a single-product company's total

---

[8]"Return on Capital Employed as a Guide to Managerial Decisions," *NAA Research Report No. 35*, p. 44.

costs are $210,000, that the total capital employed is $200,000, that the sales volume is 50,000 units, and that the desired rate of return on capital employed is 20%. The formula used and the resultant determination of the product's selling price would be:

$$\text{Price} = \frac{\text{Total Costs} + (\% \text{ Desired Return} \times \text{Total Capital Employed})}{\text{Sales Volume in Units}}$$

$$\text{Price} = \frac{\$210,000 + (20\% \times \$200,000)}{50,000 \text{ units}} = \frac{\$250,000}{50,000 \text{ units}} = \underline{\underline{\$5}}$$

Proof: Sales (50,000 units × $5)................... $250,000
       Less total costs...........................   210,000

       Net Income............................... $ 40,000

       $200,000 capital employed × 20%........... $ 40,000

Pricing procedures using capital employed as part of the pricing formula are, however, much more complex than illustrated above. The illustrations assume no change in capital employed. Actually, as prices and costs change, capital employed may be expected to change; with an increase, more cash will be required to serve the business; with higher prices, accounts receivable will be higher; and inventory costs will increase in ratio to increases in factory costs. Decreases would have the reverse effect.

A company's pricing decision based on the rate of return on capital employed, standard costs, and estimated plant capacity offers management one of the most advanced methods for control and analysis.

Conversion Cost Pricing. This pricing method attempts to direct management's attention to the amount of work or services that products require when being produced. Work and services constitute labor costs and factory overhead, respectively, and are known as "conversion costs."

Assume that a company manufactures two products, each selling for $10. The manufacturing cost for each is $9, resulting in a gross profit of $1 per unit, indicating that from a profit point of view it does not matter which product is promoted. However, a breakdown of the costs reveals the following:

Items of Cost	*Product A*	*Product B*
Direct materials................................	$ 6	$ 3
Direct labor....................................	2	4
Factory overhead...............................	1	2
Total manufacturing costs......................	$ 9	$ 9
Selling price...................................	10	10
Gross profit	$ 1	$ 1

The cost breakdown indicates that Product A requires only half the labor required by Product B. Factory overhead is, likewise, one half that required for Product B.

If it were possible to shift all efforts to Product A, a greater number of units could be produced and sold with the same gross profit per unit. Marketing costs of Product A versus Product B must also be considered. Of course, any volume increase might disturb the market equilibrium and even cause a drop in the price because of increased supply. These difficulties are discussed in the break-even and cost-volume-profit analysis chapter.

Contribution Margin and the Differential Cost Approach to Pricing. Chapter 22 ("Direct Costing and the Contribution Margin") and Chapter 25 ("Differential Cost Analysis") deal in considerable detail with this phase of costing and pricing. In direct costing, the contribution margin figure (excess of sales over variable costs) indicates a product's or a product line's contribution to the recovery of fixed costs and to profit. The fixed and variable cost classification permits an evaluation of each product by a comparison of specific contribution margins. While this contribution margin approach might be used for a firm's entire business, it is of even greater value in the analysis of its divisions, plants, products, product lines, customers, territories, etc. The latter phase was discussed in Chapter 23 ("Marketing Cost and Profitability Analysis").

The differential cost of an order is the variable cost necessary to produce the additional units, plus additional fixed costs (if any) at the new production level. If the cost of the additional units is accepted as a basis for pricing them, any price over and above total differential cost would be acceptable. This procedure is, of course, applicable only to the additional units.

To base selling prices on differential cost requires careful scrutiny of all related factors. For example, long-run sales promotion cannot be permitted to shift to a product priced on the basis of differential costs where total cost recovery and a reasonable profit will not result.

Standard Costs for Pricing. If cost estimates used for pricing purposes are prepared on the basis of the standard costs for materials, labor, and factory overhead, the task of the accountant preparing the estimate and of the executive using the data to set the price will be aided considerably. The use of standard costs in preparing cost information for pricing purposes makes costs more quickly available and reduces clerical detail. As a standard cost represents the cost that should be attained in an efficiently operating plant at normal capacity, it is essential, once the sales price has been established, that the cost department furnish up-to-the-minute information to all parties to make certain that the cost stays within the range set by the estimate. Any deviation between actual and standard costs should come to light for quick action through the accounting information system.

The use of standard costs for pricing purposes divides itself into two broad categories: (1) the use of standard costs for setting catalog prices and (2) the use of standard costs for bid prices on individual orders.

The National Association of Accountants in one of its bulletins stated that "companies can be divided into four groups with respect to the type of cost figures which they supply to pricing executives. These groups are composed of:

1. Companies which supply pricing executives with standard costs without application of any adjustments to the standards.

2. Companies in which costs supplied to the pricing executives are standard costs adjusted by the ratio of actual costs to standard costs as shown by the variance accounts.

3. Companies which use current market prices for materials, and in a few cases for labor, together with standard costs for other elements of product cost when preparing pricing costs.

4. Companies which adjust their standard costs to reflect actual costs which are anticipated during the period for which the prices are to be in effect."[9]

Where standard costs are used for bid prices, they might be based on estimates previously submitted. However, while some materials parts or labor operations might be identical with those used for another product, pricing executives need the most up-to-date information on all cost components in order to set a profitable price. Companies that must present bids adjust the costs developed from the detailed standards to approximate actual costs expected. The separation between fixed and variable expenses is considered a "must" for pricing purposes.

Use of Cost Data in Making Pricing Decisions. Regardless of the pricing method employed, an estimated cost statement is still required in order to supply management with all the costs needed for sound pricing. The cost estimate must be as reliable as possible and might take the form shown on page 895.

This estimating cost sheet makes use of the following cost principles which must be regarded as fundamental for an orderly pricing procedure:

1. Manufacturing costs detailed as to materials, labor, and overhead

2. Factory overhead cost divided into its fixed and variable elements

3. Marketing costs consisting of cost of shipping and cost of selling

[9]Research Series, No. 14, "Standard Manufacturing Costs for Pricing and Budgeting," *NAA Bulletin*, Vol. XXX, No. 3, pp. 165–166.

4. Development cost segregated to allow for a clear-cut distinction between costs to be incurred for this order and repetitive engineering costs

5. General administrative cost to include a portion of the salaries of the chief executive, his assistants, and other office personnel

6. Profit consisting of two parts:
   a. Return on invested capital, called interest
   b. Return for the risk of the enterprise

ESTIMATING COST SHEET [10]

Manufacturing cost:
Materials:

Invoice cost......................................		$1,000
Freight..		10
Receiving and handling...........................		60
Total materials cost.............................		$1,070

Producing:

Direct labor.....................................	$ 730	
Overhead — variable..............................	500	
fixed............................	1,100	
Total producing cost.............................		2,330
Provision for scrap losses		47
Total manufacturing cost		$3,447

Marketing, development, and general administrative cost:
Shipping:

Materials..	$200	
Packing & shipping		
Direct labor.................................	50	
Overhead.....................................	40	
Total shipping cost..............................	$ 290	
Selling cost @ 10% of producing cost	233	
Total marketing cost.............................		523
Development cost.................................		500
General administrative cost at 4% of producing cost...........		93
Total cost.......................................		$4,563

Profit:
Interest on invested capital:

Invested capital.................................	$61,156	
5% for normal annual interest..................	3,058	
16,200 normal hours = $.19 per hr.		
Interest on 852 hours for the job...............	$ 162	
5% provision for stockholders' risk.............	162	324
Total provision for normal profit		$4,887

Selling price for the job:

Estimated _____ Date _____ By_____			$4,887
Established ceiling...............................			5,500
Competitive price................................			None
Quoted _____ Date _____ By _____			5,500

---

[10]A. E. Grover, "Problems Involved in Pricing Postwar Products," *NAA Bulletin*, Vol. XXVII, No. 11, p. 486.

The inclusion of interest on investment requires the determination of an equitable interest rate. In the cost sheet on page 895, interest is based on an invested capital of $61,156 which represents the value of those assets to be utilized by this order. With a 5 percent rate, the interest is $3,058. An assumption that the equipment to be used on this job has an annual production volume of 16,200 hours results in an hourly rate of $.19 ($3,058 ÷ 16,200 hours). The job contemplated will use the equipment for 852 hours, resulting in an interest cost of $162 (852 hours × $.19).

The entrepreneurial risk, also based on 5 percent, results in the same amount ($162). From the estimate it is apparent that the profit resulting from interest and risk taking is $324. However, as the ceiling price is considered the competitive price, an additional $613 ($5,500 — $4,887) is added to the $324, resulting in a total profit of $937. Many authorities consider this the ideal type of pricing, because the $613 is looked upon as a cushion against orders that must be taken at a loss. It is difficult to state whether such an attitude toward a pricing procedure is always desirable and acceptable. If the trend seems to be toward a situation where costs have a distinct influence upon pricing, this type of opportunity profit is ruled out.

Adjustments of Contemplated Selling Price Because of Competition. If in the above illustration the company's competitor enters the market with an identical product priced at only $4,000, the question arises as to what cost concessions could be made. This price is $1,500 below the ceiling price and $887 below the price estimated to cover all costs and minimum profit. With the aid of the estimating cost sheet, possible concessions can be determined:

"(1) The $162 of normal interest on invested capital may be eliminated.

(2) The $162 for stockholders' risk may be eliminated.

(3) The $93 of general administrative cost may be conceded.

(4) The $233 of selling cost chargeable to this job may be eliminated.

(5) $237, or 21.5% of the $1,100 fixed overhead, may be taken out.

These concessions total $887, or approximately 18% of the total estimated selling price. If the company is operating at less than the established normal hours and the $887 represents only profit and fixed expenses, perhaps a new adjusted sales price of $4,000 is justified, as it would return all the out-of-pocket costs and a part of the fixed expenses. However, if the company is operating the plant at normal capacity, the best interests of the company can be served by refusing to bid on this type of business, provided some use of the facilities is available that will offer a greater contribution."[11]

---

[11] *Ibid.*, p. 491.

DISCUSSION QUESTIONS

1. The terminology "return on investment" has been confusing, for it has been used indiscriminately to describe two different types of financial measurement. Discuss.
2. What items are generally included in the term "capital employed"?
3. How is the return on capital employed computed?
4. Rate of return on capital employed is a common measure of management's performance. The rate can be expressed as the product of two factors: the percentage of profit to sales and the capital-employed turnover rate. What management activities are measured by each of these factors?

   (NAA adapted)

5. State two major objectives that management may have in mind when setting up a system for measuring the return on divisional capital employed.
6. In measuring the return on capital, some accountants have argued that capital employed should be measured by gross assets without any deduction for depreciation. Others believe that only net assets offer the true basis for measuring the investment. Discuss.
7. An integral part of the return-on-capital-employed equation is the percentage of profit to sales. The use of this percentage in connection with the equation involves a whole series of factors which must be taken into consideration. Name some of the factors that will affect this percentage.
8. Name and discuss the four basic methods of pricing intracompany transfers.
9. Explain the dual transfer pricing approach in intracompany transfer pricing.
10. Discuss the statement, "Price setting is truly an art."
11. What methods are available that might assist and permit the computation and determination of a sales price cost-accounting-wise?
12. Discuss profit maximization, relating total revenues with total costs.
13. Why are standard costs considered helpful in setting prices?
14. Select the correct answer for each of the following statements.
    (a) In order to evaluate the performance of each department, interdepartmental transfers of a product preferably should be made at prices (1) equal to the market price of the product; (2) set by the receiving department; (3) equal to fully allocated costs to the producing department; (4) equal to variable costs to the producing department.
    (b) In a decentralized company in which divisions may buy goods from one another, the transfer pricing system should be designed primarily to (1) increase the consolidated value of inventory; (2) prevent division managers from buying from outsiders; (3) minimize the degree of autonomy of division managers; (4) aid in the appraisal and motivation of managerial performance.
    (c) With other variables remaining constant, the rate of return on capital employed of a merchandising company will increase with a decrease in (1) sales; (2) inventory turnover; (3) the profit margin; (4) the investment in inventory.

    (AICPA adapted)

EXERCISES

1. Return on Capital Employed. During the past year the Lorraine Waterworks Company had a net income after taxes of $40,000. Net sales were $200,000, and total capital employed was $400,000.

> *Required:* (1) The capital-employed turnover rate.
> (2) The percentage of profit to sales.
> (3) The rate of return on capital employed.

2. Return on Fixed Investment. On December 31, 19—, a company's balance sheet showed:

Assets		Liabilities and Capital	
Cash..........................	$100,000	Accounts payable............	$ 70,000
Accounts receivable..........	125,000	Long-term loan..............	280,000
Inventory....................	175,000	Capital stock................	500,000
Plant and machinery.........	550,000	Retained earnings............	100,000
Total assets.................	$950,000	Total liabilities and capital....	$950,000

The company produces two products on the same set of machines. A breakdown of the cost shows:

	Product A	Product B
Materials.....................................	$10.00	$ 7.00
Labor (2 hrs. for Product A, 4 hrs. for Product B)....	4.00	8.00
Factory overhead...............................	2.00	4.00
Total...	$16.00	$19.00
Selling price...................................	$20.00	$24.00
Gross profit....................................	$ 4.00	$ 5.00
Marketing and administrative expenses.............	1.00	1.00
Net income....................................	$ 3.00	$ 4.00

Estimated sales:
> Product A................................. 15,000 units
> Product B................................. 20,000 units

Required: The rate of return on fixed investment for each product.

3. Return on Capital Employed; Minimum Price. The Aster Corporation manufactures a highly specialized alloy used in missile skins. Rising materials costs led the company to adopt the lifo method for inventory costing. In 19A the company produced 702,000 kilograms of alloy. New government contracts and other new business should increase volume by about 30%. In spite of increased costs the management felt that it could reduce the sales price from $12.30 per kilogram in 19A to $11.40 in 19B and still maintain the same rate of return on capital employed. However, prices of basic raw materials climbed higher than expected and the desired return and profit did not materialize.

Data available (000's omitted):

	19A	19B
Sales...	$8,450	$8,550
Cost of goods sold and commercial expenses.........	7,370	7,931
Aftertax net income...............................	876	896
Cash..	1,200	500
Accounts receivable..............................	1,000	1,000
Inventories..	1,750	2,300
Plant and other fixed assets......................	6,650	7,400

Required: (1) The actual rate of return on capital employed for the past two years.

(2) The minimum price that the company should have charged.

4. Rate of Return on Capital Employed; Payback Period; Product's Rate of Return. The management of the Masterson Manufacturing Company has been using the return-on-capital-employed method of measuring performance by division and product managers. Recently the management decided to extend the concept to a product performance measurement device for four product groups. The Cost Department assembled the following data:

	Product A	Product B	Product C	Product D
Investment....................	$ 500,000	$ 300,000	$ 600,000	$ 200,000
Sales volume in dollars........	2,000,000	5,000,000	3,000,000	1,800,000
Net income after taxes..........	60,000	45,000	175,000	36,000
Aftertax cash inflows..........	75,000	60,000	200,000	60,000

Required: (1) For all four products, the (a) capital-employed turnover rate; (b) percentage of profit to sales; and (c) return-on-capital-employed rate.

(2) The management is further interested in the length of time required for cash produced by the investment to repay the original cash outlay. Compute the payback period for each of the four products based on the data given above.

(3) The management is also aware of the possibility of using the discounted cash flow method which attempts to show that rate which equates the sum of the present values of a series of future cash flows to the value of the original investment. Compute the discounted cash flow rate of return for Product D assuming that (a) the product's life cycle is estimated at 10 years and (b) the effective interest rate or cost of the investment capital is 20% per year.

(Based on an article in *Management Services*)

5. Rate of Return on Capital Employed; New Sales Price. The H. D. Ransom Company has an opportunity to increase production with an increase in machinery. The company has never computed a rate of return on capital employed and is interested in finding out the present rate and also the new rate and new selling price that would result under the proposed plan.

The accountant provides the following data:

INCOME STATEMENT FOR 19—

Sales....................................			$1,200,000
Cost of goods sold:			
Direct materials...........................		$200,000	
Direct labor...............................		300,000	
Factory overhead:			
Fixed..................................	$100,000		
Variable................................	150,000	250,000	
Total cost of goods sold......................			750,000
Gross profit.................................			$ 450,000
Less commercial expenses:			
Fixed expenses............................		$150,000	
Variable expenses........................		50,000	200,000
Net income..................................			$ 250,000

Additional data:

Current production (units)......................	100,000
Current assets................................	$600,000
Fixed assets...................................	500,000
New machinery................................	200,000
Fixed factory overhead increase.................	200,000
Increase in volume............................	50%

Required (*Ignore income taxes*): (1) The capital-employed turnover rate.
(2) The percentage of profit to sales.
(3) The rate of return on capital employed.
(4) A pro-forma income statement based on the plan of expanding production facilities.
(5) Similar rates as in (1), (2), and (3) on the basis of (4).
(6) The new sales price assuming that the rate of return on capital employed computed in(3)is considered satisfactory. (Use both formulas on pages 891–892.)

6. Division Transfer Pricing. The Wallach Iron Mill produces high-grade pig iron in its single blast furnace in Bedford, Pennsylvania. Coal from nearby mines is converted into coke in company-owned ovens and 80% of the coke produced is used in the blast furnace. The management of the mill is experimenting with divisional profit reporting and control and has established the blast furnace as well as the coke producing activity as profit centers. Coke used by the blast furnace is charged to that profit center at $6 a ton which approximates the current market price less costs of marketing (including substantial freight costs). The remaining 20% of the coke produced at a normal annual volume output of 80,000 tons is sold to other mills in the area at $7.50 a ton.

Cost of coal and other variable costs of coke production amount to $4.50 a ton. Fixed costs of the coke division amount to $40,000 a year.

The blast furnace manager has found a reliable, independent coke producer who has offered to sell him coke at a fixed delivered price of $5 a ton on a long-term contract. The manager of Wallach Iron Mill's coke division claims it cannot match that price and maintain profitable operations.

Required: (1) Assuming that Wallach Iron Mill cannot increase its sales of coke to outsiders above the 20% of normal production, present calculations to guide the coke division manager in making a decision as to whether or not to accept the offer. (The blast furnace manager has authority to purchase outside.)

(2) The manager of the coke division indicates that with an expenditure of $60,000 annually for fixed productive and delivery equipment the division's entire annual normal output could be sold to outside firms at $6 a ton, f.o.b. the Wallach Iron Mill plant. Assume other marketing expenses will be $.50 per ton. The increased fixed costs would reduce variable production costs by $1.50 a ton. Present calculations to aid top management in making a decision as to whether to make the additional investment and sell the entire coke division's output to outsiders.

7. Sales Price Calculation. A standard unit product cost of the Newhart Manufacturing Company contains the following direct or variable costs:

	Per Unit
Direct materials...	$5.60
Direct labor cost (¼ hour @ $6 per hour)......................	1.50
Variable factory overhead.......................................	.40
Total direct costs..	$7.50

Fixed factory overhead is budgeted at $300,000 for a normal sales volume of 400,000 units. Factory productive capacity is 500,000 units. Marketing and administrative expenses are budgeted at $220,000.

Capital employed is considered to consist of 50% of net sales for current assets and of $450,000 for fixed assets.

Additional analysis indicates:

(a) Direct materials prices will increase $.40 per unit.
(b) An unfavorable direct labor variance of approximately 8% has been experienced for the past two years.
(c) Customers' cash discounts average about 3% of the gross sales price.

Required: A sales price which will yield a 16% return on capital employed. Ignore income taxes.

8. Contract Price Renegotiation. In 19A the Comp-Bell Company obtained a government contract for the construction of 16 space capsule components for the NASA Manned Spacecraft Center. The bid which resulted in the contract being awarded to Comp-Bell Company was broken down as follows:

BID PRICE — 16 SPACE CAPSULE COMPONENTS

Direct materials...	$12,000,000
Direct labor (163,840 hours @ $4)....:....................	655,360
Variable factory overhead (163,840 hours @ $5).............	819,200
Fixed factory overhead (163,840 hours @ $3)................	491,520
	$13,966,080
Margin to cover general overhead and profit................	3,491,000
Total contract price......................................	$17,457,080

Late in 19C, NASA terminated the contract because of project difficulties and budget cuts in its appropriations. The NASA contract renegotiation team agreed to allow the firm the full bid price for direct materials, direct labor, and variable overhead on the four capsule components already completed and delivered. These costs were to be adjusted to reflect the company's learning curve for labor time by allowing 125% of the bid hours in determining the direct labor and the factory overhead, variable and fixed. The fixed overhead rate was to be increased to $3.50 an hour to compensate for idle plant capacity resulting from the termination. In addition, the customary margin percentage based on total bid price was to be allowed plus a $10,000 penalty.

Required: The amount the Comp-Bell Company should receive in the renegotiation settlement.

PROBLEMS

27-1. Profit and Rate of Return on Capital Employed Using Various Proposals. Safe-for-Kids Toy Company manufactures two specialty children's toys marketed under the trade names of Springy and Leapy. During 19— the following costs, revenues, and capital employed by the company in the production of these two items were:

	Springy	*Leapy*
Sales price per unit......................	$ 1.50	$ 1.95
Sales in units............................	280,000	150,000
Materials costs per unit...................	$ .20	$ .30
Labor costs per unit......................	.50	.75
Variable factory overhead per unit..........	.15	.20
Variable marketing cost per unit............	.05	.10
Fixed factory overhead....................	100,000	30,000
Fixed marketing costs.....................	30,000	15,000
Variable capital employed.................	10% of sales	20% of sales
Fixed capital employed....................	$148,000	$ 91,500

Fixed administrative and other nonallocable fixed costs amounted to $28,000, and nonallocable capital employed was $25,000.

Management, dissatisfied with the return on total capital employed in 19—, is considering a number of alternatives to improve this return.

The market for Springy appears to be underdeveloped, and the consensus of opinion is that sales can be increased to 325,000 units at the same price with an increase of $9,500 in fixed advertising costs. An increase in the production of Springy will require use of some equipment previously utilized in the production of Leapy and a transfer of $10,000 of fixed capital and fixed factory overhead of $5,000 to the production of Springy.

For Leapy it would mean limiting its production to 100,000 units which could be marketed with the current sales effort at (a) an increase in price of $.15 per unit; (b) without a price increase and with a reduction in current fixed advertising cost of $9,000; or (c) with a $.05 per unit increase in price and a $7,500 reduction in current fixed advertising costs.

Required: (1) The net income before taxes and the return on capital employed for each product and in total for 19—.

(2) The net income before taxes and the return on capital employed for each product and in total under each alternative.

27-2. Measuring Operating Performance via Return on Capital Employed. The T. Tramber Corporation is composed of three autonomous manufacturing plants, X, Y, and Z. The three plants manufacture three different types of heavy machinery. Operating decisions are decentralized and are made by independent plant managers who report to a central executive staff. The executive staff is in the process of evaluating the past year's (19B) performance of the three plants. During the last months of 19A, Y's sales showed an upward trend, so the president invested additional capital during 19A in Plant Y. Now the president wants to know if the increased investment in Plant Y has paid off and if additional investments should be made in Plant Z which has had the least amount of sales. The capital employed in the three plants during 19A and 19B was:

Plant	19B	19A
X	$35,119	$23,421
Y	78,125	20,115
Z	9,361	5,742

At the executive committee meeting the controller presents the following comparative income statements which show the relation of the three plants to each other and to the base year:

	Plant	Sales Amount*	Percent of Total Sales	Costs and Expenses Amount*	Percent of Sales	Profit Amount*	Percent of Sales
Year 19A:	X	$ 44,500	44.5%	$ 38,940	87.5%	$ 5,560	12.5%
	Y	35,000	35.0	32,025	91.5	2,975	8.5
	Z	20,500	20.5	18,040	88.0	2,460	12.0
Total..........		$100,000	100.0%	$ 89,005	89.0%	$ 10,995	11.0%
Year 19B:	X	$ 59,000	29.5%	$ 52,215	88.5%	$ 6,785	11.5%
	Y	100,000	50.0	91,700	91.7	8,300	8.3
	Z	41,000	20.5	36,326	88.6	4,674	11.4
Total..........		$200,000	100.0%	$180,241	90.1%	$ 19,759	9.9%

*000's omitted.

The controller says that the income statements show that Plant Y's sales have continually increased while Plant Z's sales, expressed as a total of the company's sales, have remained the same. Therefore, the controller reasons that the investment in Plant Y was well made; and he recommends that the president consider changing Z's plant manager because of his poor performance.

Required: An analysis to prove or disprove the controller's findings.

(Based on an article in *The Journal of Accountancy*)

27-3. Rate of Return on Capital Employed. Neal Corporation's management is concerned over its current financial position and return on capital employed. In a request for assistance in analyzing these financial conditions, the controller provides the statements on page 904.

NEAL CORPORATION
STATEMENT OF WORKING CAPITAL DEFICIT
DECEMBER 31, 19A

Current liabilities....................................			$198,625
Less current assets:			
Cash..		$ 5,973	
Accounts receivable, net.............................		70,952	
Inventory...		90,200	167,125
Working capital deficit................................			$ 31,500

NEAL CORPORATION
INCOME STATEMENT
FOR THE YEAR ENDED DECEMBER 31, 19A

Sales (90,500 units)..	$751,150
Cost of goods sold...	451,000
Gross profit...	$300,150
Marketing and general expenses, including $22,980 depreciation.........	149,920
Net income before income tax....................................	$150,230
Less 50% income tax...	75,115
Net income..	$ 75,115

Additional data:

Assets other than current assets consist of land, building, and equipment with a book value of $350,000 on December 31, 19A.

Required: (1) The inventory turnover ratio.

(2) The return-on-capital-employed ratio after income tax.

(3) The rate of return on book value of total assets after income taxes based on the following data:

Sales of 100,000 units are forecast for 19B. Within this relevant range of activity, costs are estimated as follows (excluding income taxes):

	Fixed Costs	Variable Costs per Unit
Cost of goods sold.............................		$4.90
Marketing and general expenses, including $15,450 depreciation................................	$125,750	1.10
Total......................................	$125,750	$6.00

The income tax rate is expected to be 50%. Past experience indicates that current assets vary in direct proportion to sales. Management feels that in 19B the market will support a sales price of $8.40 at a sales volume of 100,000 units.

(AICPA adapted)

27-4. Product Pricing; Rate of Return on Capital Employed.   The Brynner Products Company manufactures and sells electric fans.   The market has been quite encouraging; and the management decides to increase production by 50% resulting in an increase of cash, accounts receivables, and inventories.   Some additional factory help must be hired as well as a number of sales and administrative people.   No new machinery or additional space is needed.

The management doubts the unusually high increase in net income and decides to consult the management services staff of its CPA firm.   To assist the consultant, the management supplies the following additional data and ratios:

Cash to sales 4%; receivables to sales 6%; inventory to sales 5%; a total of 15% for current assets.   Fixed assets are constant for all levels of production with $7,500,000.

The Cost Department prepared this comparative income statement:

COMPARATIVE INCOME STATEMENT
(000's omitted)

		Present 100%	Proposed 150%
Sales @ $50.00 per unit..............		$10,000	$15,000
Less cost of goods sold:			
Direct labor........................	$2,000		$2,500
Direct materials....................	4,000		5,750
Total.........................	$6,000		$8,250
Factory overhead:			
Fixed	$1,500		$2,000
Variable	500		600
Total...........................	$2,000		$2,600
Marketing and administrative expenses....	$ 750		$1,250
Total cost........................		8,750	12,100
Net income.......................		$ 1,250	$ 2,900

Required (Ignore income taxes): (1) The new unit selling price for the proposed new production level if the:
  (a) Original earnings ratio on total capital employed should be retained. (Compute the answer to 1/100th of 1%.)
  (b) Desired ratio for the return on capital employed is 17%. (Use the long form of the formula on page 891.)
  (2) Two new income statements for the 150% output based on (a) the answer to (1) (a) above and (b) the answer to (1) (b) above.
  (3) The following ratios for both income statements: (a) percentage of profit to sales; (b) capital-employed turnover rate; and (c) return on capital employed.

27-5. Transfer Pricing.   A. R. Oma, Inc. manufactures men's cologne.   The manufacturing process is basically a series of mixing operations with the addition of certain aromatic and coloring ingredients.   The finished product is packaged in a company-produced glass bottle and is packed in cases containing six bottles.

A. R. Oma feels that the sale of its product is heavily influenced by the appearance of the bottle and has therefore devoted considerable managerial effort to the production process. This has resulted in the development of certain unique bottle production processes in which management takes considerable pride.

The two areas (i.e., cologne production and bottle manufacture) have evolved over the years in an almost independent manner; in fact, a rivalry has developed between management personnel as to "which division is the most important" to the company. This attitude is probably intensified because the bottle manufacturing plant was purchased intact ten years ago, and no real interchange of management personnel or ideas (except at the top corporate level) has taken place.

Since the acquisition, all bottle production has been used by the cologne manufacturing plant. Each area is considered a separate profit center and evaluated as such. As the new corporate controller, you are responsible for the definition of a proper transfer price to use in crediting the bottle production profit center and in debiting the cologne profit center.

At your request, the Bottle Division general manager asks other bottle manufacturers to quote a price for the three possible levels demanded by the Cologne Division. These competitive prices are:

Sales Volume (In Equivalent Cases)*	Total Sales Revenue	Sales Price Per Case
2,000,000	$ 4,000,000	$2.00
4,000,000	7,000,000	1.75
6,000,000	10,000,000	1.67

*An "equivalent case" represents six bottles each.

A cost analysis of the internal bottle plant indicates that it can produce bottles at these costs:

Sales Volume (In Equivalent Cases)	Total Cost	Cost Per Case
2,000,000	$3,200,000	$1.60
4,000,000	5,200,000	1.30
6,000,000	7,200,000	1.20

The cost analyst explains that these costs represent fixed costs of $1,200,000 and variable costs of $1 per equivalent case.

These figures have caused considerable corporate discussion as to the proper price to be used in transferring bottles to the Cologne Division. This interest is heightened because a significant portion of a division manager's income is an incentive bonus based on profit-center results.

The Cologne Division has these costs in addition to the bottle costs:

Sales Volume (In Equivalent Cases)	Total Cost	Cost Per Case
2,000,000	$16,400,000	$8.20
4,000,000	32,400,000	8.10
6,000,000	48,400,000	8.07

After considerable analysis, the Marketing Research Department furnishes the following price-demand relationship for the finished product:

Sales Volume (In Equivalent Cases)	Total Sales Revenue	Sales Price Per Case
2,000,000	$25,000,000	$12.50
4,000,000	45,600,000	11.40
6,000,000	63,900,000	10.65

Required: (1) The profit for (a) the Bottle Division, (b) the Cologne Division, and (c) the company. A. R. Oma, Inc. has used market-based transfer prices in the past. Use current market prices and costs, and assume a volume of 6,000,000 cases.

(2) An explanation as to whether this production and sales level is the most profitable volume for (a) the Bottle Division, (b) the Cologne Division, and (c) the company.

(3) Assuming that A. R. Oma, Inc. uses the profit-center concept for divisional operation, (a) define a profit center, (b) discuss the conditions that should exist for the establishment of a profit center, and (c) indicate whether the two divisions should be organized as profit centers.

(NAA adapted)

27-6. Divisional Transfer Pricing. The Defco Division of Gunnco Corporation requests its Ajax Division, which operates at capacity, for a supply of Electrical Fitting #1726. The Ajax Division sells this part to its regular customers for $7.50 each. Defco, operating at 50% capacity, is willing to pay $5 each for this fitting. Defco will put the fitting into a brake unit which it manufactures on essentially a cost basis for a commercial jet plane manufacturer.

The Ajax Division produces Electrical Fitting #1726 at a variable cost of $4.25. The cost (and selling price) of the brake unit as it is being built by the Defco Division is:

Purchased parts (outside vendors)...............................	$22.50
Ajax Electrical Fitting #1726.....................................	5.00
Other variable costs...	14.00
Fixed factory overhead and administrative expenses................	8.00
Total..	$49.50

Defco believes the price concession is necessary to obtain the job.

Gunnco uses return-on-investment and dollar profits in measuring division and division manager performance.

Required: A recommendation as to whether the Ajax Division should supply Electrical Fitting #1726 to the Defco Division. (Ignore income taxes.)

(2) A discussion as to whether it would be to the short-run economic advantage of the Gunnco Corporation for the Ajax Division to supply the Defco Division with Electrical Fitting #1726 at $5 each. (Ignore income taxes.)

(3) A discussion of the organizational and managerial behavior difficulties, if any, inherent in this situation and a recommendation to Gunnco's president advising him how to handle the problem.

(NAA adapted)

27-7. Differential Analysis with Probability Estimates; Return on Investment; Net Present Value. The president of Benjamin Industries needs assistance in evaluating several financial management problems in her Home Applicances Division as summarized below.

Management wants to determine the best selling price for a new appliance that has a variable cost of $4 per unit. The sales manager has estimated these probabilities of achieving annual sales levels for various selling prices:

Sales Level (In Units)	Selling Price $4	$5	$6	$7
20,000			20%	80%
30,000		10%	40	20
40,000	50%	50	20	
50,000	50	40	20	

The Division's current profit rate is 5% on annual sales of $1,200,000. A $400,000 investment is needed to finance these sales. The company's basis for measuring divisional success is by return on investment.

Management is also considering these two alternative plans submitted by Benjamin employees for improving operations in the Home Appliances Division:

Green believes that the Division's sales volume can be doubled by greater promotional effort, but this method would lower the profit rate to 4% of sales and would require an additional $100,000 investment.

Gold favors eliminating some unprofitable appliances and improving efficiency by adding $200,000 in capital equipment. These methods would decrease the Division's sales volume by 10% but would improve the profit rate to 7%.

Black, White, and Gray — three franchised home appliance dealers — have requested short-term financing from the company. These dealers have agreed to repay the loans within three years and to pay Benjamin Industries 5% of their profit for the three-year period for the use of the funds. The table below summarizes, by dealer, the financing requested and the total remittances (principal plus 5% of profit) expected at the end of each year:

	Black	White	Gray
Financing requested	$ 80,000	$40,000	$30,000
Remittances expected at the end of:			
Year 1	$ 10,000	$25,000	$10,000
Year 2	40,000	30,000	15,000
Year 3	70,000	5,000	15,000
Total	$120,000	$60,000	$40,000

Management believes these financing requests should be granted only if the annual pretax return to the company exceeds the target internal rate of 20% on investment. Discount factors (rounded) that would provide this 20% rate of return are:

Year 1 8
Year 2 7
Year 3 6

Required: (1) A schedule of the expected differential profit for each of the selling prices proposed for the new product. Include the expected sales levels in units (weighted according to the sales manager's estimated probabilities), the expected total monetary sales, the expected variable costs, and the expected differential profit.

(2) The company's (a) current rate of return on investment in the Home Appliances Division and (b) the anticipated rates of return under the alternative suggestions made by (*1*) Green and (*2*) Gold.

(3) The net present value of the investment opportunities of financing Black, White, and Gray. Determine if the discounted cash flows expected from (a) Black, (b) White, and (c) Gray would be more or less than the amounts of Benjamin Industries' investment in loans to each of the three dealers.

(AICPA adapted)

27-8. Contribution Margin Approach to Pricing. E. Berg & Sons manufacture custom-made pleasure boats ranging in price from $10,000 to $250,000. For the past thirty years, Ed Berg, Sr. has determined each boat's selling price by estimating the costs of materials, labor, and a prorated portion of overhead and by adding 20% to these estimated costs.

For example, a recent price quotation was determined as follows:

Direct materials...................................	$ 5,000
Direct labor..	8,000
Overhead...	2,000
	$15,000
Plus 20%...	3,000
Selling price.......................................	$18,000

The overhead figure was determined by estimating total overhead costs for the year and allocating them at 25% of direct labor.

If a customer rejects the price and business is slack, Ed Berg, Sr. is often willing to reduce the markup to as little as 5% over estimated costs. Thus, average markup for the year is estimated at 15%.

Ed Berg, Jr. has just completed a pricing course and believes the company could use some of the modern techniques he has learned. The course emphasized the contribution margin approach to pricing, and Ed Berg, Jr. feels such an approach would be helpful in determining the selling prices of their custom-made pleasure boats.

Total overhead (including marketing and administrative expenses for the year) has been estimated at $150,000, of which $90,000 is fixed and the remainder is variable in direct proportion to direct labor.

Required: (1) Assuming a customer rejected the $18,000 quotation and also rejected a $15,750 quotation (5% markup) during a slack period and then countered with a $15,000 offer, (a) the difference in net income for the year between the acceptance or rejection of the offer, and (b) the minimum selling price Ed Berg, Jr. could have quoted without reducing or increasing net income.

(2) The advantages that the contribution margin approach to pricing has over the approach used by Ed Berg, Sr.

(3) The pitfalls, if any, to contribution margin pricing.

(NAA adapted)

CHAPTER **28**

LINEAR PROGRAMMING FOR PLANNING AND DECISION MAKING

Increasingly, new tools and techniques are coming into use by managers as they seek to make intelligent decisions and control operations. At the heart of management's responsibility is the best or optimum use of limited resources including money, personnel, materials, facilities, and time. *Linear programming*, a mathematical technique, permits determination of the best use which can be made of available resources. It is a valuable aid to management because it provides a systematic and efficient procedure which can be used as a guide in decision making.

A LINEAR PROGRAMMING PROBLEM

As an example, imagine the simple problem of a small machine shop that manufactures two models, standard and deluxe. Each standard model requires two hours of grinding and four hours of polishing; each deluxe model requires five hours of grinding and two hours of polishing. The manufacturer has three grinders and two polishers; therefore, in a 40-hour week there are 120 hours of grinding capacity and 80 hours of polishing capacity. There is a contribution margin of $3 on each standard model and $4 on each deluxe model and a ready market for both models. The management must decide on (1) the allocation of the available production capacity to standard and deluxe models and (2) the number of units of each model in order to maximize the total contribution margin.

To solve this linear programming problem, the symbol X is assigned to the number of standard models and Y to the number of deluxe models. The contribution margin from making X standard models and Y deluxe models then is $3X + 4Y$ dollars. The contribution margin per unit is the selling price per unit less the unit variable cost. Total contribution margin is the per unit contribution multiplied by the number of units.

The restrictions on machine capacity are expressed in this manner: To manufacture one standard unit requires two hours of grinding time, so that making X standard models uses 2X hours. Similarly, the production of Y deluxe models uses 5Y hours of grinding time. With 120 hours of grinding time available, the grinding capacity is written: $2X + 5Y \leq 120$ hours of grinding capacity per week. The limitation on polishing capacity is expressed: $4X + 2Y \leq 80$ hours per week. In summary, the relevant information is:

	Grinding Time	Polishing Time	Contribution Margin
Standard model..................	2 hours	4 hours	$3
Deluxe model....................	5 hours	2 hours	4
Plant capacity..................	120 hours	80 hours	

Two basic linear programming techniques, the graphic method and the simplex method, are described and illustrated in this chapter, using the above capacity allocation — contribution margin maximization data.

GRAPHIC METHOD — A LINEAR PROGRAMMING TECHNIQUE

Operation	Hours Available	Hours Required Per Model		Maximum Number of Models	
		Standard	Deluxe	Standard	Deluxe
Grinding.....	120	2	5	$\frac{120}{2} = 60$	$\frac{120}{5} = 24$
Polishing.....	80	4	2	$\frac{80}{4} = 20$	$\frac{80}{2} = 40$

The lowest number in each of the two columns at the extreme right measures the impact of the hours limitations. At best, the company can produce 20 standard models with a contribution margin of $60 (20 × $3) or 24 deluxe models at a contribution margin of $96 (24 × $4). Is there a better solution?

To determine production levels in order to maximize the contribution margin of $3X + $4Y when:

$$2X + 5Y \leq 120 \text{ hours grinding constraint}$$
$$4X + 2Y \leq 80 \text{ hours polishing constraint}$$

a graph is drawn with the constraints shown. The two-dimensional graphic technique is limited to problems with only two variables—in this example, standard and deluxe models. However, more than two constraints can be considered although this case uses only two, grinding and polishing.

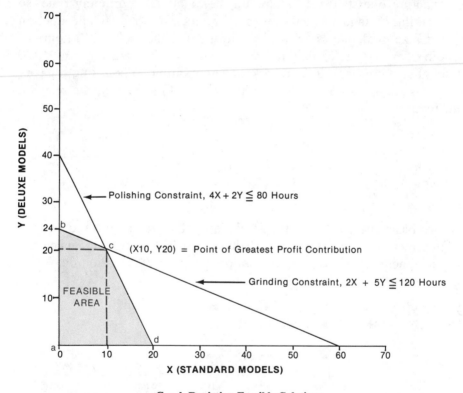

Graph Depicting Feasible Solutions

The constraints define the solution space when they are sketched on the graph:

When X = 0
    Y ≤ 24, grinding constraint
    Y ≤ 40, polishing constraint

When Y = 0
    X ≤ 60, grinding constraint
    X ≤ 20, polishing constraint

The solution space, representing the area of feasible solutions, is bounded by the *corner points* a, b, c, and d on the graph. Any combination of standard and deluxe units that falls within the solution space is a feasible solution. However, the *best* feasible solution, according to mathematical laws, is found to be at one of the four corner points. Consequently, all *corner point variables* must be tried to find the combination which maximizes the contribution margin (CM): $3X + $4Y.

The X and Y corner point values can be read from the graph, or computed. The X and Y values for the corner points b(24) and d(20) were computed in the table on page 911. And corner point c values can be computed as follows:

$$2X + 5Y = 120$$
$$4X + 2Y = 80$$

To find the value of Y, multiply the first equation by two and subtract the second equation:

$$\begin{aligned} 4X + 10Y &= 240 \\ -4X - 2Y &= -80 \\ \hline 8Y &= 160 \\ Y &= 20 \end{aligned}$$

Substitute the value of Y in the first equation:

$$2X + 5(20) = 120$$
$$2X = 20$$
$$X = 10$$

Trying values at each of the corner points:

a = (X=0, Y=0); $3 (0)+$4 (0)= $0 CM
b = (X=0, Y=24); $3 (0)+$4 (24)= $96 CM
c = (X=10, Y=20); $3 (10)+$4 (20)= $110 CM
d = (X=20, Y=0); $3 (20)+$4 (0)= $60 CM

Therefore, in order to maximize total contribution margin, the plant should schedule 10 standard models and 20 deluxe models for production.

In this example, the optimal solution uses all of the constraint resources:

2 (10) + 5 (20) = 120 hours grinding constraint
4 (10) + 2 (20) = 80 hours polishing constraint

Full utilization of all resources will occur, however, only in cases in which the optimal solution is at a point of common intersection of *all* of the constraint equations in the problem — point c in this example.

SIMPLEX METHOD — A LINEAR
PROGRAMMING TECHNIQUE

The *simplex method*[1] is considered one of the basic techniques from which many linear programming techniques are directly or indirectly derived. The simplex method is an iterative, stepwise process which approaches an optimum solution in order to reach an objective function of maximization or minimization. Matrix algebra provides the deterministic working tools from which the simplex method was developed, requiring mathematical formulation in describing the problem.

Contribution Margin Maximization. The example described earlier in this chapter attempts to determine or maximize the contribution margin of the two models — standard and deluxe — which require different operating times:

Standard model.............. 2 hours in the first or grinding operation
4 hours in the second or polishing operation

Deluxe model................ 5 hours in the first or grinding operation
2 hours in the second or polishing operation

The available time for fabricating the two models is 120 hours for the first operation (grinding) and 80 hours for the second operation (polishing). With these data, the constraints can be expressed by mathematical notation in the form of inequalities.

Initial Steps.

1. The relationships which establish the constraints or inequalities must be set up first. Letting X and Y be respectively the quantity of items of the standard model and the deluxe model that are to be manufactured, the system of inequalities, or the set of constraint equations, is:

$$2X + 5Y \leq 120$$
$$4X + 2Y \leq 80$$

   in which both X and Y must be positive values or zero ($X \geq 0$; $Y \geq 0$) for this problem.

2. The objective function is the total contribution margin the manager can obtain from the two models. A contribution margin of $3 is expected for each standard model, and $4 for each deluxe model. The objective function is CM = 3X + 4Y. The problem is now completely described by mathematical notation. These two steps were the same for the graphic method.

3. The simplex method requires the use of equations in contrast to the inequalities used by the graphic method. Therefore, the set of inequalities must be transformed into a set of equations by introducing slack variables, S_1 and S_2. The use of slack variables involves simply the addition of an

---

[1]This presentation is adapted from G. M. F. di Roccaferrera, *Introduction to Linear Programming Processes* (Cincinnati: South-Western Publishing Company, 1967).

arbitrary variable to one side of the inequality, transforming it into an equality. This arbitrary variable is called a "slack variable" since it takes up the slack in the inequality. The inequalities rewritten as equalities are:

$$2X + 5Y + S_1 = 120$$
$$4X + 2Y + S_2 = 80$$

and the objective equation becomes

Maximize: $CM = 3X + 4Y + 0S_1 + 0S_2$

in which the unit contribution margins of the fictitious products S_1 and S_2 are zero.

4. At this point the simplex method can be applied and the first matrix, or tableau, can be set up as shown below.

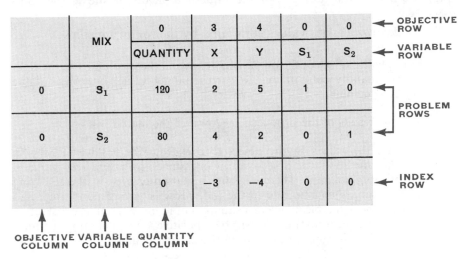

First Simplex Tableau and First Solution

Explanation and Computations for the First Tableau. The simplex method records the pertinent data in matrix, tabular form, known as the *simplex tableau.* The components of a tableau are:

The *objective row* of the matrix consists of the coefficients of the objective function, or the contribution margin per unit of the two products.

The *variable row* is made up of the notation of the variables of the problem, including slack variables.

The *problem rows* in the first tableau contain the coefficients of the equations which represent constraints upon the satisfaction of the objective function. Each constraint equation adds an additional problem row. Variables not included in a constraint are assigned zero coefficients in the problem rows. In subsequent tableaus, new problem row values will be computed.

The *objective column* receives different entries at each iteration, representing the contribution margin per unit of the variables in the solution.

The *variable column* receives different notations at each iteration, by replacement. These notations are the variables used to find the total contribution margin of the particular iteration. In the first matrix, a situation of no production is considered as a starting point in the iterative solution process. For this reason, zeros are marked in the objective column, and the slacks are recorded in the variable column. As the iterations proceed, by replacement, appropriate values and notations will be entered in the objective and variable columns.

The *quantity column* shows the constant values of the constraint equations in the first tableau; in subsequent tableaus, it shows the solution mix.

The *index row* carries values computed by the following steps:

1. Multiply the values of the quantity column and those columns to the right of the quantity column by the corresponding value, by rows, of the objective column.

2. Add the results of the products, by rows, of the matrix.

3. Subtract the values in the objective row from the results in Step 2. For this operation, the objective row is assumed to have a zero value in the quantity column. The contribution margin entered in the cell lying in the quantity column and in the index row is zero, a condition valid only for the first tableau where a situation of no production is considered. In the subsequent matrices, it will be a positive value, denoting the total contribution margin represented by the particular matrix.

Index row:

Steps 1 and 2	*Step 3*
$120(0) + 80(0) = 0$	$0 - 0 = \quad 0$
$2(0) + \quad 4(0) = 0$	$0 - 3 = -3$
$5(0) + \quad 2(0) = 0$	$0 - 4 = -4$
$1(0) + \quad 0(0) = 0$	$0 - 0 = \quad 0$
$0(0) + \quad 1(0) = 0$	$0 - 0 - \quad 0$

In this first tableau, the slack variables were introduced into the product mix, variable column, to find an initial feasible solution to the problem. It can be proven mathematically that beginning with slack variables assures a feasible solution. Hence, one possible solution might have S_1 take a value of 120 and S_2 a value of 80. This approach satisfies the constraint equation but is undesirable since the resulting contribution margin is zero.

It is a rule of the simplex method that the optimum solution has not been reached if the index row carries any negative values at the completion of an iteration. Consequently, this first tableau does not carry the optimum solution since negative values appear in its index row. A second tableau or matrix must now be prepared, step by step, according to the rules of the simplex method.

	MIX	0 QUANTITY	3 X	4 Y	0 S_1	0 S_2	
4	Y	24	0.4	1	0.2	0	← MAIN ROW
0	S_2	32	3.2	0	−0.4	1	
		96	−1.4	0	0.8	0	

This row has been replaced because 24 was the smallest positive ratio computed in Step 2.

Second Simplex Tableau and Second Solution

Explanation and Computations for the Second Tableau. The elaboration of the second tableau (above) is accomplished through these six steps:

1. Select the *key column*, the one which has the negative number with the highest absolute value in the index row; i.e., that variable whose value will increase the contribution margin the most. In the first tableau, the key column is the one formed by the values: 5, 2, and −4.

2. Select the *key row*, the row to be replaced. The key row is the one which contains the smallest positive ratio obtained by dividing the positive numbers in the problem rows of the key column into the corresponding values, by rows, of the quantity column. The smallest positive ratio identifies the equation which operates as the limiting constraint. In the first tableau, the ratios are $\frac{120}{5} = 24$ and $\frac{80}{2} = 40$. Since $\frac{120}{5}$ is the smaller of the two positive ratios, the key row is 120, 2, 5, 1, and 0.

3. Select the *key number*, which is the value found in the crossing cell of the key column and the key row. In the example, the key number is 5.

4. Compute the *main row*, which is a computed series of new values replacing the key row of the preceding tableau (in this case, the first tableau). The main row is determined by dividing each amount in Row S_1 (the row being replaced) of the preceding tableau by the key number, the amount in the Y or key column in the S_1 row; i.e., $120 \div 5 = 24$; $2 \div 5 = 2/5$ths, or 0.4; $5 \div 5 = 1$; $1 \div 5 = 1/5$th, or 0.2; $0 \div 5 = 0$. These are the new figures in the row labeled Y, the main row.

5. Compute the amounts in all other rows. In this problem new values must be determined for the S_2 row only, by the following procedure:

Old S_n Row (First Tableau) Minus (when n=2)		Old S_n Row Y (the Key) Column (when n=2)		New Y Row (Second Tableau)				Values of New S_n Row (when n=2)
80	− (	2	×	24	)	=		32
4	− (	2	×	0.4	)	=		3.2
2	− (	2	×	1	)	=		0
0	− (	2	×	0.2	)	=		−0.4
1	− (	2	×	0	)	=		1

These computations accomplish (1) the substitution of as much of the deluxe model as is consistent with constraints and (2) the removal of as much S_1 and S_2 as is necessary to provide for the insertion of Y, deluxe model, units into the solution. The $4 contribution margin of the deluxe model is placed in the objective column of the Y row.

6. Finally, compute the index row:

Steps 1 and 2	Step 3
24 (4) + 32 (0) = 96	96 − 0 = 96
0.4(4) + 3.2(0) = 1.6	1.6 − 3 = −1.4
1 (4) + 0 (0) = 4	4 − 4 = 0
0.2(4) + −0.4(0) = 0.8	0.8 − 0 = 0.8
0 (4) + 1 (0) = 0	0 − 0 = 0

This second matrix does not contain the optimum solution since a negative figure, -1.4, still remains in the index row. The contribution margin arising from this model mix is $96 [4(24) + 0(32)], which is an improvement. However, the second solution indicates that some standard models and $1.40 (or 7/5ths dollars of contribution margin) can be added for each unit of the standard model substituted in this solution.

It is interesting to reflect on the significance of $-7/5$ths, or -1.4. The original statement of the problem had promised a unit contribution margin of $3 for the standard model. Now the contribution will only increase by $1.40 per unit. The significance of the -1.4 is that it measures the net increase of the per unit contribution margin after allowing for the reduction of the deluxe model represented by Y units. That is, all the grinding hours have been committed to produce 24 deluxe models (24 units × 5 hours grinding time per unit = 120 hours capacity); the standard model cannot be made without sacrificing the deluxe model. The standard model requires 2 hours of grinding time; the deluxe model requires 5 hours of grinding time. To introduce one standard model unit into the product mix, the manufacture of 2/5ths (0.4) of one deluxe model unit must be foregone. This figure, 0.4, appears in the column headed "X" on the row representing foregone variable (deluxe) models. If more nonslack variables (i.e., more than two products) were involved, the figures for these variables, appearing in Column X, would have the same meaning as 0.4 has for the deluxe models.

Thus, the manufacturer loses 2/5ths of $4 by making 2/5ths less deluxe models but gains $3 from the additional standard model. A loss of 2/5ths of $4 = $1.60, and a gain of $3 results in a net improvement of $1.40. The final answer, already known from the graphic method illustration, adds $14 (10 standard models × 1.4) to $96, equaling $110, except that the deluxe model will then add $80 (20 units × $4) and the standard model $30 (10 units × $3). In summary, the −1.4 in the second tableau indicates the amount of increase in the contribution margin possible if one unit of the variable heading that column (X in this case) were added to the solution; and the 0.4 value in Column X represents the production of the deluxe model that must be relinquished.

	MIX	0	3	4	0	0
		QUANTITY	X	Y	S_1	S_2
4	Y	20	0	1	0.250	−0.1250
3	X	10	1	0	−0.125	0.3125
		110	0	0	0.625	0.4375

Third Simplex Tableau and Third As Well As Optimal Solution

Explanation and Computations for the Third Tableau. The third tableau (above) is computed by these steps:

1. Select the *key column.* This is the column from the second tableau, which has the negative number with the highest absolute value in the index row and is formed by the values: 0.4, 3.2, and −1.4.

2. Select the *key row*, S_2, the row to be replaced by X, which is determined as follows: from the second tableau, for Y row: 24 ÷ 0.4 = 60; for the S_2 row: 32 ÷ 3.2 = 10. Since 10 is the smaller positive ratio and comes from the S_2 row, S_2 should be replaced by X.

3. Select the *key number*, 3.2, which is the value located in the crossing cell of the key column and the key row of the preceding (second) tableau.

4. Compute the *main row.* The new X row (old S_2 row) figures are determined by dividing each amount in row S_2 of the second tableau by the amount in the X column in row S_2, the key number. The results are:

$$32 \div 3.2 = 10; \quad 3.2 \div 3.2 = 1; \quad 0 \div 3.2 = 0; \quad -0.4 \div 3.2 = -0.125;$$
$$1 \div 3.2 = 0.3125$$

5. Compute the amounts in all other rows. The new values of the Y row are:

Old Y Row (Second Tableau)	Minus	Old Y Row X (the Key) × Column		New X Row (Third Tableau)		Values of New Y Row
24	−	(0.4	×	10	) =	20
0.4	−	(0.4	×	1	) =	0
1	−	(0.4	×	0	) =	1
0.2	−	(0.4	×	−0.125	) =	0.25
0	−	(0.4	×	0.3125	) =	−0.125

6. Compute the index row:

Steps 1 and 2				Step 3		
20	(4) +	10	(3) = 110	110	− 0 =	110
0	(4) +	1	(3) = 3	3	− 3 =	0
1	(4) +	0	(3) = 4	4	− 4 =	0
0.25 (4) +	−0.125 (3) =		0.625	0.625	− 0 =	0.625
−0.125(4) +	0.3125(3) =		0.4375	0.4375	− 0 =	0.4375

There are no negative figures in the index row, which indicates that any further substitutions will not result in an increase in the contribution margin; the optimum solution has been obtained. The optimum strategy is to produce and sell 20 deluxe and 10 standard models [20($4 = $80] + [10($3) = $30] = $110, the contribution margin.

Cost Minimization. The previous problem dealt with the maximization of the contribution margin. The simplex method as well as the graphic method can also be used in problems whose objective is to *minimize variable cost.*

To illustrate a cost minimization problem, assume that:

> A pharmaceutical firm is to produce exactly 40 gallons of a mixture in which the basic ingredients A and B cost $8 per gallon and $15 per gallon, respectively. No more than 12 gallons of A can be used, and at least 10 gallons of B must be used.
>
> How much of each ingredient should be used if the firm wants to minimize cost?

This problem illustrates the three types of constraints — =, ≦, and ≧.

The cost function objective can be written as:

$$C \text{ (cost)} = 8X + 15Y; \text{ when } X = \text{gallons of ingredient A}$$
$$Y = \text{gallons of ingredient B}$$

The problem contains three constraints:

1. Forty gallons must be produced, which can be written mathematically as:

$$X + Y = 40 \text{ gallons}$$

2. No more than 12 gallons of A can be used. This constraint can be stated as:

$$X \leq 12 \text{ gallons}$$

3. At least 10 gallons of B must be used. This constraint can be written as:

$$Y \geq 10 \text{ gallons}$$

In summary form, the problem can be written as follows:

Minimize: $C = 8X + 15Y$

Subject to: $X + Y = 40$ gallons
$X \leq 12$ gallons
$Y \geq 10$ gallons

The optimum solution is obvious. Since X is cheaper, as much of it as possible should be used, i.e., 12 gallons; then Y should be used to obtain the desired total quantity of 40 gallons. Thus Y should be $40 - 12 = 28$. In more realistic problems, especially if there are many ingredients each having constraints, a solution may not be so obvious. A simple procedure is needed to generate an optimal solution no matter how complex the problem. The steps toward a solution in the cost minimization problem are similar to those taken in the contribution margin maximization case, where slack variables were introduced in order to arrive at the first and feasible solution which gave a zero contribution margin.

In the minimization problem illustration, in addition to the slack variables, a different type of variable known as an *artificial variable* is introduced. Artificial variables are of value only as computational devices; they allow two types of restrictions or constraints to be treated: the equality type and the greater-than-or-equal-to type. Artificial variables are also used in maximization problems when equality or greater-than-or-equal-to types of constraints are encountered.

Therefore, in this minimization problem with two ingredients and three constraints, a third ingredient, A_1, is introduced as an artificial variable in the first constraint, which leads to the new equality:

$$X + Y + A_1 = 40 \text{ gallons}$$

This new ingredient, A_1, must be thought of as a very expensive item; for example, $999 per gallon, making the 40 gallons cost $39,960. This high cost is noted by the symbol M. Such an answer is undesirable cost-wise; it would be an answer but certainly not the optimum solution.

Next, the second constraint is examined and a slack variable, S_1, is added to form an equation: $X + S_1 = 12$ gallons. S_1 represents the difference between 12 gallons of X and the actual number of gallons of X in the final solution.

Then the third constraint is examined, and a variable, S_2, is introduced to form an equation: $Y - S_2 = 10$ gallons. The variable, S_2, must be thought of as the difference between the actual number of gallons of Y used, reduced by S_2 to arrive at 10 gallons. For example, if Y should be 18 gallons, then S_2 would be 8 gallons ($18 - 8 = 10$ gallons). However, if Y appears in the first solution as 0, then $0 - S_2 = 10$ or $S_2 = -10$. This is not a feasible equation because -10 gallons of an ingredient is not possible. So to prevent S_2 from entering the first solution, in which as a starting point only slack and artificial variables are introduced, a second artificial variable, A_2, is utilized and, similar to A_1, a high cost is assigned to it, such as M or $999 per gallon. Thus, $Y - S_2 + A_2 = 10$ gallons.

As a rule, there must be the same number of entries in the variable (mix) column as there are constraint equations. There are three constraint equations and, before A_2 is introduced, only two slack (S_1 and S_2) and one artificial variable (A_1), of which S_2 has a negative coefficient. The introduction of the artificial variable, A_2, gives a set of four variables, two slack and two artificial, from which the three with positive coefficients can be chosen to enter into the variable column of the first tableau, thereby eliminating the use of the negative coefficient of S_2. Slack and artificial variables are introduced into the product mix (variable column) of the first tableau to find an initial feasible solution.

The new cost equation would be:

$$C = 8X + 15Y - 0S_2 + MA_1 + 0S_1 + MA_2$$

For minimizing costs, the objective function must be multiplied by -1. This transformed function enters in the first tableau as the objective row. The resulting expression is:

$$C = -8X - 15Y + 0S_2 - MA_1 - 0S_1 - MA_2$$

followed by the new constraint equations for the simplex solution

$$X + Y + A_1 = 40$$
$$X + S_1 = 12$$
$$Y - S_2 + A_2 = 10$$

The tableau format and the computations are identical with those for the maximization problem.

MIX		0	-8	-15	0	-M	0	-M
		QUANTITY	X	Y	S_2	A_1	S_1	A_2
-M	A_1	40	1	1	0	1	0	0
0	S_1	12	1	0	0	0	1	0
-M	A_2	10	0	1	-1	0	0	1
		-50M	-M+8	-2M+15	M	0	0	0

First Simplex Tableau and First Solution

Explanation and Computations for the First Tableau. The explanations of the arrangement of the tableau are identical with those given for the first tableau of the maximization model (pages 915–917). Observe that variables not included in a constraint are assigned zero coefficients in the problem rows. The index row is computed as follows:

$$
\begin{array}{ll}
\textit{Steps 1 and 2} & \textit{Step 3} \\
-M\,(40) + 0\,(12) + (-M)\,(10) = -50M & -50M - 0 \quad\quad = \quad -50M \\
-M\,(1) + 0\,(1) + (-M)\,(0) = -M & -M - (-8) = \quad -M + 8 \\
-M\,(1) + 0\,(0) + (-M)\,(1) = -2M & -2M - (-15) = -2M + 15 \\
-M\,(0) + 0\,(0) + (-M)\,(-1) = M & M - 0 \quad\quad = \quad M \\
-M\,(1) + 0\,(0) + (-M)\,(0) = -M & M - (-M) = \quad 0 \\
-M\,(0) + 0\,(1) + (-M)\,(0) = 0 & 0 - 0 \quad\quad = \quad 0 \\
-M\,(0) + 0\,(0) + (-M)\,(1) = -M & M - (-M) = \quad 0 \\
\end{array}
$$

It is the rule of the simplex method that the optimum solution has not been reached if the index row carries any negative values (except for the quantity column which denotes total cost of this solution) at the completion of an iteration. Consequently, since negative values appear in the index row, the optimum solution has not been found, and a second tableau must be set up.

Explanation and Computations for the Second Tableau. As the objective is to minimize costs, the key column is found by selecting that column

	MIX	0	−8	−15	0	−M	0	−M
		QUANTITY	X	Y	S_2	A_1	S_1	A_2
−M	A_1	30	1	0	1	1	0	−1
0	S_1	12	1	0	0	0	1	0
−15	Y	10	0	1	−1	0	0	1
		−30M−150	−M+8	0	−M+15	0	0	2M−15

Second Simplex Tableau and Second Solution

with the negative value with the highest absolute value in the index row; i.e., that variable whose value will decrease costs the most. The index row shows only two negative values: $-M + 8$ and $-2M + 15$. Observe that the quantity column value in the index row, $-50M$, is not considered. This figure denotes total cost of this solution and is negative by convention. The negative number with the highest absolute value in the index row is $-2M + 15$ and Y is, therefore, the key column.

The row to be replaced, the key row, is A_2, computed as follows:

A_1 row $40/1 = 40$

S_1 row $12/0$ is not considered (not defined mathematically)

A_2 row $10/1 = 10 =$ replaced row (smallest *positive* ratio)

Again, as in the maximization discussion, the smallest positive ratio identifies the equation which operates as the limiting constraint.

Since the key number (the crossing cell between the key column Y and the key row A_2) is 1, the values of the main row do not change.

Y Row	*A_1 Row*	*S_1 Row*
$10/1 = 10$	$40 - 1 (10) = 30$	$12 - 0 (10) = 12$
$0/1 = 0$	$1 - 1 (0) = 1$	$1 - 0 (0) = 1$
$1/1 = 1$	$1 - 1 (1) = 0$	$0 - 0 (1) = 0$
$-1/1 = -1$	$0 - 1 (-1) = 1$	$0 - 0 (-1) = 0$
$0/1 = 0$	$1 - 1 (0) = 1$	$0 - 0 (0) = 0$
$0/1 = 0$	$0 - 1 (0) = 0$	$1 - 0 (0) = 1$
$1/1 = 1$	$0 - 1 (1) = -1$	$0 - 0 (1) = 0$

Index row:

Steps 1 and 2

$$-M(\ \ 30) + 0\ (12) + (-15)(\ \ 10) = -30M - 150$$
$$-M(\ \ \ 1) + 0\ (\ 1) + (-15)(\ \ \ 0) = \ \ \ \ \ \ -M$$
$$-M(\ \ \ 0) + 0\ (\ 0) + (-15)(\ \ \ 1) = \ \ \ \ \ \ -15$$
$$-M(\ \ \ 1) + 0\ (\ 0) + (-15)(-1) = \ \ \ \ -M + 15$$
$$-M(\ \ \ 1) + 0\ (\ 0) + (-15)(\ \ \ 0) = \ \ \ \ \ \ -M$$
$$-M(\ \ \ 0) + 0\ (\ 1) + (-15)(\ \ \ 0) = \ \ \ \ \ \ \ \ \ 0$$
$$-M(-1) + 0\ (\ 0) + (-15)(\ \ \ 1) = \ \ \ \ \ M - 15$$

Step 3

$$(-30M - 150)\ \ -0\ \ \ \ \ \ \ \ \ = -30M - 150$$
$$(-M)\ \ \ \ \ \ \ \ \ \ \ \ - (-8)\ \ = \ \ \ \ \ -M + 8$$
$$(-15)\ \ \ \ \ \ \ \ \ \ \ - (-15) = \ \ \ \ \ \ \ \ \ 0$$
$$(-M + 15)\ \ \ \ \ \ -0\ \ \ \ \ \ = \ \ \ \ \ -M + 15$$
$$(-M)\ \ \ \ \ \ \ \ \ \ \ \ - (-M) = \ \ \ \ \ \ \ \ \ 0$$
$$(0)\ \ \ \ \ \ \ \ \ \ \ \ \ \ -0\ \ \ \ \ \ = \ \ \ \ \ \ \ \ \ 0$$
$$(M - 15)\ \ \ \ \ \ \ - (-M) = \ \ \ \ \ 2M - 15$$

Since negative values appear in the index row, excluding the quantity column, the optimum solution has not yet been found; and a third tableau must be set up.

Explanation and Computations for the Third Tableau. Since $-M + 8$ is the negative number with the highest absolute value in the index row of the second tableau, X is the key column.

The row to be replaced, the key row, is S_1, determined as follows:

A_1 row $30/1 = 30$
S_1 row $12/1 = 12 =$ replaced row
Y row $10/0$ (not defined mathematically)

X Row	*A₁ Row*	*Y Row*
$12/1 = 12$	$30 - 1\ (12) = \ \ 18$	$10 - 0\ (12) = \ \ 10$
$1/1 = \ \ 1$	$1 - 1\ (\ 1) = \ \ \ \ 0$	$0 - 0\ (\ 1) = \ \ \ \ 0$
$0/1 = \ \ 0$	$0 - 1\ (\ 0) = \ \ \ \ 0$	$1 - 0\ (\ 0) = \ \ \ \ 1$
$0/1 = \ \ 0$	$1 - 1\ (\ 0) = \ \ \ \ 1$	$-1 - 0\ (\ 0) = \ -1$
$0/1 = \ \ 0$	$1 - 1\ (\ 0) = \ \ \ \ 1$	$0 - 0\ (\ 0) = \ \ \ \ 0$
$1/1 = \ \ 1$	$0 - 1\ (\ 1) = -1$	$0 - 0\ (\ 1) = \ \ \ \ 0$
$0/1 = \ \ 0$	$-1 - 1\ (\ 0) = -1$	$1 - 0\ (\ 0) = \ \ \ \ 1$

	MIX	0 QUANTITY	-8 X	-15 Y	0 S_2	-M A_1	0 S_1	-M A_2
-M	A_1	18	0	0	1	1	-1	-1
-8	X	12	1	0	0	0	1	0
-15	Y	10	0	1	-1	0	0	1
		-18M-246	0	0	-M+15	0	M-8	2M-15

Third Simplex Tableau and Third Solution

Index row:

Steps 1 and 2

$$-M\ (\ 18) + (-8)\ (12) + (-15)\ (\ 10) = -18M-246$$
$$-M\ (\ \ 0) + (-8)\ (\ 1) + (-15)\ (\ \ 0) = \qquad -8$$
$$-M\ (\ \ 0) + (-8)\ (\ 0) + (-15)\ (\ \ 1) = \qquad -15$$
$$-M\ (\ \ 1) + (-8)\ (\ 0) + (-15)\ (-1) = \qquad -M+15$$
$$-M\ (\ \ 1) + (-8)\ (\ 0) + (-15)\ (\ \ 0) = \qquad -M$$
$$-M\ (-1) + (-8)\ (\ 1) + (-15)\ (\ \ 0) = \qquad M-8$$
$$-M\ (-1) + (-8)\ (\ 0) + (-15)\ (\ \ 1) = \qquad M-15$$

Step 3

$$(-18M-246)\ -\ 0 \qquad = -18M-246$$
$$-8 \qquad\quad -\ (-8)\ = \qquad\quad 0$$
$$-15 \qquad\quad -\ (-15) = \qquad\quad 0$$
$$(-M+15) \qquad -\ 0 \qquad = \quad -M+15$$
$$-M \qquad\quad -\ (-M) = \qquad\quad 0$$
$$(M-8) \qquad\quad -\ 0 \qquad = \qquad M-\ 8$$
$$(M\ -\ 15) \qquad -\ (-M) = \qquad 2M-15$$

Since a negative value, $-M + 15$, appears in the index row, excluding the quantity column, the optimum solution has not been found; and a fourth tableau must be set up.

Explanation and Computations for the Fourth Tableau. Since $-M+15$ is the only negative number in the index row of the third tableau, excluding the quantity column, S_2 is the key column.

The row to be replaced is A_1, computed as follows:

A_1 row $18/1 = 18 =$ replaced row (the smallest *positive* ratio)
X row $12/0$ (not defined mathematically)
Y row $10/-1 = -10$

	MIX	0 QUANTITY	-8 X	-15 Y	0 S_2	-M A_1	0 S1	-M A_2
0	S_2	18	0	0	1	1	-1	-1
-8	X	12	1	0	0	0	1	0
-15	Y	28	0	1	0	1	-1	0
		-516	0	0	0	M-15	7	M

Fourth Simplex Tableau and Fourth as Well As Optimal Solution

S_2 Row	X Row	Y Row
$18/1 =$ 18	$12 - 0\,(\ 18) = 12$	$10 - (-1)\,(\ 18) =$ 28
$0/1 =$ 0	$1 - 0\,(\ \ 0) =$ 1	$0 - (-1)\,(\ \ 0) =$ 0
$0/1 =$ 0	$0 - 0\,(\ \ 0) =$ 0	$1 - (-1)\,(\ \ 0) =$ 1
$1/1 =$ 1	$0 - 0\,(\ \ 1) =$ 0	$-1 - (-1)\,(\ \ 1) =$ 0
$1/1 =$ 1	$0 - 0\,(\ \ 1) =$ 0	$0 - (-1)\,(\ \ 1) =$ 1
$-1/1 = -1$	$1 - 0\,(-1) =$ 1	$0 - (-1)\,(-1) = -1$
$-1/1 = -1$	$0 - 0\,(-1) =$ 0	$1 - (-1)\,(-1) =$ 0

Index row:

Steps 1 and 2

$$0\,(\ 18) + (-8)\,(12) + (-15)\,(\ 28) = -516$$
$$0\,(\ \ 0) + (-8)\,(\ 1) + (-15)\,(\ \ 0) = -\ \ 8$$
$$0\,(\ \ 0) + (-8)\,(\ 0) + (-15)\,(\ \ 1) = -\ 15$$
$$0\,(\ \ 1) + (-8)\,(\ 0) + (-15)\,(\ \ 0) = \ \ \ \ 0$$
$$0\,(\ \ 1) + (-8)\,(\ 0) + (-15)\,(\ \ 1) = -\ 15$$
$$0\,(-1) + (-8)\,(\ 1) + (-15)\,(-1) = \ \ \ \ 7$$
$$0\,(-1) + (-8)\,(\ 0) + (-15)\,(\ \ 0) = \ \ \ \ 0$$

Step 3

$$
\begin{aligned}
-516 - 0 &= -516 \\
-8 - (-8) &= 0 \\
-15 - (-15) &= 0 \\
0 - 0 &= 0 \\
-15 - (-M) &= M - 15 \\
7 - 0 &= 7 \\
0 - (-M) &= M
\end{aligned}
$$

No negative values remain in the index row of the fourth tableau except the minimum cost figure which is negative (-516) by convention. The optimum solution has been reached:

$$
\begin{array}{lll}
\underline{\text{12 gals. of A @ \$ 8 per gal.}} &= & \$ 96 \\
\underline{+28 \text{ gals. of B @ \$15 per gal.}} &= & 420 \\
\underline{\underline{\text{40 gals. of mixture}}} &= & \underline{\underline{\$516}} \text{ (the lowest cost combination)}
\end{array}
$$

USING THE GRAPHIC METHOD TO SOLVE COST MINIMIZATION PROBLEMS

The graphic method can be applied to minimization problems in the same manner as illustrated for maximization problems. Again, the constraints define the solution space when they are plotted on the graph on page 929:

$$
\begin{aligned}
X + Y &= 40 \text{ gallons} \\
X &\le 12 \text{ gallons} \\
Y &\ge 10 \text{ gallons}
\end{aligned}
$$

The solution space indicates the area of feasible solutions represented by the line ab. Any combination of Ingredients A and B that falls within the solution space (line ab) is a feasible solution. However, the best feasible solution is found at one of the corner points, a or b. Consequently, the corner points must be tried to find the combination that minimizes costs; i.e., $\$8X + \$15Y$.

Trying values at each of the two corner points:

$$
\begin{aligned}
a &= (X = 0, Y = 40); \ \$8(0) + \$15(40) = \$600 \text{ cost} \\
b &= (X = 12, Y = 28); \ \$8(12) + \$15(28) = \$516 \text{ cost}
\end{aligned}
$$

Therefore, in order to minimize cost, the company should use 12 gallons of Ingredient A and 28 gallons of Ingredient B at a total cost of $516.

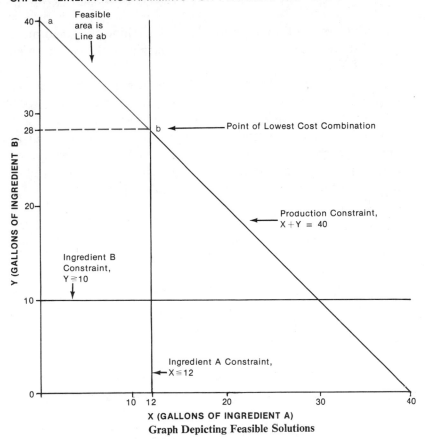

Graph Depicting Feasible Solutions

SHADOW PRICES

The determination of the optimum mix to maximize the contribution margin or to minimize cost assumes a defined set of constraints. It is useful to consider the sensitivity of the solution if a constraint is relaxed. This effect is often referred to as the *shadow price* and simply shows the additional contribution margin (if a contribution margin maximization problem) or the reduction in cost (if a cost minimization problem) resulting from relaxing a constraint. The shadow price thus sets a maximum on the *increase* over existing unit variable cost that could be incurred to acquire one more unit of a constraining factor.[2]

To present the idea of shadow prices, the value of additional grinding or polishing hours (from the contribution margin maximization problem previously discussed) can be considered. That is, what is the worth of

[2]This discussion adapted from Lanny Gordon Chasteen, "A Graphical Approach to Linear Programming Shadow Prices," *The Accounting Review*, Vol. XLVII, No. 4, pp. 819–823.

additional grinding and polishing hours? If the machine shop had more grinding or polishing hours, the contribution margin could be increased by using more of each.

The index row of the third (optimal solution) simplex tableau shows the shadow prices. The coefficients under the S_1 (grinding) and S_2 (polishing) slack variable columns give the trade-off in terms of product mix as the constraints are increased and decreased. Thus, one more hour of grinding time will increase the contribution margin by $.625, computed as follows: as one more grinding hour is made available, .25 units of Y (deluxe models) with a unit contribution margin of $4 (.25 × $4 = $1) will replace .125 units of X (standard models) with a $3 unit contribution margin (.125 × $3 = $.375) for a net of $.625 ($1 − $.375 = $.625).

If additional grinding time could be obtained at no increase in *unit* variable cost, an increase of $.625 contribution margin per grinding hour would result; and as much as $.625 more than the present *unit* variable cost of grinding time could be incurred before reaching a point at which a zero per unit contribution margin would occur. Thus, overtime hours might be considered. These observations assume that the selling price per unit remains unchanged. The $.4375 has the same meaning for each hour of polishing time.

The range of hours over which the shadow prices of $.625 and $.4375 for grinding and polishing hours are valid can be found as follows:

Step 1. For the lower limit of the range, divide each unit in the solution mix by the coefficients under the slack variable columns; i.e., the S_1 and S_2 columns. The smallest positive number that results in a column is the maximum decrease for that constraint:

Product	Units (1)	S_1 Grinding (2)	S_2 Polishing (3)	S_1 Grinding (1)÷(2)	S_2 Polishing (1)÷(3)
Y..........	20	0.250	−0.1250	80	−160
X..........	10	−0.125	0.3125	−80	32

For the grinding constraint, the decrease is 80 hours. Since the original number of hours available was 120, the lower limit is 40 hours. For the polishing constraint, the decrease is 32 hours. Since 80 hours were originally available, the lower limit is 48 hours.

Step 2. For the upper limit of the range, multiply each coefficient by −1 and repeat the Step 1 process. The smallest positive number that results in a column is the maximum increase for that constraint:

Product	Units (1)	S_1 Grinding (2)	S_2 Polishing (3)	S_1 Grinding (1)÷(2)	S_2 Polishing (1)÷(3)
Y..........	20	−0.250	0.1250	−80	160
X..........	10	0.125	−0.3125	80	− 32

For the grinding constraint, the maximum increase is 80; and since the original number of hours available was 120, the upper limit is 200 hours. For the polishing constraint, the increase is 160; and the upper limit is 240 hours (160, plus the original constraint of 80 polishing hours).

The limits occur for a constraint because increases or decreases beyond the limits will change the shadow price.

In summary, the lower and upper constraint limits for this example are:

	Lower Limit	Upper Limit
Grinding hours....................................	40	200
Polishing hours...................................	48	240

Both the constraint equations in this example are of the $\leq$ type. The same method is used for the $=$ type of constraint equation except that the coefficients under the *artificial* variable column for the $=$ equation are used in the computations. For any $\geq$ constraint equations, the method for finding the lower and upper constraint range limits differs in that the *signs* of the coefficients under the slack variable column for the $\geq$ constraint equations are changed in Step 1. With this exception, the procedure is the same.

When there is a zero shadow price (not the case in the above example), there is no defined upper limit for the $\leq$ type of constraint equation because there is already more of this constraint available than is required. There is no defined lower limit for the $\geq$ type of constraint equation because there is already more of this constraint used than is required.

The lower- and upper-limit computations apply, assuming only one constraint is to be relaxed, and provided there is a unique solution to the linear programming problem. The limits for cases in which two or more constraints are relaxed simultaneously can be computed following a methodology that is beyond the scope of this discussion.[3]

It should also be observed that the shadow price indicates the opportunity cost of using a resource (such as grinding or polishing hours) for some other purpose. For example, if an hour of grinding time could instead be used to produce some other product at a contribution margin greater than $.625 per hour, then use of the grinding hour resource in producing the alternate product would be preferable.

The described method is equally applicable to cost minimization problems.

[3]See Harvey M. Wagner, *Principles of Operations Research* (Englewood Cliffs, NJ: Prentice-Hall, Inc., 1969), pp. 132–133.

LINEAR PROGRAMMING TECHNIQUES — GENERAL OBSERVATIONS

The maximization and minimization studies, together with the exercises and problems presented in this chapter, are realistic examples of the types of problems management faces. By maximizing certain managerial objectives such as contribution margin and utilization of available labor hours or factory capacities or by minimizing functions such as costs, weight, materials mix, or time, management's goal can be determined quantitatively, and hopefully, satisfied. To find a feasible solution, it is necessary to state each situation in mathematical notations. Restrictions or constraints must confine the solution within a well-defined area and appear in the form of equations with nonnegative variables.

For the accounting community a definite similarity exists between certain managerial problems and mathematical programming techniques. Furthermore, as other chapters have pointed out, the growing need for and involvement of accounting and cost data in management's planning and decision-making processes are supported and enhanced by these techniques.

The accountant's methods for determining the most profitable or optimum use or alternative uses of long-life facilities are presented in Chapter 26 ("Capital Expenditure Planning, Evaluating, and Control"). Problems dealing with the short-run uses of facilities or with output having varying combinations of alternative input might be solved by setting down every possible combination of output in order to determine the maximum contribution margin or the minimum cost. Such a procedure, while proven feasible and acceptable, may no longer be necessary. The introduction of newer and more sophisticated decision models, particularly that of linear programming, allows the accountant to administer the implementation of these models by determining the data needed for their application. Should the cases with their data, constraints, etc., move beyond the possibility of being solved manually or by simple desk or hand calculators, then the electronic computer will aid the accountant in arriving at a correct and immediate solution.

DISCUSSION QUESTIONS

1. Linear programming models are referred to as a scientific method of solving problems. Discuss.
2. What is meant by the contribution margin per unit or the unit cost in linear programming problems?

3. Examine the graph on page 912 of this chapter and answer the following questions:
   (a) The area bounded by the corner points a, b, c, and d is called the solution space. Why?
   (b) The triangles formed by b, c, and #40 and c, d, and #60 are not part of the solution space. Why?
   (c) What does corner point "c" mean?
   (d) What is the meaning of the perpendicular line c-10 and the horizontal line c-20?

4. Describe the simplex method.

5. Examine the first simplex tableau on page 915 and discuss the components of a tableau.

6. What is the purpose of a slack variable?

7. What is the purpose of an artificial variable?

8. Formulate objective and constraint equations for a situation in which a company seeks to minimize the total cost of Raw Materials A and B. The per pound cost of A is $25 and of B, $10. The two materials are combined to form a product that must weigh 50 pounds. At least 20 pounds of A and no more than 40 pounds of B can be used.

9. A partial linear programming maximization simplex tableau for Products X and Y and Slack Variables S_1 and S_2 appears below:

MIX		0	6	7	0	0
	QUANTITY	X	Y	S_1	S_2	
7	Y	4	2/3	1	1/3	0
0	S_2	4	4/3	0	−1/3	1

   (a) Compute the index row.
   (b) Has an optimum solution been reached? Explain.
   (c) Suppose that one unit of S_1 were placed in the solution. What effect would this have on Product Y?

10. What is a shadow price? Explain its significance.

11. Beekley, Inc. manufactures Beko, Seko, and Weko and needs advice in determining the best production mix for these three products. Demand for the products is excellent, and management finds that it is unable to meet potential sales with the existing plant capacity. Each product goes through three operations: Milling, Grinding, and Painting. The effective weekly departmental capacities in minutes are: Milling, 10,000; Grinding,

14,000; and Painting, 10,000. The following information is available on the three products:

Product	Selling Price per Unit	Variable Cost per Unit	Per Unit Production Time (in Minutes)		
			Milling	Grinding	Painting
Beko..................	$5.25	$4.45	4	8	4
Seko..................	5.00	3.90	10	4	2
Weko..................	4.50	3.30	4	8	2

Select the correct answer for each of the following statements.

(a) The quantitative technique most useful in determining the best product mix would be (1) least squares analysis; (2) queuing theory; (3) linear regression; (4) linear programming.

(b) The objective function for this problem using the simplex method might be expressed as

(1) $CM = 4.45X + 3.90Y + 3.30Z + OS_1 + OS_2 + OS_3$;
(2) $CM = 5.25X + 5.00Y + 4.50Z + S_1 + S_2 + S_3$;
(3) $CM = .80X + 1.10Y + 1.20Z + S_1 + S_2 + S_3$;
(4) $CM = .80X + 1.10Y + 1.20Z + OS_1 + OS_2 + OS_3$.

(c) The requirement that total production time in the Painting Department may not exceed 10,000 minutes per week might be expressed as

(1) $4X + 2Y + 2Z \geqq 10,000$;
(2) $4X + 2Y + 2Z > 10,000$;
(3) $4X + 2Y + 2Z \leqq 10,000$;
(4) $4X + 2Y + 2Z < 10,000$.

(d) The variables S_1, S_2, and S_3 included in the answer to (b) are referred to as (1) artificial variables; (2) primary variables; (3) stochastic variables; (4) slack variables.

(e) The coefficients for X, Y, and Z included in the answer to (b) are referred to as the (1) coefficients of the objective function in the problem; (2) coefficients of the artificial variables in the problem; (3) coefficients of the constraints in the problem and represent the contribution margin for each product; (4) shadow prices of the variables in the problem.

(f) If Beekley were willing to pay $ .12 for every minute of additional grinding time that might be made available, this may be called (1) a primal restraint; (2) a slack variable; (3) a shadow price; (4) an artificial variable.

(g) A significant advantage of applying the simplex method to certain problems having many variables is that solutions may be arrived at quickly using (1) graphic analysis; (2) electronic computer routines; (3) simple algebraic methods; (4) regression analysis.

(AICPA adapted)

EXERCISES

1. Graphic Procedure. Given the constraints $2X + 6Y = 60$ and $4X + 2Y = 40$, draw a graph, then identify and compute algebraically the X, Y values of the corner points.

2. Product Mix Contribution Margin. The illustration on page 912 assumes that the market for standard and deluxe models was stable and that the $3 and $4 per unit was maintainable for at least the near future. Increased demand for the deluxe model suggests the desirability of raising the price well above the level that produced the original $4 contribution margin.

Required: (1) The product mix to be attained if deluxe models are priced to yield a $6 unit contribution margin.

(2) The product mix to be attained if deluxe models are priced to yield a $10 contribution margin.

(3) The contribution margin figure per deluxe model to make it possible to abandon production of standard units and operate at less than full capacity, but maintain maximum profits.

3. Problem Formulation and Graphic Method. A company markets two products, Alpha and Gamma. The marginal contributions per gallon are $5 for Alpha and $4 for Gamma. Both products consist of two ingredients, D and K. Alpha contains 80% of D and 20% of K while the proportions of the same ingredients in Gamma are 40% and 60%, respectively. The current inventory is 16,000 gallons of D and 6,000 gallons of K. The only company producing D and K is on strike and will neither deliver nor produce these ingredients in the foreseeable future. The company wishes to know the gallons of Alpha and Gamma that it should produce with its present stock of raw materials in order to maximize its total profit.

Required: (1) The objective function.

(2) The constraint imposed by the (a) quantity of D on hand and (b) quantity of K on hand.

(3) A graph to determine the product mix that the company should produce to maximize total profit.

(4) Requirement (3) assuming that the contribution margins per gallon are $7 for Alpha and $9 for Gamma.

(AICPA adapted)

4. Contribution Margin Maximization — Graphic Method. The Neeley Company produces two products, Nelo and Telo, in two departments, Fabricating and Finishing. The fabricating machines can be operated 100 hours per week, and the finishing machines 150 hours per week. Each unit of Nelo requires only one half as much fabricating time as Telo, but requires three times as much finishing time as Telo. Each unit of Telo requires two hours of work in each process. The contribution margin on each unit of Nelo is $8, and on each unit of Telo, $6.

Required: (1) A graph to determine the product mix that the Neeley Company should maintain to maximize the total contribution margin.

(2) The maximum weekly contribution margin figure.

5. Contribution Margin Maximization — Simplex Method. The first tableau of the simplex method is on page 936.

Required: (1) The second tableau of the simplex method.

(2) An explanation as to whether an optimum solution has been reached.

MIX		0	8	10	0	0
		QUANTITY	A	B	S_1	S_2
0	S_1	12	2	3	1	0
0	S_2	8	2	1	0	1
		0	−8	−10	0	0

6. Time Allocation; Contribution Margin Maximization — Graphic and Simplex Methods. The Virginia Doll Co. manufactures two dolls, Pattie and Suzie, in three departments: Frame Building, Stuffing, and Covering. The following data are available.

Department	Maximum Hours Available per Week	Manufacturing Time Required (Hrs.)	
		Per Pattie	Per Suzie
Frame Building........	150	1	2
Stuffing..............	300	2	5
Covering.............	200	2	2

The contribution margin is $5 per Pattie doll and $10 per Suzie doll.

Required: The optimum combination of products to maximize the total contribution margin, using both the graphic and simplex methods.

7. Materials Allocation; Contribution Margin Maximization — Graphic and Simplex Methods; Shadow Prices. Cornett Products, Inc. is compelled to curtail manufacturing due to a strike at the mill of one of its suppliers. The company still has the following inventory on hand to permit some production:

Raw material #101–2............................ 12,100 kilograms (kg.)
Raw material #102–6............................ 4,900   ”

Other data:

	Raw Materials	
	#101–2	#102–6
Required per unit of Product A.......................	.8 kg.	.2 kg.
Required per unit of Product B.......................	.3 kg.	.7 kg.
Contribution margin per unit — Product A.............	$50	
Contribution margin per unit — Product B.............	80	

Required: (1) A graphic and simplex solution regarding the number of units of Products A and B that should be produced in order to maximize the total contribution margin with the available raw materials while the supplier's employees are on strike.
(2) The shadow prices and their lower and upper constraint range limits.

(Based on an article in *The Journal of Accountancy*)

8. Contribution Margin Maximization — Simplex Method; Shadow Prices. A firm produces two products, X_1 and X_2, which pass through two facilities — b_1 and b_2, with fixed capacities of 1,000,000 and 900,000 hours, respectively. Product X_1 requires 8/10ths hour of Facility b_1 and 5/10ths hour of Facility b_2 while Product X_2 requires 5/10ths hour of Facility b_1 and one hour of Facility b_2. Each unit of Product X_1 contributes (= contribution margin) \$960, and each unit of Product X_2 contributes \$875. The entire problem can be expressed as:

$$\text{Maximize: } CM = 960X_1 + 875X_2$$

$$\text{Subject to: } 8/10X_1 + 5/10X_2 \leq 1.0$$
$$5/10X_1 + 1X_2 \leq .9$$
$$X_1, X_2 \geq 0.0$$

Required: (1) The linear programming tableaus to maximize the contribution margin.

(2) The shadow prices and their lower and upper constraint range limits.

(Based on an article in *The Accounting Review*)

9. Cost Minimization — Graphic and Simplex Methods; Shadow Prices. A company produces three products, A, B, and C, which use common Raw Materials X and Y. Raw Material X costs \$3 per ton and Raw Material Y \$4 per ton. The amount of raw materials required per product and the required weight per product is:

PRODUCT EXTRACT   (POUNDS PER TON)

Raw Material	Product A	Product B	Product C	Cost of Raw Material
X..............	4	7	1.5	\$3 per ton
Y..............	8	2	5	\$4 per ton
Minimum weight required.	32	14	15	

Required: (1) The number of tons of each raw material needed to meet the requirements at minimum cost by (a) the graphic method and (b) the simplex method.

(2) The shadow prices and their lower and upper constraint range limits.

10. Cost Minimization — Graphic and Simplex Methods; Shadow Prices. Two additives are mixed with a plastic resin prior to extension into a final product. Over a period of time, empirical relationships were developed to meet quality specifications of the final product. Within the latitude of these relationships, the quantities are varied according to their current cost. Operating costs are not affected by the proportions of the two additives in the product.

The quality relationships are:
For tensile strength............ $2A + B \geq 1.1$ } per 100 kilograms of product
For flexibility................ $A + 3B \geq 1.5$

A sells for \$8 per kg., and B for \$5 per kg.

Required: (1) The most economical (minimum cost) mixture using the (a) graphic method and (b) simplex method.

(2) The shadow prices and their lower and upper constraint range limits.

PROBLEMS

28-1. Contribution Margin Maximization — Graphic and Simplex Methods. Zeus, Inc. manufactures two kinds of leather belts — Belt A (a high-quality belt) and Belt B (of a lower quality). The respective contribution margins are $4 and $3 per belt. Production of Belt A requires twice as much time as for Belt B; and if all belts were of the Belt B type, Zeus could produce 1,000 per day. The leather supply is sufficient for only 800 belts per day (both Belt A and Belt B combined). Belt A requires a fancy buckle, and only 400 buckles per day are available for this belt.

Required: The quantity of each type belt to be produced to maximize contribution margin using (a) the graphic method and (b) the simplex method.

28-2. Capital Expenditure Decision; Maximizing Capacity — Simplex Method. The Capital Investment Committee of Farrington Products, Inc. plans to invest $150,000 in machines to produce a particular product. Three types of machines are being considered: Type A costs $1,500; Type B, $2,000; and Type C, $2,500.

A and B each require 1 worker for their operation. C, however, requires 2 workers. A produces 10 units per hour; B, 15; and C, 30. A can operate 8 hours per day; B, 7 hours; and C, 6 hours. Operators are interchangeable among the machines. One hundred operators are available. Because of limited plant facilities, a total of only 80 machines can be purchased.

Required: The quantity of each type of machine to be purchased in order to maximize production capacity, using the simplex method.

28-3. Labor and Materials Allocation; Contribution Margin Maximization — Simplex Method. Sky, Inc., manufacturer of model airplane kits, recently developed a new line of kits consisting of three models: A, B, and C.

A special feature is in the wings that are interchangeable between kits. The wings are made of molded foam plastic. A regular production run is planned for March, six months from now. The new models are now on display at several hobby stores. Four hobby wholesalers like the kits so well they have placed orders for any that can be sent within 30 days.

During a regular management meeting, the sales manager asked the president if they should try to fill the order. The production manager pointed out that only a limited supply of wings for the models had been received and the next shipment would not be for 60 days. She did not think more that 100 kits could be produced during the next 30 days. The president suggested filling the order, since the orders came from regular customers.

The production manager finds only 220 wings on hand. Furthermore, only 800 sheets of 1/32" x 3" x 12" balsa can be allocated to the run. Kits A, B, and C use 1, 2, and 3 wings each. Otherwise, an unlimited supply of the remaining materials is in stock. Kits A, B, and C use 4, 6, and 9 sheets of 1/32" x 3" x 12" balsa each.

The labor requirements for the models are:

	Number of Minutes Required		
	Model A	*Model B*	*Model C*
Die cutting................................	2	7	8
Assembling material to put in kit.............	5	6	4
Other.......................................	3	7	6

Only 570 minutes of assembly time can be allocated for the run.

Unit sales prices and costs (excluding direct labor costs) for each of the three kits are:

	Model A	Model B	Model C
Sales price...............................	$40	$50	$60
Raw materials............................	$25	$40	$46
Factory overhead costs.....................	5	3	9
Total costs...............................	$30	$43	$55
Contribution margin.......................	$10	$ 7	$ 5

The overhead costs consist of indirect labor and other variable manufacturing costs. The company has a policy of paying the workers for a 40-hour week, even if they are idle part of the time. However, the policy also includes keeping the workers as busy as possible.

Required: (1) The maximum contribution margin.
(2) The maximum production.

28-4. Contribution Margin Maximization — Graphic and Simplex Methods; Shadow Prices.
Chasteen Company manufactures two products, Alpha and Beta, that have contribution margins of $10 and $5 per unit, respectively. Each unit of Alpha requires 10 machine hours while each unit of Beta requires 4 machine hours; 100 machine hours are available. Each unit of Beta requires two units of Material Z, of which 30 units are available.

Required: (1) The units of Alpha and Beta that must be manufactured to maximize the total contribution margin, using the graphic and simplex methods.
(2) The shadow prices and their lower and upper constraint range limits.

(Based on an article in *The Accounting Review*)

28-5. Production Planning; Contribution Margin Maximization — Graphic and Simplex Methods; Shadow Prices.
Castelli Corporation manufactures two products, P_1 and P_2, in Departments I, II, and III. The following information concerning departmental hours, product hours, costs, and selling prices is available:

	P_1	P_2	Total Hours Available
Machine hours — Department I......	3	5	450
Machine hours — Department II.....	0	1	60
Machine hours — Department III....	5	4	600
Variable manufacturing costs........	$ 7	$12	
Selling price per product...........	11	22	

Required: (1) The product mix that constitutes the maximum contribution margin, using the graphic method and the simplex method.
(2) The shadow prices and their lower and upper constraint range limits.

28-6. Product Mix; Contribution Margin Maximization — Graphic and Simplex Methods; Shadow Prices. The Sanning Company manufactures two compounds, M and N. Three processing steps are needed for Compound M while two processing steps are needed for Compound N. To produce one barrel of each compound, these percentages of the daily capacities of each processing step are required:

	Percent of Daily Capacity per Barrel	
	Compound M	Compound N
Processing step 1.....................	33-1/3	50
Processing step 2.....................	66-2/3	33-1/3
Processing step 3.....................	100	0

The contribution margin of Compound M is $4 per barrel; of Compound N, $5 per barrel.

Required: (1) A graphic solution to indicate the maximum total contribution per day from the two compounds.

(2) A linear programming simplex analysis to indicate the optimal contribution per compound and the optimal utilization of the available capacities.

(3) The shadow prices and their lower and upper constraint range limits.

28-7. Scholarship Costs; Admission Policies; Cost Minimization — Simplex Method. Due to the budget squeeze, Victoria University is faced with the problem of minimizing scholarship expenditures subject to these past traditions and new agreements:

Out of a class of 1,700 freshmen, the University, for reasons of diversification, admits no more than 800 students who are children of its alumni.

The University will admit at least 250 minority-group students. (To encourage universities to admit more minority-group students, the federal government supports the schools with $800 in aid for each minority-group student admitted.

The average scholarship costs to the University before federal aid are:

$1,000 per year for a student whose parent is an alumni
$2,000 per year for a minority-group student
$1,100 per year for a nonalumni, nonminority-group student

Required: The students to be admitted and the total cost to Victoria University, using the simplex method.

28-8. Materials Requirements; Cost Minimization — Graphic and Simplex Methods; Shadow Prices. Certain animals at the San Diego Zoo must receive an adequate amount of two vitamins in their daily food supply. The minimum daily requirement of Vitamin A is 30 units; of Vitamin B, 50 units.

One pound of foodstuff X can provide 3-1/3% of the minimum daily requirements of A and 4% of B. One pound of Y will supply 10% of A and 2% of B requirements. The costs are: X, $.02 per pound; Y, $.05 per pound.

Required: (1) The least possible cost to provide for the minimum requirements of the two vitamins, using the graphic method and the simplex method.

(2) The shadow prices and their lower and upper constraint range limits.

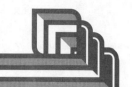

INDEX